THE ILLUSTRATED LIBRARY OF
World Poetry

Engraved by Geo E Perine, N York from Photo by Sarony

William Cullen Bryant

THE ILLUSTRATED LIBRARY OF
World Poetry

EDITED AND WITH AN INTRODUCTION
BY
WILLIAM CULLEN BRYANT

GRAMERCY BOOKS
New York

This 1999 edition is published by Gramercy Books™, an imprint of Random
House Value Publishing, Inc., 201 East 50th Street, New York, NY 10022.

Gramercy Books™ and design are trademarks of Random House
Value Publishing, Inc.

Printed in the United States of America

Random House
New York • Toronto • London • Sydney • Auckland
http://www.randomhouse.com/

Library of Congress Cataloging-in-Publication Data
Library of poetry and song.
    Library of world poetry / with an introduction
by William Cullen Bryant.
        p.   cm.
    Previously published as : Library of poetry and song.
    Includes index.
    ISBN 0-517-11892-0
    1. Poetry—Collections. I. Bryant, William Cullen Bryant,
1794–1878. II. Title.
PN6101.L5   1994
808.81—dc20   94-39050
                                           CIP

8 7 6 5 4

PREFACE.

THIS book has been prepared with the aim of gathering into a single volume the largest practicable compilation of the best Poems of the English language, making it as nearly as possible the choicest and most complete general collection of Poetry yet published.

The name "Library" which is given it indicates the principle upon which the book has been made: namely, that it might serve as a book of reference; as a comprehensive exhibit of the history, growth, and condition of poetical literature; and, more especially, as a companion, at the will of its possessor, for the varying moods of the mind.

Necessarily limited in extent, it yet contains one fifth more matter than any similar publication, presenting over fifteen hundred selections, from more than four hundred authors. It is believed that of the poetical writers acknowledged by the intelligent and cultivated to be great, none, whether English, Scotch, Irish, or American, will be found unrepresented in the volume; while many verses, of merit though not of fame, found in old books or caught out of the passing current of literature, have been here collated with those more notable. And the chief object of the collection — to present an array of good poetry so widely representative and so varied in its tone as to offer an answering chord to every mood and phase of human feeling — has been carefully kept in view, both in the selection and the arrangement of its contents. So that, in all senses, the realization of the significant title, "Library," has been an objective point.

In pursuance of this plan, the highest standard of literary criticism has not been made the only test of worth for selection, since many poems have been included, which, though less perfect than others in form, have, by some power of touching the heart, gained and maintained a sure place in the popular esteem. This policy has been followed with the more confidence, as every poem of the collection has taken its place in the book only after passing the cultured criticism of Mr. William Cullen Bryant. Although Mr. Bryant is not responsible for the classification and arrangement of the poems, yet, as he says in the very interesting "Introduction" which he has contributed, he has "used a free hand, as requested, both in excluding and adding matter, according to his judgment of what was needed." In so far, therefore, it has the sanction and authority of his widely honored name, and comes before the reading public with an indorsement second to none in the world of letters.

The Publishers desire to return their cordial thanks for the courtesy freely extended to them, by which many copyrighted American poems have been allowed to appear in this collection. In regard to a large number of them, permission has been accorded by the authors themselves; other poems, having been gathered as waifs and strays, have been necessarily used without especial authority, and where due credit is not given, or where the authorship may have been erroneously ascribed, future editions will afford opportunity for the correction, which will be gladly made. Particular acknowledgments are offered to Messrs. D. Appleton & Co. for extracts from Gen. James Grant Wilson's handsome edition of the works of Fitz-Greene Halleck, and from the poems of William Cullen Bryant; to Messrs. Harper & Brothers for a few poems of Charles G. Halpine; to Messrs. J. B. Lippincott & Co. for quotations from the writings of T. Buchanan Read; to Messrs. Charles Scribner & Co. for an extract from Dr. J. G. Holland's "Bitter-Sweet"; and more especially to the house of Messrs. Fields, Osgood, & Co., — whose good taste, liberality, and intelligent enterprise have given them an unequalled list of American poetical writers, comprising many of the most eminent poets of the land, — for their courtesy in the liberal extracts granted from the writings of Thomas Bailey Aldrich, Ralph Waldo Emerson, Oliver Wendell Holmes, Henry Wadsworth Longfellow, James Russell Lowell, Florence Percy, John Godfrey Saxe, Harriet Beecher Stowe, Edmund Clarence Stedman, Bayard Taylor, John Townsend Trowbridge, and John Greenleaf Whittier.

With these brief explanations and acknowledgments, the "Library of Poetry and Song" is placed before the public, with the hope that it will be deemed worthy of its title.

ADVERTISEMENT TO THE TWENTIETH EDITION.

(REVISED.)

THE Publishers take this opportunity of expressing their gratification at the very flattering reception given to the "Library of Poetry and Song," the best evidence of which is the fact of the 20th edition having been called for in little more than six months from the publication of the first. It has seemed to supply a real public need.

The present edition has been revised and improved in various ways, and the observations of the numerous critics of the work have been diligently consulted, with a view to make it perfect in all its details, and the recognized standard work of the kind. Many new poems have also been added.

CONTENTS.

LIST OF ILLUSTRATIONS.

INDEX OF AUTHORS.

This is love, who, deaf to prayers,
Floods with blessings unawares.
Draw, if thou canst, the mystic line,
Severing rightly his from thine,
Which is human, which divine.

R.W. Emerson.

INTRODUCTION.

So large a collection of poems as this demands of its compiler an extensive familiarity with the poetic literature of our language, both of the early and the later time, and withal so liberal a taste as not to exclude any variety of poetic merit. At the request of the Publishers I undertook to write an Introduction to the present work, and in pursuance of this design I find that I have come into a somewhat closer personal relation with the book. In its progress it has passed entirely under my revision, and, although not absolutely responsible for the compilation or its arrangement, I have, as requested, exercised a free hand both in excluding and in adding matter according to my judgment of what was best adapted to the purposes of the enterprise. Such, however, is the wide range of English verse, and such the abundance of the materials, that a compilation of this kind must be like a bouquet gathered from the fields in June, when hundreds of flowers will be left in unvisited spots, as beautiful as those which have been taken. It may happen, therefore, that many who have learned to delight in some particular poem will turn these pages, as they might those of other collections, without finding their favorite. Nor should it be matter of surprise, considering the multitude of authors from whom the compilation is made, if it be found that some are overlooked, especially the more recent, of equal merit with many whose poems appear in these pages. It may happen, also, that the compiler, in consequence of some particular association, has been sensible of a beauty and a power of awakening emotions and recalling images in certain poems which other readers will fail to perceive. It should be considered, moreover, that in poetry, as in painting, different artists have different modes of presenting their conceptions, each of which may possess its peculiar merit, yet those whose taste is formed by contemplating the productions of one class take little pleasure in any other. Crabb Robinson relates that Wordsworth once admitted to him that he did not much admire contemporary poetry, not because of its want of poetic merit, but because he had been accustomed to poetry of a different sort, and added that but for this he might have read it with pleasure. I quote from memory. It is to be hoped that every reader of this collection, however he may have been trained, will find in the great variety of its contents something conformable to his taste.

I suppose it is not necessary to give a reason for adding another to the collections of this nature, already in print. They abound in every language, for the simple reason that there is a demand for them. German literature, prolific as it is in verse, has many of them, and some of them compiled by distinguished authors. The parlor table and the winter fireside require a book which, when one is in the humor for reading poetry and knows not what author to take up, will supply exactly what he wants.

I have known persons who frankly said that they took no pleasure in reading poetry, and perhaps the number of those who make this admission would be greater were it not for the fear of appearing singular. But to the great mass of mankind poetry is really a delight and a refreshment. To many, perhaps to most, it is not requisite that it should be of the highest degree of merit. Nor, although it be true that the poems which are most famous and most highly prized are works of considerable length, can it be said that the pleasure they give is in any degree proportionate to the extent of their plan. It seems to me that it is only poems of a moderate length, or else portions of the greater works to which I refer, that produce the effect upon the mind and heart which make the charm of this kind of writing. The proper office of poetry, in filling the mind with delightful images and awakening the gentler emotions, is not accomplished on a first and rapid perusal, but requires that the words should be dwelt upon until they become in a certain sense our own, and are adopted as the utterance of our own minds. A collection such as this is intended to be furnishes for this purpose portions of the best English verse suited to any of the varying moods of its readers.

Such a work also, if sufficiently extensive, gives the reader an opportunity of comparing the poetic literature of one period with that of another ; of noting the fluctuations of taste, and how the poetic forms which are in fashion during one age are laid aside in the next ; of observing the changes which take place in our language, and the sentiments which at different periods challenge the public approbation. Specimens of the poetry of different centuries presented in this way show how the great stream of human thought in its poetic form eddies now to the right and now to the left, wearing away its banks first on one side and then on the other. Some author of more than common faculties and more than common boldness catches the public attention, and immediately he has a crowd of followers who form their taste on his and seek to divide with him the praise. Thus Cowley, with his undeniable genius, was the head of a numerous class who made poetry consist in far-fetched conceits, ideas oddly brought together, and quaint turns of thought. Pope, following close upon Dryden, and learning much from him, was the founder of a school of longer duration, which found its models in Boileau and other poets of the reign of Louis the Fourteenth, —a school in which the wit predominated over the poetry,— a school marked by striking oppositions of thought, frequent happinesses of expression, and a carefully balanced modulation, — numbers pleasing at first, but in the end fatiguing. As this school degenerated the wit almost disappeared, but there was no new infusion of poetry in its place. When Scott gave the public the *Lay of the Last Minstrel,* and other poems, which certainly, considered as mere narratives, are the best we have, carrying the reader forward without weariness and with an interest which the author never allows to subside, a crowd of imitators pressed after him, the greater part of whom are no longer read. Wordsworth had, and still has, his school ; the stamp of his example is visible on the writings of all the poets of the present day.

Even Byron showed himself, in the third canto of *Childe Harold*, to be one of his disciples, though he fiercely resented being called so. The same poet did not disdain to learn of Scott in composing his narrative poems, such as the *Bride of Abydos* and the *Giaour*, though he could never tell a story in verse without occasional tediousness. In our day the style of writing adopted by eminent living poets is often seen reflected in the verses of their younger contemporaries, — sometimes with an effect like that of a face beheld in a tarnished mirror. Thus it is that poets are formed by their influence on one another; the greatest of them are more or less indebted for what they are to their predecessors and their contemporaries.

While speaking of these changes in the public taste, I am tempted to caution the reader against the mistake often made of estimating the merit of one poet by the too easy process of comparing him with another. The varieties of poetic excellence are as great as the varieties of beauty in flowers or in the female face. There is no poet, indeed no author in any department of literature, who can be taken as a standard in judging of others; the true standard is an ideal one, and even this is not the same in all men's minds. One delights in grace, another in strength; one in a fiery vehemence and enthusiasm on the surface, another in majestic repose and the expression of feeling too deep to be noisy; one loves simple and obvious images strikingly employed, or familiar thoughts placed in a new light, another is satisfied only with novelties of thought and expression, with uncommon illustrations and images far sought. It is certain that each of these modes of treating a subject may have its peculiar merit, and that it is absurd to require of those whose genius inclines them to one that they should adopt its opposite, or to set one down as inferior to another because he is not of the same class. As well, in looking through an astronomer's telescope at that beautiful phenomenon, a double star, in which the twin flames are one of a roseate and the other of a golden tint, might we quarrel with either of them because it is not colored like its fellow. Some of the comparisons made by critics between one poet and another are scarcely less preposterous than would be a comparison between a river and a mountain.

The compiler of this collection has gone as far back as to the author who may properly be called the father of English poetry, and who wrote while our language was like the lion in Milton's account of the creation, when rising from the earth at the Divine command and

> " . . . . pawing to get free
> His hinder parts," —

for it was still clogged by the unassimilated portions of the French tongue, to which in part it owed its origin. These were to be thrown aside in after years. The versification had also one characteristic of French verse which was soon after Chaucer's time laid aside, — the mute or final *e* had in his lines the value of a syllable by itself, especially when the next word began with a consonant. But though these peculiarities somewhat embarrass the reader, he still finds in the writings of the old poet a fund of the good old English of the Saxon fireside, which makes them worthy to be studied were it only to strengthen our hold on our language. He delighted in describing natural objects which still retained their Saxon names, and this he did with great beauty and sweetness.   In the sentiments also the critics ascribe to him a degree of delicacy which one could scarcely have looked for in the age in which he wrote, though at other times he avails himself of the license then allowed.   There is no majesty, no stately march of numbers, in his poetry, still less is there of fire, rapidity, or conciseness ; the French and Italian narrative poets from whom he learned his art wrote as if the people of their time had nothing to do but to attend to long stories, and Chaucer, who translated from the French the *Romaunt of the Rose*, though a greater poet than any of those whom he took for his models, made small improvement upon them in this respect.   His *Troylus and Cryseyde*, with but little action and incident, is as long as either of the epics of Homer.   The *Canterbury Tales*, Chaucer's best things, have less of this defect ; but even there the narrative is over-minute, and the personages, as Taine, the French critic, remarks, although they talk well, talk too much.   The taste for this prolixity in narratives and conversations had a long duration in English poetry, since we find the same tediousness, to call it by its true name, in Shakespeare's *Venus and Adonis* and his *Lucrece*, written more than two hundred years later.   Yet in the mean time the old popular ballads of England and Scotland had been composed, in which the incidents follow each other in quick succession, and the briefest possible speeches are uttered by the personages. The scholars and court poets doubtless disdained to learn anything of these poets of the people, and the *Davideis* of Cowley, who lived three hundred years after Chaucer, is as remarkable for the sluggish progress of the story and the tediousness of the harangues as for any other characteristics.

Between the time of Chaucer and that of Sidney and Spenser we find little in the poetic literature of our language to detain our attention.   That age produced many obscure versifiers, and metrical romances continued to be written after the fashion of the French and Italian poets, whom Chaucer acknowledged as his masters.   During this period appeared Shelton, the poet and jester, whose special talent was facility in rhyming, who rhymed as if he could not help it, — as if he had only to put pen to paper, and the words leaped of their own accord into regular measure with an inevitable jingle at the endings.   Meantime our language was undergoing a process which gradually separated the nobler parts from the dross, rejecting the French additions for which there was no occasion, or which could not easily be made to take upon themselves the familiar forms of our tongue.   The prosody of English became also fixed in that period ; the final *e* which so perplexes the modern reader in Chaucer's verse was no longer permitted to figure as a distinct syllable.   The poets, however, still allowed themselves the liberty of sometimes making, after the French manner, two syllables of the terminations *tion* and *ion*, so that *nation* became a word of three syllables and *opinion* a word of four.   The Sonnets of Sidney, written on the Italian model, have all the grace and ingenuity of those of Petrarch.   In the *Faerie Queene* of Spenser it seems to me that we find the English language, so far as the purposes of poetry require, in a degree of perfection beyond which it has not been since carried, and, I suppose, never will be.   A vast assemblage of poetic endowments contributed to the composition of the poem, yet I think it would not be easy to name one of the same length, and the work of a genius equally great, in any language, which more fatigues the reader in a steady perusal from beginning to end. In it we have an invention ever awake, active, and apparently inexhaustible; an affluence of imagery grand, beautiful, or magnificent, as the subject may require; wise observations on human life steeped in a poetic coloring, and not without touches of pathos; a wonderful mastery of versification, and the aptest forms of expression. We read at first with admiration, yet to this erelong succeeds a sense of satiety, and we lay down the book, not unwilling, however, after an interval, to take it up with renewed admiration. I once heard an eminent poet say that he thought the second part of the *Faerie Queene* inferior to the first; yet I am inclined to ascribe the remark rather to a falling off in the attention of the reader than in the merit of the work. A poet, however, would be more likely to persevere to the end than any other reader, since in every stanza he would meet with some lesson in his art.

In that fortunate age of English literature arose a greater than Spenser. Let me only say of Shakespeare, that in his dramas, amid certain faults imputable to the taste of the English public, there is to be found every conceivable kind of poetic excellence. At the same time and immediately after him flourished a group of dramatic poets who drew their inspiration from nature and wrote with manly vigor. One would naturally suppose that their example, along with the more illustrious ones of Spenser and Shakespeare, would influence and form the taste of the succeeding age; but almost before they had ceased to claim the attention of the public, and while the eminent divines, Barrow, Jeremy Taylor, and others, wrote nobly in prose with a genuine eloquence and a fervor scarcely less than poetic, appeared the school of writers in verse whom Johnson, by a phrase the propriety of which has been disputed, calls the metaphysical poets, — a class of wits whose whole aim was to extort admiration by ingenious conceits, thoughts of such unexpectedness and singularity that one wondered how they could ever come into the mind of the author. For what they regarded as poetic effect they depended, not upon the sense of beauty or grandeur, not upon depth or earnestness of feeling, but simply upon surprise at quaint and strange resemblances, contrasts, and combinations of ideas. These were delivered for the most part in rugged diction, and in numbers so harsh as to be almost unmanageable by the reader. Cowley, a man of real genius, and of a more musical versification than his fellows, was the most distinguished example of this school. Milton, born a little before Cowley, and like him an eminent poet in his teens, is almost the only instance of escape from the infection of this vicious style; his genius was of too robust a mould for such petty employments, and he would have made, if he had condescended to them, as ill a figure as his own Samson on the stage of a mountebank. Dryden himself, in some of his earlier poems, appears as a pupil of this school; but he soon outgrew — in great part, at least — the false taste of the time, and set an example of a nobler treatment of poetic subjects.

Yet though the genius of Dryden reacted against this perversion of the art of verse, it had not the power to raise the poetry of our language to the height which it occupied in the Elizabethan age. Within a limited range he was a true poet; his imagination was far from fertile, nor had he much skill in awakening emotion, but he could treat certain subjects magnificently in verse, and often where his imagination fails him he is sustained by the vigor of his understanding and the largeness of his knowledge. He gave an example of versification in the heroic couplet, which has commanded the admiration of succeeding poets down to our time, — a versification manly, majestic, and of varied modulation, of which Pope took only a certain part as the model of his own, and, contracting its range and reducing it to more regular pauses, made it at first appear more musical to the reader, but in the end fatigued him by its monotony. Dryden drew scarcely a single image from his own observation of external nature, and Pope, though less insensible than he to natural beauty, was still merely the poet of the drawing-room. Yet he is the author of more happy lines, which have passed into the common speech and are quoted as proverbial sayings, than any author we have save Shakespeare; and, whatever may be said in his dispraise, he is likely to be quoted as long as the English is a living language. The footprints of Pope are not those of a giant, but he has left them scattered all over the field of our literature, although the fashion of writing like him has wholly passed away.

Certain faculties of the poetic mind seem to have slumbered from the time of Milton to that of Thomson, who showed the literary world of Great Britain, to its astonishment, what a profusion of materials for poetry Nature offers to him who directly consults her instead of taking his images at second-hand. Thomson's blank verse, however, is often swollen and bladdery to a painful degree. He seems to have imagined, like many other writers of his time, that blank verse could not support itself without the aid of a stilted phraseology; for that fine poem of his, in the Spenserian stanza, the *Castle of Indolence*, shows that when he wrote in rhyme he did not think it necessary to depart from a natural style.

Wordsworth is generally spoken of as one who gave to our literature that impulse which brought the poets back from the capricious forms of expression in vogue before his time to a certain fearless simplicity; for it must be acknowledged that until he arose there was scarce any English poet who did not seem in some degree to labor under the apprehension of becoming too simple and natural, — to imagine that a certain pomp of words is necessary to elevate the style and make that grand and noble which in its direct expression would be homely and trivial. Yet the poetry of Wordsworth was but the consummation of a tendency already existing and active. Cowper had already felt it in writing his *Task*, and in his longer rhymed poems had not only attempted a freer versification than that of Pope, but had clothed his thoughts in the manly English of the better age of our poetry. Percy's *Reliques* had accustomed English readers to perceive the extreme beauty of the old ballads in their absolute simplicity, and shown how much superior these were to such productions as Percy's own *Hermit of Warkworth* and Goldsmith's *Edwin and Angelina*, in their feeble elegance. Burns's inimitable Scottish poems — his English verses are tumid and wordy — had taught the same lesson. We may infer that the genius of Wordsworth was in a great degree influenced by these, just as he in his turn contributed to form the taste of those who wrote after him. It was long, however, before he reached the eminence which he now holds in the estimation of the literary world. His *Lyrical Ballads*, published about the close of the last century, were at first little read, and of those who liked them there were few who were not afraid to express their admiration. Yet his fame has slowly climbed from stage to stage until now his influence is perceived in all the English poetry of the day. If this were the place to criticise his poetry, I should say, of his more stately poems in blank verse, that they often lack compression, — that the thought suffers by too great expansion. Wordsworth was unnecessarily afraid of being epigrammatic. He abhorred what is called a point as much as Dennis is said to have abhorred a pun. Yet I must own that even his most diffuse amplifications have in them a certain grandeur that fills the mind.

At a somewhat later period arose the poet Keats, who wrote in a manner which carried the reader back to the time when those charming passages of lyrical enthusiasm were produced which we occasionally find in the plays of Shakespeare, in those of Beaumont and Fletcher, and in Milton's *Comus.* The verses of Keats are occasionally disfigured, especially in his *Endymion,* by a flatness almost childish, but in the finer passages they clothe the thought in the richest imagery and in words each of which is a poem. Lowell has justly called Keats " over-languaged," but there is scarce a word that we should be willing to part with in his *Ode to the Nightingale,* and that on a *Grecian Urn,* and the same thing may be said of the greater part of his *Hyperion.* His poems were ridiculed in the Edinburgh Review, but they survived the ridicule, and now, fifty years after their first publication, the poetry of the present day, by certain resemblances of manner, testifies to the admiration with which he is still read.

The genius of Byron was of a more vigorous mould than that of Keats ; but notwithstanding his great popularity and the number of his imitators at one time, he made a less permanent impression on the character of English poetry. His misanthropy and gloom, his scoffing vein, and the fierceness of his animosities, after the first glow of admiration was over, had a repellent effect upon readers, and made them turn to more cheerful strains. Moore had in his time many imitators, but all his gayety, his brilliant fancy, his somewhat feminine graces, and the elaborate music of his numbers, have not saved him from the fate of being imitated no more. Coleridge and Southey were of the same school with Wordsworth, and only added to the effect of his example upon our literature. Coleridge is the author of the two most perfect poetical translations which our language in his day could boast, those of Schiller's *Piccolomini* and *Death of Wallenstein,* in which the English verse falls in no respect short of the original German. Southey divides with Scott the honor of writing the first long narrative poems in our language which can be read without occasional weariness.

Of the later poets, educated in part by the generation of authors which produced Wordsworth and Byron and in part by each other, yet possessing their individual peculiarities, I should perhaps speak with more reserve. The number of those who are attempting to win a name in this walk of literature is great, and several of them have already gained, and through many years held, the public favor. To some of them will be assigned an enduring station among the eminent of their class.

There are two tendencies by which the seekers after poetic fame in our day are apt to be misled, through both the example of others and the applause of critics.

One of these is the desire to extort admiration by striking novelties of expression; and the other, the ambition to distinguish themselves by subtilties of thought, remote from the common apprehension.

With regard to the first of these I have only to say what has been often said before, that, however favorable may be the idea which this luxuriance of poetic imagery and of epithet at first gives us of the author's talent, our admiration soon exhausts itself. We feel that the thought moves heavily under its load of garments, some of which perhaps strike us as tawdry and others as ill-fitting, and we lay down the book to take it up no more.

The other mistake, if I may so call it, deserves more attention, since we find able critics speaking with high praise of passages in the poetry of the day to which the general reader is puzzled to attach a meaning. This is often the case when the words themselves seem simple enough, and keep within the range of the Saxon or household element of our language. The obscurity lies sometimes in the phrase itself, and sometimes in the recondite or remote allusion. I will not say that certain minds are not affected by this, as others are by verses in plainer English. To the few it may be genuine poetry, although it may be a riddle to the mass of readers. I remember reading somewhere of a mathematician who was affected with a sense of sublimity by the happy solution of an algebraical or geometrical problem, and I have been assured by one who devoted himself to the science of mathematics that the phenomenon is no uncommon one. Let us beware, therefore, of assigning too narrow limits to the causes which produce the poetic exaltation of mind. The genius of those who write in this manner may be freely acknowledged, but they do not write for mankind at large.

To me it seems that one of the most important requisites for a great poet is a luminous style. The elements of poetry lie in natural objects, in the vicissitudes of human life, in the emotions of the human heart, and the relations of man to man. He who can present them in combinations and lights which at once affect the mind with a deep sense of their truth and beauty is the poet for his own age and the ages that succeed it. It is no disparagement either to his skill or his power that he finds them near at hand; the nearer they lie to the common track of the human intelligence, the more certain is he of the sympathy of his own generation, and of those which shall come after him. The metaphysician, the subtile thinker, the dealer in abstruse speculations, whatever his skill in versification, misapplies it when he abandons the more convenient form of prose and perplexes himself with the attempt to express his ideas in poetic numbers.

Let me say for the poets of the present day, that in one important respect they have profited by the example of their immediate predecessors; they have learned to go directly to nature for their imagery, instead of taking it from what had once been regarded as the common stock of the guild of poets. I have often had occasion to verify this remark with no less delight than surprise on meeting in recent verse new images in their untarnished lustre, like coins fresh from the mint, unworn and unsoiled by passing from pocket to pocket. It is curious, also, to observe how a certain set of hackneyed phrases, which Leigh Hunt, I believe, was the first to ridicule, and which were once used for the convenience of rounding out a line or supplying a rhyme, have disappeared from our poetry, and how our blank verse in the hands of the most popular writers has dropped its stiff Latinisms and all the awkward distortions resorted to by those who thought that by putting a sentence out of its proper shape they were writing like Milton.

I have now brought this brief survey of the progress of our poetry down to the present time, and refer the reader, for samples of it in the different stages of its existence, to those which are set before him in this volume.

WILLIAM CULLEN BRYANT.

SEPTEMBER, 1870.

The very tones in which we spake

Had something strange I could but mark;

The leaves of memory seemed to make

A mournful rustling in the dark.

Henry W. Longfellow

POEMS OF CHILDHOOD.

These struggling tides of Life that seem
  In wayward aimless course to tend
Are eddies of the mighty stream
  That rolls to its appointed end —

William Cullen Bryant.

POEMS OF CHILDHOOD.

INFANCY.

PHILIP, MY KING.

*" Who bears upon his baby brow the round
And top of sovereignty."*

Look at me with thy large brown eyes,
   Philip, my king !
For round thee the purple shadow lies
Of babyhood's royal dignities.
Lay on my neck thy tiny hand
   With Love's invisible sceptre laden ;
I am thine Esther, to command
   Till thou shalt find thy queen-handmaiden,
     Philip, my king !

O, the day when thou goest a-wooing,
   Philip, my king !
When those beautiful lips 'gin suing,
And, some gentle heart's bars undoing,
Thou dost enter, love-crowned, and there
   Sittest love-glorified ! — Rule kindly,
Tenderly over thy kingdom fair ;
   For we that love, ah ! we love so blindly,
     Philip, my king !

I gaze from thy sweet mouth up to thy brow,
   Philip, my king !
The spirit that there lies sleeping now
May rise like a giant, and make men bow
As to one Heaven-chosen amongst his peers.
   My Saul, than thy brethren higher and fairer,
Let me behold thee in future years !
   Yet thy head needeth a circlet rarer,
     Philip, my king ; —

A wreath, not of gold, but palm. One day,
   Philip, my king !
Thou too must tread, as we trod, a way
Thorny, and cruel, and cold, and gray ;
Rebels within thee and foes without
   Will snatch at thy crown. But march on,
     glorious,
Martyr, yet monarch ! till angels shout,
   As thou sitt'st at the feet of God victorious,
     " Philip, the king ! "

                DINAH MARIA MULOCK.

CRADLE SONG.

FROM " BITTER-SWEET."

What is the little one thinking about ?
Very wonderful things, no doubt ;
   Unwritten history !
   Unfathomed mystery !
Yet he chuckles, and crows, and nods, and winks,
As if his head were as full of kinks
And curious riddles as any sphinx !
   Warped by colic, and wet by tears,
   Punctured by pins, and tortured by fears,
   Our little nephew will lose two years ;
     And he 'll never know
     Where the summers go ;
He need not laugh, for he 'll find it so.

Who can tell what a baby thinks ?
Who can follow the gossamer links
   By which the manikin feels his way
Out from the shore of the great unknown,
Blind, and wailing, and alone,
   Into the light of day ?
Out from the shore of the unknown sea,
Tossing in pitiful agony ;
Of the unknown sea that reels and rolls,
Specked with the barks of little souls, —
Barks that were launched on the other side,
And slipped from heaven on an ebbing tide !
   What does he think of his mother's eyes ?
   What does he think of his mother's hair ?
   What of the cradle-roof, that flies
Forward and backward through the air ?
   What does he think of his mother's breast,
Bare and beautiful, smooth and white,
Seeking it ever with fresh delight,
   Cup of his life, and couch of his rest ?
What does he think when her quick embrace
Presses his hand and buries his face
Deep where the heart-throbs sink and swell,
With a tenderness she can never tell,
   Though she murmur the words
   Of all the birds, —
Words she has learned to murmur well ?
   Now he thinks he 'll go to sleep !
   I can see the shadow creep

Over his eyes in soft eclipse,
Over his brow and over his lips,
Out to his little finger-tips !
Softly sinking, down he goes !
Down he goes ! down he goes !
See ! he 's hushed in sweet repose.

JOSIAH GILBERT HOLLAND.

CHOOSING A NAME.

I HAVE got a new-born sister ;
I was nigh the first that kissed her.
When the nursing-woman brought her
To papa, his infant daughter,
How papa's dear eyes did glisten ! —
She will shortly be to christen ;
And papa has made the offer,
I shall have the naming of her.

Now I wonder what would please her, —
Charlotte, Julia, or Louisa ?
Ann and Mary, they 're too common ;
Joan 's too formal for a woman ;
Jane 's a prettier name beside ;
But we had a Jane that died.
They would say, if 't was Rebecca,
That she was a little Quaker.
Edith 's pretty, but that looks
Better in old English books ;
Ellen 's left off long ago ;
Blanche is out of fashion now.
None that I have named as yet
Are so good as Margaret.
Emily is neat and fine ;
What do you think of Caroline ?
How I 'm puzzled and perplexed
What to choose or think of next !
I am in a little fever
Lest the name that I should give her
Should disgrace her or defame her ; —
I will leave papa to name her.

MARY LAMB.

BABY MAY.

CHEEKS as soft as July peaches ;
Lips whose dewy scarlet teaches
Poppies paleness ; round large eyes
Ever great with new surprise ;
Minutes filled with shadeless gladness ;
Minutes just as brimmed with sadness ;
Happy smiles and wailing cries ;
Crows, and laughs, and tearful eyes ;
Lights and shadows, swifter born
Than on wind-swept autumn corn ;
Ever some new tiny notion,

Making every limb all motion ;
Catchings up of legs and arms ;
Throwings back and small alarms ;
Clutching fingers ; straightening jerks ;
Twining feet whose each toe works ;
Kickings up and straining risings ;
Mother's ever new surprisings ;
Hands all wants and looks all wonder
At all things the heavens under ;
Tiny scorns of smiled reprovings
That have more of love than lovings ;
Mischiefs done with such a winning
Archness that we prize such sinning ;
Breakings dire of plates and glasses ;
Graspings small at all that passes ;
Pullings off of all that 's able
To be caught from tray or table ;
Silences, — small meditations
Deep as thoughts of cares for nations ;
Breaking into wisest speeches
In a tongue that nothing teaches ;
All the thoughts of whose possessing .
Must be wooed to light by guessing ;
Slumbers, — such sweet angel-seemings
That we 'd ever have such dreamings ;
Till from sleep we see thee breaking,
And we d always have thee waking ;
Wealth for which we know no measure ;
Pleasure high above all pleasure ;
Gladness brimming over gladness ;
Joy in care ; delight in sadness ;
Loveliness beyond completeness ;
Sweetness distancing all sweetness ;.
Beauty all that beauty may be ; —
That 's May Bennett ; that 's my baby.

WILLIAM C. BENNETT.

BABY BYE.

BABY Bye,
Here 's a fly ;
Let us watch him, you and I.
      How he crawls
      Up the walls,
      Yet he never falls !
I believe with six such legs ·
You and I could walk on eggs.
      There he goes
      On his toes,
      Tickling Baby's nose.

Spots of red
Dot his head ;
Rainbows on his back are spread ;
      That small speck
      Is his neck ;
      See him nod and beck.

I can show you, if you choose,
Where to look to find his shoes, —
 Three small pairs,
 Made of hairs ;
 These he always wears.

Black and brown
Is his gown ;
He can wear it upside down ;
 It is laced
 Round his waist ;
 I admire his taste.
Yet though tight his clothes are made,
He will lose them, I 'm afraid,
 If to-night
 He gets sight
 Of the candle-light.

In the sun
Webs are spun ;
What if he gets into one ?
 When it rains
 He complains
 On the window-panes.
Tongue to talk have you and I ;
God has given the little fly
 No such things,
 So he sings
 With his buzzing wings.

He can eat
Bread and meat ;
There 's his mouth between his feet.
 On his back
 Is a pack
 Like a pedler's sack.
Does the baby understand ?
Then the fly shall kiss her hand ;
 Put a crumb
 On her thumb,
 Maybe he will come.

Catch him ? No,
Let him go,
Never hurt an insect so ;
 But no doubt
 He flies out
 Just to gad about.
Now you see his wings of silk
Drabbled in the baby's milk ;
 Fie, O fie,
 Foolish fly !
 How will he get dry ?

All wet flies
Twist their thighs ;
Thus they wipe their heads and eyes ;
 Cats, you know,
 Wash just so,
 Then their whiskers grow.

Flies have hairs too short to comb,
So they fly bareheaded home ;
 But the gnat
 Wears a hat.
 Do you believe that ?

Flies can see
More than we,
So how bright their eyes must be !
 Little fly,
 Ope your eye ;
 Spiders are near by.
For a secret I can tell, —
Spiders never use flies well.
 Then away
 Do not stay.
 Little fly, good day.
    THEODORE TILTON.

WILLIE WINKIE.

WEE Willie Winkie rins through the town,
Up stairs and doon stairs, in his nicht-gown,
Tirlin' at the window, cryin' at the lock,
"Are the weans in their bed ? — for it 's now ten
 o'clock."

Hey, Willie Winkie ! are ye comin' ben ?
The cat 's singin' gay thrums to the sleepin'
 hen,
The doug 's speldered on the floor, and disna gie
 a cheep ;
But here 's a waukrife laddie, that winna fa'
 asleep.

Ony thing but sleep, ye rogue : — glow'rin' like
 the moon,
Rattlin' in an airn jug wi' an airn spoon,
Rumblin', tumblin' roun' about, crawin' like a
 cock,
Skirlin' like a kenna-what — wauknin' sleepin'
 folk !

Hey, Willie Winkie ! the wean 's in a creel !
Waumblin' aff a bodie's knee like a vera eel,
Ruggin' at the cat's lug, and ravellin' a' her
 thrums :
Hey, Willie Winkie ! — See, there he comes !

Wearie is the mither that has a storie wean,
A wee stumpie stoussie, that canna rin his
 lane,
That has a battle aye wi' sleep, before he 'll close
 an ee ;
But a kiss frae aff his rosy lips gies strength
 anew to me.
    WILLIAM MILLER.

LITTLE PUSS.

SLEEK coat, eyes of fire,
Four paws that never tire,
　　　That 's puss.

Ways playful, tail on high,
Twisting often toward the sky,
　　　That 's puss.

In the larder, stealing meat,
Patter, patter, little feet,
　　　That 's puss.

After ball, reel, or string,
Wild as any living thing,
　　　That 's puss.

Round and round, after tail,
Fast as any postal mail,
　　　That 's puss.

Curled up, like a ball,
On the door-mat in the hall,
　　　That 's puss.

Purring loud on missis' lap,
Having toast, then a nap,
　　　That 's puss.

Black as night, with talons long,
Scratching, which is very wrong,
　　　That 's puss.

From a saucer lapping milk,
Soft, as soft as washing silk,
　　　That 's puss.

Rolling on the dewy grass,
Getting wet, all in a mass,
　　　That 's puss.

Climbing tree, and catching bird,
Little twitter nevermore heard,
　　　That 's puss.

Killing fly, rat, or mouse,
As it runs about the house,
　　　That 's puss.

Pet of missis, "Itte mite,"
Never must be out of sight,
　　　That 's puss.
　　　　　　　　ANONYMOUS.

NURSE'S WATCH.

[From the "Boy's Horn of Wonders," a German Book of Nursery
Rhymes.]

THE moon it shines,
　My darling whines;
The clock strikes twelve : — God cheer
The sick, both far and near.

God knoweth all ;
　Mousy nibbles in the wall ;
The clock strikes one : — like day,
Dreams o'er thy pillow play.

　The matin-bell
　Wakes the nun in convent cell ;
The clock strikes two : — they go
To choir in a row.

　The wind it blows,
　The cock he crows ;
The clock strikes three : — the wagoner
In his straw bed begins to stir.

　The steed he paws the floor,
　Creaks the stable-door ;
The clock strikes four : — 't is plain,
The coachman sifts his grain.

　The swallow's laugh the still air shakes,
　The sun awakes ;
The clock strikes five : — the traveller must be
　　　gone,
He puts his stockings on.

　The hen is clacking,
　The ducks are quacking ;
The clock strikes six : — awake, arise,
Thou lazy hag ; come, ope thy eyes.

　Quick to the baker's run ;
　The rolls are done ;
The clock strikes seven : —
'T is time the milk were in the oven.

　Put in some butter, do,
　And some fine sugar too ;
The clock strikes eight : —
Now bring my baby's porridge straight.
　　　　　TRANSLATION OF CHARLES T. BROOKS.

BABY LOUISE.

I 'M in love with you, Baby Louise !
With your silken hair, and your soft blue eyes,
And the dreamy wisdom that in them lies,
And the faint, sweet smile you brought from the
　　　skies, —
God's sunshine, Baby Louise.

When you fold your hands, Baby Louise,
Your hands, like a fairy's, so tiny and fair,
With a pretty, innocent, saint-like air,
Are you trying to think of some angel-taught
　　　prayer
You learned above, Baby Louise ?

I'm in love with you, Baby Louise! —
Why! you never raise your beautiful head!
Some day, little one, your cheek will grow red
With a flush of delight, to hear the words said,
  "I love you," Baby Louise.

Do you hear me, Baby Louise?
I have sung your praises for nearly an hour,
And your lashes keep drooping lower and lower,
And — you've gone to sleep, like a weary flower,
  Ungrateful Baby Louise!
                                        M. E.

LULLABY.

FROM "THE PRINCESS."

SWEET and low, sweet and low,
  Wind of the western sea,
Low, low, breathe and blow,
  Wind of the western sea!
Over the rolling waters go,
Come from the dying moon, and blow,
  Blow him again to me;
While my little one, while my pretty one, sleeps.

Sleep and rest, sleep and rest,
  Father will come to thee soon;
Rest, rest, on mother's breast,
  Father will come to thee soon;
Father will come to his babe in the nest,
Silver sails all out of the west
  Under the silver moon:
Sleep, my little one, sleep, my pretty one, sleep.
                          ALFRED TENNYSON.

THE ANGEL'S WHISPER.

In Ireland they have a pretty fancy, that, when a child smiles in
its sleep, it is "talking with angels."

A BABY was sleeping;
  Its mother was weeping;
For her husband was far on the wild raging sea;
  And the tempest was swelling
  Round the fisherman's dwelling;
And she cried, "Dermot, darling, O come back
    to me!"

Her beads while she numbered,
  The baby still slumbered,
And smiled in her face as she bended her knee:
  "O, blest be that warning,
  My child, thy sleep adorning,
For I know that the angels are whispering with
    thee.

"And while they are keeping
  Bright watch o'er thy sleeping,

O, pray to them softly, my baby, with me!
  And say thou wouldst rather
  They'd watch o'er thy father!
For I know that the angels are whispering to
    thee."

  The dawn of the morning
  Saw Dermot returning,
And the wife wept with joy her babe's father to see;
  And closely caressing
  Her child with a blessing,
Said, "I knew that the angels were whispering
    with thee."
                              SAMUEL LOVER.

TO CHARLOTTE PULTENEY.

TIMELY blossom, Infant fair,
Fondling of a happy pair,
Every morn and every night
Their solicitous delight,
Sleeping, waking, still at ease,
Pleasing, without skill to please;
Little gossip, blithe and hale,
Tattling many a broken tale,
Singing many a tuneless song,
Lavish of a heedless tongue;
Simple maiden, void of art,
Babbling out the very heart,
Yet abandoned to thy will,
Yet imagining no ill,
Yet too innocent to blush;
Like the linnet in the bush
To the mother-linnet's note
Moduling her slender throat;
Chirping forth thy petty joys,
Wanton in the change of toys,
Like the linnet green, in May
Flitting to each bloomy spray;
Wearied then and glad of rest,
Like the linnet in the nest;—
This thy present happy lot,
This in time will be forgot:
Other pleasures, other cares,
Ever busy Time prepares;
And thou shalt in thy daughter see,
This picture, once, resembled thee.
                              AMBROSE PHILIPS.

TO MY INFANT SON.

THOU happy, happy elf!
(But stop, first let me kiss away that tear,)
  Thou tiny image of myself!
(My love, he's poking peas into his ear,)
Thou merry, laughing sprite,
With spirits, feather light,

Untouched by sorrow, and unsoiled by sin ;
(My dear, the child is swallowing a pin !)

Thou little tricksy Puck !
With antic toys so funnily bestuck,
Light as the singing bird that rings the air, —
(The door ! the door ! he 'll tumble down the
    stair !)
Thou darling of thy sire !
(Why, Jane, he 'll set his pinafore afire !)
    Thou imp of mirth and joy !
In love's dear chain so bright a link,
    Thou idol of thy parents ; — (Drat the boy !
There goes my ink.)

    Thou cherub, but of earth ;
Fit playfellow for fairies, by moonlight pale,
    In harmless sport and mirth,
(That dog will bite him, if he pulls his tail !)
    Thou human humming-bee, extracting honey
From every blossom in the world that blows,
    Singing in youth's Elysium ever sunny, —
(Another tumble ! That 's his precious nose !)
Thy father's pride and hope !
(He 'll break that mirror with that skipping-
    rope !)
With pure heart newly stamped from nature's
    mint,
(Where did he learn that squint ?)

Thou young domestic dove !
(He 'll have that ring off with another shove,)
Dear nursling of the hymeneal nest !
(Are these torn clothes his best ?)
Little epitome of man !
(He 'll climb upon the table, that 's his plan,)
Touched with the beauteous tints of dawning
    life,
(He 's got a knife !)
Thou enviable being !
No storms, no clouds, in thy blue sky foreseeing,
    Play on, play on,
My elfin John !
Toss the light ball, bestride the stick, —
(I knew so many cakes would make him sick !)
    With fancies buoyant as the thistle-down,
Prompting the face grotesque, and antic brisk,
With many a lamb-like frisk !
    (He 's got the scissors, snipping at your gown !)
Thou pretty opening rose !
(Go to your mother, child, and wipe your
    nose !)
Balmy and breathing music like the south,
(He really brings my heart into my mouth !)
Bold as the hawk, yet gentle as the dove ;
(I 'll tell you what, my love,
I cannot write unless he 's sent above.)
                                    THOMAS HOOD.

THE LOST HEIR.

"*O where, and O where*
Is my bonnie laddie gone ?"—OLD SONG.

ONE day, as I was going by
That part of Holborn christened High,
I heard a loud and sudden cry
    That chilled my very blood ;
And lo ! from out a dirty alley,
Where pigs and Irish wont to rally,
I saw a crazy woman sally,
    Bedaubed with grease and mud.
She turned her East, she turned her West,
Staring like Pythoness possest,
With streaming hair and heaving breast,
    As one stark mad with grief.

"O Lord ! O dear, my heart will break, I shall
    go stick stark staring wild !
Has ever a one seen anything about the streets
    like a crying lost-looking child ?
Lawk help me, I don't know where to look, or to
    run, if I only knew which way —
A Child as is lost about London streets, and es-
    pecially Seven Dials, is a needle in a
    bottle of hay.
I am all in a quiver — get out of my sight, do,
    you wretch, you little Kitty M'Nab !
You promised to have half an eye to him, you
    know you did, you dirty deceitful young
    drab.
The last time as ever I see him, poor thing, was
    with my own blessed Motherly eyes,
Sitting as good as gold in the gutter, a playing
    at making little dirt-pies.
I wonder he left the court, where he was better
    off than all the other young boys,
With two bricks, an old shoe, nine oyster-shells,
    and a dead kitten by way of toys.
When his Father comes home, and he always
    comes home as sure as ever the clock
    strikes one,
He 'll be rampant, he will, at his child being
    lost ; and the beef and the inguns not
    done !
La bless you, good folks, mind your own con-
    carns, and don't be making a mob in the
    street ;
O Sergeant M'Farlane ! you have not come across
    my poor little boy, have you, in your
    beat ?
Do, good people, move on ! don't stand staring
    at me like a parcel of stupid stuck pigs ;
Saints forbid ! but he 's p'r'aps been inviggled
    away up a court for the sake of his clothes
    by the priggs ;
He 'd a very good jacket, for certain, for I bought
    it myself for a shilling one day in Rag
    Fair ;

And his trousers considering not very much patched, and red plush, they was once his Father's best pair.

His shirt, it's very lucky I'd got washing in the tub, or that might have gone with the rest;

But he'd got on a very good pinafore with only two slits and a burn on the breast.

He'd a goodish sort of hat, if the crown was sewed in, and not quite so much jagged at the brim.

With one shoe on, and the other shoe is a boot, and not a fit, and you'll know by that if it's him.

And then he has got such dear winning ways — but O, I never, never shall see him no more!

O dear! to think of losing him just after nussing him back from death's door!

Only the very last month when the windfalls, hang 'em, was at twenty a penny!

And the threepence he'd got by grottoing was spent' in plums, and sixty for a child is too many.

And the Cholera man came and whitewashed us all, and, drat him! made a seize of our hog. —

It's no use to send the Crier to cry him about, he's such a blunderin' drunken old dog;

The last time he was fetched to find a lost child he was guzzling with his bell at the Crown,

And went and cried a boy instead of a girl, for a distracted Mother and Father about Town.

Billy — where are you, Billy, I say? come, Billy, come home, to your best of Mothers!

I'm scared when I think of them Cabroleys, they drive so, they'd run over their own Sisters and Brothers.

Or maybe he's stole by some chimbly-sweeping wretch, to stick fast in narrow flues and what not,

And be poked up behind with a picked pointed pole, when the soot has ketched, and the chimbly's red hot.

O, I'd give the whole wide world, if the world was mine, to clap my two longin' eyes on his face.

For he's my darlin' of darlin's, and if he don't soon come back, you'll see me drop stone dead on the place.

I only wish I'd got him safe in these two Motherly arms, and wouldn't I hug him and kiss him!

Lawk! I never knew what a precious he was — but a child don't not feel like a child till you miss him.

Why, there he is! Punch and Judy hunting, the young wretch, it's that Billy as sartin as sin!

But let me get him home, with a good grip of his hair, and I'm blest if he shall have a whole bone in his skin!

THOMAS HOOD.

LITTLE RED RIDING HOOD.

COME back, come back together,
  All ye fancies of the past,
Ye days of April weather,
  Ye shadows that are cast
    By the haunted hours before!
Come back, come back, my Childhood;
  Thou art summoned by a spell
From the green leaves of the wildwood,
  From beside the charmèd well,
For Red Riding Hood, the darling,
  The flower of fairy lore!

The fields were covered over
  With colors as she went;
Daisy, buttercup, and clover
  Below her footsteps bent;
    Summer shed its shining store;
She was happy as she pressed them
  Beneath her little feet;
She plucked them and caressed them;
  They were so very sweet,
  They had never seemed so sweet before,
To Red Riding Hood, the darling,
  The flower of fairy lore.

How the heart of childhood dances
  Upon a sunny day!
It has its own romances,
  And a wide, wide world have they!
    A world where Phantasie is king,
Made all of eager dreaming;
  When once grown up and tall —
Now is the time for scheming —
  Then we shall do them all!
    Do such pleasant fancies spring
For Red Riding Hood, the darling,
  The flower of fairy lore?

She seems like an ideal love,
  The poetry of childhood shown,
And yet loved with a real love,
  As if she were our own, —
    A younger sister for the heart;
Like the woodland pheasant,
  Her hair is brown and bright;
And her smile is pleasant,
  With its rosy light.
Never can the memory part

With Red Riding Hood, the darling,
  The flower of fairy lore.

Did the painter, dreaming
  In a morning hour,
Catch the fairy seeming
  Of this fairy flower?
    Winning it with eager eyes
From the old enchanted stories,
  Lingering with a long delight
On the unforgotten glories
  Of the infant sight?
    Giving us a sweet surprise
In Red Riding Hood, the darling,
  The flower of fairy lore?

Too long in the meadow staying,
  Where the cowslip bends,
With the buttercups delaying
  As with early friends,
    Did the little maiden stay.
Sorrowful the tale for us;
  We, too, loiter mid life's flowers,
A little while so glorious,
  So soon lost in darker hours.
    All love lingering on their way,
Like Red Riding Hood, the darling,
  The flower of fairy lore.
          LÆTITIA ELIZABETH LANDON.

THE CHILDREN IN THE WOOD.

Now ponder well, you parents dear,
  The words which I shall write;
A doleful story you shall hear,
  In time brought forth to light:
A gentleman, of good account,
  In Norfolk lived of late,
Whose wealth and riches did surmount
  Most men of his estate.

Sore sick he was, and like to die,
  No help then he could have;
His wife by him as sick did lie,
  And both possessed one grave.
No love between these two was lost,
  Each was to other kind;
In love they lived, in love they died,
  And left two babes behind:

The one a fine and pretty boy,
  Not passing three years old;
The other a girl, more young than he,
  And made in beauty's mould.
The father left his little son,
  As plainly doth appear,
When he to perfect age should come,
  Three hundred pounds a year, —

And to his little daughter Jane
  Five hundred pounds in gold,
To be paid down on marriage-day,
  Which might not be controlled;
But if the children chanced to die
  Ere they to age should come,
Their uncle should possess their wealth,
  For so the will did run.

"Now, brother," said the dying man,
  "Look to my children dear;
Be good unto my boy and girl,
  No friends else I have here."
With that bespake their mother dear,
  "O brother kind," quoth she,
"You are the man must bring our babes
  To wealth or misery.

"And if you keep them carefully,
  Then God will you reward;
If otherwise you seem to deal,
  God will your deeds regard."
With lips as cold as any stone
  She kissed her children small:
"God bless you both, my children dear,"
  With that the tears did fall.

Their parents being dead and gone,
  The children home he takes,
And brings them home unto his house,
  And much of them he makes.
He had not kept these pretty babes
  A twelvemonth and a day,
But, for their wealth, he did devise
  To make them both away.

He bargained with two ruffians strong,
  Which were of furious mood,
That they should take these children young,
  And slay them in a wood.
He told his wife, and all he had
  He did the children send
To be brought up in fair London,
  With one that was his friend.

Away then went these pretty babes,
  Rejoicing at that tide,
Rejoicing with a merry mind,
  They should on cock-horse ride;
They prate and prattle pleasantly,
  As they rode on the way,
To those that should their butchers be,
  And work their lives' decay,

So that the pretty speech they had
  Made Murder's heart relent;
And they that undertook the deed
  Full sore they did repent.

Yet one of them, more hard of heart,
  Did vow to do his charge,
Because the wretch that hired him
  Had paid him very large.

The other would not agree thereto,
  So here they fell at strife ;
With one another they did fight,
  About the children's life ;
And he that was of mildest mood
  Did slay the other there,
Within an unfrequented wood ;
  While babes did quake for fear.

He took the children by the hand
  When tears stood in their eye,
And bade them come and go with him,
  And look they did not cry ;
And two long miles he led them on,
  While they for food complain :
"Stay here," quoth he, "I'll bring you bread
  When I do come again."

These pretty babes, with hand in hand,
  Went wandering up and down,
But nevermore they saw the man
  Approaching from the town.
Their pretty lips with blackberries
  Were all besmeared and dyed,
And when they saw the darksome night
  They sate them down and cried.

Thus wandered these two pretty babes
  Till death did end their grief ;
In one another's arms they died,
  As babes wanting relief.
No burial this pretty pair
  Of any man receives,
Till robin redbreast, painfully,
  Did cover them with leaves.

And now the heavy wrath of God
  Upon their uncle fell ;
Yea, fearful fiends did haunt his house,
  His conscience felt an hell.
His barns were fired, his goods consumed,
  His lands were barren made ;
His cattle died within the field,
  And nothing with him stayed.

And, in the voyage of Portugal,
  Two of his sons did die ;
And, to conclude, himself was brought
  To extreme misery.
He pawned and mortgaged all his land
  Ere seven years came about ;
And now, at length, this wicked act
  Did by this means come out :

The fellow that did take in hand
  These children for to kill
Was for a robber judged to die,
  As was God's blessed will ;
Who did confess the very truth,
  The which is here expressed ;
Their uncle died while he, for debt,
  In prison long did rest.

You that executors be made,
  And overseers eke,
Of children that be fatherless,
  And infants mild and meek,
Take you example by this thing,
  And yield to each his right,
Lest God with such-like misery
  Your wicked minds requite.
                              ANONYMOUS.

A MOTHER'S LOVE.

A LITTLE in the doorway sitting,
The mother plied her busy knitting ;
And her cheek so softly smiled,
You might be sure, although her gaze
Was on the meshes of the lace,
Yet her thoughts were with her child.

But when the boy had heard her voice,
As o'er her work she did rejoice,
His became silent altogether ;
And slyly creeping by the wall,
He seized a single plume, let fall
By some wild bird of longest feather ;
And, all a-tremble with his freak,
He touched her lightly on the cheek.

O, what a loveliness her eyes
Gather in that one moment's space,
While peeping round the post she spies
Her darling's laughing face !
O, mother's love is glorifying,
On the cheek like sunset lying ;
In the eyes a moistened light,
Softer than the moon at night !
                         THOMAS BURBIDGE.

THE GAMBOLS OF CHILDREN.

Down the dimpled greensward dancing
  Bursts a flaxen-headed bevy, —
Bud-lipt boys and girls advancing,
  Love's irregular little levy.

Rows of liquid eyes in laughter,
  How they glimmer, how they quiver !
Sparkling one another after,
  Like bright ripples on a river.

Tipsy band of rubious faces,
　　Flushed with Joy's ethereal spirit,
Make your mocks and sly grimaces
　　At Love's self, and do not fear it.
　　　　　　　　　　GEORGE DARLEY.

UNDER MY WINDOW.

UNDER my window, under my window,
　　All in the Midsummer weather,
Three little girls with fluttering curls
　　Flit to and fro together : —
There's Bell with her bonnet of satin sheen,
And Maud with her mantle of silver-green,
　　And Kate with her scarlet feather.

Under my window, under my window,
　　Leaning stealthily over,
Merry and clear, the voice I hear,
　　Of each glad-hearted rover.
Ah ! sly little Kate, she steals my roses ;
And Maud and Bell twine wreaths and posies,
　　As merry as bees in clover.

Under my window, under my window,
　　In the blue Midsummer weather,
Stealing slow, on a hushed tiptoe,
　　I catch them all together : —
Bell with her bonnet of satin sheen,
And Maud with her mantle of silver-green,
　　And Kate with the scarlet feather.

Under my window, under my window,
　　And off through the orchard closes ;
While Maud she flouts, and Bell she pouts,
　　They scamper and drop their posies ;
But dear little Kate takes naught amiss,
And leaps in my arms with a loving kiss,
　　And I give her all my roses.
　　　　　　　　　　THOMAS WESTWOOD.

THE MOTHER'S HEART.

WHEN first thou camest, gentle, shy, and fond,
　　My eldest born, first hope, and dearest treasure,
My heart received thee with a joy beyond
　　All that it yet had felt of earthly pleasure ;
Nor thought that any love again might be
So deep and strong as that I felt for thee.

Faithful and true, with sense beyond thy years,
　　And natural piety that leaned to heaven ;
Wrung by a harsh word suddenly to tears,
　　Yet patient to rebuke when justly given ;
Obedient, easy to be reconciled,
And meekly cheerful ; such wert thou, my
　　child !

Not willing to be left — still by my side,
　　Haunting my walks, while summer-day was
　　　dying ;
Nor leaving in thy turn, but pleased to glide
　　Through the dark room where I was sadly
　　　lying ;
Or by the couch of pain, a sitter meek,
Watch the dim eye, and kiss the fevered cheek.

O boy ! of such as thou are oftenest made
　　Earth's fragile idols ; like a tender flower,
No strength in all thy freshness, prone to fade,
　　And bending weakly to the thunder-shower ;
Still, round the loved, thy heart found force to
　　bind,
And clung, like woodbine shaken in the wind !

Then THOU, my merry love, — bold in thy glee,
　　Under the bough, or by the firelight dancing,
With thy sweet temper, and thy spirit free, —
　　Didst come, as restless as a bird's wing glan-
　　　cing,
Full of a wild and irrepressible mirth,
Like a young sunbeam to the gladdened earth !

Thine was the shout, the song, the burst of joy,
　　Which sweet from childhood's rosy lip re-
　　　soundeth ;
Thine was the eager spirit naught could cloy,
　　And the glad heart from which all grief re-
　　　boundeth ;
And many a mirthful jest and mock reply
Lurked in the laughter of thy dark-blue eye.

And thine was many an art to win and bless,
　　The cold and stern to joy and fondness warm-
　　　ing ;
The coaxing smile, the frequent soft caress,
　　The earnest, tearful prayer all wrath disarm-
　　　ing !
Again my heart a new affection found,
But thought that love with thee had reached its
　　bound.

At length THOU camest, — thou, the last and
　　least,
　　Nicknamed "the Emperor" by thy laughing
　　　brothers,
Because a haughty spirit swelled thy breast,
　　And thou didst seek to rule and sway the
　　　others,
Mingling with every playful infant wile
A mimic majesty that made us smile.

And O, most like a regal child wert thou !
　　An eye of resolute and successful scheming !
Fair shoulders, curling lips, and dauntless brow,
　　Fit for the world's strife, not for poet's dream-
　　　ing ;

And proud the lifting of thy stately head,
And the firm bearing of thy conscious tread.

Different from both ! yet each succeeding claim
I, that all other love had been forswearing,
Forthwith admitted, equal and the same ;
  Nor injured either by this love's comparing,
Nor stole a fraction for the newer call, —
But in the mother's heart found room for all !
                        CAROLINE E. NORTON.

THE MOTHER'S HOPE.

Is there, when the winds are singing
  In the happy summer time, —
When the raptured air is ringing
  With Earth's music heavenward springing,
  Forest chirp, and village chime, —
Is there, of the sounds that float
Unsighingly, a single note
Half so sweet, and clear, and wild,
As the laughter of a child ?

Listen ! and be now delighted :
  Morn hath touched her golden strings ;
Earth and Sky their vows have plighted ;
Life and Light are reunited
  Amid countless carollings ;
Yet, delicious as they are,
There 's a sound that 's sweeter far, —
One that makes the heart rejoice
More than all, — the human voice !

Organ finer, deeper, clearer,
  Though it be a stranger's tone, —
Than the winds or waters dearer,
More enchanting to the hearer,
  For it answereth to his own.
But, of all its witching words,
Those are sweetest, bubbling wild
Through the laughter of a child.

Harmonies from time-touched towers,
  Haunted strains from rivulets,
Hum of bees among the flowers,
Rustling leaves, and silver showers, —
  These, erelong, the ear forgets ;
But in mine there is a sound
Ringing on the whole year round, —
Heart-deep laughter that I heard
Ere my child could speak a word.

Ah ! 't was heard by ear far purer,
  Fondlier formed to catch the strain, —
Ear of one whose love is surer, —
Hers, the mother, the endurer
  Of the deepest share of pain ;

Hers the deepest bliss to treasure
Memories of that cry of pleasure ;
Hers to hoard, a lifetime after,
Echoes of that infant laughter.

'T is a mother's large affection
  Hears with a mysterious sense, —
Breathings that evade detection,
Whisper faint, and fine inflection,
  Thrill in her with power intense.
Childhood's honeyed words untaught
Hiveth she in loving thought, —
Tones that never thence depart ;
For she listens — with her heart.
                        LAMAN BLANCHARD.

THE MOTHER'S STRATAGEM.

AN INFANT PLAYING NEAR A PRECIPICE.

WHILE on the cliff with calm delight she kneels,
  And the blue vales a thousand joys recall,
See, to the last, last verge her infant steals !
  O, fly — yet stir not, speak not, lest it fall. —
Far better taught, she lays her bosom bare,
And the fond boy springs back to nestle there.
        LEONIDAS of Alexandria (Greek).   Translation
                        of SAMUEL ROGERS.

THE PET LAMB.

THE dew was falling fast, the stars began to blink ;
I heard a voice ; it said, "Drink, pretty creature,
    drink ! "
And, looking o'er the hedge, before me I espied
A snow-white mountain-lamb with a maiden at
    its side.

Nor sheep nor kine were near ; the lamb was
    all alone,
And by a slender cord was tethered to a stone ;
With one knee on the grass did the little
    maiden kneel,
While to that mountain-lamb she gave its
    evening meal.

The lamb, while from her hand he thus his
    supper took,
Seemed to feast with head and ears ; and his
    tail with pleasure shook.
"Drink, pretty creature, drink ! " she said, in
    such a tone
That I almost received her heart into my own.

'T was little Barbara Lewthwaite, a child of
    beauty rare !
I watched them with delight : they were a
    lovely pair.

Now with her empty can the maiden turned away;
But ere ten yards were gone, her footsteps did
    she stay.

Right towards the lamb she looked; and from a
    shady place
I unobserved could see the workings of her face.
If nature to her tongue could measured numbers
    bring,
Thus, thought I, to her lamb that little maid
    might sing: —

"What ails thee, young one? — what? Why
    pull so at thy cord?
Is it not well with thee? — well both for bed and
    board?
Thy plot of grass is soft, and green as grass can be;
Rest, little young one, rest; what is 't that
    aileth thee?

"Thou know'st that twice a day I have brought
    thee in this can
Fresh water from the brook, as clear as ever ran;
And twice in the day, when the ground is wet
    with dew,
I bring thee draughts of milk, — warm milk it
    is, and new.

"Thy limbs will shortly be twice as stout as
    they are now;
Then I'll yoke thee to my cart like a pony in
    the plough.
My playmate thou shalt be; and when the wind
    is cold,
Our hearth shall be thy bed, our house shall be
    thy fold.

"Here thou need'st not dread the raven in the
    sky;
Night and day thou art safe, — our cottage is
    hard by.
Why bleat so after me? Why pull so at thy chain?
Sleep, and at break of day I will come to thee
    again!"

As homeward through the lane I went with lazy
    feet,
This song to myself did I oftentimes repeat;
And it seemed, as I retraced the ballad line by
    line,
That but half of it was hers, and one half of it
    was mine.

Again, and once again, did I repeat the song;
"Nay," said I, "more than half to the damsel
    must belong,
For she looked with such a look, and she spake
    with such a tone,
That I almost received her heart into my own."
          WILLIAM WORDSWORTH.

SEVEN TIMES ONE.

THERE's no dew left on the daisies and clover,
  There's no rain left in heaven.
I've said my "seven times" over and over, —
  Seven times one are seven.

I am old, — so old I can write a letter;
  My birthday lessons are done.
The lambs play always, — they know no better;
  They are only one times one.

O Moon! in the night I have seen you sailing
  And shining so round and low.
You were bright — ah, bright — but your light
    is failing;
  You are nothing now but a bow.

You Moon! have you done something wrong in
    heaven,
  That God has hidden your face?
I hope, if you have, you will soon be forgiven,
  And shine again in your place.

O velvet Bee! you're a dusty fellow, —
  You've powdered your legs with gold.
O brave marsh Mary-buds, rich and yellow,
  Give me your money to hold!

O Columbine! open your folded wrapper,
  Where two twin turtle-doves dwell!
O Cuckoo-pint! toll me the purple clapper
  That hangs in your clear green bell!

And show me your nest, with the young ones in
    it, —
  I will not steal them away:
I am old! you may trust me, linnet, linnet!
  I am seven times one to-day.
          JEAN INGELOW.

WE ARE SEVEN.

A SIMPLE child,
  That lightly draws its breath,
And feels its life in every limb,
  What should it know of death?

I met a little cottage girl:
  She was eight years old, she said;
Her hair was thick with many a curl
  That clustered round her head.

She had a rustic, woodland air,
  And she was wildly clad;
Her eyes were fair, and very fair; —
  Her beauty made me glad.

"Sisters and brothers, little maid,
    How many may you be?"
"How many? Seven in all," she said,
    And wondering looked at me.

"And where are they? I pray you tell."
    She answered, "Seven are we;
And two of us at Conway dwell,
    And two are gone to sea;

"Two of us in the churchyard lie,
    My sister and my brother;
And, in the churchyard cottage, I
    Dwell near them with my mother."

"You say that two at Conway dwell,
    And two are gone to sea,
Yet ye are seven! I pray you tell,
    Sweet maid, how this may be."

Then did the little maid reply,
    "Seven boys and girls are we;
Two of us in the churchyard lie
    Beneath the churchyard tree."

"You run about, my little maid;
    Your limbs they are alive;
If two are in the churchyard laid,
    Then ye are only five."

"Their graves are green, they may be seen,"
    The little maid replied:
"Twelve steps or more from my mother's door,
    And they are side by side.

"My stockings there I often knit;
    My kerchief there I hem;
And there upon the ground I sit,
    And sing a song to them.

"And often after sunset, sir,
    When it is light and fair,
I take my little porringer,
    And eat my supper there.

"The first that died was Sister Jane;
    In bed she moaning lay,
Till God released her of her pain;
    And then she went away.

"So in the churchyard she was laid;
    And, when the grass was dry,
Together round her grave we played,
    My brother John and I.

"And when the ground was white with snow,
    And I could run and slide,
My brother John was forced to go,
    And he lies by her side."

"How many are you, then," said I,
    "If they two are in heaven?"
Quick was the little maid's reply:
    "O Master! we are seven."

"But they are dead; those two are dead!
    Their spirits are in heaven!" —
'T was throwing words away; for still
The little maid would have her will,
    And said, "Nay, we are seven!"
                    WILLIAM WORDSWORTH.

———◆———

TO A CHILD, DURING SICKNESS.

SLEEP breathes at last from out thee,
    My little patient boy;
And balmy rest about thee
    Smooths off the day's annoy.
    I sit me down, and think
    Of all thy winning ways;
Yet almost wish, with sudden shrink,
    That I had less to praise.

Thy sidelong pillowed meekness;
    Thy thanks to all that aid;
Thy heart, in pain and weakness,
    Of fancied faults afraid;
    The little trembling hand
    That wipes thy quiet tears, —
These, these are things that may demand
    Dread memories for years.

Sorrows I've had, severe ones,
    I will not think of now;
And calmly, midst my dear ones,
    Have wasted with dry brow;
    But when thy fingers press
    And pat my stooping head,
I cannot bear the gentleness, —
    The tears are in their bed.

Ah, first-born of thy mother,
    When life and hope were new;
Kind playmate of thy brother,
    Thy sister, father too;
    My light, where'er I go;
    My bird, when prison-bound;
My hand-in-hand companion — No,
    My prayers shall hold thee round.

To say, "He has departed" —
    "His voice" — "his face" — is gone,
To feel impatient-hearted,
    Yet feel we must bear on, —
    Ah, I could not endure
    To whisper of such woe,
Unless I felt this sleep insure
    That it will not be so.

Yes, still he 's fixed, and sleeping !
  This silence too the while, —
Its very hush and creeping
  Seem whispering us a smile ;
    Something divine and dim
  Seems going by one's ear,
Like parting wings of cherubim,
  Who say, " We 've finished here."
                 LEIGH HUNT.

BABY'S SHOES.

O, THOSE little, those little blue shoes !
Those shoes that no little feet use.
  O the price were high
  That those shoes would buy,
Those little blue unused shoes !

For they hold the small shape of feet
That no more their mother's eyes meet,
  That, by God's good will,
  Years since, grew still,
And ceased from their totter so sweet.

And O, since that baby slept,
So hushed, how the mother has kept,
  With a tearful pleasure,
  That little dear treasure,
And o'er them thought and wept !

For they mind her forevermore
Of a patter along the floor ;
  And blue eyes she sees
  Look up from her knees
With the look that in life they wore.

As they lie before her there,
There babbles from chair to chair
  A little sweet face
  That 's a gleam in the place,
With its little gold curls of hair.

Then O wonder not that her heart
From all else would rather part
  Than those tiny blue shoes
  That no little feet use,
And whose sight makes such fond tears start !
          WILLIAM C. BENNETT.

OUR WEE WHITE ROSE.

ALL in our marriage garden
  Grew, smiling up to God,
A bonnier flower than ever
  Suckt the green warmth of the sod ;
O beautiful unfathomably
  Its little life unfurled ;
And crown of all things was our wee
  White Rose of all the world.

From out a balmy bosom
  Our bud of beauty grew ;
It fed on smiles for sunshine,
  On tears for daintier dew :
Aye nestling warm and tenderly,
  Our leaves of love were curled
So close and close about our wee
  White Rose of all the world.

With mystical faint fragrance
  Our house of life she filled ;
Revealed each hour some fairy tower
  Where wingéd hopes might build !
We saw — though none like us might see —
  Such precious promise pearled
Upon the petals of our wee
  White Rose of all the world.

But, evermore the halo
  Of angel-light increased,
Like the mystery of moonlight
  That folds some fairy feast.
Snow-white, snow-soft, snow-silently
  Our darling bud up-curled,
And dropt i' the grave — God's lap — our wee
  White Rose of all the world.

Our Rose was but in blossom,
  Our life was but in spring,
When down the solemn midnight
  We heard the spirits sing,
" Another bud of infancy
  With holy dews impearled ! "
And in their hands they bore our wee
  White Rose of all the world.

You scarce could think so small a thing
  Could leave a loss so large ;
Her little light such shadow fling
  From dawn to sunset's marge.
In other springs our life may be
  In bannered bloom unfurled,
But never, never match our wee
  White Rose of all the world.
          GERALD MASSEY.

PICTURES OF MEMORY.

AMONG the beautiful pictures
  That hang on Memory's wall
Is one of a dim old forest,
  That seemeth best of all ;
Not for its gnarled oaks olden,
  Dark with the mistletoe ;
Not for the violets golden
  That sprinkle the vale below ;

Not for the milk-white lilies
  That lean from the fragrant ledge,
Coquetting all day with the sunbeams,
  And stealing their golden edge ;
Not for the vines on the upland,
  Where the bright red berries rest,
Nor the pinks, nor the pale sweet cowslip,
  It seemeth to me the best.

I once had a little brother,
  With eyes that were dark and deep ;
In the lap of that old dim forest
  He lieth in peace asleep :
Light as the down of the thistle,
  Free as the winds that blow,
We roved there the beautiful summers,
  The summers of long ago ;
But his feet on the hills grew weary,
  And, one of the autumn eves,
I made for my little brother
  A bed of the yellow leaves.
Sweetly his pale arms folded
  My neck in a meek embrace,
As the light of immortal beauty
  Silently covered his face ;
And when the arrows of sunset
  Lodged in the tree-tops bright,
He fell, in his saint-like beauty,
  Asleep by the gates of light.
Therefore, of all the pictures
  That hang on Memory's wall,
The one of the dim old forest
  Seemeth the best of all.
                        ALICE CARY.

THE PET NAME.

" The name
Which from THEIR lips seemed a caress."
        MISS MITFORD'S *Dramatic Scenes.*

I HAVE a name, a little name,
  Uncadenced for the ear,
Unhonored by ancestral claim,
Unsanctified by prayer and psalm
  The solemn font anear.

It never did, to pages wove
  For gay romance, belong.
It never dedicate did move
As "Sacharissa," unto love, —
  "Orinda," unto song.

Though I write books, it will be read
  Upon the leaves of none,
And afterward, when I am dead,
Will ne'er be graved for sight or tread,
  Across my funeral-stone.

This name, whoever chance to call
  Perhaps your smile may win.
Nay, do not smile ! mine eyelids fall
Over mine eyes, and feel withal
  The sudden tears within.

Is there a leaf that greenly grows
  Where summer meadows bloom,
But gathereth the winter snows,
And changeth to the hue of those,
  If lasting till they come ?

Is there a word, or jest, or game,
  But time encrusteth round
With sad associate thoughts the same ?
And so to me my very name
  Assumes a mournful sound.

My brother gave that name to me
  When we were children twain, —
When names acquired baptismally
Were hard to utter, as to see
  That life had any pain.

No shade was on us then, save one
  Of chestnuts from the hill, —
And through the word our laugh did run
As part thereof.   The mirth being done,
  He calls me by it still.

Nay, do not smile ! I hear in it
  What none of you can hear, —
The talk upon the willow seat,
The bird and wind that did repeat
  Around, our human cheer.

I hear the birthday's noisy bliss,
  My sisters' woodland glee, —
My father's praise I did not miss,
When, stooping down, he cared to kiss
  The poet at his knee, —

And voices which, to name me, aye
  Their tenderest tones were keeping, —
To some I nevermore can say
An answer, till God wipes away
  In heaven these drops of weeping.

My name to me a sadness wears ;
  No murmurs cross my mind.
Now God be thanked for these thick tears,
Which show, of those departed years,
  Sweet memories left behind.

Now God be thanked for years enwrought
  With love which softens yet.
Now God be thanked for every thought
Which is so tender it has caught
  Earth's guerdon of regret.

Earth saddens, never shall remove,
  Affections purely given ;
And e'en that mortal grief shall prove
The immortality of love,
  And heighten it with Heaven.
          ELIZABETH BARRETT BROWNING.

MY MOTHER'S PICTURE.

OUT OF NORFOLK, THE GIFT OF MY COUSIN, ANN BODHAM.

O THAT those lips had language ! Life has passed
With me but roughly since I heard thee last.
Those lips are thine, — thy own sweet smile I see,
The same that oft in childhood solaced me ;
Voice only fails, else how distinct they say,
"Grieve not, my child ; chase all thy fears
    away !"
The meek intelligence of those dear eyes
(Blest be the art that can immortalize, —
The art that baffles time's tyrannic claim
To quench it!) here shines on me still the same.
  Faithful remembrancer of one so dear !
O welcome guest, though unexpected here !
Who bid'st me honor with an artless song,
Affectionate, a mother lost so long.
I will obey, — not willingly alone,
But gladly, as the precept were her own ;
And, while that face renews my filial grief,
Fancy shall weave a charm for my relief, —
Shall steep me in Elysian revery,
A momentary dream that thou art she.
  My mother ! when I learned that thou wast dead,
Say, wast thou conscious of the tears I shed ?
Hovered thy spirit o'er thy sorrowing son,
Wretch even then, life's journey just begun ?
Perhaps thou gavest me, though unfelt, a kiss ;
Perhaps a tear, if souls can weep in bliss —
Ah, that maternal smile ! it answers — Yes.
I heard the bell tolled on thy burial day ;
I saw the hearse that bore thee slow away ;
And, turning from my nursery window, drew
A long, long sigh, and wept a last adieu !
But was it such ? — It was. — Where thou art gone
Adieus and farewells are a sound unknown ;
May I but meet thee on that peaceful shore,
The parting word shall pass my lips no more.
Thy maidens, grieved themselves at my concern,
Oft gave me promise of thy quick return ;
What ardently I wished I long believed,
And, disappointed still, was still deceived, —
By expectation every day beguiled,
Dupe of to-morrow even from a child.
Thus many a sad to-morrow came and went,
Till, all my stock of infant sorrows spent,
I learned at last submission to my lot ;
But, though I less deplored thee, ne'er forgot.

Where once we dwelt our name is heard no more ;
Children not thine have trod my nursery floor ;
And where the gardener Robin, day by day,
Drew me to school along the public way, —
Delighted with my bawble coach, and wrapped
In scarlet mantle warm and velvet cap, —
'T is now become a history little known
That once we called the pastoral house our own.
Short-lived possession ! but the record fair,
That memory keeps of all thy kindness there,
Still outlives many a storm that has effaced
A thousand other themes, less deeply traced :
Thy nightly visits to my chamber made,
That thou mightst know me safe and warmly laid ;
Thy morning bounties ere I left my home, —
The biscuit, or confectionery plum ;
The fragrant waters on my cheeks bestowed
By thy own hand, till fresh they shone and
    glowed, —
All this, and, more endearing still than all,
Thy constant flow of love, that knew no fall, —
Ne'er roughened by those cataracts and breaks
That humor interposed too often makes ;
All this, still legible in memory's page,
And still to be so to my latest age,
Adds joy to duty, makes me glad to pay
Such honors to thee as my numbers may, —
Perhaps a frail memorial, but sincere, —
Not scorned in heaven, though little noticed here.
  Could time, his flight reversed, restore the
    hours
When, playing with thy vesture's tissued flow-
    ers, —
The violet, the pink, the jessamine, —
I pricked them into paper with a pin,
(And thou wast happier than myself the while —
Wouldst softly speak, and stroke my head and
    smile,) —
Could those few pleasant days again appear,
Might one wish bring them, would I wish them
    here ?
I would not trust my heart, — the dear delight
Seems so to be desired, perhaps I might.
But no, — what here we call our life is such,
So little to be loved, and thou so much,
That I should ill requite thee to constrain
Thy unbound spirit into bonds again.
  Thou — as a gallant bark, from Albion's coast,
(The storms all weathered and the ocean crossed,)
Shoots into port at some well-havened isle,
Where spices breathe and brighter seasons smile ;
There sits quiescent on the floods, that show
Her beauteous form reflected clear below,
While airs impregnated with incense play
Around her, fanning light her streamers gay, —
So thou, with sails how swift ! hast reached the
    shore
"Where tempests never beat nor billows roar" :

And thy loved consort on the dangerous tide
Of life long since has anchored by thy side.
But me, scarce hoping to attain that rest,
Always from port withheld, always distressed, —
Me howling blasts drive devious, tempest-tossed,
Sails ripped, seams opening wide, and compass
    lost ;
And day by day some current's thwarting force
Sets me more distant from a prosperous course.
Yet O, the thought that thou art safe, and he ! —
That thought is joy, arrive what may to me.
My boast is not that I deduce my birth
From loins enthroned, and rulers of the earth ;
But higher far my proud pretensions rise, —
The son of parents passed into the skies.
And now, farewell ! — Time, unrevoked, has run
His wonted course ; yet what I wished is done.
By contemplation's help, not sought in vain,
I seem to have lived my childhood o'er again, —
To have renewed the joys that once were mine,
Without the sin of violating thine ;
And, while the wings of fancy still are free,
And I can view this mimic show of thee,
Time has but half succeeded in his theft, —
Thyself removed, thy power to soothe me left.

WILLIAM COWPER.

THE MITHERLESS BAIRN.

[An Inverary correspondent writes : "Thom gave me the fol-
lowing narrative as to the origin of 'The Mitherless Bairn' ; I
quote his own words. 'When I was livin' in Aberdeen, I was
limping roun' the house to my garret, when I heard the greetin' o'
a wean. A lassie was thumpin' a bairn, when out cam a big
dame, bellowin' " Ye hussie, will ye lick a mitherless bairn ! " I
hobled up the stair and wrote the sang afore sleepin'.'"]

WHEN a' ither bairnies are hushed to their hame
By aunty, or cousin, or frecky grand-dame,
Wha stands last and lanely, an' naebody carin' ?
'T is the puir doited loonie, — the mitherless
    bairn !

The mitherless bairn gangs to his lane bed ;
Nane covers his cauld back, or haps his bare
    head ;
His wee hackit heelies are hard as the airn,
An' litheless the lair o' the mitherless bairn.

Aneath his cauld brow siccan dreams hover there,
O' hands that wont kindly to kame his dark hair ;
But mornin' brings clutches, a' reckless an' stern,
That lo'e nae the locks o' the mitherless bairn !

Yon sister that sang o'er his saftly rocked bed
Now rests in the mools where her mammie is
    laid ;

The father toils sair their wee bannock to earn,
An' kens na the wrangs o' his mitherless bairn.

Her spirit, that passed in yon hour o' his birth,
Still watches his wearisome wanderings on earth ;
Recording in heaven the blessings they earn
Wha couthilie deal wi' the mitherless bairn !

O, speak him na harshly, — he trembles the
    while,
He bends to your bidding, and blesses your smile ;
In their dark hour o' anguish the heartless shall
    learn
That God deals the blow, for the mitherless bairn !

WILLIAM THOM.

I REMEMBER, I REMEMBER.

I REMEMBER, I remember
    The house where I was born,
The little window where the sun
    Came peeping in at morn.
He never came a wink too soon,
    Nor brought too long a day ;
But now I often wish the night
    Had borne my breath away !

I remember, I remember
    The roses, red and white,
The violets, and the lily-cups, —
    Those flowers made of light !
The lilacs where the robin built,
    And where my brother set
The laburnum on his birthday, —
    The tree is living yet !

I remember, I remember
    Where I was used to swing,
And thought the air must rush as fresh
    To swallows on the wing ;
My spirit flew in feathers then,
    That is so heavy now,
And summer pools could hardly cool
    The fever on my brow !

I remember, I remember
    The fir-trees dark and high ;
I used to think their slender tops
    Were close against the sky.
It was a childish ignorance,
    But now 't is little joy
To know I 'm farther off from heaven
    Than when I was a boy.

THOMAS HOOD.

YOUTH.

THE ROMANCE OF THE SWAN'S NEST.

I.

LITTLE Ellie sits alone
Mid the beeches of a meadow,
 By a stream-side on the grass,
 And the trees are showering down
Doubles of their leaves in shadow,
 On her shining hair and face.

II.

She has thrown her bonnet by,
And her feet she has been dipping
 In the shallow water's flow.
 Now she holds them nakedly
In her hands all sleek and dripping,
 While she rocketh to and fro.

III.

Little Ellie sits alone,
And the smile she softly uses
 Fills the silence like a speech,
 While she thinks what shall be done, —
And the sweetest pleasure chooses
 For her future within reach.

IV.

Little Ellie in her smile
Chooses . . . "I will have a lover,
 Riding on a steed of steeds !
 He shall love me without guile,
And to *him* I will discover
 The swan's nest among the reeds.

V.

"And the steed shall be red-roan,
And the lover shall be noble,
 With an eye that takes the breath.
 And the lute he plays upon
Shall strike ladies into trouble,
 As his sword strikes men to death.

VI.

"And the steed it shall be shod
All in silver, housed in azure,
 And the mane shall swim the wind ;
 And the hoofs along the sod
Shall flash onward and keep measure
 Till the shepherds look behind.

VII.

"But my lover will not prize
All the glory that he rides in,
 When he gazes in my face.
 He will say, 'O Love, thine eyes
Build the shrine my soul abides in,
 And I kneel here for thy grace.'

VIII.

"Then, ay then — he shall kneel low,
With the red-roan steed anear him,
 Which shall seem to understand —
 Till I answer, 'Rise and go !
For the world must love and fear him
 Whom I gift with heart and hand.'

IX.

"Then he will arise so pale,
I shall feel my own lips tremble
 With a *yes* I must not say ;
 Nathless maiden-brave, 'Farewell'
I will utter, and dissemble ; —
 'Light to-morrow with to-day.'

X.

"Then he 'll ride among the hills
To the wide world past the river,
 There to put away all wrong ;
 To make straight distorted wills,
And to empty the broad quiver
 Which the wicked bear along.

XI.

"Three times shall a young foot-page
Swim the stream and climb the mountain
 And kneel down beside my feet ; —
 'Lo, my master sends this gage,
Lady, for thy pity's counting !
 What wilt thou exchange for it ?'

XII.

"And the first time, I will send
A white rosebud for a guerdon, —
 And the second time, a glove ;
 But the third time, I may bend
From my pride, and answer, 'Pardon,
 If he comes to take my love.'

XIII.

"Then the young foot-page will run, —
Then my lover will ride faster,
 Till he kneeleth at my knee :
 'I am a duke's eldest son !
Thousand serfs do call me master, —
 But, O Love, I love but *thee !*'

NATURE'S TEACHING

" Where rivulets dance their wayward round,
And beauty born of murmuring sound
Shall pass into her face."

XIV.

"He will kiss me on the mouth
Then, and lead me as a lover
   Through the crowds that praise his deeds ;
And, when soul-tied by one troth,
Unto *him* I will discover
   That swan's nest among the reeds."

XV.

Little Ellie, with her smile
Not yet ended, rose up gayly,
   Tied the bonnet, donned the shoe,
And went homeward, round a mile,
Just to see, as she did daily,
   What more eggs were with the two.

XVI.

Pushing through the elm-tree copse,
Winding up the stream, light-hearted,
   Where the osier pathway leads, —
Past the boughs she stoops — and stops.
Lo, the wild swan had deserted,
   And a rat had gnawed the reeds.

XVII.

Ellie went home sad and slow.
If she found the lover ever,
   With his red-roan steed of steeds,
Sooth I know not ! but I know
She could never show him — never,
   That swan's nest among the reeds !
         ELIZABETH BARRETT BROWNING.

SWEET STREAM, THAT WINDS—

SWEET stream, that winds through yonder glade,
Apt emblem of a virtuous maid, —
Silent and chaste she steals along,
Far from the world's gay, busy throng ;
With gentle yet prevailing force,
Intent upon her destined course ;
Graceful and useful all she does,
Blessing and blest where'er she goes ;
Pure-bosomed as that watery glass,
And Heaven reflected in her face.
         W. COWPER.

THE EDUCATION OF NATURE.

THREE years she grew in sun and shower ;
Then Nature said, "A lovelier flower
   On earth was never sown :
This child I to myself will take ;
She shall be mine, and I will make
   A lady of my own.

"Myself will to my darling be
Both law and impulse ; and with me
   The girl, in rock and plain,
In earth and heaven, in glade and bower,
Shall feel an overseeing power
   To kindle or restrain.

"She shall be sportive as the fawn
That wild with glee across the lawn
   Or up the mountain springs ;
And hers shall be the breathing balm,
And hers the silence and the calm,
   Of mute insensate things.

"The floating clouds their state shall lend
To her ; for her the willow bend ;
   Nor shall she fail to see
E'en in the motions of the storm
Grace that shall mould the maiden's form
   By silent sympathy.

"The stars of midnight shall be dear
To her ; and she shall lean her ear
   In many a secret place
Where rivulets dance their wayward round,
And beauty born of murmuring sound
   Shall pass into her face.

"And vital feelings of delight
Shall rear her form to stately height,
   Her virgin bosom swell ;
Such thoughts to Lucy I will give
While she and I together live
   Here in this happy dell."

Thus Nature spake. The work was done, —
How soon my Lucy's race was run !
   She died, and left to me
This heath, this calm and quiet scene ;
The memory of what has been,
   And nevermore will be.
         W. WORDSWORTH.

NARCISSA.

"YOUNG, gay, and fortunate !" Each yields a
   theme.
And, first, thy youth : what says it to gray hairs ?
Narcissa, I 'm become thy pupil now ; —
Early, bright, transient, chaste as morning dew,
She sparkled, was exhaled, and went to heaven.
         DR. EDWARD YOUNG.

MAIDENHOOD.

MAIDEN ! with the meek brown eyes,
In whose orbs a shadow lies
Like the dusk in evening skies !

Thou whose locks outshine the sun, —
Golden tresses wreathed in one,
As the braided streamlets run !

Standing, with reluctant feet,
Where the brook and river meet,
Womanhood and childhood fleet !

Gazing, with a timid glance,
On the brooklet's swift advance,
On the river's broad expanse !

Deep and still, that gliding stream
Beautiful to thee must seem
As the river of a dream.

Then why pause with indecision,
When bright angels in thy vision
Beckon thee to fields Elysian ?

Seest thou shadows sailing by,
As the dove, with startled eye,
Sees the falcon's shadow fly ?

Hearest thou voices on the shore,
That our ears perceive no more,
Deafened by the cataract's roar ?

O thou child of many prayers !
Life hath quicksands, Life hath snares !
Care and age come unawares !

Like the swell of some sweet tune,
Morning rises into noon,
May glides onward into June.

Childhood is the bough where slumbered
Birds and blossoms many-numbered ; —
Age, that bough with snows encumbered.

Gather, then, each flower that grows,
When the young heart overflows,
To embalm that tent of snows.

Bear a lily in thy hand ;
Gates of brass cannot withstand
One touch of that magic wand.

Bear through sorrow, wrong, and ruth,
In thy heart the dew of youth,
On thy lips the smile of truth.

O, that dew, like balm, shall steal
Into wounds that cannot heal,
Even as sleep our eyes doth seal ;

And that smile, like sunshine, dart
Into many a sunless heart,
For a smile of God thou art.

          H. W. LONGFELLOW.

THE PRETTY GIRL OF LOCH DAN.

THE shades of eve had crossed the glen
    That frowns o'er infant Avonmore,
When, nigh Loch Dan, two weary men,
    We stopped before a cottage door.

"God save all here," my comrade cries,
    And rattles on the raised latch-pin ;
"God save you kindly," quick replies
    A clear sweet voice, and asks us in.

We enter ; from the wheel she starts,
    A rosy girl with soft black eyes ;
Her fluttering court'sy takes our hearts,
    Her blushing grace and pleased surprise.

Poor Mary, she was quite alone,
    For, all the way to Glenmalure,
Her mother had that morning gone,
    And left the house in charge with her.

But neither household cares, nor yet
    The shame that startled virgins feel,
Could make the generous girl forget
    Her wonted hospitable zeal.

She brought us in a beechen bowl
    Sweet milk that smacked of mountain thyme,
Oat cake, and such a yellow roll
    Of butter, — it gilds all my rhyme !

And, while we ate the grateful food
    (With weary limbs on bench reclined),
Considerate and discreet, she stood
    Apart, and listened to the wind.

Kind wishes both our souls engaged,
    From breast to breast spontaneous ran
The mutual thought, — we stood and pledged
    THE MODEST ROSE ABOVE LOCH DAN.

"The milk we drink is not more pure,
    Sweet Mary, — bless those budding charms ! —
Than your own generous heart, I 'm sure,
    Nor whiter than the breast it warms ! "

She turned and gazed, unused to hear
    Such language in that homely glen ;
But, Mary, you have naught to fear,
    Though smiled on by two stranger-men.

Not for a crown would I alarm
    Your virgin pride by word or sign,
Nor need a painful blush disarm
    My friend of thoughts as pure as mine.

Her simple heart could not but feel
  The words we spoke were free from guile ;
She stooped, she blushed, she fixed her wheel, —
  'T is all in vain, — she can't but smile !

Just like sweet April's dawn appears
  Her modest face, — I see it yet, —
And though I lived a hundred years
  Methinks I never could forget

The pleasure that, despite her heart,
  Fills all her downcast eyes with light,
The lips reluctantly apart,
  The white teeth struggling into sight,

The dimples eddying o'er her cheek, —
  The rosy cheek that won't be still ; —
O, who could blame what flatterers speak,
  Did smiles like this reward their skill ?

For such another smile, I vow,
  Though loudly beats the midnight rain,
I 'd take the mountain-side e'en now,
  And walk to Luggelaw again !
SAMUEL FERGUSON.

THREAD AND SONG.

SWEETER and sweeter,
    Soft and low,
Neat little nymph,
    Thy numbers flow,
Urging thy thimble,
Thrift's tidy symbol,
Busy and nimble,
    To and fro ;
Prettily plying
    Thread and song,
Keeping them flying
    Late and long,
Through the stitch linger,
Kissing thy finger,
    Quick, — as it skips along.

Many an echo,
    Soft and low,
Follows thy flying
    Fancy so, —
Melodies thrilling,
Tenderly filling
Thee with their trilling,
    Come and go ;
Memory's finger,
    Quick as thine,
Loving to linger
    On the line,
Writes of another,
    Dearer than brother :
    Would that the name were mine !
J. W. PALMER.

TO THE HIGHLAND GIRL OF INVERSNAID.

SWEET Highland Girl, a very shower
Of beauty is thy earthly dower !
Twice seven consenting years have shed
Their utmost bounty on thy head ;
And these gray rocks, this household lawn,
These trees, — a veil just half withdrawn, —
This fall of water that doth make
A murmur near the silent lake,
This little bay, a quiet road
That holds in shelter thy abode ;
In truth together ye do seem
Like something fashioned in a dream ;
Such forms as from their covert peep
When earthly cares are laid asleep !
But O fair Creature ! in the light
Of common day so heavenly bright,
I bless thee, Vision as thou art,
I bless thee with a human heart :
God shield thee to thy latest years !
I neither know thee nor thy peers ;
And yet my eyes are filled with tears.

With earnest feeling I shall pray
For thee when I am far away ;
For never saw I mien or face
In which more plainly I could trace
Benignity and home-bred sense
Ripening in perfect innocence.
Here scattered like a random seed,
Remote from men, thou dost not need
The embarrassed look of shy distress,
And maidenly shamefacedness :
Thou wear'st upon thy forehead clear
The freedom of a mountaineer ;
A face with gladness overspread,
Soft smiles, by human kindness bred ;
And seemliness complete, that sways
Thy courtesies, about thee plays ;
With no restraint, but such as springs
From quick and eager visitings
Of thoughts that lie beyond the reach
Of thy few words of English speech, —
A bondage sweetly brooked, a strife
That gives thy gestures grace and life !
So have I, not unmoved in mind,
Seen birds of tempest-loving kind,
Thus beating up against the wind.

What hand but would a garland cull
For thee who art so beautiful ?
O happy pleasure ! here to dwell
Beside thee in some heathy dell ;
Adopt your homely ways and dress,
A shepherd, thou a shepherdess !
But I could frame a wish for thee
More like a grave reality :

Thou art to me but as a wave
Of the wild sea ; and I would have
Some claim upon thee, if I could,
Though but of common neighborhood.
What joy to hear thee, and to see !
Thy elder brother I would be,
Thy father, — anything to thee.

Now thanks to Heaven ! that of its grace
Hath led me to this lonely place ;
Joy have I had ; and going hence
I bear away my recompense.
In spots like these it is we prize
Our Memory, feel that she hath eyes :
Then why should I be loath to stir ?
I feel this place was made for her ;
To give new pleasure like the past,
Continued long as life shall last.
Nor am I loath, though pleased at heart,
Sweet Highland Girl ! from thee to part ;
For I, methinks, till I grow old
As fair before me shall behold
As I do now, the cabin small,
The lake, the bay, the waterfall ;
And thee, the spirit of them all !
                              W. WORDSWORTH.

A PORTRAIT.

"One name is Elizabeth." — BEN JONSON.

I WILL paint her as I see her.
    Ten times have the lilies blown
    Since she looked upon the sun.

And her face is lily-clear,
    Lily-shaped, and dropped in duty
    To the law of its own beauty.

Oval cheeks encolored faintly,
    Which a trail of golden hair
    Keeps from fading off to air ;

And a forehead fair and saintly,
    Which two blue eyes undershine,
    Like meek prayers before a shrine.

Face and figure of a child, —
    Though too calm, you think, and tender,
    For the childhood you would lend her.

Yet child-simple, undefiled,
    Frank, obedient, — waiting still
    On the turnings of your will.

Moving light, as all your things,
    As young birds, or early wheat,
    When the wind blows over it.

Only, free from flutterings
    Of loud mirth that scorneth measure, —
    Taking love for her chief pleasure.

Choosing pleasures, for the rest,
    Which come softly, — just as she,
    When she nestles at your knee.

Quiet talk she liketh best,
    In a bower of gentle looks, —
    Watering flowers, or reading books.

And her voice, it murmurs lowly,
    As a silver stream may run,
    Which yet feels, you feel, the sun.

And her smile, it seems half holy,
    As if drawn from thoughts more far
    Than our common jestings are.

And if any poet knew her,
    He would sing of her with falls
    Used in lovely madrigals.

And if any painter drew her,
    He would paint her unaware
    With a halo round the hair.

And if reader read the poem,
    He would whisper, "You have done a
    Consecrated little Una."

And a dreamer (did you show him
    That same picture) would exclaim,
    "'T is my angel, with a name !"

And a stranger, when he sees her
    In the street even, smileth stilly,
    Just as you would at a lily.

And all voices that address her
    Soften, sleeken every word,
    As if speaking to a bird.

And all fancies yearn to cover
    The hard earth whereon she passes,
    With the thymy-scented grasses.

And all hearts do pray, "God love her !" —
    Ay, and always, in good sooth,
    We may all be sure HE DOTH.
                        ELIZABETH BARRETT BROWNING.

THE CHILDREN'S HOUR.

BETWEEN the dark and the daylight,
    When night is beginning to lower,
Comes a pause in the day's occupations,
    That is known as the children's hour.

I hear in the chamber above me
    The patter of little feet,
The sound of a door that is opened,
    And voices soft and sweet.

From my study I see in the lamplight,
    Descending the broad hall stair,
Grave Alice and laughing Allegra,
    And Edith with golden hair.

A whisper and then a silence;
    Yet I know by their merry eyes
They are plotting and planning together
    To take me by surprise.

A sudden rush from the stairway,
    A sudden raid from the hall,
By three doors left unguarded,
    They enter my castle wall.

They climb up into my turret,
    O'er the arms and back of my chair;
If I try to escape, they surround me:
    They seem to be everywhere.

They almost devour me with kisses,
    Their arms about me intwine,
Till I think of the Bishop of Bingen
    In his Mouse-Tower on the Rhine.

Do you think, O blue-eyed banditti,
    Because you have scaled the wall,
Such an old mustache as I am
    Is not a match for you all?

I have you fast in my fortress,
    And will not let you depart,
But put you into the dungeon
    In the round-tower of my heart.

And there will I keep you forever,
    Yes, forever and a day,
Till the walls shall crumble to ruin,
    And moulder in dust away.
                    H. W. LONGFELLOW.

JENNY KISSED ME.

JENNY kissed me when we met,
    Jumping from the chair she sat in.
Time, you thief! who love to get
    Sweets into your list, put that in.
Say I'm weary, say I'm sad;
    Say that health and wealth have missed me;
Say I'm growing old, but add—
            Jenny kissed me!
                    LEIGH HUNT.

I FEAR THY KISSES, GENTLE MAIDEN.

I FEAR thy kisses, gentle maiden;
    Thou needest not fear mine;
My spirit is too deeply laden
    Ever to burden thine.

I fear thy mien, thy tones, thy motion;
    Thou needest not fear mine;
Innocent is the heart's devotion
    With which I worship thine.
                    P. B. SHELLEY.

THE SMACK IN SCHOOL.

A DISTRICT school, not far away,
Mid Berkshire hills, one winter's day,
Was humming with its wonted noise
Of threescore mingled girls and boys;
Some few upon their tasks intent,
But more on furtive mischief bent.
The while the master's downward look
Was fastened on a copy-book;
When suddenly, behind his back,
Rose sharp and clear a rousing smack!
As 't were a battery of bliss
Let off in one tremendous kiss!
"What 's that?" the startled master cries;
"That, thir," a little imp replies,
"Wath William Willith, if you pleathe, —
I thaw him kith Thuthanna Peathe!"
With frown to make a statue thrill,
The master thundered, "Hither, Will!"
Like wretch o'ertaken in his track,
With stolen chattels on his back,
Will hung his head in fear and shame,
And to the awful presence came, —
A great, green, bashful simpleton,
The butt of all good-natured fun.
With smile suppressed, and birch upraised,
The threatener faltered, — "I'm amazed
That you, my biggest pupil, should
Be guilty of an act so rude!
Before the whole set school to boot --
What evil genius put you to 't?"
"'T was she herself, sir," sobbed the lad,
"I did not mean to be so bad;
But when Susannah shook her curls,
And whispered, I was 'fraid of girls,
And dursn't kiss a baby's doll,
I could n't stand it, sir, at all,
But up and kissed her on the spot!
I know — boo-hoo — I ought to not,
But, somehow, from her looks — boo-hoo —
I thought she kind o' wished me to!"
                    J. W. PALMER.

OLD-SCHOOL PUNISHMENT.

OLD Master Brown brought his ferule down,
　And his face looked angry and red.
"Go, seat you there, now, Anthony Blair,
　Along with the girls," he said.
Then Anthony Blair, with a mortified air,
　With his head down on his breast,
Took his penitent seat by the maiden sweet
　That he loved, of all, the best.
And Anthony Blair seemed whimpering there,
　But the rogue only made believe ;
For he peeped at the girls with the beautiful curls,
　And ogled them over his sleeve.
　　　　　　　　　　　　　　　　ANONYMOUS.

———◆———

THE BAREFOOT BOY.

BLESSINGS on thee, little man,
Barefoot boy, with cheek of tan !
With thy turned-up pantaloons,
And thy merry whistled tunes ;
With thy red lip, redder still
Kissed by strawberries on the hill ;
With the sunshine on thy face,
Through thy torn brim's jaunty grace ;
From my heart I give thee joy, —
I was once a barefoot boy !
Prince thou art, — the grown-up man
Only is republican.
Let the million-dollared ride !
Barefoot, trudging at his side,
Thou hast more than he can buy
In the reach of ear and eye, —
Outward sunshine, inward joy :
Blessings on thee, barefoot boy !

O for boyhood's painless play,
Sleep that wakes in laughing day,
Health that mocks the doctor's rules,
Knowledge never learned of schools,
Of the wild bee's morning chase,
Of the wild-flower's time and place,
Flight of fowl and habitude
Of the tenants of the wood ;
How the tortoise bears his shell,
How the woodchuck digs his cell,
And the ground-mole sinks his well ;
How the robin feeds her young,
How the oriole's nest is hung ;
Where the whitest lilies blow,
Where the freshest berries grow,
Where the ground-nut trails its vine,
Where the wood-grape's clusters shine ;
Of the black wasp's cunning way,
Mason of his walls of clay,
And the architectural plans
Of gray hornet artisans ! —

For, eschewing books and tasks,
Nature answers all he asks ;
Hand in hand with her he walks,
Face to face with her he talks,
Part and parcel of her joy, —
Blessings on the barefoot boy !

O for boyhood's time of June,
Crowding years in one brief moon,
When all things I heard or saw,
Me, their master, waited for.
I was rich in flowers and trees,
Humming-birds and honey-bees ;
For my sport the squirrel played,
Plied the snouted mole his spade ;
For my taste the blackberry cone
Purpled over hedge and stone ;
Laughed the brook for my delight
Through the day and through the night,
Whispering at the garden wall,
Talked with me from fall to fall ;
Mine the sand-rimmed pickerel pond,
Mine the walnut slopes beyond,
Mine, on bending orchard trees,
Apples of Hesperides !
Still as my horizon grew,
Larger grew my riches too ;
All the world I saw or knew
Seemed a complex Chinese toy,
Fashioned for a barefoot boy !

O for festal dainties spread,
Like my bowl of milk and bread, —
Pewter spoon and bowl of wood,
On the door-stone, gray and rude !
O'er me, like a regal tent,
Cloudy-ribbed, the sunset bent,
Purple-curtained, fringed with gold,
Looped in many a wind-swung fold ;
While for music came the play
Of the pied frogs' orchestra ;
And, to light the noisy choir,
Lit the fly his lamp of fire.
I was monarch : pomp and joy
Waited on the barefoot boy !
Cheerily, then, my little man,
Live and laugh, as boyhood can !
Though the flinty slopes be hard,
Stubble-speared the new-mown sward,
Every morn shall lead thee through
Fresh baptisms of the dew ;
Every evening from thy feet
Shall the cool wind kiss the heat :
All too soon these feet must hide
In the prison cells of pride,
Lose the freedom of the sod,
Like a colt's for work be shod,
Made to tread the mills of toil,

Up and down in ceaseless moil :
Happy if their track be found
Never on forbidden ground ;
Happy if they sink not in
Quick and treacherous sands of sin.
Ah ! that thou couldst know thy joy,
Ere it passes, barefoot boy !

JOHN GREENLEAF WHITTIER.

BOYHOOD.

AH, then how sweetly closed those crowded days !
The minutes parting one by one like rays,
    That fade upon a summer's eve.
But O, what charm or magic numbers
Can give me back the gentle slumbers
    Those weary, happy days did leave ?
When by my bed I saw my mother kneel,
    And with her blessing took her nightly kiss ;
Whatever Time destroys, he cannot this ; —
    E'en now that nameless kiss I feel.

WASHINGTON ALLSTON.

IT NEVER COMES AGAIN.

THERE are gains for all our losses,
    There are balms for all our pain,
But when youth, the dream, departs,
It takes something from our hearts,
    And it never comes again.

We are stronger, and are better,
    Under manhood's sterner reign ;
Still we feel that something sweet
Followed youth, with flying feet,
    And will never come again.

Something beautiful is vanished,
    And we sigh for it in vain ;
We behold it everywhere,
On the earth, and in the air,
    But it never comes again.

RICHARD HENRY STODDARD.

THE DESERTED GARDEN.

I MIND me in the days departed,
    How often underneath the sun
With childish bounds I used to run
    To a garden long deserted.

The beds and walks were vanished quite ;
And wheresoe'er had struck the spade,

The greenest grasses Nature laid
    To sanctify her right.

.   .   .   .   .   .

Adventurous joy it was for me !
I crept beneath the boughs and found
A circle smooth of mossy ground
    Beneath a poplar-tree.

Old garden rose-trees hedged it in,
Bedropt with roses white,
Well satisfied with dew and light,
    And careless to be seen.

.   .   .   .   .   .

To me upon my mossy seat,
Though never a dream the roses sent
Of science or love's compliment,
    I ween they smelt as sweet.

.   .   .   .   .   .

And gladdest hours for me did glide
In silence at the rose-tree wall,
A thrush made gladness musical
    Upon the other side.

Nor he nor I did e'er incline
To peck or pluck the blossoms white.
How should I know but roses might
    Lead lives as glad as mine ?

.   .   .   .   .   .

My childhood from my life is parted,
My footstep from the moss which drew
Its fairy circle round : anew
    The garden is deserted.

Another thrush may there rehearse
The madrigals which sweetest are ;
No more for me ! — myself afar
    Do sing a sadder verse.

.   .   .   .   .   .

ELIZABETH BARRETT BROWNING.

THE OLD OAKEN BUCKET.

How dear to this heart are the scenes of my child-
        hood,
    When fond recollection presents them to view !
The orchard, the meadow, the deep-tangled wild-
        wood,
    And every loved spot which my infancy knew ;—
The wide-spreading pond, and the mill which stood
        by it,

The bridge, and the rock where the cataract fell;
The cot of my father, the dairy-house nigh it,
  And e'en the rude bucket which hung in the well.
The old oaken bucket, the iron-bound bucket,
The moss-covered bucket which hung in the well.

That moss-covered vessel I hail as a treasure;
  For often, at noon, when returned from the field,
I found it the source of an exquisite pleasure,
  The purest and sweetest that nature can yield.
How ardent I seized it, with hands that were glow-
    ing!
  And quick to the white-pebbled bottom it fell;
Then soon, with the emblem of truth overflowing,
  And dripping with coolness, it rose from the well;
The old oaken bucket, the iron-bound bucket,
The moss-covered bucket, arose from the well.

How sweet from the green mossy brim to receive it,
  As, poised on the curb, it inclined to my lips!
Not a full blushing goblet could tempt me to leave
    it,
  Though filled with the nectar that Jupiter sips.
And now, far removed from the loved situation,
  The tear of regret will intrusively swell,
As fancy reverts to my father's plantation,
  And sighs for the bucket which hangs in the well;
The old oaken bucket, the iron-bound bucket,
The moss-covered bucket which hangs in the well.
                              SAMUEL WOODWORTH.

THE OLD ARM-CHAIR.

I LOVE it, I love it! and who shall dare
To chide me for loving that old arm-chair?
I 've treasured it long as a sainted prize,
I 've bedewed it with tears, I 've embalmed it with
    sighs.
'T is bound by a thousand bands to my heart;
Not a tie will break, not a link will start;
Would you know the spell? — a mother sat there!
And a sacred thing is that old arm-chair.

In childhood's hour I lingered near
The hallowed seat with listening ear;
And gentle words that mother would give
To fit me to die, and teach me to live.
She told me that shame would never betide
With Truth for my creed, and God for my guide;
She taught me to lisp my earliest prayer,
As I knelt beside that old arm-chair.

I sat, and watched her many a day,
When her eye grew dim, and her locks were gray;

And I almost worshipped her when she smiled,
And turned from her Bible to bless her child.
Years rolled on, but the last one sped, —
My idol was shattered, my earth-star fled!
I learnt how much the heart can bear,
When I saw her die in her old arm-chair.

'T is past, 't is past! but I gaze on it now,
With quivering breath and throbbing brow:
'T was there she nursed me, 't was there she died,
And memory flows with lava tide.
Say it is folly, and deem me weak,
Whilst scalding drops start down my cheek;
But I love it, I love it, and cannot tear
My soul from a mother's old arm-chair.
                              ELIZA COOK.

WOODMAN, SPARE THAT TREE.

WOODMAN, spare that tree!
  Touch not a single bough!
In youth it sheltered me,
  And I 'll protect it now.
'T was my forefather's hand
  That placed it near his cot;
There, woodman, let it stand,
  Thy axe shall harm it not!

That old familiar tree,
  Whose glory and renown
Are spread o'er land and sea,
  And wouldst thou hew it down?
Woodman, forbear thy stroke!
  Cut not its earth-bound ties;
O, spare that aged oak,
  Now towering to the skies!

When but an idle boy
  I sought its grateful shade;
In all their gushing joy
  Here too my sisters played.
My mother kissed me here;
  My father pressed my hand —
Forgive this foolish tear,
  But let that old oak stand!

My heart-strings round thee cling,
  Close as thy bark, old friend!
Here shall the wild-bird sing,
  And still thy branches bend,
Old tree! the storm still brave!
  And, woodman, leave the spot;
While I 've a hand to save,
  Thy axe shall hurt it not.
                              GEORGE P. MORRIS

Perhaps 'twas boyish love, yet still,
O listless woman, weary lover!
To feel once more that fresh, wild thrill
I'd give — but who can live youth over?

Edmund Clarence Stedman —

An angel face : — its <u>sunny wealth of hair</u>
In radiant ripples bathed the graceful throat
<u>And dimpled shoulders</u>; round the rosy curve
Of the sweet mouth a smile seemed wandering ever;
While in the depths of azure fire that gleamed
Beneath the drooping lashes, slept a world
Of eloquent meaning, passionate yet pure —
Dreamy — subdued — but oh, how beautiful!

Edgar A Poe.

The wonders of all-ruling Providence;
The joys that from celestial Mercy flow;
Essential beauty; perfect excellence,
Ennoble and refine the native glow
The poet feels — and thence his best resource
To paint his feelings with sublimest force.

John Keats

POEMS OF THE AFFECTIONS.

Home, Sweet Home!

'Mid pleasures and palaces though we may roam
Be it ever so humble, there's no place like home!
A charm from the sky seems to hallow us there
Which, seek through the world, is ne'er met with elsewhere!

Home, home, — sweet, sweet home!
There's no place like home! there's no place like home!

John Howard Payne.

POEMS OF THE AFFECTIONS.

FRIENDSHIP.

BENEDICITE.

God's love and peace be with thee, where
Soe'er this soft autumnal air
Lifts the dark tresses of thy hair!

Whether through city casements comes
Its kiss to thee, in crowded rooms,
Or, out among the woodland blooms,

It freshens o'er thy thoughtful face,
Imparting, in its glad embrace,
Beauty to beauty, grace to grace!

Fair Nature's book together read,
The old wood-paths that knew our tread,
The maple shadows overhead, —

The hills we climbed, the river seen
By gleams along its deep ravine, —
All keep thy memory fresh and green.

Where'er I look, where'er I stray,
Thy thought goes with me on my way,
And hence the prayer I breathe to-day:

O'er lapse of time and change of scene,
The weary waste which lies between
Thyself and me, my heart I lean.

Thou lack'st not Friendship's spellword, nor
The half-unconscious power to draw
All hearts to thine by Love's sweet law.

With these good gifts of God is cast
Thy lot, and many a charm thou hast
To hold the blessèd angels fast.

If, then, a fervent wish for thee
The gracious heavens will heed from me,
What should, dear heart, its burden be?

The sighing of a shaken reed, —
What can I more than meekly plead
The greatness of our common need?

God's love, unchanging, pure, and true, —
The Paraclete white-shining through
His peace, — the fall of Hermon's dew!

With such a prayer, on this sweet day,
As thou mayst hear and I may say,
I greet thee, dearest, far away!
JOHN GREENLEAF WHITTIER.

THE POET'S FRIEND.

LORD BOLINGBROKE.

Come then, my friend! my genius! come along;
O master of the poet, and the song!
And while the muse now stoops, or now ascends,
To man's low passions, or their glorious ends,
Teach me, like thee, in various nature wise,
To fall with dignity, with temper rise;
Formed by thy converse happily to steer
From grave to gay, from lively to severe;
Correct with spirit, eloquent with ease,
Intent to reason, or polite to please.
O, while along the stream of time thy name
Expanded flies, and gathers all its fame;
Say, shall my little bark attendant sail,
Pursue the triumph, and partake the gale?
When statesmen, heroes, kings, in dust repose,
Whose sons shall blush their fathers were thy foes,
Shall then this verse to future age pretend
Thou wert my guide, philosopher, and friend!
That, urged by thee, I turned the tuneful art
From sounds to things, from fancy to the heart:
For wit's false mirror held up Nature's light;
Showed erring pride, WHATEVER IS, IS RIGHT;
That REASON, PASSION, answer one great aim;
That true SELF-LOVE and SOCIAL are the same;
That VIRTUE only makes our bliss below;
And all our knowledge is, OURSELVES TO KNOW.
ALEXANDER POPE.

A GENEROUS friendship no cold medium knows,
Burns with one love, with one resentment glows.
POPE'S ILIAD.

PARTED FRIENDS.

FRIEND after friend departs :
　Who hath not lost a friend ?
There is no union here of hearts
　That finds not here an end ;
Were this frail world our only rest,
Living or dying, none were blest.

Beyond the flight of time,
　Beyond this vale of death,
There surely is some blesséd clime
　Where life is not a breath,
Nor life's affections transient fire,
Whose sparks fly upward to expire.

There is a world above,
　Where parting is unknown ;
A whole eternity of love,
　Formed for the good alone ;
And faith beholds the dying here
Translated to that happier sphere.

Thus star by star declines,
　Till all are passed away,
As morning high and higher shines,
　To pure and perfect day ;
Nor sink those stars in empty night ;
They hide themselves in heaven's own light.
　　　　　　　　　　　JAMES MONTGOMERY.

JOSEPH RODMAN DRAKE.

[Died in New York, September, 1820.]

GREEN be the turf above thee,
　Friend of my better days !
None knew thee but to love thee,
　Nor named thee but to praise.

Tears fell, when thou wert dying,
　From eyes unused to weep,
And long, where thou art lying,
　Will tears the cold turf steep.

When hearts, whose truth was proven,
　Like thine, are laid in earth,
There should a wreath be woven
　To tell the world their worth ;

And I, who woke each morrow
　To clasp thy hand in mine,
Who shared thy joy and sorrow,
　Whose weal and woe were thine, —

It should be mine to braid it
　Around thy faded brow,

But I 've in vain essayed it,
　And feel I cannot now.

While memory bids me weep thee,
　Nor thoughts nor words are free,
The grief is fixed too deeply
　That mourns a man like thee.
　　　　　　　　　　　FITZ-GREENE HALLECK.

EARLY FRIENDSHIP.

THE half-seen memories of childish days,
When pains and pleasures lightly came and went ;
The sympathies of boyhood rashly spent
In fearful wand'rings through forbidden ways ;
The vague, but manly wish to tread the maze
Of life to noble ends, — whereon intent,
Asking to know for what man here is sent,
The bravest heart must often pause, and gaze, —
The firm resolve to seek the chosen end
Of manhood's judgment, cautious and mature, —
Each of these viewless bonds binds friend to friend
With strength no selfish purpose can secure :
My happy lot is this, that all attend
That friendship which first came, and which shall
　　last endure.
　　　　　　　　　　　AUBREY DE VERE.

FRIENDSHIP.

　HAM. Horatio, thou art e'en as just a man
As e'er my conversation coped withal.
　HOR. O my dear lord —
　HAM.　　　　　Nay, do not think I flatter :
For what advancement may I hope from thee
That no revenue hast but thy good spirits,
To feed and clothe thee ? Why should the poor
　　be flattered ?
No, let the candied tongue lick absurd pomp,
And crook the pregnant hinges of the knee,
Where thrift may follow fawning. Dost thou
　　hear ?
Since my dear soul was mistress of her choice,
And could of men distinguish, her election
Hath sealed thee for herself ; for thou hast been
As one, in suffering all, that suffers nothing, —
A man that Fortune's buffets and rewards
Hast ta'en with equal thanks ; and blessed are
　　those
Whose blood and judgment are so well co-mingled,
That they are not a pipe for Fortune's finger
To sound what stop she please : Give me that
　　man
That is not passion's slave, and I will wear him
In my heart's core, ay, in my heart of heart,
As I do thee.
　　　　　　　　　　　SHAKESPEARE.

OLD MATTHEW

A CONVERSATION.

WE talked with open heart, and tongue
 Affectionate and true,
A pair of friends, though I was young,
 And Matthew seventy-two.

We lay beneath a spreading oak,
 Beside a mossy seat ;
And from the turf a fountain broke
 And gurgled at our feet.

"Now, Matthew !" said I, "let us match
 This water's pleasant tune
With some old border-song, or catch
 That suits a summer's noon.

"Or of the church-clock and the chimes
 Sing here beneath the shade
That half-mad thing of witty rhymes
 Which you last April made !"

In silence Matthew lay, and eyed
 The spring beneath the tree ;
And thus the dear old man replied,
 The gray-haired man of glee : —

"No check, no stay, this Streamlet fears,
 How merrily it goes !
'T will murmur on a thousand years,
 And flow as now it flows.

"And here, on this delightful day,
 I cannot choose but think
How oft, a vigorous man, I lay
 Beside this fountain's brink.

"My eyes are dim with childish tears,
 My heart is idly stirred,
For the same sound is in my ears
 Which in those days I heard.

"Thus fares it still in our decay :
 And yet the wiser mind
Mourns less for what Age takes away
 Than what it leaves behind.

"The blackbird amid leafy trees,
 The lark above the hill,
Let loose their carols when they please,
 Are quiet when they will.

"With Nature never do they wage
 A foolish strife ; they see
A happy youth, and their old age
 Is beautiful and free :

"But we are pressed by heavy laws ;
 And often, glad no more,
We wear a face of joy because
 We have been glad of yore.

"If there be one who need bemoan
 His kindred laid in earth,
The household hearts that were his own, —
 It is the man of mirth.

"My days, my friend, are almost gone,
 My life has been approved,
And many love me ; but by none
 Am I enough beloved."

"Now both himself and me he wrongs,
 The man who thus complains !
I live and sing my idle songs
 Upon these happy plains :

"And, Matthew, for thy children dead
 I 'll be a son to thee ! "
At this he grasped my hand and said,
 "Alas ! that cannot be."

We rose up from the fountain-side ;
 And down the smooth descent
Of the green sheep-track did we glide ;
 And through the wood we went ;

And ere we came to Leonard's Rock
 He sang those witty rhymes
About the crazy old church-clock,
 And the bewildered chimes.
      W. WORDSWORTH.

MARTIAL FRIENDSHIP.

FROM "CORIOLANUS."

[Aufidius the Volscian to Caius Marcius Coriolanus.]

AUF.   O Marcius, Marcius !
Each word thou hast spoke hath weeded from my
   heart
A root of ancient envy. If Jupiter
Should from yond' cloud speak divine things, and
   say,
"'T is true," I 'd not believe them more than thee,
All-noble Marcius. — Let me twine
Mine arms about that body, where-against
My grainéd ash an hundred times hath broke,
And scared the moon with splinters ! Here I clip
The anvil of my sword ; and do contest
As hotly and as nobly with thy love,
As ever in ambitious strength I did
Contend against thy valor. Know thou first,
I loved the maid I married ; never man
Sighed truer breath ; but that I see thee here,

Thou noble thing ! more dances my rapt heart
Than when I first my wedded mistress saw
Bestride my threshold. Why, thou Mars ! I tell
    thee,
We have a power on foot ; and I had purpose
Once more to hew thy target from thy brawn,
Or lose mine arm for 't.   Thou hast beat me out
Twelve several times, and I have nightly since
Dreamt of encounters 'twixt thyself and me,
We have been down together in my sleep,
Unbuckling helms, fisting each other's throat,
And waked half dead with nothing.   Worthy
    Marcius,
Had we no other quarrel else to Rome, but that
Thou art thence banished, we would muster all
From twelve to seventy ; and, pouring war
Into the bowels of ungrateful Rome,
Like a bold flood o'erbear.   O, come ! go in,
And take our friendly senators by th' hands ;
Who now are here, taking their leaves of me,
Who am prepared against your territories,
Though not for Rome itself.
                    A thousand welcomes !
And more a friend than e'er an enemy ;
Yet, Marcius, that was much.
                                SHAKESPEARE.

WHEN TO THE SESSIONS OF SWEET SILENT THOUGHT.

SONNET.

WHEN to the sessions of sweet silent thought
I summon up remembrance of things past,
I sigh the lack of many a thing I sought,
And with old woes new wail my dear time's waste.
Then can I drown an eye, unused to flow,
For precious friends hid in death's dateless night,
And weep afresh love's long since cancelled woe,
And moan th' expense of many a vanished sight.
Then can I grieve at grievances foregone,
And heavily from woe to woe tell o'er
The sad account of fore-bemoanéd moan,
Which I new pay, as if not paid before ;
But if the while I think on thee, dear friend,
All losses are restored, and sorrows end.
                                SHAKESPEARE.

FRIENDS FAR AWAY.

COUNT not the hours while their silent wings
    Thus waft them in fairy flight ;
For feeling, warm from her dearest springs,
    Shall hallow the scene to-night.
And while the music of joy is here,
    And the colors of life are gay,
Let us think on those that have loved us dear,
    The Friends who are far away.

Few are the hearts that have proved the truth
    Of their early affection's vow ;
And let those few, the beloved of youth,
    Be dear in their absence now.
O, vividly in their faithful breast
    Shall the gleam of remembrance play,
Like the lingering light of the crimson west,
    When the sunbeam hath passed away !

Soft be the sleep of their pleasant hours,
    And calm be the seas they roam !
May the way they travel be strewed with flowers,
    Till it bring them in safety home !
And when we whose hearts are o'erflowing thus
    Ourselves may be doomed to stray,
May some kind orison rise for us,
    When we shall be far away !
                                HORACE TWISS.

THE MEETING OF THE SHIPS.

" We take each other by the hand, and we exchange a few
words and looks of kindness, and we rejoice together for a few
short moments ; and then days, months, years intervene, and we
see and know nothing of each other." — WASHINGTON IRVING.

Two barks met on the deep mid-sea,
    When calms had stilled the tide ;
A few bright days of summer glee
    There found them side by side.

And voices of the fair and brave
    Rose mingling thence in mirth ;
And sweetly floated o'er the wave
    The melodies of earth.

Moonlight on that lone Indian main
    Cloudless and lovely slept ;
While dancing step and festive strain
    Each deck in triumph swept.

And hands were linked, and answering eyes
    With kindly meaning shone ;
O, brief and passing sympathies,
    Like leaves together blown !

A little while such joy was cast
    Over the deep's repose,
Till the loud singing winds at last
    Like trumpet music rose.

And proudly, freely on their way
    The parting vessels bore ;
In calm or storm, by rock or bay,
    To meet — O, nevermore !

Never to blend in victory's cheer,
    To aid in hours of woe ;
And thus bright spirits mingle here,
    Such ties are formed below.
                                FELICIA HEMANS.

William Shakspere

AFTER WARD'S BRONZE STATUE IN THE CENTRAL PARK, NEW YORK.

ENGRAVED BY H.B. HALL & SONS

FORDS, HOWARD & HULBERT N.Y.

THE QUARREL OF FRIENDS.

FROM "CHRISTABEL."

ALAS ! they had been friends in youth :
But whispering tongues can poison truth ;
And constancy lives in realms above ;
    And life is thorny ; and youth is vain ;
And to be wroth with one we love
    Doth work like madness in the brain.
And thus it chanced, as I divine,
With Roland and Sir Leoline !
Each spoke words of high disdain
    And insult to his heart's best brother ;
They parted, — ne'er to meet again !
But never either found another
To free the hollow heart from paining.
They stood aloof, the scars remaining,
Like cliffs which had been rent asunder ;
    A dreary sea now flows between,
But neither heat, nor frost, nor thunder
    Shall wholly do away, I ween,
    The marks of that which once hath been.
                        S. T. COLERIDGE.

THE QUARREL OF BRUTUS AND CASSIUS.

FROM "JULIUS CÆSAR."

CAS. That you have wronged me doth appear
in this :
You have condemned and noted Lucius Pella,
For taking bribes here of the Sardians ;
Wherein my letters, praying on his side,
Because I knew the man, were slighted off.
    BRU. You wronged yourself to write in such a
        case.
CAS. In such a time as this, it is not meet
That every nice offence should bear his comment.
    BRU. Let me tell you, Cassius, you yourself
Are much condemned to have an itching palm,
To sell and mart your offices for gold,
To undeservers.
    CAS.   I an itching palm ?
You know that you are Brutus that speak this,
Or, by the gods, this speech were else your last.
    BRU. The name of Cassius honors this corrup-
        tion,
And chastisement doth therefore hide his head.
    CAS. Chastisement !
    BRU. Remember March, the ides of March re-
        member !
Did not great Julius bleed for justice' sake ?
What villain touched his body, that did stab,
And not for justice ? What ! shall one of us,
That struck the foremost man of all this world,
But for supporting robbers, — shall we now

Contaminate our fingers with base bribes,
And sell the mighty space of our large honors
For so much trash as may be graspéd thus ?
I had rather be a dog, and bay the moon,
Than such a Roman.
    CAS.   Brutus, bay not me,
I 'll not enduré it : you forget yourself,
To hedge me in ; I am a soldier, I,
Older in practice, abler than yourself
To make conditions.
    BRU.   Go to ; you are not, Cassius.
    CAS. I am.
    BRU. I say you are not.
    CAS. Urge me no more, I shall forget myself :
Have mind upon your health ; tempt me no further.
    BRU. Away, slight man !
    CAS. Is 't possible ?
    BRU.   Hear me, for I will speak.
Must I give way and room to your rash choler ?
Shall I be frighted when a madman stares ?
    CAS. O ye gods ! ye gods ! Must I endure all
        this ?
    BRU. All this ? ay, more : Fret, till your proud
        heart break ;
Go, show your slaves how choleric you are,
And make your bondmen tremble. Must I budge ?
Must I observe you ? Must I stand and crouch
Under your testy humor ? By the gods,
You shall digest the venom of your spleen,
Though it do split you ; for from this day forth
I 'll use you for my mirth, yea, for my laughter,
When you are waspish.
    CAS.   Is it come to this ?
    BRU. You say you are a better soldier :
Let it appear so ; make your vaunting true,
And it shall please me well : For mine own part,
I shall be glad to learn of noble men.
    CAS. You wrong me, every way you wrong me,
        Brutus ;
I said an elder soldier, not a better ;
Did I say, better ?
    BRU.   If you did, I care not.
    CAS. When Cæsar lived, he durst not thus
        have moved me.
    BRU. Peace, peace ! you durst not so have
        tempted him.
    CAS. I durst not ?
    BRU. No.
    CAS. What ! durst not tempt him ?
    BRU.   For your life you durst not.
    CAS. Do not presume too much upon my love ;
I may do that I shall be sorry for.
    BRU. You have done that you should be sorry
        for.
There is no terror, Cassius, in your threats ;
For I am armed so strong in honesty,
That they pass by me as the idle wind,
Which I respect not. I did send to you

For certain sums of gold, which you denied me ; —
For I can raise no money by vile means :
By Heaven, I had rather coin my heart,
And drop my blood for drachmas, than to wring
From the hard hands of peasants their vile trash,
By any indirection.   I did send
To you for gold to pay my legions,
Which you denied me : Was that done like Cassius ?
Should I have answered Caius Cassius so ?
When Marcus Brutus grows so covetous,
To lock such rascal counters from his friends,
Be ready, gods, with all your thunderbolts,
Dash him to pieces !
    Cas.   I denied you not.
    Bru. You did.
    Cas.   I did not : — he was but a fool
That brought my answer back. — Brutus hath
      rived my heart :
A friend should bear his friend's infirmities,
But Brutus makes mine greater than they are.
    Bru. I do not, till you practise them on me.
    Cas. You love me not.
    Bru.   I do not like your faults.
    Cas. A friendly eye could never see such faults.
    Bru. A flatterer's would not, though they do
      appear
As huge as high Olympus.
    Cas. Come, Antony, and young Octavius,
      come,
Revenge yourselves alone on Cassius,
For Cassius is a-weary of the world :
Hated by one he loves ; braved by his brother ;
Checked like a bondman ; all his faults observed,
Set in a note-book, learned and conned by rote,
To cast into my teeth.   O, I could weep
My spirit from mine eyes ! — There is my dagger,
And here my naked breast ; within, a heart
Dearer than Plutus' mine, richer than gold :
If that thou be'st a Roman, take it forth ;
I, that denied thee gold, will give my heart.
Strike as thou didst at Cæsar ; for I know,
When thou didst hate him worst, thou lov'dst
      him better
Than ever thou lov'dst Cassius.
    Bru.   Sheath your dagger :
Be angry when you will, it shall have scope ;
Do what you will, dishonor shall be humor.
O Cassius, you are yokéd with a lamb
That carries anger, as the flint bears fire ;
Who, much enforcéd, shows a hasty spark,
And straight is cold again.
    Cas.   Hath Cassius lived
To be but mirth and laughter to his Brutus,
When grief, and blood ill-tempered, vexeth him ?
    Bru. When I spoke that, I was ill-tempered too.
    Cas. Do you confess so much ?   Give me your
      hand.
    Bru. And my heart too.

    Cas.   O Brutus ! —
    Bru.   What 's the matter ?
    Cas. Have you not love enough to bear with
      me,
When that rash humor which my mother gave me
Makes me forgetful ?
    Bru.   Yes, Cassius ; and from henceforth,
When you are over-earnest with your Brutus,
He 'll think your mother chides, and leave you so.

     .   .   .   .
    Bru. O Cassius ! I am sick of many griefs.
    Cas. Of your philosophy you make no use,
If you give place to accidental evils.
    Bru. No man bears sorrow better : — Portia is
      dead.
    Cas. Ha ! Portia ?
    Bru. She is dead.
    Cas. How 'scaped I killing, when I crossed you
      so ? —
O insupportable and touching loss ! —
Upon what sickness ?
    Bru.   Impatient of my absence,
And grief that young Octavius with Mark Antony
Have made themselves so strong ; — for with her
      death
That tidings came ; — with this she fell distract,
And, her attendants absent, swallowed fire.
    Cas. And died so ?
    Bru. Even so.
    Cas. O ye immortal gods !

       Enter Lucius, *with wine and tapers.*

    Bru. Speak no more of her. — Give me a bowl
      of wine : —
In this I bury all unkindness, Cassius. (*Drinks.*)
    Cas. My heart is thirsty for that noble
      pledge. —
Fill, Lucius, till the wine o'erswell the cup ;
I cannot drink too much of Brutus' love. (*Drinks.*)
                    SHAKESPEARE.

THE ROYAL GUEST.

They tell me I am shrewd with other men ;
   With thee I 'm slow, and difficult of speech.
With others I may guide the car of talk :
   Thou wing'st it oft to realms beyond my reach.

If other guests should come, I 'd deck my hair,
   And choose my newest garment from the shelf ;
When thou art bidden, I would clothe my heart
   With holiest purpose, as for God himself.

For them I while the hours with tale or song,
   Or web of fancy, fringed with careless rhyme ;
But how to find a fitting lay for thee,
   Who hast the harmonies of every time ?

O friend beloved! I sit apart and dumb, —
  Sometimes in sorrow, oft in joy divine;
My lip will falter, but my prisoned heart
  Springs forth to measure its faint pulse with
    thine.

Thou art to me most like a royal guest,
  Whose travels bring him to some lowly roof,
Where simple rustics spread their festal fare
  And, blushing, own it is not good enough.

Bethink thee, then, whene'er thou com'st to me,
  From high emprise and noble toil to rest,
My thoughts are weak and trivial, matched with
    thine;
  But the poor mansion offers thee its best.
              JULIA WARD HOWE.

THE DEAD FRIEND.

FROM "IN MEMORIAM."

THE path by which we twain did go,
  Which led by tracts that pleased us well,
  Through four sweet years arose and fell,
From flower to flower, from snow to snow.

But where the path we walked began
  To slant the fifth autumnal slope,
  As we descended following Hope,
There sat the Shadow feared of man;

Who broke our fair companionship,
  And spread his mantle dark and cold,
  And wrapped thee formless in the fold,
And dulled the murmur on thy lip.

When each by turns was guide to each,
  And Fancy light from Fancy caught,
  And Thought leapt out to wed with Thought
Ere Thought could wed itself with Speech;

And all we met was fair and good,
  And all was good that Time could bring,
  And all the secret of the Spring
Moved in the chambers of the blood;

I know that this was Life, — the track
  Whereon with equal feet we fared;
  And then, as now, the day prepared
The daily burden for the back.

But this it was that made me move
  As light as carrier-birds in air;
  I loved the weight I had to bear
Because it needed help of Love:

Nor could I weary, heart or limb,
  When mighty Love would cleave in twain

The lading of a single pain,
And part it, giving half to him.

But I remained, whose hopes were dim,
  Whose life, whose thoughts were little worth
  To wander on a darkened earth,
Where all things round me breathed of him.

O friendship, equal-poised control,
  O heart, with kindliest motion warm,
  O sacred essence, other form,
O solemn ghost, O crownéd soul!

Yet none could better know than I,
  How much of act at human hands
  The sense of human will demands
By which we dare to live or die.

Whatever way my days decline,
  I felt and feel, though left alone,
  His being working in mine own,
The footsteps of his life in mine.

My pulses therefore beat again
  For other friends that once I met;
  Nor can it suit me to forget
The mighty hopes that make us men.

I woo your love: I count it crime
  To mourn for any overmuch;
  I, the divided half of such
A friendship as had mastered Time;

Which masters Time, indeed, and is
  Eternal, separate from fears:
  The all-assuming months and years
Can take no part away from this.

O days and hours, your work is this,
  To hold me from my proper place,
  A little while from his embrace,
For fuller gain of after bliss:

That out of distance might ensue
  Desire of nearness doubly sweet;
  And unto meeting when we meet,
Delight a hundred-fold accrue.

The hills are shadows, and they flow
  From form to form, and nothing stands;
  They melt like mist, the solid lands,
Like clouds they shape themselves and go.

But in my spirit will I dwell,
  And dream my dream, and hold it true;
  For though my lips may breathe adieu,
I cannot think the thing farewell.
              ALFRED TENNYSON.

COMPLIMENT AND ADMIRATION.

TO MISTRESS MARGARET HUSSEY.

MERRY Margaret,
As midsummer flower,
Gentle as falcon,
Or hawk of the tower ;
With solace and gladness,
Much mirth and no madness,
All good and no badness ;
So joyously,
So maidenly,
So womanly
Her demeaning, —
In everything
Far, far passing
That I can indite,
Or suffice to write,
Of merry Margaret,
As midsummer flower,
Gentle as falcon
Or hawk of the tower ;
As patient and as still,
And as full of good-will,
As fair Isiphil,
Coliander,
Sweet Pomander,
Good Cassander ;
Steadfast of thought,
Well made, well wrought ;
Far may be sought
Ere you can find
So courteous, so kind,
As merry Margaret,
This midsummer flower,
Gentle as falcon,
Or hawk of the tower.

JOHN SKELTON.

WHY SHOULD THIS DESERT SILENT BE?

FROM "AS YOU LIKE IT."

WHY should this desert silent be ?
For it is unpeopled ? No ;
Tongues I 'll hang on every tree,
That shall civil sayings show :
Some, how brief the life of man
Runs his erring pilgrimage ;
That the stretching of a span
Buckles in his sum of age :
Some, of violated vows

'Twixt the souls of friend and friend :
But upon the fairest boughs,
Or at every sentence' end,
Will I Rosalinda write ;
Teaching all that read to know
The quintessence of every sprite
Heaven would in little show.
Therefore Heaven nature charged
That one body should be filled
With all graces wide enlarged :
Nature presently distilled
Helen's cheek, but not her heart,
Cleopatra's majesty,
Atalanta's better part,
Sad Lucretia's modesty.
Thus Rosalind of many parts
By heavenly synod was devised ;
Of many faces, eyes, and hearts,
To have the touches dearest prized.
Heaven would that she these gifts should have,
And I to live and die her slave.

SHAKESPEARE.

PHILLIS THE FAIR.

ON a hill there grows a flower,
Fair befall the dainty sweet !
By that flower there is a bower
Where the heavenly muses meet.

In that bower there is a chair,
Fringéd all about with gold,
Where doth sit the fairest fair
That ever eye did yet behold.

It is Phillis, fair and bright,
She that is the shepherd's joy,
She that Venus did despite,
And did blind her little boy.

Who would not that face admire ?
Who would not this saint adore ?
Who would not this sight desire ?
Though he thought to see no more.

Thou that art the shepherd's queen,
Look upon thy love-sick swain ;
By thy comfort have been seen
Dead men brought to life again.

NICHOLAS BRETON

A HEALTH.

I FILL this cup to one made up
  Of loveliness alone,
A woman, of her gentle sex
  The seeming paragon;
To whom the better elements
  And kindly stars have given
A form so fair, that, like the air,
  'T is less of earth than heaven.

Her every tone is music's own,
  Like those of morning birds,
And something more than melody
  Dwells ever in her words;
The coinage of her heart are they,
  And from her lips each flows
As one may see the burdened bee
  Forth issue from the rose.

Affections are as thoughts to her,
  The measures of her hours;
Her feelings have the fragrancy,
  The freshness of young flowers;
And lovely passions, changing oft,
  So fill her, she appears
The image of themselves by turns, —
  The idol of past years!

Of her bright face one glance will trace
  A picture on the brain,
And of her voice in echoing hearts
  A sound must long remain;
But memory, such as mine of her,
  So very much endears,
When death is nigh my latest sigh
  Will not be life's, but hers.

I fill this cup to one made up
  Of loveliness alone,
A woman, of her gentle sex
  The seeming paragon.
Her health! and would on earth there stood
  Some more of such a frame,
That life might be all poetry,
  And weariness a name.
                    EDWARD COATE PINCKNEY.

THERE IS A GARDEN IN HER FACE.

FROM "AN HOURE'S RECREATION IN MUSICKE." 1606.

THERE is a garden in her face,
  Where roses and white lilies blow;
A heavenly paradise is that place,
  Wherein all pleasant fruits do grow;
There cherries grow that none may buy,
Till cherry-ripe themselves do cry.

Those cherries fairly do enclose
  Of orient pearl a double row,
Which when her lovely laughter shows,
  They look like rosebuds filled with snow;
Yet them no peer nor prince may buy,
Till cherry-ripe themselves do cry.

Her eyes like angels watch them still,
  Her brows like bended bows do stand,
Threatening with piercing frowns to kill
  All that approach with eye or hand
These sacred cherries to come nigh,
Till cherry-ripe themselves do cry.
                    RICHARD ALLISON.

THE WHITE ROSE.

SENT BY A YORKISH LOVER TO HIS LANCASTRIAN
MISTRESS.

IF this fair rose offend thy sight,
  Placed in thy bosom bare,
'T will blush to find itself less white,
  And turn Lancastrian there.

But if thy ruby lip it spy,
  As kiss it thou mayest deign,
With envy pale 't will lose its dye,
  And Yorkish turn again.
                    ANONYMOUS.

OLIVIA.

FROM "TWELFTH NIGHT."

VIOLA.   'T is beauty truly blent, whose red and
             white
Nature's own sweet and cunning hand laid on:
Lady, you are the cruel'st she alive,
If you will lead these graces to the grave,
And leave the world no copy.
                    SHAKESPEARE.

ROSALINE.

LIKE to the clear in highest sphere
Where all imperial glory shines:
Of selfsame color is her hair
Whether unfolded, or in twines:
  Heigh-ho, fair Rosaline!
Her eyes are sapphires set in snow,
Resembling heaven by every wink;
The gods do fear whenas they glow,
And I do tremble when I think
  Heigh-ho, would she were mine!

Her cheeks are like the blushing cloud
That beautifies Aurora's face,

Or like the silver crimson shroud
That Phœbus' smiling looks doth grace :
 Heigh-ho, fair Rosaline !
Her lips are like two budded roses
Whom ranks of lilies neighbor nigh,
Within which bounds she balm encloses
Apt to entice a deity :
 Heigh-ho, would she were mine !

Her neck is like a stately tower
Where Love himself imprisoned lies,
To watch for glances every hour
From her divine and sacred eyes ;
 Heigh-ho, for Rosaline !
Her paps are centres of delight,
Her breasts are orbs of heavenly frame,
Where Nature moulds the dew of light
To feed perfection with the same :
 Heigh-ho, would she were mine !

With orient pearl, with ruby red,
With marble white, with sapphire blue,
Her body every way is fed,
Yet soft in touch and sweet in view :
 Heigh-ho, fair Rosaline !
Nature herself her shape admires ;
The gods are wounded in her sight ;
And Love forsakes his heavenly fires
And at her eyes his brand doth light :
 Heigh-ho, would she were mine !

Then muse not, Nymphs, though I bemoan
The absence of fair Rosaline,
Since for a fair there 's fairer none,
Nor for her virtues so divine :
 Heigh-ho, fair Rosaline !
Heigh-ho, my heart ! would God that she were
  mine !
T. LODGE.

A VIOLET IN HER HAIR.

A VIOLET in her lovely hair,
A rose upon her bosom fair !
 But O, her eyes
A lovelier violet disclose,
And her ripe lips the sweetest rose
 That 's 'neath the skies.

A lute beneath her graceful hand
Breathes music forth at her command ;
 But still her tongue
Far richer music calls to birth
Than all the minstrel power on earth
 Can give to song.

And thus she moves in tender light,
The purest ray, where all is bright,
 Serene, and sweet ;
And sheds a graceful influence round,
That hallows e'en the very ground
 Beneath her feet !
CHARLES SWAIN.

WELCOME, WELCOME, DO I SING.

Welcome, welcome, do I sing,
Far more welcome than the spring ;
He that parteth from you never
Shall enjoy a spring forever.

LOVE that to the voice is near,
 Breaking from your ivory pale,
Need not walk abroad to hear
 The delightful nightingale.
  Welcome, welcome, then I sing, etc.

Love, that still looks on your eyes,
 Though the winter have begun
To benumb our arteries,
 Shall not want the summer's sun.
  Welcome, welcome, then I sing, etc.

Love, that still may see your cheeks,
 Where all rareness still reposes,
Is a'fool if e'er he seeks
 Other lilies, other roses.
  Welcome, welcome, then I sing, etc.

Love, to whom your soft lip yields,
 And perceives your breath in kissing,
All the odors of the fields
 Never, never shall be missing.
WILLIAM BROWNE.

PORTIA'S PICTURE.

FROM " THE MERCHANT OF VENICE."

FAIR Portia's counterfeit ? What demi-god
Hath come so near creation ? Move these eyes ?
Or whether, riding on the balls of mine,
Seem they in motion ? Here are severed lips,
Parted with sugar breath ; so sweet a bar
Should sunder such sweet friends : Here in her
  hairs
The painter plays the spider ; and hath woven
A golden mesh to entrap the hearts of men,
Faster than gnats in cobwebs : But her eyes, —
How could he see to do them ? having made one,
Methinks it should have power to steal both his,
And leave itself unfurnished.
SHAKESPEARE.

WHENAS IN SILKS MY JULIA GOES.

WHENAS in silks my Julia goes
Then, then (methinks) how sweetly flows
That liquefaction of her clothes.

Next, when I cast mine eyes and see
That brave vibration each way free ;
O, how that glittering taketh me !
R. HERRICK.

I DO NOT LOVE THEE FOR THAT FAIR.

I DO not love thee for that fair
Rich fan of thy most curious hair,
Though the wires thereof be drawn
Finer than the threads of lawn,
And are softer than the leaves
On which the subtle spider weaves.

I do not love thee for those flowers
Growing on thy cheeks, — love's bowers, —
Though such cunning them hath spread,
None can paint them white and red.
Love's golden arrows thence are shot,
Yet for them I love thee not.

I do not love thee for those soft
Red coral lips I 've kissed so oft ;
Nor teeth of pearl, the double guard
To speech whence music still is heard,
Though from those lips a kiss being taken
Might tyrants melt, and death awaken.

I do not love thee, O my fairest,
For that richest, for that rarest
Silver pillar, which stands under
Thy sound head, that globe of wonder ;
Though that neck be whiter far
Than towers of polished ivory are.
THOMAS CAREW.

THE FORWARD VIOLET THUS DID I CHIDE.

SONNET.

THE forward violet thus did I chide : —
Sweet thief, whence didst thou steal thy sweet
that smells,
If not from my love's breath ? the purple pride
Which on thy soft cheek for complexion dwells,
In my love's veins thou hast too grossly dyed.
The lily I condemnéd for thy hand,
And buds of marjoram had stol'n thy hair :
The roses fearfully on thorns did stand,
One blushing shame, another white despair ;

A third, nor red nor white, had stol'n of both,
And to this robbery had annexed thy breath ;
But, for his theft, in pride of all his growth
A vengeful canker eat him up to death.
More flowers I noted, yet I none could see,
But sweet or color it had stolen from thee.
SHAKESPEARE.

GIVE PLACE, YE LOVERS.

GIVE place, ye lovers, here before
That spent your boasts and brags in vain ;
My lady's beauty passeth more
The best of yours, I dare well sayen,
Than doth the sun the candle-light,
Or brightest day the darkest night.

And thereto hath a troth as just
As had Penelope the fair ;
For what she saith, ye may it trust,
As it by writing sealed were :
And virtues hath she many mo'
Than I with pen have skill to show.

I could rehearse, if that I would,
The whole effect of Nature's plaint,
When she had lost the perfect mould,
The like to whom she could not paint :
With wringing hands, how she did cry,
And what she said, I know it aye.

I know she swore with raging mind,
Her kingdom only set apart,
There was no loss by law of kind
That could have gone so near her heart ;
And this was chiefly all her pain ;
"She could not make the like again."

Sith Nature thus gave her the praise,
To be the chiefest work she wrought,
In faith, methink, some better ways
On your behalf might well be sought,
Than to compare, as ye have done,
To match the candle with the sun.
LORD SURREY.

YOU MEANER BEAUTIES.

YOU meaner beauties of the night,
That poorly satisfy our eyes
More by your number than your light, —
You common people of the skies,
What are you when the moon shall rise ?

You curious chanters of the wood,
That warble forth Dame Nature's lays,
Thinking your passions understood
By your weak accents, — what 's your praise
When Philomel her voice shall raise ?

You violets that first appear,
  By your pure purple mantles known,
Like the proud virgins of the year,
  As if the spring were all your own, —
  What are you when the rose is blown ?

So when my mistress shall be seen
  In form and beauty of her mind :
By virtue first, then choice, a queen, —
  Tell me, if she were not designed
  Th' eclipse and glory of her kind ?
                    SIR HENRY WOTTON.

A VISION OF BEAUTY.

IT was a beauty that I saw, —
  So pure, so perfect, as the frame
  Of all the universe were lame
To that one figure, could I draw,
Or give least line of it a law :
  A skein of silk without a knot !
  A fair march made without a halt !
  A curious form without a fault !
  A printed book without a blot !
  All beauty ! — and without a spot.
                    BEN JONSON.

WHEN IN THE CHRONICLE OF WASTED TIME.

SONNET.

WHEN in the chronicle of wasted time
I see descriptions of the fairest wights,
And beauty making beautiful old rhyme,
In praise of ladies dead, and lovely knights ;
Then, in the blazon of sweet beauty's best
Of hand, of foot, of lip, of eye, of brow,
I see their antique pen would have expressed
Even such a beauty as you master now.
So all their praises are but prophecies
Of this our time, all you prefiguring ;
And, for they looked but with divining eyes,
They had not skill enough your worth to sing ;
For we, which now behold these present days,
Have eyes to wonder, but lack tongues to praise.
                    SHAKESPEARE.

CHILD AND MAIDEN.

AH, Chloris ! could I now but sit
  As unconcerned as when
Your infant beauty could beget
  No happiness or pain !
When I the dawn used to admire,
  And praised the coming day,

I little thought the rising fire
  Would take my rest away.

Your charms in harmless childhood lay
  Like metals in a mine ;
Age from no face takes more away
  Than youth concealed in thine.
But as your charms insensibly
  To their perfection prest,
So love as unperceived did fly,
  And centred in my breast.

My passion with your beauty grew,
  While Cupid at my heart
Still as his mother favored you
  Threw a new flaming dart :
Each gloried in their wanton part ;
  To make a lover, he
Employed the utmost of his art ;
  To make a beauty, she.
                    SIR CHARLES SEDLEY.

WAITING FOR THE GRAPES.

THAT I love thee, charming maid, I a thousand
    times have said,
  And a thousand times more I have sworn it,
But 't is easy to be seen in the coldness of your
    mien
  That you doubt my affection — or scorn it.
                    Ah me !

Not a single grain of sense is in the whole of
    these pretences
  For rejecting your lover's petitions ;
Had I windows in my bosom, O how gladly I 'd
    expose 'em !
  To undo your fantastic suspicions.
                    Ah me !

You repeat I 've known you long, and you hint
    I do you wrong,
  In beginning so late to pursue ye ;
But 't is folly to look glum because people did not
    come
  Up the stairs of your nursery to woo ye.
                    Ah me !

In a grapery one walks without looking at the
    stalks,
  While the bunches are green that they 're bear-
    ing :
All the pretty little leaves that are dangling at the
    eaves
  Scarce attract e'en a moment of staring.
                    Ah me !

But when time has swelled the grapes to a richer
style of shapes,
And the sun has lent warmth to their blushes,
Then to cheer us and to gladden, to enchant us
and to madden,
Is the ripe ruddy glory that rushes.
Ah me !

O, 't is then that mortals pant while they gaze on
Bacchus' plant, —
O, 't is then, — will my simile serve ye ?
Should a damsel fair repine, though neglected like
a vine ?
Both erelong shall turn heads topsy-turvy.
Ah me !
WILLIAM MAGINN.

SHE WAS A PHANTOM OF DELIGHT.

SHE was a phantom of delight
When first she gleamed upon my sight ;
A lovely apparition, sent
To be a moment's ornament ;
Her eyes as stars of twilight fair ;
Like Twilight's, too, her dusky hair ;
But all things else about her drawn
From May-time and the cheerful dawn ;
A dancing shape, an image gay,
To haunt, to startle, and waylay.

I saw her upon nearer view,
A spirit, yet a woman too !
Her household motions light and free,
And steps of virgin-liberty ;
A countenance in which did meet
Sweet records, promises as sweet ;
A creature not too bright or good
For human nature's daily food,
For transient sorrows, simple wiles,
Praise, blame, love, kisses, tears, and smiles.

And now I see with eye serene
The very pulse of the machine ;
A being breathing thoughtful breath,
A traveller between life and death :
The reason firm, the temperate will,
Endurance, foresight, strength, and skill ;
A perfect woman, nobly planned
To warn, to comfort, and command ;
And yet a spirit still, and bright
With something of an angel-light.
W. WORDSWORTH.

BELINDA.

FROM THE "RAPE OF THE LOCK."

ON her white breast a sparkling cross she wore,
Which Jews might kiss, and Infidels adore,

Her lively looks a sprightly mind disclose,
Quick as her eyes, and as unfixed as those :
Favors to none, to all she smiles extends :
Oft she rejects, but never once offends.
Bright as the sun, her eyes the gazers strike,
And, like the sun, they shine on all alike.
Yet, graceful ease, and sweetness void of pride,
Might hide her faults, if belles had faults te
hide ;
If to her share some female errors fall,
Look on her face, and you 'll forget them all.
ALEXANDER POPE.

IF IT BE TRUE THAT ANY BEAUTEOUS THING.

IF it be true that any beauteous thing
Raises the pure and just desire of man
From earth to God, the eternal fount of all,
Such I believe my love ; for as in her
So fair, in whom I all besides forget,
I view the gentle work of her Creator,
I have no care for any other thing,
Whilst thus I love.   Nor is it marvellous,
Since the effect is not of my own power,
If the soul doth, by nature tempted forth,
Enamored through the eyes,
Repose upon the eyes which it resembleth,
And through them riseth to the Primal Love,
As to its end, and honors in admiring ;
For who adores the Maker needs must love his
work.
MICHAEL ANGELO (Italian).   Translation
of J. E. TAYLOR.

THE MIGHT OF ONE FAIR FACE.

THE might of one fair face sublimes my love,
For it hath weaned my heart from low desires ;
Nor death I heed, nor purgatorial fires.
Thy beauty, antepast of joys above,
Instructs me in the bliss that saints approve ;
For O, how good, how beautiful, must be
The God that made so good a thing as thee,
So fair an image of the heavenly Dove !

Forgive me if I cannot turn away
From those sweet eyes that are my earthly
heaven,
For they are guiding stars, benignly given
To tempt my footsteps to the upward way ;
And if I dwell too fondly in thy sight,
I live and love in God's peculiar light.
MICHAEL ANGELO (Italian).   Translation
of J. E. TAYLOR.

THE MILKING-MAID.

THE year stood at its equinox,
　And bluff the North was blowing,
A bleat of lambs came from the flocks,
　Green hardy things were growing;
I met a maid with shining locks
　Where milky kine were lowing.

She wore a kerchief on her neck,
　Her bare arm showed its dimple,
Her apron spread without a speck,
　Her air was frank and simple.

She milked into a wooden pail,
　And sang a country ditty, —
An innocent fond lovers' tale,
　That was not wise nor witty,
Pathetically rustical,
　Too pointless for the city.

She kept in time without a beat,
　As true as church-bell ringers,
Unless she tapped time with her feet,
　Or squeezed it with her fingers;
Her clear, unstudied notes were sweet
　As many a practised singer's.

I stood a minute out of sight,
　Stood silent for a minute,
To eye the pail, and creamy white
　The frothing milk within it, —

To eye the comely milking-maid,
　Herself so fresh and creamy.
"Good day to you!" at last I said;
　She turned her head to see me.
"Good day!" she said, with lifted head;
　Her eyes looked soft and dreamy.

And all the while she milked and milked
　The grave cow heavy-laden:
I've seen grand ladies, plumed and silked,
　But not a sweeter maiden;

But not a sweeter, fresher maid
　Than this in homely cotton,
Whose pleasant face and silky braid
　I have not yet forgotten.

Seven springs have passed since then, as I
　Count with a sober sorrow;
Seven springs have come and passed me by,
　And spring sets in to-morrow.

I've half a mind to shake myself
　Free, just for once, from London,
To set my work upon the shelf,
　And leave it done or undone;

To run down by the early train,
　Whirl down with shriek and whistle,
And feel the bluff north blow again,
　And mark the sprouting thistle
Set up on waste patch of the lane
　Its green and tender bristle;

And spy the scarce-blown violet banks,
　Crisp primrose-leaves and others,
And watch the lambs leap at their pranks,
　And butt their patient mothers.

Alas! one point in all my plan
　My serious thoughts demur to:
Seven years have passed for maid and man,
　Seven years have passed for her too.

Perhaps my rose is over-blown,
　Not rosy or too rosy;
Perhaps in farm-house of her own
　Some husband keeps her cosey,
Where I should show a face unknown, —
　Good by, my wayside posy!
　　　　　　CHRISTINA GEORGINA ROSSETTI.

SHE WALKS IN BEAUTY.

SHE walks in beauty, like the night
　Of cloudless climes and starry skies,
And all that's best of dark and bright
　Meets in her aspect and her eyes,
Thus mellowed to that tender light
　Which heaven to gaudy day denies.

One shade the more, one ray the less
　Had half impaired the nameless grace
Which waves in every raven tress
　Or softly lightens o'er her face,
Where thoughts serenely sweet express
　How pure, how dear their dwelling-place.

And on that cheek and o'er that brow
　So soft, so calm, yet eloquent,
The smiles that win, the tints that glow,
　But tell of days in goodness spent, —
A mind at peace with all below,
　A heart whose love is innocent.
　　　　　　LORD BYRON.

CASTARA.

LIKE the violet, which alone
　Prospers in some happy shade,
My Castara lives unknown,
　To no ruder eye betrayed;
For she's to herself untrue
Who delights i' the public view.

Eng^d by G E Perine, New York

FORDS, HOWARD & HULBERT, N.Y.

Such is her beauty as no arts
  Have enriched with borrowed grace.
Her high birth no pride imparts,
  For she blushes in her place.
Folly boasts a glorious blood, —
She is noblest being good.

Cautious, she knew never yet
  What a wanton courtship meant;
Nor speaks loud to boast her wit,
  In her silence eloquent.
Of herself survey she takes,
But 'tween men no difference makes.

She obeys with speedy will
  Her grave parents' wise commands;
And so innocent, that ill
  She nor acts, nor understands.
Women's feet run still astray
If to ill they know the way.

She sails by that rock, the court,
  Where oft virtue splits her mast;
And retiredness thinks the port,
  Where her fame may anchor cast.
Virtue safely cannot sit
Where vice is enthroned for wit.

She holds that day's pleasure best
  Where sin waits not on delight;
Without mask, or ball, or feast,
  Sweetly spends a winter's night.
O'er that darkness whence is thrust
Prayer and sleep, oft governs lust.

She her throne makes reason climb,
  While wild passions captive lie;
And each article of time,
  Her pure thoughts to heaven fly;
All her vows religious be,
And she vows her love to me.
                    WILLIAM HABINGTON.

ANSWER TO A CHILD'S QUESTION.

Do you ask what the birds say? The sparrow,
    the dove,
The linnet, and thrush say "I love, and I love!"
In the winter they're silent, the wind is so strong;
What it says I don't know, but it sings a loud
    song.
But green leaves, and blossoms, and sunny
    warm weather,
And singing and loving—all come back together.
But the lark is so brimful of gladness and love,
The green fields below him, the blue sky above,
That he sings, and he sings, and forever sings he,
"I love my Love, and my Love loves me."
                    SAMUEL COLERIDGE.

AT THE CHURCH GATE.

ALTHOUGH I enter not,
Yet round about the spot
    Ofttimes I hover;
And near the sacred gate,
With longing eyes I wait,
    Expectant of her.

The minster bell tolls out
Above the city's rout,
    And noise and humming;
They 've hushed the minster bell;
The organ 'gins to swell;
    She 's coming, coming!

My lady comes at last,
Timid and stepping fast,
    And hastening hither,
With modest eyes downcast;
She comes, — she 's here, she 's past!
    May Heaven go with her!

Kneel undisturbed, fair saint!
Pour out your praise or plaint
    Meekly and duly;
I will not enter there,
To sully your pure prayer
    With thoughts unruly.

But suffer me to pace
Round the forbidden place,
    Lingering a minute,
Like outcast spirits, who wait,
And see, through heaven's gate,
    Angels within it.
            WILLIAM MAKEPEACE THACKERAY.

VERSES WRITTEN IN AN ALBUM.

HERE is one leaf reserved for me,
From all thy sweet memorials free;
And here my simple song might tell
The feelings thou must guess so well.
But could I thus, within thy mind,
One little vacant corner find,
Where no impression yet is seen,
Where no memorial yet has been,
O, it should be my sweetest care
To write my name forever there!
                    T. MOORE.

GO, LOVELY ROSE.

  Go, lovely rose!
Tell her that wastes her time and me,
  That now she knows,
When I resemble her to thee,
How sweet and fair she seems to be:

Tell her that's young,
And shuns to have her graces spied,
That hadst thou sprung
In deserts, where no men abide,
Thou must have uncommended died.

Small is the worth
Of beauty from the light retired ;
Bid her come forth,
Suffer herself to be desired,
And not blush so to be admired.

Then die, that she
The common fate of all things rare
May read in thee ;
How small a part of time they share,
That are so wondrous, sweet, and fair.
EDMUND WALLER.

STANZA ADDED BY HENRY KIRKE WHITE.

Yet, though thou fade,
From thy dead leaves let fragrance rise ;
And teach the maid,
That goodness Time's rude hand defies,
That virtue lives when beauty dies.

———◆———

FAIRER THAN THEE.

FAIRER than thee, beloved,
Fairer than thee ! —
There is one thing, beloved,
Fairer than thee.

Not the glad sun, beloved,
Bright though it beams ;
Not the green earth, beloved,
Silver with streams ;

Not the gay birds, beloved,
Happy and free :
Yet there 's one thing, beloved,
Fairer than thee.

Not the clear day, beloved,
Glowing with light ;
Not (fairer still, beloved)
Star-crownéd night.

Truth in her might, beloved,
Grand in her sway ;
Truth with her eyes, beloved,
Clearer than day.

Holy and pure, beloved,
Spotless and free,
Is the one thing, beloved,
Fairer than thee.

Guard well thy soul, beloved ;
Truth, dwelling there,
Shall shadow forth, beloved,
Her image rare.

Then shall I deem, beloved,
That thou art she ;
And there 'll be naught, beloved,
Fairer than thee.
ANONYMOUS.

———◆———

HER LIKENESS.

A GIRL, who has so many wilful ways
She would have caused Job's patience to for-
sake him ;
Yet is so rich in all that 's girlhood's praise,
Did Job himself upon her goodness gaze,
A little better she would surely make him.

Yet is this girl I sing in naught uncommon,
And very far from angel yet, I trow.
Her faults, her sweetnesses, are purely human ;
Yet she 's more lovable as simple woman
Than any one diviner that I know.

Therefore I wish that she may safely keep
This womanhede, and change not, only grow ;
From maid to matron, youth to age, may creep,
And in perennial blessedness, still reap
On every hand of that which she doth sow.
DINAH MARIA MULOCK.

———◆———

BLACK AND BLUE EYES.

THE brilliant black eye
May in triumph let fly
All its darts without caring who feels 'em ;
But the soft eye of blue,
Though it scatter wounds too,
Is much better pleased when it heals 'em !
Dear Fanny !

The black eye may say,
" Come and worship my ray ;
By adoring, perhaps you may move me ! "
But the blue eye, half hid,
Says, from under its lid,
" I love, and am yours, if you love me ! "
Dear Fanny !

Then tell me, O why,
In that lovely blue eye,
Not a charm of its tint I discover ;
Or why should you wear
The only blue pair
That ever said " No " to a lover ?
Dear Fanny !
THOMAS MOORE.

WHY, LOVELY CHARMER?

FROM "THE HIVE."

WHY, lovely charmer, tell me why,
So very kind, and yet so shy?
Why does that cold, forbidding air
Give damps of sorrow and despair?
Or why that smile my soul subdue,
And kindle up my flames anew?

In vain you strive with all your art,
By turns to fire and freeze my heart;
When I behold a face so fair,
So sweet a look, so soft an air,
My ravished soul is charmed all o'er,
I cannot love thee less or more.

ANONYMOUS.

I PRITHEE SEND ME BACK MY HEART.

I PRITHEE send me back my heart,
Since I cannot have thine;
For if from yours you will not part,
Why then shouldst thou have mine?

Yet, now I think on 't, let it lie;
To find it were in vain;
For thou 'st a thief in either eye
Would steal it back again.

Why should two hearts in one breast lie,
And yet not lodge together?
O Love! where is thy sympathy
If thus our breasts thou sever?

But love is such a mystery,
I cannot find it out;
For when I think I 'm best resolved
Then I am most in doubt.

Then farewell care, and farewell woe;
I will no longer pine;
For I 'll believe I have her heart
As much as she has mine.

SIR JOHN SUCKLING.

IF DOUGHTY DEEDS MY LADY PLEASE.

IF doughty deeds my lady please,
Right soon I 'll mount my steed,
And strong his arm and fast his seat
That bears frae me the meed.
I 'll wear thy colors in my cap,
Thy picture at my heart,
And he that bends not to thine eye
Shall rue it to his smart!

Then tell me how to woo thee, Love;
O, tell me how to woo thee!
For thy dear sake nae care I 'll take,
Though ne'er another trow me.

If gay attire delight thine eye,
I 'll dight me in array;
I 'll tend thy chamber door all night,
And squire thee all the day.
If sweetest sounds can win thine ear,
These sounds I 'll strive to catch;
Thy voice I 'll steal to woo thysell,
That voice that nane can match.

But if fond love thy heart can gain,
I never broke a vow;
Nae maiden lays her skaith to me;
I never loved but you.
For you alone I ride the ring,
For you I wear the blue;
For you alone I strive to sing,
O, tell me how to woo!
Then tell me how to woo thee, Love;
O, tell me how to woo thee!
For thy dear sake nae care I 'll take,
Though ne'er another trow me.

GRAHAM OF GARTMORE.

MY LOVE IN HER ATTIRE.

MY Love in her attire doth show her wit,
It doth so well become her:
For every season she hath dressings fit,
For Winter, Spring, and Summer.
No beauty she doth miss
When all her robes are on:
But beauty's self she is
When all her robes are gone.

ANONYMOUS.

A SLEEPING BEAUTY.

SLEEP on! and dream of Heaven awhile!
Though shut so close thy laughing eyes,
Thy rosy lips still wear a smile,
And move, and breathe delicious sighs.

Ah! now soft blushes tinge her cheeks
And mantle o'er her neck of snow;
Ah! now she murmurs, now she speaks,
What most I wish, and fear, to know.

She starts, she trembles, and she weeps!
Her fair hands folded on her breast;
— And now, how like a saint she sleeps!
A seraph in the realms of rest!

Sleep on secure ! Above control,
  Thy thoughts belong to Heaven and thee ;
And may the secret of thy soul
  Remain within its sanctuary !
SAMUEL ROGERS.

SHE IS NOT FAIR TO OUTWARD VIEW.

SHE is not fair to outward view,
  As many maidens be ;
Her loveliness I never knew
  Until she smiled on me :
O, then I saw her eye was bright, —
A well of love, a spring of light.

But now her looks are coy and cold ;
  To mine they ne'er reply ;
And yet I cease not to behold,
  The love-light in her eye :
Her very frowns are better far
Than smiles of other maidens are !
HARTLEY COLERIDGE.

PHILLIS IS MY ONLY JOY.

PHILLIS is my only joy
  Faithless as the wind or seas ;
Sometimes coming, sometimes coy,
  Yet she never fails to please.
    If with a frown
    I am cast down,
    Phillis, smiling
    And beguiling,
Makes me happier than before.

Though, alas ! too late I find
  Nothing can her fancy fix ;
Yet the moment she is kind
  I forgive her all her tricks ;
    Which though I see,
    I can't get free ;
    She deceiving,
    I believing,
What need lovers wish for more ?
SIR CHARLES SEDLEY.

TO ALTHEA FROM PRISON.

WHEN Love with unconfinéd wings
  Hovers within my gates,
And my divine Althea brings
  To whisper at the grates ;
When I lie tangled in her hair
  And fettered to her eye,

The birds that wanton in the air
  Know no such liberty.

When flowing cups run swiftly round
  With no allaying Thames,
Our careless heads with roses crowned,
  Our hearts with loyal flames ;
When thirsty grief in wine we steep,
  When healths and draughts go free,
Fishes that tipple in the deep
  Know no such liberty.

When, linnet-like confinéd, I
  With shriller throat shall sing
The sweetness, mercy, majesty
  And glories of my King ;
When I shall voice aloud how good
  He is, how great should be,
Enlargéd winds, that curl the flood,
  Know no such liberty.

Stone walls do not a prison make,
  Nor iron bars a cage ;
Minds innocent and quiet take
  That for an hermitage :
If I have freedom in my love,
  And in my soul am free,
Angels alone, that soar above,
  Enjoy such liberty.
COLONEL RICHARD LOVELACE.

MY LITTLE SAINT.

I CARE not, though it be
By the preciser sort thought popery ;
  We poets can a license show
  For everything we do.
Hear, then, my little saint ! I 'll pray to thee.

If now thy happy mind,
Amidst its various joys, can leisure find
  To attend to anything so low
  As what I say or do,
Regard, and be what thou wast ever, — kind.

Let not the blest above
Engross thee quite, but sometimes hither rove :
  Fain would I thy sweet image see,
  And sit and talk with thee ;
Nor is it curiosity, but love.

Ah ! what delight 't would be,
Wouldst thou sometimes by stealth converse with
  me !
  How should I thy sweet commune prize,
  And other joys despise !
Come, then ! I ne'er was yet denied by thee.

I would not long detain
Thy soul from bliss, nor keep thee here in pain ;
    Nor should thy fellow-saints e'er know
    Of thy escape below :
Before thou 'rt missed, thou shouldst return again.

Sure, heaven must needs thy love,
As well as other qualities, improve :
    Come, then ! and recreate my sight
    With rays of thy pure light ;
'T will cheer my eyes more than the lamps above.

But if Fate 's so severe
As to confine thee to thy blissful sphere,
    (And by thy absence I shall know
    Whether thy state be so,)
Live happy, and be mindful of me there.

JOHN NORRIS.

A GOLDEN GIRL.

LUCY is a golden girl ;
    But a man, a *man*, should woo her !
They who seek her shrink aback,
    When they should, like storms, pursue her.

All her smiles are hid in light ;
    All her hair is lost in splendor ;
But she hath the eyes of Night
    And a heart that 's over-tender.

Yet the foolish suitors fly
    (Is 't excess of dread or duty ?)
From the starlight of her eye,
    Leaving to neglect her beauty !

Men by fifty seasons taught
    Leave her to a young beginner,
Who, without a second thought,
    Whispers, woos, and straight must win her.

Lucy is a golden girl !
    Toast her in a goblet brimming !
May the man that wins her wear
    On his heart the Rose of Women !

BARRY CORNWALL.

MY SWEET SWEETING.

FROM A MS. TEMP. HENRY VIII.

AH, my sweet sweeting ;
    My little pretty sweeting,
My sweeting will I love wherever I go ;
    She is so proper and pure,
Full, steadfast, stable, and demure,
    There is none such, you may be sure,
        As my sweet sweeting.

In all this world, as thinketh me,
Is none so pleasant to my e'e,
    That I am glad so oft to see,
        As my sweet sweeting.
When I behold my sweeting sweet,
Her face, her hands, her minion feet,
They seem to me there is none so mete,
    As my sweet sweeting.

Above all other praise must I,
And love my pretty pygsnye,
For none I find so womanly
    As my sweet sweeting.

ANONYMOUS.

THE FLOWER'S NAME.

HERE 's the garden she walked across,
    Arm in my arm, such a short while since :
Hark ! now I push its wicket, the moss
    Hinders the hinges, and makes them wince.
She must have reached this shrub ere she turned,
    As back with that murmur the wicket swung ;
For she laid the poor snail my chance foot spurned,
    To feed and forget it the leaves among.

Down this side of the gravel walk
    She went while her robe's edge brushed the box ;
And here she paused in her gracious talk
    To point me a moth on the milk-white phlox.
Roses, ranged in valiant row,
    I will never think that she passed you by !
She loves you, noble roses, I know ;
    But yonder see where the rock-plants lie !

This flower she stopped at, finger on lip, —
    Stooped over, in doubt, as settling its claim ;
Till she gave me, with pride to make no slip,
    Its soft meandering Spanish name.
What a name ! was it love or praise ?
    Speech half asleep, or song half awake ?
I must learn Spanish one of these days,
    Only for that slow sweet name's sake.

Roses, if I live and do well,
    I may bring her one of these days,
To fix you fast with as fine a spell, —
    Fit you each with his Spanish phrase.
But do not detain me now, for she lingers
    There, like sunshine over the ground ;
And ever I see her soft white fingers
    Searching after the bud she found.

Flower, you Spaniard ! look that you grow not, —
    Stay as you are, and be loved forever.
Bud, if I kiss you, 't is that you blow not, —
    Mind ! the shut pink mouth opens never !

For while thus it pouts, her fingers wrestle,
  Twinkling the audacious leaves between,
Till round they turn, and down they nestle :
  Is not the dear mark still to be seen ?

Where I find her not, beauties vanish ;
  Whither I follow her, beauties flee.
Is there no method to tell her in Spanish
  June's twice June since she breathed it with me ?
Come, bud ! show me the least of her traces.
  Treasure my lady's lightest footfall :
Ah ! you may flout and turn up your faces, —
  Roses, you are not so fair after all !
                  ROBERT BROWNING.

ON A GIRDLE.

THAT which her slender waist confined
Shall now my joyful temples bind ;
No monarch but would give his crown,
His arms might do what this hath done.

It was my heaven's extremest sphere,
The pale which held that lovely deer :
My joy, my grief, my hope, my love,
Did all within this circle move.

A narrow compass ! and yet there
Dwelt all that's good, and all that's fair.
Give me but what this ribbon bound,
Take all the rest the sun goes round !
                  EDMUND WALLER.

THE MILLER'S DAUGHTER.

IT is the miller's daughter,
  And she is grown so dear, so dear,
That I would be the jewel
  That trembles at her ear ;
For, hid in ringlets day and night,
I'd touch her neck so warm and white.

And I would be the girdle
  About her dainty, dainty waist,
And her heart would beat against me
  In sorrow and in rest ;
And I should know if it beat right,
I'd clasp it round so close and tight.

And I would be the necklace,
  And all day long to fall and rise
Upon her balmy bosom
  With her laughter or her sighs ;
And I would lie so light, so light,
I scarce should be unclasped at night.
                ALFRED TENNYSON.

THE FLOWER O' DUMBLANE.

THE sun has gane down o'er the lofty Ben Lomond,
  And left the red clouds to preside o'er the scene,
While lanely I stray in the calm summer gloamin',
  To muse on sweet Jessie, the Flower o' Dumblane.

How sweet is the brier, wi' its saft fauldin' blossom,
  And sweet is the birk, wi' its mantle o' green ;
Yet sweeter and fairer, and dear to this bosom,
  Is lovely young Jessie, the Flower o' Dumblane.

She's modest as ony, and blithe as she's bonnie, —
  For guileless simplicity marks her its ain ;
And far be the villain, divested of feeling,
  Wha'd blight in its bloom the sweet Flower o' Dumblane.

Sing on, thou sweet mavis, thy hymn to the e'ening ! —
  Thou 'rt dear to the echoes of Calderwood glen :
Sae dear to this bosom, sae artless and winning,
  Is charming young Jessie, the Flower o' Dumblane.

How lost were my days till I met wi' my Jessie !
  The sports o' the city seemed foolish and vain ;
I ne'er saw a nymph I would ca' my dear lassie
  Till charmed wi' sweet Jessie, the Flower o' Dumblane.

Though mine were the station o' loftiest grandeur,
  Amidst its profusion I'd languish in pain,
And reckon as naething the height o' its splendor,
  If wanting sweet Jessie, the Flower o' Dumblane.
                ROBERT TANNAHILL.

O, SAW YE THE LASS?

O, SAW ye the lass wi' the bonny blue een ?
Her smile is the sweetest that ever was seen ;
Her cheek like the rose is, but fresher, I ween ;
She's the loveliest lassie that trips on the green.
The home of my love is below in the valley,
Where wild-flowers welcome the wandering bee ;
But the sweetest of flowers in that spot that is seen
Is the maid that I love wi' the bonny blue een.

When night overshadows her cot in the glen,
She'll steal out to meet her loved Donald again ;
And when the moon shines on the valley so green,
I'll welcome the lass wi' the bonny blue een.
As the dove that has wandered away from his nest
Returns to the mate his fond heart loves the best,
I'll fly from the world's false and vanishing scene,
To my dear one, the lass wi' the bonny blue een.
                RICHARD RYAN.

THE LASS OF RICHMOND HILL.

ON Richmond Hill there lives a lass
　　More bright than May-day morn,
Whose charms all other maids surpass, —
　　A rose without a thorn.

This lass so neat, with smiles so sweet,
　　Has won my right good-will ;
I 'd crowns resign to call her mine,
　　Sweet lass of Richmond Hill.

Ye zephyrs gay, that fan the air,
　　And wanton through the grove,
O, whisper to my charming fair,
　　I die for her I love.

How happy will the shepherd be
　　Who calls this nymph his own !
O, may her choice be fixed on me !
　　Mine 's fixed on her alone.
　　　　　　　　　　　　　UPTON.

MARY MORISON.

O MARY, at thy window be !
It is the wished, the trysted hour !
Those smiles and glances let me see
　　That make the miser's treasure poor :
How blithely wad I bide the stoure,
　　A weary slave frae sun to sun,
Could I the rich reward secure,
　　The lovely Mary Morison.

Yestreen when to the trembling string
　　The dance gaed through the lighted ha',
To thee my fancy took its wing, —
　　I sat, but neither heard nor saw :
Though this was fair, and that was braw,
　　And yon the toast of a' the town,
I sighed, and said amang them a',
　　"Ye are na Mary Morison."

O Mary, canst thou wreck his peace
　　Wha for thy sake wad gladly dee ?
Or canst thou break that heart of his,
　　Whase only faut is loving thee ?
If love for love thou wilt na gie,
　　At least be pity to me shown ;
A thought ungentle canna be
　　The thought o' Mary Morison.
　　　　　　　　　　　ROBERT BURNS.

IN THE STILLNESS O' THE NIGHT.

DORSET DIALECT.

Ov all the housen o' the pliace
　　Ther 's gone wher I da like to call,

By dae ar night, the best ov all,
To zee my Fanny's smilén fiace ;
　　An' dere the stiately trees da grow,
　　A-rockén as the win' da blow,
　　While she da sweetly sleep below,
　　　　In the stillness o' the night.

An' dere at evemen I da goo,
　　A-hoppén auver ghiates an' bars,
　　By twinklen light o' winter stars,
When snow da clumper to my shoe ;
　　An' zometimes we da slyly catch
　　A chat, an hour upon the stratch,
　　An' piart wi' whispers at the hatch,
　　　　In the stillness o' the night.

An' zometimes she da goo to zome
Young nâighbours' housen down the pliace,
　　An' I da get a clue to triace
Her out, an' goo to zee her huome ,
　　An' I da wish a vield a mile,
　　As she da sweetly chat an' smile
　　Along the drove, or at the stile,
　　　　In the stillness o' the night.
　　　　　　　　　　　WILLIAM BARNES.

O MISTRESS MINE.

O MISTRESS mine, where are you roaming ?
O, stay and hear ! your true-love 's coming
　　That can sing both high and low ;
Trip no further, pretty sweeting,
Journeys end in lovers' meeting, —
　　Every wise man's son doth know.

What is love ? 't is not hereafter ;
Present mirth hath present laughter ;
　　What 's to come is still unsure :
In delay there lies no plenty, —
Then come kiss me, Sweet-and-twenty,
　　Youth 's a stuff will not endure.
　　　　　　　　　　　SHAKESPEARE.

THE LOW–BACKED CAR.

WHEN first I saw sweet Peggy,
　　'T was on a market day :
A low-backed car she drove, and sat
　　Upon a truss of hay ;
But when that hay was blooming grass,
　　And decked with flowers of spring,
No flower was there that could compare
　　With the blooming girl I sing.
As she sat in the low-backed car,
　　The man at the turnpike bar
　　　　Never asked for the toll,
　　　　But just rubbed his owld poll,
And looked after the low-backed car.

In battle's wild commotion,
　　The proud and mighty Mars
With hostile scythes demands his tithes
　　Of death in warlike cars ;
While Peggy, peaceful goddess,
　　Has darts in her bright eye,
That knock men down in the market town,
　　As right and left they fly ;
While she sits in her low-backed car,
Than battle more dangerous far, —
　　　　For the doctor's art
　　　　Cannot cure the heart,
That is hit from that low-backed car.

Sweet Peggy round her car, sir,
　　Has strings of ducks and geese,
But the scores of hearts she slaughters
　　By far outnumber these ;
While she among her poultry sits,
　　Just like a turtle-dove,
Well worth the cage, I do engage,
　　Of the blooming god of Love !
While she sits in her low-backed car,
The lovers come near and far,
　　　　And envy the chicken
　　　　That Peggy is pickin',
As she sits in her low-backed car.

O, I 'd rather own that car, sir,
　　With Peggy by my side,
Than a coach and four, and gold *galore*,
　　And a lady for my bride ;
For the lady would sit forninst me,
　　On a cushion made with taste,
While Peggy would sit beside me,
　　With my arm around her waist,
While we drove in the low-backed car,
To be married by Father Mahar ;
　　　　O, my heart would beat high
　　　　At her glance and her sigh, —
Though it beat in a low-backed car !
　　　　　　　　SAMUEL LOVER.

SALLY IN OUR ALLEY.

OF all the girls that are so smart
　　There 's none like pretty Sally ;
She is the darling of my heart,
　　And she lives in our alley.
There is no lady in the land
　　Is half so sweet as Sally ;
She is the darling of my heart,
　　And she lives in our alley.

Her father he makes cabbage-nets,
　　And through the streets does cry 'em ;

Her mother she sells laces long
　　To such as please to buy 'em ;
But sure such folks could ne'er beget
　　So sweet a girl as Sally !
She is the darling of my heart,
　　And she lives in our alley.

When she is by I leave my work,
　　I love her so sincerely ;
My master comes like any Turk,
　　And bangs me most severely.
But let him bang his bellyful, —
　　I 'll bear it all for Sally ;
For she 's the darling of my heart,
　　And she lives in our alley.

Of all the days that 's in the week
　　I dearly love but one day,
And that 's the day that comes betwixt
　　The Saturday and Monday ;
For then I 'm drest all in my best
　　To walk abroad with Sally ;
She is the darling of my heart,
　　And she lives in our alley.

My master carries me to church,
　　And often am I blaméd
Because I leave him in the lurch
　　As soon as text is naméd :
I leave the church in sermon-time,
　　And slink away to Sally, —
She is the darling of my heart,
　　And she lives in our alley.

When Christmas comes about again,
　　O, then I shall have money !
I 'll hoard it up, and, box and all,
　　I 'll give it to my honey ;
O, would it were ten thousand pound !
　　I 'd give it all to Sally ;
For she 's the darling of my heart,
　　And she lives in our alley.

My master and the neighbors all
　　Make game of me and Sally,
And but for her I 'd better be
　　A slave, and row a galley ;
But when my seven long years are out,
　　O, then I 'll marry Sally !
O, then we 'll wed, and then we 'll bed, —
　　But not in our alley !
　　　　　　　　HENRY CAREY.

LOVELY MARY DONNELLY.

O LOVELY Mary Donnelly, it 's you I love the
　　best !
If fifty girls were around you, I 'd hardly see the
　　rest ;

Be what it may the time of day, the place be
where it will,
Sweet looks of Mary Donnelly, they bloom before
me still.

Her eyes like mountain water that's flowing on
a rock,
How clear they are! how dark they are! and
they give me many a shock;
Red rowans warm in sunshine, and wetted with
a shower,
Could ne'er express the charming lip that has
me in its power.

Her nose is straight and handsome, her eyebrows
lifted up,
Her chin is very neat and pert, and smooth like
a china cup;
Her hair's the brag of Ireland, so weighty and
so fine, —
It's rolling down upon her neck, and gathered
in a twine.

The dance o' last Whit-Monday night exceeded
all before;
No pretty girl for miles around was missing from
the floor;
But Mary kept the belt of love, and O, but she
was gay;
She danced a jig, she sung a song, and took my
heart away!

When she stood up for dancing, her steps were
so complete,
The music nearly killed itself, to listen to her
feet;
The fiddler mourned his blindness, he heard her
so much praised,
But blessed himself he was n't deaf when once
her voice she raised.

And evermore I'm whistling or lilting what you
sung;
Your smile is always in my heart, your name be-
side my tongue.
But you've as many sweethearts as you'd count
on both your hands,
And for myself there's not a thumb or little
finger stands.

O, you're the flower of womankind, in country
or in town;
The higher I exalt you, the lower I'm cast down.
If some great lord should come this way and see
your beauty bright,
And you to be his lady, I'd own it was but right.

O, might we live together in lofty palace hall,
Where joyful music rises, and where scarlet cur-
tains fall;
O, might we live together in a cottage mean and
small,
With sods of grass the only roof, and mud the
only wall!

O lovely Mary Donnelly, your beauty's my dis-
tress;
It's far too beauteous to be mine, but I'll never
wish it less;
The proudest place would fit your face, and I am
poor and low,
But blessings be about you, dear, wherever you
may go!

WILLIAM ALLINGHAM.

THE POSIE.

O, LUVE will venture in where it daurna weel be
seen,
O, luve will venture in where wisdom ance has been!
But I will down yon river rove amang the woods
sae green:
And a' to pu' a posie to my ain dear May.

The primrose I will pu', the firstling o' the year,
And I will pu' the pink, the emblem o' my dear,
For she's the pink o' womankind, and blooms
without a peer:
And a' to be a posie to my ain dear May.

I'll pu' the budding rose, when Phœbus peeps in
view,
For it's like a balmy kiss o' her sweet bonnie mou';
The hyacinth's for constancy, wi' its unchanging
blue:
And a' to be a posie to my ain dear May.

The lily it is pure, and the lily it is fair,
And in her lovely bosom I'll place the lily there;
The daisy's for simplicity and unaffected air:
And a' to be a posie to my ain dear May.

The hawthorn I will pu', wi' its locks o' siller gray,
Where, like an aged man, it stands at break o' day;
But the songster's nest within the bush I winna
take away:
And a' to be a posie to my ain dear May.

The woodbine I will pu', when the e'ening star
is near,
And the diamond draps o' dew shall be her een
sae clear;
The violet's for modesty, which weel she fa's to
wear:
And a' to be a posie to my ain dear May.

I 'll tie the posie round wi' the silken band o' luve,
And I 'll place it in her breast, and I 'll swear by
　a' above,
That to my latest draught o' life the band shall
　ne'er remove :
And this will be a posie to my ain dear May.
ROBERT BURNS.

MARY LEE.

I HAVE traced the valleys fair
In May morning's dewy air,
　My bonny Mary Lee !
Wilt thou deign the wreath to wear,
　Gathered all for thee ?
They are not flowers of Pride,
For they graced the dingle-side ;
Yet they grew in Heaven's smile,
　My gentle Mary Lee !
Can they fear thy frowns the while
　Though offeréd by me ?

Here 's the lily of the vale,
That perfumed the morning gale,
　My fairy Mary Lee !
All so spotless and so pale,
　Like thine own purity.
And might I make it known,
'T is an emblem of my own
Love, — if I dare so name
　My esteem for thee.
Surely flowers can bear no blame,
　My bonny Mary Lee.

Here 's the violet's modest blue,
That 'neath hawthorns hides from view,
　My gentle Mary Lee,
Would show whose heart is true,
　While it thinks of thee.
While they choose each lowly spot,
The sun disdains them not ;
I 'm as lowly too, indeed,
　My charming Mary Lee ;
So I 've brought the flowers to plead,
　And win a smile from thee.

Here 's a wild rose just in bud ;
Spring's beauty in its hood,
　My bonny Mary Lee !
'T is the first in all the wood
　I could find for thee.
Though a blush is scarcely seen,
Yet it hides its worth within,
Like my love ; for I 've no power,
　My angel Mary Lee,
To speak unless the flower
　Can make excuse for me.

Though they deck no princely halls,
In bouquets for glittering balls,
　My gentle Mary Lee !
Richer hues than painted walls
　Will make them dear to thee ;
For the blue and laughing sky
Spreads a grander canopy
Than all wealth's golden skill,
　My charming Mary Lee !
Love would make them dearer still,
　That offers them to thee.

My wreathéd flowers are few,
Yet no fairer drink the dew,
　My bonny Mary Lee !
They may seem as trifles too, —
　Not, I hope, to thee ;
Some may boast a richer prize
Under pride and wealth's disguise ;
None a fonder offering bore
　Than this of mine to thee ;
And can true love wish for more ?
　Surely not, Mary Lee !
JOHN CLARE.

ANNIE LAURIE.

MAXWELTON braes are bonnie
Where early fa's the dew,
And it 's there that Annie Laurie
Gie'd me her promise true, —
Gie'd me her promise true,
Which ne'er forgot will be ;
And for bonnie Annie Laurie
I 'd lay me doune and dee.

Her brow is like the snaw drift ;
Her throat is like the swan ;
Her face it is the fairest
That e'er the sun shone on, —
That e'er the sun shone on ;
And dark blue is her ee ;
And for bonnie Annie Laurie
I 'd lay me doune and dee.

Like dew on the gowan lying
Is the fa' o' her fairy feet ;
And like the winds in summer sighing,
Her voice is low and sweet, —
Her voice is low and sweet ;
And she 's a' the world to me ;
And for bonnie Annie Laurie
I 'd lay me doune and dee.
ANONYMOUS.

LOVE.

LOVE IS A SICKNESS.

Love is a sickness full of woes,
  All remedies refusing ;
A plant that most with cutting grows,
  Most barren with best using.
    Why so ?
More we enjoy it, more it dies ;
If not enjoyed, it sighing cries
    Heigh-ho !

Love is a torment of the mind,
  A tempest everlasting ;
And Jove hath made it of a kind,
  Not well, nor full, nor fasting.
    Why so ?
More we enjoy it, more it dies ;
If not enjoyed, it sighing cries
    Heigh-ho !

SAMUEL DANIEL.

AH ! WHAT IS LOVE ?

Ah ! what is love ? It is a pretty thing,
As sweet unto a shepherd as a king,
    And sweeter too ;
For kings have cares that wait upon a crown,
And cares can make the sweetest face to frown :
    Ah then, ah then,
If country loves such sweet desires gain,
What lady would not love a shepherd swain ?

His flocks are folded ; he comes home at night
As merry as a king in his delight,
    And merrier too ;
For kings bethink them what the state require,
Where shepherds, careless, carol by the fire :
    Ah then, ah then,
If country love such sweet desires gain,
What lady would not love a shepherd swain ?

He kisseth first, then sits as blithe to eat
His cream and curd as doth the king his meat,
    And blither too ;
For kings have often fears when they sup,
Where shepherds dread no poison in their cup :
    Ah then, ah then,
If country loves such sweet desires gain,
What lady would not love a shepherd swain ?

Upon his couch of straw he sleeps as sound
As doth the king upon his beds of down,
    More sounder too ;

For cares cause kings full oft their sleep to spill,
Where weary shepherds lie and snort their fill :
    Ah then, ah then,
If country loves such sweet desires gain,
What lady would not love a shepherd swain ?

Thus with his wife he spends the year as blithe
As doth the king at every tide or syth,
    And blither too ;
For kings have wars and broils to take in hand,
When shepherds laugh, and love upon the land :
    Ah then, ah then,
If country loves such sweet desires gain,
What lady would not love a shepherd swain ?

ROBERT GREENE.

TELL ME, MY HEART, IF THIS BE LOVE.

When Delia on the plain appears,
Awed by a thousand tender fears,
I would approach, but dare not move ; —
Tell me, my heart, if this be love.

Whene'er she speaks, my ravished ear
No other voice than hers can hear ;
No other wit but hers approve ; —
Tell me, my heart, if this be love.

If she some other swain commend,
Though I was once his fondest friend,
His instant enemy I prove ; —
Tell me, my heart, if this be love.

When she is absent, I no more
Delight in all that pleased before,
The clearest spring, the shadiest grove ; —
Tell me, my heart, if this be love.

When fond of power, of beauty vain,
Her nets she spread for every swain,
I strove to hate, but vainly strove ; —
Tell me, my heart, if this be love.

GEORGE LORD LYTTELTON.

ECHOES.

How sweet the answer Echo makes
    To Music at night
When, roused by lute or horn, she wakes,
And far away o'er lawns and lakes
    Goes answering light !

Yet Love hath echoes truer far
    And far more sweet
Than e'er, beneath the moonlight's star,
Of horn or lute or soft guitar
    The songs repeat.

'T is when the sigh — in youth sincere
    And only then,
The sigh that 's breathed for one to hear —
Is by that one, that only Dear
    Breathed back again.
               THOMAS MOORE.

AH, HOW SWEET.

AH, how sweet it is to love !
    Ah, how gay is young desire !
And what pleasing pains we prove
When we first approach love's fire !
Pains of love are sweeter far
Than all other pleasures are.

Sighs which are from lovers blown
    Do but gently heave the heart :
E'en the tears they shed alone
    Cure, like trickling balm, their smart.
Lovers, when they lose their breath,
Bleed away in easy death.

Love and Time with reverence use,
    Treat them like a parting friend ;
Nor the golden gifts refuse
    Which in youth sincere they send :
For each year their price is more,
And they less simple than before.

Love, like spring-tides full and high,
    Swells in every youthful vein ;
But each tide does less supply,
    Till they quite shrink in again.
If a flow in age appear,
'T is but rain, and runs not clear.
               JOHN DRYDEN.

THE FIRE OF LOVE.

FROM THE "EXAMEN MISCELLANEUM," 1708.

THE fire of love in youthful blood,
Like what is kindled in brushwood,
    But for a moment burns ;
Yet in that moment makes a mighty noise ;
It crackles, and to vapor turns,
    And soon itself destroys.

But when crept into aged veins
It slowly burns, and then long remains,
    And with a silent heat,

Like fire in logs, it glows and warms 'em long ;
And though the flame be not so great,
    Yet is the heat as strong.
               EARL OF DORSET.

THE AGE OF WISDOM.

Ho ! pretty page, with the dimpled chin,
    That never has known the barber's shear,
All your wish is woman to win ;
This is the way that boys begin, —
    Wait till you come to forty year.

Curly gold locks cover foolish brains ;
    Billing and cooing is all your cheer, —
Sighing, and singing of midnight strains,
Under Bonnybell's window-panes, —
    Wait till you come to forty year.

Forty times over let Michaelmas pass ;
    Grizzling hair the brain doth clear ;
Then you know a boy is an ass,
Then you know the worth of a lass, —
    Once you have come to forty year.

Pledge me round ; I bid ye declare,
    All good fellows whose beards are gray, —
Did not the fairest of the fair
Common grow and wearisome ere
    Ever a month was past away ?

The reddest lips that ever have kissed,
    The brightest eyes that ever have shone,
May pray and whisper and we not list,
Or look away and never be missed, —
    Ere yet ever a month is gone.

Gillian 's dead ! God rest her bier, —
    How I loved her twenty years syne !
Marian 's married ; but I sit here,
Alone and merry at forty year,
    Dipping my nose in the Gascon wine.
        WILLIAM MAKEPEACE THACKERAY.

THE DECEIVED LOVER SUETH ONLY FOR LIBERTY.

IF chance assigned,
Were to my mind,
By every kind
    Of destiny ;
Yet would I crave
Naught else to have,
    But dearest life and liberty.

Then were I sure,
I might endure
The displeasure
    Of cruelty ;

Where now I plain
Alas ! in vain,
    Lacking my life for liberty.

For without th' one,
Th' other is gone,
And there can none
    It remedy ;
If th' one be past,
Th' other doth waste,
    And all for lack of liberty.

And so I drive,
As yet alive,
Although I strive
    With misery ;
Drawing my breath,
Looking for death,
    And loss of life for liberty.

But thou that still,
May'st at thy will,
Turn all this ill
    Adversity ;
For the repair,
Of my welfare,
    Grant me but life and liberty.

And if not so,
Then let all go
To wretched woe,
    And let me die ;
For th' one or th' other,
There is none other ;
    My death, or life with liberty.
          SIR THOMAS WYATT.

MY TRUE–LOVE HATH MY HEART.

My true-love hath my heart, and I have his,
  By just exchange one to the other given :
I hold his dear, and mine he cannot miss,
  There never was a better bargain driven :
My true-love hath my heart, and I have his.

His heart in me keeps him and me in one ;
  My heart in him his thoughts and senses
    guides :
He loves my heart, for once it was his own ;
  I cherish his because in me it bides :
My true-love hath my heart, and I have his.
          SIR PHILIP SIDNEY.

I SAW TWO CLOUDS AT MORNING.

I saw two clouds at morning,
  Tinged by the rising sun,
And in the dawn they floated on,
  And mingled into one ;

I thought that morning cloud was blessed,
It moved so sweetly to the west.

I saw two summer currents
  Flow smoothly to their meeting,
And join their course, with silent force,
  In peace each other greeting ;
Calm was their course through banks of green,
While dimpling eddies played between.

Such be your gentle motion,
  Till life's last pulse shall beat ;
Like summer's beam, and summer's stream,
  Float on, in joy, to meet
A calmer sea, where storms shall cease,
A purer sky, where all is peace.
          JOHN G. C. BRAINARD.

LOVE'S PHILOSOPHY.

THE fountains mingle with the river,
  And the rivers with the océan ;
The winds of heaven mix forever,
  With a sweet emotion ;
Nothing in the world is single ;
  All things by a law divine
In one another's being mingle : —
  Why not I with thine ?

See ! the mountains kiss high heaven,
  And the waves clasp one another ;
No sister flower would be forgiven
  If it disdained its brother ;
And the sunlight clasps the earth,
  And the moonbeams kiss the sea : —
What are all these kissings worth,
  If thou kiss not me ?
          PERCY BYSSHE SHELLEY.

THOSE EYES.

AH ! do not wanton with those eyes,
  Lest I be sick with seeing ;
Nor cast them down, but let them rise,
  Lest shame destroy their being.

Ah ! be not angry with those fires,
  For then their threats will kill me ;
Nor look too kind on my desires,
  For then my hopes will spill me.

Ah ! do not steep them in thy tears,
  For so will sorrow slay me ;
Nor spread them as distraught with fears, —
  Mine own enough betray me.
          BEN JONSON.

SWEET, BE NOT PROUD.

SWEET, be not proud of those two eyes,
Which starlike sparkle in their skies ;
Nor be you proud that you can see
All hearts your captives, yours yet free.
Be you not proud of that rich hair,
Which wantons with the lovesick air ;
Whenas that ruby which you wear,
Sunk from the tip of your soft ear,
Will last to be a precious stone
When all your world of beauty 's gone.
ROBERT HERRICK.

GREEN GROW THE RASHES O!

GREEN grow the rashes O,
  Green grow the rashes O ;
The sweetest hours that e'er I spend
  Are spent amang the lasses O.

There 's naught but care on ev'ry han',
  In every hour that passes O ;
What signifies the life o' man,
  An' 't were na for the lasses O ?

The warly race may riches chase,
  An' riches still may fly them O ;
An' though at last they catch them fast,
  Their hearts can ne'er enjoy them O.

Gie me a canny hour at e'en,
  My arms about my dearie O,
An' warly cares an' warly men
  May all gae tapsalteerie O.

For you sae douce, ye sneer at this,
  Ye 're naught but senseless asses O !
The wisest man the warl' e'er saw
  He dearly lo'ed the lasses O.

Auld Nature swears the lovely dears
  Her noblest work she classes O :
Her 'prentice han' she tried on man,
  An' then she made the lasses O.
ROBERT BURNS.

THE CHRONICLE.

MARGARITA first possessed,
If I remember well, my breast,
  Margarita first of all ;
But when awhile the wanton maid
With my restless heart had played,
  Martha took the flying ball.

Martha soon did it resign
To the beauteous Catharine.
  Beauteous Catharine gave place
(Though loath and angry she to part
With the possession of my heart)
  To Eliza's conquering face.

Eliza till this hour might reign,
Had she not evil counsels ta'en ;
  Fundamental laws she broke,
And still new favorites she chose,
Till up in arms my passions rose,
  And cast away her yoke.

Mary then, and gentle Anne,
Both to reign at once began ;
  Alternately they swayed ;
And sometimes Mary was the fair,
And sometimes Anne the crown did wear,
  And sometimes both I obeyed.

Another Mary then arose,
And did rigorous laws impose ;
  A mighty tyrant she !
Long, alas ! should I have been
Under that iron-sceptred queen,
  Had not Rebecca set me free.

When fair Rebecca set me free,
'T was then a golden time with me :
  But soon those pleasures fled ;
For the gracious princess died
In her youth and beauty's pride,
  And Judith reignéd in her stead.

One month, three days, and half an hour,
Judith held the sovereign power :
  Wondrous beautiful her face !
But so weak and small her wit,
That she to govern was unfit,
  And so Susanna took her place.

But when Isabella came,
Armed with a resistless flame,
  And the artillery of her eye,
Whilst she proudly marched about,
Greater conquests to find out,
  She beat out Susan, by the by.

But in her place I then obeyed
Black-eyed Bess, her viceroy-maid,
  To whom ensued a vacancy :
Thousand worse passions then possessed
The interregnum of my breast ;
  Bless me from such an anarchy !

Gentle Henrietta then,
And a third Mary next began ;
  Then Joan, and Jane, and Andria ;
And then a pretty Thomasine,
And then another Catharine,
  And then a long *et cætera*.

But I will briefer with them be,
Since few of them were long with me.
  An higher and a nobler strain
My present emperess does claim,
Heleonora, first of the name ;
  Whom God grant long to reign !
                    ABRAHAM COWLEY.

A DOUBT.

FROM THE THIRD BOOK OF LAWES'S AYRES.

FAIN would I love, but that I fear
I quickly should the willow wear ;
Fain would I marry, but men say
When love is tied he will away ;
Then tell me, love, what shall I do,
To cure these fears, whene'er I woo ?

The fair one she 's a mark to all,
The brown each one doth lovely call,
The black 's a pearl in fair men's eyes,
The rest will stoop at any prize ;
Then tell me, love, what shall I do,
To cure these fears whene'er I woo ?
                    DR. R. HUGHES.

WISHES FOR THE SUPPOSED MISTRESS.

WHOE'ER she be,
That not impossible She
That shall command my heart and me ;

Where'er she lie,
Locked up from mortal eye
In shady leaves of destiny :

Till that ripe birth
Of studied Fate stand forth,
And teach her fair steps to our earth ;

Till that divine
Idea take a shrine
Of crystal flesh, through which to shine :

— Meet you her, my Wishes,
Bespeak her to my blisses,
And be ye called, my absent kisses.

I wish her beauty
That owes not all its duty
To gaudy tire, or glist'ring shoe-tie :

Something more than
Taffeta or tissue can,
Or rampant feather, or rich fan.

A face that 's best
By its own beauty drest,
And can alone command the rest :

A face made up
Out of no other shop
Than what Nature's white hand sets ope.

Sydneian showers
Of sweet discourse, whose powers
Can crown old Winter's head with flowers.

Whate'er delight
Can make day's forehead bright
Or give down to the wings of night.

Soft silken hours,
Open suns, shady bowers ;
'Bove all, nothing within that lowers.

Days, that need borrow
No part of their good morrow
From a fore-spent night of sorrow :

Days, that in spite
Of darkness, by the light
Of a clear mind are day all night.

Life, that dares send
A challenge to his end,
And when it comes, say, "Welcome, friend."

I wish her store
Of worth may leave her poor
Of wishes ; and I wish — no more.

— Now, if Time knows
That Her, whose radiant brows
Weave them a garland of my vows ;

Her that dares be
What these lines wish to see :
I seek no further, it is She.

'T is She, and here
Lo ! I unclothe and clear
My wishes' cloudy character.

Such worth as this is
Shall fix my flying wishes,
And determine them to kisses.

Let her full glory,
My fancies, fly before ye ;
Be ye my fictions : — but her story.
                    R. CRASHAW.

RIVALRY IN LOVE.

OF all the torments, all the cares,
  With which our lives are curst ;
Of all the plagues a lover bears,
  Sure rivals are the worst !
By partners in each other kind,
  Afflictions easier grow ;
In love alone we hate to find
  Companions of our woe.

Sylvia, for all the pangs you see
  Are lab'ring in my breast ;
I beg not you would favor me,
  Would you but slight the rest !
How great soe'er your rigors are,
  With them alone I 'll cope ;
I can endure my own despair,
  But not another's hope.
              WILLIAM WALSH.

THE MAIDEN'S CHOICE.

GENTEEL in personage,
  Conduct, and equipage ;
Noble by heritage ;
  Generous and free ;

Brave, not romantic ;
Learned, not pedantic ;
Frolic, not frantic, —
  This must he be.

Honor maintaining,
Meanness disdaining,
Still entertaining,
  Engaging and new ;

Neat, but not finical ;
Sage, but not cynical ;
Never tyrannical,
  But ever true.
              HENRY FIELDING.

THE LOVELINESS OF LOVE.

IT is not Beauty I demand,
  A crystal brow, the moon's despair,
Nor the snow's daughter, a white hand,
  Nor mermaid's yellow pride of hair :

Tell me not of your starry eyes,
  Your lips that seem on roses fed,
Your breasts, where Cupid tumbling lies
  Nor sleeps for kissing of his bed, —

A bloomy pair of vermeil cheeks
  Like Hebe's in her ruddiest hours,
A breath that softer music speaks
  Than summer winds a-wooing flowers ; —

These are but gauds : nay, what are lips ?
  Coral beneath the ocean-stream,
Whose brink when your adventurer slips
  Full oft he perisheth on them.

And what are cheeks, but ensigns oft
  That wave hot youth to fields of blood ?
Did Helen's breast, though ne'er so soft,
  Do Greece or Ilium any good ?

Eyes can with baleful ardor burn ;
  Poison can breath, that erst perfumed ;
There 's many a white hand holds an urn
  With lovers' hearts to dust consumed.

For crystal brows there 's naught within ;
  They are but empty cells for pride ;
He who the Siren's hair would win
  Is mostly strangled in the tide.

Give me, instead of Beauty's bust,
  A tender heart, a loyal mind,
Which with temptation I would trust,
  Yet never linked with error find, —

One in whose gentle bosom I
  Could pour my secret heart of woes,
Like the care-burdened honey-fly
  That hides his murmurs in the rose, —

My earthly Comforter ! whose love
  So indefeasible might be
That, when my spirit wonned above,
  Hers could not stay, for sympathy.
              ANONYMOUS.

MY DEAR AND ONLY LOVE.

MY dear and only love, I pray,
  This noble world of thee
Be governed by no other sway
  But purest monarchie.
For if confusion have a part,
  Which virtuous souls abhore,
And hold a synod in thy heart,
  I 'll never love thee more.

Like Alexander I will reign,
  And I will reign alone,
My thoughts shall evermore disdain
  A rival on my throne.
He either fears his fate too much,
  Or his deserts are small,
That puts it not unto the touch,
  To win or lose it all.

         JAMES GRAHAM, *Earl of Montrose.*

MY CHOICE.

SHALL I tell you whom I love ?
  Hearken then awhile to me ;
And if such a woman move
  As I now shall versify,
Be assured 't is she or none,
  That I love, and love alone.

Nature did her so much right
 As she scorns the help of art.
In as many virtues dight
 As e'er yet embraced a heart.
So much good so truly tried,
Some for less were deified.

Wit she hath, without desier
 To make known how much she hath ;
And her anger flames no higher
 Than may fitly sweeten wrath.
Full of pity as may be,
Though perhaps not so to me.

Reason masters every sense,
 And her virtues grace her birth ;
Lovely as all excellence,
 Modest in her most of mirth.
Likelihood enough to prove
Only worth could kindle love.

Such she is ; and if you know
 Such a one as I have sung ;
Be she brown, or fair, or so
 That she be but somewhat young ;
Be assured 't is she, or none,
That I love, and love alone.

WILLIAM BROWNE.

LOVE NOT ME FOR COMELY GRACE.

LOVE not me for comely grace,
For my pleasing eye or face,
Nor for any outward part,
No, nor for my constant heart ;
 For those may fail or turn to ill,
 So thou and I shall sever ;
Keep therefore a true woman's eye,
And love me still, but know not why.
 So hast thou the same reason still
 To dote upon me ever.

ANONYMOUS.

HE THAT LOVES A ROSY CHEEK.

HE that loves a rosy cheek,
 Or a coral lip admires,
Or from starlike eyes doth seek
 Fuel to maintain his fires ;
As old Time makes these decay,
So his flames must waste away.

But a smooth and steadfast mind
 Gentle thoughts, and calm desires,
Hearts with equal love combined,
 Kindle never-dying fires : —
Where these are not, I despise
Lovely cheeks or lips or eyes.

T. CAREW.

LOVE ME LITTLE, LOVE ME LONG.

ORIGINALLY PRINTED IN 1569.

LOVE me little, love me long !
Is the burden of my song :
Love that is too hot and strong
 Burneth soon to waste.
Still I would not have thee cold, —
Not too backward, nor too bold ;
Love that lasteth till 't is old
 Fadeth not in haste.
Love me little, love me long !
Is the burden of my song.

If thou lovest me too much,
'T will not prove as true a touch ;
Love me little more than such, —
 For I fear the end.
I 'm with little well content,
And a little from thee sent
Is enough, with true intent
 To be steadfast, friend.

Say thou lovest me, while thou live
I to thee my love will give,
Never dreaming to deceive
 While that life endures ;
Nay, and after death, in sooth,
I to thee will keep my truth,
As now when in my May of youth :
 This my love assures.

Constant love is moderate ever,
And it will through life persever ;
Give me that with true endeavor, —
 I will it restore.
A suit of durance let it be,
For all weathers, — that for me, —
For the land or for the sea :
 Lasting evermore.

Winter's cold or summer's heat,
Autumn's tempests on it beat ;
It can never know defeat,
 Never can rebel :
Such the love that I would gain,
Such the love, I tell thee plain,
Thou must give, or woo in vain :
 So to thee — farewell !

ANONYMOUS

SONG.

SHALL I love you like the wind, love,
 That is so fierce and strong,
That sweeps all barriers from its path
 And recks not right or wrong ?
The passion of the wind, love,
 Can never last for long

Shall I love you like the fire, love,
　With furious heat and noise,
To waken in you all love's fears
　And little of love's joys?
The passion of the fire, love,
　Whate'er it finds, destroys.

I will love you like the stars, love,
　Set in the heavenly blue,
That only shine the brighter
　After weeping tears of dew;
Above the wind and fire, love,
　They love the ages through!

And when this life is o'er, love,
　With all its joys and jars,
We 'll leave behind the wind and fire
　To wage their boisterous wars, —
Then we shall only be, love,
　The nearer to the stars!
　　　　　　　R. W. RAYMOND.

A "MERCENARY" MARRIAGE.

SHE moves as light across the grass
　As moves my shadow large and tall;
And like my shadow, close yet free,
The thought of her aye follows me,
　My little maid of Moreton Hall.

No matter how or where we loved,
　Or when we 'll wed, or what befall;
I only feel she 's mine at last,
I only know I 'll hold her fast,
　Though to dust crumbles Moreton Hall.

Her pedigree — good sooth, 't is long!
　Her grim sires stare from every wall;
And centuries of ancestral grace
Revive in her sweet girlish face,
　As meek she glides through Moreton Hall.

Whilst I have — nothing; save, perhaps,
　Some worthless heaps of idle gold
And a true heart, — the which her eye
Through glittering dross spied, womanly;
　Therefore they say *her* heart was sold!

I laugh; she laughs; the hills and vales
　Laugh as we ride 'neath chestnuts tall,
Or start the deer that silent graze,
And look up, large-eyed, with soft gaze,
　At the fair maid of Moreton Hall;

We let the neighbors talk their fill,
　For life is sweet, and love is strong,
And two, close knit in marriage ties,
The whole world's shams may well despise, —
　Its folly, madness, shame, and wrong.

We are not proud, with a fool's pride,
　Nor cowards, — to be held in thrall
By pelf or lineage, rank or lands: —
One honest heart, two honest hands,
　Are worth far more than Moreton Hall.

Therefore we laugh to scorn — we two —
　The bars that weaker souls appall:
I take her hand, and hold it fast,
Knowing she 'll love me to the last,
　My dearest maid of Moreton Hall.
　　　　　　　DINAH MARIA MULOCK.

AMY'S CRUELTY.

I.

FAIR Amy of the terraced house,
　Assist me to discover
Why you who would not hurt a mouse
　Can torture so your lover.

II.

You give your coffee to the cat,
　You stroke the dog for coming,
And all your face grows kinder at
　The little brown bee's humming.

III.

But when *he* haunts your door . . . the town
　Marks coming and marks going . . .
You seem to have stitched your eyelids down
　To that long piece of sewing!

IV.

You never give a look, not you,
　Nor drop him a " Good morning,"
To keep his long day warm and blue,
　So fretted by your scorning.

V.

She shook her head : " The mouse and bee
　For crumb or flower will linger;
The dog is happy at my knee,
　The cat purrs at my finger.

VI.

" But he . . . to *him*, the least thing given
　Means great things at a distance;
He wants my world, my sun, my heaven,
　Soul, body, whole existence.

VII.

"They say love gives as well as takes;
　But I 'm a simple maiden, —
My mother's first smile when she wakes
　I still have smiled and prayed in.

VIII.

" I only know my mother's love
　Which gives all and asks nothing,

And this new loving sets the groove
  Too much the way of loathing.

IX.

" Unless he gives me all in change,
  I forfeit all things by him :
The risk is terrible and strange —
  I tremble, doubt, . . . deny him.

X.

" He 's sweetest friend, or hardest foe,
  Best angel, or worst devil ;
I either hate or . . . love him so,
  I can't be merely civil !

XI.

" You trust a woman who puts forth
  Her blossoms thick as summer's ?
You think she dreams what love is worth,
  Who casts it to new-comers ?

XII.

" Such love 's a cowslip-ball to fling,
  A moment's pretty pastime ;
I give . . . all me, if anything,
  The first time and the last time.

XIII.

" Dear neighbor of the trellised house,
  A man should murmur never,
Though treated worse than dog and mouse,
  Till doted on forever ! "
        ELIZABETH BARRETT BROWNING.

A WOMAN'S QUESTION.

BEFORE I trust my fate to thee,
  Or place my hand in thine,
Before I let thy future give
  Color and form to mine,
Before I peril all for thee,
Question thy soul to-night for me.

I break all slighter bonds, nor feel
  A shadow of regret :
Is there one link within the past
  That holds thy spirit yet ?
Or is thy faith as clear and free
As that which I can pledge to thee ?

Does there within thy dimmest dreams
  A possible future shine,
Wherein thy life could henceforth breathe,
  Untouched, unshared by mine ?
If so, at any pain or cost,
O, tell me before all is lost !

Look deeper still : if thou canst feel,
  Within thy inmost soul,

That thou hast kept a portion back,
  While I have staked the whole,
Let no false pity spare the blow,
But in true mercy tell me so.

Is there within thy heart a need
  That mine cannot fulfil ?
One chord that any other hand
  Could better wake or still ?
Speak now, lest at some future day
My whole life wither and decay.

Lives there within thy nature hid
  The demon-spirit, change,
Shedding a passing glory still
  On all things new and strange ?
It may not be thy fault alone, —
But shield my heart against thine own.

Couldst thou withdraw thy hand one day
  And answer to my claim,
That fate, and that to-day's mistake, —
  Not thou, — had been to blame ?
Some soothe their conscience thus ; but thou
Wilt surely warn and save me now.

Nay, answer *not*, — I dare not hear,
  The words would come too late ;
Yet I would spare thee all remorse,
  So comfort thee, my fate :
Whatever on my heart may fall,
Remember, I *would* risk it all !
        ADELAIDE ANNE PROCTER.

THE LADY'S "YES."

" YES," I answered you last night ;
  " No," this morning, sir, I say.
Colors seen by candle-light
  Will not look the same by day.

When the viols played their best,
  Lamps above, and laughs below,
Love me sounded like a jest,
  Fit for *yes* or fit for *no*.

Call me false or call me free,
  Vow, whatever light may shine,
No man on your face shall see
  Any grief for change on mine.

Yet the sin is on us both ;
  Time to dance is not to woo ;
Wooing light makes fickle troth.
  Scorn of *me* recoils on *you*.

Learn to win a lady's faith
  Nobly, as the thing is high,
Bravely, as for life and death,
  With a loyal gravity.

Lead her from the festive boards,
　　Point her to the starry skies,
Guard her, by your truthful words,
　　Pure from courtship's flatteries.

By your truth she shall be true,
　　Ever true, as wives of yore ;
And her *yes*, once said to you,
　　SHALL be Yes forevermore.
　　　　　ELIZABETH BARRETT BROWNING.

LOVE'S SILENCE.

BECAUSE I breathe not love to everie one,
　　Nor do not use set colors for to weare,
　　Nor nourish special locks of vowéd haire,
Nor give each speech a full point of a groane, —
The courtlie nymphs, acquainted with the moane
　　Of them who on their lips Love's standard beare,
　　"What ! he ?" say they of me. "Now I dare
　　　　sweare
He cannot love : No, no ! let him alone."
　　And think so still, — if Stella know my minde.

Profess, indeed, I do not Cupid's art ;
　　But you, faire maids, at length this true shall
　　　　finde, —
That his right badge is but worne in the hearte.
　　Dumb swans, not chattering pies, do lovers
　　　　prove :
They love indeed who quake to say they love.
　　　　　SIR PHILIP SIDNEY.

THE MAID'S REMONSTRANCE.

NEVER wedding, ever wooing,
　　Still a love-lorn heart pursuing,
Read you not the wrong you 're doing
　　In my cheek's pale hue ?
All my life with sorrow strewing,
　　Wed, or cease to woo.

Rivals banished, bosoms plighted,
　　Still our days are disunited ;
Now the lamp of hope is lighted,
　　Now half quenched appears,
Damped and wavering and benighted
　　Midst my sighs and tears.

Charms you call your dearest blessing,
　　Lips that thrill at your caressing,
Eyes a mutual soul confessing,
　　Soon you 'll make them grow
Dim, and worthless your possessing,
　　Not with age, but woe !
　　　　　THOMAS CAMPBELL.

GIVE ME MORE LOVE OR MORE
DISDAIN.

GIVE me more love or more disdain ;
　　The torrid or the frozen zone
Brings equal ease unto my pain ;
　　The temperate affords me none ;
Either extreme, of love or hate,
Is sweeter than a calm estate.

Give me a storm ; if it be love,
　　Like Danaë in a golden shower,
I swim in pleasure ; if it prove
　　Disdain, that torrent will devour
My vulture hopes ; and he 's possessed
Of heaven that 's but from hell released ;
Then crown my joys, or cure my pain ;
Give me more love or more disdain.
　　　　　THOMAS CAREW.

LOVE DISSEMBLED.

FROM "AS YOU LIKE IT."

THINK not I love him, though I ask for him ;
'T is but a peevish boy : — yet he talks well ; —
But what care I for words ? — yet words do well,
When he that speaks them pleases those that hear.
But, sure, he 's proud ; and yet his pride becomes
　　him :
He 'll make a proper man : The best thing in him
Is his complexion ; and faster than his tongue
Did make offence, his eye did heal it up.
He is not very tall ; yet for his years he 's tall ;
His leg is but so so ; and yet 't is well :
There was a pretty redness in his lip,
A little riper and more lusty red
Than that mixed in his cheek ; 't was just the
　　difference
Betwixt the constant red, and mingled damask.
There be some women, Silvius, had they marked
　　him
In parcels, as I did, would have gone near
To fall in love with him : but, for my part,
I love him not, nor hate him not ; and yet
I have more cause to hate him than to love him :
For what had he to do to chide at me ?
He said mine eyes were black, and my hair black ;
And, now I am remembered, scorned at me :
I marvel, why I answered not again :
But that 's all one ; omittance is no quittance.
　　　　　SHAKESPEARE.

THE SHEPHERD'S RESOLUTION.

SHALL I, wasting in despair,
　　Die because a woman 's fair ?
Or make pale my cheeks with care
　　'Cause another's rosy are ?

Be she fairer than the day,
Or the flowery meads in May,
  If she be not so to me,
  What care I how fair she be?

Shall my foolish heart be pined
'Cause I see a woman kind?
Or a well-disposéd nature
Joinéd with a lovely feature?
Be she meeker, kinder than
The turtle-dove or pelican,
  If she be not so to me,
  What care I how kind she be?

Shall a woman's virtues move
Me to perish for her love?
Or, her well deservings known,
Make me quite forget mine own?
Be she with that goodness blest
Which may merit name of best,
  If she be not such to me,
  What care I how good she be?

'Cause her fortune seems too high,
Shall I play the fool and die?
Those that bear a noble mind
Where they want of riches find,
Think what with them they would do
That without them dare to woo;
  And unless that mind I see,
  What care I how great she be?

Great, or good, or kind, or fair,
I will ne'er the more despair:
If she love me, this believe, —
I will die ere she shall grieve.
If she slight me when I woo,
I can scorn and let her go;
  For if she be not for me,
  What care I for whom she be?
          GEORGE WITHER.

LET NOT WOMAN E'ER COMPLAIN.

LET not woman e'er complain
  Of inconstancy in love;
Let not woman e'er complain
  Fickle man is apt to rove;
Look abroad through Nature's range,
Nature's mighty law is change;
Ladies, would it not be strange
  Man should then a monster prove?

Mark the winds, and mark the skies;
  Ocean's ebb and ocean's flow;
Sun and moon but set to rise,
  Round and round the seasons go.

Why then ask of silly man,
To oppose great Nature's plan?
We'll be constant while we can, —
You can be no more, you know.
          ROBERT BURNS.

ROSALIND'S COMPLAINT.

LOVE in my bosom like a bee,
  Doth suck his sweet;
Now with his wings he plays with me,
  Now with his feet;
Within mine eyes he makes his nest,
His bed amidst my tender breast,
My kisses are his daily feast,
And yet he robs me of my rest:
  Ah! wanton, will you?

And if I sleep, then pierceth he
  With pretty slight,
And makes his pillow of my knee,
  The livelong night;
Strike I the lute, he tunes the string,
He music plays, if I but sing:
He lends me every lovely thing,
Yet cruel, he my heart doth sting:
  Ah! wanton, will you?

Else I with roses every day
  Will whip you hence,
And bind you when you long to play,
  For your offence;
I'll shut my eyes to keep you in,
I'll make you fast it for your sin,
I'll count your power not worth a pin,
Alas! what hereby shall I win
  If he gainsay me!

What if I beat the wanton boy
  With many a rod,
He will repay me with annoy
  Because a god;
Then sit thou softly on my knee,
And let thy bower my bosom be;
Lurk in my eyes, I like of thee,
O Cupid! so thou pity me;
  Spare not, but play thee.
          THOMAS LODGE.

CUPID AND CAMPASPE.

CUPID and my Campaspe played
At cards for kisses, — Cupid paid;
He stakes his quiver, bow and arrows,
His mother's doves, and team of sparrows, —
Loses them too; then down he throws
The coral of his lip, the rose

Growing on 's cheek (but none knows how) ;
With these the crystal of his brow,
And then the dimple of his chin, —
All these did my Campaspe win.
At last he set her both his eyes ;
She won, and Cupid blind did rise.
O Love ! has she done this to thee ?
What shall, alas ! become of me ?

JOHN LYLY.

CUPID SWALLOWED.

T' OTHER day, as I was twining
Roses for a crown to dine in,
What, of all things, midst the heap,
Should I light on, fast asleep,
But the little desperate elf,
The tiny traitor, — Love himself !
By the wings I pinched him up
Like a bee, and in a cup
Of my wine I plunged and sank him ;
And what d' ye think I did ? — I drank him !
Faith, I thought him dead.   Not he !
There he lives with tenfold glee ;
And now this moment, with his wings
I feel him tickling my heart-strings.

LEIGH HUNT.

LOVE AND TIME.

Two pilgrims from the distant plain
  Come quickly o'er the mossy ground.
One is a boy, with locks of gold
  Thick curling round his face so fair ;
The other pilgrim, stern and old,
  Has snowy beard and silver hair.

The youth with many a merry trick
  Goes singing on his careless way ;
His old companion walks as quick,
  But speaks no word by night or day.
Where'er the old man treads, the grass
  Fast fadeth with a certain doom ;
But where the beauteous boy doth pass
  Unnumbered flowers are seen to bloom.

And thus before the sage, the boy
  Trips lightly o'er the blooming lands,
And proudly bears a pretty toy, —
  A crystal glass with diamond sands.
A smile o'er any brow would pass
  To see him frolic in the sun, —
To see him shake the crystal glass,
  And make the sands more quickly run.

And now they leap the streamlet o'er,
  A silver thread so white and thin,
And now they reach the open door,
  And now they lightly enter in :

"God save all here," — that kind wish flies
  Still sweeter from his lips so sweet ;
"God save you kindly," Norah cries,
  "Sit down, my child, and rest and eat."

"Thanks, gentle Norah, fair and good,
  We 'll rest awhile our weary feet ;
But though this old man needeth food,
  There 's nothing here that he can eat.
His taste is strange, he eats alone,
  Beneath some ruined cloister's cope,
Or on some tottering turret's stone,
  While I can only live on — Hope !

"A week ago, ere you were wed, —
  It was the very night before, —
Upon so many sweets I fed
  While passing by your mother's door, —
It was that dear, delicious hour
  When Owen here the nosegay brought,
And found you in the woodbine bower, —
  Since then, indeed, I 've needed naught."

A blush steals over Norah's face,
  A smile comes over Owen's brow,
A tranquil joy illumes the place,
  As if the moon were shining now ;
The boy beholds the pleasing pain,
  The sweet confusion he has done,
And shakes the crystal glass again,
  And makes the sands more quickly run.

"Dear Norah, we are pilgrims, bound
  Upon an endless path sublime ;
We pace the green earth round and round,
  And mortals call us LOVE and TIME ;
He seeks the many, I the few ;
  I dwell with peasants, he with kings.
We seldom meet ; but when we do,
  I take his glass, and he my wings.

"And thus together on we go,
  Where'er I chance or wish to lead ;
And Time, whose lonely steps are slow,
  Now sweeps along with lightning speed.
Now on our bright predestined way
  We must to other regions pass ;
But take this gift, and night and day
  Look well upon its truthful glass.

"How quick or slow the bright sands fall
  Is hid from lovers' eyes alone,
If you can see them move at all,
  Be sure your heart has colder grown.
'T is coldness makes the glass grow dry,
  The icy hand, the freezing brow ;
But warm the heart and breathe the sigh,
  And then they 'll pass you know not how."

LOVE-LETTERS IN FLOWERS

"An exquisite invention this,
Worthy of Love's most honeyed kiss. —
This art of writing billet-doux
In buds, and odors, and bright hues!"

She took the glass where Love's warm hands
  A bright impervious vapor cast,
She looks, but cannot see the sands,
  Although she feels they 're falling fast.
But cold hours came, and then, alas !
  She saw them falling frozen through,
Till Love's warm light suffused the glass,
  And hid the loos'ning sands from view !
          DENIS FLORENCE MACCARTHY.

DEATH AND CUPID.

AH ! who but oft hath marvelled why
  The gods, who rule above,
Should e'er permit the young to die,
  The old to fall in love ?

Ah ! why should hapless human kind
  Be punished out of season ? —
Pray listen, and perhaps you 'll find
  My rhyme may give the reason.

Death, strolling out one summer's day,
  Met Cupid, with his sparrows ;
And, bantering in a merry way,
  Proposed a change of arrows.

"Agreed !" quoth Cupid. "I foresee
  The queerest game of errors ;
For you the King of Hearts will be,
  And I 'll be King of Terrors ! "

And so 't was done ; — alas, the day
  That multiplied their arts ! —
Each from the other bore away
  A portion of his darts.

And that explains the reason why,
  Despite the gods above,
The young are often doomed to die,
  The old to fall in love !
          JOHN GODFREY SAXE.

LOVE–LETTERS MADE OF FLOWERS.

AN exquisite invention this,
Worthy of Love's most honeyed kiss, —
This art of writing *billet-doux*
In buds, and odors, and bright hues !
In saying all one feels and thinks
In clever daffodils and pinks ;
In puns of tulips ; and in phrases,
Charming for their truth, of daisies ;
Uttering, as well as silence may,
The sweetest words the sweetest way.
How fit too for the lady's bosom !
The place where *billet-doux* repose 'em.

What delight in some sweet spot
Combining *love* with *garden* plot,
At once to cultivate one's flowers
And one's epistolary powers !
Growing one's own choice words and fancies
In orange tubs, and beds of pansies ;
One's sighs, and passionate declarations,
In odorous rhetoric of carnations ;
Seeing how far one's stocks will reach,
Taking due care one's flowers of speech
To guard from blight as well as bathos,
And watering every day one's pathos !
A letter comes, just gathered. We
Dote on its tender brilliancy,
Inhale its delicate expressions
Of balm and pea, and its confessions
Made with as sweet a *maiden's blush*
As ever morn bedewed on bush :
('T is in reply to one of ours,
Made of the most convincing flowers.)

Then, after we have kissed its wit,
And heart, in water putting it
(To keep its remarks fresh), go round
Our little eloquent plot of ground,
And with enchanted hands compose
Our answer, — all of lily and rose,
Of tuberose and of violet,
And *little darling* (mignonette) ;
Of *look at me* and *call me to you*
(Words, that while they greet, go through you) ;
Of *thoughts*, of *flames, forget-me-not,*
Bridewort, — in short, the whole blest lot
Of vouchers for a lifelong kiss, —
And literally, breathing bliss !
          LEIGH HUNT.

THE BIRTH OF PORTRAITURE.

As once a Grecian maiden wove
  Her garland mid the summer bowers,
There stood a youth, with eyes of love,
  To watch her while she wreathed the flowers.
The youth was skilled in painting's art,
  But ne'er had studied woman's brow,
Nor knew what magic hues the heart
  Can shed o'er Nature's charm, till now.

CHORUS.

  Blest be Love, to whom we owe
  All that 's fair and bright below.

His hand had pictured many a rose,
  And sketched the rays that lit the brook ;
But what were these, or what were those,
  To woman's blush, to woman's look ?
"Oh ! if such magic power there be,
  This, this," he cried, "is all my prayer,

To paint that living light I see,
  And fix the soul that sparkles there."

His prayer as soon as breathed was heard ;
  His pallet touched by Love grew warm,
And painting saw her thus transferred
  From lifeless flowers to woman's form.
Still, as from tint to tint he stole,
  The fair design shone out the more,
And there was now a life, a soul,
  Where only colors glowed before.

Then first carnation learned to speak,
  And lilies into life were brought ;
While mantling on the maiden's cheek,
  Young roses kindled into thought :
Then hyacinths their darkest dyes
  Upon the locks of beauty threw ;
And violets transformed to eyes,
  Inshrined a soul within their blue.

CHORUS.

  Blest be Love, to whom we owe
  All that 's bright and fair below ;
  Song was cold and painting dim,
  Till song and painting learned from him.
                        THOMAS MOORE.

UP ! QUIT THY BOWER.

Up ! quit thy bower ! late wears the hour,
Long have the rooks cawed round the tower ;
O'er flower and tree loud hums the bee,
And the wild kid sports merrily.
The sun is bright, the sky is clear ;
Wake, lady, wake ! and hasten here.

Up, maiden fair ! and bind thy hair,
And rouse thee in the breezy air !
The lulling stream that soothed thy dream
Is dancing in the sunny beam.
Waste not these hours, so fresh, so gay :
Leave thy soft couch, and haste away !

Up ! Time will tell the morning bell
Its service-sound has chiméd well ;
The aged crone keeps house alone,
The reapers to the fields are gone.
Lose not these hours, so cool, so gay :
Lo ! while thou sleep'st they haste away !
                        JOANNA BAILLIE.

FOR LOVE'S SWEET SAKE.

Awake ! — the starry midnight hour
  Hangs charmed, and pauseth in its flight ;
In its own sweetness sleeps the flower,
  And the doves lie hushed in deep delight.
    Awake ! awake !
    Look forth, my love, for Love's sweet sake !

Awake ! — soft dews will soon arise
  From daisied mead and thorny brake :
Then, sweet, uncloud those eastern eyes,
  And like the tender morning break !
    Awake ! awake !
    Dawn forth, my love, for Love's sweet sake !

Awake ! — within the musk-rose bower
  I watch, pale flower of love, for thee.
Ah, come ! and show the starry hour
  What wealth of love thou hid'st from me !
    Awake ! awake !
    Show all thy love, for Love's sweet sake !

Awake ! — ne'er heed though listening night
  Steal music from thy silver voice ;
Uncloud thy beauty, rare and bright,
  And bid the world and me rejoice !
    Awake ! awake ! —
    She comes at last, for Love's sweet sake.
                        BARRY CORNWALL.

INVOCATION TO THE ANGEL.

FROM "HEAVEN AND EARTH."

            Samiasa !
I call thee, I await thee, and I love thee ;
  Many may worship thee, that will I not ;
If that thy spirit down to mine may move thee,
  Descend and share my lot !
      Though I be formed of clay,
        And thou of beams
      More bright than those of day
        On Eden's streams,
Thine immortality cannot repay
  With love more warm than mine
My love.   There is a ray
  In me, which, though forbidden yet to shine,
  I feel was lighted at thy God's and thine.
It may be hidden long : death and decay
  Our mother Eve bequeathed us, but my heart
Defies it ; though this life must pass away,
  Is *that* a cause for thee and me to part ?
Thou art immortal ; so am I : I feel —
  I feel my immortality o'ersweep
All pains, all tears, all time, all fears, and peal,
  Like the eternal thunders of the deep,
Into my ears this truth, — "Thou liv'st forever !"
                        BYRON.

FLY TO THE DESERT, FLY WITH ME.

SONG OF NOURMAHAL IN "THE LIGHT OF THE HAREM."

  "Fly to the desert, fly with me,
  Our Arab tents are rude for thee ;
  But oh ! the choice what heart can doubt
  Of tents with love or thrones without ?

"Our rocks are rough, but smiling there
Th' acacia waves her yellow hair,
Lonely and sweet, nor loved the less
For flowering in a wilderness.

"Our sands are bare, but down their slope
The silvery-footed antelope
As gracefully and gayly springs
As o'er the marble courts of kings.

"Then come, — thy Arab maid will be
The loved and lone acacia-tree,
The antelope, whose feet shall bless
With their light sound thy loneliness.

"Oh ! there are looks and tones that dart
An instant sunshine through the heart,
As if the soul that minute caught
Some treasure it through life had sought ;

"As if the very lips and eyes
Predestined to have all our sighs,
And never be forgot again,
Sparkled and spoke before as then !

"So came thy every glance and tone,
When first on me they breathed and shone ;
New, as if brought from other spheres,
Yet welcome as if loved for years !

"Then fly with me, if thou hast known
No other flame, nor falsely thrown
A gem away, that thou hadst sworn
Should ever in thy heart be worn.

"Come, if the love thou hast for me
Is pure and fresh as mine for thee, —
Fresh as the fountain underground,
When first 't is by the lapwing found.

"But if for me thou dost forsake
Some other maid, and rudely break
Her worshipped image from its base,
To give to me the ruined place ;

"Then, fare thee well ! — I 'd rather make
My bower upon some icy lake
When thawing suns begin to shine,
Than trust to love so false as thine ! "

There was a pathos in this lay,
  That even without enchantment's art
Would instantly have found its way
  Deep into Selim's burning heart ;
But breathing, as it did, a tone
To earthly lutes and lips unknown ;
With every chord fresh from the touch
Of music's spirit, 't was too much !
  Starting, he dashed away the cup, —
  Which, all the time of this sweet air,
His hand had held, untasted, up,

As if 't were fixed by magic there, —
And naming her, so long unnamed,
So long unseen, wildly exclaimed,
"O Nourmahal ! O Nourmahal !
  Hadst thou but sung this witching strain,
I could forget — forgive thee all,
  And never leave those eyes again."

The mask is off, — the charm is wrought,
And Selim to his heart has caught,
In blushes, more than ever bright,
His Nourmahal, his Harem's Light !
And well do vanished frowns enhance
The charm of every brightened glance ;
And dearer seems each dawning smile
For having lost its light awhile ;
And, happier now for all her sighs,
  As on his arm her head reposes,
She whispers him, with laughing eyes,
  "Remember, love, the Feast of Roses ! "
                              THOMAS MOORE.

———

COME INTO THE GARDEN, MAUD.

COME into the garden, Maud,
  For the black bat, night, has flown !
Come into the garden, Maud,
  I am here at the gate alone ;
And the woodbine spices are wafted abroad,
  And the musk of the roses blown.

For a breeze of morning moves,
  And the planet of Love is on high,
Beginning to faint in the light that she loves,
  On a bed of daffodil sky,
To faint in the light of the sun that she loves,
  To faint in its light, and to die.

All night have the roses heard
  The flute, violin, bassoon ;
All night has the casement jessamine stirred
  To the dancers dancing in tune, —
Till a silence fell with the waking bird,
  And a hush with the setting moon.

I said to the lily, " There is but one
  With whom she has heart to be gay.
When will the dancers leave her alone ?
  She is weary of dance and play."
Now half to the setting moon are gone,
  And half to the rising day ;
Low on the sand and loud on the stone
  The last wheel echoes away.

I said to the rose, " The brief night goes
  In babble and revel and wine.
O young lord-lover, what sighs are those
  For one that will never be thine ?
But mine, but mine," so I sware to the rose,
  "For ever and ever mine ! "

And the soul of the rose went into my blood,
  As the music clashed in the hall ;
And long by the garden lake I stood,
  For I heard your rivulet fall
From the lake to the meadow and on to the wood,
  Our wood, that is dearer than all ;

From the meadow your walks have left so sweet
  That whenever a March-wind sighs,
He sets the jewel-print of your feet
  In violets blue as your eyes,
To the woody hollows in which we meet,
  And the valleys of Paradise.

The slender acacia would not shake
  One long milk-bloom on the tree ;
The white lake-blossom fell into the lake,
  As the pimpernel dozed on the lea ;
But the rose was awake all night for your sake,
  Knowing your promise to me ;
The lilies and roses were all awake,
  They sighed for the dawn and thee.

Queen rose of the rosebud garden of girls,
  Come hither ! the dances are done ;
In gloss of satin and glimmer of pearls,
  Queen lily and rose in one ;
Shine out, little head, sunning over with curls,
  To the flowers, and be their sun.

There has fallen a splendid tear
  From the passion-flower at the gate.
She is coming, my dove, my dear ;
  She is coming, my life, my fate !
The red rose cries, "She is near, she is near" ;
  And the white rose weeps, "She is late" ;
The larkspur listens, "I hear, I hear" ;
  And the lily whispers, "I wait."

She is coming, my own, my sweet !
  Were it ever so airy a tread,
My heart would hear her and beat,
  Were it earth in an earthly bed ;
My dust would hear her and beat,
  Had I lain for a century dead ;
Would start and tremble under her feet,
  And blossom in purple and red.
                          ALFRED TENNYSON.

THE YOUNG MAY MOON.

THE young May moon is beaming, love,
The glowworm's lamp is gleaming, love,
    How sweet to rove
    Through Morna's grove,
While the drowsy world is dreaming, love !
Then awake !—the heavens look bright, my dear !
'T is never too late for delight, my dear !

And the best of all ways
  To lengthen our days
Is to steal a few hours from the night, my dear !

Now all the world is sleeping, love,
But the sage, his star-watch keeping, love,
    And I, whose star,
    More glorious far,
Is the eye from that casement peeping, love.
Then awake !—till rise of sun, my dear,
The sage's glass we 'll shun, my dear,
    Or, in watching the flight
    Of bodies of light,
He might happen to take thee for one, my dear !
                          THOMAS MOORE.

AH, SWEET KITTY NEIL !

"AH, sweet Kitty Neil ! rise up from your wheel,
  Your neat little foot will be weary from spin-
    ning ;
Come, trip down with me to the sycamore-tree ;
  Half the parish is there, and the dance is
    beginning.
The sun is gone down ; but the full harvest moon
  Shines sweetly and cool on the dew-whitened
    valley ;
While all the air rings with the soft, loving things
  Each little bird sings in the green shaded alley."

With a blush and a smile, Kitty rose up the
    while,
  Her eye in the glass, as she bound her hair,
    glancing ;
'T is hard to refuse when a young lover sues,
  So she could n't but choose to — go off to the
    dancing.
And now on the green the glad groups are seen, —
  Each gay-hearted lad with the lass of his choos-
    ing ;
And Pat, without fail, leads out sweet Kitty Neil,—
  Somehow, when he asked, she ne'er thought
    of refusing.

Now Felix Magee puts his pipes to his knee,
  And, with flourish so free, sets each couple in
    motion ;
With a cheer and a bound, the lads patter the
    ground,
  The maids move around just like swans on the
    ocean.
Cheeks bright as the rose, — feet light as the doe's,
  Now coyly retiring, now boldly advancing ;
Search the world all around from the sky to the
    ground,
  No such sight can be found as an Irish lass
    dancing !

Sweet Kate! who could view your bright eyes
   of deep blue,
   Beaming humidly through their dark lashes
     so mildly,
Your fair-turned arm, heaving breast, rounded
   form,
   Nor feel his heart warm, and his pulses throb
     wildly?
Poor Pat feels his heart, as he gazes, depart,
   Subdued by the smart of such painful yet sweet
     love;
The sight leaves his eye as he cries with a
   sigh,
   "Dance light, for my heart it lies under your
     feet, love!"
              DENIS FLORENCE MACCARTHY.

O NANCY, WILT THOU GO WITH ME?

O NANCY, wilt thou go with me,
   Nor sigh to leave the flaunting town?
Can silent glens have charms for thee,
   The lonely cot and russet gown?
No longer drest in silken sheen,
   No longer decked with jewels rare,
Say, canst thou quit each courtly scene
   Where thou wert fairest of the fair?

O Nancy! when thou 'rt far away,
   Wilt thou not cast a wish behind?
Say, canst thou face the parching ray,
   Nor shrink before the wintry wind?
O, can that soft and gentle mien
   Extremes of hardship learn to bear,
Nor sad regret each courtly scene
   Where thou wert fairest of the fair?

O Nancy! canst thou love so true,
   Through perils keen with me to go,
Or when thy swain mishap shall rue,
   To share with him the pang of woe?
Say, should disease or pain befall,
   Wilt thou assume the nurse's care,
Nor wistful those gay scenes recall
   Where thou wert fairest of the fair?

And when at last thy love shall die,
   Wilt thou receive his parting breath?
Wilt thou repress each struggling sigh,
   And cheer with smiles the bed of death?
And wilt thou o'er his breathless clay,
   Strew flowers, and drop the tender tear,
Nor then regret those scenes so gay
   Where thou wert fairest of the fair?
              THOMAS PERCY, D.D.

BEDOUIN LOVE-SONG.

FROM the Desert I come to thee,
   On a stallion shod with fire;
And the winds are left behind
   In the speed of my desire.
Under thy window I stand,
   And the midnight hears my cry:
I love thee, I love but thee!
   With a love that shall not die
     Till the sun grows cold,
     And the stars are old,
     And the leaves of the Judgment
       Book unfold!

Look from thy window, and see
   My passion and my pain!
I lie on the sands below,
   And I faint in thy disdain.
Let the night-winds touch thy brow
   With the heat of my burning sigh,
And melt thee to hear the vow
   Of a love that shall not die
     Till the sun grows cold,
     And the stars are old,
     And the leaves of the Judgment
       Book unfold!

My steps are nightly driven,
   By the fever in my breast,
To hear from thy lattice breathed
   The word that shall give me rest.
Open the door of thy heart,
   And open thy chamber door,
And my kisses shall teach thy lips
   The love that shall fade no more
     Till the sun grows cold,
     And the stars are old,
     And the leaves of the Judgment
       Book unfold!
              BAYARD TAYLOR.

COME, REST IN THIS BOSOM.

FROM "IRISH MELODIES."

COME, rest in this bosom, my own stricken deer,
Though the herd have fled from thee, thy home
   is still here;
Here still is the smile, that no cloud can o'ercast,
And a heart and a hand all thy own to the last.

Oh! what was love made for, if 't is not the same
Through joy and through torment, through glory
   and shame?
I know not, I ask not, if guilt's in that heart,
I but know that I love thee, whatever thou
   art.

Thou hast called me thy Angel in moments of bliss,
And thy Angel I 'll be, mid the horrors of this,
Through the furnace, unshrinking, thy steps to pursue,
And shield thee, and save thee, — or perish there too !

THOMAS MOORE.

THE WELCOME.

I.

COME in the evening, or come in the morning ;
Come when you 're looked for, or come without warning ;
Kisses and welcome you 'll find here before you,
And the oftener you come here the more I 'll adore you !
 Light is my heart since the day we were plighted ;
 Red is my cheek that they told me was blighted ;
 The green of the trees looks far greener than ever,
 And the linnets are singing, "True lovers don't sever ! "

II.

I 'll pull you sweet flowers, to wear if you choose them !
Or, after you 've kissed them, they 'll lie on my bosom ;
I 'll fetch from the mountain its breeze to inspire you ;
I 'll fetch from my fancy a tale that won't tire you.
 Oh ! your step's like the rain to the summer-vexed farmer,
 Or sabre and shield to a knight without armor ;
 I 'll sing you sweet songs till the stars rise above me,
 Then, wandering, I 'll wish you in silence to love me.

III.

We 'll look through the trees at the cliff and the eyrie ;
We 'll tread round the rath on the track of the fairy ;
We 'll look on the stars, and we 'll list to the river,
Till you ask of your darling what gift you can give her.
 Oh ! she 'll whisper you, — "Love, as unchangeably beaming,
 And trust, when in secret, most tunefully streaming ;
 Till the starlight of heaven above us shall quiver,
 As our souls flow in one down eternity's river."

IV.

So come in the evening, or come in the morning ;
Come when you 're looked for, or come without warning ;
Kisses and welcome you 'll find here before you,
And the oftener you come here the more I 'll adore you !
 Light is my heart since the day we were plighted ;
 Red is my cheek that they told me was blighted ;
 The green of the trees looks far greener than ever,
 And the linnets are singing, "True lovers don't sever ! "

THOMAS DAVIS.

CA' THE YOWES TO THE KNOWES.

CHORUS.

Ca' the yowes to the knowes,
Ca' them where the heather grows,
Ca' them where the burnie rowes,
 My bonnie dearie.

Hark the mavis' evening sang
Sounding Cluden's woods amang ;
Then a-faulding let us gang,
 My bonnie dearie.
  Ca' the, &c.

We 'll gae down by Clauden side,
Thro' the hazels spreading wide,
O'er the waves that sweetly glide
 To the moon sae clearly.
  Ca' the, &c.

Yonder Cluden's silent towers,
Where at moonshine midnight hours,
O'er the dewy bending flowers,
 Fairies dance sae cheerie.
  Ca' the, &c.

Ghaist nor bogle shalt thou fear :
Thou 'rt to Love and Heaven sae dear,
Nocht of ill may come thee near,
 My bonnie dearie.
  Ca' the, &c.

Fair and lovely as thou art,
Thou hast stown my very heart ;
I can die — but canna part,
 My bonnie dearie.
  Ca' the, &c.

While waters wimple to the sea ;
While day blinks in the lift sae hie ;
Till clay-cauld death shall blin' my e'e,
 Ye shall be my dearie.
  Ca' the, &c.

ROBERT BURNS.

WHISTLE, AND I'LL COME TO YOU, MY LAD.

O WHISTLE and I'll come to you, my lad,
O whistle, and I'll come to you, my lad;
Tho' father and mither and a' should gae mad,
O whistle, and I'll come to you, my lad.

But warily tent, when ye come to court me,
And come na unless the back-yett be a-jee;
Syne up the back stile, and let naebody see,
And come as ye were na' comin' to me.
And come, &c.
    O whistle, &c.

At kirk, or at market, whene'er ye meet me,
Gang by me as tho' that ye cared nae a flie;
But steal me a blink o' your bonnie black e'e,
Yet look as ye were na lookin' at me.
Yet look, &c.
    O whistle, &c.

Aye vow and protest that ye care na for me,
And whiles ye may lightly my beauty a wee;
But court nae anither, tho' jokin' ye be,
For fear that she wile your fancy frae me.
For fear, &c.
    O whistle, &c.
                ROBERT BURNS.

THE SHEPHERD TO HIS LOVE.

COME, live with me, and be my love,
And we will all the pleasures prove
That valleys, groves, hills, and fields,
Woods or steepy mountains, yields.

There we will sit upon the rocks,
Seeing the shepherds feed their flocks
By shallow rivers, to whose falls
Melodious birds sing madrigals.

There will I make thee beds of roses
With a thousand fragrant posies;
A cap of flowers, and a kirtle,
Embroidered all with leaves of myrtle;

A gown made of the finest wool,
Which from our pretty lambs we pull;
Fair-lined slippers for the cold,
With buckles of the purest gold;

A belt of straw, and ivy buds,
With coral clasps and amber studs:
And if these pleasures may thee move,
Come, live with me, and be my love.

The shepherd swains shall dance and sing
For thy delight each May morning,
If these delights thy mind may move,
Then live with me, and be my love.
             CHRISTOPHER MARLOWE.

THE NYMPH'S REPLY.

IF that the world and love were young,
And truth in every shepherd's tongue,
These pretty pleasures might me move
To live with thee and be thy love.

But time drives flocks from field to fold,
When rivers rage, and rocks grow cold;
And Philomel becometh dumb,
And all complain of cares to come.

The flowers do fade, and wanton fields
To wayward winter reckoning yields;
A honey tongue, a heart of gall,
Is fancy's spring, but sorrow's fall.

Thy gowns, thy shoes, thy beds of roses,
Thy cap, thy kirtle, and thy posies
Soon break, soon wither, soon forgotten, —
In folly ripe, in reason rotten.

Thy belt of straw and ivy buds,
Thy coral clasps and amber studs, —
All these in me no means can move
To come to thee, and be thy love.

But could youth last, and love still breed,
Had joys no date, nor age no need,
Then those delights my mind might move
To live with thee, and be thy love.
          SIR WALTER RALEIGH.

GO, HAPPY ROSE.

Go, happy Rose! and, interwove
With other flowers, bind my love!
  Tell her, too, she must not be
  Longer flowing, longer free,
  That so oft hath fettered me.

Say, if she's fretful, I have bands
Of pearl and gold to bind her hands;
  Tell her, if she struggle still,
  I have myrtle rods at will,
  For to tame, though not to kill.

Take then my blessing thus, and go,
And tell her this, — but do not so!
  Lest a handsome anger fly,
  Like a lightning from her eye,
  And burn thee up, as well as I.
          ROBERT HERRICK.

THE GROOMSMAN TO HIS MISTRESS.

I.

EVERY wedding, says the proverb,
  Makes another, soon or late;
Never yet was any marriage

Entered in the book of fate,
But the names were also written
Of the patient pair that wait.

II.

Blessings then upon the morning
When my friend, with fondest look,
By the solemn rites' permission,
To himself his mistress took,
And the destinies recorded
Other two within their book.

III.

While the priest fulfilled his office,
Still the ground the lovers eyed,
And the parents and the kinsmen
Aimed their glances at the bride;
But the groomsmen eyed the virgins
Who were waiting at her side.

IV.

Three there were that stood beside her;
One was dark, and one was fair;
But nor fair nor dark the other,
Save her Arab eyes and hair;
Neither dark nor fair I call her,
Yet she was the fairest there.

V.

While her groomsman — shall I own it?
Yes to thee, and only thee —
Gazed upon this dark-eyed maiden
Who was fairest of the three,
Thus he thought : "How blest the bridal
Where the bride were such as she!"

VI.

Then I mused upon the adage,
Till my wisdom was perplexed,
And I wondered, as the churchman
Dwelt upon his holy text,
Which of all who heard his lesson
Should require the service next.

VII.

Whose will be the next occasion
For the flowers, the feast, the wine?
Thine, perchance, my dearest lady;
Or, who knows? — it may be mine,
What if 't were — forgive the fancy —
What if 't were — both mine and thine?

THOMAS WILLIAM PARSONS.

MY EYES! HOW I LOVE YOU.

My eyes! how I love you,
You sweet little dove you!
There 's no one above you,
Most beautiful Kitty.

So glossy your hair is,
Like a sylph's or a fairy's;
And your neck, I declare, is
Exquisitely pretty!

Quite Grecian your nose is,
And your cheeks are like roses,
So delicious — O Moses!
Surpassingly sweet!

Not the beauty of tulips,
Nor the taste of mint-juleps,
Can compare with your two lips,
Most beautiful Kate!

Not the black eyes of Juno,
Nor Minerva's of blue, no,
Nor Venus's, you know,
Can equal your own!

O, how my heart prances,
And frolics and dances,
When its radiant glances
Upon me are thrown!

And now, dearest Kitty,
It 's not very pretty,
Indeed it 's a pity,
To keep me in sorrow!

So, if you 'll but chime in,
We 'll have done with our rhymin',
Swap Cupid for Hymen,
And be married to-morrow.

ANONYMOUS.

RUTH.

She stood breast high amid the corn,
Clasped by the golden light of morn,
Like the sweetheart of the sun,
Who many a glowing kiss had won.

On her cheek an autumn flush
Deeply ripened; — such a blush
In the midst of brown was born,
Like red poppies grown with corn.

Round her eyes her tresses fell, —
Which were blackest none could tell;
But long lashes veiled a light
That had else been all too bright.

And her hat, with shady brim,
Made her tressy forehead dim; —
Thus she stood amid the stooks,
Praising God with sweetest looks.

FORDS, HOWARD & HULBERT, N.Y.

Sure, I said, Heaven did not mean
Where I reap thou shouldst but glean ;
Lay thy sheaf adown and come,
Share my harvest and my home.

THOMAS HOOD.

WIDOW MACHREE.

I.

WIDOW machree, it 's no wonder you frown, —
　Och hone ! widow machree ;
Faith, it ruins your looks, that same dirty black
　　gown, —
　Och hone ! widow machree.
How altered your air,
With that close cap you wear, —
'T is destroying your hair,
　Which should be flowing free :
Be no longer a churl
Of its black silken curl, —
　Och hone ! widow machree !

II.

Widow machree, now the summer is come, —
　Och hone ! widow machree,
When everything smiles, should a beauty look
　　glum ?
　Och hone ! widow machree !
See the birds go in pairs,
And the rabbits and hares ;
Why, even the bears
　Now in couples agree ;
And the mute little fish,
Though they can't spake, they wish, —
　Och hone ! widow machree.

III.

Widow machree, and when winter comes in, —
　Och hone ! widow machree, —
To be poking the fire all alone is a sin,
　Och hone ! widow machree.
Sure the shovel and tongs
To each other belongs,
And the kettle sings songs
　Full of family glee ;
While alone with your cup
Like a hermit you sup,
　Och hone ! widow machree.

IV.

And how do you know, with the comforts I 've
　　towld, —
　Och hone ! widow machree, —
But you 're keeping some poor fellow out in the
　　cowld,
　Och hone ! widow machree !
With such sins on your head,
Sure your peace would be fled ;

Could you sleep in your bed
　Without thinking to see
Some ghost or some sprite,
That would wake you each night,
　Crying " Och hone ! widow machree ! "

V.

Then take my advice, darling widow machree, —
　Och hone ! widow machree, —
And with my advice, faith, I wish you 'd take me,
　Och hone ! widow machree !
You 'd have me to desire
Then to stir up the fire ;
And sure hope is no liar
　In whispering to me,
That the ghosts would depart
When you 'd me near your heart, —
　Och hone ! widow machree !

SAMUEL LOVER.

MAUD MULLER.

MAUD MULLER, on a summer's day,
Raked the meadow sweet with hay.

Beneath her torn hat glowed the wealth
Of simple beauty and rustic health.

Singing, she wrought, and her merry glee
The mock-bird echoed from his tree.

But, when she glanced to the far-off town,
White from its hill-slope looking down,

The sweet song died, and a vague unrest
And a nameless longing filled her breast, —

A wish, that she hardly dared to own,
For something better than she had known.

The Judge rode slowly down the lane,
Smoothing his horse's chestnut mane.

He drew his bridle in the shade
Of the apple-trees, to greet the maid,

And ask a draught from the spring that flowed
Through the meadow, across the road.

She stooped where the cool spring bubbled up,
And filled for him her small tin cup,

And blushed as she gave it, looking down
On her feet so bare, and her tattered gown.

" Thanks ! " said the Judge, " a sweeter draught
From a fairer hand was never quaffed."

He spoke of the grass and flowers and trees,
Of the singing birds and the humming bees ;

Then talked of the haying, and wondered whether
The cloud in the west would bring foul weather.

And Maud forgot her brier-torn gown,
And her graceful ankles, bare and brown,

And listened, while a pleased surprise
Looked from her long-lashed hazel eyes.

At last, like one who for delay
Seeks a vain excuse, he rode away.

Maud Muller looked and sighed : " Ah me !
That I the Judge's bride might be !

" He would dress me up in silks so fine,
And praise and toast me at his wine.

" My father should wear a broadcloth coat,
My brother should sail a painted boat.

" I 'd dress my mother so grand and gay,
And the baby should have a new toy each day.

" And I 'd feed the hungry and clothe the poor,
And all should bless me who left our door."

The Judge looked back as he climbed the hill,
And saw Maud Muller standing still :

" A form more fair, a face more sweet,
Ne'er hath it been my lot to meet.

" And her modest answer and graceful air
Show her wise and good as she is fair.

" Would she were mine, and I to-day,
Like her, a harvester of hay.

" No doubtful balance of rights and wrongs,
Nor weary lawyers with endless tongues,

" But low of cattle, and song of birds,
And health, and quiet, and loving words."

But he thought of his sister, proud and cold,
And his mother, vain of her rank and gold.

So, closing his heart, the Judge rode on,
And Maud was left in the field alone.

But the lawyers smiled that afternoon,
When he hummed in court an old love tune ;

And the young girl mused beside the well,
Till the rain on the unraked clover fell.

He wedded a wife of richest dower,
Who lived for fashion, as he for power.

Yet oft, in his marble hearth's bright glow,
He watched a picture come and go ;

And sweet Maud Muller's hazel eyes
Looked out in their innocent surprise.

Oft, when the wine in his glass was red,
He longed for the wayside well instead,

And closed his eyes on his garnished rooms,
To dream of meadows and clover blooms ;

And the proud man sighed with a secret pain,
" Ah, that I were free again !

" Free as when I rode that day
Where the barefoot maiden raked the hay."

She wedded a man unlearned and poor,
And many children played round her door.

But care and sorrow, and child-birth pain,
Left their traces on heart and brain.

And oft, when the summer sun shone hot
On the new-mown hay in the meadow lot,

And she heard the little spring brook fall
Over the roadside, through the wall,

In the shade of the apple-tree again
She saw a rider draw his rein,

And, gazing down with a timid grace,
She felt his pleased eyes read her face.

Sometimes her narrow kitchen walls
Stretched away into stately halls ;

The weary wheel to a spinnet turned,
The tallow candle an astral burned ;

And for him who sat by the chimney lug,
Dozing and grumbling o'er pipe and mug,

A manly form at her side she saw,
And joy was duty and love was law.

Then she took up her burden of life again,
Saying only, " It might have been."

Alas for maiden, alas for judge,
For rich repiner and household drudge !

God pity them both ! and pity us all,
Who vainly the dreams of youth recall ;

For of all sad words of tongue or pen,
The saddest are these : " It might have been ! '

Ah, well ! for us all some sweet hope lies
Deeply buried from human eyes ;

And, in the hereafter, angels may
Roll the stone from its grave away !
                        JOHN GREENLEAF WHITTIER.

QUAKERDOM.

THE FORMAL CALL.

THROUGH her forced, abnormal quiet
Flashed the soul of frolic riot,
And a most malicious laughter lighted up her
    downcast eyes;
    All in vain I tried each topic,
    Ranged from polar climes to tropic, —
Every commonplace I started met with yes-or-
    no replies.

For her mother — stiff and stately,
As if starched and ironed lately —
Sat erect, with rigid elbows bedded thus in curv-
    ing palms;
    There she sat on guard before us,
    And in words precise, decorous,
And most calm, reviewed the weather, and recited
    several psalms.

How without abruptly ending
This my visit, and offending
Wealthy neighbors, was the problem which em-
    ployed my mental care;
    When the butler, bowing lowly,
    Uttered clearly, stiffly, slowly,
"Madam, please, the gardener wants you," —
Heaven, I thought, has heard my prayer.

"Pardon me!" she grandly uttered;
Bowing low, I gladly muttered,
"Surely, madam!" and, relieved, I turned to
    scan the daughter's face:
    Ha! what pent-up mirth outflashes
    From beneath those pencilled lashes!
How the drill of Quaker custom yields to Na-
    ture's brilliant grace.

Brightly springs the prisoned fountain
From the side of Delphi's mountain
When the stone that weighed upon its buoyant
    life is thrust aside;
    So the long-enforced stagnation
    Of the maiden's conversation
Now imparted five-fold brilliance to its ever-
    varying tide.

Widely ranging, quickly changing,
Witty, winning, from beginning
Unto end I listened, merely flinging in a casual
    word;
    Eloquent, and yet how simple!
    Hand and eye, and eddying dimple,
Tongue and lip together made a music seen as
    well as heard.

When the noonday woods are ringing,
All the birds of summer singing,
Suddenly there falls a silence, and we know a
    serpent nigh:
    So upon the door a rattle
    Stopped our animated tattle,
And the stately mother found us prim enough to
    suit her eye.

CHARLES G. HALPINE.

THE CHESS-BOARD.

MY little love, do you remember,
Ere we were grown so sadly wise,
Those evenings in the bleak December,
Curtained warm from the snowy weather,
When you and I played chess together,
    Checkmated by each other's eyes?

Ah! still I see your soft white hand
Hovering warm o'er Queen and Knight;
    Brave Pawns in valiant battle stand;
The double Castles guard the wings;
The Bishop, bent on distant things,
Moves, sidling, through the fight.

Our fingers touch; our glances meet,
And falter; falls your golden hair
    Against my cheek; your bosom sweet
Is heaving. Down the field, your Queen
Rides slow, her soldiery all between,
    And checks me unaware.

Ah me! the little battle's done:
Disperst is all its chivalry.
Full many a move since then have we
Mid life's perplexing checkers made,
And many a game with fortune played;
    What is it we have won?
    This, this at least, — if this alone: ·

That never, never, nevermore,
As in those old still nights of yore,
    (Ere we were grown so sadly wise,)
    Can you and I shut out the skies,
Shut out the world and wintry weather,
    And eyes exchanging warmth with eyes,
Play chess, as then we played together.

ROBERT BULWER LYTTON.

WHEN YOUR BEAUTY APPEARS.

"WHEN your beauty appears,
In its graces and airs,
All bright as an angel new dropt from the skies,
At distance I gaze, and am awed by my fears,
So strangely you dazzle my eyes!

But when without art
Your kind thoughts you impart,
When your love runs in blushes through every
  vein,
When it darts from your eyes, when it pants
  at your heart,
Then I know that you 're woman again."

"There 's a passion and pride
In our sex," she replied ;
"And thus (might I gratify both) I would do, —
Still an angel appear to each lover beside,
But still be a woman for you."

THOMAS PARNELL.

THE FIRST KISS.

How delicious is the winning
Of a kiss at love's beginning,
When two mutual hearts are sighing
For the knot there 's no untying.

Yet remember, midst your wooing,
Love has bliss, but love has ruing ;
Other smiles may make you fickle,
Tears for other charms may trickle.

Love he comes, and Love he tarries,
Just as fate or fancy carries, —
Longest stays when sorest chidden,
Laughs and flies when pressed and bidden.

Bind the sea to slumber stilly,
Bind its odor to the lily,
Bind the aspen ne'er to quiver, —
Then bind Love to last forever !

Love 's a fire that needs renewal
Of fresh beauty for its fuel ;
Love's wing moults when caged and captured, —
Only free he soars enraptured.

Can you keep the bee from ranging,
Or the ring-dove's neck from changing ?
No ! nor fettered Love from dying
In the knot there 's no untying.

THOMAS CAMPBELL.

KISS ME SOFTLY.

Da me basia. — CATULLUS.

I.

KISS me softly and speak to me low, —
  Malice has ever a vigilant ear :
What if Malice were lurking near ?
    Kiss me, dear !
Kiss me softly and speak to me low.

II.

Kiss me softly and speak to me low, —
  Envy too has a watchful ear :
What if Envy should chance to hear ?
    Kiss me, dear !
Kiss me softly and speak to me low.

III.

Kiss me softly and speak to me low :
  Trust me, darling, the time is near
When lovers may love with never a fear, —
    Kiss me, dear !
Kiss me softly and speak to me low.

JOHN GODFREY SAXE.

SLY THOUGHTS.

"I saw him kiss your cheek !" —
    "'T is true."
"O Modesty !" — "'T was strictly kept :
He thought me asleep ; at least, I knew
He thought I thought he thought I slept."

COVENTRY PATMORE.

THE KISS.

1. AMONG thy fancies tell me this :
   What is the thing we call a kiss ? —
2. I shall resolve ye what it is :

   It is a creature born and bred
   Between the lips all cherry red,
   By love and warm desires fed ;
Chor. And makes more soft the bridal bed.

   It is an active flame, that flies
   First to the babies of the eyes,
   And charms them there with lullabies ;
Chor. And stills the bride too when she cries.

   Then to the chin, the cheek, the ear,
   It frisks and flies, — now here, now there ;
   'T is now far off, and then 't is near ;
Chor. And here, and there, and everywhere.

1. Has it a speaking virtue ? — 2. Yes.
1. How speaks it, say ? — 2. Do you but this :
   Part your joined lips, — then speaks your
     kiss ;
Chor. And this love's sweetest language is.

1. Has it a body ? — 2. Ay, and wings,
   With thousand rare encolorings ;
   And as it flies it gently sings ;
Chor. Love honey yields, but never stings.

ROBERT HERRICK.

KISSING 'S NO SIN.

Some say that kissing 's a sin ;
But I think it 's nane ava,
For kissing has wonn'd in this warld
Since ever that there was twa.

O, if it wasna lawfu',
Lawyers wadna allow it ;
If it wasna holy,
Ministers wadna do it.

If it wasna modest,
Maidens wadna tak' it ;
If it wasna plenty,
Puir folk wadna get it.
ANONYMOUS.

DINNA ASK ME.

O, DINNA ask me gin I lo'e ye :
Troth, I daurna tell !
Dinna ask me gin I lo'e ye, —
Ask it o' yoursel'.

O, dinna look sae sair at me,
For weel ye ken me true ;
O, gin ye look sae sair at me,
I daurna look at you.

When ye gang to yon braw braw town,
And bonnier lassies see,
O, dinna, Jamie, look at them,
Lest ye should mind na me.

For I could never bide the lass
That ye 'd lo'e mair than me ;
And O, I 'm sure my heart wad brak,
Gin ye 'd prove fause to me !
DUNLOP.

COMIN' THROUGH THE RYE.

Gin a body meet a body
Comin' through the rye,
Gin a body kiss a body,
Need a body cry ?
Every lassie has her laddie, —
Ne'er a ane hae I ;
Yet a' the lads they smile at me
When comin' through the rye.
Amang the train there is a swain
I dearly lo'e mysel' ;
But whaur his hame, or what his name,
I dinna care to tell.

Gin a body meet a body
Comin' frae the town,
Gin a body greet a body,
Need a body frown ?
Every lassie has her laddie, —
Ne'er a ane hae I ;
Yet a' the lads they smile at me
When comin' through the rye.
Amang the train there is a swain
I dearly lo'e mysel' ;
But whaur his hame, or what his name,
I dinna care to tell.
Adapted by BURNS.

KITTY OF COLERAINE.

As beautiful Kitty one morning was tripping
With a pitcher of milk, from the fair of Coleraine,
When she saw me she stumbled, the pitcher it
tumbled,
And all the sweet buttermilk watered the plain.

" O, what shall I do now ? — 't was looking at you
now !
Sure, sure, such a pitcher I 'll ne'er meet again !
'T was the pride of my dairy : O Barney M'Cleary !
You 're sent as a plague to the girls of Coleraine."

I sat down beside her, and gently did chide her,
That such a misfortune should give her such pain.
A kiss then I gave her ; and ere I did leave her,
She vowed for such pleasure she 'd break it again.

'T was hay-making season — I can't tell the rea-
son —
Misfortunes will never come single, 't is plain ;
For very soon after poor Kitty's disaster
The devil a pitcher was whole in Coleraine.
CHARLES DAWSON SHANLY.

THE DULE 'S I' THIS BONNET O' MINE.

YORKSHIRE DIALECT.

The dule 's i' this bonnet o' mine :
My ribbins 'll never be reet ;
Here, Mally, aw 'm like to be fine,
For Jamie 'll be comin' to-neet ;
He met me i' th' lone t' other day
(Aw wur gooin' for wayter to th' well),
An' he begged that aw 'd wed him i' May,
Bi th' mass, if he 'll let me, aw will !

When he took my two honds into his,
Good Lord, heaw they trembled between !
An' aw durst n't look up in his face,
Becose on him seein' my e'en.

My cheek went as red as a rose ;
　There 's never a mortal con tell
Heaw happy aw felt, — for, thae knows,
　One could n't ha' axed him theirsel'.

But th' tale wur at th' end o' my tung :
　To let it eawt would n't be reet,
For aw thought to seem forrud wur wrung ;
　So aw towd him aw 'd tell him to-neet.
But, Mally, thae knows very weel,
　Though it is n't a thing one should own,
Iv aw 'd th' pikein' o' th' world to mysel',
　Aw 'd oather ha' Jamie or noan.

Neaw, Mally, aw 've towd thae my mind ;
　What would to do iv it wur thee ?
" Aw 'd tak him just while he 'se inclined,
　An' a farrantly bargain he 'll be ;
For Jamie 's as greadly a lad
　As ever stept eawt into th' sun.
Go, jump at thy chance, an' get wed ;
　An' mak th' best o' th' job when it 's done ! "

Eh, dear ! but it 's time to be gwon :
　Aw should n't like Jamie to wait ;
Aw connut for shame be too soon,
　An' aw would n't for th' wuld be too late.
Aw 'm o' ov a tremble to th' heel :
　Dost think 'at my bonnet 'll do ?
" Be off, lass, — thae looks very weel ;
　He wants noan o' th' bonnet, thae foo ! "
　　　　　　　　　　　　　EDWIN WAUGH.

THE MOTH'S KISS, FIRST !

FROM "IN A GONDOLA."

THE Moth's kiss, first !
Kiss me as if you made believe
You were not sure, this eve,
How my face, your flower, had pursed
Its petals up ; so, here and there
You brush it, till I grow aware
Who wants me, and wide open burst.

The Bee's kiss, now !
Kiss me as if you entered gay
My heart at some noonday,
A bud that dared not disallow
The claim, so all is rendered up,
And passively its shattered cup
Over your head to sleep I bow.
　　　　　　　　　　　ROBERT BROWNING.

SUMMER DAYS.

IN summer, when the days were long,
We walked together in the wood :
　Our heart was light, our step was strong ;
Sweet flutterings were there in our blood,
　In summer, when the days were long.

We strayed from morn till evening came ;
We gathered flowers, and wove us crowns ;
　We walked mid poppies red as flame,
Or sat upon the yellow downs ;
　And always wished our life the same.

In summer, when the days were long,
We leaped the hedgerow, crossed the brook ;
　And still her voice flowed forth in song,
Or else she read some graceful book,
　In summer, when the days were long.

And then we sat beneath the trees,
With shadows lessening in the noon ;
　And in the sunlight and the breeze,
We feasted, many a gorgeous June,
　While larks were singing o'er the leas.

In summer, when the days were long,
On dainty chicken, snow-white bread,
　We feasted, with no grace but song ;
We plucked wild strawb'rries, ripe and red,
　In summer, when the days were long.

We loved, and yet we knew it not, —
For loving seemed like breathing then ;
　We found a heaven in every spot ;
Saw angels, too, in all good men ;
　And dreamed of God in grove and grot.

In summer, when the days are long,
Alone I wander, muse alone.
　I see her not ; but that old song
Under the fragrant wind is blown,
　In summer, when the days are long.

Alone I wander in the wood :
But one fair spirit hears my sighs ;
　And half I see, so glad and good,
The honest daylight of her eyes,
　That charmed me under earlier skies.

In summer, when the days are long,
I love her as we loved of old.
　My heart is light, my step is strong ;
For love brings back those hours of gold,
　In summer, when the days are long.
　　　　　　　　　　　　　ANONYMOUS.

THE WHISTLE.

"You have heard," said a youth to his sweet-
    heart, who stood,
  While he sat on a corn-sheaf, at daylight's
    decline, —
"You have heard of the Danish boy's whistle of
    wood?
I wish that that Danish boy's whistle were mine."

"And what would you do with it? — tell me,"
    she said,
  While an arch smile played over her beautiful
    face.
"I would blow it," he answered; "and then my
    fair maid
Would fly to my side, and would here take her
    place."

"Is that all you wish it for? — That may be yours
  Without any magic," the fair maiden cried:
"A favor so slight one's good nature secures";
  And she playfully seated herself by his side.

"I would blow it again," said the youth, "and
    the charm
Would work so, that not even Modesty's check
Would be able to keep from my neck your fine arm":
  She smiled, — and she laid her fine arm round
    his neck.

"Yet once more would I blow, and the music
    divine
  Would bring me the third time an exquisite
    bliss:
You would lay your fair cheek to this brown one
    of mine,
  And your lips, stealing past it, would give me
    a kiss."

The maiden laughed out in her innocent glee, —
  "What a fool of yourself with your whistle
    you 'd make!
For only consider, how silly 't would be,
  To sit there and whistle for — what you might
    take."
                   ROBERT STORY.

GENEVIEVE.

ALL thoughts, all passions, all delights,
  Whatever stirs this mortal frame,
All are but ministers of Love,
  And feed his sacred flame.

Oft in my waking dreams do I
  Live o'er again that happy hour,
When midway on the mount I lay
  Beside the ruined tower.

6

The moonshine stealing o'er the scene
Had blended with the lights of eve;
And she was there, my hope, my joy,
  My own dear Genevieve!

She leaned against the arméd man,
The statue of the arméd knight;
She stood and listened to my lay,
  Amid the lingering light.

Few sorrows hath she of her own,
My hope! my joy! my Genevieve!
She loves me best, whene'er I sing
  The songs that make her grieve.

I played a soft and doleful air,
I sang an old and moving story, —
An old rude song, that suited well
  That ruin wild and hoary.

She listened with a flitting blush,
With downcast eyes and modest grace;
For well she knew, I could not choose
  But gaze upon her face.

I told her of the Knight that wore
Upon his shield a burning brand;
And that for ten long years he wooed
  The Lady of the Land.

I told her how he pined: and ah!
The deep, the low, the pleading tone
With which I sang another's love
  Interpreted my own.

She listened with a flitting blush,
With downcast eyes, and modest grace;
And she forgave me, that I gazed
  Too fondly on her face.

But when I told the cruel scorn
That crazed that bold and lovely Knight,
And that he crossed the mountain-woods,
  Nor rested day nor night;

That sometimes from the savage den,
And sometimes from the darksome shade,
And sometimes starting up at once
  In green and sunny glade,

There came and looked him in the face
An angel beautiful and bright;
And that he knew it was a Fiend,
  This miserable Knight!

And that unknowing what he did,
He leaped amid a murderous band,
And saved from outrage worse than death
  The Lady of the Land;

And how she wept, and clasped his knees ;
And how she tended him in vain ;
And ever strove to expiate
     The scorn that crazed his brain ;

And that she nursed him in a cave,
And how his madness went away,
When on the yellow forest-leaves
     A dying man he lay ;

— His dying words — but when I reached
That tenderest strain of all the ditty,
My faltering voice and pausing harp
     Disturbed her soul with pity !

All impulses of soul and sense
Had thrilled my guileless Genevieve ;
The music and the doleful tale,
     The rich and balmy eve ;

And hopes, and fears that kindle hope,
An undistinguishable throng,
And gentle wishes long subdued,
     Subdued and cherished long.

She wept with pity and delight,
She blushed with love, and virgin shame ;
And like the murmur of a dream,
     I heard her breathe my name.

Her bosom heaved, — she stepped aside,
As conscious of my look she stept, —
Then suddenly, with timorous eye
     She fled to me and wept.

She half enclosed me with her arms,
She pressed me with a meek embrace ;
And bending back her head, looked up,
     And gazed upon my face.

'T was partly love, and partly fear,
And partly 't was a bashful art
That I might rather feel than see
     The swelling of her heart.

I calmed her fears, and she was calm,
And told her love with virgin pride ;
And so I won my Genevieve,
     My bright and beauteous Bride.
         SAMUEL TAYLOR COLERIDGE.

WHEN THE KYE COME HAME.

COME, all ye jolly shepherds,
     That whistle through the glen !
I 'll tell ye o' a secret
     That courtiers dinna ken :
What is the greatest bliss
     That the tongue o' man can name ?

'T is to woo a bonnie lassie
     When the kye come hame.
       When the kye come hame,
       When the kye come hame, —
       'Tween the gloamin' an' the mirk,
       When the kye come hame.

'T is not beneath the burgonet,
     Nor yet beneath the crown ;
'T is not on couch o' velvet,
     Nor yet in bed o' down :
'T is beneath the spreading birk,
     In the glen without the name,
Wi' a bonnie bonnie lassie,
     When the kye come hame.

There the blackbird bigs his nest,
     For the mate he lo'es to see,
And on the tapmost bough
     O, a happy bird is he !
There he pours his melting ditty,
     And love is a' the theme ;
And he 'll woo his bonnie lassie,
     When the kye come hame.

When the blewart bears a pearl,
     And the daisy turns a pea,
And the bonnie lucken gowan
     Has fauldit up his ee,
Then the lavrock, frae the blue lift,
     Draps down and thinks nae shame
To woo his bonnie lassie,
     When the kye come hame.

See yonder pawky shepherd,
     That lingers on the hill :
His yowes are in the fauld,
     And his lambs are lying still ;
Yet he downa gang to bed,
     For his heart is in a flame,
To meet his bonnie lassie
     When the kye come hame.

When the little wee bit heart
     Rises high in the breast,
And the little wee bit starn
     Rises red in the east,
O, there 's a joy sae dear
     That the heart can hardly frame !
Wi' a bonnie bonnie lassie,
     When the kye come hame.

Then since all Nature joins
     In this love without alloy,
O, wha wad prove a traitor
     To Nature's dearest joy ?
Or wha wad choose a crown,
     Wi' its perils an' its fame,
And miss his bonnie lassie,
     When the kye come hame ?
         JAMES HOGG.

ATALANTA VICTORIOUS.

FROM "ATALANTA'S RACE," IN "THE EARTHLY
PARADISE."

AND there two runners did the sign abide
Foot set to foot, — a young man slim and fair,
Crisp-haired, well knit, with firm limbs often tried
In places where no man his strength may spare ;
Dainty his thin coat was, and on his hair
A golden circlet of renown he wore,
And in his hand an olive garland bore.

But on this day with whom shall he contend ?
A maid stood by him like Diana clad
When in the woods she lists her bow to bend,
Too fair for one to look on and be glad,
Who scarcely yet has thirty summers had,
If he must still behold her from afar ;
Too fair to let the world live free from war.

She seemed all earthly matters to forget ;
Of all tormenting lines her face was clear,
Her wide gray eyes upon the goal were set
Calm and unmoved as though no soul were near ;
But her foe trembled as a man in fear,
Nor from her loveliness one moment turned
His anxious face with fierce desire that burned.

Now through the hush there broke the trum-
pet's clang
Just as the setting sun made eventide.
Then from light feet a spurt of dust there sprang,
And swiftly were they running side by side ;
But silent did the thronging folk abide
Until the turning-post was reached at last,
And round about it still abreast they passed.

But when the people saw how close they ran,
When half-way to the starting-point they were,
A cry of joy broke forth, whereat the man
Headed the white-foot runner, and drew near
Unto the very end of all his fear ;
And scarce his straining feet the ground could feel,
And bliss unhoped for o'er his heart 'gan steal.

But midst the loud victorious shouts he heard
Her footsteps drawing nearer, and the sound
Of fluttering raiment, and thereat afeard
His flushed and eager face he turned around,
And even then he felt her past him bound
Fleet as the wind, but scarcely saw her there
Till on the goal she laid her fingers fair.

There stood she breathing like a little child
Amid some warlike clamor laid asleep,
For no victorious joy her red lips smiled,
Her cheek its wonted freshness did but keep ;
No glance lit up her clear gray eyes and deep,
Though some divine thought softened all her face
As once more rang the trumpet through the place.

But her late foe stopped short amidst his course,
One moment gazed upon her piteously,
Then with a groan his lingering feet did force
To leave the spot whence he her eyes could see ;
And, changed like one who knows his time must be
But short and bitter, without any word
He knelt before the bearer of the sword ;

Then high rose up the gleaming deadly blade,
Bared of its flowers, and through the crowded place
Was silence now, and midst of it the maid
Went by the poor wretch at a gentle pace,
And he to hers upturned his sad white face ;
Nor did his eyes behold another sight
Ere on his soul there fell eternal night.

WILLIAM MORRIS.

ATALANTA CONQUERED.

FROM "ATALANTA'S RACE," IN "THE EARTHLY
PARADISE."

Now has the lingering month at last gone by,
Again are all folk round the running place,
Nor other seems the dismal pageantry
Than heretofore, but that another face
Looks o'er the smooth course ready for the race,
For now, beheld of all, Milanion
Stands on the spot he twice has looked upon.

But yet — what change is this that holds the
maid ?
Does she indeed see in his glittering eye
More than disdain of the sharp shearing blade,
Some happy hope of help and victory ?
The others seemed to say, " We come to die,
Look down upon us for a little while,
That dead, we may bethink us of thy smile."

But he — what look of mastery was this
He cast on her ? why were his lips so red ?
Why was his face so flushed with happiness ?
So looks not one who deems himself but dead,
E'en if to death he bows a willing head ;
So rather looks a god well pleased to find
Some earthly damsel fashioned to his mind.

Why must she drop her lids before his gaze,
And even as she casts adown her eyes
Redden to note his eager glance of praise,
And wish that she were clad in other guise ?
Why must the memory to her heart arise
Of things unnoticed when they first were heard,
Some lover's song, some answering maiden's word ?

What makes these longings, vague, without a
name,
And this vain pity never felt before,
This sudden languor, this contempt of fame,

This tender sorrow for the time past o'er,
These doubts that grow each minute more and
        more ?
Why does she tremble as the time grows near,
And weak defeat and woful victory fear ?

But while she seemed to hear her beating
        heart,
Above their heads the trumpet blast rang out,
And forth they sprang ; and she must play her
        part ;
Then flew her white feet, knowing not a doubt,
Though slackening once, she turned her head
        about,
But then she cried aloud and faster fled
Than e'er before, and all men deemed him
        dead.

But with no sound he raised aloft his hand,
And thence what seemed a ray of light there
        flew
And past the maid rolled on along the sand ;
Then trembling she her feet together drew,
And in her heart a strong desire there grew
To have the toy ; some god she thought had
        given
That gift to her, to make of earth a heaven.

Then from the course with eager steps she ran,
And in her odorous bosom laid the gold.
But when she turned again, the great-limbed man
Now well ahead she failed not to behold,
And mindful of her glory waxing cold,
Sprang up and followed him in hot pursuit,
Though with one hand she touched the golden
        fruit.

Note, too, the bow that she was wont to bear
She laid aside to grasp the glittering prize,
And o'er her shoulder from the quiver fair
Three arrows fell and lay before her eyes
Unnoticed, as amidst the people's cries
She sprang to head the strong Milanion,
Who now the turning-post had wellnigh won.

But as he set his mighty hand on it,
White fingers underneath his own were laid,
And white limbs from his dazzled eyes did flit,
Then he the second fruit cast by the maid,
But she ran on awhile, then as afraid
Wavered and stopped, and turned and made no stay
Until the globe with its bright fellow lay.

Then, as a troubled glance she cast around,
Now far ahead the Argive could she see,
And in her garment's hem one hand she wound
To keep the double prize, and strenuously
Sped o'er the course, and little doubt had she

To win the day, though now but scanty space
Was left betwixt him and the winning place.

Short was the way unto such wingéd feet,
Quickly she gained upon him till at last
He turned about her eager eyes to meet,
And from his hand the third fair apple cast.
She wavered not, but turned and ran so fast
After the prize that should her bliss fulfil,
That in her hand it lay ere it was still.

Nor did she rest, but turned about to win
Once more, an unblest woful victory —
And yet — and yet — why does her breath begin
To fail her, and her feet drag heavily ?
Why fails she now to see if far or nigh
The goal is ? why do her gray eyes grow dim ?
Why do these tremors run through every limb ?

She spreads her arms abroad some stay to find
Else must she fall, indeed, and findeth this,
A strong man's arms about her body twined.
Nor may she shudder now to feel his kiss,
So wrapped she is in new, unbroken bliss :
Made happy that the foe the prize hath won,
She weeps glad tears for all her glory done.
                              WILLIAM MORRIS.

THE SIESTA.

FROM THE SPANISH.

" Vientecico murmurador,
Que lo gozas y andas todo," &c.

AIRS, that wander and murmur round,
    Bearing delight where'er ye blow !
Make in the elms a lulling sound,
    While my lady sleeps in the shade below.

Lighten and lengthen her noonday rest,
    Till the heat of the noonday sun is o'er.
Sweet be her slumbers ! though in my breast
    The pain she has waked may slumber no more.
Breathing soft from the blue profound,
    Bearing delight where'er ye blow,
Make in the elms a lulling sound,
    While my lady sleeps in the shade below.

Airs ! that over the bending boughs,
    And under the shade of pendent leaves,
Murmur soft, like my timid vows
    Or the secret sighs my bosom heaves, —
Gently sweeping the grassy ground,
    Bearing delight where'er ye blow,
Make in the elms a lulling sound,
    While my lady sleeps in the shade below.
                      WILLIAM CULLEN BRYANT.

ACBAR AND NOURMAHAL.

FROM "THE LIGHT OF THE HAREM."

OH ! best of delights, as it everywhere is,
To be near the loved *one*, — what a rapture is his
Who in moonlight and music thus sweetly may
    glide
O'er the Lake of Cashmere with that *one* by his side !
If woman can make the worst wilderness dear,
Think, think what a heaven she must make of
    Cashmere !

So felt the magnificent Son of Acbar,
When from power and pomp and the trophies of war
He flew to that valley, forgetting them all
With the Light of the Harem, his young Nour-
    mahal.
When free and uncrowned as the conqueror roved
By the banks of that lake, with his only beloved,
He saw, in the wreaths she would playfully snatch
From the hedges, a glory his crown could not
    match,
And preferred in his heart the least ringlet that
    curled
Down her exquisite neck to the throne of the world !

There 's a beauty, forever unchangingly bright,
Like the long sunny lapse of a summer's day's light,
Shining on, shining on, by no shadow made tender,
Till love falls asleep in its sameness of splendor.
This *was* not the beauty, — O, nothing like this,
That to young Nourmahal gave such magic of bliss,
But that loveliness, ever in motion, which plays
Like the light upon autumn's soft shadowy days,
Now here and now there, giving warmth as it flies
From the lips to the cheek, from the cheek to the
    eyes,
Now melting in mist and now breaking in gleams,
Like the glimpses a saint has of heaven in his
    dreams !
When pensive, it seemed as if that very grace,
That charm of all others, was born with her face ;
And when angry, — for even in the tranquillest
    climes
Light breezes will ruffle the flowers sometimes, —
The short, passing anger but seemed to awaken
New beauty, like flowers that are sweetest when
    shaken.
If tenderness touched her, the dark of her eye
At once took a darker, a heavenlier dye,
From the depth of whose shadow, like holy re-
    vealings
From innermost shrines, came the light of her
    feelings !
Then her mirth — O, 't was sportive as ever
    took wing
From the heart with a burst like the wild-bird
    in spring, —

Illumed by a wit that would fascinate sages,
Yet playful as Peris just loosed from their cages.
While her laugh, full of life, without any control
But the sweet one of gracefulness, rung from her
    soul ;
And where it most sparkled no glance could dis-
    cover,
In lip, cheek, or eyes, for she brightened all over, —
Like any fair lake that the breeze is upon,
When it breaks into dimples, and laughs in the sun.
Such, such were the peerless enchantments that
    gave
Nourmahal the proud Lord of the East for her
    slave ;
And though bright was his Harem, — a living
    parterre
Of the flowers of this planet, — though treasures
    were there,
For which Solomon's self might have given all
    the store
That the navy from Ophir e'er winged to his shore,
Yet dim before *her* were the smiles of them all,
And the Light of his Harem was young Nourmahal !
                              THOMAS MOORE.

MEETING.

THE gray sea, and the long black land ;
And the yellow half-moon large and low ;
And the startled little waves, that leap
In fiery ringlets from their sleep,
As I gain the cove with pushing prow,
And quench its speed in the slushy sand.

Then a mile of warm, sea-scented beach ;
Three fields to cross, till a farm appears :
A tap at the pane, the quick sharp scratch
And blue spurt of a lighted match,
And a voice less loud, through its joys and fears,
Than the two hearts, beating each to each.
                              ROBERT BROWNING.

THE LADY'S LOOKING-GLASS.

CELIA and I, the other day,
Walked o'er the sand-hills to the sea :
The setting sun adorned the coast,
His beams entire his fierceness lost :
And on the surface of the deep
The winds lay only not asleep :
The nymphs did, like the scene, appear
Serenely pleasant, calmly fair ;
Soft felt her words as flew the air.
With secret joy I heard her say
That she would never miss one day
A walk so fine, a sight so gay,

But, O the change ! The winds grow high,
Impending tempests charge the sky,
The lightning flies, the thunder roars,
The big waves lash the frightened shores.
Struck with the horror of the sight,
She turns her head and wings her flight ;
And, trembling, vows she 'll ne'er again
Approach the shore or view the main.

"Once more at least look back," said I,
"Thyself in that large glass descry :
When thou art in good humor drest,
When gentle reason rules thy breast,
The sun upon the calmest sea
Appears not half so bright as thee :
'T is then that with delight I rove
Upon the boundless depth of love :
I bless my chain, I hand my oar,
Nor think on all I left on shore.

" But when vain doubt and groundless fear
Do that dear foolish bosom tear ;
When the big lip and watery eye
Tell me the rising storm is nigh ;
'T is then thou art yon angry main
Deformed by winds and dashed by rain ;
And the poor sailor that must try
Its fury labors less than I.
Shipwrecked, in vain to land I make,
While love and fate still drive me back :
Forced to dote on thee thy own way,
I chide thee first, and then obey :
Wretched when from thee, vexed when nigh,
I with thee, or without thee, die."
MATTHEW PRIOR.

THE BELLE OF THE BALL.

YEARS, years ago, ere yet my dreams
Had been of being wise or witty,
Ere I had done with writing themes,
Or yawned o'er this infernal Chitty, —
Years, years ago, while all my joys
Were in my fowling-piece and filly ;
In short, while I was yet a boy,
I fell in love with Laura Lilly.

I saw her at the county ball ;
There, when the sounds of flute and fiddle
Gave signal sweet in that old hall
Of hands across and down the middle,
Hers was the subtlest spell by far
Of all that sets young hearts romancing :
She was our queen, our rose, our star ;
And then she danced, —O Heaven ! her dancing.

Dark was her hair ; her hand was white ;
Her voice was exquisitely tender ;
Her eyes were full of liquid light ;
I never saw a waist so slender ;
Her every look, her every smile,
Shot right and left a score of arrows :
I thought 't was Venus from her isle,
And wondered where she 'd left her sparrows.

She talked of politics or prayers,
Of Southey's prose or Wordsworth's sonnets,
Of danglers or of dancing bears,
Of battles or the last new bonnets ;
By candle-light, at twelve o'clock, —
To me it mattered not a tittle, —
If those bright lips had quoted Locke,
I might have thought they murmured Little.

Through sunny May, through sultry June,
I loved her with a love eternal ;
I spoke her praises to the moon,
I wrote them to the Sunday Journal.
My mother laughed ; I soon found out
That ancient ladies have no feeling :
My father frowned ; but how should gout
See any happiness in kneeling ?

She was the daughter of a dean, —
Rich, fat, and rather apoplectic ;
She had one brother just thirteen,
Whose color was extremely hectic ;
Her grandmother for many a year,
Had fed the parish with her bounty ;
Her second cousin was a peer,
And lord-lieutenant of the county.

But titles and the three-per-cents,
And mortgages, and great relations,
And India bonds, and tithes and rents,
O, what are they to love's sensations ?
Black eyes, fair forehead, clustering locks, —
Such wealth, such honors Cupid chooses ;
He cares as little for the stocks
As Baron Rothschild for the muses.

She sketched ; the vale, the wood, the beach,
Grew lovelier from her pencil's shading :
She botanized ; I envied each
Young blossom in her boudoir fading :
She warbled Handel ; it was grand, —
She made the Catilina jealous :
She touched the organ ; I could stand
For hours and hours to blow the bellows.

She kept an album too, at home,
Well filled with all an album's glories, —
Paintings of butterflies and Rome,
Patterns for trimmings, Persian stories,

Soft songs to Julia's cockatoo,
  Fierce odes to famine and to slaughter,
And autographs of Prince Leeboo,
  And recipes for elder water.

And she was flattered, worshipped, bored ;
  Her steps were watched, her dress was noted ;
Her poodle-dog was quite adored ;
  Her sayings were extremely quoted.
She laughed, — and every heart was glad,
  As if the taxes were abolished ;
She frowned, — and every look was sad,
  As if the opera were demolished.

She smiled on many just for fun, —
  I knew that there was nothing in it ;
I was the first, the only one,
  Her heart had thought of for a minute.
I knew it, for she told me so,
  In phrase which was divinely moulded ;
She wrote a charming hand, — and O,
  How sweetly all her notes were folded !

Our love was most like other loves, —
  A little glow, a little shiver,
A rosebud and a pair of gloves,
  And " Fly Not Yet," upon the river ;
Some jealousy of some one's heir,
  Some hopes of dying broken-hearted ;
A miniature, a lock of hair,
  The usual vows, — and then we parted.

We parted : months and years rolled by ;
  We met again four summers after.
Our parting was all sob and sigh,
  Our meeting was all mirth and laughter !
For in my heart's most secret cell
  There had been many other lodgers ;
And she was not the ball-room's belle,
  But only Mrs. — Something — Rogers !
                    WINTHROP MACKWORTH PRAED.

THE FRIAR OF ORDERS GRAY.

IT was a friar of orders gray
  Walked forth to tell his beads ;
And he met with a lady fair
  Clad in a pilgrim's weeds.

" Now Christ thee save, thou reverend friar ;
  I pray thee tell to me,
If ever at yon holy shrine
  My true-love thou didst see."

" And how should I know your true-love
  From many another one ? "
" O, by his cockle hat, and staff,
  And by his sandal shoon.

" But chiefly by his face and mien,
  That were so fair to view ;
His flaxen locks that sweetly curled,
  And eyes of lovely blue."

" O lady, he 's dead and gone !
  Lady, he 's dead and gone !
And at his head a green grass turf,
  And at his heels a stone.

" Within these holy cloisters long
  He languished, and he died,
Lamenting of a lady's love,
  And 'plaining of her pride.

" Here bore him barefaced on his bier
  Six proper youths and tall,
And many a tear bedewd his grave
  Within yon kirk-yard wall."

" And art thou dead, thou gentle youth ?
  And art thou dead and gone ?
And didst thou die for love of me ?
  Break, cruel heart of stone ! "

" O weep not, lady, weep not so ;
  Some ghostly comfort seek ;
Let not vain sorrow rive thy heart,
  Nor tears bedew thy cheek."

" O do not, do not, holy friar,
  My sorrow now reprove ;
For I have lost the sweetest youth
  That e'er won lady's love.

" And now, alas ! for thy sad loss
  I 'll evermore weep and sigh :
For thee I only wished to live,
  For thee I wish to die."

" Weep no more, lady, weep no more,
  Thy sorrow is in vain ;
For violets plucked, the sweetest showers
  Will ne'er make grow again.

" Our joys as wingéd dreams do fly ;
  Why then should sorrow last ?
Since grief but aggravates thy loss,
  Grieve not for what is past."

" O say not so, thou holy friar ;
  I pray thee, say not so ;
For since my true-love died for me,
  'T is meet my tears should flow.

" And will he never come again ?
  Will he ne'er come again ?
Ah ! no he is dead and laid in his grave,
  Forever to remain.

"His cheek was redder than the rose;
  The comeliest youth was he!
But he is dead and laid in his grave:
  Alas, and woe is me!"

"Sigh no more, lady, sigh no more,
  Men were deceivers ever:
One foot on sea and one on land,
  To one thing constant never.

"Hadst thou been fond, he had been false,
  And left thee sad and heavy;
For young men ever were fickle found,
  Since summer trees were leafy."

"Now say not so, thou holy friar,
  I pray thee say not so;
My love he had the truest heart, —
  O, he was ever true!

"And art thou dead, thou much-loved youth,
  And didst thou die for me?
Then farewell home; for evermore
  A pilgrim I will be.

"But first upon my true-love's grave
  My weary limbs I'll lay,
And thrice I'll kiss the green-grass turf
  That wraps his breathless clay."

"Yet stay, fair lady: rest awhile
  Beneath this cloister wall;
See through the hawthorn blows the cold wind,
  And drizzly rain doth fall."

"O stay me not, thou holy friar,
  O stay me not, I pray;
No drizzly rain that falls on me
  Can wash my fault away."

"Yet stay, fair lady, turn again,
  And dry those pearly tears;
For see, beneath this gown of gray
  Thy own true-love appears.

"Here forced by grief and hopeless love,
  These holy weeds I sought;
And here, amid these lonely walls,
  To end my days I thought.

"But haply, for my year of grace
  Is not yet passed away,
Might I still hope to win thy love,
  No longer would I stay."

"Now farewell grief, and welcome joy
  Once more unto my heart;
For since I have found thee, lovely youth,
  We nevermore will part."
    Adapted by THOMAS PERCY.

PYGMALION AND THE IMAGE.

FROM "THE EARTHLY PARADISE."

ARGUMENT.

A Man of Cyprus, a Sculptor named Pygmalion, made an Image of a Woman, fairer than any that had yet been seen, and in the end came to love his own handiwork as though it had been alive: wherefore, praying to Venus for help, he obtained his end, for she made the Image alive indeed, and a Woman, and Pygmalion wedded her.

AT Amathus, that from the southern side
Of Cyprus looks across the Syrian sea,
There did in ancient time a man abide
Known to the island-dwellers, for that he
Had wrought most godlike works in imagery,
And day by day still greater honor won,
Which man our old books call Pygmalion.

   .   .   .   .

The lessening marble that he worked upon,
A woman's form now imaged doubtfully,
And in such guise the work had he begun,
Because when he the untouched block did see
In wandering veins that form there seemed to be,
Whereon he cried out in a careless mood,
"O lady Venus, make this presage good!

"And then this block of stone shall be thy maid,
And, not without rich golden ornament,
Shall bide within thy quivering myrtle-shade."
So spoke he, but the goddess, well content,
Unto his hand such godlike mastery sent,
That like the first artificer he wrought,
Who made the gift that woe to all men brought.

And yet, but such as he was wont to do,
At first indeed that work divine he deemed,
And as the white chips from the chisel flew
Of other matters languidly he dreamed,
For easy to his hand that labor seemed.
And he was stirred with many a troubling thought,
And many a doubt perplexed him as he wrought.

And yet, again, at last there came a day
When smoother and more shapely grew the stone,
And he, grown eager, put all thought away
But that which touched his craftsmanship alone,
And he would gaze at what his hands had done,
Until his heart with boundless joy would swell
That all was wrought so wonderfully well.

Yet long it was ere he was satisfied,
And with his pride that by his mastery
This thing was done, whose equal far and wide
In no town of the world a man could see,
Came burning longing that the work should be
E'en better still, and to his heart there came
A strange and strong desire he could not name.

   .   .   .   .

The night seemed long, and long the twilight
    seemed,
A vain thing seemed his flowery garden fair ;
Though through the night still of his work he
    dreamed,
And though his smooth-stemmed trees so nigh it
    were,
That thence he could behold the marble hair ;
Naught was enough, until with steel in hand
He came before the wondrous stone to stand.

Blinded with tears, his chisel up he caught,
And, drawing near, and sighing, tenderly
Upon the marvel of the face he wrought,
E'en as he used to pass the long days by ;
But his sighs changed to sobbing presently,
And on the floor the useless steel he flung,
And, weeping loud, about the image clung.

"Alas !" he cried, "why have I made thee then,
That thus thou mockest me ? I know indeed
That many such as thou are loved of men,
Whose passionate eyes poor wretches still will lead
Into their net, and smile to see them bleed ;
But these the Gods made, and this hand made thee
Who wilt not speak one little word to me."

Then from the image did he draw aback
To gaze on it through tears : and you had said,
Regarding it, that little did it lack
To be a living and most lovely maid ;
Naked it was, its unbound locks were laid
Over the lovely shoulders ; with one hand
Reached out, as to a lover, did it stand,

The other held a fair rose over-blown ;
No smile was on the parted lips, the eyes
Seemed as if even now great love had shown
Unto them something of its sweet surprise,
Yet saddened them with half-seen mysteries,
And still midst passion maiden-like she seemed,
As though of love unchanged for aye she dreamed.

Reproachfully beholding all her grace,
Pygmalion stood, until he grew dry-eyed,
And then at last he turned away his face
As if from her cold eyes his grief to hide ;
And thus a weary while did he abide,
With nothing in his heart but vain desire,
The ever-burning, unconsuming fire.

No word indeed the moveless image said,
But with the sweet grave eyes his hands had
    wrought
Still gazed down on his bowed imploring head,
Yet his own words some solace to him brought,
Gilding the net wherein his soul was caught

With something like to hope, and all that day
Some tender words he ever found to say ;

And still he felt as something heard him speak ;
Sometimes he praised her beauty, and sometimes
Reproached her in a feeble voice and weak,
And at the last drew forth a book of rhymes,
Wherein were writ the tales of many climes,
And read aloud the sweetness hid therein
Of lovers' sorrows and their tangled sin.

And when the sun went down, the frankincense
Again upon the altar-flame he cast
That through the open window floating thence
O'er the fresh odors of the garden passed ;
And so another day was gone at last,
And he no more his lovelorn watch could keep,
But now for utter weariness must sleep.

But the next morn, e'en while the incense-smoke
At sunrising curled round about her head,
Sweet sound of songs the wonted quiet broke
Down in the street, and he by something led,
He knew not what, must leave his prayer unsaid,
And through the freshness of the morn must see
The folk who went with that sweet minstrelsy ;

Damsels and youths in wonderful attire,
And in their midst upon a car of gold
An image of the Mother of Desiré,
Wrought by his hands in days that seemed grown
    old,
Though those sweet limbs a garment did enfold.
Colored like flame, en-wrought with precious
    things,
Most fit to be the prize of striving kings.

Then he remembered that the manner was
That fair-clad priests the lovely Queen should take
Thrice in the year, and through the city pass,
And with sweet songs the dreaming folk awake ;
And through the clouds a light there seemed to
    break
When he remembered all the tales well told
About her glorious kindly deeds of old.

So his unfinished prayer he finished not,
But, kneeling, once more kissed the marble feet,
And, while his heart with many thoughts waxed
    hot,
He clad himself with fresh attire and meet
For that bright service, and with blossoms sweet
Entwined with tender leaves he crowned his head,
And followed after as the goddess led.

So there he stood, that help from her to gain,
Bewildered by that twilight midst of day ;
Downcast with listening to the joyous strain
He had no part in, hopeless with delay

Of all the fair things he had meant to say :
Yet, as the incense on the flame he cast,
From stammering lips and pale these words there
    passed, —

"O thou forgotten help, dost thou yet know
What thing it is I need, when even I,
Bent down before thee in this shame and woe,
Can frame no set of words to tell thee why
I needs must pray, O help me or I die !
Or slay me, and in slaying take from me
Even a dead man's feeble memory.

Yet soon, indeed, before his door he stood,
And, as a man awaking from a dream,
Seemed waked from his old folly ; naught seemed
    good
In all the things that he before had deemed
At least worth life, and on his heart there streamed
Cold light of day, — he found himself alone,
Reft of desire, all love and madness gone.

Thus to his chamber at the last he came,
And, pushing through the sti'l half-opened door,
He stood within ; but there, for very shame
Of all the things that he had done before,
Still kept his eyes bent down upon the floor,
Thinking of all that he had done and said
Since he had wrought that luckless marble maid.

Yet soft his thoughts were, and the very place
Seemed perfumed with some nameless heavenly air.
So gaining courage, did he raise his face
Unto the work his hands had made so fair,
And cried aloud to see the niche all bare
Of that sweet form, while through his heart again
There shot a pang of his old yearning pain.

Yet while he stood, and knew not what to do
With yearning, a strange thrill of hope there came,
A shaft of new desire now pierced him through,
And therewithal a soft voice called his name,
And when he turned, with eager eyes aflame,
He saw betwixt him and the setting sun
The lively image of his lovéd one.

He trembled at the sight, for though her eyes,
Her very lips, were such as he had made,
And though her tresses fell but in such guise
As he had wrought them, now was she arrayed
In that fair garment that the priests had laid
Upon the goddess on that very morn,
Dyed like the setting sun upon the corn.

Speechless he stood, but she now drew anear,
Simple and sweet as she was wont to be,
And once again her silver voice rang clear,
Filling his soul with great felicity,
And thus she spoke, " Wilt thou not come to me,

O dear companion of my new-found life,
For I am called thy lover and thy wife ?

She reached her hand to him, and with kind eyes
Gazed into his ; but he the fingers caught
And drew her to him, and midst ecstasies
Passing all words, yea, well nigh passing thought,
Felt that sweet breath that he so long had sought,
Felt the warm life within her heaving breast
As in his arms his living love he pressed.

But as his cheek touched hers he heard her say,
"Wilt thou not speak, O love ? why dost thou weep ?
Art thou then sorry for this long-wished day,
Or dost thou think perchance thou wilt not keep
This that thou holdest, but in dreamy sleep ?
Nay, let us do the bidding of the Queen,
And hand in hand walk through thy garden green ;

"Then shalt thou tell me, still beholding me,
Full many things whereof I wish to know,
And as we walk from whispering tree to tree
Still more familiar to thee shall I grow,
And such things shalt thou say unto me now
As when thou deemedst thou wast quite alone,
A madman kneeling to a thing of stone."

But at that word a smile lit up his eyes
And therewithal he spake some loving word,
And she at first looked up in grave surprise
When his deep voice and musical she heard,
And clung to him as somewhat grown afeard ;
Then cried aloud and said, "O mighty one !
What joy with thee to look upon the sun !"

Then into that fair garden did they pass,
And all the story of his love he told,
And as the twain went o'er the dewy grass,
Beneath the risen moon could he behold
The bright tears trickling down, then, waxen bold,
He stopped and said, " Ah, love, what meaneth
    this ?
Seest thou how tears still follow earthly bliss ?"

Then both her white arms round his neck she
    threw,
And sobbing said, "O love, what hurteth me ?
When first the sweetness of my life I knew,
Not this I felt, but when I first saw thee
A little pain and great felicity
Rose up within me, and thy talk e'en now
Made pain and pleasure ever greater grow."

"O sweet," he said, "this thing is even love,
Whereof I told thee ; that all wise men fear,
But yet escape not ; nay, to gods above,
Unless the old tales lie, it draweth near.
But let my happy ears, I pray thee, hear
Thy story too, and how thy blessed birth
Has made a heaven of this once lonely earth."

" My sweet," she said, " as yet I am not wise,
Or stored with words, aright the tale to tell,
But listen : when I opened first mine eyes
I stood within the niche thou knowest well,
And from mine hand a heavy thing there fell
Carved like these flowers, nor could I see things
    clear,
And but a strange confused noise could hear.

" At last mine eyes could see a woman fair,
But awful as this round white moon o'erhead,
So that I trembled when I saw her there,
For with my life was born some touch of dread,
And therewithal I heard her voice that said,
' Come down, and learn to love and be alive,
For thee, a well-prized gift, to-day I give.'

" Then on the floor I stepped, rejoicing much,
Not knowing why, not knowing aught at all,
Till she reached out her hand my breast to touch,
And when her fingers thereupon did fall,
Thought came unto my.life, and therewithal
I knew her for a goddess, and began
To murmur in some tongue unknown to man.

" And then indeed not in this guise was I,
No sandals had I, and no saffron gown,
But naked as thou knowest utterly,
E'en as my limbs beneath thine hand had grown,
And this fair perfumed robe then fell adown
Over the goddess' feet and swept the ground,
And round her loins a glittering belt was bound.

" But when the stammering of my tongue she
    heard
Upon my trembling lips her hand she laid,
And spoke again, ' Nay, say not any word,
All that thine heart would say I know unsaid,
Who even now thine heart and voice have made ;
But listen rather, for thou knowest now
What these words mean, and still wilt wiser grow.

" ' Thy body, lifeless till I gave it life,
A certain man, my servant, well hath wrought,
I give thee to him as his love and wife,
With all thy dowry of desire and thought,
Since this his yearning heart hath ever sought ;
Now from my temple is he on the way,
Deeming to find thee e'en as yesterday ;

" ' Bide thou his coming by the bed-head there,
And when thou seest him set his eyes upon
Thine empty niche, and hear'st him cry for care,
Then call him by his name, Pygmalion,
And certainly thy lover hast thou won ;
But when he stands before thee silently,
Say all these words that I shall teach to thee.'

" With that she said what first I told thee, love,
And then went on, ' Moreover thou shalt say
That I, the daughter of almighty Jove,

Have wrought for him this long-desired day ;
In sign whereof, these things that pass away,
Wherein mine image men have well arrayed,
I give thee for thy wedding gear, O maid.'

" Therewith her raiment she put off from her,
And laid bare all her perfect loveliness,
And, smiling on me, came yet more anear,
And on my mortal lips her lips did press,
And said, ' Now herewith shalt thou love no less
Than Psyche loved my son in days of old ;
Farewell, of thee shall many a tale be told.'

" And even with that last word was she gone,
How, I know not, and I my limbs arrayed
In her fair gifts, and waited thee alone —
Ah, love, indeed the word is true she said,
For now I love thee so, I grow afraid
Of what the gods upon our heads may send —
I love thee so, I think upon the end."

What words he said ? How can I tell again
What words they said beneath the glimmering
    light,
Some tongue they used unknown to loveless men
As each to each they told their great delight,
Until for stillness of the growing night
Their soft sweet murmuring words seemed grow-
    ing loud,
And dim the moon grew, hid by fleecy cloud.
                          WILLIAM MORRIS.

———◆———

JAMES FITZ–JAMES AND ELLEN.
FROM " THE LADY OF THE LAKE."

A FOOTSTEP struck her ear,
And Snowdoun's graceful Knight was near.
She turned the hastier, lest again
The prisoner should renew his strain.
" O welcome, brave Fitz-James ! " she said ;
" How may an almost orphan maid
Pay the deep debt " — " O, say not so !
To me no gratitude you owe.
Not mine, alas ! the boon to give,
And bid thy noble father live ;
I can but be thy guide, sweet maid,
With Scotland's King thy suit to aid.
No tyrant he, though ire and pride
May lead his better mood aside.
Come, Ellen, come ; 't is more than time,
He holds his court at morning prime."
With beating heart and bosom wrung,
As to a brother's arm she clung.
Gently he dried the falling tear,
And gently whispered hope and cheer ;
Her faltering steps half led, half stayed,
Through gallery fair and high arcade,
Till, at his touch, its wings of pride
A portal arch unfolded wide.

Within 't was brilliant all and light,
A thronging scene of figures bright;
It glowed on Ellen's dazzled sight,
As when the setting sun has given
Ten thousand hues to summer even,
And from their tissue fancy frames
Aerial knights and fairy dames.
Still by Fitz-James her footing stayed;
A few faint steps she forward made,
Then slow her drooping head she raised,
And fearful round the presence gazed:
For him she sought who owned this state,
The dreaded prince whose will was fate!
She gazed on many a princely port
Might well have ruled a royal court;
On many a splendid garb she gazed, —
Then turned bewildered and amazed,
For all stood bare; and in the room
Fitz-James alone wore cap and plume.
To him each lady's look was lent,
On him each courtier's eye was bent,
Midst furs and silks and jewels sheen
He stood, in simple Lincoln green,
The centre of the glittering ring, —
And Snowdoun's Knight is Scotland's King!

As wreath of snow, on mountain breast,
Slides from the rock that gave it rest,
Poor Ellen glided from her stay,
And at the Monarch's feet she lay;
No word her choking voice commands:
She showed the ring, she clasped her hands.
O, not a moment could he brook,
The generous prince, that suppliant look!
Gently he raised her, and the while
Checked with a glance the circle's smile;
Graceful, but grave, her brow he kissed,
And bade her terrors be dismissed: —
"Yes, fair; the wandering poor Fitz-James
The fealty of Scotland claims.
To him thy woes, thy wishes bring;
He will redeem his signet-ring.
Ask naught for Douglas; yester even
His prince and he have much forgiven:
Wrong hath he had from slanderous tongue,
I, from his rebel kinsmen, wrong.
We would not to the vulgar crowd
Yield what they craved with clamor loud;
Calmly we heard and judged his cause,
Our council aided and our laws.
I stanched thy father's death-feud stern,
With stout De Vaux and gray Glencairn;
And Bothwell's Lord henceforth we own
The friend and bulwark of our Throne.
But, lovely infidel, how now?
What clouds thy misbelieving brow?
Lord James of Douglas, lend thine aid;
Thou must confirm this doubting maid."

Then forth the noble Douglas sprung,
And on his neck his daughter hung.
The Monarch drank, that happy hour,
The sweetest, holiest draught of Power,
When it can say, with godlike voice,
Arise, sad Virtue, and rejoice!
Yet would not James the general eye
On nature's raptures long should pry:
He stepped between — "Nay, Douglas, nay,
Steal not my proselyte away!
The riddle 't is my right to read,
That brought this happy chance to speed.
Yes, Ellen, when disguised I stray
In life's more low but happier way.
'T is under name which veils my power,
Nor falsely veils, — for Stirling's tower
Of yore the name of Snowdoun claims,
And Normans call me James Fitz-James,
Thus watch I o'er insulted laws,
Thus learn to right the injured cause."
Then, in a tone apart and low,
"Ah, little trait'ress! none must know
What idle dream, what lighter thought,
What vanity full dearly bought,
Joined to thine eye's dark witchcraft, drew
My spell-bound steps to Benvenue,
In dangerous hour, and all but gave
Thy Monarch's life to mountain glaive!"
Aloud he spoke, — "Thou still dost hold
That little talisman of gold,
Pledge of my faith, Fitz-James's ring;
What seeks fair Ellen of the King?"
Full well the conscious maiden guessed,
He probed the weakness of her breast;
But with that consciousness there came
A lightening of her fears for Græme,
And more she deemed the monarch's ire
Kindled 'gainst him, who, for her sire,
Rebellious broadsword boldly drew;
And, to her generous feeling true,
She craved the grace of Roderick Dhu.
"Forbear thy suit; the King of kings
Alone can stay life's parting wings.
I know his heart, I know his hand,
Have shared his cheer, and proved his brand;
My fairest earldom would I give
To bid Clan-Alpine's Chieftain live! —
Hast thou no other boon to crave?
No other captive friend to save?"
Blushing, she turned her from the King,
And to the Douglas gave the ring,
As if she wished her sire to speak
The suit that stained her glowing cheek.
"Nay, then, my pledge has lost its force,
And stubborn justice holds her course.

"Malcolm, come forth!" — And, at the word
Down knelt the Græme to Scotland's Lord.

"For thee, rash youth, no suppliant sues,
From thee may Vengeance claim her dues,
Who, nurtured underneath our smile,
Hast paid our care by treacherous wile,
And sought, amid thy faithful clan,
A refuge for an outlawed man,
Dishonoring thus thy loyal name, —
Fetters and warder for the Græme!"
His chain of gold the King unstrung,
The links o'er Malcolm's neck he flung,
Then gently drew the glittering band,
And laid the clasp on Ellen's hand.

SIR WALTER SCOTT.

FETCHING WATER FROM THE WELL.

EARLY on a sunny morning, while the lark was
    singing sweet,
Came, beyond the ancient farm-house, sounds of
    lightly tripping feet.
'T was a lowly cottage maiden going, — why, let
    young hearts tell, —
With her homely pitcher laden, fetching water
    from the well.
Shadows lay athwart the pathway, all along the
    quiet lane,
And the breezes of the morning moved them to
    and fro again.
O'er the sunshine, o'er the shadow, passed the
    maiden of the farm,
With a charméd heart within her, thinking of
    no ill nor harm.
Pleasant, surely, were her musings, for the nod-
    ding leaves in vain
Sought to press their bright'ning image on her
    ever-busy brain.
Leaves and joyous birds went by her, like a dim,
    half-waking dream ;
And her soul was only conscious of life's gladdest
    summer gleam.
At the old lane's shady turning lay a well of water
    bright,
Singing, soft, its hallelujah to the gracious morn-
    ing light.
Fern-leaves, broad and green, bent o'er it where
    its silv'ry droplets fell,
And the fairies dwelt beside it, in the spotted
    foxglove bell.
Back she bent the shading fern-leaves, dipt the
    pitcher in the tide, —
Drew it, with the dripping waters flowing o'er its
    glazéd side.
But before her arm could place it on her shiny,
    wavy hair,
By her side a youth was standing ! — Love re-
    joiced to see the pair !

Tones of tremulous emotion trailed upon the morn-
    ing breeze,
Gentle words of heart-devotion whispered 'neath
    the ancient trees.
But the holy, blessed secrets it becomes me not
    to tell :
Life had met another meaning, fetching water
    from the well !
Down the rural lane they sauntered.   He the bur-
    den-pitcher bore ;
She, with dewy eyes downlooking, grew more beau-
    teous than before !
When they neared the silent homestead, up he
    raised the pitcher light ;
Like a fitting crown he placed it on her hair of
    wavelets bright :
Emblems of the coming burdens that for love of
    him she 'd bear,
Calling every burden blessed, if his love but light-
    ed there.
Then, still waving benedictions, further, further
    off he drew,
While his shadow seemed a glory that across the
    pathway grew.
Now about her household duties silently the maid-
    en went,
And an ever-radiant halo o'er her daily life was
    blent.
Little knew the aged matron as her feet like music
    fell,
What abundant treasure found she fetching water
    from the well !

ANONYMOUS.

A MAIDEN WITH A MILKING-PAIL.

I.

WHAT change has made the pastures sweet,
And reached the daisies at my feet,
    And cloud that wears a golden hem ?
This lovely world, the hills, the sward, —
They all look fresh, as if our Lord
    But yesterday had finished them.

And here 's the field with light aglow :
How fresh its boundary lime-trees show !
    And how its wet leaves trembling shine !
Between their trunks come through to me
The morning sparkles of the sea,
    Below the level browzing line.

I see the pool, more clear by half
Than pools where other waters laugh
    Up at the breasts of coot and rail.
There, as she passed it on her way,
I saw reflected yesterday
    A maiden with a milking-pail.

There, neither slowly nor in haste, —
One hand upon her slender waist,
   The other lifted to her pail, —
She, rosy in the morning light,
Among the water-daisies white,
   Like some fair sloop appeared to sail.

Against her ankles as she trod
The lucky buttercups did nod :
   I leaned upon the gate to see.
The sweet thing looked, but did not speak ;
A dimple came in either cheek,
   And all my heart was gone from me.

Then, as I lingered on the gate,
And she came up like coming fate,
   I saw my picture in her eyes, —
Clear dancing eyes, more black than sloes !
Cheeks like the mountain pink, that grows
   Among white-headed majesties !

I said, " A tale was made of old
That I would fain to thee unfold.
   Ah ! let me, — let me tell the tale."
But high she held her comely head :
" I cannot heed it now," she said,
   " For carrying of the milking-pail."

She laughed.   What good to make ado ?
I held the gate, and she came through,
   And took her homeward path anon.
From the clear pool her face had fled ;
It rested on my heart instead,
   Reflected when the maid was gone.

With happy youth, and work content,
So sweet and stately, on she went,
   Right careless of the untold tale.
Each step she took I loved her more,
And followed to her dairy door
   The maiden with the milking-pail.

II.

For hearts where wakened love doth lurk,
How fine, how blest a thing is work !
   For work does good when reasons fail, —
Good ; yet the axe at every stroke
The echo of a name awoke, —
   Her name is Mary Martindale.

I 'm glad that echo was not heard
Aright by other men.   A bird
   Knows doubtless what his own notes tell ;
And I know not, — but I can say
I felt as shamefaced all that day
   As if folks heard her name right well.

And when the west began to glow
I went — I could not choose but go —
   To that same dairy on the hill ;

And while sweet Mary moved about
Within, I came to her without,
   And leaned upon the window-sill.

The garden border where I stood
Was sweet with pinks and southernwood.
   I spoke, — her answer seemed to fail.
I smelt the pinks, — I could not see.
The dusk came down and sheltered me.
   And in the dusk she heard my tale.

And what is left that I should tell ?
I begged a kiss, — I pleaded well :
   The rosebud lips did long decline ;
But yet, I think — I think 't is true —
That, leaned at last into the dew,
   One little instant they were mine !

O life ! how dear thou hast become !
She laughed at dawn, and I was dumb !
   But evening counsels best prevail.
Fair shine the blue that o'er her spreads,
Green be the pastures where she treads,
   The maiden with the milking-pail !
                    JEAN INGELOW

THE MILKMAID'S SONG.

TURN, turn, for my cheeks they burn,
Turn by the dale, my Harry !
Fill pail, fill pail,
He has turned by the dale,
And there by the stile waits Harry.
Fill, fill,
Fill pail, fill,
For there by the stile waits Harry !
The world may go round, the world may stand still
But I can milk and marry,
Fill pail,
I can milk and marry.

Wheugh, wheugh !
O, if we two
Stood down there now by the water,
I know who 'd carry me over the ford
As brave as a soldier, as proud as a lord,
Though I don't live over the water.
Wheugh, wheugh ! he 's whistling through,
He 's whistling " The Farmer's Daughter."
Give down, give down,
My crumpled brown !
He shall not take the road to the town,
For I 'll meet him beyond the water.
Give down, give down,
My crumpled brown !
And send me to my Harry.
The folk o' towns
May have silken gowns,

But I can milk and marry,
Fill pail,
I can milk and marry.

Wheugh, wheugh ! he has whistled through
He has whistled through the water.
Fill, fill, with a will, a will,
For he 's whistled through the water,
And he 's whistling down
The way to the town,
And it 's not "The Farmer's Daughter ! "
Churr, churr ! goes the cockchafer,
The sun sets over the water,
Churr, churr ! goes the cockchafer,
I 'm too late for my Harry !
And, O, if he goes a-soldiering,
The cows they may low, the bells they may
    ring,
But I 'll neither milk nor marry,
Fill pail,
Neither milk nor marry.

My brow beats on thy flank, Fill pail,
Give down, good wench, give down !
I know the primrose bank, Fill pail,
Between him and the town.
Give down, good wench, give down, Fill pail,
And he shall not reach the town !
Strain, strain ! he 's whistling again,
He 's nearer by half a mile.
More, more ! O, never before
Were you such a weary while !
Fill, fill ! he 's crossed the hill,
I can see him down by the stile,
He 's passed the hay, he 's coming this way,
He 's coming to me, my Harry !
Give silken gowns to the folk o' towns,
He 's coming to me, my Harry !
There 's not so grand a dame in the land,
That she walks to-night with Harry !
Come late, come soon, come sun, come moon,
O, I can milk and marry,
Fill pail,
I can milk and marry.

Wheugh, wheugh ! he has whistled through,
My Harry ! my lad ! my lover !
Set the sun and fall the dew,
Heigh-ho, merry world, what 's to do
That you 're smiling over and over ?
Up on the hill and down in the dale,
And along the tree-tops over the vale
Shining over and over,
Low in the grass and high on the bough,
Shining over and over,
O world, have you ever a lover ?
You were so dull and cold just now,
O world, have you ever a lover ?

I could not see a leaf on the tree,
And now I could count them, one, two, three,
Count them over and over,
Leaf from leaf like lips apart,
Like lips apart for a lover.
And the hillside beats with my beating heart,
And the apple-tree blushes all over,
And the May bough touched me and made me
    start,
And the wind breathes warm like a lover.

Pull, pull ! and the pail is full,
And milking 's done and over.
Who would not sit here under the tree ?
What a fair fair thing 's a green field to see !
Brim, brim, to the rim, ah me !
I have set my pail on the daisies !
It seems so light, — can the sun be set ?
The dews must be heavy, my cheeks are wet.
I could cry to have hurt the daisies !
Harry is near, Harry is near,
My heart 's as sick as if he were here,
My lips are burning, my cheeks are wet,
He has n't uttered a word as yet,
But the air 's astir with his praises.
My Harry !
The air 's astir with your praises.

He has scaled the rock by the pixy's stone,
He 's among the kingcups, — he picks me one,
I love the grass that I tread upon
When I go to my Harry !
He has jumped the brook, he has climbed the
    knowe,
There 's never a faster foot I know,
But still he seems to tarry.
O Harry ! O Harry ! my love, my pride,
My heart is leaping, my arms are wide !
Roll up, roll up, you dull hillside,
Roll up, and bring my Harry !
They may talk of glory over the sea,
But Harry 's alive, and Harry 's for me,
My love, my lad, my Harry !
Come spring, come winter, come sun, come
    snow,
What cares Dolly, whether or no,
While I can milk and marry ?
Right or wrong, and wrong or right,
Quarrel who quarrel, and fight who fight,
But I 'll bring my pail home every night
To love, and home, and Harry !
We 'll drink our can, we 'll eat our cake,
There 's beer in the barrel, there 's bread in the
    bake,
The world may sleep, the world may wake,
But I shall milk and marry,
And marry,
I shall milk and marry.

SYDNEY DOBELL.

AUF WIEDERSEHEN ! *

SUMMER.

THE little gate was reached at last,
   Half hid in lilacs down the lane ;
She pushed it wide, and, as she past,
A wistful look she backward cast,
   And said, "*Auf wiedersehen !*"

With hand on latch, a vision white
   Lingered reluctant, and again
Half doubting if she did aright,
Soft as the dews that fell that night,
   She said, "*Auf wiedersehen !*"

The lamp's clear gleam flits up the stair ;
   I linger in delicious pain ;
Ah, in that chamber, whose rich air
To breathe in thought I scarcely dare,
   Thinks she, "*Auf wiedersehen !*"

'T is thirteen years : once more I press
   The turf that silences the lane ;
I hear the rustle of her dress,
I smell the lilacs, and — ah yes,
   I hear, "*Auf wiedersehen !*"

Sweet piece of bashful maiden art !
   The English words had seemed too fain,
But these — they drew us heart to heart,
Yet held us tenderly apart ;
   She said, "*Auf wiedersehen !*"
              JAMES RUSSELL LOWELL.

SWEET MEETING OF DESIRES.

I GREW assured, before I asked,
   That she 'd be mine without reserve,
And in her unclaimed graces basked
   At leisure, till the time should serve, —
With just enough of dread to thrill
   The hope, and make it trebly dear :
Thus loath to speak the word, to kill
   Either the hope or happy fear.

Till once, through lanes returning late,
   Her laughing sisters lagged behind ;
And ere we reached her father's gate,
   We paused with one presentient mind ;
And, in the dim and perfumed mist
   Their coming stayed, who, blithe and free,
And very women, loved to assist
   A lover's opportunity.

Twice rose, twice died, my trembling word ;
   To faint and frail cathedral chimes
Spake time in music, and we heard
   The chafers rustling in the limes.
Her dress, that touched me where I stood,
   The warmth of her confided arm ;

        * Till we meet again !

Her bosom's gentle neighborhood ;
   Her pleasure in her power to charm ;

Her look, her love, her form, her touch !
   The least seemed most by blissful turn, —
Blissful but that it pleased too much,
   And taught the wayward soul to yearn.
It was as if a harp with wires
   Was traversed by the breath I drew ;
And O, sweet meeting of desires !
   She, answering, owned that she loved too.
              COVENTRY PATMORE.

ZARA'S EAR-RINGS.

FROM THE SPANISH.

"MY ear-rings ! my ear-rings ! they 've dropt into
   the well,
And what to say to Muça, I cannot, cannot tell."
'T was thus, Granada's fountain by, spoke Albu-
   harez' daughter, —
"The well is deep, far down they lie, beneath the
   cold blue water.
To me did Muça give them, when he spake his sad
   farewell,
And what to say when he comes back, alas ! I can-
   not tell.

"My ear-rings ! my ear-rings ! they were pearls
   in silver set,
That when my Moor was far away, I ne'er should
   him forget,
That I ne'er to other tongue should list, nor smile
   on other's tale,
But remember he my lips had kissed, pure as those
   ear-rings pale.
When he comes back, and hears that I have dropped
   them in the well,
O, what will Muca think of me, I cannot, cannot tell.

"My ear-rings ! my ear-rings ! he 'll say they
   should have been,
Not of pearl and of silver, but of gold and glitter-
   ing sheen,
Of jasper and of onyx, and of diamond shining clear,
Changing to the changing light, with radiance
   insincere ;
That changeful mind unchanging gems are not
   befitting well, —
Thus will he think, — and what to say, alas ! I can-
   not tell.

"He 'll think when I to market went I loitered by
   the way ;
He 'll think a willing ear I lent to all the lads
   might say ;
He 'll think some other lover's hand, among my
   tresses noosed,
From the ears where he had placed them my rings
   of pearl unloosed ;

He'll think when I was sporting so beside this
    marble well,
My pearls fell in, — and what to say, alas ! I can-
    not tell.

"He'll say I am a woman, and we are all the same ;
He'll say I loved when he was here to whisper of
    his flame —
But when he went to Tunis my virgin troth had
    broken,
And thought no more of Muça, and cared not for
    his token.
My ear-rings ! my ear-rings ! O, luckless, luckless
    well !
For what to say to Muça, alas ! I cannot tell.

"I'll tell the truth to Muça, and I hope he will
    believe,
That I have thought of him at morning, and
    thought of him at eve ;
That musing on my lover, when down the sun was
    gone,
His ear-rings in my hand I held, by the fountain
    all alone ;
And that my mind was o'er the sea, when from my
    hand they fell,
And that deep his love lies in my heart, as they lie
    in the well."   JOHN GIBSON LOCKHART.

FATIMA AND RADUAN.

FROM THE SPANISH.

"Diamante falso y fingido,
Engastado en pedernal," &c.

"FALSE diamond set in flint ! hard heart in
    haughty breast !
By a softer, warmer bosom the tiger's couch is prest.
Thou art fickle as the sea, thou art wandering as
    the wind,
And the restless ever-mounting flame is not more
    hard to bind.
If the tears I shed were tongues, yet all too few
    would be
To tell of all the treachery that thou hast shown
    to me.
Oh ! I could chide thee sharply, — but every maiden
    knows
That she who chides her lover forgives him ere he
    goes.

"Thou hast called me oft the flower of all Grenada's
    maids,
Thou hast said that by the side of me the first and
    fairest fades ;
And they thought thy heart was mine, and it
    seemed to every one
That what thou didst to win my love, for love of
    me was done.

Alas ! if they but knew thee, as mine it is to know,
They well might see another mark to which thine
    arrows go ;
But thou giv'st little heed, — for I speak to one
    who knows
That she who chides her lover, forgives him ere
    he goes.

"It wearies me, mine enemy, that I must weep
    and bear
What fills thy heart with triumph, and fills my
    own with care.
Thou art leagued with those that hate me, and ah !
    thou know'st I feel
That cruel words as surely kill as sharpest blades
    of steel.
'T was the doubt that thou wert false that wrung
    my heart with pain ;
But, now I know thy perfidy, I shall be well again.
I would proclaim thee as thou art — but every
    maiden knows
That she who chides her lover, forgives him ere he
    goes."

Thus Fatima complained to the valiant Raduan,
Where underneath the myrtles Alhambra's foun-
    tains ran :
The Moor was inly moved, and blameless as he was,
He took her white hand in his own, and pleaded
    thus his cause :
"O lady, dry those star-like eyes, — their dimness
    does me wrong ;
If my heart be made of flint, at least 't will keep
    thy image long ;
Thou hast uttered cruel words, — but I grieve the
    less for those,
Since she who chides her lover forgives him ere
    he goes."   WILLIAM CULLEN BRYANT.

SOMEBODY.

SOMEBODY's courting somebody,
    Somewhere or other to-night ;
Somebody's whispering to somebody,
Somebody's listening to somebody,
    Under this clear moonlight.

Near the bright river's flow,
Running so still and slow,
Talking so soft and low,
    She sits with somebody.

Pacing the ocean's shore,
Edged by the foaming roar,
Words never used before
    Sound sweet to somebody.

Under the maple-tree
Deep though the shadow be,

Plain enough they can see,
Bright eyes has somebody.

No one sits up to wait,
Though she is out so late,
All know she's at the gate,
Talking with somebody.

Tiptoe to parlor door,
Two shadows on the floor,
Moonlight, reveal no more,
Susy and somebody.

Two, sitting side by side,
Float with the ebbing tide,
"Thus, dearest, may we glide
Through life," says somebody.

Somewhere, somebody,
Makes love to somebody,
To-night.
ANONYMOUS.

THE SPINNING-WHEEL SONG.

MELLOW the moonlight to shine is beginning;
Close by the window young Eileen is spinning;
Bent o'er the fire, her blind grandmother, sitting,
Is croaning, and moaning, and drowsily knit-
ting, —
"Eileen, achora, I hear some one tapping."
"'T is the ivy, dear mother, against the glass
flapping."
"Eileen, I surely hear somebody sighing."

"'T is the sound, mother dear, of the summer
wind dying."
Merrily, cheerily, noisily whirring,
Swings the wheel, spins the reel, while the foot's
stirring;
Sprightly, and lightly, and airily ringing,
Thrills the sweet voice of the young maiden
singing.

"What's that noise that I hear at the window,
I wonder?"
"'T is the little birds chirping the holly-bush
under."
"What makes you be shoving and moving your
stool on,
And singing all wrong that old song of 'The
Coolun'?"
There's a form at the casement, — the form of
her true-love, —
And he whispers, with face bent, "I'm waiting
for you, love;
Get up on the stool, through the lattice step
lightly,
We'll rove in the grove while the moon's shin-
ing brightly."

Merrily, cheerily, noisily whirring,
Swings the wheel, spins the reel, while the foot's
stirring;
Sprightly, and lightly, and airily ringing,
Thrills the sweet voice of the young maiden
singing.

The maid shakes her head, on her lip lays her
fingers,
Steals up from her seat, — longs to go, and yet
lingers;
A frightened glance turns to her drowsy grand-
mother,
Puts one foot on the stool, spins the wheel with
the other.
Lazily, easily, swings now the wheel round;
Slowly and lowly is heard now the reel's sound;
Noiseless and light to the lattice above her
The maid steps, — then leaps to the arms of her
lover.
Slower — and slower — and slower the wheel
swings;
Lower — and lower — and lower the reel rings;
Ere the reel and the wheel stop their ringing and
moving,
Through the grove the young lovers by moon-
light are roving.
JOHN FRANCIS WALLER.

A SPINSTER'S STINT.

SIX skeins and three, six skeins and three!
Good mother, so you stinted me,
And here they be, — ay, six and three!

Stop, busy wheel! stop, noisy wheel!
Long shadows down my chamber steal,
And warn me to make haste and reel.

'T is done, — the spinning work complete,
O heart of mine, what makes you beat
So fast and sweet, so fast and sweet.

I must have wheat and pinks, to stick
My hat from brim to ribbon, thick, —
Slow hands of mine, be quick, be quick!

One, two, three stars along the skies
Begin to wink their golden eyes, —
I'll leave my thread all knots and ties.

O moon, so red! O moon, so red!
Sweetheart of night, go straight to bed;
Love's light will answer in your stead.

A-tiptoe, beckoning me, he stands, —
Stop trembling, little foolish hands,
And stop the bands, and stop the bands!
ALICE CARY.

OTHELLO'S DEFENCE.

OTHELLO. Most potent, grave, and reverend
    signiors,
My very noble and approved good masters, —
That I have ta'en away this old man's daughter,
It is most true ; true, I have married her :
The very head and front of my offending
Hath this extent, no more. Rude am I in my
    speech,
And little blessed with the soft phrase of peace ;
For since these arms of mine had seven years' pith,
Till now, some nine moons wasted, they have used
Their dearest action in the tented field ;
And little of this great world can I speak,
More than pertains to feats of broil and battle ;
And therefore little shall I grace my cause,
In speaking for myself. Yet, by your gracious
    patience,
I will a round unvarnished tale deliver
Of my whole course of love ; what drugs, what
    charms,
What conjuration, and what mighty magic, —
For such proceeding I am charged withal, —
I won his daughter.
    BRABANTIO. A maiden never bold ;
Of spirit so still and quiet, that her motion
Blushed at herself ; and she — in spite of nature,
Of years, of country, credit, everything, —
To fall in love with what she feared to look on !
It is a judgment maimed, and most imperfect,
That will confess perfection so could err
Against all rules of nature ; and must be driven
To find out practices of cunning hell,
Why this should be. I therefore vouch again,
That with some mixtures powerful o'er the blood,
Or with some dram conjured to this effect,
He wrought upon her.

OTH.   I 'll present
How I did thrive in this fair lady's love,
And she in mine.
Her father loved me ; oft invited me ;
Still questioned me the story of my life,
From year to year ; — the battles, sieges, fortunes,
That I have passed.
I ran it through, even from my boyish days,
To th' very moment that he bade me tell it :
Wherein I spake of most disastrous chances,
Of moving accidents by flood and field ;
Of hair-breadth 'scapes i' the imminent deadly
    breach ;
Of being taken by the insolent foe,
And sold to slavery ; of my redemption thence,
And portance in my travel's history :
Wherein of antres vast, and deserts idle,
Rough quarries, rocks, and hills whose heads
    touch heaven,

It was my hint to speak, — such was the process ;
And of the Cannibals that each other eat,
The Anthropophagi, and men whose heads
Do grow beneath their shoulders. This to hear,
Would Desdemona seriously incline :
But still the house affairs would draw her thence ;
Which ever as she could with haste despatch,
She 'd come again, and with a greedy ear
Devour up my discourse. Which I observing,
Took once a pliant hour ; and found good means
To draw from her a prayer of earnest heart,
That I would all my pilgrimage dilate,
Whereof by parcels she had something heard,
But not intentively : I did consent ;
And often did beguile her of her tears,
When I did speak of some distressful stroke,
That my youth suffered. My story being done,
She gave me for my pains a world of sighs :
She swore, — in faith 't was strange, 't was pass-
    ing strange ;
'T was pitiful, 't was wondrous pitiful :
She wished she had not heard it, yet she wished
That Heaven had made her such a man : she
    thanked me ;
And bade me, if I had a friend that loved her,
I should teach him how to tell my story,
And that would woo her. Upon this hint, I spake :
She loved me for the dangers I had passed ;
And I loved her that she did pity them.
This only is the witchcraft I have used :
Here comes the lady, let her witness it.

Enter DESDEMONA, IAGO, *and Attendants.*

DUKE. I think this tale would win my daugh-
    ter too. —
Good Brabantio,
Take up this mangled matter at the best :
Men do their broken weapons rather use,
Than their bare hands.
    BRA.   I pray you hear her speak :
If she confess that she was half the wooer,
Destruction on my head, if my bad blame
Light on the man ! — Come hither, gentle mistress :
Do you perceive in all this noble company,
Where most you owe obedience ?
    DES.   My noble father,
I do perceive here a divided duty :
To you I am bound for life and education ;
My life and education both do learn me
How to respect you ; you are the lord of duty,
I am hitherto your daughter : but here 's my
    husband ;
And so much duty as my mother showed
To you, preferring you before her father,
So much I challenge that I may profess
Due to the Moor my lord.
    BRA.   God be with you ! — I have done.
                           SHAKESPEARE.

THE GARDEN SCENE.

FROM "ROMEO AND JULIET."

ROMEO. He jests at scars that never felt a wound.

(JULIET *appears above, at a window.*)

But, soft ! what light through yonder window breaks ?
It is the east, and Juliet is the sun ! —
Arise, fair sun, and kill the envious moon,
Who is already sick and pale with grief,
That thou, her maid, art far more fair than she :
Be not her maid, since she is envious ;
Her vestal livery is but sick and green,
And none but fools do wear it ; cast it off. —
It is my lady ; O, it is my love !
O that she knew she were ! —
She speaks, yet she says nothing : What of that ?
Her eye discourses, I will answer it. —
I am too bold, 't is not to me she speaks :
Two of the fairest stars in all the heaven,
Having some business, do entreat her eyes
To twinkle in their spheres till they return.
What if her eyes were there, they in her head ?
The brightness of her cheek would shame those stars,
As daylight doth a lamp ; her eyes in heaven
Would through the airy region stream so bright,
That birds would sing, and think it were not night.
See, how she leans her cheek upon her hand !
O, that I were a glove upon that hand,
That I might touch that cheek !

JULIET.   Ah me !

ROM.   She speaks : —
O, speak again, bright angel ! for thou art
As is glorious to this night, being o'er my head,
As is a wingéd messenger of heaven
Unto the white-upturnéd wondering eyes
Of mortals, that fall back to gaze on him,
When he bestrides the lazy-pacing clouds,
And sails upon the bosom of the air.

JUL. O Romeo, Romeo ! wherefore art thou Romeo ?
Deny thy father, and refuse thy name ;
Or, if thou wilt not, be but sworn my love,
And I 'll no longer be a Capulet.

ROM. [*Aside.*] Shall I hear more, or shall I speak at this ?

JUL. 'T is but thy name, that is my enemy ; —
Thou art thyself though, not a Montague.
What 's Montague ? it is nor hand, nor foot,
Nor arm, nor face, nor any other part
Belonging to a man. O, be some other name !
What 's in a name ? that which we call a rose
By any other name would smell as sweet ;
So Romeo would, were he not Romeo called,

Retain that dear perfection which he owes,
Without that title. — Romeo, doff thy name ;
And for that name, which is no part of thee,
Take all myself.

ROM.   I take thee at thy word :
Call me but love, and I 'll be new baptized ;
Henceforth I never will be Romeo.

JUL. What man art thou, that, thus bescreened in night,
So stumblest on my counsel ?

ROM.   By a name
I know not how to tell thee who I am :
My name, dear saint, is hateful to myself,
Because it is an enemy to thee :
Had I it written, I would tear the word.

JUL. My ears have not yet drunk a hundred words
Of that tongue's utterance, yet I know the sound :
Art thou not Romeo, and a Montague ?

ROM. Neither, fair saint, if either thee dislike.

JUL. How cam'st thou hither, tell me, and wherefore ?
The orchard walls are high, and hard to climb ;
And the place death, considering who thou art,
If any of my kinsmen find thee here.

ROM. With love's light wings did I o'erperch these walls ;
For stony limits cannot hold love out :
And what love can do, that dares love attempt ;
Therefore thy kinsmen are no let to me.

JUL. If they do see thee, they will murder thee.

ROM. Alack ! there lies more peril in thine eye,
Than twenty of their swords ; look thou but sweet,
And I am proof against their enmity.

JUL. I would not for the world they saw thee here.

ROM. I have night's cloak to hide me from their sight ;
And, but thou love me, let them find me here :
My life were better ended by their hate,
Than death proroguéd, wanting of thy love.

JUL. By whose direction found'st thou out this place ?

ROM. By love, who first did prompt me to inquire :
He lent me counsel, and I lent him eyes.
I am no pilot ; yet wert thou as far
As that vast shore washed with the farthest sea,
I would adventure for such merchandise.

JUL. Thou know'st the mask of night is on my face ;
Else would a maiden blush bepaint my cheek,
For that which thou hast heard me speak to-night.
Fain would I dwell on form, fain, fain deny
What I have spoke ; but farewell compliment !
Dost thou love me ? I know, thou wilt say, Ay ;
And I will take thy word ; yet, if thou swear'st,

Thou mayst prove false : at lover's perjuries,
They say, Jove laughs.   O gentle Romeo,
If thou dost love, pronounce it faithfully :
Or if thou think'st I am too quickly won,
I 'll frown and be perverse, and say thee nay,
So thou wilt woo ; but, else, not for the world.
In truth, fair Montague, I am too fond ;
And therefore thou mayst think my 'havior light :
But trust me, gentleman, I 'll prove more true
Than those that have more cunning to be strange.
I should have been more strange, I must confess,
But that thou overheard'st, ere I was ware,
My true love 's passion : therefore, pardon me ;
And not impute this yielding to light love,
Which the dark night hath so discoveréd.

Rom. Lady, by yonder blessed moon I swear,
That tips with silver all these fruit-tree tops —

Jul. O, swear not by the moon, th' inconstant
moon,
That monthly changes in her circled orb,
Lest that thy love prove likewise variable.

Rom. What shall I swear by ?

Jul.   Do not swear at all ;
Or, if thou wilt, swear by thy gracious self,
Which is the god of my idolatry,
And I 'll believe thee.

Rom.   If my heart's dear love —

Jul. Well, do not swear : although I joy in thee,
I have no joy of this contract to-night :
It is too rash, too unadvised, too sudden ;
Too like the lightning, which doth cease to be,
Ere one can say, It lightens.   Sweet, good night !
This bud of love, by summer's ripening breath,
May prove a beauteous flower when next we meet.
Good night, good night ! as sweet repose and rest
Come to thy heart as that within my breast !

Rom. O, wilt thou leave me so unsatisfied ?

Jul. What satisfaction canst thou have to-
night?

Rom. Th' exchange of thy love's faithful vow
for mine.

Jul. I gave thee mine before thou didst re-
quest it :
And yet I would it were to give again.

Rom. Wouldst thou withdraw it ? for what
purpose, love ?

Jul. But to be frank, and give it thee again.
And yet I wish but for the thing I have :
My bounty is as boundless as the sea,
My love is deep ; the more I give to thee,
The more I have, for both are infinite.
                    [Nurse calls within.]
I hear some noise within.   Dear love, adieu ! —
Anon, good nurse ! — Sweet Montague, be true.
Stay but a little, I will come again. [Exit above.

Rom. O blesséd, blesséd night ! I am afeard,
Being in night, all this is but a dream,
Too flattering-sweet to be substantial.

(Re-enter Juliet, above.)

Jul. Three words, dear Romeo, and good night,
indeed.
If that thy bent of love be honorable,
Thy purpose marriage, send me word to-morrow
By one that I 'll procure to come to thee,
Where, and what time, thou wilt perform the rite ;
And all my fortunes at thy foot I 'll lay,
And follow thee, my lord, throughout the world.

Nurse. [Within.] Madam !

Jul. I come anon : — But if thou mean'st not
well,
I do beseech thee, —

Nurse. [Within.] Madam !

Jul.   By and by ; I come : —
To cease thy suit, and leave me to my grief :
To-morrow will I send.

Rom.   So thrive my soul, —

Jul. A thousand times good night ! [Exit above.

Rom. A thousand times the worse, to want
thy light. —
Love goes toward love, as school-boys from their
books ;
But love from love, toward school with heavy looks.
                              [Retiring.]

(Re-enter Juliet, above.)

Jul. Hist ! Romeo, hist ! — O, for a falconer's
voice,
To lure this tercel-gentle back again !
Bondage is hoarse, and may not speak aloud ;
Else would I tear the cave where echo lies,
And make her airy tongue more hoarse than mine
With repetition of my Romeo's name.

Rom. It is my soul, that calls upon my name :
How silver-sweet sound lovers' tongues by night,
Like softest music to attending ears !

Jul. Romeo !

Rom.   My dear !

Jul.   At what o'clock to-morrow
Shall I send to thee ?

Rom.   At the hour of nine.

Jul. I will not fail : 't is twenty years till then.
I have forgot why I did call thee back.

Rom. Let me stand here till thou remember it.

Jul. I shall forget, to have thee still stand there,
Remembering how I love thy company.

Rom. And I 'll still stay, to have thee still forget,
Forgetting any other home but this.

Jul. 'T is almost morning ; I would have thee
gone :
And yet no farther than a wanton's bird ;
Who lets it hop a little from her hand,
Like a poor prisoner in his twisted gyves,
And with a silk thread plucks it back again,
So loving-jealous of his liberty.

Rom. I would I were thy bird.

Jul.   Sweet, so would I :
Yet I should kill thee with much cherishing.

Good night, good night ! parting is such sweet
    sorrow,
That I shall say good night, till it be morrow.
                      [*Exit above.*
  ROM. Sleep dwell upon thine eyes, peace in
    thy breast ! —
Would I were sleep and peace, so sweet to rest !
Hence will I to my ghostly father's cell,
His help to crave, and my dear hap to tell.
                      SHAKESPEARE.

THE COURTIN'.

GOD makes sech nights, all white an' still
    Fur 'z you can look or listen.
Moonshine an' snow on field an' hill,
    All silence an' all glisten.

Zekle crep' up quite unbeknown
    An' peeked in thru' the winder,
An' there sot Huldy all alone,
    'Ith no one nigh to hender.

A fireplace filled the room's one side
    With half a cord o' wood in —
There warn't no stoves (tell comfort died)
    To bake ye to a puddin'.

The wa'nut logs shot sparkles out
    Towards the pootiest, bless her,
An' leetle flames danced all about
    The chiny on the dresser.

Agin the chimbley crook-necks hung,
    An' in amongst 'em rusted
The ole queen's arm thet gran'ther Young
    Fetched back from Concord busted.

The very room, coz she was in,
    Seemed warm from floor to ceilin',
An' she looked full ez rosy agin
    Ez the apples she was peelin'.

'T was kin' o' kingdom-come to look
    On sech a blessèd cretur,
A dogrose blushin' to a brook
    Ain't modester nor sweeter.

He was six foot o' man, A 1,
    Clean grit an' human natur';
None could n't quicker pitch a ton
    Nor dror a furrer straighter.

He 'd sparked it with full twenty gals,
    Hed squired 'em, danced 'em, druv 'em,
Fust this one, an' then thet, by spells —
    All is, he could n't love 'em.

But long o' her his veins 'ould run
    All crinkly like curled maple,

The side she breshed felt full o' sun
    Ez a south slope in Ap'il.

She thought no v'ice hed sech a swing
    Ez hisn in the choir ;
My ! when he made Ole Hundred ring,
    She *knowed* the Lord was nigher.

An' she 'd blush scarlet, right in prayer,
    When her new meetin'-bunnet
Felt somehow thru' its crown a pair
    O' blue eyes sot upon it.

Thet night, I tell ye, she looked *some* !
    She seemed to 've gut a new soul,
For she felt sartin-sure he 'd come,
    Down to her very shoe-sole.

She heered a foot, an' knowed it tu,
    A-raspin' on the scraper, —
All ways to once her feelin's flew
    Like sparks in burnt-up paper.

He kin' o' l'itered on the mat,
    Some doubtfle o' the sekle,
His heart kep' goin' pity-pat,
    But hern went pity Zekle.

An' yit she gin her cheer a jerk
    Ez though she wished him furder,
An' on her apples kep' to work,
    Parin' away like murder.

"You want to see my Pa, I s'pose ?"
    "Wal . . . no . . . I come dasignin'" —
"To see my Ma ? She 's sprinklin' clo'es
    Agin to-morrer's i'nin'."

To say why gals acts so or so,
    Or don't, 'ould be presumin' ;
Mebby to mean *yes* an' say *no*
    Comes nateral to women.

He stood a spell on one foot fust,
    Then stood a spell on t' other,
An' on which one he felt the wust
    He could n't ha' told ye nuther.

Says he, "I 'd better call agin " ;
    Says she, "Think likely, Mister " ;
Thet last word pricked him like a pin,
    An' . . . Wal, he up an' kist her.

When Ma bimeby upon 'em slips,
    Huldy sot pale ez ashes,
All kin' o' smily roun' the lips
    An' teary roun' the lashes.

For she was jes' the quiet kind
    Whose naturs never vary,
Like streams that keep a summer mind
    Snowhid in Jenooary.

The blood clost roun' her heart felt glued
   Too tight for all expressin',
Tell mother see how metters stood,
   And gin 'em both her blessin'.

Then her red come back like the tide
   Down to the Bay o' Fundy,
An' all I know is they was cried
   In meetin' come nex' Sunday.
          JAMES RUSSELL LOWELL.

THE LAIRD O' COCKPEN.

THE laird o' Cockpen he 's proud and he 's great,
His mind is ta'en up with the things o' the state ;
He wanted a wife his braw house to keep,
But favor wi' wooin' was fashious to seek.

Down by the dyke-side a lady did dwell,
At his table-head he thought she 'd look well ;
M'Lish's ae daughter o' Claverse-ha' Lee,
A penniless lass wi' a lang pedigree.

His wig was weel pouthered, and as gude as new ;
His waistcoat was white, his coat it was blue ;
He put on a ring, a sword, and cocked hat,
And wha could refuse the Laird wi' a' that ?

He took the gray mare, and rade cannily —
And rapped at the yett o' Claverse-ha' Lee :
"'Gae tell Mistress Jean to come speedily ben,
She 's wanted to speak to the Laird o' Cockpen."

Mistress Jean was makin' the elder-flower wine :
"And what brings the Laird at sic a like time ?"
She put aff her apron, and on her silk gown,
Her mutch wi' red ribbons, and gaed awa' down.

And when she cam' ben, he bowed fu' low,
And what was his errand he soon let her know ;
Amazed was the Laird when the lady said "Na" ;
And wi' a laigh curtsey she turned awa'.

Dumbfoundered he was — nae sigh did he gie ;
He mounted his mare — he rade cannily ;
And aften he thought, as he gaed through the glen,
She 's daft to refuse the Laird o' Cockpen.

And now that the Laird his exit had made,
Mistress Jean she reflected on what she had said ;
"Oh ! for ane I 'll get better, it 's waur I 'll get ten,
I was daft to refuse the Laird o' Cockpen."

Next time that the Laird and the lady were seen,
They were gaun arm-in-arm to the kirk on the
   green.
Now she sits in the ha' like a weel-tappit hen —
But as yet there 's nae chickens appeared at Cock-
   pen.
          LADY NAIRN.

THE LITTLE MILLINER.

MY girl hath violet eyes and yellow hair,
A soft hand, like a lady's, small and fair,
A sweet face pouting in a white straw bonnet,
A tiny foot, and little boot upon it ;
And all her finery to charm beholders
Is the gray shawl drawn tight around her shoulders,
The plain stuff-gown and collar white as snow,
And sweet red petticoat that peeps below.
But gladly in the busy town goes she,
Summer and winter, fearing nobodie ;
She pats the pavement with her fairy feet,
With fearless eyes she charms the crowded street ;
And in her pocket lie, in lieu of gold,
A lucky sixpence and a thimble old.

We lodged in the same house a year ago :
She on the topmost floor, I just below, —
She, a poor milliner, content and wise,
I, a poor city clerk, with hopes to rise ;
And, long ere we were friends, I learnt to love
The little angel on the floor above.
For, every morn, ere from my bed I stirred,
Her chamber door would open, and I heard, —
And listened, blushing, to her coming down,
And palpitated with her rustling gown,
And tingled while her foot went downward slow,
Creaked like a cricket, passed, and died below ;
Then peeping from the window, pleased and sly,
I saw the pretty shining face go by,
Healthy and rosy, fresh from slumber sweet, —
A sunbeam in the quiet morning street.

And every night, when in from work she tript,
Red to the ears I from my chamber slipt,
That I might hear upon the narrow stair
Her low "Good evening," as she passed me there.
And when her door was closed, below sat I,
And hearkened stilly as she stirred on high, —
Watched the red firelight shadows in the room,
Fashioned her face before me in the gloom,
And heard her close the window, lock the door,
Moving about more lightly than before,
And thought, "She is undressing now !" and O,
My cheeks were hot, my heart was in a glow !
And I made pictures of her, — standing bright
Before the looking-glass in bed-gown white,
Unbinding in a knot her yellow hair,
Then kneeling timidly to say a prayer ;
Till, last, the floor creaked softly overhead,
'Neath bare feet tripping to the little bed, —
And all was hushed.   Yet still I hearkened on,
Till the faint sounds about the streets were gone ;
And saw her slumbering with lips apart,
One little hand upon her little heart,
The other pillowing a face that smiled
In slumber like the slumber of a child,
The bright hair shining round the small white ear,

The soft breath stealing visible and clear,
And mixing with the moon's, whose frosty gleam
Made round her rest a vaporous light of dream.

How free she wandered in the wicked place,
Protected only by her gentle face !
She saw bad things — how could she choose but
  see ? —
She heard of wantonness and misery ;
The city closed around her night and day,
But lightly, happily, she went her way.
Nothing of evil that she saw or heard
Could touch a heart so innocently stirred, —
By simple hopes that cheered it through the storm,
And little flutterings that kept it warm.
No power had she to reason out her needs,
To give the whence and wherefore of her deeds ;
But she was good and pure amid the strife,
By virtue of the joy that was her life.
Here, where a thousand spirits daily fall,
Where heart and soul and senses turn to gall,
She floated, pure as innocent could be,
Like a small sea-bird on a stormy sea,
Which breasts the billows, wafted to and fro,
Fearless, uninjured, while the strong winds blow,
While the clouds gather, and the waters roar,
And mighty ships are broken on the shore.

.   .   .   .   .

'T was when the spring was coming, when the
  snow
Had melted, and fresh winds began to blow,
And girls were selling violets in the town,
That suddenly a fever struck me down.
The world was changed, the sense of life was pained,
And nothing but a shadow-land remained ;
Death came in a dark mist and looked at me,
I felt his breathing, though I could not see,
But heavily I lay and did not stir,
And had strange images and dreams of her.
Then came a vacancy : with feeble breath,
I shivered under the cold touch of Death,
And swooned among strange visions of the dead,
When a voice called from heaven, and he fled ;
And suddenly I wakened, as it seemed,
From a deep sleep wherein I had not dreamed.

And it was night, and I could see and hear,
And I was in the room I held so dear,
And unaware, stretched out upon my bed,
I hearkened for a footstep overhead.

But all was hushed. I looked around the room,
And slowly made out shapes amid the gloom.
The wall was reddened by a rosy light,
A faint fire flickered, and I knew 't was night,
Because below there was a sound of feet
Dying away along the quiet street, —
When, turning my pale face and sighing low,
I saw a vision in the quiet glow :

A little figure, in a cotton gown,
Looking upon the fire and stooping down,
Her side to me, her face illumed, she eyed
Two chestnuts burning slowly, side by side, —
Her lips apart, her clear eyes strained to see,
Her little hands clasped tight around her knee,
The firelight gleaming on her golden head,
And tinting her white neck to rosy red,
Her features bright, and beautiful, and pure,
With childish fear and yearning half demure.

O sweet, sweet dream ! I thought, and strained
  mine eyes,
Fearing to break the spell with words and sighs.
Softly she stooped, her dear face sweetly fair,
And sweeter since a light like love was there,
Brightening, watching, more and more elate,
As the nuts glowed together in the grate,
Crackling with little jets of fiery light,
Till side by side they turned to ashes white, —
Then up she leapt, her face cast off its fear
For rapture that itself was radiance clear,
And would have clapped her little hands in glee,
But, pausing, bit her lips and peeped at me,
And met the face that yearned on her so whitely,
And gave a cry and trembled, blushing brightly,
While, raised on elbow, as she turned to flee,
"Polly !" I cried, — and grew as red as she !

It was no dream ! for soon my thoughts were
  clear,
And she could tell me all, and I could hear :
How in my sickness friendless I had lain,
How the hard people pitied not my pain ;
How, in despite of what bad people said,
She left her labors, stopped beside my bed,
And nursed me, thinking sadly I would die ;
How, in the end, the danger passed me by ;
How she had sought to steal away before
The sickness passed, and I was strong once more.
By fits she told the story in mine ear,
And troubled all the telling with a fear
Lest by my cold man's heart she should be chid,
Lest I should think her bold in what she did ;
But, lying on my bed, I dared to say,
How I had watched and loved her many a day,
How dear she was to me, and dearer still
For that strange kindness done while I was ill,
And how I could but think that Heaven above
Had done it all to bind our lives in love.
And Polly cried, turning her face away,
And seemed afraid, and answered "yea" nor
  "nay" ;
Then stealing close, with little pants and sighs,
Looked on my pale thin face and earnest eyes,
And seemed in act to fling her arms about
My neck, then, blushing, paused, in fluttering
  doubt,

Last, sprang upon my heart, sighing and sob-
bing, —
That I might feel how gladly hers was throbbing!

Ah! ne'er shall I forget until I die
How happily the dreamy days went by,
While I grew well, and lay with soft heart-beats,
Heark'ning the pleasant murmur from the streets,
And Polly by me like a sunny beam,
And life all changed, and love a drowsy dream!
'T was happiness enough to lie and see
The little golden head bent droopingly
Over its sewing, while the still time flew,
And my fond eyes were dim with happy dew!
And then, when I was nearly well and strong,
And she went back to labor all day long,
How sweet to lie alone with half-shut eyes,
And hear the distant murmurs and the cries,
And think how pure she was from pain and
sin, —
And how the summer days were coming in!
Then, as the sunset faded from the room,
To listen for her footstep in the gloom,
To pant as it came stealing up the stair,
To feel my whole life brighten unaware
When the soft tap came to the door, and when
The door was opened for her smile again!
Best, the long evenings! — when, till late at night,
She sat beside me in the quiet light,
And happy things were said and kisses won,
And serious gladness found its vent in fun.
Sometimes I would draw close her shining head,
And pour her bright hair out upon the bed,
And she would laugh, and blush, and try to scold,
While "Here," I cried, "I count my wealth in
gold!"

Once, like a little sinner for transgression,
She blushed upon my breast, and made confession:
How, when that night I woke and looked around,
I found her busy with a charm profound, —
One chestnut was herself, my girl confessed,
The other was the person she loved best,
And if they burned together side by side,
He loved her, and she would become his bride;
And burn indeed they did, to her delight, —
And had the pretty charm not proven right?
Thus much, and more, with timorous joy, she
said,
While her confessor, too, grew rosy red, —
And close together pressed two blissful faces,
As I absolved the sinner, with embraces.

And here is winter come again, winds blow,
The houses and the streets are white with snow;
And in the long and pleasant eventide,
Why, what is Polly making at my side?
What but a silk gown, beautiful and grand,
We bought together lately in the Strand!

What but a dress to go to church in soon,
And wear right queenly 'neath a honey-moon!
And who shall match her with her new straw
bonnet,
Her tiny foot and little boot upon it,
Embroidered petticoat and silk gown new,
And shawl she wears as few fine ladies do?
And she will keep, to charm away all ill,
The lucky sixpence in her pocket still;
And we will turn, come fair or cloudy weather,
To ashes, like the chestnuts, close together!
ROBERT BUCHANAN.

WIDOW MALONE.

DID you hear of the Widow Malone,
Ohone!
Who lived in the town of Athlone,
Alone!
O, she melted the hearts
Of the swains in them parts:
So lovely the Widow Malone,
Ohone!
So lovely the Widow Malone.

Of lovers she had a full score,
Or more,
And fortunes they all had galore,
In store;
From the minister down
To the clerk of the Crown
All were courting the Widow Malone,
Ohone!
All were courting the Widow Malone.

But so modest was Mistress Malone,
'T was known
That no one could see her alone,
Ohone!
Let them ogle and sigh,
They could ne'er catch her eye,
So bashful the Widow Malone,
Ohone!
So bashful the Widow Malone.

Till one Misther O'Brien, from Clare,
(How quare!
It 's little for blushing they care
Down there.)
Put his arm round her waist, —
Gave ten kisses at laste, —
"O," says he, "you 're my Molly Malone,
My own!
O," says he, "you 're my Molly Malone!"

And the widow they all thought so shy,
My eye!
Ne'er thought of a simper or sigh, —
For why?

But, "Lucius," says she,
  "Since you 've now made so free,
You may marry your Mary Malone,
      Ohone !
You may marry your Mary Malone."

There 's a moral contained in my song,
      Not wrong ;
And one comfort, it 's not very long,
      But strong, —
If for widows you die,
  Learn to kiss, not to sigh ;
For they 're all like sweet Mistress Malone,
      Ohone !
O, they 're all like sweet Mistress Malone !
          CHARLES LEVER.

JWOHNNY, GIT OOT !

CUMBERLAND DIALECT.

"GIT oot wid the', Jwohnny, — thou 's no' but
  a fash ;
Thou 'll come till thou raises a desperate clash.
Thou 's Here every day, just to put yan aboot ;
An' thou moiders yan terribly, — Jwohnny, git
  oot !

"What says t'é ? I 's bonnie ? Whey ! that 's
  nowte 'at 's new.
Thou 's wantin' a sweetheart ? Thou 's had a gay
  few !
An' thou 's cheatit them, yan efter t'udder, nèa
  doobt ;
But I 's nŭt to be cheatit sàa, — Jwohnny, git
  oot !

"There 's planty o' lads, i' beàth Lamplugh an'
  Dean,
As yabble as thee, an' as weel to be seen ;
An' I med tak my pick amang o' there aboot :
Does t'é think I 'd have thee, than ? Hut !
  Jwohnny, git oot !

"What ? Nŭt yan amang them 'at likes mé sae
  weel ?
Whey, min, — there 's Dick Walker an' Jona-
  than Peel
'At ola 's foorsett mé i' t' lonnings aboot ;
An' beàth want to sweetheart mé, — Jwohnny,
  git oot !

"What ? Thou *will* hev a kiss ? — Ah ! but
  tak 't if thou dăr ! '
I tell the' I 'll squeel, if thou tries to cŭ' năr.
Tak care o' my collar ! — thou byspel, I 'll shoot !
Nay, thou *sha' n't* hev anudder ! — Noo, Jwohn-
  ny, git oot !

"Git oot wid the', Jwohnny ! — thou 's tewt me
  reet sair ;
Thou 's brocken my comb, an' thou 's toozelt my
  hair.
I will n't be kisst, thou unmannerly loot !
Was t'ere iver sec impidence ? Jwohnny, git oot !

"Git oot wid the', Jwohnny ! — I tell the' be
  deùn :
Does t'é think I 'll tak' up wid Ann Dixon's
  oald sheùn ?
Thou ma' gã' till Ann Dixon, an' pu' her aboot ;
But thou s'all n't pu' me, sàa, — Jwohnny, git
  oot ! "

Well ! that 's sent him off, — an' I 'm sorry it
  hes ;
He med ken 'at yan niver means hoaf 'at yan
  says.
He 's a reet canny fellow, however I floot,
An' it 's growin' o' wark to say "Jwohnny, git
  oot ! "
          ANONYMOUS.

DUNCAN GRAY CAM' HERE TO WOO.

DUNCAN Gray cam' here to woo —
    Ha, ha ! the wooing o't !
On blythe Yule night when we were fu' —
    Ha, ha ! the wooing o't !
Maggie coost her head fu' high,
Looked asklent and unco skeigh,
Gart poor Duncan stand abeigh —
    Ha, ha ! the wooing o't !

Duncan fleeched and Duncan prayed —
    Ha, ha ! the wooing o't !
Meg was deaf as Ailsa craig —
    Ha, ha ! the wooing o't !
Duncan sighed baith out and in,
Grat his een baith bleer't and blin',
Spak o' lowpin o'er a linn —
    Ha, ha ! the wooing o't !

Time and chance are but a tide —
    Ha, ha ! the wooing o't !
Slighted love is sair to bide —
    Ha, ha ! the wooing o't !
Shall I, like a fool, quoth he,
For a haughty hizzie dee ?
She may gae to — France for me !
    Ha, ha ! the wooing o't !

How it comes let doctors tell —
    Ha, ha ! the wooing o't !
Meg grew sick as he grew heal —
    Ha, ha ! the wooing o't !
Something in her bosom wrings, —
For relief a sigh she brings ;
And O, her een they speak sic things !
    Ha, ha ! the wooing o't !

Duncan was a lad o' grace —
    Ha, ha ! the wooing o't !
Maggie's was a piteous case —
    Ha, ha ! the wooing o't !
Duncan could na be her death :
Swelling pity smoored his wrath.
Now they 're crouse and canty baith,
    Ha, ha ! the wooing o't !

ROBERT BURNS.

RORY O'MORE ;

OR, GOOD OMENS.

I.

YOUNG Rory O'More courted Kathleen Bawn ;
He was bold as the hawk, and she soft as the dawn ;
He wished in his heart pretty Kathleen to please,
And he thought the best way to do that was to
    tease.
"Now, Rory, be aisy," sweet Kathleen would cry,
Reproof on her lip, but a smile in her eye ;
"With your tricks, I don't know, in throth, what
    I'm about ;
Faith you've teazed till I've put on my cloak
    inside out."
"Och ! jewel," says Rory, "that same is the way
You've thrated my heart for this many a day ;
And 't is plazed that I am, and why not, to be sure ?
For 't is all for good luck," says bold Rory O'More.

II.

"Indeed, then," says Kathleen, "don't think of
    the like,
For I half gave a promise to soothering Mike ;
The ground that I walk on he loves, I'll be
    bound"—
"Faith !" says Rory, "I'd rather love you than
    the ground."
"Now, Rory, I'll cry if you don't let me go :
Sure I dream ev'ry night that I'm hating you
    so ! "
"Och !" says Rory, "that same I'm delighted to
    hear,
For dhrames always go by conthraries, my dear.
Och ! jewel, keep dhraming that same till you
    die,
And bright morning will give dirty night the black
    lie !
And 't is plazed that I am, and why not, to be
    sure ?
Since 't is all for good luck, " says bold Rory
    O'More.

III.

"Arrah, Kathleen, my darlint, you've teazed me
    enough ;
Sure, I've thrashed, for your sake, Dinny Grimes
    and Jim Duff ;

And I've made myself, drinking your health,
    quite a baste,
So I think, after that, I may talk to the priest."
Then Rory, the rogue, stole his arm round her
    neck,
So soft and so white, without freckle or speck ;
And he looked in her eyes, that were beaming
    with light,
And he kissed her sweet lips — Don't you think
    he was right ?
"Now Rory, leave off, sir — you'll hug me no
    more, —
That's eight times to-day you have kissed me
    before."
"Then here goes another," says he, "to make sure,
For there's luck in odd numbers," says Rory
    O'More.

SAMUEL LOVER.

KISSING HER HAIR.

KISSING her hair, I sat against her feet :
Wove and unwove it, — wound, and found it sweet ;
Made fast therewith her hands, drew down her eyes,
Deep as deep flowers, and dreamy like dim skies ;
With her own tresses bound, and found her fair, —
    Kissing her hair.

Sleep were no sweeter than her face to me, —
Sleep of cold sea-bloom under the cold sea :
What pain could get between my face and hers ?
What new sweet thing would Love not relish worse ?
Unless, perhaps, white Death had kissed me
    there, —
    Kissing her hair.

ALGERNON CHARLES SWINBURNE.

WHEN THE SULTAN GOES TO ISPAHAN.

WHEN the Sultan Shah-Zaman
Goes to the city Ispahan,
Even before he gets so far
As the place where the clustered palm-trees are,
At the last of the thirty palace-gates,
The Pet of the Harem, *Rose in Bloom,*
Orders a feast in his favorite room, —
Glittering squares of colored ice,
Sweetened with syrups, tinctured with spice ;
Creams, and cordials, and sugared dates ;
Syrian apples, Othmanee quinces,
Limes, and citrons, and apricots ;
And wines that are known to Eastern princes.
And Nubian slaves, with smoking pots
Of spiced meats, and costliest fish,
And all that the curious palate could wish,
Pass in and out of the cedarn doors.

Scattered over mosaic floors
Are anemones, myrtles, and violets ;
And a musical fountain throws its jets
Of a hundred colors into the air.
The dark sultana loosens her hair,
And stains with the henna plant the tips
Of her pearly nails, and bites her lips
Till they bloom again ; but alas, *that* rose
Not for the Sultan buds and blows !
    Not for the Sultan Shah-Zaman
    When he goes to the city Ispahan.

Then at a wave of her sunny hand,
The dancing girls of Samarcand
Float in like mists from Fairy-land !
And to the low voluptuous swoons
Of music, rise and fall the moons
Of their full brown bosoms. Orient blood
Runs in their veins, shines in their eyes ;
And there in this Eastern paradise,
Filled with the fumes of sandal-wood,
And Khoten musk, and aloes, and myrrh,
Sits *Rose in Bloom* on a silk divan,
Sipping the wines of Astrackhan ;
And her Arab lover sits with her.
    That 's when the Sultan Shah-Zaman
    Goes to the city Ispahan.

Now, when I see an extra light
Flaming, flickering on the night,
From my neighbor's casement opposite,
I know as well as I know to pray,
I know as well as a tongue can say,
    That the innocent Sultan Shah-Zaman
    Has gone to the city Ispahan.
           THOMAS BAILEY ALDRICH.

BONNIE WEE THING.

BONNIE wee thing ! cannie wee thing !
  Lovely wee thing ! wert thou mine,
I wad wear thee in my bosom,
  Lest my jewel I should tine.
Wishfully I look, and languish,
  In that bonnie face o' thine ;
And my heart it stounds wi' anguish,
  Lest my wee thing be na mine.

Wit and grace, and love and beauty,
  In ae constellation shine ;
To adore thee is my duty,
  Goddess o' this soul o' mine !
Bonnie wee thing, cannie wee thing,
  Lovely wee thing, wert thou mine,
I wad wear thee in my bosom,
  Lest my jewel I should tine.
           ROBERT BURNS.

THE LUTE-PLAYER.

FROM "HASSAN BEN KHALED."

" ' MUSIC !' they shouted, echoing my demand,
And answered with a beckon of his hand
The gracious host, whereat a maiden, fair
As the last star that leaves the morning air,
Came down the leafy paths. Her veil revealed
The beauty of her face, which, half concealed
Behind its thin blue folds, showed like the moon
Behind a cloud that will forsake it soon.
Her hair was braided darkness, but the glance
Of lightning eyes shot from her countenance,
And showed her neck, that like an ivory tower
Rose o'er the twin domes of her marble breast.
Were all the beauty of this age compressed
Into one form, she would transcend its power.
Her step was lighter than the young gazelle's,
And as she walked, her anklet's golden bells
Tinkled with pleasure, but were quickly mute
With jealousy, as from a case she drew
With snowy hands the pieces of her lute,
And took her seat before me. As it grew
To perfect shape, her lovely arms she bent
Around the neck of the sweet instrument,
Till from her soft caresses it awoke
To consciousness, and thus its rapture spoke :
' I was a tree within an Indian vale,
When first I heard the love-sick nightingale
Declare his passion ; every leaf was stirred
With the melodious sorrow of the bird,
And when he ceased, the song remained with me.
Men came anon, and felled the harmless tree,
But from the memory of the songs I heard,
The spoiler saved me from the destiny
Whereby my brethren perished. O'er the sea
I came, and from its loud, tumultuous moan
I caught a soft and solemn undertone ;
And when I grew beneath the maker's hand
To what thou seest, he sang (the while he planned)
The mirthful measures of a careless heart,
And of my soul his songs became a part.
Now they have laid my head upon a breast
Whiter than marble, I am wholly blest.
The fair hands smite me, and my strings com-
    plain
With such melodious cries, they smite again,
Until, with passion and with sorrow swayed,
My torment moves the bosom of the maid,
Who hears it speak her own. I am the voice
Whereby the lovers languish or rejoice ;
And they caress me, knowing that my strain
Alone can speak the language of their pain.'

" Here ceased the fingers of the maid to stray
Over the strings ; the sweet song died away
In mellow, drowsy murmurs, and the lute
Leaned on her fairest bosom, and was mute.

Better than wine that music was to me ;
Not the lute only felt her hands, but she
Played on my heart-strings, till the sounds be-
came
Incarnate in the pulses of my frame.
Speech left my tongue, and in my tears alone
Found utterance. With stretched arms I im-
plored
Continuance, whereat her fingers poured
A tenderer music, answering the tone
Her parted lips released, the while her throat
Throbbed, as a heavenly bird were fluttering
there,
And gave her voice the wonder of his note.
' His brow,' she sang, ' is white beneath his
hair ;
The fertile beard is soft upon his chin,
Shading the mouth that nestles warm within,
As a rose nestles in its leaves ; I see
His eyes, but cannot tell what hue they be,
For the sharp eyelash, like a sabre, speaks
The martial law of Passion ; in his cheeks
The quick blood mounts, and then as quickly
goes,
Leaving a tint like marble when a rose
Is held beside it ; — bid him veil his eyes,
Lest all my soul should unto mine arise,
And he behold it ! ' As she sang, her glance
Dwelt on my face ; her beauty, like a lance,
Transfixed my heart. I melted into sighs,
Slain by the arrows of her beauteous eyes.
' Why is her bosom made ' (I cried) ' a snare ?
Why does a single ringlet of her hair
Hold my heart captive ? ' ' Would you know ? '
she said ;
' It is that you are mad with love, and chains
Were made for madmen.' Then she raised her
head
With answering love, that led to other strains,
Until the lute, which shared with her the
smart,
Rocked as in storm upon her beating heart.
Thus to its wires she made impassioned cries :
' I swear it by the brightness of his eyes ;
I swear it by the darkness of his hair ;
By the warm bloom his limbs and bosom wear ;
By the fresh pearls his rosy lips enclose ;
By the calm majesty of his repose ;
By smiles I coveted, and frowns I feared,
And by the shooting myrtles of his beard, —
I swear it, that from him the morning drew
Its freshness, and the moon her silvery hue,
The sun his brightness, and the stars their
fire,
And musk and camphor all their odorous breath :
And if he answer not my love's desire,
Day will be night to me, and Life be Death ! ' "

BAYARD TAYLOR.

I ARISE FROM DREAMS OF THEE.

SERENADE.

I ARISE from dreams of thee
    In the first sweet sleep of night,
When the winds are breathing low,
    And the stars are shining bright.
I arise from dreams of thee,
    And a spirit in my feet
Has led me — who knows how ? —
    To thy chamber-window, sweet !

The wandering airs they faint
    On the dark, the silent stream, —
The champak odors fail
    Like sweet thoughts in a dream ;
The nightingale's complaint,
    It dies upon her heart,
As I must die on thine,
    O, beloved as thou art !

O, lift me from the grass !
    I die, I faint, I fail !
Let thy love in kisses rain
    On my lips and eyelids pale.
My cheek is cold and white, alas !
    My heart beats loud and fast :
Oh ! press it close to thine again,
    Where it will break at last !

PERCY BYSSHE SHELLEY.

HER SHADOW,

BENDING between me and the taper,
    While o'er the harp her white hands strayed,
The shadows of her waving tresses
    Above my hand were gently swayed.

With every graceful movement waving,
    I marked their undulating swell ;
I watched them while they met and parted,
    Curled close or widened, rose or fell.

I laughed in triumph and in pleasure —
    So strange the sport, so undesigned !
Her mother turned and asked me, gravely,
    "What thought was passing through my mind ?"

'T is Love that blinds the eyes of mothers ;
    'T is Love that makes the young maids fair !
She touched my hand ; my rings she counted ;
    Yet never felt the shadows there.

Keep, gamesome Love, beloved Infant,
    Keep ever thus all mothers blind ;
And make thy dedicated virgins,
    In substance as in shadow, kind !

AUBREY DE VERE.

SMILE AND NEVER HEED ME.

THOUGH, when other maids stand by,
I may deign thee no reply,
Turn not then away, and sigh, —
    Smile, and never heed me !
If our love, indeed, be such
As must thrill at every touch,
Why should others learn as much ? —
    Smile, and never heed me !

Even if, with maiden pride,
I should bid thee quit my side,
Take this lesson for thy guide, —
    Smile, and never heed me !
But when stars and twilight meet,
And the dew is falling sweet,
And thou hear'st my coming feet, —
    Then — thou then — mayst heed me !
                CHARLES SWAIN

SONNETS FROM THE PORTUGUESE.

Go from me. Yet I feel that I shall stand
Henceforward in thy shadow. Nevermore
Alone upon the threshold of my door
Of individual life, I shall command
The uses of my soul, nor lift my hand
Serenely in the sunshine as before,
Without the sense of that which I forbore, . . .
Thy touch upon the palm. The widest land
Doom takes to part us, leaves thy heart in mine
With pulses that beat double. What I do
And what I dream include thee, as the wine
Must taste of its own grapes. And when I sue
God for myself, He hears that name of thine,
And sees within my eyes the tears of two.

THE face of all the world is changed, I think,
Since first I heard the footsteps of thy soul
Move still, O still, beside me, as they stole
Betwixt me and the dreadful outer brink
Of obvious death, where I, who thought to sink,
Was caught up into love, and taught the whole
Of life in a new rhythm. The cup of dole
God gave for baptism, I am fain to drink,
And praise its sweetness, Sweet, with thee anear.
The names of country, heaven, are changed away
For where thou art or shall be, there or here ;
And this . . . this lute and song . . . loved yesterday,
(The singing angels know) are only dear,
Because thy name moves right in what they say.

INDEED this very love which is my boast,
And which, when rising up from breast to brow,
Doth crown me with a ruby large enow
To draw men's eyes and prove the inner cost, . . .
This love even, all my worth, to the uttermost,
I should not love withal, unless that thou
Hadst set me an example, shown me how,
When first thine earnest eyes with mine were
    crossed,
And love called love. And thus, I cannot speak
Of love even, as a good thing of my own.
Thy soul hath snatched up mine all faint and weak,
And placed it by thee on a golden throne, —
And that I love (O soul, we must be meek !)
Is by thee only, whom I love alone.

IF thou must love me, let it be for naught
Except for love's sake only. Do not say
"I love her for her smile . . . her look . . . her way
Of speaking gently, — for a trick of thought
That falls in well with mine, and certes brought
A sense of pleasant ease on such a day."
For these things in themselves, beloved, may
Be changed, or change for thee, — and love so
    wrought,
May be unwrought so. Neither love me for
Thine own dear pity's wiping my cheeks dry, —
A creature might forget to weep, who bore
Thy comfort long, and lose thy love thereby.
But love me for love's sake, that evermore
Thou mayst love on, through love's eternity.

I NEVER gave a lock of hair away
To a man, Dearest, except this to thee,
Which now upon my fingers thoughtfully
I ring out to the full brown length and say
"Take it." My day of youth went yesterday ;
My hair no longer bounds to my foot's glee.
Nor plant I it from rose or myrtle tree,
As girls do, any more. It only may
Now shade on two pale cheeks, the mark of tears,
Taught drooping from the head that hangs aside
Through sorrow's trick. I thought the funeral-
    shears
Would take this first, but Love is justified, —
Take it thou, . . . finding pure, from all those years,
The kiss my mother left here when she died.

THE soul's Rialto hath its merchandise ;
I barter curl for curl upon that mart,
And from my poet's forehead to my heart,
Receive this lock which outweighs argosies, —
As purely black, as erst, to Pindar's eyes,
The dim purpureal tresses gloomed athwart
The nine white Muse-brows. For this counterpart,
Thy bay-crown's shade, Beloved, I surmise,
Still lingers on thy curl, it is so black !
Thus, with a fillet of smooth-kissing breath,
I tie the shadow safe from gliding back,
And lay the gift where nothing hindereth,
Here on my heart, as on thy brow, to lack
No natural heat till mine grows cold in death.

Elizabeth Barrett Browning

FORDS, HOWARD & HULBERT, N.Y.

Say over again, and yet once over again,
That thou dost love me. Though the word repeated
Should seem "a cuckoo-song," as thou dost treat it,
Remember, never to the hill or plain,
Valley and wood, without her cuckoo-strain,
Comes the fresh spring in all her green completed.
Beloved, I, amid the darkness greeted
By a doubtful spirit-voice, in that doubt's pain
Cry: "Speak once more — thou lovest!" Who can fear
Too many stars, though each in heaven shall roll,—
Too many flowers, though each shall crown the year?
Say thou dost love me, love me, love me,—toll
The silver iterance!—only minding, dear,
To love me also in silence, with thy soul.

* * *

Is it indeed so? If I lay here dead,
Wouldst thou miss any life in losing mine?
And would the sun for thee more coldly shine,
Because of grave-damps falling round my head?
I marvelled, my Belovéd, when I read
Thy thought so in the letter. I am thine—
But . . . so much to thee? Can I pour thy wine
While my hands tremble? Then my soul, instead
Of dreams of death, resumes life's lower range.
Then, love me, Love! look on me . . . breathe on me!
As brighter ladies do not count it strange,
For love, to give up acres and degree,
I yield the grave for thy sake, and exchange
My near sweet view of Heaven, for earth with thee!

* * *

My letters! all dead paper, . . . mute and white!—
And yet they seem alive and quivering
Against my tremulous hands which loose the string
And let them drop down on my knee to-night.
This said, . . . he wished to have me in his sight
Once, as a friend: this fixed a day in spring
To come and touch my hand . . . a simple thing,
Yet I wept for it! this, . . . the paper 's light . . .
Said, Dear, I love thee; and I sank and quailed
As if God's future thundered on my past.
This said, I am thine,—and so its ink has paled
With lying at my heart that beat too fast.
And this . . . O Love, thy words have ill availed,
If what this said, I dared repeat at last!

* * *

I think of thee! my thoughts do twine and bud
About thee, as wild vines, about a tree,
Put out broad leaves, and soon there 's naught to see
Except the straggling green which hides the wood.
Yet, O my palm-tree, be it understood
I will not have my thoughts instead of thee

Who art dearer, better! rather instantly
Renew thy presence. As a strong tree should,
Rustle thy boughs and set thy trunk all bare,
And let these bands of greenery which insphere thee
Drop heavily down, . . . burst, shattered, everywhere!
Because, in this deep joy to see and hear thee
And breathe within thy shadow a new air,
I do not think of thee,—I am too near thee.

* * *

The first time that the sun rose on thine oath
To love me, I looked forward to the moon
To slacken all those bonds which seemed too soon
And quickly tied to make a lasting troth.
Quick-loving hearts, I thought, may quickly loathe;
And, looking on myself, I seemed not one
For such man's love!—more like an out of tune
Worn viol, a good singer would be wroth
To spoil his song with, and which, snatched in haste
Is laid down at the first ill-sounding note.
I did not wrong myself so, but I placed
A wrong on thee. For perfect strains may float
Neath master-hands, from instruments defaced,—
And great souls, at one stroke, may do and doat.

* * *

First time he kissed me, he but only kissed
The fingers of this hand wherewith I write;
And, ever since, it grew more clean and white,
Slow to world-greetings, quick with its "O list!"
When the angels speak. A ring of amethyst
I could not wear here, plainer to my sight
Than that first kiss. The second passed in height
The first, and sought the forehead, and half missed,
Half falling on the hair. O, beyond meed!
That was the chrism of love, which love's own crown,
With sanctifying sweetness, did precede.
The third upon my lips was folded down
In perfect, purple state; since when, indeed,
I have been proud, and said, "My love, my own!"

* * *

How do I love thee? Let me count the ways.
I love thee to the depth and breadth and height
My soul can reach, when feeling out of sight
For the ends of Being and ideal Grace.
I love thee to the level of every day's
Most quiet need, by sun and candlelight.
I love thee freely, as men strive for Right;
I love thee purely, as they turn from Praise.
I love thee with the passion put to use
In my old griefs, and with my childhood's faith.
I love thee with a love I seemed to lose
With my lost saints,—I love thee with the breath,
Smiles, tears, of all my life!—and, if God choose,
I shall but love thee better after death.

ELIZABETH BARRETT BROWNING.

BURD HELEN.

[" This beautiful tale of woman's love," wrote Dr. Robert Chambers in 1829, — "beautiful in the pathos of its simple and touching narrative, and equally beautiful in the pathos of its simple and touching language, was first published by Percy, as an English ballad, under the title of " Childe Waters."]

LORD JOHN stood in his stable door,
    Said he was boun' to ride :
Burd Helen stood in her bouir door,
    Said she 'd run by his side.

"The corn is turning ripe, Lord John ;
    The nuts are growing fu' :
An' ye are boun' for your ain countrie ;
    Fain wad I go with you."

"Wi' me, Helen ! wi' me, Helen !
    What wad ye do wi' me ?
I 've mair need o' a little foot-page,
    Than of the like o' thee."

"O, I will be your little foot-boy,
    To wait upon your steed ;
And I will be your little foot-page,
    Your leish of hounds to lead."

"But my hounds will eat the breid o' wheat,
    And ye the dust and bran ;
Then will ye sit and sigh, Helen,
    That e'er ye lo'ed a man."

"O, your dogs may eat the gude wheat-breid,
    And I the dust and bran ;
Yet will I sing and say, weel 's me,
    That e'er I lo'ed a man ! "

"O, better ye 'd stay at hame, Helen,
    And sew your silver seam ;
For my house is in the far Hielands,
    And ye 'll ha'e puir welcome hame."

"I winna stay, Lord John," she said,
    "To sew my silver seam ;
Though your house is in the far Hielands,
    And I 'll ha'e puir welcome hame."

"Then if you 'll be my foot-page, Helen,
    As you tell unto me,
Then you must cut your gown of green
    An inch abune your knee.

"So you must cut your yellow locks
    An inch abune your e'e ;
You must tell no man what is my name :
    My foot-page then you 'll be."

Then he has luppen* on his white steed,
    And straight awa' did ride ;
Burd Helen, dressed in men's array,
    She ran fast by his side.

* Leapt.

And he was ne'er sae lack * a knicht,
    As ance wad bid her ride ;
And she was ne'er sae mean a May,
    As ance wad bid him bide.

Lord John he rade, Burd Helen ran,
    A livelong summer-day ;
Until they cam to Clyde-water,
    Was filled frae bank to brae.

"Seest thou yon water, Helen," said he,
    "That flows from bank to brim ? "
"I trust to God, Lord John," she said,
    "You ne'er will see me swim ! "

But he was ne'er sae lack a knicht,
    As ance wad bid her ride ;
Nor did he sae much as reach his hand,
    To help her ower the tide.

The firsten step that she wade in,
    She wadit to the knee ;
"Ochone, alas," quo' that ladye fair,
    "This water 's no for me ! "

The second step that she wade in,
    She steppit to the middle :
Then, sighing, said that fair ladye,
    "I 've wet my gowden girdle."

The thirden step that she wade in,
    She steppit to the neck ;
When that the bairn that she was wi',
    For cauld began to quake.

"Lie still, my babe ; lie still, my babe ;
    Lie still as lang 's ye may :
Your father, that rides on horseback high,
    Cares little for us twae."

And when she cam to the other side,
    She sat down on a stane ;
Says, "Them that made me, help me now ;
    For I am far frae hame !

"O, tell me this, now, good Lord John ;
    In pity tell to me ;
How far is it to your lodging,
    Where we this nicht maun be ? "

"O, dinna ye see yon castle, Helen,
    Stands on yon sunny lea ?
There ye'se get ane o' my mother's men :
    Ye'se get nae mair o' me."

"O, weel see I your bonnie castell
    Stands on yon sunny lea ;
But I 'se hae nane o' your mother's men,
    Though I never get mair o' thee."

* Little.

"But there is in yon castle, Helen,
 That stands on yonder lea,
There is a lady in yon castle,
 Will sinder* you and me."

"I wish nae ill to that ladye,
 She comes na in my thocht :
But I wish the maid maist o' your love,
 That dearest has you bocht."

When he cam to the porter's yett,†
 He tirled at the pin ; ‡
And wha sae ready as the bauld porter,
 To open and let him in ?

Many a lord and lady bright
 Met Lord John in the closs ;
But the bonniest lady among them a'
 Was hauding Lord John's horse.

Four and twenty gay ladyes
 Led him through bouir and ha' ;
But the fairest lady that was there
 Led his horse to the sta'.

Then up bespak Lord John's sister ;
 These were the words spak she :
"You have the prettiest foot-page, brother,
 My eyes did ever see —

"But that his middle is sae thick,
 His girdle sae wond'rous hie :
Let him, I pray thee, good Lord John,
 To chamber go with me."

"It is not fit for a little foot-page,
 That has run through moss and mire,
To go into chamber with any ladye
 That wears so rich attire.

"It were more meet for a little foot-page,
 That has run through moss and mire,
To take his supper upon his knee,
 And sit doun by the kitchen fire."

When bells were rung, and mass was sung,
 And a' men boun' to meat,
Burd Helen was, at the bye-table, §
 Amang the pages set.

"O, eat and drink, my bonnie boy,
 The white breid and the beer."
"The never a bit can I eat or drink ;
 My heart 's sae fu' o' fear."

"O, eat and drink, my bonnie boy,
 The white breid and the wine."
"O the never a bit can I eat or drink ;
 My heart 's sae fu' o' pyne." ‖

But out and spak Lord John his mother,
 And a skeely * woman was she :
"Where met ye, my son, wi' that bonnie boy,
 That looks sae sad on thee ?

"Sometimes his cheek is rosy red,
 And sometimes deidly wan :
He 's liker a woman grit wi' child,
 Than a young lord's serving man."

"O, it maks me laugh, my mother dear,
 Sic words to hear frae thee ;
He is a squire's ae dearest son,
 That for love has followed me.

"Rise up, rise up, my bonnie boy ;
 Gi'e my horse corn and hay."
"O that I will, my master deir,
 As quickly as I may."

She took the hay aneath her arm,
 The corn intill her hand ;
But atween the stable door and the sta'
 Burd Helen made a stand.

"O room ye round, my bonnie broun steids ;
 O room ye near the wa' ;
For the pain that strikes through my twa sides,
 I fear, will gar me fa'."

She leaned her back again' the wa' ;
 Strong travail came her on ;
And, e'en among the great horse' feet,
 She has brought forth her son.

When bells were rung, and mass was sung,
 And a' men boun' for bed,
Lord John's mother and sister gay
 In ae bouir they were laid.

Lord John hadna weel got aff his claes,
 Nor was he weel laid doun,
Till his mother heard a bairn greet,
 And a woman's heavy moan.

"Win up, win up, Lord John," she said ;
 "Seek neither stockings nor shoen :
For I ha'e heard a bairn loud greet,
 And a woman's heavy moan !"

"Richt hastilie he rase him up,
 Socht neither hose nor shoen ;
And he 's doen him to the stable door,
 By the lee licht o' the mune.

"O, open the door, Burd Helen," he said,
 "O, open and let me in ;
I want to see if my steed be fed,
 Or my greyhounds fit to rin."

"O lullaby, my own deir child !
   Lullaby, deir child, deir !
I wold thy father were a king,
   Thy mother laid on a bier ! "

"O, open the door, Burd Helen," he says,
   "O, open the door to me ;
Or, as my sword hangs by my gair,*
   I 'll gar it gang in three ! "

"That never was my mother's custome,
   And I hope it 's ne'er be mine ;
A knicht into her companie,
   When she dries a' her pyne."

He hit the door then wi' his foot,
   Sae did he wi' his knee ;
Till door o' deal, and locks o' steel,
   In splinders he gart * flee.

"An askin', an askin', Lord John," she says,
   "An askin' ye 'll grant me ;
The meanest maid about your house,
   To bring a drink to me.

"An askin', an askin', my dear Lord John,
   An askin' ye 'll grant me ;
The warsten bouir in a' your touirs,
   For thy young son and me ! "

"I grant, I grant your askins, Helen,
   An' that and mair frae me ;
The very best bouir in a' my touirs,
   For my young son and thee.

"O, have thou comfort, fair Helen.
   Be of good cheer, I pray ;
And your bridal and your kirking baith
   Shall stand upon ae day."

And he has ta'en her Burd Helen,
   And rowed her in the silk ;
And he has ta'en his ain young son,
   And washed him in the milk.

And there was ne'er a gayer bridegroom,
   Nor yet a blyther bride,
As they, Lord John and Lady Helen,
   Neist day to kirk did ride.
                                   ANONYMOUS.

THE MISTRESS.

If he 's capricious, she 'll be so ;
   But, if his duties constant are,
She lets her loving favor glow
   As steady as a tropic star.
Appears there naught for which to weep,

She 'll weep for naught for his dear sake ;
She clasps her sister in her sleep ;
   Her love in dreams is most awake.
Her soul, that once with pleasure shook
   Did any eyes her beauty own,
Now wonders how they dare to look
   On what belongs to him alone.
The indignity of taking gifts
   Exhilarates her loving breast ;
A rapture of submission lifts
   Her life into celestial rest.
There 's nothing left of what she was, —
   Back to the babe the woman dies ;
And all the wisdom that she has
   Is to love him for being wise.
She 's confident because she fears ;
   And, though discreet when he 's away,
If none but her dear despot hears,
   She 'll prattle like a child at play.
Perchance, when all her praise is said,
   He tells the news, — a battle won —
On either side ten thousand dead —
   Describing how the whole was done :
She thinks, "He 's looking on my face !
   I am his joy ; whate'er I do,
He sees such time-contenting grace
   In that, he 'd have me always so ! "
And, evermore, for either's sake,
   To the sweet folly of the dove
She joins the cunning of the snake,
   To rivet and exalt his love.
Her mode of candor is deceit ;
   And what she thinks from what she 'll say,
(Although I 'll never call her cheat,)
   Lies far as Scotland from Cathay.
Without his knowledge he was won, —
   Against his nature kept devout ;
She 'll never tell him how 't was done,
   And he will never find it out.
If, sudden, he suspects her wiles,
   And hears her forging chain and trap,
And looks, — she sits in simple smiles,
   Her two hands lying in her lap !
Her secret (privilege of the Bard,
   Whose fancy is of either sex)
Is mine ; but let the darkness guard
   Mysteries that light would more perplex.
                              COVENTRY PATMORE.

BELIEVE ME, IF ALL THOSE ENDEARING YOUNG CHARMS.

BELIEVE me, if all those endearing young charms,
   Which I gaze on so fondly to-day,
Were to change by to-morrow, and fleet in my arms,
   Like fairy-gifts fading away !

---

* Side.   † Made or forced to.

Thou wouldst still be adored, as this moment thou
    art,
  Let thy loveliness fade as it will,
And around the dear ruin each wish of my heart
  Would entwine itself verdantly still.

It is not while beauty and youth are thine own,
  And thy cheeks unprofaned by a tear,
That the fervor and faith of a soul may be known,
  To which time will but make thee more dear !
O the heart that has truly loved never forgets,
  But as truly loves on to the close,
As the sunflower turns to her god when he sets
The same look which she turned when he rose !
        THOMAS MOORE *("Irish Melodies")*.

WERE I AS BASE AS IS THE LOWLY PLAIN.

WERE I as base as is the lowly plain,
And you, my Love, as high as heaven above,
Yet should the thoughts of me your humble
    swain
Ascend to heaven, in honor of my Love.

Were I as high as heaven above the plain,
And you, my Love, as humble and as low
As are the deepest bottoms of the main,
Whereso'er you were, with you my Love should
    go.

Were you the earth, dear Love, and I the skies,
My love should shine on you like to the sun,
And look upon you with ten thousand eyes
Till heaven waxed blind, and till the world were
    done.

Whereso'er I am, below, or else above you,
Whereso'er you are, my heart shall truly love you.
        JOSHUA SYLVESTER.

LOCHINVAR.

O, YOUNG Lochinvar is come out of the west,
Through all the wide Border his steed was the
    best ;
And, save his good broadsword, he weapon had
    none,
He rode all unarmed, and he rode all alone.
So faithful in love, and so dauntless in war,
There never was knight like the young Lochin-
    var.

He stayed not for brake, and he stopped not for
    stone,
He swam the Eske River where ford there was
    none ;
But, ere he alighted at Netherby gate,

The bride had consented, the gallant came late ;
For a laggard in love, and a dastard in war,
Was to wed the fair Ellen of brave Lochinvar.

So boldly he entered the Netherby Hall,
Among bridesmen, and kinsmen, and brothers,
    and all.
Then spoke the bride's father, his hand on his
    sword
(For the poor craven bridegroom said never a
    word),
" O, come ye in peace here, or come ye in war,
Or to dance at our bridal, young Lord Lochin-
    var ?"

" I long wooed your daughter, my suit you de-
    nied ; —
Love swells like the Solway, but ebbs like its
    tide, —
And now I am come, with this lost love of mine,
To lead but one measure, drink one cup of wine,
There are maidens in Scotland more lovely by far,
That would gladly be bride to the young Loch-
    invar."

The bride kissed the goblet ; the knight took it
    up,
He quaffed off the wine, and threw down the cup.
She looked down to blush, and she looked up to
    sigh,
With a smile on her lips, and a tear in her eye.
He took her soft hand, ere her mother could
    bar, —
" Now tread we a measure," said young Lochinvar.

So stately his form, and so lovely her face,
That never a hall such a galliard did grace ;
While her mother did fret, and her father did
    fume,
And the bridegroom stood dangling his bonnet
    and plume ;
And the bridemaidens whispered, " 'T were bet-
    ter by far
To have matched our fair cousin with young
    Lochinvar."

One touch to her hand, and one word in her ear,
When they reached the hall-door, and the charger
    stood near ;
So light to the croupe the fair lady he swung,
So light to the saddle before her he sprung ;
" She is won ! we are gone ! over bank, bush,
    and scaur ;
They 'll have fleet steeds that follow," quoth
    young Lochinvar.

There was mounting 'mong Græmes of the Neth-
    erby clan ;
Forsters, Fenwicks, and Musgraves, they rode
    and they ran ;

There was racing and chasing on Cannobie Lee,
But the lost bride of Netherby ne'er did they see.
So daring in love, and so dauntless in war,
Have ye e'er heard of gallant like young Lochin-
    var ?   SIR WALTER SCOTT.

THE SLEEPING BEAUTY.

FROM "THE DAY DREAM."

YEAR after year unto her feet,
    She lying on her couch alone,
Across the purple coverlet,
    The maiden's jet-black hair has grown ;
On either side her trancéd form
    Forth streaming from a braid of pearl ;
The slumb'rous light is rich and warm,
    And moves not on the rounded curl.

The silk star-broidered coverlid
    Unto her limbs itself doth mould,
Languidly ever ; and amid
    Her full black ringlets, downward rolled,
Glows forth each softly shadowed arm,
    With bracelets of the diamond bright.
Her constant beauty doth inform
    Stillness with love, and day with light.

She sleeps ; her breathings are not heard
    In palace chambers far apart.
The fragrant tresses are not stirred
    That lie upon her charméd heart.
She sleeps ; on either hand upswells
    The gold-fringed pillow lightly prest ;
She sleeps, nor dreams, but ever dwells
    A perfect form in perfect rest.
                        ALFRED TENNYSON.

THE REVIVAL OF THE "SLEEPING BEAUTY."

FROM "THE DAY DREAM."

A TOUCH, a kiss ! the charm was snapt.
    There rose a noise of striking clocks ;
And feet that ran, and doors that clapt,
    And barking dogs, and crowing cocks ;
A fuller light illumined all ;
    A breeze through all the garden swept ;
A sudden hubbub shook the hall ;
    And sixty feet the fountain leapt.

The hedge broke in, the banner blew,
    The butler drank, the steward scrawled,
The fire shot up, the martin flew,
    The parrot screamed, the peacock squalled ;

The maid and page renewed their strife ;
    The palace banged, and buzzed and clackt ;
And all the long-pent stream of life
    Dashed downward in a cataract.

And last of all the king awoke,
    And in his chair himself upreared,
And yawned, and rubbed his face, and spoke :
    " By holy rood, a royal beard !
How say you ? we have slept, my lords ;
    My beard has grown into my lap."
The barons swore, with many words,
    'T was but an after-dinner's nap.

" Pardy ! " returned the king, " but still
    My joints are something stiff or so.
My lord, and shall we pass the bill
    I mentioned half an hour ago ? "
The chancellor, sedate and vain,
    In courteous words returned reply ;
But dallied with his golden chain,
    And, smiling, put the question by.
                        ALFRED TENNYSON.

THE "SLEEPING BEAUTY" DEPARTS WITH HER LOVER.

FROM "THE DAY DREAM."

AND on her lover's arm she leant,
    And round her waist she felt it fold ;
And far across the hills they went
    In that new world which is the old.
Across the hills, and far away
    Beyond their utmost purple rim,
And deep into the dying day,
    The happy princess followed him.

" I 'd sleep another hundred years,
    O love, for such another kiss ! "
" O wake forever, love," she hears,
    " O love, 't was such as this and this."
And o'er them many a sliding star,
    And many a merry wind was borne,
And, streamed through many a golden bar,
    The twilight melted into morn.

" O eyes long laid in happy sleep ! "
    " O happy sleep, that lightly fled ! "
" O happy kiss, that woke thy sleep ! "
    " O love, thy kiss would wake the dead ! "
And o'er them many a flowing range
    Of vapor buoyed the crescent bark ;
And, rapt through many a rosy change,
    The twilight died into the dark.

" A hundred summers ! can it be ?
    And whither goest thou, tell me where ! "
" O, seek my father's court with me,
    For there are greater wonders there."

And o'er the hills, and far away
  Beyond their utmost purple rim,
Beyond the night, across the day,
  Through all the world she followed him.
ALFRED TENNYSON.

THE EVE OF ST. AGNES.

I.

ST. AGNES' EVE, — ah, bitter chill it was
The owl, for all his feathers, was a-cold ;
The hare limped trembling through the frozen
    grass,
And silent was the flock in woolly fold :
Numb were the beadman's fingers while he told
His rosary, and while his frosted breath,
Like pious incense from a censer old,
Seemed taking flight for heaven without a death,
Past the sweet virgin's picture, while his prayer
    he saith.

II.

His prayer he saith, this patient, holy man ;
Then takes his lamp, and riseth from his knees,
And back returneth, meagre, barefoot, wan,
Along the chapel aisle by slow degrees ;
The sculptured dead, on each side seem to freeze,
Emprisoned in black, purgatorial rails ;
Knights, ladies, praying in dumb orat'ries,
He passed by ; and his weak spirit fails
To think how they may ache in icy hoods and mails.

III.

Northward he turneth through a little door,
And scarce three steps, ere music's golden tongue
Flattered to tears this aged man and poor ;
But no, — already had his death-bell rung ;
The joys of all his life were said and sung ;
His was harsh penance on St. Agnes' Eve ;
Another way he went, and soon among
Rough ashes sat he for his soul's reprieve,
And all night kept awake, for sinners' sake to
    grieve.

IV.

That ancient beadsman heard the prelude soft :
And so it chanced, for many a door was wide,
From hurry to and fro.   Soon, up aloft,
The silver, snarling trumpets 'gan to chide ;
The level chambers, ready with their pride,
Were glowing to receive a thousand guests ;
The carved angels, ever eager-eyed,
Stared, where upon their heads the cornice rests,
With hair blown back, and wings put crosswise
    on their breasts.

V.

At length burst in the argent revelry,
With plume, tiara, and all rich array,
Numerous as shadows haunting fairily

The brain, new-stuffed, in youth, with triumphs
    gay
Of old romance.   These let us wish away ;
And turn, sole-thoughted, to one lady there,
Whose heart had brooded, all that wintry day,
On love, and winged St. Agnes' saintly care,
As she had heard old dames full many times de-
    clare.

VI.

They told her how, upon St. Agnes' Eve,
Young virgins might have visions of delight,
And soft adorings from their loves receive
Upon the honeyed middle of the night,
If ceremonies due they did aright ;
As, supperless to bed they must retire,
And couch supine their beauties, lily white ;
Nor look behind, nor sideways, but require
Of heaven with upward eyes for all that they
    desire.

VII.

Full of this whim was thoughtful Madeline ;
The music, yearning like a god in pain,
She scarcely heard ; her maiden eyes divine,
Fixed on the floor, saw many a sweeping train
Pass by, — she heeded not at all ; in vain
Came many a tiptoe, amorous cavalier,
And back retired ; not cooled by high disdain,
But she saw not ; her heart was otherwhere ;
She sighed for Agnes' dreams, the sweetest of the
    year.

VIII.

She danced along with vague, regardless eyes,
Anxious her lips, her breathing quick and short ;
The hallowed hour was near at hand ; she sighs
Amid the timbrels, and the thronged resort
Of whisperers in anger, or in sport ;
Mid looks of love, defiance, hate, and scorn,
Hoodwinked with fairy fancy ; all amort
Save to St. Agnes and her lambs unshorn,
And all the bliss to be before to-morrow morn.

IX.

So, purposing each moment to retire,
She lingered still.   Meantime, across the moors,
Had come young Porphyro, with heart on fire
For Madeline.   Beside the portal doors,
Buttressed from moonlight, stands he, and im-
    plores
All saints to give him sight of Madeline ;
But for one moment in the tedious hours,
That he might gaze and worship all unseen ;
Perchance speak, kneel, touch, kiss, — in sooth
    such things have been.

X.

He ventures in ; let no buzzed whisper tell ;
All eyes be muffled, or a hundred swords
Will storm his heart, love's feverous citadel ;

For him, those chambers held barbarian hordes,
Hyena foemen, and hot-blooded lords,
Whose very dogs would execrations howl
Against his lineage ; not one breast affords
Him any mercy, in that mansion foul,
Save one old beldame, weak in body and in soul.

XI.

Ah, happy chance ! the aged creature came,
Shuffling along with ivory-headed wand,
To where he stood, hid from the torch's flame,
Behind a broad hall-pillar, far beyond
The sound of merriment and chorus bland.
He startled her ; but soon she knew his face,
And grasped his fingers in her palsied hand,
Saying, " Mercy, Porphyro ! hie thee from this place ;
They are all here to-night, the whole bloodthirsty race !

XII.

" Get hence ! get hence ! there 's dwarfish Hildebrand ;
He had a fever late, and in the fit
He cursed thee and thine, both house and land ;
Then there 's that old Lord Maurice, not a whit
More tame for his gray hairs — Alas me ! flit !
Flit like a ghost away ! " — " Ah, gossip dear,
We 're safe enough ; here in this arm-chair sit,
And tell me how " — " Good saints, not here, not here ;
Follow me, child, or else these stones will be thy bier."

XIII.

He followed through a lowly arched way,
Brushing the cobwebs with his lofty plume ;
And as she muttered " Well-a — well-a-day ! "
He found him in a little moonlight room,
Pale, latticed, chill, and silent as a tomb.
" Now tell me where is Madeline," said he,
" O, tell me, Angela, by the holy loom
Which none but secret sisterhood may see,
When they St. Agnes' wool are weaving piously."

XIV.

" St. Agnes ! Ah ! it is St. Agnes' Eve, —
Yet men will murder upon holy days ;
Thou must hold water in a witch's sieve,
And be liege-lord of all the elves and fays,
To venture so. It fills me with amaze
To see thee, Porphyro ! — St. Agnes' Eve !
God's help ! my lady fair the conjurer plays
This very night ; good angels her deceive !
But let me laugh awhile, I 've mickle time to grieve."

XV.

Feebly she laugheth in the languid moon,
While Porphyro upon her face doth look,
Like puzzled urchin on an aged crone
Who keepeth closed a wondrous riddle-book,
As spectacled she sits in chimney nook.
But soon his eyes grew brilliant, when she told
His lady's purpose ; and he scarce could brook
Tears, at the thought of those enchantments cold,
And Madeline asleep in lap of legends old.

XVI.

Sudden a thought came like a full-blown rose,
Flushing his brow, and in his pained heart
Made purple riot ; then doth he propose
A stratagem, that makes the beldame start :
" A cruel man and impious thou art !
Sweet lady, let her pray, and sleep and dream
Alone with her good angels, far apart
From wicked men like thee. Go, go ! I deem
Thou canst not surely be the same that thou didst seem."

XVII.

" I will not harm her, by all saints I swear ! "
Quoth Porphyro ; " O, may I ne'er find grace
When my weak voice shall whisper its last prayer,
If one of her soft ringlets I displace,
Or look with ruffian passion in her face ;
Good Angela, believe me by these tears ;
Or I will, even in a moment's space,
Awake, with horrid shout, my foemen's ears,
And beard them, though they be more fanged than wolves and bears."

XVIII.

" Ah ! why wilt thou affright a feeble soul ?
A poor, weak, palsy-stricken, church-yard thing,
Whose passing-bell may ere the midnight toll ;
Whose prayers for thee, each morn and evening,
Were never missed." Thus plaining, doth she bring
A gentler speech from burning Porphyro ;
So woful, and of such deep sorrowing,
That Angela gives promise she will do
Whatever he shall wish, betide her weal or woe.

XIX.

Which was, to lead him, in close secrecy,
Even to Madeline's chamber, and there hide
Him in a closet, of such privacy
That he might see her beauty unespied,
And win perhaps that night a peerless bride ;
While legioned fairies paced the coverlet,
And pale enchantment held her sleepy-eyed.
Never on such a night have lovers met,
Since Merlin paid his demon all the monstrous debt.

XX.

" It shall be as thou wishest," said the dame ;
" All cates and dainties shall be stored there
Quickly on this feast-night ; by the tambour frame

Her own lute thou wilt see ; no time to spare,
For I am slow and feeble, and scarce dare
On such a catering trust my dizzy head.
Wait here, my child, with patience kneel in
　　prayer
The while. Ah ! thou must needs the lady wed,
Or may I never leave my grave among the dead."

XXI.

So saying, she hobbled off with busy fear.
The lover's endless minutes slowly passed :
The dame returned, and whispered in his ear
To follow her ; with aged eyes aghast
From fright of dim espial. Safe at last,
Through many a dusky gallery, they gain
The maiden's chamber, silken, hushed and
　　chaste ;
Where Porphyro took covert, pleased amain.
His poor guide hurried back with agues in her
　　brain.

XXII.

Her faltering hand upon the balustrade,
Old Angela was feeling for the stair,
When Madeline, St. Agnes' charmed maid,
Rose, like a missioned spirit, unaware ;
With silver taper's light, and pious care,
She turned, and down the aged gossip led
To a safe level matting. Now prepare,
Young Porphyro, for gazing on that bed !
She comes, she comes again, like a ring-dove
　　frayed and fled.

XXIII.

Out went the taper as she hurried in ;
Its little smoke, in pallid moonshine, died ;
She closed the door, she panted, all akin
To spirits of the air, and visions wide ;
No uttered syllable, or, woe betide !
But to her heart, her heart was voluble,
Paining with eloquence her balmy side ;
As though a tongueless nightingale should swell
Her throat in vain, and die, heart-stifled in her
　　dell.

XXIV.

A casement high and triple-arched there was,
All garlanded with carven imageries
Of fruits, and flowers, and bunches of knot-grass,
And diamonded with panes of quaint device,
Innumerable of stains and splendid dyes,
As are the tiger-moth's deep-damasked wings ;
And in the midst, 'mong thousand heraldries,
And twilight saints, and dim emblazonings,
A shielded scutcheon blushed with blood of
　　queens and kings.

XXV.

Full on this casement shone the wintry moon,
And threw warm gules on Madeline's fair breast,
As down she knelt for heaven's grace and boon ;

Rose-bloom fell on her hands, together prest,
And on her silver cross soft amethyst,
And on her hair a glory, like a saint ;
She seemed a splendid angel, newly drest,
Save wings, for heaven. Porphyro grew faint :
She knelt, so pure a thing, so free from mortal
　　taint.

XXVI.

Anon his heart revives ; her vespers done,
Of all its wreathed pearls her hair she frees ;
Unclasps her warmed jewels one by one ;
Loosens her fragrant bodice ; by degrees
Her rich attire creeps rustling to her knees ;
Half hidden, like a mermaid in sea-weed,
Pensive awhile she dreams awake, and sees,
In fancy, fair St. Agnes in her bed,
But dares not look behind, or all the charm is
　　fled.

XXVII.

Soon, trembling in her soft and chilly nest,
In sort of wakeful swoon, perplexed she lay,
Until the poppied warmth of sleep oppressed
Her soothed limbs, and soul fatigued away ;
Flown like a thought, until the morrow-day ;
Blissfully havened both from joy and pain ;
Clasped like a missal where swart Paynims pray ;
Blinded alike from sunshine and from rain,
As though a rose should shut, and be a bud again.

XXVIII.

Stolen to this paradise, and so entranced,
Porphyro gazed upon her empty dress,
And listened to her breathing, if it chanced
To wake into a slumberous tenderness ;
Which when he heard, that minute did he bless,
And breathed himself ; then from the closet crept,
Noiseless as fear in a wide wilderness,
And over the hushed carpet, silent, stept,
And 'tween the curtains peeped, where, lo ! — how
　　fast she slept.

XXIX.

Then by the bedside, where the faded moon
Made a dim, silver twilight, soft he set
A table, and, half anguished, threw thereon
A cloth of woven crimson, gold, and jet : —
O for some drowsy Morphean amulet !
The boisterous, midnight, festive clarion,
The kettle-drum, and far-heard clarionet,
Affray his ears, though but in dying tone : —
The hall-door shuts again, and all the noise is gone.

XXX.

And still she slept an azure-lidded sleep,
In blanched linen, smooth, and lavendered ;
While he from forth the closet brought a heap
Of candied apple, quince, and plum, and gourd ;
With jellies soother than the creamy curd,

And lucent syrops, tinct with cinnamon ;
Manna and dates, in argosy transferred
From Fez ; and spiced dainties, every one,
From silken Samarcand to cedared Lebanon.

XXXI.

These delicates he heaped with glowing hand
On golden dishes and in baskets bright
Of wreathed silver.   Sumptuous they stand
In the retired quiet of the night,
Filling the chilly room with perfume light. —
" And now, my love, my seraph fair awake !
Thou art my heaven, and I thine eremite ;
Open thine eyes, for meek St. Agnes' sake,
Or I shall drowse beside thee, so my soul doth ache."

XXXII.

Thus whispering, his warm, unnervéd arm
Sank in her pillow.   Shaded was her dream
By the dusk curtains ; — 't was a midnight charm
Impossible to melt as iced stream :
The lustrous salvers in the moonlight gleam ;
Broad golden fringe upon the carpet lies ;
It seemed he never, never could redeem
From such a steadfast spell his lady's eyes ;
So mused awhile, entoiled in woofed phantasies.

XXXIII.

Awakening up, he took her hollow lute, —
Tumultuous, — and, in chords that tenderest be,
He played an ancient ditty, long since mute,
In Provence called "La belle dame sans mercy" ;
Close to her ear touching the melody ; —
Wherewith disturbed, she uttered a soft moan ;
He ceased — she panted quick — and suddenly
Her blue affrayed eyes wide open shone ;
Upon his knees he sank, pale as smooth-sculptured
stone.

XXXIV.

Her eyes were open, but she still beheld,
Now wide awake, the vision of her sleep.
There was a painful change, that nigh expelled
The blisses of her dream so pure and deep ;
At which fair Madeline began to weep,
And moan forth witless words with many a sigh ;
While still her gaze on Porphyro would keep.
Who knelt, with joined hands and piteous eye,
Fearing to move or speak, she looked so dreamingly.

XXXV.

"Ah, Porphyro !" said she, "but even now
Thy voice was at sweet tremble in mine ear,
Made tunable with every sweetest vow ;
And those sad eyes were spiritual and clear ;
How changed thou art ! how pallid, chill, and
drear !
Give me that voice again, my Porphyro,
Those looks immortal, those complainings dear !

O, leave me not in this eternal woe,
For if thou diest, my love, I know not where to go."

XXXVI.

Beyond a mortal man impassioned far
At these voluptuous accents, he arose,
Ethereal, flushed, and like a throbbing star
Seen mid the sapphire heaven's deep repose ;
Into her dream he melted, as the rose
Blendeth its odor with the violet, —
Solution sweet ; meantime the frost-wind blows
Like love's alarum pattering the sharp sleet
Against the window-panes ; St. Agnes' moon hath
set.

XXXVII.

'T is dark ; quick pattereth the flaw-blown sleet ;
"This is no dream, my bride, my Madeline !"
'T is dark ; the iced gusts still rave and beat :
"No dream, alas ! alas ! and woe is mine !
Porphyro will leave me here to fade and pine. —
Cruel ! what traitor could thee hither bring ?
I curse not, for my heart is lost in thine,
Though thou forsakest a deceived thing ; —
A dove forlorn and lost, with sick, unpruned wing."

XXXVIII.

" My Madeline ! sweet dreamer ! lovely bride !
Say, may I be for aye thy vassal blest ?
Thy beauty's shield, heart-shaped and vermeil
dyed ?
Ah, silver shrine, here will I take my rest
After so many hours of toil and quest,
A famished pilgrim, — saved by miracle.
Though I have found, I will not rob thy nest,
Saving of thy sweet self ; if thou think'st well
To trust, fair Madeline, to no rude infidel.

XLI.

They glide, like phantoms, into the wide hall !
Like phantoms to the iron porch they glide,
Where lay the porter, in uneasy sprawl,
With a huge empty flagon by his side ;
The wakeful bloodhound rose, and shook his hide,
But his sagacious eye an inmate owns ;
By one, and one, the bolts full easy slide ;
The chains lie silent on the footworn stones ;
The key turns, and the door upon its hinges groans.

XLII.

And they are gone ! ay, ages long ago
These lovers fled away into the storm.
That night the baron dreamt of many a woe,
And all his warrior-guests, with shade and form
Of witch, and demon, and large coffin-worm,
Were long be-nightmared.   Angela the old
Died palsy-twitched, with meagre face deform ;
The beadsman, after thousand aves told,
For aye unsought-for slept among his ashes cold.
                                        JOHN KEATS.

MARRIAGE.

THOU HAST SWORN BY THY GOD, MY JEANIE.

THOU hast sworn by thy God, my Jeanie,
  By that pretty white hand o' thine,
And by a' the lowing stars in heaven,
  That thou wad aye be mine !
And I hae sworn by my God, my Jeanie,
  And by that kind heart o' thine,
By a' the stars sown thick owre heaven,
  That thou shalt aye be mine ?

Then foul fa' the hands that wad loose sic bands,
  And the heart that wad part sic luve !
But there 's nae hand can loose my band,
  But the finger o' Him abuve.
Though the wee, wee cot maun be my bield,
  And my claithing ne'er sae mean,
I wad lap me up rich i' the faulds o' luve, —
  Heaven's armfu' o' my Jean.

Her white arm wad be a pillow for me,
  Fu' safter than the down ;
And Luve wad winnow owre us his kind, kind
    wings,
  And sweetly I 'd sleep, and soun'.
Come here to me, thou lass o' my luve !
  Come here and kneel wi' me !
The morn is fu' o' the presence o' God,
  And I canna pray without thee.

The morn wind is sweet 'mang the beds o' new
    flowers,
  The wee birds sing kindlie and hie ;
Our gudeman leans owre his kale-yard dike,
  And a blythe auld bodie is he.
The Beuk maun be ta'en whan the carle comes
    hame,
  Wi' the holy psalmodie ;
And thou maun speak o' me to thy God,
  And I will speak o' thee.
                              ALLAN CUNNINGHAM.

THE BRIDE.

Lo ! where she comes along with portly pace,
Like Phœbe from her chamber of the east,
Arising forth to run her mighty race,
Clad all in white, that seems a virgin best.
So well it her beseems, that ye would ween
Some angel she had been.
Her long, loose yellow locks, like golden wire,
Sprinkled with pearl, and pearling flowers atween,
Do like a golden mantle her attire ;
And being crownéd with a garland green,
Seem like some maiden queen.
Her modest eyes, abashéd to behold
So many gazers as on her do stare,
Upon the lowly ground affixéd are ;
Ne dare lift up her countenance too bold,
But blush to hear her praises sung so loud,
So far from being proud.
Nathless do ye still loud her praises sing,
That all the woods may answer, and your echo ring.

Tell me, ye merchants' daughters, did ye see
So fair a creature in your town before ?
So sweet, so lovely, and so mild as she,
Adorned with Beauty's grace and Virtue's store ?
Her goodly eyes like sapphires, shining bright,
Her forehead ivory white,
Her cheeks like apples which the sun hath rudded,
Her lips like cherries charming men to bite,
Her breast like to a bowl of cream uncrudded,
Her paps like lilies budded,
Her snowy neck like to a marble tower ;
And all her body like a palace fair,
Ascending up with many a stately stair
To Honor's seat and Chastity's sweet bower.
Why stand ye still, ye virgins, in amaze,
Upon her so to gaze,
Whilst ye forget your former lay to sing,
To which the woods did answer, and your echo ring.
                              EDMUND SPENSER.

LOVE.

THERE are who say the lover's heart
  Is in the loved one's merged ;
O, never by love's own warm art
  So cold a plea was urged !
No ! — hearts that love hath crowned or crossed,
  Love fondly knits together ;
But not a thought or hue is lost
  That made a part of either.

It is an ill-told tale that tells
  Of "hearts by love made one" ;
He grows who near another's dwells
  More conscious of his own ;
In each spring up new thoughts and powers
  That, mid love's warm, clear weather,
Together tend like climbing flowers,
  And, turning, grow together.

Such fictions blink love's better part,
  Yield up its half of bliss ;
The wells are in the neighbor heart
  When there is thirst in this :
There findeth love the passion-flowers
  On which it learns to thrive,
Makes honey in another's bowers,
  But brings it home to hive.

Love's life is in its own replies, —
  To each low beat it beats,
Smiles back the smiles, sighs back the sighs,
  And every throb repeats.
Then, since one loving heart still throws
  Two shadows in love's sun,
How should two loving hearts compose
  And mingle into one ?

THOMAS KIBBLE HERVEY.

ADAM DESCRIBING EVE.

MINE eyes he closed, but open left the cell
Of fancy, my internal sight, by which
Abstract, as in a trance, methought I saw,
Though sleeping, where I lay, and saw the shape
Still glorious before whom awake I stood ;
Who, stooping, opened my left side, and took
From thence a rib, with cordial spirits warm,
And life-blood streaming fresh ; wide was the
    wound,
But suddenly with flesh filled up and healed :
The rib he formed and fashioned with his hands ;
Under his forming hands a creature grew,
Manlike, but different sex, so lovely fair,
That what seemed fair in all the world seemed
    now
Mean, or in her summed up, in her contained
And in her looks, which from that time infused
Sweetness into my heart, unfelt before,
And into all things from her air inspired
The spirit of love and amorous delight.
She disappeared, and left me dark ; I waked
To find her, or forever to deplore
Her loss, and other pleasures all abjure :
When out of hope, behold her, not far off,
Such as I saw her in my dream, adorned
With what all earth or Heaven could bestow
To make her amiable.   On she came,
Led by her heavenly Maker, though unseen,
And guided by his voice, nor uninformed
Of nuptial sanctity and marriage rites :
Grace was in all her steps, Heaven in her eye,
In every gesture dignity and love.
I, overjoyed, could not forbear aloud :
  "This turn hath made amends ; thou hast
    fulfilled
Thy words, Creator bounteous and benign,

Giver of all things fair, but fairest this
Of all thy gifts, nor enviest.   I now see
Bone of my bone, flesh of my flesh, myself
Before me ; Woman is her name, of man
Extracted : for this cause he shall forego
Father and mother, and to his wife adhere ;
And they shall be one flesh, one heart, one soul.'
  She heard me thus, and though divinely
    brought,
Yet innocence and virgin modesty,
Her virtue and the conscience of her worth,
That would be wooed, and not unsought be
    won,
Not obvious, not obtrusive, but retired,
The more desirable ; or, to say all,
Nature herself, though pure of sinful thought,
Wrought in her so, that, seeing me, she turned :
I followed her ; she what was honor knew,
And with obsequious majesty approved
My pleaded reason.   To the nuptial bower
I led her blushing like the morn : all Heaven,
And happy constellations on that hour
Shed their selectest influence ; the earth
Gave sign of gratulation, and each hill ;
Joyous the birds ; fresh gales and gentle airs
Whispered it to the woods, and from their
    wings
Flung rose, flung odors from the spicy shrub,
Disporting, till the amorous bird of night
Sung spousal, and bid haste the evening star
On his hill-top, to light the bridal lamp.
.   .   .   .

            When I approach
Her loveliness, so absolute she seems,
And in herself complete, so well to know
Her own, that what she wills to do or say
Seems wisest, virtuousest, discreetest, best ;
All higher knowledge in her presence falls
Degraded, wisdom in discourse with her
Loses discountenanced, and like folly shows ;
Authority and reason on her wait,
As one intended first, not after made
Occasionally ; and, to consummate all,
Greatness of mind and nobleness their seat
Build in her loveliest, and create an awe
About her, as a guard angelic placed."
.   .   .   .

Neither her outside formed so fair, nor aught
In procreation common to all kinds,
.   .   .   .

So much delights me, as those graceful acts,
Those thousand decencies that daily flow
From all her words and actions, mixed with love
And sweet compliance, which declare unfeigned
Union of mind, or in us both one soul ;
Harmony to behold in wedded pair
More grateful than harmonious sound to the ear.

MILTON.

ALICE.

FROM "ALICE AND UNA."

I.

ALICE was a chieftain's daughter,
And though many suitors sought her,
She so loved Glengariff's water
That she let her lovers pine.
  Her eye was beauty's palace,
  And her cheek an ivory chalice,
  Through which the blood of Alice
Gleamed soft as rosiest wine,
And her lips like lusmore blossoms which the
      fairies intertwine, —
And her heart a golden mine.

II.

She was gentler and shyer
Than the light fawn which stood by her,
And her eyes emit a fire
Soft and tender as her soul ;
  Love's dewy light doth drown her,
  And the braided locks that crown her .
  Than autumn's trees are browner,
When the golden shadows roll
Through the forests in the evening, when cathe-
      dral turrets toll,
And the purple sun advanceth to its goal.

III.

Her cottage was a dwelling
All regal homes excelling,
But, ah ! beyond the telling
Was the beauty round it spread, —
  The wave and sunshine playing,
  Like sisters each arraying,
  Far down the sea-plants swaying
Upon their coral bed,
And languid as the tresses on a sleeping maiden's
      head,
When the summer breeze is dead.

IV.

Need we say that Maurice loved her,
And that no blush reproved her,
When her throbbing bosom moved her
To give the heart she gave ?
  That by dawn-light and by twilight,
  And, O blessed moon, by thy light, —
  When the twinkling stars on high light
The wanderer o'er the wave, —
His steps unconscious led him where Glengariff's
      waters lave
Each mossy bank and cave.

V.

The sun his gold is flinging,
The happy birds are singing,
And bells are gayly ringing
Along Glengariff's sea ;
  And crowds in many a galley
  To the happy marriage rally
  Of the maiden of the valley
And the youth of Céim-an-eich ;
Old eyes with joy are weeping, as all ask on
      bended knee,
A blessing, gentle Alice, upon thee.

DENIS FLORENCE MACCARTHY.

TO A LADY BEFORE MARRIAGE.

O, FORMED by Nature, and refined by Art,
With charms to win, and sense to fix the heart !
By thousands sought, Clotilda, canst thou free
Thy crowd of captives and descend to me ?
Content in shades obscure to waste thy life,
A hidden beauty and a country wife ?
O, listen while thy summers are my theme !
Ah ! soothe thy partner in his waking dream !
In some small hamlet on the lonely plain,
Where Thames through meadows rolls his mazy
      train,
Or where high Windsor, thick with greens arrayed,
Waves his old oaks, and spreads his ample shade,
Fancy has figured out our calm retreat ;
Already round the visionary seat
Our limes begin to shoot, our flowers to spring,
The brooks to murmur, and the birds to sing.
Where dost thou lie, thou thinly peopled green,
Thou nameless lawn, and village yet unseen,
Where sons, contented with their native ground,
Ne'er travelled further than ten furlongs round,
And the tanned peasant and his ruddy bride
Were born together, and together died,
Where early larks best tell the morning light,
And only Philomel disturbs the night ?
Midst gardens here my humble pile shall rise,
With sweets surrounded of ten thousand dyes ;
All savage where th' embroidered gardens end,
The haunt of echoes, shall my woods ascend ;
And oh ! if Heaven th' ambitious thought approve,
A rill shall warble 'cross the gloomy grove, —
A little rill, o'er pebbly beds conveyed,
Gush down the steep, and glitter through the glade.
What cheering scents these bordering banks exhale!
How loud that heifer lows from yonder vale !
That thrush how shrill ! his note so clear, so high,
He drowns each feathered minstrel of the sky.
Here let me trace beneath the purpled morn
The deep-mouthed beagle and the sprightly horn,
Or lure the trout with well-dissembled flies,
Or fetch the fluttering partridge from the skies.
Nor shall thy hand disdain to crop the vine,
The downy peach, or flavored nectarine ;
Or rob the beehive of its golden hoard,
And bear th' unbought luxuriance to thy board.

Sometimes my books by day shall kill the hours,
While from thy needle rise the silken flowers,
And thou, by turns, to ease my feeble sight,
Resume the volume, and deceive the night.
O, when I mark thy twinkling eyes opprest,
Soft whispering, let me warn my love to rest ;
Then watch thee, charmed, while sleep locks every
          sense,
And to sweet Heaven commend thy innocence.
Thus reigned our fathers o'er the rural fold,
Wise, hale, and honest, in the days of old ;
Till courts arose, where substance pays for show,
And specious joys are bought with real woe.
                              THOMAS TICKELL.

O, LAY THY HAND IN MINE, DEAR!

O, LAY thy hand in mine, dear !
    We 're growing old ;
But Time hath brought no sign, dear,
    That hearts grow cold.
'T is long, long since our new love
    Made life divine ;
But age enricheth true love,
    Like noble wine.

And lay thy cheek to mine, dear, ·
    And take thy rest ;
Mine arms around thee twine, dear,
    And make thy nest.
A many cares are pressing
    On this dear head ;
But Sorrow's hands in blessing
    Are surely laid.

O, lean thy life on mine, dear !
    'T will shelter thee.
Thou wert a winsome vine, dear,
    On my young tree :
And so, till boughs are leafless,
    And songbirds flown,
We 'll twine, then lay us, griefless,
    Together down.
                              GERALD MASSEY.

THE BRIDE.

FROM A BALLAD UPON A WEDDING.

THE maid, and thereby hangs a tale,
For such a maid no Whitsun-ale
    Could ever yet produce :

No grape that 's kindly ripe could be
So round, so plump, so soft as she,
    Nor half so full of juice.

Her finger was so small, the ring
Would not stay on which they did bring, —
    It was too wide a peck ;
And, to say truth, — for out it must, —
It looked like the great collar — just —
    About our young colt's neck.

Her feet beneath her petticoat,
Like little mice, stole in and out,
    As if they feared the light ;
But O, she dances such a way !
No sun upon an Easter-day
    Is half so fine a sight.

Her cheeks so rare a white was on,
No daisy makes comparison ;
    Who sees them is undone ; ·
For streaks of red were mingled there,
Such as are on a Cath'rine pear,
    The side that 's next the sun.

Her lips were red ; and one was thin,
Compared to that was next her chin.
    Some bee had stung it newly ;
But, Dick, her eyes so guard her face,
I durst no more upon them gaze,
    Than on the sun in July.

Her mouth so small, when she does speak,
Thou 'dst swear her teeth her words did break,
    That they might passage get ;
But she so handled still the matter,
They came as good as ours, or better,
    And are not spent a whit.
                              SIR JOHN SUCKLING.

HEBREW WEDDING.

To the sound of timbrels sweet
Moving slow our solemn feet,
We have borne thee on the road
To the virgin's blest abode ;
With thy yellow torches gleaming,
And thy scarlet mantle streaming,
And the canopy above
Swaying as we slowly move.

Thou hast left the joyous feast,
And the mirth and wine have ceased ;
And now we set thee down before
The jealously unclosing door,
That the favored youth admits
Where the veiléd virgin sits
In the bliss of maiden fear,
Waiting our soft tread to hear,

And the music's brisker din
At the bridegroom's entering in,
Entering in, a welcome guest,
To the chamber of his rest.

CHORUS OF MAIDENS.

Now the jocund song is thine,
Bride of David's kingly line ;
How thy dove-like bosom trembleth,
And thy shrouded eye resembleth
Violets, when the dews of eve
A moist and tremulous glitter leave

On the bashful sealéd lid !
Close within the bride-veil hid,
Motionless thou sitt'st and mute ;
Save that at the soft salute
Of each entering maiden friend,
Thou dost rise and softly bend.

Hark ! a brisker, merrier glee !
The door unfolds, — 't is he ! 't is he !
Thus we lift our lamps to meet him,
Thus we touch our lutes to greet him.
Thou shalt give a fonder meeting,
Thou shalt give a tenderer greeting.
                    HENRY HART MILMAN.

WIFE, CHILDREN, AND FRIENDS.

WHEN the black-lettered list to the gods was pre-
    sented
  (The list of what fate for each mortal intends),
At the long string of ills a kind goddess relented,
  And slipped in three blessings, — wife, children,
    and friends.

In vain surely Pluto maintained he was cheated,
  For justice divine could not compass its ends.
The scheme of man's penance he swore was defeated,
  For earth becomes heaven with — wife, children,
    and friends.

If the stock of our bliss is in stranger hands vested,
  The fund ill secured, oft in bankruptcy ends ;
But the heart issues bills which are never protested,
  When drawn on the firm of — wife, children,
    and friends.

The day-spring of youth still unclouded by sorrow,
  Alone on itself for enjoyment depends ;
But drear is the twilight of age if it borrow
  No warmth from the smile of — wife, children,
    and friends.
                    WILLIAM ROBERT SPENCER.

MARRIAGE.

FROM "HUMAN LIFE."

THEN before All they stand, — the holy vow
And ring of gold, no fond illusions now,
Bind her as his. Across the threshold led,
And every tear kissed off as soon as shed,
His house she enters, — there to be a light,
Shining within, when all without is night ;
A guardian angel o'er his life presiding,
Doubling his pleasures and his cares dividing,
Winning him back when mingling in the throng,
Back from a world we love, alas ! too long,
To fireside happiness, to hours of ease,
Blest with that charm, the certainty to please.
How oft her eyes read his ; her gentle mind
To all his wishes, all his thoughts inclined ;
Still subject, — ever on the watch to borrow
Mirth of his mirth and sorrow of his sorrow !
The soul of music slumbers in the shell,
Till waked and kindled by the master's spell,
And feeling hearts — touch them but rightly —
    pour
A thousand melodies unheard before !
                    SAMUEL ROGERS.

CONNUBIAL LIFE.

FROM "THE SEASONS."

BUT happy they ! the happiest of their kind !
Whom gentler stars unite, and in one fate
Their hearts, their fortunes, and their beings blend.
'T is not the coarser tie of human laws,
Unnatural oft, and foreign to the mind,
That binds their peace, but harmony itself,
Attuning all their passions into love ;
Where friendship full-exerts her softest power,
Perfect esteem enlivened by desire
Ineffable, and sympathy of soul ;
Thought meeting thought, and will preventing
    will,
With boundless confidence : for naught but love
Can answer love, and render bliss secure.
Meantime a smiling offspring rises round,
And mingles both their graces. By degrees,
The human blossom blows ; and every day,
Soft as it rolls along, shows some new charm,
The father's lustre and the mother's bloom.
Then infant reason grows apace, and calls
For the kind hand of an assiduous care.
Delightful task ! to rear the tender thought,
To teach the young idea how to shoot,
To pour the fresh instruction o'er the mind,
To breathe the enlivening spirit, and to fix
The generous purpose in the glowing breast.
O, speak the joy ! ye whom the sudden tear

Surprises often, while you look around,
And nothing strikes your eye but sights of bliss,
All various Nature pressing on the heart ;
An elegant sufficiency, content,
Retirement, rural quiet, friendship, books,
Ease and alternate labor, useful life,
Progressive virtue, and approving Heaven.
These are the matchless joys of virtuous love ;
And thus their moments fly.   The Seasons thus,
As ceaseless round a jarring world they roll,
Still find them happy ; and consenting Spring
Sheds her own rosy garland on their heads :
Till evening comes at last, serene and mild ;
When after the long vernal day of life,
Enamored more, as more remembrance swells
With many a proof of recollected love,
Together down they sink in social sleep ;
Together freed, their gentle spirits fly
To scenes where love and bliss immortal reign.
JAMES THOMSON.

THE BANKS OF THE LEE.

Air, "A TRIP TO THE COTTAGE."

O THE banks of the Lee, the banks of the Lee,
And love in a cottage for Mary and me !
There 's not in the land a lovelier tide,
And I 'm sure that there's no one so fair as my bride.
　　She 's modest and meek,
　　There 's a down on her cheek,
　　And her skin is as sleek
　　　　As a butterfly's wing ;
　　Then her step would scarce show
　　On the fresh-fallen snow,
　　And her whisper is low,
　　　　But as clear as the spring.
O the banks of the Lee, the banks of the Lee,
And love in a cottage for Mary and me !
I know not how love is happy elsewhere,
I know not how any but lovers are there.

O, so green is the grass, so clear is the stream,
So mild is the mist and so rich is the beam,
That beauty should never to other lands roam,
But make on the banks of our river its home !
　　When, dripping with dew,
　　The roses peep through,
　　'T is to look in at you
　　　　They are growing so fast ;
　　While the scent of the flowers
　　Must be hoarded for hours,
　　'T is poured in such showers
　　　　When my Mary goes past.
O the banks of the Lee, the banks of the Lee,
And love in a cottage for Mary and me !
O, Mary for me, Mary for me,
And 't is little I 'd sigh for the banks of the Lee !
THOMAS DAVIS.

MY WIFE 'S A WINSOME WEE THING.

　　SHE is a winsome wee thing,
　　She is a handsome wee thing,
　　She is a bonnie wee thing,
　　This sweet wee wife o' mine.

　　I never saw a fairer,
　　I never lo'ed a dearer,
　　And neist my heart I 'll wear her,
　　For fear my jewel tine.

　　She is a winsome wee thing,
　　She is a handsome wee thing,
　　She is a bonnie wee thing,
　　This sweet wee wife o' mine.

　　The warld's wrack we share o't,
　　The warstle and the care o't :
　　Wi' her I 'll blythely bear it,
　　And think my lot divine.
ROBERT BURNS.

SONNETS.

MY Love, I have no fear that thou shouldst die ;
Albeit I ask no fairer life than this,
Whose numbering-clock is still thy gentle kiss,
While Time and Peace with hands unlockéd fly, —
Yet care I not where in Eternity
We live and love, well knowing that there is
No backward step for those who feel the bliss
Of Faith as their most lofty yearnings high :
Love hath so purified my being's core,
Meseems I scarcely should be startled, even,
To find, some morn, that thou hadst gone before ;
Since, with thy love, this knowledge too was
　　given,
Which each calm day doth strengthen more and
　　more,
That they who love are but one step from Heaven.

I CANNOT think that thou shouldst pass away,
Whose life to mine is an eternal law,
A piece of nature that can have no flaw,
A new and certain sunrise every day ;
But, if thou art to be another ray
About the Sun of Life, and art to live
Free from all of thee that was fugitive,
The debt of Love I will more fully pay,
Not downcast with the thought of thee so high,
But rather raised to be a nobler man,
And more divine in my humanity,
As knowing that the waiting eyes which scan
My life are lighted by a purer being,
And ask meek, calm-browed deeds, with it agree-
ing.

THE BANKS OF THE LEE.

" So green is the grass, so clear is the stream,
So mild is the mist and so rich is the beam,
That beauty should never to other lands roam,
But make on the banks of our river its home ! "

THERE never yet was flower fair in vain,
Let classic poets rhyme it as they will ;
The seasons toil that it may blow again,
And summer's heart doth feel its every ill ;
Nor is a true soul ever born for naught :
Wherever any such hath lived and died,
There hath been something for true freedom
  wrought,
Some bulwark levelled on the evil side :
Toil on, then, Greatness ! thou art in the right,
However narrow souls may call thee wrong :
Be as thou wouldst be in thine own clear sight,
And so thou wilt in all the world's erelong :
For worldlings cannot, struggle as they may,
From man's great soul one great thought hide away.

I THOUGHT our love at full, but I did err ;
Joy's wreath drooped o'er mine eyes ; I could not
  see
That sorrow in our happy world must be
Love's deepest spokesman and interpreter ?
But, as a mother feels her child first stir
Under her heart, so felt I instantly
Deep in my soul another bond to thee
Thrill with that life we saw depart from her ;
O mother of our angel child ! twice dear !
Death knits as well as parts, and still, I wis,
Her tender radince shall infold us here,
Even as the light, borne up by inward bliss,
Threads the void glooms of space without a fear,
To print on farthest stars her pitying kiss.
                        JAMES RUSSELL LOWELL.

POSSESSION.

I.

" IT was our wedding-day
A month ago," dear heart, I hear you say.
If months, or years, or ages since have passed,
I know not : I have ceased to question Time.
I only know that once there pealed a chime
Of joyous bells, and then I held you fast,
And all stood back, and none my right denied,
And forth we walked : the world was free and wide
Before us. Since that day
I count my life : the Past is washed away.

II.

It was no dream, that vow :
It was the voice that woke me from a dream, —
A happy dream, I think ; but I am waking now,
And drink the splendor of a sun supreme
That turns the mist of former tears to gold.
Within these arms I hold
The fleeting promise, chased so long in vain :

Ah, weary bird ! thou wilt not fly again :
Thy wings are clipped, thou canst no more de-
  part, —
Thy nest is builded in my heart !

III.

I was the crescent ; thou
The silver phantom of the perfect sphere,
Held in its bosom : in one glory now
Our lives united shine, and many a year —
Not the sweet moon of bridal only — we
One lustre, ever at the full, shall be :
One pure and rounded light, one planet whole,
One life developed, one completed soul !
For I in thee, and thou in me,
Unite our cloven halves of destiny.

IV.

God knew his chosen time.
He bade me slowly ripen to my prime,
And from my boughs withheld the promised fruit,
Till storm and sun gave vigor to the root.
Secure, O Love ! secure
Thy blessing is : I have thee day and night :
Thou art become my blood, my life, my light :
God's mercy thou, and therefore shalt endure.
                        BAYARD TAYLOR.

THE DAY RETURNS, MY BOSOM BURNS.

THE day returns, my bosom burns,
  The blissful day we twa did meet ;
Though winter wild in tempest toiled,
  Ne'er summer sun was half sae sweet.
Than a' the pride that loads the tide,
  And crosses o'er the sultry line, —
Than kingly robes, and crowns and globes,
  Heaven gave me more ; it made thee mine.

While day and night can bring delight,
  Or nature aught of pleasure give, —
While joys above my mind can move,
  For thee and thee alone I live ;
When that grim foe of life below
  Comes in between to make us part,
The iron hand that breaks our band,
  It breaks my bliss, — it breaks my heart.
                        ROBERT BURNS.

THE POET'S BRIDAL-DAY SONG.

O, MY love 's like the steadfast sun,
  Or streams that deepen as they run ;
Nor hoary hairs, nor forty years,
Nor moments between sighs and tears,
Nor nights of thought, nor days of pain,
Nor dreams of glory dreamed in vain,

Nor mirth, nor sweetest song that flows
To sober joys and soften woes,
Can make my heart or fancy flee,
One moment, my sweet wife, from thee.

Even while I muse, I see thee sit
In maiden bloom and matron wit;
Fair, gentle as when first I sued,
Ye seem, but of sedater mood;
Yet my heart leaps as fond for thee
As when, beneath Arbigland tree,
We stayed and wooed, and thought the moon
Set on the sea an hour too soon;
Or lingered mid the falling dew,
When looks were fond and words were few.

Though I see smiling at thy feet
Five sons and ae fair daughter sweet,
And time, and care, and birthtime woes
Have dimmed thine eye and touched thy rose,
To thee, and thoughts of thee, belong
Whate'er charms me in tale or song.
When words descend like dews, unsought,
With gleams of deep, enthusiast thought,
And fancy in her heaven flies free,
They come, my love, they come from thee.

O, when more thought we gave, of old,
To silver, than some give to gold,
'T was sweet to sit and ponder o'er
How we should deck our humble bower;
'T was sweet to pull, in hope, with thee,
The golden fruit of fortune's tree;
And sweeter still to choose and twine
A garland for that brow of thine, —
A song-wreath which may grace my Jean,
While rivers flow, and woods grow green.

At times there come, as come there ought,
Grave moments of sedater thought,
When fortune frowns, nor lends our night
One gleam of her inconstant light;
And hope, that decks the peasant's bower,
Shines like a rainbow through the shower;
O then I see, while seated nigh,
A mother's heart shine in thine eye,
And proud resolve and purpose meek,
Speak of thee more than words can speak.
I think this wedded wife of mine,
The best of all that 's not divine.

ALLAN CUNNINGHAM.

THE POET'S SONG TO HIS WIFE.

How many summers, love,
  Have I been thine?
How many days, thou dove,
  Hast thou been mine?

Time, like the wingéd wind
  When 't bends the flowers,
Hath left no mark behind,
  To count the hours!

Some weight of thought, though loath,
  On thee he leaves;
Some lines of care round both
  Perhaps he weaves;
Some fears, — a soft regret
  For joys scarce known;
Sweet looks we half forget; —
  All else is flown!

Ah! — With what thankless heart
  I mourn and sing!
Look, where our children start,
  Like sudden spring!
With tongues all sweet and low
  Like a pleasant rhyme,
They tell how much I owe
  To thee and time!

BARRY CORNWALL.

IF THOU WERT BY MY SIDE, MY LOVE

IF thou wert by my side, my love,
  How fast would evening fail
In green Bengala's palmy grove,
  Listening the nightingale!

If thou, my love, wert by my side,
  My babies at my knee,
How gayly would our pinnace glide
  O'er Gunga's mimic sea!

I miss thee at the dawning gray,
  When, on our deck reclined,
In careless ease my limbs I lay
  And woo the cooler wind.

I miss thee when by Gunga's stream
  My twilight steps I guide,
But most beneath the lamp's pale beam
  I miss thee from my side.

I spread my books, my pencil try,
  The lingering noon to cheer,
But miss thy kind, approving eye,
  Thy meek, attentive ear.

But when at morn and eve the star
  Beholds me on my knee,
I feel, though thou art distant far,
  Thy prayers ascend for me.

Then on! then on! where duty leads,
  My course be onward still,
O'er broad Hindostan's sultry meads,
  O'er bleak Almorah's hill.

That course nor Delhi's kingly gates,
Nor mild Malwah detain ;
For sweet the bliss us both awaits
By yonder western main.

Thy towers, Bombay, gleam bright, they say,
Across the dark blue sea ;
But ne'er were hearts so light and gay
As then shall meet in thee !
REGINALD HEBER.

JOHN ANDERSON, MY JO.

John Anderson, my jo, John,
When we were first acquent,
Your locks were like the raven,
Your bonnie brow was brent ;
But now your brow is beld, John,
· Your locks are like the snaw ;
But blessings on your frosty pow,
John Anderson, my jo.

John Anderson, my jo, John,
We clamb the hill thegither ;
And mony a canty day, John,
We've had wi' ane anither.
Now we maun totter down, John,
But hand in hand we'll go :
And sleep thegither at the foot,
John Anderson, my jo.
ROBERT BURNS.

THE WORN WEDDING-RING.

Your wedding-ring wears thin, dear wife ; ah,
summers not a few,
Since I put it on your finger first, have passed
o'er me and you ;
And, love, what changes we have seen, — what
cares and pleasures, too, —
Since you became my own dear wife, when this
old ring was new !

O, blessings on that happy day, the happiest of
my life,
When, thanks to God, your low, sweet "Yes"
made you my loving wife !
Your heart will say the same, I know ; that
day's as dear to you, —
That day that made me yours, dear wife, when
this old ring was new.

How well do I remember now your young sweet
face that day !
How fair you were, how dear you were, my
tongue could hardly say ;

Nor how I doated on you ; O, how proud I was
of you !
But did I love you more than now, when this
old ring was new ?

No — no ! no fairer were you then than at this
hour to me ;
And, dear as life to me this day, how could you
dearer be ?
As sweet your face might be that day as now it
is, 't is true ;
But did I know your heart as well when this old
ring was new ?

O partner of my gladness, wife, what care, what
grief is there
For me you would not bravely face, with me
you would not share ?
O, what a weary want had every day, if wanting
you,
Wanting the love that God made mine when
this old ring was new !

Years bring fresh links to bind us, wife, — young
voices that are here ;
Young faces round our fire that make their
mother's yet more dear ;
Young loving hearts your care each day makes
yet more like to you,
More like the loving heart made mine when this
old ring was new.

And blessed be God ! all he has given are with
us yet ; around
Our table every precious life lent to us still is
found.
Though cares we've known, with hopeful hearts
the worst we've struggled through ;
Blessed be his name for all his love since this
old ring was new !

The past is dear, its sweetness still our memo-
ries treasure yet ;
The griefs we've borne, together borne, we would
not now forget.
Whatever, wife, the future brings, heart unto
heart still true,
We'll share as we have shared all else since this
old ring was new.

And if God spare us 'mongst our sons and daugh-
ters to grow old,
We know his goodness will not let your heart
or mine grow cold.

Your aged eyes will see in mine all they 've still
　　shown to you,
And mine in yours all they have seen since this
　　old ring was new.

And O, when death shall come at last to bid me
　　to my rest,
May I die looking in those eyes, and resting on
　　that breast ;
O, may my parting gaze be blessed with the dear
　　sight of you,
Of those fond eyes, — fond as they were when
　　this old ring was new !

WILLIAM COX BENNETT.

MARIE BHAN ASTOR.

"FAIR MARY, MY TREASURE."

I.

In a valley far away
　　With my Maire bhan astór,
Short would be the summer-day,
　　Ever loving more and more ;
Winter days would all grow long,
　　With the light her heart would pour,
With her kisses and her song,
　　And her loving mait go leór.
　　　　Fond is Maire bhan astór,
　　　　Fair is Maire bhan astór,
　　　　Sweet as ripple on the shore,
　　　　Sings my Maire bhan astór.

II.

O, her sire is very proud,
　　And her mother cold as stone ;
But her brother bravely vowed
　　She should be my bride alone ;
For he knew I loved her well,
　　And he knew she loved me too,
So he sought their pride to quell,
　　But 't was all in vain to sue.
　　　　True is Maire bhan astór,
　　　　Tried is Maire bhan astór,
　　　　Had I wings I 'd never soar
　　　　From my Maire bhan astór.

III.

There are lands where manly toil
　　Surely reaps the crop it sows,
Glorious woods and teeming soil,
　　Where the broad Missouri flows ;
Through the trees the smoke shall rise,
　　From our hearth with mait go leór,
There shall shine the happy eyes
　　Of my Maire bhan astór.

Mild is Maire bhan astór,
Mine is Maire bhan astór,
Saints will watch about the door
Of my Maire bhan astór.

THOMAS DAVIS.

ADAM TO EVE.

O fairest of creation, last and best
Of all God's works, creature in whom excelled
Whatever can to sight or thought be formed,
Holy, divine, good, amiable, or sweet !
How art thou lost, how on a sudden lost,
Defaced, deflowered, and now to death devote !
Rather, how hast thou yielded to transgress
The strict forbiddance, how to violate
The sacred fruit forbidden ! Some curséd fraud
Of enemy hath beguiled thee, yet unknown,
And me with thee hath ruined, for with thee
Certain my resolution is to die.
How can I live without thee, how forego
Thy sweet converse, and love so dearly joined,
To live again in these wild woods forlorn ?
Should God create another Eve, and I
Another rib afford, yet loss of thee
Would never from my heart ; no, no, I feel
The link of nature draw me : flesh of flesh,
Bone of my bone thou art, and from thy state
Mine never shall be parted, bliss or woe.

．　　．　　．　　．　　．

However, I with thee have fixed my lot,
Certain to undergo like doom ; if death
Consort with thee, death is to me as life ;
So forcible within my heart I feel
The bond of nature draw me to my own,
My own in thee, for what thou art is mine ;
Our state cannot be severed, we are one,
One flesh ; to lose thee were to lose myself.

MILTON.

PORTIA AND BRUTUS.

FROM " JULIUS CÆSAR."

Portia. Brutus, my lord !
　Brutus. Portia, what mean you ? Wherefore
　　rise you now ?
It is not for your health thus to commit
Your weak condition to the raw-cold morning.
　Por. Nor for yours neither. You have un-
　　gently, Brutus,
Stole from my bed : And yesternight, at supper,
You suddenly arose, and walked about,
Musing, and sighing, with your arms across ;
And when I asked you what the matter was,
You stared upon me with ungentle looks :
I urged you further ; then you scratched your head,

And too impatiently stamped with your foot :
Yet I insisted, yet you answered not ;
But, with an angry wafture of your hand,
Gave sign for me to leave you : So I did ;
Fearing to strengthen that impatience,
Which seemed too much enkindled ; and withal
Hoping it was but an effect of humor,
Which sometime hath his hour with every
   man.
It will not let you eat, nor talk, nor sleep,
And, could it work so much upon your shape,
As it hath much prevailed on your condition,
I should not know you, Brutus. Dear my lord,
Make me acquainted with your cause of grief.
   BRU. I am not well in health, and that is
all.
   POR. Brutus is wise, and were he not in health,
He would embrace the means to come by it.
   BRU. Why, so I do : — good Portia, go to bed.
   POR. Is Brutus sick, — and is it physical
To walk unbraced, and suck up the humors
Of the dank morning ? What, is Brutus sick, —
And will he steal out of his wholesome bed,
To dare the vile contagion of the night,
And tempt the rheumy and unpurgéd air
To add unto his sickness ? No, my Brutus ;
You have some sick offence within your mind,
Which, by the right and virtue of my place,
I ought to know of : And upon my knees
I charm you, by my once commended beauty,
By all your vows of love, and that great vow
Which did incorporate and make us one,
That you unfold to me, yourself, your half,
Why you are heavy ; and what men to-night
Have had resort to you, — for here have been
Some six or seven, who did hide their faces
Even from darkness.
   BRU.   Kneel not, gentle Portia.
   POR. I should not need, if you were gentle
   Brutus.
Within the bond of marriage, tell me, Brutus,
Is it expected, I should know no secrets
That appertain to you ? Am I yourself
But, as it were, in sort or limitation, —
To keep with you at meals, comfort your bed,
And talk to you sometimes ? Dwell I but in the
   suburbs
Of your good pleasure ? If it be no more,
Portia is Brutus' harlot, not his wife.
   BRU. You are my true and honorable wife ;
As dear to me, as are the ruddy drops
That visit my sad heart.
   POR. If this were true, then should I know
   this secret.
I grant I am a woman ; but, withal,
A woman that Lord Brutus took to wife :
I grant I am a woman ; but, withal,
A woman well-reputed, Cato's daughter.

Think you, I am no stronger than my sex,
Being so fathered, and so husbanded ?
Tell me your counsels, I will not disclose them.
                    SHAKESPEARE.

LORD WALTER'S WIFE.

I.

"BUT why do you go ?" said the lady, while both
   saté under the yew,
And her eyes were alive in their depth, as the
   kraken beneath the sea-blue.

II.

"Because I fear you," he answered ; — "because
   you are far too fair,
And able to strangle my soul in a mesh of your
   gold-colored hair."

III.

"O that," she said, "is no reason ! Such knots
   are quickly undone,
And too much beauty, I reckon, is nothing but
   too much sun."

IV.

"Yet farewell so," he answered ; — "the sun-
   stroke 's fatal at times.
I value your husband, Lord Walter, whose gallop
   rings still from the limes."

V.

"O that," she said, "is no reason. You smell
   a rose through a fence :
If two should smell it, what matter ? who grum-
   bles, and where 's the pretence ?"

VI.

"But I," he replied, "have promised another,
   when love was free,
To love her alone, alone, who alone and afar loves
   me."

VII.

"Why, that," she said, "is no reason. Love 's
   always free, I am told.
Will you vow to be safe from the headache on
   Tuesday, and think it will hold ?"

VIII.

"But you," he replied, "have a daughter, a
   young little child, who was laid
In your lap to be pure ; so I leave you : the an-
   gels would make me afraid."

IX.

"O that," she said, "is no reason. The angels
   keep out of the way ;
And Dora, the child, observes nothing, although
   you should please me and stay."

x.

At which he rose up in his anger, — "Why, now,
    you no longer are fair !
Why, now, you no longer are fatal, but ugly and
    hateful, I swear."

XI.

At which she laughed out in her scorn, —"These
    men ! O, these men overnice,
Who are shocked if a color not virtuous is frankly
    put on by a vice."

XII.

Her eyes blazed upon him — "And *you !* You
    bring us your vices so near
That we smell them ! You think in our presence
    a thought 't would defame us to hear !

XIII.

"What reason had you, and what right, — I ap-
    peal to your soul from my life, —
To find me too fair as a woman ? Why, sir, I am
    pure, and a wife.

XIV.

"Is the day-star too fair up above you ? It burns
    you not. Dare you imply
I brushed you more close than the star does, when
    Walter had set me as high ?

XV.

"If a man finds a woman too fair, he means sim-
    ply adapted too much
To uses unlawful and fatal. The praise ! — shall
    I thank you for such ?

XVI.

"Too fair ? — not unless you misuse us ! and surely
    if, once in a while,
You attain to it, straightway you call us no longer
    too fair, but too vile.

XVII.

"A moment, — I pray your attention ! — I have
    a poor word in my head
I must utter, though womanly custom would set
    it down better unsaid.

XVIII.

"You grew, sir, pale to impertinence, once when
    I showed you a ring.
You kissed my fan when I dropped it. No mat-
    ter ! I 've broken the thing.

XIX.

"You did me the honor, perhaps, to be moved at
    my side now and then
In the senses, — a vice, I have heard, which is
    common to beasts and some men.

XX.

"Love 's a virtue for heroes ! — as white as the
    snow on high hills,
And immortal as every great soul is that strug-
    gles, endures, and fulfils.

XXI.

"I love my Walter profoundly, — you, Maude,
    though you faltered a week,
For the sake of . . . what was it ? an eyebrow ? or,
    less still, a mole on a cheek ?

XXII.

"And since, when all 's said, you 're too noble to
    stoop to the frivolous cant
About crimes irresistible, virtues that swindle,
    betray, and supplant,

XXIII.

"I determined to prove to yourself that, whate'er
    you might dream or avow
By illusion, you wanted precisely no more of me
    than you have now.

XXIV.

"There ! Look me full in the face ! — in the face.
    Understand, if you can,
That the eyes of such women as I am are clean
    as the palm of a man.

XXV.

"Drop his hand, you insult him. Avoid us for
    fear we should cost you a scar, —
You take us for harlots, I tell you, and not for
    the women we are.

XXVI.

"You wronged me : but then I considered . . .
    there 's Walter ! And so at the end,
I vowed that he should not be mulcted, by me,
    in the hand of a friend.

XXVII.

"Have I hurt you indeed ? We are quits then.
    Nay, friend of my Walter, be mine !
Come, Dora, my darling, my angel, and help me
    to ask him to dine."

          ELIZABETH BARRETT BROWNING.

THE WELL OF ST. KEYNE.

["In the Parish of St. Neots, Cornwall, is a well, arched over
with the robes of four kinds of trees, — withy, oak, elm, and ash, —
and dedicated to St. Keyne. The reported virtue of the water is
this, that, whether husband or wife first drink thereof, they get the
mastery thereby." — FULLER.]

A WELL there is in the West country,
    And a clearer one never was seen ;
There is not a wife in the West country
    But has heard of the well of St. Keyne.

Home Sweet Home !

'Mid pleasures and palaces though we may roam
Be it ever so humble, there's no place like home !
A charm from the sky seems to hallow us there
Which, seek through the world, is ne'er met with elsewhere !

Home, home, — sweet, sweet home ! —
There's no place like home ! there's no place like home !

John Howard Payne.

The sun is tired with onward flight,
Our ships the tree no eye will miss;
But God will know a little ancle ships
And God his angels out with this

H. H.

[Helen Hunt Jackson.]

An oak and an elm tree stand beside,
  And behind does an ash-tree grow,
And a willow from the bank above
  Droops to the water below.

A traveller came to the well of St. Keyne;
  Pleasant it was to his eye,
For from cock-crow he had been travelling,
  And there was not a cloud in the sky.

He drank of the water so cool and clear,
  For thirsty and hot was he,
And he sat down upon the bank,
  Under the willow-tree.

There came a man from the nighboring town
  At the well to fill his pail,
On the well-side he rested it,
  And bade the stranger hail.

"Now art thou a bachelor, stranger?" quoth he,
  "For an if thou hast a wife,
The happiest draught thou hast drank this day
  That ever thou didst in thy life.

"Or has your good woman, if one you have,
  In Cornwall ever been?
For an if she have, I'll venture my life
  She has drank of the well of St. Keyne."

"I have left a good woman who never was here,"
  The stranger he made reply;
"But that my draught should be better for that,
  I pray you answer me why."

"St. Keyne," quoth the countryman, "many a time
  Drank of this crystal well,
And before the angel summoned her
  She laid on the water a spell.

"If the husband of this gifted well
  Shall drink before his wife,
A happy man thenceforth is he,
  For he shall be master for life.

"But if the wife should drink of it first,
  Heaven help the husband then!"
The stranger stooped to the well of St. Keyne,
  And drank of the waters again.

"You drank of the well, I warrant, betimes?"
  He to the countryman said.
But the countryman smiled as the stranger spake,
  And sheepishly shook his head.

"I hastened, as soon as the wedding was done,
  And left my wife in the porch.
But i' faith, she had been wiser than me,
  For she took a bottle to church."
                                        ROBERT SOUTHEY.

HOME.

HOME, SWEET HOME.

FROM THE OPERA OF "CLARI, THE MAID OF MILAN."

MID pleasures and palaces though we may roam,
Be it ever so humble there's no place like home!
A charm from the skies seems to hallow us here,
Which, seek through the world, is ne'er met with
    elsewhere.
  Home! home! sweet, sweet home!
  There's no place like home!

An exile from home, splendor dazzles in vain!
O, give me my lowly thatched cottage again!
The birds singing gayly that came at my call;—
Give me them! and the peace of mind dearer
    than all!
  Home! home, &c.
                        JOHN HOWARD PAYNE.

GILLE MACHREE.

ENGLISH, — "BRIGHTENER OF MY HEART."

  Gille machree,
    Sit down by me,
  We now are joined and ne'er shall sever;

    This hearth's our own,
    Our hearts are one,
  And peace is ours forever!

    When I was poor,
    Your father's door
  Was closed against your constant lover,
    With care and pain,
    I tried in vain
  My fortunes to recover.
I said, "To other lands I'll roam,
  Where Fate may smile on me, love";
I said, "Farewell, my own old home!"
  And I said, "Farewell to thee, love!"
    Sing *Gille machree,* &c.

    I might have said,
    My mountain maid,
  Come live with me, your own true lover;
    I know a spot,
    A silent cot,
  Your friends can ne'er discover,
Where gently flows the waveless tide
  By one small garden only;

Where the heron waves his wings so wide,
  And the linnet sings so lonely !
    Sing *Gille machree*, &c.

    I might have said,
    My mountain maid,
A father's right was never given
    True hearts to curse
    With tyrant force
That have been blest in heaven.
But then, I said, " In after years,
  When thoughts of home shall find her !
My love may mourn with secret tears
  Her friends thus left behind her."
    Sing *Gille machree*, &c.

    O no, I said,
    My own dear maid,
For me, though all forlorn, forever,
    That heart of thine
    Shall ne'er repine
O'er slighted duty, — never.
From home and thee though wandering far,
  A dreary fate be mine, love ;
I 'd rather live in endless war,
  Than buy my peace with thine, love.
    Sing *Gille machree*, &c.

    Far, far away,
    By night and day,
I toiled to win a golden treasure ;
    And golden gains
    Repaid my pains
In fair and shining measure.
I sought again my native land,
  Thy father welcomed me, love ;
I poured my gold into his hand,
  And my guerdon found in thee, love ;
    Sing *Gille machree*
    Sit down by me,
We now are joined, and ne'er shall sever ;
    This hearth 's our own,
    Our hearts are one,
And peace is ours forever.
             GERALD GRIFFIN.

A WISH.

MINE be a cot beside the hill ;
A bee-hive's hum shall soothe my ear ;
A willowy brook that turns a mill,
With many a fall shall linger near.

The swallow, oft, beneath my thatch
Shall twitter from her clay-built nest ;
Oft shall the pilgrim lift the latch,
And share my meal, a welcome guest.

Around my ivied porch shall spring
Each fragrant flower that drinks the dew ;
And Lucy, at her wheel, shall sing
In russet gown and apron blue.

The village-church among the trees,
Where first our marriage-vows were given,
With merry peals shall swell the breeze
And point with taper spire to heaven.
             SAMUEL ROGERS.

THE QUIET LIFE.

HAPPY the man, whose wish and care
A few paternal acres bound,
Content to breathe his native air
    In his own ground.

Whose herds with milk, whose fields with bread,
Whose flocks supply him with attire ;
Whose trees in summer yield him shade,
    In winter, fire.

Blest, who can unconcern'dly find
Hours, days, and years slide soft away
In health of body, peace of mind,
    Quiet by day,

Sound sleep by night ; study and ease
Together mixed ; sweet recreation,
And innocence, which most does please
    With meditation.

Thus let me live, unseen, unknown ;
Thus unlamented let me die ;
Steal from the world, and not a stone
    Tell where I lie.
            ALEXANDER POPE.

A SONG FOR THE "HEARTH AND HOME."

DARK is the night, and fitful and drearily
  Rushes the wind like the waves of the sea :
Little care I, as here I sit cheerily,
  Wife at my side and my baby on knee.
    King, king, crown me the king :
    Home is the kingdom, and Love is the king !

Flashes the firelight upon the dear faces,
  Dearer and dearer and onward we go,
Forces the shadow behind us, and places
  Brightness around us with warmth in the glow.
    King, king, crown me the king :
    Home is the kingdom, and Love is the king !

Flashes the lovelight, increasing the glory,
  Beaming from bright eyes with warmth of the
    soul,
Telling of trust and content the sweet story,
  Lifting the shadows that over us roll.
    King, king, crown me the king:
    Home is the kingdom, and Love is the king!

Richer than miser with perishing treasure,
  Served with a service no conquest could bring;
Happy with fortune that words cannot measure,
  Light-hearted I on the hearthstone can sing.
    King, king, crown me the king:
    Home is the kingdom, and Love is the king.
        REV. WILLIAM RANKIN DURYEA.

A SHEPHERD'S LIFE.

FROM "THIRD PART OF HENRY VI."

KING HENRY. O God! methinks, it were a
    happy life,
To be no better than a homely swain;
To sit upon a hill, as I do now,
To carve out dials quaintly, point by point,
Thereby to see the minutes how they run;
How many make the hour full complete;
How many hours bring about the day;
How many days will finish up the year;
How many years a mortal man may live.
When this is known, then to divide the times, —
So many hours must I tend my flock;
So many hours must I take my rest;
So many hours must I contemplate;
So many hours must I sport myself;
So many days my ewes have been with young;
So many weeks ere the poor fools will yean;
So many years ere I shall shear the fleece:
So minutes, hours, days, weeks, months, and years,
Passed over to the end they were created,
Would bring white hairs unto a quiet grave.
Ah, what a life were this! how sweet! how lovely!
Gives not the hawthorn bush a sweeter shade
To shepherds, looking on their silly sheep,
Than doth a rich embroidered canopy
To kings that fear their subjects' treachery?
        SHAKESPEARE.

THE MEANS TO ATTAIN HAPPY LIFE.

MARTIAL, the things that do attain
  The happy life be these, I find, —
The riches left, not got with pain;
  The fruitful ground, the quiet mind,

The equal friend; no grudge, no strife;
  No charge of rule, nor governance;

Without disease, the healthful life;
  The household of continuance;

The mean diet, no delicate fare;
  True wisdom joined with simpleness;
The night dischargéd of all care,
  Where wine the wit may not oppress;

The faithful wife, without debate;
  Such sleeps as may beguile the night;
Contented with thine own estate,
  Ne wish for death, ne fear his might.
        LORD SURREY.

THE FIRESIDE.

DEAR Chloe, while the busy crowd,
The vain, the wealthy, and the proud,
  In folly's maze advance;
Though singularity and pride
Be called our choice, we'll step aside,
  Nor join the giddy dance.

From the gay world we'll oft retire
To our own family and fire,
  Where love our hours employs;
No noisy neighbor enters here,
No intermeddling stranger near,
  To spoil our heartfelt joys.

If solid happiness we prize,
Within our breast this jewel lies,
  And they are fools who roam;
The world hath nothing to bestow, —
From our own selves our bliss must flow,
  And that dear hut, our home.

Our portion is not large, indeed;
But then how little do we need,
  For nature's calls are few;
In this the art of living lies,
To want no more than may suffice,
  And make that little do.

We'll therefore relish with content
Whate'er kind Providence has sent,
  Nor aim beyond our power;
For, if our stock be very small,
'T is prudence to enjoy it all,
  Nor lose the present hour.

To be resigned when ills betide,
Patient when favors are denied,
  And pleased with favors given, —
Dear Chloe, this is wisdom's part,
This is that incense of the heart,
  Whose fragrance smells to heaven.
        NATHANIEL COTTON.

A WINTER'S EVENING HYMN TO MY FIRE.

O THOU of home the guardian Lar,
And when our earth hath wandered far
Into the cold, and deep snow covers
The walks of our New England lovers,
Their sweet secluded evening-star !
'T was with thy rays the English Muse
Ripened her mild domestic hues :
'T was by thy flicker that she conned
The fireside wisdom that enrings
With light from heaven familiar things ;
By thee she found the homely faith
In whose mild eyes thy comfort stay'th,
When Death, extinguishing his torch,
Gropes for the latch-string in the porch ;
The love that wanders not beyond
His earliest nest, but sits and sings
While children smooth his patient wings :
Therefore with thee I love to read
Our brave old poets : at thy touch how stirs
Life in the withered words ! how swift recede
Time's shadows ! and how glows again
Through its dead mass the incandescent verse,
As when upon the anvils of the brain
It glittering lay, cyclopically wrought
By the fast-throbbing hammers of the poet's
        thought !
Thou murmurest, too, divinely stirred,
The aspirations unattained,
The rhythms so rathe and delicate,
They bent and strained
And broke, beneath the sombre weight
Of any airiest mortal word.

As who would say, " 'T is those, I ween,
Whom lifelong armor-chafe makes lean
        That win the laurel " ;
While the gray snow-storm, held aloof,
To softest outline rounds the roof,
Or the rude North with baffled strain
Shoulders the frost-starred window-pane !
Now the kind nymph to Bacchus borne
By Morpheus' daughter, she that seems
Gifted upon her natal morn
By him with fire, by her with dreams,
Nicotia, dearer to the Muse
Than all the grapes' bewildering juice,
We worship, unforbid of thee ;
And, as her incense floats and curls
In airy spires and wayward whirls,
Or poises on its tremulous stalk
A flower of frailest revery,
So winds and loiters, idly free,
The current of unguided talk,
Now laughter-rippled, and now caught
In smooth dark pools of deeper thought.

Meanwhile thou mellowest every word,
A sweetly unobtrusive third :
For thou hast magic beyond wine,
To unlock natures each to each ;
The unspoken thought thou canst divine ;
Thou fillest the pauses of the speech
With whispers that to dream-land reach,
And frozen fancy-springs unchain
In Arctic outskirts of the brain ;
Sun of all inmost confidences !
To thy rays doth the heart unclose
Its formal calyx of pretences,
That close against rude day's offences,
And open its shy midnight rose.

                        JAMES RUSSELL LOWELL.

HOMESICK FOR THE COUNTRY.

I 'D kind o' like to have a cot
Fixed on some sunny slope ; a spot
    Five acres more or less,
With maples, cedars, cherry-trees,
And poplars whitening in the breeze.

'T would suit my taste, I guess,
To have the porch with vines o'erhung,
    With bells of pendant woodbine swung,
    In every bell a bee ;
And round my latticed window spread
A clump of roses, white and red.

To solace mine and me,
I kind o' think I should desire
To hear around the lawn a choir
    Of wood-birds singing sweet ;
And in a dell I 'd have a brook,
Where I might sit and read my book.

Such should be my retreat,
Far from the city's crowd and noise :
There would I rear the girls and boys,
    (I have some two or three.)
And if kind Heaven should bless my store
With five or six or seven more,
    How happy I would be !
                        ANONYMOUS.

I KNEW BY THE SMOKE THAT SO GRACEFULLY CURLED.

I KNEW by the smoke that so gracefully curled
    Above the green elms, that a cottage was near,
And I said, " If there 's peace to be found in the
        world,
    A heart that is humble might hope for it here ! "

It was noon, and on flowers that languished around
  In silence reposed the voluptuous bee ;
Every leaf was at rest, and I heard not a sound
  But the woodpecker tapping the hollow beech-
    tree.

And "Here in this lone little wood," I exclaimed,
  "With a maid who was lovely to soul and to
    eye,
Who would blush when I praised her, and weep if
  I blamed,
    How blest could I live, and how calm could I
    die !

" By the shade of yon sumach, whose red berry
  dips
  In the gush of the fountain, how sweet to
    recline,
And to know that I sighed upon innocent lips,
  Which had never been sighed on by any but
    mine !"

                                    THOMAS MOORE.

HOME.

FROM "THE TRAVELLER."

BUT where to find that happiest spot below,
Who can direct, when all pretend to know ?
The shudd'ring tenant of the frigid zone
Boldly proclaims that happiest spot his own ;
Extols the treasures of his stormy seas,
And his long nights of revelry and ease :
The naked negro, panting at the line,
Boasts of his golden sands and palmy wine,
Basks in the glare, or stems the tepid wave,
And thanks his gods for all the good they gave.
Such is the patriot's boast, where'er we roam,
His first, best country, ever is at home.
And yet, perhaps, if countries we compare,
And estimate the blessings which they share,
Though patriots flatter, still shall wisdom find
An equal portion dealt to all mankind ;
As different good, by art or nature given,
To different nations makes their blessing even.
                              OLIVER GOLDSMITH.

THE HOMES OF ENGLAND.

The stately Homes of England,
How beautiful they stand !
Amidst their tall ancestral trees,
O'er all the pleasant land ;
The deer across their greensward bound
Through shade and sunny gleam,
And the swan glides past them with the sound
Of some rejoicing stream.

The merry Homes of England !
Around their hearths by night,
What gladsome looks of household love
Meet in the ruddy light.
There woman's voice flows forth in song,
Or childish tale is told ;
Or lips move tunefully along
Some glorious page of old.

The blessed Homes of England !
How softly on their bowers
Is laid the holy quietness
That breathes from Sabbath hours !
Solemn, yet sweet, the church-bell's chime
Floats through their woods at morn ;
All other sounds, in that still time,
Of breeze and leaf are born.

The cottage Homes of England !
By thousands on her plains,
They are smiling o'er the silvery brooks,
And round the hamlet-fanes.
Through glowing orchards forth they peep,
Each from its nook of leaves ;
And fearless there the lowly sleep,
As the bird beneath their eaves.

The free, fair Homes of England !
Long, long in hut and hall,
May hearts of native proof be reared
To guard each hallowed wall !
And green forever be the groves,
And bright the flowery sod,
Where first the child's glad spirit loves
Its country and its God.
                                MRS. HEMANS.

FILIAL AND FRATERNAL LOVE.

FILIAL LOVE.

FROM "CHILDE HAROLD."

THERE is a dungeon in whose dim drear light
What do I gaze on ? Nothing : look again !
Two forms are slowly shadowed on my sight, —
Two insulated phantoms of the brain :
It is not so ; I see them full and plain, —
An old man and a female young and fair,
Fresh as a nursing mother, in whose vein
The blood is nectar : but what doth she there,
With her unmantled neck, and bosom white and
    bare ?

Full swells the deep pure fountain of young life,
Where *on* the heart and *from* the heart we took
Our first and sweetest nurture, when the wife,
Blest into mother, in the innocent look,
Or even the piping cry of lips that brook
No pain and small suspense, a joy perceives
Man knows not, when from out its cradled nook
She sees her little bud put forth its leaves —
What may the fruit be yet ? I know not — Cain
    was Eve's.

But here youth offers to old age the food,
The milk of his own gift : it is her sire
To whom she renders back the debt of blood
Born with her birth.   No ! he shall not expire
While in those warm and lovely veins the fire
Of health and holy feeling can provide
Great Nature's Nile, whose deep stream rises
    higher
Than Egypt's river ; — from that gentle side
Drink, drink and live, old man ! Heaven's realm
    holds no such tide.

The starry fable of the milky-way
Has not thy story's purity ; it is
A constellation of a sweeter ray,
And sacred Nature triumphs more in this
Reverse of her decree, than in the abyss
Where sparkle distant worlds : — O, holiest
    nurse !
No drop of that clear stream its way shall miss
To thy sire's heart, replenishing its source
With life, as our freed souls rejoin the universe.
                                        BYRON.

———

TO AUGUSTA.

HIS SISTER, AUGUSTA LEIGH.

MY sister ! my sweet sister ! if a name
    Dearer and purer were, it should be thine,

Mountains and seas divide us, but I claim
    No tears, but tenderness to answer mine :
Go where I will, to me thou art the same, —
    A loved regret which I would not resign.
There yet are two things in my destiny, —
A world to roam through, and a home with thee.

The first were nothing, — had I still the last,
    It were the haven of my happiness ;
But other claims and other ties thou hast,
    And mine is not the wish to make them less.
A strange doom is thy father's son's, and past
    Recalling, as it lies beyond redress ;
Reversed for him our grandsire's fate of yore, —
He had no rest at sea, nor I on shore.

If my inheritance of storms hath been
    In other elements, and on the rocks
Of perils, overlooked or unforeseen,
    I have sustained my share of worldly shocks,
The fault was mine ; nor do I seek to screen
    My errors with defensive paradox ;
I have been cunning in mine overthrow,
The careful pilot of my proper woe.

Mine were my faults, and mine be their reward,
    My whole life was a contest, since the day
That gave me being gave me that which marred
    The gift, — a fate, or will, that walked astray :
And I at times have found the struggle hard,
    And thought of shaking off my bonds of clay :
But now I fain would for a time survive,
If but to see what next can well arrive.

Kingdoms and empires in my little day
    I have outlived, and yet I am not old ;
And when I look on this, the petty spray
    Of my own years of trouble, which have rolled
Like a wild bay of breakers, melts away :
    Something — I know not what — does still
        uphold
A spirit of slight patience ; — not in vain,
Even for its own sake, do we purchase pain.

Perhaps the workings of defiance stir
    Within me, — or perhaps of cold despair,
Brought on when ills habitually recur, —
    Perhaps a kinder clime, or purer air,
(For even to this may change of soul refer,
    And with light armor we may learn to bear,)
Have taught me a strange quiet, which was not
The chief companion of a calmer lot.

I feel almost at times as I have felt
  In happy childhood; trees, and flowers, and
      brooks,
Which do remember me of where I dwelt,
  Ere my young mind was sacrificed to books,
Come as of yore upon me, and can melt
  My heart with recognition of their looks;
And even at moments I could think I see
Some living thing to love, — but none like thee.

Here are the Alpine landscapes which create
  A fund for contemplation; — to admire
Is a brief feeling of a trivial date;
  But something worthier do such scenes inspire.
Here to be lonely is not desolate,
  For much I view which I could most desire,
And, above all, a lake I can behold
Lovelier, not dearer, than our own of old.

O that thou wert but with me! — but I grow
  The fool of my own wishes, and forget
The solitude which I have vaunted so
  Has lost its praise in this but one regret;
There may be others which I less may show;
  I am not of the plaintive mood, and yet
I feel an ebb in my philosophy,
And the tide rising in my altered eye.

I did remind thee of our own dear Lake,
  By the old Hall which may be mine no more.
Leman's is fair? but think not I forsake
  The sweet remembrance of a dearer shore;
Sad havoc Time must with my memory make,
  Ere *that* or *thou* can fade these eyes before;
Though, like all things which I have loved, they are
Resigned forever, or divided far.

The world is all before me; I but ask
  Of Nature that with which she will comply, —
It is but in her summer's sun to bask,
  To mingle with the quiet of her sky,
To see her gentle face without a mask,
  And never gaze on it with apathy.
She was my early friend, and now shall be
My sister, — till I look again on thee.

I can reduce all feelings but this one;
  And that I would not; for at length I see
Such scenes as those wherein my life begun.
  The earliest, — even the only paths for me, —
Had I but sooner learnt the crowd to shun,
  I had been better than I now can be;
The passions which have torn me would have slept:
I had not suffered, and *thou* hadst not wept.

With false Ambition what had I to do?
  Little with Love, and least of all with Fame!
And yet they came unsought, and with me grew,
  And made me all which they can make, — a name.

Yet this was not the end I did pursue;
  Surely I once beheld a nobler aim.
But all is over; I am one the more
To baffled millions which have gone before.

And for the future, this world's future may
  From me demand but little of my care;
I have outlived myself by many a day:
  Having survived so many things that were;
My years have been no slumber, but the prey
  Of ceaseless vigils; for I had the share
Of life which might have filled a century,
Before its fourth in time had passed me by.

And for the remnant which may be to come,
  I am content; and for the past I feel
Not thankless, — for within the crowded sum
  Of struggles, happiness at times would steal,
And for the present, I would not benumb
  My feelings farther. — Nor shall I conceal
That with all this I still can look around,
And worship Nature with a thought profound.

For thee, my own sweet sister, in thy heart
  I know myself secure, as thou in mine:
We were and are — I am, even as thou art —
  Beings who ne'er each other can resign;
It is the same, together or apart,
  From life's commencement to its slow decline
We are intwined, — let death come slow or fast,
The tie which bound the first endures the last!
                  BYRON.

BERTHA IN THE LANE.

PUT the broidery-frame away,
  For my sewing is all done!
The last thread is used to-day,
  And I need not join it on.
Though the clock stands at the noon,
  I am weary! I have sewn,
Sweet, for thee, a wedding-gown.

Sister, help me to the bed,
  And stand near me, dearest-sweet!
Do not shrink nor be afraid,
  Blushing with a sudden heat!
No one standeth in the street! —
  By God's love I go to meet,
Love I thee with love complete.

Lean thy face down! drop it in
  These two hands, that I may hold
'Twixt their palms thy cheek and chin,
  Stroking back the curls of gold.
'T is a fair, fair face, in sooth, —
  Larger eyes and redder mouth
Than mine were in my first youth!

Thou art younger by seven years —
　Ah ! so bashful at my gaze
That the lashes, hung with tears,
　Grow too heavy to upraise ?
I would wound thee by no touch
Which thy shyness feels as such, —
Dost thou mind me, dear, so much ?

Have I not been nigh a mother
　To thy sweetness, — tell me, dear ?
Have we not loved one another
　Tenderly, from year to year ?
Since our dying mother mild
Said, with accents undefiled,
" Child, be mother to this child ! "

Mother, mother, up in heaven,
　Stand up on the jasper sea,
And be witness I have given
　All the gifts required of me ; —
Hope that blessed me, bliss that crowned,
Love that left me with a wound,
Life itself, that turned around !

Mother, mother, thou art kind,
　Thou art standing in the room,
In a molten glory shrined,
　That rays off into the gloom !
But thy smile is bright and bleak,
Like cold waves, — I cannot speak ;
I sob in it, and grow weak.

Ghostly mother, keep aloof
　One hour longer from my soul,
For I still am thinking of
　Earth's warm-beating joy and dole !
On my finger is a ring
Which I still see glittering,
When the night hides everything.

Little sister, thou art pale !
　Ah, I have a wandering brain ;
But I lose that fever-bale,
　And my thoughts grow calm again.
Lean down closer, closer still !
I have words thine ear to fill,
And would kiss thee at my will.

Dear, I heard thee in the spring,
　Thee and Robert, through the trees,
When we all went gathering
　Boughs of May-bloom for the bees.
Do not start so ! think instead
How the sunshine overhead
Seemed to trickle through the shade.

What a day it was, that day !
　Hills and vales did openly
Seem to heave and throb away,

At the sight of the great sky ;
And the silence, as it stood
In the glory's golden flood,
Audibly did bud, — and bud !

Through the winding hedge-rows green,
　How we wandered, I and you, —
With the bowery tops shut in,
　And the gates that showed the view ;
How we talked there ! thrushes soft
Sang our pauses out, or oft
Bleatings took them from the croft.

Till the pleasure, grown too strong,
　Left me muter evermore ;
And, the winding road being long,
　I walked out of sight, before ;
And so, wrapt in musings fond,
Issued (past the wayside pond)
On the meadow-lands beyond.

I sat down beneath the beech
　Which leans over to the lane,
And the far sound of your speech
　Did not promise any pain ;
And I blessed you, full and free,
With a smile stooped tenderly
O'er the May-flowers on my knee.

But the sound grew into word
　As the speakers drew more near —
Sweet, forgive me that I heard
　What you wished me not to hear.
Do not weep so, do not shake —
O, I heard thee, Bertha, make
Good true answers for my sake.

Yes, and he too ! let him stand
　In thy thoughts, untouched by blame.
Could he help it, if my hand
　He had claimed with hasty claim !
That was wrong perhaps, but then
Such things be — and will, again !
Women cannot judge for men.

Had he seen thee, when he swore
　He would love but me alone ?
Thou wert absent, — sent before
　To our kin in Sidmouth town.
When he saw thee, who art best
Past compare, and loveliest,
He but judged thee as the rest.

Could we blame him with grave words,
　Thou and I, dear, if we might ?
Thy brown eyes have looks like birds
　Flying straightway to the light ;
Mine are older. — Hush ! — look out —
Up the street ! Is none without ?
How the poplar swings about !

And that hour — beneath the beach —
  When I listened in a dream,
And he said, in his deep speech,
  That he owed me all esteem —
Each word swam in on my brain
With a dim, dilating pain,
Till it burst with that last strain.

I fell flooded with a dark,
  In the silence of a swoon ;
When I rose, still, cold, and stark,
  There was night, — I saw the moon ;
And the stars, each in its place,
And the May-blooms on the grass,
Seemed to wonder what I was.

And I walked as if apart
  From myself when I could stand,
And I pitied my own heart,
  As if I held it in my hand
Somewhat coldly, with a sense
Of fulfilled benevolence,
And a " Poor thing" negligence.

And I answered coldly too,
  When you met me at the door ;
And I only heard the dew
  Dripping from me to the floor ;
And the flowers I bade you see
Were too withered for the bee, —
As my life, henceforth, for me.

Do not weep so — dear — heart-warm !
  It was best as it befell !
If I say he did me harm,
  I speak wild, — I am not well.
All his words were kind and good, —
He esteemed me !   Only blood
Runs so faint in womanhood.

Then I always was too grave,
  Liked the saddest ballads sung,
With that look, besides, we have
  In our faces who die young.
I had died, dear, all the same, —
Life's long, joyous, jostling game
Is too loud for my meek shame.

We are so unlike each other,
  Thou and I, that none could guess
We were children of one mother,
  But for mutual tenderness.
Thou art rose-lined from the cold,
And meant, verily, to hold
Life's pure pleasures manifold.

I am pale as crocus grows
  Close beside a rose-tree's root !
Whosoe'er would reach the rose,
  Treads the crocus underfoot ;

I like May-bloom on thorn-tree,
  Thou like merry summer-bee !
Fit, that I be plucked for thee.

Yet who plucks me ? — no one mourns ;
  I have lived my season out,
And now die of my own thorns,
  Which I could not live without.
Sweet, be merry !   How the light
Comes and goes !   If it be night,
Keep the candles in my sight.

Are there footsteps at the door ?
  Look out quickly.   Yea, or nay ?
Some one might be waiting for
  Some last word that I might say.
Nay ?   So best ! — So angels would
Stand off clear from deathly road,
Not to cross the sight of God.

Colder grow my hands and feet, —
  When I wear the shroud I made,
Let the folds lie straight and neat,
  And the rosemary be spread,
That if any friend should come,
(To see thee, sweet !) all the room
May be lifted out of gloom.

And, dear Bertha, let me keep
  On my hand this little ring,
Which at nights, when others sleep,
  I can still see glittering.
Let me wear it out of sight,
In the grave, — where it will light
All the dark up, day and night.

On that grave drop not a tear !
  Else, though fathom-deep the place,
Through the woollen shroud I wear
  I shall feel it on my face.
Rather smile there, blessed one,
Thinking of me in the sun, —
Or forget me, smiling on !

Art thou near me ? nearer ? so !
  Kiss me close upon the eyes,
That the earthly light may go
  Sweetly as it used to rise,
When I watched the morning gray
Strike, betwixt the hills, the way
He was sure to come that day.

So — no more vain words be said !
  The hosannas nearer roll !
Mother, smile now on thy dead, —
  I am death-strong in my soul !
Mystic Dove alit on cross,
Guide the poor bird of the snows
Through the snow-wind above loss !

Jesus, victim, comprehending
  Love's divine self-abnegation,
Cleanse my love in its self-spending,
  And absorb the poor libation !
Wind my thread of life up higher,
  Up through angels' hands of fire ! —
I aspire while I expire ! —

ELIZABETH BARRETT BROWNING.

HOMESICK.

COME to me, O my Mother ! come to me,
Thine own son slowly dying far away !
Through the moist ways of the wide ocean, blown
By great invisible winds, come stately ships
To this calm bay for quiet anchorage ;
They come, they rest awhile, they go away,
But, O my Mother, never comest thou !
The snow is round thy dwelling, the white snow,
That cold soft revelation pure as light,
And the pine-spire is mystically fringed,
Laced with incrusted silver.   Here — ah me ! —
The winter is decrepit, underborn,
A leper with no power but his disease.
Why am I from thee, Mother, far from thee ?
Far from the frost enchantment, and the woods
Jewelled from bough to bough ? O home, my
    home !
O river in the valley of my home,
With mazy-winding motion intricate,
Twisting thy deathless music underneath
The polished ice-work, — must I nevermore
Behold thee with familiar eyes, and watch
Thy beauty changing with the changeful day,
Thy beauty constant to the constant change ?

DAVID GRAY.

THE ABSENT SOLDIER SON.

FROM "THE ROMAN."

LORD, I am weeping. As Thou wilt, O Lord,
Do with him as Thou wilt ; but O my God,
Let him come back to die ! Let not the fowls
O' the air defile the body of my child,
My own fair child, that when he was a babe,
I lift up in my arms and gave to Thee !
Let not his garment, Lord, be vilely parted,
Nor the fine linen which these hands have spun
Fall to the stranger's lot ! Shall the wild bird,
That would have pilfered of the ox, this year
Disdain the pens and stalls ? Shall her blind
    young,
That on the fleck and moult of brutish beasts
Had been too happy, sleep in cloth of gold
Whereof each thread is to this beating heart

As a peculiar darling ?   Lo, the flies
Hum o'er him ! Lo, a feather from the crow
Falls in his parted lips ! Lo, his dead eyes
See not the raven ! Lo, the worm, the worm
Creeps from his festering corse ! My God ! my
    God !

O Lord, Thou doest well.   I am content.
If Thou have need of him he shall not stay.
But as one calleth to a servant, saying
"At such a time be with me," so, O Lord,
Call him to Thee ! O, bid him not in haste
Straight whence he standeth. Let him lay aside
The soiléd tools of labor.   Let him wash
His hands of blood.   Let him array himself
Meet for his Lord, pure from the sweat and fume
Of corporal travail ! Lord, if he must die,
Let him die here. O, take him where Thou gavest !

And even as once I held him in my womb
Till all things were fulfilled, and he came forth,
So, O Lord, let me hold him in my grave
Till the time come, and Thou, who settest when
The hinds shall calve, ordain a better birth ;
And as I looked and saw my son, and wept
For joy, I look again and see my son,
And weep again for joy of him and Thee !

SIDNEY DOBELL.

THE FAREWELL

OF A VIRGINIA SLAVE MOTHER TO HER DAUGHTERS SOLD INTO SOUTHERN BONDAGE.

GONE, gone, — sold and gone,
  To the rice-swamp dank and lone.
Where the slave-whip ceaseless swings,
Where the noisome insect stings,
Where the fever demon strews
Poison with the falling dews,
Where the sickly sunbeams glare
Through the hot and misty air, —
  Gone, gone, — sold and gone,
  To the rice-swamp dank and lone,
From Virginia's hill and waters, —
Woe is me, my stolen daughters !

Gone, gone, — sold and gone,
  To the rice-swamp dank and lone.
There no mother's eye is near them,
There no mother's ear can hear them ;
Never, when the torturing lash
Seams their back with many a gash,
Shall a mother's kindness bless them,
Or a mother's arms caress them.
  Gone, gone, — sold and gone,
  To the rice-swamp dank and lone,
From Virginia's hills and waters, —
Woe is me, my stolen daughters !

Gone, gone, — sold and gone,
To the rice-swamp dank and lone.
O, when weary, sad, and slow,
From the fields at night they go,
Faint with toil, and racked with pain,
To their cheerless homes again,
There no brother's voice shall greet them, —
There no father's welcome meet them.
    Gone, gone, — sold and gone,
    To the rice-swamp dank and lone,
    From Virginia's hills and waters, —
    Woe is me, my stolen daughters !

Gone, gone, — sold and gone,
To the rice-swamp dank and lone,
From the tree whose shadow lay
On their childhood's place of play, —
From the cool spring where they drank, —
Rock, and hill, and rivulet bank, —
From the solemn house of prayer,
And the holy counsels there, —
    Gone, gone, — sold and gone,
    To the rice-swamp dank and lone,
    From Virginia's hills and waters, —
    Woe is me, my stolen daughters !

Gone, gone, — sold and gone,
To the rice-swamp dank and lone, —
Toiling through the weary day,
And at night the spoiler's prey.
O that they had earlier died,
Sleeping calmly, side by side,
Where the tyrant's power is o'er,
And the fetter galls no more !
    Gone, gone, — sold and gone,
    To the rice-swamp dank and lone,
    From Virginia's hills and waters, —
    Woe is me, my stolen daughters !

Gone, gone, — sold and gone,
To the rice-swamp dank and lone.
By the holy love He beareth, —
By the bruised reed He spareth, —
O, may He, to whom alone
All their cruel wrongs are known,
Still their hope and refuge prove,
With a more than mother's love.
    Gone, gone, — sold and gone,
    To the rice-swamp dank and lone,
    From Virginia's hills and waters, —
    Woe is me, my stolen daughters !
                    JOHN GREENLEAF WHITTIER.

PARTING.

AS SHIPS BECALMED.

As ships becalmed at eve, that lay
    With canvas drooping, side by side,
Two towers of sail, at dawn of day
    Are scarce long leagues apart descried.

When fell the night, up sprang the breeze,
    And all the darkling hours they plied ;
Nor dreamt but each the selfsame seas
    By each was cleaving, side by side :

E'en so — but why the tale reveal
    Of those whom, year by year unchanged,
Brief absence joined anew, to feel,
    Astounded, soul from soul estranged ?

At dead of night their sails were filled,
    And onward each rejoicing steered ;
Ah ! neither blame, for neither willed
    Or wist what first with dawn appeared.

To veer, how vain ! On, onward strain,
    Brave barks ! — in light, in darkness too !
Through winds and tides one compass guides :
    To that and your own selves be true.

But O blithe breeze ! and O great seas !
    Though ne'er that earliest parting past,
On your wide plain they join again,
    Together lead them home at last.

One port, methought, alike they sought, —
    One purpose hold where'er they fare ;
O bounding breeze, O rushing seas,
    At last, at last, unite them there.
                    ARTHUR HUGH CLOUGH.

AE FOND KISS BEFORE WE PART.

Ae fond kiss and then we sever !
Ae fareweel, alas ! forever !
Deep in heart-wrung tears I 'll pledge thee ;
Warring sighs and groans I 'll wage thee.
Who shall say that fortune grieves him,
While the star of hope she leaves him ?
Me, nae cheerfu' twinkle lights me ;
Dark despair around benights me.

I 'll ne'er blame my partial fancy —
Naething could resist my Nancy :
But to see her was to love her,
Love but her, and love forever.

Had we never loved sae kindly,
Had we never loved sae blindly,
Never met — or never parted,
We had ne'er been broken-hearted.

Fare thee weel, thou first and fairest !
Fare thee weel, thou best and dearest !
Thine be ilka joy and treasure,
Peace, enjoyment, love, and pleasure !
Ae fond kiss, and then we sever !
Ae fareweel, alas ! forever !
Deep in heart-wrung tears I 'll pledge thee ;
Warring sighs and groans I 'll wage thee.
ROBERT BURNS.

O MY LUVE'S LIKE A RED, RED ROSE.

O MY Luve 's like a red, red rose
    That 's newly sprung in June :
O my Luve 's like the melodie
    That 's sweetly played in tune.
As fair art thou, my bonnie lass,
    So deep in luve am I :
And I will luve thee still, my dear,
    Till a' the seas gang dry :

Till a' the seas gang dry, my Dear,
    And the rocks melt wi' the sun ;
I will luve thee still, my dear,
    While the sands o' life shall run.
And fare thee weel, my only Luve !
    And fare thee weel awhile !
And I will come again, my Luve,
    Tho' it were ten thousand mile.
ROBERT BURNS.

THE KISS, DEAR MAID.

THE kiss, dear maid ! thy lip has left
    Shall never part from mine,
Till happier hours restore the gift
    Untainted back to thine.

Thy parting glance, which fondly beams,
    An equal love may see :
The tear that from thine eyelid streams
    Can weep no change in me.

I ask no pledge to make me blest
    In gazing when alone ;
Nor one memorial for a breast
    Whose thoughts are all thine own.

Nor need I write — to tell the tale
    My pen were doubly weak :
O, what can idle words avail,
    Unless the heart could speak ?

By day or night, in weal or woe,
    That heart, no longer free,
Must bear the love it cannot show,
    And silent, ache for thee.
BYRON.

MAID OF ATHENS, ERE WE PART.

Ζώη μοῦ σάς ἀγαπῶ.*

MAID of Athens, ere we part,
Give, O give me back my heart !
Or, since that has left my breast,
Keep it now, and take the rest !
Hear my vow before I go,
Ζώη μοῦ σάς ἀγαπῶ.

By those tresses unconfined,
Wooed by each Ægean wind ;
By those lids whose jetty fringe
Kiss thy soft cheeks' blooming tinge ;
By those wild eyes like the roe,
Ζώη μοῦ σάς ἀγαπῶ.

By that lip I long to taste ;
By that zone-encircled waist ;
By all the token-flowers that tell
What words can never speak so well ;
By love's alternate joy and woe,
Ζώη μοῦ σάς ἀγαπῶ.

Maid of Athens ! I am gone.
Think of me, sweet ! when alone.
Though I fly to Istambol,
Athens holds my heart and soul :
Can I cease to love thee ? No !
Ζώη μοῦ σάς ἀγαπῶ.
BYRON.

THE HEATH THIS NIGHT MUST BE MY BED.

SONG OF THE YOUNG HIGHLANDER SUMMONED FROM THE SIDE OF HIS BRIDE BY THE "FIERY CROSS" OF RODERICK DHU.

THE heath this night must be my bed,
The bracken curtain for my head,
My lullaby the warder's tread,
    Far, far from love and thee, Mary ;
To-morrow eve, more stilly laid
My couch may be my bloody plaid,
My vesper song, thy wail, sweet maid !
    It will not waken me, Mary !

I may not, dare not, fancy now
The grief that clouds thy lovely brow,

* My life, I love thee.

I dare not think upon thy vow,
　And all it promised me, Mary.
No fold regret must Norman know ;
When bursts Clan-Alpine on the foe,
His heart must be like bended bow,
　His foot like arrow free, Mary.

A time will come with feeling fraught !
For, if I fall in battle fought,
Thy hapless lover's dying thought
　Shall be a thought on thee, Mary.
And if returned from conquered foes,
How blithely will the evening close,
How sweet the linnet sing repose,
　To my young bride and me, Mary !
　　　　　　　SIR WALTER SCOTT.

　　　　　——◆——

TO LUCASTA,

ON GOING TO THE WARS.

TELL me not, sweet, I am unkinde,
　That from the nunnerie
Of thy chaste breast and quiet minde,
　To warre and armes I flee.

True, a new mistresse now I chase,—
　The first foe in the field ;
And with a stronger faith imbrace
　A sword, a horse, a shield.

Yet this inconstancy is such
　As you, too, should adore ;
I could not love thee, deare, so much,
　Loved I not honor more.
　　　　　　　RICHARD LOVELACE.

　　　　　——◆——

ADIEU, ADIEU ! OUR DREAM OF LOVE—

ADIEU, adieu ! our dream of love
　Was far too sweet to linger long ;
Such hopes may bloom in bowers above,
　But here they mock the fond and young.

We met in hope, we part in tears !
　Yet O, 't is sadly sweet to know
That life, in all its future years,
　Can reach us with no heavier blow !
　　　　　．　　．　　．　　．
The hour is come, the spell is past ;
　Far, far from thee, my only love,
Youth's earliest hope, and manhood's last,
　My darkened spirit turns to rove.

Adieu, adieu ! O, dull and dread
　Sinks on the ear that parting knell !
Hope and the dreams of love lie dead, —
　To them and thee, farewell, farewell !
　　　　　　　THOMAS K. HERVEY.

BLACK-EYED SUSAN.

ALL in the Downs the fleet was moored,
　The streamers waving in the wind,
When black eyed Susan came aboard ;
　"O, where shall I my true-love find ?
Tell me, ye jovial sailors, tell me true
If my sweet William sails among the crew."

William, who high upon the yard
　Rocked with the billow to and fro,
Soon as her well-known voice he heard
　He sighed, and cast his eyes below :
The cord slides swiftly through his glowing hands,
And quick as lightning on the deck he stands.

So the sweet lark, high poised in air,
　Shuts close his pinions to his breast
If chance his mate's shrill call he hear,
　And drops at once into her nest : —
The noblest captain in the British fleet
Might envy William's lip those kisses sweet.

"O Susan, Susan, lovely dear,
　My vows shall ever true remain ;
Let me kiss off that falling tear ;
　We only part to meet again.
Change as ye list, ye winds ; my heart shall be
The faithful compass that still points to thee.

"Believe not what the landmen say
　Who tempt with doubts thy constant mind :
They 'll tell thee sailors, when away,
　In every port a mistress find :
Yes, yes, believe them when they tell thee so,
For Thou art present wheresoe'er I go.

"If to fair India's coast we sail,
　Thy eyes are seen in diamonds bright,
Thy breath is Afric's spicy gale,
　Thy skin is ivory so white.
Thus every beauteous object that I view
Wakes in my soul some charm of lovely Sue.

"Though battle call me from thy arms,
　Let not my pretty Susan mourn ;
Though cannons roar, yet safe from harms
　William shall to his dear return.
Love turns aside the balls that round me fly,
Lest precious tears should drop from Susan's eye."

The boatswain gave the dreadful word,
　The sails their swelling bosom spread ;
No longer must she stay aboard ;
　They kissed, she sighed, he hung his head.
Her lessening boat unwilling rows to land ;
"Adieu !" she cries ; and waved her lily hand.
　　　　　　　JOHN GAY.

PARTING LOVERS.

SIENNA.

I.

I LOVE thee, love thee, Giulio !
 Some call me cold, and some demure,
And if thou hast ever guessed that so
 I love thee . . . well ; — the proof was poor,
 And no one could be sure.

II.

Before thy song (with shifted rhymes
 To suit my name) did I undo
The persian ? If it moved sometimes,
 Thou hast not seen a hand push through
 A flower or two.

III.

My mother listening to my sleep
 Heard nothing but a sigh at night, —
The short sigh rippling on the deep, —
 When hearts run out of breath and sight
 Of men, to God's clear light.

IV.

When others named thee, . . . thought thy brows
 Were straight, thy smile was tender, . . . " Here
He comes between the vineyard-rows !" —
 I said not " Ay," — nor waited, Dear,
 To feel thee step too near.

V.

I left such things to bolder girls,
 Olivia or Clotilda.   Nay,
When that Clotilda through her curls
 Held both thine eyes in hers one day,
 I marvelled, let me say.

VI.

I could not try the woman's trick :
 Between us straightway fell the blush
Which kept me separate, blind, and sick.
 A wind came with thee in a flush,
 As blown through Horeb's bush.

VII.

But now that Italy invokes
 Her young men to go forth and chase
The foe or perish, — nothing chokes
 My voice, or drives me from the place :
 I look thee in the face.

VIII.

I love thee ! it is understood,
 Confest : I do not shrink or start !
No blushes : all my body's blood
 Has gone to greaten this poor heart,
 That, loving, we may part.

IX.

Our Italy invokes the youth.
 To die if need be.   Still there 's room,
Though earth is strained with dead, in truth.
 Since twice the lilies were in bloom
 They have not grudged a tomb.

X.

And many a plighted maid and wife
 And mother, who can say since then
" My country," cannot say through life
 " My son," "my spouse," "my flower of men,"
 And not weep dumb again.

XI.

Heroic males the country bears,
 But daughters give up more than sons.
Flags wave, drums beat, and unawares
 You flash your souls out with the guns,
 And take your heaven at once !

XII.

But _we_, — we empty heart and home
 Of life's life, love ! we bear to think
You 're gone, . . . to feel you may not come, . . .
 To hear the door-latch stir and clink
 Yet no more you, . . . nor sink.

XIII.

Dear God ! when Italy is one
 And perfected from bound to bound, . . .
Suppose (for my share) earth 's undone
 By one grave in 't ! as one small wound
 May kill a man, 't is found !

XIV.

What then ? If love's delight must end,
 At least we 'll clear its truth from flaws.
I love thee, love thee, sweetest friend !
 Now take my sweetest without pause,
 To help the nation's cause.

XV.

And thus of noble Italy
 We 'll both be worthy.   Let her show
The future how we made her free,
 Not sparing life, nor Giulio,
 Nor this . . . this heart-break. Go !
    ELIZABETH BARRETT BROWNING.

———◆———

HERO TO LEANDER.

O, GO not yet, my love,
 The night is dark and vast ;
The white moon is hid in her heaven above,
 And the waves climb high and fast.
O, kiss me, kiss me, once again,
 Lest thy kiss should be the last.

O kiss me ere we part ;
Grow closer to my heart.
My heart is warmer surely than the bosom of the
    main.
O joy ! O bliss of blisses !
    My heart of hearts art thou.
Come, bathe me with thy kisses,
    My eyelids and my brow.
Hark how the wild rain hisses,
    And the loud sea roars below.

Thy heart beats through thy rosy limbs,
    So gladly doth it stir ;
Thine eye in drops of gladness swims.
    I have bathed thee with the pleasant myrrh ;
Thy locks are dripping balm ;
Thou shalt not wander hence to-night,
    I 'll stay thee with my kisses.
To-night the roaring brine
    Will rend thy golden tresses ;
The ocean with the morrow light
    Will be both blue and calm ;
And the billow will embrace thee with a kiss as
    soft as mine.

No Western odors wander
    On the black and moaning sea,
And when thou art dead, Leander,
    My soul must follow thee !
O, go not yet, my love,
    Thy voice is sweet and low ;
The deep salt wave breaks in above
    Those marble steps below.
The turret-stairs are wet
    That lead into the sea.
Leander ! go not yet.
The pleasant stars have set :
O, go not, go not yet,
    Or I will follow thee.
                        ALFRED TENNYSON.

——◆——

THE PARTING LOVERS.

She says, " The cock crows, — hark ! "
He says, " No ! still 't is dark."

She says, " The dawn grows bright,"
He says " O no, my Light."

She says, " Stand up and say,
Gets not the heaven gray ? "

He says, " The morning star
Climbs the horizon's bar."

She says, " Then quick depart :
Alas ! you now must start ;

But give the cock a blow
Who did begin our woe ! "
        ANONYMOUS (Chinese). Translation
        of WILLIAM R. ALGER.

——◆——

THE PARTING OF ROMEO AND JULIET.

JULIET. Wilt thou be gone ? it is not yet near
        day :
It was the nightingale, and not the lark,
That pierced the fearful hollow of thine ear ;
Nightly she sings on yon pomegranate tree :
Believe me, love, it was the nightingale.
    ROMEO. It was the lark, the herald of the
        morn,
No nightingale : look, love, what envious streaks
Do lace the severing clouds in yonder east :
Night's candles are burnt out, and jocund day
Stands tiptoe on the misty mountain tops.
I must be gone and live, or stay and die.
    JULIET. Yon light is not daylight, I know
        it, I :
It is some meteor, that the sun exhales,
To be to thee this night a torch-bearer,
And light thee on thy way to Mantua :
Therefore stay yet, — thou need'st not be gone.
    ROMEO. Let me be ta'en, let me be put to
        death ;
I am content, so thou wilt have it so.
I 'll say, yon gray is not the morning's eye,
'T is but the pale reflex of Cynthia's brow ;
Nor that is not the lark, whose notes do beat
The vaulty heaven so high above our heads :
I have more care to stay than will to go ; —
Come, death, and welcome ! Juliet wills it so. —
How is 't, my soul ? let 's talk, it is not day.
    JULIET. It is, it is, hie hence, be gone, away !
It is the lark that sings so out of tune,
Straining harsh discords, and unpleasing sharps.
Some say, the lark makes sweet division ;
This doth not so, for she divideth us :
Some say, the lark and loathéd toad change
        eyes :
O, now I would they had changed voices too !
Since arm from arm that voice doth us affray,
Hunting thee hence, with hunts-up to the day.
O, now be gone ; more light and light it grows.
    ROMEO. More light and light, — more dark
        and dark our woes.
    JULIET. Then, window, let day in, and let
        life out.
    ROMEO. Farewell, farewell ! one kiss, and I 'll
        descend.   (Descends.)
    JULIET. Art thou gone so ? my love ! my
        lord ! my friend !
I must hear from thee every day i' the hour,
For in a minute there are many days :

Oh ! by this count I shall be much in years,
Ere I again behold my Romeo.
   ROMEO. Farewell ! I will omit no opportunity
That may convey my greetings, love, to thee.
   JULIET. O, think'st thou we shall ever meet
     again ?
   ROMEO. I doubt it not ; and all these woes
     shall serve
For sweet discourses in our time to come.
                     SHAKESPEARE.

AS SLOW OUR SHIP.

As slow our ship her foamy track
  Against the wind was cleaving,
Her trembling pennant still looked back
  To that dear isle 't was leaving.
So loath we part from all we love,
  From all the links that bind us ;
So turn our hearts, as on we rove,
  To those we 've left behind us !

When, round the bowl, of vanished years
  We talk with joyous seeming, —
With smiles that might as well be tears,
  So faint, so sad their beaming ;
While memory brings us back again
  Each early tie that twined us,
O, sweet 's the cup that circles then
  To those we 've left behind us !

And when, in other climes, we meet
  Some isle or vale enchanting,
Where all looks flowery, wild, and sweet,
  And naught but love is wanting ;
We think how great had been our bliss
  If Heaven had but assigned us
To live and die in scenes like this,
  With some we 've left behind us !

As travellers oft look back at eve
  When eastward darkly going,
To gaze upon that light they leave
  Still faint behind them glowing, —
So, when the close of pleasure's day
  To gloom hath near consigned us,
We turn to catch one fading ray
  Of joy that 's left behind us.
                  THOMAS MOORE.

ADIEU, ADIEU ! MY NATIVE SHORE.

ADIEU, adieu ! my native shore
  Fades o'er the waters blue ;
The night-winds sigh, the breakers roar,
  And shrieks the wild sea-mew.

Yon sun that sets upon the sea
  We follow in his flight ;
Farewell awhile to him and thee,
  My native Land — Good Night !

A few short hours, and he will rise
  To give the morrow birth ;
And I shall hail the main and skies,
  But not my mother earth.
Deserted is my own good hall,
  Its hearth is desolate ;
Wild weeds are gathering on the wall ;
  My dog howls at the gate.
                  BYRON.

LOCHABER NO MORE.

FAREWELL to Lochaber ! and farewell, my Jean,
Where heartsome with thee I hae mony day been !
For Lochaber no more, Lochaber no more,
We 'll maybe return to Lochaber no more !
These tears that I shed they are a' for my dear,
And no for the dangers attending on war,
Though borne on rough seas to a far bloody shore,
Maybe to return to Lochaber no more.

Though hurricanes rise, and rise every wind,
They 'll ne'er make a tempest like that in my mind ;
Though loudest of thunder on louder waves roar,
That 's naething like leaving my love on the shore.
To leave thee behind me my heart is sair pained ;
By ease that 's inglorious no fame can be gained ;
And beauty and love 's the reward of the brave,
And I must deserve it before I can crave.

Then glory, my Jeany, maun plead my excuse ;
Since honor commands me, how can I refuse ?
Without it I ne'er can have merit for thee,
And without thy favor I 'd better not be.
I gae then, my lass, to win honor and fame,
And if I should luck to come gloriously hame,
I 'll bring a heart to thee with love running o'er,
And then I 'll leave thee and Lochaber no more.
                  ALLAN RAMSAY.

MY OLD KENTUCKY HOME.

NEGRO SONG.

THE sun shines bright in our old Kentucky home ;
  'T is summer, the darkeys are gay ;
The corn top 's ripe and the meadow 's in the bloom,
  While the birds make music all the day ;
The young folks roll on the little cabin floor,
  All merry, all happy, all bright ;
By 'm by hard times comes a knockin' at the door, —
  Then, my old Kentucky home, good night !

CHORUS.

Weep no more, my lady ; O, weep no more
    to-day !
We 'll sing one song for my old Kentucky
    home,
For our old Kentucky home far away.

They hunt no more for the possum and the coon,
    On the meadow, the hill, and the shore ;
They sing no more by the glimmer of the moon,
    On the bench by the old cabin door ;
The day goes by, like a shadow o'er the heart,
    With sorrow where all was delight ;
The time has come, when the darkeys have to part,
    Then, my old Kentucky home, good night !
        Weep no more, my lady, &c.

The head must bow, and the back will have to bend,
    Wherever the darkey may go ;
A few more days, and the troubles all will end,
    In the field where the sugar-cane grow ;
A few more days to tote the weary load,
    No matter it will never be light ;
A few more days till we totter on the road,
    Then, my old Kentucky home, good night !
        Weep no more, my lady, &c.

ANONYMOUS.

FAREWELL! IF EVER FONDEST PRAYER.

FAREWELL ! if ever fondest prayer
    For other's weal availed on high,
Mine will not all be lost in air,
    But waft thy name beyond the sky.
'T were vain to speak, to weep, to sigh :
    Oh ! more than tears of blood can tell,
When wrung from guilt's expiring eye,
    Are in that word — Farewell ! — Farewell !

These lips are mute, these eyes are dry :
    But in my breast and in my brain
Awake the pangs that pass not by,
    The thought that ne'er shall sleep again.
My soul nor deigns nor dares complain,
    Though grief and passion there rebel :
I only know we loved in vain —
    I only feel — Farewell ! — Farewell !

BYRON.

FARE THEE WELL! AND IF FOREVER.

FARE thee well ! and if forever,
    Still forever, fare thee well ;
Even though unforgiving, never
    'Gainst thee shall my heart rebel.

Would that breast were bared before thee
    Where thy head so oft hath lain,
While that placid sleep came o'er thee
    Which thou ne'er canst know again :

Would that breast, by thee glanced over,
    Every inmost thought could show !
Then thou wouldst at last discover
    'T was not well to spurn it so.

Though the world for this commend thee, —
    Though it smile upon the blow,
Even its praises must offend thee,
    Founded on another's woe :

Though my many faults defaced me,
    Could no other arm be found,
Than the one which once embraced me,
    To inflict a cureless wound ?

Yet, O yet, thyself deceive not :
    Love may sink by slow decay,
But by sudden wrench, believe not
    Hearts can thus be torn away ;

Still thine own its life retaineth, —
    Still must mine, though bleeding, beat ;
And the undying thought which paineth
    Is — that we no more may meet.

These are words of deeper sorrow
    Than the wail above the dead ;
Both shall live, but every morrow
    Wake us from a widowed bed.

And when thou wouldst solace gather,
    When our child's first accents flow,
Wilt thou teach her to say "Father !"
    Though his care she must forego ?

When her little hands shall press thee,
    When her lip to thine is pressed,
Think of him whose prayer shall bless thee,
    Think of him thy love had blessed !

Should her lineaments resemble
    Those thou nevermore mayst see,
Then thy heart will softly tremble
    With a pulse yet true to me.

All my faults perchance thou knowest,
    All my madness none can know ;
All my hopes, where'er thou goest,
    Wither, yet with thee they go.

Every feeling hath been shaken ;
    Pride which not a world could bow,
Bows to thee, — by thee forsaken,
    Even my soul forsakes me now ;

But 't is done ; all words are idle, —
    Words from me are vainer still ;
But the thoughts we cannot bridle
    Force their way without the will.

Fare thee well ! — thus disunited,
  Torn from every nearer tie,
Seared in heart, and lone, and blighted,
  More than this I scarce can die.

BYRON.

WHEN WE TWO PARTED.

WHEN we two parted
In silence and tears,
Half broken-hearted,
To sever for years,
Pale grew thy cheek and cold,
Colder thy kiss :
Truly that hour foretold
Sorrow to this !

The dew of the morning
Sunk chill on my brow ;
It felt like the warning
Of what I feel now.
Thy vows are all broken,
And light is thy fame :
I hear thy name spoken
And share in its shame.

They name thee before me,
A knell to mine ear ;
A shudder comes o'er me —
Why wert thou so dear ?
They know not I knew thee
Who knew thee too well :
Long, long shall I rue thee
Too deeply to tell.

In secret we met :
In silence I grieve
That thy heart could forget,
Thy spirit deceive.
If I should meet thee
After long years,
How should I greet thee ? —
With silence and tears.

BYRON.

COME, LET US KISSE AND PARTE.

SINCE there's no helpe, — come, let us kisse and
    parte,
  Nay, I have done, — you get no more of me ;
And I am glad, — yea, glad with all my hearte,
  That thus so cleanly I myselfe can free.
Shake hands forever ! — cancel all our vows ;
  And when we meet at any time againe,
Be it not seene in either of our brows,
  That we one jot of former love retaine.

Now — at the last gaspe of Love's latest breath —
  When, his pulse failing, Passion speechless lies ;

When Faith is kneeling by his bed of death,
  And Innocence is closing up his eyes,
Now ! if thou wouldst — when all have given
    him over —
  From death to life thou might'st him yet re-
    cover.

MICHAEL DRAYTON.

FAREWELL ! THOU ART TOO DEAR.

FAREWELL ! thou art too dear for my possessing,
And like enough thou know'st thy estimate :
The charter of thy worth gives thee releasing ;
My bonds in thee are all determinate.
For how do I hold thee but by thy granting ?
And for that riches where is my deserving ?
The cause of this fair gift in me is wanting,
And so my patent back again is swerving.
Thyself thou gav'st, thy own worth then not
    knowing,
Or me, to whom thou gav'st it, else mistaking ;
So thy great gift, upon misprision growing,
Comes home again, on better judgment making.
  Thus have I had thee, as a dream doth flatter ;
In sleep a king, but, waking, no such matter.

SHAKESPEARE.

AN EARNEST SUIT

TO HIS UNKIND MISTRESS NOT TO FORSAKE HIM.

AND wilt thou leave me thus ?
Say nay ! say nay ! for shame !
To save thee from the blame
Of all my grief and grame.
And wilt thou leave me thus ?
  Say nay ! say nay !

And wilt thou leave me thus,
That hath loved thee so long,
In wealth and woe among ?
And is thy heart so strong
As for to leave me thus ?
  Say nay ! say nay !

And wilt thou leave me thus,
That hath given thee my heart,
Never for to depart,
Neither for pain nor smart ?
And wilt thou leave me thus ?
  Say nay ! say nay !

And wilt thou leave me thus,
And have no more pity
Of him that loveth thee ?
Alas ! thy cruelty !
And wilt thou leave me thus ?
  Say nay ! say nay !

SIR THOMAS WYAT.

WE PARTED IN SILENCE.

WE parted in silence, we parted by night,
  On the banks of that lonely river;
Where the fragrant limes their boughs unite,
  We met — and we parted forever!
The night-bird sung, and the stars above
  Told many a touching story,
Of friends long passed to the kingdom of love,
Where the soul wears its mantle of glory.

We parted in silence, — our cheeks were wet
  With the tears that were past controlling;
We vowed we would never, no, never forget,
  And those vows at the time were consoling;
But those lips that echoed the sounds of mine
  Are as cold as that lonely river;
And that eye, that beautiful spirit's shrine,
  Has shrouded its fires forever.

And now on the midnight sky I look,
  And my heart grows full of weeping;
Each star is to me a sealéd book,
  Some tale of that loved one keeping.
We parted in silence, — we parted in tears,
  On the banks of that lonely river:
But the odor and bloom of those bygone years
  Shall hang o'er its waters forever.

                              MRS. CRAWFORD.

--◆--

PEACE! WHAT CAN TEARS AVAIL?

PEACE! what can tears avail?
She lies all dumb and pale,
  And from her eye
The spirit of lovely life is fading, —
  And she must die!
Why looks the lover wroth, — the friend upbraid-
    ing?
  Reply, reply!

Hath she not dwelt too long
Midst pain, and grief, and wrong?
  Then why not die?
Why suffer again her doom of sorrow,
  And hopeless lie?
Why nurse the trembling dream until to-morrow?
  Reply, reply!

Death! Take her to thine arms,
In all her stainless charms!
  And with her fly
To heavenly haunts, where, clad in brightness,
  The angels lie!
Wilt bear her there, O death! in all her whiteness?
  Reply, reply!

                              BARRY CORNWALL.

HANG UP HIS HARP; HE'LL WAKE NO MORE!

HIS young bride stood beside his bed,
  Her weeping watch to keep;
Hush! hush! he stirred not, — was he dead,
  Or did he only sleep?

His brow was calm, no change was there,
  No sigh had filled his breath;
O, did he wear that smile so fair
  In slumber or in death?

"Reach down his harp," she wildly cried,
  "And if one spark remain,
Let him but hear 'Loch Erroch's Side";
  He'll kindle at the strain.

"That tune e'er held his soul in thrall;
  It never breathed in vain;
He'll waken as its echoes fall,
  Or never wake again."

The strings were swept. 'T was sad to hear
  Sweet music floating there;
For every note called forth a tear
  Of anguish and despair.

"See! see!" she cried, "the tune is o'er
  No opening eye, no breath;
Hang up his harp; he'll wake no more;
  He sleeps the sleep of death."

                              ELIZA COOK.

--◆--

THE DYING GERTRUDE TO WALDE-GRAVE.

FROM "GERTRUDE OF WYOMING."

CLASP me a little longer on the brink
Of fate! while I can feel thy dear caress;
And when this heart hath ceased to beat, — O,
    think,
And let it mitigate thy woe's excess,
That thou hast been to me all tenderness,
And friend to more than human friendship just.
Oh! by that retrospect of happiness,
And by the hopes of an immortal trust,
God shall assuage thy pangs, when I am laid in
    dust!

Go, Henry, go not back, when I depart,
The scene thy bursting tears too deep will move,
Where my dear father took thee to his heart,
And Gertrude thought it ecstasy to rove
With thee, as with an angel, through the grove
Of peace, imagining her lot was cast
In heaven; for ours was not like earthly love.

And must this parting be our very last ?
No ! I shall love thee still, when death itself is
    past.

Half could I bear, methinks, to leave this
    earth, —
And thee, more loved than aught beneath the sun,
If I had lived to smile but on the birth
Of one dear pledge ; — but shall there then be
    none,
In future time, — no gentle little one,
To clasp thy neck, and look, resembling me ?
Yet seems it, even while life's last pulses run,
A sweetness in the cup of death to be,
Lord of my bosom's love ! to die beholding thee !
                         THOMAS CAMPBELL.

THE MOURNER.

YES ! there are real mourners, — I have seen
A fair sad girl, mild, suffering, and serene ;
Attention (through the day) her duties claimed,
And to be useful as resigned she aimed :
Neatly she drest, nor vainly seemed t' expect
Pity for grief, or pardon for neglect ;
But when her wearied parents sunk to sleep,
She sought her place to meditate and weep ;
Then to her mind was all the past displayed,
That faithful memory brings to sorrow's aid :
For then she thought on one regretted youth,
Her tender trust, and his unquestioned truth ;
In every place she wandered, where they 'd been,
And sadly-sacred held the parting scene,
Where last for sea he took his leave ; that place
With double interest would she nightly trace !
Happy he sailed, and great the care she took,
That he should softly sleep and smartly look ;
White was his better linen, and his check
Was made more trim than any on the deck ;
And every comfort men at sea can know,
Was hers to buy, to make, and to bestow :
For he to Greenland sailed, and much she told,
How he should guard against the climate's cold ;
Yet saw not danger ; dangers he 'd withstood,
Nor could she trace the fever in his blood.
His messmates smiled at flushings on his cheek,
And he too smiled, but seldom would he speak ;
For now he found the danger, felt the pain,
With grievous symptoms he could not explain.
He called his friend, and prefaced with a sigh
A lover's message, — "Thomas, I must die ;
Would I could see my Sally, and could rest
My throbbing temples on her faithful breast,
And gazing go ! — if not, this trifle take,
And say, till death I wore it for her sake :
Yes ! I must die — blow on, sweet breeze, blow
    on,

Give me one look before my life be gone,
Oh ! give me that, and let me not despair,
One last fond look ! — and now repeat the
    prayer."
He had his wish, had more : I will not paint
The lovers' meeting ; she beheld him faint, —
With tender fears, she took a nearer view,
Her terrors doubling as her hopes withdrew ;
He tried to smile ; and, half succeeding, said,
"Yes ! I must die " — and hope forever fled.
Still long she nursed him ; tender thoughts
    meantime
Were interchanged, and hopes and views sublime.
To her he came to die, and every day
She took some portion of the dread away ;
With him she prayed, to him his Bible read,
Soothed the faint heart, and held the aching
    head :
She came with smiles the hour of pain to cheer,
Apart she sighed ; alone, she shed the tear ;
Then, as if breaking from a cloud, she gave
Fresh light, and gilt the prospect of the grave.
One day she lighter seemed, and they forgot
The care, the dread, the anguish of their lot ;
They spoke with cheerfulness, and seemed to
    think,
Yet said not so — "Perhaps he will not sink."
A sudden brightness in his look appeared,
A sudden vigor in his voice was heard ; —
She had been reading in the Book of Prayer,
And led him forth, and placed him in his chair ;
Lively he seemed, and spake of all he knew,
The friendly many, and the favorite few ;
Nor one that day did he to mind recall,
But she has treasured, and she loves them all ;
When in her way she meets them, they appear
Peculiar people, — death has made them dear.
He named his friend, but then his hand she prest,
And fondly whispered, "Thou must go to rest."
"I go," he said ; but as he spoke, she found
His hand more cold, and fluttering was the
    sound ;
Then gazed affrighted ; but she caught a last,
A dying look of love, and all was past !
She placed a decent stone his grave above,
Neatly engraved, — an offering of her love :
For that she wrought, for that forsook her bed,
Awake alike to duty and the dead ;
She would have grieved, had friends presumed to
    spare
The least assistance, — 't was her proper care.
Here will she come, and on the grave will sit,
Folding her arms, in long abstracted fit :
But if observer pass, will take her round,
And careless seem, for she would not be found ;
Then go again, and thus her hours employ,
While visions please her, and while woes destroy.
                         GEORGE CRABBE.

MARINE VIEW.

"Blown out and in by summer gales,
The stately ships, with crowded sails."

ABSENCE.

TO HER ABSENT SAILOR.

FROM "THE TENT ON THE BEACH."

HER window opens to the bay,
On glistening light or misty gray,
And there at dawn and set of day
    In prayer she kneels:
"Dear Lord!" she saith, "to many a home
From wind and wave the wanderers come;
I only see the tossing foam
    Of stranger keels.

"Blown out and in by summer gales,
The stately ships, with crowded sails,
And sailors leaning o'er their rails,
    Before me glide;
They come, they go, but nevermore,
Spice-laden from the Indian shore,
I see his swift-winged Isidore
    The waves divide.

"O thou! with whom the night is day
And one the near and far away,
Look out on yon gray waste, and say
    Where lingers he.
Alive, perchance, on some lone beach
Or thirsty isle beyond the reach
Of man, he hears the mocking speech
    Of wind and sea.

"O dread and cruel deep, reveal
The secret which thy waves conceal,
And, ye wild sea-birds, hither wheel
    And tell your tale.
Let winds that tossed his raven hair
A message from my lost one bear, —
Some thought of me, a last fond prayer
    Or dying wail!

"Come, with your dreariest truth shut out
The fears that haunt me round about;
O God! I cannot bear this doubt
    That stifles breath.
The worst is better than the dread;
Give me but leave to mourn my dead
Asleep in trust and hope, instead
    Of life in death!"

It might have been the evening breeze
That whispered in the garden trees,
It might have been the sound of seas
    That rose and fell;

But, with her heart, if not her ear,
The old loved voice she seemed to hear:
"I wait to meet thee: be of cheer
    For all is well!"
        JOHN GREENLEAF WHITTIER.

TO LUCASTA.

IF to be absent were to be
    Away from thee;
Or that, when I am gone,
    You or I were alone;
Then, my Lucasta, might I crave
Pity from blustering wind or swallowing wave.

But I'll not sigh one blast or gale
    To swell my sail,
Or pay a tear to 'suage
    The foaming blue-god's rage;
For, whether he will let me pass
Or no, I'm still as happy as I was.

Though seas and lands be 'twixt us both,
    Our faith and troth,
Like-separated souls,
    All time and space controls:
Above the highest sphere we meet,
Unseen, unknown; and greet as angels greet.

So, then, we do anticipate
    Our after-fate,
And are alive i' th' skies,
    If thus our lips and eyes
Can speak like spirits unconfined
In heaven, — their earthly bodies left behind.
        COLONEL RICHARD LOVELACE.

OF A' THE AIRTS THE WIND CAN BLAW.

OF a' the airts the wind can blaw,
    I dearly like the west;
For there the bonnie lassie lives,
    The lassie I lo'e best.
There wild woods grow, and rivers row,
    And monie a hill 's between;
But day and night my fancy's flight
    Is ever wi' my Jean.

I see her in the dewy flowers,
    I see her sweet and fair;

I hear her in the tunefu' birds,
  I hear her charm the air ;
There 's not a bonnie flower that springs
  By fountain, shaw, or green, —
There 's not a bonnie bird that sings,
  But minds me of my Jean.

ROBERT BURNS.

LOVE'S MEMORY.

FROM "ALL 'S WELL THAT ENDS WELL."

I AM undone : there is no living, none,
If Bertram be away.   It were all one,
That I should love a bright particular star,
And think to wed it, he is so above me :
In his bright radiance and collateral light
Must I be comforted, not in his sphere.
The ambition in my love thus plagues itself :
The hind that would be mated by the lion
Must die for love.   'T was pretty, though a plague,
To see him ev'ry hour ; to sit and draw
His arched brows, his hawking eye, his curls,
In our heart's table, — heart too capable
Of every line and trick of his sweet favor :
But now he 's gone, and my idolatrous fancy
Must sanctify his relics.

SHAKESPEARE.

THE SUN UPON THE LAKE IS LOW.

THE sun upon the lake is low,
  The wild birds hush their song,
The hills have evening's deepest glow,
  Yet Leonard tarries long.
Now all whom varied toil and care
  From home and love divide,
In the calm sunset may repair
  Each to the loved one's side.

The noble dame on turret high,
  Who waits her gallant knight,
Looks to the western beam to spy
  The flash of armor bright.
The village maid, with hand on brow
  The level ray to shade,
Upon the footpath watches now
  For Colin's darkening plaid.

Now to their mates the wild swans row,
  By day they swam apart,
And to the thicket wanders slow
  The hind beside the hart.
The woodlark at his partner's side
  Twitters his closing song, —
All meet whom day and care divide,
  But Leonard tarries long !

SIR WALTER SCOTT.

O, SAW YE BONNIE LESLEY?

O, SAW ye bonnie Lesley
  As she gaed o'er the border ?
She 's gane, like Alexander,
  To spread her conquests farther.

To see her is to love her,
  And love but her forever ;
For nature made her what she is,
  And ne'er made sic anither !

Thou art a queen, fair Lesley, ~
  Thy subjects we, before thee ;
Thou art divine, fair Lesley,
  The hearts o' men adore thee.

The deil he could na scaith thee,
  Or aught that wad belang thee ;
He 'd look into thy bonnie face,
  And say 'I canna wrang thee !'

The Powers aboon will tent thee ;
  Misfortune sha' na steer thee ;
Thou 'rt like themselves sae lovely
  That ill they 'll ne'er let near thee.

Return again, fair Lesley,
  Return to Caledonie !
That we may brag we hae a lass
  There 's nane again sae bonnie.

ROBERT BURNS.

JEANIE MORRISON.

I 've wandered east, I 've wandered west,
  Through mony a weary way ;
But never, never can forget
  The luve o' life's young day !
The fire that 's blawn on Beltane e'en
  May weel be black gin Yule ;
But blacker fa' awaits the heart
  Where first fond luve grows cule.

O dear, dear Jeanie Morrison,
  The thochts o' bygane years
Still fling their shadows ower my path,
  And blind my een wi' tears :
They blind my een wi' saut, saut tears,
  And sair and sick I pine,
As memory idly summons up
  The blithe blinks o' langsyne.

'T was then we luvit ilk ither weel,
  'T was then we twa did part ;
Sweet time — sad time ! twa bairns at scule,
  Twa bairns, and but ae heart !

'T was then we sat on ae laigh bink,
　To leir ilk ither lear ;
And tones and looks and smiles were shed,
　Remembered evermair.

I wonder, Jeanie, aften yet,
　When sitting on that bink,
Cheek touchin' cheek, loof locked in loof,
　What our wee heads could think.
When baith bent doun ower ae braid page,
　Wi' ae buik on our knee,
Thy lips were on thy lesson, but
　My lesson was in thee.

O, mind ye how we hung our heads,
　How cheeks brent red wi' shame,
Whene'er the scule-weans, laughin', said
　We cleeked thegither hame ?
And mind ye o' the Saturdays,
　(The scule then skail't at noon,)
When we ran off to speel the braes, —
　The broomy braes o' June ?

My head rins round and round about, —
　My heart flows like a sea,
As ane by ane the thochts rush back
　O' scule-time, and o' thee.
O mornin' life ! O mornin' luve !
　O lichtsome days and lang,
When hinnied hopes around our hearts
　Like simmer blossoms sprang !

O, mind ye, luve, how aft we left
　The deavin' dinsome toun,
To wander by the green burnside,
　And hear its waters croon ?
The simmer leaves hung ower our heads,
　The flowers burst round our feet,
And in the gloamin' o' the wood
　The throssil whusslit sweet ;

The throssil whusslit in the wood,
　The burn sang to the trees, —
And we, with nature's heart in tune,
　Concerted harmonies ;
And on the knowe abune the burn
　For hours thegither sat
In the silentness o' joy, till baith
　Wi' very gladness grat.

Ay, ay, dear Jeanie Morrison,
　Tears trickled doun your cheek
Like dew-beads on a rose, yet nane
　Had ony power to speak !
That was a time, a blessed time,
　When hearts were fresh and young,
When freely gushed all feelings forth,
　Unsyllabled — unsung !

I marvel, Jeanie Morrison,
　Gin I hae been to thee
As closely twined wi' earliest thochts
　As ye hae been to me ?
O, tell me gin their music fills
　Thine ear as it does mine !
O, say gin e'er your heart grows grit
　Wi' dreamings o' langsyne ?

I 've wandered east, I 've wandered west,
　I 've borne a weary lot ;
But in my wanderings, far or near,
　Ye never were forgot.
The fount that first burst frae this heart
　Still travels on its way ;
And channels deeper, as it rins,
　The luve o' life's young day.

O dear, dear Jeanie Morrison,
　Since we were sindered young
I 've never seen your face nor heard
　The music o' your tongue ;
But I could hug all wretchedness,
　And happy could I die,
Did I but ken your heart still dreamed
　O' bygone days and me !

WILLIAM MOTHERWELL.

LOVE.

FROM "THE TRIUMPH OF TIME."

THERE lived a singer in France of old
　By the tideless, dolorous, midland sea.
In a land of sand and ruin and gold
　There shone one woman, and none but she.
And finding life for her love's sake fail,
Being fain to see her, he bade set sail,
Touched land, and saw her as life grew cold,
　And praised God, seeing ; and so died he.

Died, praising God for his gift and grace :
　For she bowed down to him weeping, and said,
"Live" ; and her tears were shed on his face
　Or ever the life in his face was shed.
The sharp tears fell through her hair, and stung
Once, and her close lips touched him and clung
Once, and grew one with his lips for a space ;
　And so drew back, and the man was dead.

O brother, the gods were good to you.
　Sleep, and be glad while the world endures.
Be well content as the years wear through ;
　Give thanks for life, and the loves and lures ;
Give thanks for life, O brother, and death,
For the sweet last sound of her feet, her breath,
For gifts she gave you, gracious and few,
　Tears and kisses, that lady of yours.

Rest, and be glad of the gods ; but I,
  How shall I praise them, or how take rest ?
There is not room under all the sky
  For me that know not of worst or best,
Dream or desire of the days before,
Sweet things or bitterness, any more.
Love will not come to me now though I die,
  As love came close to you, breast to breast.

I shall never be friends again with roses ;
  I shall loathe sweet tunes, where a note grown
      strong
Relents and recoils, and climbs and closes,
  As a wave of the sea turned back by song.
There are sounds where the soul's delight takes fire,
Face to face with its own desire ;
A delight that rebels, a desire that reposes ;
  I shall hate sweet music my whole life long.

The pulse of war and passion of wonder,
  The heavens that murmur, the sounds that
      shine,
The stars that sing and the loves that thunder,
  The music burning at heart like wine,
An armed archangel whose hands raise up
All senses mixed in the spirit's cup,
Till flesh and spirit are molten in sunder, —
  These things are over, and no more mine.

These were a part of the playing I heard
  Once, ere my love and my heart were at strife ;
Love that sings and hath wings as a bird,
  Balm of the wound and heft of the knife.
Fairer than earth is the sea, and sleep
Than overwatching of eyes that weep,
Now time has done with his one sweet word,
  The wine and leaven of lovely life.

I shall go my ways, tread out my measure,
  Fill the days of my daily breath
With fugitive things not good to treasure,
  Do as the world doth, say as it saith ;
But if we had loved each other — O sweet,
Had you felt, lying under the palms of your feet,
The heart of my heart, beating harder with pleasure
  To feel you tread it to dust and death —

Ah, had I not taken my life up and given
  All that life gives and the years let go,
The wine and money, the balm and leaven,
  The dreams reared high and the hopes brought
     low,
Come life, come death, not a word be said ;
Should I lose you living, and vex you dead ?
I shall never tell you on earth ; and in heaven,
  If I cry to you then, will you hear or know ?
            ALGERNON CHARLES SWINBURNE.

DAY, IN MELTING PURPLE DYING

DAY, in melting purple dying ;
Blossoms, all around me sighing ;
Fragrance, from the lilies straying ;
Zephyr, with my ringlets playing ;
    Ye but waken my distress ;
    I am sick of loneliness !

Thou, to whom I love to hearken,
Come, ere night around me darken ;
Though thy softness but deceive me,
Say thou 'rt true, and I 'll believe thee ;
    Veil, if ill, thy soul's intent,
    Let me think it innocent !

Save thy toiling, spare thy treasure ;
All I ask is friendship's pleasure ;
Let the shining ore lie darkling, —
Bring no gem in lustre sparkling ;
    Gifts and gold are naught to me,
    I would only look on thee !

Tell to thee the high-wrought feeling,
Ecstasy but in revealing ;
Paint to thee the deep sensation,
Rapture in participation ;
    Yet but torture, if comprest
    In a lone, unfriended breast.

Absent still ! Ah ! come and bless me !
Let these eyes again caress thee.
Once in caution, I could fly thee ;
Now, I nothing could deny thee.
    In a look if death there be,
    Come, and I will gaze on thee !
            MARIA BROOKS

BY THE ALMA RIVER.

WILLIE, fold your little hands ;
  Let it drop, — that "soldier" toy ;
Look where father's picture stands, —
  Father, that here kissed his boy
Not a month since, — father kind,
Who this night may (never mind
Mother's sob, my Willie dear)
Cry out loud that He may hear
Who is God of battles, — cry,
"God keep father safe this day
  By the Alma River !"

Ask no more, child. Never heed
  Either Russ, or Frank, or Turk ;
Right of nations, trampled creed,
  Chance-poised victory's bloody work ;
Any flag i' the wind may roll
On thy heights, Sevastopol !

Willie, all to you and me
Is that spot, whate'er it be,
Where he stands — no other word —
Stands — God sure the child's prayers heard —
 Near the Alma River.

Willie, listen to the bells
 Ringing in the town to-day;
That's for victory. No knell swells
 For the many swept away, —
Hundreds, thousands. Let us weep,
We, who need not, —just to keep
Reason clear in thought and brain
Till the morning comes again;
Till the third dread morning tell
Who they were that fought and —*fell*
 By the Alma River.

Come, — we'll lay us down, my child;
 Poor the bed is, — poor and hard;
But thy father, far exiled,
 Sleeps upon the open sward,
Dreaming of us two at home;
Or, beneath the starry dome,
Digs out trenches in the dark,
Where he buries — Willie, mark! —
Where *he buries* those who died
Fighting — fighting at his side —
 By the Alma River.

Willie, Willie, go to sleep;
 God will help us, O my boy!
He will make the dull hours creep
 Faster, and send news of joy;
When I need not shrink to meet
Those great placards in the street,
That for weeks will ghastly stare
In some eyes — child, say that prayer
Once again, — a different one, —
Say, "O God! Thy will be done
 By the Alma River."

    DINAH MARIA MULOCK.

THE WIFE TO HER HUSBAND.

LINGER not long. Home is not home without thee:
 Its dearest tokens do but make me mourn.
O, let its memory, like a chain about thee,
 Gently compel and hasten thy return!

Linger not long. Though crowds should woo thy
  staying,
 Bethink thee, can the mirth of thy friends,
  though dear,
Compensate for the grief thy long delaying
 Costs the fond heart that sighs to have thee here?

Linger not long. How shall I watch thy coming,
 As evening shadows stretch o'er moor and dell;
When the wild bee hath ceased her busy humming,
 And silence hangs on all things like a spell!

How shall I watch for thee, when fears grow
  stronger,
 As night grows dark and darker on the hill!
How shall I weep, when I can watch no longer!
 Ah! art thou absent, art thou absent still?

Yet I should grieve not, though the eye that seeth
  me
 Gazeth through tears that make its splendor dull;
For oh! I sometimes fear when thou art with me,
 My cup of happiness is all too full.

Haste, haste thee home to thy mountain dwelling,
 Haste, as a bird unto its peaceful nest!
Haste, as a skiff, through tempests wide and
  swelling,
 Flies to its haven of securest rest!

    ANONYMOUS.

ABSENCE.

WHAT shall I do with all the days and hours
 That must be counted ere I see thy face?
How shall I charm the interval that lowers
 Between this time and that sweet time of grace?

Shall I in slumber steep each weary sense, —
 Weary with longing? Shall I flee away
Into past days, and with some fond pretence
 Cheat myself to forget the present day?

Shall love for thee lay on my soul the sin
 Of casting from me God's great gift of time?
Shall I, these mists of memory locked within,
 Leave and forget life's purposes sublime?

O, how or by what means may I contrive
 To bring the hour that brings thee back more
  near?
How may I teach my drooping hope to live
 Until that blessed time, and thou art here?

I'll tell thee; for thy sake I will lay hold
 Of all good aims, and consecrate to thee,
In worthy deeds, each moment that is told
 While thou, beloved one! art far from me.

For thee I will arouse my thoughts to try
 All heavenward flights, all high and holy strains;
For thy dear sake I will walk patiently
 Through these long hours, nor call their min-
  utes pains.

I will this dreary blank of absence make
 A noble task-time; and will therein strive
To follow excellence, and to o'ertake
 More good than I have won since yet I live.

So may this doomed time build up in me
 A thousand graces, which shall thus be thine;
So may my love and longing hallowed be,
 And thy dear thought an influence divine.

    FRANCES ANNE KEMBLE.

DISAPPOINTMENT AND ESTRANGEMENT.

THE COURSE OF TRUE LOVE.

FROM "MIDSUMMER NIGHT'S DREAM."

FOR aught that ever I could read,
Could ever hear by tale or history,
The course of true love never did run smooth:
But, either it was different in blood,
Or else misgrafïëd in respect of years;
Or else it stood upon the choice of friends;
Or, if there were a sympathy in choice,
War, death, or sickness did lay siege to it,
Making it momentary as a sound,
Swift as a shadow, short as any dream;
Brief as the lightning in the collied night,
That, in a spleen, unfolds both heaven and earth,
And ere a man hath power to say, — Behold!
The jaws of darkness do devour it up:
So quick bright things come to confusion.

SHAKESPEARE.

THE BANKS O' DOON.

YE banks and braes o' bonnie Doon,
    How can ye bloom sae fresh and fair?
How can ye chant, ye little birds,
    And I sae weary, fu' o' care?
Thou 'lt break my heart, thou warbling bird,
    That wantons through the flowering thorn;
Thou minds me o' departed joys,
    Departed — never to return.

Aft hae I roved by bonnie Doon,
    To see the rose and woodbine twine;
And ilka bird sang o' its luve,
    And, fondly, sae did I o' mine.
Wi' lightsome heart I pou'd a rose,
    Fu' sweet upon its thorny tree;
And my fause luver stole my rose,
    But ah! he left the thorn wi' me.

ROBERT BURNS.

AULD ROBIN GRAY.

WHEN the sheep are in the fauld, and the kye at
        hame,
And a' the warld to sleep are gane;
The waes o' my heart fa' in showers frae my ee,
When my gudeman lies sound by me.

Young Jamie loo'd me weel, and socht me for his
        bride;
But, saving a croun, he had naething else beside.
To mak that croun a pund, young Jamie gaed to
        sea;
And the croun and the pund were baith for me!

He hadna been awa a week but only twa,
When my mother she fell sick, and the cow was
        stown awa;
My father brak his arm, and young Jamie at the
        sea, —
And auld Robin Gray cam' a-courtin' me.

My father cou'dna work, and my mother cou'dna
        spin;
I toiled day and nicht, but their bread I cou'dna
        win;
Auld Rob maintained them baith, and, wi' tears
        in his ee,
Said, "Jenny, for their sakes, O marry me!"

My heart it said nay, for I looked for Jamie
        back;
But the wind it blew high, and the ship it was a
        wrack;
The ship it was a wrack! Why didna Jamie
        dee?
Or why do I live to say, Wae 's me?

My father argued sair, — my mother didna speak,
But she lookit in my face till my heart was like
        to break;
Sae they gied him my hand, though my heart
        was in the sea;
And auld Robin Gray was gudeman to me.

I hadna been a wife, a week but only four,
When, sitting sae mournfully at the door,
I saw my Jamie's wraith, for I cou'dna think it he,
Till he said, "I 'm come back for to marry thee!"

O sair, sair did we greet, and muckle did we say;
We took but ae kiss, and we tore ourselves away:
I wish I were dead, but I 'm no like to dee;
And why do I live to say, Wae 's me?

I gang like a ghaist, and I carena to spin;
I daurna think on Jamie, for that wad be a sin;
But I 'll do my best a gude wife to be,
For auld Robin Gray is kind unto me.

LADY ANNE BARNARD.

AULD ROB MORRIS.

THERE 's auld Rob Morris that wons in yon glen,
He 's the king o' guid fellows and wale of auld
men :
He has gowd in his coffers, he has owsen and kine,
And ae bonnie lassie, his darling and mine.

She 's fresh as the morning, the fairest in May ;
She 's sweet as the ev'ning amang the new hay ;
As blythe and as artless as the lambs on the lea,
And dear to my heart as the light to my e'e.

But O, she 's an heiress, auld Robin 's a laird,
And my daddie has naught but a cot-house and
yard ;
A wooer like me maunna hope to come speed,
The wounds I must hide that will soon be my
dead.

The day comes to me, but delight brings me
nane :
The night comes to me, but my rest it is gane ;
I wander my lane like a night-troubled ghaist,
And I sigh as my heart it wad burst in my breast.

O, had she but been of a lower degree,
I then might hae hoped she wad smiled upon
me !
O, how past describing had then been my bliss,
As now my distraction no words can express !
ROBERT BURNS.

CLAUDE MELNOTTE'S APOLOGY AND DEFENCE.

PAULINE, by pride
Angels have fallen ere thy time ; by pride, —
That sole alloy of thy most lovely mould —
The evil spirit of a bitter love
And a revengeful heart, had power upon thee.
From my first years my soul was filled with thee ;
I saw thee midst the flowers the lowly boy
Tended, unmarked by thee, — a spirit of bloom,
And joy and freshness, as spring itself
Were made a living thing, and wore thy shape !
I saw thee, and the passionate heart of man
Entered the breast of the wild-dreaming boy ;
And from that hour I grew — what to the last
I shall be — thine adorer ! Well, this love,
Vain, frantic, — guilty, if thou wilt, became
A fountain of ambition and bright hope ;
I thought of tales that by the winter hearth
Old gossips tell, — how maidens sprung from
kings
Have stooped from their high sphere ; how Love,
like Death,
Levels all ranks, and lays the shepherd's crook

Beside the sceptre. Thus I made my home
In the soft palace of a fairy Future !
My father died ; and I, the peasant-born,
Was my own lord. Then did I seek to rise
Out of the prison of my mean estate ;
And, with such jewels as the exploring mind
Brings from the caves of Knowledge, buy my
ransom
From those twin jailers of the daring heart, —
Low birth and iron fortune. Thy bright image,
Glassed in my soul, took all the hues of glory,
And lured me on to those inspiring toils
By which man masters men ! For thee, I grew
A midnight student o'er the dreams of sages !
For thee, I sought to borrow from each Grace
And every Muse such attributes as lend
Ideal charms to Love. I thought of thee,
And passion taught me poesy, — of thee,
And on the painter's canvas grew the life
Of beauty ! — Art became the shadow
Of the dear starlight of thy haunting eyes !
Men called me vain, — some, mad, — I heeded
not ;
But still toiled on, hoped on, — for it was sweet,
If not to win, to feel more worthy, thee !

. . . . .

At last, in one mad hour, I dared to pour
The thoughts that burst their channels into song,
And sent them to thee, — such a tribute, lady,
As beauty rarely scorns, even from the meanest.
The name — appended by the burning heart
That longed to show its idol what bright things
It had created — yea, the enthusiast's name,
That should have been thy triumph, was thy
scorn !
That very hour — when passion, turned to wrath,
Resembled hatred most ; when thy disdain
Made my whole soul a chaos — in that hour
The tempters found me a revengeful tool
For their revenge ! Thou hadst trampled on the
worm, —
It turned, and stung thee !
LORD EDWARD BULWER LYTTON.

LEFT BEHIND.

IT was the autumn of the year ;
The strawberry-leaves were red and sear ;
October's airs were fresh and chill,
When, pausing on the windy hill,
The hill that overlooks the sea,
You talked confidingly to me, —
Me whom your keen, artistic sight
Has not yet learned to read aright,
Since I have veiled my heart from you,
And loved you better than you knew.

You told me of your toilsome past ;
The tardy honors won at last,
The trials borne, the conquests gained,
The longed-for boon of Fame attained ;
I knew that every victory
But lifted you away from me,
That every step of high emprise
But left me lowlier in your eyès ;
I watched the distance as it grew,
And loved you better than you knew.

You did not see the bitter trace
Of anguish sweep across my face ;
You did not hear my proud heart beat,
Heavy and slow, beneath your feet ;
You thought of triumphs still unwon,
Of glorious deeds as yet undone ;
And I, the while you talked to me,
I watched the gulls float lonesomely,
Till lost amid the hungry blue,
And loved you better than you knew.

You walk the sunny side of fate ;
The wise world smiles, and calls you great ;
The golden fruitage of success
Drops at your feet in plenteousness ;
And you have blessings manifold :
Renown and power and friends and gold,
They build a wall between us twain,
Which may not be thrown down again,
Alas ! for I, the long years through,
Have loved you better than you knew.

Your life's proud aim, your art's high truth,
Have kept the promise of your youth ;
And while you won the crown, which now
Breaks into bloom upon your brow,
My soul cried strongly out to you
Across the ocean's yearning blue,
While, unremembered and afar,
I watched you, as I watch a star
Through darkness struggling into view,
And loved you better than you knew.

I used to dream in all these years
Of patient faith and silent tears,
That Love's strong hand would put aside
The barriers of place and pride,
Would reach the pathless darkness through,
And draw me softly up to you ;
But that is past. If you should stray
Beside my grave, some future day,
Perchance the violets o'er my dust
Will half betray their buried trust,
And say, their blue eyes full of dew,
"She loved you better than you knew."

FLORENCE PERCY.

LINDA TO HAFED.

FROM "THE FIRE-WORSHIPPERS."

"How sweetly," said the trembling maid,
Of her own gentle voice afraid,
So long had they in silence stood,
Looking upon that moonlight flood, —
"How sweetly does the moonbeam smile
To-night upon yon leafy isle !
Oft in my fancy's wanderings,
I 've wished that little isle had wings,
And we, within its fairy bowers,
  Were wafted off to seas unknown,
Where not a pulse should beat but ours,
  And we might live, love, die alone !
Far from the cruel and the cold, —
  Where the bright eyes of angels only
Should come around us, to behold
  A paradise so pure and lonely !
Would this be world enough for thee ?" —
Playful she turned, that he might see
  The passing smile her cheek put on ;
But when she marked how mournfully
  His eyes met hers, that smile was gone ;
And, bursting into heartfelt tears,
"Yes, yes," she cried, "my hourly fears,
My dreams, have boded all too right, —
We part — forever part — to-night !
I knew, I knew it *could* not last, —
'T was bright, 't was heavenly, but 'tis past !
O, ever thus, from childhood's hour,
  I 've seen my fondest hopes decay ;
I never loved a tree or flower
  But 't was the first to fade away.
I never nursed a dear gazelle,
  To glad me with its soft black eye,
But when it came to know me well,
  And love me, it was sure to die !
Now, too, the joy most like divine
  Of all I ever dreamt or knew,
To see thee, hear thee, call thee mine, —
  O misery ! must I lose *that* too ?

THOMAS MOORE.

UNREQUITED LOVE.

FROM "TWELFTH NIGHT."

VIOLA. Ay, but I know, —
DUKE. What dost thou know ?
VIOLA. Too well what love women to men may
        owe :
In faith, they are as true of heart as we.
My father had a daughter loved a man,
As it might be, perhaps, were I a woman,
I should your lordship.
DUKE. And what 's her history ?

Eng⁴ by Geo. E. Perine, New York.

FORDS, HOWARD & HULBERT, N.Y.

VIOLA. A blank, my lord. She never told her love,
But let concealment, like a worm i' the bud,
Feed on her damask cheek; she pined in thought;
And, with a green and yellow melancholy,
She sat like Patience on a monument,
Smiling at grief. Was not this love, indeed?
We men may say more, swear more: but, indeed,
Our shows are more than will; for still we prove
Much in our vows, but little in our love.
SHAKESPEARE.

LOCKSLEY HALL.

COMRADES, leave me here a little, while as yet
't is early morn, —
Leave me here, and when you want me, sound
upon the bugle horn.

'T is the place, and all around it, as of old, the
curlews call,
Dreary gleams about the moorland, flying over
Locksley Hall:

Locksley Hall, that in the distance overlooks the
sandy tracts,
And the hollow ocean-ridges roaring into
cataracts.

Many a night from yonder ivied casement, ere I
went to rest,
Did I look on great Orion sloping slowly to the
west.

Many a night I saw the Pleiads, rising through
the mellow shade,
Glitter like a swarm of fire-flies tangled in a silver
braid.

Here about the beach I wandered, nourishing a
youth sublime
With the fairy tales of science, and the long
result of time;

When the centuries behind me like a fruitful
land reposed;
When I clung to all the present for the promise
that it closed;

When I dipt into the future far as human eye
could see, —
Saw the vision of the world, and all the wonder
that would be.

In the spring a fuller crimson comes upon the
robin's breast;
In the spring the wanton lapwing gets himself
another crest;

In the spring a livelier iris changes on the
burnished dove;
In the spring a young man's fancy lightly turns
to thoughts of love.

Then her cheek was pale and thinner than should
be for one so young,
And her eyes on all my motions with a mute
observance hung.

And I said, "My cousin Amy, speak, and speak
the truth to me;
Trust me, cousin, all the current of my being
sets to thee."

On her pallid cheek and forehead came a color
and a light,
As I have seen the rosy red flushing in the
northern night.

And she turned, — her bosom shaken with a
sudden storm of sighs;
All the spirit deeply dawning in the dark of
hazel eyes, —

Saying, "I have hid my feelings, fearing they
should do me wrong";
Saying, "Dost thou love me, cousin?" weeping,
"I have loved thee long."

Love took up the glass of time, and turned it in
his glowing hands;
Every moment, lightly shaken, ran itself in
golden sands.

Love took up the harp of life, and smote on all
the chords with might;
Smote the chord of self, that, trembling, passed
in music out of sight.

Many a morning on the moorland did we hear the
copses ring,
And her whisper thronged my pulses with the
fulness of the spring.

Many an evening by the waters did we watch the
stately ships,
And our spirits rushed together at the touching
of the lips.

O my cousin, shallow-hearted! O my Amy,
mine no more!
O the dreary, dreary moorland! O the barren,
barren shore!

False than all fancy fathoms, false than all songs
have sung, —
Puppet to a father's threat, and servile to a
shrewish tongue!

Is it well to wish thee happy ? — having known
    me ; to decline
On a range of lower feelings and a narrower heart
    than mine !

Yet it shall be : thou shalt lower to his level day
    by day,
What is fine within thee growing coarse to sym-
    pathize with clay.

As the husband is, the wife is ; thou art mated
    with a clown,
And the grossness of his nature will have weight
    to drag thee down.

He will hold thee, when his passion shall have
    spent its novel force,
Something better than his dog, a little dearer than
    his horse.

What is this ? his eyes are heavy, — think not
    they are glazed with wine.
Go to him ; it is thy duty, — kiss him ; take his
    hand in thine.

It may be my lord is weary, that his brain is
    overwrought, —
Soothe him with thy finer fancies, touch him with
    thy lighter thought.

He will answer to the purpose, easy things to un-
    derstand, —
Better thou wert dead before me, though I slew
    thee with my hands.

Better thou and I were lying, hidden from the
    heart's disgrace,
Rolled in one another's arms, and silent in a last
    embrace.

Cursed be the social wants that sin against the
    strength of youth !
Cursed be the social lies that warp us from the
    ' living truth !

Cursed be the sickly forms that err from honest
    nature's rule !
Cursed be the gold that gilds the straitened fore-
    head of the fool !

Well — 't is well that I should bluster ! — Hadst
    thou less unworthy proved,
Would to God — for I had loved thee more than
    ever wife was loved.

Am I mad, that I should cherish that which bears
    but bitter fruit ?
I will pluck it from my bosom, though my heart
    be at the root.

Never ! though my mortal summers to such length
    of years should come
As the many-wintered crow that leads the clang-
    ing rookery home.

Where is comfort ? in division of the records of
    the mind ?
Can I part her from herself, and love her, as I
    knew her, kind ?

I remember one that perished ; sweetly did she
    speak and move ;
Such a one do I remember, whom to look at was
    to love.

Can I think of her as dead, and love her for the
    love she bore ?
No, — she never loved me truly ; love is love for-
    evermore.

Comfort ? comfort scorned of devils ! this is truth
    the poet sings,
That a sorrow's crown of sorrow is remembering
    happier things.

Drug thy memories, lest thou learn it, lest thy
    heart be put to proof,
In the dead, unhappy night, and when the rain
    is on the roof.

Like a dog, he hunts in dreams ; and thou art
    staring at the wall,
Where the dying night-lamp flickers, and the
    shadows rise and fall.

Then a hand shall pass before thee, pointing to
    his drunken sleep,
To thy widowed marriage-pillows, to the tears
    that thou wilt weep.

Thou shalt hear the " Never, never," whispered
    by the phantom years,
And a song from out the distance in the ringing
    of thine ears ;

And an eye shall vex thee, looking ancient kind-
    ness on thy pain.
Turn thee, turn thee on thy pillow ; get thee to
    thy rest again.

Nay, but nature brings thee solace ; for a tender
    voice will cry ;
'T is a purer life than thine, a lip to drain thy
    trouble dry.

Baby lips will laugh me down ; my latest rival
    brings thee rest, —
Baby fingers, waxen touches, press me from the
    mother's breast.

O, the child too clothes the father with a dearness not his due.
Half is thine and half is his : it will be worthy of the two.

O, I see thee old and formal, fitted to thy petty part,
With a little hoard of maxims preaching down a daughter's heart.

"They were dangerous guides the feelings—she herself was not exempt—
Truly, she herself had suffered "— Perish in thy self-contempt !

Overlive it—lower yet—be happy ! wherefore should I care ?
I myself must mix with action, lest I wither by despair.

What is that which I should turn to, lighting upon days like these ?
Every door is barred with gold, and opens but to golden keys.

Every gate is thronged with suitors, all the markets overflow.
I have but an angry fancy : what is that which I should do ?

I had been content to perish, falling on the foeman's ground,
When the ranks are rolled in vapor, and the winds are laid with sound.

But the jingling of the guinea helps the hurt that honor feels,
And the nations do but murmur, snarling at each other's heels.

Can I but relive in sadness ? I will turn that earlier page.
Hide me from my deep emotion, O thou wondrous mother-age !

Make me feel the wild pulsation that I felt before the strife,
When I heard my days before me, and the tumult of my life ;

Yearning for the large excitement that the coming years would yield,
Eager-hearted as a boy when first he leaves his father's field,

And at night along the dusky highway near and nearer drawn,
Sees in heaven the light of London flaring like a dreary dawn ;

And his spirit leaps within him to be gone before him then,
Underneath the light he looks at, in among the throngs of men ;

Men, my brothers, men the workers, ever reaping something new :
That which they have done but earnest of the things that they shall do :

For I dipt into the future, far as human eye could see,
Saw the vision of the world, and all the wonder that would be ;

Saw the heavens fill with commerce, argosies of magic sails,
Pilots of the purple twilight, dropping down with costly bales ;

Heard the heavens fill with shouting, and there rained a ghastly dew
From the nations' airy navies grappling in the central blue ;

Far along the world-wide whisper of the southwind rushing warm,
With the standards of the peoples plunging through the thunder-storm ;

Till the war-drum throbbed no longer, and the battle-flags were furled
In the parliament of man, the federation of the world.

There the common sense of most shall hold a fretful realm in awe,
And the kindly earth shall slumber, lapt in universal law.

So I triumphed ere my passion sweeping through me left me dry,
Left me with the palsied heart, and left me with the jaundiced eye ;

Eye, to which all order festers, all things here are out of joint.
Science moves, but slowly slowly, creeping on from point to point :

Slowly comes a hungry people, as a lion, creeping nigher,
Glares at one that nods and winks behind a slowly dying fire.

Yet I doubt not through the ages one increasing purpose runs,
And the thoughts of men are widened with the process of the suns.

What is that to him that reaps not harvest of his
　　youthful joys,
Though the deep heart of existence beat forever
　　like a boy's?

Knowledge comes, but wisdom lingers; and I
　　linger on the shore,
And the individual withers, and the world is more
　　and more.

Knowledge comes, but wisdom lingers, and he
　　bears a laden breast,
Full of sad experience moving toward the still-
　　ness of his rest.

Hark! my merry comrades call me, sounding on
　　the bugle horn, —
They to whom my foolish passion were a target
　　for their scorn;

Shall it not be scorn to me to harp on such a
　　mouldered string?
I am shamed through all my nature to have loved
　　so slight a thing.

Weakness to be wroth with weakness! woman's
　　pleasure, woman's pain —
Nature made them blinder motions bounded in a
　　shallower brain;

Woman is the lesser man, and all thy passions,
　　matched with mine,
Are as moonlight unto sunlight, and as water
　　unto wine —

Here at least, where nature sickens, nothing.　Ah
　　for some retreat
Deep in yonder shining Orient, where my life
　　began to beat!

Where in wild Mahratta-battle fell my father,
　　evil-starred;
I was left a trampled orphan, and a selfish uncle's
　　ward.

Or to burst all links of habit, — there to wander
　　far away,
On from island unto island at the gateways of the
　　day, —

Larger constellations burning, mellow moons and
　　happy skies,
Breadths of tropic shade and palms in cluster,
　　knots of Paradise.

Never comes the trader, never floats an European
　　flag, —
Slides the bird o'er lustrous woodland, swings the
　　trailer from the crag, —

Droops the heavy-blossomed bower, hangs the
　　heavy-fruited tree, —
Summer isles of Eden lying in dark-purple spheres
　　of sea.

There, methinks, would be enjoyment more than
　　in this march of mind —
In the steamship, in the railway, in the thoughts
　　that shake mankind.

There the passions, cramped no longer, shall have
　　scope and breathing-space;
I will take some savage woman, she shall rear my
　　dusky race.

Iron-jointed, supple-sinewed, they shall dive, and
　　they shall run,
Catch the wild goat by the hair, and hurl their
　　lances in the sun,

Whistle back the parrot's call, and leap the rain-
　　bows of the brooks,
Not with blinded eyesight poring over miserable
　　books —

Fool, again the dream, the fancy! but I know my
　　words are wild,
But I count the gray barbarian lower than the
　　Christian child.

I, to herd with narrow foreheads, vacant of our
　　glorious gains,
Like a beast with lower pleasures, like a beast
　　with lower pains!

Mated with a squalid savage, — what to me were
　　sun or clime?
I, the heir of all the ages, in the foremost files of
　　time, —

I, that rather held it better men should perish
　　one by one,
Than that earth should stand at gaze like Joshua's
　　moon in Ajalon!

Not in vain the distance beacons.　Forward,
　　forward let us range;
Let the great world spin forever down the ring-
　　ing grooves of change.

Through the shadow of the globe we sweep into
　　the younger day:
Better fifty years of Europe than a cycle of
　　Cathay.

Mother-age, (for mine I knew not,) help me as
　　when life begun, —
Rift the hills, and roll the waters, flash the light-
　　nings, weigh the sun, —

O, I see the crescent promise of my spirit hath
   not set ;
Ancient founts of inspiration well through all my
   fancy yet.

Howsoever these things be, a long farewell to
   Locksley Hall !
Now for me the woods may wither, now for me the
   roof-tree fall.

Comes a vapor from the margin, blackening over
   heath and holt,
Cramming all the blast before it, in its breast a
   thunderbolt.

Let it fall on Locksley Hall, with rain or hail, or
   fire or snow ;
For the mighty wind arises, roaring seaward, and
   I go.   ALFRED TENNYSON.

ONLY A WOMAN.

"She loves with love that cannot tire :
  And if, ah, woe ! she loves alone,
Through passionate duty love flames higher,
  As grass grows taller round a stone."
      COVENTRY PATMORE.

So, the truth 's out. I 'll grasp it like a snake, —
It will not slay me. My heart shall not break
Awhile, if only for the children's sake.

For his, too, somewhat. Let him stand unblamed ;
None say, he gave me less than honor claimed,
Except — one trifle scarcely worth being named —

The *heart*. That 's gone. The corrupt dead might
   be
As easily raised up, breathing, — fair to see,
As he could bring his whole heart back to me.

I never sought him in coquettish sport,
Or courted him as silly maidens court,
And wonder when the longed-for prize falls short.

I only loved him, — any woman would :
But shut my love up till he came and sued,
Then poured it o'er his dry life like a flood.

I was so happy I could make him blest ! —
So happy that I was his first and best,
As he mine, — when he took me to his breast.

Ah me ! if only then he had been true !
If for one little year, a month or two,
He had given me love for love, as was my due !

Or had he told me, ere the deed was done,
He only raised me to his heart's dear throne —
Poor substitute — because the queen was gone !

O, had he whispered, when his sweetest kiss
Was warm upon my mouth in fancied bliss,
He had kissed another woman even as this, —

It were less bitter ! Sometimes I could weep
To be thus cheated, like a child asleep ; —
Were not my anguish far too dry and deep.

So I built my house upon another's ground ;
Mocked with a heart just caught at the rebound, —
A cankered thing that looked so firm and sound.

And when that heart grew colder, — colder still,
I, ignorant, tried all duties to fulfil,
Blaming my foolish pain, exacting will,

All, — anything but *him*. It was to be
The full draught others drink up carelessly
Was made this bitter Tantalus-cup for me.

I say again, — he gives me all I claimed,
I and my children never shall be shamed :
He is a just man, — he will live unblamed.

Only — O God, O God, to cry for bread,
And get a stone ! Daily to lay my head
Upon a bosom where the old love 's dead !

Dead ? — Fool ! It never lived. It only stirred
Galvanic, like an hour-cold corpse. None heard :
So let me bury it without a word.

He 'll keep that other woman from my sight.
I know not if her face be foul or bright ;
I only know that it was his delight —

As his was mine ; I only know he stands
Pale, at the touch of their long-severed hands,
Then to a flickering smile his lips commands,

Lest I should grieve, or jealous anger show.
He need not. When the ship 's gone down, I trow,
We little reck whatever wind may blow.

And so my silent moan begins and ends,
No world's laugh or world's taunt, no pity of
   friends
Or sneer of foes, with this my torment blends.

None knows, — none heeds. I have a little pride ;
Enough to stand up, wifelike, by his side,
With the same smile as when I was his bride.

And I shall take his children to my arms ;
They will not miss these fading, worthless charms ;
Their kiss — ah ! unlike his — all pain disarms.

And haply as the solemn years go by,
He will think sometimes, with regretful sigh,
The other woman was less true than I.
      DINAH MARIA MULOCK.

IN A YEAR.

NEVER any more
    While I live,
Need I hope to see his face
    As before.
Once his love grown chill,
    Mine may strive, —
Bitterly we re-embrace,
    Single still.

Was it something said,
    Something done,
Vexed him ? was it touch of hand,
    Turn of head ?
Strange ! that very way
    Love begun.
I as little understand
    Love's decay.

When I sewed or drew,
    I recall
How he looked as if I sang
    — Sweetly too.
If I spoke a word,
    First of all
Up his cheek the color sprang,
    Then he heard.

Sitting by my side,
    At my feet,
So he breathed the air I breathed,
    Satisfied !
I, too, at love's brim
    Touched the sweet.
I would die if death bequeathed
    Sweet to him.

"Speak, — I love thee best ! "
    He exclaimed, —
" Let thy love my own foretell."
    I confessed :
" Clasp my heart on thine
    Now unblamed,
Since upon thy soul as well
    Hangeth mine ! "

Was it wrong to own,
    Being truth ?
Why should all the giving prove
    His alone ?
I had wealth and ease,
    Beauty, youth, —
Since my lover gave me love,
    I gave these.

That was all I meant,
    — To be just,
And the passion I had raised
    To content.

Since he chose to change
    Gold for dust,
If I gave him what he praised,
    Was it strange ?

Would he loved me yet,
    On and on,
While I found some way undreamed,
    — Paid my debt !
Gave more life and more,
    Till, all gone,
He should smile, "She never seemed
    Mine before.

"What — she felt the while,
    Must I think ?
Love 's so different with us men,"
    He should smile.
" Dying for my sake —
    White and pink !
Can't we touch these bubbles then
    But they break ?"

Dear, the pang is brief.
    Do thy part,
Have thy pleasure.   How perplext
    Grows belief !
Well, this cold clay clod
    Was man's heart.
Crumble it, — and what comes next ?
    Is it God ?
                    ROBERT BROWNING.

ENOCH ARDEN AT THE WINDOW.

BUT Enoch yearned to see her face again ;
" If I might look on her sweet face again
And know that she is happy."   So the thought
Haunted and harassed him, and drove him forth
At evening when the dull November day
Was growing duller twilight, to the hill.
There he sat down gazing on all below :
There did a thousand memories roll upon him,
Unspeakable for sadness.   By and by
The ruddy square of comfortable light,
Far-blazing from the rear of Philip's house,
Allured him, as the beacon-blaze allures
The bird of passage, till he madly strikes
Against it, and beats out his weary life.

For Philip's dwelling fronted on the street,
The latest house to landward ; but behind,
With one small gate that opened on the waste,
Flourished a little garden square and walled :
And in it throve an ancient evergreen,
A yewtree, and all round it ran a walk
Of shingle, and a walk divided it :
But Enoch shunned the middle walk and stole

Up by the wall, behind the yew ; and thence
That which he better might have shunned, if griefs
Like his have worse or better, Enoch saw.

For cups and silver on the burnished board
Sparkled and shone ; so genial was the hearth ;
And on the right hand of the hearth he saw
Philip, the slighted suitor of old times,
Stout, rosy, with his babe across his knees ;
And o'er her second father stoopt a girl,
A later but a loftier Annie Lee,
Fair-haired and tall, and from her lifted hand
Dangled a length of ribbon and a ring
To tempt the babe, who reared his creasy arms,
Caught at and ever missed it, and they laughed :
And on the left hand of the hearth he saw
The mother glancing often toward her babe,
But turning now and then to speak with him,
Her son, who stood beside her tall and strong,
And saying that which pleased him, for he smiled.

Now when the dead man come to life beheld
His wife his wife no more, and saw the babe
Hers, yet not his, upon the father's knee,
And all the warmth, the peace, the happiness,
And his own children tall and beautiful,
And him, that other, reigning in his place,
Lord of his rights and of his children's love, —
Then he, though Miriam Lane had told him all,
Because things seen are mightier than things heard,
Staggered and shook, holding the branch, and feared
To send abroad a shrill and terrible cry,
Which in one moment, like the blast of doom,
Would shatter all the happiness of the hearth.

He therefore turning softly like a thief,
Lest the harsh shingle should grate underfoot,
And feeling all along the garden-wall,
Lest he should swoon and tumble and be found,
Crept to the gate, and opened it, and closed,
As lightly as a sick man's chamber-door,
Behind him, and came out upon the waste.

And there he would have knelt, but that his knees
Were feeble, so that falling prone he dug
His fingers into the wet earth, and prayed.
ALFRED TENNYSON.

LOVE'S YOUNG DREAM.

O THE days are gone when beauty bright
    My heart's chain wove !
When my dream of life, from morn till night,
    Was love, still love !

New hope may bloom,
    And days may come,
Of milder, calmer beam,
But there 's nothing half so sweet in life
    As love's young dream !
O, there 's nothing half so sweet in life
    As love's young dream !

Though the bard to purer fame may soar,
    When wild youth 's past ;
Though he win the wise, who frowned before,
    To smile at last ;
    He 'll never meet
    A joy so sweet
In all his noon of fame
As when first he sung to woman's ear
    His soul-felt flame,
And at every close she blushed to hear
    The one loved name !

O, that hallowed form is ne'er forgot,
    Which first love traced ;
Still it lingering haunts the greenest spot
    On memory's waste !
    'T was odor fled
    As soon as shed ;
    'T was morning's winged dream ;
'T was a light that ne'er can shine again
    On life's dull stream !
O, 't was a light that ne'er can shine again
    On life's dull stream !
        THOMAS MOORE ("Irish Melodies").

WHEN THE LAMP IS SHATTERED.

WHEN the lamp is shattered
The light in the dust lies dead ;
When the cloud is scattered,
The rainbow's glory is shed.
When the lute is broken,
Sweet tones are remembered not ;
When the lips have spoken,
Loved accents are soon forgot.

As music and splendor
Survive not the lamp and the lute,
The heart's echoes render
No song when the spirit is mute, —
No song but sad dirges,
Like the wind through a ruined cell,
Or the mournful surges
That ring the dead seaman's knell.

When hearts have once mingled,
Love first leaves the well-built nest ;
The weak one is singled
To endure what it once possesst.

O Love ! who bewailest
The frailty of all things here,
Why choose you the frailest
For your cradle, your home, and your bier ?

Its passions will rock thee
As the storms rock the ravens on high ;
Bright reason will mock thee
Like the sun from a wintry sky.
From thy nest every rafter
Will rot, and thine eagle home
Leave thee naked to laughter,
When leaves fall and cold winds come.

PERCY BYSSHE SHELLEY.

MARY, I BELIEVED THEE TRUE.

MARY, I believed thee true,
   And I was blest in thus believing ;
But now I mourn that e'er I knew
   A girl so fair and so deceiving.
Few have ever loved like me ;
   O, I have loved thee too sincerely !
And few have e'er deceived like thee,
   Alas ! deceived me too severely.
       Fare thee well !

Fare thee well ! yet think awhile
   On one whose bosom seems to doubt thee ;
Who now would rather trust that smile,
   And die with thee than live without thee.
Fare thee well ! I 'll think on thee,
   Thou leav'st me many a bitter token ;
For see, distracting woman, see
   My peace is gone, my heart is broken.
       Fare thee well !

THOMAS MOORE.

HAD I A CAVE.

HAD I a cave on some wild, distant shore,
Where the winds howl to the waves' dashing roar,
   There would I weep my woes,
   There seek my lost repose,
   Till grief my eyes should close,
     Ne'er to wake more !

Falsest of womankind ! canst thou declare
All thy fond-plighted vows, — fleeting as air ?
   To thy new lover hie,
   Laugh o'er thy perjury,
   Then in thy bosom try
     What peace is there !

ROBERT BURNS.

TAKE, O, TAKE THOSE LIPS AWAY.

FROM "MEASURE FOR MEASURE."

TAKE, O, take those lips away,
   That so sweetly were forsworn ;
And those eyes, the break of day,
   Lights that do mislead the morn ;
But my kisses bring again,
Seals of love, but sealed in vain.

Hide, O, hide those hills of snow
   Which thy frozen bosom bears,
On whose tops the pinks that grow
   Are of those that April wears !
But first set my poor heart free,
Bound in those icy chains by thee.

SHAKESPEARE and JOHN FLETCHER.

I LOVED A LASS, A FAIR ONE.

I LOVED a lass, a fair one,
   As fair as e'er was seen ;
She was indeed a rare one,
   Another Sheba Queen ;
But fool as then I was,
   I thought she loved me too,
But now, alas ! sh' 'as left me,
   Falero, lero, loo.

Her hair like gold did glister,
   Each eye was like a star,
She did surpass her sister
   Which past all others far ;
She would me honey call,
   She 'd, O — she 'd kiss me too,
But now, alas ! sh' 'as left me,
   Falero, lero, loo.

In summer time to Medley,
   My love and I would go, —
The boatmen there stood ready
   My love and I to row ;
For cream there would we call,
   For cakes, and for prunes too,
But now, alas ! sh' 'as left me,
   Falero, lero, loo.

Many a merry meeting
   My love and I have had ;
She was my only sweeting,
   She made my heart full glad :
The tears stood in her eyes,
   Like to the morning dew,
But now, alas ! sh' 'as left me,
   Falero, lero, loo.

And as abroad we walked,
   As lovers' fashion is,
Oft as we sweetly talked,
   The sun would steal a kiss;
The wind upon her lips
   Likewise most sweetly blew,
But now, alas! sh' 'as left me,
   Falero, lero, loo.

Her cheeks were like the cherry,
   Her skin as white as snow,
When she was blithe and merry,
   She angel-like did show;
Her waist exceeding small,
   The fives did fit her shoe,
But now, alas! sh' 'as left me,
   Falero, lero, loo.

In summer time or winter,
   She had her heart's desire;
I still did scorn to stint her,
   From sugar, sack, or fire;
The world went round about,
   No cares we ever knew,
But now, alas! sh' 'as left me,
   Falero, lero, loo.

As we walked home together
   At midnight through the town,
To keep away the weather, —
   O'er her I'd cast my gown;
No cold my love should feel,
   Whate'er the heavens could do,
But now, alas! sh' 'as left me,
   Falero, lero, loo.

Like doves we would be billing,
   And clip and kiss so fast,
Yet she would be unwilling
   That I should kiss the last;
They 're Judas kisses now,
   Since that they proved untrue;
For now, alas! sh' 'as left me,
   Falero, lero, loo.

To maiden's vows and swearing,
   Henceforth no credit give,
You may give them the hearing, —
   But never them believe;
They are as false as fair,
   Unconstant, frail, untrue;
For mine, alas! hath left me,
   Falero, lero, loo.

'T was I that paid for all things,
   'T was other drank the wine;
I cannot now recall things,
   Live but a fool to pine:

'T was I that beat the bush,
   The birds to others flew,
For she, alas! hath left me,
   Falero, lero, loo.

If ever that Dame Nature,
   For this false lover's sake,
Another pleasing creature
   Like unto her would make;
Let her remember this,
   To make the other true,
For this, alas! hath left me,
   Falero, lero, loo.

No riches now can raise me,
   No want makes me despair,
No misery amaze me,
   Nor yet for want I care;
I have lost a world itself,
   My earthly heaven, adieu!
Since she, alas! hath left me,
   Falero, lero, loo.
GEORGE WITHER.

WHY SO PALE AND WAN —

WHY so pale and wan, fond lover?
   Pr'y thee, why so pale? —
Will, when looking well can't move her,
   Looking ill prevail?
   Pr'y thee, why so pale?

Why so dull and mute, young sinner?
   Pr'y thee, why so mute?
Will, when speaking well can't win her,
   Saying nothing do 't?
   Pr'y thee, why so mute?

Quit, quit, for shame! this will not move,
   This cannot take her:
If of herself she will not love,
   Nothing can make her:
   The devil take her!
SIR JOHN SUCKLING.

ALAS! HOW LIGHT A CAUSE MAY MOVE —

FROM "THE LIGHT OF THE HAREM."

ALAS! how light a cause may move
Dissension between hearts that love! —
Hearts that the world in vain has tried,
And sorrow but more closely tied;
That stood the storm when waves were rough,
Yet in a sunny hour fall off,
Like ships that have gone down at sea,
When heaven was all tranquillity!

A something light as air, — a look,
  A word unkind or wrongly taken, —
O, love that tempests never shook,
  A breath, a touch like this has shaken !
And ruder words will soon rush in
To spread the breach that words begin ;
And eyes forget the gentle ray
They wore in courtship's smiling day ;
And voices lose the tone that shed
A tenderness round all they said ;
Till fast declining, one by one,
The sweetnesses of love are gone,
And hearts, so lately mingled, seem
Like broken clouds, — or like the stream,
That smiling left the mountain's brow,
  As though its waters ne'er could sever,
Yet, ere it reach the plain below,
  Breaks into floods that part forever.

O you, that have the charge of Love,
  Keep him in rosy bondage bound,
As in the Fields of Bliss above
  He sits, with flowerets fettered round ; —
Loose not a tie that round him clings,
Nor ever let him use his wings ;
For even an hour, a minute's flight
Will rob the plumes of half their light.
Like that celestial bird, — whose nest
  Is found beneath far Eastern skies, —
Whose wings, though radiant when at rest,
  Lose all their glory when he flies !
                              THOMAS MOORE.

AUX ITALIENS.

At Paris it was, at the opera there ;
  And she looked like a queen in a book that
    night,
With the wreath of pearl in her raven hair,
  And the brooch on her breast so bright.

Of all the operas that Verdi wrote,
  The best, to my taste, is the Trovatore ;
And Mario can soothe, with a tenor note,
  The souls in purgatory.

The moon on the tower slept soft as snow ;
  And who was not thrilled in the strangest way,
As we heard him sing, while the gas burned low,
  " Non ti scordar di me ?"

The emperor there, in his box of state,
  Looked grave ; as if he had just then seen
The red flag wave from the city gate,
  Where his eagles in bronze had been.

The empress, too, had a tear in her eye :
  You'd have said that her fancy had gone back
    again,

For one moment, under the old blue sky,
  To the old glad life in Spain.

Well ! there in our front-row box we sat
  Together, my bride betrothed and I ;
My gaze was fixed on my opera hat,
  And hers on the stage hard by.

And both were silent, and both were sad ; —
  Like a queen she leaned on her full white arm,
With that regal, indolent air she had ;
  So confident of her charm !

I have not a doubt she was thinking then
  Of her former lord, good soul that he was,
Who died the richest and roundest of men,
  The Marquis of Carabas.

I hope that, to get to the kingdom of heaven,
  Through a needle's eye he had not to pass ;
I wish him well for the jointure given
  To my lady of Carabas.

Meanwhile, I was thinking of my first love
  As I had not been thinking of aught for years ;
Till over my eyes there began to move
  Something that felt like tears.

I thought of the dress that she wore last time,
  When we stood 'neath the cypress-trees together,
In that lost land, in that soft clime,
  In the crimson evening weather ;

Of that muslin dress (for the eve was hot) ;
  And her warm white neck in its golden chain ;
And her full soft hair, just tied in a knot,
  And falling loose again ;

And the jasmine flower in her fair young breast ;
  (O the faint, sweet smell of that jasmine flower !)
And the one bird singing alone to his nest ;
  And the one star over the tower.

I thought of our little quarrels and strife,
  And the letter that brought me back my ring ;
And it all seemed then, in the waste of life,
  Such a very little thing !

For I thought of her grave below the hill,
  Which the sentinel cypress-tree stands over :
And I thought, "Were she only living still,
  How I could forgive her and love her !"

And I swear, as I thought of her thus, in that hour,
  And of how, after all, old things are best,
That I smelt the smell of that jasmine flower
  Which she used to wear in her breast.

It smelt so faint, and it smelt so sweet,
  It made me creep, and it made me cold !
Like the scent that steals from the crumbling sheet
  Where a mummy is half unrolled.

And I turned and looked : she was sitting there,
In a dim box over the stage ; and drest
In that muslin dress, with that full soft hair,
And that jasmine in her breast !

I was here, and she was there ;
And the glittering horse-shoe curved between :—
From my bride betrothed, with her raven hair
And her sumptuous scornful mien,

To my early love with her eyes downcast,
And over her primrose face the shade,
(In short, from the future back to the past,)
There was but a step to be made.

To my early love from my future bride
One moment I looked. Then I stole to the door,
I traversed the passage ; and down at her side
I was sitting, a moment more.

My thinking of her, or the music's strain,
Or something which never will be exprest,
Had brought her back from the grave again,
With the jasmine in her breast.

She is not dead, and she is not wed !
But she loves me now, and she loved me then !
And the very first word that her sweet lips said,
My heart grew youthful again.

The marchioness there, of Carabas,
She is wealthy, and young, and handsome still ;
And but for her . . . . well, we 'll let that pass ;
She may marry whomever she will.

But I will marry my own first love,
With her primrose face, for old things are best ;
And the flower in her bosom, I prize it above
The brooch in my lady's breast.

The world is filled with folly and sin,
And love must cling where it can, I say :
For beauty is easy enough to win ;
But one is n't loved every day.

And I think, in the lives of most women and men,
There 's a moment when all would go smooth
and even,
If only the dead could find out when
To come back and be forgiven.

But O the smell of that jasmine flower !
And O that music ! and O the way
That voice rang out from the donjon tower,
Non ti scordar di me,
Non ti scordar di me !

ROBERT BULWER LYTTON.

TRANSIENT BEAUTY.

THE GIAOUR.

As, rising on its purple wing,
The insect-queen of Eastern spring,
O'er emerald meadows of Kashmeer,
Invites the young pursuer near,
And leads him on from flower to flower,
A weary chase and wasted hour,
Then leaves him, as it soars on high,
With panting heart and tearful eye ;
So Beauty lures the full-grown child,
With hue as bright, and wind as wild ;
A chase of idle hopes and fears,
Begun in folly, closed in tears.
If won, to equal ills betrayed,
Woe waits the insect and the maid :
A life of pain, the loss of peace,
From infant's play and man's caprice ;
The lovely toy, so fiercely sought,
Hath lost its charm by being caught ;
For every touch that wooed its stay
Hath brushed its brightest hues away,
Till, charm and hue and beauty gone,
'T is left to fly or fall alone.
With wounded wing or bleeding breast,
Ah ! where shall either victim rest ?
Can this with faded pinion soar
From rose to tulip as before ?
Or Beauty, blighted in an hour,
Find joy within her broken bower ?
No ; gayer insects fluttering by
Ne'er droop the wing o'er those that die,
And lovelier things have mercy shown
To every failing but their own,
And every woe a tear can claim,
Except an erring sister's shame.

BYRON.

WOMAN'S INCONSTANCY.

I LOVED thee once, I 'll love no more,
Thine be the grief as is the blame ;
Thou art not what thou wast before,
What reason I should be the same ?
He that can love unloved again,
Hath better store of love than brain :
God send me love my debts to pay,
While unthrifts fool their love away.

Nothing could have my love o'erthrown,
If thou hadst still continued mine ;
Yea, if thou hadst remained thy own,
I might perchance have yet been thine.
But thou thy freedom did recall,
That if thou might elsewhere inthrall ;
And then how could I but disdain
A captive's captive to remain ?

When new desires had conquered thee,
    And changed the object of thy will,
It had been lethargy in me,
    Not constancy, to love thee still.
        Yea, it had been a sin to go
        And prostitute affection so,
Since we are taught no prayers to say
To such as must to others pray.

Yet do thou glory in thy choice,
    Thy choice of his good fortune boast ;
I\'ll neither grieve nor yet rejoice,
    To see him gain what I have lost ;
        The height of my disdain shall be,
        To laugh at him, to blush for thee ;
To love thee still, but go no more
A begging to a beggar's door.

SIR ROBERT AYTON.

THE ORIGIN OF THE HARP.

'T IS believed that this harp which I wake now
        for thee
Was a siren of old who sung under the sea ;
And who often at eve through the bright billow
        roved
To meet on the green shore a youth whom she loved.

But she loved him in vain, for he left her to weep,
And in tears all the night her gold ringlets to
        steep,
Till Heaven looked with pity on true love so warm,
And changed to this soft harp the sea-maiden's
        form !

Still her bosom rose fair — still her cheek smiled
        the same —
While her sea-beauties gracefully curled round
        the frame ;
And her hair, shedding tear-drops from all its
        bright rings,
Fell over her white arm, to make the gold strings !

Hence it came that this soft harp so long hath
        been known
To mingle love's language with sorrow's sad tone ;
Till *thou* didst divide them, and teach the fond lay
To be love when I 'm near thee and grief when away !

THOMAS MOORE (" *Irish Melodies* ").

WHERE SHALL THE LOVER REST?

    WHERE shall the lover rest
      Whom the fates sever
    From his true maiden's breast
      Parted forever ?

Where, through groves deep and high
    Sounds the far billow,
Where early violets die
    Under the willow.
        Eleu loro
Soft shall be his pillow.

There, through the summer day
    Cool streams are laving :
There, while the tempests sway,
    Scarce are boughs waving ;
There thy rest shalt thou take,
    Parted forever,
Never again to wake
    Never, O never !
        Eleu loro
    Never, O never !

Where shall the traitor rest,
    He, the deceiver,
Who could win maiden's breast,
    Ruin, and leave her ?
In the lost battle,
    Borne down by the flying,
Where mingles war's rattle
    With groans of the dying ;
        Eleu loro
There shall he be lying.

Her wing shall the eagle flap
    O'er the false-hearted ;
His warm blood the wolf shall lap
    Ere life be parted :
Shame and dishonor sit
    By his grave ever ;
Blessing shall hallow it
    Never, O never !
        Eleu loro
    Never, O never !

SIR WALTER SCOTT.

THE MOTHER'S LAST SONG.

SLEEP ! — The ghostly winds are blowing !
No moon abroad, no star is glowing ;
The river is deep, and the tide is flowing
To the land where you and I are going !
        We are going afar,
        Beyond moon or star,
To the land where the sinless angels are !

I lost my heart to your heartless sire
('T was melted away by his looks of fire),
Forgot my God, and my father's ire,
All for the sake of a man's desire ;
        But now we 'll go
        Where the waters flow,
And make us a bed where none shall know.

The world is cruel, the world is untrue ;
Our foes are many, our friends are few ;
No work, no bread, however we sue !
What is there left for me to do,
    But fly, — fly
    From the cruel sky,
And hide in the deepest deeps, — and die ?
            BARRY CORNWALL.

WALY, WALY, BUT LOVE BE BONNY.

O, WALY, waly up the bank,
  And waly, waly down the brae,
And waly, waly yon burn side,
  Where I and my love wont to gae.

I leaned my back unto an aik,
  I thought it was a trusty tree ;
But first it bowed, and syne it brak —
  Sae my true love did lightly me !

O, waly, waly, but love be bonny,
  A little time while it is new ;
But when 't is auld it waxeth cauld,
  And fades away like the morning dew.

O, wherefore should I busk my head ?
  Or wherefore should I kame my hair ?
For my true love has me forsook,
  And says he 'll never love me mair.

Now Arthur-Seat shall be my bed ;
  The sheets shall ne'er be fyled by me ;
Saint Anton's well shall be my drink,
  Since my true love has forsaken me.

Martinmas wind, when wilt thou blaw,
  And shake the green leaves off the tree ?
O gentle death, when wilt thou come ?
  For of my life I 'm weary.

'T is not the frost that freezes fell,
  Nor blawing snaw's inclemency ;
'T is not sic cauld that makes me cry,
  But my love 's heart grown cauld to me.

When we came in by Glasgow town,
  We were a comely sight to see ;
My love was clad in the black velvet,
  And I my sell in cramasie.

But had I wist, before I kissed,
  That love had been sae ill to win,
I 'd locked my heart in a case of gold,
  And pinned it with a silver pin.

O, O, if my young babe were born,
  And set upon the nurse's knee,
And I my sell were dead and gane,
  And the green grass growin' over me !
            ANONYMOUS.

LADY ANN BOTHWELL'S LAMENT.

A SCOTTISH SONG.

BALOW, my babe, ly stil and sleipe !
It grieves me sair to see thee weipe ;
If thou 'st be silent, I 'se be glad,
Thy maining maks my heart ful sad.
Balow, my boy, thy mither's joy !
Thy father breides me great annoy.
    Balow, my babe, ly stil and sleipe !
    It grieves me sair to see thee weipe.

When he began to court my luve,
And with his sugred words to muve,
His faynings fals, and flattering cheire,
To me that time did not appeire :
But now I see, most cruell hee,
Cares neither for my babe nor mee.
    Balow, my babe, ly stil and sleipe !
    It grieves me sair to see thee weipe.

Ly stil, my darlinge, sleipe awhile,
And when thou wakest sweitly smile :
But smile not, as thy father did,
To cozen maids ; nay, God forbid !
But yette I feire, thou wilt gae neire,
Thy fatheris hart and face to beire.
    Balow, my babe, ly stil and sleipe !
    It grieves me sair to see thee weipe.

I cannae chuse, but ever will
Be luving to thy father stil :
Whair-eir he gae, whair-eir he ryde,
My luve with him maun stil abyde :
In weil or wae, whair-eir he gae,
Mine hart can neir depart him frae.
    Balow, my babe, ly stil and sleipe !
    It grieves me sair to see thee weipe.

But doe not, doe not, prettie mine,
To faynings fals thine hart incline ;
Be loyal to thy luver trew,
And nevir change hir for a new ;
If gude or faire, of hir have care,
For women's banning's wonderous sair.
    Balow, my babe, ly stil and sleipe !
    It grieves me sair to see thee weipe.

Bairne, sin thy cruel father is gane,
Thy winsome smiles maun eise my paine ;
My babe and I 'll together live,
He 'll comfort me when cares doe grieve ;
My babe and I right saft will ly,
And quite forget man's cruelty.
    Balow, my babe, ly stil and sleipe !
    It grieves me sair to see thee weipe.

Farweil, farweil, thou falsest youth
That ever kist a woman's mouth !

I wish all maids be warned by mee,
Nevir to trust man's curtesy ;
For if we doe but chance to bow,
They 'll use us than they care not how.
    Balow, my babe, ly stil and sleipe !
    It grieves me sair to see thee weipe.
                ANONYMOUS.

MY HEID IS LIKE TO REND, WILLIE.

My heid is like to rend, Willie,
  My heart is like to break ;
I 'm wearin' aff my feet, Willie,
  I 'm dyin' for your sake !
O, lay your cheek to mine, Willie,
  Your hand on my briest-bane, —
O, say ye 'll think on me, Willie,
  When I am deid and gane !

It 's vain to comfort me, Willie,
  Sair grief maun ha'e its will ;
But let me rest upon your briest
  To sab and greet my fill.
Let me sit on your knee, Willie,
  Let me shed by your hair,
And look into the face, Willie,
  I never sall see mair !

I 'm sittin' on your knee, Willie,
  For the last time in my life, —
A puir heart-broken thing, Willie,
  A mither, yet nae wife.
Ay, press your hand upon my heart,
  And press it mair and mair,
Or it will burst the silken twine,
  Sae strang is its despair.

O, wae 's me for the hour, Willie,
  When we thegither met, —
O, wae 's me for the time, Willie,
  That our first tryst was set !
O, wae 's me for the loanin' green
  Where we were wont to gae, —
And wae 's me for the destinie
  That gart me luve thee sae !

O, dinna mind my words, Willie,
  I downa seek to blame ;
But O, it 's hard to live, Willie,
  And dree a warld's shame !
Het tears are hailin' ower your cheek,
  And hailin' ower your chin :
Why weep ye sae for worthlessness,
  For sorrow, and for sin ?

I 'm weary o' this warld, Willie,
  And sick wi' a' I see,
I canna live as I ha'e lived,
  Or be as I should be.
But fauld unto your heart, Willie,
  The heart that still is thine,
And kiss ance mair the white, white cheek
  Ye said was red langsyne.

A stoun' gaes through my heid, Willie,
  A sair stoun' through my heart ;
O, haud me up and let me kiss
  Thy brow ere we twa pairt.
Anither, and anither yet ! —
  How fast my life-strings break ! —
Fareweel ! fareweel ! through yon kirk-yard
  Step lichtly for my sake !

The lav'rock in the lift, Willie,
  That lilts far ower our heid,
Will sing the morn as merrilie
  Abune the clay-cauld deid ;
And this green turf we 're sittin' on,
  Wi' dew-draps shimmerin' sheen,
Will hap the heart that luvit thee
  As warld has seldom seen.

But O, remember me, Willie,
  On land where'er ye be ;
And O, think on the leal, leal heart,
  That ne'er luvit ane but thee !
And O, think on the cauld, cauld mools
  That file my yellow hair,
That kiss the cheek, and kiss the chin
  Ye never sall kiss mair !
            WILLIAM MOTHERWELL.

BEREAVEMENT AND DEATH.

RESIGNATION.

THERE is no flock, however watched and tended,
But one dead lamb is there !
There is no fireside, howsoe'er defended,
But has one vacant chair !

The air is full of farewells to the dying,
And mournings for the dead ;
The heart of Rachel, for her children crying,
Will not be comforted !

Let us be patient ! These severe afflictions
Not from the ground arise,
But oftentimes celestial benedictions
Assume this dark disguise.

We see but dimly through the mists and vapors ;
Amid these earthly damps
What seem to us but sad, funereal tapers
May be heaven's distant lamps.

There is no Death ! What seems so is transition :
This life of mortal breath
Is but a suburb of the life elysian,
Whose portal we call Death.

She is not dead, — the child of our affection, —
But gone unto that school
Where she no longer needs our poor protection,
And Christ himself doth rule.

In that great cloister's stillness and seclusion,
By guardian angels led,
Safe from temptation, safe from sin's pollution,
She lives whom we call dead.

Day after day we think what she is doing
In those bright realms of air ;
Year after year, her tender steps pursuing,
Behold her grown more fair.

Thus do we walk with her, and keep unbroken
The bond which nature gives,
Thinking that our remembrance, though unspoken,
May reach her where she lives.

Not as a child shall we again behold her ;
For when with raptures wild
In our embraces we again enfold her,
She will not be a child :

But a fair maiden, in her Father's mansion,
Clothed with celestial grace ;
And beautiful with all the soul's expansion
Shall we behold her face.

And though, at times, impetuous with emotion
And anguish long suppressed,
The swelling heart heaves moaning like the ocean,
That cannot be at rest, —

We will be patient, and assuage the feeling
We may not wholly stay ;
By silence sanctifying, not concealing,
The grief that must have way.
HENRY WADSWORTH LONGFELLOW.

BURIED TO-DAY.

February 23, 1858.

BURIED to-day.
When the soft green buds are bursting out,
And up on the south-wind comes a shout
Of village boys and girls at play
In the mild spring evening gray.

Taken away
Sturdy of heart and stout of limb,
From eyes that drew half their light from him,
And put low, low underneath the clay,
In his spring, — on this spring day.

Passes away,
All the pride of boy-life begun,
All the hope of life yet to run ;
Who dares to question when One saith "Nay."
Murmur not, — only pray.

Enters to-day
Another body in churchyard sod,
Another soul on the life in God.
HIS Christ was buried — and lives alway :
Trust Him, and go your way.
DINAH MARIA MULOCK.

UNVEIL THY BOSOM, FAITHFUL TOMB.

UNVEIL thy bosom, faithful tomb ;
Take this new treasure to thy trust,
And give these sacred relics room
To slumber in the silent dust.

Nor pain, nor grief, nor anxious fear,
  Invade thy bounds ; no mortal woes
Can reach the peaceful sleeper here,
  While angels watch the soft repose.

So Jesus slept ; God's dying Son
  Passed through the grave, and blest the bed :
Rest here, blest saint, till from his throne
  The morning break, and pierce the shade.

Break from his throne, illustrious morn ;
  Attend, O earth, his sovereign word ;
Restore thy trust ; a glorious form
  Shall then arise to meet the Lord.

DR. ISAAC WATTS.

GRIEF FOR THE DEAD.

O HEARTS that never cease to yearn !
  O brimming tears that ne'er are dried !
The dead, though they depart, return
  As though they had not died !

The living are the only dead ;
  The dead live, — nevermore to die ;
And often, when we mourn them fled,
  They never were so nigh !

And though they lie beneath the waves,
  Or sleep within the churchyard dim,
(Ah ! through how many different graves
  God's children go to him !) —

Yet every grave gives up its dead
  Ere it is overgrown with grass ;
Then why should hopeless tears be shed,
  Or need we cry, " Alas " ?

Or why should Memory, veiled with gloom,
  And like a sorrowing mourner craped,
Sit weeping o'er an empty tomb,
  Whose captives have escaped ?

'T is but a mound, — and will be mossed
  Whene'er the summer grass appears ;
The loved, though wept, are never lost ;
  We only lose — our tears !

Nay, Hope may whisper with the dead
  By bending forward where they are ;
But Memory, with a backward tread,
  Communes with them afar.

The joys we lose are but forecast,
  And we shall find them all once more ;
We look behind us for the Past,
  But lo ! 't is all before !

ANONYMOUS.

LINES

TO THE MEMORY OF "ANNIE," WHO DIED AT MILAN,
JUNE 6, 1860.

" Jesus saith unto her, Woman, why weepest thou ? whom seek-
est thou ? She, supposing him to be the gardener, saith unto him,
Sir, if thou have borne him hence, tell me where thou hast laid
him." — JOHN xx. 15.

IN the fair gardens of celestial peace
  Walketh a gardener in meekness clad ;
Fair are the flowers that wreathe his dewy locks,
  And his mysterious eyes are sweet and sad.

Fair are the silent foldings of his robes,
  Falling with saintly calmness to his feet ;
And when he walks, each floweret to his will
  With living pulse of sweet accord doth beat.

Every green leaf thrills to its tender heart,
  In the mild summer radiance of his eye ;
No fear of storm, or cold, or bitter frost,
  Shadows the flowerets when their sun is nigh.

And all our pleasant haunts of earthly love
  Are nurseries to those gardens of the air ;
And his far-darting eye, with starry beam,
  Watching the growing of his treasures there.

We call them ours, o'erwept with selfish tears,
  O'erwatched with restless longings night and
    day ;
Forgetful of the high, mysterious right
  He holds to bear our cherished plants away.

But when some sunny spot in those bright fields
  Needs the fair presence of an added flower,
Down sweeps a starry angel in the night :
  At morn the rose has vanished from our bower.

Where stood our tree, our flower, there is a grave !
  Blank, silent, vacant ; but in worlds above,
Like a new star outblossomed in the skies,
  The angels hail an added flower of love.

Dear friend, no more upon that lonely mound,
  Strewed with the red and yellow autumn leaf,
Drop thou the tear, but raise the fainting eye
  Beyond the autumn mists of earthly grief.

Thy garden rosebud bore within its breast
  Those mysteries of color, warm and bright,
That the bleak climate of this lower sphere
  Could never waken into form and light.

Yes, the sweet Gardener hath borne her hence,
  Nor must thou ask to take her thence away ;
Thou shalt behold her, in some coming hour,
  Full blossomed in his fields of cloudless day.

HARRIET BEECHER STOWE.

CALM ON THE BOSOM OF THY GOD.

CALM on the bosom of thy God,
  Young spirit ! rest thee now.
Even while with us thy footstep trod,
  His seal was on thy brow.

Dust, to its narrow house beneath !
  Soul, to its place on high ! —
They that have seen thy look in death
  No more may fear to die.

Lone are the paths, and sad the bowers,
  Whence thy meek smile is gone ;
But O, a brighter home than ours
  In heaven is now thine own !
      FELICIA HEMANS.

LIFE ! I KNOW NOT WHAT THOU ART.

LIFE ! I know not what thou art,
But know that thou and I must part ;
And when, or how, or where we met
I own to me 's a secret yet.

Life ! we 've been long together
Through pleasant and through cloudy weather,
'T is hard to part when friends are dear, —
Perhaps 't will cost a sigh, a tear ;
— Then steal away, give little warning,
Choose thine own time ;
Say not Good Night, — but in some brighter clime
Bid me Good Morning.
      A. L. BARBAULD.

NOW AND AFTERWARDS.

"Two hands upon the breast, and labor is past."
      RUSSIAN PROVERB.

"Two hands upon the breast,
  And labor 's done ;
Two pale feet crossed in rest, —
  The race is won ;
Two eyes with coin-weights shut,
  And all tears cease ;
Two lips where grief is mute,
  Anger at peace" :
So pray we oftentimes, mourning our lot ;
God in his kindness answereth not.

"Two hands to work addrest
  Aye for his praise ;
Two feet that never rest
  Walking his ways ;
Two eyes that look above
  Through all their tears ;
12

Two lips still breathing love,
  Not wrath, nor fears" :
So pray we afterwards, low on our knees ;
Pardon those erring prayers ! Father, hear these !
      DINAH MARIA MULOCK.

FOOTSTEPS OF ANGELS.

WHEN the hours of day are numbered,
  And the voices of the night
Wake the better soul that slumbered
  To a holy, calm delight, —

Ere the evening lamps are lighted,
  And, like phantoms grim and tall,
Shadows from the fitful firelight
  Dance upon the parlor wall ;

Then the forms of the departed
  Enter at the open door, —
The beloved ones, the true-hearted,
  Come to visit me once more :

He, the young and strong, who cherished
  Noble longings for the strife,
By the roadside fell and perished,
  Weary with the march of life !

They, the holy ones and weakly,
  Who the cross of suffering bore,
Folded their pale hands so meekly,
  Spake with us on earth no more !

And with them the being beauteous
  Who unto my youth was given,
More than all things else to love me,
  And is now a saint in heaven.

With a slow and noiseless footstep
  Comes that messenger divine,
Takes the vacant chair beside me,
  Lays her gentle hand in mine ;

And she sits and gazes at me
  With those deep and tender eyes,
Like the stars, so still and saint-like,
  Looking downward from the skies.

Uttered not, yet comprehended,
  Is the spirit's voiceless prayer,
Soft rebukes, in blessings ended,
  Breathing from her lips of air.

O, though oft depressed and lonely,
  All my fears are laid aside
If I but remember only
  Such as these have lived and died !
      HENRY WADSWORTH LONGFELLOW

MY MOTHER'S BIBLE.

THIS book is all that's left me now, —
　Tears will unbidden start, —
With faltering lip and throbbing brow
　I press it to my heart.
For many generations past
　Here is our family tree ;
My mother's hands this Bible clasped,
　She, dying, gave it me.

Ah ! well do I remember those
　Whose names these records bear ;
Who round the hearthstone used to close,
　After the evening prayer,
And speak of what these pages said
　In tones my heart would thrill !
Though they are with the silent dead,
　Here are they living still !

My father read this holy book
　To brothers, sisters, dear ;
How calm was my poor mother's look,
　Who loved God's word to hear !
Her angel face, — I see it yet !
　What thronging memories come !
Again that little group is met
　Within the halls of home !

Thou truest friend man ever knew,
　Thy constancy I've tried ;
When all were false, I found thee true,
　My counsellor and guide.
The mines of earth no treasures give
　That could this volume buy ;
In teaching me the way to live,
　It taught me how to die !
　　　　　　　GEORGE P. MORRIS.

GOD'S-ACRE.

I LIKE that ancient Saxon phrase which calls
　The burial-ground God's-Acre ! It is just ;
It consecrates each grave within its walls,
　And breathes a benison o'er the sleeping dust.

God's-Acre ! Yes, that blessed name imparts
　Comfort to those who in the grave have sown
The seed that they had garnered in their hearts,
　Their bread of life, alas ! no more their own.

Into its furrows shall we all be cast,
　In the sure faith that we shall rise again
At the great harvest, when the archangel's blast
　Shall winnow, like a fan, the chaff and grain.

Then shall the good stand in immortal bloom,
　In the fair gardens of that second birth ;
And each bright blossom mingle its perfume
　With that of flowers which never bloomed on
　　　earth.

With thy rude ploughshare, Death, turn up the
　sod,
　And spread the furrow for the seed we sow ;
This is the field and Acre of our God,
　This is the place where human harvests grow !
　　　　　　　HENRY WADSWORTH LONGFELLOW.

FOR CHARLIE'S SAKE.

THE night is late, the house is still ;
The angels of the hour fulfil
Their tender ministries, and move
From couch to couch in cares of love.
They drop into thy dreams, sweet wife,
The happiest smile of Charlie's life,
And lay on baby's lips a kiss,
Fresh from his angel-brother's bliss ;
And, as they pass, they seem to make
A strange, dim hymn, "For Charlie's sake."

My listening heart takes up the strain,
And gives it to the night again,
Fitted with words of lowly praise,
And patience learned of mournful days,
And memories of the dead child's ways.

His will be done, His will be done !
Who gave and took away my son,
In "the far land" to shine and sing
Before the Beautiful, the King,
Who every day doth Christmas make,
All starred and belled for Charlie's sake.

For Charlie's sake I will arise ;
I will anoint me where he lies,
And change my raiment, and go in
To the Lord's house, and leave my sin
Without, and seat me at his board,
Eat, and be glad, and praise the Lord.
For wherefore should I fast and weep,
And sullen moods of mourning keep ?
I cannot bring him back, nor he,
For any calling, come to me.
The bond the angel Death did sign,
God sealed — for Charlie's sake, and mine.
　　　　　　　JOHN WILLIAMSON PALMER.

UNDER THE CROSS.

I CANNOT, cannot say,
Out of my bruised and breaking heart,
Storm-driven along a thorn-set way,
　While blood-drops start
From every pore, as I drag on,
　"Thy will, O God, be done !"

I thought, but yesterday,
My will was one with God's dear will ;
And that it would be sweet to say,
  Whatever ill
My happy state should smite upon,
  "Thy will, my God, be done !"

But I was weak and wrong,
Both weak of soul and wrong of heart ;
And Pride alone in me was strong,
  With cunning art
To cheat me in the golden sun,
  To say, "God's will be done !"

O shadow drear and cold,
That frights me out of foolish pride ;
O flood, that through my bosom rolled
  Its billowy tide ;
I said, till ye your power made known,
  "God's will, not mine, be done !"

Now, faint and sore afraid,
Under my cross, heavy and rude,
My idols in the ashes laid,
  Like ashes strewed,
The holy words my pale lips shun,
  "O God, thy will be done !"

Pity my woes, O God,
And touch my will with thy warm breath ;
Put in my trembling hand thy rod,
  That quickens death ;
That my dead faith may feel thy sun,
  And say, "Thy will be done !"
W. C. R.

SOFTLY WOO AWAY HER BREATH.

Softly woo away her breath,
  Gentle death !
Let her leave thee with no strife,
  Tender, mournful, murmuring life !
She hath seen her happy day, —
  She hath had her bud and blossom ;
Now she pales and shrinks away,
  Earth, into thy gentle bosom !

She hath done her bidding here,
  Angels dear !
Bear her perfect soul above,
  Seraph of the skies, — sweet love !
Good she was, and fair in youth ;
  And her mind was seen to soar,
And her heart was wed to truth :
  Take her, then, forevermore, —
  Forever — evermore !
BARRY CORNWALL.

THE ANGEL OF PATIENCE.

A FREE PARAPHRASE OF THE GERMAN.

To weary hearts, to mourning homes,
God's meekest Angel gently comes :
No power has he to banish pain,
Or give us back our lost again ;
And yet in tenderest love our dear
And heavenly Father sends him here.

There 's quiet in that Angel's glance,
There 's rest in his still countenance !
He mocks no grief with idle cheer,
Nor wounds with words the mourner's ear ;
But ills and woes he may not cure
He kindly trains us to endure.

Angel of Patience ! sent to calm
Our feverish brows with cooling palm ;
To lay the storms of hope and fear,
And reconcile life's smile and tear ;
The throbs of wounded pride to still,
And make our own our Father's will !

O thou who mournest on thy way,
With longings for the close of day ;
He walks with thee, that Angel kind,
And gently whispers, " Be resigned :
Bear up, bear on, the end shall tell
The dear Lord ordereth all things well !"
JOHN GREENLEAF WHITTIER.

OVER THE RIVER.

Over the river they beckon to me,
  Loved ones who 've crossed to the farther side,
The gleam of their snowy robes I see,
  But their voices are lost in the dashing tide.
There 's one with ringlets of sunny gold,
  And eyes the reflection of heaven's own blue ;
He crossed in the twilight gray and cold,
  And the pale mist hid him from mortal view.
We saw not the angels who met him there,
  The gates of the city we could not see :
Over the river, over the river,
  My brother stands waiting to welcome me.

Over the river the boatman pale
  Carried another, the household pet ;
Her brown curls waved in the gentle gale,
  Darling Minnie ! I see her yet.
She crossed on her bosom her dimpled hands,
  And fearlessly entered the phantom bark ;
We felt it glide from the silver sands,
  And all our sunshine grew strangely dark ;
We know she is safe on the farther side,
  Where all the ransomed and angels be :

Over the river, the mystic river,
  My childhood's idol is waiting for me.

For none return from those quiet shores,
  Who cross with the boatman cold and pale ;
We hear the dip of the golden oars,
  And catch a gleam of the snowy sail ;
And lo ! they have passed from our yearning hearts,
  They cross the stream and are gone for aye.
We may not sunder the veil apart
  That hides from our vision the gates of day ;
We only know that their barks no more
  May sail with us o'er life's stormy sea ;
Yet somewhere, I know, on the unseen shore,
  They watch, and beckon, and wait for me.

And I sit and think, when the sunset's gold
  Is flushing river and hill and shore,
I shall one day stand by the water cold,
  And list for the sound of the boatman's oar ;
I shall watch for a gleam of the flapping sail,
  I shall hear the boat as it gains the strand,
I shall pass from sight with the boatman pale,
  To the better shore of the spirit land.
I shall know the loved who have gone before,
  And joyfully sweet will the meeting be,
When over the river, the peaceful river,
  The angel of death shall carry me.
              NANCY AMELIA WOODBURY PRIEST.

THOU ART GONE TO THE GRAVE.

THOU art gone to the grave, — we no longer deplore thee,
  Though sorrows and darkness encompass the tomb ;
The Saviour has passed through its portals before thee,
  And the lamp of his love is thy guide through the gloom.

Thou art gone to the grave, — we no longer behold thee,
  Nor tread the rough path of the world by thy side ;
But the wide arms of mercy are spread to enfold thee,
  And sinners may hope, since the Sinless has died.

Thou art gone to the grave, — and, its mansion forsaking,
  Perhaps thy tried spirit in doubt lingered long,
But the sunshine of heaven beamed bright on thy waking,
  And the song which thou heard'st was the seraphim's song.

Thou art gone to the grave, — but 't were wrong to deplore thee,
  When God was thy ransom, thy guardian, thy guide ;
He gave thee, and took thee, and soon will restore thee,
  Where death hath no sting, since the Saviour hath died.   REGINALD HEBER.

THE PLEASURES OF HEAVEN.

THERE all the happy souls that ever were,
Shall meet with gladness in one theatre ;
And each shall know there one another's face,
By beatific virtue of the place.
There shall the brother with the sister walk,
And sons and daughters with their parents talk ;
But all of God : they still shall have to say,
But make him all in all their theme that day :
That happy day that never shall see night !
Where he will be all beauty to the sight ;
Wine or delicious fruits unto the taste ;
A music in the ears will ever last ;
Unto the scent, a spicery or balm ;
And to the touch, a flower, like soft as palm.
He will all glory, all perfection, be,
God in the Union and the Trinity !
That holy, great, and glorious mystery
Will there revealéd be in majesty,
By light and comfort of spiritual grace ;
The vision of our Saviour face to face,
In his humanity ! to hear him preach
The price of our redemption, and to teach,
Through his inherent righteousness in death,
The safety of our souls and forfeit breath !
What fulness of beatitude is here !
What love with mercy mixéd doth appear !
To style us friends, who were by nature foes !
Adopt us heirs by grace, who were of those
Had lost ourselves ; and prodigally spent
Our native portions and possesséd rent !
Yet have all debts forgiven us ; an advance
By imputed right to an inheritance
In his eternal kingdom, where we sit
Equal with angels, and co-heirs of it.
              BEN JONSON.

I WOULD NOT LIVE ALWAY.

I WOULD not live alway ; I ask not to stay
Where storm after storm rises dark o'er the way ;
The few lurid mornings that dawn on us here
Are enough for life's joys, full enough for its cheer.

I would not live alway ; no, — welcome the tomb !
Since Jesus hath lain there, I dread not its gloom ;
There sweet be my rest till he bid me arise,
To hail him in triumph descending the skies.

Who, who would live alway, away from his God, —
Away from yon heaven, that blissful abode,
Where rivers of pleasure flow bright o'er the plains,
And the noontide of glory eternally reigns?

There saints of all ages in harmony meet,
Their Saviour and brethren transported to greet;
While anthems of rapture unceasingly roll,
And the smile of the Lord is the feast of the soul.

WM. A. MUHLENBERG.

BEYOND THE SMILING AND THE WEEPING.

BEYOND the smiling and the weeping
  I shall be soon;
Beyond the waking and the sleeping,
Beyond the sowing and the reaping,
  I shall be soon.
    Love, rest, and home!
    Sweet hope!
    Lord, tarry not, but come.

Beyond the blooming and the fading
  I shall be soon;
Beyond the shining and the shading,
Beyond the hoping and the dreading,
  I shall be soon.
    Love, rest, and home!

Beyond the rising and the setting
  I shall be soon;
Beyond the calming and the fretting,
Beyond remembering and forgetting,
  I shall be soon.
    Love, rest, and home!

Beyond the gathering and the strowing
  I shall be soon;
Beyond the ebbing and the flowing,
Beyond the coming and the going,
  I shall be soon.
    Love, rest, and home!

Beyond the parting and the meeting
  I shall be soon;
Beyond the farewell and the greeting,
Beyond this pulse's fever beating,
  I shall be soon.
    Love, rest, and home!

Beyond the frost chain and the fever
  I shall be soon;
Beyond the rock waste and the river,
Beyond the ever and the never,
  I shall be soon.
    Love, rest, and home!
    Sweet hope!
    Lord, tarry not, but come.

HORATIUS BONAR.

THE LAND O' THE LEAL.

I 'M wearing awa', Jean,
Like snaw when its thaw, Jean,
I 'm wearing awa'
  To the land o' the leal.
There 's nae sorrow there, Jean,
There 's neither cauld nor care, Jean,
The day is aye fair ·
  In the land o' the leal.

Ye were aye leal and true, Jean;
Your task 's ended noo, Jean,
And I 'll welcome you
  To the land o' the leal.
Our bonnie bairn 's there, Jean,
She was baith guid and fair, Jean,
O, we grudged her right sair
  To the land o' the leal!

Then dry that tearfu' e'e, Jean,
My soul·langs to be free, Jean,
And angels wait on me
  To the land o' the leal!
Now fare ye weel, my ain Jean,
This warld's care is vain, Jean;
We 'll meet and aye be fain
  In the land o' the leal.

LADY NAIRN.

UNDER THE VIOLETS.

HER hands are cold; her face is white;
  No more her pulses come and go;
Her eyes are shut to life and light; —
  Fold the white vesture, snow on snow,
  And lay her where the violets blow.

But not beneath a graven stone,
  To plead for tears with alien eyes;
A slender cross of wood alone
  Shall say, that here a maiden lies
  In peace beneath the peaceful skies.

And gray old trees of hugest limb
  Shall wheel their circling shadows round,
To make the scorching sunlight dim
  That drinks the greenness from the ground,
  And drop their dead leaves on her mound.

When o'er their boughs the squirrels run,
  And through their leaves the robins call,
And, ripening in the autumn sun,
  The acorns and the chestnuts fall,
  Doubt not that she will heed them all.

For her the morning choir shall sing
  Its matins from the branches high,
And every minstrel-voice of spring,

That trills beneath the April sky,
  Shall greet her with its earliest cry.

When, turning round their dial-track,
  Eastward the lengthening shadows pass,
Her little mourners, clad in black,
  The crickets, sliding through the grass,
  Shall pipe for her an evening mass.

At last the rootléts of the trees
  Shall find the prison where she lies,
And bear the buried dust they seize
  In leaves and blossoms to the skies.
  So may the soul that warmed it rise !

If any, born of kindlier blood,
  Should ask, What maiden lies below ?
Say only this : A tender bud,
  That tried to blossom in the snow,
  Lies withered where the violets blow.
            OLIVER WENDELL HOLMES.

SELECTIONS FROM "IN MEMORIAM."

GRIEF UNSPEAKABLE.

I SOMETIMES hold it half a sin
  To put in words the grief I feel :
  For words, like Nature, half reveal
And half conceal the Soul within.

But, for the unquiet heart and brain,
  A use in measured language lies ;
  The sad mechanic exercise,
Like dull narcotics, numbing pain.

In words, like weeds, I 'll wrap me o'er,
  Like coarsest clothes against the cold ;
  But that large grief which these enfold
Is given in outline and no more.

DEAD, IN A FOREIGN LAND.

FAIR ship, that from the Italian shore
  Sailest the placid ocean-plains
  With my lost Arthur's loved remains,
Spread thy full wings, and waft him o'er.

So draw him home to those that mourn
  In vain ; a favorable speed
  Ruffle thy mirrored mast, and lead
Through prosperous floods his holy urn.

All night no ruder air perplex
  Thy sliding keel, till Phosphor, bright
  As our pure love, through early light
Shall glimmer on the dewy decks.

Sphere all your lights around, above ;
  Sleep, gentle heavens, before the prow ;
  Sleep, gentle winds, as he sleeps now,
My friend, the brother of my love ;

My Arthur, whom I shall not see
  Till all my widowed race be run ;
  Dear as the mother to the son,
More than my brothers are to me.

THE PEACE OF SORROW.

CALM is the morn without a sound,
  Calm as to suit a calmer grief,
  And only through the faded leaf
The chestnut pattering to the ground :

Calm and deep peace on this high wold
  And on these dews that drench the furze,
  And all the silvery gossamers
That twinkle into green and gold :

Calm and still light on yon great plain
  That sweeps with all its autumn bowers,
  And crowded farms and lessening towers,
To mingle with the bounding main :

Calm and deep peace in this wide air,
  These leaves that redden to the fall ;
  And in my heart, if calm at all,
If any calm, a calm despair :

Calm on the seas, and silver sleep,
  And waves that sway themselves in rest,
  And dead calm in that noble breast
Which heaves but with the heaving deep.

TIME AND ETERNITY.

IF Sleep and Death be truly one,
  And every spirit's folded bloom
  Through all its intervital gloom
In some long trance should slumber on ;

Unconscious of the sliding hour,
  Bare of the body, might it last,
  And silent traces of the past
Be all the color of the flower :

So then were nothing lost to man ;
  So that still garden of the souls
  In many a figured leaf enrolls
The total world since life began ;

And love will last as pure and whole
  As when he loved me here in Time,
  And at the spiritual prime
Rewaken with the dawning soul.

PERSONAL RESURRECTION.

THAT each, who seems a separate whole,
  Should move his rounds, and fusing all
  The skirts of self again, should fall
Remerging in the general Soul,

Is faith as vague as all unsweet :
   Eternal form shall still divide
   The eternal soul from all beside ;
And I shall know him when we meet :

And we shall sit at endless feast,
   Enjoying each the other's good :
   What vaster dream can hit the mood
Of Love on earth ? He seeks at least

Upon the last and sharpest height,
   Before the spirits fade away,
   Some landing-place to clasp and say,
"Farewell ! We lose ourselves in light."

SPIRITUAL COMPANIONSHIP.

Do we indeed desire the dead
   Should still be near us at our side ?
   Is there no baseness we would hide ?
No inner vileness that we dread ?

Shall he for whose applause I strove,
   I had such reverence for his blame,
   See with clear eye some hidden shame,
And I be lessened in his love ?

I wrong the grave with fears untrue :
   Shall love be blamed for want of faith ?
   There must be wisdom with great Death :
The dead shall look me through and through.

Be near us when we climb or fall :
   Ye watch, like God, the rolling hours
   With larger other eyes than ours,
To make allowance for us all.

MOONLIGHT MUSINGS.

When on my bed the moonlight falls,
   I know that in thy place of rest,
   By that broad water of the west,
There comes a glory on the walls ;

Thy marble bright in dark appears,
   As slowly steals a silver flame
   Along the letters of thy name,
And o'er the number of thy years.

The mystic glory swims away ;
   From off my bed the moonlight dies :
   And, closing eaves of wearied eyes,
I sleep till dusk is dipt in gray :

And then I know the mist is drawn
   A lucid veil from coast to coast,
   And in the dark church, like a ghost,
Thy tablet glimmers to the dawn.

DEATH IN LIFE'S PRIME.

So many worlds, so much to do,
   So little done, such things to be,
   How know I what had need of thee,
For thou wert strong as thou wert true ?

The fame is quenched that I foresaw,
   The head hath missed an earthly wreath :
   I curse not nature, no, nor death ;
For nothing is that errs from law.

We pass ; the path that each man trod
   Is dim, or will be dim, with weeds :
   What fame is left for human deeds
In endless age ? It rests with God.

O hollow wraith of dying fame,
   Fade wholly, while the soul exults,
   And self-enfolds the large results
Of force that would have forged a name.

THE POET'S TRIBUTE.

What hope is here for modern rhyme
   To him who turns a musing eye
   On songs, and deeds, and lives, that lie
Foreshortened in the tract of time ?

These mortal lullabies of pain
   May bind a book, may line a box,
   May serve to curl a maiden's locks :
Or when a thousand moons shall wane

A man upon a stall may find,
   And, passing, turn the page that tells
   A grief, then changed to something else,
Sung by a long-forgotten 'mind.

But what of that ? My darkened ways
   Shall ring with music all the same ;
   To breathe my loss is more than fame,
To utter love more sweet than praise.
            ALFRED TENNYSON.

THEY ARE ALL GONE.

They are all gone into the world of light,
   And I alone sit lingering here !
Their very memory is fair and bright,
   And my sad thoughts doth clear ;

It glows and glitters in my cloudy breast,
   Like stars upon some gloomy grove, —
Or those faint beams in which this hill is drest
   After the sun's remove.

I see them walking in an air of glory,
   Whose light doth trample on my days, —
My days which are at best but dull and hoary,
   Mere glimmering and decays.

O holy hope ! and high humility, —
   High as the heavens above !
These are your walks, and you have showed them
      me
   To kindle my cold love.

Dear, beauteous death, — the jewel of the just, —
　Shining nowhere but in the dark !
What mysteries do lie beyond thy dust,
　Could man outlook that mark !

He that hath found some fledged bird's nest may
　　know,
　At first sight, if the bird be flown ;
But what fair dell or grove he sings in now,
　That is to him unknown.

And yet, as angels in some brighter dreams
　Call to the soul when man doth sleep,
So some strange thoughts transcend our wonted
　　themes,
　And into glory peep.

If a star were confined into a tomb,
　Her captive flames must needs burn there,
But when the hand that locked her up gives room,
　She 'll shine through all the sphere.

O Father of eternal life, and all
　Created glories under thee !
Resume thy spirit from this world of thrall
　Into true liberty.

Either disperse these mists, which blot and fill
　My perspective still as they pass ;
Or else remove me hence unto that hill
　Where I shall need no glass.
　　　　　　　　　　HENRY VAUGHAN.

THE FIRST SNOW-FALL.

THE snow had begun in the gloaming,
　And busily all the night
Had been heaping field and highway
　With a silence deep and white.

Every pine and fir and hemlock
　Wore ermine too dear for an earl,
And the poorest twig on the elm-tree
　Was ridged inch deep with pearl.

From sheds new-roofed with Carrara
　Came Chanticleer's muffled crow,
The stiff rails were softened to swan's-down,
　And still fluttered down the snow.

I stood and watched by the window
　The noiseless work of the sky,
And the sudden flurries of snow-birds,
　Like brown leaves whirling by.

I thought of a mound in sweet Auburn
　Where a little headstone stood ;
How the flakes were folding it gently,
　As did robins the babes in the wood.

Up spoke our own little Mabel,
　Saying, "Father, who makes it snow ?"
And I told of the good All-father
　Who cares for us here below.

Again I looked at the snow-fall,
　And thought of the leaden sky
That arched o'er our first great sorrow,
　When that mound was heaped so high.

I remembered the gradual patience
　That fell from that cloud like snow,
Flake by flake, healing and hiding
　The scar of our deep-plunged woe.

And again to the child I whispered,
　"The snow that husheth all,
Darling, the merciful Father
　Alone can make it fall !"

Then, with eyes that saw not, I kissed her ;
　And she, kissing back, could not know
That *my* kiss was given to her sister,
　Folded close under deepening snow.
　　　　　　　　　　JAMES RUSSELL LOWELL.

THE REAPER AND THE FLOWERS.

THERE is a Reaper whose name is Death,
　And, with his sickle keen,
He reaps the bearded grain at a breath,
　And the flowers that grow between.

"Shall I have naught that is fair ?" saith he ;
　"Have naught but the bearded grain ?
Though the breath of these flowers is sweet to me,
　I will give them all back again."

He gazed at the flowers with tearful eyes,
　He kissed their drooping leaves ;
It was for the Lord of Paradise
　He bound them in his sheaves.

"My Lord has need of these flowerets gay,
　The Reaper said, and smiled ;
"Dear tokens of the earth are they,
　Where he was once a child.

"They shall all bloom in fields of light,
　Transplanted by my care,
And saints, upon their garments white,
　These sacred blossoms wear."

And the mother gave, in tears and pain,
　The flowers she most did love ;
She knew she should find them all again
　In the fields of light above.

O, not in cruelty, not in wrath,
 The Reaper came that day ;
'T was an angel visited the green earth,
 And took the flowers away.
HENRY WADSWORTH LONGFELLOW.

Lord of the living and the dead,
 Our Saviour dear !
We lay in silence at thy feet
 This sad, sad year.
HARRIET BEECHER STOWE.

"ONLY A YEAR."

ONE year ago, — a ringing voice,
 A clear blue eye,
And clustering curls of sunny hair,
 Too fair to die.

Only a year, — no voice, no smile,
 No glance of eye,
No clustering curls of golden hair,
 Fair but to die !

One year ago, — what loves, what schemes
 Far into life !
What joyous hopes, what high resolves,
 What generous strife !

The silent picture on the wall,
 The burial-stone,
Of all that beauty, life, and joy
 Remain alone !

One year, — one year, — one little year,
 And so much gone !
And yet the even flow of life
 Moves calmly on.

The grave grows green, the flowers bloom fair,
 Above that head ;
No sorrowing tint of leaf or spray
 Says he is dead.

No pause or hush of merry birds,
 That sing above,
Tells us how coldly sleeps below
 The form we love.

Where hast thou been this year, beloved ?
 What hast thou seen, —
What visions fair, what glorious life ?
 Where thou hast been ?

The veil ! the veil ! so thin, so strong !
 'Twixt us and thee ;
The mystic veil ! when shall it fall,
 That we may see ?

Not dead, not sleeping, not even gone,
 But present still,
And waiting for the coming hour
 Of God's sweet will.

MY CHILD.

I CANNOT make him dead !
 His fair sunshiny head
Is ever bounding round my study chair ;
 Yet when my eyes, now dim
 With tears, I turn to him,
The vision vanishes, — he is not there !

I walk my parlor floor,
 And, through the open door,
I hear a footfall on the chamber stair ;
 I 'm stepping toward the hall
 To give the boy a call ;
And then bethink me that — he is not there !

I thread the crowded street ;
 A satchelled lad I meet,
With the same beaming eyes and colored hair ;
 And, as he 's running by,
 Follow him with my eye,
Scarcely believing that — he is not there !

I know his face is hid
 Under the coffin lid ;
Closed are his eyes ; cold is his forehead fair ;
 My hand that marble felt ;
 O'er it in prayer I knelt ;
Yet my heart whispers that — he is not there !

I cannot make him dead !
 When passing by the bed,
So long watched over with parental care,
 My spirit and my eye
 Seek him inquiringly,
Before the thought comes that — he is not there !

When, at the cool gray break
 Of day, from sleep I wake,
With my first breathing of the morning air
 My soul goes up, with joy,
 To Him who gave my boy ;
Then comes the sad thought that — he is not there !

When at the day's calm close,
 Before we seek repose,
I 'm with his mother, offering up our prayer ;
 Whate'er I may be saying,
 I am in spirit praying
For our boy's spirit, though — he is not there !

Not there ! — Where, then, is he ?
The form I used to see
Was but the raiment that he used to wear.
The grave, that now doth press
Upon that cast-off dress,
Is but his wardrobe locked ; — he is not there !

He lives ! — In all the past
He lives ; nor, to the last,
Of seeing him again will I despair ;
In dreams I see him now ;
And, on his angel brow,
I see it written, " Thou shalt see me *there !*

Yes, we all live to God !
Father, thy chastening rod
So help us, thine afflicted ones, to bear,
That, in the spirit land,
Meeting at thy right hand,
'T will be our heaven to find that — he is there !
JOHN PIERPONT.

SWEET DAY.

SWEET day, so cool, so calm, so bright,
The bridall of the earth and skie :
The dew shall weep thy fall to-night ;
     For thou must die.

Sweet rose, whose hue angrie and brave
Bids the rash gazer wipe his eye,
Thy root is ever in its grave,
     And thou must die.

Sweet spring, full of sweet dayes and roses,
A box where sweets compacted lie,
My musick shows ye have your closes,
     And all must die.

Onely a sweet and vertuous soul,
Like seasoned timber, never gives ;
But though the whole world turn to coal,
     Then chiefly lives.
GEORGE HERBERT.

MAN'S MORTALITY.

LIKE as the damask rose you see,
Or like the blossom on the tree,
Or like the dainty flower in May,
Or like the morning of the day,
Or like the sun, or like the shade,
Or like the gourd which Jonas had, —
E'en such is man ; — whose thread is spun,
Drawn out, and cut, and so is done. —
The rose withers, the blossom blasteth,
The flower fades, the morning hasteth,

The sun sets, the shadow flies,
The gourd consumes, — and man he dies !

Like to the grass that 's newly sprung,
Or like a tale that 's new begun,
Or like the bird that 's here to-day,
Or like the pearléd dew of May,
Or like an hour, or like a span,
Or like the singing of a swan, —
E'en such is man ; — who lives by breath,
Is here, now there, in life and death. —
The grass withers, the tale is ended,
The bird is flown, the dew 's ascended.
The hour is short, the span is long,
The swan 's near death, — man's life is done !
SIMON WASTELL.

IF THOU WILT EASE THINE HEART.

DIRGE.

IF thou wilt ease thine heart
Of love, and all its smart, —
    Then sleep, dear, sleep !
And not a sorrow
   Hang any tear on your eyelashes ;
    Lie still and deep,
   Sad soul, until the sea-wave washes
The rim o' the sun to-morrow,
    In eastern sky.

But wilt thou cure thine heart
Of love, and all its smart, —
    Then die, dear, die !
'T is deeper, sweeter,
   Than on a rose bank to lie dreaming
    With folded eye ;
   And then alone, amid the beaming
Of love's stars, thou 'lt meet her
    In eastern sky.
THOMAS LOVELL BEDDOES.

DEATH.

THE GIAOUR.

HE who hath bent him o'er the dead
Ere the first day of death is fled,
The first dark day of nothingness,
The last of danger and distress,
(Before Decay's effacing fingers
Have swept the lines where beauty lingers,)
And marked the mild angelic air,
The rapture of repose, that 's there,
The fixed yet tender traits that streak
The languor of the placid cheek,
And — but for that sad shrouded eye,

That fires not, wins not, weeps not now,
And but for that chill, changeless brow,
Where cold Obstruction's apathy
Appalls the gazing mourner's heart,
As if to him it could impart
The doom he dreads, yet dwells upon ;
Yes, but for these and these alone,
Some moments, ay, one treacherous hour,
He still might doubt the tyrant's power ;
So fair, so calm, so softly sealed,
The first, last look by death revealed !
Such is the aspect of this shore ;
'T is Greece, but living Greece no more !
So coldly sweet, so deadly fair,
We start, for soul is wanting there.
Hers is the loveliness in death,
That parts not quite with parting breath ;
But beauty with that fearful bloom,
That hue which haunts it to the tomb,
Expression's last receding ray,
A gilded halo hovering round decay,
The farewell beam of Feeling past away ;
Spark of that flame, perchance of heavenly birth,
Which gleams, but warms no more its cherished
        earth !   BYRON.

DEATH'S FINAL CONQUEST.

[These verses are said to have "chilled the heart" of Oliver Cromwell.]

THE glories of our birth and state
    Are shadows, not substantial things ;
There is no armor against fate, —
    Death lays his icy hands on kings ;
        Sceptre and crown
        Must tumble down,
And in the dust be equal made
With the poor crooked scythe and spade.

Some men with swords may reap the field,
    And plant fresh laurels where they kill ;
But their strong nerves at last must yield, —
    They tame but one another still ;
        Early or late
        They stoop to fate,
And must give up their murmuring breath,
When they, pale captives, creep to death.

The garlands wither on your brow, —
    Then boast no more your mighty deeds ;
Upon death's purple altar, now,
    See where the victor victim bleeds !
        All heads must come
        To the cold tomb, —
Only the actions of the just
Smell sweet, and blossom in the dust.
                                JAMES SHIRLEY.

LIFE.

LIKE to the falling of a star,
Or as the flights of eagles are,
Or like the fresh spring's gaudy hue,
Or silver drops of morning dew,
Or like a wind that chafes the flood,
Or bubbles which on water stood, —
E'en such is man, whose borrowed light
Is straight called in, and paid to-night.
The wind blows out, the bubble dies,
The spring entombed in autumn lies,
The dew dries up, the star is shot,
The flight is past, — and man forgot !
                                HENRY KING.

THE GRAVE.

THERE is a calm for those who weep,
A rest for weary pilgrims found,
They softly lie and sweetly sleep
        Low in the ground.

The storm that wrecks the winter sky
No more disturbs their deep repose,
Than summer-evening's latest sigh
        That shuts the rose.

I long to lay this painful head
And aching heart beneath the soil,
To slumber in that dreamless bed
        From all my toil.

For Misery stole me at my birth,
And cast me helpless on the wild :
I perish ; — O my Mother Earth,
        Take home thy Child !

On thy dear lap these limbs reclined,
Shall gently moulder into thee ;
Nor leave one wretched trace behind
        Resembling me.

Hark ! a strange sound affrights mine ear,
My pulse, — my brain runs wild, — I rave ;
— Ah ! who art thou whose voice I hear ?
        — "I am the Grave !

"The Grave, that never spake before,
Hath found at length a tongue to chide :
O listen !" "I will speak no more : —
        Be silent, Pride !"

"Art thou a Wretch of hope forlorn,
The victim of consuming care ?
Is thy distracted conscience torn
        By fell despair ?

" A bruiséd reed he will not break ;
Afflictions all his children feel ;
He wounds them for his mercy's sake,
　　　　　He wounds to heal.

·　　　·　　　·　　　·

"There is a calm for those who weep,
A rest for weary Pilgrims found ;
And while the mouldering ashes sleep
　　　　　Low in the ground,

" The Soul, of origin divine,
God's glorious image, freed from clay,
In heaven's eternal sphere shall shine,
　　　　　A star of day.

" The Sun is but a spark of fire,
A transient meteor in the sky ;
The Soul, immortal as its Sire,
　　　　　Shall never die."
　　　　　　　　JAMES MONTGOMERY.

WE WATCHED HER BREATHING.

WE watched her breathing through the night,
　Her breathing soft and low,
As in her breast the wave of life
　Kept heaving to and fro.

So silently we seemed to speak,
　So slowly moved about,
As we had lent her half our powers
　To eke her living out.

Our very hopes belied our fears,
　Our fears our hopes belied, —
We thought her dying when she slept,
　And sleeping when she died.

For when the morn came dim and sad,
　And chill with early showers,
Her quiet eyelids closed, — she had
　Another morn than ours.
　　　　　　　　THOMAS HOOD.

A DEATH-BED.

HER suffering ended with the day ;
　Yet lived she at its close,
And breathed the long, long night away
　In statue-like repose.

But when the sun, in all his state,
　Illumed the eastern skies,
She passed through glory's morning-gate,
　And walked in Paradise !
　　　　　　　　JAMES ALDRICH.

O, SNATCHED AWAY IN BEAUTY'S BLOOM !

O, SNATCHED away in beauty's bloom !
On thee shall press no ponderous tomb ;
But on thy turf shall roses rear
Their leaves, the earliest of the year,
And the wild cypress wave in tender gloom :
And oft by yon blue gushing stream
Shall Sorrow lean her drooping head,
And feed deep thought with many a dream,
And lingering pause and lightly tread ;
Fond wretch ! as if her step disturbed the dead !

Away ! we know that tears are vain,
That Death nor heeds nor hears distress :
Will this unteach us to complain ?
Or make one mourner weep the less ?
And thou, who tell'st me to forget,
Thy looks are wan, thine eyes are wet.
　　　　　　　　BYRON.

TO MARY IN HEAVEN.

[Composed by Burns, in September, 1789, on the anniversary of the day on which he heard of the death of his early love, Mary Campbell.]

THOU lingering star, with lessening ray,
　That lov'st to greet the early morn,
Again thou usher'st in the day
　My Mary from my soul was torn.
O Mary ! dear departed shade !
　Where is thy place of blissful rest ?
See'st thou thy lover lowly laid ?
　Hear'st thou the groans that rend his breast ?

That sacred hour can I forget, —
　Can I forget the hallowed grove,
Where by the winding Ayr we met
　To live one day of parting love !
Eternity will not efface
　Those records dear of transports past ;
Thy image at our last embrace ;
　Ah ! little thought we 't was our last !

Ayr, gurgling, kissed his pebbled shore,
　O'erhung with wild woods, thickening green ;
The fragrant birch, and hawthorn hoar,
　Twined amorous round the raptured scene ;
The flowers sprang wanton to be prest,
　The birds sang love on every spray, —
Till soon, too soon, the glowing west
　Proclaimed the speed of wingéd day.

Still o'er these scenes my memory wakes,
　And fondly broods with miser care !
Time but the impression stronger makes,
　As streams their channels deeper wear.

My Mary ! dear departed shade !
  Where is thy place of blissful rest ?
See'st thou thy lover lowly laid ?
  Hear'st thou the groans that rend his breast ?
           ROBERT BURNS.

FOR ANNIE.

THANK Heaven ! the crisis, —
  The danger is past,
And the lingering illness
  Is over at last, —
And the fever called " Living"
  Is conquered at last.

Sadly, I know,
  I am shorn of my strength,
And no muscle I move
  As I lie at full length —
But no matter ! — I feel
  I am better at length.

And I rest so composedly
  Now, in my bed,
That any beholder
  Might fancy me dead, —
Might start at beholding me,
  Thinking me dead.

The moaning and groaning,
  The sighing and sobbing,
Are quieted now,
  With that horrible throbbing
At heart, — ah, that horrible,
  Horrible throbbing !

The sickness, the nausea,
  The pitiless pain,
Have ceased, with the fever
  That maddened my brain, —
With the fever called " Living"
  That burned in my brain.

And O, of all tortures
  That torture the worst
Has abated, — the terrible
  Torture of thirst
For the napthaline river
  Of Passion accurst !
I have drunk of a water
  That quenches all thirst, —

Of a water that flows
  With a lullaby sound,
From a spring but a very few
  Feet under ground, —
From a cavern not very far
  Down under ground.

And ah ! let it never
  Be foolishly said
That my room it is gloomy
  And narrow my bed ;
For man never slept
  In a different bed, —
And, to *sleep*, you must slumber
  In just such a bed.

My tantalized spirit
  Here blandly reposes,
Forgetting, or never
  Regretting, its roses, —
Its old agitations
  Of myrtles and roses :

For now, while so quietly
  Lying, it fancies
A holier odor
  About it, of pansies, —
A rosemary odor,
  Commingled with pansies,
With rue and the beautiful
  Puritan pansies.

And so it lies happily,
  Bathing in many
A dream of the truth
  And the beauty of Annie, —
Drowned in a bath
  Of the tresses of Annie.

She tenderly kissed me,
  She fondly caressed,
And then I fell gently
  To sleep on her breast, —
Deeply to sleep
  From the heaven of her breast.

When the light was extinguished,
  She covered me warm,
And she prayed to the angels
  To keep me from harm, —
To the queen of the angels
  To shield me from harm.

And I lie so composedly
  Now in my bed,
(Knowing her love,)
  That you fancy me dead ;
And I rest so contentedly
  Now in my bed,
(With her love at my breast,)
  That you fancy me dead, —
That you shudder to look at me,
  Thinking me dead :

But my heart it is brighter
  Than all of the many
Stars in the sky ;
  For it sparkles with Annie, —

It glows with the light
    Of the love of my Annie,
With the thought of the light
    Of the eyes of my Annie.
                        EDGAR ALLAN POE.

THE FAIREST THING IN MORTAL EYES.

[Addressed to his deceased wife, who died in childbed at the age of twenty-two.]

To make my lady's obsequies
    My love a minster wrought,
And, in the chantry, service there
    Was sung by doleful thought;
The tapers were of burning sighs,
    That light and odor gave;
And sorrows, painted o'er with tears,
    Enluminéd her grave;
And round about, in quaintest guise,
Was carved: " Within this tomb there lies
The fairest thing in mortal eyes."

Above her lieth spread a tomb
    Of gold and sapphires blue:
The gold doth show her blessedness,
    The sapphires mark her true;
For blessedness and truth in her
    Were livelily portrayed,
When gracious God with both his hands
    Her goodly substance made.
He framed her in such wondrous wise,
She was, to speak without disguise,
The fairest thing in mortal eyes.

No more, no more! my heart doth faint
    When I the life recall
Of her who lived so free from taint,
    So virtuous deemed by all, —
That in herself was so complete
    I think that she was ta'en
By God to deck his paradise,
    And with his saints to reign;
Whom while on earth each one did prize,
The fairest thing in mortal eyes.

But naught our tears avail, or cries;
    All soon or late in death shall sleep;
    Nor living wight long time may keep
The fairest thing in mortal eyes.
        CHARLES, DUKE OF ORLEANS (French). Trans-
        lation of HENRY FRANCIS CARY.

DIRGE FOR A YOUNG GIRL.

UNDERNEATH the sod low-lying,
    Dark and drear,
Sleepeth one who left, in dying,
    Sorrow here.

Yes, they 're ever bending o'er her
    Eyes that weep;
Forms, that to the cold grave bore her,
    Vigils keep.

When the summer moon is shining
    Soft and fair,
Friends she loved in tears are twining
    Chaplets there.

Rest in peace, thou gentle spirit,
    Throned above, —
Souls like thine with God inherit
    Life and love!
                        JAMES T. FIELDS.

FEAR NO MORE THE HEAT O' THE SUN.

FROM "CYMBELINE."

FEAR no more the heat o' the sun,
    Nor the furious winter's rages;
Thou thy worldly task hast done,
    Home art gone, and ta'en thy wages:
Golden lads and girls all must,
As chimney-sweepers, come to dust.

Fear no more the frown o' the great,
    Thou art past the tyrant's stroke;
Care no more to clothe, and eat;
    To thee the reed is as the oak:
The sceptre, learning, physic, must
All follow this, and come to dust.

Fear no more the lightning flash
    Nor the all-dreaded thunder-stone;
Fear not slander, censure rash;
    Thou hast finished joy and moan:
All lovers young, all lovers must,
Consign to thee, and come to dust.
                        SHAKESPEARE.

ROCK ME TO SLEEP.

BACKWARD, turn backward, O Time, in your
        flight,
Make me a child again just for to-night!
Mother come back from the echoless shore,
Take me again to your heart as of yore;
Kiss from my forehead the furrows of care,
Smooth the few silver threads out of my hair;
Over my slumbers your loving watch keep; —
Rock me to sleep, mother, — rock me to sleep!

Backward, flow backward, O tide of the years!
I am so weary of toil and of tears, —
Toil without recompense, tears all in vain, —
Take them, and give me my childhood again!

I have grown weary of dust and decay, —
Weary of flinging my soul-wealth away ;
Weary of sowing for others to reap ; —
Rock me to sleep, mother, — rock me to sleep !

Tired of the hollow, the base, the untrue,
Mother, O mother, my heart calls for you !
Many a summer the grass has grown green,
Blossomed, and faded our faces between,
Yet with strong yearning and passionate pain
Long I to-night for your presence again.
Come from the silence so long and so deep ; —
Rock me to sleep, mother, — rock me to sleep !

Over my heart, in the days that are flown,
No love like mother-love ever has shone ;
No other worship abides and endures, —
Faithful, unselfish, and patient like yours :
None like a mother can charm away pain
From the sick soul and the world-weary brain.
Slumber's soft calms o'er my heavy lids creep ; —
Rock me to sleep, mother, — rock me to sleep !

Come, let your brown hair, just lighted with
        gold,
Fall on your shoulders again as of old ;
Let it drop over my forehead to-night,
Shading my faint eyes away from the light ;
For with its sunny-edged shadows once more
Haply will throng the sweet visions of yore ;
Lovingly, softly, its bright billows sweep ; —
Rock me to sleep, mother, — rock me to sleep !

Mother, dear mother, the years have been
        long
Since I last listened your lullaby song :
Sing, then, and unto my soul it shall seem
Womanhood's years have been only a dream.
Clasped to your heart in a loving embrace,
With your light lashes just sweeping my face,
Never hereafter to wake or to weep ; —
Rock me to sleep, mother, — rock me to sleep !
                                    FLORENCE PERCY.

CASA WAPPY.

THE CHILD'S PET NAME, CHOSEN BY HIMSELF.

AND hast thou sought thy heavenly home,
    Our fond, dear boy, —
The realms where sorrow dare not come,
    Where life is joy ?
Pure at thy death as at thy birth,
Thy spirit caught no taint from earth ;
Even by its bliss we mete our dearth,
    Casa Wappy !

Despair was in our last farewell,
    As closed thine eye ;
Tears of our anguish may not tell
    When thou didst die ;
Words may not paint our grief for thee ;
Sighs are but bubbles on the sea
Of our unfathomed agony ;
    Casa Wappy !

Thou wert a vision of delight,
    To bless us given ;
Beauty embodied to our sight,
    A type of heaven !
So dear to us thou wert, thou art
Even less thine own self, than a part
Of mine, and of thy mother's heart,
    Casa Wappy !

Thy bright, brief day knew no decline,
    'T was cloudless joy ;
Sunrise and night alone were thine,
    Beloved boy !
This moon beheld thee blithe and gay ;
That found thee prostrate in decay ;
And ere a third shone, clay was clay,
    Casa Wappy !

Gem of our hearth, our household pride,
    Earth's undefiled,
Could love have saved, thou hadst not died,
    Our dear, sweet child !
Humbly we bow to Fate's decree ;
Yet had we hoped that Time should see
Thee mourn for us, not us for thee,
    Casa Wappy !

We mourn for thee when blind, blank night
    The chamber fills ;
We pine for thee when morn's first light
    Reddens the hills :
The sun, the moon, the stars, the sea,
All — to the wallflower and wild pea —
Are changed ; we saw the world through thee,
    Casa Wappy !

And though, perchance, a smile may gleam
    Of casual mirth,
It doth not own, whate'er may seem,
    An inward birth ;
We miss thy small step on the stair ;
We miss thee at thine evening prayer ;
All day we miss thee, — everywhere, —
    Casa Wappy !

Snows muffled earth when thou didst go,
    In life's spring-bloom,
Down to the appointed house below, —
    The silent tomb.

But now the green leaves of the tree,
The cuckoo, and "the busy bee,"
Return, — but with them bring not thee,
  Casa Wappy !

'T is so ; but can it be — while flowers
    Revive again —
Man's doom, in death that we and ours
    For aye remain ?
O, can it be, that o'er the grave
The grass renewed should yearly wave,
Yet God forget our child to save ? —
    Casa Wappy !

It cannot be ; for were it so
    Thus man could die,
Life were a mockery, thought were woe,
    And truth a lie ;
Heaven were a coinage of the brain ;
Religion frenzy, virtue vain,
And all our hopes to meet again,
    Casa Wappy !

Then be to us, O dear, lost child !
    With beam of love,
A star, death's uncongenial wild
    Smiling above !
Soon, soon thy little feet have trod
The skyward path, the seraph's road,
That led thee back from man to God,
    Casa Wappy !

Yet 't is sweet balm to our despair,
    Fond, fairest boy,
That heaven is God's, and thou art there,
    With him in joy ;
There past are death and all its woes ;
There beauty's stream forever flows ;
And pleasure's day no sunset knows,
    Casa Wappy !

Farewell, then, — for a while, farewell, —
    Pride of my heart !
It cannot be that long we dwell,
    Thus torn apart.
Time's shadows like the shuttle flee ;
And dark howe'er life's night may be,
Beyond the grave I 'll meet with thee,
    Casa Wappy !
                    DAVID MACBETH MOIR.

MOTHER AND POET.

TURIN, — AFTER NEWS FROM GAETA. 1861.

[This was Laura Savio of Turin, a poetess and patriot, whose
sons were killed at Ancona and Gaeta.]

I.

DEAD ! one of them shot by the sea in the east,
  And one of them shot in the west by the sea.

Dead ! both my boys ! When you sit at the feast
  And are wanting a great song for Italy free,
    Let none look at me !

II.

Yet I was a poetess only last year,
  And good at my art, for a woman, men said.
But this woman, this, who is agonized here,
  The east sea and west sea rhyme on in her head
    Forever instead.

III.

What art can a woman be good at ? O, vain !
  What art is she good at, but hurting her breast
With the milk teeth of babes, and a smile at the
    pain ?
  Ah, boys, how you hurt ! you were strong as
      you pressed,
    And I proud by that test.

IV.

What art 's for a woman ! To hold on her knees
  Both darlings ! to feel all their arms round her
      throat
Cling, struggle a little ! to sew by degrees
  And 'broider the long-clothes and neat little coat!
    To dream and to dote.

V.

To teach them. . . . . It stings there. I made them
    indeed
  Speak plain the word "country," I taught
      them, no doubt,
That a country 's a thing men should die for at need.
  I prated of liberty, rights, and about
    The tyrant turned out.

VI.

And when their eyes flashed . . . . O my beautiful
    eyes ! . . . .
  I exulted ! nay, let them go forth at the wheels
Of the guns, and denied not. — But then the sur-
    prise,
  When one sits quite alone ! — Then one weeps,
      then one kneels !
    — God ! · how the house feels !

VII.

At first happy news came, in gay letters moiled
  With my kisses, of camp-life, and glory, and how
They both loved me, and soon, coming home to
    be spoiled,
  In return would fan off every fly from my brow
    With their green laurel-bough.

VIII.

Then was triumph at Turin. "Ancona was free !"
  And some one came out of the cheers in the street
With a face pale as stone, to say something to me.
  — My Guido was dead ! — I fell down at his feet,
    While they cheered in the street.

IX.

I bore it ; — friends soothed me : my grief looked
  sublime
As the ransom of Italy.   One boy remained
To be leant on and walked with, recalling the time
When the first grew immortal, while both of us
  strained
To the height he had gained.

X.

And letters still came, — shorter, sadder, more
  strong,
Writ now but in one hand. " I was not to faint.
One loved me for two . . . would be with me erelong :
And ' Viva Italia ' he died for, our saint,
Who forbids our complaint."

XI.

My Nanni would add " he was safe, and aware
Of a presence that turned off the balls . . . was
  imprest
It was Guido himself, who knew what I could bear,
And how 't was impossible, quite dispossessed,
To live on for the rest."

XII.

On which without pause up the telegraph line
Swept smoothly the next news from Gaeta : —
  " Shot.
Tell his mother." Ah, ah, " his," "their" mother ;
  not " mine."
No voice says "my mother" again to me. What !
  You think Guido forgot ?

XIII.

Are souls straight so happy that, dizzy with heaven,
They drop earth's affections, conceive not of woe ?
I think not.   Themselves were too lately forgiven
Through that love and sorrow which reconciled so
  The above and below.

XIV.

O Christ of the seven wounds, who look'dst
  through the dark
To the face of thy mother ! consider, I pray,
How we common mothers stand desolate, mark,
Whose sons, not being Christs, die with eyes
  turned away,
  And no last word to say !

XV.

Both boys dead ! but that's out of nature.   We all
Have been patriots, yet each house must always
  keep one.
T were imbecile hewing out roads to a wall.
And when Italy 's made, for what end is it done
  If we have not a son ?

XVI.

Ah, ah, ah ! when Gaeta 's taken, what then ?
When the fair wicked queen sits no more at her
  sport
Of the fire-balls of death crashing souls out of men ?
When your guns at Cavalli with final retort
  Have cut the game short, —

XVII.

When Venice and Rome keep their new jubilee,
When your flag takes all heaven for its white,
  green, and red,
When you have your country from mountain to sea,
When King Victor has Italy's crown on his head,
  (And I have my dead,)

XVIII.

What then ? Do not mock me. Ah, ring your
  bells low,
And burn your lights faintly ! — My country
  is there,
Above the star pricked by the last peak of snow,
My Italy 's there, — with my brave civic pair,
  To disfranchise despair.

XIX.

Forgive me. Some women bear children in
  strength,
And bite back the cry of their pain in self-scorn.
But the birth-pangs of nations will wring us at
  length
Into such wail as this ! — and we sit on forlorn
  When the man-child is born.

XX.

Dead ! one of them shot by the sea in the west,
And one of them shot in the east by the sea !
Both ! both my boys ! — If in keeping the feast
You want a great song for your Italy free,
  Let none look at me !
ELIZABETH BARRETT BROWNING.

THE TWO APRIL MORNINGS.

WE walked along, while bright and red
  Uprose the morning sun ;
And Matthew stopped, he looked, and said,
  " The will of God be done ! "

A village schoolmaster was he,
  With hair of glittering gray ;
As blithe a man as you could see
  On a spring holiday.

And on that morning, through the grass
  And by the steaming rills
We travelled merrily, fo pass
  A day among the hills.

" Our work," said I, "was well begun ;
  Then from thy breast what thought,
Beneath so beautiful a sun,
  So sad a sigh has brought ? "

A second time did Matthew stop ;
  And, fixing still his eye
Upon the eastern mountain-top,
  To me he made reply :

"Yon cloud with that long purple cleft
  Brings fresh into my mind
A day like this, which I have left
  Full thirty years behind.

"And just above yon slope of corn
  Such colors, and no other,
Were in the sky that April morn,
  Of this the very brother.

"With rod and line I sued the sport
  Which that sweet season gave,
And, coming to the church, stopped short
  Beside my daughter's grave.

"Nine summers had she scarcely seen,
  The pride of all the vale ;
And then she sang ; — she would have been
  A very nightingale.

"Six feet in earth my Emma lay ;
  And yet I loved her more —
For so it seemed — than till that day
  I e'er had loved before.

"And, turning from her grave, I met
  Beside the churchyard yew
A blooming girl, whose hair was wet
  With points of morning dew.

"A basket on her head she bare ;
  Her brow was smooth and white :
To see a child so very fair,
  It was a pure delight !

"No fountain from its rocky cave
  E'er tripped with foot so free ;
She seemed as happy as a wave
  That dances on the sea.

"There came from me a sigh of pain
  Which I could ill confine ;
I looked at her, and looked again :
  And did not wish her mine !"

— Matthew is in his grave, yet now
  Methinks I see him stand
As at that moment, with a bough
  Of wilding in his hand.
                WILLIAM WORDSWORTH.

HESTER.

WHEN maidens such as Hester die,
  Their place ye may not well supply,
  Though ye among a thousand try,
    With vain endeavor.

A month or more hath she been dead,
Yet cannot I by force be led
To think upon the wormy bed
    And her together.

A springy motion in her gait,
A rising step, did indicate
Of pride and joy no common rate,
    That flushed her spirit ;

I know not by what name beside
I shall it call ; — if 't was not pride,
It was a joy to that allied,
    She did inherit.

Her parents held the Quaker rule,
Which doth the human feeling cool ;
But she was trained in nature's school,
    Nature had blessed her.

A waking eye, a prying mind,
A heart that stirs, is hard to bind ;
A hawk's keen sight ye cannot blind, —
    Ye could not Hester.

My sprightly neighbor, gone before
To that unknown and silent shore !
Shall we not meet as heretofore
    Some summer morning,

When from thy cheerful eyes a ray
Hath struck a bliss upon the day, —
A bliss that would not go away, —
    A sweet forewarning ?
                CHARLES LAMB.

THE LOST LOVE.

SHE dwelt among the untrodden ways
  Beside the springs of Dove ;
A maid whom there were none to praise,
  And very few to love.

A violet by a mossy stone
  Half hidden from the eye !
— Fair as a star, when only one
  Is shining in the sky.

She lived unknown, and few could know
  When Lucy ceased to be ;
But she is in her grave, and O
  The difference to me !
                WILLIAM WORDSWORTH.

THE LOST SISTER.

THEY waked me from my sleep, I knew not why,
And bade me hasten where a midnight lamp
Gleamed from an inner chamber.   There she lay,

With brow so pale, who yester-morn breathed
    forth
Through joyous smiles her superflux of bliss
Into the hearts of others. By her side
Her hoary sire, with speechless sorrow, gazed
Upon the stricken idol, — all dismayed
Beneath his God's rebuke. And she who nursed
That fair young creature at her gentle breast,
And oft those sunny locks had decked with
    buds
Of rose and jasmine, shuddering wiped the dews
Which death distils.
                    The sufferer just had given
Her long farewell, and for the last, *last* time
Touched with cold lips his cheek who led so
    late
Her footsteps to the altar, and received
In the deep transport of an ardent heart
Her vow of love. And she had striven to press
That golden circlet with her bloodless hand
Back on his finger, which he kneeling gave
At the bright bridal morn. So there she lay
In calm endurance, like the smitten lamb
Wounded in flowery pastures, from whose breast
The dreaded bitterness of death had passed.
— But a faint wail disturbed the silent scene,
And in its nurse's arms a new-born babe
Was borne in utter helplessness along,
Before that dying eye.
                  Its gathered film
Kindled one moment with a sudden glow
Of tearless agony, — and fearful pangs,
Racking the rigid features, told how strong
A mother's love doth root itself. One cry
Of bitter anguish, blent with fervent prayer,
Went up to Heaven, — and, as its cadence sank,
Her spirit entered there.
                Morn after morn
Rose and retired ; yet still as in a dream
I seemed to move. The certainty of loss
Fell not *at once* upon me. Then I wept
As weep the sisterless. — For thou wert fled,
My only, my beloved, my sainted one, —
Twin of my spirit ! and my numbered days
Must wear the sable of that midnight hour
Which rent thee from me.
                 LYDIA H. SIGOURNEY.

GO TO THY REST.

Go to thy rest, fair child !
Go to thy dreamless bed,
While yet so gentle, undefiled,
    With blessings on thy head.

Fresh roses in thy hand,
Buds on thy pillow laid,
Haste from this dark and fearful land,
    Where flowers so quickly fade.

Ere sin had seared the breast,
Or sorrow woke the tear,
Rise to thy throne of changeless rest,
    In yon celestial sphere !

Because thy smile was fair,
Thy lip and eye so bright,
Because thy loving cradle-care
    Was such a dear delight,

Shall love, with weak embrace,
Thy upward wing detain ?
No ! gentle angel, seek thy place
    Amid the cherub train.
                 ANONYMOUS.

HISTORY OF A LIFE.

DAY dawned ; within a curtained room,
Filled to faintness with perfume,
A lady lay at point of doom.
Day closed ; a child had seen the light :
But, for the lady fair and bright,
She rested in undreaming night.
Spring rose ; the lady's grave was green ;
And near it, oftentimes, was seen
A gentle boy with thoughtful mien.
Years fled ; he wore a manly face,
And struggled in the world's rough race,
And won at last a lofty place.
And then he died ! behold before ye
Humanity's poor sum and story ;
Life — Death — and all that is of Glory.
                 BARRY CORNWALL.

O, WHY SHOULD THE SPIRIT OF MORTAL BE PROUD?

[The following poem was a particular favorite with Mr. Lincoln.
Mr. F. B. Carpenter, the artist, writes that while engaged in paint-
ing his picture at the White House, he was alone one evening with the
President in his room, when he said : " There is a poem which has
been a great favorite with me for years, which was first shown to
me when a young man by a friend, and which I afterwards saw
and cut from a newspaper and learned by heart. I would," he
continued, " give a great deal to know who wrote it, but have never
been able to ascertain."]

O, WHY should the spirit of mortal be proud ?
Like a swift-fleeting meteor, a fast-flying cloud,
A flash of the lightning, a break of the wave,
Man passes from life to his rest in the grave.

The leaves of the oak and the willow shall fade,
Be scattered around and together be laid ;
And the young and the old, and the low and the
    high,
Shall moulder to dust and together shall lie.

The infant a mother attended and loved,
The mother that infant's affection who proved ;
The husband that mother and infant who blessed,
Each, all, are away to their dwellings of rest.

The maid on whose cheek, on whose brow, in
    whose eye,
Shone beauty and pleasure,—her triumphs are by ;
And the memory of those who loved her and praised,
Are alike from the minds of the living erased.

The hand of the king that the sceptre hath borne ;
The brow of the priest that the mitre hath worn ;
The eye of the sage and the heart of the brave,
Are hidden and lost in the depth of the grave.

The peasant, whose lot was to sow and to reap ;
The herdsman, who climbed with his goats up the
    steep ;
The beggar, who wandered in search of his bread,
Have faded away like the grass that we tread.

The saint who enjoyed the communion of heaven,
The sinner who dared to remain unforgiven,
The wise and the foolish, the guilty and just,
Have quietly mingled their bones in the dust.

So the multitude goes, like the flowers or the weed
That withers away to let others succeed ;
So the multitude comes, even those we behold,
To repeat every tale that has often been told.

For we are the same our fathers have been ;
We see the same sights our fathers have seen,—
We drink the same stream and view the same sun,
Aud run the same course our fathers have run.

The thoughts we are thinking our fathers would
    think ;
From the death we are shrinking our fathers would
    shrink,
To the life we are clinging they also would cling ;
But it speeds for us all, like a bird on the wing.

They loved, but the story we cannot unfold ;
They scorned, but the heart of the haughty is cold ;
They grieved, but no wail from their slumbers
    will come ;
They joyed, but the tongue of their gladness is
    dumb.

They died, ay ! they died : and we things that
    are now,
Who walk on the turf that lies over their brow,

Who make in their dwelling a transient abode,
Meet the things that they met on their pilgrimage
    road.

Yea ! hope and despondency, pleasure and pain,
We mingle together in sunshine and rain ;
And the smiles and the tears, the song and the
    dirge,
Still follow each other, like surge upon surge.

'Tis the wink of an eye, 'tis the draught of a breath,
From the blossom of health to the paleness of death,
From the gilded saloon to the bier and the shroud,—
O, why should the spirit of mortal be proud ?

WILLIAM KNOX.

ELEONORA.

ELEGY ON THE COUNTESS OF ABINGDON.

No single virtue we could most commend,
Whether the wife, the mother, or the friend ;
For she was all, in that supreme degree,
That as no one prevailed, so all was she.
The several parts lay hidden in the piece ;
The occasion but exerted that, or this.
A wife as tender, and as true withal,
As the first woman was before her fall :
Made for the man, of whom she was a part ;
Made to attract his eyes, and keep his heart.
A second Eve, but by no crime accursed ;
As beauteous, not as brittle, as the first.
Had she been first, still Paradise had been,
And death had found no entrance by her sin.
So she not only had preserved from ill
Her sex and ours, but lived their pattern still.
    Love and obedience to her lord she bore ;
She much obeyed him, but she loved him more :
Not awed to duty by superior sway,
But taught by his indulgence to obey.
Thus we love God, as author of our good.

.   .   .   .   .

    Yet unemployed no minute slipped away ;
Moments were precious in so short a stay.
The haste of Heaven to have her was so great
That some were single acts, though each complete ;
But every act stood ready to repeat.
    Her fellow-saints with busy care will look
For her blest name in fate's eternal book ;
And, pleased to be outdone, with joy will see
Numberless virtues, endless charity :
But more will wonder at so short an age,
To find a blank beyond the thirtieth page :
And with a pious fear begin to doubt
The piece imperfect, and the rest torn out.
But 'twas her Saviour's time ; and could there be
A copy near the original, 'twas she.

As precious gums are not for lasting fire,
They but perfume the temple, and expire ;
So was she soon exhaled, and vanished hence, —
A short sweet odor, of a vast expense.
She vanished, we can scarcely say she died ;
For but a now did heaven and earth divide :
She passed serenely with a single breath ;
This moment perfect health, the next was death :
One sigh did her eternal bliss assure ;
So little penance needs, when souls are almost pure.
As gentle dreams our waking thoughts pursue ;
Or, one dream passed, we slide into a new ;
So close they follow, such wild order keep,
We think ourselves awake, and are asleep :
So softly death succeeded life in her :
She did but dream of heaven, and she was there.

No pains she suffered, nor expired with noise ;
Her soul was whispered out with God's still voice ;
As an old friend is beckoned to a feast,
And treated like a long-familiar guest.
He took her as he found, but found her so,
As one in hourly readiness to go :
E'en on that day, in all her trim prepared ;
As early notice she from heaven had heard,
And some descending courier from above
Had given her timely warning to remove ;
Or counselled her to dress the nuptial room,
For on that night the bridegroom was to come.
He kept his hour, and found her where she lay
Clothed all in white, the livery of the day.

JOHN DRYDEN.

———◆———

FAREWELL TO THEE, ARABY'S DAUGHTER.

FROM "THE FIRE-WORSHIPPERS."

FAREWELL, — farewell to thee, Araby's daughter !
(Thus warbled a Peri beneath the dark sea ;)
No pearl ever lay under Oman's green water
More pure in its shell than thy spirit in thee.

O, fair as the sea-flower close to thee growing,
How light was thy heart till love's witchery
came,
Like the wind of the south o'er a summer lute
blowing,
And hushed all its music and withered its frame !

But long, upon Araby's green sunny highlands,
Shall maids and their lovers remember the doom
Of her who lies sleeping among the Pearl Islands,
With naught but the sea-star to light up her
tomb.

And still, when the merry date-season is burning,
And calls to the palm-groves the young and the
old,
The happiest there, from their pastime returning
At sunset, will weep when thy story is told.

The young village maid, when with flowers she
dresses
Her dark-flowing hair for some festival day,
Will think of thy fate till, neglecting her tresses,
She mournfully turns from the mirror away.

Nor shall Iran, beloved of her hero ! forget thee, —
Though tyrants watch over her tears as they
start,
Close, close by the side of that hero she 'll set thee,
Embalmed in the innermost shrine of her heart.

Farewell ! — be it ours to embellish thy pillow
With everything beauteous that grows in the
deep ;
Each flower of the rock and each gem of the billow
Shall sweeten thy bed and illumine thy sleep.

Around thee shall glisten the loveliest amber
That ever the sorrowing sea-bird has wept ;
With many a shell, in whose hollow-wreathed
chamber,
We, Peris of ocean, by moonlight have slept.

We 'll dive where the gardens of coral lie darkling,
And plant all the rosiest stems at thy head ;
We 'll seek where the sands of the Caspian are
sparkling,
And gather their gold to strew over thy bed.

Farewell ! — farewell ! — until pity's sweet foun-
tain
Is lost in the hearts of the fair and the brave,
They 'll weep for the Chieftain who died on that
mountain,
They 'll weep for the Maiden who sleeps in the
wave.

THOMAS MOORE.

———◆———

FAIR HELEN OF KIRKCONNELL.

[" A lady of the name of Helen Irving or Bell (for this is disputed by the two clans), daughter of the laird of Kirkconnell, in Dumfries-shire, and celebrated for her beauty, was beloved by two gentle-men in the neighborhood. The name of the favored sulter was Adam Fleming of Kirkpatrick ; that of the other has escaped tra-dition, although it has been alleged that he was a Bell of Blacket House. The addresses of the latter were, however, favored by the friends of the lady, and the lovers were therefore obliged to meet in secret, and by night, in the churchyard of Kirkconnell, a romantic spot surrounded by the river Kirtle. During one of these private interviews, the jealous and despised lover suddenly ap-peared on the opposite bank of the stream, and levelled his carabine at the breast of his rival. Helen threw herself before her lover, received in her bosom the bullet, and died in his arms. A desperate and mortal combat ensued between Fleming and the murderer, in which the latter was cut to pieces. Other accounts say that Fleming pursued his enemy to Spain, and slew him in the streets of Madrid." — SIR WALTER SCOTT.]

I WISH I were where Helen lies !
Night and day on me she cries ;
O that I were where Helen lies,
On fair Kirkconnell lee !

Curst be the heart that thought the thought,
And curst the hand that fired the shot,
When in my arms burd Helen dropt,
　And died to succor me !

O, think ye na my heart was sair,
When my love dropt down and spake nae mair !
There did she swoon wi' meikle care,
　On fair Kirkconnell lee.

As I went down the water-side,
None but my foe to be my guide,
None but my foe to be my guide,
　On fair Kirkconnell lee, —

I lighted down, my sword did draw,
I hacked him in pieces sma,
I hacked him in pieces sma,
　For her sake that died for me.

O Helen fair, beyond compare !
I 'll make a garland of thy hair,
Shall bind my heart forevermair
　Until the day I dee !

O that I were where Helen lies !
Night and day on me she cries ;
Out of my bed she bids me rise,
　Says, "Haste, and come to me !"

O Helen fair ! O Helen chaste !
If I were with thee I were blest,
Where thou lies low, and takes thy rest,
　On fair Kirkconnell lee.

I wish my grave were growing green ;
A winding-sheet drawn ower my een,
And I in Helen's arms lying
　On fair Kirkconnell lee.

I wish I were where Helen lies !
Night and day on me she cries,
And I am weary of the skies,
　For her sake that died for me !
　　　　　　　ANONYMOUS.

A ROUGH RHYME ON A ROUGH MATTER.

THE ENGLISH GAME LAWS.

THE merry brown hares came leaping
　Over the crest of the hill,
Where the clover and corn lay sleeping,
　Under the moonlight still.

Leaping late and early,
　Till under their bite and their tread,
The swedes, and the wheat, and the barley
　Lay cankered, and trampled, and dead.

A poacher's widow sat sighing
　On the side of the white chalk bank,
Where, under the gloomy fir-woods,
　One spot in the lea throve rank.

She watched a long tuft of clover,
　Where rabbit or hare never ran,
For its black sour haulm covered over
　The blood of a murdered man.

She thought of the dark plantation,
　And the hares, and her husband's blood,
And the voice of her indignation
　Rose up to the throne of God.

"I am long past wailing and whining, —
　I have wept too much in my life :
I 've had twenty years of pining
　As an English laborer's wife.

"A laborer in Christian England,
　Where they cant of a Saviour's name,
And yet waste men's lives, like the vermin's,
　For a few more brace of game.

"There 's blood on your new foreign shrubs, squire,
　There 's blood on your pointer's feet ;
There 's blood on the game you sell, squire,
　And there 's blood on the game you eat.

"You have sold the laboring man, squire,
　Both body and soul to shame,
To pay for your seat in the House, squire,
　And to pay for the feed of your game.

"You made him a poacher yourself, squire,
　When you 'd give neither work nor meat,
And your barley-fed hares robbed the garden
　At our starving children's feet.

"When, packed in one reeking chamber,
　Man, maid, mother, and little ones lay ;
While the rain pattered in on the rotten bride-bed,
　And the walls let in the day.

"When we lay in the burning fever,
　On the mud of the cold clay floor,
Till you parted us all for three months, squire,
　At the cursed workhouse door.

"We quarrelled like brutes, and who wonders ?
　What self-respect could we keep,
Worse housed than your hacks and your pointers,
　Worse fed than your hogs and your sheep ?

"Our daughters, with base-born babies,
　Have wandered away in their shame ;
If your misses had slept, squire, where they did,
　Your misses might do the same.

THE POACHER'S GAME.

" There 's blood on your foreign shrubs, squire,
There 's blood on your pointer's feet :
There 's blood on the game you sell, squire,
And there 's blood on the game you eat."

"Can your lady patch hearts that are breaking,
  With handfuls of coals and rice,
Or by dealing out flannel and sheeting
  A little below cost price?

"You may tire of the jail and the workhouse,
  And take to allotments and schools,
But you've run up a debt that will never
  Be repaid us by penny-club rules.

"In the season of shame and sadness,
  In the dark and dreary day,
When scrofula, gout, and madness
  Are eating your race away;

"When to kennels and liveried varlets
  You have cast your daughters' bread,
And, worn out with liquor and harlots,
  Your heir at your feet lies dead;

"When your youngest, the mealy-mouthed
  rector,
Lets your soul rot asleep to the grave,
You will find in your God the protector
  Of the freeman you fancied your slave."

She looked at the tuft of clover,
  And wept till her heart grew light;
And at last, when her passion was over,
  Went wandering into the night.

But the merry brown hares came leaping
  Over the uplands still,
Where the clover and corn lay sleeping
  On the side of the white chalk hill.

                          CHARLES KINGSLEY.

"THEY 'RE DEAR FISH TO ME."

THE farmer's wife sat at the door,
  A pleasant sight to see;
And blithesome were the wee, wee bairns
  That played around her knee.

When, bending 'neath her heavy creel,
  A poor fish-wife came by,
And, turning from the toilsome road,
  Unto the door drew nigh.

She laid her burden on the green,
  And spread its scaly store,
With trembling hands and pleading words
  She told them o'er and o'er.

But lightly laughed the young guidwife,
  " We 're no sae scarce o' cheer;
Tak' up your creel, and gang your ways, —
  I 'll buy nae fish sae dear."

Bending beneath her load again,
  A weary sight to see;
Right sorely sighed the poor fish-wife,
  "They 're dear fish to me!

"Our boat was oot ae fearfu' night,
  And when the storm blew o'er,
My husband, and my three brave sons,
  Lay corpses on the shore.

"I 've been a wife for thirty years,
  A childless widow three;
I maun buy them now to sell again, —
  They 're dear fish to me!"

The farmer's wife turned to the door, —
  What was 't upon her cheek?
What was there rising in her breast,
  That then she scarce could speak?

She thought upon her ain guidman,
  Her lightsome laddies three;
The woman's words had pierced her heart, —
  "They 're dear fish to me!"

"Come back," she cried, with quivering voice,
  And pity's gathering tear;
"Come in, come in, my poor woman,
  Ye 're kindly welcome here.

"I kentna o' your aching heart,
  Your weary lot to dree;
I 'll ne'er forget your sad, sad words:
  'They 're dear fish to me!'"

Ay, let the happy-hearted learn
  To pause ere they deny
The meed of honest toil, and think
  How much their gold may buy, —

How much of manhood's wasted strength,
  What woman's misery, —
What breaking hearts might swell the cry:
  "They 're dear fish to me!"

                          ANONYMOUS.

HOME THEY BROUGHT HER WARRIOR DEAD.

FROM "THE PRINCESS."

HOME they brought her warrior dead:
  She nor swooned, nor uttered cry;
All her maidens, watching, said,
  "She must weep or she will die."

Then they praised him, soft and low,
  Called him worthy to be loved,
Truest friend and noblest foe;
  Yet she neither spoke nor moved.

Stole a maiden from her place,
　Lightly to the warrior stept,
Took the face-cloth from the face ,
　Yet she neither moved nor wept.

Rose a nurse of ninety years,
　Set his child upon her knee, —
Like summer tempest came her tears, —
　"Sweet my child, I live for thee."
ALFRED TENNYSON.

THE FLOWER OF FINAE.

A BRIGADE BALLAD.

[Early in the eighteenth century the flower of the Catholic youth
of Ireland were drawn away to recruit the ranks of the Irish Bri-
gade in the service of the King of France. These recruits were
popularly known as " Wild Geese." Few returned.]

BRIGHT red is the sun on the waves of Lough
　　Sheelin,
A cool gentle breeze from the mountain is stealing,
While fair round its islets the small ripples play,
But fairer than all is the Flower of Finae.

Her hair is like night, and her eyes like gray
　　morning,
She trips on the heather as if its touch scorning,
Yet her heart and her lips are as mild as May day,
Sweet Eily MacMahon, the Flower of Finae.

But who down the hillside than red deer runs
　　fleeter ?
And who on the lake side is hastening to greet her ?
Who but Fergus O'Farrell, the fiery and gay,
The darling and pride of the Flower of Finae.

One kiss and one clasp, and one wild look of glad-
　　ness ;
Ah ! why do they change on a sudden to sadness, —
He has told his hard fortune, nor more he can stay,
He must leave his poor Eily to pine at Finae.

For Fergus O'Farrell was true to his sire-land,
And the dark hand of tyranny drove him from
　　Ireland ;
He joins the Brigade, in the wars far away,
But he vows he'll come back to the Flower of Finae.

He fought at Cremona, — she hears of his story ;
He fought at Cassano, — she 's proud of his glory,
Yet sadly she sings " Shule Aroon " all the day,
"O, come, come, my darling, come home to Finae."

Eight long years have passed, till she 's nigh
　　broken-hearted,
Her reel, and her rock, and her flax she has
　　parted ;
She sails with the "Wild Geese" to Flanders away,
And leaves her sad parents alone in Finae.

Lord Clare on the field of Ramillies is charging,
Before him the Sasanach squadrons enlarging, —
Behind him the Cravats their sections display, —
Beside him rides Fergus and shouts for Finae.

On the slopes of La Judoigne the Frenchmen are
　　flying,
Lord Clare and his squadrons the foe still defying,
Outnumbered, and wounded, retreat in array ;
And bleeding rides Fergus and thinks of Finae.

In the cloisters of Ypres a banner is swaying,
And by it a pale weeping maiden is praying ;
That flag 's the sole trophy of Ramillies' fray,
This nun is poor Eily, the Flower of Finae.
THOMAS DAVIS.

SHULE AROON.

[The following old Irish ballad has reference to the same event.]

I WOULD I were on yonder hill,
'T is there I 'd sit and cry my fill,
And every tear would turn a mill,
　Is go de tu mo murnin slàn.

　　Shule, shule, shule aroon,
　　Shule go succir, agus shule go cuin,
　　Shule go den durrus augus eligh glum,
　　Is go de tu mo murnin slàn.

I 'll sell my rock, I 'll sell my reel,
I 'll sell my only spinning-wheel,
To buy for my love a sword of steel,
　Is go de tu mo murnin slàn.

I 'll dye my petticoats, — dye them red,
And round the world I 'll beg my bread,
Until my parents shall wish me dead,
　Is go de tu mo murnin slàn.

I wish, I wish, I wish in vain,
I wish I had my heart again,
And vainly think I 'd not complain,
　Is go de tu mo murnin slàn.

But now my love has gone to France,
To try his fortune to advance,
If he e'er come back 't is but a chance,
　Is go de tu mo murnin slàn.
ANONYMOUS.

THE MAID'S LAMENT.

I LOVED him not ; and yet, now he is gone,
　I feel I am alone.
I checked him while he spoke ; yet could he speak,
　Alas ! I would not check.

For reasons not to love him once I sought,
    And wearied all my thought
To vex myself and him : I now would give
    My love, could he but live
Who lately lived for me, and when he found
    'T was vain, in holy ground
He hid his face amid the shades of death !
    I waste for him my breath
Who wasted his for me ; but mine returns,
    And this lone bosom burns
With stifling heat, heaving it up in sleep,
    And waking me to weep
Tears that had melted his soft heart : for years
    Wept he as bitter tears !
"Merciful God !" such was his latest prayer,
    "These may she never share !"
Quieter is his breath, his breast more cold
    Than daisies in the mould,
Where children spell athwart the churchyard gate
    His name and life's brief date.
Pray for him, gentle souls, whoe'er ye be,
    And O, pray, too, for me !
                WALTER SAVAGE LANDOR.

THE LANDLADY'S DAUGHTER.

THREE students were travelling over the Rhine ;
They stopped when they came to the landlady's
    sign ;
"Good landlady, have you good beer and wine ?
And where is that dear little daughter of thine?"

"My beer and wine are fresh and clear ;
My daughter she lies on the cold death-bier !"
And when to the chamber they made their way,
There, dead, in a coal-black shrine, she lay.

The first he drew near, and the veil gently raised,
And on her pale face he mournfully gazed :
"Ah ! wert thou but living yet," he said,
"I 'd love thee from this time forth, fair maid !"

The second he slowly put back the shroud,
And turned him away and wept aloud :
"Ah ! that thou liest in the cold death-bier !
Alas ! I have loved thee for many a year !"

The third he once more uplifted the veil,
And kissed her upon her mouth so pale :
"Thee loved I always ; I love still but thee ;
And thee will I love through eternity !"
        UHLAND. Translation of J. S. DWIGHT.

HIGHLAND MARY.

YE banks and braes and streams around
    The castle o' Montgomery,

Green be your woods, and fair your flowers,
    Your waters never drumlie !
There simmer first unfauld her robes,
    And there the langest tarry ;
For there I took the last fareweel
    O' my sweet Highland Mary.

How sweetly bloomed the gay green birk,
    How rich the hawthorn's blossom,
As underneath their fragrant shade
    I clasped her to my bosom !
The golden hours on angel wings
    Flew o'er me and my dearie ;
For dear to me as light and life
    Was my sweet Highland Mary.

Wi' mony a vow and locked embrace
    Our parting was fu' tender ;
And pledging aft to meet again,
    We tore oursels asunder ;
But, O, fell death's untimely frost,
    That nipt my flower sae early !
Now green 's the sod, and cauld 's the clay,
    That wraps my Highland Mary !

O pale, pale now, those rosy lips,
    I aft hae kissed sae fondly !
And closed for aye the sparkling glance
    That dwelt on me sae kindly ;
And mouldering now in silent dust
    That heart that lo'ed me dearly !
But still within my bosom's core
    Shall live my Highland Mary.
                ROBERT BURNS.

THY BRAES WERE BONNY.

THY braes were bonny, Yarrow stream !
    When first on them I met my lover ;
Thy braes how dreary, Yarrow stream !
    When now thy waves his body cover.

Forever now, O Yarrow stream !
    Thou art to me a stream of sorrow ;
For never on thy banks shall I
    Behold my love, the flower of Yarrow.

He promised me a milk-white steed,
    To bear me to his father's bowers ;
He promised me a little page,
    To 'squire me to his father's towers ;
He promised me a wedding-ring, —
    The wedding-day was fixed to-morrow ;
Now he is wedded to his grave,
    Alas, his watery grave, in Yarrow !

Sweet were his words when last we met ;
    My passion I as freely told him !
Clasped in his arms, I little thought
    That I should nevermore behold him !

Scarce was he gone, I saw his ghost;
　It vanished with a shriek of sorrow;
Thrice did the water-wraith ascend,
　And gave a doleful groan through Yarrow.

His mother from the window looked
　With all the longing of a mother;
His little sister weeping walked
　The greenwood path to meet her brother.
They sought him east, they sought him west,
　They sought him all the forest thorough;
They only saw the cloud of night,
　They only heard the roar of Yarrow!

No longer from thy window look,
　Thou hast no son, thou tender mother!
No longer walk, thou lovely maid;
　Alas, thou hast no more a brother!
No longer seek him east or west,
　And search no more the forest thorough;
For, wandering in the night so dark,
　He fell a lifeless corse in Yarrow.

The tear shall never leave my cheek,
　No other youth shall be my marrow;
I 'll seek thy body in the stream,
　And then with thee I 'll sleep in Yarrow.
　　　　　　　　　　　JOHN LOGAN.

WILLY DROWNED IN YARROW.

Down in yon garden sweet and gay
　Where bonnie grows the lily,
I heard a fair maid sighing say,
　"My wish be wi' sweet Willie!

"Willie's rare, and Willie's fair,
　And Willie's wondrous bonny;
And Willie hecht to marry me
　Gin e'er he married ony.

"O gentle wind, that bloweth south,
　From where my Love repaireth,
Convey a kiss frae his dear mouth
　And tell me how he fareth!

"O, tell sweet Willie to come doun
　And hear the mavis singing,
And see the birds on ilka bush
　And leaves around them hinging.

"The lav'rock there, wi' her white breast
　And gentle throat sae narrow;
There 's sport eneuch for gentlemen
　On Leader haughs and Yarrow.

"O, Leader haughs are wide and braid,
　And Yarrow haughs are bonny;
There Willie hecht to marry me
　If e'er he married ony.

"But Willie 's gone, whom I thought on,
　And does not hear me weeping;
Draws many a tear frae true love's e'e
　When other maids are sleeping.

"Yestreen I made my bed fu' braid,
　The night I 'll mak' it narrow,
For a' the livelang winter night
　I lie twined o' my marrow.

"O, came ye by yon water-side?
　Pou'd you the rose or lily?
Or came you by yon meadow green,
　Or saw you my sweet Willie?"

She sought him up, she sought him down,
　She sought him braid and narrow;
Syne, in the cleaving of a craig,
　She found him drowned in Yarrow!
　　　　　　　　　　　ANONYMOUS.

MARY'S DREAM.

THE moon had climbed the highest hill
　Which rises o'er the source of Dee,
And from the eastern summit shed
　Her silver light on tower and tree,
When Mary laid her down to sleep,
　Her thoughts on Sandy far at sea,
When, soft and slow, a voice was heard,
　Saying, "Mary, weep no more for me!"

She from her pillow gently raised
　Her head, to ask who there might be,
And saw young Sandy shivering stand,
　With visage pale, and hollow e'e.
"O Mary dear, cold is my clay;
　It lies beneath a stormy sea.
Far, far from thee I sleep in death;
　So, Mary, weep no more for me!

"Three stormy nights and stormy days
　We tossed upon the raging main;
And long we strove our bark to save,
　But all our striving was in vain.
Even then, when horror chilled my blood,
　My heart was filled with love for thee:
The storm is past, and I at rest;
　So, Mary, weep no more for me!

"O maiden dear, thyself prepare;
　We soon shall meet upon that shore,
Where love is free from doubt and care,
　And thou and I shall part no more!"
Loud crowed the cock, the shadow fled,
　No more of Sandy could she see;
But soft the passing spirit said,
　"Sweet Mary, weep no more for me!"
　　　　　　　　　　　JOHN LOWE.

EVELYN HOPE.

BEAUTIFUL Evelyn Hope is dead!
  Sit and watch by her side an hour.
That is her book-shelf, this her bed;
  She plucked that piece of geranium-flower,
Beginning to die, too, in the glass.
  Little has yet been changed, I think;
The shutters are shut, — no light may pass
  Save two long rays through the hinge's chink.

Sixteen years old when she died!
  Perhaps she had scarcely heard my name, —
It was not her time to love; beside,
  Her life had many a hope and aim,
Duties enough and little cares;
  And now was quiet, now astir, —
Till God's hand beckoned unawares,
  And the sweet white brow is all of her.

Is it too late, then, Evelyn Hope?
  What! your soul was pure and true;
The good stars met in your horoscope,
  Made you of spirit, fire, and dew;
And just because I was thrice as old,
  And our paths in the world diverged so wide,
Each was naught to each, must I be told?
  We were fellow-mortals, — naught beside?

No, indeed! for God above
  Is great to grant as mighty to make,
And creates the love to reward the love;
  I claim you still, for my own love's sake!
Delayed, it may be, for more lives yet,
  Through worlds I shall traverse, not a few;
Much is to learn and much to forget
  Ere the time be come for taking you.

But the time will come — at last it will —
  When, Evelyn Hope, what meant, I shall say,
In the lower earth, — in the years long still, —
  That body and soul so gay?
Why your hair was amber I shall divine,
  And your mouth of your own geranium's red, —
And what you would do with me, in fine,
  In the new life come in the old one's stead.

I have lived, I shall say, so much since then,
  Given up myself so many times,
Gained me the gains of various men,
  Ransacked the ages, spoiled the climes;
Yet one thing — one — in my soul's full scope,
  Either I missed or itself missed me, —
And I want and find you, Evelyn Hope!
  What is the issue? let us see!

I loved you, Evelyn, all the while;
  My heart seemed full as it could hold, —

There was place and to spare for the frank young
    smile,
  And the red young mouth, and the hair's young
    gold.
So, hush! I will give you this leaf to keep;
  See, I shut it inside the sweet, cold hand.
There, that is our secret! go to sleep;
  You will wake, and remember, and understand.
                                    ROBERT BROWNING.

LAMENT OF THE IRISH EMIGRANT.

I 'M sittin' on the stile, Mary,
  Where we sat side by side
On a bright May mornin' long ago,
  When first you were my bride;
The corn was springin' fresh and green,
  And the lark sang loud and high;
And the red was on your lip, Mary,
  And the love-light in your eye.

The place is little changed, Mary;
  The day is bright as then;
The lark's loud song is in my ear,
  And the corn is green again;
But I miss the soft clasp of your hand,
  And your breath, warm on my cheek;
And I still keep list'nin' for the words
  You nevermore will speak.

'T is but a step down yonder lane,
  And the little church stands near, —
The church where we were wed, Mary;
  I see the spire from here.
But the graveyard lies between, Mary,
  And my step might break your rest, —
For I 've laid you, darling, down to sleep,
  With your baby on your breast.

I 'm very lonely now, Mary,
  For the poor make no new friends;
But, O, they love the better still
  The few our Father sends!
And you were all I had, Mary, —
  My blessin' and my pride;
There 's nothing left to care for now,
  Since my poor Mary died.

Yours was the good, brave heart, Mary,
  That still kept hoping on,
When the trust in God had left my soul,
  And my arm's young strength was gone;
There was comfort ever on your lip,
  And the kind look on your brow, —
I bless you, Mary, for that same,
  Though you cannot hear me now.

I thank you for the patient smile
  When your heart was fit to break, —

When the hunger pain was gnawin' there,
   And you hid it for my sake ;
I bless you for the pleasant word,
   When your heart was sad and sore, —
O, I 'm thankful you are gone, Mary,
   Where grief can't reach you more !

I 'm biddin' you a long farewell,
   My Mary — kind and true !
But I 'll not forget you, darling,
   In the land I 'm goin' to ;
They say there 's bread and work for all,
   And the sun shines always there, —
But I 'll not forget old Ireland,
   Were it fifty times as fair !

And often in those grand old woods
   I 'll sit, and shut my eyes,
And my heart will travel back again
   To the place where Mary lies ;
And I 'll think I see the little stile
   Where we sat side by side,
And the springin' corn, and the bright May morn,
   When first you were my bride.
                LADY DUFFERIN.

GINEVRA.

IF ever you should come to Modena,
Where among other trophies may be seen
Tassoni's bucket (in its chain it hangs (72)
Within that reverend tower, the Guirlandina),
Stop at a Palace near the Reggio-gate,
Dwelt in of old by one of the Orsini.
Its noble gardens, terrace above terrace,
And rich in fountains, statues, cypresses,
Will long detain you ; but, before you go,
Enter the house — forget it not, I pray —
And look awhile upon a picture there.

'T is of a Lady in her earliest youth,
The last of that illustrious family ;
Done by Zampieri (73) — but by whom I care not.
He who observes it, ere he passes on,
Gazes his fill, and comes and comes again,
That he may call it up when far away.

She sits inclining forward as to speak,
Her lips half open, and her finger up,
As though she said "Beware !" her vest of gold
Broidered with flowers, and clasped from head to
    foot,
An emerald stone in every golden clasp ;
And on her brow, fairer than alabaster,
A coronet of pearls.
              But then her face,
So lovely, yet so arch, so full of mirth,
The overflowings of an innocent heart, —

It haunts me still, though many a year has fled,
Like some wild melody !
                  Alone it hangs
Over a mouldering heirloom, its companion,
An oaken chest, half eaten by the worm,
But richly carved by Antony of Trent
With Scripture stories from the Life of Christ, —
A chest that came from Venice, and had held
The ducal robes of some old Ancestor,
That by the way — it may be true or false —
But don't forget the picture ; and you will not
When you have heard the tale they told me there.

She was an only child, — her name Ginevra,
The joy, the pride, of an indulgent Father ;
And in her fifteenth year became a bride,
Marrying an only son, Francesco Doria,
Her playmate from her birth, and her first love.

Just as she looks there in her bridal dress,
She was all gentleness, all gayety,
Her pranks the favorite theme of every tongue.
But now the day was come, the day, the hour ;
Now, frowning, smiling, for the hundredth time,
The nurse, that ancient lady, preached decorum ;
And, in the lustre of her youth, she gave
Her hand, with her heart in it, to Francesco.

Great was the joy ; but at the Nuptial Feast,
When all sate down, the Bride herself was wanting,
Nor was she to be found ! Her father cried,
"'T is but to make a trial of our love !"
And filled his glass to all ; but his hand shook,
And soon from guest to guest the panic spread.
'T was but that instant she had left Francesco,
Laughing and looking back, and flying still,
Her ivory tooth imprinted on his finger.
But now, alas, she was not to be found ;
Nor from that hour could anything be guessed,
But that she was not !
              Weary of his life,
Francesco flew to Venice, and, embarking,
Flung it away in battle with the Turk.
Orsini lived, — and long might you have seen
An old man wandering as in quest of something,
Something he could not find, he knew not what.
When he was gone, the house remained awhile
Silent and tenantless, — then went to strangers.

Full fifty years were past, and all forgotten,
When on an idle day, a day of search
Mid the old lumber in the Gallery,
That mouldering chest was noticed ; and 't was said
By one as young, as thoughtless as Ginevra,
"Why not remove it from its lurking-place ?"
'T was done as soon as said ; but on the way
It burst, it fell ; and lo, a skeleton,
With here and there a pearl, an emerald stone,
A golden clasp, clasping a shred of gold.

All else had perished, — save a wedding-ring,
And a small seal, her mother's legacy,
Engraven with a name, the name of both,
" Ginevra."

      There then had she found a grave !
Within that chest had she concealed herself,
Fluttering with joy, the happiest of the happy ;
When a spring-lock, that lay in ambush there,
Fastened her down forever !

SAMUEL ROGERS.

THE MISTLETOE BOUGH.

THE mistletoe hung in the castle hall,
The holly branch shone on the old oak wall ;
And the baron's retainers were blithe and gay,
And keeping their Christmas holiday.
The baron beheld with a father's pride
His beautiful child, young Lovell's bride ;
While she with her bright eyes seemed to be
The star of the goodly company.

" I 'm weary of dancing now," she cried ;
" Here tarry a moment, — I 'll hide, I 'll hide !
And, Lovell, be sure thou 'rt first to trace
The clew to my secret lurking-place."
Away she ran, — and her friends began
Each tower to search, and each nook to scan ;
And young Lovell cried, "O, where dost thou hide?
I 'm lonesome without thee, my own dear bride."

They sought her that night ! and they sought her
    next day !
And they sought her in vain when a week passed
    away !
In the highest, the lowest, the loneliest spot,
Young Lovell sought wildly, — but found her not.
And years flew by, and their grief at last
Was told as a sorrowful tale long past ;
And when Lovell appeared, the children cried,
" See ! the old man weeps for his fairy bride."

At length an oak chest, that had long lain hid,
Was found in the castle, — they raised the lid,
And a skeleton form lay mouldering there
In the bridal wreath of that lady fair !
O, sad was her fate ! — in sportive jest
She hid from her lord in the old oak chest.
It closed with a spring ! — and, dreadful doom,
The bride lay clasped in her living tomb !

THOMAS HAYNES BAYLY.

THE DISAPPOINTED LOVER.

I WILL go back to the great sweet mother,
Mother and lover of men, the sea.

I will go down to her, I and none other,
    Close with her, kiss her, and mix her with me ;
Cling to her, strive with her, hold her fast.
O fair white mother, in days long past
Born without sister, born without brother,
    Set free my soul as thy soul is free.

O fair green-girdled mother of mine,
    Sea, that art clothed with the sun and the rain,
Thy sweet hard kisses are strong like wine,
    Thy large embraces are keen like pain !
Save me and hide me with all thy waves,
Find me one grave of thy thousand graves,
Those pure cold populous graves of thine,
    Wrought without hand in a world without stain.

I shall sleep, and move with the moving ships,
    Change as the winds change, veer in the tide ;
My lips will feast on the foam of thy lips,
    I shall rise with thy rising, with thee subside.
Sleep, and not know if she be, if she were,
Filled full with life to the eyes and hair,
As a rose is fulfilled to the rose-leaf tips
    With splendid summer and perfume and pride.

This woven raiment of nights and days,
    Were it once cast off and unwound from me,
Naked and glad would I walk in thy ways,
    Alive and aware of thy waves and thee ;
Clear of the whole world, hidden at home,
Clothed with the green, and crowned with the foam,
A pulse of the life of thy straits and bays,
    A vein in the heart of the streams of the sea.

ALGERNON CHARLES SWINBURNE.

ANNABEL LEE.

IT was many and many a year ago,
    In a kingdom by the sea,
That a maiden lived, whom you may know
    By the name of Annabel Lee ;
And this maiden she lived with no other thought
    Than to love, and be loved by me.

I was a child and she was a child,
    In this kingdom by the sea ;
But we loved with a love that was more than love,
    I and my Annabel Lee, —
With a love that the wingéd seraphs of heaven
    Coveted her and me.

And this was the reason that long ago,
    In this kingdom by the sea,
A wind blew out of a cloud, chilling
    My beautiful Annabel Lee ;

So that her high-born kinsmen came,
  And bore her away from me,
To shut her up in a sepulchre,
  In this kingdom by the sea.

The angels, not so happy in heaven,
  Went envying her and me.
Yes ! that was the reason (as all men know)
  In this kingdom by the sea,
That the wind came out of the cloud by night,
  Chilling and killing my Annabel Lee.

But our love it was stronger by far than the love
  Of those who were older than we,
  Of many far wiser than we ;
And neither the angels in heaven above,
  Nor the demons down under the sea,
Can ever dissever my soul from the soul
  Of the beautiful Annabel Lee.

For the moon never beams without bringing me
    dreams
  Of the beautiful Annabel Lee,
And the stars never rise but I feel the bright eyes
  Of the beautiful Annabel Lee.
And so, all the night-tide I lie down by the side
Of my darling, my darling, my life, and my bride,
  In her sepulchre there by the sea,
  In her tomb by the sounding sea.
                              EDGAR ALLAN POE.

MINSTREL'S SONG.

O, SING unto my roundelay !
  O, drop the briny tear with me !
Dance no more at holiday ;
  Like a running river be.
    My love is dead,
    Gone to his death-bed,
    All under the willow-tree.

Black his hair as the winter night,
  White his neck as the summer snow,
Ruddy his face as the morning light ;
  Cold he lies in the grave below.
    My love is dead, &c.

Sweet his tongue as the throstle's note ;
  Quick in dance as thought can be ;
Deft his tabor, cudgel stout ;
  O, he lies by the willow-tree !
    My love is dead, &c.

Hark ! the raven flaps his wing
  In the briered dell below ;
Hark ! the death-owl loud doth sing
  To the nightmares as they go.
    My love is dead, &c.

See ! the white moon shines on high ;
  Whiter is my true-love's shroud,
Whiter than the morning sky,
  Whiter than the evening cloud.
    My love is dead, &c.

Here, upon my true-love's grave
  Shall the barren flowers be laid,
Nor one holy saint to save
  All the coldness of a maid.
    My love is dead, &c.

With my hands I 'll bind the briers
  Round his holy corse to gre ;
Ouphant fairy, light your fires ;
  Here my body still shall be.
    My love is dead, &c.

Come, with acorn-cup and thorn,
  Drain my heart's blood away ;
Life and all its good I scorn,
  Dance by night, or feast by day.
    My love is dead, &c.

Water-witches, crowned with reytes,
  Bear me to your lethal tide.
I die ! I come ! my true-love waits.
  Thus the damsel spake, and died.
                          THOMAS CHATTERTON.

THE DIRTY OLD MAN.

A LAY OF LEADENHALL.

[A singular man, named Nathaniel Bentley, for many years kept a large hardware shop in Leadenhall Street, London. He was best known as Dirty Dick (Dick, for alliteration's sake, probably), and his place of business as the Dirty Warehouse. He died about the year 1809. These verses accord with the accounts respecting himself and his house.]

IN a dirty old house lived a Dirty Old Man ;
Soap, towels, or brushes were not in his plan.
For forty long years, as the neighbors declared,
His house never once had been cleaned or repaired.

'T was a scandal and shame to the business-like
    street,
One terrible blot in a ledger so neat :
The shop full of hardware, but black as a hearse,
And the rest of the mansion a thousand times worse.

Outside, the old plaster, all spatter and stain,
Looked spotty in sunshine and streaky in rain ;
The window-sills sprouted with mildewy grass,
And the panes from being broken were known to
    be glass.

On the rickety signboard no learning could spell
The merchant who sold, or the goods he 'd to
    sell :

But for house and for man a new title took growth,
Like a fungus, — the Dirt gave its name to them
   both.

Within, there were carpets and cushions of dust,
The wood was half rot, and the metal half rust,
Old curtains, half cobwebs, hung grimly aloof ;
'T was a Spiders' Elysium from cellar to roof.

There, king of the spiders, the Dirty Old Man
Lives busy and dirty as ever he can ;
With dirt on his fingers and dirt on his face,
For the Dirty Old Man thinks the dirt no disgrace.

From his wig to his shoes, from his coat to his shirt,
His clothes are a proverb, a marvel of dirt ;
The dirt is pervading, unfading, exceeding, —
Yet the Dirty Old Man has both learning and
   breeding.

Fine dames from their carriages, noble and fair,
Have entered his shop, less to buy than to stare ;
And have afterwards said, though the dirt was
   so frightful,
The Dirty Man's manners were truly delightful.

Upstairs might they venture, in dirt and in gloom,
To peep at the door of the wonderful room
Such stories are told about, none of them true ! —
The keyhole itself has no mortal seen through.

That room, — forty years since, folk settled and
   decked it.
The luncheon 's prepared, and the guests are ex-
   pected.
The handsome young host he is gallant and gay,
For his love and her friends will be with him to-day.

With solid and dainty the table is drest,
The wine beams its brightest, the flowers bloom
   their best ;
Yet the host need not smile, and no guests will
   appear,
For his sweetheart is dead, as he shortly shall hear.

Full forty years since turned the key in that door.
'T is a room deaf and dumb mid the city's uproar.
The guests, for whose joyance that table was spread,
May now enter as ghosts, for they 're every one dead.

Through a chink in the shutter dim lights come
   and go ;
The seats are in order, the dishes a-row :
But the luncheon was wealth to the rat and the
   mouse
Whose descendants have long left the Dirty Old
   House.

Cup and platter are masked in thick layers of dust ;
The flowers fallen to powder, the wine swathed in
   crust ;

A nosegay was laid before one special chair,
And the faded blue ribbon that bound it lies there.

The old man has played out his parts in the scene.
Wherever he now is, I hope he 's more clean.
Yet give we a thought free of scoffing or ban
To that Dirty Old House and that Dirty Old Man.
              WILLIAM ALLINGHAM.

LAMENT OF THE BORDER WIDOW.

[This ballad relates to the execution of Cockburne of Hender-
land, a border freebooter, hanged over the gate of his own tower by
James V. in his famous expedition, in 1529, against the marauders
of the border. In a deserted burial-place near the ruins of the cas-
tle, the monument of Cockburne and his lady is still shown. The
following inscription is still legible, though defaced : —
"HERE LYES PERYS OF COKBURNE AND HIS WYFE
        MARJORY."
           SIR WALTER SCOTT.]

MY love he built me a bonnie bower,
  And clad it a' wi' lily flower ;
A brawer bower ye ne'er did see,
  Than my true-love he built for me.

There came a man, by middle day,
  He spied his sport, and went away ;
And brought the king that very night,
  Who brake my bower, and slew my knight.

He slew my knight, to me sae dear ;
  He slew my knight, and poin'd his gear :
My servants all for life did flee,
  And left me in extremitie.

I sewed his sheet, making my mane ;
  I watched the corpse mysell alane ;
I watched his body night and day ;
  No living creature came that way.

I took his body on my back,
  And whiles I gaed, and whiles I sat ;
I digged a grave, and laid him in,
  And happed him with the sod sae green.

But think na ye my heart was sair,
  When I laid the moul' on his yellow hair ?
O, think na ye my heart was wae,
  When I turned about, away to gae ?

Nae living man I 'll love again,
  Since that my lively knight is slain ;
Wi' ae lock o' his yellow hair
  I 'll chain my heart forevermair.
              ANONYMOUS.

THE KING OF DENMARK'S RIDE.

WORD was brought to the Danish king
     (Hurry !)
That the love of his heart lay suffering,
And pined for the comfort his voice would bring ;
     (O, ride as though you were flying !)

Better he loves each golden curl
On the brow of that Scandinavian girl
Than his rich crown jewels of ruby and pearl:
　And his rose of the isles is dying!

Thirty nobles saddled with speed;
　　(Hurry!)
Each one mounting a gallant steed
Which he kept for battle and days of need;
　　(O, ride as though you were flying!)
Spurs were struck in the foaming flank;
Worn-out chargers staggered and sank;
Bridles were slackened, and girths were burst;
But ride as they would, the king rode first,
For his rose of the isles lay dying!

His nobles are beaten, one by one;
　　(Hurry!)
They have fainted, and faltered, and homeward
　　gone;
His little fair page now follows alone,
　　For strength and for courage trying!
The king looked back at that faithful child;
Wan was the face that answering smiled;
They passed the drawbridge with clattering din,
Then he dropped; and only the king rode in
　Where his rose of the isles lay dying!

The king blew a blast on his bugle horn;
　　(Silence!)
No answer came; but faint and forlorn
An echo returned on the cold gray morn,
　　Like the breath of a spirit sighing.
The castle portal stood grimly wide;
None welcomed the king from that weary ride;
For dead, in the light of the dawning day,
The pale sweet form of the welcomer lay,
　Who had yearned for his voice while dying!

The panting steed, with a drooping crest,
　　Stood weary.
The king returned from her chamber of rest,
The thick sobs choking in his breast;
　　And, that dumb companion eying,
The tears gushed forth which he strove to check;
He bowed his head on his charger's neck:
"O steed, that every nerve didst strain,
Dear steed, our ride hath been in vain
　To the halls where my love lay dying!"

　　　　　　　　　　CAROLINE NORTON.

HIGH-TIDE ON THE COAST OF LIN-
COLNSHIRE.

THE old mayor climbed the belfry tower,
　The ringers ran by two, by three;
"Pull! if ye never pulled before;
　Good ringers, pull your best," quoth hee.

"Play uppe, play uppe, O Boston bells!
Ply all your changes, all your swells!
　Play uppe *The Brides of Enderby!*"

Men say it was a "stolen tyde,"—
　The Lord that sent it, he knows all,
But in myne ears doth still abide
　The message that the bells let fall;
And there was naught of strange, beside
The flights of mews and peewits pied,
　By millions crouched on the old sea-wall.

I sat and spun within the doore;
　My thread brake off, I raised myne eyes:
The level sun, like ruddy ore,
　Lay sinking in the barren skies;
And dark against day's golden death
She moved where Lindis wandereth!—
My sonne's faire wife, Elizabeth.

"Cusha! Cusha! Cusha!" calling,
Ere the early dews were falling,
Farre away I heard her song.
"Cusha! Cusha!" all along;
Where the reedy Lindis floweth,
　　Floweth, floweth,
From the meads where melick groweth,
Faintly came her milking-song.

"Cusha! Cusha! Cusha!" calling,
"For the dews will soone be falling;
Leave your meadow grasses mellow,
　　Mellow, mellow!
Quit your cowslips, cowslips yellow!
Come uppe, Whitefoot! come uppe, Lightfoot!
Quit the stalks of parsley hollow,
　　Hollow, hollow!
Come uppe, Jetty! rise and follow;
From the clovers lift your head!
Come uppe, Whitefoot! come uppe, Lightfoot!
Come uppe, Jetty! rise and follow,
Jetty, to the milking-shed."

If it be long—ay, long ago—
　When I beginne to think howe long,
Againe I hear the Lindis flow,
　Swift as an arrowe, sharpe and strong;
And all the aire, it seemeth mee,
Bin full of floating bells (sayth shee),
That ring the tune of *Enderby*.

Alle fresh the level pasture lay,
　And not a shadowe mote be seene,
Save where, full fyve good miles away,
　The steeple towered from out the greene,
And lo! the great bell farre and wide
Was heard in all the country side
That Saturday at eventide.

The swannerds, where their sedges are,
    Moved on in sunset's golden breath ;
The shepherde lads I heard afarre,
    And my sonne's wife, Elizabeth ;
Till, floating o'er the grassy sea,
Came downe that kyndly message free,
The Brides of Mavis Enderby.

Then some looked uppe into the sky,
    And all along where Lindis flows
To where the goodly vessels lie,
    And where the lordly steeple shows.
They sayde, " And why should this thing be,
What danger lowers by land or sea ?
They ring the tune of *Enderby.*

" For evil news from Mablethorpe,
    Of pyrate galleys, warping down, —
For shippes ashore beyond the scorpe,
    They have not spared to wake the towne ;
But while the west bin red to see,
And storms be none, and pyrates flee,
Why ring *The Brides of Enderby ?*

I looked without, and lo ! my sonne
    Came riding downe with might and main ;
He raised a shout as he drew on,
    Till all the welkin rang again :
" Elizabeth ! Elizabeth ! "
(A sweeter woman ne'er drew breath
Than my sonne's wife, Elizabeth.)

" The olde sea-wall " (he cryed) " is downe !
    The rising tide comes on apace ;
And boats adrift in yonder towne
    Go sailing uppe the market-place ! "
He shook as one that looks on death :
" God save you, mother ! " straight he sayth ;
" Where is my wife, Elizabeth ? "

" Good sonne, where Lindis winds away
    With her two bairns I marked her long ;
And ere yon bells beganne to play,
    Afar I heard her milking-song."
He looked across the grassy sea,
To right, to left, Ho, *Enderby !*
They rang *The Brides of Enderby.*

With that he cried and beat his breast ;
    For lo ! along the river's bed
A mighty eygre reared his crest,
    And uppe the Lindis raging sped.
It swept with thunderous noises loud, —
Shaped like a curling snow-white cloud,
Or like a demon in a shroud.

And rearing Lindis, backward pressed,
    Shook all her trembling bankes amaine ;
Then madly at the eygre's breast
    Flung uppe her weltering walls again.

Then bankes came downe with ruin and rout, —
Then beaten foam flew round about, —
Then all the mighty floods were out.

So farre, so fast, the eygre drave,
    The heart had hardly time to beat
Before a shallow seething wave
    Sobbed in the grasses at oure feet :
The feet had hardly time to flee
Before it brake against the knee, —
And all the world was in the sea.

Upon the roofe we sate that night ;
    The noise of bells went sweeping by ;
I marked the lofty beacon light
    Stream from the church tower, red and high, —
A lurid mark, and dread to see ;
And awsome bells they were to mee,
That in the dark rang *Enderby.*

They rang the sailor lads to guide,
    From roofe to roofe who fearless rowed ;
And I, — my sonne was at my side,
    And yet the ruddy beacon glowed ;
And yet he moaned beneath his breath,
" O, come in life, or come in death !
O lost ! my love, Elizabeth ! "

And didst thou visit him no more ?
    Thou didst, thou didst, my daughter deare,
The waters laid thee at his doore
    Ere yet the early dawn was clear :
Thy pretty bairns in fast embrace,
The lifted sun shone on thy face,
Downe drifted to thy dwelling-place.

That *flow* strewed wrecks about the grass,
    That *ebbe* swept out the flocks to sea, —
A fatal *ebbe* and *flow,* alas !
    To manye more than myne and mee ;
But each will mourne his own (she sayth)
And sweeter woman ne'er drew breath
Than my sonne's wife, Elizabeth.

I shall never hear her more
By the reedy Lindis shore,
    " Cusha ! Cusha ! Cusha ! " calling,
Ere the early dews be falling ;
I shall never hear her song,
    " Cusha ! Cusha ! " all along,
Where the sunny Lindis floweth,
        Goeth, floweth,
From the meads where melick groweth,
Where the water, winding down,
Onward floweth to the town.

I shall never see her more,
Where the reeds and rushes quiver,
        Shiver, quiver,
Stand beside the sobbing river, —

Sobbing, throbbing, in its falling,
   To the sandy, lonesome shore ;
I shall never hear her calling,
   "Leave your meadow grasses mellow,
         Mellow, mellow !
Quit your cowslips, cowslips yellow !
Come uppe, Whitefoot ! come uppe, Lightfoot !
Quit your pipes of parsley hollow,
         Hollow, hollow !
Come uppe, Lightfoot ! rise and follow ;
         Lightfoot ! Whitefoot !
From your clovers lift the head ;
Come uppe, Jetty ! follow, follow,
Jetty, to the milking-shed ! "
                              JEAN INGELOW.

THE MERRY LARK.

THE merry, merry lark was up and singing,
   And the hare was out and feeding on the lea,
And the merry, merry bells below were ringing,
   When my child's laugh rang through me.
Now the hare is snared and dead beside the
         snowyard,
   And the lark beside the dreary winter sea,
And my baby in his cradle in the churchyard
   Waiteth there until the bells bring me.
                           CHARLES KINGSLEY.

THE MORNING-GLORY.

WE wreathed about our darling's head
   The morning-glory bright ;
Her little face looked out beneath
   So full of life and light,
So lit as with a sunrise,
   That we could only say,
"She is the morning-glory true,
   And her poor types are they."

So always from that happy time
   We called her by their name,
And very fitting did it seem, —
   For sure as morning came,
Behind her cradle bars she smiled
   To catch the first faint ray,
As from the trellis smiles the flower
   And opens to the day.

But not so beautiful they rear
   Their airy cups of blue,
As turned her sweet eyes to the light,
   Brimmed with sleep's tender dew ;
And not so close their tendrils fine
   Round their supports are thrown,
As those dear arms whose outstretched plea
   Clasped all hearts to her own.

We used to think how she had come,
   Even as comes the flower,
The last and perfect added gift
   To crown Love's morning hour ;
And how in her was imaged forth
   The love we could not say,
As on the little dewdrops round
   Shines back the heart of day.

.   .   .   .   .

The morning-glory's blossoming
   Will soon be coming round, —
We see their rows of heart-shaped leaves
   Upspringing from the ground ;
The tender things the winter killed
   Renew again their birth,
But the glory of our morning
   Has passed away from earth.

Earth ! in vain our aching eyes
   Stretch over thy green plain !
Too harsh thy dews, too gross thine air,
   Her spirit to sustain ;
But up in groves of Paradise
   Full surely we shall see
Our morning-glory beautiful
   Twine round our dear Lord's knee.
                        MARIA WHITE LOWELL.

THE TOMB OF CYRUS.

A VOICE from stately Babylon, a mourner's rising
      cry,
And Lydia's marble palaces give back their deep
      reply ;
And like the sounds of distant winds o'er ocean's
      billows sent,
Ecbatana, thy storied walls send forth the wild
      lament.

For he, the dreaded arbiter, a dawning empire's
      trust,
The eagle child of victory, the great, the wise, the
      just,
Assyria's famed and conquering sword, and Media's
      regal strength,
Hath bowed his head to earth beneath a mightier
      hand at length.

And darkly through a sorrowing land Euphrates
      winds along,
And Cydnus with its silver wave hath heard the
      funeral song ;
And through the wide and sultry East, and through
      the frozen North,
The tabret and the harp are hushed, — the wail of
      grief goes forth.

There is a solitary tomb, with rankling weeds o'er-
grown,
A single palm bends mournfully beside the mould-
ering stone
Amidst whose leaves the passing breeze with fit-
ful gust and slow
Seems sighing forth a feeble dirge for him who
sleeps below.

Beside, its sparkling drops of foam a desert foun-
tain showers ;
And, floating calm, the lotus wreathes its red and
scented flowers,
Here lurks the mountain fox unseen beside the
vulture's nest ;
And steals the wild hyena forth, in lone and silent
quest.

Is this deserted resting-place the couch of fallen
might ?
And ends the path of glory thus, and fame's in-
spiring light ?
Chief of a progeny of kings renowned and feared
afar,
How is thy boasted name forgot, and dimmed thine
honor's star !

Approach, — what saith the graven verse ? "Alas
for human pride !
Dominion's envied gifts were mine, nor earth
her praise denied.
Thou traveller, if a suppliant's voice find echo in
thy breast,
O, envy not the little dust that hides my mortal
rest !" ANONYMOUS.

HELVELLYN.

A BARKING sound the shepherd hears,
A cry as of a dog or fox ;
He halts, and searches with his eyes
Among the scattered rocks ;
And now at distance can discern
A stirring in a brake of fern ;
And instantly a dog is seen,
Glancing through that covert green.

The dog is not of mountain breed ;
Its motions, too, are wild and shy, —
With something, as the shepherd thinks,
Unusual in its cry ;
Nor is there any one in sight
All round, in hollow or on height ;
Nor shout nor whistle strikes his ear.
What is the creature doing here ?

It was a cove, a huge recess,
That keeps, till June, December's snow ;
A lofty precipice in front,
A silent tarn below !
Far in the bosom of Helvellyn,

Remote from public road or dwelling,
Pathway, or cultivated land, —
From trace of human foot or hand.

There sometimes doth a leaping fish
Send through the tarn a lonely cheer ;
The crags repeat the raven's croak
In symphony austere ;
Thither the rainbow comes, the cloud,
And mists that spread the flying shroud ;
And sunbeams ; and the sounding blast,
That, if it could, would hurry past,
But that enormous barrier holds it fast.

Not free from boding thoughts, awhile
The shepherd stood ; then makes his way
O'er rocks and stones, following the dog
As quickly as he may ;
Nor far had gone before he found
A human skeleton on the ground.
The appalled discoverer with a sigh
Looks round to learn the history.

From those abrupt and perilous rocks
The man had fallen, that place of fear !
At length upon the shepherd's mind
It breaks, and all is clear.
He instantly recalled the name,
And who he was, and whence he came ;
Remembered, too, the very day
On which the traveller passed this way.

But hear a wonder, for whose sake
This lamentable tale I tell !
A lasting monument of words
This wonder merits well.
The dog, which still was hovering nigh,
Repeating the same timid cry,
This dog had been through three months' space
A dweller in that savage place.

Yes, proof was plain, that, since the day
When this ill-fated traveller died,
The dog had watched about the spot,
Or by his master's side.
How nourished here through such long time
He knows who gave that love sublime,
And gave that strength of feeling, great
Above all human estimate !
WILLIAM WORDSWORTH.

HELVELLYN.

[In the spring of 1805 a young gentleman of talents, and of a most
amiable disposition, perished by losing his way on the mountain
Helvellyn. His remains were not discovered till three months af-
terwards, when they were found guarded by a faithful terrier, his
constant attendant during frequent solitary rambles through the
wilds of Cumberland and Westmoreland.]

I CLIMBED the dark brow of the mighty Helvellyn,
Lakes and mountains beneath me gleamed
misty and wide :

All was still, save, by fits, when the eagle was
　　yelling,
And starting around me the echoes replied.
On the right, Striden Edge round the Red Tarn
　　was bending,
And Catchedicam its left verge was defending,
One huge nameless rock in the front was ascending,
　　When I marked the sad spot where the wan-
　　　derer had died.

Dark green was that spot mid the brown mountain
　　heather,
　　Where the Pilgrim of Nature lay stretched in
　　　decay,
Like the corpse of an outcast abandoned to weather,
　　Till the mountain winds wasted the tenantless
　　　clay.
Nor yet quite deserted, though lonely extended,
For, faithful in death, his mute favorite attended,
The much-loved remains of her master defended,
　　And chased the hill-fox and the raven away.

How long didst thou think that his silence was
　　slumber?
　　When the wind waved his garment, how oft
　　　didst thou start?
How many long days and long nights didst thou
　　number
　　Ere he faded before thee, the friend of thy heart?
And, O, was it meet that—no requiem read
　　o'er him,
No mother to weep, and no friend to deplore
　　him,
And thou, little guardian, alone stretched before
　　him—
　　Unhonored the Pilgrim from life should depart?

When a prince to the fate of the Peasant has
　　yielded,
　　The tapestry waves dark round the dim-lighted
　　　hall,
With 'scutcheons of silver the coffin is shielded,
　　And pages stand mute by the canopied pall:
Through the courts, at deep midnight, the
　　torches are gleaming;
In the proudly arched chapel the banners are
　　beaming;
Far adown the long aisle sacred music is stream-
　　ing,
　　Lamenting a Chief of the People should fall.

But meeter for thee, gentle lover of nature,
　　To lay down thy head like the meek mountain
　　　lamb,
When, wildered, he drops from some cliff huge
　　in stature,
　　And draws his last sob by the side of his
　　　dam.

And more stately thy couch by this desert lake
　　lying,
Thy obsequies sung by the gray plover flying,
With one faithful friend but to witness thy dying,
　　In the arms of Helvellyn and Catchedicam.
　　　　　　　　　　　　　SIR WALTER SCOTT.

CŒUR DE LION AT THE BIER OF HIS FATHER.

[The body of Henry the Second lay in state in the abbey-church of Fontevraud, where it was visited by Richard Cœur de Lion, who on beholding it, was struck with horror and remorse, and bitterly reproached himself for that rebellious conduct which had been the means of bringing his father to an untimely grave.]

TORCHES were blazing clear,
　　Hymns pealing deep and slow,
Where a king lay stately on his bier
　　In the church of Fontevraud.
Banners of battle o'er him hung,
　　And warriors slept beneath,
And light, as noon's broad light was flung
　　On the settled face of death.

On the settled face of death
　　A strong and ruddy glare,
Though dimmed at times by the censer's breath,
　　Yet it fell still brightest there;
As if each deeply furrowed trace
　　Of earthly years to show,—
Alas! that sceptred mortal's race
　　Had surely closed in woe!

The marble floor was swept
　　By many a long dark stole,
As the kneeling priests, round him that slept,
　　Sang mass for the parted soul;
And solemn were the strains they poured
　　Through the stillness of the night,
With the cross above, and the crown and sword,
　　And the silent king in sight.

There was heard a heavy clang,
　　As of steel-girt men the tread,
And the tombs and the hollow pavement rang
　　With a sounding thrill of dread;
And the holy chant was hushed awhile,
　　As, by the torch's flame,
A gleam of arms up the sweeping aisle
　　With a mail-clad leader came.

He came with haughty look,
　　An eagle glance and clear;
But his proud heart through its breastplate shook
　　When he stood beside the bier!
He stood there still with a drooping brow,
　　And clasped hands o'er it raised;—
For his father lay before him low,
　　It was Cœur de Lion gazed!

And silently he strove
With the workings of his breast ;
But there 's more in late repentant love
Than steel may keep suppressed !
And his tears brake forth, at last, like rain, —
Men held their breath in awe,
For his face was seen by his warrior-train,
And he recked not that they saw.

He looked upon the dead,
And sorrow seemed to lie,
A weight of sorrow, even like lead,
Pale on the fast-shut eye.
He stooped, — and kissed the frozen cheek,
And the heavy hand of clay,
Till bursting words — yet all too weak —
Gave his soul's passion way.

"O father ! is it vain,
This late remorse and deep ?
Speak to me, father ! once again,
I weep, — behold, I weep !
Alas ! my guilty pride and ire !
Were but this work undone,
I would give England's crown, my sire !
To hear thee bless thy son.

"Speak to me ! mighty grief
Ere now the dust hath stirred !
Hear me, but hear me ! — father, chief,
My king ! I *must* be heard !
Hushed, hushed, — how is it that I call,
And that thou answerest not ?
When was it thus, woe, woe for all
The love my soul forgot !

"Thy silver hairs I see,
So still, so sadly bright !
And father, father ! but for me,
They had not been so white !
I bore thee down, high heart ! at last,
No longer couldst thou strive ; —
O, for one moment of the past
To kneel and say, — 'Forgive !'

"Thou wert the noblest king
On royal throne ere seen ;
And thou didst wear in knightly ring,
Of all, the stateliest mien ;
And thou didst prove, where spears are proved,
In war, the bravest heart, —
O, ever the renowned and loved
Thou wert, — and *there* thou art !

"Thou that my boyhood's guide
Didst take fond joy to be ! —
The times I 've sported at thy side,
And climbed thy parent knee !

And there before the blessed shrine,
My sire ! I see thee lie, —
How will that sad still face of thine
Look on me till I die !"
FELICIA HEMANS.

BERNARDO DEL CARPIO.

[Bernardo del Carpio, a Spanish warrior and grandee, having made many ineffectual efforts to procure the release of his father, the Count Saldana, declared war against King Alphonso of Asturias. Being successful, the king agreed to terms by which he rendered up his prisoner to Bernardo, in exchange for the castle of Carpio and the captives confined therein. When the warrior pressed forward to greet his father, whom he had not seen for many years, he found a corpse on horseback.]

I.

THE warrior bowed his crested head, and tamed
    his heart of fire,
And sued the haughty king to free his long-im-
    prisoned sire :
"I bring thee here my fortress-keys, I bring my
    captive train,
I pledge thee faith, my liege, my lord ! O, break
    my father's chain ! "

II.

"*Rise ! rise !* even now thy father comes, a ran-
    somed man this day !
Mount thy good horse ; and thou and I will meet
    him on his way.
Then lightly rose that loyal son, and bounded on
    his steed,
And urged, as if with lance in rest, the charger's
    foamy speed.

III.

And, lo, from far, as on they pressed, there came
    a glittering band,
With one that midst them stately rode, as a leader
    in the land :
"Now haste, Bernardo, haste ! for there, in very
    truth, is he,
The father whom thy faithful heart hath yearned
    so long to see.

IV.

His dark eye flashed, his proud breast heaved,
    his cheek's hue came and went ;
He reached that gray-haired chieftain's side, and
    there, dismounting, bent ;
A lowly knee to earth he bent, his father's hand
    he took, —
What was there in its touch that all his fiery spirit
    shook ?

V.

That hand was cold, — a frozen thing, — it
    dropped from his like lead !
He looked up to the face above, — the face was
    of the dead !

A plume waved o'er the noble brow, — the brow
    was fixed and white ;
He met, at last, his father's eyes, — but in them
    was no sight !

VI.

Up from the ground he sprang and gazed ; but
    who could paint that gaze ?
They hushed their very hearts that saw its hor-
    ror and amaze :
They might have chained him, as before that stony
    form he stood ;
For the power was stricken from his arm, and
    from his lip the blood.

VII.

"Father !" at length, he murmured low, and
    wept like childhood then :
Talk not of grief till thou hast seen the tears of
    warlike men !
He thought on all his glorious hopes, and all his
    young renown ;
He flung his falchion from his side, and in the
    dust sat down.

VIII.

Then covering with his steel-gloved hands his
    darkly mournful brow, —
"No more, there is no more," he said, "to lift
    the sword for now ;
My king is false, — my hope betrayed ! My fa-
    ther, — O the worth,
The glory, and the loveliness are passed away
    from earth !

IX.

"I thought to stand where banners waved, my
    sire, beside thee, yet ;
I would that there our kindred blood on Spain's
    free soil had met !
Thou wouldst have known my spirit, then ; for
    thee my fields were won ;
And thou hast perished in thy chains, as though
    thou hadst no son !"

X.

Then, starting from the ground once more, he
    seized the monarch's rein,
Amidst the pale and wildered looks of all the
    courtier train ;
And with a fierce, o'ermastering grasp, the rear-
    ing war-horse led,
And sternly set them face to face, — the king be-
    fore the dead :

XI.

"Came I not forth, upon thy pledge, my father's
    hand to kiss ?
Be still, and gaze thou on, false king ! and tell
    me what is this ?

The voice, the glance, the heart I sought, — give
    answer, where are they ?
If thou wouldst clear thy perjured soul, send life
    through this cold clay ;

XII.

"Into these glassy eyes put light ; — be still !
    keep down thine ire !
Bid these white lips a blessing speak, — this earth
    is not my sire :
Give me back him for whom I strove, — for whom
    my blood was shed.
Thou canst not ? — and a king ! — his dust be
    mountains on thy head !"

XIII.

He loosed the steed, — his slack hand fell ; upon
    the silent face
He cast one long, deep, troubled look, then turned
    from that sad place.
His hope was crushed, his after fate untold in
    martial strain :
His banner led the spears no more amidst the
    hills of Spain.   FELICIA HEMANS.

THE CORONATION OF INEZ DE CASTRO.

THERE was music on the midnight :
    From a royal fane it rolled,
And a mighty bell, each pause between,
    Sternly and slowly tolled.
Strange was their mingling in the sky,
    It hushed the listener's breath ;
For the music spoke of triumph high,
    The lonely bell, of death.

There was hurrying through the midnight,
    A sound of many feet ;
But they fell with a muffled fearfulness
    Along the shadowy street :
And softer, fainter, grew their tread
    As it neared the minster gate,
Whence a broad and solemn light was shed
    From a scene of royal state.

Full glowed the strong red radiance
    In the centre of the nave,
Where the folds of a purple canopy
    Swept down in many a wave ;
Loading the marble pavement old
    With a weight of gorgeous gloom,
For something lay midst their fretted gold
    Like a shadow of the tomb.

And within that rich pavilion,
    High on a glittering throne,

A woman's form sat silently,
　Midst the glare of light alone.
Her jewelled robes fell strangely still, —
　The drapery on her breast
Seemed with no pulse beneath to thrill,
　So stonelike was its rest !

But a peal of lordly music
　Shook e'en the dust below,
When the burning gold of the diadem
　Was set on her pallid brow !
Then died away that haughty sound,
　And from the encircling band
Stepped prince and chief, midst the hush profound,
　With homage to her hand.

Why passed a faint, cold shuddering
　Over each martial frame,
As one by one, to touch that hand,
　Noble and leader came ?
Was not the settled aspect fair ?
　Did not a queenly grace,
Under the parted ebon hair,
　Sit on the pale still face ?

Death ! death ! canst *thou* be lovely
　Unto the eye of life ?
Is not each pulse of the quick high breast
　With thy cold mien at strife ?
— It was a strange and fearful sight,
　The crown upon that head,
The glorious robes, and the blaze of light,
　All gathered round the Dead !

And beside her stood in silence
　One with a brow as pale,
And white lips rigidly compressed,
　Lest the strong heart should fail :
King Pedro, with a jealous eye,
　Watching the homage done,
By the land's flower and chivalry,
　To her, his martyred one.

But on the face he looked not,
　Which once his star had been ;
To every form his glance was turned,
　Save of the breathless queen ;
Though something, won from the grave's embrace,
　Of her beauty still was there,
Its hues were all of that shadowy place,
　It was not for *him* to bear.

Alas ! the crown, the sceptre,
　The treasures of the earth,
And the priceless love that poured those gifts,
　Alike of wasted worth !
The rites are closed ; — bear back the dead
　Unto the chamber deep !

Lay down again the royal head,
　Dust with the dust to sleep !

There is music on the midnight, —
　A requiem sad and slow,
As the mourners through the sounding aisle
　In dark procession go ;
And the ring of state, and the starry crown,
　And all the rich array,
Are borne to the house of silence down,
　With her, that queen of clay.

And tearlessly and firmly
　King Pedro led the train ;
But his face was wrapt in his folding robe,
　When they lowered the dust again.
'T is hushed at last the tomb above,
　Hymns die, and steps depart :
Who called thee strong as Death, O Love ?
　Mightier thou wast and art.
　　　　　FELICIA HEMANS.

INDIAN DEATH-SONG.

THE sun sets in night, and the stars shun the day;
But glory remains when their lights fade away.
Begin, you tormentors ! your threats are in vain,
For the sons of Alknomook will never complain.

Remember the arrows he shot from his bow ;
Remember your chiefs by his hatchet laid low !
Why so slow ? do you wait till I shrink from the
　pain ?
No ! the son of Alknomook shall never complain.

Remember the wood where in ambush we lay,
And the scalps which we bore from your nation
　away.
Now the flame rises fast, you exult in my pain ;
But the son of Alknomook can never complain.

I go to the land where my father is gone ;
His ghost shall rejoice in the fame of his son.
Death comes, like a friend, to relieve me from
　pain ;
And thy son, O Alknomook ! has scorned to com-
　plain.　　　PHILIP FRENEAU.

THE FEMALE CONVICT.

SHE shrank from all, and her silent mood
Made her wish only for solitude :
Her eye sought the ground, as it could not brook,
For innermost shame, on another's to look ;
And the cheerings of comfort fell on her ear
Like deadliest words, that were curses to hear ! —

She still was young, and she had been fair ;
But weather-stains, hunger, toil, and care,
That frost and fever that wear the heart,
Had made the colors of youth depart
From the sallow cheek, save over it came
The burning flush of the spirit's shame.

They were sailing o'er the salt sea-foam,
Far from her country, far from her home ;
And all she had left for her friends to keep
Was a name to hide and a memory to weep !
And her future held forth but the felon's lot, —
To live forsaken, to die forgot !
She could not weep, and she could not pray,
But she wasted and withered from day to day,
Till you might have counted each sunken vein,
When her wrist was prest by the iron chain ;
And sometimes I thought her large dark eye
Had the glisten of red insanity.

She called me once to her sleeping-place,
A strange, wild look was upon her face,
Her eye flashed over her cheek so white,
Like a gravestone seen in the pale moonlight,
And she spoke in a low, unearthly tone, —
The sound from mine ear hath never gone ! —
"I had last night the loveliest dream :
My own land shone in the summer beam,
I saw the fields of the golden grain,
I heard the reaper's harvest strain ;
There stood on the hills the green pine-tree,
And the thrush and the lark sang merrily.
A long and a weary way I had come ;
But I stopped, methought, by mine own sweet home.
I stood by the hearth, and my father sat there,
With pale, thin face, and snow-white hair !
The Bible lay open upon his knee,
But he closed the book to welcome me.
He led me next where my mother lay,
And together we knelt by her grave to pray,
And heard a hymn it was heaven to hear,
For it echoed one to my young days dear.
This dream has waked feelings long, long since fled,
And hopes which I deemed in my heart were dead !
— We have not spoken, but still I have hung
On the Northern accents that dwell on thy tongue.
To me they are music, to me they recall
The things long hidden by Memory's pall !
Take this long curl of yellow hair,
And give it my father, and tell him my prayer,
My dying prayer, was for him." . . . .

Next day

Upon the deck a coffin lay ;
They raised it up, and like a dirge
The heavy gale swept o'er the surge ;
The corpse was cast to the wind and wave, —
The convict has found in the green sea a grave.

LÆTITIA E. LANDON.

GRIEF.

FROM " HAMLET, PRINCE OF DENMARK."

QUEEN. Good Hamlet, cast thy nighted color
    off,
And let thine eye look like a friend on Denmark.
Do not, forever, with thy veiléd lids
Seek for thy noble father in the dust :
Thou know'st 't is common, — all that live must
    die,
Passing through nature to eternity.
  HAMLET. Ay, madam, it is common.
  QUEEN.   If it be,
Why seems it so particular with thee ?
  HAM. Seems, madam ! nay, it is ; I know not
    seems.
'T is not alone my inky cloak, good mother,
Nor customary suits of solemn black,
Nor windy suspiration of forced breath,
No, nor the fruitful river in the eye,
Nor the dejected havior of the visage,
Together with all forms, modes, shows of grief,
That can denote me truly : these, indeed, seem,
For they are actions that a man might play :
But I have that within, which passeth show ;
These, but the trappings and the suits of woe.
                              SHAKESPEARE.

SOLILOQUY ON DEATH.

FROM "HAMLET, PRINCE OF DENMARK."

HAMLET. To be, or not to be, — that is the
    question : —
Whether 't is nobler in the mind to suffer
The slings and arrows of outrageous fortune,
Or to take arms against a sea of troubles,
And, by opposing, end them ? — To die, — to
    sleep ; —
No more ; and, by a sleep, to say we end
The heart-ache, and the thousand natural shocks
That flesh is heir to, — 't is a consummation
Devoutly to be wished.   To die, — to sleep ; —
To sleep ! perchance to dream : — ay, there 's the
    rub ;
For in that sleep of death what dreams may come,
When we have shuffled off this mortal coil,
Must give us pause : there 's the respect
That makes calamity of so long life ;
For who would bear the whips and scorns of time,
The oppressor's wrong, the proud man's contumely,
The pangs of despised love, the law's delay,
The insolence of office, and the spurns
That patient merit of the unworthy takes,
When he himself might his quietus make
With a bare bodkin ? who would fardels bear,
To grunt and sweat under a weary life,
But that the dread of something after death, —

That undiscovered country, from whose bourn
No traveller returns, — puzzles the will,
And makes us rather bear those ills we have,
Than fly to others that we know not of?
Thus conscience does make cowards of us all;
And thus the native hue of resolution
Is sicklied o'er with the pale cast of thought;
And enterprises of great pith and moment,
With this regard, their currents turn awry,
And lose the name of action.   SHAKESPEARE.

THE HUSBAND AND WIFE'S GRAVE.

HUSBAND and wife! no converse now ye hold,
As once ye did in your young days of love,
On its alarms, its anxious hours, delays,
Its silent meditations and glad hopes,
Its fears, impatience, quiet sympathies;
Nor do ye speak of joy assured, and bliss
Full, certain, and possessed.   Domestic cares
Call you not now together.   Earnest talk
On what your children may be moves you not.
Ye lie in silence, and an awful silence;
Not like to that in which ye rested once
Most happy, — silence eloquent, when heart
With heart held speech, and your mysterious
          frames,
Harmonious, sensitive, at every beat
Touched the soft notes of love.

                              A stillness deep,
Insensible, unheeding, folds you round,
And darkness, as a stone, has sealed you in;
Away from all the living, here ye rest,
In all the nearness of the narrow tomb,
Yet feel ye not each other's presence now; —
Dread fellowship! — together, yet alone.
   Is this thy prison-house, thy grave, then, Love?
And doth death cancel the great bond that holds
Commingling spirits? Are thoughts that know no
          bounds,
But, self-inspired, rise upward, searching out
The Eternal Mind, the Father of all thought, —
Are they become mere tenants of a tomb? —
Dwellers in darkness, who the illuminate realms
Of uncreated light have visited and lived? —
Lived in the dreadful splendor of that throne
Which One, with gentle hand the veil of flesh
Lifting that hung 'twixt man and it, revealed
In glory? — throne before which even now
Our souls, moved by prophetic power, bow down
Rejoicing, yet at their own natures awed? —
Souls that thee know by a mysterious sense,
Thou awful unseen Presence, — are they quenched?
Or burn they on, hid from our mortal eyes
By that bright day which ends not, as the sun
His robe of light flings round the glittering stars?

And do our loves all perish with our frames?
Do those that took their root and put forth buds,
And then soft leaves unfolded in the warmth
Of mutual hearts, grow up and live in beauty,
Then fade and fall, like fair, unconscious flowers?
Are thoughts and passions that to the tongue give
          speech,
And make it set forth winning harmonies,
That to the cheek do give its living glow,
And vision in the eye the soul intense
With that for which there is no utterance, —
Are these the body's accidents, no more? —
To live in it, and when that dies go out
Like the burnt taper's flame?

                              O listen, man!
A voice within us speaks the startling word,
"Man, thou shalt never die!" celestial voices
Hymn it around our souls; according harps,
By angel fingers touched when the mild stars
Of morning sang together, sound forth still
The song of our great immortality;
Thick-clustering orbs, and this our fair domain,
The tall, dark mountains and the deep-toned seas,
Join in this solemn, universal song.
   O listen, ye, our spirits! drink it in
From all the air! 'T is in the gentle moonlight;
Is floating in day's setting glories; Night,
Wrapped in her sable robe, with silent step
Comes to our bed and breathes it in our ears; —
Night and the dawn, bright day and thoughtful eve,
As one great mystic instrument, are touched
By an unseen, living Hand, and conscious chords
Quiver with joy in this great jubilee.
The dying hear it; and, as sounds of earth
Grow dull and distant, wake their passing souls
To mingle in this heavenly harmony.

Why is it that I linger round this tomb?
What holds it?   Dust that cumbered those I
          mourn.
They shook it off, and laid aside earth's robes,
And put on those of light.   They 're gone to dwell
In love, — their God's and angels'?   Mutual love,
That bound them here, no longer needs a speech
For full communion; nor sensations strong,
Within the breast, their prison, strive in vain
To be set free, and meet their kind in joy.
Changed to celestials, thoughts that rise in each
By natures new impart themselves, though silent.
Each quickening sense, each throb of holy love,
Affections sanctified, and the full glow
Of being, which expand and gladden one,
By union all mysterious, thrill and live
In both immortal frames; — sensation all,
And thought, pervading, mingling sense and
          thought!
Ye paired, yet one! wrapt in a consciousness
Twofold, yet single, — this is love, this life!

Why call we, then, the square-built monument,
The upright column, and the low-laid slab
Tokens of death, memorials of decay ?
Stand in this solemn, still assembly, man,
And learn thy proper nature ; for thou seest
In these shaped stones and lettered tables figures
Of life.   Then be they to thy soul as those
Which he who talked on Sinai's mount with God
Brought to the old Judeans ; — types are these
Of thine eternity.

          I thank thee, Father,
That at this simple grave on which the dawn
Is breaking, emblem of that day which hath
No close, thou kindly unto my dark mind
Hast sent a sacred light, and that away
From this green hillock, whither I had come
In sorrow, thou art leading me in joy.
                RICHARD HENRY DANA.

DE PROFUNDIS.

I.

THE face which, duly as the sun,
Rose up for me with life begun,
To mark all bright hours of the day
With hourly love, is dimmed away, —
And yet my days go on, go on.

II.

The tongue which, like a stream, could run
Smooth music from the roughest stone,
And every morning with "Good day"
Make each day good, is hushed away, —
And yet my days go on, go on.

III.

The heart which, like a staff, was one
For mine to lean and rest upon,
The strongest on the longest day
With steadfast love, is caught away, —
And yet my days go on, go on.

IV.

And cold before my summer 's done,
And deaf in Nature's general tune,
And fallen too low for special fear,
And here, with hope no longer here, —
While the tears drop, my days go on.

V.

The world goes whispering to its own,
"This anguish pierces to the bone";
And tender friends go sighing round,
"What love can ever cure this wound ?"
My days go on, my days go on.

VI.

The past rolls forward on the sun
And makes all night.   O dreams begun,

Not to be ended !   Ended bliss,
And life that will not end in this !
My days go on, my days go on.

VII.

Breath freezes on my lips to moan :
As one alone, once not alone,
I sit and knock at Nature's door,
Heart-bare, heart-hungry, very poor,
Whose desolated days go on.

VIII.

I knock and cry, — Undone, undone !
Is there no help, no comfort, — none ?
No gleaning in the wide wheat-plains
Where others drive their loaded wains ?
My vacant days go on, go on.

IX.

This Nature, though the snows be down,
Thinks kindly of the bird of June :
The little red hip on the tree
Is ripe for such.   What is for me,
Whose days so winterly go on ?

X.

No bird am I, to sing in June,
And dare not ask an equal boon.
Good nests and berries red are Nature's
To give away to better creatures, —
And yet my days go on, go on.

XI.

I ask less kindness to be done, —
Only to loose these pilgrim-shoon,
(Too early worn and grimed) with sweet
Cool deathly touch to these tired feet,
Till days go out which now go on.

   .   .   .   .   .

XIV.

From gracious Nature have I won
Such liberal bounty ? may I run
So, lizard-like, within her side,
And there be safe, who now am tried
By days that painfully go on ?

XV.

— A Voice reproves me thereupon,
More sweet than Nature's when the drone
Of bees is sweetest, and more deep
Than when the rivers overleap
The shuddering pines, and thunder on.

XVI.

God's Voice, not Nature's.   Night and noon
He sits upon the great white throne
And listens for the creatures' praise.
What babble we of days and days ?
The Day-spring he, whose days go on.

XVII.

He reigns above, he reigns alone ;
Systems burn out and leave his throne :
Fair mists of seraphs melt and fall
Around him, changeless amid all, —
Ancient of Days, whose days go on.

XVIII.

He reigns below, he reigns alone,
And, having life in love foregone
Beneath the crown of sovran thorns,
He reigns the jealous God.   Who mourns
Or rules with him, while days go on ?

XIX.

By anguish which made pale the sun,
I hear him charge his saints that none
Among his creatures anywhere
Blaspheme against him with despair,
However darkly days go on.

XX.

Take from my head the thorn-wreath brown !
No mortal grief deserves that crown.
O supreme Love, chief Misery,
The sharp regalia are for Thee
Whose days eternally go on !

XXI.

For us, — whatever 's undergone,
Thou knowest, willest what is done.
Grief may be joy misunderstood ;
Only the Good discerns the good,
I trust thee while my days go on.

XXII.

Whatever 's lost, it first was won :
We will not struggle nor impugn.
Perhaps the cup was broken here,
That Heaven's new wine might show more clear.
I praise thee while my days go on.

XXIII.

I praise thee while my days go on ;
I love thee while my days go on ;
Through dark and dearth, through fire and frost,
With emptied arms and treasure lost,
I thank thee while my days go on.

ELIZABETH BARRETT BROWNING.

ELEGY WRITTEN IN A COUNTRY CHURCHYARD.

THE curfew tolls the knell of parting day ;
  The lowing herd winds slowly o'er the lea,
The ploughman homeward plods his weary way,
  And leaves the world to darkness and to me.

Now fades the glimmering landscape on the sight,
  And all the air a solemn stillness holds,
Save where the beetle wheels his droning flight,
  And drowsy tinklings lull the distant folds ;

Save that, from yonder ivy-mantled tower,
  The moping owl does to the moon complain
Of such as, wandering near her secret bower,
  Molest her ancient, solitary reign.

Beneath those rugged elms, that yew-tree's shade,
  Where heaves the turf in many a mouldering heap,
Each in his narrow cell forever laid,
  The rude forefathers of the hamlet sleep.

The breezy call of incense-breathing morn,
  The swallow twittering from the straw-built shed,
The cock's shrill clarion, or the echoing horn,
  No more shall rouse them from their lowly bed.

For them no more the blazing hearth shall burn,
  Or busy housewife ply her evening care ;
No children run to lisp their sire's return,
  Or climb his knees the envied kiss to share.

Oft did the harvest to their sickle yield,
  Their furrow oft the stubborn glebe has broke ;
How jocund did they drive their team afield !
  How bowed the woods beneath their sturdy stroke !

Let not ambition mock their useful toil,
  Their homely joys, and destiny obscure ;
Nor grandeur hear with a disdainful smile
  The short and simple annals of the poor.

The boast of heraldry, the pomp of power,
  And all that beauty, all that wealth e'er gave,
Await alike the inevitable hour ;
  The paths of glory lead but to the grave.

Nor you, ye proud, impute to these the fault,
  If memory o'er their tomb no trophies raise,
Where, through the long-drawn aisle and fretted vault,
  The pealing anthem swells the note of praise.

Can storied urn, or animated bust,
  Back to its mansion call the fleeting breath ?
Can honor's voice provoke the silent dust,
  Or flattery soothe the dull, cold ear of death ?

Perhaps in this neglected spot is laid
  Some heart once pregnant with celestial fire ;
Hands that the rod of empire might have swayed,
  Or waked to ecstasy the living lyre ;

But knowledge to their eyes her ample page,
  Rich with the spoils of time, did ne'er unroll ;
Chill penury repressed their noble rage,
  And froze the genial current of the soul.

Full many a gem of purest ray serene
 The dark, unfathomed caves of ocean bear ;
Full many a flower is born to blush unseen,
 And waste its sweetness on the desert air.

Some village Hampden, that, with dauntless
  breast,
 The little tyrant of his fields withstood ;
Some mute, inglorious Milton here may rest ;
 Some Cromwell, guiltless of his country's blood.

The applause of listening senates to command,
 The threats of pain and ruin to despise,
To scatter plenty o'er a smiling land,
 And read their history in a nation's eyes,

Their lot forbade ; nor circumscribed alone
 Their growing virtues, but their crimes con-
  fined ;
Forbade to wade through slaughter to a throne,
 And shut the gates of mercy on mankind ;

The struggling pangs of conscious truth to hide,
 To quench the blushes of ingenuous shame,
Or heap the shrine of luxury and pride
 With incense kindled at the muse's flame.

Far from the madding crowd's ignoble strife,
 Their sober wishes never learned to stray ;
Along the cool, sequestered vale of life
 They kept the noiseless tenor of their way.

Yet even these bones from insult to protect,
 Some frail memorial still erected nigh,
With uncouth rhymes and shapeless sculpture
  decked,
 Implores the passing tribute of a sigh.

Their name, their years, spelt by the unlettered
  muse,
 The place of fame and elegy supply ;
And many a holy text around she strews,
 That teach the rustic moralist to die.

For who, to dumb forgetfulness a prey,
 This pleasing, anxious being e'er resigned,
Left the warm precincts of the cheerful day,
 Nor cast one longing, lingering look behind ?

On some fond breast the parting soul relies,
 Some pious drops the closing eye requires ;
E'en from the tomb the voice of Nature cries,
 E'en in our ashes live their wonted fires.

For thee, who, mindful of the unhonored dead,
 Dost in these lines their artless tale relate ;
If chance, by lonely contemplation led,
 Some kindred spirit shall inquire thy fate,

Haply some hoary-headed swain may say : —
 " Oft have we seen him, at the peep of dawn,
Brushing with hasty steps the dews away,
 To meet the sun upon the upland lawn.

" There at the foot of yonder nodding beech,
 That wreathes its old, fantastic roots so high,
His listless length at noontide would he stretch,
 And pore upon the brook that babbles by.

" Hard by yon wood, now smiling as in scorn,
 Muttering his wayward fancies, he would rove ;
Now drooping, woful-wan, like one forlorn,
 Or crazed with care, or crossed in hopeless
  love.

" One morn I missed him on the customed hill,
 Along the heath, and near his favorite tree ;
Another came, — nor yet beside the rill,
 Nor up the lawn, nor at the wood was he ;

" The next, with dirges due, in sad array,
 Slow through the church-way path we saw him
  borne ; —
Approach and read (for thou canst read) the lay
 Graved on the stone beneath yon aged thorn."

THE EPITAPH.

Here rests his head upon the lap of earth
 A youth to fortune and to fame unknown ;
Fair science frowned not on his humble birth,
 And melancholy marked him for her own.

Large was his bounty, and his soul sincere ;
 Heaven did a recompense as largely send ;
He gave to misery (all he had) a tear,
 He gained from heaven ('t was all he wished) a
  friend.

No further seek his merits to disclose,
 Or draw his frailties from their dread abode, —
(There they alike in trembling hope repose,)
 The bosom of his Father and his God.
        THOMAS GRAY.

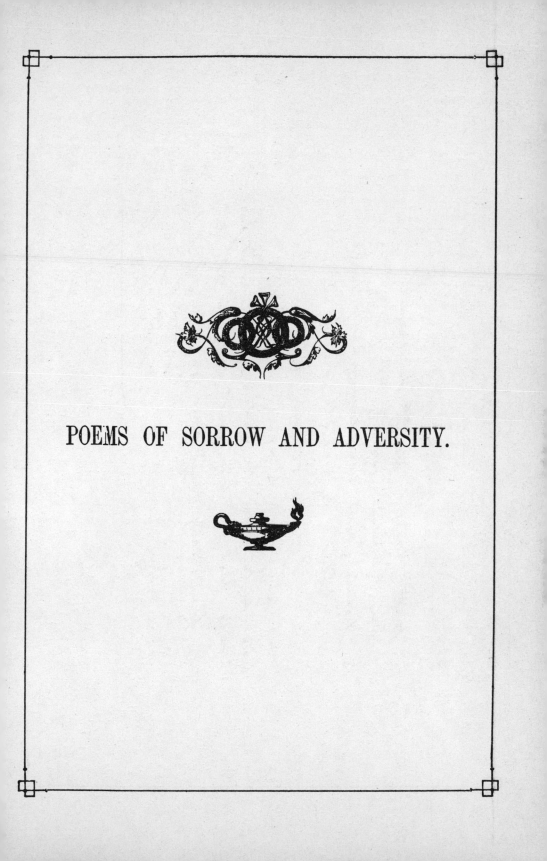

POEMS OF SORROW AND ADVERSITY.

With fingers weary and worn
With eyelids heavy and red
A woman sate in unwomanly rags
Plying her needle & thread —
Stitch, stitch, stitch,
In poverty, hunger, & dirt,
And still with a voice of dolorous pitch
Would that its tone could reach the Rich!
She sang this Song of the Shirt!

Thos. Hood

POEMS OF SORROW AND ADVERSITY.

RETROSPECTION.

FROM "THE PRINCESS."

TEARS, idle tears, I know not what they mean.
Tears from the depth of some divine despair
Rise in the heart, and gather to the eyes,
In looking on the happy autumn fields,
And thinking of the days that are no more.

Fresh as the first beam glittering on a sail,
That brings our friends up from the under world;
Sad as the last which reddens over one
That sinks with all we love below the verge, —
So sad, so fresh, the days that are no more.

Ah, sad and strange as in dark summer dawns
The earliest pipe of half-awakened birds
To dying ears, when unto dying eyes
The casement slowly grows a glimmering square;
So sad, so strange, the days that are no more.

Dear as remembered kisses after death,
And sweet as those by hopeless fancy feigned
On lips that are for others; deep as love,
Deep as first love, and wild with all regret, —
O Death in Life, the days that are no more.
                              ALFRED TENNYSON.

TWO WOMEN.

THE shadows lay along Broadway,
  'T was near the twilight-tide,
And slowly there a lady fair
  Was walking in her pride.
Alone walked she; but, viewlessly,
  Walked spirits at her side.

Peace charmed the street beneath her feet,
  And Honor charmed the air;
And all astir looked kind on her,
  And called her good as fair, —
For all God ever gave to her
  She kept with chary care.

She kept with care her beauties rare
  From lovers warm and true,
For her heart was cold to all but gold,
  And the rich came not to woo, —
But honored well are charms to sell
  If priests the selling do.

Now walking there was one more fair, —
  A slight girl, lily-pale;
And she had unseen company
  To make the spirit quail, —
'Twixt Want and Scorn she walked forlorn,
  And nothing could avail.

No mercy now can clear her brow
  For this world's peace to pray;
For, as love's wild prayer dissolved in air,
  Her woman's heart gave way! —
But the sin forgiven by Christ in heaven
  By man is cursed alway!
              NATHANIEL PARKER WILLIS.

THE DREAMER.

FROM "POEMS BY A SEAMSTRESS."

NOT in the laughing bowers,
Where by green swinging elms a pleasant shade
At summer's noon is made,
    And where swift-footed hours
    Steal the rich breath of enamored flowers,
Dream I. Nor where the golden glories be,
At sunset, laving o'er the flowing sea;
And to pure eyes the faculty is given
To trace a smooth ascent from Earth to Heaven!

    Not on a couch of ease,
With all the appliances of joy at hand, —
Soft light, sweet fragrance, beauty at command;
    Viands that might a godlike palate please,
    And music's soul-creative ecstasies,
Dream I. Nor gloating o'er a wide estate,
Till the full, self-complacent heart elate,
Well satisfied with bliss of mortal birth,
Sighs for an immortality on Earth!

But where the incessant din
Of iron hands, and roars of brazen throats,
Join their unmingled notes,
    While the long summer day is pouring in,
    Till day is gone, and darkness doth begin,
Dream I, — as in the corner where I lie,
On wintry nights, just covered from the sky ! —
Such is my fate, — and, barren though it seem,
Yet, thou blind, soulless scorner, yet I dream !

    And yet I dream, —
Dream what, were men more just, I might have been,
How strong, how fair, how kindly and serene,
Glowing of heart, and glorious of mien ;
The conscious crown to Nature's blissful scene,
In just and equal brotherhood to glean,
With all mankind, exhaustless pleasure keen, —
    Such is my dream !

    And yet I dream, —
I, the despised of fortune, lift mine eyes,
Bright with the lustre of integrity,
In unappealing wretchedness, on high,
And the last rage of Destiny defy ;
Resolved alone to live, — alone to die,
    Nor swell the tide of human misery !

    And yet I dream, —
Dream of a sleep where dreams no more shall come,
My last, my first, my only welcome home !
Rest, unbeheld since Life's beginning stage,
Sole remnant of my glorious heritage,
Unalienable, I shall find thee yet,
And in thy soft embrace the past forget.
    Thus do I dream !
                                    ANONYMOUS.

MOAN, MOAN, YE DYING GALES.

    MOAN, moan, ye dying gales !
    The saddest of your tales
        Is not so sad as life ;
    Nor have you e'er began
    A theme so wild as man,
        Or with such sorrow rife.

    Fall, fall, thou withered leaf !
    Autumn sears not like grief,
        Nor kills such lovely flowers ;
    More terrible the storm,
    More mournful the deform,
        When dark misfortune lowers.

    Hush ! hush ! thou trembling lyre,
    Silence, ye vocal choir,
        And thou, mellifluous lute,
    For man soon breathes his last,
    And all his hope is past,
        And all his music mute.

Then, when the gale is sighing,
And when the leaves are dying,
    And when the song is o'er,
O, let us think of those
Whose lives are lost in woes,
    Whose cup of grief runs o'er.
                                    HENRY NEELE.

HENCE, ALL YE VAIN DELIGHTS.

HENCE, all ye vain delights,
As short as are the nights
Wherein you spend your folly !
There 's naught in this life sweet,
If man were wise to see 't,
    But only melancholy,
    O, sweetest melancholy !

Welcome, folded arms, and fixed eyes,
A sigh that piercing mortifies,
A look that 's fastened to the ground,
A tongue chained up without a sound !

Fountain-heads and pathless groves,
Places which pale passion loves !
Moonlight walks, when all the fowls
Are warmly housed save bats and owls !
A midnight bell, a parting groan !
These are the sounds we feed upon.
Then stretch our bones in a still gloomy valley ;
Nothing 's so dainty sweet as lovely melancholy.
                                BEAUMONT and FLETCHER.

BLOW, BLOW, THOU WINTER WIND.

FROM "AS YOU LIKE IT."

    BLOW, blow, thou winter wind,
    Thou art not so unkind
        As man's ingratitude ;
    Thy tooth is not so keen,
    Because thou art not seen,
        Although thy breath be rude.
Heigh-ho ! sing heigh-ho ! unto the green holly :
Most friendship is feigning, most loving mere folly :
    Then, heigh-ho ! the holly !
        This life is most jolly !

    Freeze, freeze, thou bitter sky,
    Thou dost not bite so nigh
        As benefits forgot :
    Though thou the waters warp,
    Thy sting is not so sharp
        As friend remembered not.
Heigh-ho ! sing heigh-ho ! unto the green holly :
Most friendship is feigning, most loving mere folly :
    Then, heigh-ho ! the holly !
        This life is most jolly !
                                    SHAKESPEARE.

A LAMENT.

O WORLD ! O Life ! O Time !
On whose last steps I climb,
  Trembling at that where I had stood before ;
When will return the glory of your prime ?
  No more, — O nevermore !

Out of the day and night
A joy has taken flight :
  Fresh spring, and summer, and winter hoar
Move my faint heart with grief, but with delight
  No more, — O nevermore !

PERCY BYSSHE SHELLEY.

SPRING IT IS CHEERY.

  SPRING it is cheery,
  Winter is dreary,
Green leaves hang, but the brown must fly ;
  When he 's forsaken,
  Withered and shaken,
What can an old man do but die ?

  Love will not clip him,
  Maids will not lip him,
Maud and Marian pass him by ;
  Youth it is sunny,
  Age has no honey, —
What can an old man do but die ?

  June it was jolly,
  O for its folly !
A dancing leg and a laughing eye !
  Youth may be silly,
  Wisdom is chilly, —
What can an old man do but die ?

  Friends they are scanty,
  Beggars are plenty,
If he has followers, I know why ;
  Gold 's in his clutches,
  (Buying him crutches !) —
What can an old man do but die ?

THOMAS HOOD.

WHEN SHALL WE ALL MEET AGAIN ?

  WHEN shall we all meet again ?
  When shall we all meet again ?
  Oft shall glowing hope expire,
  Oft shall wearied love retire,
  Oft shall death and sorrow reign,
  Ere we all shall meet again.

  Though in distant lands we sigh,
  Parched beneath a hostile sky ;

Though the deep between us rolls,
Friendship shall unite our souls.
  Still in Fancy's rich domain
  Oft shall we all meet again.

  When the dreams of life are fled,
  When its wasted lamps are dead ;
  When in cold oblivion's shade,
  Beauty, power, and fame are laid ;
  Where immortal spirits reign,
  There shall we all meet again.

ANONYMOUS.

THE LAST LEAF.

  I SAW him once before,
  As he passed by the door ;
    And again
  The pavement-stones resound
  As he totters o'er the ground
    With his cane.

  They say that in his prime,
  Ere the pruning-knife of time
    Cut him down,
  Not a better man was found
  By the crier on his round
    Through the town.

  But now he walks the streets,
  And he looks at all he meets
    So forlorn ;
  And he shakes his feeble head,
  That it seems as if he said,
  " They are gone."

  The mossy marbles rest
  On the lips that he has pressed
    In their bloom ;
  And the names he loved to hear
  Have been carved for many a year
    On the tomb.

  My grandmamma has said —
  Poor old lady ! she is dead
    Long ago —
  That he had a Roman nose,
  And his cheek was like a rose
    In the snow.

  But now his nose is thin,
  And it rests upon his chin
    Like a staff ;
  And a crook is in his back,
  And a melancholy crack
    In his laugh.

  I know it is a sin
  For me to sit and grin
    At him here,

But the old three-cornered hat,
And the breeches, — and all that,
   Are so queer !

And if I should live to be
The last leaf upon the tree
   In the spring,
Let them smile, as I do now,
At the old forsaken bough
   Where I cling.

        OLIVER WENDELL HOLMES.

THE APPROACH OF AGE.

FROM "TALES OF THE HALL."

SIX years had passed, and forty ere the six,
When Time began to play his usual tricks :
The locks once comely in a virgin's sight,
Locks of pure brown, displayed the encroaching
    white ;
The blood, once fervid, now to cool began,
And Time's strong pressure to subdue the man.
I rode or walked as I was wont before,
But now the bounding spirit was no more ;
A moderate pace would now my body heat,
A walk of moderate length distress my feet.
I showed my stranger guest those hills sublime,
But said, "The view is poor, we need not climb."
At a friend's mansion I began to dread
The cold neat parlor and the gay glazed bed ;
At home I felt a more decided taste,
And must have all things in my order placed.
I ceased to hunt ; my horses pleased me less, —
My dinner more ; I learned to play at chess.
I took my dog and gun, but saw the brute
Was disappointed that I did not shoot.
My morning walks I now could bear to lose,
And blessed the shower that gave me not to
    choose.
In fact, I felt a languor stealing on ;
The active arm, the agile hand, were gone ;
Small daily actions into habits grew,
And new dislike to forms and fashions new.
I loved my trees in order to dispose ;
I numbered peaches, looked how stocks arose ;
Told the same story oft, — in short, began to prose.

        GEORGE CRABBE.

TOMMY 'S DEAD.

YOU may give over plough, boys,
You may take the gear to the stead,
All the sweat o' your brow, boys,
Will never get beer and bread.
The seed 's waste, I know, boys,

There 's not a blade will grow, boys,
'T is cropped out, I trow, boys,
And Tommy 's dead.

Send the colt to fair, boys,
He 's going blind, as I said,
My old eyes can't bear, boys,
To see him in the shed ;
The cow 's dry and spare, boys,
She 's neither here nor there, boys,
I doubt she 's badly bred ;
Stop the mill to-morn, boys,
There 'll be no more corn, boys,
Neither white nor red ;
There 's no sign of grass, boys,
You may sell the goat and the ass, boys,
The land 's not what it was, boys,
And the beasts must be fed :
You may turn Peg away, boys,
You may pay off old Ned,
We 've had a dull day, boys,
And Tommy 's dead.

Move my chair on the floor, boys,
Let me turn my head :
She 's standing there in the door, boys,
Your sister Winifred !
Take her away from me, boys,
Your sister Winifred !
Move me round in my place, boys,
Let me turn my head,
Take her away from me, boys,
As she lay on her death-bed,
The bones of her thin face, boys,
As she lay on her death-bed !
I don't know how it be, boys,
When all 's done and said,
But I see her looking at me, boys,
Wherever I turn my head ;
Out of the big oak tree, boys,
Out of the garden-bed,
And the lily as pale as she, boys,
And the rose that used to be red.

There 's something not right, boys,
But I think it 's not in my head,
I 've kept my precious sight, boys, —
The Lord be hallowéd !
Outside and in
The ground is cold to my tread,
The hills are wizen and thin,
The sky is shrivelled and shred,
The hedges down by the loan
I can count them bone by bone,
The leaves are open and spread,
But I see the teeth of the land,
And hands like a dead man's hand,
And the eyes of a dead man's head.

There 's nothing but cinders and sand,
The rat and the mouse have fed,
And the summer 's empty and cold ;
Over valley and wold
Wherever I turn my head
There 's a mildew and a mould,
The sun 's going out overhead,
And I 'm very old,
And Tommy 's dead.

What am I staying for, boys,
You 're all born and bred,
'T is fifty years and more, boys,
Since wife and I were wed,
And she 's gone before, boys,
And Tommy 's dead.

She was always sweet, boys,
Upon his curly head,
She knew she 'd never see 't, boys,
And she stole off to bed ;
I 've been sitting up alone, boys,
For he 'd come home, he said,
But it 's time I was gone, boys,
For Tommy 's dead.

Put the shutters up, boys,
Bring out the beer and bread,
Make haste and sup, boys,
For my eyes are heavy as lead ;
There 's something wrong i' the cup, boys,
There 's something ill wi' the bread,
I don't care to sup, boys,
And Tommy 's dead.

I 'm not right, I doubt, boys,
I 've such a sleepy head,
I shall nevermore be stout, boys,
You may carry me to bed.
What are you about, boys ?
The prayers are all said,
The fire 's raked out, boys,
And Tommy 's dead.

The stairs are too steep, boys,
You may carry me to the head,
The night 's dark and deep, boys,
Your mother 's long in bed,
'T is time to go to sleep, boys,
And Tommy 's dead.

I 'm not used to kiss, boys,
You may shake my hand instead.
All things go amiss, boys,
You may lay me where she is, boys,
And I 'll rest my old head :
'T is a poor world, this, boys,
And Tommy 's dead.

SIDNEY DOBELL.

OFT IN THE STILLY NIGHT.

OFT in the stilly night
Ere slumber's chain has bound me,
Fond Memory brings the light
Of other days around me :
The smiles, the tears,
Of boyhood's years,
The words of love then spoken ;
The eyes that shone,
Now dimmed and gone,
The cheerful hearts now broken !
Thus in the stilly night
Ere slumber's chain has bound me,
Sad Memory brings the light
Of other days around me.

When I remember all
The friends so linked together
I 've seen around me fall
Like leaves in wintry weather,
I feel like one
Who treads alone
Some banquet-hall deserted,
Whose lights are fled,
Whose garlands dead,
And all but he departed !
Thus in the stilly night
Ere slumber's chain has bound me,
Sad Memory brings the light
Of other days around me.

THOMAS MOORE.

ROSALIE.

O, POUR upon my soul again
That sad, unearthly strain
That seems from other worlds to plain !
Thus falling, falling from afar,
As if some melancholy star
Had mingled with her light her sighs,
And dropped them from the skies.

No, never came from aught below
This melody of woe,
That makes my heart to overflow,
As from a thousand gushing springs
Unknown before ; that with it brings
This nameless light — if light it be —
That veils the world I see.

For all I see around me wears
The hue of other spheres ;
And something blent of smiles and tears
Comes from the very air I breathe.
O, nothing, sure, the stars beneath,
Can mould a sadness like to this, —
So like angelic bliss !

So, at that dreamy hour of day,
   When the last lingering ray
Stops on the highest cloud to play, —
So thought the gentle Rosalie
As on her maiden revery
First fell the strain of him who stole
   In music to her soul.
                    WASHINGTON ALLSTON.

THE RAINY DAY.

THE day is cold, and dark, and dreary;
It rains, and the wind is never weary;
The vine still clings to the mouldering wall,
But at every gust the dead leaves fall,
   And the day is dark and dreary.

My life is cold, and dark, and dreary;
It rains, and the wind is never weary;
My thoughts still cling to the mouldering Past,
But the hopes of youth fall thick in the blast,
   And the days are dark and dreary.

Be still, sad heart! and cease repining;
Behind the clouds is the sun still shining;
Thy fate is the common fate of all,
Into each life some rain must fall,
   Some days must be dark and dreary.
                    HENRY WADSWORTH LONGFELLOW.

BLIGHTED LOVE.

FLOWERS are fresh, and bushes green,
   Cheerily the linnets sing;
Winds are soft, and skies serene;
   Time, however, soon shall throw
      Winter's snow
O'er the buxom breast of Spring!

Hope, that buds in lover's heart,
   Lives not through the scorn of years;
Time makes love itself depart;
   Time and scorn congeal the mind, —
      Looks unkind
Freeze affection's warmest tears.

Time shall make the bushes green;
   Time dissolve the winter snow;
Winds be soft, and skies serene;
   Linnets sing their wonted strain.
      But again
Blighted love shall never blow!
            LUIS DE CAMOENS (Portuguese). Translation
                    of LORD STRANGFORD.

THOSE EVENING BELLS.

THOSE evening bells! those evening bells!
How many a tale their music tells
Of youth, and home, and that sweet time
When last I heard their soothing chime!

Those joyous hours are passed away;
And many a heart that then was gay
Within the tomb now darkly dwells,
And hears no more those evening bells.

And so 't will be when I am gone, —
That tuneful peal will still ring on;
While other bards shall walk these dells,
And sing your praise, sweet evening bells.
                    THOMAS MOORE.

THE SUN IS WARM, THE SKY IS CLEAR.

STANZAS WRITTEN IN DEJECTION NEAR NAPLES.

THE sun is warm, the sky is clear,
The waves are dancing fast and bright,
Blue isles and snowy mountains wear
The purple noon's transparent light:
The breath of the moist air is light
Around its unexpanded buds;
Like many a voice of one delight, —
The winds', the birds', the ocean-floods', —
The City's voice itself is soft like Solitude's.

I see the Deep's untrampled floor
With green and purple sea-weeds strown;
I see the waves upon the shore
Like light dissolved in star-showers thrown:
I sit upon the sands alone;
The lightning of the noontide ocean
Is flashing round me, and a tone
Arises from its measured motion, —
How sweet, did any heart now share in my emotion!

Alas! I have nor hope nor health,
Nor peace within nor calm around,
Nor that Content surpassing wealth
The sage in meditation found,
And walked with inward glory crowned, —
Nor fame, nor power, nor love, nor leisure;
Others I see whom these surround;
Smiling they live, and call life pleasure;
To me that cup has been dealt in another measure.

Yet now despair itself is mild
Even as the winds and waters are;
I could lie down like a tired child,
And weep away the life of care
Which I have borne, and yet must bear,

Till death like sleep might steal on me,
And I might feel in the warm air
My cheek grow cold, and hear the sea
Breathe o'er my dying brain its last monotony.

PERCY BYSSHE SHELLEY.

BYRON'S LATEST VERSES.

[Missolonghi, January 23, 1824. On this day I completed my thirty-sixth year.]

'T IS time this heart should be unmoved,
Since others it has ceased to move ;
Yet, though I cannot be beloved,
  Still let me love.

My days are in the yellow leaf,
The flowers and fruits of love are gone,
The worm, the canker, and the grief,
  Are mine alone.

The fire that in my bosom preys
Is like to some volcanic isle,
No torch is kindled at its blaze,
  A funeral pile.

The hope, the fear, the jealous care,
The exalted portion of the pain
And power of love, I cannot share,
  But wear the chain.

But 't is not here, — it is not here,
Such thoughts should shake my soul, nor now
Where glory seals the hero's bier,
  Or binds his brow.

The sword, the banner, and the field,
Glory and Greece about us see ;
The Spartan borne upon his shield
  Was not more free.

Awake ! not Greece, — she is awake !
Awake, my spirit ! think through whom
My life-blood tastes its parent lake,
  And then strike home !

Tread those reviving passions down,
Unworthy manhood ! unto thee,
Indifferent should the smile or frown
  Of beauty be.

If thou regrett'st thy youth, — why live ?
The land of honorable death
Is here, — up to the field, and give
  Away thy breath !

Seek out — less often sought than found —
A soldier's grave, for thee the best ;
Then look around, and choose thy ground,
  And take thy rest !

BYRON.

OLD.

By the wayside, on a mossy stone,
 Sat a hoary pilgrim, sadly musing ;
Oft I marked him sitting there alone,
 All the landscape, like a page, perusing ;
  Poor, unknown,
By the wayside, on a mossy stone.

Buckled knee and shoe, and broad-brimmed hat ;
 Coat as ancient as the form 't was folding ;
Silver buttons, queue, and crimped cravat ;
 Oaken staff his feeble hand upholding ;
  There he sat !
Buckled knee and shoe, and broad-brimmed hat.

Seemed it pitiful he should sit there,
 No one sympathizing, no one heeding,
None to love him for his thin gray hair,
 And the furrows all so mutely pleading
  Age and care :
Seemed it pitiful he should sit there.

It was summer, and we went to school,
 Dapper country lads and little maidens ;
Taught the motto of the "Dunce's Stool," —
 Its grave import still my fancy ladens, —
  "Here 's a fool !"
It was summer, and we went to school.

When the stranger seemed to mark our play,
 Some of us were joyous, some sad-hearted,
I remember well, too well, that day !
 Oftentimes the tears unbidden started
  Would not stay
When the stranger seemed to mark our play.

One sweet spirit broke the silent spell,
 O, to me her name was always Heaven !
She besought him all his grief to tell,
 (I was then thirteen, and she eleven,)
  Isabel !
One sweet spirit broke the silent spell.

"Angel," said, he sadly, "I am old ;
 Earthly hope no longer hath a morrow ;
Yet, why I sit here thou shalt be told."
 Then his eye betrayed a pearl of sorrow,
  Down it rolled !
"Angel," said he sadly, "I am old.

"I have tottered here to look once more
 On the pleasant scene where I delighted
In the careless, happy days of yore,
 Ere the garden of my heart was blighted
  To the core :
I have tottered here to look once more.

"All the picture now to me how dear !
 E'en this gray old rock where I am seated,

Is a jewel worth my journey here ;
   Ah that such a scene must be completed
      With a tear !
All the picture now to me how dear !

"Old stone school-house ! — it is still the same ;
   There 's the very step I so oft mounted ;
There 's the window creaking in its frame,
   And the notches that I cut and counted
      For the game.
Old stone school-house, it is still the same.

"In the cottage yonder I was born ;
   Long my happy home, that humble dwelling ;
There the fields of clover, wheat, and corn ;
   There the spring with limpid nectar swelling ;
      Ah, forlorn !
In the cottage yonder I was born.

"Those two gateway sycamores you see
   Then were planted just so far asunder
That long well-pole from the path to free,
   And the wagon to pass safely under ;
      Ninety-three !
Those two gateway sycamores you see.

"There 's the orchard where we used to climb
   When my mates and I were boys together,
Thinking nothing of the flight of time,
   Fearing naught but work and rainy weather ;
      Past its prime !
There 's the orchard where we used to climb.

"There the rude, three-cornered chestnut-rails,
   Round the pasture where the flocks were grazing,
Where, so sly, I used to watch for quails
   In the crops of buckwheat we were raising ;
      Traps and trails !
There the rude, three-cornered chestnut-rails.

"There 's the mill that ground our yellow grain ;
   Pond and river still serenely flowing ;
Cot there nestling in the shaded lane,
   Where the lily of my heart was blowing.
      Mary Jane !
There 's the mill that ground our yellow grain.

"There 's the gate on which I used to swing,
   Brook, and bridge, and barn, and old red stable ;
But alas ! no more the morn shall bring
   That dear group around my father's table ;
      Taken wing !
There 's the gate on which I used to swing.

"I am fleeing, — all I loved have fled.
   Yon green meadow was our place for playing ;
That old tree can tell of sweet things said
   When around it Jane and I were straying ;
      She is dead !
I am fleeing, — all I loved have fled.

"Yon white spire, a pencil on the sky,
   Tracing silently life's changeful story,
So familiar to my dim old eye,
   Points me to seven that are now in glory
      There on high !
Yon white spire, a pencil on the sky.

"Oft the aisle of that old church we trod,
   Guided thither by an angel mother ;
Now she sleeps beneath its sacred sod ;
   Sire and sisters, and my little brother,
      Gone to God !
Oft the aisle of that old church we trod.

"There I heard of Wisdom's pleasant ways ;
   Bless the holy lesson ! — but, ah, never
Shall I hear again those songs of praise,
   Those sweet voices silent now forever !
      Peaceful days !
There I heard of Wisdom's pleasant ways.

"There my Mary blest me with her hand
   When our souls drank in the nuptial blessing,
Ere she hastened to the spirit-land,
   Yonder turf her gentle bosom pressing ;
      Broken band !
There my Mary blest me with her hand.

"I have come to see that grave once more,
   And the sacred place where we delighted,
Where we worshipped, in the days of yore,
   Ere the garden of my heart was blighted
      To the core !
I have come to see that grave once more.

"Angel," said he sadly, "I am old ;
   Earthly hope no longer hath a morrow,
Now, why I sit here thou hast been told."
   In his eye another pearl of sorrow,
      Down it rolled !
"Angel," said he sadly, "I am old."

By the wayside, on a mossy stone,
   Sat the hoary pilgrim, sadly musing ;
Still I marked him sitting there alone,
   All the landscape, like a page, perusing ;
      Poor, unknown !
By the wayside, on a mossy stone.

RALPH HOYT.

THE OLD FAMILIAR FACES.

I HAVE had playmates, I have had companions,
In my days of childhood, in my joyful school-days ;
All, all are gone, the old familiar faces.

I have been laughing, I have been carousing,
Drinking late, sitting late, with my bosom cronies ;
All, all are gone, the old familiar faces.

I loved a Love once, fairest among women :
Closed are her doors on me, I must not see her, —
All, all are gone, the old familiar faces.

I have a friend, a kinder friend has no man :
Like an ingrate, I left my friend abruptly ;
Left him, to muse on the old familiar faces.

Ghost-like I paced round the haunts of my child-
hood,
Earth seemed a desert I was bound to traverse,
Seeking to find the old familiar faces.

Friend of my bosom, thou more than a brother,
Why wert not thou born in my father's dwell-
ing ?
So might we talk of the old familiar faces.

How some they have died, and some they have
left me,
And some are taken from me ; all are departed ;
All, all are gone, the old familiar faces.

CHARLES LAMB.

THE BURIED FLOWER.

In the silence of my chamber,
  When the night is still and deep,
And the drowsy heave of ocean
  Mutters in its charméd sleep,

Oft I hear the angel voices
  That have thrilled me long ago, —
Voices of my lost companions,
  Lying deep beneath the snow.

Where are now the flowers we tended ?
  Withered, broken, branch and stem ;
Where are now the hopes we cherished ?
  Scattered to the winds with them.

For ye, too, were flowers, ye dear ones !
  Nursed in hope and reared in love,
Looking fondly ever upward
  To the clear blue heaven above ;

Smiling on the sun that cheered us,
  Rising lightly from the rain,
Never folding up your freshness
  Save to give it forth again.

O, 't is sad to lie and reckon
  All the days of faded youth,
All the vows that we believed in,
  All the words we spoke in truth.

Severed, — were it severed only
  By an idle thought of strife,
Such as time may knit together ;
  Not the broken chord of life !

O, I fling my spirit backward,
  And I pass o'er years of pain ;
All I loved is rising round me,
  All the lost returns again.

Brighter, fairer far than living,
  With no trace of woe or pain,
Robed in everlasting beauty,
  Shall I see thee once again,

By the light that never fadeth,
  Underneath eternal skies,
When the dawn of resurrection
  Breaks o'er deathless Paradise.

WILLIAM EDMONSTOWNE AYTOUNE.

AFAR IN THE DESERT.

Afar in the desert I love to ride,
With the silent Bush-boy alone by my side,
When the sorrows of life the soul o'ercast,
And, sick of the present, I cling to the past ;
When the eye is suffused with regretful tears,
From the fond recollections of former years ;
And shadows of things that have long since fled
Flit over the brain, like the ghosts of the dead, —
Bright visions of glory that vanished too soon ;
Day-dreams, that departed ere manhood's noon ;
Attachments by fate or falsehood reft ;
Companions of early days lost or left ;
And my native land, whose magical name
Thrills to the heart like electric flame ;
The home of my childhood ; the haunts of my
    prime ;
All the passions and scenes of that rapturous time
When the feelings were young, and the world
    was new,
Like the fresh bowers of Eden unfolding to view ;
All, all now forsaken, forgotten, foregone !
And I, a lone exile remembered of none,
My high aims abandoned, my good acts un-
    done,
Aweary of all that is under the sun,
With that sadness of heart which no stranger
    may scan, —
I fly to the desert afar from man.

Afar in the desert I love to ride,
With the silent Bush-boy alone by my side.,
When the wild turmoil of this wearisome life,
With its scenes of oppression, corruption, and
    strife,

The proud man's frown, and the base man's fear,
The scorner's laugh, and the sufferer's tear,
And malice, and meanness, and falsehood, and folly,
Dispose me to musing and dark melancholy ;
When my bosom is full, and my thoughts are high,
And my soul is sick with the bondman's sigh, —
O, then there is freedom, and joy, and pride,
Afar in the desert alone to ride !
There is rapture to vault on the champing steed,
And to bound away with the eagle's speed,
With the death-fraught firelock in my hand, —
The only law of the Desert Land !

Afar in the desert I love to ride,
With the silent Bush-boy alone by my side,
Away, away from the dwellings of men,
By the wild deer's haunt, by the buffalo's glen ;
By valleys remote where the oribi plays,
Where the gnu, the gazelle, and the hartèbeest graze,
And the kudu and eland unhunted recline
By the skirts of gray forest o'erhung with wild vine ;
Where the elephant browses at peace in his wood,
And the river-horse gambols unscared in the flood,
And the mighty rhinoceros wallows at will
In the fen where the wild ass is drinking his fill.

Afar in the desert I love to ride,
With the silent Bush-boy alone by my side,
O'er the brown karroo, where the bleating cry
Of the springbok's fawn sounds plaintively ;
And the timorous quagga's shrill whistling neigh
Is heard by the fountain at twilight gray ;
Where the zebra wantonly tosses his mane,
With wild hoof scouring the desolate plain ;
And the fleet-footed ostrich over the waste
Speeds like a horseman who travels in haste,
Hieing away to the home of her rest,
Where she and her mate have scooped their nest,
Far hid from the pitiless plunderer's view
In the pathless depths of the parched karroo.

Afar in the desert I love to ride,
With the silent Bush-boy alone by my side,
Away, away, in the wilderness vast
Where the white man's foot hath never passed,
And the quivered Coranna or Bechuan
Hath rarely crossed with his roving clan, —
A region of emptiness, howling and drear,
Which man hath abandoned from famine and fear ;
Which the snake and the lizard inhabit alone,
With the twilight bat from the yawning stone ;

Where grass, nor herb, nor shrub takes root,
Save poisonous thorns that pierce the foot ;
And the bitter-melon, for food and drink,
Is the pilgrim's fare by the salt lake's brink ;
A region of drought, where no river glides,
Nor rippling brook with osiered sides ;
Where sedgy pool, nor bubbling fount,
Nor tree, nor cloud, nor misty mount,
Appears, to refresh the aching eye ;
But the barren earth and the burning sky,
And the blank horizon, round and round,
Spread, — void of living sight or sound.
And here, while the night-winds round me sigh,
And the stars burn bright in the midnight sky,
As I sit apart by the desert stone,
Like Elijah at Horeb's cave, alone,
"A still small voice" comes through the wild
(Like a father consoling his fretful child),
Which banishes bitterness, wrath, and fear,
Saying, — Man is distant, but God is near !

THOMAS PRINGLE.

SELECTIONS FROM "PARADISE LOST."

EVE'S LAMENT.

O UNEXPECTED stroke, worse than of death !
Must I thus leave thee, Paradise ? thus leave
Thee, native soil ! these happy walks and shades,
Fit haunt of gods ? where I had hope to spend,
Quiet, though sad, the respite of that day
That must be mortal to us both.   O flowers,
That never will in other climate grow,
My early visitation, and my last
At even, which I bred up with tender hand
From the first opening bud, and gave ye names !
Who now shall rear ye to the sun, or rank
Your tribes, and water from the ambrosial fount ?
Thee, lastly, nuptial bower ! by me adorned
With what to sight or smell was sweet, from thee
How shall I part, and whither wander down
Into a lower world, to this obscure
And wild ? how shall we breathe in other air
Less pure, accustomed to immortal fruits ?

THE DEPARTURE FROM PARADISE.

ADAM TO MICHAEL.

. . . . GENTLY hast thou told
Thy message, which might else in telling wound,
And in performing end us.   What besides
Of sorrow, and dejection, and despair
Our frailty can sustain, thy tidings bring ;
Departure from this happy place, our sweet
Recess, and only consolation left,
Familiar to our eyes, all places else

Jo: Milton

Inhospitable appear and desolate,
Nor knowing us nor known ; and if by prayer
Incessant I could hope to change the will
Of Him who all things can, I would not cease
To weary him with my assiduous cries.
But prayer against his absolute decree
No more avails than breath against the wind,
Blown stifling back on him that breathes it forth ;
Therefore to his great bidding I submit.
This most afflicts me, that, departing hence,
As from his face I shall be hid, deprived
His blessèd countenance, here I could frequent
With worship place by place where he vouch-
    safed
Presence divine, and to my sons relate,
On this mount he appeared ; under this tree
Stood visible ; among these pines his voice
I heard ; here with him at this fountain talked :
So many grateful altars I would rear
Of grassy turf, and pile up every stone
Of lustre from the brook, in memory
Or monument to ages, and thereon
Offer sweet-smelling gums, and fruits, and flowers.
In yonder nether world where shall I seek
His bright appearances, or footstep trace ?
For though I fled him angry, yet, recalled
To life prolonged and promised race, I now
Gladly behold though but his utmost skirts
Of glory, and far off his steps adore.

.   .   .   .   .

Henceforth I learn that to obey is best,
And love with fear the only God, to walk
As in his presence, ever to observe
His providence, and on him sole depend,
Merciful over all his works, with good
Still overcoming evil, and by small
Accomplishing great things, by things deemed
    weak
Subverting worldly strong and worldly wise
By simply meek ; that suffering for truth's sake
Is fortitude to highest victory,
And to the faithful death the gate of life :
Taught this by his example, whom I now
Acknowledge my Redeemer ever blest.

EVE TO ADAM.

. . . . WITH sorrow and heart's distress
Wearied, I fell asleep.   But now lead on ;
In me is no delay ; with thee to go,
Is to stay here ; without thee here to stay,
Is to go hence unwilling ; thou to me
Art all things under heaven, all places thou,
Who for my wilful crime art banished hence.
This further consolation, yet secure,
I carry hence ; though all by me is lost,
Such favor I unworthy am vouchsafed,
By me the promised Seed shall all restore.

THE DEPARTURE.

IN either hand the hastening angel caught
Our lingering parents, and to the eastern gate
Led them direct, and down the cliff as fast
To the subjected plain ; then disappeared.
They, looking back, all the eastern side beheld
Of Paradise, so late their happy seat,
Waved over by that flaming brand ; the gate
With dreadful faces thronged and fiery arms.
Some natural tears they dropt, but wiped them
    soon ;
The world was all before them, where to choose
Their place of rest, and Providence their guide.
They, hand in hand, with wandering steps and
    slow,
Through Eden took their solitary way.
                                        MILTON.

———◇———

PATIENCE AND SORROW.

FROM "KING LEAR."

KENT. Did your letters pierce the queen to any
    demonstration of grief ?
GENTLEMAN. Ay, sir ; she took them, read
    them in my presence ;
And now and then an ample tear trilled down
Her delicate cheek , it seemed she was a queen
Over her passion ; who, most rebel-like,
Sought to be king o'er her.
KENT.   O, then it moved her.
GENT. Not to a rage : patience and sorrow strove
Who should express her goodliest. You have seen
Sunshine and rain at once ; her smiles and tears
Were like a better way : those happy smilets,
That played on her ripe lip, seemed not to know
What guests were in her eyes ; which parted thence,
As pearls from diamonds dropped. — In brief,
    sorrow
Would be a rarity most beloved, if all
Could so become it.   SHAKESPEARE.

———◇———

FLORENCE VANE.

I LOVED thee long and dearly,
    Florence Vane ;
My life's bright dream and early
    Hath come again;
I renew in my fond vision
    My heart's dear pain,
My hopes and thy derision,
    Florence Vane !

The ruin, lone and hoary,
    The ruin old,
Where thou didst hark my story,
    At even told,

That spot, the hues elysian
    Of sky and plain
I treasure in my vision,
    Florence Vane!

Thou wast lovelier than the roses
    In their prime ;
Thy voice excelled the closes
    Of sweetest rhyme ;
Thy heart was as a river
    Without a main,
Would I had loved thee never,
    Florence Vane.

But fairest, coldest wonder !
    Thy glorious clay
Lieth the green sod under ;
    Alas the day !
And it boots not to remember
    Thy disdain,
To quicken love's pale ember,
    Florence Vane !

The lilies of the valley
    By young graves weep,
The daisies love to dally
    Where maidens sleep,
May their bloom, in beauty vying,
    Never wane
Where thine earthly part is lying,
    Florence Vane.
                        PHILIP P. COOKE.

MAN WAS MADE TO MOURN.

A DIRGE.

I.

WHEN chill November's surly blast
    Made fields and forests bare,
One evening, as I wandered forth
    Along the banks of Ayr,
I spied a man whose aged step
    Seemed weary, worn with care ;
His face was furrowed o'er with years,
    And hoary was his hair.

II.

"Young stranger, whither wanderest thou ?"
    Began the reverend sage ;
"Does thirst of wealth thy step constrain,
    Or youthful pleasures rage ?
Or haply, prest with cares and woes,
    Too soon thou hast began
To wander forth, with me, to mourn
    The miseries of man !

III.

The sun that overhangs yon moors,
    Outspreading far and wide,
Where hundreds labor to support
    A haughty lordling's pride, —
I 've seen yon weary winter sun
    Twice forty times return ;
And every time has added proofs
    That man was made to mourn.

IV.

O man, while in thy early years,
    How prodigal of time !
Mispending all thy precious hours,
    Thy glorious youthful prime !
Alternate follies take the sway :
    Licentious passions burn ;
Which tenfold force gives Nature's law,
    That man was made to mourn.

V.

Look not alone on youthful prime,
    Or manhood's active might ;
Man then is useful to his kind,
    Supported in his right ;
But see him on the edge of life,
    With cares and sorrows worn,
Then age and want, O ill-matched pair !
    Show man was made to mourn.

VI.

A few seem favorites of fate,
    In pleasure's lap carest ;
Yet think not all the rich and great
    Are likewise truly blest.
But, O, what crowds in every land
    Are wretched and forlorn !
Through weary life this lesson learn, —
    That man was made to mourn.

VII.

Many and sharp the numerous ills,
    Inwoven with our frame,
More pointed still we make ourselves,
    Regret, remorse, and shame !
And man, whose heaven-erected face
    The smiles of love adorn,
Man's inhumanity to man
    Makes countless thousands mourn !

VIII.

See yonder poor, o'erlabored wight,
    So abject, mean, and vile,
Who begs a brother of the earth
    To give him leave to toil ;
And see his lordly fellow-worm
    The poor petition spurn.
Unmindful though a weeping wife
    And helpless offspring mourn.

IX.

If I 'm designed yon lordling's slave, —
  By Nature's law designed, —
Why was an independent wish
  E'er planted in my mind ?
If not, why am I subject to
  His cruelty or scorn ?
Or why has man the will and power
  To make his fellow mourn ?

X.

Yet let not this too much, my son,
  Disturb thy youthful breast :
This partial view of human-kind
  Is surely not the last !
The poor, oppresséd, honest man
  Had never, sure, been born,
Had there not been some recompense
  To comfort those that mourn !

XI.

O Death ! the poor man's dearest friend,
  The kindest and the best !
Welcome the hour my aged limbs
  Are laid with thee at rest.
The great, the wealthy, fear thy blow,
  From pomp and pleasure torn ;
But O, a blest relief to those
  That weary-laden mourn !
              ROBERT BURNS.

LOVE NOT.

LOVE not, love not ! ye hapless sons of clay !
Hope's gayest wreaths are made of earthly flow-
  ers, —
Things that are made to fade and fall away
Ere they have blossomed for a few short hours.
        Love not !

Love not ! the thing ye love may change ;
The rosy lip may cease to smile on you,
The kindly-beaming eye grow cold and strange,
The heart still warmly beat, yet not be true.
        Love not !

Love not ! the thing you love may die, —
May perish from the gay and gladsome earth ;
The silent stars, the blue and smiling sky,
Beam o'er its grave, as once upon its birth.
        Love not !

Love not ! O warning vainly said
In present hours as in years gone by !
Love flings a halo round the dear ones' head,
Faultless, immortal, till they change or die.
        Love not !
           CAROLINE NORTON.

SAMSON AGONISTES.

SAMSON.

A LITTLE onward lend thy guiding hand
To these dark steps, a little farther on ;
For yonder bank hath choice of sun or shade :
There I am wont to sit, when any chance
Relieves me from my task of servile toil,
Daily in the common prison else enjoined me,
Where I a prisoner, chained, scarce freely draw
The air imprisoned also, close and damp,
Unwholesome draught ; but here I feel amends,
The breath of heaven fresh blowing, pure and
  sweet,
With day-spring born : here leave me to respire.
This day a solemn feast the people hold
To Dagon, their sea-idol, and forbid
Laborious works : unwillingly this rest
Their superstition yields me ; hence with leave
Retiring from the popular noise, I seek
This unfrequented place to find some ease, —
Ease to the body some, none to the mind
From restless thoughts, that, like a deadly swarm
Of hornets armed, no sooner found alone,
But rush upon me thronging, and present
Times past, what once I was, and what am now.
O, wherefore was my birth from Heaven foretold
Twice by an angel, who at last in sight
Of both my parents all in flames ascended
From off the altar, where an offering burned,
As in a fiery column, charioting
His godlike presence, and from some great act
Or benefit revealed to Abraham's race ?
Why was my breeding ordered and prescribed
As of a person separate to God,
Designed for great exploits, if I must die
Betrayed, captived, and both my eyes put out,
Made of my enemies the scorn and gaze ;
To grind in brazen fetters under task
With this Heaven-gifted strength ? O glorioùs
  strength,
Put to the labor of a beast, debased
Lower than bondslave ! Promise was that I
Should Israel from Philistian yoke deliver ;
Ask for this great deliverer now, and find him
Eyeless in Gaza, at the mill with slaves,
Himself in bonds under Philistian yoke !
   .   .   .
O loss of sight, of thee I most complain !
Blind among enemies, O, worse than chains,
Dungeon, or beggary, or decrepit age !
Light, the prime work of God, to me is extinct,
And all her various objects of delight
Annulled, which might in part my grief have eased.
Inferior to the vilest now become
Of man or worm ; the vilest here excel me :
They creep, yet see ; I dark in light exposed
To daily fraud, contempt, abuse, and wrong,

Within doors or without, still as a fool,
In power of others, never in my own ;
Scarce half I seem to live, dead more than half.
O dark, dark, dark, amid the blaze of noon,
Irrecoverably dark, total eclipse,
Without all hope of day !

MILTON.

THE MANIAC.

STAY, jailer, stay, and hear my woe !
  She is not mad who kneels to thee ;
For what I 'm now too well I know,
  And what I was, and what should be.
I 'll rave no more in proud despair ;
  My language shall be mild, though sad ;
But yet I firmly, truly swear,
  I am not mad, I am not mad !

My tyrant husband forged the tale
  Which chains me in this dismal cell ;
My fate unknown my friends bewail, —
  O jailer, haste that fate to tell !
O, haste my father's heart to cheer !
  His heart at once 't will grieve and glad
To know, though kept a captive here,
  I am not mad, I am not mad !

He smiles in scorn, and turns the key ;
  He quits the grate ; I knelt in vain ;
His glimmering lamp still, still I see, —
  'T is gone ! and all is gloom again.
Cold, bitter cold ! — No warmth ! no light !
  Life, all thy comforts once I had ;
Yet here I 'm chained, this freezing night,
  Although not *mad ; no, no, — not mad !*

'T is sure some dream, some vision vain ;
  What ! *I*, the child of rank and wealth, —
Am *I* the wretch who clanks this chain,
  Bereft of freedom, friends, and health ?
Ah ! while I dwell on blessings fled,
  Which nevermore my heart must glad,
How aches my heart, how burns my head ;
  But 't is not *mad ; no, 't is not mad !*

Hast thou, my child, forgot, ere this,
  A mother's face, a mother's tongue ?
She 'll ne'er forget your parting kiss,
  Nor round her neck how fast you clung ;
Nor how with her you sued to stay ;
  Nor how that suit your sire forbade ;
Nor how — I 'll drive such thoughts away ;
  They 'll *make* me mad, they 'll *make* me mad !

His rosy lips, how sweet they smiled !
  His mild blue eyes, how bright they shone !
None ever bore a lovelier child,
  And art thou now forever gone ?

And must I never see thee more,
  My pretty, pretty, pretty lad ?
I will be free ! unbar the door !
  I am not mad ; I am not mad !

O, hark ! what mean those yells and cries ?
  His chain some furious madman breaks ;
He comes, — I see his glaring eyes ;
  Now, now, my dungeon-grate he shakes.
Help ! Help ! — He 's gone ! — O, fearful woe,
  Such screams to hear, such sights to see !
My brain, my brain, — I know, I know
  I am *not* mad, but soon *shall* be.

Yes, soon ; — for, lo yon ! — while I speak, —
  Mark how yon demon's eyeballs glare !
He sees me ; now, with dreadful shriek,
  He whirls a serpent high in air.
Horror ! — the reptile strikes his tooth
  Deep in my heart, so crushed and sad ;
Ay, laugh, ye fiends ; — I feel the truth ;
  Your task is done, — I 'M MAD ! I 'M MAD !

GEORGE MONK LEWIS.

ODE TO A NIGHTINGALE.

[Written in the spring of 1819, when suffering from physical depression, the precursor of his death, which happened soon after.]

MY heart aches, and a drowsy numbness pains
  My sense, as though of hemlock I had drunk ;
Or emptied some dull opiate to the drains
  One minute past, and Lethe-ward had sunk.
'T is not through envy of thy happy lot,
  But being too happy in thy happiness,
That thou, light-wingéd Dryad of the trees,
    In some melodious plot
Of beechen green, and shadows numberless,
Singest of Summer in full-throated ease.

O for a draught of vintage
  Cooled a long age in the deep-delvéd earth,
Tasting of Flora and the country green,
  Dance, and Provençal song, and sunburned
    mirth !
O for a beaker full of the warm South,
  Full of the true, the blushful Hippocrene,
With beaded bubbles winking at the brim,
    And purple-stainéd mouth, —
  That I might drink, and leave the world un-
    seen,
And with thee fade away into the forest dim.

Fade far away, dissolve, and quite forget
  What thou among the leaves hast never
    known,
The weariness, the fever, and the fret :
  Here, where men sit and hear each other
    groan,

Where palsy shakes a few sad, last gray hairs,
  Where youth grows pale, and spectre-thin, and
    dies,
Where but to think is to be full of sorrow
  And leaden-eyed despairs,
Where beauty cannot keep her lustrous eyes,
Or new love pine at them beyond to-morrow.

Away ! away ! for I will fly to thee !
  Not charioted by Bacchus and his pards,
But on the viewless wings of poesy,
  Though the dull brain perplexes and retards
Already with thee tender is the night,
  And haply the queen-moon is on her throne,
    Clustered around by all her starry fays ;
      But here there is no light,
Save what from heaven is with the breezes
    blown
Through verdurous glooms and winding mossy
    ways.

I cannot see what flowers are at my feet,
  Nor what soft incense hangs upon the boughs ;
But, in embalméd darkness guess each sweet
  Wherewith the seasonable month endows
The grass, the thicket, and the fruit-tree wild, —
  White hawthorn and the pastoral eglantine ;
Fast-fading violets, covered up in leaves ;
  And mid-May's oldest child,
The coming musk-rose, full of dewy wine,
The murmurous haunt of bees on summer eves.

Darkling I listen ; and for many a time
  I have been half in love with easeful Death,
Called him soft names in many a muséd rhyme,
  To take into the air my quiet breath ;
Now, more than ever, seems it rich to die,
  To cease upon the midnight, with no pain,
While thou art pouring forth thy soul abroad,
    In such an ecstasy !
  Still wouldst thou sing, and I have ears in
    vain, —
To thy high requiem become a sod.

Thou wast not born for death, immortal bird !
  No hungry generations tread thee down ;
The voice I hear this passing night was heard
  In ancient days by emperor and clown :
Perhaps the self-same song that found a path
  Through the sad heart of Ruth, when, sick for
    home,
She stood in tears amid the alien corn ;
  The same that ofttimes hath
Charmed magic casements opening on the foam
Of perilous seas, in fairy lands forlorn.

Forlorn ! the very word is like a bell,
  To toll me back from thee to my sole self !
Adieu ! the Fancy cannot cheat so well
  As she is famed to do, deceiving elf.

Adieu ! adieu ! thy plaintive anthem fades
  Past the near meadows, over the still stream,
Up the hillside ; and now 't is buried deep
  In the next valley-glades :
Was it a vision or a waking dream ?
Fled is that music, — do I wake or sleep ?
                                    JOHN KEATS.

THE PALMER.

FROM "MARMION."

WHENAS the Palmer came in hall,
No lord, nor knight, was there more tall,
Or had a statelier step withal,
  Or looked more high and keen ;
For no saluting did he wait,
But strode across the hall of state,
And fronted Marmion where he sate,
  As he his peer had been.
But his gaunt frame was worn with toil ;
His cheek was sunk, alas the while !
And when he struggled at a smile,
His eye looked haggard wild :
Poor wretch ! the mother that him bare,
If she had been in presence there,
In his wan face and sunburned hair
  She had not known her child.
Danger, long travel, want, or woe,
Soon change the form that best we know, —
For deadly fear can time outgo,
  And blanch at once the hair ;
Hard toil can roughen form and face,
And want can quench the eye's bright grace,
Nor does old age a wrinkle trace,
  More deeply than despair.
Happy whom none of these befall,
But this poor Palmer knew them all.
                              SIR WALTER SCOTT.

WOOLSEY'S FALL.

FROM "HENRY VIII."

FAREWELL, a long farewell, to all my greatness !
This is the state of man : to-day he puts forth
The tender leaves of hope ; to-morrow blossoms,
And bears his blushing honors thick upon him :
The third day comes a frost, a killing frost ;
And—when he thinks, good easy man, full surely
His greatness is a ripening — nips his root,
And then he falls, as I do.   I have ventured,
Like little wanton boys that swim on bladders,
This many summers in a sea of glory ;
But far beyond my depth : my high-blown pride
At length broke under me ; and now has left me,
Weary and old with service, to the mercy
Of a rude stream, that must forever hide me.

Vain pomp and glory of this world, I hate ye :
I feel my heart new opened. O, how wretched
Is that poor man that hangs on princes' favors !
There is, betwixt that smile we would aspire to,
That sweet aspect of princes, and their ruin,
More pangs and fears than wars or women have :
And when he falls, he falls like Lucifer,
Never to hope again.

SHAKESPEARE.

CARDINAL WOLSEY'S SPEECH TO CROMWELL.

FROM "HENRY VIII."

CROMWELL, I did not think to shed a tear
In all my miseries ; but thou hast forced me,
Out of thy honest truth, to play the woman.
Let 's dry our eyes : and thus far hear me, Cromwell ;
And — when I am forgotten, as I shall be,
And sleep in dull cold marble, where no mention
Of me more must be heard of — say, I taught thee,
Say, Wolsey — that once trod the ways of glory,
And sounded all the depths and shoals of honor —
Found thee a way, out of his wreck, to rise in ;
A sure and safe one, though thy master missed it.
Mark but my fall, and that that ruined me.
Cromwell, I charge thee, fling away ambition :
By that sin fell the angels ; how can man, then,
The image of his Maker, hope to win by 't ?
Love thyself last : cherish those hearts that hate thee :
Corruption wins not more than honesty.
Still in thy right hand carry gentle peace,
To silence envious tongues. Be just, and fear not :
Let all the ends thou aim'st at be thy country's,
Thy God's, and truth's ; then if thou fall'st, O Cromwell !
Thou fall'st a blessed martyr.
Serve the king ; and — pr'ythee, lead me in :
There take an inventory of all I have,
To the last penny ; 't is the king's : my robe,
And my integrity to heaven, is all
I dare now call mine own. O Cromwell, Cromwell !
Had I but served my God with half the zeal
I served my king, he would not in mine age
Have left me naked to mine enemies !

SHAKESPEARE.

DEATH OF THE WHITE FAWN.

THE wanton troopers, riding by,
Have shot my fawn, and it will die.
Ungentle men ! they cannot thrive
Who killed thee. Thou ne'er didst, alive,
Them any harm ; alas ! nor could
Thy death yet do them any good.
I 'm sure I never wished them ill, —

Nor do I for all this, nor will ;
But if my simple prayers may yet
Prevail with Heaven to forget
Thy murder, I will join my tears,
Rather than fail. But, O my fears !
It cannot die so. Heaven's king
Keeps register of everything ;
And nothing may we use in vain ;
Even beasts must be with justice slain, —
Else men are made their deodands.
Though they should wash their guilty hands
In this warm life-blood, which doth part
From thine and wound me to the heart,
Yet could they not be clean, — their stain
Is dyed in such a purple grain ;
There is not such another in
The world to offer for their sin.

Inconstant Sylvio ! when yet
I had not found him counterfeit,
One morning (I remember well),
Tied in this silver chain and bell,
Gave it to me ; nay, and I know
What he said then, — I 'm sure I do :
Said he, " Look how your huntsman here
Hath taught a fawn to hunt his dear ! "
But Sylvio soon had me beguiled, —
This waxed tame, while he grew wild ;
And, quite regardless of my smart,
Left me his fawn, but took his heart.

Thenceforth I set myself to play
My solitary time away
With this ; and, very well content,
Could so mine idle life have spent.
For it was full of sport, and light
Of foot and heart, and did invite
Me to its game. It seemed to bless
Itself in me ; how could I less
Than love it ? O, I cannot be
Unkind t' a beast that loveth me !

Had it lived long, I do not know
Whether it, too, might have done so
As Sylvio did, — his gifts might be
Perhaps as false, or more, than he.
For I am sure, for aught that I
Could in so short a time espy,
Thy love was far more better than
The love of false and cruel man.

With sweetest milk, and sugar, first
I it at mine own fingers nursed ;
And as it grew, so every day
It waxed more white and sweet than they
It had so sweet a breath ! and oft
I blushed to see its foot more soft
And white — shall I say than my hand ?
Nay, any lady's of the land.
It is a wondrous thing how fleet
'T was on those little silver feet !
With what a pretty, skipping grace

It oft would challenge me the race !
And when 't had left me far away,
'T would stay, and run again, and stay ;
For it was nimbler much than hinds,
And trod as if on the four winds.
    I have a garden of my own, —
But so with roses overgrown,
And lilies, that you would it guess
To be a little wilderness ;
And all the springtime of the year
It only lovéd to be there.
Among the beds of liiies I
Have sought it oft, where it should lie ;
Yet could not, till itself would rise,
Find it, although before mine eyes ;
For in the flaxen lilies' shade
It like a bank of lilies laid.
Upon the roses it would feed,
Until its lips even seemed to bleed ;
And then to me 't would boldly trip,
And print those roses on my lip.
But all its chief delight was still
On roses thus itself to fill ;
And its pure virgin limbs to fold
In whitest sheets of lilies cold.
Had it lived long, it would have been
Lilies without, roses within.
    O, help ! O, help ! I see it faint,
And die as calmly as a saint !
See how it weeps ! the tears do come,
Sad, slowly, dropping like a gum.
So weeps the wounded balsam ; so
The holy frankincense doth flow ;
The brotherless Heliades
Melt in such amber tears as these,
    I in a golden phial will
Keep these two crystal tears, and fill
It, till it do o'erflow with mine ;
Then place it in Diana's shrine.
    Now my sweet fawn is vanished to
Whither the swans and turtles go,
In fair Elysium to endure,
With milk-white lambs, and ermines pure.
O, do not run too fast ! for I
Will but bespeak thy grave — and die.
    First, my unhappy statue shall
Be cut in marble ; and withal,
Let it be weeping too.   But there
The engraver sure his art may spare ;
For I so truly thee bemoan
That I shall weep, though I be stone,
Until my tears, still dropping, wear
My breast, themselves engraving there.
There at my feet shalt thou be laid,
Of purest alabaster made ;
For I would have thine image be
White as I can, though not as thee.
                    ANDREW MARVELL.

FAREWELL, LIFE.

WRITTEN DURING SICKNESS, APRIL, 1845.

FAREWELL, life ! my senses swim,
And the world is growing dim ;
Thronging shadows cloud the light,
Like the advent of the night, —
Colder, colder, colder still,
Upward steals a vapor chill ;
Strong the earthy odor grows, —
I smell the mould above the rose !

Welcome, life ! the spirit strives !
Strength returns and hope revives ;
Cloudy fears and shapes forlorn
Fly like shadows at the morn, —
O'er the earth there comes a bloom ;
Sunny light for sullen gloom,
Warm perfume for vapor cold, —
I smell the rose above the mould !
                    THOMAS HOOD.

THE MAY QUEEN.

I.

You must wake and call me early, call me early,
        mother dear ;
To-morrow 'll be the happiest time of all the glad
        new-year, —
Of all the glad new-year, mother, the maddest,
        merriest day ;
For I 'm to be Queen o' the May, mother, I 'm to
        be Queen o' the May.

II.

There 's many a black, black eye, they say, but
        none so bright as mine ;
There 's Margaret and Mary, there 's Kate and
        Caroline ;
But none so fair as little Alice in all the land,
        they say :
So I 'm to be Queen o' the May, mother, I 'm to
        be Queen o' the May.

III.

I sleep so sound all night, mother, that I shall
        never wake,
If you do not call me loud when the day begins
        to break ;
But I must gather knots of flowers and buds, and
        garlands gay ;
For I 'm to be Queen o' the May, mother, I 'm to
        be Queen o' the May.

IV.

As I came up the valley, whom think ye should
        I see
But Robin leaning on the bridge beneath the
        hazel-tree ?

He thought of that sharp look, mother, I gave
  him yesterday, —
But I 'm to be Queen o' the May, mother, I 'm to
  be Queen o' the May.

V.

He thought I was a ghost, mother, for I was all
  in white ;
And I ran by him without speaking, like a flash
  of light.
They call me cruel-hearted, but I care not what
  they say,
For I 'm to be Queen o' the May, mother, I 'm to
  be Queen o' the May.

VI.

They say he 's dying all for love, — but that can
  never be ;
They say his heart is breaking, mother, — what
  is that to me ?
There 's many a bolder lad 'll woo me any sum-
  mer day ;
And I 'm to be Queen o' the May, mother, I 'm to
  be Queen o' the May.

VII.

Little Effie shall go with me to-morrow to the
  green,
And you 'll be there, too, mother, to see me made
  the Queen ;
For the shepherd lads on every side 'll come from
  far away ;
And I 'm to be Queen o' the May, mother, I 'm to
  be Queen o' the May.

VIII.

The honeysuckle round the porch has woven its
  wavy bowers,
And by the meadow-trenches blow the faint sweet
  cuckoo-flowers ;
And the wild marsh-marigold shines like fire in
  swamps and hollows gray ;
And I 'm to be Queen o' the May, mother, I 'm to
  be Queen o' the May.

IX.

The night-winds come and go, mother, upon the
  meadow-grass,
And the happy stars above them seem to brighten
  as they pass ;
There will not be a drop of rain the whole of the
  livelong day ;
And I 'm to be Queen o' the May, mother, I 'm to
  be Queen o' the May.

X.

All the valley, mother, 'll be fresh and green and
  still,
And the cowslip and the crowfoot are over all the
  hill,

And the rivulet in the flowery dale 'll merrily
  glance and play,
For I 'm to be Queen o' the May, mother, I 'm to
  be Queen o' the May.

XI.

So you must wake and call me early, call me
  early, mother dear ;
To-morrow 'll be the happiest time of all the glad
  new-year ;
To-morrow 'll be of all the year the maddest,
  merriest day,
For I 'm to be Queen o' the May, mother, I 'm
  to be Queen o' the May.

NEW YEAR'S EVE.

I.

IF you 're waking, call me early, call me early,
  mother dear,
For I would see the sun rise upon the glad new-
  year.
It is the last new-year that I shall ever see, —
Then you may lay me low i' the mould, and think
  no more of me.

II.

To-night I saw the sun set, — he set and left be-
  hind
The good old year, the dear old time, and all my
  peace of mind ;
And the new-year's coming up, mother ; but I
  shall never see
The blossom on the blackthorn, the leaf upon the
  tree.

III.

Last May we made a crown of flowers ; we had
  a merry day, —
Beneath the hawthorn on the green they made
  me Queen of May ;
And we danced about the May-pole and in the
  hazel copse,
Till Charles's Wain came out above the tall white
  chimney-tops.

IV.

There 's not a flower on all the hills, — the frost
  is on the pane ;
I only wish to live till the snowdrops come again.
I wish the snow would melt and the sun come
  out on high, —
I long to see a flower so before the day I die.

V.

The building rook 'll caw from the windy tall
  elm-tree,
And the tufted plover pipe along the fallow lea,
And the swallow 'll come back again with sum-
  mer o'er the wave,
But I shall lie alone, mother, within the mould-
  ering grave.

VI.

Upon the chancel-casement, and upon that grave
of mine,
In the early, early morning the summer sun 'll
shine,
Before the red cock crows from the farm upon
the hill, —
When you are warm-asleep, mother, and all the
world is still.

VII.

When the flowers come, again, mother, beneath
the waning light
You 'll never see me more in the long gray fields
at night ;
When from the dry dark wold the summer airs
blow cool
On the oat-grass and the sword-grass, and the
bulrush in the pool.

VIII.

You 'll bury me, my mother, just beneath the
hawthorn shade,
And you 'll come sometimes and see me where I
am lowly laid.
I shall not forget you, mother ; I shall hear you
when you pass,
With your feet above my head in the long and
pleasant grass.

IX.

I have been wild and wayward, but you 'll forgive
me now ;
You 'll kiss me, my own mother, upon my cheek
and brow ;
Nay, nay, you must not weep, nor let your grief
be wild ;
You should not fret for me, mother, — you have
another child.

X.

If I can, I 'll come again, mother, from out my
resting-place ;
Though you 'll not see me, mother, I shall look
upon your face ;
Though I cannot speak a word, I shall hearken
what you say,
And be often, often with you when you think I 'm
far away.

XI.

Good night ! good night ! when I have said good
night forevermore,
And you see me carried out from the threshold
of the door,
Don't let Effie come to see me till my grave be
growing green, —
She 'll be a better child to you than ever I have
been.

XII.

She 'll find my garden tools upon the granary
floor.
Let her take 'em, — they are hers ; I shall never
garden more.
But tell her, when I 'm gone, to train the rose-
bush that I set
About the parlor window and the box of mignon-
ette.

XIII.

Good night, sweet mother ! Call me before the
day is born.
All night I lie awake, but I fall asleep at morn ;
But I would see the sun rise upon the glad new-
year, —
So, if you 're waking, call me, call me early, mother
dear

CONCLUSION.

I.

I thought to pass away before, and yet alive I
am ;
And in the fields all round I hear the bleating of
the lamb.
How sadly, I remember, rose the morning of the
year !
To die before the snowdrop came, and now the
violet 's here.

II.

O, sweet is the new violet, that comes beneath the
skies ;
And sweeter is the young lamb's voice to me that
cannot rise ;
And sweet is all the land about, and all the flowers
that blow ;
And sweeter far is death than life, to me that long
to go.

III.

It seemed so hard at first, mother, to leave the
blessed sun,
And now it seems as hard to stay ; and yet, His
will be done !
But still I think it can't be long before I find re-
lease ;
And that good man, the clergyman, has told me
words of peace.

IV.

O, blessings on his kindly voice, and on his silver
hair !
And blessings on his whole life long, until he meet
me there !
O, blessings on his kindly heart and on his silver
head !
A thousand times I blest him, as he knelt beside
my bed.

16

V.

He taught me all the mercy, for he showed me
all the sin ;
Now, though my lamp was lighted late, there's
One will let me in.
Nor would I now be well, mother, again, if that
could be ;
For my desire is but to pass to Him that died for
me.

VI.

I did not hear the dog howl, mother, or the
death-watch beat, —
There came a sweeter token when the night and
morning meet ;
But sit beside my bed, mother, and put your
hand in mine,
And Effie on the other side, and I will tell the
sign.

VII.

All in the wild March-morning I heard the
angels call, —
It was when the moon was setting, and the dark
was over all ;
The trees began to whisper, and the wind began
to roll,
And in the wild March-morning I heard them
call my soul.

VIII.

For, lying broad awake, I thought of you and
Effie dear ;
I saw you sitting in the house, and I no longer
here ;
With all my strength I prayed for both, — and so
I felt resigned,
And up the valley came a swell of music on the
wind.

IX.

I thought that it was fancy, and I listened in my
bed ;
And then did something speak to me, — I know
not what was said ;
For great delight and shuddering took hold of all
my mind,
And up the valley came again the music on the
wind.

X.

But you were sleeping ; and I said, "It's not
for them, — it's mine" ;
And if it comes three times, I thought, I take it
for a sign.
And once again it came, and close beside the
window-bars ;
Then seemed to go right up to heaven and die
among the stars.

XI.

So now I think my time is near ; I trust it is.
I know
The blessed music went that way my soul will
have to go.
And for myself, indeed, I care not if I go to-day ;
But Effie, you must comfort her when I am past
away.

XII.

And say to Robin a kind word, and tell him not
to fret ;
There's many worthier than I, would make him
happy yet.
If I had lived — I cannot tell — I might have
been his wife ;
But all these things have ceased to be, with my
desire of life.

XIII.

O, look ! the sun begins to rise ! the heavens are
in a glow ;
He shines upon a hundred fields, and all of them
I know.
And there I move no longer now, and there his
light may shine, —
Wild flowers in the valley for other hands than
mine.

XIV.

O, sweet and strange it seems to me, that ere this
day is done
The voice that now is speaking may be beyond
the sun, —
Forever and forever with those just souls and
true, —
And what is life, that we should moan ? why
make we such ado ?

XV.

Forever and forever, all in a blessed home,
And there to wait a little while till you and
Effie come, —
To lie within the light of God, as I lie upon your
breast, —
And the wicked cease from troubling, and the
weary are at rest.

ALFRED TENNYSON.

HOME, WOUNDED.

WHEEL me into the sunshine,
Wheel me into the shadow,
There must be leaves on the woodbine,
Is the king-cup crowned in the meadow ?

Wheel me down to the meadow,
Down to the little river,
In sun or in shadow

I shall not dazzle or shiver,
I shall be happy anywhere,
Every breath of the morning air
Makes me throb and quiver.

Stay wherever you will,
By the mount or under the hill,
Or down by the little river :
Stay as long as you please,
Give me only a bud from the trees,
Or a blade of grass in morning dew,
Or a cloudy violet clearing to blue,
I could look on it forever.

Wheel, wheel through the sunshine,
Wheel, wheel through the shadow ;
There must be odors round the pine,
There must be balm of breathing kine,
Somewhere down in the meadow.
Must I choose ? Then anchor me there
Beyond the beckoning poplars, where
The larch is snooding her flowery hair
With wreaths of morning shadow.

Among the thickest hazels of the brake
Perchance some nightingale doth shake
His feathers, and the air is full of song ;
In those old days when I was young and strong,
He used to sing on yonder garden tree,
Beside the nursery.
Ah, I remember how I loved to wake,
And find him singing on the self-same bough
(I know it even now)
Where, since the flit of bat,
In ceaseless voice he sat,
Trying the spring night over, like a tune,
Beneath the vernal moon ;
And while I listed long,
Day rose, and still he sang,
And all his stanchless song,
As something falling unaware,
Fell out of the tall trees he sang among,
Fell ringing down the ringing morn, and rang, —
Rang like a golden jewel down a golden stair.

My soul lies out like a basking hound, —
A hound that dreams and dozes ;
Along my life my length I lay,
I fill to-morrow and yesterday,
I am warm with the suns that have long since set,
I am warm with the summers that are not yet,
And like one who dreams and dozes
Softly afloat on a sunny sea,
Two worlds are whispering over me,
And there blows a wind of roses
From the backward shore to the shore before,
From the shore before to the backward shore,
And like two clouds that meet and pour
Each through each, till core in core

A single self reposes,
The nevermore with the evermore
Above me mingles and closes ;
As my soul lies out like the basking hound,
And wherever it lies seems happy ground,
And when, awakened by some sweet sound,
A dreamy eye uncloses,
I see a blooming world around,
And I lie amid primroses, —
Years of sweet primroses,
Springs of fresh primroses,
Springs to be, and springs for me
Of distant dim primroses.

O to lie a-dream, a-dream,
To feel I may dream and to know you deem
My work is done forever,
And the palpitating fever,
That gains and loses, loses and gains,
And beats the hurrying blood on the brunt of a
        thousand pains,
Cooled at once by that blood-let
Upon the parapet ;
And all the tedious taskéd toil of the difficult long
        endeavor
Solved and quit by no more fine
Than these limbs of mine,
Spanned and measured once for all
By that right hand I lost,
Bought up at so light a cost
As one bloody fall
On the soldier's bed,
And three days on the ruined wall
Among the thirstless dead.

O to think my name is crost
From duty's muster-roll ;
That I may slumber though the clarion call,
And live the joy of an embodied soul
Free as a liberated ghost.
O to feel a life of deed
Was emptied out to feed
That fire of pain that burned so brief awhile, —
That fire from which I come, as the dead come
Forth from the irreparable tomb,
Or as a martyr on his funeral pile
Heaps up the burdens other men do bear
Through years of segregated care,
And takes the total load
Upon his shoulders broad,
And steps from earth to God.

O to think, through good or ill,
Whatever I am you 'll love me still ;
O to think, though dull I be,
You that are so grand and free,
You that are so bright and gay,
Will pause to hear me when I will,
As though my head were gray ;

And though there 's little I can say,
Each will look kind with honor while he
  hears.
And to your loving ears
My thoughts will halt with honorable scars,
And when my dark voice stumbles with the
  weight
Of what it doth relate
(Like that blind comrade, — blinded in the
  wars, —
Who bore the one-eyed brother that was lame),
You 'll remember 't is the same
That cried " Follow me,"
Upon a summer's day ;
And I shall understand with unshed tears
This great reverence that I see,
And bless the day, — and thee,
Lord God of victory !

And she,
Perhaps, O even she
May look as she looked when I knew her
In those old days of childish sooth,
Ere my boyhood dared to woo her.
I will not seek nor sue her,
For I 'm neither fonder nor truer
Than when she slighted my lovelorn youth,
My giftless, graceless, guinealess truth,
And I only lived to rue her.
But I 'll never love another,
And, in spite of her lovers and lands,
She shall love me yet, my brother !

As a child that holds by his mother,
While his mother speaks his praises,
Holds with eager hands,
And ruddy and silent stands
In the ruddy and silent daisies,
And hears her bless her boy,
And lifts a wondering joy,
So I 'll not seek nor sue her,
But I 'll leave my glory to woo her,
And I 'll stand like a child beside,
And from behind the purple pride
I 'll lift my eyes unto her,
And I shall not be denied.
And you will love her, brother dear,
And perhaps next year you 'll bring me here
All through the balmy April tide,
And she will trip like spring by my side,
And be all the birds to my ear.
And here all three we 'll sit in the sun,
And see the Aprils one by one,
Primrosed Aprils on and on,
Till the floating prospect closes
In golden glimmers that rise and rise,
And perhaps are gleams of Paradise,
And perhaps too far for mortal eyes,

New springs of fresh primroses,
Springs of earth's primroses,
Springs to be and springs for me
Of distant dim primroses.
                              SIDNEY DOBELL.

THE BLIND BOY.

O, SAY what is that thing called Light,
  Which I must ne'er enjoy ?
What are the blessings of the sight,
  O, tell your poor blind boy !

You talk of wondrous things you see,
  You say the sun shines bright ;
I feel him warm, but how can he
  Or make it day or night ?

My day or night myself I make
  Whene'er I sleep or play ;
And could I ever keep awake
  With me 't were always day.

With heavy sighs I often hear
  You mourn my hapless woe ;
But sure with patience I can bear
  A loss I ne'er can know.

Then let not what I cannot have
  My cheer of mind destroy :
Whilst thus I sing, I am a king,
  Although a poor blind boy.
                              COLLEY CIBBER.

DIVERSITY OF FORTUNE.

FROM " MISS KILMANSEGG."

WHAT different dooms our birthdays bring !
For instance, one little manikin thing
  Survives to wear many a wrinkle ;
While death forbids another to wake,
And a son that it took nine moons to make
  Expires without even a twinkle :

Into this world we come like ships,
Launched from the docks, and stocks, and slips,
  For fortune fair or fatal ;
And one little craft is cast away
In its very first trip in Babbicome Bay,
  While another rides safe at Port Natal.

What different lots our stars accord !
This babe to be hailed and wooed as a lord !
  And that to be shunned like a leper !
One, to the world's wine, honey, and corn,
Another, like Colchester native, born
  To its vinegar only, and pepper.

One is littered under a roof
Neither wind nor water proof, —
    That's the prose of Love in a cottage, —
A puny, naked, shivering wretch,
The whole of whose birthright would not fetch,
Though Robins himself drew up the sketch,
    The bid of "a mess of pottage."

Born of Fortunatus's kin,
Another comes tenderly ushered in
    To a prospect all bright and burnished :
No tenant he for life's back slums, —
He comes to the world as a gentleman comes
    To a lodging ready furnished.

And the other sex — the tender — the fair —
What wide reverses of fate are there !
Whilst Margaret, charmed by the Bulbul rare,
    In a garden of Gul reposes,
Poor Peggy hawks nosegays from street to street
Till — think of that, who find life so sweet ! —
    She hates the smell of roses !
                                    THOMAS HOOD.

SIMON LEE, THE OLD HUNTSMAN.

IN the sweet shire of Cardigan,
    Not far from pleasant Ivor Hall,
An old man dwells, — a little man,
    I 've heard he once was tall.
Full five-and-thirty years he lived
    A running huntsman merry ;
And still the centre of his cheek
    Is red as a ripe cherry.

No man like him the horn could sound,
    And hill and valley rang with glee,
When Echo bandied round and round
    The halloo of Simon Lee.
In those proud days he little cared
    For husbandry or tillage ;
To blither tasks did Simon rouse
    The sleepers of the village.

He all the country could outrun,
    Could leave both man and horse behind ;
And often, ere the chase was done,
    He reeled and was stone blind.
And still there 's something in the world
    At which his heart rejoices ;
For when the chiming hounds are out,
    He dearly loves their voices.

But O the heavy change ! — bereft
    Of health, strength, friends and kindred, see
Old Simon to the world is left
    In liveried poverty :

His master 's dead, and no one now
    Dwells in the Hall of Ivor ;
Men, dogs, and horses, all are dead ;
    He is the sole survivor.

And he is lean and he is sick,
    His body dwindled and awry
Rests upon ankles swollen and thick ;
    His legs are thin and dry.
He has no son, he has no child ;
    His wife, an aged woman,
Lives with him, near the waterfall,
    Upon the village common.

Beside their moss-grown hut of clay,
    Not twenty paces from the door,
A scrap of land they have, but they
    Are poorest of the poor.
This scrap of land he from the heath
    Enclosed when he was stronger ;
But what avails the land to them
    Which he can till no longer ?

Oft, working by her husband's side,
    Ruth does what Simon cannot do ;
For she, with scanty cause for pride,
    Is stouter of the two.
And, though you with your utmost skill
    From labor could not wean them,
'T is little, very little, all
    That they can do between them.

Few months of life has he in store
    As he to you will tell,
For still, the more he works, the more
    Do his weak ankles swell.
My gentle reader, I perceive
    How patiently you 've waited,
And now I fear that you expect
    Some tale will be related.

O reader ! had you in your mind
    Such stores as silent thought can bring,
O gentle reader ! you would find
    A tale in everything.
What more I have to say is short,
    And you must kindly take it :
It is no tale ; but should you think,
    Perhaps a tale you 'll make it.

One summer day I chanced to see
    This old man doing all he could
To unearth the root of an old tree,
    A stump of rotten wood.
The mattock tottered in his hand ;
    So vain was his endeavor
That at the root of the old tree
    He might have worked forever.

"You 're overtasked, good Simon Lee,
  Give me your tool," to him I said ;
And at the word right gladly he
  Received my proffered aid.
I struck, and with a single blow
  The tangled root I severed,
At which the poor old man so long
  And vainly had endeavored.

The tears into his eyes were brought,
  And thanks and praises seemed to run
So fast out of his heart, I thought
  They never would have done.
— I 've heard of hearts unkind, kind deeds
  With coldness still returning ;
Alas ! the gratitude of men
  Has oftener left me mourning.

WILLIAM WORDSWORTH.

LONDON CHURCHES.

I STOOD, one Sunday morning,
  Before a large church door,
The congregation gathered
  And carriages a score, —
From one out stepped a lady
  I oft had seen before.

Her hand was on a prayer-book,
  And held a vinaigrette ;
The sign of man's redemption
  Clear on the book was set, —
But above the Cross there glistened
  A golden Coronet.

For her the obsequious beadle
  The inner door flung wide,
Lightly, as up a ball-room,
  Her footsteps seemed to glide, —
There might be good thoughts in her
  For all her evil pride.

But after her a woman
  Peeped wistfully within,
On whose wan face was graven
  Life 's hardest discipline, —
The trace of the sad trinity
  Of weakness, pain, and sin.

The few free-seats were crowded
  Where she could rest and pray ;
With her worn garb contrasted
  Each side in fair array, —
"God's house holds no poor sinners,"
  She sighed, and crept away.

RICHARD MONCKTON MILNES.

THE ORPHANS.

MY chaise the village inn did gain,
  Just as the setting sun's last ray
Tipped with refulgent gold the vane
  Of the old church across the way.

Across the way I silent sped,
  The time till supper to beguile,
In moralizing o'er the dead
  That mouldered round the ancient pile.

There many a humble green grave showed
  Where want and pain and toil did rest ;
And many a flattering stone I viewed
  O'er those who once had wealth possest.

A faded beech its shadow brown
  Threw o'er a grave where sorrow slept,
On which, though scarce with grass o'ergrown,
  Two ragged children sat and wept.

A piece of bread between them lay,
  Which neither seemed inclined to take,
And yet they looked so much a prey
  To want, it made my heart to ache.

"My little children, let me know
  Why you in such distress appear,
And why you wasteful from you throw
  That bread which many a one might cheer ?"

The little boy, in accents sweet,
  Replied, while tears each other chased, —
"Lady ! we 've not enough to eat,
  Ah ! if we had, we should not waste.

"But Sister Mary 's naughty grown,
  And will not eat, whate'er I say,
Though sure I am the bread 's her own,
  For she has tasted none to-day."

"Indeed," the wan, starved Mary said,
  "Till Henry eats, I 'll eat no more,
For yesterday I got some bread,
  He 's had none since the day before."

My heart did swell, my bosom heave,
  I felt as though deprived of speech ;
Silent I sat upon the grave,
  And clasped the clay-cold hand of each.

With looks of woe too sadly true,
  With looks that spoke a grateful heart,
The shivering boy then nearer drew,
  And did his simple tale impart :

"Before my father went away,
  Enticed by bad men o'er the sea,
Sister and I did naught but play, —
  We lived beside yon great ash-tree.

"But then poor mother did so cry,
　And looked so changed, I cannot tell;
She told us that she soon should die,
　And bade us love each other well.

"She said that when the war was o'er,
　Perhaps we might our father see;
But if we never saw him more,
　That God our father then would be!

"She kissed us both, and then she died,
　And we no more a mother have;
Here many a day we've sat and cried
　Together at poor mother's grave.

"But when my father came not here,
　I thought if we could find the sea,
We should be sure to meet him there,
　And once again might happy be.

"We hand in hand went many a mile,
　And asked our way of all we met;
And some did sigh, and some did smile,
　And we of some did victuals get.

"But when we reached the sea and found
　'T was one great water round us spread,
We thought that father must be drowned,
　And cried, and wished we both were dead.

"So we returned to mother's grave,
　And only longed with her to be;
For Goody, when this bread she gave,
　Said father died beyond the sea.

"Then since no parent we have here,
　We'll go and search for God around;
Lady, pray, can you tell us where
　That God, our Father, may be found?

"He lives in heaven, our mother said,
　And Goody says that mother's there;
So, if she knows we want his aid,
　I think perhaps she'll send him here."

I clasped the prattlers to my breast,
　And cried, "Come, both, and live with me;
I'll clothe you, feed you, give you rest,
　And will a second mother be.

"And God shall be your Father still,
　'T was he in mercy sent me here,
To teach you to obey his will,
　Your steps to guide, your hearts to cheer."
ANONYMOUS.

THE ORPHAN BOY'S TALE.

STAY, lady, stay, for mercy's sake,
　And hear a helpless orphan's tale;

Ah, sure my looks must pity wake, —
　'T is want that makes my cheek so pale;
Yet I was once a mother's pride,
　And my brave father's hope and joy;
But in the Nile's proud fight he died,
　And I am now an orphan boy!

Poor, foolish child! how pleased was I,
　When news of Nelson's victory came,
Along the crowded streets to fly,
　To see the lighted windows flame!
To force me home my mother sought, —
　She could not bear to hear my joy;
For with my father's life 't was bought, —
　And made me a poor orphan boy!

The people's shouts were long and loud;
　My mother, shuddering, closed her ears;
"Rejoice! REJOICE!" still cried the crowd, —
　My mother answered with her tears!
"O, why do tears steal down your cheek,"
　Cried I, "while others shout for joy?"
She kissed me; and in accents weak,
　She called me her poor orphan boy!

"What is an orphan boy?" I said;
　When suddenly she gasped for breath,
And her eyes closed! I shrieked for aid,
　But ah! her eyes were closed in death.
My hardships since I will not tell;
　But now, no more a parent's joy,
Ah! lady, I have learned too well
　What 't is to be an orphan boy!

O, were I by your bounty fed!
　Nay, gentle lady, do not chide;
Trust me, I mean to earn my bread, —
　The sailor's orphan boy has pride.
Lady, you weep; what is 't you say?
　You'll give me clothing, food, employ?
Look down, dear parents! look and see
　Your happy, happy orphan boy!
MRS. OPIE.

LITTLE NED.

ALL that is like a dream. It don't seem true!
Father was gone, and mother left, you see,
To work for little brother Ned and me;
And up among the gloomy roofs we grew, —
Locked in full oft, lest we should wander out,
With nothing but a crust o' bread to eat,
While mother chared for poor folk round about,
Or sold cheap odds and ends from street to street.
Yet, Parson, there were pleasures fresh and fair,
To make the time pass happily up there, —
A steamboat going past upon the tide,
A pigeon lighting on the roof close by,

The sparrows teaching little ones to fly,
The small white moving clouds, that we espied,
    And thought were living, in the bit of sky, —
    With sights like these right glad were Ned and
        I ;
And then we loved to hear the soft rain calling,
    Pattering, pattering, upon the tiles,
And it was fine to see the still snow falling,
    Making the house-tops white for miles on miles,
And catch it in our little hands in play,
And laugh to feel it melt and slip away !
But I was six, and Ned was only three,
And thinner, weaker, wearier than me ;
    And one cold day, in winter-time, when mother
Had gone away into the snow, and we
    Sat close for warmth and cuddled one another,
He put his little head upon my knee,
And went to sleep, and would not stir a limb,
    But looked quite strange and old ;
And when I shook him, kissed him, spoke to him,
    He smiled, and grew so cold.
Then I was frightened, and cried out, and none
    Could hear me ; while I sat and nursed his head,
Watching the whitened window, while the sun
    Peeped in upon his face, and made it red.
And I began to sob, — till mother came,
Knelt down, and screamed, and named the good
        God's name,
    And told me he was dead.
And when she put his nightgown on, and, weep-
        ing,
    Placed him among the rags upon his bed,
I thought that Brother Ned was only sleeping,
    And took his little hand, and felt no fear.
    But when the place grew gray and cold and
        drear,
And the round moon over the roofs came creeping,
    And put a silver shade
All round the chilly bed where he was laid,
    I cried, and was afraid.
                            ROBERT BUCHANAN.

THE SONG OF THE SHIRT.

WITH fingers weary and worn,
    With eyelids heavy and red,
A woman sat, in unwomanly rags,
    Plying her needle and thread, —
        Stitch ! stitch ! stitch !
In poverty, hunger, and dirt ;
    And still with a voice of dolorous pitch
She sang the "Song of the Shirt !"

"Work ! work ! work !
    While the cock is crowing aloof !
And work — work — work
    Till the stars shine through the roof !

It 's, O, to be a slave
    Along with the barbarous Turk,
Where woman has never a soul to save,
    If this is Christian work !

"Work — work — work !
    Till the brain begins to swim !
Work — work — work
    Till the eyes are heavy and dim !
Seam, and gusset, and band,
    Band, and gusset, and seam, —
Till over the buttons I fall asleep,
    And sew them on in a dream !

"O men with sisters dear !
    O men with mothers and wives !
It is not linen you 're wearing out,
    But human creatures' lives !
        Stitch — stitch — stitch,
In poverty, hunger, and dirt, —
Sewing at once, with a double thread,
    A shroud as well as a shirt !

"But why do I talk of death, —
    That phantom of grisly bone ?
I hardly fear his terrible shape,
    It seems so like my own —
    It seems so like my own
Because of the fasts I keep ;
O God ! that bread should be so dear,
    And flesh and blood so cheap !

"Work — work — work !
    My labor never flags ;
And what are its wages ? A bed of straw,
    A crust of bread — and rags,
That shattered roof — and this naked floor —
    A table — a broken chair —
And a wall so blank my shadow I thank
    For sometimes falling there !

"Work — work — work !
    From weary chime to chime !
Work — work — work
    As prisoners work for crime !
Band, and gusset, and seam,
    Seam, and gusset, and band, —
Till the heart is sick and the brain benumbed,
    As well as the weary hand.

"Work — work — work !
    In the dull December light !
And work — work — work
    When the weather is warm and bright !
While underneath the eaves
    The brooding swallows cling,
As if to show me their sunny backs,
    And twit me with the Spring.

"O but to breathe the breath
  Of the cowslip and primrose sweet, —
With the sky above my head,
  And the grass beneath my feet !
For only one short hour
  To feel as I used to feel,
Before I knew the woes of want
  And the walk that costs a meal !

"O but for one short hour, —
  A respite, however brief !
No blesséd leisure for love or hope,
  But only time for grief !
A little weeping would ease my heart ;
  But in their briny bed
My tears must stop, for every drop
  Hinders needle and thread !"

With fingers weary and worn,
  With eyelids heavy and red,
A woman sat, in unwomanly rags,
  Plying her needle and thread, —
    Stitch ! stitch ! stitch !
In poverty, hunger, and dirt ;
And still with a voice of dolorous pitch —
Would that its tone could reach the rich ! —
She sang this "Song of the Shirt !"
            THOMAS HOOD.

NEW YEAR'S EVE.

LITTLE Gretchen, little Gretchen wanders up and
  down the street ;
The snow is on her yellow hair, the frost is on
  her feet.
The rows of long, dark houses without look cold
  and damp,
By the struggling of the moonbeam, by the flicker
  of the lamp.
The clouds ride fast as horses, the wind is from
  the north,
But no one cares for Gretchen, and no one looketh
  forth.
Within those dark, damp houses are merry faces
  bright,
And happy hearts are watching out the old year's
  latest night.

With the little box of matches she could not sell
  all day,
And the thin, tattered mantle the wind blows
  every way,
She clingeth to the railing, she shivers in the
  gloom, —
There are parents sitting snugly by the firelight
  in the room ;
And children with grave faces are whispering one
  another

Of presents for the new year, for father or for
  mother.
But no one talks to Gretchen, and no one hears
  her speak,
No breath of little whisperers comes warmly to
  her cheek.

    .   .   .   .

Her home is cold and desolate ; no smile, no food,
  no fire,
But children clamorous for bread, and an
  impatient sire.
So she sits down in an angle where two great
  houses meet,
And she curleth up beneath her for warmth her
  little feet ;
And she looketh on the cold wall, and on the
  colder sky,
And wonders if the little stars are bright fires up
  on high.
She hears the clock strike slowly, up in a church-
  tower,
With such a sad and solemn tone, telling the
  midnight hour.

And she remembered her of tales her mother used
  to tell,
And of the cradle-songs she sang, when summer's
  twilight fell ;
Of good men and of angels, and of the Holy
  Child,
Who was cradled in a manger when winter was
  most wild ;
Who was poor, and cold, and hungry, and deso-
  late and lone ;
And she thought the song had told he was ever
  with his own ;
And all the poor and hungry and forsaken ones
  are his, —
"How good of him to look on me in such a place
  as this !"

Colder it grows and colder, but she does not feel
  it now,
For the pressure on her heart, and the weight
  upon her brow ;
But she struck one little match on the wall so
  cold and bare,
That she might look around her, and see if he
  were there.

    .   .   .   .

There were blood-drops on his forehead, a spear-
  wound in his side,
And cruel nail-prints in his feet, and in his hands
  spread wide.
And he looked upon her gently, and she felt that
  he had known
Pain, hunger, cold, and sorrow, — ay, equal to
  her own.

And he pointed to the laden board and to the
    Christmas tree,
Then up to the cold sky, and said, "Will Gretchen
    come with me?"
The poor child felt her pulses fail, she felt her
    eyeballs swim,
And a ringing sound was in her ears, like her
    dead mother's hymn:
And she folded both her thin white hands and
    turned from that bright board,
And from the golden gifts, and said, "With thee,
    with thee, O Lord!"
The chilly winter morning breaks up in the dull
    skies
On the city wrapt in vapor, on the spot where
    Gretchen lies.

In her scant and tattered garments, with her back
    against the wall,
She sitteth cold and rigid, she answers to no call.
They have lifted her up fearfully, they shuddered
    as they said,
"It was a bitter, bitter night! the child is frozen
    dead."
The angels sang their greeting for one more
    redeemed from sin;
Men said, "It was a bitter night; would no one
    let her in?"
And they shivered as they spoke of her, and
    sighed. They could not see
How much of happiness there was after that
    misery.
                                        ANONYMOUS.

----◆----

THE BRIDGE OF SIGHS.

"Drowned! drowned!"—HAMLET.

ONE more unfortunate,
Weary of breath,
Rashly importunate,
Gone to her death!

Take her up tenderly,
Lift her with care!
Fashioned so slenderly,
Young, and so fair!

Look at her garments
Clinging like cerements,
Whilst the wave constantly
Drips from her clothing;
Take her up instantly,
Loving, not loathing!

Touch her not scornfully!
Think of her mournfully,
Gently and humanly, —
Not of the stains of her;
All that remains of her
Now is pure womanly.

Make no deep scrutiny
Into her mutiny,
Rash and undutiful;
Past all dishonor,
Death has left on her
Only the beautiful.

Still, for all slips of hers, —
One of Eve's family, —
Wipe those poor lips of hers,
Oozing so clammily.

Loop up her tresses
Escaped from the comb, —
Her fair auburn tresses, —
Whilst wonderment guesses
Where was her home?

Who was her father?
Who was her mother?
Had she a sister?
Had she a brother?
Or was there a dearer one
Still, and a nearer one
Yet, than all other?

Alas! for the rarity
Of Christian charity
Under the sun!
O, it was pitiful!
Near a whole city full,
Home she had none.

Sisterly, brotherly,
Fatherly, motherly
Feelings had changed, —
Love, by harsh evidence,
Thrown from its eminence;
Even God's providence
Seeming estranged.

Where the lamps quiver
So far in the river,
With many a light
From window and casement,
From garret to basement,
She stood, with amazement,
Houseless by night.

The bleak wind of March
Made her tremble and shiver;
But not the dark arch,
Or the black flowing river;
Mad from life's history,
Glad to death's mystery,
Swift to be hurled —
Anywhere, anywhere
Out of the world!

In she plunged boldly, —
No matter how coldly

The rough river ran —
Over the brink of it !
Picture it, — think of it !
Dissolute man !
Lave in it, drink of it,
Then, if you can !

Take her up tenderly,
Lift her with care !
Fashioned so slenderly,
Young, and so fair !

Ere her limbs, frigidly,
Stiffen too rigidly,
Decently, kindly,
Smooth and compose them ;
And her eyes, close them,
Staring so blindly !
Dreadfully staring
Through muddy impurity,
As when with the daring
Last look of despairing
Fixed on futurity.

Perishing gloomily,
Spurred by contumely,
Cold inhumanity,
Burning insanity,
Into her rest !
Cross her hands humbly,
As if praying dumbly,
Over her breast !

Owning her weakness,
Her evil behavior,
And leaving, with meekness,
Her sins to her Saviour !
                    THOMAS HOOD.

BEAUTIFUL SNOW.

O THE snow, the beautiful snow,
Filling the sky and the earth below !
Over the house-tops, over the street,
Over the heads of the people you meet,
          Dancing,
               Flirting,
                    Skimming along.
Beautiful snow ! it can do nothing wrong.
Flying to kiss a fair lady's cheek ;
Clinging to lips in a frolicsome freak.
Beautiful snow, from the heavens above,
Pure as an angel and fickle as love !

O the snow, the beautiful snow !
How the flakes gather and laugh as they go !
Whirling about in its maddening fun,
It plays in its glee with every one.
          Chasing,
               Laughing,
                    Hurrying by,

It lights up the face and it sparkles the eye ;
And even the dogs, with a bark and a bound,
Snap at the crystals that eddy around.
The town is alive, and its heart in a glow
To welcome the coming of beautiful snow.

How the wild crowd goes swaying along,
Hailing each other with humor and song !
How the gay sledges like meteors flash by, —
Bright for a moment, then lost to the eye.
          Ringing,
               Swinging,
                    Dashing they go
Over the crest of the beautiful snow :
Snow so pure when it falls from the sky,
To be trampled in mud by the crowd rushing by ;
To be trampled and tracked by the thousands of feet
Till it blends with the horrible filth in the street.

Once I was pure as the snow, — but I fell :
Fell, like the snow-flakes, from heaven — to hell :
Fell, to be tramped as the filth of the street :
Fell, to be scoffed, to be spit on, and beat.
          Pleading,
               Cursing,
                    Dreading to die,
Selling my soul to whoever would buy,
Dealing in shame for a morsel of bread,
Hating the living and fearing the dead.
Merciful God ! have I fallen so low ?
And yet I was once like this beautiful snow !

Once I was fair as the beautiful snow,
With an eye like its crystals, a heart like its glow ;
Once I was loved for my innocent grace, —
Flattered and sought for the charm of my face.
          Father,
               Mother,
                    Sisters all,
God, and myself I have lost by my fall.
The veriest wretch that goes shivering by
Will take a wide sweep, lest I wander too nigh ;
For of all that is on or about me, I know
There is nothing that's pure but the beautiful snow.

How strange it should be that this beautiful snow
Should fall on a sinner with nowhere to go !
How strange it would be, when the night comes
          again,
If the snow and the ice struck my desperate brain !
          Fainting,
               Freezing,
                    Dying alone,
Too wicked for prayer, too weak for my moan
To be heard in the crash of the crazy town,
Gone mad in its joy at the snow's coming down ;
To lie and to die in my terrible woe,
With a bed and a shroud of the beautiful snow !
                    JAMES W. WATSON.

THE PAUPER'S DEATH-BED.

TREAD softly, — bow the head, —
   In reverent silence bow, —
No passing bell doth toll,
Yet an immortal soul
   Is passing now.

Stranger ! however great,
   With lowly reverence bow ;
There 's one in that poor shed —
One by that paltry bed —
   Greater than thou.

Beneath that beggar's roof,
   Lo ! Death doth keep his state.
Enter, no crowds attend ;
Enter, no guards defend
   This palace gate.

That pavement, damp and cold,
   No smiling courtiers tread ;
One silent woman stands,
Lifting with meagre hands
   A dying head.

No mingling voices sound, —
   An infant wail alone ;
A sob suppressed, — again
That short deep gasp, and then —
   The parting groan.

O change ! O wondrous change !
   Burst are the prison bars, —
This moment *there* so low,
So agonized, and now
   Beyond the stars.

O change ! stupendous change !
   There lies the soulless clod ;
The sun eternal breaks,
The new immortal wakes, —
   Wakes with his God.
                  CAROLINE BOWLES.

THE PAUPER'S DRIVE.

THERE 's a grim one-horse hearse in a jolly round
   trot, —
To the churchyard a pauper is going, I wot ;
The road it is rough, and the hearse has no springs ;
And hark to the dirge which the mad driver sings :
   Rattle his bones over the stones !
   He 's only a pauper whom nobody owns !

O, where are the mourners ? Alas ! there are none ;
He has left not a gap in the world, now he 's gone, —

Not a tear in the eye of child, woman, or man ;
To the grave with his carcass as fast as you can :
   Rattle his bones over the stones !
   He 's only a pauper whom nobody owns !

What a jolting, and creaking, and splashing, and
   din !
The whip, how it cracks ! and the wheels, how they
   spin !
How the dirt, right and left, o'er the hedges is
   hurled ! —
The pauper at length makes a noise in the world !
   Rattle his bones over the stones !
   He 's only a pauper whom nobody owns !

Poor pauper defunct ! he has made some approach
To gentility, now that he 's stretched in a coach !
He 's taking a drive in his carriage at last ;
But it will not be long, if he goes on so fast :
   Rattle his bones over the stones !
   He 's only a pauper whom nobody owns !

You bumpkins ! who stare at your brother con-
   veyed,
Behold what respect to a cloddy is paid !
And be joyful to think, when by death you 're
   laid low,
You 've a chance to the grave like a gemman to go !
   Rattle his bones over the stones !
   He 's only a pauper whom nobody owns !

But a truce to this strain ; for my soul it is sad,
To think that a heart in humanity clad
Should make, like the brutes, such a desolate end,
And depart from the light without leaving a friend !
   Bear soft his bones over the stones !
   Though a pauper, he 's one whom his Maker yet
   owns !   THOMAS NOEL.

FOR A' THAT AND A' THAT.

Is there for honest poverty
   Wha hangs his head, and a' that ?
The coward slave, we pass him by ;
   We dare be poor for a' that.
For a' that and a' that,
   Our toils obscure, and a' that ;
The rank is but the guinea's stamp, —
   The man 's the gowd for a' that.

What though on hamely fare we dine,
   Wear hoddin gray, and a' that ;
Gie fools their silks, and knaves their wine, —
   A man 's a man for a' that.
For a' that, and a' that,
   Their tinsel show, and a' that ;
The honest man, though e'er sae poor,
   Is king o' men for a' that.

Ye see yon birkie ca'd a lord,
　Wha struts, and stares, and a' that, —
Though hundreds worship at his word,
　He 's but a coof for a' that ;
For a' that, and a' that,
　His riband, star, and a' that ;
The man of independent mind,
　He looks and laughs at a' that.

A prince can mak a belted knight,
　A marquis, duke, and a' that ;
But an honest man 's aboon his might, —
　Guid faith, he maunna fa' that !
For a' that, and a' that,
　Their dignities, and a' that ;
The pith o' sense, and pride o' worth,
　Are higher ranks than a' that.

Then let us pray that come it may, —
　As come it will for a' that, —
That sense and worth, o'er a' the earth,
　May bear the gree, and a' that.
For a' that, and a' that,
　It 's coming yet, for a' that, —
When man to man, the warld o'er,
　Shall brothers be for a' that !
　　　　　　　　　ROBERT BURNS.

SONNET.

A GOOD that never satisfies the mind,
A beauty fading like the April flowers,
A sweet with floods of gall that runs combined,
A pleasure passing ere in thought made ours,
An honor that more fickle is than wind,
A glory at opinion's frown that lowers,
A treasury which bankrupt time devours,
A knowledge than grave ignorance more blind,
A vain delight our equals to command,
A style of greatness, in effect a dream,
A swelling thought of holding sea and land,
A servile lot, decked with a pompous name, —
Are the strange ends we toil for here below,
Till wisest death make us our errors know.
　　　　　　　　　WILLIAM DRUMMOND.

THE DIRGE.

WHAT is the existence of man's life
But open war, or slumbered strife ?
Where sickness to his sense presents
The combat of the elements ;
And never feels a perfect peace,
Till death's cold hand signs his release.

It is a storm where the hot blood
Outvies in rage the boiling flood ;

And each loud passion of the mind
Is like a furious gust of wind,
Which bears his bark with many a wave,
Till he casts anchor in the grave.

It is a flower which buds and grows
And withers as the leaves disclose.;
Whose spring and fall faint seasons keep,
Like fits of waking before sleep ;
Then shrinks into that fatal mould
Where its first being was enrolled.

It is a dream whose seeming truth
Is moralized in age and youth ;
Where all the comforts he can share
As wandering as his fancies are ;
Till in the mist of dark decay
The dreamer vanish quite away.

It is a dial which points out
The sunset as it moves about ;
And shadows out in lines of night
The subtle stages of time's flight,
Till all-obscuring earth hath laid
The body in perpetual shade.

It is a weary interlude,
Which doth short joys, long woes include ;
The world the stage, the prologue tears,
The acts vain hopes and varied fears ;
The scene shuts up with loss of breath,
And leaves no epilogue but death.
　　　　　　　　　HENRY KING.

THE END OF THE PLAY.

THE play is done, — the curtain drops,
　Slow falling to the prompter's bell ;
A moment yet the actor stops,
　And looks around, to say farewell.
It is an irksome word and task ;
　And, when he 's laughed and said his say,
He shows, as he removes the mask,
　A face that 's anything but gay.

One word, ere yet the evening ends, —
　Let 's close it with a parting rhyme ;
And pledge a hand to all young friends,
　As fits the merry Christmas time ;
On life's wide scene you, too, have parts
　That fate erelong shall bid you play ;
Good night ! — with honest, gentle hearts
　A kindly greeting go alway !

Good night ! — I 'd say the griefs, the joys,
　Just hinted in this mimic page,
The triumphs and defeats of boys,
　Are but repeated in our age ;

I 'd say your woes were not less keen,
  Your hopes more vain, than those of men, —
Your pangs or pleasures of fifteen
  At forty-five played o'er again.

I 'd say we suffer and we strive
  Not less nor more as men than boys, —
With grizzled beards at forty-five,
  As erst at twelve in corduroys ;
And if, in time of sacred youth,
  We learned at home to love and pray,
Pray Heaven that early love and truth
  May never wholly pass away.

And in the world, as in the school,
  I 'd say how fate may change and shift, —
The prize be sometimes with the fool,
  The race not always to the swift :
The strong may yield, the good may fall,
  The great man be a vulgar clown,
The knave be lifted over all,
  The kind cast pitilessly down.

Who knows the inscrutable design ?
  Blessed be He who took and gave !
Why should your mother, Charles, not mine,
  Be weeping at her darling's grave ;
We bow to Heaven that willed it so,
  That darkly rules the fate of all,
That sends the respite or the blow,
  That 's free to give or to recall.

This crowns his feast with wine and wit, —
  Who brought him to that mirth and state ?
His betters, see, below him sit,
  Or hunger hopeless at the gate.
Who bade the mud from Dives' wheel
  To spurn the rags of Lazarus ?

Come, brother, in that dust we 'll kneel,
  Confessing Heaven that ruled it thus.

So each shall mourn, in life's advance,
  Dear hopes, dear friends, untimely killed ;
Shall grieve for many a forfeit chance
  And longing passion unfulfilled.
Amen ! — whatever fate be sent,
  Pray God the heart may kindly glow,
Although the head with cares be bent,
  And whitened with the winter snow.

Come wealth or want, come good or ill,
  Let young and old accept their part,
And bow before the awful will,
  And bear it with an honest heart.
Who misses, or who wins the prize, —
  Go, lose or conquer as you can ;
But if you fail, or if you rise,
  Be each, pray God, a gentleman.

A gentleman, or old or young !
  (Bear kindly with my humble lays ;)
The sacred chorus first was sung
  Upon the first of Christmas days ;
The shepherds heard it overhead, —
  The joyful angels raised it then :
Glory to Heaven on high, it said,
  And peace on earth to gentle men !

My song, save this, is little worth ;
  I lay the weary pen aside,
And wish you health and love and mirth,
  As fits the solemn Christmas-tide.
As fits the holy Christmas birth,
  Be this, good friends, our carol still, —
Be peace on earth, be peace on earth,
  To men of gentle will.
                    WILLIAM MAKEPEACE THACKERAY.

POEMS OF RELIGION

The angel wrote, and vanish'd.—The next night
It came again, with a great wakening light,
And shew'd the names whom love of God had bless'd,
And lo! Ben Adhem's name led all the rest.

       Leigh Hunt

———•———

Here on this blest Thanksgiving Night,
We raise to Thee our grateful voice;
For what thou doest, Lord, is right,
And thus believing, we rejoice.

       L. G. Hallam

POEMS OF RELIGION.

MY GOD, I LOVE THEE.

My God, I love thee! not because
  I hope for heaven thereby;
Nor because those who love thee not
  Must burn eternally.

Thou, O my Jesus, thou didst me
  Upon the cross embrace!
For me didst bear the nails and spear,
  And manifold disgrace.

And griefs and torments numberless,
  And sweat of agony,
Yea, death itself, — and all for one
  That was thine enemy.

Then why, O blessed Jesus Christ,
  Should I not love thee well?
Not for the hope of winning heaven,
  Nor of escaping hell!

Not with the hope of gaining aught,
  Not seeking a reward;
But as thyself hast lovéd me,
  O everlasting Lord!

E'en so I love thee, and will love,
  And in thy praise will sing, —
Solely because thou art my God,
  And my eternal King.
        St. Francis Xavier (Latin). Translation
          of Edward Caswell.

EMPLOYMENT.

If as a flowre doth spread and die,
  Thou wouldst extend me to some good,
Before I were by frost's extremitie
      Nipt in the bud,

The sweetnesse and the praise were thine;
  But the extension and the room
Which in thy garland I should fill were mine
      At thy great doom.

17

For as thou dost impart thy grace,
  The greater shall our glorie be.
The measure of our joyes is in this place,
      The stuffe with thee.

Let me not languish, then, and spend
  A life as barren to thy praise
As is the dust, to which that life doth tend,
      But with delaies.

All things are busie; only I
  Neither bring hony with the bees,
Nor flowres to make that, nor the husbandrie
      To water these.

I am no link of thy great chain,
  But all my companie is a weed.
Lord, place me in thy consort; give one strain
      To my poore reed.
              George Herbert.

THE NEW JERUSALEM.

O mother dear, Jerusalem,
  When shall I come to thee?
When shall my sorrows have an end, —
  Thy joys when shall I see?

O happy harbor of God's saints!
  O sweet and pleasant soil!
In thee no sorrow can be found,
  Nor grief, nor care, nor toil.

No dimly cloud o'ershadows thee,
  Nor gloom, nor darksome night;
But every soul shines as the sun,
  For God himself gives light.

Thy walls are made of precious stone,
  Thy bulwarks diamond-square,
Thy gates are all of orient pearl, —
  O God! if I were there!

O my sweet home, Jerusalem!
  Thy joys when shall I see? —
The King sitting upon thy throne,
  And thy felicity?

Thy gardens and thy goodly walks
　　Continually are green,
Where grow such sweet and pleasant flowers
　　As nowhere else are seen.

Quite through the streets with pleasing sound
　　The flood of life doth flow ;
And on the banks, on every side,
　　The trees of life do grow.

These trees each month yield ripened fruit ;
　　Forevermore they spring,
And all the nations of the earth
　　To thee their honors bring.

Jerusalem, God's dwelling-place
　　Full sore I long to see ;
O that my sorrows had an end,
　　That I might dwell in thee !

I long to see Jerusalem,
　　The comfort of us all ;
For thou art fair and beautiful, —
　　None ill can thee befall.

No candle needs, no moon to shine,
　　No glittering star to light ;
For Christ the King of Righteousness
　　Forever shineth bright.

O, passing happy were my state,
　　Might I be worthy found
To wait upon my God and King,
　　His praises there to sound !

Jerusalem ! Jerusalem !
　　Thy joys fain would I see ;
Come quickly, Lord, and end my grief,
　　And take me home to thee !
　　　　　　　　DAVID DICKSON.

DROP, DROP, SLOW TEARS.

DROP, drop, slow tears,
　　And bathe those beauteous feet
Which brought from heaven
　　The news and prince of peace !
Cease not, wet eyes,
　　His mercies to entreat ;
To cry for vengeance
　　Sin doth never cease ;
In your deep floods
　　Drown all my faults and fears ;
Nor let his eye
　　See sin but through my tears.
　　　　　　　PHINEAS FLETCHER.

DARKNESS IS THINNING.

DARKNESS is thinning ; shadows are retreating ;
Morning and light are coming in their beauty.
Suppliant seek we, with an earnest outcry,
　　　　　God the Almighty !

So that our Master, having mercy on us,
May repel languor, may bestow salvation,
Granting us, Father, of thy loving kindness
　　　　　Glory hereafter !

This of his mercy, ever-blesséd Godhead,
Father, and Son, and Holy Spirit, give us, —
Whom through the wide world celebrate forever
　　　　　Blessing and glory !
　　　ST. GREGORY THE GREAT (Latin). Translation
　　　　　of J. M. NEALE.

I LOVE, AND HAVE SOME CAUSE—

I LOVE, and have some cause to love, the earth, —
　　She is my Maker's creature, therefore good ;
She is my mother, for she gave me birth ;
　　She is my tender nurse, she gives me food :
　　But what 's a creature, Lord, compared with
　　　　thee ?
　　Or what 's my mother or my nurse to me ?

I love the air, — her dainty sweets refresh
　　My drooping soul, and to new sweets invite me ;
Her shrill-mouthed choir sustain me with their
　　　flesh,
　　And with their polyphonian notes delight me :
　　But what 's the air, or all the sweets that she
　　Can bless my soul withal, compared to thee ?

I love the sea, — she is my fellow-creature,
　　My careful purveyor ; she provides me store ;
She walls me round ; she makes my diet greater ;
　　She wafts my treasure from a foreign shore :
　　But, Lord of oceans, when compared with thee,
　　What is the ocean or her wealth to me ?

To heaven's high city I direct my journey,
　　Whose spangled suburbs entertain mine eye, —
Mine eye, by contemplation's great attorney,
　　Transcends the crystal pavement of the sky :
　　But what is heaven, great God, compared to
　　　thee ?
　　Without thy presence, heaven 's no heaven to
　　　me.

Without thy presence, earth gives no refection ;
　　Without thy presence, sea affords no treasure ;
Without thy presence, air 's a rank infection ;
　　Without thy presence, heaven 's itself no
　　　pleasure :

If not possessed, if not enjoyed in thee,
What's earth, or sea, or air, or heaven to me?

The highest honors that the world can boast
Are subjects far too low for my desire;
The brightest beams of glory are, at most,
But dying sparkles of thy living fire;
The loudest flames that earth can kindle be
But nightly glow-worms if compared to thee.

Without thy presence, wealth is bags of cares;
Wisdom but folly; joy, disquiet, sadness;
Friendship is treason, and delights are snares;
Pleasures but pain, and mirth but pleasing
madness, —
Without thee, Lord, things be not what they be,
Nor have their being, when compared with thee.

In having all things, and not thee, what have I?
Not having thee, what have my labors got?
Let me enjoy but thee, what further crave I?
And having thee alone, what have I not?
I wish nor sea, nor land, nor would I be
Possessed of heaven, heaven unpossessed of
thee!

FRANCIS QUARLES.

TWO WENT UP TO THE TEMPLE TO PRAY.

Two went to pray? O, rather say,
One went to brag, the other to pray;

One stands up close and treads on high,
Where the other dares not lend his eye;

One nearer to God's altar trod,
The other to the altar's God.

RICHARD CRASHAW.

THE VALEDICTION.

THE silly lambs to-day
Pleasantly skip and play,
Whom butchers mean to slay,
Perhaps to-morrow;
In a more brutish sort
Do careless sinners sport,
Or in dead sleep still snort,
As near to sorrow;
Till life, not well begun,
Be sadly ended,
And the web they have spun
Can ne'er be mended.

What is the time that's gone,
And what is that to come?
Is it not now as none?
The present stays not.

Time posteth, O, how fast!
Unwelcome death makes haste;
None can call back what's past, —
Judgment delays not;
Though God bring in the light,
Sinners awake not, —
Because hell's out of sight,
They sin forsake not.

Man walks in a vain show;
They know, yet will not know;
Sit still when they should go, —
But run for shadows,
While they might taste and know
The living streams that flow,
And crop the flowers that grow,
In Christ's sweet meadows.
Life's better slept away
Than as they use it;
In sin and drunken play
Vain men abuse it.

RICHARD BAXTER.

THE BIRD LET LOOSE.

THE bird let loose in eastern skies,
When hastening fondly home,
Ne'er stoops to earth her wing, nor flies
Where idle warblers roam;
But high she shoots through air and light,
Above all low delay,
Where nothing earthly bounds her flight,
Nor shadow dims her way.

So grant me, God, from every care
And stain of passion free,
Aloft, through Virtue's purer air,
To hold my course to thee!
No sin to cloud, no lure to stay
My soul, as home she springs; —
Thy sunshine on her joyful way,
Thy freedom in her wings!

THOMAS MOORE.

THE PILGRIMAGE.

GIVE me my scallop-shell of quiet,
My staff of faith to walk upon;
My scrip of joy, immortal diet;
My bottle of salvation;
My gown of glory, hope's true gauge,
And thus I'll take my pilgrimage!
Blood must be my body's 'balmer,
No other balm will there be given;
Whilst my soul, like quiet palmer,
Travelleth towards the land of Heaven;

Over the silver mountains
Where spring the nectar fountains.
There will I kiss the bowl of bliss,
And drink mine everlasting fill
Upon every milken hill.
My soul will be a-dry before,
But after, it will thirst no more.
Then by that happy, blissful day,
More peaceful pilgrims I shall see,
That have cast off their rags of clay,
And walk apparelled fresh like me.
I 'll take them first to quench their thirst,
And taste of nectar's suckets
At those clear wells where sweetness dwells
Drawn up by saints in crystal buckets.
And when our bottles and all we
Are filled with immortality,
Then the blest paths we 'll travel,
Strewed with rubies thick as gravel, —
Ceilings of diamonds, sapphire floors,
High walls of coral, and pearly bowers.
From thence to Heaven's bribeless hall,
Where no corrupted voices brawl ;
No conscience molten into gold,
No forged accuser, bought or sold,
No cause deferred, no vain-spent journey,
For there Christ is the King's Attorney ;
Who pleads for all without degrees,
And he hath angels, but no fees ;
And when the grand twelve-million jury
Of our sins, with direful fury,
'Gainst our souls black verdicts give,
Christ pleads his death, and then we live.
Be thou my speaker, taintless pleader,
Unblotted lawyer, true proceeder !
Thou giv'st salvation even for alms, —
Not with a bribéd lawyer's palms.
And this is mine eternal plea
To Him that made heaven, earth, and sea,
That since my flesh must die so soon,
And want a head to dine next noon,
Just at the stroke when my veins start and
     spread,
Set on my soul an everlasting head :
Then am I, like a palmer, fit
To tread those blest paths which before I writ.
Of death and judgment, heaven and hell,
Who oft doth think, must needs die well.

SIR WALTER RALEIGH.

A TRUE LENT.

Is this a fast, — to keep
     The larder lean,
          And clean
From fat of veals and sheep ?

Is it to quit the dish
     Of flesh, yet still
          To fill
The platter high with fish ?

Is it to fast an hour,
     Or ragged to go,
          Or show
A downcast look, and sour ?

No ! 't is a fast to dole
     Thy sheaf of wheat,
          And meat,
Unto the hungry soul.

It is to fast from strife,
     From old debate
          And hate, —
To circumcise thy life.

To show a heart grief-rent ;
     To starve thy sin,
          Not bin, —
And that 's to keep thy lent.

ROBERT HERRICK.

I WOULD I WERE AN EXCELLENT DIVINE —

I would I were an excellent divine
     That had the Bible at my fingers' ends ;
That men might hear out of this mouth of mine
     How God doth make his enemies his friends ;
Rather than with a thundering and long prayer
Be led into presumption, or despair.

This would I be, and would none other be,
     But a religious servant of my God ;
And know there is none other God but he,
     And willingly to suffer mercy's rod, —
Joy in his grace, and live but in his love,
And seek my bliss but in the world above.

And I would frame a kind of faithful prayer,
     For all estates within the state of grace,
That careful love might never know despair,
     Nor servile fear might faithful love deface ;
And this would I both day and night devise
To make my humble spirit's exercise.

And I would read the rules of sacred life ;
     Persuade the troubled soul to patience ;
The husband care, and comfort to the wife,
     To child and servant due obedience ;
Faith to the friend, and to the neighbor peace,
That love might live, and quarrels all might cease.

Prayer for the health of all that are diseased,
  Confession unto all that are convicted,
And patience unto all that are displeased,
  And comfort unto all that are afflicted,
And mercy unto all that have offended,
  And grace to all, that all may be amended.
NICHOLAS BRETON.

ADAM'S MORNING HYMN IN PARADISE.

THESE are thy glorious works, Parent of good,
Almighty, thine this universal frame,
Thus wondrous fair ; thyself how wondrous then !
Unspeakable, who sitt'st above these heavens
To us invisible, or dimly seen
In these thy lowest works ; yet these declare
Thy goodness beyond thought, and power divine.
Speak, ye who best can tell, ye sons of light,
Angels ; for ye behold him, and with songs
And choral symphonies, day without night,
Circle his throne rejoicing ; ye in Heaven,
On earth join, all ye creatures, to extol
Him first, him last, him midst, and without end.
Fairest of stars, last in the train of night,
If better thou belong not to the dawn,
Sure pledge of day, that crown'st the smiling
    morn
With thy bright circlet, praise him in thy sphere,
While day arises, that sweet hour of prime.
Thou sun, of this great world both eye and soul,
Acknowledge him thy greater ; sound his praise
In thy eternal course, both when thou climb'st,
And when high noon hast gained, and when thou
    fall'st.
Moon, that now meets the orient sun, now fliest,
With the fixed stars, fixed in their orb that flies,
And ye five other wandering fires that move
In mystic dance not without song, resound
His praise, who out of darkness called up light.
Air, and ye elements, the eldest birth
Of Nature's womb, that in quaternion run
Perpetual circle, multiform, and mix
And nourish all things, let your ceaseless change
Vary to our great Maker still new praise.
Ye mists and exhalations, that now rise
From hill or steaming lake, dusky or gray,
Till the sun paint your fleecy skirts with gold,
In honor to the world's great Author rise,
Whether to deck with clouds the uncolored sky,
Or wet the thirsty earth with falling showers,
Rising or falling, still advance his praise.
His praise, ye winds, that from four quarters blow,
Breathe soft or loud ; and wave your tops, ye
    pines,
With every plant, in sign of worship wave.
Fountains, and ye that warble, as ye flow,
Melodious murmurs, warbling tune his praise.
Join voices, all ye living souls ; ye birds,
That singing up to Heaven-gate ascend,
Bear on your wings and in your notes his praise.
Ye that in waters glide, and ye that walk
The earth, and stately tread, or lowly creep,
Witness if I be silent, morn or even,
To hill or valley, fountain or fresh shade,
Made vocal by my song, and taught his praise.
Hail, universal Lord ! be bounteous still
To give us only good ; and if the night
Have gathered aught of evil, or concealed,
Disperse it, as now light dispels the dark.
MILTON.

PRAISE.

To write a verse or two is all the praise
      That I can raise ;
  Mend my estate in any wayes,
      Thou shalt have more.

I go to church ; help me to wings, and I
      Will thither flie ;
  Or, if I mount unto the skie,
      I will do more.

Man is all weakness e: there is no such thing
      As Prince or King :
  His arm is short ; yet with a sling
      He may do more.

A herb destilled, and drunk, may dwell next doore,
      On the same floore,
  To a brave soul : Exalt the poore,
      They can do more.

O, raise me then ! poore bees, that work all day,
      Sting my delay,
  Who have a work, as well as they,
      And much, much more.
GEORGE HERBERT.

UP HILL.

DOES the road wind up hill all the way ?
  Yes, to the very end.
Will the day's journey take the whole long day ?
  From morn to night, my friend.

But is there for the night a resting-place ?
  A roof for when the slow dark hours begin ?
May not the darkness hide it from my face ?
  You cannot miss that inn.

Shall I meet other wayfarers at night ?
  Those who have gone before.

Then must I knock, or call when just in sight ?
  They will not keep you standing at that door.

Shall I find comfort, travel-sore and weak ?
  Of labor you shall find the sum.
Will there be beds for me and all who seek ?
  Yea, beds for all who come.
                        CHRISTINA G. ROSSETTI.

TO HEAVEN APPROACHED A SUFI SAINT.

To heaven approached a Sufi Saint,
  From groping in the darkness late,
And, tapping timidly and faint,
  Besought admission at God's gate.

Said God, "Who seeks to enter here ?"
  "'T is I, dear Friend," the Saint replied,
And trembling much with hope and fear.
  "If it be *thou*, without abide."

Sadly to earth the poor Saint turned,
  To bear the scourging of life's rods ;
But aye his heart within him yearned
  To mix and lose its love in God's.

He roamed alone through weary years,
  By cruel men still scorned and mocked,
Until from faith's pure fires and tears
  Again he rose, and modest knocked.

Asked God, "Who now is at the door ?"
  "It is thyself, beloved Lord,"
Answered the Saint, in doubt no more,
  But clasped and rapt in his reward.
          DSCHELLALEDDIN RUMI (Persian). Translation
                  of WILLIAM R. ALGER.

THE DYING CHRISTIAN TO HIS SOUL.

VITAL spark of heavenly flame !
Quit, O, quit this mortal frame !
Trembling, hoping, lingering, flying,
O the pain, the bliss of dying !
Cease, fond nature, cease thy strife,
And let me languish into life !

Hark ! they whisper ; angels say,
Sister spirit, come away !
What is this absorbs me quite ?
Steals my senses, shuts my sight,
Drowns my spirits, draws my breath ?
Tell me, my soul, can this be death ?

The world recedes ; it disappears !
Heaven opens on my eyes ! my ears

With sounds seraphic ring :
Lend, lend your wings ! I mount ! I fly !
O Grave ! where is thy victory ?
  O Death ! where is thy sting ?
                        ALEXANDER POPE.

PRAYER BY MARY, QUEEN OF HUNGARY.

[Translation.]

O GOD ! though sorrow be my fate,
And the world's hate
    For my heart's faith pursue me,
My peace they cannot take away ;
From day to day
    Thou dost anew imbue me ;
Thou art not far ; a little while
Thou hid'st thy face with brighter smile
    Thy father-love to show me.

Lord, not my will, but thine, be done ;
If I sink down
    When men to terrors leave me,
Thy father-love still warms my breast,
All 's for the best ;
    Shall man have power to grieve me
When bliss eternal is my goal,
And thou the keeper of my soul,
Who never will deceive me ?

Thou art my shield, as saith the Word.
Christ Jesus, Lord,
    Thou standest pitying by me,
And lookest on each grief of mine
As if 't were thine :
    What then though foes may try me,
Though thorns be in my path concealed ?
World, do thy worst ! God is my shield !
    And will be ever nigh me.

DIES IRÆ.

DAY of wrath, that day of burning,
All shall melt, to ashes turning,
All foretold by seers discerning.

O, what fear it shall engender
When the Judge shall come in splendor,
Strict to mark and just to render !

Trumpet-scattered sound of wonder,
Rending sepulchres asunder,
Shall resistless summons thunder.

All aghast then Death shall shiver,
And great Nature's frame shall quiver,
When the graves their dead deliver.

Think, O Jesus, for what reason
Thou enduredst earth's spite and treason,
Nor me lose in that dread season.

Seeking me thy worn feet hasted,
On the cross thy soul death tasted,
Let such labor not be wasted.

Righteous Judge of retribution,
Grant me perfect absolution,
Ere that day of execution.

Culprit-like, I — heart all broken,
On my cheek shame's crimson token —
Plead the pardoning word be spoken.

Mid the sheep a place decide me,
And from goats on left divide me,
Standing on the right beside thee.

When the accursed away are driven,
To eternal burnings given,
Call me with the blest to heaven.

I beseech thee, prostrate lying,
Heart as ashes, contrite, sighing,
Care for me when I am dying.

On that awful day of wailing,
When man, rising, stands before thee,
Spare the culprit, God of glory !
Translated by ABR. COLES, M. D.

LITANY.

SAVIOUR, when in dust to thee
Low we bow the adoring knee ;
When, repentant, to the skies
Scarce we lift our weeping eyes, —
O, by all thy pains and woe
Suffered once for man below,
Bending from thy throne on high,
Hear our solemn litany !

By thy helpless infant years ;
By thy life of want and tears ;
By thy days of sore distress
In the savage wilderness ;
By the dread mysterious hour
Of the insulting tempter's power, —
Turn, O, turn a favoring eye,
Hear our solemn litany !

By the sacred griefs that wept
O'er the grave where Lazarus slept ;
By the boding tears that flowed
Over Salem's loved abode ;

By the anguished sigh that told
Treachery lurked within the fold, —
From thy seat above the sky
Hear our solemn litany !

By thine hour of dire despair ;
By thine agony of prayer ;
By the cross, the wail, the thorn,
Piercing spear, and torturing scorn ;
By the gloom that veiled the skies
O'er the dreadful sacrifice, —
Listen to our humble cry,
Hear our solemn litany !

By thy deep expiring groan ;
By the sad sepulchral stone ;
By the vault whose dark abode
Held in vain the rising God !
O, from earth to heaven restored,
Mighty, reascended Lord, —
Listen, listen to the cry
Of our solemn litany !
SIR ROBERT GRANT.

THE HOLY SPIRIT.

IN the hour of my distress,
When temptations me oppress,
And when I my sins confess,
Sweet Spirit, comfort me !

When I lie within my bed,
Sick at heart, and sick in head,
And with doubts discomforted,
Sweet Spirit, comfort me !

When the house doth sigh and weep,
And the world is drowned in sleep,
Yet mine eyes the watch do keep,
Sweet Spirit, comfort me !

When the artless doctor sees
No one hope but of his fees,
And his skill runs on the lees,
Sweet Spirit, comfort me !

When his potion and his pill,
His or none or little skill,
Meet for nothing, but to kill, —
Sweet Spirit, comfort me !

When the passing bell doth toll,
And the Furies, in a shoal,
Come to fright a parting soul,
Sweet Spirit, comfort me !

When the tapers now burn blue,
And the comforters are few,
And that number more than true,
Sweet Spirit, comfort me !

When the priest his last hath prayed,
And I nod to what is said
Because my speech is now decayed,
    Sweet Spirit, comfort me !

When, God knows, I 'm tost about
Either with despair or doubt,
Yet before the glass be out,
    Sweet Spirit, comfort me !

When the tempter me pursu'th
With the sins of all my youth,
And half damns me with untruth,
    Sweet Spirit, comfort me !

When the flames and hellish cries
Fright mine ears, and fright mine eyes,
And all terrors me surprise,
    Sweet Spirit, comfort me !

When the judgment is revealed,
And that opened which was sealed, —
When to thee I have appealed,
    Sweet Spirit, comfort me !
               ROBERT HERRICK.

THE MARTYRS' HYMN.

FLUNG to the heedless winds,
  Or on the waters cast,
The martyrs' ashes, watched,
  Shall gathered be at last ;
And from that scattered dust,
  Around us and abroad,
Shall spring a plenteous seed
  Of witnesses for God.

The Father hath received
  Their latest living breath ;
And vain is Satan's boast
  Of victory in their death ;
Still, still, though dead, they speak,
  And, trumpet-tongued, proclaim
To many a wakening land
  The one availing name.
        MARTIN LUTHER. Translation
          of W. J. FOX.

THE FIGHT OF FAITH.

[One of the victims of the persecuting Henry VIII., the author
was burnt to death at Smithfield in 1546. The following was made
and sung by her while a prisoner in Newgate.]

LIKE as the armed Knighte,
Appointed to the fielde,
With this world wil I fight,
And faith shal be my shilde.

Faith is that weapon stronge,
Which wil not faile at nede ;
My foes therefore amonge,
Therewith wil I procede.

As it is had in strengthe,
And forces of Christes waye,
It wil prevaile at lengthe,
Though all the devils saye *naye.*

Faithe of the fathers olde
Obtained right witnèss,
Which makes me vérye bolde
To fear no worldes distress.

I now rejoice in harte,
And hope bides me do so ;
For Christ wil take my part,
And ease me of my wo.

Thou sayst, Lord, whoso knocke,
To them wilt thou attende ;
Undo, therefore, the locke,
And thy stronge power sende.

More enemies now I have
Than heeres upon my head ;
Let them not me deprave,
But fight thou in my steade.

On thee my care I cast,
For all their cruell spight ;
I set not by their hast,
For thou art my delight.

I am not she that list
My anker to let fall
For every drislinge mist ;
My shippe 's substancial.

Not oft I use to wright
In prose, nor yet in ryme ;
Yet wil I shewe one sight,
That I sawe in my time.

I sawe a royall throne,
Where Justice shulde have sitte ;
But in her steade was One
Of moody cruell witte.

Absorpt was rightwisness,
As by the raginge floude ;
Sathan, in his excess
Sucte up the guiltlesse bloude.

Then thought I, — Jesus, Lorde,
When thou shalt judge us all,
Harde is it to recorde
On these men what will fall.

THE BLIND MILTON

"They also serve who only stand and wait."

Yet, Lorde, I thee desire,
For that they doe to me,
Let them not taste the hire
Of their iniquitie.
                    ANNE ASKEWE.

SERVANT OF GOD, WELL DONE.

[Verses occasioned by the sudden death of the Rev. Thomas Taylor, who had preached the previous evening.]

"SERVANT of God, well done;
    Rest from thy loved employ;
The battle fought, the victory won,
    Enter thy Master's joy."
The voice at midnight came;
    He started up to hear,
A mortal arrow pierced his frame:
    He fell, — but felt no fear.

Tranquil amidst alarms,
    It found him in the field,
A veteran slumbering on his arms,
    Beneath his red-cross shield:
His sword was in his hand,
    Still warm with recent fight;
Ready that moment, at command,
    Through rock and steel to smite.

At midnight came the cry,
    "To meet thy God prepare!"
He woke, — and caught his Captain's eye;
    Then, strong in faith and prayer,
His spirit, with a bound,
    Burst its encumbering clay;
His tent, at sunrise, on the ground,
    A darkened ruin lay.

The pains of death are past,
    Labor and sorrow cease;
And life's long warfare closed at last,
    His soul is found in peace.
Soldier of Christ! well done;
    Praise be thy new employ;
And while eternal ages run,
    Rest in thy Saviour's joy.
                    JAMES MONTGOMERY.

ON HIS BLINDNESS.

WHEN I consider how my light is spent
Ere half my days, in this dark world and wide,
And that one talent, which is death to hide,
Lodged with me useless, though my soul more bent
To serve therewith my Maker, and present
My true account, lest he returning chide;
"Doth God exact day-labor, light denied?"
I fondly ask: But Patience, to prevent

That murmur, soon replies, "God doth not need
    Either man's work or his own gifts; who best
Bear his mild yoke, they serve him best: his state
Is kingly; thousands at his bidding speed,
    And post o'er land and ocean without rest;
    They also serve who only stand and wait."
                    MILTON.

SAID I NOT SO.

SAID I not so, — that I would sin no more?
    Witness, my God, I did;
Yet I am run again upon the score:
    My faults cannot be hid.

What shall I do? — Make vows and break them still?
    'T will be but labor lost;
My good cannot prevail against mine ill:
    The business will be crost.

O, say not so; thou canst not tell what strength
    Thy God may give thee at the length.
Renew thy vows, and if thou keep the last,
    Thy God will pardon all that's past.
Vow while thou canst; while thou canst vow, thou mayst
    Perhaps perform it when thou thinkest least.

Thy God hath not denied thee all,
    Whilst he permits thee but to call.
Call to thy God for grace to keep
    Thy vows; and if thou break them, weep.
Weep for thy broken vows, and vow again:
Vows made with tears cannot be still in vain.
        Then once again
    I vow to mend my ways;
        Lord, say Amen,
    And thine be all the praise,
                    GEORGE HERBERT

ON JORDAN'S STORMY BANKS.

ON Jordan's stormy banks I stand,
    And cast a wishful eye
To Canaan's fair and happy land,
    Where my possessions lie.

O the transporting, rapturous scene
    That rises to my sight!
Sweet fields arrayed in living green,
    And rivers of delight.

There generous fruits, that never fail,
    On trees immortal grow;
There rock, and hill, and brook, and vale
    With milk and honey flow.

O'er all those wide-extended plains
  Shines one eternal day ;
There God the Son forever reigns,
  And scatters night away.

No chilling winds, or poisonous breath,
  Can reach that healthful shore ;
Sickness and sorrow, pain and death,
  Are felt and feared no more.

When shall I reach that happy place,
  And be forever blest ?
When shall I see my Father's face,
  And in his bosom rest ?

Filled with delight, my raptured soul
  Would here no longer stay :
Though Jordan's waves around me roll,
  Fearless I 'd launch away.
CHARLES WESLEY.

HEAVEN.

O BEAUTEOUS God ! uncircumscribed treasure
Of an eternal pleasure !
Thy throne is seated far
Above the highest star,
Where thou preparest a glorious place,
Within the brightness of thy face,
For every spirit
To inherit
That builds his hopes upon thy merit,
And loves thee with a holy charity.
What ravished heart, seraphic tongue, or eyes
Clear as the morning rise,
Can speak, or think, or see
That bright eternity,
Where the great King's transparent throne
Is of an entire jasper stone ?
There the eye
O' the chrysolite,
And a sky
Of diamonds, rubies, chrysoprase, —
And above all thy holy face, —
Makes an eternal charity.
When thou thy jewels up dost bind, that day
Remember us, we pray, —
That where the beryl lies,
And the crystal 'bove the skies,
There thou mayest appoint us place
Within the brightness of thy face, —
And our soul
In the scroll
Of life and blissfulness enroll,
That we may praise thee to eternity. Allelujah !
JEREMY TAYLOR.

THE SPIRIT-LAND.

FATHER ! thy wonders do not singly stand,
Nor far removed where feet have seldom strayed ;
Around us ever lies the enchanted land,
In marvels rich to thine own sons displayed ;
In finding thee are all things round us found ;
In losing thee are all things lost beside ;
Ears have we, but in vain strange voices sound ;
And to our eyes the vision is denied ;
We wander in the country far remote,
Mid tombs and ruined piles in death to dwell ;
Or on the records of past greatness dote,
And for a buried soul the living sell ;
While on our path bewildered falls the night
That ne'er returns us to the fields of light.
JONES VERY.

THERE IS A LAND OF PURE DELIGHT.

THERE is a land of pure delight,
  Where saints immortal reign ;
Infinite day excludes the night,
  And pleasures banish pain.

There everlasting spring abides,
  And never-withering flowers ;
Death, like a narrow sea, divides
  This heavenly land from ours.

Sweet fields beyond the swelling flood
  Stand dressed in living green ;
So to the Jews old Canaan stood,
  While Jordan rolled between.

But timorous mortals start and shrink
  To cross this narrow sea,
And linger shivering on the brink,
  And fear to launch away.

O, could we make our doubts remove,
  Those gloomy doubts that rise,
And see the Canaan that we love
  With unbeclouded eyes, —

Could we but climb where Moses stood,
  And view the landscape o'er,
Not Jordan's stream, nor death's cold flood,
  Should fright us from the shore.
ISAAC WATTS.

HEAVEN.

BEYOND these chilling winds and gloomy skies,
  Beyond death's cloudy portal,
There is a land where beauty never dies,
  Where love becomes immortal ;

A land whose life is never dimmed by shade,
  Whose fields are ever vernal ;
Where nothing beautiful can ever fade,
  But blooms for aye eternal.

We may not know how sweet its balmy air,
  How bright and fair its flowers ;
We may not hear the songs that echo there,
  Through those enchanted bowers.

The city's shining towers we may not see
  With our dim earthly vision,
For Death, the silent warder, keeps the key
  That opes the gates elysian.

But sometimes, when adown the western sky
  A fiery sunset lingers,
Its golden gates swing inward noiselessly,
  Unlocked by unseen fingers.

And while they stand a moment half ajar,
  Gleams from the inner glory
Stream brightly through the azure vault afar
  And half reveal the story.

O land unknown ! O land of love divine !
  Father, all-wise, eternal !
O, guide these wandering, wayworn feet of mine
  Into those pastures vernal !
                              ANONYMOUS.

"ONLY WAITING."

[A very aged man in an almshouse was asked what he was doing now. He replied, "Only waiting."]

ONLY waiting till the shadows
  Are a little longer grown,
Only waiting till the glimmer
  Of the day's last beam is flown ;
Till the night of earth is faded
  From the heart, once full of day ;
Till the stars of heaven are breaking
  Through the twilight soft and gray.

Only waiting till the reapers
  Have the last sheaf gathered home,
For the summer time is faded,
  And the autumn winds have come.
Quickly, reapers ! gather quickly
  The last ripe hours of my heart,
For the bloom of life is withered,
  And I hasten to depart.

Only waiting till the angels
  Open wide the mystic gate,
At whose feet I long have lingered,
  Weary, poor, and desolate.
Even now I hear the footsteps,
  And their voices far away ;

If they call me I am waiting,
  Only waiting to obey.

Only waiting till the shadows
  Are a little longer grown,
Only waiting till the glimmer
  Of the day's last beam is flown.
Then from out the gathered darkness,
  Holy, deathless stars shall rise,
By whose light my soul shall gladly
  Tread its pathway to the skies.
                              ANONYMOUS.

THE SOUL.

COME, Brother, turn with me from pining
        thought
And all the inward ills that sin has wrought ;
Come, send abroad a love for all who live,
And feel the deep content in turn they give.
Kind wishes and good deeds, — they make not
        poor ;
They 'll home again, full laden, to thy door ;
The streams of love flow back where they begin,
For springs of outward joys lie deep within.
  Even let them flow, and make the places glad
Where dwell thy fellow-men. Shouldst thou be sad,
And earth seem bare, and hours, once happy, press
Upon thy thoughts, and make thy loneliness
More lonely for the past, thou then shalt hear
The music of those waters running near ;
And thy faint spirit drink the cooling stream,
And thine eye gladden with the playing beam
That now upon the water dances, now
Leaps up and dances in the hanging bough.
  Is it not lovely ? Tell me, where doth dwell
The power that wrought so beautiful a spell ?
In thine own bosom, Brother ? Then as thine
Guard with a reverent fear this power divine.
  And if, indeed, 't is not the outward state,
But temper of the soul by which we rate
Sadness or joy, even let thy bosom move
With noble thoughts and wake thee into love,
And let each feeling in thy breast be given
An honest aim, which, sanctified by Heaven,
And springing into act, new life imparts,
Till beats thy frame as with a thousand hearts.
  Sin clouds the mind's clear vision,
Around the self-starved soul has spread a dearth.
The earth is full of life ; the living Hand
Touched it with life ; and all its forms expand
With principles of being made to suit
Man's varied powers and raise him from the brute.
And shall the earth of higher ends be full, —
Earth which thou tread'st, — and thy poor mind
        be dull ?
Thou talk of life, with half thy soul asleep ?

Thou "living dead man," let thy spirit leap
Forth to the day, and let the fresh air blow
Through thy soul's shut-up mansion. Wouldst
    thou know
Something of what is life, shake off this death ;
Have thy soul feel the universal breath
With which all nature 's quick, and learn to be
Sharer in all that thou dost touch or see ;
Break from thy body's grasp, thy spirit's trance ;
Give thy soul air, thy faculties expanse ;
Love, joy, even sorrow, — yield thyself to all !
They make thy freedom, groveller, not thy thrall.
Knock off the shackles which thy spirit bind
To dust and sense, and set at large the mind !
Then move in sympathy with God's great whole,
And be like man at first, a LIVING SOUL.
RICHARD HENRY DANA.

SIT DOWN, SAD SOUL.

SIT down, sad soul, and count
    The moments flying ;
Come, tell the sweet amount
    That 's lost by sighing !
How many smiles ? — a score ?
Then laugh, and count no more ;
    For day is dying !

Lie down, sad soul, and sleep,
    And no more measure
The flight of time, nor weep
    The loss of leisure ;
But here, by this lone stream,
Lie down with us, and dream
    Of starry treasure !

We dream ; do thou the same ;
    We love, — forever ;
We laugh, yet few we shame, —
    The gentle never.
Stay, then, till sorrow dies ;
Then — hope and happy skies
    Are thine forever !
BARRY CORNWALL.

TELL ME, YE WINGED WINDS.

TELL me, ye wingéd winds,
    That round my pathway roar,
Do ye not know some spot
    Where mortals weep no more ?
Some lone and pleasant dell,
    Some valley in the west,
Where, free from toil and pain,
    The weary soul may rest ?
The loud wind dwindled to a whisper low,
And sighed for pity as it answered, — "No."

Tell me, thou mighty deep,
    Whose billows round me play,
Know'st thou some favored spot,
    Some island far away,
Where weary man may find
    The bliss for which he sighs, —
Where sorrow never lives,
    And friendship never dies ?
The loud waves, rolling in perpetual flow,
Stopped for a while, and sighed to answer, —
    "No."

And thou, serenest moon,
    That, with such lovely face,
Dost look upon the earth,
    Asleep in night's embrace ;
Tell me, in all thy round
    Hast thou not seen some spot
Where miserable man
    May find a happier lot ?
Behind a cloud the moon withdrew in woe,
And a voice, sweet but sad, responded, — "No."

Tell me, my secret soul,
    O, tell me, Hope and Faith,
Is there no resting-place
    From sorrow, sin, and death ?
Is there no happy spot
    Where mortals may be blessed,
Where grief may find a balm,
    And weariness a rest ?
Faith, Hope, and Love, best boons to mortals given,
Waved their bright wings, and whispered, —
    "Yes, in heaven !"
CHARLES MACKAY.

O, WHERE SHALL REST BE FOUND?

O, WHERE shall rest be found, —
    Rest for the weary soul ?
'T were vain the ocean depths to sound,
    Or pierce to either pole.

The world can never give
    The bliss for which we sigh :
'T is not the whole of life to live,
    Nor all of death to die.

Beyond this vale of tears
    There is a life above,
Unmeasured by the flight of years ;
    And all that life is love.

There is a death whose pang
    Outlasts the fleeting breath :
O, what eternal horrors hang
    Around the second death !

Lord God of truth and grace,
  Teach us that death to shun,
Lest we be banished from thy face,
  And evermore undone.
                      JAMES MONTGOMERY.

THERE IS AN HOUR OF PEACEFUL REST.

THERE is an hour of peaceful rest,
  To mourning wanderers given ;
There is a joy for souls distressed,
A balm for every wounded breast ;
  'T is found above, — in heaven.

There is a soft, a downy bed,
  'T is fair as breath of even ;
A couch for weary mortals spread,
Where they may rest the aching head,
  And find repose, — in heaven.

There is a home for weary souls
  By sin and sorrow driven ;
When tossed on life's tempestuous shoals,
Where storms arise, and ocean rolls,
  And all is drear, — but heaven.

There Faith lifts up her cheerful eye,
  To brighter prospects given,
And views the tempest passing by,
The evening shadows quickly fly,
  And all serene, — in heaven.

There fragrant flowers immortal bloom,
  And joys supreme are given ;
There rays divine disperse the gloom ;
Beyond the confines of the tomb
  Appears the dawn of heaven.
                      W. B. TAPPAN.

NOTHING BUT LEAVES.

NOTHING but leaves ; the spirit grieves
  Over a wasted life ;
Sin committed while conscience slept,
Promises made but never kept,
  Hatred, battle, and strife ;
    Nothing but leaves !

Nothing but leaves ; no garnered sheaves
  Of life's fair, ripened grain ;
Words, idle words, for earnest deeds ;
We sow our seeds, — lo ! tares and weeds ;
  We reap,, with toil and pain,
    Nothing but leaves !

Nothing but leaves ; memory weaves
  No veil to screen the past :
As we retrace our weary way,
Counting each lost and misspent day,
  We find, sadly, at last,
    Nothing but leaves !

And shall we meet the Master so,
  Bearing our withered leaves ?
The Saviour looks for perfect fruit ;
We stand before him, humbled, mute ;
  Waiting the words he breathes, —
    " Nothing but leaves ? "
                      ANONYMOUS.

GREENWOOD CEMETERY.

How calm they sleep beneath the shade
  Who once were weary of the strife,
And bent, like us, beneath the load
    Of human life !

The willow hangs with sheltering grace
  And benediction o'er their sod,
And Nature, hushed, assures the soul
    They rest in God.

O weary hearts, what rest is here,
  From all that curses yonder town !
So deep the peace, I almost long
    To lay me down.

For, O, it will be blest to sleep,
  Nor dream, nor move, that silent night,
Till wakened in immortal strength
    And heavenly light !
                      CRAMMOND KENNEDY.

THE UNIVERSAL PRAYER.

FATHER of all ! in every age,
  In every clime adored,
By saint, by savage, and by sage,
  Jehovah, Jove, or Lord !

Thou great First Cause, least understood,
  Who all my sense confined
To know but this, that thou art good,
  And that myself am blind ;

Yet gave me, in this dark estate,
  To see the good from ill ;
And, binding nature fast in fate,
  Left free the human will.

What conscience dictates to be done,
  Or warns me not to do,
This, teach me more than hell to shun,
  That, more than heaven pursue.

What blessings thy free bounty gives
  Let me not cast away ;
For God is paid when man receives,
  To enjoy is to obey.

Yet not to earth's contracted span
  Thy goodness let me bound,
Or think thee Lord alone of man,
  When thousand worlds are round :

Let not this weak, unknowing hand
  Presume thy bolts to throw,
And deal damnation round the land
  On each I judge thy foe.

If I am right, thy grace impart
  Still in the right to stay ;
If I am wrong, O, teach my heart
  To find that better way !

Save me alike from foolish pride,
  Or impious discontent,
At aught thy wisdom has denied,
  Or aught thy goodness lent.

Teach me to feel another's woe,
  To hide the fault I see ;
That mercy I to others show,
  That mercy show to me.

Mean though I am, not wholly so,
  Since quickened by thy breath ;
O, lead me wheresoe'er I go,
  Through this day's life or death !

This day be bread and peace my lot ;
  All else beneath the sun,
Thou know'st if best bestowed or not,
  And let thy will be done.

To thee, whose temple is all space,
  Whose altar, earth, sea, skies !
One chorus let all Being raise !
  All Nature's incense rise !
                    ALEXANDER POPE.

WRESTLING JACOB.

FIRST PART.

COME, O thou Traveller unknown,
  Whom still I hold, but cannot see ;
My company before is gone,
  And I am left alone with thee ;
With thee all night I mean to stay,
And wrestle till the break of day.

I need not tell thee who I am ;
  My sin and misery declare ;
Thyself hast called me by my name ;
  Look on thy hands, and read it there ;

But who, I ask thee, who art thou ?
  Tell me thy name, and tell me now.

In vain thou strugglest to get free ;
  I never will unloose my hold :
Art thou the Man that died for me ?
  The secret of thy love unfold ;
Wrestling, I will not let thee go
Till I thy name, thy nature know.

Wilt thou not yet to me reveal
  Thy new, unutterable name ?
Tell me, I still beseech thee, tell ;
  To know it now resolved I am ;
Wrestling, I will not let thee go
Till I thy name, thy nature know.

What though my shrinking flesh complain
  And murmur to contend so long,
I rise superior to my pain ;
  When I am weak, then am I strong !
And when my all of strength shall fail,
I shall with the God-man prevail.

SECOND PART.

YIELD to me now, for I am weak,
  But confident in self-despair ;
Speak to my heart, in blessings speak ;
  Be conquered by my instant prayer ;
Speak, or thou never hence shalt move,
And tell me if thy name be Love.

'T is love ! 't is love ! Thou diedst for me ;
  I hear thy whisper in my heart ;
The morning breaks, the shadows flee ;
  Pure, universal love thou art ;
To me, to all, thy bowels move ;
Thy nature and thy name is Love.

My prayer hath power with God ; the grace
  Unspeakable I now receive ;
Through faith I see thee face to face ;
  I see thee face to face and live !
In vain I have not wept and strove ;
Thy nature and thy name is Love.

I know thee, Saviour, who thou art,
  Jesus, the feeble sinner's friend ;
Nor wilt thou with the night depart,
  But stay and love me to the end ;
Thy mercies never shall remove ;
Thy nature and thy name is Love.

The Sun of Righteousness on me
  Hath rose, with healing in his wings ;
Withered my nature's strength ; from thee
  My soul its life and succor brings ;
My help is all laid up above ;
Thy nature and thy name is Love.

Contented now upon my thigh
  I halt till life's short journey end ;
All helplessness, all weakness, I
  On thee alone for strength depend ;
Nor have I power from thee to move ;
  Thy nature and thy name is Love.

Lame as I am, I take the prey ;
  Hell, earth, and sin with ease o'ercome ;
I leap for joy, pursue my way,
  And, as a bounding hart, fly home ;
Through all eternity to prove
  Thy nature and thy name is Love.
                    CHARLES WESLEY.

O GOD! OUR HELP IN AGES PAST.

O God ! our help in ages past,
  Our hope for years to come,
Our shelter from the stormy blast,
  And our eternal home !

Before the hills in order stood,
  Or earth received her frame,
From everlasting thou art God,
  To endless years the same.

A thousand ages in thy sight
  Are like an evening gone ;
Short as the watch that ends the night
  Before the rising sun.

Time, like an ever-rolling stream,
  Bears all its sons away ;
They fly, forgotten, as a dream
  Dies at the opening day.

O God ! our help in ages past,
  Our hope for years to come,
Be thou our guide while troubles last,
  And our eternal home !
                    ISAAC WATTS.

A MIGHTY FORTRESS IS OUR GOD.

EIN' FESTE BURG IST UNSER GOTT.

A MIGHTY fortress is our God,
  A bulwark never failing ;
Our helper he amid the flood
  Of mortal ills prevailing.
For still our ancient foe
Doth seek to work us woe ;
His craft and power are great,
And, armed with equal hate,
  On earth is not his equal.

Did we in our own strength confide,
  Our striving would be losing ;
Were not the right man on our side,
  The man of God's own choosing.

Dost ask who that may be ?
Christ Jesus, it is he,
Lord Sabaoth his name,
From age to age the same,
  And he must win the battle.
            MARTIN LUTHER. Translation
                  of F. H. HEDGE.

JEWISH HYMN IN JERUSALEM.

God of the thunder ! from whose cloudy seat
  The fiery winds of Desolation flow ;
Father of vengeance ! that with purple feet
  Like a full wine-press tread'st the world below ;
The embattled armies wait thy sign to slay,
Nor springs the beast of havoc on his prey,
Nor withering Famine walks his blasted way,
  Till thou hast marked the guilty land for woe.

God of the rainbow ! at whose gracious sign
  The billows of the proud their rage suppress ;
Father of mercies ! at one word of thine
  An Eden blooms in the waste wilderness,
And fountains sparkle in the arid sands,
And timbrels ring in maidens' glancing hands,
And marble cities crown the laughing lands,
  And pillared temples rise thy name to bless.

O'er Judah's land thy thunders broke, O Lord !
  The chariots rattled o'er her sunken gate,
Her sons were wasted by the Assyrian's sword,
  Even her foes wept to see her fallen state ;
And heaps her ivory palaces became,
Her princes wore the captive's garb of shame,
Her temples sank amid the smouldering flame,
  For thou didst ride the tempest cloud of fate.

O'er Judah's land thy rainbow, Lord, shall beam,
  And the sad City lift her crownless head,
And songs shall wake and dancing footsteps gleam
  In streets where broods the silence of the dead.
The sun shall shine on Salem's gilded towers,
On Carmel's side our maidens cull the flowers
To deck at blushing eve their bridal bowers,
  And angel feet the glittering Sion tread.

Thy vengeance gave us to the stranger's hand,
  And Abraham's children were led forth for
        slaves.
With fettered steps we left our pleasant land,
  Envying our fathers in their peaceful graves.
The strangers' bread with bitter tears we steep,
And when our weary eyes should sink to sleep,
In the mute midnight we steal forth to weep,
  Where the pale willows shade Euphrates' waves.

The born in sorrow shall bring forth in joy ;
  Thy mercy, Lord, shall lead thy children home ;

He that went forth a tender prattling boy
  Yet, ere he die, to Salem's streets shall come ;
And Canaan's vines for us their fruit shall bear,
And Hermon's bees their honeyed stores prepare,
And we shall kneel again in thankful prayer,
  Where o'er the cherub-seated God full blazed
    the irradiate throne.

HENRY HART MILMAN.

WHEN JORDAN HUSHED HIS WATERS STILL.

WHEN Jordan hushed his waters still,
And silence slept on Zion's hill,
When Bethlehem's shepherds, through the night,
Watched o'er their flocks by starry light, —

Hark ! from the midnight hills around,
A voice of more than mortal sound
In distant hallelujahs stole,
Wild murmuring o'er the raptured soul.

On wheels of light, on wings of flame,
The glorious hosts of Zion came ;
High heaven with songs of triumph rung,
While thus they struck their harps and sung :

"O Zion, lift thy raptured eye ;
The long-expected hour is nigh ;
The joys of nature rise again ;
The Prince of Salem comes to reign.

"See, Mercy, from her golden urn,
Pours a rich stream to them that mourn ;
Behold, she binds, with tender care,
The bleeding bosom of despair.

He comes to cheer the trembling heart ;
Bids Satan and his host depart ;
Again the day-star gilds the gloom,
Again the bowers of Eden bloom."

THOMAS CAMPBELL.

THE MOTHER'S HYMN.

"Blessed art thou among women."

LORD, who ordainest for mankind
  Benignant toils and tender cares,
We thank thee for the ties that bind
  The mother to the child she bears.

We thank thee for the hopes that rise
  Within her heart, as, day by day,
The dawning soul, from those young eyes,
  Looks with a clearer, steadier ray.

And, grateful for the blessing given
  With that dear infant on her knee,
She trains the eye to look to heaven,
  The voice to lisp a prayer to thee.

Such thanks the blessed Mary gave
  When from her lap the Holy Child,
Sent from on high to seek and save
  The lost of earth, looked up and smiled.

All-Gracious ! grant to those who bear
  A mother's charge the strength and light
To guide the feet that own their care
  In ways of Love and Truth and Right.

WILLIAM CULLEN BRYANT.

MORTALS, AWAKE ! WITH ANGELS JOIN.

MORTALS, awake ! with angels join,
  And chant the solemn lay ;
Joy, love, and gratitude combine
  To hail the auspicious day.

In heaven the rapturous song began,
  And sweet seraphic fire
Through all the shining legions ran,
  And strung and tuned the lyre.

Swift through the vast expanse it flew,
  And loud the echo rolled ;
The theme, the song, the joy, was new,
  'T was more than heaven could hold.

Down through the portals of the sky
  Th' impetuous torrent ran ;
And angels flew, with eager joy,
  To bear the news to man.

Hark ! the cherubic armies shout,
  And glory leads the song ;
"Good-will and peace" are heard throughout
  The harmonious angel throng.

Hail, Prince of life ! forever hail,
  Redeemer, Brother, Friend !
Though earth and time and life should fail,
  Thy praise shall never end.

MEDLEY.

HOW SWEET THE NAME OF JESUS SOUNDS !

How sweet the name of Jesus sounds
  In a believer's ear !
It soothes his sorrows, heals his wounds,
  And drives away his fear.

It makes the wounded spirit whole,
  And calms the troubled breast ;
'T is manna to the hungry soul,
  And for the weary, rest.

By thee my prayers acceptance gain,
  Although with sin defiled ;
Satan accuses me in vain,
  And I am owned a child.

Jesus ! my Shepherd, Guardian, Friend,
  My Prophet, Priest, and King ;
My Lord, my Life, my Way, my End,
  Accept the praise I bring.

Weak is the effort of my heart,
  And cold my warmest thought ;
But when I see thee as thou art,
  I 'll praise thee as I ought.

Till then I would thy love proclaim
  With every fleeting breath ;
And may the music of thy name
  Refresh my soul in death !
                    JOHN NEWTON.

----◆----

NOW TO THE HAVEN OF THY BREAST.

Now to the haven of thy breast,
  O Son of man, I fly ;
Be thou my refuge and my rest,
  For O, the storm is high !

Protect me from the furious blast,
  My shield and shelter be ;
Hide me, my Saviour, till o'erpast
  The storm of sin I see.

As welcome as the water-spring
  Is to a barren place,
Jesus, descend on me, and bring
  Thy sweet, refreshing grace.

As o'er a parched and weary land
  A rock extends its shade,
So hide me, Saviour, with thy hand,
  And screen my naked head.

In all the times of my distress
  Thou hast my succor been ;
And, in my utter helplessness,
  Restraining me from sin,

How swift to save me didst thou move,
  In every trying hour !
O, still protect me with thy love,
  And shield me with thy power !
                    CHARLES WESLEY.

JESUS, LOVER OF MY SOUL.

Jesus, lover of my soul,
  Let me to thy bosom fly,
While the nearer waters roll,
  While the tempest still is high !
Hide me, O my Saviour, hide,
  Till the storm of life is past ;
Safe into thy haven guide,
  O, receive my soul at last !

Other refuge have I none,
  Hangs my helpless soul on thee ;
Leave, ah ! leave me not alone,
  Still support and comfort me.
All my trust on thee is stayed,
  All my help from thee I bring ;
Cover my defenceless head
  With the shadow of thy wing.

Wilt thou not regard my call ?
  Wilt thou not regard my prayer ?
Lo ! I sink, I faint, I fall, —
  Lo ! on thee I cast my care ;
Reach me out thy gracious hand,
  While I of thy strength receive !
Hoping against hope I stand, —
  Dying, and behold I live.

Thou, O Christ, art all I want ;
  More than all in thee I find ;
Raise the fallen, cheer the faint,
  Heal the sick, and lead the blind,
Just and holy is thy name,
  I am all unrighteousness ;
False and full of sin I am,
  Thou art full of truth and grace.

Plenteous grace with thee is found, —
  Grace to cover all my sin ;
Let the healing streams abound,
  Make and keep me pure within.
Thou of life the fountain art,
  Freely let me take of thee ;
Spring thou up within my heart,
  Rise to all eternity.
                    CHARLES WESLEY.

----◆----

SWEETEST SAVIOUR, IF MY SOUL—

Sweetest Saviour, if my soul
  Were but worth the having,
Quickly should I then controll
  Any thought of waving.
But when all my care and pains
Cannot give the name of gains
To thy wretch so full of stains,
What delight or hope remains ?

What (childe), is the balance thine,
Thine the poise and measure ?
If I say, Thou shalt be mine,
Finger not my treasure.
What the gains in having thee
Do amount to, onely he
Who for man was sold can see,
That transferred the accounts to me.

But as I can see no merit
Leading to this favour :
So the way to fit me for it
Is beyond my savour.
As the reason then is thine,
So the way is none of mine :
I disclaim the whole designe ;
Sinne disclaims and I resigne.

That is all, if that I could
Get without repining ;
And my clay my creature would
Follow my resigning :
That as I did freely part
With my glorie and desert,
Left all joyes to feel all smart —
Ah ! no more : thou break'st my heart.
GEORGE HERBERT.

JUST AS I AM.

JUST as I am, — without one plea,
But that thy blood was shed for me,
And that thou bid'st me come to thee, —
O Lamb of God, I come ! I come !

Just as I am, — and waiting not
To rid my soul of one dark blot,
To thee whose blood can cleanse each spot, —
O Lamb of God, I come ! I come !

Just as I am, — though tossed about
With many a conflict, many a doubt,
Fightings within, and fears without, —
O Lamb of God, I come ! I come !

Just as I am, — poor, wretched, blind ;
Sight, riches, healing of the mind,
Yea, all I need, in thee to find, —
O Lamb of God, I come ! I come !

Just as I am, — thou wilt receive ;
Wilt welcome, pardon, cleanse, relieve ;
Because thy promise I believe, —
O Lamb of God, I come ! I come !

Just as I am, — thy love unknown
Has broken every barrier down ;
Now, to be thine, yea, thine alone, —
O Lamb of God, I come ! I come !
ANONYMOUS.

ROCK OF AGES, CLEFT FOR ME.

ROCK of Ages, cleft for me,
Let me hide myself in thee !
Let the water and the blood,
From thy riven side which flowed,
Be of sin the double cure, —
Cleanse me from its guilt and power.

Not the labors of my hands
Can fulfil thy law's demands ;
Could my zeal no respite know,
Could my tears forever flow,
All for sin could not atone, —
Thou must save, and thou alone.

Nothing in my hand I bring,
Simply to thy cross I cling ;
Naked, come to thee for dress,
Helpless, look to thee for grace ;
Foul, I to the fountain fly, —
Wash me, Saviour, or I die.

While I draw this fleeting breath,
When my eye-strings break in death,
When I soar to worlds unknown,
See thee on thy judgment-throne,
Rock of Ages, cleft for me,
Let me hide myself in thee !
AUGUSTUS MONTAGUE TOPLADY.

WHEN GATHERING CLOUDS AROUND I VIEW.

WHEN gathering clouds around I view,
And days are dark, and friends are few,
On Him I lean who not in vain
Experienced every human pain ;
He sees my wants, allays my fears,
And counts and treasures up my tears.

If aught should tempt my soul to stray
From heavenly wisdom's narrow way,
To fly the good I would pursue,
Or do the sin I would not do,
Still he who felt temptation's power
Shall guard me in that dangerous hour.

If wounded love my bosom swell,
Deceived by those I prized too well,
He shall his pitying aid bestow
Who felt on earth severer woe,
At once betrayed, denied, or fled,
By those who shared his daily bread.

If vexing thoughts within me rise,
And sore dismayed my spirit dies,
Still he who once vouchsafed to bear
The sickening anguish of despair

Shall sweetly soothe, shall gently dry,
The throbbing heart, the streaming eye.

When sorrowing o'er some stone I bend,
Which covers what was once a friend,
And from his voice, his hand, his smile,
Divides me for a little while,
Thou, Saviour, mark'st the tears I shed,
For thou didst weep o'er Lazarus dead.

And O, when I have safely past
Through every conflict but the last,
Still, still unchanging, watch beside
My painful bed, — for thou hast died;
Then point to realms of cloudless day,
And wipe the latest tear away.

SIR ROBERT GRANT.

"THOU HAST PUT ALL THINGS UNDER HIS FEET."

O NORTH, with all thy vales of green !
    O South, with all thy palms !
From peopled towns and fields between
    Uplift the voice of psalms.
Raise, ancient East ! the anthem high,
And let the youthful West reply.

Lo ! in the clouds of heaven appears
    God's well-beloved Son.
He brings a train of brighter years,
    His kingdom is begun.
He comes a guilty world to bless
With mercy, truth, and righteousness.

O Father ! haste the promised hour,
    When at his feet shall lie
All rule, authority, and power,
    Beneath the ample sky ;
When he shall reign from pole to pole,
The Lord of every human soul ;

When all shall heed the words he said,
    Amid their daily cares,
And by the loving life he led
    Shall strive to pattern theirs :
And he who conquered Death shall win
The mightier conquest over Sin.

WILLIAM CULLEN BRYANT.

O, HAPPY DAY THAT FIXED MY CHOICE !

O, HAPPY day that fixed my choice
    On thee, my Saviour and my God !
Well may this glowing heart rejoice,
    And tell its raptures all abroad.

'T is done, the great transaction 's done !
    I am my Lord's, and he is mine ;
He drew me, and I followed on,
    Charmed to confess the voice divine.

Now rest my long-divided heart,
    Fixed on this blissful centre, rest ;
Nor ever from thy Lord depart,
    With him of every good possessed.

High Heaven, that heard the solemn vow,
    That vow renewed shall daily hear ;
Till in life's latest hour I bow,
    And bless in death a bond so dear.

PHILIP DODDRIDGE.

HOPEFULLY WAITING.

" Blessed are they who are homesick, for they shall come at last
to their Father's house."— HEINRICH STILLING.

NOT as you meant, O learned man, and good !
    Do I accept thy words of truth and rest ;
    God, knowing all, knows what for me is best.
And gives me what I need, not what he could,
            Nor always as I would !
I shall go to the Father's house, and see
    Him and the Elder Brother face to face, —
What day or hour I know not.   Let me be
    Steadfast in work, and earnest in the race,
        Not as a homesick child who all day long
        Whines at its play, and seldom speaks in song

If for a time some loved one goes away,
    And leaves us our appointed work to do,
    Can we to him or to ourselves be true
In mourning his departure day by day,
            And so our work delay ?
Nay, if we love and honor, we shall make
    The absence brief by doing well our task, —
Not for ourselves, but for the dear One's sake !
    And at his coming only of him ask
        Approval of the work, which most was done,
        Not for ourselves, but our Beloved One !

Our Father's house, I know, is broad and grand ;
    In it how many, many mansions are !
    And far beyond the light of sun or star,
Four little ones of mine through that fair land
        Are walking hand in hand !
Think you I love not, or that I forget
    These of my loins ?   Still this world is fair,
And I am singing while my eyes are wet
    With weeping in this balmy summer air :
        Yet I 'm not homesick, and the children *here*
        Have need of me, and so my way is clear.

I would be joyful as my days go by,
    Counting God's mercies to me.   He who bore

Life's heaviest cross is mine forevermore,
And I who wait his coming, shall not I
　　　On his sure word rely ?
And if sometimes the way be rough and steep,
　　Be heavy for the grief he sends to me,
Or at my waking I would only weep,
　　Let me remember these are things to be,
　　　To work his blessed will until he come
　　And take my hand, and lead me safely home.
　　　　　　　　　　　A. D. F. RANDOLPH.

IS THIS ALL ?

FROM "HYMNS OF FAITH AND PEACE."

Sometimes I catch sweet glimpses of His face,
　　　But that is all.
Sometimes he looks on me, and seems to smile,
　　　But that is all.
Sometimes he speaks a passing word of peace,
　　　But that is all.
Sometimes I think I hear his loving voice
　　　Upon me call.

And is this all he meant when thus he spoke,
　　　"Come unto me" ?
Is there no deeper, more enduring rest
　　　In him for thee ?
Is there no steadier light for thee in him ?
　　　O, come and see !

O, come and see ! O, look, and look again !
　　　All shall be right ;
O, taste his love, and see that it is good,
　　　Thou child of night !
O, trust thou, trust thou in his grace and power !
　　　Then all is bright.

Nay, do not wrong him by thy heavy thoughts,
　　　But love his love.
Do thou full justice to his tenderness,
　　　His mercy prove ;
Take him for what he is ; O, take him all,
　　　And look above !

Then shall thy tossing soul find anchorage
　　　And steadfast peace ;
Thy love shall rest on his ; thy weary doubts
　　　Forever cease.
Thy heart shall find in him and in his grace
　　　Its rest and bliss !

Christ and his love shall be thy blessed all
　　　Forevermore !
Christ and his light shall shine on all thy ways
　　　Forevermore !
Christ and his peace shall keep thy troubled soul
　　　Forevermore !
　　　　　　　　　　　HORATIUS BONAR.

O DEAREST LAMB, TAKE THOU MY HEART !

O DEAREST Lamb, take thou my heart !
　　Where can such sweetness be
As I have tasted in thy love,
　　As I have found in thee ?

If there 's a fervor in my soul,
　　And fervor sure there is,
Now it shall be at thy control,
　　And but to serve thee rise.

If love, that mildest flame, can rest
　　In hearts so hard as mine,
Come, gentle Saviour, to my breast,
　　Its love shall all be thine.

Now the gay world with treacherous art
　　Shall tempt my heart in vain ;
I have conveyed away that heart,
　　Ne'er to return again.

'T is heaven on earth to taste his love,
　　To feel his quickening grace,
And all the heaven I hope above
　　Is but to see his face.
　　　　　MORAVIAN COLLECTION OF HYMNS.

THE DYING SAVIOUR.

O SACRED Head, now wounded,
　　With grief and shame weighed down ;
Now scornfully surrounded
　　With thorns, thy only crown ;
O sacred Head, what glory,
　　What bliss, till now was thine !
Yet, though despised and gory,
　　I joy to call thee mine.

O noblest brow and dearest,
　　In other days the world
All feared when thou appearedst ;
　　What shame on thee is hurled !
How art thou pale with anguish,
　　With sore abuse and scorn !
How does that visage languish
　　Which once was bright as morn !

What language shall I borrow,
　　To thank thee, dearest Friend,
For this thy dying sorrow,
　　Thy pity without end !
O, make me thine forever,
　　And should I fainting be,
Lord, let me never, never,
　　Outlive my love to thee.

If I, a wretch, should leave thee,
  O Jesus, leave not me !
In faith may I receive thee,
  When death shall set me free.
When strength and comfort languish,
  And I must hence depart,
Release me then from anguish,
  By thine own wounded heart.

Be near when I am dying,
  O, show thy cross to me !
And for my succor flying,
  Come, Lord, to set me free.
These eyes new faith receiving,
  From Jesus shall not move ;
For he who dies believing
  Dies safely — through thy love.
                    PAUL GERHARDT.

———◆———

MARY TO HER SAVIOUR'S TOMB —

MARY to her Saviour's tomb
  Hasted at the early dawn ;
Spice she brought, and rich perfume, —
  But the Lord she loved was gone.
For a while she weeping stood,
  Struck with sorrow and surprise,
Shedding tears, a plenteous flood,
  For her heart supplied her eyes.

Jesus, who is always near,
  Though too often unperceived,
Comes his drooping child to cheer,
  Kindly asking why she grieved.
Though at first she knew him not, —
  When he called her by her name,
Then her griefs were all forgot,
  For she found he was the same.

Grief and sighing quickly fled
  When she heard his welcome voice ;
Just before she thought him dead,
  Now he bids her heart rejoice.
What a change his word can make,
  Turning darkness into day !
You who weep for Jesus' sake,
  He will wipe your tears away.

He who came to comfort her
  When she thought her all was lost
Will for your relief appear,
  Though you now are tempest-tossed.
On his word your burden cast,
  On his love your thoughts employ ;
Weeping for a while may last,
  But the morning brings the joy.
                    JOHN NEWTON.

THE ASCENSION OF CHRIST.

" BRIGHT portals of the sky,
  Embossed with sparkling stars ;
Doors of eternity,
  With diamantine bars,
  Your arras rich uphold ;
Loose all your bolts and springs,
  Ope wide your leaves of gold ;
That in your roofs may come the King of kings.

" Scarfed in a rosy cloud,
  He doth ascend the air ;
Straight doth the Moon him shroud
  With her resplendent hair ;
  The next encrystalled light
Submits to him its beams ;
  And he doth trace the height
Of that fair lamp which flames of beauty streams.

" The choirs of happy souls,
  Waked with that music sweet,
Whose descant care controls,
  Their Lord in triumph meet ;
  The spotless spirits of light
His trophies do extol,
  And, arched in squadrons bright,
Greet their great Victor in his capitol.

" O glory of the Heaven !
  O sole delight of Earth !
To thee all power be given,
  God's uncreated birth ;
  Of mankind lover true,
Endurer of his wrong,
  Who dost the world renew,
Still be thou our salvation, and our song."
From top of Olivet such notes did rise,
When man's Redeemer did transcend the skies.
                    WILLIAM DRUMMOND.

———◆———

TREMBLING, BEFORE THINE AWFUL THRONE —

TREMBLING, before thine awful throne,
O Lord ! in dust my sins I own :
Justice and Mercy for my life
Contend ! — O, smile, and heal the strife.

The Saviour smiles ! upon my soul
New tides of hope tumultuous roll,
His voice proclaims my pardon found,
Seraphic transport wings the sound !

Earth has a joy unknown in heaven, —
The new-born peace of sins forgiven !
Tears of such pure and deep delight,
Ye angels ! never dimmed your sight.

Ye saw of old on chaos rise
The beauteous pillars of the skies ;
Ye know where morn exulting springs,
And evening folds her drooping wings.

Bright heralds of th' Eternal Will,
Abroad his errands ye fulfil ;
Or, throned in floods of beamy day,
Symphonious, in his presence play.

Loud is the song, the heavenly plain
Is shaken by the choral strain,
And dying echoes, floating far,
Draw music from each chiming star.

But I amid your choirs shall shine,
And all your knowledge will be mine ;
Ye on your harps must lean to hear
A secret chord that *mine* will bear.

THOMAS HILLHOUSE.

NEARER, MY GOD, TO THEE.

NEARER, my God, to thee,
Nearer to thee !
E'en though it be a cross
That raiseth me ;
Still all my song shall be, —
Nearer, my God, to thee,
Nearer to thee !

Though, like the wanderer,
The sun gone down,
Darkness be over me,
My rest a stone ;
Yet in my dreams I 'd be
Nearer, my God, to thee,
Nearer to thee !

There let the way appear
Steps unto heaven ;
All that thou sendest me
In mercy given ;
Angels to beckon me
Nearer, my God, to thee,
Nearer to thee !

Then with my waking thoughts,
Bright with thy praise,
Out of my stony griefs
Bethel I 'll raise ;
So by my woes to be
Nearer, my God, to thee,
Nearer to thee !

Or if on joyful wing,
Cleaving the sky,
Sun, moon, and stars forgot,
Upward I fly ;

Still all my song shall be, —
Nearer, my God, to thee,
Nearer to thee.

SARAH F. ADAMS.

FROM THE RECESSES OF A LOWLY SPIRIT.

FROM the recesses of a lowly spirit,
Our humble prayer ascends ; O Father ! hear it.
Upsoaring on the wings of awe and meekness,
Forgive its weakness !

We see thy hand, — it leads us, it supports us ;
We hear thy voice, — it counsels and it courts us ;
And then we turn away ; and still thy kindness
Forgives our blindness.

O, how long-suffering, Lord ! but thou delightest
To win with love the wandering : thou invitest,
By smiles of mercy, not by frowns or terrors,
Man from his errors.

Father and Saviour ! plant within each bosom
The seeds of holiness, and bid them blossom
In fragrance and in beauty bright and vernal,
And spring eternal.

JOHN BOWRING.

PRAISE TO GOD, IMMORTAL PRAISE.

PRAISE to God, immortal praise,
For the love that crowns our days, —
Bounteous source of every joy,
Let thy praise our tongues employ !

For the blessings of the field,
For the stores the gardens yield,
For the vine's exalted juice,
For the generous olive's use ;

Flocks that whiten all the plain,
Yellow sheaves of ripened grain,
Clouds that drop their fattening dews,
Suns that temperate warmth diffuse ;

All that Spring, with bounteous hand,
Scatters o'er the smiling land ;
All that liberal Autumn pours
From her rich o'erflowing stores :

These to thee, my God, we owe, —
Source whence all our blessings flow !
And for these my soul shall raise
Grateful vows and solemn praise.

Yet should rising whirlwinds tear
From its stem the ripening ear,

Should the fig-tree's blasted shoot
Drop her green untimely fruit, —

Should the vine put forth no more,
Nor the olive yield her store, —
Though the sickening flocks should fall,
And the herds desert the stall, —

Should thine altered hand restrain
The early and the latter rain,
Blast each opening bud of joy,
And the rising year destroy ; —

Yet to thee my soul should raise
Grateful vows and solemn praise,
And, when every blessing's flown,
Love thee — for thyself alone.

ANNA LÆTITIA BARBAULD.

WHEN ALL THY MERCIES, O MY GOD!

WHEN all thy mercies, O my God !
My rising soul surveys,
Transported with the view, I 'm lost
In wonder, love, and praise.

O, how shall words with equal warmth
The gratitude declare
That glows within my ravished heart ? —
But thou canst read it there !

Thy providence my life sustained,
And all my wants redrest,
When in the silent womb I lay,
And hung upon the breast.

To all my weak complaints and cries
Thy mercy lent an ear,
Ere yet my feeble thoughts had learnt
To form themselves in prayer.

Unnumbered comforts to my soul
Thy tender care bestowed,
Before my infant heart conceived
From whom those comforts flowed.

When in the slippery paths of youth
With heedless steps I ran,
Thine arm unseen conveyed me safe,
And led me up to man.

Through hidden dangers, toils, and deaths,
It gently cleared my way,
And through the pleasing snares of vice, —
More to be feared than they.

When worn with sickness oft hast thou
With health renewed my face ;
And, when in sins and sorrows sunk,
Revived my soul with grace.

Thy bounteous hand with worldly bliss
Has made my cup run o'er,
And in a kind and faithful friend
Has doubled all my store.

Ten thousand thousand precious gifts
My daily thanks employ ;
Nor is the least a cheerful heart,
That tastes those gifts with joy.

Through every period of my life
Thy goodness I 'll pursue ;
And after death, in distant worlds,
The glorious theme renew.

When nature fails, and day and night
Divide thy works no more,
My ever-grateful heart, O Lord,
Thy mercy shall adore.

Through all eternity to thee
A joyful song I 'll raise ;
For O, eternity 's too short
To utter all thy praise !

JOSEPH ADDISON.

THE MINISTRY OF ANGELS!

AND is there care in heaven ?   And is there love
In heavenly spirits to these creatures base,
That may compassion of their evils move ?
There is : — else much more wretched were the
case
Of men then beasts : but O the exceeding grace
Of Highest God ! that loves his creatures so,
And all his workes with mercy doth embrace,
That blessed angels he sends to and fro,
To serve to wicked man, to serve his wicked foe !

How oft do they their silver bowers leave,
To come to succour us that succour want !
How oft do they with goldon pinions cleave
The flitting skyes, like flying pursuivant,
Against fowle feendes to ayd us militant !
They for us fight, they watch, and dewly ward,
And their bright squadrons round about us plant;
And all for love, and nothing for reward ;
O, why should heavenly God to men have such
regard !

EDMUND SPENSER.

ETERNAL SOURCE OF EVERY JOY!

ETERNAL Source of every joy !
Well may thy praise our lips employ,
While in thy temple we appear
Whose goodness crowns the circling year.

While as the wheels of nature roll,
Thy hand supports the steady pole ;
The sun is taught by thee to rise,
And darkness when to veil the skies.

The flowery spring at thy command
Embalms the air, and paints the land ;
The summer rays with vigor shine
To raise the corn, and cheer the vine.

Thy hand in autumn richly pours
Through all our coasts redundant stores ;
And winters, softened by thy care,
No more a face of horror wear.

Seasons, and months, and weeks, and days
Demand successive songs of praise ;
Still be the cheerful homage paid
With opening light and evening shade.

Here in thy house shall incense rise,
As circling Sabbaths bless our eyes ;
Still will we make thy mercies known
Around thy board, and round our own.

O, may our more harmonious tongues
In worlds unknown pursue the songs ;
And in those brighter courts adore,
Where days and years revolve no more.
                            PHILIP DODDRIDGE.

THE SPACIOUS FIRMAMENT ON HIGH.

[This hymn originally appeared in the Spectator, and is thence
popularly, but erroneously, supposed to have been composed by
ADDISON.]

THE spacious firmament on high,
   With all the blue ethereal sky,
And spangled heavens, a shining frame,
   Their great Original proclaim ;
The unwearied sun, from day to day,
   Does his Creator's power display,
And publishes to every land
   The work of an Almighty hand.

Soon as the evening shades prevail,
   The moon takes up the wondrous tale,
And nightly to the listening earth
   Repeats the story of her birth ;
While all the stars that round her burn,
And all the planets in their turn,
Confirm the tidings as they roll,
   And spread the truth from pole to pole.

What though, in solemn silence, all
   Move round the dark terrestrial ball ?
What though no *real* voice or sound
   Amid their radiant orbs be found ?

In *Reason's* ear they all rejoice,
And utter forth a glorious voice,
Forever singing, as they shine,
" *The Hand that made us is divine !*"
                            ANDREW MARVELL.

LORD ! WHEN THOSE GLORIOUS LIGHTS I SEE.

HYMN AND PRAYER FOR THE USE OF BELIEVERS.

LORD ! when those glorious lights I see
   With which thou hast adorned the skies,
Observing how they movéd be,
   And how their splendor fills mine eyes,
Methinks it is too large a grace,
   But that thy love ordained it so, —
That creatures in so high a place
   Should servants be to man below.

The meanest lamp now shining there
   In size and lustre doth exceed
The noblest of thy creatures here,
   And of our friendship hath no need.
Yet these upon mankind attend
   For secret aid or public light ;
And from the world's extremest end
   Repair unto us every night.

O, had that stamp been undefaced
   Which first on us thy hand had set,
How highly should we have been graced,
   Since we are so much honored yet !
Good God, for what but for the sake
   Of thy beloved and only Son,
Who did on him our nature take,
   Were these exceeding favors done !

As we by him have honored been,
   Let us to him due honors give ;
Let his uprightness hide our sin,
   And let us worth from him receive.
Yea, so let us by grace improve
   What thou by nature doth bestow,
That to thy dwelling-place above
   We may be raiséd from below.
                            GEORGE WITHER.

HYMN.

BEFORE SUNRISE, IN THE VALE OF CHAMOUNI.

HAST thou a charm to stay the morning-star
In his steep course ? So long he seems to pause
On thy bald, awful head, O sovereign Blanc !
The Arve and Arveiron at thy base
Rave ceaselessly ; but thou, most awful Form,
Risest from forth thy silent sea of pines
How silently ! Around thee and above

Deep is the air and dark, substantial, black, —
An ebon mass.   Methinks thou piercest it,
As with a wedge! But when I look again,
It is thine own calm home, thy crystal shrine,
Thy habitation from eternity!
O dread and silent Mount! I gazed upon thee,
Till thou, still present to the bodily sense,
Didst vanish from my thought.   Entranced in
     prayer
I worshipped the Invisible alone.

Yet, like some sweet beguiling melody,
So sweet we know not we are listening to it,
Thou, the mean while, wast blending with my
     thought, —
Yea, with my life and life's own secret joy, —
Till the dilating soul, enrapt, transfused,
Into the mighty vision passing, there,
As in her natural form, swelled vast to Heaven!

Awake, my soul! not only passive praise
Thou owest! not alone these swelling tears,
Mute thanks, and secret ecstasy! Awake,
Voice of sweet song! Awake, my heart, awake!
Green vales and icy cliffs, all join my hymn.

Thou first and chief, sole sovereign of the vale!
O, struggling with the darkness all the night,
And visited all night by troops of stars,
Or when they climb the sky or when they sink, —
Companion of the morning-star at dawn,
Thyself Earth's rosy star, and of the dawn
Co-herald, — wake, O, wake, and utter praise!
Who sank thy sunless pillars deep in earth?
Who filled thy countenance with rosy light?
Who made thee parent of perpetual streams?

And you, ye five wild torrents fiercely glad!
Who called you forth from night and utter death,
From dark and icy caverns called you forth,
Down those precipitous, black, jagged rocks,
Forever shattered and the same forever?
Who gave you your invulnerable life,
Your strength, your speed, your fury, and your joy,
Unceasing thunder and eternal foam?
And who commanded (and the silence came),
Here let the billows stiffen, and have rest?

Ye ice-falls! ye that from the mountain's brow
Adown enormous ravines slope amain, — .
Torrents, methinks, that heard a mighty voice,
And stopped at once amid their maddest plunge!
Motionless torrents! silent cataracts!
Who made you glorious as the gates of Heaven
Beneath the keen full moon? Who bade the sun
Clothe you with rainbows? Who, with living
     flowers
Of loveliest blue, spread garlands at your feet?
God! — let the torrents, like a shout of nations,

Answer! and let the ice-plains echo, God!
God! sing, ye meadow-streams, with gladsome
     voice!
Ye pine-groves, with your soft and soul-like
     sounds!
And they too have a voice, yon piles of snow,
And in their perilous fall shall thunder, God!
Ye living flowers that skirt the eternal frost!
Ye wild goats sporting round the eagle's nest!
Ye eagles, playmates of the mountain-storm!
Ye lightnings, the dread arrows of the clouds!
Ye signs and wonders of the elements!
Utter forth God, and fill the hills with praise!

Thou, too, hoar Mount! with thy sky-pointing
     peaks,
Oft from whose feet the avalanche, unheard,
Shoots downward, glittering through the pure
     serene,
Into the depth of clouds that veil thy breast, —
Thou too again, stupendous Mountain! thou
That as I raise my head, awhile bowed low
In adoration, upward from thy base
Slow travelling with dim eyes suffused with tears,
Solemnly seemest, like a vapory cloud,
To rise before me, — Rise, O, ever rise!
Rise like a cloud of incense, from the Earth!
Thou kingly Spirit throned among the hills,
Thou dread ambassador from Earth to Heaven,
Great Hierarch! tell thou the silent sky,
And tell the stars, and tell yon rising sun,
Earth, with her thousand voices, praises God.
                SAMUEL TAYLOR COLERIDGE.

THOU ART, O GOD—

" The day is thine, the night also is thine : thou hast prepared
the light and the sun. Thou hast set all the borders of the earth :
thou hast made summer and winter." — PSALM lxxiv. 16, 17.

THOU art, O God, the life and light
   Of all this wondrous world we see;
Its glow by day, its smile by night,
   Are but reflections caught from thee.
Where'er we turn thy glories shine,
And all things fair and bright are thine!

When day, with farewell beam, delays
   Among the opening clouds of even,
And we can almost think we gaze
   Through golden vistas into heaven, —
Those hues that make the sun's decline
So soft, so radiant, Lord! are thine.

When night, with wings of starry gloom,
   O'ershadows all the earth and skies,
Like some dark, beauteous bird, whose plume
   Is sparkling with unnumbered eyes, —
That sacred gloom, those fires divine,
So grand, so countless, Lord! are thine.

When youthful spring around us breathes,
  Thy Spirit warms her fragrant sigh ;
And every flower the summer wreathes
  Is born beneath that kindling eye.
Where'er we turn, thy glories shine,
And all things fair and bright are thine !
                              THOMAS MOORE.

THE HEAVENS DECLARE THY GLORY, LORD !

PSALM XIX.

THE heavens declare thy glory, Lord !
  In every star thy wisdom shines ;
But when our eyes behold thy word,
  We read thy name in fairer lines.

The rolling sun, the changing light,
  And nights and days thy power confess ;
But the blest volume thou hast writ
  Reveals thy justice and thy grace.

Sun, moon, and stars convey thy praise
  Round the whole earth, and never stand ;
So when thy truth began its race
  It touched and glanced on every land.

Nor shall thy spreading gospel rest
  Till through the world thy truth has run ;
Till Christ has all the nations blest
  That see the light or feel the sun.

Great Sun of Righteousness, arise !
  Bless the dark world with heavenly light !
Thy gospel makes the simple wise, —
  Thy laws are pure, thy judgments right.

Thy noblest wonders here we view,
  In souls renewed and sins forgiven ;
Lord, cleanse my sins, my soul renew,
  And make thy word my guide to heaven !
                              ISAAC WATTS.

GOD MOVES IN A MYSTERIOUS WAY.

GOD moves in a mysterious way
  His wonders to perform ;
He plants his footsteps in the sea,
  And rides upon the storm.

Deep in unfathomable mines
  Of never-failing skill
He treasures up his bright designs,
  And works his sovereign will.

Ye fearful saints, fresh courage take !
  The clouds ye so much dread
Are big with mercy, and shall break
  In blessings on your head.

Judge not the Lord by feeble sense,
  But trust him for his grace ;
Behind a frowning providence
  He hides a smiling face.

His purposes will ripen fast,
  Unfolding every hour ;
The bud may have a bitter taste,
  But sweet will be the flower.

Blind unbelief is sure to err,
  And scan his work in vain ;
God is his own interpreter,
  And he will make it plain.
                              WILLIAM COWPER.

THROUGH LIFE'S VAPORS DIMLY SEEING.

THROUGH life's vapors dimly seeing,
  Who but longs for light to break !
Othe feverish dream of being !
  When, O, when shall we awake?
O the hour when this material
  Shall have vanished as a cloud, —
When amid the wide ethereal
  All the invisible shall crowd, —

And the naked soul, surrounded
  With realities unknown,
Triumph in the view unbounded,
  Feel herself with God alone !
In that sudden, strange transition,
  By what new and finer sense
Shall she grasp the mighty vision,
  And receive its influence ?

Angels, guard the new immortal,
  Through the wonder-teeming space,
To the everlasting portal,
  To the spirit's resting-place.
Till the trump, which shakes creation,
  Through the circling heavens shall roll,
Till the day of consummation,
  Till the bridal of the soul.

Jesus, blessed Mediator !
  Thou the airy path hast trod ;
Thou the Judge, the Consummator !
  Shepherd of the fold of God !
Can I trust a fellow-being ?
  Can I trust an angel's care ?
O thou merciful All-seeing !
  Beam around my spirit there.

Blessed fold ! no foe can enter ;
  And no friend departeth thence ;
Jesus is their sun, their centre,
  And their shield Omnipotence.

Blessed ! for the Lamb shall feed them,
  All their tears shall wipe away,
To the living fountains lead them,
  Till fruition's perfect day.

Lo ! it comes, that day of wonder !
  Louder chorals shake the skies ;
Hades' gates are burst asunder ;
  See ! the new-clothed myriads rise.
Thought ! repress thy weak endeavor ;
  Here must reason prostrate fall ;
O the ineffable Forever !
  And the eternal All in All !

CONDER.

SOUND THE LOUD TIMBREL.

MIRIAM'S SONG.

"And Miriam the prophetess, the sister of Aaron, took a timbrel in her hand ; and all the women went out after her with timbrels and with dances." — EXOD. XV. 20.

SOUND the loud timbrel o'er Egypt's dark sea !
Jehovah has triumphed, — his people are free !
Sing, — for the pride of the tyrant is broken,
  His chariots, his horsemen, all splendid and
    brave, —
How vain was their boasting ! the Lord hath but
    spoken,
  And chariots and horsemen are sunk in the wave.
Sound the loud timbrel o'er Egypt's dark sea !
Jehovah has triumphed, — his people are free !

Praise to the Conqueror, praise to the Lord !
His word was our arrow, his breath was our sword.
Who shall return to tell Egypt the story
  Of those she sent forth in the hour of her pride ?
For the Lord hath looked out from his pillar of
    glory,
  And all her brave thousands are dashed in the
    tide.
Sound the loud timbrel o'er Egypt's dark sea !
Jehovah has triumphed, — his people are free !

THOMAS MOORE.

CHILDREN OF GOD, WHO, FAINT AND SLOW—

CHILDREN of God, who, faint and slow,
  Your pilgrim-path pursue,
In strength and weakness, joy and woe,
  To God's high calling true ! —

Why move ye thus, with lingering tread,
  A doubting, mournful band ?
Why faintly hangs the drooping head ?
  Why fails the feeble hand ?

O, weak to know a Saviour's power,
  To feel a Father's care !
A moment's toil, a passing shower,
  Is all the grief ye share.

The orb of light, though clouds awhile
  May hide his noontide ray,
Shall soon in lovelier beauty smile
  To gild the closing day, —

And, bursting through the dusky shroud
  That dared his power invest,
Ride throned in light, o'er every cloud,
  Triumphant to his rest.

Then, Christian, dry the falling tear,
  The faithless doubt remove ;
Redeemed at last from guilt and fear,
  O, wake thy heart to love !

BOWDLER.

I STAND ON ZION'S MOUNT.

I STAND on Zion's mount,
  And view my starry crown ;
No power on earth my hope can shake,
  Nor hell can thrust me down.

The lofty hills and towers,
  That lift their heads on high,
Shall all be levelled low in dust, —
  Their very names shall die.

The vaulted heavens shall fall,
  Built by Jehovah's hands ;
But firmer than the heavens the Rock
  Of my salvation stands.

CHARLES SWAIN.

THE LORD MY PASTURE SHALL PRE-PARE.

PSALM XXIII.

THE Lord my pasture shall prepare,
And feed me with a shepherd's care ;
His presence shall my wants supply,
And guard me with a watchful eye ;
My noonday walks he shall attend,
And all my midnight hours defend.

When in the sultry glebe I faint,
Or on the thirsty mountains pant,
To fertile vales and dewy meads,
My weary, wandering steps he leads,
Where peaceful rivers soft and slow
Amid the verdant landscape flow.

Though in the paths of death I tread,
With gloomy horrors overspread,
My steadfast heart shall fear no ill ;
For thou, O Lord, art with me still :
Thy friendly crook shall give me aid,
And guide me through the dreadful shade.

Though in a bare and rugged way,
Through devious lonely wilds I stray,
Thy bounty shall my pains beguile ;
The barren wilderness shall smile,
With sudden greens and herbage crowned,
And streams shall murmur all around.
                              JOSEPH ADDISON.

AMAZING, BEAUTEOUS CHANGE!

AMAZING, beauteous change !
A world created new !
My thoughts with transport range,
The lovely scene to view ;
    In all I trace,
    Saviour divine,
    The work is thine, —
    Be thine the praise !

See crystal fountains play
Amidst the burning sands ;
The river's winding way
Shines through the thirsty lands ;
    New grass is seen,
    And o'er the meads
    Its carpet spreads
    Of living green.

Where pointed brambles grew,
Intwined with horrid thorn,
Gay flowers, forever new,
The painted fields adorn, —
    The blushing rose
    And lily there,
    In union fair
    Their sweets disclose.

Where the bleak mountain stood
All bare and disarrayed,
See the wide-branching wood
Diffuse its grateful shade ;
    Tall cedars nod,
    And oaks and pines,
    And elms and vines
    Confess the God.

The tyrants of the plain
Their savage chase give o'er, —
No more they rend the slain,
And thirst for blood no more ;
    But infant hands
    Fierce tigers stroke,

And lions yoke
In flowery bands.

O, when, Almighty Lord !
Shall these glad scenes arise,
To verify thy word,
And bless our wondering eyes ?
    That earth may raise,
    With all its tongues,
    United songs
    Of ardent praise.
                              PHILIP DODDRIDGE.

O, HOW THE THOUGHT OF GRACE ATTRACTS !

O, HOW the thought of God attracts
    And draws the heart from earth,
And sickens it of passing shows
    And dissipating mirth !

God only is the creature's home,
    Though long and rough the road ;
Yet nothing less can satisfy
    The love that longs for God.

O, utter but the name of God
    Down in your heart of hearts,
And see how from the world at once
    All tempting light departs.

A trusting heart, a yearning eye,
    Can win their way above ;
If mountains can be moved by faith,
    Is there less power in love ?

How little of that road, my soul,
    How little hast thou gone !
Take heart, and let the thought of God
    Allure thee farther on.

Dole not thy duties out to God,
    But let thy hand be free ;
Look long at Jesus ; his sweet blood,
    How was it dealt to thee ?

The perfect way is hard to flesh ;
    It is not hard to love ;
If thou wert sick for want of God
    How swiftly wouldst thou move !
                              FABER.

BEFORE JEHOVAH'S AWFUL THRONE.

BEFORE Jehovah's awful throne,
    Ye nations, bow with sacred joy ;
Know that the Lord is God alone ;
    He can create, and he destroy.

His sovereign power, without our aid,
  Made us of clay, and formed us men ;
And when, like wandering sheep, we strayed,
  He brought us to his fold again.

We are his people ; we his care, —
  Our souls, and all our mortal frame ;
What lasting honors shall we rear,
  Almighty Maker, to thy name ?

We 'll crowd thy gates with thankful songs ;
  High as the heaven our voices raise ;
And Earth, with her ten thousand tongues,
  Shall fill thy courts with sounding praise.

Wide as the world is thy command ;
  Vast as eternity thy love ;
Firm as a rock thy truth shall stand
  When rolling years shall cease to move.
              ISAAC WATTS.

AND LET THIS FEEBLE BODY DIE.

AND let this feeble body fail,
  And let it faint or die ;
My soul shall quit this mournful vale,
  And soar to worlds on high ;
Shall join the disembodied saints,
  And find its long-sought rest,
That only bliss for which it pants,
  In the Redeemer's breast.

In hope of that immortal crown
  I now the cross sustain ;
And gladly wander up and down,
  And smile at toil and pain.
I suffer on my threescore years,
  Till my Deliverer come,
And wipe away his servant's tears,
  And take his exile home.

O, what hath Jesus bought for me ?
  Before my ravished eye,
Rivers of life divine I see,
  And trees of Paradise !
I see a world of spirits bright,
  Who taste the pleasures there !
They all are robed in spotless white,
  And conquering palms they bear.

O, what are all my sufferings here,
  If, Lord, thou count me meet
With that enraptured host to appear,
  And worship at thy feet !
Give joy or grief, give ease or pain ;
  Take life or friends away,
But let me find them all again
  In that eternal day.
            CHARLES WESLEY.

THE SABBATH.

How still the morning of the hallowed day !
Mute is the voice of rural labor, hushed
The plough-boy's whistle and the milkmaid's
    song.
The scythe lies glittering in the dewy wreath
Of tedded grass, mingled with fading flowers,
That yestermorn bloomed waving in the breeze ;
Sounds the most faint attract the ear, — the
    hum
Of early bee, the trickling of the dew,
The distant bleating, midway up the hill.
Calmness sits throned on yon unmoving cloud.
To him who wanders o'er the upland leas
The blackbird's note comes mellower from the
    dale ;
And sweeter from the sky the gladsome lark
Warbles his heaven-tuned song ; the lulling brook
Murmurs more gently down the deep-worn glen ;
While from yon lowly roof, whose circling
    smoke
O'ermounts the mist, is heard at intervals
The voice of psalms, the simple song of praise.
With dovelike wings Peace o'er yon village
    broods ;
The dizzying mill-wheel rests ; the anvil's din
Hath ceased ; all, all around is quietness.
Less fearful on this day, the limping hare
Stops, and looks back, and stops, and looks on
    man,
Her deadliest foe. The toilworn horse, set free,
Unheedful of the pasture, roams at large ;
And as his stiff, unwieldly bulk he rolls,
His iron-armed hoofs gleam in the morning ray.
            JAMES GRAHAME.

THE MEETING.

THE elder folk shook hands at last,
Down seat by seat the signal passed.
To simple ways like ours unused,
Half solemnized and half amused,
With long-drawn breath and shrug, my guest
His sense of glad relief expressed.
Outside the hills lay warm in sun ;
The cattle in the meadow-run
Stood half-leg deep ; a single bird
The green repose above us stirred.
"What part or lot have you," he said,
"In these dull rites of drowsy-head ?
Is silence worship ? Seek it where
It soothes with dreams the summer air,
Not in this close and rude-benched hall,
But where soft lights and shadows fall,
And all the slow, sleep-walking hours
Glide soundless over grass and flowers !

From time and place and form apart,
Its holy ground the human heart,
Nor ritual-bound nor templeward
Walks the free spirit of the Lord !
Our common Master did not pen
His followers up from other men ;
His service liberty indeed,
He built no church, he framed no creed ;
But while the saintly Pharisee
Made broader his phylactery,
As from the synagogue was seen
The dusty-sandalled Nazarene
Through ripening cornfields lead the way
Upon the awful Sabbath day,
His sermons were the healthful talk
That shorter made the mountain-walk,
His wayside texts were flowers and birds,
Where mingled with his gracious words
The rustle of the tamarisk-tree
And ripple-wash of Galilee."

"Thy words are well, O friend," I said ;
"Unmeasured and unlimited,
With noiseless slide of stone to stone,
The mystic Church of God has grown.
Invisible and silent stands
The temple never made with hands,
Unheard the voices still and small
Of its unseen confessional.
He needs no special place of prayer
Whose hearing ear is everywhere ;
He brings not back the childish days
That ringed the earth with stones of praise,
Roofed Karnak's hall of gods, and laid
The plinths of Philæ's colonnade.
Still less he owns the selfish good
And sickly growth of solitude, —
The worthless grace that, out of sight,
Flowers in the desert anchorite ;
Dissevered from the suffering whole,
Love hath no power to save a soul.
Not out of Self, the origin
And native air and soil of sin,
The living waters spring and flow,
The trees with leaves of healing grow.

"Dream not, O friend, because I seek
This quiet shelter twice a week,
I better deem its pine-laid floor
Than breezy hill or sea-sung shore ;
But nature is not solitude ;
She crowds us with her thronging wood ;
Her many hands reach out to us,
Her many tongues are garrulous ;
Perpetual riddles of surprise
She offers to our ears and eyes ;
She will not leave our senses still,
But drags them captive at her will ;

And, making earth too great for heaven,
She hides the Giver in the given.

"And so I find it well to come
For deeper rest to this still room,
For here the habit of the soul
Feels less the outer world's control ;
The strength of mutual purpose pleads
More earnestly our common needs ;
And from the silence multiplied
By these still forms on either side,
The world that time and sense have known
Falls off and leaves us God alone.

"Yet rarely through the charmed repose
Unmixed the stream of motive flows,
A flavor of its many springs,
The tints of earth and sky it brings ;
In the still waters needs must be
Some shade of human sympathy ;
And here, in its accustomed place,
I look on memory's dearest face ;
The blind by-sitter guesseth not
What shadow haunts that vacant spot ;
No eyes save mine alone can see
The love wherewith it welcomes me !
And still, with those alone my kin,
In doubt and weakness, want and sin,
I bow my head, my heart I bare
As when that face was living there,
And strive (too oft, alas ! in vain)
The peace of simple trust to gain,
Fold fancy's restless wings, and lay
The idols of my heart away.

"Welcome the silence all unbroken,
Nor less the words of fitness spoken, —
Such golden words as hers for whom
Our autumn flowers have just made room ;
Whose hopeful utterance through and through
The freshness of the morning blew ;
Who loved not less the earth that light
Fell on it from the heavens in sight,
But saw in all fair forms more fair
The Eternal beauty mirrored there.
Whose eighty years but added grace
And saintlier meaning to her face, —
The look of one who bore away
Glad tidings from the hills of day,
While all our hearts went forth to meet
The coming of her beautiful feet !
Or haply hers whose pilgrim tread
Is in the paths where Jesus led ;
Who dreams her childhood's sabbath dream
By Jordan's willow-shaded stream,
And, of the hymns of hope and faith,
Sung by the monks of Nazareth,
Hears pious echoes, in the call
To prayer, from Moslem minarets fall,

Repeating where His works were wrought
The lesson that her Master taught,
Of whom an elder Sibyl gave,
The prophecies of Cumæ's cave !

"I ask no organ's soulless breath
To drone the themes of life and death,
No altar candle-lit by day,
No ornate wordsman's rhetoric-play,
No cool philosophy to teach
Its bland audacities of speech
To doubled-tasked idolaters,
Themselves their gods and worshippers,
No pulpit hammered by the fist
Of loud-asserting dogmatist,
Who borrows for the hand of love
The smoking thunderbolts of Jove.
I know how well the fathers taught,
What work the later schoolmen wrought ;
I reverence old-time faith and men,
But God is near us now as then ;
His force of love is still unspent,
His hate of sin as imminent ;
And still the measure of our needs
Outgrows the cramping bounds of creeds ;
The manna gathered yesterday
Already savors of decay ;
Doubts to the world's child-heart unknown
Question us now from star and stone ;
Too little or too much we know,
And sight is swift and faith is slow ;
The power is lost to self-deceive
With shallow forms of make-believe.
We walk at high noon, and the bells
Call to a thousand oracles,
But the sound deafens, and the light
Is stronger than our dazzled sight ;
The letters of the sacred Book
Glimmer and swim beneath our look ;
Still struggles in the Age's breast
With deepening agony of quest
The old entreaty : ' Art thou He,
Or look we for the Christ to be ?'

"God should be most where man is least ;
So, where is neither church nor priest,
And never rag of form or creed
To clothe the nakedness of need, —
Where farmer-folk in silence meet, —
I turn my bell-unsummoned feet ;
I lay the critic's glass aside,
I tread upon my lettered pride,
And, lowest-seated, testify
To the oneness of humanity ;
Confess the universal want,
And share whatever Heaven may grant.
He findeth not who seeks his own,
The soul is lost that 's saved alone.
Not on one favored forehead fell
Of old the fire-tongued miracle,
But flamed o'er all the thronging host
The baptism of the Holy Ghost ;
Heart answers heart : in one desire
The blending lines of prayer aspire ;
'Where, in my name, meet two or three,
Our Lord hath said, ' I there will be !'

"So sometimes comes to soul and sense
The feeling which is evidence
That very near about us lies
The realm of spiritual mysteries.
The sphere of the supernal powers
Impinges on this world of ours.
The low and dark horizon lifts,
To light the scenic terror shifts ;
The breath of a diviner air
Blows down the answer of a prayer : —
That all our sorrow, pain, and doubt
A great compassion clasps about,
And law and goodness, love and force,
Are wedded fast beyond divorce.
Then duty leaves to love its task,
The beggar Self forgets to ask ;
With smile of trust and folded hands,
The passive soul in waiting stands
To feel, as flowers the sun and dew,
The One true Life its own renew.

"So, to the calmly gathered thought
The innermost of truth is taught,
The mystery dimly understood,
That love of God is love of good,
And, chiefly, its divinest trace
In Him of Nazareth's holy face ;
That to be saved is only this, —
Salvation from our selfishness,
From more than elemental fire,
The soul's unsanctified desire,
From sin itself, and not the pain
That warns us of its chafing chain ;
That worship's deeper meaning lies
In mercy, and not sacrifice,
Not proud humilities of sense
And posturing of penitence,
But love's unforced obedience ;
That Book and Church and Day are given
For man, not God, — for earth, not heaven, —
The blessed means to holiest ends,
Not masters, but benignant friends ;
That the dear Christ dwells not afar,
The king of some remoter star,
But flamed o'er all the thronging host
The baptism of the Holy Ghost ;
Heart answers heart : in one desire
The blending lines of prayer aspire ;
'Where, in my name, meet two or three,'
Our Lord hath said, ' I there will be !'"

JOHN GREENLEAF WHITTIER.

A PRAYER FOR LIFE.

. . . . .

O FATHER, let me not die young !
Earth's beauty asks a heart and tongue
To give true love and praises to her worth ;
 Her sins and judgment-sufferings call
For fearless martyrs to redeem thy Earth
  From her disastrous fall.
For though her summer hills and vales might
  seem
The fair creation of a poet's dream, —
  Ay, of the Highest Poet,
Whose wordless rhythms are chanted by the
  gyres
  Of constellate star-choirs,
That with deep melody flow and overflow it, —
  The sweet Earth, — very sweet, despite
The rank grave-smell forever drifting in
 Among the odors from her censers white
Of wave-swung lilies and of wind-swung roses, —
 The Earth sad-sweet is deeply attaint with sin !
  The pure air, which encloses
  Her and her starry kin,
Still shudders with the unspent palpitating
Of a great Curse, that to its utmost shore
  Thrills with a deadly shiver
  Which has not ceased to quiver
Down all the ages, nathless the strong beating
 Of Angel-wings, and the defiant roar
 Of Earth's Titanic thunders.

    Fair and sad,
In sin and beauty, our beloved Earth
Has need of all her sons to make her glad ;
 Has need of martyrs to refire the hearth
Of her quenched altars, — of heroic men
With Freedom's sword, or Truth's supernal pen,
To shape the worn-out mould of nobleness again.
And she has need of Poets who can string
 Their harps with steel to catch the lightning's
  fire,
 And pour her thunders from the clanging wire,
 To cheer the hero, mingling with his cheer,
 Arouse the laggard in the battle's rear,
Daunt the stern wicked, and from discord wring
 Prevailing harmony, while the humblest soul
Who keeps the tune the warder angels sing
  In golden choirs above,
 And only wears, for crown and aureole,
 The glow-worm light of lowliest human
  love,
Shall fill with low, sweet undertones the
  chasms
 Of silence, 'twixt the booming thunder-
  spasms.
And Earth has need of Prophets fiery-lipped
And deep-souled, to announce the glorious
  dooms

Writ on the silent heavens in starry script,
 And flashing fitfully from her shuddering
  tombs, —
Commissioned Angels of the new-born Faith,
 To teach the immortality of Good,
The soul's God-likeness, Sin's coeval death,
 And Man's indissoluble Brotherhood.

Yet never an age, when God has need of him,
 Shall want its Man, predestined by that
  need,
 To pour his life in fiery word or deed, —
The strong Archangel of the Elohim !
 Earth's hollow want is prophet of his com-
  ing :
 In the low murmur of her famished cry,
 And heavy sobs breathed up despairingly,
  Ye hear the near invisible humming
Of his wide wings that fan the lurid sky
Into cool ripples of new life and hope,
While far in its dissolving ether ope
Deeps beyond deeps, of sapphire calm, to cheer
With Sabbath gleams the troubled Now and
  Here.

  Father ! thy will be done,
  Holy and righteous One !
  Though the reluctant years
May never crown my throbbing brows with
  white,
Nor round my shoulders turn the golden light
Of my thick locks to wisdom's royal ermine :
  Yet by the solitary tears,
 Deeper than joy or sorrow, — by the thrill,
Higher than hope or terror, whose quick germen,
 In those hot tears to sudden vigor sprung,
Sheds, even now, the fruits of graver age, —
 By the long wrestle in which inward ill
Fell like a trampled viper to the ground, —
 By all that lifts me o'er my outward peers
  To that supernal stage
Where soul dissolves the bonds by Nature
  bound, —
 Fall when I may, by pale disease unstrung,
Or by the hand of fratricidal rage,
  I cannot now die young !
      ANONYMOUS.

THE GREENWOOD SHRIFT.

GEORGE III. AND A DYING WOMAN IN WINDSOR FOREST.

OUTSTRETCHED beneath the leafy shade
Of Windsor forest's deepest glade,
  A dying woman lay ;
Three little children round her stood,
And there went up from the greenwood
  A woful wail that day.

"O mother!" was the mingled cry,
"O mother, mother! do not die,
    And leave us all alone."
"My blessed babes!" she tried to say,
But the faint accents died away
    In a low sobbing moan.

And then, life struggling hard with death,
And fast and strong she drew her breath,
    And up she raised her head;
And, peering through the deep wood maze
With a long, sharp, unearthly gaze,
    "Will she not come?" she said.

Just then, the parting boughs between,
A little maid's light form was seen,
    All breathless with her speed;
And, following close, a man came on
(A portly man to look upon),
    Who led a panting steed.

"Mother!" the little maiden cried,
Or e'er she reached the woman's side,
    And kissed her clay-cold cheek, —
"I have not idled in the town,
But long went wandering up and down,
    The minister to seek.

"They told me here, they told me there, —
I think they mocked me everywhere';
    And when I found his home,
And begged him on my bended knee
To bring his book and come with me,
    Mother! he would not come.

"I told him how you dying lay,
And could not go in peace away
    Without the minister;
I begged him, for dear Christ his sake,
But O, my heart was fit to break, —
    Mother! he would not stir.

"So, though my tears were blinding me,
I ran back, fast as fast could be,
    To come again to you;
And here — close by — this squire I met,
Who asked (so mild) what made me fret;
    And when I told him true, —

"'I will go with you, child,' he said,
'God sends me to this dying bed,' —
    Mother, he's here, hard by."
While thus the little maiden spoke,
The man, his back against an oak,
    Looked on with glistening eye.

The bridle on his neck hung free,
With quivering flank and trembling knee,
    Pressed close his bonny bay;

A statelier man, a statelier steed,
Never on greensward paced, I rede,
    Than those stood there that day.

So, while the little maiden spoke,
The man, his back against an oak,
    Looked on with glistening eye
And folded arms, and in his look
Something that, like a sermon-book,
    Preached, — "All is vanity."

But when the dying woman's face
Turned toward him with a wishful gaze,
    He stepped to where she lay;
And, kneeling down, bent over her,
Saying, "I am a minister,
    My sister! let us pray."

And well, withouten book or stole,
(God's words were printed on his soul!)
    Into the dying ear
He breathed, as 't were an angel's strain,
The things that unto life pertain,
    And death's dark shadows clear.

He spoke of sinners' lost estate,
In Christ renewed, regenerate, —
    Of God's most blest decree,
That not a single soul should die
Who turns repentant, with the cry
    "Be merciful to me."

He spoke of trouble, pain, and toil,
Endured but for a little while
    In patience, faith, and love, —
Sure, in God's own good time, to be
Exchanged for an eternity
    Of happiness above.

Then, as the spirit ebbed away,
He raised his hands and eyes to pray
    That peaceful it might pass;
And then — the orphans' sobs alone
Were heard, and they knelt, every one,
    Close round on the green grass.

Such was the sight their wandering eyes
Beheld, in heart-struck, mute surprise,
    Who reined their coursers back,
Just as they found the long astray,
Who, in the heat of chase that day,
    Had wandered from their track.

But each man reined his pawing steed,
And lighted down, as if agreed,
    In silence at his side;
And there, uncovered all, they stood, —
It was a wholesome sight and good
    That day for mortal pride.

For of the noblest of the land
Was that deep-hushed, bareheaded band ;
   And, central in the ring,
By that dead pauper on the ground,
Her ragged orphans clinging round,
   Knelt their anointed king.
ROBERT and CAROLINE SOUTHEY.

ABDIEL.

FROM "PARADISE LOST."

. . . . THE seraph Abdiel, faithful found
Among the faithless, faithful only he ;
Among inumerable false, unmoved,
Unshaken, unseduced, unterrified,
His loyalty he kept, his love, his zeal ;
Nor number, nor example with him wrought
To swerve from truth, or change his constant mind,
Though single. From amidst them forth he passed,
Long way through hostile scorn, which he sus-
tained
Superior, nor of violence feared aught ;
And with retorted scorn his back he turned
On those proud towers to swift destruction doomed.
MILTON.

THE REAPER'S DREAM.

THE road was lone ; the grass was dank
With night-dews on the briery bank
Whereon a weary reaper sank.
His garb was old ; his visage tanned ;
The rusty sickle in his hand
Could find no work in all the land.

He saw the evening's chilly star
Above his native vale afar ;
A moment on the horizon's bar
It hung, then sank, as with a sigh ;
And there the crescent moon went by,
An empty sickle down the sky.

To soothe his pain, Sleep's tender palm
Laid on his brow its touch of balm ;
His brain received the slumberous calm ;
And soon that angel without name,
Her robe a dream, her face the same,
The giver of sweet visions came.

She touched his eyes ; no longer sealed,
They saw a troop of reapers wield
Their swift blades in a ripened field.
At each thrust of their snowy sleeves
A thrill ran through the future sheaves
Rustling like rain on forest leaves.

They were not brawny men who bowed,
With harvest-voices rough and loud,
But spirits, moving as a cloud.
Like little lightnings in their hold,
The silver sickles manifold
Slid musically through the gold.

O, bid the morning stars combine
To match the chorus clear and fine,
That rippled lightly down the line, —
A cadence of celestial rhyme,
The language of that cloudless clime,
To which their shining hands kept time !

Behind them lay the gleaming rows,
Like those long clouds the sunset shows
On amber meadows of repose ;
But, like a wind, the binders bright
Soon followed in their mirthful might,
And swept them into sheaves of light.

Doubling the splendor of the plain,
There rolled the great celestial wain,
To gather in the fallen grain.
Its frame was built of golden bars ;
Its glowing wheels were lit with stars ;
The royal Harvest's car of cars.

The snowy yoke that drew the load,
On gleaming hoofs of silver trode ;
And music was its only goad.
To no command of word or beck
It moved, and felt no other check
Than one white arm laid on the neck, —

The neck, whose light was overwound
With bells of lilies, ringing round
Their odors till the air was drowned :
The starry foreheads meekly borne,
With garlands looped from horn to horn,
Shone like the many-colored morn.

The field was cleared. Home went the bands,
Like children, linking happy hands,
While singing through their father's lands ;
Or, arms about each other thrown,
With amber tresses backward blown,
They moved as they were music's own.

The vision brightening more and more,
He saw the garner's glowing door,
And sheaves, like sunshine, strew the floor, —
The floor was jasper, — golden flails,
Swift-sailing as a whirlwind sails,
Throbbed mellow music down the vales.

He saw the mansion, — all repose, —
Great corridors and porticos,
Propped with the columns, shining rows ;

Eng^d by Geo E. Perine New York.

Robert Burns

FORDS, HOWARD & HULBERT, N.Y.

And these — for beauty was the rule —
The polished pavements, hard and cool,
Redoubled, like a crystal pool.

And there the odorous feast was spread ;
The fruity fragrance widely shed
Seemed to the floating music wed.
Seven angels, like the Pleiad seven,
Their lips to silver clarions given,
Blew welcome round the walls of heaven.

In skyey garments, silky thin,
The glad retainers floated in
A thousand forms, and yet no din :
And from the visage of the Lord,
Like splendor from the Orient poured,
A smile illumined all the board.

Far flew the music's circling sound ;
Then floated back, with soft rebound,
To join, not mar, the converse round, —
Sweet notes, that, melting, still increased,
Such as ne'er cheered the bridal feast
Of king in the enchanted East.

Did any great door ope or close,
It seemed the birth-time of repose,
The faint sound died where it arose ;
And they who passed from door to door,
Their soft feet on the polished floor
Met their soft shadows, — nothing more.

Then once again the groups were drawn
Through corridors, or down the lawn,
Which bloomed in beauty like a dawn.
Where countless fountains leapt alway,
Veiling their silver heights in spray,
The choral people held their way.

There, midst the brightest, brightly shone
Dear forms he loved in years agone, —
The earliest loved, — the earliest flown.
He heard a mother's sainted tongue,
A sister's voice, who vanished young,
While one still dearer sweetly sung !

No further might the scene unfold ;
The gazer's voice could not withhold ;
The very rapture made him bold :
He cried aloud, with claspéd hands,
"O happy fields ! O happy bands !
Who reap the never-failing lands.

"O master of these broad estates,
Behold, before your very gates
A worn and wanting laborer waits !
Let me but toil amid your grain,
Or be a gleaner on the plain,
So I may leave these fields of pain !

"A gleaner, I will follow far,
With never look or word to mar,
Behind the Harvest's yellow car ;
All day my hand shall constant be,
And every happy eve shall see
The precious burden borne to thee !"

At morn some reapers neared the place,
Strong men, whose feet recoiled apace ;
Then gathering round the upturned face,
They saw the lines of pain and care,
Yet read in the expression there
The look as of an answered prayer.
                        THOMAS BUCHANAN READ.

——◆——

THE RELIGION OF HUDIBRAS.

. . . . HE was of that stubborn crew
Of errant saints, whom all men grant
To be the true church militant ;
Such as do build their faith upon
The holy text of pike and gun ;
Decide all controversies by
Infallible artillery,
And prove their doctrine orthodox
By apostolic blows and knocks ;
Call fire, and sword, and desolation
A godly, thorough Reformation,
Which always must be carried on
And still be doing, never done ;
As if religion were intended
For nothing else but to be mended.
A sect whose chief devotion lies
In odd perverse antipathies ;
In falling out with that or this,
And finding somewhat still amiss ;
More peevish, cross, and splenetic,
Than dog distract, or monkey sick ;
That with more care keep holiday
The wrong, than others the right way ;
Compound for sins they are inclined to,
By damning those they have no mind to ;
Still so perverse and opposite,
As if they worshipped God for spite ;
The self-same thing they will abhor
One way, and long another for.
                        SAMUEL BUTLER.

——◆——

THE COTTER'S SATURDAY NIGHT.

INSCRIBED TO R. AIKEN, ESQ.

" Let not ambition mock their useful toil,
    Their homely joys and destiny obscure ;
Nor grandeur hear, with a disdainful smile,
    The short but simple annals of the poor." — GRAY.

I.

MY loved, my honored, much-respected friend,
No mercenary bard his homage pays :

With honest pride I scorn each selfish end ;
　My dearest meed, a friend's esteem and praise.
To you I sing, in simple Scottish lays,
　The lowly train in life's sequestered scene ;
The native feelings strong, the guileless ways ;
　What Aiken in a cottage would have been ;
Ah ! though his worth unknown, far happier
　　there, I ween.

II.

November chill blaws loud wi' angry sugh ;
　The shortening winter-day is near a close ;
The miry beasts retreating frae the pleugh,
　The blackening trains o' craws to their repose ;
The toilworn cotter frae his labor goes,
This night his weekly moil is at an end, —
Collects his spades, his mattocks, and his hoes, —
　Hoping the morn in ease and rest to spend,
And weary, o'er the moor, his course does home-
　　ward bend.

III.

At length his lonely cot appears in view,
　Beneath the shelter of an aged tree ;
Th' expectant wee things, toddlin', stacher
　　through
To meet their dad, wi' flichterin' noise an' glee.
His wee bit ingle, blinking bonnily,
　His clean hearthstane, his thriftie wifie's
　　smile,
The lisping infant prattling on his knee,
　Does a' his weary carking cares beguile,
And makes him quite forget his labor and his toil.

IV.

Belyve the elder bairns come drapping in,
　At service out amang the farmers roun' ;
Some ca' the pleugh, some herd, some tentie rin
　A cannie errand to a neibor town ;
Their eldest hope, their Jenny, woman grown,
　In youthfu' bloom, love sparkling in her e'e,
Comes hame, perhaps, to shew a bra' new gown,
　Or deposit her sair-won penny-fee,
To help her parents dear, if they in hardship be.

V.

Wi' joy unfeigned brothers and sisters meet,
　An' each for other's weelfare kindly spiers :
The social hours, swift-winged, unnoticed fleet ;
　Each tells the uncos that he sees or hears ;
The parents, partial, eye their hopeful years ;
　Anticipation forward points the view.
The mother, wi' her needle an' her shears,
　Gars auld claes look amaist as weel 's the new ;
The father mixes a' wi' admonition due.

VI.

Their master's an' their mistress's command,
　The younkers a' are warnéd to obey ;
And mind their labors wi' an eydent hand,
　And ne'er, though out o' sight, to jauk or play ;

"An' O, be sure to fear the Lord alway !
　An' mind your duty, duly, morn an' night !
Lest in temptation's path ye gang astray,
　Implore his counsel and assisting might ;
They never sought in vain that sought the Lord
　　aright !"

VII.

But, hark ! a rap comes gently to the door.
　Jenny, wha kens the meaning o' the same,
Tells how a neibor lad cam o'er the moor,
　To do some errands and convoy her hame.
The wily mother sees the conscious flame
　Sparkle in Jenny's e'e, and flush her cheek ;
Wi' heart-struck anxious care inquires his
　　name,
　While Jenny hafflins is afraid to speak ;
Weel pleased the mother hears it 's nae wild, worth-
　　less rake.

VIII.

Wi' kindly welcome, Jenny brings him ben ;
　A strappin' youth ; he taks the mother's e'e ;
Blithe Jenny sees the visit 's no ill ta'en ;
　The father cracks of horses, pleughs, and kye.
The youngster's artless heart o'erflows wi' joy,
　But blate and lathefu', scarce can weel behave ;
The mother, wi' a woman's wiles, can spy
　What makes the youth sae bashfu' an' sae
　　grave ;
Weel pleased to think her bairn 's respected like
　　the lave.

IX.

O happy love ! where love like this is found !
　O heartfelt raptures ! bliss beyond compare !
I 've pacéd much this weary mortal round,
　And sage experience bids me this declare : —
If Heaven a draught of heavenly pleasure spare,
　One cordial in this melancholy vale,
'T is when a youthful, loving, modest pair
　In other's arms breathe out the tender tale,
Beneath the milk-white thorn that scents the even-
　　ing gale.

X.

Is there, in human form, that bears a heart,
　A wretch, a villain, lost to love and truth,
That can, with studied, sly, ensnaring art,
　Betray sweet Jenny's unsuspecting youth ?
Curse on his perjured arts ! dissembling smooth !
　Are honor, virtue, conscience, all exiled ?
Is there no pity, no relenting ruth,
　Points to the parents fondling o'er their child,
Then paints the ruined maid, and their distrac-
　　tion wild ?

XI.

But now the supper crowns their simple board,
　The halesome parritch, chief o' Scotia's food ;

The soupe their only hawkie does afford,
That 'yont the hallan snugly chows her cood ;
The dame brings forth, in complimental mood,
To grace the lad, her weel-hained kebbuck fell,
An' aft he 's prest, an' aft he ca's it guid ;
The frugal wifie, garrulous, will tell,
How 't was a towmond auld, sin' lint was i' the
 bell.

XII.

The cheerfu' supper done, wi' serious face,
They, round the ingle, form a circle wide ;
The sire turns o'er, wi' patriarchal grace,
The big ha'-Bible, ance his father's pride ;
His bonnet reverently is laid aside,
His lyart haffets wearing thin an' bare :
Those strains that once did sweet in Zion glide,
He wales a portion with judicious care ;
And " Let us worship God ! " he says with solemn
 air.

XIII.

They chant their artless notes in simple guise ;
They tune their hearts, by far the noblest aim :
Perhaps " Dundee's " wild-warbling measures
 rise,
Or plaintive " Martyrs," worthy of the name ;
Or noble " Elgin" beets the heavenward flame,
The sweetest far of Scotia's holy lays :
Compared with these, Italian trills are tame ;
The tickled ears no heartfelt raptures raise ;
Nae unison hae they with our Creator's praise.

XIV.

The priest-like father reads the sacred page, —
How Abram was the friend of God on high ;
Or Moses bade eternal warfare wage
With Amalek's ungracious progeny,
Or how the royal bard did groaning lie
Beneath the stroke of Heaven's avenging ire ;
Or Job's pathetic plaint, and wailing cry ;
Or rapt Isaiah's wild, seraphic fire ;
Or other holy seers that tune the sacred lyre.

XV.

Perhaps the Christian volume is the theme, —
How guiltless blood for guilty man was shed ;
How He, who bore in heaven the second name,
Had not on earth whereon to lay his head :
How his first followers and servants sped ;
The precepts sage they wrote to many a land ;
How he, who lone in Patmos banishéd,
Saw in the sun a mighty angel stand,
And heard great Bab'lon's doom pronounced by
 Heaven's command.

XVI.

Then, kneeling down, to heaven's eternal King,
The saint, the father, and the husband prays :

Hope " springs exulting on triumphant wing,"
That thus they all shall meet in future days ;
There ever bask in uncreated rays,
No more to sigh, or shed the bitter tear,
Together hymning their Creator's praise,
In such society, yet still more dear ;
While circling Time moves round in an eternal
 sphere.

XVII.

Compared with this, how poor Religion's pride,
In all the pomp of method and of art,
When men display to congregations wide,
Devotion's every grace, except the heart !
The Power, incensed, the pageant will desert,
The pompous strain, the sacerdotal stole ;
But, haply, in some cottage far apart,
May hear, well pleased, the language of the
 soul ;
And in his Book of Life the inmates poor enroll.

XVIII.

Then homeward all take off their several way ;
The youngling cottagers retire to rest :
The parent-pair their secret homage pay,
And proffer up to heaven the warm request,
That He who stills the raven's clamorous nest,
And decks the lily fair in flowery pride,
Would, in the way his wisdom sees the best,
For them and for their little ones provide ;
But, chiefly, in their hearts with grace divine pre-
 side.

XIX.

From scenes like these old Scotia's grandeur
 springs,
That makes her loved at home, revered abroad ;
Princes and lords are but the breath of kings,
 " An honest man 's the noblest work of God ! "
And certes, in fair Virtue's heavenly road,
The cottage leaves the palace far behind :
What is a lordling's pomp ? — a cumbrous load,
Disguising oft the wretch of human kind,
Studied in arts of hell, in wickedness refined !

XX.

O Scotia ! my dear, my native soil !
For whom my warmest wish to Heaven is
 sent,
Long may thy hardy sons of rustic toil
Be blest with health, and peace, and sweet
 content !
And, O, may Heaven their simple lives prevent
From luxury's contagion, weak and vile !
Then, howe'er crowns and coronets be rent,
A virtuous populace may rise the while,
And stand a wall of fire around their much-loved
 isle.

XXI.

O Thou ! who poured the patriotic tide,
  That streamed through Wallace's undaunted
     heart ;
Who dared to nobly stem tyrannic pride,
Or nobly die, the second glorious part,
(The patriot's God peculiarly thou art,
  His friend, inspirer, guardian, and reward !)
O, never, never Scotia's realm desert ;
  But still the patriot and the patriot bard
In bright succession raise, her ornament and guard!
ROBERT BURNS.

EVENING HYMN.

GLORY to thee, my God, this night,
For all the blessings of the light ;
Keep me, O, keep me, King of kings,
Beneath thy own almighty wings !

Forgive me, Lord, for thy dear Son,
The ill that I this day have done ;
That with the world, myself, and thee
I, ere I sleep, at peace may be.

Teach me to live, that I may dread
The grave as little as my bed ;
To die, that this vile body may
Rise glorious at the judgment-day.

O, may my soul on thee repose,
And may sweet sleep mine eyelids close, —
Sleep, that may me more vigorous make
To serve my God when I awake !

When in the night I sleepless lie,
My soul with heavenly thoughts supply ;
Let no ill dreams disturb my rest,
No powers of darkness me molest.

Praise God, from whom all blessings flow ;
Praise him, all creatures here below ;
Praise him above, ye heavenly host ;
Praise Father, Son, and Holy Ghost.
KEN.

FROM ALL THAT DWELL—

PSALM CXVII.

FROM all that dwell below the skies
Let the Creator's praise arise ;
Let the Redeemer's name be sung
Through every land, by every tongue.

Eternal are thy mercies, Lord,
Eternal truth attends thy word ;
Thy praise shall sound from shore to shore,
Till suns shall rise and set no more.
ISAAC WATTS.

POEMS OF NATURE.

Tears, idle tears, I know not what they mean,
Tears from the depth of some divine despair
Rise in the heart & gather to the eyes
In looking on the happy Autumn fields,
And thinking on the days that are no more.

A Tennyson

POEMS OF NATURE.

WORLDLINESS.

THE World is too much with us ; late and soon,
　Getting and spending, we lay waste our powers ;
　Little we see in nature that is ours ;
We have given our hearts away, a sordid boon !

This sea that bares her bosom to the moon,
　The winds that will be howling at all hours
　And are up-gathered now like sleeping flowers,
For this, for everything, we are out of tune ;

It moves us not. — Great God ! I 'd rather be
　A Pagan suckled in a creed outworn, —
So might I, standing on this pleasant lea,
　Have glimpses that would make me less forlorn ;
Have sight of Proteus rising from the sea ;
　Or hear old Triton blow his wreathéd horn.
　　　　　　　　　WILLIAM WORDSWORTH.

DAYBREAK.

A WIND came up out of the sea,
And said, "O mists, make room for me !"

It hailed the ships, and cried, "Sail on,
Ye mariners, the night is gone."

And hurried landward far away,
Crying, "Awake ! it is the day."

It said unto the forest, "Shout !
Hang all your leafy banners out !"

It touched the wood-bird's folded wing,
And said, "O bird, awake and sing !"

And o'er the farms, "O chanticleer,
Your clarion blow ; the day is near !"

It whispered to the fields of corn,
"Bow down, and hail the coming morn !"

It shouted through the belfry-tower,
"Awake, O bell ! proclaim the hour."

It crossed the churchyard with a sigh,
And said, "Not yet ! in quiet lie."
　　　　　　　　HENRY WADSWORTH LONGFELLOW.

INVOCATION TO LIGHT.

HAIL, holy Light, offspring of Heaven first-born !
Or of the Eternal coeternal beam
May I express thee unblamed ? since God is light,
And never but in unapproachéd light
Dwelt from eternity, dwelt then in thee,
Bright effluence of bright essence increate.
Or hear'st thou rather pure ethereal stream,
Whose fountain who shall tell ? before the sun,
Before the heavens, thou wert, and at the voice
Of God, as with a mantle, didst invest
The rising world of waters dark and deep,
Won from the void and formless infinite.
Thee I revisit now with bolder wing,
Escaped the Stygian pool, though long detained
In that obscure sojourn, while in my flight
Through utter and through middle darkness borne,
With other notes than to the Orphean lyre,
I sung of Chaos and eternal Night,
Taught by the heavenly Muse to venture down
The dark descent, and up to reascend,
Though hard and rare : thee I revisit safe,
And feel thy sovereign vital lamp ; but thou
Revisitest not these eyes, that roll in vain
To find thy piercing ray, and find no dawn ;
So thick a drop serene hath quenched their orbs,
Or dim suffusion veiled. Yet not the more
Cease I to wander where the Muses haunt
Clear spring, or shady grove, or sunny hill,
Smit with the love of sacred song ; but chief
Thee, Sion, and the flowery brooks beneath,
That wash thy hallowed feet, and warbling flow,
Nightly I visit : nor sometimes forget
Those other two equalled with me in fate,
So were I equalled with them in renown,
Blind Thamyris and blind Mæonides,
And Tiresias and Phineus, prophets old :
Then feed on thoughts that voluntary move
Harmonious numbers ; as the wakeful bird
Sings darkling, and in shadiest covert hid
Tunes her nocturnal note. Thus with the year
Seasons return, but not to me returns
Day, or the sweet approach of even or morn,
Or sight of vernal bloom, or summer's rose,

Or flocks, or herds, or human face divine ;
But cloud, instead, and ever-during dark,
Surrounds me, from the cheerful ways of men
Cut off, and for the book of knowledge fair
Presented with a universal blank
Of nature's works, to me expunged and rased,
And wisdom at one entrance quite shut out.
So much the rather thou, celestial Light,
Shine inward, and the mind through all her powers
Irradiate ; there plant eyes, all mist from thence
Purge and disperse, that I may see and tell
Of things invisible to mortal sight.
                                          MILTON.

PACK CLOUDS AWAY.

PACK clouds away, and welcome day,
   With night we banish sorrow ;
Sweet air, blow soft ; mount, lark, aloft,
   To give my love good morrow.
Wings from the wind to please her mind,
   Notes from the lark I 'll borrow :
Bird, prune thy wing ; nightingale, sing,
   To give my love good morrow.
   To give my love good morrow,
   Notes from them all I 'll borrow.

Wake from thy nest, robin redbreast,
   Sing, birds, in every furrow ;
And from each hill let music shrill
   Give my fair love good morrow.
Blackbird and thrush in every bush,
   Stare, linnet, and cock-sparrow,
You pretty elves, amongst yourselves,
   Sing my fair love good morrow.
   To give my love good morrow,
   Sing, birds, in every furrow.
                                    THOMAS HEYWOOD.

MORNING.

FROM "THE MINSTREL."

BUT who the melodies of morn can tell ?
The wild brook babbling down the mountain
      side ;
The lowing herd ; the sheepfold's simple bell ;
The pipe of early shepherd dim descried
In the lone valley ; echoing far and wide
The clamorous horn along the cliffs above ;
The hollow murmur of the ocean tide ;
The hum of bees, the linnet's lay of love,
And the full choir that wakes the universal grove.

The cottage curs at early pilgrim bark ;
Crowned with her pail the tripping milkmaid
      sings ;

The whistling ploughman stalks afield ; and,
      hark !
Down the rough slope the ponderous wagon
      rings ;
Through rustling corn the hare astonished
      springs ;
Slow tolls the village-clock the drowsy hour ;
The partridge bursts away on whirring wings ;
Deep mourns the turtle in sequestered bower,
And shrill lark carols clear from her aerial tower.
                                    JAMES BEATTIE.

THE SABBATH MORNING.

WITH silent awe I hail the sacred morn,
That slowly wakes while all the fields are still !
A soothing calm on every breeze is borne ;
A graver murmur gurgles from the rill ;
And echo answers softer from the hill ;
And softer sings the linnet from the thorn :
The skylark warbles in a tone less shrill.
Hail, light serene ! hail, sacred Sabbath morn !
The rooks float silent by in airy drove ;
The sun a placid yellow lustre throws ;
The gales that lately sighed along the grove
Have hushed their downy wings in dead repose ;
The hovering rack of clouds forgets to move, —
So smiled the day when the first morn arose !
                                    DR. JOHN LEYDEN.

REVE DU MIDI.

WHEN o'er the mountain steeps
   The hazy noontide creeps,
And the shrill cricket sleeps
   Under the grass ;
When soft the shadows lie,
And clouds sail o'er the sky,
And the idle winds go by,
With the heavy scent of blossoms as they pass, —

Then, when the silent stream
   Lapses as in a dream,
And the water-lilies gleam
   Up to the sun ;
When the hot and burdened day
Rests on its downward way,
When the moth forgets to play,
And the plodding ant may dream her work is
      done, —

Then, from the noise of war
And the din of earth afar,
Like some forgotten star
   Dropt from the sky, —
The sounds of love and fear,

All voices sad and clear,
Banished to silence drear, —
The willing thrall of trances sweet I lie.

Some melancholy gale
Breathes its mysterious tale,
Till the rose's lips grow pale
With her sighs;
And o'er my thoughts are cast
Tints of the vanished past,
Glories that faded fast,
Renewed to splendor in my dreaming eyes.

As poised on vibrant wings,
Where its sweet treasure swings,
The honey-lover clings
To the red flowers, —
So, lost in vivid light,
So, rapt from day and night,
I linger in delight,
Enraptured o'er the vision-freighted hours.

ROSE TERRY.

NOONTIDE.

BENEATH a shivering canopy reclined,
Of aspen-leaves that wave without a wind,
I love to lie, when lulling breezes stir
The spiry cones that tremble on the fir;
Or wander mid the dark-green fields of broom,
When peers in scattered tufts the yellow bloom;
Or trace the path with tangling furze o'errun,
When bursting seed-bells crackle in the sun,
And pittering grasshoppers, confus'dly shrill,
Pipe giddily along the glowing hill:
Sweet grasshopper, who lov'st at noon to lie
Serenely in the green-ribbed clover's eye,
To sun thy filmy wings and emerald vest,
Unseen thy form, and undisturbed thy rest,
Oft have I listening mused the sultry day,
And wondered what thy chirping song might say,
When naught was heard along the blossomed lea,
To join thy music, save the listless bee.

DR. JOHN LEYDEN.

ON A BEAUTIFUL DAY.

O UNSEEN Spirit! now a calm divine
Comes forth from thee, rejoicing earth and air!
Trees, hills, and houses, all distinctly shine,
And thy great ocean slumbers everywhere.

The mountain ridge against the purple sky
Stands clear and strong, with darkened rocks
and dells,
And cloudless brightness opens wide and high
A home aerial, where thy presence dwells.

The chime of bells remote, the murmuring sea,
The song of birds in whispering copse and wood,
The distant voice of children's thoughtless glee,
And maiden's song, are all one voice of good.

Amid the leaves' green mass a sunny play
Of flash and shadow stirs like inward life;
The ship's white sail glides onward far away,
Unhaunted by a dream of storm or strife.

JOHN STERLING.

THE MIDGES DANCE ABOON THE BURN.

THE midges dance aboon the burn;
The dews begin to fa';
The pairtricks down the rushy holm
Set up their e'ening ca'.
Now loud and clear the blackbird's sang
Rings through the briery shaw,
While, flitting gay, the swallows play
Around the castle wa'.

Beneath the golden gloamin' sky
The mavis mends her lay;
The redbreast pours his sweetest strains
To charm the lingering day;
While weary yeldrins seem to wail
Their little nestlings torn,
The merry wren, frae den to den,
Gaes jinking through the thorn.

The roses fauld their silken leaves,
The foxglove shuts its bell;
The honeysuckle and the birk
Spread fragrance through the dell.
Let others crowd the giddy court
Of mirth and revelry,
The simple joys that nature yields
Are dearer far to me.

ROBERT TANNAHILL.

THE EVENING WIND.

SPIRIT that breathest through my lattice: thou
That cool'st the twilight of the sultry day!
Gratefully flows thy freshness round my brow;
Thou hast been out upon the deep at play,
Riding all day the wild blue waves till now,
Roughening their crests, and scattering high
their spray,
And swelling the white sail. I welcome thee
To the scorched land, thou wanderer of the sea!

Nor I alone, — a thousand bosoms round
Inhale thee in the fulness of delight;
And languid forms rise up, and pulses bound
Livelier, at coming of the wind of night;

And languishing to hear thy welcome sound,
  Lies the vast inland, stretched beyond the sight.
Go forth into the gathering shade ; go forth, —
God's blessing breathed upon the fainting earth !

Go, rock the little wood-bird in his nest ;
  Curl the still waters, bright with stars ; and rouse
The wide old wood from his majestic rest,
  Summoning, from the innumerable boughs,
The strange deep harmonies that haunt his breast.
  Pleasant shall be thy way where meekly bows
The shutting flower, and darkling waters pass,
And where the o'ershadowing branches sweep the
  grass.

Stoop o'er the place of graves, and softly sway
  The sighing herbage by the gleaming stone
That they who near the churchyard willows stray,
  And listen in the deepening gloom, alone,
May think of gentle souls that passed away,
  Like thy pure breath, into the vast unknown,
Sent forth from heaven among the sons of men,
And gone into the boundless heaven again.

The faint old man shall lean his silver head
  To feel thee ; thou shalt kiss the child asleep,
And dry the moistened curls that overspread
  His temples, while his breathing grows more
    deep ;
And they who stand about the sick man's bed
  Shall joy to listen to thy distant sweep,
And softly part his curtains to allow
Thy visit, grateful to his burning brow.

Go, — but the circle of eternal change,
  Which is the life of nature, shall restore,
With sounds and scents from all thy mighty range,
  Thee to thy birthplace of the deep once more.
Sweet odors in the sea air, sweet and strange,
  Shall tell the homesick mariner of the shore ;
And, listening to thy murmur, he shall deem
He hears the rustling leaf and running stream.
                     WILLIAM CULLEN BRYANT.

THE EVENING STAR.

STAR that bringest home the bee,
And sett'st the weary laborer free !
If any star shed peace, 't is thou,
  That send'st it from above,
Appearing when heaven's breath and brow
  Are sweet as hers we love.

Come to the luxuriant skies,
Whilst the landscape's odors rise,
Whilst far-off lowing herds are heard,
  And songs, when toil is done,
From cottages whose smoke unstirred
  Curls yellow in the sun.

Star of love's soft interviews,
Parted lovers on thee muse ;
Their remembrancer in heaven
  Of thrilling vows thou art,
Too delicious to be riven
  By absence from the heart.
                     THOMAS CAMPBELL.

CAPE-COTTAGE AT SUNSET.

WE stood upon the ragged rocks,
  When the long day was nearly done ;
The waves had ceased their sullen shocks,
  And lapped our feet with murmuring tone,
And o'er the bay in streaming locks
  Blew the red tresses of the sun.

Along the west the golden bars
  Still to a deeper glory grew ;
Above our heads the faint, few stars
  Looked out from the unfathomed blue ;
And the fair city's clamorous jars
  Seemed melted in that evening hue.

O sunset sky ! O purple tide !
  O friends to friends that closer pressed !
Those glories have in darkness died,
  And ye have left my longing breast.
I could not keep you by my side,
  Nor fix that radiance in the west.
                     W. B. GLAZIER.

SUNSET.

IF solitude hath ever led thy steps
  To the wild ocean's echoing shore,
    And thou hast lingered there
    Until the sun's broad orb
  Seemed resting on the burnished wave,
    Thou must have marked the lines
  Of purple gold, that motionless
    Hung o'er the sinking sphere :
Thou must have marked the billowy clouds,
  Edged with intolerable radiancy,
    Towering like rocks of jet
  Crowned with a diamond wreath.
    And yet there is a moment,
    When the sun's highest point
Peeps like a star o'er ocean's western edge,
When those far clouds of feathery gold,
  Shaded with deepest purple, gleam
  Like islands on a dark-blue sea ;
Then has thy fancy soared above the earth,
    And furled its wearied wing
    Within the Fairy's fane.

Yet not the golden islands
Gleaming in yon flood of light,
  Nor the feathery curtains
Stretching o'er the sun's bright couch,
  Nor the burnished ocean's waves
    Paving that gorgeous dome,
So fair, so wonderful a sight
As Mab's ethereal palace could afford.
Yet likest evening's vault, that fairy Hall !
  Heaven, low resting on the wave, it spread
    Its floors of flashing light,
    Its vast and azure dome,
    Its fertile golden islands
    Floating on a silver sea ;
Whilst suns their mingling beamings darted
Through clouds of circumambient darkness,
  And pearly battlements around
  Looked o'er the immense of heaven.
PERCY BYSSHE SHELLEY.

EVENING.

FROM "DON JUAN."

AVE Maria ! o'er the earth and sea,
That heavenliest hour of heaven is worthiest thee !

Ave Maria ! blessed be the hour,
  The time, the clime, the spot, where I so oft
Have felt that moment in its fullest power
  Sink o'er the earth so beautiful and soft,
While swung the deep bell in the distant tower
  Or the faint dying day hymn stole aloft,
And not a breath crept through the rosy air,
And yet the forest leaves seemed stirred with
    prayer.

Ave Maria ! 't is the hour of prayer !
  Ave Maria ! 't is the hour of love !
Ave Maria ! may our spirits dare
  Look up to thine and to thy Son's above !
Ave Maria ! O that face so fair !
  Those downcast eyes beneath the Almighty
    dove, —
What though 't is but a pictured image ? —
    strike, —
That painting is no idol, — 't is too like.

Sweet hour of twilight ! in the solitude
  Of the pine forest, and the silent shore
Which bounds Ravenna's immemorial wood,
  Rooted where once the Adrian wave flowed o'er
To where the last Cæsarean fortress stood,
  Evergreen forest ; which Boccaccio's lore
And Dryden's lay made haunted ground to me,
How have I loved the twilight hour and thee !

The shrill cicalas, people of the pine,
  Making their summer lives one ceaseless song,
Were the sole echoes, save my steed's and mine,

And vesper bells that rose the boughs along ;
The spectre huntsman of Onesti's line,
  His hell-dogs, and their chase, and the fair throng
Which learned from this example not to fly
From a true lover, — shadowed my mind's eye.

O Hesperus ! thou bringest all good things, —
  Home to the weary, to the hungry cheer,
To the young bird the parent's brooding wings,
  The welcome stall to the o'erlabored steer ;
Whate'er of peace about our hearthstone clings,
  Whate'er our household gods protect of dear,
Are gathered round us by thy look of rest ;
Thou bring'st the child, too, to the mother's breast.

Soft hour ! which wakes the wish and melts the
    heart
  Of those who sail the seas, on the first day
When they from their sweet friends are torn apart ;
  Or fills with love the pilgrim on his way,
As the far bell of vesper makes him start,
  Seeming to weep the dying day's decay :
Is this a fancy which our reason scorns ?
Ah ! surely nothing dies but something mourns.
BYRON.

EVENING IN PARADISE.

Now came still evening on, and twilight gray
Had in her sober livery all things clad ;
Silence accompanied ; for beast and bird,
They to their grassy couch, these to their nests,
Were slunk, all but the wakeful nightingale ;
She all night long her amorous descant sung.
Silence was pleased : now glowed the firmament
With living sapphires ; Hesperus, that led
The starry host, rode brightest, till the moon,
Rising in clouded majesty, at length
Apparent queen, unveiled her peerless light,
And o'er the dark her silver mantle threw.
  When Adam thus to Eve : "Fair consort, the
    hour
Of night, and all things now retired to rest,
Mind us of like repose, since God hath set
Labor and rest, as day and night, to men
Successive ; and the timely dew of sleep,
Now falling with soft slumberous weight, inclines
Our eyelids.   Other creatures all day long
Rove idle, unemployed, and less need rest ;
Man hath his daily work of body or mind
Appointed, which declares his dignity,
And the regard of Heaven on all his ways ;
While other animals unactive range,
And of their doings God takes no account.
To-morrow, ere fresh morning streak the east
With first approach of light, we must be risen,
And at our pleasant labor, to reform
Yon flowery arbors, yonder alleys green,

Our walk at noon, with branches overgrown,
That mock our scant manuring, and require
More hands than ours to lop their wanton growth.
Those blossoms also, and those dropping gums,
That lie bestrewn, unsightly and unsmooth,
Ask riddance, if we mean to tread with ease ;
Meanwhile, as Nature wills, night bids us rest."
　To whom thus Eve with perfect beauty adorned :
" My author and disposer, what thou bidd'st
Unargued I obey ; so God ordains ;
God is thy law, thou mine ; to know no more
Is woman's happiest knowledge and her praise.
With thee conversing I forget all time ;
All seasons and their change, all please alike.
Sweet is the breath of morn, her rising sweet,
With charm of earliest birds ; pleasant the sun,
When first on this delightful land he spreads
His orient beams, on herb, tree, fruit, and flower,
Glistering with dew ; fragrant the fertile earth
After soft showers ; and sweet the coming on
Of grateful evening mild ; then silent night,
With this her solemn bird, and this fair moon,
And these the gems of heaven, her starry train :
But neither breath of morn, when she ascends
With charm of earliest birds ; nor rising sun
On this delightful land ; nor herb, fruit, flower,
Glistering with dew ; nor fragrance after showers,
Nor grateful evening mild ; nor silent night
With this her solemn bird, nor walk by moon,
Or glittering starlight, without thee is sweet."
　Thus talking, hand in hand alone they passed
On to their blissful bower.

MILTON.

TO NIGHT.

SWIFTLY walk over the western wave,
　　Spirit of Night !
Out of the misty eastern cave,
Where, all the long and lone daylight,
Thou wovest dreams of joy and fear
Which make thee terrible and dear, —
　　Swift be thy flight !

Wrap thy form in a mantle gray,
　　Star-inwrought ;
Blind with thine hair the eyes of Day,
Kiss her until she be wearied out ;
Then wander o'er city and sea and land,
Touching all with thine opiate wand, —
　　Come, long-sought !

When I arose and saw the dawn,
　　I sighed for thee ;
When light rode high, and the dew was gone,
And noon lay heavy on flower and tree,
And the weary Day turned to her rest,
Lingering like an unloved guest,
　　I sighed for thee !

Thy brother Death came, and cried,
　　" Wouldst thou me ? "
Thy sweet child Sleep, the filmy-eyed,
　　Murmured like a noontide bee,
" Shall I nestle near thy side ?
Wouldst thou me ? " — And I replied,
　　" No, not thee ! "

Death will come when thou art dead,
　　Soon, too soon, —
Sleep will come when thou art fled ;
Of neither would I ask the boon
I ask of thee, beloved Night, —
Swift be thine approaching flight,
　　Come soon, soon !

PERCY BYSSHE SHELLEY.

NIGHT.

MYSTERIOUS Night ! when our first parent knew
Thee, from report divine, and heard thy name,
Did he not tremble for this lovely frame, —
This glorious canopy of light and blue ?
Yet, 'neath a curtain of translucent dew,
Bathed in the rays of the great setting flame,
Hesperus, with the host of heaven, came,
And lo ! creation widened in man's view.
Who could have thought such darkness lay con-
　　cealed
Within thy beams, O Sun ! or who could find,
Whilst fly and leaf and insect stood revealed,
That to such countless orbs thou mad'st us blind !
Why do we then shun death with anxious strife ?
If light can thus deceive, wherefore not life ?

BLANCO WHITE.

NIGHT.

How beautiful this night ! the balmiest sigh
Which vernal zephyrs breathe in evening's ear
Were discord to the speaking quietude
That wraps this moveless scene.　Heaven's ebon
　　vault,
Studded with stars unutterably bright,
Through which the moon's unclouded grandeur
　　rolls,
Seems like a canopy which love has spread
To curtain her sleeping world.　Yon gentle hills,
Robed in a garment of untrodden snow ;
Yon darksome rocks, whence icicles depend,
So stainless that their white and glittering spires
Tinge not the moon's pure beam ; yon castle steep,
Whose banner hangeth o'er the timeworn tower
So idly that rapt fancy deemeth it
A metaphor of peace — all form a scene
Where musing solitude might love to lift

Her soul above this sphere of earthliness ;
Where silence undisturbed might watch alone,
So cold, so bright, so still.

        The orb of day
In southern climes o'er ocean's waveless field
Sinks sweetly smiling : not the faintest breath
Steals o'er the unruffled deep ; the clouds of eve
Reflect unmoved the lingering beam of day ;
And vesper's image on the western main
Is beautifully still. To-morrow comes :
Cloud upon cloud, in dark and deepening mass,
Rolls o'er the blackened waters ; the deep roar
Of distant thunder mutters awfully ;
Tempest unfolds its pinion o'er the gloom
That shrouds the boiling surge ; the pitiless fiend,
With all his winds and lightnings, tracks his prey ;
The torn deep yawns, — the vessel finds a grave
Beneath its jagged gulf.
          PERCY BYSSHE SHELLEY.

NIGHT.

FROM "CHILDE HAROLD."

'T IS night, when Meditation bids us feel
We once have loved, though love is at an end :
The heart, lone mourner of its baffled zeal,
  Though friendless now, will dream it had a
    friend.
Who with the weight of years would wish to bend,
When Youth itself survives young Love and joy ?
Alas ! when mingling souls forget to blend,
Death hath but little left him to destroy !
Ah ! happy years ! once more who would not be
  a boy ?

Thus bending o'er the vessel's laving side,
To gaze on Dian's wave-reflected sphere,
The soul forgets her schemes of Hope and Pride,
And flies unconscious o'er each backward year.
None are so desolate but something dear,
Dearer than self, possesses or possessed
A thought, and claims the homage of a tear ;
A flashing pang ! of which the weary breast
Would still, albeit in vain, the heavy heart divest.

To sit on rocks, to muse o'er flood and fell,
To slowly trace the forest's shady scene,
Where things that own not man's dominion
    dwell,
And mortal foot hath ne'er or rarely been ;
To climb the trackless mountain all unseen,
With the wild flock that never needs a fold ;
Alone o'er steeps and foaming falls to lean, —
This is not solitude ; 't is but to hold
Converse with Nature's charms, and view her
  stores unrolled.

But midst the crowd, the hum, the shock of men,
To hear, to see, to feel, and to possess,
And roam along, the world's tired denizen,
With none who bless us, none whom we can bless ;
Minions of splendor shrinking from distress !
None that, with kindred consciousness endued,
If we were not, would seem to smile the less
Of all that flattered, followed, sought, and sued ;
This is to be alone ; this, this is solitude !
          BYRON.

NIGHT.

NIGHT is the time for rest :
  How sweet, when labors close,
To gather round an aching breast
  The curtain of repose,
Stretch the tired limbs, and lay the head
Down on our own delightful bed !

Night is the time for dreams :
  The gay romance of life,
When truth that is, and truth that seems,
  Mix in fantastic strife ;
Ah ! visions, less beguiling far
Than waking dreams by daylight are !

Night is the time for toil :
  To plough the classic field,
Intent to find the buried spoil
  Its wealthy furrows yield ;
Till all is ours that sages taught,
That poets sang, and heroes wrought.

Night is the time to weep :
  To wet with unseen tears
Those graves of Memory, where sleep
  The joys of other years ;
Hopes, that were Angels at their birth,
But died when young, like things of earth.

Night is the time to watch :
  O'er ocean's dark expanse,
To hail the Pleiades, or catch
  The full moon's earliest glance,
That brings into the homesick mind
All we have loved and left behind.

Night is the time for care :
  Brooding on hours misspent,
To see the spectre of Despair
  Come to our lonely tent ;
Like Brutus, midst his slumbering host,
Summoned to die by Cæsar's ghost.

Night is the time to think :
  When, from the eye, the soul
Takes flight ; and on the utmost brink
  Of yonder starry pole

Discerns beyond the abyss of night
The dawn of uncreated light.

Night is the time to pray:
  Our Saviour oft withdrew
To desert mountains far away;
  So will his follower do,
Steal from the throng to haunts untrod,
And commune there alone with God.

Night is the time for Death:
  When all around is peace,
Calmly to yield the weary breath,
  From sin and suffering cease,
Think of heaven's bliss, and give the sign
To parting friends; — such death be mine.
                    JAMES MONTGOMERY.

———◆———

HYMN TO THE NIGHT.

'Ασπασίη, τρίλλιστος.

I HEARD the trailing garments of the Night
  Sweep through her marble halls!
I saw her sable skirts all fringed with light
  From the celestial walls!

I felt her presence, by its spell of might,
  Stoop o'er me from above;
The calm, majestic presence of the Night,
  As of the one I love.

I heard the sounds of sorrow and delight,
  The manifold, soft chimes,
That fill the haunted chambers of the Night,
  Like some old poet's rhymes.

From the cool cisterns of the midnight air
  My spirit drank repose;
The fountain of perpetual peace flows there, —
  From those deep cisterns flows.

O holy Night! from thee I learn to bear
  What man has borne before!
Thou layest thy finger on the lips of Care,
  And they complain no more.

Peace! Peace! Orestes-like I breathe this prayer!
  Descend with broad-winged flight,
The welcome, the thrice-prayed for, the most fair,
  The best-beloved Night!
                    HENRY WADSWORTH LONGFELLOW.

———◆———

SPRING.

FROM "IN MEMORIAM."

DIP down upon the northern shore,
  O sweet new-year, delaying long:
  Thou doest expectant Nature wrong;
Delaying long, delay no more.

What stays thee from the clouded noons,
  Thy sweetness from its proper place?
  Can trouble live with April days,
Or sadness in the summer moons?

Bring orchis, bring the foxglove spire,
  The little speedwell's darling blue,
  Deep tulips dashed with fiery dew,
Laburnums, dropping-wells of fire.

O thou, new-year, delaying long,
  Delayest the sorrow in my blood,
  That longs to burst a frozen bud,
And flood a fresher throat with song.

      .   .   .   .   .

Now fades the last long streak of snow;
  Now bourgeons every maze of quick
  About the flowering squares, and thick
By ashen roots the violets blow.

Now rings the woodland loud and long,
  The distance takes a lovelier hue,
  And drowned in yonder living blue
The lark becomes a sightless song.

Now dance the lights on lawn and lea,
  The flocks are whiter down the vale,
  And milkier every milky sail
On winding stream or distant sea;

Where now the seamew pipes, or dives
  In yonder greening gleam, and fly
  The happy birds, that change their sky
To build and brood, that live their lives

From land to land; and in my breast
  Spring wakens too; and my regret
  Becomes an April violet,
And buds and blossoms like the rest.
                    ALFRED TENNYSON.

———◆———

DIE DOWN, O DISMAL DAY!

DIE down, O dismal day, and let me live;
And come, blue deeps, magnificently strewn
With colored clouds, — large, light, and fugitive, —
By upper winds through pompous motions blown.
Now it is death in life, — a vapor dense
Creeps round my window, till I cannot see
The far snow-shining mountains, and the glens
Shagging the mountain tops. O God! make free
This barren shackled earth, so deadly cold, —
Breathe gently forth thy spring, till winter flies
In rude amazement, fearful and yet bold,
While she performs her customed charities;
I weigh the loaded hours till life is bare, —
O God, for one clear day, a snowdrop, and sweet air!
                    DAVID GRAY.

SUMMER LONGINGS.

AH ! my heart is weary waiting,
 Waiting for the May, —
Waiting for the pleasant rambles
Where the fragrant hawthorn-brambles,
 With the woodbine alternating,
 Scent the dewy way.
 Ah ! my heart is weary waiting,
 Waiting for the May.

Ah ! my heart is sick with longing,
 Longing for the May, —
Longing to escape from study,
To the young face fair and ruddy,
 And the thousand charms belonging
 To the summer's day.
 Ah ! my heart is sick with longing,
 Longing for the May.

Ah ! my heart is sore with sighing,
 Sighing for the May, —
Sighing for their sure returning,
When the summer beams are burning,
 Hopes and flowers that, dead or dying,
 All the winter lay.
 Ah ! my heart is sore with sighing,
 Sighing for the May.

Ah ! my heart is pained with throbbing,
 Throbbing for the May, —
Throbbing for the seaside billows,
Or the water-wooing willows ;
 Where, in laughing and in sobbing,
 Glide the streams away.
 Ah ! my heart, my heart is throbbing.
 Throbbing for the May.

Waiting sad, dejected, weary,
 Waiting for the May :
Spring goes by with wasted warnings, —
Moonlit evenings, sunbright mornings, —
Summer comes, yet dark and dreary
Life still ebbs away ;
 Man is ever weary, weary,
 Waiting for the May !
 DENIS FLORENCE MAC-CARTHY.

WHEN THE HOUNDS OF SPRING.

WHEN the hounds of spring are on winter's traces,
 The mother of months in meadow or plain
Fills the shadows and windy places
 With lisp of leaves and ripple of rain ;
And the brown bright nightingale amorous
Is half assuaged for Itylus,
For the Thracian ships and the foreign faces ;
 The tongueless vigil, and all the pain.

Come with bows bent and with emptying of
 quivers,
 Maiden most perfect, lady of light,
With a noise of winds and many rivers,
 With a clamor of waters, and with might ;
Bind on thy sandals, O thou most fleet,
Over the splendor and speed of thy feet !
For the faint east quickens, the wan west shivers,
 Round the feet of the day and the feet of the
 night.

Where shall we find her, how shall we sing to her,
 Fold our hands round her knees and cling ?
O that man's heart were as fire and could spring
 to her,
 Fire, or the strength of the streams that spring !
For the stars and the winds are unto her
As raiment, as songs of the harp-player ;
For the risen stars and the fallen cling to her,
 And the southwest-wind and the west-wind
 sing.

For winter's rains and ruins are over,
 And all the season of snows and sins ;
The days dividing lover and lover,
 The light that loses, the night that wins ;
And time remembered is grief forgotten,
And frosts are slain and flowers begotten,
And in green underwood and cover
 Blossom by blossom the spring begins.

The full streams feed on flower of rushes,
 Ripe grasses trammel a travelling foot,
The faint fresh flame of the young year flushes
 From leaf to flower and flower to fruit ;
And fruit and leaf are as gold and fire,
And the oat is heard above the lyre,
And the hooféd heel of a satyr crushes
 The chestnut-husk at the chestnut-root.

And Pan by noon and Bacchus by night,
 Fleeter of foot than the fleet-foot kid,
Follows with dancing and fills with delight
 The Mænad and the Bassarid ;
And soft as lips that laugh and hide,
The laughing leaves of the trees divide,
And screen from seeing and leave in sight
 The god pursuing, the maiden hid.

The ivy falls with the Bacchanal's hair
 Over her eyebrows shading her eyes ;
The wild vine slipping down leaves bare
 Her bright breast shortening into sighs ;
The wild vine slips with the weight of its leaves,
But the berried ivy catches and cleaves
To the limbs that glitter, the feet that scare
 The wolf that follows, the fawn that flies.
 ALGERNON CHARLES SWINBURNE.

THE WINTER BEING OVER.

THE winter being over,
In order comes the spring,
Which doth green herbs discover,
And cause the birds to sing.
The night also expired,
Then comes the morning bright,
Which is so much desired
By all that love the light.
    This may learn
    Them that mourn,
To put their grief to flight :
The spring succeedeth winter,
And day must follow night.

He therefore that sustaineth
Affliction or distress
Which every member paineth,
And findeth no release, —
Let such therefore despair not,
But on firm hope depend,
Whose griefs immortal are not,
And therefore must have end.
    They that faint
    With complaint
Therefore are to blame ;
They add to their afflictions,
And amplify the same.

For if they could with patience
Awhile possess the mind,
By inward consolations
They might refreshing find,
To sweeten all their crosses
That little time they 'dure ;
So might they gain by losses,
And sharp would sweet procure.
    But if the mind
    Be inclined
To unquietness,
That only may be called
The worst of all distress.

He that is melancholy,
Detesting all delight,
His wits by sottish folly
Are ruinated quite.
Sad discontent and murmurs
To him are incident ;
Were he possessed of honors,
He could not be content.
    Sparks of joy
    Fly away ;
Floods of care arise ;
And all delightful motion
In the conception dies.

But those that are contented
However things do fall,
Much anguish is prevented,
And they soon freed from all.
They finish all their labors
With much felicity ;
Their joy in trouble savors
Of perfect piety.
    Cheerfulness
    Doth express
A settled pious mind,
Which is not prone to grudging,
From murmuring refined.
        ANN COLLINS.

SPRING.

WRITTEN WHILE A PRISONER IN ENGLAND.

THE Time hath laid his mantle by
  Of wind and rain and icy chill,
And dons a rich embroidery
  Of sunlight poured on lake and hill.

No beast or bird in earth or sky,
  Whose voice doth not with gladness thrill;
For Time hath laid his mantle by
  Of wind and rain and icy chill.

River and fountain, brook and rill,
Bespangled o'er with livery gay
Of silver droplets, wind their way.
All in their new apparel vie,
.For Time hath laid his mantle by.
        CHARLES OF ORLEANS.

RETURN OF SPRING.

[Translation.]

GOD shield ye, heralds of the spring,
Ye faithful swallows, fleet of wing,
    Houps, cuckoos, nightingales,
Turtles, and every wilder bird,
That make your hundred chirpings heard
    Through the green woods and dales.

God shield ye, Easter daisies all,
Fair roses, buds, and blossoms small,
    And he whom erst the gore
Of Ajax and Narciss did print,
Ye wild thyme, anise, balm, and mint,
    I welcome ye once more.

God shield ye, bright embroidered train
Of butterflies, that on the plain
    Of each sweet herblet sip ;
And ye, new swarms of bees, that go
Where the pink flowers and yellow grow
    To kiss them with your lip.

A hundred thousand times I call
A hearty welcome on ye all ;
   This season how I love —
This merry din on every shore —
For winds and storms, whose sullen roar
   Forbade my steps to rove.

PIERRE RONSARD (French).

MARCH.

THE cock is crowing,
The stream is flowing,
The small birds twitter,
The lake doth glitter,
The green field sleeps in the sun ;
The oldest and youngest
Are at work with the strongest ;
The cattle are grazing,
Their heads never raising ;
There are forty feeding like one !

Like an army defeated
The snow hath retreated,
And now doth fare ill
On the top of the bare hill ;
The plough-boy is whooping — anon — anon !
There 's joy on the mountains ;
There 's life in the fountains ;
Small clouds are sailing,
Blue sky prevailing ;
The rain is over and gone !

WILLIAM WORDSWORTH.

SONG OF SPRING.

LAUD the first spring daisies ;
Chant aloud their praises ;
Send the children up
To the high hill's top ;
Tax not the strength of their young hands
To increase your lands.
Gather the primroses,
Make handfuls into posies ;
Take them to the little girls who are at work in
   mills :
Pluck the violets blue, —
Ah, pluck not a few !
Knowest thou what good thoughts from Heaven
   the violet instils ?

Give the children holidays,
(And let these be jolly days,)
Grant freedom to the children in this joyous
   spring ;
Better men, hereafter,

Shall we have, for laughter
Freely shouted to the woods, till all the echoes ring.
Send the children up
To the high hill's top,
Or deep into the wood's recesses,
To woo spring's caresses.

See, the birds together,
In this splendid weather,
Worship God (for he is God of birds as well as
   men) ;
And each feathered neighbor
Enters on his labor, —
Sparrow, robin, redpole, finch, the linnet, and the
   wren.
As the year advances,
Trees their naked branches
Clothe, and seek your pleasure in their green ap-
   parel.
Insect and wild beast
Keep no Lent, but feast ;
Spring breathes upon the earth, and their joy 's
   increased,
And the rejoicing birds break forth in one loud
   carol.

Ah, come and woo the spring ;
List to the birds that sing ;
Pluck the primroses ; pluck the violets ;
Pluck the daisies,
Sing their praises ;
Friendship with the flowers some noble thought
   begets.
Come forth and gather these sweet elves,
(More witching are they than the fays of old,)
Come forth and gather them yourselves ;
Learn of these gentle flowers whose worth is more
   than gold.

Come, come into the wood ;
Pierce into the bowers
Of these gentle flowers,
Which, not in solitude
Dwell, but with each other keep society :
And with a simple piety,
Are ready to be woven into garlands for the good.
Or, upon summer earth,
To die, in virgin worth ;
Or to be strewn before the bride,
And the bridegroom, by her side.

Come forth on Sundays ;
Come forth on Mondays ;
Come forth on any day ;
Children, come forth to play : —
Worship the God of Nature in your childhood ;
Worship him at your tasks with best endeavor ;
Worship him in your sports ; worship him ever ;

Worship him in the wildwood ;
Worship him amidst the flowers ;
In the greenwood bowers ;
Pluck the buttercups, and raise
Your voices in his praise !
                                EDWARD YOUL.

SPRING.

AGAIN the violet of our early days
Drinks beauteous azure from the golden sun,
And kindles into fragrance at his blaze ;
The streams, rejoiced that winter's work is done,
Talk of to-morrow's cowslips, as they run.
Wild apple, thou art blushing into bloom !
Thy leaves are coming, snowy-blossomed thorn !
Wake, buried lily ! spirit, quit thy tomb !
And thou shade-loving hyacinth, be born !
Then, haste, sweet rose ! sweet woodbine, hymn
        the morn,
Whose dewdrops shall illume with pearly light
Each grassy blade that thick embattled stands
From sea to sea, while daisies infinite
Uplift in praise their little glowing hands,
O'er every hill that under heaven expands.
                            EBENEZER ELLIOTT.

SPRING.

Lo ! where the rosy-bosomed Hours,
    Fair Venus' train, appear,
Disclose the long-expecting flowers
    And wake the purple year !
The Attic warbler pours her throat
Responsive to the cuckoo's note,
The untaught harmony of spring :
While, whispering pleasure as they fly,
Cool zephyrs through the clear blue sky
    Their gathered fragrance fling.

Where'er the oak's thick branches stretch
    A broader, browner shade,
Where'er the rude and moss-grown beech
    O'er-canopies the glade,
Beside some water's rushy brink
With me the Muse shall sit, and think
(At ease reclined in rustic state)
How vain the ardor of the crowd,
How low, how little are the proud,
    How indigent the great !

Still is the toiling hand of care ;
    The panting herds repose :
Yet hark, how through the peopled air
    The busy murmur glows !
The insect youth are on the wing,

Eager to taste the honeyed spring
And float amid the liquid noon :
Some lightly o'er the current skim,
Some show their gayly gilded trim
    Quick-glancing to the sun.

To Contemplation's sober eye
    Such is the race of man ;
And they that creep, and they that fly
    Shall end where they began.
Alike the busy and the gay
But flutter through life's little day,
In Fortune's varying colors drest :
Brushed by the hand of rough mischance
Or chilled by age, their airy dance
    They leave, in dust to rest.

Methinks I hear in accents low
    The sportive kind reply :
Poor moralist ! and what art thou ?
    A solitary fly !
Thy joys no glittering female meets,
No hive hast thou of hoarded sweets,
No painted plumage to display ;
On hasty wings thy youth is flown ;
Thy sun is set, thy spring is gone, —
    We frolic while 't is May.
                                THOMAS GRAY.

SWEETLY BREATHING, VERNAL AIR.

SWEETLY breathing, vernal air,
That with kind warmth doth repair
Winter's ruins ; from whose breast
All the gums and spice of the East
Borrow their perfumes ; whose eye
Gilds the morn, and clears the sky ;
Whose dishevelled tresses shed
Pearls upon the violet bed ;
On whose brow, with calm smiles drest
The halcyon sits and builds her nest ;
Beauty, youth, and endless spring
Dwell upon thy rosy wing !

Thou, if stormy Boreas throws
Down whole forests when he blows,
With a pregnant, flowery birth,
Canst refresh the teeming earth.
If he nip the early bud,
If he blast what 's fair or good,
If he scatter our choice flowers,
If he shake our halls or bowers,
If his rude breath threaten us,
Thou canst stroke great Æolus,
And from him the grace obtain,
To bind him in an iron chain.
                            THOMAS CAREW.

SPRING.

BEHOLD the young, the rosy Spring
Gives to the breeze her scented wing,
While virgin graces, warm with May,
Fling roses o'er her dewy way.
The murmuring billows of the deep
Have languished into silent sleep ;
And mark ! the flitting sea-birds lave
Their plumes in the reflecting wave ;
While cranes from hoary winter fly
To flutter in a kinder sky.
Now the genial star of day
Dissolves the murky clouds away,
And cultured field and winding stream
Are freshly glittering in his beam.
　Now the earth prolific swells
With leafy buds and flowery bells ;
Gemming shoots the olive twine ;
Clusters bright festoon the vine ;
All along the branches creeping,
Through the velvet foliage peeping,
Little infant fruits we see
Nursing into luxury.

ANACREON (Greek). Translation
of THOMAS MOORE.

SPRING, THE SWEET SPRING.

SPRING, the sweet spring, is the year's pleasant
　king ;
Then blooms each thing, then maids dance in a ring,
Cold doth not sting, the pretty birds do sing,
　Cuckoo, jug-jug, pu-we, to-witta-woo !

The palm and may make country houses gay,
Lambs frisk and play, the shepherds pipe all day,
And we hear aye birds tune this merry lay,
　Cuckoo, jug-jug, pu-we, to-witta-woo !

The fields breathe sweet, the daisies kiss our feet,
Young lovers meet, old wives a sunning sit,
In every street these tunes our ears do greet,
　Cuckoo, jug-jug, pu-we, to-witta-woo !
　　Spring ! the sweet spring !

T. NASH.

THE INVITATION.

BEST and brightest, come away,
Fairer far than this fair day,
Which, like thee, to those in sorrow
Comes to bid a sweet good-morrow
To the rough year just awake
In its cradle on the brake.
The brightest hour of unborn spring
Through the winter wandering,

Found, it seems, the halcyon morn
To hoar February born ;
Bending from heaven, in azure mirth,
It kissed the forehead of the earth,
And smiled upon the silent sea,
And bade the frozen streams be free,
And waked to music all their fountains,
And breathed upon the frozen mountains,
And like a prophetess of May
Strewed flowers upon the barren way,
Making the wintry world appear
Like one on whom thou smilest, dear.

Away, away, from men and towns,
To the wild wood and the downs, —
To the silent wilderness
Where the soul need not repress
Its music, lest it should not find
An echo in another's mind,
While the touch of nature's art
Harmonizes heart to heart.

Radiant Sister of the Day,
Awake ! arise ! and come away !
To the wild woods and the plains,
To the pools where winter rains
Image all their roof of leaves,
Where the pine its garland weaves
Of sapless green, and ivy dun,
Round stems that never kiss the sun,
Where the lawns and pastures be
And the sand-hills of the sea,
Where the melting hoar-frost wets
The daisy-star that never sets,
And wind-flowers and violets
Which yet join not scent to hue
Crown the pale year weak and new ;
When the night is left behind
In the deep east, dim and blind,
And the blue noon is over us,
And the multitudinous
Billows murmur at our feet,
Where the earth and ocean meet,
And all things seem only one
In the universal sun.

PERCY BYSSHE SHELLEY.

TO AURELIA.

SEE, the flowery spring is blown,
Let us leave the smoky town ;
From the mall, and from the ring,
Every one has taken wing ;
Chloe, Strephon, Corydon,
To the meadows all are gone.
What is left you worth your stay ?
Come, Aurelia, come away.

Come, Aurelia, come and see
What a lodge I 've dressed for thee ;
But the seat you cannot see,
'T is so hid with jessamy,
With the vine that o'er the walls,
And in every window crawls ;
Let us there be blithe and gay !
Come, Aurelia, come away.

Come with all thy sweetest wiles,
With thy graces and thy smiles ;
Come, and we will merry be,
Who shall be so blest as we ?
We will frolic all the day,
Haste, Aurelia, while we may :
Ay ! and should not life be gay ?
Yes, Aurelia, — come away.
                              JOHN DYER.

MAY MORNING.

Now the bright morning star, day's harbinger,
Comes dancing from the east, and leads with her
The flowery May, who from her green lap throws
The yellow cowslip and the pale primrose.
Hail, bounteous May ! that doth inspire
Mirth and youth and warm desire ;
Woods and groves are of thy dressing,
Hill and dale doth boast thy blessing.
Thus we salute thee with our early song,
And welcome thee, and wish thee long.
                              MILTON.

MAY.

I FEEL a newer life in every gale ;
    The winds that fan the flowers,
And with their welcome breathings fill the sail,
    Tell of serener hours, —
    Of hours that glide unfelt away
    Beneath the sky of May.

The spirit of the gentle south-wind calls
    From his blue throne of air,
And where his whispering voice in music falls,
    Beauty is budding there ;
    The bright ones of the valley break
    Their slumbers, and awake.

The waving verdure rolls along the plain,
    And the wide forest weaves,
To welcome back its playful mates again,
    A canopy of leaves ;
    And from its darkening shadow floats
    A gush of trembling notes.

Fairer and brighter spreads the reign of May ;
    The tresses of the woods
With the light dallying of the west-wind play ;
    And the full-brimming floods,
    As gladly to their goal they run,
    Hail the returning sun.
                    JAMES GATES PERCIVAL.

THEY COME! THE MERRY SUMMER MONTHS.

THEY come ! the merry summer months of
    beauty, song, and flowers ;
They come ! the gladsome months that bring
    thick leafiness to bowers.
Up, up, my heart ! and walk abroad ; fling cark
    and care aside ;
Seek silent hills, or rest thyself where peaceful
    waters glide ;
Or, underneath the shadow vast of patriarchal
    tree,
Scan through its leaves the cloudless sky in rapt
    tranquillity.

The grass is soft, its velvet touch is grateful to
    the hand ;
And, like the kiss of maiden love, the breeze is
    sweet and bland ;
The daisy and the buttercup are nodding cour-
    teously ;
It stirs their blood with kindest love, to bless
    and welcome thee ;
And mark how with thine own thin locks —
    they now are silvery gray —
That blissful breeze is wantoning, and whisper-
    ing, "Be gay !"

There is no cloud that sails along the ocean of
    yon sky
But hath its own winged mariners to give it
    melody ;
Thou seest their glittering fans outspread, all
    gleaming like red gold ;
And hark ! with shrill pipe musical, their merry
    course they hold.
God bless them all, those little ones, who, far
    above this earth,
Can make a scoff of its mean joys, and vent a
    nobler mirth.

But soft ! mine ear upcaught a sound, — from
    yonder wood it came !
The spirit of the dim green glade did breathe his
    own glad name ; —
Yes, it is he ! the hermit bird, that, apart from
    all his kind,

"*The dripping rock, the mountain's misty top,
Swell on the sight, and brighten with the dawn.*"

Slow spells his beads monotonous to the soft
    western wind ;
Cuckoo ! Cuckoo ! he sings again, — his notes are
    void of art ;
But simplest strains do soonest sound the deep
    founts of the heart.

Good Lord ! it is a gracious boon for thought-
    crazed wight like me,
To smell again these summer flowers beneath this
    summer tree !
To suck once more in every breath their little
    souls away,
And feed my fancy with fond dreams of youth's
    bright summer day,
When, rushing forth like untamed colt, the reck-
    less, truant boy
Wandered through greenwoods all day long, a
    mighty heart of joy !

I 'm sadder now, — I have had cause ; but O,
    I 'm proud to think
That each pure joy-fount, loved of yore, I yet
    delight to drink ; —
Leaf, blossom, blade, hill, valley, stream, the
    calm, unclouded sky,
Still mingle music with my dreams, as in the
    days gone by.
When summer's loveliness and light fall round
    me dark and cold,
I 'll bear indeed life's heaviest curse, — a heart
    that hath waxed old !
WILLIAM MOTHERWELL.

SUMMER MORNING.

FROM "THE SEASONS."

SHORT is the doubtful empire of the night ;
And soon, observant of approaching day,
The meek-eyed morn appears, mother of dews,
At first faint gleaming in the dappled east, —
Till far o'er ether spreads the widening glow,
And, from before the lustre of her face,
White break the clouds away.   With quickened
    step,
Brown night retires.   Young day pours in apace,
And opens all the lawny prospect wide.
The dripping rock, the mountain's misty top,
Swell on the sight, and brighten with the dawn.
Blue, through the dusk, the smoking currents
    shine ;
And from the bladed field the fearful hare
Limps, awkward ; while along the forest glade
The wild deer trip, and often turning gaze
At early passenger.   Music awakes,
The native voice of undissembled joy ;
And thick around the woodland hymns arise.

Roused by the cock, the soon-clad shepherd leaves
His mossy cottage, where with peace he dwells ;
And from the crowded fold, in order, drives
His flock, to taste the verdure of the morn.
JAMES THOMSON.

SONG OF THE SUMMER WINDS.

UP the dale and down the bourne,
    O'er the meadow swift we fly ;
Now we sing, and now we mourn,
    Now we whistle, now we sigh.

By the grassy-fringéd river,
    Through the murmuring reeds we sweep ;
Mid the lily-leaves we quiver,
    To their very hearts we creep.

Now the maiden rose is blushing
    At the frolic things we say,
While aside her cheek we 're rushing,
    Like some truant bees at play.

Through the blooming groves we rustle,
    Kissing every bud we pass, —
As we did it in the bustle,
    Scarcely knowing how it was.

Down the glen, across the mountain,
    O'er the yellow heath we roam,
Whirling round about the fountain,
    Till its little breakers foam.

Bending down the weeping willows,
    While our vesper hymn we sigh ;
Then unto our rosy pillows
    On our weary wings we hie.

There of idlenesses dreaming,
    Scarce from waking we refrain,
Moments long as ages deeming
    Till we 're at our play again.
GEORGE DARLEY.

RAIN IN SUMMER.

How beautiful is the rain !
After the dust and heat,
In the broad and fiery street,
In the narrow lane,
How beautiful is the rain !

How it clatters along the roofs,
Like the tramp of hoofs !
How it gushes and struggles out
From the throat of the overflowing spout !

Across the window-pane
It pours and pours ;
And swift and wide,
With a muddy tide,
Like a river down the gutter roars
The rain, the welcome rain !

The sick man from his chamber looks
At the twisted brooks ;
He can feel the cool
Breath of each little pool ;
His fevered brain
Grows calm again,
And he breathes a blessing on the rain.

From the neighboring school
Come the boys,
With more than their wonted noise
And commotion ;
And down the wet streets
Sail their mimic fleets,
Till the treacherous pool
Ingulfs them in its whirling
And turbulent ocean.

In the country, on every side,
Where far and wide,
Like a leopard's tawny and spotted hide,
Stretches the plain,
To the dry grass and the drier grain
How welcome is the rain !

In the furrowed land
The toilsome and patient oxen stand ;
Lifting the yoke-encumbered head,
With their dilated nostrils spread,
They silently inhale
The clover-scented gale,
And the vapors that arise
From the well-watered and smoking soil.
For this rest in the furrow after toil
Their large and lustrous eyes
Seem to thank the Lord,
More than man's spoken word.

Near at hand,
From under the sheltering trees,
The farmer sees
His pastures, and his fields of grain,
As they bend their tops
To the numberless beating drops
Of the incessant rain.
He counts it as no sin
That he sees therein
Only his own thrift and gain.

These, and far more than these,
The Poet sees !
He can behold
Aquarius old

Walking the fenceless fields of air ;
And from each ample fold
Of the clouds about him rolled
Scattering everywhere
The showery rain,
As the farmer scatters his grain.

He can behold
Things manifold
That have not yet been wholly told, —
Have not been wholly sung nor said.
For his thought, that never stops,
Follows the water-drops
Down to the graves of the dead,
Down through chasms and gulfs profound,
To the dreary fountain-head
Of lakes and rivers underground ;
And sees them, when the rain is done,
On the bridge of colors seven
Climbing up once more to heaven,
Opposite the setting sun.

Thus the Seer,
With vision clear,
    Sees forms appear and disappear,
In the perpetual round of strange,
Mysterious change
From birth to death, from death to birth,
From earth to heaven, from heaven to earth;
Till glimpses more sublime
Of things, unseen before,
Unto his wondering eyes reveal
The Universe, as an immeasurable wheel
Turning forevermore
In the rapid and rushing river of Time.
                HENRY WADSWORTH LONGFELLOW

———◆———

A JUNE DAY.

Who has not dreamed a world of bliss
On a bright sunny noon like this,
Couched by his native brook's green maze,
With comrade of his boyish days,
While all around them seemed to be
Just as in joyous infancy ?
Who has not loved at such an hour,
Upon that heath, in birchen bower,
Lulled in the poet's dreamy mood,
Its wild and sunny solitude ?
While o'er the waste of purple ling
You mark a sultry glimmering ;
Silence herself there seems to sleep,
Wrapped in a slumber long and deep,
Where slowly stray those lonely sheep
Through the tall foxglove's crimson bloom,
And gleaming of the scattered broom.
Love you not, then, to list and hear

Engraved by Geo. E. Perine.

FORDS, HOWARD & HULBERT, N.Y.

The crackling of the gorse-flowers near,
Pouring an orange-scented tide
Of fragrance o'er the desert wide?
To hear the buzzard's whimpering shrill,
Hovering above you high and still?
The twittering of the bird that dwells
Among the heath's delicious bells?
While round your bed, o'er fern and blade,
Insects in green and gold arrayed,
The sun's gay tribes have lightly strayed;
And sweeter sound their humming wings
Than the proud minstrel's echoing strings.

WILLIAM HOWITT.

SUMMER MOODS.

I LOVE at eventide to walk alone,
Down narrow glens, o'erhung with dewy thorn,
Where, from the long grass underneath, the snail,
Jet black, creeps out, and sprouts his timid horn.
I love to muse o'er meadows newly mown,
Where withering grass perfumes the sultry air;
Where bees search round, with sad and weary
    drone,
In vain, for flowers that bloomed but newly
    there;
While in the juicy corn the hidden quail
Cries, "Wet my foot"; and, hid as thoughts
    unborn,
The fairy-like and seldom-seen land-rail
Utters "Craik, craik," like voices underground,
Right glad to meet the evening's dewy veil,
And see the light fade into gloom around.

JOHN CLARE.

SIGNS OF RAIN.

FORTY REASONS FOR NOT ACCEPTING AN INVITATION OF
A FRIEND TO MAKE AN EXCURSION WITH HIM.

1 THE hollow winds begin to blow;
2 The clouds look black, the glass is low,
3 The soot falls down, the spaniels sleep,
4 And spiders from their cobwebs peep.
5 Last night the sun went pale to bed,
6 The moon in halos hid her head;
7 The boding shepherd heaves a sigh,
8 For see a rainbow spans the sky.
9 The walls are damp, the ditches smell,
10 Closed is the pink-eyed pimpernel.
11 Hark how the chairs and tables crack!
12 Old Betty's nerves are on the rack;
13 Loud quacks the duck, the peacocks cry,
14 The distant hills are seeming nigh.
15 How restless are the snorting swine!
16 The busy flies disturb the kine;

17 Low o'er the grass the swallow wings,
18 The cricket, too, how sharp he sings,
19 Puss on the hearth, with velvet paws,
20 Sits wiping o'er her whiskered jaws,
21 Through the clear streams the fishes rise,
22 And nimbly catch the incautious flies.
23 The glow-worms, numerous and light,
24 Illumed the dewy dell last night,
25 At dusk the squalid toad was seen,
26 Hopping and crawling o'er the green,
27 The whirling dust the wind obeys,
28 And in the rapid eddy plays;
29 The frog has changed his yellow vest,
30 And in a russet coat is dressed.
31 Though June, the air is cold and still,
32 The mellow blackbird's voice is shrill;
33 My dog, so altered in his taste,
34 Quits mutton-bones on grass to feast;
35 And see yon rooks, how odd their flight,
36 They imitate the gliding kite,
37 And seem precipitate to fall,
38 As if they felt the piercing ball.
39 'T will surely rain; I see with sorrow,
40 Our jaunt must be put off to-morrow.

ANONYMOUS.

SUMMER STORM.

UNTREMULOUS in the river clear,
Toward the sky's image, hangs the imaged bridge;
    So still the air that I can hear
The slender clarion of the unseen midge;
    Out of the stillness, with a gathering creep,
Like rising wind in leaves, which now decreases,
Now lulls, now swells, and all the while increases,
    The huddling trample of a drove of sheep
Tilts the loose planks, and then as gradually ceases
    In dust on the other side; life's emblem deep,
A confused noise between two silences,
Finding at last in dust precarious peace.
On the wide marsh the purple-blossomed grasses
    Soak up the sunshine; sleeps the brimming
        tide
Save when the wedge-shaped wake in silence passes
    Of some slow water-rat, whose sinuous glide
Wavers the long green sedge's shade from side
        to side;
But up the west, like a rock-shivered surge,
    Climbs a great cloud edged with sun-whitened
        spray;
Huge whirls of foam boil toppling o'er its verge,
    And falling still it seems, and yet it climbs alway.

    Suddenly all the sky is hid
    As with the shutting of a lid,
One by one great drops are falling
    Doubtful and slow,

Down the pane they are crookedly crawling,
    And the wind breathes low ;
Slowly the circles widen on the river,
    Widen and mingle, one and all ;
Here and there the slenderer flowers shiver,
    Struck by an icy rain-drop's fall.

Now on the hills I hear the thunder mutter,
    The wind is gathering in the west ;
The upturned leaves first whiten and flutter,
    Then droop to a fitful rest ;
Up from the stream with sluggish flap
    Struggles the gull and floats away ;
Nearer and nearer rolls the thunder-clap, —
    We shall not see the sun go down to-day :
Now leaps the wind on the sleepy marsh,
    And tramples the grass with terrified feet,
The startled river turns leaden and harsh,
    You can hear the quick heart of the tempest beat.

Look ! look ! that livid flash !
And instantly follows the rattling thunder,
As if some cloud-crag, split asunder,
    Fell, splintering with a ruinous crash,
On the Earth, which crouches in silence under ;
    And now a solid gray wall of rain
Shuts off the landscape, mile by mile ;
    For a breath's space I see the blue wood again,
And, ere the next heart-beat, the wind-hurled pile,
    That seemed but now a league aloof,
Bursts crackling o'er the sun-parched roof ;
Against the windows the storm comes dashing,
Through tattered foliage the hail tears crashing,
    The blue lightning flashes,
    The rapid hail clashes,
    The white waves are tumbling,
    And, in one baffled roar,
    Like the toothless sea mumbling
    A rock-bristled shore,
    The thunder is rumbling
    And crashing and crumbling, —
Will silence return nevermore ?

    Hush ! Still as death,
    The tempest holds his breath
As from a sudden will ;
The rain stops short, but from the eaves
You see it drop, and hear it from the leaves,
    All is so bodingly still ;
    Again, now, now, again
Plashes the rain in heavy gouts,
    The crinkled lightning
    Seems ever brightening,
    And loud and long
Again the thunder shouts
    His battle-song, —
    One quivering flash,
    One wildering crash,

Followed by silence dead and dull,
    As if the cloud, let go,
    Leapt bodily below
To whelm the earth in one mad overthrow,
    And then a total lull.

    Gone, gone, so soon !
No more my half-crazed fancy there
    Can shape a giant in the air,
    No more I see his streaming hair,
The writhing portent of his form ; —
    The pale and quiet moon
    Makes her calm forehead bare,
And the last fragments of the storm,
Like shattered rigging from a fight at sea,
Silent and few, are drifting over me.
                JAMES RUSSELL LOWELL.

A SUMMER EVENING.

How fine has the day been! how bright was the sun!
How lovely and joyful the course that he run,
Though he rose in a mist when his race he begun,
    And there followed some droppings of rain !
But now the fair traveller 's come to the west,
His rays are all gold, and his beauties are best :
He paints the sky gay as he sinks to his rest,
    And foretells a bright rising again.

Just such is the Christian ; his course he begins,
Like the sun in a mist, when he mourns for his sins,
And melts into tears ; then he breaks out and
    shines,
    And travels his heavenly way :
But when he comes nearer to finish his race,
Like a fine setting sun, he looks richer in grace,
And gives a sure hope, at the end of his days,
    Of rising in brighter array.   ISAAC WATTS.

MOONLIGHT IN SUMMER.

Low on the utmost boundary of the sight,
The rising vapors catch the silver light ;
Thence fancy measures, as they parting fly,
Which first will throw its shadow on the eye,
Passing the source of light ; and thence away,
Succeeded quick by brighter still than they.
For yet above these wafted clouds are seen
(In a remoter sky still more serene)
Others, detached in ranges through the air,
Spotless as snow, and countless as they 're fair ;
Scattered immensely wide from east to west,
The beauteous semblance of a flock at rest.
These, to the raptured mind, aloud proclaim
Their mighty Shepherd's everlasting name ;

And thus the loiterer's utmost stretch of soul
Climbs the still clouds, or passes those that roll,
And loosed imagination soaring goes
High o'er his home and all his little woes.
ROBERT BLOOMFIELD.

A SUMMER EVENING'S MEDITATION.

" One sun by day, by night ten thousand shine." — YOUNG.

'T is past, — the sultry tyrant of the South
Has spent his short-lived rage ; more grateful hours
Move silent on ; the skies no more repel
The dazzled sight, but, with mild maiden beams
Of tempered lustre, court the cherished eye
To wander o'er their sphere ; where, hung aloft,
Dian's bright crescent, like a silver bow,
New strung in heaven, lifts its beamy horns
Impatient for the night, and seems to push
Her brother down the sky. Fair Venus shines
Even in the eye of day ; with sweetest beam
Propitious shines, and shakes a trembling flood
Of softened radiance with her dewy locks.
The shadows spread apace ; while meekened Eve,
Her cheek yet warm with blushes, slow retires
Through the Hesperian gardens of the West,
And shuts the gates of Day. 'T is now the hour
When Contemplation, from her sunless haunts,
The cool damp grotto, or the lonely depth
Of unpierced woods, where wrapt in solid shade
She mused away the gaudy hours of noon,
And fed on thoughts unripened by the sun,
Moves forward and with radiant finger points
To yon blue concave swelled by breath divine,
Where, one by one, the living eyes of heaven
Awake, quick kindling o'er the face of ether
One boundless blaze ; ten thousand trembling
    fires,
And dancing lustres, where the unsteady eye,
Restless and dazzled, wanders unconfined
O'er all this field of glories ; spacious field,
And worthy of the Master : He whose hand
With hieroglyphics elder than the Nile
Inscribed the mystic tablet ; hung on high
To public gaze, and said, Adore, O man !
The finger of thy God. From what pure wells
Of milky light, what soft o'erflowing urn,
Are all these lamps so filled ? — these friendly
    lamps,
Forever streaming o'er the azure deep
To point our path, and light us to our home.
How soft they slide along their lucid spheres !
And, silent as the foot of Time, fulfil
Their destined courses. Nature's self is hushed,
And but a scattered leaf, which rustles through
The thick-wove foliage, not a sound is heard
To break the midnight air ; though the raised ear,
Intently listening, drinks in every breath.

How deep the silence, yet how loud the praise !
But are they silent all ? or is there not
A tongue in every star that talks with man,
And wooes him to be wise ? nor wooes in vain :
This dead of midnight is the noon of thought,
And Wisdom mounts her zenith with the stars.
At this still hour the self-collected soul
Turns inward, and beholds a stranger there
Of high descent, and more than mortal rank ;
An embryo God ; a spark of fire divine,
Which must burn on for ages, when the sun
(Fair transitory creature of a day !)
Has closed his golden eye, and, wrapt in shades,
Forgets his wonted journey through the East.

Ye citadels of light, and seats of gods !
Perhaps my future home, from whence the soul,
Revolving periods past, may oft look back,
With recollected tenderness, on all
The various busy scenes she left below,
Its deep-laid projects and its strange events,
As on some fond and doting tale that soothed
Her infant hours, — O, be it lawful now
To tread the hallowed circle of your courts,
And with mute wonder and delighted awe
Approach your burning confines. Seized in
    thought,
On Fancy's wild and roving wing I sail,
From the green borders of the peopled earth,
And the pale moon, her duteous, fair attendant ;
From solitary Mars ; from the vast orb
Of Jupiter, whose huge gigantic bulk
Dances in ether like the lightest leaf ;
To the dim verge, the suburbs of the system,
Where cheerless Saturn midst his watery moons
Girt with a lucid zone, in gloomy pomp,
Sits like an exiled monarch : fearless thence
I launch into the trackless deeps of space,
Where, burning round, ten thousand suns appear,
Of elder beam, which ask no leave to shine
Of our terrestrial star, nor borrow light
From the proud regent of our scanty day ;
Sons of the morning, first-born of creation,
And only less than Him who marks their track
And guides their fiery wheels. Here must I stop,
Or is there aught beyond ? What hand unseen
Impels me onward through the glowing orbs
Of habitable nature, far remote,
To the dread confines of eternal night,
To solitudes of waste unpeopled space,
The deserts of creation, wide and wild ;
Where embryo systems and unkindled suns
Sleep in the womb of chaos ? Fancy droops,
And Thought, astonished, stops her bold career.
But, O thou mighty Mind ! whose powerful word
Said, "Thus let all things be," and thus they
    were,
Where shall I seek thy presence ? how unblamed
Invoke thy dread perfection ?

Have the broad eyelids of the morn beheld thee ?
Or does the beamy shoulder of Orion
Support thy throne ? O, look with pity down
On erring, guilty man ; not in thy names
Of terror clad ; not with those thunders armed
That conscious Sinai felt, when fear appalled
The scattered tribes ; thou hast a gentler voice,
That whispers comfort to the swelling heart,
Abashed, yet longing to behold her Maker !
But now my soul, unused to stretch her powers
In flight so daring, drops her weary wing,
And seeks again the known accustomed spot,
Drest up with sun and shade and lawns and
    streams,
A mansion fair and spacious for its guests,
And all replete with wonders.   Let me here,
Content and grateful, wait the appointed time,
And ripen for the skies : the hour will come
When all these splendors bursting on my sight
Shall stand unveiled, and to my ravished sense
Unlock the glories of the world unknown.
          ANNA LÆTITIA BARBAULD.

THE LATTER RAIN.

THE latter rain, — it falls in anxious haste
Upon the sun-dried fields and branches bare,
Loosening with searching drops the rigid waste
As if it would each root's lost strength repair ;
But not a blade grows green as in the spring ;
No swelling twig puts forth its thickening leaves ;
The robins only mid the harvests sing,
Pecking the grain that scatters from the sheaves ;
The rain falls still, — the fruit all ripened drops,
It pierces chestnut-burr and walnut-shell ;
The furrowed fields disclose the yellow crops ;
Each bursting pod of talents used can tell ;
And all that once received the early rain
Declare to man it was not sent in vain.
          JONES VERY.

AUTUMN.

THE autumn is old ;
The sear leaves are flying ;
He hath gathered up gold,
And now he is dying :
Old age, begin sighing !

The vintage is ripe ;
The harvest is heaping ;
But some that have sowed
Have no riches for reaping : —
Poor wretch, fall a-weeping !

The year 's in the wane ;
There is nothing adorning ;

The night has no eve,
And the day has no morning ;
Cold winter gives warning.

The rivers run chill ;
The red sun is sinking ;
And I am grown old,
And life is fast shrinking ;
Here 's enow for sad thinking !
          THOMAS HOOD.

AUTUMN.

THE warm sun is failing ; the bleak wind is
    wailing ;
The bare boughs are sighing ; the pale flowers
    are dying ;
    And the Year
On the earth, her death-bed, in shroud of leaves
    dead,
    Is lying.
    Come, months, come away,
    From November to May ;
    In your saddest array
    Follow the bier
    Of the dead, cold Year,
And like dim shadows watch by her sepulchre.

The chill rain is falling ; the nipt worm is
    crawling ;
The rivers are swelling ; the thunder is knelling
    For the year ;
The blithe swallows are flown, and the lizards
    each gone
    To his dwelling ;
    Come, months, come away ;
    Put on white, black, and gray ;
    Let your light sisters play, —
    Ye, follow the bier
    Of the dead, cold Year,
And make her grave green with tear on tear.
          PERCY BYSSHE SHELLEY

INDIAN SUMMER.

FROM gold to gray
Our mild sweet day
Of Indian summer fades too soon ;
    But tenderly
    Above the sea
Hangs, white and calm, the hunter's moon.

    In its pale fire,
    The village spire
Shows like the zodiac's spectral lance ;
    The painted walls
    Whereon it falls
Transfigured stand in marble trance !
          JOHN GREENLEAF WHITTIER.

INDIAN SUMMER.

WHEN leaves grow sear all things take sombre hue ;
The wild winds waltz no more the woodside
        through,
And all the faded grass is wet with dew.

A gauzy nebula films the pensive sky,
The golden bee supinély buzzes by,
In silent flocks the bluebirds southward fly.

The forests' cheeks are crimsoned o'er with shame,
The cynic frost enlaces every lane,
The ground with scarlet blushes is aflame !

The one we love grows lustrous-eyed and sad,
With sympathy too thoughtful to be glad,
While all the colors round are running mad.

The sunbeams kiss askant the sombre hill,
The naked woodbine climbs the window-sill,
The breaths that noon exhales are faint and chill.

The ripened nuts drop downward day by day,
Sounding the hollow tocsin of decay,
And bandit squirrels smuggle them away.

Vague sighs and scents pervade the atmosphere,
Sounds of invisible stirrings hum the ear,
The morning's lash reveals a frozen tear.

The hermit mountains gird themselves with mail,
Mocking the threshers with an echo flail,
The while the afternoons grow crisp and pale.

Inconstant Summer to the tropics flees,
And, as her rose-sails catch the amorous breeze,
Lo ! bare, brown Autumn trembles to her knees !

The stealthy nights encroach upon the days,
The earth with sudden whiteness is ablaze,
And all her paths are lost in crystal maze !

Tread lightly where the dainty violets blew,
Where the spring winds their soft eyes open flew ;
Safely they sleep the churlish winter through.

Though all life's portals are indiced with woe,
And frozen pearls are all the world can show,
Feel ! Nature's breath is warm beneath the snow.

Look up ! dear mourners ! Still the blue expanse,
Serenely tender, bends to catch thy glance,
Within thy tears sibyllic sunbeams dance !

With blooms full-sapped again will smile the land.
The fall is but the folding of His hand,
Anon with fuller glories to expand.

The dumb heart hid beneath the pulseless tree
Will throb again ; and then the torpid bee
Upon the ear will drone his drowsy glee.

So shall the truant bluebirds backward fly,
And all loved things that vanish or that die
Return to us in some sweet By-and-By !
                                ANONYMOUS.

NO !

No sun — no moon !
No morn — no noon —
No dawn — no dust — no proper time of day —
No sky — no earthly view —
No distance looking blue —
No road — no street — no "t'other side the
        way" —
No end to any Row —
No indications where the Crescents go —
No top to any steeple —
No recognitions of familiar people —
        No courtesies for showing 'em —
        No knowing 'em !
No travelling at all — no locomotion,
No inkling of the way — no notion —
        "No go" — by land or ocean —
No mail — no post —
No news from any foreign coast —
No park — no ring — no afternoon gentility —
        No company — no nobility —
No warmth, no cheerfulness, no healthful ease,
No comfortable feel in any member —
No shade, no shine, no butterflies, no bees,
No fruits, no flowers, no leaves, no birds,
        November !
                                THOMAS HOOD.

WINTER SONG.

SUMMER joys are o'er ;
Flowerets bloom no more,
Wintry winds are sweeping ;
Through the snow-drifts peeping,
        Cheerful evergreen
        Rarely now is seen.

Now no pluméd throng
Charms the wood with song ;
Ice-bound trees are glittering ;
Merry snow-birds, twittering,
        Fondly strive to cheer
        Scenes so cold and drear.

Winter, still I see
Many charms in thee, —
Love thy chilly greeting,
Snow-storms fiercely beating,
        And the dear delights
        Of the long, long nights.
        LUDWIG HÜLTY (German). Translation of
                CHARLES T. BROOKS.

WINTER.

FROM "THE WINTER MORNING WALK."

'T is morning ; and the sun, with ruddy orb
Ascending, fires the horizon ; while the clouds,
That crowd away before the driving wind,
More ardent as the disk emerges more,
Resemble most some city in a blaze,
Seen through the leafless wood. His slanting ray
Slides ineffectual down the snowy vale,
And, tingeing all with his own rosy hue,
From every herb and every spiry blade
Stretches a length of shadow o'er the field.
Mine, spindling into longitude immense,
In spite of gravity, and sage remark
That I myself am but a fleeting shade,
Provokes me to a smile. With eye askance
I view the muscular proportioned limb
Transformed to a lean shank. The shapeless pair,
As they designed to mock me, at my side
Take step for step ; and, as I near approach
The cottage, walk along the plastered wall,
Preposterous sight ! the legs without the man.
The verdure of the plain lies buried deep
Beneath the dazzling deluge ; and the bents,
And coarser grass, upspearing o'er the rest,
Of late unsightly and unseen, now shine
Conspicuous, and in bright apparel clad,
And, fledged with icy feathers, nod superb.
The cattle mourn in corners, where the fence
Screens them, and seem half petrified to sleep
In unrecumbent sadness. There they wait
Their wonted fodder ; not, like hungering man,
Fretful if unsupplied ; but silent, meek,
And, patient of the slow-paced swain's delay.
He from the stack carves out the accustomed load,
Deep plunging, and again deep plunging oft,
His broad keen knife into the solid mass :
Smooth as a wall the upright remnant stands,
With such undeviating and even force
He severs it away : no needless care
Lest storms should overset the leaning pile
Deciduous, or its own unbalanced weight.
Forth goes the woodman, leaving unconcerned
The cheerful haunts of men, to wield the axe
And drive the wedge in yonder forest drear,
From morn to eve his solitary task.
Shaggy and lean and shrewd with pointed ears,
And tail cropped short, half lurcher and half cur,
His dog attends him. Close behind his heel
Now creeps he slow ; and now, with many a frisk
Wide-scampering, snatches up the drifted snow
With ivory teeth, or ploughs it with his snout ;
Then shakes his powdered coat, and barks for joy.

Now from the roost, or from the neighboring pale,
Where, diligent to catch the first faint gleam
Of smiling day, they gossiped side by side,
Come trooping at the housewife's well-known call
The feathered tribes domestic. Half on wing,
And half on foot, they brush the fleecy flood,
Conscious and fearful of too deep a plunge.
The sparrows peep, and quit the sheltering eaves
To seize the fair occasion. Well they eye
The scattered grain, and thievishly resolved
To escape the impending famine, often scared
As oft return, a pert voracious kind.
Clean riddance quickly made, one only care
Remains to each, the search of sunny nook,
Or shed impervious to the blast. Resigned
To sad necessity, the cock foregoes
His wonted strut, and, wading at their head
With well-considered steps, seems to resent
His altered gait and stateliness retrenched.
How find the myriads, that in summer cheer
The hills and valleys with their ceaseless songs,
Due sustenance, or where subsist they now ?
Earth yields them naught ; the imprisoned worm
    is safe
Beneath the frozen clod ; all seeds of herbs
Lie covered close ; and berry-bearing thorns,
That feed the thrush (whatever some suppose),
Afford the smaller minstrels no supply.
The long protracted rigor of the year
Thins all their numerous flocks. In chinks and
    holes
Ten thousand seek an unmolested end,
As instinct prompts ; self-buried ere they die.
                              WILLIAM COWPER.

WINTER WALK AT NOON.

THE night was winter in his roughest mood,
The morning sharp and clear. But now at noon
Upon the southern side of the slant hills,
And where the woods fence off the northern blast,
The season smiles, resigning all its rage,
And has the warmth of May. The vault is blue
Without a cloud, and white without a speck
The dazzling splendor of the scene below.
Again the harmony comes o'er the vale ;
And through the trees I view the embattled tower,
Whence all the music. I again perceive
The soothing influence of the wafted strains,
And settle in soft musings as I tread
The walk, still verdant, under oaks and elms,
Whose outspread branches overarch the glade.

No noise is here, or none that hinders thought.
The redbreast warbles still, but is content
With slender notes, and more than half sup-
    pressed :
Pleased with his solitude, and flitting light
From spray to spray, where'er he rests he shakes
From many a twig the pendent drops of ice,
That tinkle in the withered leaves below.

Stillness, accompanied with sounds so soft,
Charms more than silence.   Meditation here
May think down hours to moments.   Here the
    heart
May give a useful lesson to the head,
And Learning wiser grow without his books.
                              WILLIAM COWPER.

WINTER SCENES.

THE keener tempests rise : and fuming dun
From all the livid east, or piercing north,
Thick clouds ascend ; in whose capacious womb
A vapory deluge lies, to snow congealed.
Heavy they roll their fleecy world along ;
And the sky saddens with the gathered storm.
Through the hushed air the whitening shower
    descends
At first thin wavering ; till at last the flakes
Fall broad and wide and fast, dimming the day
With a continual flow.   The cherished fields
Put on their winter robe of purest white.
'T is brightness all ; save where the new snow
    melts
Along the mazy current.   Low the woods
Bow their hoar head ; and, ere the languid sun
Faint from the west emits his evening ray,
Earth's universal face, deep hid and chill,
Is one wide dazzling waste, that buries wide
The works of man.   Drooping, the laborer-ox
Stands covered o'er with snow, and then demands
The fruit of all his toil.   The fowls of heaven,
Tamed by the cruel season, crowd around
The winnowing store, and claim the little boon
Which Providence assigns them.   One alone,
The redbreast, sacred to the household gods,
Wisely regardful of the embroiling sky,
In joyless fields and thorny thickets leaves
His shivering mates, and pays to trusted man
His annual visit.   Half afraid, he first
Against the window beats ; then, brisk, alights
On the warm hearth ; then, hopping o'er the
    floor,
Eyes all the smiling family askance,
And pecks, and starts, and wonders where he is :
Till, more familiar grown, the table-crumbs
Attract his slender feet.   The foodless wilds
Pour forth their brown inhabitants.   The hare,
Though timorous of heart, and hard beset
By death in various forms, dark snares, and dogs,
And more unpitying man, the garden seeks,
Urged on by fearless Want.   The bleating kind
Eye the bleak heaven, and next the glistening
    earth,
With looks of dumb despair ; then, sad dispersed,
Dig for the withered herb through heaps of snow.
                              JAMES THOMSON.

WHEN ICICLES HANG BY THE WALL.

FROM "LOVE'S LABOR 'S LOST."

WHEN icicles hang by the wall,
    And Dick the shepherd blows his nail,
And Tom bears logs into the hall,
    And milk comes frozen home in pail,
When blood is nipped, and ways be foul,
Then nightly sings the staring owl,
        To-who ;
To-whit, to-who, a merry note,
While greasy Joan doth keel the pot.

When all aloud the wind doth blow,
    And coughing drowns the parson's saw,
And birds sit brooding in the snow,
    And Marian's nose looks red and raw,
When roasted crabs hiss in the bowl,
Then nightly sings the staring owl,
        To-who ;
To-whit, to-who, a merry note,
While greasy Joan doth keel the pot.
                              SHAKESPEARE.

THE SNOW-STORM.

ANNOUNCED by all the trumpets of the sky,
Arrives the snow ; and, driving o'er the fields,
Seems nowhere to alight ; the whited air
Hides hills and woods, the river, and the heaven,
And veils the farm-house at the garden's end.
The sled and traveller stopped, the courier's feet
Delayed, all friends shut out, the housemates
    sit
Around the radiant fireplace, enclosed
In a tumultuous privacy of storm.
    Come see the north-wind's masonry.
Out of an unseen quarry, evermore
Furnished with tile, the fierce artificer
Curves his white bastions with projected roof
Round every windward stake or tree or door ;
Speeding, the myriad-handed, his wild work
So fanciful, so savage ; naught cares he
For number or proportion.   Mockingly,
On coop or kennel he hangs Parian wreaths ;
A swan-like form invests the hidden thorn ;
Fills up the farmer's lane from wall to wall,
Maugre the farmer's sighs ; and at the gate
A tapering turret overtops the work.
And when his hours are numbered, and the world
Is all his own, retiring as he were not,
Leaves, when the sun appears, astonished Art
To mimic in slow structures, stone by stone,
Built in an age, the mad wind's night-work,
The frolic architecture of the snow.
                              RALPH WALDO EMERSON.

THE SNOW-SHOWER.

STAND here by my side and turn, I pray,
  On the lake below thy gentle eyes ;
The clouds hang over it, heavy and gray,
  And dark and silent the water lies ;
And out of that frozen mist the snow
In wavering flakes begins to flow ;
      Flake after flake
They sink in the dark and silent lake.

See how in a living swarm they come
  From the chambers beyond that misty veil ;
Some hover awhile in air, and some
  Rush prone from the sky like summer hail.
All, dropping swiftly or settling slow,
Meet, and are still in the depths below ;
      Flake after flake
Dissolved in the dark and silent lake.

Here delicate snow-stars, out of the cloud,
  Come floating downward in airy play,
Like spangles dropped from the glistening crowd
  That whiten by night the Milky Way ;
There broader and burlier masses fall ;
The sullen water buries them all, —
      Flake after flake, —
All drowned in the dark and silent lake.

And some, as on tender wings they glide
  From their chilly birth-cloud, dim and gray,
Are joined in their fall, and, side by side,
  Come clinging along their unsteady way ;
As friend with friend, or husband with wife,
Makes hand in hand the passage of life ;
      Each mated flake
Soon sinks in the dark and silent lake.

Lo ! while we are gazing, in swifter haste
  Stream down the snows, till the air is white,
As, myriads by myriads madly chased,
  They fling themselves from their shadowy
      height.
The fair, frail creatures of middle sky,
What speed they make, with their grave so nigh ;
      Flake after flake
To lie in the dark and silent lake !

I see in thy gentle eyes a tear ;
  They turn to me in sorrowful thought ;
Thou thinkest of friends, the good and dear,
  Who were for a time, and now are not ;
Like these fair children of cloud and frost,
That glisten a moment and then are lost, —
      Flake after flake, —
All lost in the dark and silent lake.

Yet look again, for the clouds divide ;
  A gleam of blue on the water lies ;
And far away, on the mountain-side,
  A sunbeam falls from the opening skies.

But the hurrying host that flew between
The cloud and the water no more is seen ;
      Flake after flake
At rest in the dark and silent lake.
                WILLIAM CULLEN BRYANT.

SNOW. — A WINTER SKETCH.

THE blessed morn has come again ;
      The early gray
Taps at the slumberer's window-pane,
      And seems to say,
Break, break from the enchanter's chain,
      Away, away !

'T is winter, yet there is no sound
      Along the air
Of winds along their battle-ground ;
      But gently there
The snow is falling, — all around
      How fair, how fair !
                RALPH HOYT.

SNOW-FLAKES.

OUT of the bosom of the Air,
  Out of the cloud-folds of her garments shaken,
Over the woodlands brown and bare,
  Over the harvest-fields forsaken,
      Silent and soft and slow
      Descends the snow.

Even as our cloudy fancies take
  Suddenly shape in some divine expression,
Even as the troubled heart doth make
  In the white countenance confession,
      The troubled sky reveals
      The grief it feels.

This is the poem of the air,
  Slowly in silent syllables recorded ;
This is the secret of despair,
  Long in its cloudy bosom hoarded,
      Now whispered and revealed
      To wood and field.
                HENRY WADSWORTH LONGFELLOW.

A SNOW-STORM.

SCENE IN A VERMONT WINTER

I.

'T IS a fearful night in the winter time,
  As cold as it ever can be ;
The roar of the blast is heard like the chime
  Of the waves on an angry sea.

The moon is full ; but her silver light
The storm dashes out with its wings to-night ;
And over the sky from south to north
Not a star is seen, as the wind comes forth
  In the strength of a mighty glee.

II.

All day had the snow come down, — all day
  As it never came down before ;
And over the hills, at sunset, lay
  Some two or three feet, or more ;
The fence was lost, and the wall of stone ;
The windows blocked and the well-curbs gone ;
The haystack had grown to a mountain lift,
And the wood-pile looked like a monster drift,
  As it lay by the farmer's door.

The night sets in on a world of snow,
  While the air grows sharp and chill,
And the warning roar of a fearful blow
  Is heard on the distant hill ;
And the norther, see ! on the mountain peak
In his breath how the old trees writhe and shriek !
He shouts on the plain, ho-ho ! ho-ho !
He drives from his nostrils the blinding snow,
  And growls with a savage will.

III.

Such a night as this to be found abroad,
  In the drifts and the freezing air,
Sits a shivering dog, in the field, by the road,
  With the snow in his shaggy hair.
He shuts his eyes to the wind and growls ;
He lifts his head, and moans and howls ;
Then crouching low, from the cutting sleet,
His nose is pressed on his quivering feet, —
  Pray, what does the dog do there ?

A farmer came from the village plain, —
  But he lost the travelled way ;
And for hours he trod with might and main
  A path for his horse and sleigh ;
But colder still the cold winds blew,
And deeper still the deep drifts grew,
And his mare, a beautiful Morgan brown,
At last in her struggles floundered down,
  Where a log in a hollow lay.

In vain, with a neigh and a frenzied snort,
  She plunged in the drifting snow,
While her master urged, till his breath grew short,
  With a word and a gentle blow ;
But the snow was deep, and the tugs were tight ;
His hands were numb and had lost their might ;
So he wallowed back to his half-filled sleigh,
And strove to shelter himself till day,
  With his coat and the buffalo.

21

IV.

He has given the last faint jerk of the rein,
  To rouse up his dying steed ;
And the poor dog howls to the blast in vain
  For help in his master's need.
For a while he strives with a wistful cry
To catch a glance from his drowsy eye,
And wags his tail if the rude winds flap
The skirt of the buffalo over his lap,
  And whines when he takes no heed.

V.

The wind goes down and the storm is o'er, —
  'T is the hour of midnight, past ;
The old trees writhe and bend no more
  In the whirl of the rushing blast.
The silent moon with her peaceful light
Looks down on the hills with snow all white,
And the giant shadow of Camel's Hump,
The blasted pine and the ghostly stump,
  Afar on the plain are cast.

But cold and dead by the hidden log
  Are they who came from the town, —
The man in his sleigh, and his faithful dog,
  And his beautiful Morgan brown, —
In the wide snow-desert, far and grand,
With his cap on his head and the reins in his
    hand, —
The dog with his nose on his master's feet,
And the mare half seen through the crusted sleet,
  Where she lay when she floundered down.
                CHARLES GAMAGE EASTMAN.

O WINTER, WILT THOU NEVER GO!

O WINTER ! wilt thou never, never go !
O summer ! but I weary for thy coming,
Longing once more to hear the Luggie flow,
And frugal bees, laboriously humming.
Now the east-wind diseases the infirm,
And must crouch in corners from rough weather ;
Sometimes a winter sunset is a charm, —
When the fired clouds, compacted, blaze together,
And the large sun dips red behind the hills.
I, from my window, can behold this pleasure ;
And the eternal moon what time she fills
Her orb with argent, treading a soft measure,
With queenly motions of a bridal mood,
Through the white spaces of infinitude.
                DAVID GRAY.

FROM "HYMN ON THE SEASONS."

THESE, as they change, Almighty Father, these
Are but the varied God. The rolling year

Is full of thee.   Forth in the pleasing spring
Thy beauty walks, thy tenderness and love.
Wide flush the fields ; the softening air is balm ;
Echo the mountains round ; the forest smiles ;
And every sense and every heart is joy.
Then comes thy glory in the summer months,
With light and heat refulgent.   Then thy sun
Shoots full perfection through the swelling year ;
And oft thy voice in dreadful thunder speaks,
And oft at dawn, deep noon, or falling eve,
By brooks and groves in hollow-whispering gales.
Thy bounty shines in autumn unconfined,
And spreads a common feast for all that lives.
In winter awful thou ! with clouds and storms
Around thee thrown, tempest o'er tempest rolled,
Majestic darkness !   On the whirlwind's wing
Riding sublime, thou bid'st the world adore,
And humblest nature with thy northern blast.

Mysterious round ! what skill, what force divine,
Deep felt, in these appear ! a simple train,
Yet so delightful mixed, with such kind art,
Such beauty and beneficence combined ;
Shade, unperceived, so softening into shade ;
And all so forming an harmonious whole,
That, as they still succeed, they ravish still.
But wandering oft, with brute unconscious gaze,
Man marks not thee, marks not the mighty hand,
That, ever busy, wheels the silent spheres ;
Works in the secret deep ; shoots, steaming,
      thence
The fair profusion that o'erspreads the spring ;
Flings from the sun direct the flaming day ;
Feeds every creature ; hurls the tempest forth ;
And, as on earth this grateful change revolves,
With transport touches all the springs of life.

   Nature, attend ! join every living soul,
Beneath the spacious temple of the sky,
In adoration join ; and, ardent, raise
One general song ! To Him, ye vocal gales,
Breathe soft, whose spirit in your freshness
      breathes ;
O, talk of him in solitary glooms !
Where, o'er the rock, the scarcely waving pine
Fills the brown shade with a religious awe.
And ye whose bolder note is heard afar,
Who shake the astonished world, lift high to
      heaven
The impetuous song, and say from whom you
      rage.
His praise, ye brooks, attune, ye trembling rills ;
And let me catch it as I muse along.
Ye headlong torrents, rapid, and profound ;
Ye softer floods, that lead the humid maze
Along the vale ; and thou, majestic main,
A secret world of wonders in thyself,
Sound his stupendous praise, — whose greater
      voice
Or bids you roar, or bids your roarings fall.

Soft roll your incense, herbs, and fruits, and
      flowers,
In mingled clouds to him, — whose sun exalts,
Whose breath perfumes you, and whose pencil
      paints.
Ye forests bend, ye harvests wave, to him ;
Breathe your still song into the reaper's heart,
As home he goes beneath the joyous moon.
Ye that keep watch in heaven, as earth asleep
Unconscious lies, effuse your mildest beams,
Ye constellations, while your angels strike,
Amid the spangled sky, the silver lyre.
Great source of day ! best image here below
Of thy Creator, ever pouring wide,
From world to world, the vital ocean round,
On Nature write with every beam his praise.
The thunder rolls : be hushed the prostrate
      world ;
While cloud to cloud returns the solemn hymn.
Bleat out afresh, ye hills ; ye mossy rocks,
Retain the sound ; the broad responsive low,
Ye valleys, raise ; for the great Shepherd reigns,
And his unsuffering kingdom yet will come.
Ye woodlands all, awake : a boundless song
Burst from the groves ; and when the restless day,
Expiring, lays the warbling world asleep,
Sweetest of birds ! sweet Philomela, charm
The listening shades, and teach the night his
      praise.
Ye chief, for whom the whole creation smiles,
At once the head, the heart, and tongue of all,
Crown the great hymn ! in swarming cities vast,
Assembled men to the deep organ join
The long-resounding voice, oft breaking clear,
At solemn pauses, through the swelling bass ;
And, as each mingling flame increases each,
In one united ardor rise to heaven.
Or if you rather choose the rural shade,
And find a fane in every sacred grove,
There let the shepherd's flute, the virgin's lay,
The prompting seraph, and the poet's lyre,
Still sing the God of seasons as they roll.
For me, when I forget the darling theme,
Whether the blossom blows, the summer ray
Russets the plain, inspiring Autumn gleams,
Or winter rises in the blackening east,
Be my tongue mute, — my fancy paint no more,
And, dead to joy, forget my heart to beat !

   Should fate command me to the farthest verge
Of the green earth, to distant barbarous climes,
Rivers unknown to song, — where first the sun
Gilds Indian mountains, or his setting beam
Flames on the Atlantic isles, — 't is naught to me :
Since God is ever present, ever felt,
In the void waste as in the city full ;
And where he vital spreads there must be joy.
When even at last the solemn hour shall come,
And wing my mystic flight to future worlds,

Engᵈ by H.B. Hall & Sons, New York.

Wm Wordsworth

FORDS, HOWARD & HULBERT N.Y.

I cheerful will obey ; there, with new powers,
Will rising wonders sing : I cannot go
Where Universal Love not smiles around,
Sustaining all yon orbs, and all their suns ;
From seeming evil still educing good,
And better thence again, and better still,
In infinite progression.   But I lose
Myself in him, in light ineffable !
Come, then, expressive Silence, muse his praise.
JAMES THOMSON.

THE RAINBOW.

MY heart leaps up when I behold
    A rainbow in the sky ;
So was it when my life began,
So is it now I am a man,
So be it when I shall grow old,
    Or let me die !
The Child is father of the Man ;
And I could wish my days to be
Bound each to each by natural piety.
WILLIAM WORDSWORTH.

NEW ENGLAND IN WINTER.

FROM "SNOW-BOUND."

THE sun that brief December day
Rose cheerless over hills of gray,
And, darkly circled, gave at noon
A sadder light than waning moon.
Slow tracing down the thickening sky
Its mute and ominous prophecy,
A portent seeming less than threat,
It sank from sight before it set.
A chill no coat, however stout,
Of homespun stuff could quite shut out,
A hard, dull bitterness of cold,
    That checked, mid-vein, the circling race
    Of life-blood in the sharpened face,
The coming of the snow-storm told.
The wind blew east : we heard the roar
Of Ocean on his wintry shore,
And felt the strong pulse throbbing there
Beat with low rhythm our inland air.

Meanwhile we did our nightly chores, —
Brought in the wood from out of doors,
Littered the stalls, and from the mows
Raked down the herd's-grass for the cows ;
Heard the horse whinnying for his corn ;
And, sharply clashing horn on horn,
Impatient down the stanchion rows
The cattle shake their walnut bows ;
While, peering from his early perch
Upon the scaffold's pole of birch,

The cock his crested helmet bent
And down his querulous challenge sent.

Unwarmed by any sunset light
The gray day darkened into night,
A night made hoary with the swarm
And whirl-dance of the blinding storm,
As zigzag wavering to and fro
Crossed and recrossed the wingéd snow :
And ere the early bed-time came
The white drift piled the window-frame,
And through the glass the clothes-line posts
Looked in like tall and sheeted ghosts.

So all night long the storm roared on :
The morning broke without a sun ;
In tiny spherule traced with lines
Of Nature's geometric signs,
In starry flake, and pellicle,
All day the hoary meteor fell ;
And, when the second morning shone,
We looked upon a world unknown,
On nothing we could call our own.
Around the glistening wonder bent
The blue walls of the firmament,
No cloud above, no earth below, —
A universe of sky and snow !
The old familiar sights of ours
Took marvellous shapes ; strange domes and towers
Rose up where sty or corn-crib stood,
Or garden wall, or belt of wood ;
A smooth white mound the brush-pile showed,
A fenceless drift what once was road ;
The bridle-post an old man sat
With loose-flung coat and high cocked hat ;
The well-curb had a Chinese roof ;
And even the long sweep, high aloof,
In its slant splendor, seemed to tell
Of Pisa's leaning miracle.

A prompt, decisive man, no breath
Our father wasted : "Boys, a path !"
Well pleased, (for when did farmer boy
Count such a summons less than joy ?)
Our buskins on our feet we drew ;
    With mittened hands, and caps drawn low,
    To guard our necks and ears from snow,
We cut the solid whiteness through.
And, where the drift was deepest, made
A tunnel walled and overlaid
With dazzling crystal : we had read
Of rare Aladdin's wondrous cave,
And to our own his name we gave,
With many a wish the luck were ours
To test his lamp's supernal powers.
We reached the barn with merry din,
And roused the prisoned brutes within.
The old horse thrust his long head out,

And grave with wonder gazed about ;
The cock his lusty greeting said,
And forth his speckled harem led ;
The oxen lashed their tails, and hooked,
And mild reproach of hunger looked ;
The hornéd patriarch of the sheep,
Like Egypt's Amun roused from sleep,
Shook his sage head with gesture mute,
And emphasized with stamp of foot.

All day the gusty north-wind bore
The loosening drift its breath before ;
Low circling round its southern zone,
The sun through dazzling snow-mist shone.
No church-bell lent its Christian tone
To the savage air, no social smoke
Curled over woods of snow-hung oak.
A solitude made more intense
By dreary-voicéd elements,
The shrieking of the mindless wind,
The moaning tree-boughs swaying blind,
And on the glass the unmeaning beat
Of ghostly finger-tips of sleet.
Beyond the circle of our hearth
No welcome sound of toil or mirth
Unbound the spell, and testified
Of human life and thought outside.
We minded that the sharpest ear
The buried brooklet could not hear,
The music of whose liquid lip
Had been to us companionship,
And, in our lonely life, had grown
To have an almost human tone.
As night drew on, and, from the crest
Of wooded knolls that ridged the west,
The sun, a snow-blown traveller, sank
From sight beneath the smothering bank,
We piled, with care, our nightly stack
Of wood against the chimney-back, —
The oaken log, green, huge, and thick,
And on its top the stout back-stick ;
The knotty forestick laid apart,
And filled between with curious art
The ragged brush ; then, hovering near,
We watched the first red blaze appear,
Heard the sharp crackle, caught the gleam
On whitewashed wall and sagging beam,
Until the old, rude-furnished room
Burst, flower-like, into rosy bloom ;
While radiant with a mimic flame
Outside the sparkling drift became,
And through the bare-boughed lilac-tree
Our own warm hearth seemed blazing free.
The crane and pendent trammels showed,
The Turks' heads on the andirons glowed ;
While childish fancy, prompt to tell
The meaning of the miracle,
Whispered the old rhyme : " *Under the tree,*

When fire outdoors burns merrily,
There the witches are making tea."

The moon above the eastern wood
Shone at its full ; the hill-range stood
Transfigured in the silver flood,
Its blown snows flashing cold and keen,
Dead white, save where some sharp ravine
Took shadow, or the sombre green
Of hemlocks turned to pitchy black
Against the whiteness at their back.
For such a world and such a night
Most fitting that unwarming light,
Which only seemed where'er it fell
To make the coldness visible.

Shut in from all the world without,
We sat the clean-winged hearth about.
Content to let the north-wind roar
In baffled rage at pane and door,
While the red logs before us beat
The frost-line back with tropic heat ;
And ever, when a louder blast
Shook beam and rafter as it passed,
The merrier up its roaring draught
The great throat of the chimney laughed,
The house-dog on his paws outspread
Laid to the fire his drowsy head,
The cat's dark silhouette on the wall
A couchant tiger's seemed to fall ;
And, for the winter fireside meet,
Between the andirons' straddling feet,
The mug of cider simmered slow,
The apples sputtered in a row,
And, close at hand, the basket stood
With nuts from brown October's wood.
                    JOHN GREENLEAF WHITTIER

A DROP OF DEW.

See how the orient dew,
Shed from the bosom of the morn
    Into the blowing roses,
(Yet careless of its mansion new
For the clear region where 't was born)
    Round in itself encloses,
And in its little globe's extent
Frames, as it can, its native element.
    How it the purple flower does slight,
        Scarce touching where it lies ;
    But gazing back upon the skies,
        Shines with a mournful light,
            Like its own tear,
Because so long divided from the sphere ;
    Restless it rolls, and unsecure,
        Trembling, lest it grow impure ;
Till the warm sun pities its pain,

And to the skies exhales it back again.
  So the soul, that drop, that ray,
Of the clear fountain of eternal day,
Could it within the human flower be seen,
  Remembering still its former height,
  Shuns the sweet leaves and blossoms green,
  And, recollecting its own light,
Does, in its pure and circling thoughts, express
The greater heaven in a heaven less.
    In how coy a figure wound,
    Every way it turns away;
    So the world excluding round,
    Yet receiving in the day.
    Dark beneath, but bright above;
    Here disdaining, there in love.
  How loose and easy hence to go !
  How girt and ready to ascend !
  Moving but on a point below,
  It all about does upwards bend.
Such did the manna's sacred dew distil,
White and entire, although congealed and chill, —
Congealed on earth, but does, dissolving, run
Into the glories of the Almighty sun.
ANDREW MARVELL.

NATURE.

The bubbling brook doth leap when I come by,
Because my feet find measure with its call ;
The birds know when the friend they love is nigh,
For I am known to them, both great and small.
The flower that on the lonely hillside grows
Expects me there when spring its bloom has given ;
And many a tree and bush my wanderings knows,
And e'en the clouds and silent stars of heaven ;
For he who with his Maker walks aright,
Shall be their lord as Adam was before ;
His ear shall catch each sound with new delight,
Each object wear the dress that then it wore ;
And he, as when erect in soul he stood,
Hear from his Father's lips that all is good.
JONES VERY.

UNDER THE GREENWOOD TREE.

FROM "AS YOU LIKE IT."

Under the greenwood tree
  Who loves to lie with me,
And tune his merry note
  Unto the sweet bird's throat,
Come hither, come hither, come hither :
    Here shall he see
    No enemy,
But winter and rough weather.

Who doth ambition shun,
  And loves to live i' the sun,
Seeking the food he eats,
  And pleased with what he gets,
Come hither, come hither, come hither ·
    Here shall he see
    No enemy,
But winter and rough weather.

JAQUES. I 'll give you a verse to this note,
that I made yesterday in despite of my invention.
AMIENS. And I 'll sing it.
JAQ. Thus it goes : —

    If it do come to pass,
    That any man turn ass,
    Leaving his wealth and ease,
    A stubborn will to please,
  Ducdame, ducdame, ducdame ।
    Here shall he see
    Gross fools as he,
  An if he will come to me.

AMI. What 's that "ducdame" ?
JAQ. 'T is a Greek invocation, to call fools
into a circle. I 'll go sleep, if I can ; if I cannot,
I 'll rail against all the first-born of Egypt.
SHAKESPEARE.

THE GREENWOOD.

O, when 't is summer weather,
And the yellow bee, with fairy sound,
The waters clear is humming round,
And the cuckoo sings unseen,
And the leaves are waving green, —
    O, then 't is sweet,
    In some retreat,
To hear the murmuring dove,
With those whom on earth alone we love,
And to wind through the greenwood together.

But when 't is winter weather,
    And crosses grieve,
    And friends deceive,
    And rain and sleet
    The lattice beat, —
    O, then 't is sweet
    To sit and sing
Of the friends with whom, in the days of spring,
We roamed through the greenwood together.
WILLIAM LISLE BOWLES.

RETIREMENT.

INSCRIPTION IN A HERMITAGE.

Beneath this stony roof reclined,
I soothe to peace my pensive mind ;
And while, to shade my lowly cave,
Embowering elms their umbrage wave,

And while the maple dish is mine, —
The beechen cup, unstained with wine, —
I scorn the gay licentious crowd,
Nor heed the toys that deck the proud.

Within my limits, lone and still,
The blackbird pipes in artless trill ;
Fast by my couch, congenial guest,
The wren has wove her mossy nest ;
From busy scenes and brighter skies,
To lurk with innocence, she flies,
Here hopes in safe repose to dwell,
Nor aught suspects the sylvan cell.

At morn I take my customed round,
To mark how buds yon shrubby mound,
And every opening primrose count,
That trimly paints my blooming mount ;
Or o'er the sculptures, quaint and rude,
That grace my gloomy solitude,
I teach in winding wreaths to stray
Fantastic ivy's gadding spray.

At eve, within yon studious nook,
I ope my brass-embosséd book,
Portrayed with many a holy deed
Of martyrs, crowned with heavenly meed.
Then, as my taper waxes dim,
Chant, ere I sleep, my measured hymn,
And, at the close, the gleams behold
Of parting wings, be-dropt with gold.

While such pure joys my bliss create,
Who but would smile at guilty state ?
Who but would wish his holy lot
In calm oblivion's humble grot ?
Who but would cast his pomp away,
To take my staff, and amice gray ;
And to the world's tumultuous stage
Prefer the blameless hermitage ?

                 THOMAS WARTON.

COME TO THESE SCENES OF PEACE.

COME to these scenes of peace,
Where, to rivers murmuring,
The sweet birds all the summer sing,
Where cares and toil and sadness cease !
Stranger, does thy heart deplore
Friends whom thou wilt see no more ?
Does thy wounded spirit prove
Pangs of hopeless, severed love ?
Thee the stream that gushes clear,
Thee the birds that carol near,
Shall soothe, as silent thou dost lie
And dream of their wild lullaby ;
Come to bless these scenes of peace,
Where cares and toil and sadness cease.

           WILLIAM LISLE BOWLES.

SEE, O SEE!

SEE, O see !
How every tree,
Every bower,
Every flower,
A new life gives to others' joys ;
While that I
Grief-stricken lie,
Nor can meet
With any sweet
But what faster mine destroys.
What are all the senses' pleasures
When the mind has lost all measures ?

Hear, O hear !
How sweet and clear
The nightingale
And water's fall
In concert join for others' ear ;
While to me,
For harmony,
Every air
Echoes despair,
And every drop provokes a tear.
What are all the senses' pleasures
When the soul has lost all measures ?

                 LORD BRISTOL.

DOVER CLIFF.

FROM "KING LEAR."

COME on, sir ; here's the place : stand still.
    How fearful
And dizzy 't is, to cast one's eyes so low !
The crows and choughs that wing the midway air
Show scarce so gross as beetles : half-way down
Hangs one that gathers samphire, — dreadful
      trade !
Methinks he seems no bigger than his head :
The fishermen, that walk upon the beach,
Appear like mice ; and yon tall anchoring bark,
Diminished to her cock ; her cock, a buoy
Almost too small for sight ; the murmuring surge,
That on the unnumbered idle pebbles chafes,
Cannot be heard so high. — I 'll look no more ;
Lest my brain turn, and the deficient sight
Topple down headlong.   SHAKESPEARE.

THE OCEAN.

SONNET.

THE ocean at the bidding of the moon
Forever changes with his restless tide :
Flung shoreward now, to be regathered soon
With kingly pauses of reluctant pride,

And semblance of return.   Anon from home
He issues forth anew, high ridged and free, —
The gentlest murmur of his seething foam
Like armies whispering where great echoes be.
O, leave me here upon this beach to rove,
Mute listener to that sound so grand and lone !
A glorious sound, deep drawn, and strongly
    thrown,
And reaching those on mountain heights above,
To British ears, (as who shall scorn to own ?)
A tutelar fond voice, a saviour tone of love.
CHARLES TENNYSON.

SONG OF THE BROOK.

I COME from haunts of coot and hern :
    I make a sudden sally
And sparkle out among the fern,
    To bicker down a valley.

By thirty hills I hurry down,
    Or slip between the ridges,
By twenty thorps, a little town,
    And half a hundred bridges.

Till last by Philip's farm I flow
    To join the brimming river,
For men may come and men may go,
    But I go on forever.

I chatter over stony ways,
    In little sharps and trebles,
I bubble into eddying bays,
    I babble on the pebbles.

With many a curve my banks I fret
    By many a field and fallow,
And many a fairy foreland set
    With willow-weed and mallow.

I chatter, chatter, as I flow
    To join the brimming river ;
For men may come and men may go,
    But I go on forever.

I wind about, and in and out,
    With here a blossom sailing,
And here and there a lusty trout,
    And here and there a grayling,

And here and there a foamy flake
    Upon me, as I travel
With many a silvery waterbreak
    Above the golden gravel,

And draw them all along, and flow
    To join the brimming river,
For men may come and men may go,
    But I go on forever.

I steal by lawns and grassy plots :
    I slide by hazel covers ;
I move the sweet forget-me-nots
    That grow for happy lovers.

I slip, I slide, I gloom, I glance,
    Among my skimming swallows !
I make the netted sunbeam dance
    Against my sandy shallows.

I murmur under moon and stars
    In brambly wildernesses ;
I linger by my shingly bars ;
    I loiter round my cresses ;

And out again I curve and flow
    To join the brimming river,
For men may come and men may go,
    But I go on forever.
ALFRED TENNYSON.

GRONGAR HILL.

[The Vale of the Towy embraces, in its winding course of fifteen miles, some of the loveliest scenery of South Wales.   If it be less cultivated than the Vale of Usk, its woodland views are more romantic and frequent.   The neighborhood is historic and poetic ground.   From Grongar Hill the eye discovers traces of a Roman Camp ; Golden Grove, the home of Jeremy Taylor, is on the opposite side of the river ; Merlin's chair recalls Spenser ; and a farm-house near the foot of Llangumnor Hill brings back the memory of its once genial occupant, Richard Steele.   Spenser places the cave of Merlin among the dark woods of Dinevawr.]

SILENT nymph, with curious eye !
Who, the purple evening, lie
On the mountain's lonely van,
Beyond the noise of busy man,
Painting fair the form of things,
While the yellow linnet sings,
Or the tuneful nightingale
Charms the forest with her tale, —
Come, with all thy various hues,
Come, and aid thy sister Muse.
Now, while Phœbus, riding high,
Gives lustre to the land and sky,
Grongar Hill invites my song, —
Draw the landscape bright and strong ;
Grongar, in whose mossy cells
Sweetly musing Quiet dwells ;
Grongar, in whose silent shade,
For the modest Muses made,
So oft I have, the evening still,
At the fountain of a rill,
Sat upon a flowery bed,
With my hand beneath my head,
While strayed my eyes o'er Towy's flood,
Over mead and over wood,
From house to house, from hill to hill,
Till Contemplation had her fill.
About his checkered sides I wind,

And leave his brooks and meads behind,
And groves and grottos where I lay,
And vistas shooting beams of day.
Wide and wider spreads the vale,
As circles on a smooth canal.
The mountains round, unhappy fate !
Sooner or later, of all height,
Withdraw their summits from the skies,
And lessen as the others rise.
Still the prospect wider spreads,
Adds a thousand woods and meads ;
Still it widens, widens still,
And sinks the newly risen hill.

Now I gain the mountain's brow ;
What a landscape lies below !
No clouds, no vapors intervene ;
But the gay, the open scene
Does the face of Nature show
In all the hues of heaven's bow !
And, swelling to embrace the light,
Spreads around beneath the sight.

Old castles on the cliffs arise,
Proudly towering in the skies ;
Rushing from the woods, the spires
Seem from hence ascending fires ;
Half his beams Apollo sheds
On the yellow mountain-heads,
Gilds the fleeces of the flocks,
And glitters on the broken rocks.

Below me trees unnumbered rise,
Beautiful in various dyes :
The gloomy pine, the poplar blue,
The yellow beech, the sable yew,
The slender fir that taper grows,
The sturdy oak with broad-spread boughs ;
And beyond, the purple grove,
Haunt of Phyllis, queen of love !
Gaudy as the opening dawn,
Lies a long and level lawn,
On which a dark hill, steep and high,
Holds and charms the wandering eye ;
Deep are his feet in Towy's flood :
His sides are clothed with waving wood ;
And ancient towers crown his brow,
That cast an awful look below ;
Whose ragged walls the ivy creeps,
And with her arms from falling keeps ;
So both, a safety from the wind
In mutual dependence find.
'T is now the raven's bleak abode ;
'T is now the apartment of the toad ;
And there the fox securely feeds ;
And there the poisonous adder breeds,
Concealed in ruins, moss, and weeds ;
While, ever and anon, there fall
Huge heaps of hoary, mouldered wall ;
Yet Time has seen — that lifts the low
And level lays the lofty brow —

Has seen this broken pile complete,
Big with the vanity of state.
But transient is the smile of Fate !
A little rule, a little sway,
A sunbeam in a winter's day,
Is all the proud and mighty have
Between the cradle and the grave.

And see the rivers, how they run
Through woods and meads, in shade and sun
Sometimes swift, sometimes slow, —
Wave succeeding wave, they go
A various journey to the deep,
Like human life to endless sleep !
Thus is Nature's vesture wrought
To instruct our wandering thought ;
Thus she dresses green and gay
To disperse our cares away.

Ever charming, ever new,
When will the landscape tire the view !
The fountain's fall, the river's flow ;
The woody valleys, warm and low ;
The windy summit, wild and high,
Roughly rushing on the sky ;
The pleasant seat, the ruined tower,
The naked rock, the shady bower ;
The town and village, dome and farm, —
Each gives each a double charm,
As pearls upon an Ethiop's arm.

See on the mountain's southern side,
Where the prospect opens wide,
Where the evening gilds the tide,
How close and small the hedges lie ;
What streaks of meadow cross the eye !
A step, methinks, may pass the stream,
So little distant dangers seem ;
So we mistake the Future's face,
Eyed through Hope's deluding glass ;
As yon summits, soft and fair,
Clad in colors of the air,
Which to those who journey near,
Barren, brown, and rough appear ;
Still we tread the same coarse way, —
The present 's still a cloudy day.

O, may I with myself agree,
And never covet what I see ;
Content me with an humble shade,
My passions tamed, my wishes laid ;
For while our wishes wildly roll,
We banish quiet from the soul.
'T is thus the busy beat the air,
And misers gather wealth and care.

Now, even now, my joys run high,
As on the mountain turf I lie ;
While the wanton Zephyr sings,
And in the vale perfumes his wings ;
While the waters murmur deep ;
While the shepherd charms his sheep ;
While the birds unbounded fly,

And with music fill the sky,
Now, even now, my joys run high.
  Be full, ye courts ; be great who will ;
Search for Peace with all your skill ;
Open wide the lofty door,
Seek her on the marble floor.
In vain you search ; she is not here !
In vain you search the domes of Care !
Grass and flowers Quiet treads,
On the meads and mountain-heads,
Along with Pleasure, — close allied,
Ever by each other's side ;
And often, by the murmuring rill,
Hears the thrush, while all is still
Within the groves of Grongar Hill.
                              JOHN DYER.

AFTON WATER.

FLOW gently, sweet Afton, among thy green braes,
Flow gently, I 'll sing thee a song in thy praise ;
My Mary 's asleep by thy murmuring stream,
Flow gently, sweet Afton, disturb not her dream.

Thou stock-dove whose echo resounds through
    the glen,
Ye wild whistling blackbirds in yon thorny den,
Thou green-crested lapwing, thy screaming for-
    bear,
I charge you disturb not my slumbering fair.

How lofty, sweet Afton, thy neighboring hills,
Far marked with the courses of clear winding rills ;
There daily I wander as noon rises high,
My flocks and my Mary's sweet cot in my eye.

How pleasant thy banks and green valleys below,
Where wild in the woodlands the primroses blow ;
There oft as mild evening weeps over the lea,
The sweet-scented birk shades my Mary and me.

Thy crystal stream, Afton, how lovely it glides,
And winds by the cot where my Mary resides ;
How wanton thy waters her snowy feet lave,
As, gathering sweet flowerets, she stems thy clear
    wave.

Flow gently, sweet Afton, among thy green braes,
Flow gently, sweet river, the theme of my lays ;
My Mary 's asleep by thy murmuring stream,
Flow gently, sweet Afton, disturb not her dream.
                          ROBERT BURNS.

THE SHADED WATER.

WHEN that my mood is sad, and in the noise
  And bustle of the crowd I feel rebuke,
I turn my footsteps from its hollow joys
  And sit me down beside this little brook ;

The waters have a music to mine ear
It glads me much to hear.

It is a quiet glen, as you may see,
  Shut in from all intrusion by the trees,
That spread their giant branches, broad and free,
  The silent growth of many centuries ;
And make a hallowed time for hapless moods,
A sabbath of the woods.

Few know its quiet shelter, — none, like me,
  Do seek it out with such a fond desire,
Poring in idlesse mood on flower and tree,
  And listening as the voiceless leaves respire, —
When the far-travelling breeze, done wandering,
Rests here his weary wing.

And all the day, with fancies ever new,
  And sweet companions from their boundless
      store,
Of merry elves bespangled all with dew,
  Fantastic creatures of the old-time lore,
Watching their wild but unobtrusive play,
I fling the hours away.

A gracious couch — the root of an old oak
  Whose branches yield it moss and canopy —
Is mine, and, so it be from woodman's stroke
  Secure, shall never be resigned by me ;
It hangs above the stream that idly flies,
Heedless of any eyes.

There, with eye sometimes shut, but upward bent,
  Sweetly I muse through many a quiet hour,
While every sense on earnest mission sent,
  Returns, thought laden, back with bloom and
      flower
Pursuing, though rebuked by those who moil,
A profitable toil.

And still the waters trickling at my feet
  Wind on their way with gentlest melody,
Yielding sweet music, which the leaves repeat,
  Above them, to the gay breeze gliding by, —
Yet not so rudely as to send one sound
Through the thick copse around.

Sometimes a brighter cloud than all the rest
  Hangs o'er the archway opening through the
      trees,
Breaking the spell that, like a slumber, pressed
  On my worn spirit its sweet luxuries, —
And with awakened vision upward bent,
I watch the firmament.

How like — its sure and undisturbed retreat,
  Life's sanctuary at last, secure from storm —
To the pure waters trickling at my feet
  The bending trees that overshade my form !
So far as sweetest things of earth may seem
Like those of which we dream.

Such, to my mind, is the philosophy
  The young bird teaches, who, with sudden flight,
Sails far into the blue that spreads on high,
  Until I lose him from my straining sight, —
With a most lofty discontent to fly,
Upward, from earth to sky.
WILLIAM GILMORE SIMMS.

YARROW UNVISITED.

FROM Stirling Castle we had seen
  The mazy Forth unravelled ;
Had trod the banks of Clyde and Tay,
  And with the Tweed had travelled ;
And when we came to Clovenford,
  Then said my " winsome Marrow,"
" Whate'er betide, we 'll turn aside,
  And see the braes of Yarrow."

" Let Yarrow folk, frae Selkirk town,
  Who have been buying, selling,
Go back to Yarrow ; 't is their own, —
  Each maiden to her dwelling !
On Yarrow's banks let herons feed,
  Hares couch, and rabbits burrow !
But we will downward with the Tweed,
  Nor turn aside to Yarrow.

" There 's Galla Water, Leader Haughs,
  Both lying right before us ;
And Dryborough, where with chiming Tweed
  The lintwhites sing in chorus ;
There 's pleasant Teviot-dale, a land
  Made blithe with plough and harrow :
Why throw away a needful day
  To go in search of Yarrow ?

" What 's Yarrow but a river bare,
  That glides the dark hills under ?
There are a thousand such elsewhere,
  As worthy of your wonder."
Strange words they seemed, of slight and scorn ;
  My true-love sighed for sorrow,
And looked me in the face, to think
  I thus could speak of Yarrow !

" O, green," said I, " are Yarrow's holms,
  And sweet is Yarrow flowing !
Fair hangs the apple frae the rock,
  But we will leave it growing.
O'er hilly path and open strath
  We 'll wander Scotland thorough ;
But, though so near, we will not turn
  Into the dale of Yarrow.

" Let beeves and homebred kine partake
  The sweets of Burn Mill meadow ;
The swan still on St. Mary's Lake
  Float double, swan and shadow !

We will not see them ; will not go
  To-day, nor yet to-morrow ;
Enough, if in our hearts we know
  There 's such a place as Yarrow.

" Be Yarrow stream unseen, unknown !
  It must, or we shall rue it :
We have a vision of our own ;
  Ah ! why should we undo it ?
The treasured dreams of times long past,
  We 'll keep them, winsome Marrow !
For when we 're there, although 't is fair,
  'T will be another Yarrow !

" If Care with freezing years should come,
  And wandering seem but folly, —
Should we be loath to stir from home,
  And yet be melancholy, —
Should life be dull, and spirits low,
  'T will soothe us in our sorrow,
That earth has something yet to show, —
  The bonny holms of Yarrow !"
WILLIAM WORDSWORTH.

YARROW VISITED.

AND is this — Yarrow ? — This the stream
  Of which my fancy cherished,
So faithfully, a waking dream ?
  An image that hath perished !
O that some minstrel's harp were near,
  To utter notes of gladness,
And chase this silence from the air,
  That fills my heart with sadness !

Yet why ? — a silvery current flows
  With uncontrolled meanderings ;
Nor have these eyes by greener hills
  Been soothed in all my wanderings.
And, through her depths, St. Mary's Lake
  Is visibly delighted ;
For not a feature of those hills
  Is in the mirror slighted.

A blue sky bends o'er Yarrow vale,
  Save where that pearly whiteness
Is round the rising sun diffused, —
  A tender, hazy brightness ;
Mild dawn of promise ! that excludes
  All profitless dejection ;
Though not unwilling here to admit
  A pensive recollection.

Where was it that the famous Flower
  Of Yarrow Vale lay bleeding ?
His bed perchance was yon smooth mound
  On which the herd is feeding ;

And haply from this crystal pool,
　Now peaceful as the morning,
The water-wraith ascended thrice,
　And gave his doleful warning.

Delicious is the lay that sings
　The haunts of happy lovers, —
The path that leads them to the grove,
　The leafy grove that covers ;
And pity sanctifies the verse
　That paints, by strength of sorrow,
The unconquerable strength of love :
　Bear witness, rueful Yarrow !

But thou, that didst appear so fair
　To fond imagination,
Dost rival in the light of day
　Her delicate creation.
Meek loveliness is round thee spread, —
　A softness still and holy,
The grace of forest charms decayed,
　And pastoral melancholy.

That region left, the vale unfolds
　Rich groves of lofty stature,
With Yarrow winding through the pomp
　Of cultivated nature ;
And, rising from those lofty groves,
　Behold a ruin hoary !
The shattered front of Newark's towers,
　Renowned in border story.

Fair scenes for childhood's opening bloom,
　For sportive youth to stray in ;
For manhood to enjoy his strength,
　And age to wear away in !
Yon cottage seems a bower of bliss,
　A covert for protection
Of tender thoughts, that nestle there, —
　The brood of chaste affection.

How sweet, on this autumnal day,
　The wildwood fruits to gather,
And on my true-love's forehead plant
　A crest of blooming heather !
And what if I inwreathed my own !
　'T were no offence to reason ;
The sober hills thus deck their brows
　To meet the wintry season.

I see, — but not by sight alone,
　Loved Yarrow, have I won thee ;
A ray of fancy still survives, —
　Her sunshine plays upon thee !
Thy ever-youthful waters keep
　A course of lively pleasure ;
And gladsome notes my lips can breathe,
　Accordant to the measure.

The vapors linger round the heights ;
　They melt, and soon must vanish ;
One hour is theirs, nor more is mine, —
　Sad thought, which I would banish
But that I know, where'er I go,
　Thy genuine image, Yarrow,
Will dwell with me, to heighten joy,
　And cheer my mind in sorrow.
　　　　　　　　WILLIAM WORDSWORTH.

THE BUGLE.

FROM "THE PRINCESS."

THE splendor falls on castle walls
　And snowy summits old in story :
The long light shakes across the lakes,
　And the wild cataract leaps in glory.
Blow, bugle, blow, set the wild echoes flying,
Blow, bugle ; answer, echoes, dying, dying, dying.

O hark ! O hear ! how thin and clear,
　And thinner, clearer, farther going !
O sweet and far, from cliff and scar,
　The horns of Elfland faintly blowing !
Blow, let us hear the purple glens replying :
Blow, bugle ; answer, echoes, dying, dying, dying.

O love, they die in yon rich sky,
　They faint on hill or field or river ·
Our echoes roll from soul to soul,
　And grow forever and forever.
Blow, bugle, blow, set the wild echoes flying,
And answer, echoes, answer, dying, dying, dying.
　　　　　　　　ALFRED TENNYSON.

THE RHINE.

FROM "CHILDE HAROLD."

THE castled crag of Drachenfels
　Frowns o'er the wide and winding Rhine,
Whose breast of waters broadly swells
　Between the banks which bear the vine,
And hills all rich with blossomed trees,
　And fields which promise corn and wine,
And scattered cities crowning these,
　Whose far white walls along them shine,
Have strewed a scene, which I should see
With double joy wert *thou* with me.

And peasant girls with deep-blue eyes,
　And hands which offer early flowers,
Walk smiling o'er this paradise ;
　Above, the frequent feudal towers
Through green leaves lift their walls of gray,
　And many a rock which steeply lowers,

And noble arch in proud decay,
  Look o'er this vale of vintage-bowers ;
But one thing want these banks of Rhine, —
Thy gentle hand to clasp in mine!

I send the lilies given to me :
  Though long before thy hand they touch
I know that they must withered be,
  But yet reject them not as such ;
For I have cherished them as dear,
  Because they yet may meet thine eye,
And guide thy soul to mine even here,
  When thou behold'st them drooping nigh,
And know'st them gathered by the Rhine,
And offered from my heart to thine !

The river nobly foams and flows,
  The charm of this enchanted ground,
And all its thousand turns disclose
  Some fresher beauty varying round :
The haughtiest breast its wish might bound
  Through life to dwell delighted here ;
Nor could on earth a spot be found
  To nature and to me so dear,
Could thy dear eyes in following mine
Still sweeten more these banks of Rhine ?
                                        BYRON.

ON THE RHINE.

'T WAS morn, and beautiful the mountain's
    brow —
  Hung with the clusters of the bending vine —
  Shone in the early light, when on the Rhine
We sailed and heard the waters round the prow
In murmurs parting ; varying as we go,
Rocks after rocks come forward and retire,
As some gray convent wall or sunlit spire
Starts up along the banks, unfolding slow.
Here castles, like the prisons of despair,
  Frown as we pass ! — there, on the vineyard's
    side,
  The bursting sunshine pours its streaming
    tide ;
While Grief, forgetful amid scenes so fair,
Counts not the hours of a long summer's day,
Nor heeds how fast the prospect winds away.
                          WILLIAM LISLE BOWLES.

ALPINE HEIGHTS.

On Alpine heights the love of God is shed ;
  He paints the morning red,
  The flowerets white and blue,
  And feeds them with his dew.
On Alpine heights a loving Father dwells.

On Alpine heights, o'er many a fragrant heath,
  The loveliest breezes breathe ;
  So free and pure the air,
  His breath seems floating there.
On Alpine heights a loving Father dwells.

On Alpine heights, beneath his mild blue eye,
  Still vales and meadows lie ;
  The soaring glacier's ice
  Gleams like a paradise.
On Alpine heights a loving Father dwells.

Down Alpine heights the silvery streamlets flow ;
  There the bold chamois go ;
  On giddy crags they stand,
  And drink from his own hand.
On Alpine heights a loving Father dwells.

On Alpine heights, in troops all white as snow,
  The sheep and wild goats go ;
  There, in the solitude,
  He fills their hearts with food.
On Alpine heights a loving Father dwells.

On Alpine heights the herdsman tends his herd ;
  His Shepherd is the Lord ;
  For he who feeds the sheep
  Will sure his offspring keep.
On Alpine heights a loving Father dwells.
                      KRUMMACHER (German). Translation
                          of CHARLES T. BROOKS.

THE GREAT ST. BERNARD.

NIGHT was again descending, when my mule,
That all day long had climbed among the clouds,
Higher and higher still, as by a stair
Let down from heaven itself, transporting me,
Stopped, to the joy of both, at that low door
So near the summit of the Great St. Bernard ;
That door which ever on its hinges moved
To them that knocked, and nightly sends abroad
Ministering spirits.   Lying on the watch,
Two dogs of grave demeanor welcomed me,
All meekness, gentleness, though large of limb ;
And a lay-brother of the Hospital,
Who, as we toiled below, had heard by fits
The distant echoes gaining on his ear,
Came and held fast my stirrup in his hand,
While I alighted.

On the same rock beside it stood the church,
Reft of its cross, not of its sanctity ;
The vesper-bell, for 't was the vesper-hour,
Duly proclaiming through the wilderness,
" All ye who hear, whatever be your work,
Stop for an instant, — move your lips in prayer ! "
And just beneath it, in that dreary dale,

If dale it might be called so near to heaven,
A little lake, where never fish leaped up,
Lay like a spot of ink amid the snow ;
A star, the only one in that small sky,
On its dead surface glimmering. 'T was a scene
Resembling nothing I had left behind,
As though all worldly ties were now dissolved ; —
And to incline the mind still more to thought,
To thought and sadness, on the eastern shore
Under a beetling cliff stood half in shadow
A lonely chapel destined for the dead,
For such as, having wandered from their way,
Had perished miserably. Side by side,
Within they lie, a mournful company
All in their shrouds, no earth to cover them ;
Their features full of life, yet motionless
In the broad day, nor soon to suffer change,
Though the barred windows, barred against the
        wolf,
Are always open !   SAMUEL ROGERS.

THE RECOLLECTION.

Now the last day of many days
All beautiful and bright as thou,
The loveliest and the last, is dead,
Rise, Memory, and write its praise !
Up, do thy wonted work ! come, trace
The epitaph of glory fled,
For now the earth has changed its face,
A frown is on the heaven's brow.

We wandered to the pine forest
    That skirts the ocean's foam ;
The lightest wind was in its nest,
    The tempest in its home.
The whispering waves were half asleep,
    The clouds were gone to play,
And on the bosom of the deep
    The smile of Heaven lay ;
It seemed as if the hour were one
    Sent from beyond the skies,
Which scattered from above the sun
    A light of Paradise !

We paused amid the pines that stood
    The giants of the waste,
Tortured by storms to shapes as rude
    As serpents interlaced, —
And soothed by every azure breath
    That under heaven is blown
To harmonies and hues beneath,
    As tender as its own :
Now all the tree-tops lay asleep
    Like green waves on the sea,
As still as in the silent deep
    The ocean-woods may be.

How calm it was ! — the silence there
    By such a chain was bound,
That even the busy woodpecker
    Made stiller by her sound
The inviolable quietness ;
    The breath of peace we drew
With its soft motion made not less
    The calm that round us grew.
There seemed from the remotest seat
    Of the wide mountain waste
To the soft flower beneath our feet
    A magic circle traced,
A spirit interfused around,
    A thrilling silent life ;
To momentary peace it bound
    Our mortal nature's strife ; —
And still I felt the centre of
    The magic circle there
Was one fair Form that filled with love
    The lifeless atmosphere.

We paused beside the pools that lie
    Under the forest bough ;
Each seemed as 't were a little sky
    Gulfed in a world below ;
A firmament of purple light
    Which in the dark earth lay,
More boundless than the depth of night
    And purer than the day, —
In which the lovely forests grew
    As in the upper air,
More perfect both in shape and hue
    Than any spreading there.
There lay the glade and neighboring lawn,
    And through the dark green wood
The white sun twinkling like the dawn
    Out of a speckled cloud.
Sweet views which in our world above
    Can never well be seen
Were imaged by the water's love
    Of that fair forest green :
And all was interfused beneath
    With an Elysian glow,
An atmosphere without a breath,
    A softer day below.

Like one beloved, the scene had lent
    To the dark water's breast
Its every leaf and lineament
    With more than truth exprest ;
Until an envious wind crept by,
    Like an unwelcome thought
Which from the mind's too faithful eye
    Blots one dear image out.
— Though thou art ever fair and kind,
    The forests ever green,
Less oft is peace in Shelley's mind
    Than calm in waters seen !
                    PERCY BYSSHE SHELLEY.

TO THE WEST-WIND.

O WILD west-wind, thou breath of autumn's be-
  ing,
Thou from whose unseen presence the leaves dead
Are driven, like ghosts from an enchanter fleeing,
Yellow, and black, and pale, and hectic red,
Pestilence-stricken multitudes : O thou
Who chariotest to their dark wintry bed
The wingéd seeds, where they lie cold and low,
Each like a corpse within its grave, until
Thine azure sister of the spring shall blow
Her clarion o'er the dreaming earth, and fill
(Driving sweet buds like flocks to feed in air)
With living hues and odors plain and hill :
Wild spirit, which art moving everywhere ;
Destroyer and preserver ; hear, O hear !

Thou on whose stream, mid the steep sky's
  commotion,
Loose clouds like earth's decaying leaves are shed,
Shook from the tangled boughs of heaven and
  ocean,
Angels of rain and lightning ; there are spread
On the blue surface of thine airy surge,
Like the bright hair uplifted from the head
Of some fierce Mænad, even from the dim verge
Of the horizon to the zenith's height,
The locks of the approaching storm. Thou dirge
Of the dying year, to which this closing night
Will be the dome of a vast sepulchre,
Vaulted with all thy congregated might
Of vapors, from whose solid atmosphere
Black rain and fire and hail will burst : O hear !

Thou who didst waken from his summer dreams
The blue Mediterranean, where he lay
Lulled by the coil of his crystalline streams
Beside a pumice isle in Baiæ's bay,
And saw in sleep old palaces and towers
Quivering within the wave's intenser day,
All overgrown with azure moss and flowers
So sweet, the sense faints picturing them ! Thou
For whose path the Atlantic's level powers
Cleave themselves into chasms, while far below
The sea-blooms and the oozy woods which wear
The sapless foliage of the ocean know
Thy voice, and suddenly grow gray with fear,
And tremble, and despoil themselves : O hear !

If I were a dead leaf thou mightest bear ;
If I were a swift cloud to fly with thee ;
A wave to pant beneath thy power, and share
The impulse of thy strength, only less free
Than thou, O uncontrollable ! If even
I were as in my boyhood, and could be
The comrade of thy wanderings over heaven,
As then, when to outstrip the skyey speed

Scarce seemed a vision, I would ne'er have striven
As thus with thee in prayer in my sore need.
O, lift me as a wave, a leaf, a cloud !
I fall upon the thorns of life ! I bleed !
A heavy weight of hours has chained and bowed
One too like thee : tameless and swift and proud.

Make me thy lyre, even as the forest is :
What if my leaves are falling like its own !
The tumult of thy mighty harmonies
Will take from both a deep autumnal tone,
Sweet though in sadness. Be thou, spirit fierce,
My spirit ! be thou me, impetuous one !
Drive my dead thoughts over the universe
Like withered leaves to quicken a new birth ;
And, by the incantation of this verse,
Scatter, as from an unextinguished hearth
Ashes and sparks, my words among mankind !
Be through my lips to unawakened earth
The trumpet of a prophecy ! O wind,
If winter comes, can spring be far behind ?
PERCY BYSSHE SHELLEY.

WHAT THE WINDS BRING.

WHICH is the wind that brings the cold ?
  The north-wind, Freddy, and all the snow ;
And the sheep will scamper into the fold
  When the north begins to blow.

Which is the wind that brings the heat ?
  The south-wind, Katy ; and corn will grow,
And peaches redden for you to eat,
  When the south begins to blow.

Which is the wind that brings the rain ?
  The east-wind, Arty ; and farmers know
That cows come shivering up the lane
  When the east begins to blow.

Which is the wind that brings the flowers ?
  The west-wind, Bessy ; and soft and low
The birdies sing in the summer hours
  When the west begins to blow.
EDMUND CLARENCE STEDMAN.

A VIEW ACROSS THE ROMAN CAMPAGNA.

1861.

I.

OVER the dumb campagna-sea,
  Out in the offing through mist and rain,
St. Peter's Church heaves silently
  Like a mighty ship in pain,
Facing the tempest with struggle and strain.

II.

Motionless waifs of ruined towers,
  Soundless breakers of desolate land !
The sullen surf of the mist devours
  That mountain-range upon either hand,
  Eaten away from its outline grand.

III.

And over the dumb campagna-sea
  Where the ship of the Church heaves on to wreck,
Alone and silent as God must be
  The Christ walks ! — Ay, but Peter's neck
  Is stiff to turn on the foundering deck.

IV.

Peter, Peter, if such be thy name,
  Now leave the ship for another to steer,
And proving thy faith evermore the same
  Come forth, tread out through the dark and drear,
  Since He who walks on the sea is here !

V.

Peter, Peter ! — he does not speak, —
  He is not as rash as in old Galilee.
Safer a ship, though it toss and leak,
  Than a reeling foot on a rolling sea !
  — And he's got to be round in the girth, thinks
    he.

VI.

Peter, Peter ! — he does not stir, —
  His nets are heavy with silver fish :
He reckons his gains, and is keen to infer,
  . . "The broil on the shore, if the Lord should
    wish, —
  But the sturgeon goes to the Cæsar's dish."

VII.

Peter, Peter, thou fisher of men,
  Fisher of fish wouldst thou live instead, —
Haggling for pence with the other Ten,
  Cheating the market at so much a head,
  Griping the bag of the traitor dead ?

VIII.

At the triple crow of the Gallic cock
  Thou weep'st not, thou, though thine eyes be
    dazed :
What bird comes next in the tempest shock ?
  . . Vultures ! See, — as when Romulus gazed,
  To inaugurate Rome for a world amazed !
                ELIZABETH BARRETT BROWNING.

THE DESCENT.

  . . . . My mule refreshed, his bells
Jingled once more, the signal to depart,
And we set out in the gray light of dawn,
Descending rapidly, — by waterfalls
Fast frozen, and among huge blocks of ice
That in their long career had stopt midway ;
At length, unchecked, unbidden, he stood still,
And all his bells were muffled. Then my guide,
Lowering his voice, addressed me : "Through
    this chasm
On, and say nothing, — for a word, a breath,
Stirring the air, may loosen and bring down
A winter's snow, — enough to overwhelm
The horse and foot that, night and day, defiled
Along this path to conquer at Marengo.
                SAMUEL ROGERS.

VIEW FROM THE EUGANEAN HILLS,
    NORTH ITALY.

Many a green isle needs must be
In the deep wide sea of misery,
Or the mariner, worn and wan,
Never thus could voyage on
Day and night, and night and day,
Drifting on his dreary way,
With the solid darkness black
Closing round his vessel's track ;
Whilst above, the sunless sky,
Big with clouds, hangs heavily,
And behind the tempest fleet
Hurries on with lightning feet,
Riving sail and cord and plank
Till the ship has almost drank
Death from the o'er-brimming deep ;
And sinks down, down, like that sleep
When the dreamer seems to be
Weltering through eternity ;
And the dim low line before
Of a dark and distant shore
Still recedes, as ever still
Longing with divided will,
But no power to seek or shun,
He is ever drifted on
O'er the unreposing wave,
To the haven of the grave.

Ay, many flowering islands lie
In the waters of wide agony :
To such a one this morn was led
My bark, by soft winds piloted.
— Mid the mountains Euganean
I stood listening to the pæan
With which the legioned rooks did hail
The sun's uprise majestical :
Gathering round with wings all hoar,
Through the dewy mist they soar
Like gray shades, till the eastern heaven
Bursts, and then, as clouds of even,
Flecked with fire and azure, lie
In the unfathomable sky,
So their plumes of purple grain

Starred with drops of golden rain
Gleam above the sunlight woods,
As in silent multitudes
On the morning's fitful gale
Through the broken mist they sail ;
And the vapors cloven and gleaming
Follow down the dark steep streaming,
Till all is bright and clear and still
Round the solitary hill.

Beneath is spread like a green sea
The waveless plain of Lombardy,
Bounded by the vaporous air,
Islanded by cities fair ;
Underneath day's azure eyes,
Ocean's nursling, Venice, lies, —
A peopled labyrinth of walls,
Amphitrite's destined halls,
Which her hoary sire now paves
With his blue and beaming waves.
Lo ! the sun upsprings behind,
Broad, red, radiant, half reclined
On the level quivering line
Of the waters crystalline ;
And before that chasm of light,
As within a furnace bright,
Column, tower, and dome, and spire
Shine like obelisks of fire,
Pointing with inconstant motion
From the altar of dark ocean
To the sapphire-tinted skies ;
As the flames of sacrifice
From the marble shrines did rise
As to pierce the dome of gold
Where Apollo spoke of old.

Sun-girt city ! thou hast been
Ocean's child, and then his queen ;
Now is come a darker day,
And thou soon must be his prey,
If the power that raised thee here
Hallow so thy watery bier.
A less drear ruin then than now
With thy conquest-branded brow
Stooping to the slave of slaves
From thy throne among the waves,
Wilt thou be, when the sea-mew
Flies, as once before it flew,
O'er thine isles depopulate,
And all is in its ancient state,
Save where many a palace-gate,
With green sea-flowers overgrown
Like a rock of ocean's own,
Topples o'er the abandoned sea
As the tides change sullenly.
The fisher on his watery way
Wandering at the close of day
Will spread his sail and seize his oar
Till he pass the gloomy shore,

Lest thy dead should, from their sleep
Bursting o'er the starlight deep,
Lead a rapid mask of death
O'er the waters of his path.

Noon descends around me now :
'T is the noon of autumn's glow,
When a soft and purple mist
Like a vaporous amethyst,
Or an air-dissolvéd star
Mingling light and fragrance, far
From the curved horizon's bound
To the point of heaven's profound,
Fills the overflowing sky ;
And the plains that silent lie
Underneath ; the leaves unsodden
Where the infant frost has trodden
With his morning-wingéd feet,
Whose bright print is gleaming yet ;
And the red and golden vines
Piercing with their trellised lines
The rough, dark-skirted wilderness ;
The dun and bladed grass no less,
Pointing from this hoary tower
In the windless air ; the flower
Glimmering at my feet ; the line
Of the olive-sandalled Apennine
In the south dimly islanded ;
And the Alps, whose snows are spread
High between the clouds and sun ;
And of living things each one ;
And my spirit, which so long
Darkened this swift stream of song, —
Interpenetrated lie
By the glory of the sky ;
Be it love, light, harmony,
Odor, or the soul of all
Which from heaven like dew doth fall,
Or the mind which feeds this verse
Peopling the lone universe.

Noon descends, and after noon -
Autumn's evening meets me soon,
Leading the infantine moon
And that one star, which to her
Almost seems to minister
Half the crimson light she brings
From the sunset's radiant springs :
And the soft dreams of the morn
(Which like wingéd winds had borne
To that silent isle, which lies
Mid remembered agonies,
The frail bark of this lone being)
Pass, to other sufferers fleeing,
And its ancient pilot, Pain,
Sits beside the helm again.
Other flowering isles must be
In the sea of life and agony ;

Thomas Moore

FORDS, HOWARD & HULBERT, N.Y.

Other spirits float and flee
O'er that gulf ; even now, perhaps,
On some rock the wild wave wraps,
With folding winds they waiting sit
For my bark, to pilot it
To some calm and blooming cove,
Where for me, and those I love,
May a windless bower be built,
Far from passion, pain, and guilt,
In a dell mid lawny hills
Which the wild sea-murmur fills,
And soft sunshine, and the sound
Of old forests echoing round,
And the light and smell divine
Of all flowers that breathe and shine.
— We may live so happy there,
That the spirits of the air,
Envying us, may even entice
To our healing paradise
The polluting multitude ;
But their rage would be subdued
By that clime divine and calm,
And the winds whose wings rain balm
On the uplifted soul, and leaves
Under which the bright sea heaves ;
While each breathless interval
In their whisperings musical
The inspired soul supplies
With its own deep melodies ;
And the love which heals all strife
Circling, like the breath of life,
All things in that sweet abode
With its own mild brotherhood.
They, not it, would change ; and soon
Every sprite beneath the moon
Would repent its envy vain,
And the earth grow young again !
                    PERCY BYSSHE SHELLEY.

THE ORIENT.

FROM "THE BRIDE OF ABYDOS."

KNOW ye the land where the cypress and myrtle
  Are emblems of deeds that are done in their
    clime,
Where the rage of the vulture, the love of the
    turtle,
  Now melt into sorrow, now madden to crime ?
Know ye the land of the cedar and vine,
Where the flowers ever blossom, the beams ever
    shine :
Where the light wings of Zephyr, oppressed with
    perfume,
Wax faint o'er the gardens of Gúl in her bloom !
Where the citron and olive are fairest of fruit,
And the voice of the nightingale never is mute,
Where the tints of the earth, and the hues of the sky,

In color though varied, in beauty may vie,
And the purple of ocean is deepest in dye ;
Where the virgins are soft as the roses they twine,
And all, save the spirit of man, is divine ?
'T is the clime of the East ; 't is the land of the
    Sun, —
Can he smile on such deeds as his children have
    done ?
O, wild as the accents of lover's farewell
Are the hearts which they bear and the tales
    which they tell !
                    BYRON.

SYRIA.

FROM "PARADISE AND THE PERI."

  Now, upon Syria's land of roses
Softly the light of eve reposes,
And, like a glory, the broad sun
Hangs over sainted Lebanon ;
Whose head in wintry grandeur towers,
  And whitens with eternal sleet,
While summer, in a vale of flowers,
  Is sleeping rosy at his feet.

To one who looked from upper air
O'er all the enchanted regions there,
How beauteous must have been the glow,
The life, how sparkling from below !
Fair gardens, shining streams, with ranks
Of golden melons on their banks,
More golden where the sunlight falls ; —
Gay lizards, glittering on the walls
Of ruined shrines, busy and bright
As they were all alive with light ;
And, yet more splendid, numerous flocks
Of pigeons, settling on the rocks,
With their rich restless wings, that gleam
Variously in the crimson beam
Of the warm west, — as if inlaid
With brilliants from the mine, or made
Of tearless rainbows, such as span
The unclouded skies of Peristan !
And then, the mingling sounds that come,
Of shepherd's ancient reed, with hum
Of the wild bees of Palestine,
  Banqueting through the flowery vales ; —
And, Jordan, those sweet banks of thine,
  And woods, so full of nightingales !
                    THOMAS MOORE.

THE VALE OF CASHMERE.

FROM "THE LIGHT OF THE HAREM."

WHO has not heard of the Vale of Cashmere,
  With its roses the brightest that earth ever
    gave,

22

Its temples, and grottos, and fountains as clear
  As the love-lighted eyes that hang over their
    wave ?

O, to see it at sunset, — when warm o'er the lake
  Its splendor at parting a summer eve throws,
Like a bride, full of blushes, when lingering to
  take
    A last look of her mirror at night ere she
    goes ! —
When the shrines through the foliage are gleam-
  ing half shown,
And each hallows the hour by some rites of its
  own.
Here the music of prayer from a minaret swells,
  Here the Magian his urn full of perfume is
    swinging,
And here, at the altar, a zone of sweet bells
    Round the waist of some fair Indian dancer is
    ringing.
Or to see it by moonlight, — when mellowly
  shines
The light o'er its palaces, gardens, and shrines ;
When the waterfalls gleam like a quick fall of
  stars,
And the nightingale's hymn from the Isle of
  Chenars
Is broken by laughs and light echoes of feet
From the cool shining walks where the young
  people meet.
Or at morn, when the magic of daylight awakes
A new wonder each minute as slowly it breaks,
Hills, cupolas, fountains, called forth every one
Out of darkness, as they were just born of the
  sun.
When the spirit of fragrance is up with the day,
From his harem of night-flowers stealing away ;
And the wind, full of wantonness, wooes like a
  lover
The young aspen-trees till they tremble all over.
When the east is as warm as the light of first
  hopes,
  And day, with its banner of radiance unfurled,
Shines in through the mountainous portal that
  opes,
    Sublime, from that valley of bliss to the world !
             THOMAS MOORE.

NATURE'S CHAIN.

FROM THE "ESSAY ON MAN."

Look round our world ; behold the chain of love
Combining all below and all above,
See plastic nature working to this end,
The single atoms each to other tend,
Attract, attracted to, the next in place,
Formed and impelled its neighbor to embrace.
See matter next, with various life endued,
Press to one centre still, the general good.
See dying vegetables life sustain,
See live dissolving vegetate again :
All forms that perish other forms supply
(By turns we catch the vital breath, and die) ;
Like bubbles on the sea of matter borne,
They rise, they break, and to that sea return.
Nothing is foreign ; parts relate to whole ;
One all-extending, all-preserving Soul
Connects each being, greatest with the least ;
Made beast in aid of man, and man of beast ;
All served, all serving ; nothing stands alone ;
The chain holds on, and where it ends, unknown.
  Has God, thou fool ! worked solely for thy good,
Thy joy, thy pastime, thy attire, thy food ?
Who for thy table feeds the wanton fawn,
For him as kindly spread the flowery lawn.
Is it for thee the lark ascends and sings ?
Joy tunes his voice, joy elevates his wings.
Is it for thee the linnet pours his throat ?
Loves of his own and raptures swell the note.
The bounding steed you pompously bestride
Shares with his lord the pleasure and the pride.
Is thine alone the seed that strews the plain ?
The birds of heaven shall vindicate their grain.
Thine the full harvest of the golden year ?
Part pays, and justly, the deserving steer :
The hog that ploughs not, nor obeys thy call,
Lives on the labors of this lord of all.
  Know, nature's children all divide her care ;
The fur that warms a monarch warmed a bear.
While man exclaims, "See all things for my use !"
"See man for mine !" replies a pampered goose :
And just as short of reason he must fall
Who thinks all made for one, not one for all.
  Grant that the powerful still the weak control ;
Be man the wit and tyrant of the whole ·
Nature that tyrant checks ; he only knows,
And helps, another creature's wants and woes.
Say, will the falcon, stooping from above,
Smit with her varying plumage, spare the dove ?
Admires the jay the insect's gilded wings ?
Or hears the hawk when Philomela sings ?
Man cares for all : to birds he gives his woods,
To beasts his pastures, and to fish his floods ;
For some his interest prompts him to provide,
For more his pleasure, yet for more his pride :
All feed on one vain patron, and enjoy
The extensive blessing of his luxury.
That very life his learned hunger craves,
He saves from famine, from the savage saves ;
Nay, feasts the animal he dooms his feast,
And, till he ends the being, makes it blest ;
Which sees no more the stroke, or feels the pain,
Than favored man by touch ethereal slain.
The creature had his feast of life before ;
Thou too must perish when thy feast is o'er !
             ALEXANDER POPE.

THE LION'S RIDE.

[Translation.]

THE lion is the desert's king; through his domain so wide
Right swiftly and right royally this night he means to ride.
By the sedgy brink, where the wild herds drink, close couches the grim chief;
The trembling sycamore above whispers with every leaf.

At evening, on the Table Mount, when ye can see no more
The changeful play of signals gay; when the gloom is speckled o'er
With kraal fires; when the Caffre wends home through the lone karroo;
When the boshbok in the thicket sleeps, and by the stream the gnu;

Then bend your gaze across the waste, — what see ye? The giraffe,
Majestic, stalks towards the lagoon, the turbid lymph to quaff;
With outstretched neck and tongue adust, he kneels him down to cool
His hot thirst with a welcome draught from the foul and brackish pool.

A rustling sound, a roar, a bound, — the lion sits astride
Upon his giant courser's back. Did ever king so ride?
Had ever king a steed so rare, caparisons of state
To match the dappled skin whereon that rider sits elate?

In the muscles of the neck his teeth are plunged with ravenous greed;
His tawny mane is tossing round the withers of the steed.
Up leaping with a hollow yell of anguish and surprise,
Away, away, in wild dismay, the camel-leopard flies.

His feet have wings; see how he springs across the moonlit plain!
As from their sockets they would burst, his glaring eyeballs strain;
In thick black streams of purling blood, full fast his life is fleeting;
The stillness of the desert hears his heart's tumultuous beating.

Like the cloud that, through the wilderness, the path of Israel traced, —
Like an airy phantom, dull and wan, a spirit of the waste, —

From the sandy sea uprising, as the water-spout from ocean,
A whirling cloud of dust keeps pace with the courser's fiery motion.

Croaking companion of their flight, the vulture whirs on high;
Below, the terror of the fold, the panther fierce and sly,
And hyenas foul, round graves that prowl, join in the horrid race;
By the footprints wet with gore and sweat, their monarch's course they trace.

They see him on his living throne, and quake with fear, the while
With claws of steel he tears piecemeal his cushion's painted pile.
On! on! no pause, no rest, giraffe, while life and strength remain!
The steed by such a rider backed may madly plunge in vain.

Reeling upon the desert's verge, he falls, and breathes his last;
The courser, stained with dust and foam, is the rider's fell repast.
O'er Madagascar, eastward far, a faint flush is descried: —
Thus nightly, o'er his broad domain, the king of beasts doth ride.

FERDINAND FREILIGRATH (German).

THE BLOOD HORSE.

GAMARRA is a dainty steed,
Strong, black, and of a noble breed,
Full of fire, and full of bone,
With all his line of fathers known;
Fine his nose, his nostrils thin,
But blown abroad by the pride within!
His mane is like a river flowing,
And his eyes like embers glowing
In the darkness of the night,
And his pace as swift as light.

Look, — how round his straining throat
Grace and shifting beauty float;
Sinewy strength is in his reins,
And the red blood gallops through his veins, —
Richer, redder, never ran
Through the boasting heart of man.
He can trace his lineage higher
Than the Bourbon dare aspire, —
Douglas, Guzman, or the Guelph,
Or O'Brien's blood itself!

He, who hath no peer, was born
Here, upon a red March morn ;
But his famous fathers dead
Were Arabs all, and Arab-bred,
And the last of that great line
Trod like one of a race divine !
And yet, — he was but friend to one,
Who fed him at the set of sun
By some lone fountain fringed with green ;
With him, a roving Bedouin,
He lived (none else would he obey
Through all the hot Arabian day),
And died untamed upon the sands
Where Balkh amidst the desert stands !

BARRY CORNWALL.

LAMBS AT PLAY.

SAY, ye that know, ye who have felt and seen
Spring's morning smiles, and soul-enlivening
    green, —
Say, did you give the thrilling transport way,
Did your eye brighten, when young lambs at play
Leaped o'er your path with animated pride,
Or gazed in merry clusters by your side ?
Ye who can smile — to wisdom no disgrace —
At the arch meaning of a kitten's face ;
If spotless innocence and infant mirth
Excites to praise, or gives reflection birth ;
In shades like these pursue your favorite joy,
Midst nature's revels, sports that never cloy.
A few begin a short but vigorous race,
And indolence, abashed, soon flies the place :
Thus challenged forth, see thither, one by one,
From every side, assembling playmates run ;
A thousand wily antics mark their stay,
A starting crowd, impatient of delay ;
Like the fond dove from fearful prison freed,
Each seems to say, "Come, let us try our speed " ;
Away they scour, impetuous, ardent, strong,
The green turf trembling as they bound along
Adown the slope, then up the hillock climb,
Where every mole-hill is a bed of thyme,
Then, panting, stop ; yet scarcely can refrain,
A bird, a leaf, will set them off again :
Or, if a gale with strength unusual blow,
Scattering the wild-brier roses into snow,
Their little limbs increasing efforts try ;
Like the torn flower, the fair assemblage fly.
Ah, fallen rose ! sad emblem of their doom ;
Frail as thyself, they perish while they bloom !

ROBERT BLOOMFIELD.

FOLDING THE FLOCKS.

SHEPHERDS all, and maidens fair,
Fold your flocks up ; for the air

'Gins to thicken, and the sun
Already his great course hath run.
See the dew-drops, how they kiss
Every little flower that is ;
Hanging on their velvet heads,
Like a string of crystal beads.
See the heavy clouds low falling
And bright Hesperus down calling
The dead night from underground ;
At whose rising, mists unsound,
Damps and vapors, fly apace,
And hover o'er the smiling face
Of these pastures ; where they come,
Striking dead both bud and bloom.
Therefore from such danger lock
Every one his lovéd flock ;
And let your dogs lie loose without,
Lest the wolf come as a scout
From the mountain, and ere day,
Bear a lamb or kid away ;
Or the crafty, thievish fox,
Break upon your simple flocks.
To secure yourself from these,
Be not too secure in ease ;
So shall you good shepherds prove,
And deserve your master's love.
Now, good night ! may sweetest slumbers
And soft silence fall in numbers
On your eyelids.   So farewell :
Thus I end my evening knell.

BEAUMONT and FLETCHER.

TO A MOUSE,

ON TURNING HER UP IN HER NEST WITH THE PLOUGH NOVEMBER, 1785.

WEE, sleekit, cow'rin', tim'rous beastie,
O, what a panic 's in thy breastie !
Thou need na start awa' sae hasty,
    Wi' bickering brattle !
I wad be laith to rin an' chase thee,
    Wi' murd'ring pattle !

I 'm truly sorry man's dominion
Has broken nature's social union,
An' justifies that ill opinion
    Which makes thee startle
At me, thy poor earth-born companion,
    An' fellow-mortal !

I doubt na, whyles, but thou may thieve ;
What then ? poor beastie, thou maun live !
A daimen icker in a thrave
    'S a sma' request ;
I 'll get a blessin' wi' the laive,
    And never miss 't !

Thy wee bit housie, too, in ruin !
Its silly wa's the win's are strewin' !
An' naething now to big a new ane
    O' foggage green !
An' bleak December's winds ensuin',
      Baith snell and keen !

Thou saw the fields laid bare an' waste,
An' weary winter comin' fast,
An' cozie here, beneath the blast,
    Thou thought to dwell,
Till, crash ! the cruel coulter past
    Out through thy cell.

That wee bit heap o' leaves an' stibble
Has cost thee mony a weary nibble !
Now thou 's turned out for a' thy trouble,
    But house or hald,
To thole the winter's sleety dribble,
    An' cranreuch cauld !

But, Mousie, thou art no thy lane,
In proving foresight may be vain :
The best-laid schemes o' mice an' men
    Gang aft a-gley,
An' lea'e us naught but grief and pain,
    For promised joy.

Still thou art blest, compared wi' me !
The present only toucheth thee :
But, och ! I backward cast my e'e
    On prospects drear ;
An' forward, though I canna see,
    I guess an' fear.
              ROBERT BURNS.

THE SONGSTERS.

FROM "THE SEASONS."

    .... UPSPRINGS the lark,
Shrill-voiced and loud, the messenger of morn :
Ere yet the shadows fly, he mounted sings
Amid the dawning clouds, and from their haunts
Calls up the tuneful nations. Every copse
Deep-tangled, tree irregular, and bush
Bending with dewy moisture, o'er the heads
Of the coy quiristers that lodge within,
Are prodigal of harmony. The thrush
And woodlark, o'er the kind-contending throng
Superior heard, run through the sweetest length
Of notes ; when listening Philomela deigns
To let them joy, and purposes, in thought
Elate, to make her night excel their day.
The blackbird whistles from the thorny brake ;
The mellow bullfinch answers from the grove ;
Nor are the linnets, o'er the flowering furze
Poured out profusely, silent : joined to these
Innumerous songsters, in the freshening shade

Of new-sprung leaves, their modulations mix
Mellifluous. The jay, the rook, the daw,
And each harsh pipe, discordant heard alone,
Aid the full concert ; while the stockdove breathes
A melancholy murmur through the whole.
  'T is love creates their melody, and all
This waste of music is the voice of love ;
That even to birds and beasts the tender arts
Of pleasing teaches.
              JAMES THOMSON.

DOMESTIC BIRDS.

FROM "THE SEASONS."

    .... THE careful hen
Calls all her chirping family around,
Fed and defended by the fearless cock,
Whose breast with ardor flames, as on he walks,
Graceful, and crows defiance. In the pond
The finely checkered duck before her train
Rows garrulous. The stately-sailing swan
Gives out her snowy plumage to the gale ;
And, arching proud his neck, with oary feet
Bears forward fierce, and guards his osier-isle,
Protective of his young. The turkey nigh,
Loud-threatening, reddens ; while the peacock
    spreads
His every-colored glory to the sun,
And swims in radiant majesty along.
O'er the whole homely scene, the cooing dove
Flies thick in amorous chase, and wanton rolls
The glancing eye, and turns the changeful neck.
              JAMES THOMSON.

THE BELFRY PIGEON.

ON the cross-beam under the Old South bell
The nest of a pigeon is builded well.
In summer and winter that bird is there,
Out and in with the morning air ;
I love to see him track the street,
With his wary eye and active feet ;
And I often watch him as he springs,
Circling the steeple with easy wings,
Till across the dial his shade has passed,
And the belfry edge is gained at last ;
'T is a bird I love, with its brooding note,
And the trembling throb in its mottled throat ;
There 's a human look in its swelling breast,
And the gentle curve of its lowly crest ;
And I often stop with the fear I feel, —
He runs so close to the rapid wheel.
  Whatever is rung on that noisy bell, —
Chime of the hour, or funeral knell, —
The dove in the belfry must hear it well.
When the tongue swings out to the midnight moon,

When the sexton cheerly rings for noon,
When the clock strikes clear at morning light,
When the child is waked with "nine at night,"
When the chimes play soft in the Sabbath air,
Filling the spirit with tones of prayer, —
Whatever tale in the bell is heard,
He broods on his folded feet unstirred,
Or, rising half in his rounded nest,
He takes the time to smooth his breast,
Then drops again, with filméd eyes,
And sleeps as the last vibration dies.

   Sweet bird ! I would that I could be
A hermit in the crowd like thee !
With wings to fly to wood and glen,
Thy lot, like mine, is cast with men ;
And daily, with unwilling feet,
I tread, like thee, the crowded street,
But, unlike me, when day is o'er,
Thou canst dismiss the world, and soar ;
Or, at a half-felt wish for rest,
Canst smooth the feathers on thy breast,
And drop, fórgetful, to thy nest.

   I would that in such wings of gold
I could my weary heart upfold ;
I would I could look down unmoved
(Unloving as I am unloved),
And while the world throngs on beneath,
Smooth down my cares and calmly breathe ;
And never sad with others' sadness,
And never glad with others' gladness,
Listen, unstirred, to knell or chime,
And, lapped in quiet, bide my time.
NATHANIEL PARKER WILLIS.

TO THE CUCKOO.

HAIL, beauteous stranger of the grove !
  Thou messenger of spring !
Now heaven repairs thy rural seat,
  And woods thy welcome sing.

Soon as the daisy decks the green,
  Thy certain voice we hear.
Hast thou a star to guide thy path,
  Or mark the rolling year ?

Delightful visitant ! with thee
  I hail the time of flowers,
And hear the sound of music sweet
  From birds among the bowers.

The school-boy, wandering through the wood
  To pull the primrose gay,
Starts, thy most curious voice to hear,
  And imitates thy lay.

What time the pea puts on the bloom,
  Thou fliest thy vocal vale,
An annual guest in other lands,
  Another spring to hail.

Sweet bird ! thy bower is ever green,
  Thy sky is ever clear ;
Thou hast no sorrow in thy song,
  No winter in thy year !

O, could I fly, I 'd fly with thee !
We 'd make, with joyful wing,
  Our annual visit o'er the globe,
  Attendants on the spring.
JOHN LOGAN.

TO THE CUCKOO.

O BLITHE new-comer ! I have heard,
  I hear thee and rejoice.
O cuckoo ! shall I call thee bird,
  Or but a wandering voice ?

While I am lying on the grass
  Thy twofold shout I hear ;
From hill to hill it seems to pass,
  At once far off and near.

Though babbling only to the vale
  Of sunshine and of flowers,
Thou bringest unto me a tale
  Of visionary hours.

Thrice welcome, darling of the spring !
  Even yet thou art to me
No bird, but an invisible thing,
  A voice, a mystery ;

The same whom in my school-boy days
  I listened to ; that cry
Which made me look a thousand ways,
  In bush and tree and sky.

To seek thee did I often rove
  Through woods and on the green ;
And thou wert still a hope, a love ;
  Still longed for, never seen.

And I can listen to thee yet ;
  Can lie upon the plain
And listen, till I do beget
  That golden time again.

O blesséd bird ! the earth we pace
  Again appears to be
An unsubstantial, fairy place ;
  That is fit home for thee !
WILLIAM WORDSWORTH.

THE SKYLARK.

BIRD of the wilderness,
Blithesome and cumberless,
Sweet be thy matin o'er moorland and lea !
Emblem of happiness,
Blest is thy dwelling-place, —
O to abide in the desert with thee !
Wild is thy lay and loud
Far in the downy cloud,
Love gives it energy, love gave it birth.
Where, on thy dewy wing,
Where art thou journeying ?
Thy lay is in heaven, thy love is on earth.
O'er fell and fountain sheen,
O'er moor and mountain green,
O'er the red streamer that heralds the day,
Over the cloudlet dim,
Over the rainbow's rim,
Musical cherub, soar, singing, away !
Then, when the gloaming comes,
Low in the heather blooms
Sweet will thy welcome and bed of love be !
Emblem of happiness,
Blest is thy dwelling-place,
O to abide in the desert with thee !

JAMES HOGG.

TO THE SKYLARK.

HAIL to thee, blithe spirit !
Bird thou never wert,
That from heaven, or near it,
Pourest thy full heart
In profuse strains of unpremeditated art.

Higher still and higher
From the earth thou springest,
Like a cloud of fire ;
The blue deep thou wingest,
And singing still dost soar, and soaring ever
singest.

In the golden lightning
Of the setting sun,
O'er which clouds are brightening,
Thou dost float and run ;
Like an embodied joy whose race is just begun.

The pale purple even
Melts around thy flight ;
Like a star of heaven,
In the broad daylight
Thou art unseen, but yet I hear thy shrill delight.

Keen as are the arrows
Of that silver sphere,
Whose intense lamp narrows
In the white dawn clear,
Until we hardly see, we feel that it is there.

All the earth and air
With thy voice is loud,
As, when night is bare,
From one lonely cloud
The moon rains out her beams, and heaven is
overflowed.

What thou art we know not ;
What is most like thee ?
From rainbow clouds there flow not
Drops so bright to see,
As from thy presence showers a rain of melody.

Like a poet hidden
In the light of thought,
Singing hymns unbidden,
Till the world is wrought
To sympathy with hopes and fears it heeded
not ;

Like a high-born maiden
In a palace tower,
Soothing her love-laden
Soul in secret hour
With music sweet as love, which overflows her
bower ;

Like a glow-worm golden,
In a dell of dew,
Scattering unbeholden
Its aerial hue
Among the flowers and grass which screen it from
the view ;

Like a rose embowered
In its own green leaves,
By warm winds deflowered,
Till the scent it gives
Makes faint with too much sweet these heavy-
wingéd thieves.

Sound of vernal showers
On the twinkling grass,
Rain-awakened flowers,
All that ever was
Joyous and fresh and clear thy music doth sur-
pass.

Teach us, sprite or bird,
What sweet thoughts are thine ;
I have never heard
Praise of love or wine
That panted forth a flood of rapture so divine.

Chorus hymeneal,
Or triumphant chant,
Matched with thine, would be all
But an empty vaunt, —
A thing wherein we feel there is some hidden
want.

What objects are the fountains
　Of thy happy strain ?
What fields, or waves, or mountains ?
　What shapes of sky or plain ?
What love of thine own kind ? What ignorance of
　　pain ?

With thy clear, keen joyance
　Languor cannot be ;
Shades of annoyance
　Never come near thee ;
Thou lovest, but ne'er knew love's sad satiety.

Waking, or asleep,
　Thou of death must deem
Things more true and deep
　Than we mortals dream,
Or how could thy notes flow in such a crystal
　　stream ?

We look before and after,
　And pine for what is not ;
Our sincerest laughter
　With some pain is fraught ;
Our sweetest songs are those that tell of saddest
　　thought.

Yet if we could scorn
　Hate and pride and fear,
If we were things born
　Not to shed a tear,
I know not how thy joy we ever should come near.

Better than all measures
　Of delightful sound,
Better than all treasures
　That in books are found,
Thy skill to poet were, thou scorner of the ground !

Teach me half the gladness
　That thy brain must know,
Such harmonious madness
　From my lips would flow,
The world should listen then, as I am listening now.
　　　　　　　　　PERCY BYSSHE SHELLEY.

HARK, HARK ! THE LARK —

HARK, hark ! the lark at heaven's gate sings,
　And Phœbus 'gins arise,
His steeds to water at those springs
　On chaliced flowers that lies ;
And winking Mary-buds begin
　To ope their golden eyes ;
With everything that pretty bin,
　My lady sweet, arise ;
　　Arise, arise !
　　　　　　　　　　SHAKESPEARE.

TO THE SKYLARK.

ETHEREAL minstrel ! pilgrim of the sky !
　Dost thou despise the earth where cares abound ?
Or, while the wings aspire, are heart and eye
　Both with thy nest upon the dewy ground ?
Thy nest, which thou canst drop into at will,
Those quivering wings composed, that music still !

To the last point of vision, and beyond,
　Mount, daring warbler ! — that love-prompted
　　strain,
'Twixt thee and thine a never-failing bond,
　Thrills not the less the bosom of the plain ;
Yet mightst thou seem, proud privilege ! to sing
All independent of the leafy spring.

Leave to the nightingale her shady wood ;
　A privacy of glorious light is thine,
Whence thou dost pour upon the world a flood
　Of harmony, with instinct more divine ;
Type of the wise, who soar, but never roam, —
True to the kindred points of Heaven and Home !
　　　　　　　　　WILLIAM WORDSWORTH.

THE THRUSH.

SWEET bird ! that sing'st away the early hours
Of winters past or coming, void of care ;
Well pleased with delights which present are,
Fair seasons, budding sprays, sweet-smelling
　　flowers, —
To rocks, to springs, to rills, from leafy bowers
Thou thy Creator's goodness dost declare,
And what dear gifts on thee he did not spare,
A stain to human sense in sin that lowers.
What soul can be so sick which by thy songs
(Attired in sweetness) sweetly is not driven
Quite to forget earth's turmoils, spites, and
　　wrongs,
And lift a reverent eye and thought to heaven !
Sweet, artless songster ! thou my mind dost raise
To airs of spheres, — yes, and to angels' lays.
　　　　　　　　　WILLIAM DRUMMOND.

THE ENGLISH ROBIN.

SEE yon robin on the spray ;
　Look ye how his tiny form
Swells, as when his merry lay
　Gushes forth amid the storm.

Though the snow is falling fast,
　Specking o'er his coat with white, —
Though loud roars the chilly blast,
　And the evening 's lost in night, —

Yet from out the darkness dreary
  Cometh still that cheerful note ;
Praiseful aye, and never weary,
  Is that little warbling throat.

Thank him for his lesson's sake,
  Thank God's gentle minstrel there,
Who, when storms make others quake,
  Sings of days that brighter were.
                                    HARRISON WEIR.

THE HEATH-COCK.

GOOD morrow to thy sable beak
And glossy plumage dark and sleek,
Thy crimson moon and azure eye,
Cock of the heath, so wildly shy :
I see thee slyly cowering through
That wiry web of silvery dew,
That twinkles in the morning air,
Like casements of my lady fair.

A maid there is in yonder tower,
Who, peeping from her early bower,
Half shows, like thee, her simple wile,
Her braided hair and morning smile.
The rarest things, with wayward will,
Beneath the covert hide them still ;
The rarest things to break of day
Look shortly forth, and shrink away.

A fleeting moment of delight
I sunned me in her cheering sight ;
As short, I ween, the time will be
That I shall parley hold with thee.
Through Snowdon's mist red beams the day,
The climbing herd-boy chants his lay,
The gnat-flies dance their sunny ring, —
Thou art already on the wing.
                                    JOANNA BAILLIE.

THE BOBOLINK.

BOBOLINK ! that in the meadow,
Or beneath the orchard's shadow,
Keepest up a constant rattle
Joyous as my children's prattle,
Welcome to the north again !
Welcome to mine ear thy strain,
Welcome to mine eye the sight
Of thy buff, thy black and white.
Brighter plumes may greet the sun
By the banks of Amazon ;
Sweeter tones may weave the spell
Of enchanting Philomel ;
But the tropic bird would fail,
And the English nightingale,

If we should compare their worth
With thine endless, gushing mirth.

When the ides of May are past,
June and summer nearing fast,
While from depths of blue above
Comes the mighty breath of love,
Calling out each bud and flower
With resistless, secret power, —
Waking hope and fond desire,
Kindling the erotic fire, —
Filling youths' and maidens' dreams
With mysterious, pleasing themes ;
Then, amid the sunlight clear
Floating in the fragrant air,
Thou dost fill each heart with pleasure
By thy glad ecstatic measure.

A single note, so sweet and low,
Like a full heart's overflow,
Forms the prelude ; but the strain
Gives no such tone again,
For the wild and saucy song
Leaps and skips the notes among,
With such quick and sportive play,
Ne'er was madder, merrier lay.

Gayest songster of the spring !
Thy melodies before me bring
Visions of some dream-built land,
Where, by constant zephyrs fanned,
I might walk the livelong day,
Embosomed in perpetual May.
Nor care nor fear thy bosom knows ;
For thee a tempest never blows ;
But when our northern summer 's o'er,
By Delaware's or Schuylkill's shore
The wild rice lifts its airy head,
And royal feasts for thee are spread.
And when the winter threatens there,
Thy tireless wings yet own no fear,
But bear thee to more southern coasts,
Far beyond the reach of frosts.

Bobolink ! still may thy gladness
Take from me all taints of sadness ;
Fill my soul with trust unshaken
In that Being who has taken
Care for every living thing,
In summer, winter, fall, and spring.
                                    THOMAS HILL.

ROBERT OF LINCOLN.

MERRILY swinging on brier and weed,
  Near to the nest of his little dame,
Over the mountain-side or mead,
  Robert of Lincoln is telling his name :

Bob-o'-link, bob-o'-link,
　Spink, spank, spink ;
Snug and safe is that nest of ours,
Hidden among the summer flowers.
　　　Chee, chee, chee.

Robert of Lincoln is gayly dressed,
　Wearing a bright black wedding coat ;
White are his shoulders and white his crest,
　Hear him call in his merry note :
　Bob-o'-link, bob-o'-link,
　Spink, spank, spink ;
Look, what a nice new coat is mine,
Sure there was never a bird so fine.
　　　Chee, chee, chee.

Robert of Lincoln's Quaker wife,
　Pretty and quiet, with plain brown wings,
Passing at home a patient life,
　Broods in the grass while her husband sings :
　Bob-o'-link, bob-o'-link,
　Spink, spank, spink ;
Brood, kind creature ; you need not fear
Thieves and robbers while I am here.
　　　Chee, chee, chee.

Modest and shy as a nun is she,
　One weak chirp is her only note,
Braggart and prince of braggarts is he,
　Pouring boasts from his little throat :
　Bob-o'-link, bob-o'-link,
　Spink, spank, spink ;
Never was I afraid of man ;
Catch me, cowardly knaves, if you can.
　　　Chee, chee, chee.

Six white eggs on a bed of hay,
　Flecked with purple, a pretty sight !
There as the mother sits all day,
　Robert is singing with all his might :
　Bob-o'-link, bob-o'-link,
　Spink, spank, spink ;
Nice good wife, that never goes out,
Keeping house while I frolic about.
　　　Chee, chee, chee.

Soon as the little ones chip the shell
　Six wide mouths are open for food ;
Robert of Lincoln bestirs him well,
　Gathering seed for the hungry brood.
　Bob-o'-link, bob-o'-link,
　Spink, spank, spink ;
This new life is likely to be
Hard for a gay young fellow like me.
　　　Chee, chee, chee.

Robert of Lincoln at length is made
　Sober with work, and silent with care ;
Off is his holiday garment laid,
　Half forgotten that merry air,

Bob-o'-link, bob-o'-link,
　Spink, spank, spink ;
Nobody knows but my mate and I
Where our nest and our nestlings lie.
　　　Chee, chee, chee.

Summer wanes ; the children are grown ;
　Fun and frolic no more he knows ;
Robert of Lincoln 's a humdrum crone ;
　Off he flies, and we sing as he goes :
　Bob-o'-link, bob-o'-link,
　Spink, spank, spink ;
When you can pipe that merry old strain,
Robert of Lincoln, come back again.
　　　Chee, chee, chee.
　　　　　WILLIAM CULLEN BRYANT.

PERSEVERANCE.

A SWALLOW in the spring
Came to our granary, and 'neath the eaves
Essayed to make a nest, and there did bring
　Wet earth and straw and leaves.

Day after day she toiled
With patient art, but ere her work was crowned,
Some sad mishap the tiny fabric spoiled,
　And dashed it to the ground.

She found the ruin wrought,
But not cast down, forth from the place she flew,
And with her mate fresh earth and grasses brought
　And built her nest anew.

But scarcely had she placed
The last soft feather on its ample floor,
When wicked hand, or chance, again laid waste
　And wrought the ruin o'er.

But still her heart she kept,
And toiled again, — and last night, hearing calls,
I looked, — and lo ! three little swallows slept
　Within the earth-made walls.

What truth is here, O man !
Hath hope been smitten in its early dawn ?
Have clouds o'ercast thy purpose, trust, or plan ?
　Have faith, and struggle on !
　　　　　R. S. S. ANDROS.

THE SWALLOW.

THE gorse is yellow on the heath,
　The banks with speedwell flowers are gay,
The oaks are budding ; and beneath,
The hawthorn soon will bear the wreath,
　The silver wreath of May.

The welcome guest of settled spring,
    The swallow too is come at last ;
Just at sunset, when thrushes sing,
I saw her dash with rapid wing,
    And hailed her as she passed.

Come, summer visitant, attach
    To my reed-roof your nest of clay,
And let my ear your music catch,
Low twittering underneath the thatch,
    At the gray dawn of day.

As fables tell, an Indian sage,
    The Hindustani woods among,
Could in his desert hermitage,
As if 't were marked in written page,
    Translate the wild bird's song.

I wish I did his power possess,
    That I might learn, fleet bird, from thee,
What our vain systems only guess,
And know from what wild wilderness
    You came across the sea.
                        CHARLOTTE SMITH.

THE WINGED WORSHIPPERS.

[Addressed to two swallows that flew into the Chauncy Place Church during divine service.]

GAY, guiltless pair,
What seek ye from the fields of heaven ?
    Ye have no need of prayer,
    Ye have no sins to be forgiven.

Why perch ye here,
Where mortals to their Maker bend ?
    Can your pure spirits fear
The God ye never could offend ?

Ye never knew
The crimes for which we come to weep.
    Penance is not for you,
Blessed wanderers of the *upper deep*.

To you 't is given
To wake sweet Nature's untaught lays ;
    Beneath the arch of heaven
To chirp away a life of praise.

Then spread each wing
Far, far above, o'er lakes and lands,
    And join the choirs that sing
In yon blue dome not reared with hands.

Or, if ye stay,
To note the consecrated hour,
    Teach me the airy way,
And let me try your envied power.

Above the crowd
On upward wings could I but fly,
    I 'd bathe in yon bright cloud,
And seek the stars that gem the sky.

'T were heaven indeed
Through fields of trackless light to soar,
    On Nature's charms to feed,
And Nature's own great God adore.
                        CHARLES SPRAGUE.

THE DEPARTURE OF THE SWALLOW.

AND is the swallow gone ?
    Who beheld it ?
    Which way sailed it ?
Farewell bade it none ?

No mortal saw it go ; —
    But who doth hear
    Its summer cheer
As it flitteth to and fro ?

So the freed spirit flies !
    From its surrounding clay
    It steals away
Like the swallow from the skies.

Whither ? wherefore doth it go ?
    'T is all unknown ;
    We feel alone
That a void is left below.
                        WILLIAM HOWITT.

DEPARTURE OF THE SWALLOWS.
[Translation.]

THE rain-drops plash, and the dead leaves fall,
    On spire and cornice and mould ;
The swallows gather, and twitter and call,
" We must follow the summer, come one, come all,
    For the winter is now so cold."

Just listen awhile to the wordy war,
    As to whither the way shall tend,
Says one, " I know the skies are fair
And myriad insects float in air
    Where the ruins of Athens stand.

" And every year when the brown leaves fall,
    In a niche of the Parthenon
I build my nest on the corniced wall,
In the trough of a devastating ball
    From the Turk's besieging gun."

Says another, " My cosey home I fit
    On a Smyrna *grande café*,
Where over the threshold Hadjii sit,
And smoke their pipes and their coffee sip,
    Dreaming the hours away."

Another says, "I prefer the nave
  Of a temple of Baalbec ;
There my little ones lie when the palm-trees wave,
And, perching near on the architrave,
  I fill each open beak."

"Ah !" says the last, "I build *my* nest
  Far up on the Nile's green shore,
Where Memnon raises his stony crest,
And turns to the sun as he leaves his rest,
  But greets him with song no more.

"In his ample neck is a niche so wide,
  And withal so deep and free,
A thousand swallows their nests can hide,
And a thousand little ones rear beside, —
  Then come to the Nile with me."

They go, they go, to the river and plain,
  To ruined city and town,
They leave me alone with the cold again,
Beside the tomb where my joys are lain,
  With hope like the swallows flown.
                  GAUTIER (French).

A DOUBTING HEART.

WHERE are the swallows fled ?
    Frozen and dead
Perchance upon some bleak and stormy shore.
    O doubting heart !
  Far over purple seas
  They wait, in sunny ease,
  The balmy southern breeze
To bring them to their northern homes once more.

Why must the flowers die ?
    Prisoned they lie
In the cold tomb, heedless of tears or rain.
    O doubting heart !
  They only sleep below
  The soft white ermine snow
  While winter winds shall blow,
To breathe and smile upon you soon again.

The sun has hid its rays
    These many days ;
Will dreary hours never leave the earth ?
    O doubting heart !
  The stormy clouds on high
  Veil the same sunny sky
  That soon, for spring is nigh,
Shall wake the summer into golden mirth.

Fair hope is dead, and light
    Is quenched in night ;
What sound can break the silence of despair ?
    O doubting heart !

The sky is overcast,
  Yet stars shall rise at last,
  Brighter for darkness past,
And angels' silver voices stir the air.
            ADELAIDE ANNE PROCTER.

THE NIGHTINGALE.

THE rose looks out in the valley,
  And thither will I go !
To the rosy vale, where the nightingale
  Sings his song of woe.

The virgin is on the river-side,
  Culling the lemons pale :
Thither, — yes ! thither will I go,
  To the rosy vale, where the nightingale
  Sings his song of woe.

The fairest fruit her hand hath culled,
  'T is for her lover all :
Thither, — yes ! thither will I go,
  To the rosy vale, where the nightingale
  Sings his song of woe.

In her hat of straw, for her gentle swain,
  She has placed the lemons pale :
Thither, — yes ! thither will I go,
  To the rosy vale, where the nightingale
  Sings his song of woe.
        GIL VICENTE (Portuguese). Translation
           of JOHN BOWRING.

THE NIGHTINGALE.

PRIZE thou the nightingale,
Who soothes thee with his tale,
And wakes the woods around ;
A singing feather he, — a winged and wandering
    sound ;

Whose tender carolling
Sets all ears listening
Unto that living lyre,
Whence flow the airy notes his ecstasies inspire ;

Whose shrill, capricious song
Breathes like a flute along,
With many a careless tone, —
Music of thousand tongues, formed by one tongue
    alone.

O charming creature rare !
Can aught with thee compare ?
Thou art all song, — thy breast
Thrills for one month o' the year, — is tranquil
    all the rest.

THE NIGHTINGALE.

" With its cool trees, and night,
And the sweet, tranquil Thames,
And moonshine, and the dew."

Thee wondrous we may call, —
Most wondrous this of all,
That such a tiny throat
Should wake so loud a sound, and pour so loud
   a note.

   MARIA TESSELSCHADE VISSCHER (Dutch). Translation
   of JOHN BOWRING.

PHILOMELA.

HARK ! ah, the nightingale !
The tawny-throated !
Hark ! from that moonlit cedar what a burst !
What triumph ! hark, — what pain !
O wanderer from a Grecian shore,
Still — after many years, in distant lands —
Still nourishing in thy bewildered brain
That wild, unquenched, deep-sunken, Old-World
   pain, —
   Say, will it never heal ?
And can this fragrant lawn,
With its cool trees, and night,
And the sweet, tranquil Thames,
And moonshine, and the dew,
To thy racked heart and brain
   Afford no balm ?

   Dost thou to-night behold,
Here, through the moonlight on this English
   grass,
The unfriendly palace in the Thracian wild ?
   Dost thou again peruse,
With hot cheeks and seared eyes,
The too clear web, and thy dumb sister's shame ?
   Dost thou once more essay
Thy flight ; and feel come over thee,
Poor fugitive ! the feathery change ;
Once more ; and once more make resound,
With love and hate, triumph and agony,
Lone Daulis, and the high Cephisian vale ?

Listen, Eugenia, —
How thick the bursts come crowding through
   the leaves !
Again — thou hearest !
Eternal passion !
Eternal pain !
               MATTHEW ARNOLD.

ADDRESS TO THE NIGHTINGALE.

As it fell upon a day,
In the merry month of May,
Sitting in a pleasant shade
Which a grove of myrtles made,
Beasts did leap, and birds did sing,
Trees did grow, and plants did spring ;

Everything did banish moan,
Save the nightingale alone.
She, poor bird, as all forlorn,
Leaned her breast up-till a thorn ;
And there sung the dolefull'st ditty
That to hear it was great pity.
Fie, fie, fie ! now would she cry ;
Teru, teru, by and by ;
That, to hear her so complain,
Scarce I could from tears refrain ;
For her griefs, so lively shown,
Made me think upon mine own.
Ah ! (thought I) thou mourn'st in vain ;
None takes pity on thy pain ;
Senseless trees, they cannot hear thee ;
Ruthless bears, they will not cheer thee ;
King Pandion, he is dead ;
All thy friends are lapped in lead :
All thy fellow-birds do sing,
Careless of thy sorrowing !
Whilst as fickle Fortune smiled,
Thou and I were both beguiled,
Every one that flatters thee
Is no friend in misery.
Words are easy, like the wind ;
Faithful friends are hard to find.
Every man will be thy friend
Whilst thou hast wherewith to spend ;
But, if stores of crowns be scant,
No man will supply thy want.
If that one be prodigal,
Bountiful they will him call ;
And, with such-like flattering,
" Pity but he were a king."
If he be addict to vice,
Quickly him they will entice ;
But if Fortune once do frown,
Then farewell his great renown :
They that fawned on him before,
Use his company no more.
He that is thy friend indeed,
He will help thee in thy need ;
If thou sorrow, he will weep,
If thou wake, he cannot sleep.
Thus, of every grief in heart,
He with thee doth bear a part.
These are certain signs to know
Faithful friend from flattering foe.
               RICHARD BARNFIELD.

THE MOTHER NIGHTINGALE.

I HAVE seen a nightingale
On a sprig of thyme bewail,
Seeing the dear nest, which was
Hers alone, borne off, alas !
By a laborer ; I heard,

For this outrage, the poor bird
Say a thousand mournful things
To the wind, which, on its wings,
To the Guardian of the sky
Bore her melancholy cry,
Bore her tender tears. She spake
As if her fond heart would break:
One while in a sad, sweet note,
Gurgled from her straining throat,
She enforced her piteous tale,
Mournful prayer and plaintive wail;
One while, with the shrill dispute
Quite outwearied, she was mute;
Then afresh, for her dear brood,
Her harmonious shrieks renewed.
Now she winged it round and round;
Now she skimmed along the ground;
Now from bough to bough, in haste,
The delighted robber chased,
And, alighting in his path,
Seemed to say, 'twixt grief and wrath,
"Give me back, fierce rustic rude,
Give me back my pretty brood,"
And I heard the rustic still
Answer, "That I never will."

ESTEVAN MANUEL DE VILLEGAS (Spanish).
Translation of THOMAS ROSCOE.

MUSIC'S DUEL.

Now westward Sol had spent the richest beams
Of noon's high glory, when, hard by the streams
Of Tiber, on the scene of a green plat,
Under protection of an oak, there sat
A sweet lute's-master, in whose gentle airs
He lost the day's heat and his own hot cares.
Close in the covert of the leaves there stood
A nightingale, come from the neighboring wood
(The sweet inhabitant of each glad tree,
Their muse, their siren, harmless siren she):
There stood she listening, and did entertain
The music's soft report, and mould the same
In her own murmurs; that whatever mood
His curious fingers lent, her voice made good.
The man perceived his rival, and her art;
Disposed to give the light-foot lady sport,
Awakes his lute, and 'gainst the fight to come
Informs it in a sweet præludium
Of closer strains, and e'er the war begin,
He lightly skirmishes on every string
Charged with a flying touch; and straightway she
Carves out her dainty voice as readily
Into a thousand sweet distinguished tones,
And reckons up in soft divisions
Quick volumes of wild notes, to let him know,
By that shrill taste, she could do something too.

His nimble hand's instinct then taught each
    string
A capering cheerfulness, and made them sing
To their own dance; now negligently rash
He throws his arm, and with a long-drawn dash
Blends all together; then distinctly trips
From this to that, then quick returning skips,
And snatches this again, and pauses there.
She measures every measure, everywhere
Meets art with art; sometimes, as if in doubt
Not perfect yet, and fearing to be out,
Trails her plain ditty in one long-spun note,
Through the sleek passage of her open throat,
A clear, unwrinkled song; then doth she point it
With tender accents, and severely joint it
By short diminutives, that being reared
In controverting warbles, evenly shared,
With her sweet self she wrangles: he, amazed
That from so small a channel should be raised
The torrent of a voice whose melody
Could melt into such sweet variety,
Strains higher yet, that, tickled with rare art,
The tattling strings, each breathing in his part,
Most kindly do fall out: the grumbling bass
In surly groans disdains the treble's grace;
The high-percht treble chirps at this, and chides,
Until his finger (moderator) hides
And closes the sweet quarrel, rousing all,
Hoarse, shrill, at once; as when the trumpets call
Hot Mars to the harvest of death's field, and woo
Men's hearts into their hands; this lesson too
She gives them back; her supple breast thrills out
Sharp airs, and staggers in a warbling doubt
Of dallying sweetness, hovers o'er her skill,
And folds in waved notes, with a trembling bill,
The pliant series of her slippery song;
Then starts she suddenly into a throng
Of short thick sobs, whose thundering volleys float,
And roll themselves over her lubric throat
In panting murmurs, stilled out of her breast;
That ever-bubbling spring, the sugared nest
Of her delicious soul, that there does lie
Bathing in streams of liquid melody;
Music's best seed-plot; when in ripened airs
A golden-headed harvest fairly rears
His honey-dropping tops ploughed by her breath
Which there reciprocally laboreth
In that sweet soil it seems a holy quire,
Sounded to the name of great Apollo's lyre;
Whose silver roof rings with the sprightly notes
Of sweet-lipped angel-imps, that swill their throats
In cream of morning Helicon, and then
Prefer soft anthems to the ears of men,
To woo them from their beds, still murmuring
That men can sleep while they their matins sing
(Most divine service), whose so early lay
Prevents the eyelids of the blushing day.
There might you hear her kindle her soft voice

In the close murmur of a sparkling noise ;
And lay the groundwork of her hopeful song,
Still keeping in the forward stream so long,
Till a sweet whirlwind (striving to get out)
Heaves her soft bosom, wanders round about,
And makes a pretty earthquake in her breast,
Till the fledged notes at length forsake their nest,
Fluttering in wanton shoals, and to the sky,
Winged with their own wild echoes, prattling fly.
She opes the floodgate, and lets loose a tide
Of streaming sweetness, which in state doth ride
On the waved back of every swelling strain,
Rising and falling in a pompous train ;
And while she thus discharges a shrill peal
Of flashing airs, she qualifies their zeal
With the cool epode of a graver note ;
Thus high, thus low, as if her silver throat
Would reach the brazen voice of war's hoarse bird ;
Her little soul is ravished, and so poured
Into loose ecstasies, that she is placed
Above herself, music's enthusiast.

Shame now and anger mixed a double stain
In the musician's face : "Yet, once again,
Mistress, I come : now reach a strain, my lute,
Above her mock, or be forever mute.
Or tune a song of victory to me,
Or to thyself sing thine own obsequy."
So said, his hands sprightly as fire he flings,
And with a quavering coyness tastes the strings.
The sweet-lipped sisters musically frighted,
Singing their fears are fearfully delighted ;
Trembling as when Apollo's golden hairs
Are fanned and frizzled in the wanton airs
Of his own breath, which, married to his lyre,
Doth tune the spheres, and make heaven's self
          look higher ;
From this to that, from that to this he flies,
Feels music's pulse in all her arteries ;
Caught in a net which there Apollo spreads,
His fingers struggle with the vocal threads,
Following those little rills, he sinks into
A sea of Helicon ; his hand does go
Those parts of sweetness which with nectar drop,
Softer than that which pants in Hebe's cup.
The humorous strings expound his learned touch
By various glosses ; now they seem to grutch
And murmur in a buzzing din, then jingle
In shrill-toned accents striving to be single ;
Every smooth turn, every delicious stroke
Gives life to some new grace ; thus doth he invoke
Sweetness by all her names ; thus, bravely thus
(Fraught with a fury so harmonious)
The lute's light genius now does proudly rise,
Heaved on the surges of swoll'n rhapsodies ;
Whose flourish (meteor-like) doth curl the air
With flash of high-born fancies, here and there
Dancing in lofty measures, and anon
Creeps on the soft touch of a tender tone,

Whose trembling murmurs, melting in wild airs,
Run to and fro, complaining his sweet cares ;
Because those precious mysteries that dwell
In music's ravished soul he dare not tell,
But whisper to the world ; thus do they vary,
Each string his note, as if they meant to carry
Their master's blest soul (snatched out at his ears
By a strong ecstasy) through all the spheres
Of music's heaven ; and seat it there on high,
In the empyrean of pure harmony.
At length (after so long, so loud a strife
Of all the strings, still breathing the best life
Of blest variety, attending on
His fingers' fairest evolution,
In many a sweet rise, many as sweet a fall)
A full-mouthed diapason swallows all.

This done, he lists what she would say to this ;
And she, although her breath's late exercise
Had dealt too roughly with her tender throat,
Yet summons all her sweet powers for a note.
Alas ! in vain ! for while (sweet soul) she tries
To measure all those wild diversities
Of chattering strings, by the small size of one
Poor simple voice, raised in a natural tone ;
She fails, and failing grieves, and grieving dies :
She dies, and leaves her life the victor's prize,
Falling upon his lute : O, fit to have
(That lived so sweetly), dead, so sweet a grave !
                                    RICHARD CRASHAW.

BIRDS.

FROM "THE PELICAN ISLAND."

— BIRDS, the free tenants of land, air, and ocean,
Their forms all symmetry, their motions grace ;
In plumage, delicate and beautiful,
Thick without burden, close as fishes' scales,
Or loose as full-blown poppies to the breeze ;
With wings that might have had a soul within
          them,
They bore their owners by such sweet enchantment.
— Birds, small and great, of endless shapes and
          colors,
Here flew and perched, there swam and dived at
          pleasure ;
Watchful and agile, uttering voices wild
And harsh, yet in accordance with the waves
Upon the beach, the winds in caverns moaning,
Or winds and waves abroad upon the water.
Some sought their food among the finny shoals,
Swift darting from the clouds, emerging soon
With slender captives glittering in their beaks ;
These in recesses of steep crags constructed
Their eyries inaccessible, and trained
Their hardy broods to forage in all weathers :
Others, more gorgeously apparelled, dwelt
Among the woods, on nature's dainties feeding,

Herbs, seeds, and roots ; or, ever on the wing,
Pursuing insects through the boundless air :
In hollow trees or thickets these concealed
Their exquisitely woven nests ; where lay
Their callow offspring, quiet as the down
On their own breasts, till from her search the dam
With laden bill returned, and shared the meal
Among her clamorous suppliants, all agape ;
Then, cowering o'er them with expanded wings,
She felt how sweet it is to be a mother.
Of these, a few, with melody untaught,
Turned all the air to music within hearing,
Themselves unseen ; while bolder quiristers
On loftiest branches strained their clarion-pipes,
And made the forest echo to their screams
Discordant, — yet there was no discord there,
But tempered harmony ; all tones combining,
In the rich confluence of ten thousand tongues,
To tell of joy and to inspire it.   Who
Could hear such concert, and not join in chorus ?
Not I.   JAMES MONTGOMERY.

THE PELICAN.

FROM "THE PELICAN ISLAND."

AT early dawn I marked them in the sky,
Catching the morning colors on their plumes ;
Not in voluptuous pastime revelling there,
Among the rosy clouds, while orient heaven
Flamed like the opening gates of Paradise,
Whence issued forth the angel of the sun,
And gladdened nature with returning day :
— Eager for food, their searching eyes they fixed
On ocean's unrolled volume, from an height
That brought immensity within their scope ;
Yet with such power of vision looked they down,
As though they watched the shell-fish slowly
          gliding
O'er sunken rocks, or climbing trees of coral.
On indefatigable wing upheld,
Breath, pulse, existence, seemed suspended in
          them :
They were as pictures painted on the sky ;
Till suddenly, aslant, away they shot,
Like meteors changed from stars to gleams of
          lightning,
And struck upon the deep, where, in wild play,
Their quarry floundered, unsuspecting harm ;
With terrible voracity, they plunged
Their heads among the affrighted shoals, and beat
A tempest on the surges with their wings,
Till flashing clouds of foam and spray concealed
          them.
Nimbly they seized and secreted their prey,
Alive and wriggling in the elastic net,
Which Nature hung beneath their grasping beaks,

Till, swollen with captures, the unwieldy burden
Clogged their slow flight, as heavily to land
These mighty hunters of the deep returned.
There on the cragged cliffs they perched at ease,
Gorging their hapless victims one by one ;
Then, full and weary, side by side they slept,
Till evening roused them to the chase again.

      .   .   .   .   .   .

Love found that lonely couple on their isle,
And soon surrounded them with blithe compan-
          ions.
The noble birds, with skill spontaneous, framed
A nest of reeds among the giant-grass,
That waved in lights and shadows o'er the soil.
There, in sweet thraldom, yet unweening why,
The patient dam, who ne'er till now had known
Parental instinct, brooded o'er her eggs,
Long ere she found the curious secret out,
That life was hatching in their brittle shells.
Then, from a wild rapacious bird of prey,
Tamed by the kindly process, she became
That gentlest of all living things, — a mother ;
Gentlest while yearning o'er her naked young,
Fiercest when stirred by anger to defend them.
Her mate himself the softening power confessed,
Forgot his sloth, restrained his appetite,
And ranged the sky and fished the stream for her.
Or, when o'erwearied Nature forced her off
To shake her torpid feathers in the breeze,
And bathe her bosom in the cooling flood,
He took her place, and felt through every nerve,
While the plump nestlings throbbed against his
          heart,
The tenderness that makes the vulture mild ;
Yea, half unwillingly his post resigned,
When, homesick with the absence of an hour,
She hurried back, and drove him from her seat
With pecking bill and cry of fond distress,
Answered by him with murmurs of delight,
Whose gutturals harsh to her were love's own
          music.
Then, settling down, like foam upon the wave,
White, flickering, effervescent, soon subsiding,
Her ruffled pinions smoothly she composed ;
And, while beneath the comfort of her wings,
Her crowded progeny quite filled the nest,
The halcyon sleeps not sounder, when the wind
Is breathless, and the sea without a curl,
— Nor dreams the halcyon of serener days,
Or nights more beautiful with silent stars,
Than, in that hour, the mother pelican,
When the warm tumults of affection sunk
Into calm sleep, and dreams of what they were.
— Dreams more delicious than reality.
— He sentinel beside her stood, and watched
With jealous eye the raven in the clouds,
And the rank sea-mews wheeling round the cliffs.
Woe to the reptile then that ventured nigh !

The snap of his tremendous bill was like
Death's scythe, down - cutting everything it
    struck.
The heedless lizard, in his gambols, peeped
Upon the guarded nest, from out the flowers,
But paid the instant forfeit of his life ;
Nor could the serpent's subtlety elude
Capture, when gliding by, nor in defence
Might his malignant fangs and venom save him.

    Erelong the thriving brood outgrew their cra-
    dle,
Ran through the grass, and dabbled in the
    pools ;
No sooner denizens of earth than made
Free both of air and water ; day by day,
New lessons, exercises, and amusements
Employed the old to teach, the young to learn.
Now floating on the blue lagoon behold them ;
The sire and dam in swan-like beauty steering,
Their cygnets following through the foamy wake,
Picking the leaves of plants, pursuing insects,
Or catching at the bubbles as they broke :
Till on some minor fry, in reedy shallows,
With flapping pinions and unsparing beaks,
The well-taught scholars plied their double art,
To fish in troubled waters, and secure
The petty captives in their maiden pouches ;
Then hurried with their banquet to the shore,
With feet, wings, breast, half swimming and
    half flying.
But when their pens grew strong to fight the
    storm,
And buffet with the breakers on the reef,
The parents put them to severer proof ;
On beetling rocks the little ones were mar-
    shalled ;
There, by endearments, stripes, example, urged
To try the void convexity of heaven,
And plough the ocean's horizontal field.
Timorous at first they fluttered round the verge,
Balanced and furled their hesitating wings,
Then put them forth again with steadier aim ;
Now, gaining courage as they felt the wind
Dilate their feathers, fill their airy frames
With buoyancy that bore them from their feet,
They yielded all their burden to the breeze,
And sailed and soared where'er their guardians
    led ;
Ascending, hovering, wheeling, or alighting,
They searched the deep in quest of nobler game
Than yet their inexperience had encountered ;
With these they battled in that element,
Where wings or fins were equally at home,
Till, conquerors in many a desperate strife,
They dragged their spoils to land, and gorged at
    leisure.
                JAMES MONTGOMERY.

TO A BIRD

THAT HAUNTED THE WATERS OF LAAKEN IN THE WINTER.

O MELANCHOLY bird, a winter's day
  Thou standest by the margin of the poor,
    And, taught by God, dost thy whole being school
To patience, which all evil can allay.
God has appointed thee the fish thy prey,
  And given thyself a lesson to the fool
    Unthrifty, to submit to moral rule,
And his unthinking course by thee to weigh.
  There need not schools nor the professor's chair,
Though these be good, true wisdom to impart :
  He who has not enough for these to spare,
Of time or gold, may yet amend his heart,
  And teach his soul by brooks and rivers fair, —
Nature is always wise in every part.
                LORD THURLOW.

TO A WATERFOWL.

WHITHER, midst falling dew,
While glow the heavens with the last steps of day,
Far, through their rosy depths, dost thou pursue
    Thy solitary way ?

    Vainly the fowler's eye
Might mark thy distant flight to do thee wrong,
As, darkly painted on the crimson sky,
    Thy figure floats along.

    Seek'st thou the plashy brink
Of weedy lake, or marge of river wide,
Or where the rocking billows rise and sink
    On the chafed ocean side ?

    There is a Power whose care
Teaches thy way along that pathless coast, —
The desert and illimitable air, —
    Lone wandering, but not lost.

    All day thy wings have fanned,
At that far height, the cold, thin atmosphere,
Yet stoop not, weary, to the welcome land,
    Though the dark night is near.

    And soon that toil shall end ;
Soon shalt thou find a summer home, and rest,
And scream among thy fellows ; reeds shall bend,
    Soon, o'er thy sheltered nest.

    Thou 'rt gone, the abyss of heaven
Hath swallowed up thy form ; yet, on my heart
Deeply hath sunk the lesson thou hast given,
    And shall not soon depart :

He who, from zone to zone,
Guides through the boundless sky thy certain
flight,
In the long way that I must tread alone,
Will lead my steps aright.
WILLIAM CULLEN BRYANT.

THE STORMY PETREL.

A THOUSAND miles from land are we,
Tossing about on the stormy sea, —
From billow to bounding billow cast,
Like fleecy snow on the stormy blast.
The sails are scattered abroad like weeds ;
The strong masts shake like quivering reeds ;
The mighty cables and iron chains,
The hull, which all earthly strength disdains, —
They strain and they crack ; and hearts like stone
Their natural, hard, proud strength disown.

Up and down ! — up and down !
From the base of the wave to the billow's crown,
And amidst the flashing and feathery foam
The stormy petrel finds a home, —
A home, if such a place may be
For her who lives on the wide, wide sea,
On the craggy ice, in the frozen air,
And only seeketh her rocky lair
To warm her young, and to teach them to spring
At once o'er the waves on their stormy wing !

O'er the deep ! — o'er the deep !
Where the whale and the shark and the sword-
fish sleep, —
Outflying the blast and the driving rain,
The petrel telleth her tale — in vain ;
For the mariner curseth the warning bird
Which bringeth him news of the storm unheard !
Ah ! thus does the prophet of good or ill
Meet hate from the creatures he serveth still ;
Yet he ne'er falters, — so, petrel, spring
Once more o'er the waves on thy stormy wing !
BARRY CORNWALL.

LINES TO THE STORMY PETREL.

THE lark sings for joy in her own loved land,
In the furrowed field, by the breezes fanned ;
And so revel we
In the furrowed sea,
As joyous and glad as the lark can be.

On the placid breast of the inland lake,
The wild duck delights her pastime to take ;
But the petrel braves
The wild ocean waves,
His wing in the foaming billow he laves.

The halcyon loves in the noontide beam
To follow his sport on the tranquil stream
He fishes at ease
In the summer breeze,
But we go angling in stormiest seas.

No song-note have we but a piping cry,
That blends with the storm when the wind is high.
When the land-birds wail
We sport in the gale,
And merrily over the ocean we sail.
ANONYMOUS.

THE OWL.

IN the hollow tree, in the old gray tower,
The spectral owl doth dwell ;
Dull, hated, despised, in the sunshine hour,
But at dusk he 's abroad and well !
Not a bird of the forest e'er mates with him ;
All mock him outright by day ;
But at night, when the woods grow still and dim,
The boldest will shrink away !
O, when the night falls, and roosts the fowl,
Then, then, is the reign of the horned owl !

And the owl hath a bride, who is fond and bold,
And loveth the wood's deep gloom ;
And, with eyes like the shine of the moonstone cold,
She awaiteth her ghastly groom ;
Not a feather she moves, not a carol she sings,
As she waits in her tree so still ;
But when her heart heareth his flapping wings,
She hoots out her welcome shrill !
O, when the moon shines, and dogs do howl,
Then, then, is the joy of the horned owl !

Mourn not for the owl, nor his gloomy plight !
The owl hath his share of good :
If a prisoner he be in the broad daylight,
He is lord in the dark greenwood !
Nor lonely the bird, nor his ghastly mate,
They are each unto each a pride ;
Thrice fonder, perhaps, since a strange, dark fate
Hath rent them from all beside !
So, when the night falls, and dogs do howl,
Sing, ho ! for the reign of the horned owl !
We know not alway
Who are kings by day,
But the king of the night is the bold brown owl !
BARRY CORNWALL.

TO THE HUMBLE-BEE.

BURLY, dozing humble-bee !
Where thou art is clime for me ;
Let them sail for Porto Rique,
Far-off heats through seas to seek,

I will follow thee alone,
Thou animated torrid zone !
Zigzag steerer, desert cheerer,
Let me chase thy waving lines ;
Keep me nearer, me thy hearer,
Singing over shrubs and vines.

Insect lover of the sun,
Joy of thy dominion !
Sailor of the atmosphere ;
Swimmer through the waves of air,
Voyager of light and noon,
Epicurean of June !
Wait, I prithee, till I come
Within earshot of thy hum, —
All without is martyrdom,

When the south-wind, in May days,
With a net of shining haze
Silvers the horizon wall ;
And, with softness touching all,
Tints the human countenance
With the color of romance ;
And infusing subtle heats
Turns the sod to violets, —
Thou in sunny solitudes,
Rover of the underwoods,
The green silence dost displace
With thy mellow breezy bass.

Hot midsummer's petted crone,
Sweet to me thy drowsy tone
Tells of countless sunny hours,
Long days, and solid banks of flowers ;
Of gulfs of sweetness without bound,
In Indian wildernesses found ;
Of Syrian peace, immortal leisure,
Firmest cheer, and birdlike pleasure.

Aught unsavory or unclean
Hath my insect never seen ;
But violets, and bilberry bells,
Maple sap, and daffodels,
Grass with green flag half-mast high,
Succory to match the sky,
Columbine with horn of honey,
Scented fern, and agrimony,
Clover, catchfly, adder's-tongue,
And brier-roses, dwelt among :
All beside was unknown waste,
All was picture as he passed.
Wiser far than human seer,
Yellow-breeched philosopher,
Seeing only what is fair,
Sipping only what is sweet,
Thou dost mock at fate and care,
Leave the chaff and take the wheat.
When the fierce northwestern blast
Cools sea and land so far and fast, —

Thou already slumberest deep ;
Woe and want thou canst outsleep ;
Want and woe, which torture us,
Thy sleep makes ridiculous.

RALPH WALDO EMERSON.

A SOLILOQUY.

OCCASIONED BY THE CHIRPING OF A GRASSHOPPER.

HAPPY insect ! ever blest
With a more than mortal rest,
Rosy dews the leaves among,
Humble joys, and gentle song !
Wretched poet ! ever curst
With a life of lives the worst,
Sad despondence, restless fears,
Endless jealousies and tears.
In the burning summer thou
Warblest on the verdant bough,
Meditating cheerful play,
Mindless of the piercing ray ;
Scorched in Cupid's fervors, I
Ever weep and ever die.
Proud to gratify thy will,
Ready Nature waits thee still ;
Balmy wines to thee she pours,
Weeping through the dewy flowers,
Rich as those by Hebe given
To the thirsty sons of heaven.
Yet, alas, we both agree.
Miserable thou like me !
Each, alike, in youth rehearses
Gentle strains and tender verses ;
Ever wandering far from home,
Mindless of the days to come
(Such as aged Winter brings
Trembling on his icy wings),
Both alike at last we die ;
Thou art starved, and so am I !

WALTER HARTE.

THE GRASSHOPPER.

HAPPY insect, what can be
In happiness compared to thee ?
Fed with nourishment divine,
The dewy morning's gentle wine !
Nature waits upon thee still,
And thy verdant cup does fill ;
'T is filled wherever thou dost tread,
Nature self 's thy Ganymede.
Thou dost drink and dance and sing,
Happier than the happiest king !
All the fields which thou dost see,
All the plants belong to thee ;
All the summer hours produce,

Fertile made with early juice.
Man for thee does sow and plough,
Farmer he, and landlord thou !
Thou dost innocently enjoy,
Nor does thy luxury destroy.
The shepherd gladly heareth thee,
More harmonious than he.
Thee country hinds with gladness hear,
Prophet of the ripened year !
Thee Phœbus loves, and does inspire ;
Phœbus is himself thy sire.
To thee, of all things upon earth,
Life is no longer than thy mirth.
Happy insect ! happy thou,
Dost neither age nor winter know ;
But when thou 'st drunk and danced and sung
Thy fill, the flowery leaves among,
(Voluptuous and wise withal,
Epicurean animal !)
Sated with thy summer feast,
Thou retir'st to endless rest.

ANACREON (Greek).   Translation of
ABRAHAM COWLEY.

THE GRASSHOPPER AND CRICKET.

THE poetry of earth is never dead ;
When all the birds are faint with the hot sun
And hide in cooling trees, a voice will run
From hedge to hedge about the new-mown mead.
That is the grasshopper's, — he takes the lead
In summer luxury, — he has never done
With his delights ; for, when tired out with fun,
He rests at ease beneath some pleasant weed.
The poetry of earth is ceasing never.
On a lone winter evening, when the frost
Has wrought a silence, from the stove there shrills
The cricket's song, in warmth increasing ever,
And seems, to one in drowsiness half lost,
The grasshopper's among some grassy hills.

JOHN KEATS.

THE GRASSHOPPER AND CRICKET.

GREEN little vaulter in the sunny grass,
Catching your heart up at the feel of June, —
Sole voice that 's heard amidst the lazy noon
When even the bees lag at the summoning brass ;
And you, warm little housekeeper, who class
With those who think the candles come too soon,
Loving the fire, and with your tricksome tune
Nick the glad silent moments as they pass !

O sweet and tiny cousins, that belong,
One to the fields, the other to the hearth,

Both have your sunshine ; both, though small,
    are strong
At your clear hearts ; and both seem given to
    earth
To sing in thoughtful ears this natural song, —
In doors and out, summer and winter, mirth.

LEIGH HUNT.

THE CRICKET.

LITTLE inmate, full of mirth,
Chirping on my kitchen hearth,
Wheresoe'er be thine abode
Always harbinger of good,
Pay me for thy warm retreat
With a song more soft and sweet ;
In return thou shalt receive
Such a strain as I can give.

Thus thy praise shall be expressed,
Inoffensive, welcome guest !
While the rat is on the scout,
And the mouse with curious snout,
With what vermin else infest
Every dish, and spoil the best ;
Frisking thus before the fire,
Thou hast all thy heart's desire.

Though in voice and shape they be
Formed as if akin to thee,
Thou surpassest, happier far,
Happiest grasshoppers that are ;
Theirs is but a summer's song, —
Thine endures the winter long,
Unimpaired and shrill and clear,
Melody throughout the year.

WILLIAM COWPER

KATYDID.

I LOVE to hear thine earnest voice,
    Wherever thou art hid,
Thou testy little dogmatist,
    Thou pretty Katydid !
Thou mindest me of gentlefolks, —
    Old gentlefolks are they, —
Thou say'st an undisputed thing
    In such a solemn way.

Thou art a female, Katydid !
    I know it by the trill
That quivers through thy piercing notes,
    So petulant and shrill.
I think there is a knot of you
    Beneath the hollow tree, —
A knot of spinster Katydids, —
    Do Katydids drink tea ?

O, tell me where did Katy live,
    And what did Katy do?
And was she very fair and young,
    And yet so wicked too?
Did Katy love a naughty man,
    Or kiss more cheeks than one?
I warrant Katy did no more
    Than many a Kate has done.
          OLIVER WENDELL HOLMES.

TO A LOUSE,

ON SEEING ONE ON A LADY'S BONNET AT CHURCH.

HA! whare ye gaun, ye crawlin' ferlie?
Your impudence protects you sairly:
I canna say but ye strunt rarely
    Owre gauze an' lace;
Though, faith! I fear ye dine but sparely
    On sic a place.

Ye ugly, creepin', blastit wonner,
Detested, shunned by saunt an' sinner,
How dare you set your fit upon her,
    Sae fine a lady?
Gae somewhere else, and seek your dinner
    On some poor body.

Swith, in some beggar's haffet squattle;
There ye may creep and sprawl and sprattle
Wi' ither kindred, jumping cattle,
    In shoals and nations:
Whare horn nor bane ne'er daur unsettle
    Your thick plantations.

Now haud you there, ye 're out o' sight,
Below the fatt'rels, snug an' tight;
Na, faith ye yet! ye 'll no be right
    Till ye 've got on it,
The very tapmost tow'ring height
    O' Miss's bonnet.

My sooth; right bauld ye set your nose out,
As plump and gray as ony grozet;
O for some rank, mercurial rozet,
    Or fell, red smeddum!
I 'd gie you sic a hearty dose o't,
    Wad dress your droddum!

I wad na been surprised to spy
You on an auld wife's flannen toy;
Or aiblins some bit duddie boy,
    On 's wyliecoat;
But Miss's fine Lunardi, fie!
    How daur ye do 't?

O Jenny, dinna toss your head,
An' set your beauties a' abroad!

Ye little ken what cursèd speed
    The blastie 's makin'!
Thae winks and finger-ends, I dread,
    Are notice takin'!

O wad some power the giftie gie us
To see oursel's as others see us!
It wad frae monie a blunder free us,
    And foolish notion:
What airs in dress an' gait wad lea'e us,
    And ev'n devotion!
          ROBERT BURNS.

REMONSTRANCE WITH THE SNAILS.

YE little snails,
    With slippery tails,
    Who noiselessly travel
    Along this gravel,
By a silvery path of slime unsightly,
I learn that you visit my pea-rows nightly.
Felonious your visit, I guess!
    And I give you this warning,
    That, every morning,
        I 'll strictly examine the pods;
    And if one I hit on,
    With slaver or spit on,
        Your next meal will be with the gods.

I own you 're a very ancient race,
    And Greece and Babylon were amid;
You have tenanted many a royal dome,
    And dwelt in the oldest pyramid;
The source of the Nile!—O, you have been there!
    In the ark was your floodless bed;
On the moonless night of Marathon
    You crawled o'er the mighty dead;
        But still, though I reverence your ancestries,
    I don't see why you should nibble my peas.

The meadows are yours,—the hedgerow and brook,
    You may bathe in their dews at morn;
By the aged sea you may sound your *shells,*
    On the mountains erect your *horn;*
The fruits and the flowers are your rightful dowers,
    Then why—in the name of wonder—
Should my six pea-rows be the only cause
    To excite your midnight plunder?

I have never disturbed your slender shells;
    You have hung round my aged walk;
And each might have sat, till he died in his fat,
    Beneath his own cabbage-stalk;
But now you must fly from the soil of your sires;
    Then put on your liveliest crawl,
And think of your poor little snails at home,
    Now orphans or emigrants all.

Utensils domestic and civil and social
  I give you an evening to pack up ;
But if the moon of this night does not rise on your
      flight,
  To-morrow I 'll hang each man Jack up.
You 'll think of my peas and your thievish tricks,
  With tears of slime, when crossing the *Styx*.
                                        ANONYMOUS.

A FOREST HYMN.

THE groves were God's first temples.   Ere man
      learned
To hew the shaft, and lay the architrave,
And spread the roof above them, — ere he framed
The lofty vault, to gather and roll back
The sound of anthems ; in the darkling wood,
Amidst the cool and silence, he knelt down,
And offered to the Mightiest solemn thanks
And supplication.   For his simple heart
Might not resist the sacred influences
Which, from the stilly twilight of the place,
And from the gray old trunks that high in heaven
Mingled their mossy boughs, and from the sound
Of the invisible breath that swayed at once
All their green tops, stole over him, and bowed
His spirit with the thought of boundless power
And inaccessible majesty.   Ah, why
Should we, in the world's riper years, neglect
God's ancient sanctuaries, and adore
Only among the crowd, and under roofs
That our frail hands have raised ? Let me, at least,
Here, in the shadow of this aged wood,
Offer one hymn, — thrice happy if it find
Acceptance in his ear.

              Father, thy hand
Hath reared these venerable columns, thou
Didst weave this verdant roof.   Thou didst look
      down
Upon the naked earth, and forthwith rose
All these fair ranks of trees.   They in thy sun
Budded, and shook their green leaves in thy breeze,
And shot towards heaven. The century-living crow,
Whose birth was in their tops, grew old and died
Among their branches, till at last they stood,
As now they stand, massy and tall and dark,
Fit shrine for humble worshipper to hold
Communion with his Maker.   These dim vaults,
These winding aisles, of human pomp or pride
Report not.   No fantastic carvings show
The boast of our vain race to change the form
Of thy fair works.   But thou art here, — thou fill'st
The solitude.   Thou art in the soft winds
That run along the summit of these trees
In music ; thou art in the cooler breath
That from the inmost darkness of the place

Comes, scarcely felt; the barky trunks, the ground,
The fresh moist ground, are all instinct with thee.
Here is continual worship ; — nature, here,
In the tranquillity that thou dost love,
Enjoys thy presence.   Noiselessly around,
From perch to perch, the solitary bird
Passes ; and yon clear spring, that, midst its herbs,
Wells softly forth and wandering steeps the roots
Of half the mighty forest, tells no tale
Of all the good it does.   Thou hast not left
Thyself without a witness, in these shades,
Of thy perfections.   Grandeur, strength, and grace
Are here to speak of thee.   This mighty oak, —
By whose immovable stem I stand and seem
Almost annihilated, — not a prince,
In all that proud old world beyond the deep,
E'er wore his crown as loftily as he
Wears the green coronal of leaves with which
Thy hand has graced him.   Nestled at his root
Is beauty, such as blooms not in the glare
Of the broad sun.   That delicate forest flower
With scented breath, and look so like a smile,
Seems, as it issues from the shapeless mould,
An emanation of the indwelling Life,
A visible token of the upholding Love,
That are the soul of this wide universe.

My heart is awed within me when I think
Of the great miracle that still goes on,
In silence, round me, — the perpetual work
Of thy creation, finished, yet renewed
Forever.   Written on thy works I read
The lesson of thy own eternity.
Lo ! all grow old and die ; but see again,
How on the faltering footsteps of decay
Youth presses, — ever gay and beautiful youth
In all its beautiful forms.   These lofty trees
Wave not less proudly that their ancestors
Moulder beneath them.   O, there is not lost
One of Earth's charms ! upon her bosom yet,
After the flight of untold centuries,
The freshness of her far beginning lies,
And yet shall lie.   Life mocks the idle hate
Of his arch-enemy Death, — yea, seats himself
Upon the tyrant's throne, the sepulchre,
And of the triumphs of his ghastly foe
Makes his own nourishment.   For he came forth
From thine own bosom, and shall have no end.

There have been holy men who hid themselves
Deep in the woody wilderness, and gave
Their lives to thought and prayer, till they outlived
The generation born with them, nor seemed
Less aged than the hoary trees and rocks
Around them ; — and there have been holy men
Who deemed it were not well to pass life thus.
But let me often to these solitudes
Retire, and in thy presence reassure

My feeble virtue. Here its enemies,
The passions, at thy plainer footsteps shrink
And tremble, and are still. O God! when thou
Dost scare the world with tempests, set on fire
The heavens with falling thunderbolts, or fill,
With all the waters of the firmament,
The swift dark whirlwind that uproots the woods
And drowns the villages; when, at thy call,
Uprises the great deep, and throws himself
Upon the continent, and overwhelms
Its cities, — who forgets not, at the sight
Of these tremendous tokens of thy power,
His pride, and lays his strifes and follies by?
O, from these sterner aspects of thy face
Spare me and mine, nor let us need the wrath
Of the mad unchained elements to teach
Who rules them. Be it ours to meditate,
In these calm shades, thy milder majesty,
And to the beautiful order of thy works
Learn to conform the order of our lives.

WILLIAM CULLEN BRYANT.

THE BRAVE OLD OAK.

A song to the oak, the brave old oak,
  Who hath ruled in the greenwood long;
Here 's health and renown to his broad green crown,
  And his fifty arms so strong.
There 's fear in his frown when the sun goes down,
  And the fire in the west fades out;
And he showeth his might on a wild midnight,
  When the storm through his branches shout.

    Then here 's to the oak, the brave old oak,
      Who stands in his pride alone;
    And still flourish he, a hale green tree,
      When a hundred years are gone!

In the days of old, when the spring with cold
  Had brightened his branches gray,
Through the grass at his feet crept maidens sweet,
  To gather the dew of May.
And on that day to the rebeck gay
  They frolicked with lovesome swains;
They are gone, they are dead, in the churchyard
      laid,
    But the tree it still remains.
      Then here 's, &c.

He saw the rare times when the Christmas chimes
  Was a merry sound to hear,
When the squire's wide hall and the cottage small
  Were filled with good English cheer.
Now gold hath the sway we all obey,
  And a ruthless king is he;
But he never shall send our ancient friend
    To be tossed on the stormy sea.
      Then here 's, &c.

H. F. CHORLEY.

THE ARAB TO THE PALM.

Next to thee, O fair gazelle,
O Beddowee girl, beloved so well;

Next to the fearless Nedjidee,
Whose fleetness shall bear me again to thee;

Next to ye both, I love the palm,
With his leaves of beauty, his fruit of balm;

Next to ye both, I love the tree
Whose fluttering shadow wraps us three
With love and silence and mystery!

Our tribe is many, our poets vie
With any under the Arab sky;
Yet none can sing of the palm but I.

The marble minarets that begem
Cairo's citadel-diadem
Are not so light as his slender stem.

He lifts his leaves in the sunbeam's glance,
As the Almehs lift their arms in dance, —

A slumberous motion, a passionate sign,
That works in the cells of the blood like wine.

Full of passion and sorrow is he,
Dreaming where the beloved may be.

And when the warm south-winds arise,
He breathes his longing in fervid sighs,

Quickening odors, kisses of balm,
That drop in the lap of his chosen palm.

The sun may flame, and the sands may stir,
But the breath of his passion reaches her.

O tree of love, by that love of thine,
Teach me how I shall soften mine!

Give me the secret of the sun,
Whereby the wooed is ever won!

If I were a king, O stately tree,
A likeness, glorious as might be,
In the court of my palace I 'd build for thee!

With a shaft of silver, burnished bright,
And leaves of beryl and malachite;

With spikes of golden bloom ablaze,
And fruits of topaz and chrysoprase.

And there the poets, in thy praise,
Should night and morning frame new lays, —

New measures sung to tunes divine;
But none, O palm, should equal mine!

BAYARD TAYLOR.

THE PALM-TREE.

Is it the palm, the cocoa-palm,
On the Indian Sea, by the isles of balm ?
Or is it a ship in the breezeless calm?

A ship whose keel is of palm beneath,
Whose ribs of palm have a palm-bark sheath,
And a rudder of palm it steereth with.

Branches of palm are its spars and rails,
Fibres of palm are its woven sails,
And the rope is of palm that idly trails !

What does the good ship bear so well ?
The cocoa-nut with its stony shell,
And the milky sap of its inner cell.

What are its jars, so smooth and fine,
But hollowed nuts, filled with oil and wine,
And the cabbage that ripens under the Line ?

Who smokes his nargileh, cool and calm ?
The master, whose cunning and skill could charm
Cargo and ship from the bounteous palm.

In the cabin he sits on a palm-mat soft,
From a beaker of palm his drink is quaffed,
And a palm thatch shields from the sun aloft !

His dress is woven of palmy strands,
And he holds a palm-leaf scroll in his hands,
Traced with the Prophet's wise commands !

The turban folded about his head
Was daintily wrought of the palm-leaf braid,
And the fan that cools him of palm was made.

Of threads of palm was the carpet spun
Whereon he kneels when the day is done,
And the foreheads of Islam are bowed as one !

To him the palm is a gift divine,
Wherein all uses of man combine, —
House and raiment and food and wine !

And, in the hour of his great release,
His need of the palm shall only cease
With the shroud wherein he lieth in peace.

"Allah il Allah !" he sings his psalm,
On the Indian Sea, by the isles of balm ;
"Thanks to Allah, who gives the palm !"
JOHN GREENLEAF WHITTIER.

THE HOLLY-TREE.

O READER ! hast thou ever stood to see
The holly-tree ?
The eye that contemplates it well perceives
Its glossy leaves

Ordered by an intelligence so wise
As might confound the atheist's sophistries.

Below, a circling fence, its leaves are seen
Wrinkled and keen ;
No grazing cattle, through their prickly round,
Can reach to wound ;
But as they grow where nothing is to fear,
Smooth and unarmed the pointless leaves appear.

I love to view these things with curious eyes,
And moralize ;
And in this wisdom of the holly-tree
Can emblems see
Wherewith, perchance, to make a pleasant rhyme,
One which may profit in the after-time.

Thus, though abroad, perchance, I might appear
Harsh and austere, —
To those who on my leisure would intrude,
Reserved and rude ;
Gentle at home amid my friends I'd be,
Like the high leaves upon the holly-tree.

And should my youth, as youth is apt, I know,
Some harshness show,
All vain asperities I, day by day,
Would wear away,
Till the smooth temper of my age should be
Like the high leaves upon the holly-tree.

And as, when all the summer trees are seen
So bright and green,
The holly-leaves their fadeless hues display
Less bright than they ;
But when the bare and wintry woods we see,
What then so cheerful as the holly-tree ?

So, serious should my youth appear among
The thoughtless throng ;
So would I seem, amid the young and gay,
More grave than they ;
That in my age as cheerful I might be
As the green winter of the holly-tree.
ROBERT SOUTHEY.

THE GRAPE-VINE SWING.

LITHE and long as the serpent train,
Springing and clinging from tree to tree,
Now darting upward, now down again,
With a twist and a twirl that are strange to see ;
Never took serpent a deadlier hold,
Never the cougar a wilder spring,
Strangling the oak with the boa's fold,
Spanning the beech with the condor's wing.

Yet no foe that we fear to seek, —
The boy leaps wild to thy rude embrace ;

Thy bulging arms bear as soft a cheek
  As ever on lover's breast found place ;
On thy waving train is a playful hold
  Thou shalt never to lighter grasp persuade ;
While a maiden sits in thy drooping fold,
  And swings and sings in the noonday shade !

O giant strange of our southern woods,
  I dream of thee still in the well-known spot,
Though our vessel strains o'er the ocean floods,
  And the northern forest beholds thee not ;
I think of thee still with a sweet regret,
  As the cordage yields to my playful grasp, —
Dost thou spring and cling in our woodlands yet ?
Does the maiden still swing in thy giant clasp ?
WILLIAM GILMORE SIMMS.

FAIR PLEDGES OF A FRUITFUL TREE.

FAIR pledges of a fruitful tree,
  Why do ye fall so fast ?
  Your date is not so past
But you may stay yet here awhile
  To blush and gently smile,
    And go at last.

What ! were ye born to be
  An hour or half's delight,
  And so to bid good night ?
'T is pity Nature brought ye forth,
  Merely to show your worth,
    And lose you quite.

But you are lovely leaves, where we
  May read how soon things have
  Their end, though ne'er so brave ;
And after they have shown their pride
  Like you awhile, they glide
    Into the grave.
ROBERT HERRICK.

ALMOND BLOSSOM.

BLOSSOM of the almond-trees,
April's gift to April's bees,
Birthday ornament of spring,
Flora's fairest daughterling ; —
Coming when no flowerets dare
Trust the cruel outer air,
When the royal king-cup bold
Dares not don his coat of gold,
And the sturdy blackthorn spray
Keeps his silver for the May ; —
Coming when no flowerets would,
Save thy lowly sisterhood,
Early violets, blue and white,
Dying for their love of light.

Almond blossom, sent to teach us
That the spring days soon will reach us,
Lest, with longing over-tried,
We die as the violets died, —
Blossom, clouding all the tree
With thy crimson broidery,
Long before a leaf of green
On the bravest bough is seen, —
Ah ! when winter winds are swinging
All thy red bells into ringing,
With a bee in every bell,
Almond bloom, we greet thee well.
EDWIN ARNOLD.

THE PLANTING OF THE APPLE-TREE.

COME, let us plant the apple-tree.
Cleave the tough greensward with the spade ;
Wide let its hollow bed be made ;
There gently lay the roots, and there
Sift the dark mould with kindly care,
  And press it o'er them tenderly,
As round the sleeping infant's feet
We softly fold the cradle-sheet ;
  So plant we the apple-tree.

What plant we in this apple-tree ?
Buds, which the breath of summer days
Shall lengthen into leafy sprays ;
Boughs where the thrush, with crimson breast,
Shall haunt, and sing, and hide her nest ;
  We plant, upon the sunny lea,
A shadow for the noontide hour,
A shelter from the summer shower,
  When we plant the apple-tree.

What plant we in this apple-tree ?
Sweets for a hundred flowery springs
To load the May-wind's restless wings,
When, from the orchard row, he pours
Its fragrance through our open doors ;
  A world of blossoms for the bee,
Flowers for the sick girl's silent room,
For the glad infant sprigs of bloom,
  We plant with the apple-tree.

What plant we in this apple-tree ?
Fruits that shall swell in sunny June,
And redden in the August noon,
And drop, when gentle airs come by,
That fan the blue September sky,
  While children come, with cries of glee,
And seek them where the fragrant grass
Betrays their bed to those who pass,
  At the foot of the apple-tree.

And when, above this apple-tree,
The winter stars are quivering bright,
And winds go howling through the night,

Girls, whose young eyes o'erflow with mirth,
Shall peel its fruit by cottage hearth,
    And guests in prouder homes shall see,
    Heaped with the grape of Cintra's vine
And golden orange of the Line,
    The fruit of the apple-tree.

The fruitage of this apple-tree
Winds and our flag of stripe and star,
Shall bear to coasts that lie afar,
    Where men shall wonder at the view,
    And ask in what fair groves they grew;
And sojourners beyond the sea
Shall think of childhood's careless day
And long, long hours of summer play,
    In the shade of the apple-tree.

Each year shall give this apple-tree
A broader flush of roseate bloom,
A deeper maze of verdurous gloom,
    And loosen, when the frost-clouds lower,
    The crisp brown leaves in thicker shower.
The years past shall come and pass, but we
Shall hear no longer, where we lie,
The summer's songs, the autumn's sigh,
    In the boughs of the apple-tree.

And time shall waste this apple-tree.
O, when its aged branches throw
Thin shadows on the ground below,
    Shall fraud and force and iron will
    Oppress the weak and helpless still?
What shall the tasks of mercy be,
Amid the toils, the strifes, the tears
Of those who live when length of years
    Is wasting this apple-tree?

"Who planted this old apple-tree?"
The children of that distant day
Thus to some aged man shall say;
    And, gazing on its mossy stem,
    The gray-haired man shall answer them:
"A poet of the land was he,
Born in the rude but good old times;
'T is said he made some quaint old rhymes
    On planting the apple-tree."
                    WILLIAM CULLEN BRYANT.

THE MAIZE.

"That precious seed into the furrow cast
Earliest in springtime crowns the harvest last."
                    PHŒBE CAREY.

A song for the plant of my own native West,
    Where nature and freedom reside,
By plenty still crowned, and by peace ever blest,
    To the corn! the green corn of her pride!

In climes of the East has the olive been sung,
    And the grape been the theme of their lays,
But for thee shall a harp of the backwoods be
        strung,
    Thou bright, ever beautiful maize!

Afar in the forest the rude cabins rise,
    And send up their pillars of smoke,
And the tops of their columns are lost in the skies,
    O'er the heads of the cloud-kissing oak;
Near the skirt of the grove, where the sturdy arm
        swings
    The axe till the old giant sways,
And echo repeats every blow as it rings,
    Shoots the green and the glorious maize!

There buds of the buckeye in spring are the first,
    And the willow's gold hair then appears,
And snowy the cups of the dogwood that burst
    By the red bud, with pink-tinted tears.
And striped the bolls which the poppy holds up
    For the dew, and the sun's yellow rays,
And brown is the pawpaw's shade-blossoming cup,
    In the wood, near the sun-loving maize!

When through the dark soil the bright steel of
        the plough
    Turns the mould from its unbroken bed,
The ploughman is cheered by the finch on the
        bough,
    And the blackbird doth follow his tread.
And idle, afar on the landscape descried,
    The deep-lowing kine slowly graze,
And nibbling the grass on the sunny hillside
    Are the sheep, hedged away from the maize.

With springtime and culture, in martial array
    It waves its green broadswords on high,
And fights with the gale, in a fluttering fray,
    And the sunbeams, which fall from the sky;
It strikes its green blades at the zephyrs at noon,
    And at night at the swift-flying fays,
Who ride through the darkness the beams of the
        moon,
    Through the spears and the flags of the Maize!

When the summer is fierce still its banners are
        green,
    Each warrior's long beard groweth red,
His emerald-bright sword is sharp-pointed and
        keen,
    And golden his tassel-plumed head.
As a host of armed knights set a monarch at
        naught,
    They defy the day-god to his gaze,
And, revived every morn from the battle that's
        fought,
    Fresh stand the green ranks of the maize!

But brown comes the autumn, and sear grows
    the corn,
  And the woods like a rainbow are dressed,
And but for the cock and the noontide horn
  Old Time would be tempted to rest.
The humming bee fans off a shower of gold
  From the mullein's long rod as it sways,
And dry grow the leaves which protecting infold
  The ears of the well-ripened maize !

At length Indian Summer, the lovely, doth come,
  With its blue frosty nights, and days still,
When distantly clear sounds the waterfall's hum,
  And the sun smokes ablaze on the hill !
A dim veil hangs over the landscape and flood,
  And the hills are all mellowed in haze,
While fall, creeping on like a monk 'neath his
    hood,
  Plucks the thick-rustling wealth of the maize.

And the heavy wains creak to the barns large
    and gray,
  Where the treasure securely we hold,
Housed safe from the tempest, dry - sheltered
    away,
  Our blessing more precious than gold !
And long for this manna that springs from the
    sod
  Shall we gratefully give Him the praise,
The source of all bounty, our Father and God,
  Who sent us from heaven the maize !
               WILLIAM W. FOSDICK.

THE POTATO.

I 'M a careless potato, and care not a pin
  How into existence I came ;
If they planted me drill-wise, or dibbled me in,
  To me 't is exactly the same.
The bean and the pea may more loftily tower,
  But I care not a button for them ;
Defiance I nod with my beautiful flower
  When the earth is hoed up to my stem.
               THOMAS MOORE.

THE PUMPKIN.

On the banks of the Xenil the dark Spanish maiden
Comes up with the fruit of the tangled vine laden ;
And the Creole of Cuba laughs out to behold
Through orange-leaves shining the broad spheres
  of gold ;
Yet with dearer delight from his home in the North,
On the fields of his harvest the Yankee looks forth,
Where crook-necks are coiling and yellow fruit
  shines,
And the sun of September melts down on his vines.

Ah ! on Thanksgiving Day, when from East and
    from West,
From North and from South come the pilgrim
    and guest,
When the gray-haired New-Englander sees round
    his board
The old broken links of affection restored,
When the care-wearied man seeks his mother once
    more,
And the worn matron smiles where the girl smiled
    before,
What moistens the lip, and what brightens the eye ?
What calls back the past like the rich pumpkin-
    pie ?

O, — fruit loved of boyhood ! — the old days re-
    calling,
When wood-grapes were purpling and brown nuts
    were falling !
When wild, ugly faces we carved in its skin,
Glaring out through the dark with a candle within !
When we laughed round the corn-heap, with hearts
    all in tune,
Our chair a broad pumpkin, — our lantern the
    moon,
Telling tales of the fairy who travelled like steam
In a pumpkin-shell coach, with two rats for her
    team !

Then thanks for thy present ! — none sweeter or
    better
E'er smoked from an oven or circled a platter !
Fairer hands never wrought at a pastry more fine,
Brighter eyes never watched o'er its baking, than
    thine !
And the prayer, which my mouth is too full to
    express,
Swells my heart that thy shadow may never be less,
That the days of thy lot may be lengthened below,
And the fame of thy worth like a pumpkin-vine
    grow,
And thy life be as sweet, and its last sunset sky
Golden-tinted and fair as thy own pumpkin-pie !
          JOHN GREENLEAF WHITTIER.

HYMN TO THE FLOWERS.

DAY-STARS ! that ope your frownless eyes to twin-
    kle
  From rainbow galaxies of earth's creation,
And dew-drops on her lonely altars sprinkle
    As a libation.

Ye matin worshippers ! who bending lowly
  Before the uprisen sun, God's lidless eye,
Throw from your chalices a sweet and holy
    Incense on high.

Ye bright mosaics ! that with storied beauty,
The floor of Nature's temple tessellate,
What numerous emblems of instructive duty
Your forms create !

'Neath cloistered boughs, each floral bell that
swingeth
And tolls its perfume on the passing air,
Makes Sabbath in the fields, and ever ringeth
A call to prayer.

Not to the domes where crumbling arch and column
Attest the feebleness of mortal hand,
But to that fane, most catholic and solemn,
Which God hath planned ;

To that cathedral, boundless as our wonder,
Whose quenchless lamps the sun and moon
supply ;
Its choir the winds and waves, its organ thunder,
Its dome the sky.

There, as in solitude and shade I wander
Through the green aisles, or stretched upon the
sod,
Awed by the silence, reverently ponder
The ways of God,

Your voiceless lips, O flowers ! are living preach-
ers,
Each cup a pulpit, every leaf a book,
Supplying to my fancy numerous teachers
From loneliest nook.

Floral Apostles ! that in dewy splendor
" Weep without woe, and blush without a
crime,"
O, may I deeply learn, and ne'er surrender
Your lore sublime !

" Thou wert not, Solomon, in all thy glory,
Arrayed," the lilies cry, " in robes like ours !
How vain your grandeur ! ah, how transitory
Are human flowers !"

In the sweet-scented pictures, heavenly artist !
With which thou paintest Nature's wide-spread
hall,
What a delightful lesson thou impartest
Of love to all !

Not useless are ye, flowers ! though made for
pleasure ;
Blooming o'er field and wave, by day and night,
From every source your sanction bids me treasure
Harmless delight.

Ephemeral sages ! what instructors hoary
For such a world of thought could furnish scope ?
Each fading calyx a *memento mori*,
Yet fount of hope.

Posthumous glories ! angel-like collection !
Upraised from seed or bulb interred in earth,
Ye are to me a type of resurrection
And second birth.

Were I in churchless solitudes remaining,
Far from all voice of teachers and divines,
My soul would find, in flowers of God's ordaining,
Priests, sermons, shrines !

HORACE SMITH.

FLOWERS.

I WILL not have the mad Clytie,
Whose head is turned by the sun ;
The tulip is a courtly quean,
Whom, therefore, I will shun ;
The cowslip is a country wench,
The violet is a nun ; —
But I will woo the dainty rose,
The queen of every one.

The pea is but a wanton witch,
In too much haste to wed,
And clasps her rings on every hand ;
The wolfsbane I should dread ;
Nor will I dreary rosemarye,
That always mourns the dead ; —
But I will woo the dainty rose,
With her cheeks of tender red.

The lily is all in white, like a saint,
And so is no mate for me ;
And the daisy's cheek is tipped with a blush,
She is of such low degree ;
Jasmine is sweet, and has many loves,
And the broom 's betrothed to the bee ; —
But I will plight with the dainty rose,
For fairest of all is she.

THOMAS HOOD.

THE ROSE.

FROM "HASSAN BEN KHALED."

" THEN took the generous host
A basket filled with roses.   Every guest
Cried, ' Give me roses !' and he thus addressed
His words to all : ' He who exalts them most
In song, he only shall the roses wear.'
Then sang a guest : ' The rose's cheeks are fair ;
It crowns the purple bowl, and no one knows
If the rose colors it, or it the rose.'
And sang another : ' Crimson is its hue,
And on its breast the morning's crystal dew
Is changed to rubies.'   Then a third replied :
' It blushes in the sun's enamored sight,

As a young virgin on her wedding night,
When from her face the bridegroom lifts the veil.'
When all had sung their songs, I, Hassan, tried.
'The rose,' I sang, 'is either red or pale,
Like maidens whom the flame of passion burns,
And love or jealousy controls, by turns.
Its buds are lips preparing for a kiss ;
Its open flowers are like the blush of bliss
On lovers' cheeks ; the thorns its armor are,
And in its centre shines a golden star,
As on a favorite's cheek a sequin glows ; —
And thus the garden's favorite is the rose.'
"The master from his open basket shook
The roses on my head."

BAYARD TAYLOR.

THE MOSS ROSE.

[Translation.]

THE angel of the flowers, one day,
Beneath a rose-tree sleeping lay, —
That spirit to whose charge 't is given
To bathe young buds in dews of heaven,
Awaking from his light repose,
The angel whispered to the rose :
"O fondest object of my care,
Still fairest found, where all are fair ;
For the sweet shade thou giv'st to me
Ask what thou wilt, 't is granted thee."
"Then," said the rose, with deepened glow,
"On me another grace bestow."
The spirit paused, in silent thought, —
What grace was there that flower had not ?
'T was but a moment, — o'er the rose
A veil of moss the angel throws,
And, robed in nature's simplest weed,
Could there a flower that rose exceed ?

KRUMMACHER.

THE ROSE.

FROM "THE LADY OF THE LAKE."

"THE rose is fairest when 't is budding new,
    And hope is brightest when it dawns from
        fears ;
The rose is sweetest washed with morning dew,
    And love is loveliest when embalmed in tears.
O wilding rose, whom fancy thus endears,
    I bid your blossoms in my bonnet wave,
Emblem of hope and love through future years ! "
    Thus spoke young Norman, heir of Arman-
        dave,
    What time the sun arose on Vennachar's broad
        wave.

SIR WALTER SCOTT.

'T IS THE LAST ROSE OF SUMMER.

'T IS the last rose of summer,
    Left blooming alone ;
All her lovely companions
    Are faded and gone ;
No flower of her kindred,
    No rosebud, is nigh
To reflect back her blushes,
    Or give sigh for sigh !

I 'll not leave thee, thou lone one !
    To pine on the stem ;
Since the lovely are sleeping,
    Go, sleep thou with them ;
Thus kindly I scatter
    Thy leaves o'er the bed
Where thy mates of the garden
    Lie scentless and dead.

So soon may I follow,
    When friendships decay,
And from love's shining circle
    The gems drop away !
When true hearts lie withered,
    And fond ones are flown,
O, who would inhabit
    This bleak world alone ?

THOMAS MOORE ("*Irish Melodies*").

TO THE FRINGED GENTIAN.

THOU blossom, bright with autumn dew,
And colored with the heaven's own blue,
That openest when the quiet light
Succeeds the keen and frosty night ;

Thou comest not when violets lean
O'er wandering brooks and springs unseen,
Or columbines, in purple dressed,
Nod o'er the ground-bird's hidden nest.

Thou waitest late, and com'st alone,
When woods are bare and birds are flown,
And frosts and shortening days portend
The aged Year is near his end.

Then doth thy sweet and quiet eye
Look through its fringes to the sky,
Blue — blue — as if that sky let fall
A flower from its cerulean wall.

I would that thus, when I shall see
The hour of death draw near to me,
Hope, blossoming within my heart,
May look to heaven as I depart.

WILLIAM CULLEN BRYANT.

THE EARLY PRIMROSE.

MILD offspring of a dark and sullen sire!
Whose modest form, so delicately fine,
    Was nursed in whirling storms
    And cradled in the winds.

Thee, when young Spring first questioned Winter's sway,
And dared the sturdy blusterer to the fight,
    Thee on this bank he threw
    To mark his victory.

In this low vale the promise of the year,
Serene, thou openest to the nipping gale,
    Unnoticed and alone,
    Thy tender elegance.

So Virtue blooms, brought forth amid the storms
Of chill adversity; in some lone walk
    Of life she rears her head,
    Obscure and unobserved;

While every bleaching breeze that on her blows
Chastens her spotless purity of breast,
    And hardens her to bear
    Serene the ills of life.
              HENRY KIRKE WHITE.

THE RHODORA.

LINES ON BEING ASKED, WHENCE IS THE FLOWER?

IN May, when sea-winds pierced our solitudes,
I found the fresh rhodora in the woods
Spreading its leafless blooms in a damp nook,
To please the desert and the sluggish brook:
The purple petals fallen in the pool
Made the black waters with their beauty gay, —
Here might the red-bird come his plumes to cool,
   And court the flower that cheapens his array.
Rhodora! if the sages ask thee why
This charm is wasted on the marsh and sky,
Dear, tell them, that if eyes were made for seeing,
Then beauty is its own excuse for being.
   Why thou wert there, O rival of the rose!
I never thought to ask; I never knew,
   But in my simple ignorance suppose
The selfsame Power that brought me there brought you.
              RALPH WALDO EMERSON.

THE BROOM-FLOWER.

O THE broom, the yellow broom!
   The ancient poet sung it,
And dear it is on summer days
   To lie at rest among it.

I know the realms where people say
   The flowers have not their fellow;
I know where they shine out like suns,
   The crimson and the yellow.

I know where ladies live enchained
   In luxury's silken fetters,
And flowers as bright as glittering gems
   Are used for written letters.

But ne'er was flower so fair as this,
   In modern days or olden;
It groweth on its nodding stem
   Like to a garland golden.

And all about my mother's door
   Shine out its glittering bushes,
And down the glen, where clear as light
   The mountain-water gushes.

Take all the rest; but give me this,
   And the bird that nestles in it, —
I love it, for it loves the broom, —
   The green and yellow linnet.

Well, call the rose the queen of flowers,
   And boast of that of Sharon,
Of lilies like to marble cups,
   And the golden rod of Aaron:

I care not how these flowers may be
   Beloved of man and woman;.
The broom it is the flower for me,
   That groweth on the common.

O the broom, the yellow broom!
   The ancient poet sung it,
And dear it is on summer days
   To lie at rest among it.
             MARY HOWITT.

VIOLETS.

WELCOME, maids of honor!
   You do bring
   In the Spring,
And wait upon her.

She has virgins many,
   Fresh and fair;
   Yet you are
More sweet than any.

Y' are the maiden Posies,
   And, so graced,
   To be placed,
'Fore damask roses.

Yet though thus respected,
     By and by
     Ye do lie,
Poor girls, neglected.

ROBERT HERRICK.

THE VIOLET.

O FAINT, delicious, springtime violet !
     Thine odor, like a key,
Turns noiselessly in memory's wards to let
     A thought of sorrow free.

The breath of distant fields upon my brow
     Blows through that open door
The sound of wind-borne bells, more sweet and
          low,
     And sadder than of yore.

It comes afar, from that beloved place,
     And that beloved hour,
When life hung ripening in love's golden grace,
     Like grapes above a bower.

A spring goes singing through its reedy grass ;
     The lark sings o'er my head,
Drowned in the sky — O, pass, ye visions, pass !
     I would that I were dead ! —

Why hast thou opened that forbidden door,
     From which I ever flee ?
O vanished joy ! O love, that art no more,
     Let my vexed spirit be !

O violet ! thy odor through my brain
     Hath searched, and stung to grief
This sunny day, as if a curse did stain
     Thy velvet leaf.

WILLIAM W. STORY.

TO THE DAISY.

WITH little here to do or see
Of things that in the great world be,
Sweet daisy ! oft I talk to thee.
     For thou art worthy,
Thou unassuming commonplace
Of nature, with that homely face,
And yet with something of a grace
     Which love makes for thee !

Oft on the dappled turf at ease
I sit and play with similes,
Loose types of things through all degrees,
     Thoughts of thy raising ;
And many a fond and idle name
I give to thee, for praise or blame,
As is the humor of the game,
     While I am gazing.

A nun demure, of lowly port ;
Or sprightly maiden, of Love's court,
In thy simplicity the sport
     Of all temptations ;
A queen in crown of rubies drest ;
A starveling in a scanty vest, —
Are all, as seems to suit thee best,
     Thy appellations.

A little Cyclops, with one eye
Staring to threaten and defy,
That thought comes next, — and instantly
     The freak is over,
The shape will vanish, and behold !
A silver shield with boss of gold
That spreads itself, some fairy bold
     In fight to cover.

I see thee glittering from afar, —
And then thou art a pretty star,
Not quite so fair as many are
     In heaven above thee !
Yet like a star, with glittering crest,
Self-poised in air thou seem'st to rest ; —
May peace come never to his nest
     Who shall reprove thee !

Sweet flower ! for by that name at last,
When all my reveries are past,
I call thee, and to that cleave fast,
     Sweet, silent creature !
That breath'st with me in sun and air,
Do thou, as thou art wont, repair
My heart with gladness, and a share
     Of thy meek nature !

WILLIAM WORDSWORTH.

THE DAISY.

STAR of the mead ! sweet daughter of the day,
Whose opening flower invites the morning ray,
From the moist cheek and bosom's chilly fold
To kiss the tears of eve, the dew-drops cold !
Sweet daisy, flower of love, when birds are paired,
'T is sweet to see thee, with thy bosom bared,
Smiling in virgin innocence serene,
Thy pearly crown above thy vest of green.
The lark with sparkling eye and rustling wing
Rejoins his widowed mate in early spring,
And as he prunes his plumes of russet hue,
Swears on thy maiden blossom to be true.
Oft have I watched thy closing buds at eve,
Which for the parting sunbeams seemed to grieve ;
And when gay morning gilt the dew-bright plain,
Seen them unclasp their folded leaves again ;
Nor he who sung "The daisy is so sweet !"
More dearly loved thy pearly form to greet.

When on his scarf the knight the daisy bound,
And dames to tourneys shone with daisies crowned,
And fays forsook the purer fields above,
To hail the daisy, flower of faithful love.

DR. LEYDEN.

TO A MOUNTAIN DAISY,

ON TURNING ONE DOWN WITH THE PLOUGH, IN APRIL,
1786.

WEE, modest, crimson-tippéd flower,
Thou 's met me in an evil hour,
For I maun crush amang the stoure
    Thy slender stem ;
To spare thee now is past my power,
    Thou bonny gem.

Alas ! it 's no thy neibor sweet,
The bonny lark, companion meet,
Bending thee 'mang the dewy weet,
    Wi' speckled breast,
When upward springing, blithe, to greet
    The purpling east.

Cauld blew the bitter biting north
Upon thy early, humble birth ;
Yet cheerfully thou glinted forth
    Amid the storm,
Scarce reared above the parent earth
    Thy tender form.

The flaunting flowers our gardens yield,
High sheltering woods and wa's maun shield :
But thou beneath the random bield
    O' clod or stane,
Adorns the histie stibble-field,
    Unseen, alane.

There, in thy scanty mantle clad,
Thy snawie bosom sunward spread,
Thou lifts thy unassuming head
    In humble guise ;
But now the share uptears thy bed,
    And low thou lies !

Such is the fate of artless maid,
Sweet floweret of the rural shade !
By love's simplicity betrayed,
    And guileless trust,
Till she, like thee, all soiled, is laid
    Low i' the dust.

Such is the fate of simple bard,
On life's rough ocean luckless starred !
Unskilful he to note the card
    Of prudent lore,
Till billows rage, and gales blow hard,
    And whelm him o'er !

Such fate to suffering worth is given,
Who long with wants and woes has striven,
By human pride or cunning driven
    To misery's brink,
Till wrenched of every stay but Heaven,
    He, ruined, sink !

Even thou who mourn'st the daisy's fate,
That fate is thine, — no distant date :
Stern Ruin's ploughshare drives, elate,
    Full on thy bloom,
Till crushed beneath the furrow's weight,
    Shall be thy doom !

ROBERT BURNS.

THE DAISY.

THERE is a flower, a little flower
    With silver crest and golden eye,
That welcomes every changing hour,
    And weathers every sky.

The prouder beauties of the field
    In gay but quick succession shine ;
Race after race their honors yield,
    They flourish and decline.

But this small flower, to Nature dear,
    While moons and stars their courses run,
Inwreathes the circle of the year,
    Companion of the sun.

It smiles upon the lap of May,
    To sultry August spreads its charm,
Lights pale October on his way,
    And twines December's arm.

The purple heath and golden broom
    On moory mountains catch the gale ;
O'er lawns the lily sheds perfume,
    The violet in the vale.

But this bold floweret climbs the hill,
    Hides in the forest, haunts the glen,
Plays on the margin of the rill,
    Peeps round the fox's den.

Within the garden's cultured round
    It shares the sweet carnation's bed ;
And blooms on consecrated ground
    In honor of the dead.

The lambkin crops its crimson gem ;
    The wild bee murmurs on its breast ;
The blue-fly bends its pensile stem
    Light o'er the skylark's nest.

'T is Flora's page, — in every place,
  In every season, fresh and fair ;
It opens with perennial grace,
  And blossoms everywhere.

On waste and woodland, rock and plain,
  Its humble buds unheeded rise ;
The rose has but a summer reign ;
  The daisy never dies !
                    JAMES MONTGOMERY.

DAFFODILS.

I WANDERED lonely as a cloud
  That floats on high o'er vales and hills,
When all at once I saw a crowd, —
  A host of golden daffodils
Beside the lake, beneath the trees,
Fluttering and dancing in the breeze.

Continuous as the stars that shine
  And twinkle on the Milky Way,
They stretched in never-ending line
  Along the margin of a bay :
Ten thousand saw I, at a glance,
Tossing their heads in sprightly dance.

The waves beside them danced, but they
  Outdid the sparkling waves in glee ;
A poet could not but be gay
  In such a jocund company ;
I gazed — and gazed — but little thought
What wealth the show to me had brought.

For oft, when on my couch I lie,
  In vacant or in pensive mood,
They flash upon that inward eye
  Which is the bliss of solitude ;
And then my heart with pleasure fills,
And dances with the daffodils.
                    WILLIAM WORDSWORTH.

DAFFODILS.

FAIR daffodils, we weep to see
  You haste away so soon ;
As yet the early-rising sun
  Has not attained its noon.
    Stay, stay,
  Until the hastening day
    Has run
  But to the even-song ;
And, having prayed together, we
  Will go with you along.

We have short time to stay as you,
  We have as short a spring ;

As quick a growth, to meet decay,
  As you or anything.
    We die,
  As your hours do, and dry
    Away,
  Like to the summer's rain,
Or as the pearls of morning's dew,
  Ne'er to be found again.
                    ROBERT HERRICK.

THE VOICE OF THE GRASS.

HERE I come creeping, creeping everywhere ;
  By the dusty roadside,
  On the sunny hillside,
  Close by the noisy brook,
  In every shady nook,
I come creeping, creeping everywhere.

Here I come creeping, smiling everywhere ;
  All round the open door,
  Where sit the aged poor ;
  Here where the children play,
  In the bright and merry May,
I come creeping, creeping everywhere.

Here I come creeping, creeping everywhere ;
  In the noisy city street
  My pleasant face you 'll meet,
  Cheering the sick at heart
  Toiling his busy part, —
Silently creeping, creeping everywhere.

Here I come creeping, creeping everywhere ;
  You cannot see me coming,
  Nor hear my low sweet humming ;
  For in the starry night,
  And the glad morning light,
I come quietly creeping everywhere.

Here I come creeping, creeping everywhere ;
  More welcome than the flowers
  In summer's pleasant hours ;
  The gentle cow is glad,
  And the merry bird not sad,
To see me creeping, creeping everywhere.

Here I come creeping, creeping everywhere ;
  When you 're numbered with the dead
  In your still and narrow bed,
  In the happy spring I 'll come
  And deck your silent home, —
Creeping, silently creeping everywhere.

Here I come creeping, creeping everywhere ;
  My humble song of praise
  Most joyfully I raise
  To Him at whose command
  I beautify the land,
Creeping, silently creeping everywhere.
                    SARAH ROBERTS.

THE IVY GREEN.

O, A DAINTY plant is the ivy green,
  That creepeth o'er ruins old !
Of right choice food are his meals, I ween,
  In his cell so lone and cold.
The walls must be crumbled, the stones decayed,
  To pleasure his dainty whim ;
And the mouldering dust that years have made
  Is a merry meal for him.
      Creeping where no life is seen,
      A rare old plant is the ivy green.

Fast he stealeth on, though he wears no wings,
  And a stanch old heart has he !
How closely he twineth, how tight he clings
  To his friend, the huge oak-tree !
And slyly he traileth along the ground,
  And his leaves he gently waves,
And he joyously twines and hugs around
  The rich mould of dead men's graves.
      Creeping where no life is seen,
      A rare old plant is the ivy green.

Whole ages have fled, and their works decayed,
  And nations scattered been ;
But the stout old ivy shall never fade
  From its hale and hearty green.
The brave old plant in its lonely days
  Shall fatten upon the past ;
For the stateliest building man can raise
  Is the ivy's food at last.
      Creeping where no life is seen,
      A rare old plant is the ivy green.
                        CHARLES DICKENS.

THE DEATH OF THE FLOWERS.

THE melancholy days are come, the saddest of
  the year,
Of wailing winds, and naked woods, and meadows
  brown and sear.
Heaped in the hollows of the grove, the autumn
  leaves lie dead ;
They rustle to the eddying gust, and to the rab-
  bit's tread.
The robin and the wren are flown, and from the
  shrubs the jay,
And from the wood-top calls the crow through all
  the gloomy day.

Where are the flowers, the fair young flowers, that
  lately sprang and stood
In brighter light and softer airs, a beauteous
  sisterhood ?
Alas ! they all are in their graves ; the gentle race
  of flowers

Are lying in their lowly beds with the fair and
  good of ours.
The rain is falling where they lie ; but the cold
  November rain
Calls not from out the gloomy earth the lovely
  ones again.

The wind-flower and the violet, they perished long
  ago,
And the brier-rose and the orchis died amid the
  summer glow ;
But on the hill the golden-rod, and the aster in
  the wood,
And the yellow sunflower by the brook in au-
  tumn beauty stood,
Till fell the frost from the clear cold heaven, as
  falls the plague on men,
And the brightness of their smile was gone from
  upland, glade, and glen.

And now, when comes the calm mild day, as still
  such days will come,
To call the squirrel and the bee from out their
  winter home ;
When the sound of dropping nuts is heard, though
  all the trees are still,
And twinkle in the smoky light the waters of the
  rill,
The south-wind searches for the flowers whose
  fragrance late he bore,
And sighs to find them in the wood and by the
  stream no more.

And then I think of one who in her youthful
  beauty died,
The fair meek blossom that grew up and faded
  by my side.
In the cold moist earth we laid her, when the
  forests cast the leaf,
And we wept that one so lovely should have a
  life so brief ;
Yet not unmeet it was that one, like that young
  friend of ours,
So gentle and so beautiful, should perish with the
  flowers.
                WILLIAM CULLEN BRYANT.

THE USE OF FLOWERS.

GOD might have bade the earth bring forth
  Enough for great and small,
The oak-tree and the cedar-tree,
  Without a flower at all.
We might have had enough, enough
  For every want of ours,
For luxury, medicine, and toil,
  And yet have had no flowers.

AUTUMN DAYS.

" When the sound of dropping nuts is heard, though all the trees are still,
And twinkle in the smoky light the waters of the rill."

Then wherefore, wherefore were they made,
  All dyed with rainbow-light,
All fashioned with supremest grace
  Upspringing day and night : —
Springing in valleys green and low,
  And on the mountains high,
And in the silent wilderness
  Where no man passes by ?

Our outward life requires them not, —
  Then wherefore had they birth ?—
To minister delight to man,
  To beautify the earth ;
To comfort man, — to whisper hope,
  Whene'er his faith is dim,
For who so careth for the flowers
  Will care much more for him !
                        MARY HOWITT.

BETROTHED ANEW.

The sunlight fills the trembling air,
  And balmy days their guerdons bring ;
The Earth again is young and fair,
  And amorous with musky Spring.

The golden nurslings of the May
  In splendor strew the spangled green,
And hues of tender beauty play,
  Entangled where the willows lean.

Mark how the rippled currents flow ;
  What lustres on the meadows lie !
And hark ! the songsters come and go,
  And trill between the earth and sky.

Who told us that the years had fled,
  Or borne afar our blissful youth ?
Such joys are all about us spread,
  We know the whisper was not truth.

The birds that break from grass and grove
  Sing every carol that they sung
When first our veins were rich with love,
  And May her mantle round us flung.

O fresh-lit dawn ! immortal life !
  O Earth's betrothal, sweet and true,
With whose delights our souls are rife,
  And aye their vernal vows renew !

Then, darling, walk with me this morn ;
  Let your brown tresses drink its sheen ;
These violets, within them worn,
  Of floral fays shall make you queen.

What though there comes a time of pain
  When autumn winds forbode decay ?
The days of love are born again ;
  That fabled time is far away !

And never seemed the land so fair
  As now, nor birds such notes to sing,
Since first within your shining hair
  I wove the blossoms of the spring.
              EDMUND CLARENCE STEDMAN.

THE STORY OF A SUMMER DAY.

O PERFECT Light, which shaid away
  The darkness from the light,
And set a ruler o'er the day,
  Another o'er the night ;

Thy glory, when the day forth flies,
  More vively does appear,
Than at midday unto our eyes
  The shining sun is clear.

The shadow of the earth anon
  Removes and drawis by,
While in the east, when it is gone,
  Appears a clearer sky.

Which soon perceive the little larks,
  The lapwing and the snipe,
And time their songs, like Nature's clerks,
  O'er meadow, muir, and stripe.

Our hemisphere is polished clean,
  And lightened more and more ;
While everything is clearly seen,
  Which seemed dim before ;

Except the glistering astres bright,
  Which all the night were clear,
Offuskéd with a greater light
  No longer do appear.

The golden globe incontinent
  Sets up his shining head,
And o'er the earth and firmament
  Displays his beams abroad.

For joy the birds with boulden throats
  Against his visage sheen
Take up their kindly music notes
  In woods and gardens green.

The dew upon the tender crops,
  Like pearles white and round,
Or like to melted silver drops,
  Refreshes all the ground.

The misty reek, the clouds of rain
  From tops of mountains skails,
Clear are the highest hills and plain,
  The vapors take the vales.

The ample heaven, of fabric sure,
  In cleanness does surpass
The crystal and the silver pure,
  Or clearest polished glass.

The time so tranquil is and still,
  That nowhere shall ye find,
Save on a high and barren hill,
  The air of peeping wind.

All trees and simples, great and small,
  That balmy leaf do bear,
Than they were painted on a wall,
  No more they move or steir.

Calm is the deep and purple sea,
  Yea, smoother than the sand ;
The waves, that weltering wont to be,
  Are stable like the land.

So silent is the cessile air,
  That every cry and call,
The hills and dales and forest fair
  Again repeats them all.

The flourishes and fragrant flowers,
  Through Phœbus' fostering heat,
Refreshed with dew and silver showers,
  Cast up an odor sweet.

The cloggéd busy humming bees,
  That never think to drone,
On flowers and flourishes of trees,
  Collect their liquor brown.

The sun, most like a speedy post,
  With ardent course ascends ;
The beauty of the heavenly host
  Up to our zenith tends ;

Not guided by a Phaëthon,
  Not trainéd in a chair,
But by the high and holy One,
  Who does all where empíre.

The burning beams down from his face
  So fervently can beat,
That man and beast now seek a place
  To save them from the heat.

The herds beneath some leafy tree,
  Amidst the flowers they lie ;
The stable ships upon the sea
  Tend up their sails to dry.

With gilded eyes and open wings,
  The cock his courage shows ;
With claps of joy his breast he dings,
  And twenty times he crows.

The dove with whistling wings so blue,
  The winds can fast collect,
Her purple pens turn many a hue
  Against the sun direct.

Now noon is went ; gone is midday,
  The heat does slake at last,
The sun descends down west away,
  For three o'clock is past.

The rayons of the sun we see
  Diminish in their strength,
The shade of every tower and tree
  Extended is in length.

Great is the calm, for everywhere
  The wind is settling down,
The reek throws right up in the air
  From every tower and town.

The gloaming comes, the day is spent,
  The sun goes out of sight,
And painted is the occident
  With purple sanguine bright.

The scarlet nor the golden thread,
  Who would their beauty try,
Are nothing like the color red
  And beauty of the sky.

Our west horizon circular,
  From time the sun be set,
Is all with rubies, as it were,
  Or roses red o'erfret.

What pleasure were to walk and see,
  Endlong a river clear,
The perfect form of every tree
  Within the deep appear.

O, then it were a seemly thing,
  While all is still and calm,
The praise of God to play and sing
  With cornet and with shalm !

All laborers draw home at even,
  And can to other say,
Thanks to the gracious God of heaven,
  Which sent this summer day.
                    ALEXANDER HUME.

The Prairie States-

A newer "Garden of Creation,"
—no primal solitude:
Dense, joyous, modern, populous
millions, cities and farms,
With iron interlaced, composite,
tied, many in one,
By all the "world contributed"—
Freedom's and Law's and Thrift's "society,"
The crown and teeming "Paradise," so
far, of Time's accumulations,
To justify the "Past."

Walt Whitman

POEMS OF PEACE AND WAR.

Close his eyes; his work is done!
What to him is friend or foeman,
Rise of moon or set of sun,
Hand of man or kiss of woman?
Lay him low, lay him low,
In the clover or the snow!
What cares he? he cannot know;
Lay him low!

Geo. H. Boker.

POEMS OF PEACE AND WAR.

ODE TO PEACE.

DAUGHTER of God ! that sit'st on high
Amid the dances of the sky,
And guidest with thy gentle sway
The planets on their tuneful way ;
 Sweet Peace ! shall ne'er again
The smile of thy most holy face,
From thine ethereal dwelling-place,
Rejoice the wretched, weary race
 Of discord-breathing men ?
Too long, O gladness-giving Queen !
Thy tarrying in heaven has been ;
Too long o'er this fair blooming world
The flag of blood has been unfurled,
 Polluting God's pure day ;
Whilst, as each maddening people reels,
War onward drives his scythéd wheels,
And at his horses' bloody heels
 Shriek Murder and Dismay.

Oft have I wept to hear the cry
Of widow wailing bitterly ;
To see the parent's silent tear
For children fallen beneath the spear ;
 And I have felt so sore
The sense of human guilt and woe,
That I, in Virtue's passioned glow,
Have cursed (my soul was wounded so)
 The shape of man I bore !
Then come from thy serene abode,
Thou gladness-giving child of God !
And cease the world's ensanguined strife,
And reconcile my soul to life ;
 For much I long to see,
Ere I shall to the grave descend,
Thy hand its blessed branch extend,
And to the world's remotest end
 Wave Love and Harmony !
     WILLIAM TENNENT.

HYMN OF PEACE.

ANGEL of Peace, thou hast wandered too long !
 Spread thy white wings to the sunshine of love !
Come while our voices are blended in song, —
 Fly to our ark like the storm-beaten dove,
Fly to our ark on the wings of the dove,
 Speed o'er the far-sounding billows of song,
Crowned with thine olive-leaf garland of love ;
 Angel of Peace, thou hast waited too long !

Brothers, we meet on this altar of thine,
 Mingling the gifts we have gathered for thee,
Sweet with the odors of myrtle and pine,
 Breeze of the prairie and breath of the sea !
Meadow and mountain, and forest and sea !
 Sweet is the fragrance of myrtle and pine,
Sweeter the incense we offer to thee,
 Brothers, once more round this altar of thine !

Angels of Bethlehem, answer the strain !
 Hark ! a new birth-song is filling the sky !
Loud as the storm-wind that tumbles the main,
 Bid the full breath of the organ reply ;
Let the loud tempest of voices reply ;
 Roll its longsurge like the earth-shaking main !
Swell the vast song till it mounts to the sky !
 Angels of Bethlehem, echo the strain !
     OLIVER WENDELL HOLMES.

THE BATTLE-FIELD.

ONCE this soft turf, this rivulet's sands,
 Were trampled by a hurrying crowd,
And fiery hearts and arméd hands
 Encountered in the battle-cloud.

Ah ! never shall the land forget
 How gushed the life-blood of her brave, —
Gushed, warm with hope and courage yet,
 Upon the soil they fought to save.

Now all is calm and fresh and still ;
 Alone the chirp of flitting bird,
And talk of children on the hill,
 And bell of wandering kine, are heard.

No solemn host goes trailing by
 The black-mouthed gun and staggering wain ;

Men start not at the battle-cry, —
    O, be it never heard again !

Soon rested those who fought ; but thou
    Who minglest in the harder strife
For truths which men receive not now,
    Thy warfare only ends with life.

A friendless warfare ! lingering long
    Through weary day and weary year ;
A wild and many-weaponed throng
    Hang on thy front and flank and rear.

Yet nerve thy spirit to the proof,
    And blench not at thy chosen lot ;
The timid good may stand aloof,
    The sage may frown, — yet faint thou not.

Nor heed the shaft too surely cast,
    The foul and hissing bolt of scorn ;
For with thy side shall dwell, at last,
    The victory of endurance born.

Truth, crushed to earth, shall rise again, —
    The eternal years of God are hers ;
But Error, wounded, writhes in pain,
    And dies among his worshippers.

Yea, though thou lie upon the dust,
    When they who helped thee flee in fear,
Die full of hope and manly trust,
    Like those who fell in battle here !

Another hand thy sword shall wield,
    Another hand the standard wave,
Till from the trumpet's mouth is pealed
    The blast of triumph o'er thy grave.
                    WILLIAM CULLEN BRYANT.

THE SOLDIER'S RETURN.

How sweet it was to breathe that cooler air,
And take possession of my father's chair !
Beneath my elbow, on the solid frame,
Appeared the rough initials of my name,
Cut forty years before !   The same old clock
Struck the same bell, and gave my heart a shock
I never can forget.   A short breeze sprung,
And while a sigh was trembling on my tongue,
Caught the old dangling almanacs behind,
And up they flew like banners in the wind ;
Then gently, singly, down, down, down they went,
And told of twenty years that I had spent
Far from my native land.   That instant came
A robin on the threshold ; though so tame,
At first he looked distrustful, almost shy,
And cast on me his coal-black steadfast eye,
And seemed to say, — past friendship to renew, —

"Ah ha ! old worn-out soldier, is it you ?"
While thus I mused, still gazing, gazing still,
On beds of moss that spread the window-sill,
I deemed no moss my eyes had ever seen
Had been so lovely, brilliant, fresh, and green,
And guessed some infant hand had placed it there,
And prized its hue, so exquisite, so rare.
Feelings on feelings mingling, doubling rose ;
My heart felt everything but calm repose ;
I could not reckon minutes, hours, nor years,
But rose at once, and bursted into tears ;
Then, like a fool, confused, sat down again,
And thought upon the past with shame and pain ;
I raved at war and all its horrid cost,
And glory's quagmire, where the brave are lost.
On carnage, fire, and plunder long I mused,
And cursed the murdering weapons I had used.
    Two shadows then I saw, two voices heard,
One bespoke age, and one a child's appeared.
In stepped my father with convulsive start,
And in an instant clasped me to his heart.
Close by him stood a little blue-eyed maid ;
And stooping to the child, the old man said,
"Come hither, Nancy, kiss me once again ;
This is your uncle Charles, come home from Spain."
The child approached, and with her fingers light
Stroked my old eyes, almost deprived of sight.
But why thus spin my tale, — thus tedious be ?
Happy old soldier ! what 's the world to me ?
                    ROBERT BLOOMFIELD.

SOLDIER, REST! THY WARFARE O'ER.

FROM "THE LADY OF THE LAKE."

Soldier, rest ! thy warfare o'er,
    Sleep the sleep that knows not breaking ;
Dream of battled fields no more,
    Days of danger, nights of waking.
In our isle's enchanted hall,
    Hands unseen thy couch are strewing,
Fairy strains of music fall,
    Every sense in slumber dewing,
Soldier, rest ! thy warfare o'er,
Dream of fighting fields no more ;
Sleep the sleep that knows not breaking,
Morn of toil, nor night of waking.

No rude sound shall reach thine ear,
    Armor's clang, or war-steed champing,
Trump nor pibroch summon here
    Mustering clan, or squadron tramping.
Yet the lark's shrill fife may come
    At the daybreak from the fallow,
And the bittern sound his drum,
    Booming from the sedgy shallow.
Ruder sounds shall none be near,
Guards nor warders challenge here ;

Here 's no war-steed's neigh and champing,
Shouting clans or squadrons stamping.

Huntsman, rest ! thy chase is done,
  While our slumbérous spells assail ye,
Dream not, with the rising sun,
  Bugles here shall sound reveillé.
Sleep ! the deer is in his den ;
  Sleep ! thy hounds are by thee lying ;
Sleep ! nor dream in yonder glen
  How thy gallant steed lay dying.
Huntsman, rest ! thy chase is done,
Think not of the rising sun,
For, at dawning to assail ye,
Here no bugles sound reveillé.

SIR WALTER SCOTT.

DRIVING HOME THE COWS.

Out of the clover and blue-eyed grass
  He turned them into the river-lane ;
One after another he let them pass,
  Then fastened the meadow bars again.

Under the willows, and over the hill,
  He patiently followed their sober pace ;
The merry whistle for once was still,
  And something shadowed the sunny face.

Only a boy ! and his father had said
  He never could let his youngest go ;
Two already were lying dead
  Under the feet of the trampling foe.

But after the evening work was done,
  And the frogs were loud in the meadow-swamp,
Over his shoulder he slung his gun
  And stealthily followed the foot-path damp.

Across the clover and through the wheat
  With resolute heart and purpose grim,
Though cold was the dew on his hurrying feet,
  And the blind bat's flitting startled him.

Thrice since then had the lanes been white,
  And the orchards sweet with apple-bloom ;
And now, when the cows came back at night,
  The feeble father drove them home.

For news had come to the lonely farm
  That three were lying where two had lain ;
And the old man's tremulous, palsied arm
  Could never lean on a son's again.

The summer day grew cool and late,
  He went for the cows when the work was done ;
But down the lane, as he opened the gate,
  He saw them coming one by one, —

Brindle, Ebony, Speckle, and Bess,
  Shaking their horns in the evening wind ;
Cropping the buttercups out of the grass, —
  But who was it following close behind ?

Loosely swung in the idle air
  The empty sleeve of army blue ;
And worn and pale, from the crisping hair,
  Looked out a face that the father knew.

For Southern prisons will sometimes yawn,
  And yield their dead unto life again ;
And the day that comes with a cloudy dawn
  In golden glory at last may wane.

The great tears sprang to their meeting eyes ;
  For the heart must speak when the lips are dumb ;
And under the silent evening skies
  Together they followed the cattle home.

ANONYMOUS.

THE BATTLE OF BLENHEIM.

[The battle of Blenheim in Bavaria was fought August 13, 1704, between the troops of the English and Austrians on one side, under the Duke of Marlborough and Prince Eugene, and the French and Bavarians on the other side, led by Marshal Tallart and the Elector of Bavaria. The latter party was defeated, and the schemes of Louis XIV. of France were materially checked thereby.

I.

It was a summer evening, —
  Old Kaspar's work was done,
And he before his cottage door
  Was sitting in the sun ;
And by him sported on the green
His little grandchild Wilhelmine.

II.

She saw her brother Peterkin
  Roll something large and round,
Which he beside the rivulet,
  In playing there, had found ;
He came to ask what he had found
That was so large and smooth and round.

III.

Old Kaspar took it from the boy,
  Who stood expectant by ;
And then the old man shook his head,
  And, with a natural sigh, —
"'T is some poor fellow's skull," said he,
"Who fell in the great victory.

IV.

"I find them in the garden,
  For there 's many hereabout ;
And often, when I go to plough,
  The ploughshare turns them out ;
For many thousand men," said he,
"Were slain in the great victory."

V.

"Now tell us what 't was all about,"
  Young Peterkin he cries ;
And little Wilhelmine looks up
  With wonder-waiting eyes, —
"Now tell us all about the war,
And what they fought each other for.'

VI.

"It was the English," Kaspar cried,
  "Who put the French to rout ;
But what they fought each other for
  I could not well make out ;
But everybody said," quoth he,
"That 't was a famous victory.

VII.

"My father lived at Blenheim then,
  Yon little stream hard by ;
They burnt his dwelling to the ground,
  And he was forced to fly ;
So with his wife and child he fled,
Nor had he where to rest his head.

VIII.

"With fire and sword the country round
  Was wasted far and wide ;
And many a childing mother there,
  And new-born baby died ;
But things like that, you know, must be
At every famous victory.

IX.

"They say it was a shocking sight
  After the field was won, —
For many thousand bodies here
  Lay rotting in the sun ;
But things like that, you know, must be
After a famous victory.

X.

"Great praise the Duke of Marlborough won,
  And our good Prince Eugene."
"Why, 't was a very wicked thing !"
  Said little Wilhelmine.
"Nay, nay, my little girl !" quoth he,
"It was a famous victory.

XI.

"And everybody praised the duke
  Who this great fight did win."
"But what good came of it at last ?"
  Quoth little Peterkin.
"Why, that I cannot tell," said he ;
"But 't was a famous victory."
                              ROBERT SOUTHEY.

TUBAL CAIN.

OLD Tubal Cain was a man of might,
  In the days when earth was young ;
By the fierce red light of his furnace bright,
  The strokes of his hammer rung :
And he lifted high his brawny hand
  On the iron glowing clear,
Till the sparks rushed out in scarlet showers,
  As he fashioned the sword and the spear.
And he sang : "Hurrah for my handiwork !
  Hurrah for the spear and the sword !
Hurrah for the hand that shall wield them well,
  For he shall be king and lord."

To Tubal Cain came many a one,
  As he wrought by his roaring fire,
And each one prayed for a strong steel blade
  As the crown of his desire :
And he made them weapons sharp and strong,
  Till they shouted loud for glee,
And gave him gifts of pearl and gold,
  And spoils of the forest free.
And they sang : "Hurrah for Tubal Cain,
  Who hath given us strength anew !
Hurrah for the smith, hurrah for the fire,
  And hurrah for the metal true !"

But a sudden change came o'er his heart,
  Ere the setting of the sun,
And Tubal Cain was filled with pain
  For the evil he had done ;
He saw that men, with rage and hate,
  Made war upon their kind,
That the land was red with the blood they shed,
  In their lust for carnage blind.
And he said : "Alas ! that ever I made,
  Or that skill of mine should plan,
The spear and the sword for men whose joy
  Is to slay their fellow-man !"

And for many a day old Tubal Cain
  Sat brooding o'er his woe ;
And his hand forbore to smite the ore,
  And his furnace smouldered low.
But he rose at last with a cheerful face,
  And a bright courageous eye,
And bared his strong right arm for work,
  While the quick flames mounted high.
And he sang : "Hurrah for my handiwork !"
  And the red sparks lit the air ;
"Not alone for the blade was the bright steel
      made," —
  And he fashioned the first ploughshare.

And men, taught wisdom from the past,
  In friendship joined their hands,
Hung the sword in the hall, the spear on the wall,
  And ploughed the willing lands ;

And sang : " Hurrah for Tubal Cain !
  Our stanch good friend is he ;
And for the ploughshare and the plough
  To him our praise shall be.
But while oppression lifts its head,
  Or a tyrant would be lord,
Though we may thank him for the plough,
  We 'll not forget the sword ! "

CHARLES MACKAY.

BARCLAY OF URY.

UP the streets of Aberdeen,
By the kirk and college green,
  Rode the laird of Ury ;
Close behind him, close beside,
Foul of mouth and evil-eyed,
  Pressed the mob in fury.

Flouted him the drunken churl,
Jeered at him the serving-girl,
  Prompt to please her master ;
And the begging carlin, late
Fed and clothed at Ury's gate,
  Cursed him as he passed her.

Yet with calm and stately mien
Up the streets of Aberdeen
  Came he slowly riding ;
And to all he saw and heard
Answering not with bitter word,
  Turning not for chiding.

Came a troop with broadswords swinging,
Bits and bridles sharply ringing,
  Loose and free and froward :
Quoth the foremost, " Ride him down !
Push him ! prick him ! Through the town
  Drive the Quaker coward ! "

But from out the thickening crowd
Cried a sudden voice and loud :
  " Barclay ! Ho ! a Barclay ! "
And the old man at his side
Saw a comrade, battle-tried,
  Scarred and sunburned darkly ;

Who, with ready weapon bare,
Fronting to the troopers there,
  Cried aloud : " God save us !
Call ye coward him who stood
Ankle-deep in Lutzen's blood,
  With the brave Gustavus ? "

" Nay, I do not need thy sword,
Comrade mine," said Ury's lord ;
  " Put it up, I pray thee.
Passive to his holy will,
Trust I in my Master still,
  Even though he slay me.

" Pledges of thy love and faith,
Proved on many a field of death,
  Not by me are needed."
Marvelled much that henchman bold,
That his laird, so stout of old,
  Now so meekly pleaded.

" Woe 's the day," he sadly said,
With a slowly shaking head,
  And a look of pity ;
" Ury's honest lord reviled,
Mock of knave and sport of child,
  In his own good city !

" Speak the word, and, master mine,
As we charged on Tilly's line,
  And his Walloon lancers,
Smiting through their midst, we 'll teach
Civil look and decent speech
  To these boyish prancers ! "

" Marvel not, mine ancient friend, —
Like beginning, like the end ! "
  Quoth the laird of Ury ;
" Is the sinful servant more
Than his gracious Lord who bore
  Bonds and stripes in Jewry ?

" Give me joy that in his name
I can bear, with patient frame,
  All these vain ones offer ;
While for them he suffered long,
Shall I answer wrong with wrong,
  Scoffing with the scoffer ?

" Happier I, with loss of all, —
Hunted, outlawed, held in thrall,
  With few friends to greet me, —
Than when reeve and squire were seen
Riding out from Aberdeen
  With bared heads to meet me ;

" When each goodwife, o'er and o'er,
Blessed me as I passed her door ;
  And the snooded daughter,
Through her casement glancing down,
Smiled on him who bore renown
  From red fields of slaughter.

" Hard to feel the stranger's scoff,
Hard the old friends' falling off,
  Hard to learn forgiving ;
But the Lord his own rewards,
And his love with theirs accords
  Warm and fresh and living.

" Through this dark and stormy night
Faith beholds a feeble light
  Up the blackness streaking ;

Knowing God's own time is best,
In a patient hope I rest
  For the full day-breaking!"

So the laird of Ury said,
Turning slow his horse's head
  Towards the Tolbooth prison,
Where, through iron gates, he heard
Poor disciples of the Word
  Preach of Christ arisen!

Not in vain, confessor old,
Unto us the tale is told
  Of thy day of trial!
Every age on him who strays
From its broad and beaten ways
  Pours its sevenfold vial.

Happy he whose inward ear
Angel comfortings can hear,
  O'er the rabble's laughter;
And, while hatred's fagots burn,
Glimpses through the smoke discern
  Of the good hereafter.

Knowing this, — that never yet
Share of truth was vainly set
  In the world's wide fallow;
After hands shall sow the seed,
After hands from hill and mead
  Reap the harvests yellow.

Thus, with somewhat of the seer,
Must the moral pioneer
  From the future borrow, —
Clothe the waste with dreams of grain,
And, on midnight's sky of rain,
  Paint the golden morrow!
                JOHN GREENLEAF WHITTIER.

THE SOLDIER'S DREAM.

OUR bugles sang truce, — for the night-cloud had
    lowered,
And the sentinel stars set their watch in the sky;
And thousands had sunk on the ground over-
    powered,
  The weary to sleep, and the wounded to die.

When reposing that night on my pallet of straw,
By the wolf-scaring fagot that guarded the slain;
At the dead of the night a sweet vision I saw,
  And thrice ere the morning I dreamt it again.

Methought from the battle-field's dreadful array,
  Far, far I had roamed on a desolate track:
'T was autumn, — and sunshine arose on the way
  To the home of my fathers, that welcomed me
    back.

I flew to the pleasant fields traversed so oft
  In life's morning march, when my bosom was
    young;
I heard my own mountain-goats bleating aloft,
  And knew the sweet strain that the corn-
    reapers sung.

Then pledged we the wine-cup, and fondly I
    swore,
  From my home and my weeping friends never
    to part;
My little ones kissed me a thousand times o'er,
  And my wife sobbed aloud in her fulness of
    heart.

"Stay, stay with us, — rest, thou art weary and
    worn";
  And fain was their war-broken soldier to
    stay; —
But sorrow returned with the dawning of morn,
  And the voice in my dreaming ear melted away.
                THOMAS CAMPBELL.

THE DRUMMER-BOY'S BURIAL.

ALL day long the storm of battle through the
    startled valley swept;
All night long the stars in heaven o'er the slain
    sad vigils kept.

O the ghastly upturned faces gleaming whitely
    through the night!
O the heaps of mangled corses in that dim sepul-
    chral light!

One by one the pale stars faded, and at length
    the morning broke;
But not one of all the sleepers on that field of
    death awoke.

Slowly passed the golden hours of that long bright
    summer day,
And upon that field of carnage still the dead
    unburied lay.

Lay there stark and cold, but pleading with a
    dumb, unceasing prayer,
For a little dust to hide them from the staring
    sun and air.

But the foeman held possession of that hard-
    won battle-plain,
In unholy wrath denying even burial to our slain.

Once again the night dropped round them, —
    night so holy and so calm
That the moonbeams hushed the spirit, like the
    sound of prayer or psalm.

On a couch of trampled grasses, just apart from all
    the rest,
Lay a fair young boy, with small hands meekly
    folded on his breast.

Death had touched him very gently, and he lay
    as if in sleep ;
Even his mother scarce had shuddered at that
    slumber calm and deep.

For a smile of wondrous sweetness lent a radiance
    to the face,
And the hand of cunning sculptor could have
    added naught of grace

To the marble limbs so perfect in their passion-
    less repose,
Robbed of all save matchless purity by hard,
    unpitying foes.

And the broken drum beside him all his life's
    short story told :
How he did his duty bravely till the death-tide
    o'er him rolled.

Midnight came with ebon garments and a diadem
    of stars,
While right upward in the zenith hung the fiery
    planet Mars.

Hark ! a sound of stealthy footsteps and of voices
    whispering low,
Was it nothing but the young leaves, or the
    brooklet's murmuring flow ?

Clinging closely to each other, striving never to
    look round
As they passed with silent shudder the pale
    corses on the ground,

Came two little maidens, — sisters, — with a
    light and hasty tread,
And a look upon their faces, half of sorrow, half
    of dread.

And they did not pause nor falter till, with
    throbbing hearts, they stood
Where the drummer-boy was lying in that
    partial solitude.

They had brought some simple garments from
    their wardrobe's scanty store,
And two heavy iron shovels in their slender
    hands they bore.

Then they quickly knelt beside him, crushing
    back the pitying tears,
For they had no time for weeping, nor for any
    girlish fears.

And they robed the icy body, while no glow of
    maiden shame
Changed the pallor of their foreheads to a flush
    of lambent flame.

For their saintly hearts yearned o'er it in that
    hour of sorest need,
And they felt that Death was holy, and it sanc-
    tified the deed.

But they smiled and kissed each other when
    their new strange task was o'er,
And the form that lay before them its unwonted
    garments wore.

Then with slow and weary labor a small grave
    they hollowed out,
And they lined it with the withered grass and
    leaves that lay about.

But the day was slowly breaking ere their holy
    work was done,
And in crimson pomp the morning again heralded
    the sun.

And then those little maidens — they were
    children of our foes —
Laid the body of our drummer-boy to undis-
    turbed repose.'   ANONYMOUS.

NOT ON THE BATTLE-FIELD.

"To fall on the battle-field fighting for my dear country, — that
would not be hard." — THE NEIGHBORS.

O NO, no, — let me lie
Not on a field of battle when I die !
    Let not the iron tread
Of the mad war-horse crush my helméd head ;
    Nor let the reeking knife,
That I have drawn against a brother's life,
    Be in my hand when Death
Thunders along, and tramples me beneath
    His heavy squadron's heels,
Or gory felloes of his cannon's wheels.

    From such a dying bed,
Though o'er it float the stripes of white and red,
    And the bald eagle brings
The clustered stars upon his wide-spread wings
    To sparkle in my sight,
O, never let my spirit take her flight !

    I know that beauty's eye
Is all the brighter where gay pennants fly,
    And brazen helmets dance,
And sunshine flashes on the lifted lance ;
    I know that bards have sung,
And people shouted till the welkin rung,
    In honor of the brave
Who on the battle-field have found a grave ;

I know that o'er their bones
Have grateful hands piled monumental stones.
    Some of those piles I 've seen :
The one at Lexington upon the green
    Where the first blood was shed,
And to my country's independence led ;
    And others, on our shore,
The " Battle Monument " at Baltimore,
    And that on Bunker's Hill.
Ay, and abroad, a few more famous still ;
    Thy " tomb," Themistocles,
That looks out yet upon the Grecian seas,
    And which the waters kiss
That issue from the gulf of Salamis.
    And thine, too, have I seen,
Thy mound of earth, Patroclus, robed in green,
    That, like a natural knoll,
Sheep climb and nibble over as they stroll,
    Watched by some turbaned boy,
Upon the margin of the plain of Troy.
    Such honors grace the bed,
I know, whereon the warrior lays his head,
    And hears, as life ebbs out,
The conquered flying, and the conqueror's shout ;
    But as his eye grows dim,
What is a column or a mound to him ?
    What, to the parting soul,
The mellow note of bugles ? What the roll
    Of drums ? No, let me die
Where the blue heaven bends o'er me lovingly,
    And the soft summer air,
As it goes by me, stirs my thin white hair,
    And from my forehead dries
The death-damp as it gathers, and the skies
    Seem waiting to receive
My soul to their clear depths ! Or let me leave
    The world when round my bed
Wife, children, weeping friends are gathered,
    And the calm voice of prayer
And holy hymning shall my soul prepare
    To go and be at rest
With kindred spirits, — spirits who have blessed
    The human brotherhood
By labors, cares, and counsels for their good.

JOHN PIERPONT.

THE DESTRUCTION OF SENNACHERIB.

The Assyrian came down like the wolf on the fold,
And his cohorts were gleaming in purple and gold ;
And the sheen of their spears was like stars on
    the sea,
When the blue wave rolls nightly on deep Galilee.

Like the leaves of the forest when summer is green,
That host with their banners at sunset were seen ;

Like the leaves of the forest when Autumn hath
    blown,
That host on the morrow lay withered and strown.

For the Angel of Death spread his wings on the
    blast,
And breathed in the face of the foe as he passed ;
And the eyes of the sleepers waxed deadly and
    chill,
And their hearts but once heaved, and forever
    grew still !

And there lay the steed with his nostrils all wide,
But through it there rolled not the breath of his
    pride :
And the foam of his gasping lay white on the turf,
And cold as the spray of the rock-beating surf.

And there lay the rider distorted and pale,
With the dew on his brow and the rust on his mail ;
And the tents were all silent, the banners alone,
The lances unlifted, the trumpet unblown.

And the widows of Ashur are loud in their wail,
And the idols are broke in the temple of Baal ;
And the might of the Gentile, unsmote by the
    sword,
Hath melted like snow in the glance of the Lord !

BYRON.

WAR.

        Ah ! whence yon glare,
That fires the arch of heaven ?—that dark red smoke
Blotting the silver moon ? The stars are quenched
In darkness, and pure and spangling snow
Gleams faintly through the gloom that gathers
    round !
Hark to that roar, whose swift and deafening peals
In countless echoes through the mountains ring,
Startling pale midnight on her starry throne !
Now swells the intermingling din ; the jar
Frequent and frightful of the bursting bomb ;
The falling beam, the shriek, the groan, the shout,
The ceaseless clangor, and the rush of men
Inebriate with rage ; — loud, and more loud
The discord grows ; till pale death shuts the scene,
And o'er the conqueror and the conquered draws
His cold and bloody shroud. — Of all the men
Whom day's departing beam saw blooming there,
In proud and vigorous health ; of all the hearts
That beat with anxious life at sunset there,
How few survive, how few are beating now !
All is deep silence, like the fearful calm
That slumbers in the storm's portentous pause ;
Save when the frantic wail of widowed love
Comes shuddering on the blast, or the faint moan
With which some soul bursts from the frame of clay
Wrapt round its struggling powers.

The gray morn
Dawns on the mournful scene ; the sulphurous smoke
Before the icy wind slow rolls away,
And the bright beams of frosty morning dance
Along the spangling snow.   There tracks of blood
Even to the forest's depth, and scattered arms,
And lifeless warriors, whose hard lineaments
Death's self could change not, mark the dreadful path
Of the outsallying victors ; far behind,
Black ashes note where their proud city stood.
Within yon forest is a gloomy glen, —
Each tree which guards its darkness from the day
Waves o'er a warrior's tomb.

War is the statesman's game, the priest's delight,
The lawyer's jest, the hired assassin's trade,
And to those royal murderers whose mean thrones
Are bought by crimes of treachery and gore,
The bread they eat, the staff on which they lean.
Guards, garbed in blood-red livery, surround
Their palaces, participate the crimes
That force defends, and from a nation's rage
Secure the crown, which all the curses reach
That famine, frenzy, woe, and penury breathe.
These are the hired bravos who defend
The tyrant's throne.
PERCY BYSSHE SHELLEY.

THE PICKET-GUARD.

"ALL quiet along the Potomac," they say,
"Except now and then a stray picket
Is shot, as he walks on his beat, to and fro,
By a rifleman hid in the thicket.
'T is nothing : a private or two, now and then,
Will not count in the news of the battle ;
Not an officer lost, — only one of the men,
Moaning out, all alone, the death rattle."

All quiet along the Potomac to-night,
Where the soldiers lie peacefully dreaming ;
Their tents in the rays of the clear autumn moon,
Or the light of the watch-fires, are gleaming.
A tremulous sigh, as the gentle night-wind
Through the forest leaves softly is creeping ;
While stars up above, with their glittering eyes,
Keep guard, — for the army is sleeping.

There 's only the sound of the lone sentry's tread
As he tramps from the rock to the fountain,
And he thinks of the two in the low trundle-bed,
Far away in the cot on the mountain.
His musket falls slack ; his face, dark and grim,
Grows gentle with memories tender,

As he mutters a prayer for the children asleep,
For their mother, — may Heaven defend her !

The moon seems to shine just as brightly as then,
That night when the love yet unspoken
Leaped up to his lips, — when low, murmured vows
Were pledged to be ever unbroken ;
Then drawing his sleeve roughly over his eyes,
He dashes off tears that are welling,
And gathers his gun closer up to its place,
As if to keep down the heart-swelling.

He passes the fountain, the blasted pine-tree, —
The footstep is lagging and weary ;
Yet onward he goes, through the broad belt of light,
Toward the shades of the forest so dreary.
Hark ! was it the night-wind that rustled the leaves?
Was it moonlight so wondrously flashing ?
It looked like a rifle : "Ha ! Mary, good by !"
And the life-blood is ebbing and plashing.

All quiet along the Potomac to-night, —
No sound save the rush of the river ;
While soft falls the dew on the face of the dead, —
The picket 's off duty forever.
MRS. ETHEL LYNN BEERS.

CIVIL WAR.

"RIFLEMAN, shoot me a fancy shot
Straight at the heart of yon prowling vidette ;
Ring me a ball in the glittering spot
That shines on his breast like an amulet !"

"Ah, captain ! here goes for a fine-drawn bead,
There 's music around when my barrel 's in tune !"
Crack ! went the rifle, the messenger sped,
And dead from his horse fell the ringing dragoon.

"Now, rifleman, steal through the bushes, and snatch
From your victim some trinket to handsel first blood ;
A button, a loop, or that luminous patch
That gleams in the moon like a diamond stud !"

"O captain ! I staggered, and sunk on my track,
When I gazed on the face of that fallen vidette,
For he looked so like you, as he lay on his back,
That my heart rose upon me, and masters me yet.

"But I snatched off the trinket, — this locket of gold ;
An inch from the centre my lead broke its way,
Scarce grazing the picture, so fair to behold,
Of a beautiful lady in bridal array."

"Ha ! rifleman, fling me the locket ! — 't is she,
  My brother's young bride, — and the fallen
      dragoon
Was her husband — Hush ! soldier, 't was
      Heaven's decree,
  We must bury him there, by the light of the
      moon !

"But, hark ! the far bugles their warnings unite ;
  War is a virtue, — weakness a sin ;
There 's a lurking and loping around us to-night ;
  Load again, rifleman, keep your hand in !"
                                    ANONYMOUS.

LEFT ON THE BATTLE–FIELD.

WHAT, was it a dream ? am I all alone
  In the dreary night and the drizzling rain ?
Hist ! — ah, it was only the river's moan ;
  They have left me behind with the mangled
      slain.

Yes, now I remember it all too well !
  We met, from the battling ranks apart ;
Together our weapons flashed and fell,
  And mine was sheathed in his quivering heart.

In the cypress gloom, where the deed was done,
  It was all too dark to see his face ;
But I heard his death-groans, one by one,
  And he holds me still in a cold embrace.

He spoke but once, and I could not hear
  The words he said, for the cannon's roar ;
But my heart grew cold with a deadly fear, —
  O God ! I had heard that voice before !

Had heard it before at our mother's knee,
  When we lisped the words of our evening prayer !
My brother ! would I had died for thee, —
  This burden is more than my soul can bear !

I pressed my lips to his death-cold cheek,
  And begged him to show me, by word or sign,
That he knew and forgave me : he could not speak,
  But he nestled his poor cold face to mine.

The blood flowed fast from my wounded side,
  And then for a while I forgot my pain,
And over the lakelet we seemed to glide
  In our little boat, two boys again.

And then, in my dream, we stood alone
  On a forest path where the shadows fell ;
And I heard again the tremulous tone,
  And the tender words of his last farewell.

But that parting was years, long years ago,
  He wandered away to a foreign land ;
And our dear old mother will never know
  That he died to-night by his brother's hand.

*   *   *   *   *

The soldiers who buried the dead away
Disturbed not the clasp of that last embrace,
But laid them to sleep till the judgment-day,
  Heart folded to heart, and face to face.
                              SARAH T. BOLTON.

MY AUTUMN WALK.

ON woodlands ruddy with autumn
    The amber sunshine lies ;
I look on the beauty round me,
    And tears come into my eyes.

For the wind that sweeps the meadows
    Blows out of the far Southwest,
Where our gallant men are fighting,
    And the gallant dead are at rest.

The golden-rod is leaning,
    And the purple aster waves
In a breeze from the land of battles,
    A breath from the land of graves.

Full fast the leaves are dropping
    Before that wandering breath ;
As fast, on the field of battle,
    Our brethren fall in death.

Beautiful over my pathway
    The forest spoils are shed ;
They are spotting the grassy hillocks
    With purple and gold and red.

Beautiful is the death-sleep
    Of those who bravely fight
In their country's holy quarrel,
    And perish for the Right.

But who shall comfort the living,
    The light of whose homes is gone :
The bride that, early widowed,
    Lives broken-hearted on ;

The matron whose sons are lying
    In graves on a distant shore ;
The maiden, whose promised husband
    Comes back from the war no more ?

I look on the peaceful dwellings
    Whose windows glimmer in sight,
With croft and garden and orchard
    That bask in the mellow light ;

And I know that, when our couriers
  With news of victory come,
They will bring a bitter message
  Of hopeless grief to some.

Again I turn to the woodlands,
  And I shudder as I see
The mock-grape's * blood-red banner
  Hung out on the cedar-tree ;

And I think of days of slaughter,
  And the night-sky red with flames,
On the Chattahoochee's meadows,
  And the wasted banks of the James.

O for the fresh spring-season,
  When the groves are in their prime,
And far away in the future
  Is the frosty autumn-time !

O for that better season,
  When the pride of the foe shall yield,
And the hosts of God and Freedom
  March back from the well-won field ;

And the matron shall clasp her first-born
  With tears of joy and pride ;
And the scarred and war-worn lover
  Shall claim his promised bride !

The leaves are swept from the branches ;
  But the living buds are there,
With folded flower and foliage,
  To sprout in a kinder air.

WILLIAM CULLEN BRYANT.

October, 1864.

BINGEN ON THE RHINE.

A SOLDIER of the Legion lay dying in Algiers,
There was lack of woman's nursing, there was
    dearth of woman's tears ;
But a comrade stood beside him, while his life-
    blood ebbed away,
And bent, with pitying glances, to hear what he
    might say.
The dying soldier faltered, and he took that com-
    rade's hand,
And he said, " I nevermore shall see my own,
    my native land ;
Take a message, and a token, to some distant
    friends of mine,
For I was born at Bingen, — at Bingen on the
    Rhine.

* *Ampelopis*, mock-grape. I have here literally trans-
lated the botanical name of the Virginia creeper, an ap-
pellation too cumbrous for verse.

" Tell my brothers and companions, when they
    meet and crowd around,
To hear my mournful story, in the pleasant
    vineyard ground,
That we fought the battle bravely, and when the
    day was done,
Full many a corse lay ghastly pale beneath the
    setting sun ;
And, mid the dead and dying, were some grown
    old in wars, —
The death-wound on their gallant breasts, the
    last of many scars ;
And some were young, and suddenly beheld life's
    morn decline, —
And one had come from Bingen, — fair Bingen
    on the Rhine.

" Tell my mother that her other son shall com-
    fort her old age ;
For I was still a truant bird, that thought his
    home a cage.
For my father was a soldier, and even as a
    child
My heart leaped forth to hear him tell of strug-
    gles fierce and wild ;
And when he died, and left us to divide his
    scanty hoard,
I let them take whate'er they would, — but kept
    my father's sword ;
And with boyish love I hung it where the bright
    light used to shine,
On the cottage wall at Bingen, — calm Bingen
    on the Rhine.

" Tell my sister not to weep for me, and sob with
    drooping head,
When the troops come marching home again
    with glad and gallant tread,
But to look upon them proudly, with a calm and
    steadfast eye,
For her brother was a soldier too, and not afraid
    to die ;
And if a comrade seek her love, I ask her in my
    name
To listen to him kindly, without regret or shame,
And to hang the old sword in its place (my fa-
    ther's sword and mine)
For the honor of old Bingen, — dear Bingen on
    the Rhine.

" There 's another, — not a sister ; in the happy
    days gone by
You 'd have known her by the merriment that
    sparkled in her eye ;
Too innocent for coquetry, — too fond for idle
    scorning, —
O friend ! I fear the lightest heart makes some-
    times heaviest mourning !

Tell her the last night of my life (for, ere the moon
    be risen,
My body will be out of pain, my soul be out of
    prison), —
I dreamed I stood with *her*, and saw the yellow
    sunlight shine
On the vine-clad hills of Bingen, — fair Bingen on
    the Rhine.

"I saw the blue Rhine sweep along, — I heard,
    or seemed to hear,
The German songs we used to sing, in chorus
    sweet and clear ;
And down the pleasant river, and up the slant-
    ing hill,
The echoing chorus sounded, through the evening
    calm and still ;
And her glad blue eyes were on me, as we passed,
    with friendly talk,
Down many a path beloved of yore, and well-
    remembered walk !
And her little hand lay lightly, confidingly in
    mine, —
But we 'll meet no more at Bingen, — loved Bin-
    gen on the Rhine."

His trembling voice grew faint and hoarse, — his
    grasp was childish weak, —
His eyes put on a dying look, — he sighed and
    ceased to speak ;
His comrade bent to lift him, but the spark of
    life had fled, —
The soldier of the Legion in a foreign land is dead !
And the soft moon rose up slowly, and calmly
    she looked down
On the red sand of the battle-field, with bloody
    corses strewn ;
Yes, calmly on that dreadful scene her pale light
    seemed to shine,
As it shone on distant Bingen, — fair Bingen on
    the Rhine.

CAROLINE E. NORTON.

THE TRUMPETS OF DOOLKARNEIN.

[In Eastern history are two Iskanders, or Alexanders, who are sometimes confounded, and both of whom are called Doolkarnein, or the Two-Horned, in allusion to their subjugation of East and West, horns being an Oriental symbol of power.

One of these heroes is Alexander of Macedon ; the other a conqueror of more ancient times, who built the marvellous series of ramparts on Mount Caucasus, known in fable as the wall of Gog and Magog. that is to say, of the people of the North. It reached from the Euxine Sea to the Caspian, where its flanks originated the subsequent appellation of the Caspian Gates.]

WITH awful walls, far glooming, that possessed
    The passes 'twixt the snow-fed Caspian foun-
    tains,
Doolkarnein, the dread lord of East and West,
    Shut up the northern nations in their moun-
    tains ;

And upon platforms where the oak-trees grew,
    Trumpets he set, huge beyond dreams of won-
    der,
Craftily purposed, when his arms withdrew,
    To make him thought still housed there, like
    the thunder :
And it so fell ; for when the winds blew right,
They woke their trumpets to their calls of might.

Unseen, but heard, their calls the trumpets blew,
    Ringing the granite rocks, their only bearers,
Till the long fear into religion grew,
    And nevermore those heights had human darers.
Dreadful Doolkarnein was an earthly god ;
    His walls but shadowed forth his mightier
    frowning ;
Armies of giants at his bidding trod
    From realm to realm, king after king dis-
    crowning ;
When thunder spoke, or when the earthquake
    stirred,
Then, muttering in accord, his host was heard.

But when the winters marred the mountain
    shelves,
    And softer changes came with vernal mornings,
Something had touched the trumpets' lofty selves,
    And less and less rang forth their sovereign
    warnings ;
Fewer and feebler ; as when silence spreads
    In plague-struck tents, where haughty chiefs,
    left dying,
Fail by degrees upon their angry beds,
    Till, one by one, ceases the last stern sighing.
One by one, thus, their breath the trumpets
    drew,
Till now no more the imperious music blew.

Is he then dead ? Can great Doolkarnein die ?
    Or can his endless hosts elsewhere be needed ?
Were the great breaths that blew his minstrelsy
    Phantoms, that faded as himself receded ?
Or is he angered ? Surely he still comes ;
    This silence ushers the dread visitation ;
Sudden will burst the torrent of his drums,
    And then will follow bloody desolation.
So did fear dream ; though now, with not a sound
To scare good hope, summer had twice crept round.

Then gathered in a band, with lifted eyes,
    The neighbors, and those silent heights as-
    cended.
Giant, nor aught blasting their bold emprise,
    They met, though twice they halted, breath
    suspended :
Once, at a coming like a god's in rage
    With thunderous leaps, — but 't was the piled
    snow, falling ;

And once, when in the woods an oak, for age,
  Fell dead, the silence with its groan appalling.
At last they came where still, in dread array,
As though they still might speak, the trumpets lay.

Unhurt they lay, like caverns above ground,
  The rifted rocks, for hands, about them clinging,
Their tubes as straight, their mighty mouths as
    round
  And firm as when the rocks were first set ring-
    ing.
Fresh from their unimaginable mould
  They might have seemed, save that the storms
    had stained them
With a rich rust, that now, with gloomy gold
  In the bright sunshine, beauteously engrained
    them.
Breathless the gazers looked, nigh faint for awe,
Then leaped, then laughed. What was it now
    they saw?

Myriads of birds. Myriads of birds, that filled
  The trumpets all with nests and nestling voices!
The great, huge, stormy music had been stilled
  By the soft needs that nursed those small, sweet
    noises!
O thou Doolkarnein, where is now thy wall?
  Where now thy voice divine and all thy forces?
Great was thy cunning, but its wit was small
  Compared with nature's least and gentlest
    courses.
Fears and false creeds may fright the realms
    awhile;
But heaven and earth abide their time, and smile.
                            LEIGH HUNT.

THE KNIGHT'S TOMB.

WHERE is the grave of Sir Arthur O'Kellyn?
Where may the grave of that good man be?—
By the side of a spring, on the breast of Helvellyn,
Under the twigs of a young birch-tree!
The oak that in summer was sweet to hear,
And rustled its leaves in the fall of the year,
And whistled and roared in the winter alone,
Is gone,—and the birch in its stead is grown.—
The knight's bones are dust,
And his good sword rust;—
His soul is with the saints, I trust.
                    SAMUEL TAYLOR COLERIDGE.

DIRGE FOR A SOLDIER.

CLOSE his eyes; his work is done!
  What to him is friend or foeman,
Rise of moon or set of sun,
  Hand of man or kiss of woman?

Lay him low, lay him low,
In the clover or the snow!
What cares he? he cannot know;
  Lay him low!

Fold him in his country's stars,
  Roll the drum and fire the volley!
What to him are all our wars?—
  What but death bemocking folly?
Lay him low, lay him low,
In the clover or the snow!

Leave him to God's watching eye;
  Trust him to the hand that made him.
Mortal love weeps idly by;
  God alone has power to aid him.
Lay him low, lay him low,
In the clover or the snow!
What cares he? he cannot know;
  Lay him low!
                    GEORGE HENRY BOKER.

THE PRIVATE OF THE BUFFS.

LAST night, among his fellow roughs,
  He jested, quaffed, and swore;
A drunken private of the Buffs,
  Who never looked before.
To-day, beneath the foeman's frown,
  He stands in Elgin's place,
Ambassador from Britain's crown,
  And type of all her race.

Poor, reckless, rude, low-born, untaught,
  Bewildered, and alone,
A heart, with English instinct fraught,
  He yet can call his own.
Ay, tear his body limb from limb,
  Bring cord or axe or flame,
He only knows that not through him
  Shall England come to shame.

Far Kentish hop-fields round him seemed,
  Like dreams, to come and go;
Bright leagues of cherry-blossom gleamed,
  One sheet of living snow;
The smoke above his father's door
  In gray soft eddyings hung;
Must he then watch it rise no more,
  Doomed by himself so young?

Yes, honor calls!—with strength like steel
  He put the vision by;
Let dusky Indians whine and kneel,
  An English lad must die.

And thus, with eyes that would not shrink,
　With knee to man unbent,
Unfaltering on its dreadful brink,
　To his red grave he went.

Vain mightiest fleets of iron framed,
　Vain those all-shattering guns,
Unless proud England keep untamed
　The strong heart of her sons ;
So let his name through Europe ring, —
　A man of mean estate,
Who died, as firm as Sparta's king,
　Because his soul was great.
　　　　　　SIR FRANCIS HASTINGS DOYLE.

CAVALRY SONG.

FROM " ALICE OF MONMOUTH."

OUR good steeds snuff the evening air,
　Our pulses with their purpose tingle ;
The foeman's fires are twinkling there ;
　He leaps to hear our sabres jingle !
　　HALT !
Each carbine send its whizzing ball :
Now, cling ! clang ! forward all,
　Into the fight !

Dash on beneath the smoking dome :
　Through level lightnings gallop nearer !
One look to Heaven ! No thoughts of home :
　The guidons that we bear are dearer.
　　CHARGE !
Cling ! clang ! forward all !
Heaven help those whose horses fall :
　Cut left and right !

They flee before our fierce attack !
　They fall ! they spread in broken surges.
Now, comrades, bear our wounded back,
　And leave the foeman to his dirges.
　　WHEEL !
The bugles sound the swift recall :
Cling ! clang ! backward all !
　Home, and good night !
　　　　　　EDMUND CLARENCE STEDMAN.

THE BALLAD OF AGINCOURT.

FAIR stood the wind for France,
　When we our sails advance,
　Nor now to prove our chance
　　Longer will tarry ;
　But putting to the main,
　At Kaux, the mouth of Seine,
　With all his martial train,
　　Landed King Harry.

And taking many a fort,
Furnished in warlike sort,
Marched towards Agincourt
　In happy hour, —
Skirmishing day by day
With those that stopped his way,
Where the French general lay
　With all his power,

Which in his height of pride,
King Henry to deride,
His ransom to provide
　To the king sending ;
Which he neglects the while,
As from a nation vile,
Yet, with an angry smile,
　Their fall portending.

And turning to his men,
Quoth our brave Henry then :
Though they to one be ten,
　Be not amazed ;
Yet have we well begun, —
Battles so bravely won
Have ever to the sun
　By fame been raised.

And for myself, quoth he,
This my full rest shall be ;
England ne'er mourn for me,
　Nor more esteem me.
Victor I will remain,
Or on this earth lie slain ;
Never shall she sustain
　Loss to redeem me.

Poitiers and Cressy tell,
When most their pride did swell,
Under our swords they fell ;
　No less our skill is
Than when our grandsire great,
Claiming the regal seat,
By many a warlike feat
　Lopped the French lilies.

The Duke of York so dread
The eager vaward led ;
With the main Henry sped,
　Amongst his henchmen.
Excester had the rear, —
A braver man not there :
O Lord ! how hot they were
　On the false Frenchmen !

They now to fight are gone ;
Armor on armor shone ;
Drum now to drum did groan, —
　To hear was wonder ;

That with the cries they make
The very earth did shake ;
Trumpet to trumpet spake,
    Thunder to thunder.

Well it thine age became,
O noble Erpingham !
Which did the signal aim
    To our hid forces ;
When, from a meadow by,
Like a storm suddenly,
The English archery
    Struck the French horses,

With Spanish yew so strong,
Arrows a cloth-yard long,
That like to serpents stung,
    Piercing the weather ;
None from his fellow starts,
But playing manly parts,
And like true English hearts,
    Stuck close together.

When down their bows they threw,
And forth their bilboes drew,
And on the French they flew,
    Not one was tardy ;
Arms were from shoulders sent ;
Scalps to the teeth were rent ;
Down the French peasants went ;
    Our men were hardy.

This while our noble king,
His broadsword brandishing,
Down the French host did ding,
    As to o'erwhelm it ;
And many a deep wound lent,
His arms with blood besprent,
And many a cruel dent
    Bruiséd his helmet.

Glo'ster, that duke so good,
Next of the royal blood,
For famous England stood,
    With his brave brother, —
Clarence, in steel so bright,
Though but a maiden knight,
Yet in that furious fight
    Scarce such another.

Warwick in blood did wade ;
Oxford the foe invade,
And cruel slaughter made,
    Still as they ran up.
Suffolk his axe did ply ;
Beaumont and Willoughby
Bare them right doughtily,
    Ferrers and Fanhope.

Upon St. Crispin's day
Fought was this noble fray,
Which fame did not delay
    To England to carry ;
O, when shall Englishmen
With such acts fill a pen,
Or England breed again
    Such a King Harry !
                    MICHAEL DRAYTON.

HOTSPUR'S DESCRIPTION OF A FOP.

FROM "KING HENRY IV.," PART I.

BUT I remember, when the fight was done,
When I was dry with rage and extreme toil,
Breathless and faint, leaning upon my sword,
Came there a certain lord, neat, trimly dressed,
Fresh as a bridegroom ; and his chin, new reaped,
Showed like a stubble-land at harvest-home ;
He was perfumed like a milliner ;
And 'twixt his finger and his thumb he held
A pouncet-box, which ever and anon
He gave his nose, and took 't away again ; —
Who, therewith angry, when it next came there,
Took it in snuff :—and still he smiled and talked ;
And as the soldiers bore dead bodies by,
He called them untaught knaves, unmannerly,
To bring a slovenly unhandsome corse
Betwixt the wind and his nobility.
With many holiday and lady terms
He questioned me ; among the rest, demanded
My prisoners in your majesty's behalf.
I then, all smarting, with my wounds being cold,
To be so pestered with a popinjay,
Out of my grief and my impatience,
Answered neglectingly, I know not what, —
He should, or he should not ; for he made me mad
To see him shine so brisk, and smell so sweet,
And talk so like a waiting gentlewoman,
Of guns, and drums, and wounds, — God save the
        mark ! —
And telling me, the sovereign'st thing on earth
Was parmaceti for an inward bruise ;
And that it was great pity, so it was,
That villanous saltpetre should be digged
Out of the bowels of the harmless earth,
Which many a good tall fellow had destroyed
So cowardly ; and, but for these vile guns,
He would himself have been a soldier.
                    SHAKESPEARE.

MARMION AND DOUGLAS.

NOT far advanced was morning day,
When Marmion did his troop array
    To Surrey's camp to ride ;
He had safe-conduct for his band,

Beneath the royal seal and hand,
　And Douglas gave a guide :
The ancient Earl, with stately grace,
Would Clara on her palfrey place,
And whispered in an undertone,
" Let the hawk stoop, his prey is flown." —
The train from out the castle drew,
But Marmion stopped to bid adieu : —
" Though something I might plain," he said,
" Of cold respect to stranger guest,
Sent hither by your king's behest,
　While in Tantallon's towers I stayed,
Part we in friendship from your land,
And, noble Earl, receive my hand." —
But Douglas round him drew his cloak,
Folded his arms, and thus he spoke : —
" My manors, halls, and bowers shall still
Be open, at my sovereign's will,
To each one whom he lists, howe'er
Unmeet to be the owner's peer.
My castles are my king's alone,
From turret to foundation-stone, —
The hand of Douglas is his own ;
And never shall in friendly grasp
The hand of such as Marmion clasp." —

Burned Marmion's swarthy cheek like fire,
And shook his very frame for ire,
　And — " This to me !" he said, —
" An 't were not for thy hoary beard,
Such hand as Marmion's had not spared
　To cleave the Douglas' head !
And, first, I tell thee, haughty Peer,
He who does England's message here,
Although the meanest in her state,
May well, proud Angus, be thy mate :
And, Douglas, more I tell thee here,
　Even in thy pitch of pride,
Here in thy hold, thy vassals near,
(Nay, never look upon your lord,
And lay your hands upon your sword,)
I tell thee, thou 'rt defied !
And if thou said'st I am not peer
To any lord in Scotland here,
Lowland or Highland, far or near,
　Lord Angus, thou hast lied !" —
On the Earl's cheek the flush of rage
O'ercame the ashen hue of age :
Fierce he broke forth, — " And dar'st thou then
To beard the lion in his den,
　The Douglas in his hall ?
And hop'st thou hence unscathed to go ?
No, by St. Bride of Bothwell, no !
Up drawbridge, grooms, — what, Warder, ho !
　Let the portcullis fall." —
Lord Marmion turned, — well was his need ! —
And dashed the rowels in his steed,
Like arrow through the archway sprung ;

The ponderous grate behind him rung :
To pass there was such scanty room,
The bars, descending, razed his plume.

The steed along the drawbridge flies,
Just as it trembled on the rise ;
Not lighter does the swallow skim
Along the smooth lake's level brim ;
And when Lord Marmion reached his band,
He halts, and turns with clenched hand,
And shout of loud defiance pours,
And shook his gauntlet at the towers.
" Horse ! horse !" the Douglas cried, " and
　　chase !"
But soon he reined his fury's pace :
" A royal messenger he came,
Though most unworthy of the name.

. 　 . 　 . 　 . 　 .

St. Mary, mend my fiery mood !
Old age ne'er cools the Douglas blood,
I thought to slay him where he stood.
'T is pity of him too," he cried ;
" Bold can he speak, and fairly ride :
I warrant him a warrior tried."
With this his mandate he recalls,
And slowly seeks his castle halls.
　　　　　　　　SIR WALTER SCOTT.

————

MARMION AT FLODDEN FIELD.

[The battle was fought in September, 1513, between the forces of
England and Scotland.　The latter were worsted, and King James
slain with eight thousand of his men.　Lord Surrey commanded the
English troops.]

A MOMENT then Lord Marmion stayed,
And breathed his steed, his men arrayed,
　Then forward moved his band,
Until, Lord Surrey's rear-guard won,
He halted by a cross of stone,
That, on a hillock standing lone,
　Did all the field command.

Hence might they see the full array
Of either host for deadly fray ;
Their marshalled lines stretched east and west,
　And fronted north and south,
And distant salutation past
　From the loud cannon-mouth ;
Not in the close successive rattle
That breathes the voice of modern battle,
　But slow and far between. —
The hillock gained, Lord Marmion stayed :
" Here, by this cross," he gently said,
　" You well may view the scene ;
Here shalt thou tarry, lovely Clare :
O, think of Marmion in thy prayer ! —
Thou wilt not ? — well, — no less my care
Shall, watchful, for thy weal prepare. —

You, Blount and Eustace, are her guard,
 With ten picked archers of my train ;
With England if the day go hard,
 To Berwick speed amain. —
But, if we conquer, cruel maid,
My spoils shall at your feet be laid,
 When here we meet again."
He waited not for answer there,
And would not mark the maid's despair,
 Nor heed the discontented look
From either squire : but spurred amain,
And, dashing through the battle-plain,
 His way to Surrey took.

 . . . . .

Blount and Fitz-Eustace rested still
 With Lady Clare upon the hill ;
On which (for far the day was spent)
The western sunbeams now were bent.
The cry they heard, its meaning knew,
Could plain their distant comrades view ;
Sadly to Blount did Eustace say,
" Unworthy office here to stay !
No hope of gilded spurs to-day. —
But, see ! look up, — on Flodden bent
The Scottish foe has fired his tent." —
 And sudden, as he spoke,
From the sharp ridges of the hill,
All downward to the banks of Till
 Was wreathed in sable smoke.
Volumed and vast, and rolling far,
The cloud enveloped Scotland's war,
 As down the hill they broke ;
Nor martial shout, nor minstrel tone,
Announced their march ; their tread alone,
At times their warning trumpet blown,
 At times a stifled hum,
Told England, from his mountain-throne
 King James did rushing come. —
Scarce could they hear or see their foes,
Until at weapon-point they close. —
They close in clouds of smoke and dust,
With sword-sway and with lance's thrust ;
 And such a yell was there,
Of sudden and portentous birth,
As if men fought upon the earth
 And fiends in upper air :
O life and death were in the shout,
Recoil and rally, charge and rout,
 And triumph and despair.
Long looked the anxious squires ; their eye
Could in the darkness naught descry.

At length the freshening western blast
Aside the shroud of battle cast ;
And, first, the ridge of mingled spears
Above the brightening cloud appears ;
And in the smoke the pennons flew,
As in the storm the white sea-mew.

Then marked they, dashing broad and far,
The broken billows of the war,
And pluméd crests of chieftains brave
Floating like foam upon the wave ;
 But naught distinct they see :
Wide raged the battle on the plain ;·
Spears shook, and falchions flashed amain ;
Fell England's arrow-flight like rain ;
Crests rose, and stooped, and rose again,
 Wild and disorderly.
Amid the scene of tumult, high
They saw Lord Marmion's falcon fly :
And stainless Tunstall's banner white,
And Edmund Howard's lion bright,
Still bear them bravely in the fight ;
 Although against them come,
Of gallant Gordons many a one,
And many a stubborn Highlandman,
And many a rugged Border clan,
 With Huntley and with Home.

Far on the left, unseen the while,
Stanley broke Lennox and Argyle ;·
Though there the western mountaineer
Rushed with bare bosom on the spear,
And flung the feeble targe aside,
And with both hands the broadsword plied,
'T was vain : — But Fortune, on the right,
With fickle smile, cheered Scotland's fight.
Then fell that spotless banner white,
 The Howard's lion fell ;
Yet still Lord Marmion's falcon flew
With wavering flight, while fiercer grew
 Around the battle-yell.
The Border slogan rent the sky !
A Home ! a Gordon ! was the cry :
Loud were the clanging blows ;
Advanced, — forced back, — now low, now nigh,
 The pennon sunk and rose ;
As bends the bark's mast in the gale,
When rent are rigging, shrouds, and sail,
 It wavered mid the foes.
No longer Blount the view could bear : —
" By heaven and all its saints, I swear,
 I will not see it lost !
Fitz-Eustace, you with Lady Clare
May bid your beads, and patter prayer, —
 I gallop to the host."
And to the fray he rode amain,
Followed by all the archer train.
The fiery youth, with desperate charge,
Made, for a space, an opening large, —
 The rescued banner rose, —
But darkly closed the war around,
Like pine-tree, rooted from the ground,
 It sunk among the foes.
Then Eustace mounted too ; — yet stayed,
As loath to leave the helpless maid,

When, fast as shaft can fly,
Bloodshot his eyes, his nostrils spread,
The loose rein dangling from his head,
Housing and saddle bloody red,
   Lord Marmion's steed rushed by ;
And Eustace, maddening at the sight,
   A look and sign to Clara cast,
   To mark he would return in haste,
Then plunged into the fight.

Ask me not what the maiden feels,
   Left in that dreadful hour alone :
Perchance her reason stoops or reels ;
   Perchance a courage, not her own,
   Braces her mind to desperate tone. —
The scattered van of England wheels ; —
   She only said, as loud in air
   The tumult roared, " Is Wilton there ? " —
   They fly, or, maddened by despair,
   Fight but to die, — " Is Wilton there ? "
With that, straight up the hill there rode
   Two horsemen drenched with gore,
And in their arms, a helpless load,
   A wounded knight they bore.
His hand still strained the broken brand ;
His arms were smeared with blood and sand.
Dragged from among the horses' feet,
With dinted shield, and helmet beat,
The falcon-crest and plumage gone,
Can that be haughty Marmion ! . . . .
Young Blount his armor did unlace,
And, gazing on his ghastly face,
   Said, — " By St. George, he 's gone !
That spear-wound has our master sped, —
And see the deep cut on his head !
   Good night to Marmion." —
" Unnurtured Blount ! thy brawling cease :
He opes his eyes," said Eustace ; " peace ! "

When, doffed his casque, he felt free air,
Around 'gan Marmion wildly stare : —
" Where 's Harry Blount ? Fitz-Eustace where ?
Linger ye here, ye hearts of hare !
Redeem my pennon, — charge again !
Cry — ' Marmion to the rescue ! ' — vain !
Last of my race, on battle-plain
That shout shall ne'er be heard again ! —
Yet my last thought is England's : — fly,
   To Dacre bear my signet-ring :
   Tell him his squadrons up to bring : —
Fitz-Eustace, to Lord Surrey hie ;
   Tunstall lies dead upon the field,
   His life-blood stains the spotless shield :
   Edmund is down ; — my life is reft ; —
   The Admiral alone is left.
   Let Stanley charge with spur of fire, —
   With Chester charge, and Lancashire,
   Full upon Scotland's central host,

Or victory and England 's lost. —
Must I bid twice ? — hence, varlets ! fly !
Leave Marmion here alone — to die."
They parted, and alone he lay :
Clare drew her from the sight away,
Till pain wrung forth a lowly moan,
And half he murmured, — " Is there none,
   Of all my halls have nurst,
Page, squire, or groom, one cup to bring,
Of blessed water from the spring,
   To slake my dying thirst ? "

O woman ! in our hours of ease,
Uncertain, coy, and hard to please,
   And variable as the shade
By the light quivering aspen made ;
When pain and anguish wring the brow,
A ministering angel thou ! —
Scarce were the piteous accents said,
When, with the Baron's casque, the maid
   To the nigh streamlet ran :
Forgot were hatred, wrongs, and fears ;
The plaintive voice alone she hears,
   Sees but the dying man.
She stooped her by the runnel's side,
   But in abhorrence backward drew ;
For, oozing from the mountain's side,
Where raged the war, a dark-red tide
   Was curdling in the streamlet blue.
Where shall she turn ! — behold her mark
   A little fountain cell,
Where water, clear as diamond-spark,
   In a stone basin fell.
Above, some half-worn letters say,
𝔇𝔯𝔦𝔫𝔨. 𝔴𝔢𝔞𝔯𝔶. 𝔭𝔦𝔩𝔤𝔯𝔦𝔪. 𝔡𝔯𝔦𝔫𝔨. 𝔞𝔫𝔡. 𝔭𝔯𝔞𝔶.
𝔉𝔬𝔯. 𝔱𝔥𝔢. 𝔨𝔦𝔫𝔡. 𝔰𝔬𝔲𝔩. 𝔬𝔣. 𝔖𝔶𝔟𝔦𝔩. 𝔊𝔯𝔢𝔶.
𝔚𝔥𝔬. 𝔟𝔲𝔦𝔩𝔱. 𝔱𝔥𝔦𝔰. 𝔠𝔯𝔬𝔰𝔰. 𝔞𝔫𝔡. 𝔴𝔢𝔩𝔩.
She filled the helm, and back she hied,
And with surprise and joy espied
   A monk supporting Marmion's head ;
A pious man whom duty brought
To dubious verge of battle fought,
   To shrive the dying, bless the dead.

Deep drank Lord Marmion of the wave,
And, as she stooped his brow to lave, —
" Is it the hand of Clare," he said,
" Or injured Constance, bathes my head ? "
   Then, as remembrance rose, —
" Speak not to me of shrift or prayer !
   I must redress her woes.
Short space, few words, are mine to spare ;
Forgive and listen, gentle Clare ! " —
   "Alas ! " she said, " the while, —
O, think of your immortal weal !
In vain for Constance is your zeal ;
   She — died at Holy Isle." —
Lord Marmion started from the ground,

As light as if he felt no wound ;
Though in the action burst the tide
In torrents from his wounded side.
" Then it was truth ! " he said, — " I knew
That the dark presage must be true. —
I would the Fiend, to whom belongs
The vengeance due to all her wrongs,
  Would spare me but a day !
For wasting fire, and dying groan,
And priests slain on the altar stone,
  Might bribe him for delay.
It may not be ! — this dizzy trance, —
Curse on yon base marauder's lance,
And doubly cursed my failing brand !
A sinful heart makes feeble hand."
Then, fainting, down on earth he sunk,
Supported by the trembling monk.

With fruitless labor, Clara bound,
And strove to stanch the gushing wound :
The monk, with unavailing cares,
Exhausted all the Church's prayers.
Ever, he said, that, close and near,
A lady's voice was in his ear,
And that the priest he could not hear,
  For that she ever sung,
" *In the lost battle, borne down by the flying,*
Where mingles war's rattle with groans of the
    dying ! "
  So the notes rung : —
" Avoid thee, Fiend ! — with cruel hand,
Shake not the dying sinner's sand ! —
O, look, my son, upon yon sign
Of the Redeemer's grace divine :
  O, think on faith and bliss ! —
By many a death-bed I have been,
And many a sinner's parting seen,
  But never aught like this."
The war, that for a space did fail,
Now trebly thundering swelled the gale,
  And — STANLEY ! was the cry : —
A light on Marmion's visage spread,
And fired his glazing eye :
With dying hand above his head
He shook the fragment of his blade,
  And shouted " Victory ! —
Charge, Chester, charge ! On, Stanley, on ! "
Were the last words of Marmion.
                          SIR WALTER SCOTT.

———◆———

THE HEART OF THE BRUCE.

IT was upon an April morn,
  While yet the frost lay hoar,
We heard Lord James's bugle-horn
  Sound by the rocky shore.

Then down we went, a hundred knights,
  All in our dark array,
And flung our armor in the ships
  That rode within the bay.

We spoke not as the shore grew less,
  But gazed in silence back,
Where the long billows swept away
  The foam behind our track.

And aye the purple hues decayed
  Upon the fading hill,
And but one heart in all that ship
  Was tranquil, cold, and still.

The good Lord Douglas paced the deck,
  And O, his face was wan !
Unlike the flush it used to wear
  When in the battle-van. —

" Come hither, come hither, my trusty knight,
  Sir Simon of the Lee ;
There is a freit lies near my soul
  I fain would tell to thee.

" Thou know'st the words King Robert spoke
  Upon his dying day :
How he bade take his noble heart
  And carry it far away ;

" And lay it in the holy soil
  Where once the Saviour trod,
Since he might not bear the blessed Cross.
  Nor strike one blow for God.

" Last night as in my bed I lay,
  I dreamed a dreary dream : —
Methought I saw a Pilgrim stand
  In the moonlight's quivering beam.

" His robe was of the azure dye,
  Snow-white his scattered hairs,
And even such a cross he bore
  As good St. Andrew bears.

" ' Why go ye forth, Lord James,' he said,
  ' With spear and belted brand ?
Why do you take its dearest pledge
  From this our Scottish land ?

" ' The sultry breeze of Galilee
  Creeps through its groves of palm,
The olives on the Holy Mount
  Stand glittering in the calm.

" ' But 't is not there that Scotland's heart
  Shall rest by God's decree,
Till the great angel calls the dead
  To rise from earth and sea !

" ' Lord James of Douglas, mark my rede !
　　That heart shall pass once more
In fiery fight against the foe,
　　As it was wont of yore.

" ' And it shall pass beneath the Cross,
　　And save King Robert's vow ;
But other hands shall bear it back,
　　Not, James of Douglas, thou ! '

" Now, by thy knightly faith, I pray,
　　Sir Simon of the Lee, —
For truer friend had never man
　　Than thou hast been to me, —

" If ne'er upon the Holy Land
　　'T is mine in life to tread,
Bear thou to Scotland's kindly earth
　　The relics of her dead."

The tear was in Sir Simon's eye
　　As he wrung the warrior's hand, —
" Betide me weal, betide me woe,
　　I 'll hold by thy command.

" But if in battle-front, Lord James,
　　'T is ours once more to ride,
Nor force of man, nor craft of fiend,
　　Shall cleave me from thy side ! "

And aye we sailed and aye we sailed
　　Across the weary sea,
Until one morn the coast of Spain
　　Rose grimly on our lee.

And as we rounded to the port,
　　Beneath the watch-tower's wall,
We heard the clash of the atabals,
　　And the trumpet's wavering call.

" Why sounds yon Eastern music here
　　So wantonly and long,
And whose the crowd of arméd men
　　That round yon standard throng ? "

" The Moors have come from Africa
　　To spoil and waste and slay,
And King Alonzo of Castile
　　Must fight with them to-day."

" Now shame it were," cried good Lord James,
　　" Shall never be said of me
That I and mine have turned aside
　　From the Cross in jeopardie !

" Have down, have down, my merry men all, —
　　Have down unto the plain ;
We 'll let the Scottish lion loose
　　Within the fields of Spain ! "

" Now welcome to me, noble lord,
　　Thou and thy stalwart power ;
Dear is the sight of a Christian knight,
　　Who comes in such an hour !

" Is it for bond or faith you come,
　　Or yet for golden fee ?
Or bring ye France's lilies here,
　　Or the flower of Burgundie ? "

" God greet thee well, thou valiant king,
　　Thee and thy belted peers, —
Sir James of Douglas am I called,
　　And these are Scottish spears.

" We do not fight for bond or plight,
　　Nor yet for golden fee ;
But for the sake of our blessed Lord,
　　Who died upon the tree.

" We bring our great King Robert's heart
　　Across the weltering wave,
To lay it in the holy soil
　　Hard by the Saviour's grave.

" True pilgrims we, by land or sea,
　　Where danger bars the way ;
And therefore are we here, Lord King,
　　To ride with thee this day ! "

The King has bent his stately head,
　　And the tears were in his eyne, —
" God's blessing on thee, noble knight,
　　For this brave thought of thine !

" I know thy name full well, Lord James ;
　　And honored may I be,
That those who fought beside the Bruce
　　Should fight this day for me !

" Take thou the leading of the van,
　　And charge the Moors amain ;
There is not such a lance as thine
　　In all the host of Spain ! "

The Douglas turned towards us then,
　　O, but his glance was high ! —
" There is not one of all my men
　　But is as bold as I.

" There is not one of all my knights
　　But bears as true a spear, —
Then onward, Scottish gentlemen,
　　And think King Robert 's here ! "

The trumpets blew, the cross-bolts flew,
　　The arrows flashed like flame,
As spur in side, and spear in rest,
　　Against the foe we came.

And many a bearded Saracen
  Went down, both horse and man ;
For through their ranks we rode like corn,
  So furiously we ran !

But in behind our path they closed,
  Though fain to let us through,
For they were forty thousand men,
  And we were wondrous few.

We might not see a lance's length,
  So dense was their array,
But the long fell sweep of the Scottish blade
  Still held them hard at bay.

"Make in ! make in !" Lord Douglas cried, —
  "Make in, my brethren dear !
Sir William of St. Clair is down ;
  We may not leave him here !"

But thicker, thicker grew the swarm,
  And sharper shot the rain,
And the horses reared amid the press,
  But they would not charge again.

"Now Jesu help thee," said Lord James,
  "Thou kind and true St. Clair !
An' if I may not bring thee off,
  I 'll die beside thee there !"

Then in his stirrups up he stood,
  So lion-like and bold,
And held the precious heart aloft
  All in its case of gold.

He flung it from him, far ahead,
  And never spake he more,
But — "Pass thou first, thou dauntless heart,
  As thou wert wont of yore !"

The roar of fight rose fiercer yet,
  And heavier still the stour,
Till the spears of Spain came shivering in,
  And swept away the Moor.

"Now praised be God, the day is won !
  They fly o'er flood and fell, —
Why dost thou draw the rein so hard,
  Good knight, that fought so well ?"

"O, ride ye on, Lord King !" he said,
  "And leave the dead to me,
For I must keep the dreariest watch
  That ever I shall dree !

"There lies, above his master's heart,
  The Douglas, stark and grim ;
And woe is me I should be here,
  Not side by side with him !

"The world grows cold, my arm is old,
  And thin my lyart hair,
And all that I loved best on earth
  Is stretched before me there.

"O Bothwell banks ! that bloom so bright
  Beneath the sun of May,
The heaviest cloud that ever blew
  Is bound for you this day.

"And Scotland ! thou mayst veil thy head
  In sorrow and in pain :
The sorest stroke upon thy brow
  Hath fallen this day in Spain !

"We 'll bear them back unto our ship,
  We 'll bear them o'er the sea,
And lay them in the hallowed earth
  Within our own countrie.

"And be thou strong of heart, Lord King,
  For this I tell thee sure,
The sod that drank the Douglas' blood
  Shall never bear the Moor !"

The King he lighted from his horse,
  He flung his brand away,
And took the Douglas by the hand,
  So stately as he lay.

"God give thee rest, thou valiant soul !
  That fought so well for Spain ;
I 'd rather half my land were gone,
  So thou wert here again !"

We bore the good Lord James away,
  And the priceless heart we bore,
And heavily we steered our ship
  Towards the Scottish shore.

No welcome greeted our return,
  Nor clang of martial tread,
But all were dumb and hushed as death
  Before the mighty dead.

We laid our chief in Douglas Kirk,
  The heart in fair Melrose ;
And woful men were we that day, —
  God grant their souls repose !
                WILLIAM EDMONDSTOUNE AYTOUN.

GATHERING SONG OF DONALD THE
          BLACK.

PIBROCH of Donuil Dhu,
  Pibroch of Donuil,
Wake thy wild voice anew,
  Summon Clan Conuil.

Come away, come away,
  Hark to the summons!
Come in your war array,
  Gentles and commons.

Come from deep glen, and
  From mountain so rocky;
The war-pipe and pennon
  Are at Inverlocky.
Come every hill-plaid, and
  True heart that wears one,
Come every steel blade, and
  Strong hand that bears one.

Leave untended the herd,
  The flock without shelter;
Leave the corpse uninterred,
  The bride at the altar;
Leave the deer, leave the steer,
  Leave nets and barges;
Come with your fighting gear,
  Broadswords and targes.

Come as the winds come when
  Forests are rended;
Come as the waves come when
  Navies are stranded;
Faster come, faster come,
  Faster and faster,
Chief, vassal, page and groom,
  Tenant and master.

Fast they come, fast they come;
  See how they gather!
Wide waves the eagle plume
  Blended with heather.
Cast your plaids, draw your blades,
  Forward each man set!
Pibroch of Donuil Dhu,
  Knell for the onset!
        SIR WALTER SCOTT.

SONG OF CLAN-ALPINE.

HAIL to the Chief who in triumph advances!
  Honored and blessed be the evergreen Pine!
Long may the tree, in his banner that glances,
  Flourish, the shelter and grace of our line!
    Heaven send it happy dew,
    Earth lend it sap anew,
Gayly to bourgeon, and broadly to grow,
    While every highland glen
    Sends our shout back again,
  "Roderigh Vich Alpine dhu, ho! ieroe!"

Ours is no sapling, chance-sown by the fountain,
  Blooming at Beltane, in winter to fade;
When the whirlwind has stripped every leaf on
    the mountain,
  The more shall Clan-Alpine exult in her shade.

Moored in the rifted rock,
  Proof to the tempest's shock,
Firmer he roots him the ruder it blow;
  Menteith and Breadalbane, then,
  Echo his praise again,
  "Roderigh Vich Alpine dhu, ho! ieroe!"

Proudly our pibroch has thrilled in Glen Fruin,
  And Bannachar's groans to our slogan replied;
Glen Luss and Ross-dhu, they are smoking in ruin,
  And the best of Loch-Lomond lie dead on her
    side.
    Widow and Saxon maid
    Long shall lament our raid,
Think of Clan-Alpine with fear and with woe;
    Lennox and Leven-glen
    Shake when they hear again,
  "Roderigh Vich Alpine dhu, ho! ieroe!"

Row, vassals, row, for the pride of the Highlands!
  Stretch to your oars for the evergreen Pine!
O that the rosebud that graces yon islands
  Were wreathed in a garland around him to twine!
    O that some seedling gem,
    Worthy such noble stem,
Honored and blessed in their shadow might
    grow!
    Loud should Clan-Alpine then
    Ring from her deepmost glen,
  "Roderigh Vich Alpine dhu, ho! ieroe!"
        SIR WALTER SCOTT.

THE FIERY CROSS OF CLAN-ALPINE.

'T WAS all prepared;—and from the rock
A goat, the patriarch of the flock,
Before the kindling pile was laid,
And pierced by Roderick's ready blade.
Patient the sickening victim eyed
The life-blood ebb in crimson tide,
Down his clogged beard and shaggy limb,
Till darkness glazed his eyeballs dim.
The grisly priest, with murmuring prayer,
A slender crosslet framed with care,
A cubit's length in measure due;
The shaft and limbs were rods of yew,
Whose parents in Inch-Cailliach wave
Their shadows o'er Clan-Alpine's grave,
And, answering Lomond's breezes deep,
Soothe many a chieftain's endless sleep.
The Cross, thus formed, he held on high,
With wasted hand and haggard eye,
And strange and mingled feelings woke,
While his anathema he spoke:—

"Woe to the clansman who shall view
This symbol of sepulchral yew,
Forgetful that its branches grew

Where weep the heavens their holiest dew
　On Alpine's dwelling low !
Deserter of his Chieftain's trust,
He ne'er shall mingle with their dust,
But, from his sires and kindred thrust,
Each clansman's execration just
　Shall doom him wrath and woe."
He paused ; — the word the vassals took,
With forward step and fiery look,
On high their naked brands they shook,
Their clattering targets wildly strook ;
　And first in murmur low,
Then, like the billow in his course,
That far to seaward finds his source,
And flings to shore his mustered force,
Burst, with loud roar, their answer hoarse,
　"Woe to the traitor, woe !"
Ben-an's gray scalp the accents knew,
The joyous wolf from covert drew,
The exulting eagle screamed afar, —
They knew the voice of Alpine's war.

The shout was hushed on lake and fell,
The monk resumed his muttered spell :
Dismal and low its accents came,
The while he scathed the Cross with flame ;
And the few words that reached the air,
Although the holiest name was there,
Had more of blasphemy than prayer.
But when he shook above the crowd
Its kindled points, he spoke aloud : —
"Woe to the wretch who fails to rear
At this dread sign the ready spear !
For, as the flames this symbol sear,
His home, the refuge of his fear,
　A kindred fate shall know ;
Far o'er its roof the volumed flame
Clan-Alpine's vengeance shall proclaim,
While maids and matrons on his name
Shall call down wretchedness and shame,
　And infamy and woe "
Then rose the cry of females, shrill
As goshawk's whistle on the hill,
Denouncing misery and ill,
Mingled with childhood's babbling trill
　Of curses stammered slow ;
Answering, with imprecation dread,
"Sunk be his home in embers red !
And curséd be the meanest shed
That e'er shall hide the houseless head
　We doom to want and woe ! "
A sharp and shrieking echo gave,
Coir-Uriskin, thy goblin cave !
And the gray pass where birches wave,
　On Beala-nam-bo.

Then deeper paused the priest anew,
And hard his laboring breath he drew,

While, with set teeth and clenchéd hand,
And eyes that glowed like fiery brand,
He meditated curse more dread,
And deadlier, on the clansman's head,
Who, summoned to his Chieftain's aid,
The signal saw and disobeyed.
The crosslet's points of sparkling wood
He quenched among the bubbling blood,
And, as again the sign he reared,
Hollow and hoarse his voice was heard :
"When flits this Cross from man to man,
Vich-Alpine's summons to his clan,
Burst be the ear that fails to heed !
Palsied the foot that shuns to speed !
May ravens tear the careless eyes,
Wolves make the coward heart their prize !
As sinks that blood-stream in the earth,
So may his heart's-blood drench his hearth !
As dies in hissing gore the spark,
Quench thou his light, Destruction dark !
And be the grace to him denied,
Bought by this sign to all beside ! "
He ceased ; no echo gave again
The murmur of the deep Amen.

Then Roderick, with impatient look,
From Brian's hand the symbol took :
"Speed, Malise, speed ! " he said, and gave
The crosslet to his henchman brave.
"The muster-place be Lanrick mead, —
Instant the time, — speed, Malise, speed ! "
Like heath-bird, when the hawks pursue,
A barge across Loch-Katrine flew ;
High stood the henchman on the prow,
So rapidly the bargemen row,
The bubbles, where they launched the boat,
Were all unbroken and afloat,
Dancing in foam and ripple still,
When it had neared the mainland hill ;
And from the silver beach's side
Still was the prow three fathom wide,
When lightly bounded to the land
The messenger of blood and brand.

. . . . . .

Fast as the fatal symbol flies,
In arms the huts and hamlets rise ;
From winding glen, from upland brown,
They poured each hardy tenant down.
Nor slacked the messenger his pace ;
He showed the sign, he named the place,
And, pressing forward like the wind,
Left clamor and surprise behind.
The fisherman forsook the strand,
The swarthy smith took dirk and brand ;
With changed cheer, the mower blithe
Left in the half-cut swath his scythe ;
The herds without a keeper strayed,
The plough was in mid-furrow stayed,

The falc'ner tossed his hawk away,
The hunter left the stag at bay ;
Prompt at the signal of alarms,
Each son of Alpine rushed to arms ;
So swept the tumult and affray
Along the margin of Achray.
Alas, thou lovely lake ! that e'er
Thy banks should echo sounds of fear !
The rocks, the bosky thickets, sleep
So stilly on thy bosom deep,
The lark's blithe carol from the cloud
Seems for the scene too gayly loud.

SIR WALTER SCOTT.

MARCH, MARCH, ETTRICK AND TEVIOTDALE.

MARCH, march, Ettrick and Teviotdale !
Why the deil dinna ye march forward in order?
March, march, Eskdale and Liddesdale !
All the Blue Bonnets are over the Border !
    Many a banner spread
    Flutters above your head,
Many a crest that is famous in story.
    Mount and make ready, then,
    Sons of the mountain glen,
Fight for the Queen and our old Scottish glory !

Come from the hills where your hirsels are grazing ;
    Come from the glen of the buck and the roe ;
Come to the crag where the beacon is blazing ;
    Come with the buckler, the lance, and the bow.
    Trumpets are sounding ;
    War-steeds are bounding ;
Stand to your arms, then, and march in good order,
    England shall many a day
    Tell of the bloody fray,
When the Blue Bonnets came over the Border.

SIR WALTER SCOTT.

GO WHERE GLORY WAITS THEE.

Go where glory waits thee,
But, while fame elates thee,
    O, still remember me !
When the praise thou meetest
To thine ear is sweetest,
    O, then remember me !
Other arms may press thee,
Dearer friends caress thee,
All the joys that bless thee,
    Sweeter far may be ;
But when friends are nearest,
And when joys are dearest,
    O, then remember me !

When at eve thou rovest
By the star thou lovest,
    O, then remember me !
Think, when home returning,
Bright we've seen it burning,
    O, thus remember me !
Oft as summer closes,
On its lingering roses,
    Once so loved by thee,
Think of her who wove them,
Her who made thee love them,
    O, then remember me !

When, around thee dying,
Autumn leaves are lying,
    O, then remember me !
And, at night, when gazing
On the gay hearth blazing,
    O, still remember me !
Then should music, stealing
All the soul of feeling,
To thy heart appealing,
    Draw one tear from thee ;
Then let memory bring thee
Strains I used to sing thee, —
    O, then remember me !

THOMAS MOORE (" Irish Melodies ").

THE BATTLE - SONG OF GUSTAVUS ADOLPHUS.

[Translation.]

FEAR not, O little flock ! the foe
Who madly seeks your overthrow,
    Dread not his rage and power ;
What though your courage sometimes faints ?
His seeming triumph o'er God's saints
    Lasts but a little hour.

Be of good cheer ; your cause belongs
To Him who can avenge your wrongs,
    Leave it to him, our Lord.
Though hidden now from all our eyes,
He sees the Gideon who shall rise
    To save us, and his word.

As true as God's own word is true,
Not earth or hell with all their crew
    Against us shall prevail.
A jest and by-word are they grown ;
God is with us, we are his own,
    Our victory cannot fail.

Amen, Lord Jesus ; grant our prayer !
Great Captain, now thine arm make bare ;
    Fight for us once again !

So shall the saints and martyrs raise
A mighty chorus to thy praise,
World without end! Amen.
MICHAEL ALTENBURG (German).

HOW THEY BROUGHT THE GOOD NEWS FROM GHENT TO AIX.

I SPRANG to the stirrup, and Joris and he ;
I galloped, Dirck galloped, we galloped all three ;
"Good speed!" cried the watch as the gate-bolts undrew,
"Speed!" echoed the wall to us galloping through.
Behind shut the postern, the lights sank to rest,
And into the midnight we galloped abreast.

Not a word to each other ; we kept the great pace, —
Neck by neck, stride by stride, never changing our place ;
I turned in my saddle and made its girths tight,
Then shortened each stirrup and set the pique right,
Rebuckled the check-strap, chained slacker the bit,
Nor galloped less steadily Roland a whit.

'T was a moonset at starting ; but while we drew near
Lokeren, the cocks crew and twilight dawned clear ;
At Boom a great yellow star came out to see ;
At Düffeld 't was morning as plain as could be ;
And from Mecheln church-steeple we heard the half-chime, —
So Joris broke silence with "Yet there is time!"

At Aerschot up leaped of a sudden the sun,
And against him the cattle stood black every one,
To stare through the mist at us galloping past ;
And I saw my stout galloper Roland at last,
With resolute shoulders, each butting away
The haze, as some bluff river headland its spray ;

And his low head and crest, just one sharp ear bent back
For my voice, and the other pricked out on his track ;
And one eye's black intelligence, — ever that glance
O'er its white edge at me, his own master, askance ;
And the thick heavy spume-flakes, which aye and anon
His fierce lips shook upward in galloping on.

By Hasselt Dirck groaned ; and cried Joris, "Stay spur!
Your Roos galloped bravely, the fault's not in her ;
We'll remember at Aix," — for one heard the quick wheeze
Of her chest, saw the stretched neck, and staggering knees,
And sunk tail, and horrible heave of the flank,
As down on her haunches she shuddered and sank.

So we were left galloping, Joris and I,
Past Looz and past Tongres, no cloud in the sky ;
The broad sun above laughed a pitiless laugh ;
'Neath our feet broke the brittle, bright stubble like chaff ;
Till over by Dalhem a dome-spire sprang white,
And "Gallop," gasped Joris, "for Aix is in sight!"

"How they'll greet us!" — and all in a moment his roan
Rolled neck and croup over, lay dead as a stone ;
And there was my Roland to bear the whole weight
Of the news which alone could save Aix from her fate,
With his nostrils like pits full of blood to the brim,
And with circles of red for his eye-sockets' rim.

Then I cast loose my buff-coat, each holster let fall,
Shook off both my jack-boots, let go belt and all,
Stood up in the stirrup, leaned, patted his ear,
Called my Roland his pet name, my horse without peer, —
Clapped my hands, laughed and sung, any noise, bad or good,
Till at length into Aix Roland galloped and stood.

And all I remember is friends flocking round,
As I sate with his head 'twixt my knees on the ground ;
And no voice but was praising this Roland of mine,
As I poured down his throat our last measure of wine,
Which (the burgesses voted by common consent)
Was no more than his due who brought good news from Ghent.
ROBERT BROWNING.

INCIDENT OF THE FRENCH CAMP.

I.

You know we French stormed Ratisbon :
  A mile or so away,
On a little mound, Napoleon
  Stood on our storming-day ;
With neck out-thrust, you fancy how,
  Legs wide, arms locked behind,
As if to balance the prone brow,
  Oppressive with its mind.

II.

Just as perhaps he mused, " My plans
  That soar, to earth may fall,
Let once my army-leader Lannes
  Waver at yonder wall," —
Out 'twixt the battery-smokes there flew
  A rider, bound on bound
Full-galloping ; nor bridle drew
  Until he reached the mound.

III.

Then off there flung in smiling joy,
  And held himself erect
By just his horse's mane, a boy :
  You hardly could suspect,
(So tight he kept his lips compressed,
  Scarce any blood came through,)
You looked twice ere you saw his breast
  Was all but shot in two.

IV.

" Well," cried he, " Emperor, by God's grace
  We 've got you Ratisbon !
The marshal 's in the market-place,
  And you 'll be there anon
To see your flag-bird flap his vans
  Where I, to heart's desire,
Perched him !" The chief's eye flashed ; his plans
  Soared up again like fire.

V.

The chief's eye flashed ; but presently
  Softened itself, as sheathes
A film the mother-eagle's eye
  When her bruised eaglet breathes :
" You 're wounded !" " Nay," his soldier's pride
  Touched to the quick, he said :
" I 'm killed, sire !" And, his chief beside,
  Smiling, the boy fell dead.

ROBERT BROWNING.

HOHENLINDEN.

On Linden, when the sun was low,
All bloodless lay the untrodden snow,
And dark as winter was the flow
  Of Iser, rolling rapidly.

But Linden saw another sight
When the drum beat, at dead of night,
Commanding fires of death to light
  The darkness of her scenery.

By torch and trumpet fast arrayed,
Each horseman drew his battle-blade,
And furious every charger neighed,
  To join the dreadful revelry.

Then shook the hills with thunder riven,
Then rushed the steed to battle driven,
And louder than the bolts of heaven
  Far flashed the red artillery.

But redder yet that light shall glow
On Linden's hills of stainéd snow,
And bloodier yet the torrent flow
  Of Iser, rolling rapidly.

'T is morn, but scarce yon level sun
Can pierce the war-clouds, rolling dun,
Where furious Frank and fiery Hun
  Shout in their sulphurous canopy.

The combat deepens. On, ye brave,
Who rush to glory, or the grave !
Wave, Munich ! all thy banners wave,
  And charge with all thy chivalry !

Few, few shall part where many meet !
The snow shall be their winding-sheet,
And every turf beneath their feet
  Shall be a soldier's sepulchre.

THOMAS CAMPBELL.

THE NOBLEMAN AND THE PEN-SIONER.

" Old man, God bless you ! does your pipe taste
  sweetly ?
  A beauty, by my soul !
A red clay flower-pot, rimmed with gold so neatly !
  What ask you for the bowl ?"

" O sir, that bowl for worlds I would not part with ;
  A brave man gave it me,
Who won it — now what think you ? — of a bashaw
  At Belgrade's victory.

" There, sir, ah ! there was booty worth the
  showing, —
  Long life to Prince Eugene !
Like after-grass you might have seen us mowing
  The Turkish ranks down clean."

" Another time I 'll hear your story ; —
  Come, old man, be no fool ;
Take these two ducats, — gold for glory, —
  And let me have the bowl !"

"I'm a poor churl, as you may say, sir;
　My pension 's all I 'm worth :
Yet I 'd not give that bowl away, sir,
　For all the gold on earth.

"Just hear now ! Once, as we hussars, all merry,
　Hard on the foe's rear pressed,
A blundering rascal of a janizary
　Shot through our captain's breast.

"At once across my horse I hove him, —
　The same would he have done, —
And from the smoke and tumult drove him
　Safe to a nobleman.

"I nursed him, and, before his end, bequeathing
　His money and this bowl
To me, he pressed my hand, just ceased his
　　breathing,
　And so he died, brave soul !

"The money thou must give mine host, — so
　　thought I, —
　Three plunderings suffered he :
And, in remembrance of my old friend, brought I
　The pipe away with me.

"Henceforth in all campaigns with me I bore it,
　In flight or in pursuit ;
It was a holy thing, sir, and I wore it
　Safe-sheltered in my boot.

"This very limb, I lost it by a shot, sir,
　Under the walls of Prague :
First at my precious pipe, be sure, I caught, sir,
　And then picked up my leg."

"You move me even to tears, old sire :
　What was the brave man's name ?
Tell me, that I, too, may admire,
　And venerate his fame."

"They called him only the brave Walter ;
　His farm lay near the Rhine." —
"God bless your old eyes ! 't was my father,
　And that same farm is mine.

"Come, friend, you 've seen some stormy weather,
　With me is now your bed ;
We 'll drink of Walter's grapes together,
　And eat of Walter's bread."

"Now, — done ! I march in, then, to-morrow ;
　You 're his true heir, I see ;
And when I die, your thanks, kind master,
　The Turkish pipe shall be."

PFEFFEL. Translation of
CHARLES T. BROOKS.

THE SWORD SONG.

FROM THE GERMAN OF KÖRNER.

[Charles Theodore Körner was a young German soldier, scholar, poet, and patriot. He was born at Dresden in the autumn of 1791, and fell in battle for his country at the early age of twenty-two. The "Sword Song," so called, was written in his pocket-book only two hours before he fell, during a halt in a wood previous to the engagement, and was read by him to a comrade just as the signal was given for battle. This bold song represents the soldier chiding his sword, which, under the image of his iron bride, is impatient to come forth from her chamber, the scabbard, and be wedded to him on the field of battle, where each soldier shall press the blade to his lips.

Körner fell in an engagement with superior numbers near a thicket in the neighborhood of Rosenburg. He had advanced in pursuit of the flying foe too far beyond his comrades. They buried him under an old oak on the site of the battle, and carved his name on the trunk.]

SWORD, on my left side gleaming,
What means thy bright eye's beaming ?
It makes my spirit dance
To see thy friendly glance.
　　Hurrah !

"A valiant rider bears me ;
A free-born German wears me :
That makes my eye so bright ;
That is the sword's delight."
　　Hurrah !

Yes, good sword, I *am* free,
And love thee heartily,
And clasp thee to my side,
E'en as a plighted bride.
　　Hurrah !

"And I to thee, by Heaven,
My light steel life have given ;
When shall the knot be tied ?
When wilt thou take thy bride ?"
　　Hurrah !

The trumpet's solemn warning
Shall hail the bridal morning.
When cannon-thunders wake
Then my true-love I take.
　　Hurrah !

"O blessed, blessed meeting !
My heart is wildly beating :
Come, bridegroom, come for me ;
My garland waiteth thee."
　　Hurrah !

Why in the scabbard rattle,
So wild, so fierce for battle ?
What means this restless glow ?
My sword, why clatter so ?
　　Hurrah !

"Well may thy prisoner rattle ;
My spirit yearns for battle.

Rider, 't is war's wild glow
That makes me tremble so."
      Hurrah !

Stay in thy chamber near,
My love ; what wilt thou here ?
Still in thy chamber bide :
Soon, soon I take my bride.
      Hurrah !

" Let me not longer wait :
Love's garden blooms in state,
With roses bloody-red,
And many a bright death-bed."
      Hurrah !

Now, then, come forth, my bride !
Come forth, thou rider's pride !
Come out, my good sword, come !
Forth to thy father's home !
      Hurrah !

" O, in the field to prance
The glorious wedding dance !
How, in the sun's bright beams,
Bride-like the clear steel gleams !"
      Hurrah !

Then forward, valiant fighters !
And forward, German riders !
And when the heart grows cold,
Let each his love infold.
      Hurrah !

Once on the left it hung,
And stolen glances flung ;
Now clearly on your right
Doth God each fond bride plight.
      Hurrah !

Then let your hot lips feel
That virgin cheek of steel ;
One kiss, — and woe betide
Him who forsakes the bride.
      Hurrah !

Now let the loved one sing ;
Now let the clear blade ring,
Till the bright sparks shall fly,
Heralds of victory !
      Hurrah !

For, hark ! the trumpet's warning
Proclaims the marriage morning ;
It dawns in festal pride ;
Hurrah, thou Iron Bride !
      Hurrah !
            Translation of CHARLES T. BROOKS.

THE TURKISH CAMP.

BEFORE CORINTH.

'T is midnight : on the mountains brown
The cold round moon shines deeply down ;
Blue roll the waters, blue the sky
Spreads like an ocean hung on high,
Bespangled with those isles of light,
So wildly, spiritually bright ;
Who ever gazed upon them shining,
And turned to earth without repining,
Nor wished for wings to flee away,
And mix with their eternal ray ?
The waves on either shore lay there,
Cælm, clear, and azure as the air :
And scarce their foam the pebbles shook,
But murmured meekly as the brook.
The winds were pillowed on the waves ;
The banners drooped along their staves,
And, as they fell around them furling,
Above them shone the crescent curling ;
And that deep silence was unbroke,
Save where the watch his signal spoke,
Save where the steed neighed oft and shrill,
And echo answered from the hill,
And the wide hum of that wild host
Rustled like leaves from coast to coast,
As rose the Muezzin's voice in air
In midnight call to wonted prayer ;
It rose, that chanted mournful strain,
Like some lone spirit's o'er the plain :
'T was musical, but sadly sweet,
Such as when winds and harp-strings meet,
And take a long unmeasured tone,
To mortal minstrelsy unknown.
It seemed to those within the wall
A cry prophetic of their fall :
It struck even the besieger's ear
With something ominous and drear,
An undefined and sudden thrill,
Which makes the heart a moment still,
Then beat with quicker pulse, ashamed
Of that strange sense its silence framed ;
Such as a sudden passing-bell
Wakes, though but for a stranger's knell.
                              BYRON.

WATERLOO.

FROM "CHILDE HAROLD."

THERE was a sound of revelry by night,
And Belgium's capital had gathered then
Her beauty and her chivalry, and bright
The lamps shone o'er fair women and brave men ;
A thousand hearts beat happily ; and when

Music arose with its voluptuous swell,
Soft eyes looked love to eyes which spake again,
And all went merry as a marriage-bell ;
But hush ! hark ! a deep sound strikes like a rising knell !

Did ye not hear it ? — No ; 't was but the wind,
Or the car rattling o'er the stony street ;
On with the dance ! let joy be unconfined !
No sleep till morn when Youth and Pleasure meet
To chase the glowing Hours with flying feet, —
But, hark ! — that heavy sound breaks in once more,
As if the clouds its echo would repeat ;
And nearer, clearer, deadlier than before !
Arm ! arm ! it is — it is — the cannon's opening roar !

Within a windowed niche of that high hall
Sate Brunswick's fated chieftain ; he did hear
That sound the first amidst the festival,
And caught its tone with Death's prophetic ear;
And when they smiled because he deemed it near,
His heart more truly knew that peal too well
Which stretched his father on a bloody bier,
And roused the vengeance blood alone could quell :
He rushed into the field, and, foremost fighting, fell.

Ah ! then and there was hurrying to and fro,
And gathering tears, and tremblings of distress,
And cheeks all pale which but an hour ago
Blushed at the praise of their own loveliness ;
And there were sudden partings, such as press
The life from out young hearts, and choking sighs
Which ne'er might be repeated : who would guess
If evermore should meet those mutual eyes,
Since upon night so sweet such awful morn could rise !

And there was mounting in hot haste : the steed,
The mustering squadron, and the clattering car,
Went pouring forward with impetuous speed,
And swiftly forming in the ranks of war ;
And the deep thunder peal on peal afar ;
And near, the beat of the alarming drum
Roused up the soldier ere the morning star ;
While thronged the citizens with terror dumb,
Or whispering with white lips, — " The foe ! they come ! they come ! "

And wild and high the "Cameron's gathering" rose,
The war-note of Lochiel, which Albyn's hills

Have heard, — and heard, too, have her Saxon foes :
How in the noon of night that pibroch thrills
Savage and shrill !   But with the breath which fills
Their mountain pipe, so fill the mountaineers
With the fierce native daring which instils
The stirring memory of a thousand years,
And Evan's, Donald's fame rings in each clansman's ears !

And Ardennes waves above them her green leaves,
Dewy with nature's tear-drops, as they pass,
Grieving, if aught inanimate e'er grieves,
Over the unreturning brave, — alas !
Ere evening to be trodden like the grass
Which now beneath them, but above shall grow
In its next verdure, when this fiery mass
Of living valor, rolling on the foe,
And burning with high hope, shall moulder cold and low.

Last noon beheld them full of lusty life,
Last eve in Beauty's circle proudly gay,
The midnight brought the signal sound of strife,
The morn the marshalling in arms, — the day
Battle's magnificently stern array !
The thunder-clouds close o'er it, which when rent
The earth is covered thick with other clay,
Which her own clay shall cover, heaped and pent,
Rider and horse, — friend, foe, — in one red burial blent !

Their praise is hymned by loftier harps than mine ;
Yet one I would select from that proud throng,
Partly because they blend me with his line,
And partly that I did his sire some wrong,
And partly that bright names will hallow song !
And his was of the bravest, and when showered
The death-bolts deadliest the thinned files along,
Even where the thickest of war's tempest lowered,
They reached no nobler breast than thine, young, gallant Howard !

There have been tears and breaking hearts for thee,
And mine were nothing, had I such to give ;
But when I stood beneath the fresh green tree,
Which living waves where thou didst cease to live,
And saw around me the wide field revive
With fruits and fertile promise, and the Spring
Come forth her work of gladness to contrive,

With all her reckless birds upon the wing,
I turned from all she brought to those she could
    not bring.

I turned to thee, to thousands, of whom each
And one as all a ghastly gap did make
In his own kind and kindred, whom to teach
Forgetfulness were mercy for their sake ;
The Archangel's trump, not glory's, must awake
Those whom they thirst for ; though the sound
    of Fame
May for a moment soothe, it cannot slake
The fever of vain longing, and the name
So honored but assumes a stronger, bitterer claim.

They mourn, but smile at length ; and, smiling,
    mourn :
The tree will wither long before it fall ;
The hull drives on, though mast and sail be torn ;
The roof-tree sinks, but moulders on the hall
In massy hoariness ; the ruined wall
Stands when its wind-worn battlements are
    gone ;
The bars survive the captive they inthrall ;
The day drags through though storms keep out
    the sun ;
And thus the heart will break, yet brokenly live on ;

Even as a broken mirror, which the glass
In every fragment multiplies, and makes
A thousand images of one that was
The same, and still the more, the more it breaks ;
And thus the heart will do which not forsakes,
Living in shattered guise, and still, and cold,
And bloodless, with its sleepless sorrow aches,
Yet withers on till all without is old,
Showing no visible sign, for such things are untold.
                                        BYRON.

THE CHARGE AT WATERLOO.

ON came the whirlwind, — like the last
But fiercest sweep of tempest-blast ;
On came the whirlwind, — steel-gleams broke
Like lightning through the rolling smoke ;
    The war was waked anew.
Three hundred cannon-mouths roared loud,
And from their throats, with flash and cloud,
    Their showers of iron threw.
Beneath their fire, in full career,
Rushed on the ponderous cuirassier,
The lancer couched his ruthless spear,
And, hurrying as to havoc near,
    The cohorts' eagles flew.
In one dark torrent, broad and strong,
The advancing onset rolled along,
Forth harbingered by fierce acclaim,

That, from the shroud of smoke and flame,
Pealed wildly the imperial name.
But on the British heart were lost
The terrors of the charging host ;
For not an eye the storm that viewed
Changed its proud glance of fortitude,
Nor was one forward footstep stayed,
As dropped the dying and the dead.
Fast as their ranks the thunders tear,
Fast they renewed each serried square ;
And on the wounded and the slain
Closed their diminished files again,
Till from their lines scarce spears' lengths three,
Emerging from the smoke they see
Helmet and plume and panoply.
    Then waked their fire at once !
Each musketeer's revolving knell
As fast, as regularly fell,
As when they practise to display
Their discipline on festal day.
    Then down went helm and lance,
Down were the eagle-banners sent,
Down reeling steeds and riders went,
Corselets were pierced and pennons rent ;
    And, to augment the fray,
Wheeled full against their staggering flanks,
The English horsemen's foaming ranks
    Forced their resistless way.
Then to the musket-knell succeeds
The clash of swords, the neigh of steeds ;
As plies the smith his clanging trade,
Against the cuirass rang the blade ;
And while amid their close array
The well-served cannon rent their way,
And while amid their scattered band
Raged the fierce rider's bloody brand,
Recoiled in common rout and fear
Lancer and guard and cuirassier,
Horsemen and foot, — a mingled host, —
Their leaders fallen, their standards lost.
                            SIR WALTER SCOTT.

THE MARCH TO MOSCOW.

THE Emperor Nap he would set out
    For a summer excursion to Moscow ;
The fields were green and the sky was blue ;
        Morbleu ! Parbleu !
    What a pleasant excursion to Moscow !

Four hundred thousand men and more,
        Heigh-ho, for Moscow !
There were marshals by dozens and dukes by the
        score,
        Princes a few, and kings one or two,
While the fields are so green and the sky so blue,
        Morbleu ! Parbleu !
    What a pleasant excursion to Moscow !

There was Junot and Augereau,
    Heigh-ho, for Moscow !
Dombrowsky and Poniatowsky,
General Rapp and Emperor Nap,
    Nothing would do,
While the fields were so green and the sky so blue,
    Morbleu ! Parbleu !
But they must be marched to Moscow.

But the Russians they stoutly turned to,
    All on the road to Moscow,
Nap had to fight his way all through,
They could fight, but they could not parley-vous,
But the fields were green, and the sky was blue,
    Morbleu ! Parbleu !
And so he got to Moscow.

They made the place too hot for him,
    For they set fire to Moscow;
To get there had cost him much ado,
And then no better course he knew,
While the fields were green and the sky was blue,
    Morbleu ! Parbleu !
Than to march back again from Moscow.

The Russians they stuck close to him,
    All on the road from Moscow ;
There was Tormazow and Gomalow,
And all the others that end in *ow ;*
Rajefsky and Noverefsky,
And all the others that end in *efsky ;*
Schamscheff, Souchosaneff, and Schepeleff,
    And all the others that end in *eff ;*
Wasiltschecoff, Kostomaroff, and Theoglokoff,
    And all the others that end in *off ;*
Milaravoditch, and Juladovitch, and Karatch-
      kowitch,
    And all the others that end in *itch ;*
Oscharoffsky, and Rostoffsky, Kasatichkoffsky,
    And all the others that end in *offsky ;*
And Platoff he played them off,
And Markoff he marked them off,
And Tutchkoff he touched them off,
And Kutusoff he cut them off,
And Woronzoff he worried them off,
And Dochtoroff he doctored them off,
And Rodinoff he flogged them off ;
    And last of all an Admiral came,
    A terrible man, with a terrible name,
A name which you all must know very well,
Nobody can speak, and nobody can spell.

They stuck close to Nap with all their might,
They were on the left and on the right,
Behind and before, and by day and by night ;
Nap would rather parley-vous than fight ;
    But parley-vous would no more do,
    Morbleu ! Parbleu !
For they remembered Moscow !

And then came on the frost and snow,
    All on the road from Moscow !
The Emperor Nap found, as he went,
That he was not quite omnipotent ;
And worse and worse the weather grew,
The fields were so white and the sky so blue,
    Morbleu ! Ventrebleu !
What a terrible journey from Moscow !

The devil take the hindmost,
    All on the road from Moscow !
Quoth Nap, who thought it small delight,
To fight all day and to freeze all night ;
And so, not knowing what else to do,
When the fields were so white and the sky so blue,
    Morbleu ! Parbleu !
He stole away, I tell you true,
    All by himself from Moscow.

               ROBERT SOUTHEY.

RODERICK IN BATTLE.

FROM "RODERICK, THE LAST OF THE GOTHS."

WITH that he fell upon the old man's neck ;
Then vaulted in the saddle, gave the reins,
And soon rejoined the host.   On, comrades, on !
Victory and Vengeance ! he exclaimed, and took
The lead on that good charger, he alone
Horsed for the onset.   They, with one consent,
Gave all their voices to the inspiring cry,
Victory and Vengeance ! and the hills and rocks
Caught the prophetic shout and rolled it round.
Count Pedro's people heard amid the heat
Of battle, and returned the glad acclaim.
The astonished Mussulmen, on all sides charged,
Heard that tremendous cry ; yet manfully
They stood, and everywhere, with gallant front,
Opposed in fair array the shock of war.
Desperately they fought, like men expert in arms,
And knowing that no safety could be found
Save from their own right hands.   No former day
Of all his long career had seen their chief
Approved so well ; nor had Witiza's sons
Ever before this hour achieved in fight
Such feats of resolute valor.   Sisibert
Beheld Pelayo in the field afoot,
And twice essayed beneath his horse's feet
To thrust him down.   Twice did the prince evade
The shock, and twice upon his shield received
The fratricidal sword.   Tempt me no more,
Son of Witiza, cried the indignant chief,
Lest I forget what mother gave thee birth !
Go meet thy death from any hand but mine !
He said, and turned aside.   Fitliest from me !
Exclaimed a dreadful voice, as through the throng
Orelio forced his way : fitliest from me
Receive the rightful death too long withheld !

'T is Roderick strikes the blow! And as he spake,
Upon the traitor's shoulder fierce he drove
The weapon, well bestowed. He in the seat
Tottered and fell. The avenger hastened on
In search of Ebba; and in the heat of fight
Rejoicing, and forgetful of all else,
Set up his cry, as he was wont in youth, —
Roderick the Goth! — his war-cry known so well.
Pelayo eagerly took up the word,
And shouted out his kinsman's name beloved, —
Roderick the Goth! Roderick and Victory!
Roderick and Vengeance! Odoar gave it forth;
Urban repeated it, and through his ranks
Count Pedro sent the cry. Not from the field
Of his great victory, when Witiza fell,
With louder acclamations had that name
Been borne abroad upon the winds of heaven.
The unreflecting throng, who yesterday,
If it had passed their lips, would with a curse
Have clogged it, echoed it as if it came
From some celestial voice in the air, revealed
To be the certain pledge of all their hopes.
Roderick the Goth! Roderick and Victory!
Roderick and Vengeance! O'er the field it spread,
All hearts and tongues uniting in the cry;
Mountains and rocks and vales re-echoed round;
And he, rejoicing in his strength, rode on,
Laying on the Moors with that good sword, and smote,
And overthrew, and scattered, and destroyed,
And trampled down; and still at every blow
Exultingly he sent the war-cry forth,
Roderick the Goth! Roderick and Victory!
Roderick and Vengeance!
　　　　　　　　Thus he made his way,
Smiting and slaying, through the astonished ranks,
Till he beheld, where, on a fiery barb,
Ebba, performing well a soldier's part,
Dealt to the right and left his deadly blows.
With mutual rage they met. The renegade
Displays a cimeter, the splendid gift
Of Walid from Damascus sent; its hilt
Embossed with gems, its blade of perfect steel,
Which, like a mirror sparkling to the sun
With dazzling splendor, flashed. The Goth objects
His shield, and on its rim received the edge
Driven from its aim aside, and of its force
Diminished. Many a frustrate stroke was dealt
On either part, and many a foin and thrust
Aimed and rebated; many a deadly blow,
Straight or reverse, delivered and repelled,
Roderick at length with better speed hath reached
The apostate's turban, and through all its folds

The true Cantabrian weapon making way
Attained his forehead. "Wretch!" the avenger cried,
"It comes from Roderick's hand! Roderick the Goth!
Who spared, who trusted thee, and was betrayed!
Go tell thy father now how thou hast sped
With all thy treasons!" Saying thus, he seized
The miserable, who, blinded now with blood,
Reeled in the saddle; and with sidelong step
Backing Orelio, drew him to the ground.
He shrieking, as beneath the horse's feet
He fell, forgot his late-learnt creed, and called
On Mary's name. The dreadful Goth passed on,
Still plunging through the thickest war, and still
Scattering, where'er he turned, the affrighted ranks.
　　　　　　　　ROBERT SOUTHEY.

———◆———

THE LORD OF BUTRAGO.

"YOUR horse is faint, my King, my lord! your gallant horse is sick, —
His limbs are torn, his breast is gored, on his eye the film is thick;
Mount, mount on mine, O, mount apace, I pray thee, mount and fly!
Or in my arms I 'll lift your Grace, — their trampling hoofs are nigh!

"My King, my King! you 're wounded sore,
　— the blood runs from your feet;
But only lay a hand before, and I 'll lift you to your seat;
Mount, Juan, for they gather fast! — I hear their coming cry, —
Mount, mount, and ride for jeopardy, — I 'll save you though I die!

"Stand, noble steed! this hour of need, — be gentle as a lamb;
I 'll kiss the foam from off thy mouth, — thy master dear I am, —
Mount, Juan, mount; whate'er betide, away the bridle fling,
And plunge the rowels in his side. — My horse shall save my King!

"Nay, never speak; my sires, Lord King, received their land from yours,
And joyfully their blood shall spring, so be it thine secures;
If I should fly, and thou, my King, be found among the dead,
How could I stand 'mong gentlemen, such scorn on my gray head!

"Castile's proud dames shall never point the
    finger of disdain,
And say there's one that ran away when our
    good lords were slain !
I leave Diego in your care, — you'll fill his
    father's place ;
Strike, strike the spur, and never spare, — God's
    blessing on your Grace ! "

So spake the brave Montanez, Butrago's lord was
    he ;
And turned him to the coming host in steadfast-
    ness and glee ;
He flung himself among them, as they came
    down the hill, —
He died, God wot ! but not before his sword had
    drunk its fill.   JOHN GIBSON LOCKHART.

HUDIBRAS' SWORD AND DAGGER.

His puissant sword unto his side
Near his undaunted heart was tied,
With basket hilt that would hold broth,
And serve for fight and dinner both.
In it he melted lead for bullets
To shoot at foes, and sometimes pullets,
To whom he bore so fell a grutch
He ne'er gave quarter to any such.
The trenchant blade, Toledo trusty,
For want of fighting was grown rusty,
And ate into itself, for lack
Of somebody to hew and hack.
The peaceful scabbard, where it dwelt,
The rancor of its edge had felt ;
For of the lower end two handful
It had devoured, it was so manful ;
And so much scorned to lurk in case,
As if it durst not show its face.

.   .   .   .   .

This sword a dagger had, his page,
That was but little for his age,
And therefore waited on him so
As dwarfs unto knight-errants do.
It was a serviceable dudgeon,
Either for fighting or for drudging.
When it had stabbed or broke a head,
It would scrape trenchers or chip bread,
Toast cheese or bacon, though it were
To bait a mouse-trap 't would not care ;
'T would make clean shoes, and in the earth
Set leeks and onions, and so forth :
It had been 'prentice to a brewer,
Where this and more it did endure ;
But left the trade, as many more
Have lately done on the same score.
    SAMUEL BUTLER.

MALBROUCK.

MALBROUCK, the prince of commanders,
Is gone to the war in Flanders ;
His fame is like Alexander's ;
    But when will he come home ?

Perhaps at Trinity feast ; or
Perhaps he may come at Easter.
Egad ! he had better make haste, or
    We fear he may never come.

For Trinity feast is over,
And has brought no news from Dover ;
And Easter is past, moreover,
    And Malbrouck still delays.

Milady in her watch-tower
Spends many a pensive hour,
Not knowing why or how her
    Dear lord from England stays.

While sitting quite forlorn in
That tower, she spies returning
A page clad in deep mourning,
    With fainting steps and slow.

"O page, prithee, come faster !
What news do you bring of your master ?
I fear there is some disaster, —
    Your looks are so full of woe."

"The news I bring, fair lady,"
With sorrowful accent said he,
"Is one you are not ready
    So soon, alas ! to hear.

"But since to speak I'm hurried,"
Added this page quite flurried,
"Malbrouck is dead and buried ! "
    — And here he shed a tear.

"He's dead ! he's dead as a herring !
For I beheld his berring,
And four officers transferring
    His corpse away from the field.

"One officer carried his sabre ;
And he carried it not without labor,
Much envying his next neighbor,
    Who only bore a shield.

"The third was helmet-bearer, —
That helmet which on its wearer
Filled all who saw with terror,
    And covered a hero's brains.

"Now, having got so far, I
Find that — by the Lord Harry ! —
The fourth is left nothing to carry ; —
    So there the thing remains."
    ANONYMOUS (French). Translation
    of MAHONY.

THE BROADSWORDS OF SCOTLAND.

Now there 's peace on the shore, now there 's calm
    on the sea,
Fill a glass to the heroes whose swords kept us
    free,
Right descendants of Wallace, Montrose, and
    Dundee.
    O the broadswords of old Scotland !
    And O the old Scottish broadswords !

Old Sir Ralph Abercromby, the good and the
    brave, —
Let him flee from our board, let him sleep with
    the slave,
Whose libation comes slow while we honor his
    grave.
    O the broadswords of old Scotland ! etc.

Though he died not, like him, amid victory's
    roar,
Though disaster and gloom wove his shroud on
    the shore,
Not the less we remember the spirit of Moore.
    O the broadswords of old Scotland ! etc.

Yea, a place with the fallen the living shall claim ;
We 'll intwine in one wreath every glorious name,
The Gordon, the Ramsay, the Hope, and the
    Graham,
    All the broadswords of old Scotland ! etc.

Count the rocks of the Spey, count the groves of
    the Forth,
Count the stars in the clear, cloudless heaven of
    the north ;
Then go blazon their numbers, their names, and
    their worth,
    All the broadswords of old Scotland ! etc.

The highest in splendor, the humblest in place,
Stand united in glory, as kindred in race,
For the private is brother in blood to his Grace.
    O the broadswords of old Scotland ! etc.

Then sacred to each and to all let it be,
Fill a glass to the heroes whose swords kept us
    free,
Right descendants of Wallace, Montrose, and
    Dundee.
    O the broadswords of old Scotland ! etc.
            JOHN GIBSON LOCKHART.

MONTEREY.

WE were not many, — we who stood
    Before the iron sleet that day ;
Yet many a gallant spirit would

Give half his years if but he could
    Have been with us at Monterey.

Now here, now there, the shot it hailed
    In deadly drifts of fiery spray,
Yet not a single soldier quailed
When wounded comrades round them wailed
    Their dying shout at Monterey.

And on, still on our column kept,
    Through walls of flame, its withering way ;
Where fell the dead, the living stept,
Still charging on the guns which swept
    The slippery streets of Monterey.

The foe himself recoiled aghast,
    When, striking where he strongest lay,
We swooped his flanking batteries past,
And, braving full their murderous blast,
    Stormed home the towers of Monterey.

Our banners on those turrets wave,
    And there our evening bugles play ;
Where orange boughs above their grave,
Keep green the memory of the brave
    Who fought and fell at Monterey.

We are not many, — we who pressed
    Beside the brave who fell that day ;
But who of us has not confessed
He 'd rather share their warrior rest
    Than not have been at Monterey ?
            CHARLES FENNO HOFFMAN.

BALAKLAVA.

O THE charge at Balaklava !
    O that rash and fatal charge !
Never was a fiercer, braver,
Than that charge at Balaklava,
    On the battle's bloody marge !
All the day the Russian columns,
    Fortress-huge, and blazing banks,
Poured their dread destructive volumes
    On the French and English ranks, —
    On the gallant allied ranks !
Earth and sky seemed rent asunder
By the loud incessant thunder !
When a strange but stern command —
Needless, heedless, rash command —
Came to Lucan's little band, —
Scarce six hundred men and horses
Of those vast contending forces : —
"England 's lost unless you save her !
Charge the pass at Balaklava ! "
    O that rash and fatal charge,
    On the battle's bloody marge !

Far away the Russian Eagles
　　Soar o'er smoking hill and dell,
And their hordes, like howling beagles,
　　Dense and countless, round them yell !
Thundering cannon, deadly mortar,
Sweep the field in every quarter !
Never, since the days of Jesus,
Trembled so the Chersonesus !
　　Here behold the Gallic Lilies —
　　Stout St. Louis' golden Lilies —
　　Float as erst at old Ramillies !
　　And beside them, lo ! the Lion !
　　With her trophied Cross, is flying !
Glorious standards ! — shall they waver
On the field of Balaklava ?
No, by Heavens ! at that command —
Sudden, rash, but stern command —
Charges Lucan's little band !
　　　　Brave Six Hundred ! lo ! they charge,
　　　　On the battle's bloody marge !

Down yon deep and skirted valley,
　　Where the crowded cannon play, —
Where the Czar's fierce cohorts rally,
Cossack, Calmuck, savage Kalli, —
　　Down that gorge they swept away !
Down that new Thermopylæ,
Flashing swords and helmets see !
Underneath the iron shower,
　　To the brazen cannon's jaws,
Heedless of their deadly power,
　　Press they without fear or pause, —
　　To the very cannon's jaws !
Gallant Nolan, brave as Roland
　　At the field of Roncesvalles,
　　Dashes down the fatal valley,
Dashes on the bolt of death,
Shouting with his latest breath,
"Charge, then, gallants ! do not waver,
Charge the pass at Balaklava !"
　　　　O that rash and fatal charge,
　　　　On the battle's bloody marge !

Now the bolts of volleyed thunder
Rend that little band asunder,
Steed and rider wildly screaming,
　　Screaming wildly, sink away ;
Late so proudly, proudly gleaming,
　　Now but lifeless clods of clay, —
　　Now but bleeding clods of clay !
Never, since the days of Jesus,
Saw such sight the Chersonesus !
Yet your remnant, brave Six Hundred,
Presses onward, onward, onward,
　　Till they storm the bloody pass, —
　　Till, like brave Leonidas,
　　They storm the deadly pass !
Sabring Cossack, Calmuck, Kalli,
In that wild shot-rended valley, —

Drenched with fire and blood, like lava,
Awful pass at Balaklava !
　　　　O that rash and fatal charge,
　　　　On that battle's bloody marge !

For now Russia's rallied forces,
Swarming hordes of Cossack horses,
Trampling o'er the reeking corses,
　　Drive the thinned assailants back,
　　Drive the feeble remnant back,
　　O'er their late heroic track !
Vain, alas ! now rent and sundered,
Vain your struggles, brave Two Hundred !
Thrice your number lie asleep,
In that valley dark and deep.
Weak and wounded you retire
From that hurricane of fire, —
That tempestuous storm of fire, —
But no soldiers, firmer, braver,
　　Ever trod the field of fame,
Than the Knights of Balaklava, —
　　Honor to each hero's name !
Yet their country long shall mourn
For her rank so rashly shorn, —
So gallantly, but madly shorn
　　　　In that fierce and fatal charge,
　　　　On the battle's bloody marge.
　　　　　　　　ALEXANDER B. MEEK.

DEATH OF ARTHUR.

So all day long the noise of battle rolled
Among the mountains by the winter sea ;
Until King Arthur's Table, man by man,
Had fallen in Lyonesse about their lord,
King Arthur : then, because his wound was deep,
The bold Sir Bedivere uplifted him,
And bore him to a chapel nigh the field,
A broken chancel with a broken cross,
That stood on a dark strait of barren land.
On one side lay the Ocean, and on one
Lay a great water, and the moon was full.

Then spake King Arthur to Sir Bedivere :
"The sequel of to-day unsolders all
The goodliest fellowship of famous knights
Whereof this world holds record. Such a sleep
They sleep — the men I loved. I think that we
Shall nevermore, at any future time,
Delight our souls with talk of knightly deeds,
Walking about the gardens and the halls
Of Camelot, as in the days that were.
I perish by this people which I made, —
Though Merlin sware that I should come again
To rule once more ; but let what will be, be.
I am so deeply smitten through the helm
That without help I cannot last till morn.
Thou therefore take my brand Excalibur,

Which was my pride : for thou rememberest how
In those old days, one summer noon, an arm
Rose up from out the bosom of the lake,
Clothed in white samite, mystic, wonderful,
Holding the sword — and how I rowed across
And took it, and have worn it, like a king ;
And, wheresoever I am sung or told
In after-time, this also shall be known :
But now delay not : take Excalibur,
And fling him far into the middle mere —
Watch what thou seëst, and lightly bring me
    word."

To him replied the bold Sir Bedivere :
"It is not meet, Sir King, to leave thee thus,
Aidless, alone, and smitten through the helm —
A little thing may harm a wounded man ;
Yet I thy hest will all perform at full,
Watch what I see, and lightly bring thee word."

So saying, from the ruined shrine he stept
And in the moon athwart the place of tombs,
Where lay the mighty bones of ancient men,
Old knights, and over them the sea-wind sang
Shrill, chill, with flakes of foam. He, stepping
    down
By zigzag paths, and juts of pointed rock,
Came on the shining levels of the lake.

There drew he forth the brand Excalibur
And o'er him, drawing it, the winter moon,
Brightening the skirts of a long cloud, ran forth
And sparkled keen with frost against the hilt :
For all the haft twinkled with diamond sparks,
Myriads of topaz-lights, and jacinth-work
Of subtlest jewelry. He gazed so long
That both his eyes were dazzled as he stood,
This way and that dividing the swift mind,
In act to throw : but at the last it seemed
Better to leave Excalibur concealed
There in the many-knotted water-flags,
That whistled stiff and dry about the marge.
So strode he back slow to the wounded King.

Then spake King Arthur to Sir Bedivere :
"Hast thou performed my mission which I gave?
What is it thou hast seen ? or what hast heard ?"

And answer made the bold Sir Bedivere :
"I heard the ripple washing in the reeds,
And the wild water lapping on the crag."

To whom replied King Arthur, faint and pale :
"Thou hast betrayed thy nature and thy name,
Not rendering true answer, as beseemed
Thy fëalty, nor like a noble knight :
For surer sign had followed, either hand,
Or voice, or else a motion of the mere.
This is a shameful thing for men to lie.

Yet now, I charge thee, quickly go again,
As thou art lief and dear, and do the thing
I bade thee, watch, and lightly bring me word."

Then went Sir Bedivere the second time
Across the ridge, and paced beside the mere,
Counting the dewy pebbles, fixed in thought ;
But when he saw the wonder of the hilt,
How curiously and strangely chased, he smote
His palms together, and he cried aloud : —

"And if indeed I cast the brand away,
Surely a precious thing, one worthy note,
Should thus be lost forever from the earth,
Which might have pleased the eyes of many men.
What good should follow this, if this were done ?
What harm, undone ? deep harm to disobey,
Seeing obedience is the bond of rule.
Were it well to obey then, if a king demand
An act unprofitable, against himself ?
The King is sick, and knows not what he does.
What record, or what relic of my lord
Should be to after-time, but empty breath
And rumors of a doubt ? but were this kept,
Stored in some treasure-house of mighty kings,
Some one might show it at a joust of arms,
Saying, 'King Arthur's sword, Excalibur,
Wrought by the lonely maiden of the Lake.
Nine years she wrought it, sitting in the deeps
Upon the hidden bases of the hills.'
So might some old man speak in the after-time
To all the people, winning reverence.
But now much honor and much fame were lost."

So spake he, clouded with his own conceit,
And hid Excalibur the second time,
And so strode back slow to the wounded King.

Then spoke King Arthur, breathing heavily :
"What is it thou hast seen ? or what hast heard ?"

And answer made the bold Sir Bedivere :
"I heard the water lapping on the crag,
And the long ripple washing in the reeds."

To whom replied King Arthur, much in wrath :
"Ah, miserable and unkind, untrue,
Unknightly, traitor-hearted ! Woe is me !
Authority forgets a dying king,
Laid widowed of the power in his eye
That bowed the will. I see thee what thou art,
For thou, the latest-left of all my knights
In whom should meet the offices of all,
Thou wouldst betray me for the precious hilt ;
Either from lust of gold, or like a girl
Valuing the giddy pleasure of the eyes.
Yet, for a man may fail in duty twice,
And the third time may prosper, get thee hence :
But, if thou spare to fling Excalibur,
I will arise and slay thee with my hands."

Then quickly rose Sir Bedivere, and ran,
And, leaping down the ridges lightly, plunged
Among the bulrush-beds, and clutched the sword,
And strongly wheeled and threw it. The great
    brand
Made lightnings in the splendor of the moon,
And flashing round and round, and whirled in an
    arch,
Shot like a streamer of the northern morn,
Seen where the moving isles of winter shock
By night, with noises of the northern sea.
So flashed and fell the brand Excalibur:
But ere he dipt the surface, rose an arm
Clothed in white samite, mystic, wonderful,
And caught him by the hilt, and brandished him
Three times, and drew him under in the mere.
And lightly went the other to the King.

Then spoke King Arthur, drawing thicker
    breath :
"Now see I by thine eyes that this is done.
Speak out : what is it thou hast heard, or seen ?"

And answer made the bold Sir Bedivere :
"Sir King, I closed mine eyelids, lest the gems
Should-blind my purpose, for I never saw,
Nor shall see, here or elsewhere, till I die,
Not though I live three lives of mortal men,
So great a miracle as yonder hilt,
Then with both hands I flung him, wheeling him ;
But when I looked again, behold an arm,
Clothed in white samite, mystic, wonderful,
That caught him by the hilt, and brandished him
Three times, and drew him under in the mere."

And answer made King Arthur, breathing hard :
"My end draws nigh ; 't is time that I were gone.
Make broad thy shoulders to receive my weight,
And bear me to the margin ; yet I fear
My wound hath taken cold, and I shall die."

So saying, from the pavement he half rose,
Slowly, with pain, reclining on his arm,
And looking wistfully with wide blue eyes
As in a picture. Him Sir Bedivere
Remorsefully regarded through his tears,
And would have spoken, but he found not words ;
Then took with care, and kneeling on one knee,
O'er both his shoulders drew the languid hands,
And rising bore him through the place of tombs.

But, as he walked, King Arthur panted hard,
Like one that feels a nightmare on his bed
When all the house is mute. So sighed the King,
Muttering and murmuring at his ear "Quick,
    quick !
I fear it is too late, and I shall die."
But the other swiftly strode from ridge to ridge,

Clothed with his breath, and looking, as he walked,
Larger than human on the frozen hills.
He heard the deep behind him, and a cry
Before. His own thought drove him like a goad.
Dry clashed his harness in the icy caves
And barren chasms, and all to left and right
The bare black cliff clanged round him, as he based
His feet on juts of slippery crag that rang
Sharp-smitten with the dint of arméd heels —
And on a sudden, lo ! the level lake,
And the long glories of the winter moon.

Then saw they how there hove a dusky barge,
Dark as a funeral scarf from stem to stern,
Beneath them ; and descending they were ware
That all the decks were dense with stately forms,
Black-stoled, black-hooded, like a dream, — by
    these
Three Queens with crowns of gold, — and from
    them rose
A cry that shivered to the tingling stars,
And, as it were one voice, an agony
Of lamentation, like a wind that shrills
All night in a waste land, where no one comes,
Or hath come, since the making of the world.

Then murmured Arthur, "Place me in the
    barge" ;
So to the barge they came. There those three
    Queens
Put forth their hands, and took the King, and
    wept.
But she that rose the tallest of them all,
And fairest, laid his head upon her lap,
And loosed the shattered casque, and chafed his
    hands,
And called him by his name, complaining loud,
And dropping bitter tears against his brow
Striped with dark blood : for all his face was
    white
And colorless, and like the withered moon
Smote by the fresh beam of the springing east ;
And all his greaves and cuisses dashed with drops
Of onset ; and the light and lustrous curls —
That made his forehead like a rising sun
High from the dais-throne — were parched with
    dust ;
Or, clotted into points and hanging loose,
Mixed with the knightly growth that fringed
    his lips.
So like a shattered column lay the King ;
Not like that Arthur, who, with lance in rest,
From spur to plume a star of tournament,
Shot through the lists at Camelot, and charged
Before the eyes of ladies and of kings.

Then loudly cried the bold Sir Bedivere :
"Ah ! my Lord Arthur, whither shall I go ?
Where shall I hide my forehead and my eyes ?

For now I see the true old times are dead,
When every morning brought a noble chance,
And every chance brought out a noble knight.
Such times have been not since the light that led
The holy Elders with the gift of myrrh.
But now the whole Round Table is dissolved
Which was an image of the mighty world ;
And I, the last, go forth companionless,
And the days darken round me, and the years,
Among new men, strange faces, other minds."

And slowly answered Arthur from the barge :
"The old order changeth, yielding place to new,
And God fulfils himself in many ways,
Lest one good custom should corrupt the world.
Comfort thyself: what comfort is in me ?
I have lived my life, and that which I have done
May He within himself make pure ! but thou,
If thou shouldst never see my face again,
Pray for my soul.   More things are wrought by
     prayer
Than this world dreams of.   Wherefore, let thy
     voice
Rise like a fountain for me night and day.
For what are men better than sheep or goats
That nourish a blind life within the brain,
If, knowing God, they lift not hands of prayer
Both for themselves and those who call them
     friend ?
For so the whole round earth is every way
Bound by gold chains about the feet of God.
But now farewell.   I am going a long way
With these thou seëst, — if indeed I go
(For all my mind is clouded with a doubt) —
To the island-valley of Avilion ;
Where falls not hail, or rain, or any snow,
Nor ever wind blows loudly ; but it lies
Deep-meadowed, happy, fair with orchard-lawns
And bowery hollows crowned with summer sea,
Where I will heal me of my grievous wound."

So said he, and the barge with oar and sail
Moved from the brink, like some full-breasted
     swan,
That, fluting a wild carol ere her death,
Ruffles her pure cold plume, and takes the flood
With swarthy webs.   Long stood Sir Bedivere
Revolving many memories, till the hull
Looked one black dot against the verge of dawn,
And on the mere the wailing died away.
                              ALFRED TENNYSON.

THE SALLY OF THE CID FROM THE CASTLE OF ALCOCES.

FROM "THE POEM OF THE CID."

THEY fain would sally forth, but he, the noble Cid,
Accounted it as rashness, and constantly forbid.

The fourth week was beginning, the third already
     past,
The Cid and his companions they are now agreed
     at last.
"The water is cut off, the bread is wellnigh
     spent,
To allow us to depart by night the Moors will
     not consent ;
To combat with them in the field our numbers
     are but few ;
Gentlemen, tell me your minds ; what do you
     think to do ?"
Minaya Alvar Fañez answered him again :
"We are come here from fair Castile to live like
     banished men ;
There are here six hundred of us, beside some
     nine or ten.
It is by fighting with the Moors that we have
     earned our bread ;
In the name of God that made us, let nothing
     more be said,
Let us sally forth upon them by the dawn of
     day."
The Cid replied, "Minaya, I approve of what
     you say,
You have spoken for the best, and had done so
     without doubt."
The Moors that were within the town they took
     and turned them out,
That none should know their secret ; they
     labored all that night ;
They were ready for the combat with the morning
     light.
The Cid was in his armor mounted at their head ;
He spoke aloud amongst them ; you shall hear
     the words he said :
"We must all sally forth ! There cannot a man
     be spared,
Two footmen only at the gates to close them and
     keep guard ;
If we are slain in battle, they will bury us here
     in peace,
If we survive and conquer, our riches will increase.
And you, Pero Bermuez, the standard you must
     bear ;
Advance it like a valiant man, evenly and fair,
But do not venture forward before I give com-
     mand."
Bermuez took the standard, he went and kist
     his hand.
The gates were then thrown open, and forth at
     once they rushed.
The outposts of the Moorish host back to the
     camp were pushed ;
The camp was all in tumult, and there was such
     a thunder
Of cymbals and of drums, as if earth would
     cleave in sunder.

There you might see the Moors arming themselves in haste,
And the two main battles how they were forming fast ;
Horsemen and footmen mixt, a countless troop and vast.
The Moors are moving forward, the battle soon must join.
"My men, stand here in order, ranged upon a line !
Let not a man move from his rank before I give the sign."
Pero Bermuez heard the word, but he could not refrain.
He held the banner in his hand, he gave his horse the rein ;
"You see yon foremost squadron there, the thickest of the foes,
Noble Cid, God be your aid, for there your banner goes !
Let him that serves and honors it show the duty that he owes."
Earnestly the Cid called out, "For Heaven's sake, be still !"
Bermuez cried, "I cannot hold," so eager was his will.
He spurred his horse and drove him on amid the Moorish rout ;
They strove to win the banner, and compast him about ;
Had not his armor been so true, he had lost either life or limb.
The Cid called out again, "For Heaven's sake, succor him !"
Their shields before their breasts, forth at once they go,
Their lances in the rest levelled fair and low,
Their banners and their crests waving in a row,
Their heads all stooping down toward the saddle-bow.
The Cid was in the midst, his shout was heard afar,
"I am Rui Diaz, the Champion of Bivar ;
Strike amongst them, gentlemen, for sweet mercy's sake !"
There where Bermuez fought amidst the foe they brake,
Three hundred bannered knights, — it was a gallant show :
Three hundred Moors they killed, a man with every blow ;
When they wheeled and turned, as many more lay slain,
You might see them raise their lances and level them again ;
There you might see the breastplates, how they were cleft in twain,

And many a Moorish shield lie shattered on the plain,
The pennons that were white marked with a crimson stain,
The horses running wild whose riders had been slain.
The Christians call upon St. James, the Moors upon Mahound, —
There were thirteen hundred of them slain on a little spot of ground.
Minaya Alvar Fañez smote with all his might,
He went as he was wont, and was foremost in the fight ;
There was Galin Garcia, of courage firm and clear ;
Felez Munioz, the Cid's own cousin dear ;
Antolinez of Burgos, a hardy knight and keen,
Munio Gustioz, his pupil that had been ;
The Cid on his gilded saddle above them all was seen ;
There was Martin Munioz that ruled in Montmayor ;
There were Alvar Fañez and Alvar Salvador ; —
These were the followers of the Cid, with many others more,
In rescue of Bermuez and the standard that he bore.
Minaya is dismounted, his courser has been slain,
He fights upon his feet, and smites with might and main.
The Cid came all in haste to help him to horse again.
He saw a Moor well mounted, thereof he was full fain ;
Through the girdle at a stroke he cast him to the plain ;
He called to Minaya Fañez and reached him out the rein,
"Mount and ride, Minaya, you are my right hand ;
We shall have need of you to-day, these Moors will not disband !"
Minaya leapt upon the horse, his sword was in his hand,
Nothing that came near him could resist him or withstand ;
All that fall within his reach he despatches as he goes.
The Cid rode to King Fariz, and struck at him three blows ;
The third was far the best, it forced the blood to flow :
The stream ran from his side, and stained his arms below ;
The King caught round the rein, and turned his back to go.
The Cid has won the battle with that single blow.

By an anonymous translator in the appendix to SOUTHEY'S translation of "The Chronicle of the Cid."

The Mother who conceals her grief
While to her heart her son she presses,
Then breathes a few brave words and brief,
Kissing the fair hair-brows she blesses,—
With no one near her except God,
To know the pain that weighs upon her,
Sheds holy blood as e'er the sod
Received on Freedom's field of honor.

T. Buchanan Read

POEMS OF TEMPERANCE AND LABOR.

Believe me still, as thou e'en hast been
The steadfast lover of my fellowman;
My weakness, errors, failures whatso'
Thy sense the truth that all men kind was too,—
Free will, blood redeemed too, trequest by ones;
Each fellow both one land in body run time,!

John C. Whitten

POEMS OF TEMPERANCE AND LABOR.

MORAL COSMETICS.

Ye who would have your features florid,
Lithe limbs, bright eyes, unwrinkled forehead,
From age's devastation horrid,
    Adopt this plan, —
'T will make, in climate cold or torrid,
    A hale old man.

Avoid in youth luxurious diet,
Restrain the passions' lawless riot ;
Devoted to domestic quiet,
    Be wisely gay ;
So shall ye, spite of age's fiat,
    Resist decay.

Seek not in Mammon's worship pleasure,
But find your richest, dearest treasure
In God, his word, his work, not leisure :
    The mind, not sense,
Is the sole scale by which to measure
    Your opulence.

This is the solace, this the science,
Life's purest, sweetest, best appliance,
That disappoints not man's reliance,
    Whate'er his state ;
But challenges, with calm defiance,
    Time, fortune, fate.
               HORACE SMITH.

ADVICE.

Take the open air,
    The more you take the better ;
Follow Nature's laws
    To the very letter.
Let the doctors go
    To the Bay of Biscay,
Let alone the gin,
    The brandy, and the whiskey.
Freely exercise,
    Keep your spirits cheerful ;
Let no dread of sickness
    Make you ever fearful.

Eat the simplest food,
    Drink the pure, cold water,
Then you will be well,
    Or at least you *oughter*.
               ANONYMOUS.

A FAREWELL TO TOBACCO.

May the Babylonish curse
Straight confound my stammering verse,
If I can a passage see
In this word-perplexity,
Or a fit expression find,
Or a language to my mind
(Still the phrase is wide or scant),
To take leave of thee, great plant !
Or in any terms relate
Half my love, or half my hate ;
For I hate, yet love, thee so,
That, whichever thing I show,
The plain truth will seem to be
A constrained hyperbole,
And the passion to proceed
More for a mistress than a weed.

Sooty retainer to the vine !
Bacchus's black servant, negro fine !
Sorcerer ! that mak'st us dote upon
Thy begrimed complexion,
And, for thy pernicious sake,
More and greater oaths to break
Than reclaiméd lovers take
'Gainst women ! Thou thy siege dost lay
Much, too, in the female way,
While thou suck'st the laboring breath
Faster than kisses, or than death.

Thou in such a cloud dost bind us
That our worst foes cannot find us,
And ill fortune, that would thwart us,
Shoots at rovers, shooting at us ;
While each man, through thy heightening steam,
Does like a smoking Etna seem ;
And all about us does express

(Fancy and wit in richest dress)
A Sicilian fruitfulness.

Thou through such a mist dost show us
That our best friends do not know us,
And, for those allowed features
Due to reasonable creatures,
Liken'st us to fell chimeras,
Monsters, — that who see us, fear us ;
Worse than Cerberus or Geryon,
Or, who first loved a cloud, Ixion.

Bacchus we know, and we allow
His tipsy rites.   But what art thou,
That but by reflex canst show
What his deity can do, —
As the false Egyptian spell
Aped the true Hebrew miracle ?
Some few vapors thou mayst raise,
The weak brain may serve to amaze ;
But to the reins and nobler heart
Canst nor life nor heat impart.

Brother of Bacchus, later born !
The old world was sure forlorn,
Wanting thee, that aidest more
The god's victories than, before,
All his panthers, and the brawls
Of his piping Bacchanals.
These, as stale, we disallow,
Or judge of thee meant : only thou
His true Indian conquest art ;
And, for ivy round his dart,
The reformed god now weaves
A finer thyrsus of thy leaves.

Scent to match thy rich perfume
Chemic art did ne'er presume, —
Through her quaint alembic strain,
None so sovereign to the brain.
Nature, that did in thee excel,
Framed again no second smell.
Roses, violets, but toys
For the smaller sort of boys,
Or for greener damsels meant ;
Thou art the only manly scent.

Stinkingest of the stinking kind !
Filth of the mouth and fog of the mind !
Africa, that brags her foyson,
Breeds no such prodigious poison !
Henbane, nightshade, both together,
Hemlock, aconite—

Nay, rather,
Plant divine, of rarest virtue !
Blisters on the tongue would hurt you !
'T was but in a sort I blamed thee ;
None e'er prospered who defamed thee ;

Irony all, and feigned abuse,
Such as perplext lovers use
At a need, when, in despair
To paint forth their fairest fair,
Or in part but to express
That exceeding comeliness
Which their fancies doth so strike,
They borrow language of dislike ;
And, instead of dearest Miss,
Jewel, honey, sweetheart, bliss,
And those forms of old admiring,
Call her cockatrice and siren,
Basilisk, and all that 's evil,
Witch, hyena, mermaid, devil,
Ethiop, wench, and blackamoor,
Monkey, ape, and twenty more, —
Friendly trait'ress, loving foe, —
Not that she is truly so,
But no other way they know,
A contentment to express
Borders so upon excess
That they do not rightly wot
Whether it be from pain or not.

Or, as men, constrained to part
With what 's nearest to their heart,
While their sorrow 's at the height
Lose discrimination quite,
And their hasty wrath let fall,
To appease their frantic gall,
On the darling thing, whatever,
Whence they feel it death to sever,
Though it be, as they, perforce,
Guiltless of the sad divorce.

For I must (nor let it grieve thee,
Friendliest of plants, that I must) leave thee.
For thy sake, tobacco, I
Would do anything but die,
And but seek to extend my days
Long enough to sing thy praise.
But, as she who once hath been
A king's consort is a queen
Ever after, nor will bate
Any tittle of her state
Though a widow, or divorced, —
So I, from thy converse forced,
The old name and style retain,
A right Catherine of Spain ;
And a seat, too, 'mongst the joys
Of the blest tobacco boys ;
Where, though I, by sour physician,
Am debarred the full fruition
Of thy favors, I may catch
Some collateral sweets, and snatch
Sidelong odors, that give life
Like glances from a neighbor's wife ;
And still live in the by-places

And the suburbs of thy graces ;
And in thy borders take delight,
An unconquered Canaanite.

CHARLES LAMB.

GO, FEEL WHAT I HAVE FELT.

[By a young lady who was told that she was a monomaniac in her hatred of alcoholic liquors.]

Go, feel what I have felt,
   Go, bear what I have borne ;
Sink 'neath a blow a father dealt,
   And the cold, proud world's scorn.
Thus struggle on from year to year,
Thy sole relief the scalding tear.

Go, weep as I have wept
   O'er a loved father's fall ;
See every cherished promise swept,
   Youth's sweetness turned to gall ;
Hope's faded flowers strewed all the way
That led me up to woman's day.

Go, kneel as I have knelt ;
   Implore, beseech, and pray,
Strive the besotted heart to melt,
   The downward course to stay ;
Be cast with bitter curse aside, —
Thy prayers burlesqued, thy tears defied.

Go, stand where I have stood,
   And see the strong man bow ;
With gnashing teeth, lips bathed in blood,
   And cold and livid brow ;
Go, catch his wandering glance, and see
There mirrored his soul's misery.

Go, hear what I have heard, —
   The sobs of sad despair,
As memory's feeling fount hath stirred,
   And its revealings there
Have told him what he might have been,
Had he the drunkard's fate foreseen.

Go to my mother's side,
   And her crushed spirit cheer ;
Thine own deep anguish hide,
   Wipe from her cheek the tear ;
Mark her dimmed eye, her furrowed brow,
The gray that streaks her dark hair now,
The toil-worn frame, the trembling limb,
And trace the ruin back to him
Whose plighted faith, in early youth,
Promised eternal love and truth,
But who, forsworn, hath yielded up
This promise to the deadly cup,
And led her down from love and light,
From all that made her pathway bright,

And chained her there mid want and strife,
That lowly thing, — a drunkard's wife !
And stamped on childhood's brow, so mild,
That withering blight, — a drunkard's child !

Go, hear, and see, and feel, and know
   All that my soul hath felt and known,
Then look within the wine-cup's glow ;
   See if its brightness can atone ;
Think if its flavor you would try,
If all proclaimed, — 'T is drink and die.

Tell me I hate the bowl, —
   Hate is a feeble word ;
I loathe, abhor, my very soul
   By strong disgust is stirred
Whene'er I see, or hear, or tell
Of the DARK BEVERAGE OF HELL !

ANONYMOUS.

THE VAGABONDS.

WE are two travellers, Roger and I.
   Roger 's my dog : — come here, you scamp !
Jump for the gentlemen, — mind your eye !
   Over the table, — look out for the lamp ! —
The rogue is growing a little old ;
   Five years we 've tramped through wind and weather,
And slept out-doors when nights were cold,
   And ate and drank — and starved together.

We 've learned what comfort is, I tell you !
   A bed on the floor, a bit of rosin,
A fire to thaw our thumbs (poor fellow !
   The paw he holds up there 's been frozen),
Plenty of catgut for my fiddle
   (This out-door business is bad for the strings),
Then a few nice buckwheats hot from the griddle,
   And Roger and I set up for kings !

No, thank ye, sir, — I never drink ;
   Roger and I are exceedingly moral, —
Are n't we, Roger ? — see him wink ! —
   Well, something hot, then, — we won't quarrel.
He 's thirsty too, — see him nod his head !
   What a pity, sir, that dogs can't talk !
He understands every word that 's said, —
   And he knows good milk from water-and-chalk.

The truth is, sir, now I reflect,
   I 've been so sadly given to grog,
I wonder I 've not lost the respect
   (Here 's to you, sir !) even of my dog.
But he sticks by through thick and thin ;
   And this old coat, with its empty pockets,
And rags that smell of tobacco and gin,
   He 'll follow while he has eyes in his sockets.

There is n't another creature living
  Would do it, and prove, through every disaster,
So fond, so faithful, and so forgiving
  To such a miserable, thankless master !
No, sir ! — see him wag his tail and grin !
  By George ! it makes my old eyes water ! —
That is, there 's something in this gin
  That chokes a fellow.   But no matter !

We 'll have some music, if you 're willing,
  And Roger (hem ! what a plague a cough is,
    sir !)
Shall march a little.   Start, you villain !
  Stand straight ! 'Bout face ! Salute your offi-
    cer !
Put up that paw ! Dress ! Take your rifle !
  (Some dogs have arms, you see !) Now hold
    your
Cap while the gentlemen give a trifle,
  To aid a poor old patriot soldier !

March ! Halt ! Now show how the rebel shakes
  When he stands up to hear his sentence.
Now tell us how many drams it takes
  To honor a jolly new acquaintance.
Five yelps, — that 's five ; he 's mighty knowing !
  The night 's before us, fill the glasses ! —
Quick, sir ! I 'm ill, — my brain is going !
  Some brandy, — thank you, — there ! — it
    passes !

Why not reform ? That 's easily said ;
  But I 've gone through such wretched treat-
    ment,
Sometimes forgetting the taste of bread,
  And scarce remembering what meat meant,
That my poor stomach 's past reform ;
  And there are times when, mad with thinking,
I 'd sell out heaven for something warm
  To prop a horrible inward sinking.

Is there a way to forget to think ?
  At your age, sir, home, fortune, friends,
A dear girl's love, — but I took to drink, —
  The same old story ; you know how it ends.
If you could have seen these classic features, —
  You need n't laugh, sir ; they were not then
Such a burning libel on God's creatures ;
  I was one of your handsome men !

If you had seen her, so fair and young,
  Whose head was happy on this breast !
If you could have heard the songs I sung
  When the wine went round, you would n't have
    guessed
That ever I, sir, should be straying
  From door to door, with fiddle and dog,
Ragged and penniless, and playing
  To you to-night for a glass of grog !

She 's married since, — a parson's wife ;
  'T was better for her that we should part, —
Better the soberest, prosiest life
  Than a blasted home and a broken heart.
I have seen her ? Once : I was weak and spent
  On the dusty road, a carriage stopped ;
But little she dreamed, as on she went,
  Who kissed the coin that her fingers dropped !

You 've set me talking, sir ; I 'm sorry ;
  It makes me wild to think of the change !
What do you care for a beggar's story ?
  Is it amusing ? you find it strange ?
I had a mother so proud of me !
  'T was well she died before — Do you know
If the happy spirits in heaven can see
  The ruin and wretchedness here below ?

Another glass, and strong, to deaden
  This pain ; then Roger and I will start.
I wonder, has he such a lumpish, leaden,
  Aching thing in place of a heart ?
He is sad sometimes, and would weep, if he could,
  No doubt, remembering things that were, —
A virtuous kennel, with plenty of food,
  And himself a sober, respectable cur.

I 'm better now ; that glass was warming.
  You rascal ! limber your lazy feet !
We must be fiddling and performing
  For supper and bed, or starve in the street.
Not a very gay life to lead, you think ?
  But soon we shall go where lodgings are free,
And the sleepers need neither victuals nor
    drink ; —
  The sooner the better for Roger and me !
                              J. T. TROWBRIDGE.

THE POOR MAN AND THE FIEND.

A FIEND once met a humble man
  At night, in the cold dark street,
And led him into a palace fair,
  Where music circled sweet ;
And light and warmth cheered the wanderer's
    heart,
  From frost and darkness screened,
Till his brain grew mad-beneath the joy,
  And he worshipped before the fiend.

Ah ! well if he ne'er had knelt to that fiend,
  For a taskmaster grim was he ;
And he said, " One half of thy life on earth
  I enjoin thee to yield to me ;
And when, from rising till set of sun,
  Thou hast toiled in the heat or snow,
Let thy gains on mine altar an offering be " ;
  And the poor man ne'er said " No ! "

The poor man had health, more dear than gold ;
   Stout bone and muscle strong,
That neither faint nor weary grew,
   To toil the June day long ;
And the fiend, his god, cried hoarse and loud,
   "Thy strength thou must forego,
Or thou no worshipper art of mine" ;
   And the poor man ne'er said "No !"

Three children blest the poor man's home, —
   Stray angels dropped on earth, —
The fiend beheld their sweet blue eyes,
   And he laughed in fearful mirth :
"Bring forth thy little ones," quoth he,
   "My godhead wills it so !
I want an evening sacrifice" ;
   And the poor man ne'er said "No !"

A young wife sat by the poor man's fire,
   Who, since she blushed a bride,
Had gilded his sorrow, and brightened his joys,
   His guardian, friend, and guide.
Foul fall the fiend ! he gave command,
   "Come, mix the cup of woe,
Bid thy young wife drain it to the dregs" ;
   And the poor man ne'er said "No !"

O, misery now for this poor man !
   O, deepest of misery !
Next the fiend his godlike reason took,
   And amongst beasts fed he ;
And when the sentinel mind was gone,
   He pilfered his soul also ;
And — marvel of marvels ! — he murmured not ;
   The poor man ne'er said "No !"

Now, men and matrons in your prime,
   Children and grandsires old,
Come listen, with soul as well as ear,
   This saying whilst I unfold ;
O, listen ! till your brain whirls round,
   And your heart is sick to think,
That in England's isle all this befell,
   And the name of the fiend was — DRINK !
             REV. MR. MACLELLAN.

THE HAPPY HEART.

ART thou poor, yet hast thou golden slumbers ?
   O sweet content !
Art thou rich, yet is thy mind perplexed ?
   O punishment !
Dost thou laugh to see how fools are vexed
To add to golden numbers, golden numbers ?
O sweet content ! O sweet, O sweet content !
   Work apace, apace, apace, apace ;
   Honest labor bears a lovely face ;
Then hey nonny nonny, hey nonny nonny !

Canst drink the waters of the crispéd spring ?
   O sweet content !
Swimm'st thou in wealth, yet sink'st in thine
     own tears ?
   O punishment !
Then he that patiently want's burden bears
No burden bears, but is a king, a king !
O sweet content ! O sweet, O sweet content !
   Work apace, apace, apace, apace ;
   Honest labor bears a lovely face ;
Then hey nonny nonny, hey nonny nonny !
             T. DECKER.

SWEET IS THE PLEASURE.

SWEET is the pleasure
   Itself cannot spoil !
Is not true leisure
   One with true toil ?

Thou that wouldst taste it,
   Still do thy best ;
Use it, not waste it, —
   Else 't is no rest.

Wouldst behold beauty
   Near thee ? all round ?
Only hath duty
   Such a sight found.

Rest is not quitting
   The busy career ;
Rest is the fitting
   Of self to its sphere.

'T is the brook's motion,
   Clear without strife,
Fleeing to ocean
   After its life.

Deeper devotion
   Nowhere hath knelt ;
Fuller emotion
   Heart never felt.

'T is loving and serving
   The highest and best ;
'T is onwards ! unswerving, —
   And that is true rest.
          JOHN SULLIVAN DWIGHT.

THE VILLAGE BLACKSMITH.

UNDER a spreading chestnut-tree
   The village smithy stands ;
The smith, a mighty man is he,
   With large and sinewy hands ;
And the muscles of his brawny arms
   Are strong as iron bands.

His hair is crisp and black and long ;
 His face is like the tan ;
His brow is wet with honest sweat, —
 He earns whate'er he can ;
And looks the whole world in the face,
 For he owes not any man.

Week in, week out, from morn till night,
 You can hear his bellows blow ;
You can hear him swing his heavy sledge,
 With measured beat and slow,
Like sexton ringing the village bell,
 When the evening sun is low.

And children, coming home from school,
 Look in at the open door ;
They love to see the flaming forge,
 And hear the bellows roar,
And catch the burning sparks that fly
 Like chaff from a threshing-floor.

He goes on Sunday to the church,
 And sits among his boys ;
He hears the parson pray and preach,
 He hears his daughter's voice,
Singing in the village choir,
 And it makes his heart rejoice.

It sounds to him like her mother's voice,
 Singing in Paradise !
He needs must think of her once more,
 How in the grave she lies ;
And with his hard, rough hand he wipes
 A tear out of his eyes.

Toiling, rejoicing, sorrowing,
 Onward through life he goes ;
Each morning sees some task begin,
 Each evening sees it close ;
Something attempted, something done,
 Has earned a night's repose.

Thanks, thanks to thee, my worthy friend,
 For the lesson thou hast taught !
Thus at the flaming forge of life
 Our fortunes must be wrought ;
Thus on its sounding anvil shaped
 Each burning deed and thought !
   HENRY WADSWORTH LONGFELLOW.

THE HUSBANDMAN.

EARTH, of man the bounteous mother,
 Feeds him still with corn and wine ;
He who best would aid a brother
 Shares with him these gifts divine.

Many a power within her bosom,
 Noiseless, hidden, works beneath ;
Hence are seed and leaf and blossom,
 Golden ear, and clustered wreath.

These to swell with strength and beauty
 Is the royal task of man ;
Man 's a king ; his throne is duty,
 Since his work on earth began.

Bud and harvest, bloom and vintage, —
 These, like man, are fruits of earth ;
Stamped in clay, a heavenly mintage,
 All from dust receive their birth.

Barn and mill, and wine-vat's treasures,
 Earthly goods for earthly lives, —
These are Nature's ancient pleasures,
 These her child from her derives.

What the dream but vain rebelling,
 If from earth we sought to flee ?
'T is our stored and ample dwelling ;
 'T is from it the skies we see.

Wind and frost, and hour and season,
 Land and water, sun and shade, —
Work with these, as bids thy reason,
 For they work thy toil to aid.

Sow thy seed and reap in gladness !
 Man himself is all a seed ;
Hope and hardship, joy and sadness, —
 Slow the plant to ripeness lead.
    JOHN STERLING.

THE USEFUL PLOUGH.

A COUNTRY life is sweet !
In moderate cold and heat,
 To walk in the air how pleasant and fair !
In every field of wheat,
 The fairest of flowers adorning the bowers,
And every meadow's brow ;
 So that I say, no courtier may
 Compare with them who clothe in gray,
And follow the useful plough.

They rise with the morning lark,
And labor till almost dark,
 Then, folding their sheep, they hasten to sleep ;
While every pleasant park
 Next morning is ringing with birds that
  are singing,
On each green, tender bough.
 With what content and merriment
Their days are spent whose minds are bent
 To follow the useful plough !
    ANONYMOUS.

HONEST TOIL.

"*These are the hands whose sturdy labor brings*
The peasant's food, the golden pomp of kings."

THE GOOD OLD PLOUGH.

AS SUNG BY THE HUTCHINSONS.

LET them sing who may of the battle fray,
　And the deeds that have long since past ;
Let them chant in praise of the tar whose days,
　Are spent on the ocean vast.
I would render to these all the worship you please,
　I would honor them even now ;
But I 'd give far more from my heart's full store
　To the cause of the Good Old Plough.

Let them laud the notes that in music float
　Through the bright and glittering hall ;
While the amorous twirl of the hair's bright curl
　Round the shoulder of beauty fall.
But dearer to me is the song from the tree,
　And the rich and blossoming bough ;
O, these are the sweets which the rustic greets
　As he follows the Good Old Plough !

Full many there be that daily we see,
　With a selfish and hollow pride,
Who the ploughman's lot, in his humble cot,
　With a scornful look deride ;
But I 'd rather take, aye, a hearty shake
　From his hand than to wealth I 'd bow ;
For the honest grasp of his hand's rough clasp,
　Has stood by the Good Old Plough.

All honor be, then, to these gray old men,
　When at last they are bowed with toil !
Their warfare then o'er, they battle no more,
　For they 've conquered the stubborn soil.
And the chaplet each wears is his silver hairs ;
　And ne'er shall the victor's brow
With a laurel crown to the grave go down
　Like the sons of the Good Old Plough.
ANONYMOUS.

TO THE HARVEST MOON.

PLEASING 't is, O modest Moon !
Now the night is at her noon,
'Neath thy sway to musing lie,
While around the zephyrs sigh,
Fanning soft the sun-tanned wheat,
Ripened by the summer's heat ;
Picturing all the rustic's joy
When boundless plenty greets his eye,
　And thinking soon,
　O modest Moon !
How many a female eye will roam
　Along the road,
　To see the load,
The last dear load of harvest-home.

'Neath yon lowly roof he lies,
The husbandman, with sleep-sealed eyes :
He dreams of crowded barns, and round
The yard he hears the flail resound ;
O, may no hurricane destroy
His visionary views of joy !
God of the winds ! O, hear his humble prayer,
And while the Moon of Harvest shines, thy
　blustering whirlwind spare !
HENRY KIRKE WHITE.

THE PLOUGHMAN.

CLEAR the brown path to meet his coulter's gleam !
Lo ! on he comes, behind his smoking team,
With toil's bright dew-drops on his sunburnt brow,
The lord of earth, the hero of the plough !

First in the field before the reddening sun,
Last in the shadows when the day is done,
Line after line, along the bursting sod,
Marks the broad acres where his feet have trod ;
Still where he treads the stubborn clods divide,
The smooth, fresh furrow opens deep and wide ;
Matted and dense the tangled turf upheaves,
Mellow and dark the ridgy cornfield cleaves ;
Up the steep hillside, where the laboring train
Slants the long track that scores the level plain,
Through the moist valley, clogged with oozing clay,
The patient convoy breaks its destined way ;
At every turn the loosening chains resound,
The swinging ploughshare circles glistening round,
Till the wide field one billowy waste appears,
And wearied hands unbind the panting steers.

These are the hands whose sturdy labor brings
The peasant's food, the golden pomp of kings ;
This is the page whose letters shall be seen,
Changed by the sun to words of living green ;
This is the scholar whose immortal pen
Spells the first lesson hunger taught to men ;
These are the lines that heaven-commanded Toil
Shows on his deed, — the charter of the soil !

O gracious Mother, whose benignant breast
Wakes us to life, and lulls us all to rest,
How thy sweet features, kind to every clime,
Mock with their smile the wrinkled front of Time !
We stain thy flowers, — they blossom o'er the dead ;
We rend thy bosom, and it gives us bread ;
O'er the red field that trampling strife has torn,
Waves the green plumage of thy tasselled corn ;
Our maddening conflicts scar thy fairest plain,
Still thy soft answer is the growing grain.
Yet, O our Mother, while uncounted charms
Steal round our hearts in thine embracing arms,
Let not our virtues in thy love decay,
And thy fond sweetness waste our strength away.

No, by these hills whose banners now displayed
In blazing cohorts Autumn has arrayed ;
By yon twin summits, on whose splintery crests
The tossing hemlocks hold the eagles' nests ;
By these fair plains the mountain circle screens,
And feeds with streamlets from its dark ravines, —
True to their home, these faithful arms shall toil
To crown with peace their own untainted soil ;
And, true to God, to freedom, to mankind,
If her chained bandogs Faction shall unbind,
These stately forms, that, bending even now,
Bowed their strong manhood to the humble plough,
Shall rise erect, the guardians of the land,
The same stern iron in the same right hand,
Till o'er their hills the shouts of triumph run ;
The sword has rescued what the ploughshare won !
                              OLIVER WENDELL HOLMES.

THE FARMER'S BOY.

WHERE noble Grafton spreads his rich domains,
Round Euston's watered vale and sloping plains,
Where woods and groves in solemn grandeur rise,
Where the kite brooding unmolested flies,
The woodcock and the painted pheasant race,
And skulking foxes, destined for the chase ;
There Giles, untaught and unrepining, strayed
Through every copse and grove and winding
    glade ;
There his first thoughts to Nature's charms in-
    clined,
That stamps devotion on the inquiring mind.
A little farm his generous master tilled,
Who with peculiar grace his station filled ;
By deeds of hospitality endeared,
Served from affection, for his worth revered.
A happy offspring blest his plenteous board,
His fields were fruitful, and his barns well stored,
And fourscore ewes he fed, a sturdy team,
And lowing kine that grazed beside the stream ;
Unceasing industry he kept in view,
And never lacked a job for Giles to do.

Fled now the sullen murmurs of the north,
The splendid raiment of the Spring peeps forth ;
Her universal green and the clear sky
Delight still more and more the gazing eye.
Wide o'er the fields, in rising moisture strong,
Shoots up the simple flower, or creeps along
The mellowed soil, imbibing fairer hues,
Or sweets from frequent showers and evening dews ;
That summon from their sheds the slumbering
    ploughs,
While health impregnates every breeze that blows.
No wheels support the diving, pointed share ;
No groaning ox is doomed to labor there ;

No helpmates teach the docile steed his road
(Alike unknown the ploughboy and the goad) ;
But unassisted, through each toilsome day,
With smiling brow the ploughman cleaves his way,
Draws his fresh parallels, and, widening still,
Treads slow the heavy dale, or climbs the hill.
Strong on the wing his busy followers play,
Where writhing earthworms meet the unwelcome
    day,
Till all is changed, and hill and level down
Assume a livery of sober brown ;
Again disturbed when Giles with wearying strides
From ridge to ridge the ponderous harrow guides,
His heels deep sinking, every step he goes,
Till dirt adhesive loads his clouted shoes.
Welcome, green headland ! firm beneath his feet ;
Welcome, the friendly bank's refreshing seat ;
There, warm with toil, his panting horses browse
Their sheltering canopy of pendent boughs ;
Till rest delicious chase each transient pain,
And new-born vigor swell in every vein.
Hour after hour and day to day succeeds,
Till every clod and deep-drawn furrow spreads
To crumbling mould, — a level surface clear,
And strewed with corn to crown the rising year ;
And o'er the whole Giles, once transverse again,
In earth's moist bosom buries up the grain.
The work is done ; no more to man is given ;
The grateful farmer trusts the rest to Heaven.

.   .   .   .   .

His simple errand done, he homeward hies ;
Another instantly his place supplies.
The clattering dairy-maid immersed in steam,
Singing and scrubbing midst her milk and cream,
Bawls out, " Go fetch the cows ! " — he hears no
    more ;
For pigs and ducks and turkeys throng the
    door,
And sitting hens for constant war prepared, —
A concert strange to that which late he heard.
Straight to the meadow then he whistling goes ;
With well-known halloo calls his lazy cows ;
Down the rich pasture heedlessly they graze,
Or hear the summons with an idle gaze ;
For well they know the cow-yard yields no more
Its tempting fragrance, nor its wintry store.
Reluctance marks their steps, sedate and slow,
The right of conquest all the law they know ;
The strong press on, the weak by turns succeed,
And one superior always takes the lead,
Is ever foremost wheresoe'er they stray,
Allowed precedence, undisputed sway ;
With jealous pride her station is maintained,
For many a broil that post of honor gained.
At home, the yard affords a grateful scene,
For spring makes e'en a miry cow-yard clean.
Thence from its chalky bed behold conveyed
The rich manure that drenching winter made,

Which, piled near home, grows green with many
    a weed,
A promised nutriment for autumn's seed.
Forth comes the maid, and like the morning smiles;
The mistress too, and followed close by Giles.
A friendly tripod forms their humble seat,
With pails bright scoured and delicately sweet.
Where shadowing elms obstruct the morning ray
Begins the work, begins the simple lay ;
The full-charged udder yields its willing stream
While Mary sings some lover's amorous dream ;
And crouching Giles beneath a neighboring tree
Tugs o'er his pail, and chants with equal glee ;
Whose hat with battered brim, of nap so bare,
From the cow's side purloins a coat of hair, —
A mottled ensign of his harmless trade,
An unambitious, peaceable cockade.
As unambitious, too, that cheerful aid
The mistress yields beside her rosy maid ;
With joy she views her plenteous reeking store,
And bears a brimmer to the dairy door.
Her cows dismissed, the luscious mead to roam,
Till eve again recall them loaded home.
ROBERT BLOOMFIELD.

THE SONG OF THE FORGE.

CLANG, clang ! the massive anvils ring ;
Clang, clang ! a hundred hammers swing ;
Like the thunder-rattle of a tropic sky,
The mighty blows still multiply, —
Clang, clang !
Say, brothers of the dusky brow,
What are your strong arms forging now ?

Clang, clang ! — we forge the coulter now, —
The coulter of the kindly plough.
Sweet Mary mother, bless our toil !
May its broad furrow still unbind
To genial rains, to sun and wind,
The most benignant soil !

Clang, clang ! — our coulter's course shall be
On many a sweet and sheltered lea,
By many a streamlet's silver tide ;
Amidst the song of morning birds,
Amidst the low of sauntering herds,
Amidst soft breezes, which do stray
Through woodbine hedges and sweet May,
Along the green hill's side.

When regal Autumn's bounteous hand
With wide-spread glory clothes the land, —
When to the valleys, from the brow
Of each resplendent slope, is rolled
A ruddy sea of living gold, —
We bless, we bless the plough.

Clang, clang ! — again, my mates, what grows
Beneath the hammer's potent blows ?
Clink, clank ! — we forge the giant chain,
Which bears the gallant vessel's strain
Midst stormy winds and adverse tides ;
Secured by this, the good ship braves
The rocky roadstead, and the waves
Which thunder on her sides.

Anxious no more, the merchant sees
The mist drive dark before the breeze,
The storm-cloud on the hill ;
Calmly he rests, — though far away,
In boisterous climes, his vessel lay, —
Reliant on our skill.

Say on what sands these links shall sleep,
Fathoms beneath the solemn deep ?
By Afric's pestilential shore ;
By many an iceberg, lone and hoar ;
By many a balmy western isle,
Basking in spring's perpetual smile ;
By stormy Labrador.

Say, shall they feel the vessel reel,
When to the battery's deadly peal
The crashing broadside makes reply ;
Or else, as at the glorious Nile,
Hold grappling ships, that strive the while
For death or victory ?

Hurrah ! — cling, clang ! — once more, what glows,
Dark brothers of the forge, beneath
The iron tempest of your blows,
The furnace's red breath ?

Clang, clang ! — a burning torrent, clear
And brilliant of bright sparks, is poured
Around, and up in the dusky air,
As our hammers forge the sword.

The sword ! — a name of dread ; yet when
Upon the freeman's thigh 't is bound, —
While for his altar and his hearth,
While for the land that gave him birth,
The war-drums roll, the trumpets sound, —
How sacred is it then !

Whenever for the truth and right
It flashes in the van of fight, —
Whether in some wild mountain pass,
As that where fell Leonidas ;
Or on some sterile plain and stern,
A Marston, or a Bannockburn ;
Or amidst crags and bursting rills,
The Switzer's Alps, gray Tyrol's hills ;
Or as, when sunk the Armada's pride,
It gleams above the stormy tide, —

Still, still, whene'er the battle word
Is liberty, when men do stand
For justice and their native land, —
Then Heaven bless the sword !
                              ANONYMOUS.

THE FORGING OF THE ANCHOR.

COME, see the Dolphin's anchor forged ; 't is at a
    white heat now :
The billows ceased, the flames decreased ; though
    on the forge's brow
The little flames still fitfully play through the
    sable mound ;
And fitfully you still may see the grim smiths
    ranking round,
All clad in leathern panoply, their broad hands
    only bare ;
Some rest upon their sledges here, some work
    the windlass there.

The windlass strains the tackle-chains, the black
    mound heaves below,
And red and deep a hundred veins burst out at
    every throe ;
It rises, roars, rends all outright, — O Vulcan,
    what a glow !
'T is blinding white, 't is blasting bright, the
    high sun shines not so !
The high sun sees not, on the earth, such fiery
    fearful show, —
The roof-ribs swarth, the candent hearth, the
    ruddy, lurid row
Of smiths that stand, an ardent band, like men
    before the foe ;
As, quivering through his fleece of flame, the
    sailing monster slow
Sinks on the anvil, — all about the faces fiery
    grow,
" Hurrah ! " they shout, " leap out, leap out " :
    bang, bang, the sledges go ;
Hurrah ! the jetted lightnings are hissing high
    and low ;
A hailing fount of fire is struck at every squash-
    ing blow ;
The leathern mail rebounds the hail ; the rattling
    cinders strew
The ground around ; at every bound the swelter-
    ing fountains flow ;
And thick and loud the swinking crowd, at every
    stroke, pant " Ho ! "

Leap out, leap out, my masters ; leap out and
    lay on load !
Let 's forge a goodly anchor, a bower, thick and
    broad ;

For a heart of oak is hanging on every blow, I bode,
And I see the good ship riding, all in a perilous
    road ;
The low reef roaring on her lee, the roll of ocean
    poured
From stem to stern, sea after sea, the mainmast
    by the board ;
The bulwarks down, the rudder gone, the boats
    stove at the chains,
But courage still, brave mariners, the bower still
    remains,
And not an inch to flinch he deigns save when
    ye pitch sky-high,
Then moves his head, as though he said, "Fear
    nothing, — here am I ! "
Swing in your strokes in order, let foot and hand
    keep time,
Your blows make music sweeter far than any
    steeple's chime !
But while ye swing your sledges, sing ; and let
    the burden be,
The Anchor is the Anvil King, and royal crafts-
    men we ;
Strike in, strike in, the sparks begin to dull
    their rustling red !
Our hammers ring with sharper din, our work
    will soon be sped ;
Our anchor soon must change his bed of fiery
    rich array
For a hammock at the roaring bows, or an oozy
    couch of clay ;
Our anchor soon must change the lay of merry
    craftsmen here,
For the Yeo-heave-o, and the Heave-away, and
    the sighing seaman's cheer ;
When, weighing slow, at eve they go far, far
    from love and home,
And sobbing sweethearts, in a row, wail o'er the
    ocean foam.

In livid and obdurate gloom, he darkens down
    at last.
A shapely one he is, and strong as e'er from cat
    was cast.
A trusted and trustworthy guard, if thou hadst
    life like me,
What pleasures would thy toils reward beneath
    the deep green sea !
O deep sea-diver, who might then behold such
    sights as thou ?
The hoary monsters' palaces ! methinks what joy
    't were now
To go plump plunging down amid the assembly
    of the whales,
And feel the churned sea round me boil beneath
    their scourging tails !

SAMUEL FERGUSON.

LABOR SONG.

FROM "THE BELL-FOUNDER."

Ah ! little they know of true happiness, they
    whom satiety fills,
Who, flung on the rich breast of luxury, eat of
    the rankness that kills.
Ah ! little they know of the blessedness toil-
    purchased slumber enjoys
Who, stretched on the hard rack of indolence,
    taste of the sleep that destroys ;
Nothing to hope for, or labor for ; nothing to sigh
    for, or gain ;
Nothing to light in its vividness, lightning-like,
    bosom and brain ;
Nothing to break life's monotony, rippling it o'er
    with its breath :
Nothing but dulness and lethargy, weariness,
    sorrow, and death !

But blesséd that child of humanity, happiest man
    among men,
Who, with hammer or chisel or pencil, with rud-
    der or ploughshare or pen,
Laboreth ever and ever with hope through the
    morning of life,
Winning home and its darling divinities, — love-
    worshipped children and wife.
Round swings the hammer of industry, quickly
    the sharp chisel rings,
And the heart of the toiler has throbbings that stir
    not the bosom of kings, —
He the true ruler and conqueror, he the true king
    of his race,
Who nerveth his arm for life's combat, and looks
    the strong world in the face.
                    DENIS FLORENCE MAC-CARTHY.

A LANCASHIRE DOXOLOGY.

[" Some cotton has lately been imported into Farringdon, where
the mills have been closed for a considerable time. The people,
who were previously in the deepest distress, went out to meet the
cotton : the women wept over the bales and kissed them, and
finally sang the Doxology over them." — *Spectator* of May 14, 1863.]

" PRAISE God from whom all blessings flow,"
Praise him who sendeth joy and woe.
The Lord who takes, the Lord who gives,
O praise him, all that dies, and lives.

He opens and he shuts his hand,
But why we cannot understand :
Pours and dries up his mercies' flood,
And yet is still All-perfect Good.

We fathom not the mighty plan,
The mystery of God and man ;

We women, when afflictions come,
We only suffer and are dumb.

And when, the tempest passing by,
He gleams out, sunlike, through our sky,
We look up, and through black clouds riven
We recognize the smile of Heaven.

Ours is no wisdom of the wise,
We have no deep philosophies ;
Childlike we take both kiss and rod,
For he who loveth knoweth God.
                    DINAH MARIA MULOCK.

TO LABOR IS TO PRAY.

PAUSE not to dream of the future before us ;
Pause not to weep the wild cares that come o'er us ;
Hark how Creation's deep, musical chorus,
    Unintermitting, goes up into heaven !
Never the ocean wave falters in flowing ;
Never the little seed stops in its growing ;
More and more richly the rose heart keeps glow-
    ing,
    Till from its nourishing stem it is riven.

" Labor is worship !" the robin is singing ;
" Labor is worship !" the wild bee is ringing ;
Listen ! that eloquent whisper, upspringing,
    Speaks to thy soul from out nature's great
        heart.
From the dark cloud flows the life-giving shower ;
From the rough sod blows the soft-breathing
    flower ;
From the small insect, the rich coral bower ;
    Only man, in the plan, shrinks from his part.

Labor is life ! 't is the still water faileth ;
Idleness ever despaireth, bewaileth ;
Keep the watch wound, or the dark rust assaileth ;
    Flowers droop and die in the stillness of noon.
Labor is glory ! — the flying cloud lightens ;
Only the waving wing changes and brightens ,
Idle hearts only the dark future frightens ,
    Play the sweet keys, wouldst thou keep them
        in tune !

Labor is rest — from the sorrows that greet us ;
Rest from all petty vexations that meet us ;
Rest from sin-promptings that ever entreat us ;
    Rest from world-sirens that lure us to ill.
Work, — and pure slumbers shall wait on thy
        pillow ;
Work, — thou shalt ride o'er Care's coming billow ;
Lie not down 'neath Woe's weeping willow,
    Work with a stout heart and resolute will !

Labor is health! Lo, the husbandman reaping,
How through his veins goes the life-current
    leaping!
How his strong arm in its stalworth pride sweep-
    ing,
  True as a sunbeam the swift sickle guides.
Labor is wealth, — in the sea the pearl groweth;
Rich the queen's robe from the cocoon floweth;
From the fine acorn the strong forest bloweth;
  Temple and statue the marble block hides.

Droop not! though shame, sin, and anguish are
    round thee!
Bravely fling off the cold chain that hath bound
    thee!
Look to the pure heaven smiling beyond thee!
  Rest not content in thy darkness, — a clod!
Work for some good, be it ever so slowly!
Cherish some flower, be it ever so lowly!
Labor! — all labor is noble and holy;
  Let thy great deed be thy prayer to thy God.
                              FRANCES S. OSGOOD.

THE POOR MAN'S LABOR.

My mother sighed, the stream of pain
  Flowed fast and chilly o'er her brow;
My father prayed, nor prayed in vain;
  Sweet Mercy, cast a glance below.
"My husband dear," the sufferer cried,
  "My pains are o'er, behold your son."
"Thank Heaven, sweet partner," he replied;
  "The poor boy's labor's then begun."

Alas! the hapless life she gave
  By fate was doomed to cost her own;
For soon she found an early grave,
  Nor stayed her partner long alone.
They left their orphan here below,
  A stranger wild beneath the sun,
This lesson sad to learn from woe, —
  The poor man's labor's never done.

No parent's hand, with pious care,
  My childhood's devious steps to guide;
Or bid my venturous youth beware
  The griefs that smote on every side.

'T was still a round of changing woe,
  Woe never ending, still begun,
That taught my bleeding heart to know
  The poor man's labor's never done.

Soon dies the faltering voice of fame;
  The vow of love's too warm to last;
And friendship, what a faithless dream!
  And, wealth, how soon thy glare is past!
But sure one hope remains to save, —
  The longest course must soon be run,
And in the shelter of the grave
  The poor man's labor must be done.
                        JOHN PHILPOT CURRAN.

GOOD NIGHT.

Good night!
  To each weary, toil-worn wight,
Now the day so sweetly closes,
Every aching brow reposes
  Peacefully till morning light.
    Good night!

Home to rest!
  Close the eye and calm the breast;
Stillness through the streets is stealing,
And the watchman's horn is pealing,
  And the night calls softly, "Haste!
    Home to rest!"

Sweetly sleep!
  Eden's breezes round ye sweep.
O'er the peace-forsaken lover
Let the darling image hover,
  As he lies in transport deep.
    Sweetly sleep!

So, good night!
  Slumber on till morning light;
Slumber till another morrow
Brings its stores of joy and sorrow;
  Fearless, in the Father's sight,
    Slumber on. Good night.
          KÖRNER. Translation of
          CHARLES T. BROOKS.

POEMS OF PATRIOTISM AND FREEDOM.

Thy sacred leaves, fair Freedom's flower,
Shall ever float on dome and tower,
To all their heavenly colors true
In blackening frost or crimson dew,
And God love us as we love thee,
Thrice holy Flower of Liberty!

  Then hail the banner of the free,
  The starry Flower of Liberty!

  Oliver Wendell Holmes

POEMS OF PATRIOTISM AND FREEDOM.

BREATHES THERE THE MAN—

BREATHES there the man with soul so dead
Who never to himself hath said,
  This is my own, my native land !
Whose heart hath ne'er within him burned,
As home his footsteps he hath turned
  From wandering on a foreign strand !
If such there breathe, go, mark him well ;
For him no minstrel raptures swell ;
High though his titles, proud his name,
Boundless his wealth as wish can claim,
Despite those titles, power, and pelf,
The wretch, concentred all in self,
Living, shall forfeit fair renown,
And, doubly dying, shall go down
To the vile dust from whence he sprung,
Unwept, unhonored, and unsung.
SIR WALTER SCOTT.

MY COUNTRY.

THERE is a land, of every land the pride,
Beloved by Heaven o'er all the world beside,
Where brighter suns dispense serener light,
And milder moons imparadise the night ;
A land of beauty, virtue, valor, truth,
Time-tutored age, and love-exalted youth:
The wandering mariner, whose eye explores
The wealthiest isles, the most enchanting shores,
Views not a realm so bountiful and fair,
Nor breathes the spirit of a purer air.
In every clime, the magnet of his soul,
Touched by remembrance, trembles to that pole ;
For in this land of Heaven's peculiar race,
The heritage of nature's noblest grace,
There is a spot of earth supremely blest,
A dearer, sweeter spot than all the rest,
Where man, creation's tyrant, casts aside
His sword and sceptre, pageantry and pride,
While in his softened looks benignly blend
The sire, the son, the husband, brother, friend.
Here woman reigns ; the mother, daughter, wife,
Strew with fresh flowers the narrow way of life :

In the clear heaven of her delightful eye,
An angel-guard of love and graces lie ;
Around her knees domestic duties meet,
And fireside pleasures gambol at her feet.
"Where shall that land, that spot of earth be
    found ?"
Art thou a man ?—a patriot ?—look around ;
O, thou shalt find, howe'er thy footsteps roam,
That land *thy* country, and that spot *thy* home !
  .   .   .   .   .
Man, through all ages of revolving time,
Unchanging man, in every varying clime,
Deems his own land of every land the pride,
Beloved by Heaven o'er all the world beside ;
His home the spot of earth supremely blest,
A dearer, sweeter spot than all the rest.
JAMES MONTGOMERY.

HOW SLEEP THE BRAVE—

How sleep the brave, who sink to rest
By all their country's wishes blessed !
When Spring, with dewy fingers cold,
Returns to deck their hallowed mould,
She there shall dress a sweeter sod
Than Fancy's feet have ever trod.

By fairy hands their knell is rung ;
By forms unseen their dirge is sung ;
There Honor comes, a pilgrim gray,
To bless the turf that wraps their clay ;
And Freedom shall awhile repair,
To dwell a weeping hermit there !
WILLIAM COLLINS.

THE BRAVE AT HOME.

I.

THE maid who binds her warrior's sash
  With smile that well her pain dissembles,
The while beneath her drooping lash
  One starry tear-drop hangs and trembles,

Though Heaven alone records the tear,
　And Fame shall never know her story,
Her heart has shed a drop as dear
　As e'er bedewed the field of glory !

II.

The wife who girds her husband's sword,
　Mid little ones who weep or wonder,
And bravely speaks the cheering word,
　What though her heart be rent asunder,
Doomed nightly in her dreams to hear
　The bolts of death around him rattle,
Hath shed as sacred blood as e'er
　Was poured upon the field of battle !

III.

The mother who conceals her grief
　While to her breast her son she presses,
Then breathes a few brave words and brief,
　Kissing the patriot brow she blesses,
With no one but her secret God
　To know the pain that weighs upon her,
Sheds holy blood as e'er the sod
　Received on Freedom's field of honor !
　　　　　　　　THOMAS BUCHANAN READ.

THE DEATH OF LEONIDAS.

IT was the wild midnight, — a storm was on the
　sky ;
The lightning gave its light, and the thunder
　echoed by.
The torrent swept the glen, the ocean lashed the
　shore ;
Then rose the Spartan men, to make their bed in
　gore !

Swift from the deluged ground three hundred took
　the shield ;
Then, in silence, gathered round the leader of the
　field !
All up the mountain's side, all down the woody
　vale,
All by the rolling tide waved the Persian banners
　pale.

And foremost from the pass, among the slumber-
　ing band,
Sprang King Leonidas, like the lightning's living
　brand.
Then double darkness fell, and the forest ceased
　its moan ;
But there came a clash of steel, and a distant dy-
　ing groan.

Anon, a trumpet blew, and a fiery sheet burst high,
That o'er the midnight threw a blood-red canopy.

A host glared on the hill ; a host glared by the bay ;
But the Greeks rushed onward still, like leopards
　in their play.

The air was all a yell, and the earth was all a flame,
Where the Spartan's bloody steel on the silken
　turbans came ;
And still the Greek rushed on where the fiery
　torrent rolled,
Till like a rising sun shone Xerxes' tent of gold.

They found a royal feast, his midnight banquet,
　there ;
And the treasures of the East lay beneath the
　Doric spear.
Then sat to the repast the bravest of the brave !
That feast must be their last, that spot must be
　their grave.

Up rose the glorious rank, to Greece one cup
　poured high,
Then hand in hand they drank, "To immortal-
　ity !"
Fear on King Xerxes fell, when, like spirits from
　the tomb,
With shout and trumpet knell, he saw the war-
　riors come.

But down swept all his power, with chariot and
　with charge ;
Down poured the arrows' shower, till sank the
　Spartan targe.
Thus fought the Greek of old ! thus will he fight
　again !
Shall not the selfsame mould bring forth the self-
　same men ?
　　　　　　　　GEORGE CROLY.

PERICLES AND ASPASIA.

THIS was the ruler of the land
　When Athens was the land of fame ;
This was the light that led the band
　When each was like a living flame ;
The centre of earth's noblest ring, —
Of more than men the more than king.

Yet not by fetter, nor by spear,
　His sovereignty was held or won :
Feared — but alone as freemen fear,
　Loved — but as freemen love alone,
He waved the sceptre o'er his kind
By nature's first great title, — mind !

Resistless words were on his tongue, —
　Then eloquence first flashed below ;
Full armed to life the portent sprung, —
　Minerva from the thunderer's brow !

And his the sole, the sacred hand
That shook her ægis o'er the land.

And throned immortal by his side,
  A woman sits with eye sublime, —
Aspasia, all his spirit's bride ;
  But, if their solemn love were crime,
Pity the beauty and the sage, —
  Their crime was in their darkened age

He perished, but his wreath was won, —
  He perished in his height of fame ;
Then sunk the cloud on Athens' sun,
  Yet still she conquered in his name.
Filled with his soul, she could not die ;
  Her conquest was posterity !
GEORGE CROLY.

HORATIUS AT THE BRIDGE.

LARS PORSENA of Clusium,
  By the nine gods he swore
That the great house of Tarquin
  Should suffer wrong no more.
By the nine gods he swore it,
  And named a trysting-day,
And bade his messengers ride forth,
East and west and south and north,
  To summon his array.

East and west and south and north
  The messengers ride fast,
And tower and town and cottage
  Have heard the trumpet's blast.
Shame on the false Etruscan
  Who lingers in his home,
When Porsena of Clusium
  Is on the march for Rome !

There be thirty chosen prophets,
  The wisest of the land,
Who alway by Lars Porsena
  Both morn and evening stand.
Evening and morn the thirty
  Have turned the verses o'er,
Traced from the right on linen white
  By mighty seers of yore ;

And with one voice the thirty
  Have their glad answer given :
"Go forth, go forth, Lars Porsena, —
  Go forth, beloved of heaven !
Go, and return in glory
  To Clusium's royal dome,
And hang round Nurscia's altars
  The golden shields of Rome !"

And now hath every city
  Sent up her tale of men ;
The foot are fourscore thousand,
  The horse are thousands ten.
Before the gates of Sutrium
  Is met the great array ;
A proud man was Lars Porsena
  Upon the trysting-day.

Now, from the rock Tarpeian,
  Could the wan burghers spy
The line of blazing villages
  Red in the midnight sky.
The fathers of the city,
  They sat all night and day,
For every hour some horseman came
  With tidings of dismay.

I wis, in all the senate
  There was no heart so bold
But sore it ached, and fast it beat,
  When that ill news was told.
Forthwith up rose the consul,
  Up rose the fathers all ;
In haste they girded up their gowns,
  And hied them to the wall.

They held a council, standing
  Before the river-gate ;
Short time was there, ye well may guess,
  For musing or debate.
Outspake the consul roundly :
  "The bridge must straight go down ;
For, since Janiculum is lost,
  Naught else can save the town."

Just then a scout came flying,
  All wild with haste and fear :
"To arms ! to arms ! sir consul, —
  Lars Porsena is here."
On the low hills to westward
  The consul fixed his eye,
And saw the swarthy storm of dust
  Rise fast along the sky.

But the consul's brow was sad,
  And the consul's speech was low,
And darkly looked he at the wall,
  And darkly at the foe :
"Their van will be upon us
  Before the bridge goes down ;
And if they once may win the bridge,
  What hope to save the town ?"

Then outspake brave Horatius,
  The captain of the gate :
"To every man upon this earth
  Death cometh soon or late.

And how can man die better
  Than facing fearful odds
For the ashes of his fathers
  And the temples of his gods?

"And for the tender mother
  Who dandled him to rest,
And for the wife who nurses
  His baby at her breast,
And for the holy maidens
  Who feed the eternal flame, —
To save them from false Sextus
  That wrought the deed of shame?

"Hew down the bridge, sir consul,
  With all the speed ye may;
I, with two more to help me,
  Will hold the foe in play, —
In yon strait path a thousand
  May well be stopped by three.
Now who will stand on either hand,
  And keep the bridge with me?"

Then outspake Spurius Lartius, —
  A Ramnian proud was he:
"Lo, I will stand at thy right hand,
  And keep the bridge with thee."
And outspake strong Herminius, —
  Of Titian blood was he:
"I will abide on thy left side,
  And keep the bridge with thee."

The three stood calm and silent,
  And looked upon the foes,
And a great shout of laughter
  From all the vanguard rose;
And forth three chiefs came spurring
  Before that deep array;
To earth they sprang, their swords they drew,
And lifted high their shields, and flew
  To win the narrow way.

Aunus, from green Tifernum,
  Lord of the hill of vines;
And Seius, whose eight hundred slaves
  Sicken in Ilva's mines;
And Picus, long to Clusium
  Vassal in peace and war,
Who led to fight his Umbrian powers
From that gray crag where, girt with towers,
The fortress of Nequinum lowers
  O'er the pale waves of Nar.

Stout Lartius hurled down Aunus
  Into the stream beneath;
Herminius struck at Seius,
  And clove him to the teeth;

At Picus brave Horatius
  Darted one fiery thrust,
And the proud Umbrian's gilded arms
  Clashed in the bloody dust.

Then Ocnus of Falerii
  Rushed on the Roman three;
And Lausulus of Urgo,
  The rover of the sea;
And Aruns of Volsinium,
  Who slew the great wild boar, —
The great wild boar that had his den
Amidst the reeds of Cosa's fen,
And wasted fields, and slaughtered men,
  Along Albinia's shore.

Herminius smote down Aruns;
  Lartius laid Ocnus low;
Right to the heart of Lausulus
  Horatius sent a blow:
"Lie there," he cried, "fell pirate!
  No more, aghast and pale,
From Ostia's walls the crowd shall mark
The track of thy destroying bark;
No more Campania's hinds shall fly
To woods and caverns, when they spy
  Thy thrice-accursèd sail!"

But now no sound of laughter
  Was heard among the foes;
A wild and wrathful clamor
  From all the vanguard rose.
Six spears' lengths from the entrance,
  Halted that deep array,
And for a space no man came forth
  To win the narrow way.

But, hark! the cry is Astur:
  And lo! the ranks divide;
And the great lord of Luna
  Comes with his stately stride.
Upon his ample shoulders
  Clangs loud the fourfold shield,
And in his hand he shakes the brand
  Which none but he can wield.

He smiled on those bold Romans,
  A smile serene and high;
He eyed the flinching Tuscans,
  And scorn was in his eye.
Quoth he, "The she-wolf's litter
  Stand savagely at bay;
But will ye dare to follow,
  If Astur clears the way?"

Then, whirling up his broadsword
  With both hands to the height,
He rushed against Horatius,
  And smote with all his might.

With shield and blade Horatius
  Right deftly turned the blow.
The blow, though turned, came yet too nigh ;
It missed his helm, but gashed his thigh.
The Tuscans raised a joyful cry
  To see the red blood flow.

He reeled, and on Herminius
  He leaned one breathing-space,
Then, like a wild-cat mad with wounds,
  Sprang right at Astur's face.
Through teeth and skull and helmet
  So fierce a thrust he sped,
The good sword stood a handbreadth out
  Behind the Tuscan's head.

And the great lord of Luna
  Fell at that deadly stroke,
As falls on Mount Avernus
  A thunder-smitten oak.
Far o'er the crashing forest
  The giant arms lie spread ;
End the pale augurs, muttering low,
  Gaze on the blasted head.

On Astur's throat Horatius
  Right firmly pressed his heel,
And thrice and four times tugged amain,
  Ere he wrenched out the steel.
"And see," he cried, "the welcome,
  Fair guests, that waits you here !
What noble Lucumo comes next
  To taste our Roman cheer ?"

But at his haughty challenge
  A sullen murmur ran,
Mingled with wrath and shame and dread,
  Along that glittering van.
There lacked not men of prowess,
  Nor men of lordly race,
For all Etruria's noblest
  Were round the fatal place.

But all Etruria's noblest
  Felt their hearts sink to see
On the earth the bloody corpses,
  In the path the dauntless three ;
And from the ghastly entrance,
  Where those bold Romans stood,
All shrank, — like boys who, unaware,
Ranging a wood to start a hare,
Come to the mouth of the dark lair
Where, growling low, a fierce old bear
  Lies amidst bones and blood.

Was none who would be foremost
  To lead such dire attack ;
But those behind cried " Forward ! "
  And those before cried " Back ! "

And backward now, and forward,
  Wavers the deep array ;
And on the tossing sea of steel
To and fro the standards reel,
And the victorious trumpet-peal
  Dies fitfully away.

Yet one man for one moment
  Strode out before the crowd ;
Well known was he to all the three,
  And they gave him greeting loud :
"Now welcome, welcome, Sextus !
  Now welcome to thy home !
Why dost thou stay, and turn away ?
  Here lies the road to Rome."

Thrice looked he at the city ;
  Thrice looked he at the dead ;
And thrice came on in fury,
  And thrice turned back in dread ;
And, white with fear and hatred,
  Scowled at the narrow way
Where, wallowing in a pool of blood,
  The bravest Tuscans lay.

But meanwhile axe and lever
  Have manfully been plied ;
And now the bridge hangs tottering
  Above the boiling tide.
"Come back, come back, Horatius !"
  Loud cried the fathers all, —
"Back, Lartius ! back, Herminius !
  Back, ere the ruin fall ! "

Back darted Spurius Lartius, —
  Herminius darted back ;
And, as they passed, beneath their feet
  They felt the timbers crack.
But when they turned their faces,
  And on the farther shore
Saw brave Horatius stand alone,
  They would have crossed once more ;

But with a crash like thunder
  Fell every loosened beam,
And, like a dam, the mighty wreck
  Lay right athwart the stream ;
And a long shout of triumph
  Rose from the walls of Rome,
As to the highest turret-tops
  Was splashed the yellow foam.

And like a horse unbroken,
  When first he feels the rein,
The furious river struggled hard,
  And tossed his tawny mane,
And burst the curb, and bounded,

Rejoicing to be free ;
And whirling down, in fierce career,
Battlement and plank and pier,
Rushed headlong to the sea.

Alone stood brave Horatius,
But constant still in mind, —
Thrice thirty thousand foes before,
And the broad flood behind.
"Down with him !" cried false Sextus,
With a smile on his pale face ;
"Now yield thee," cried Lars Porsena,
"Now yield thee to our grace !"

Round turned he, as not deigning
Those craven ranks to see ;
Naught spake he to Lars Porsena,
To Sextus naught spake he ;
But he saw on Palatinus
The white porch of his home ;
And he spake to the noble river
That rolls by the towers of Rome :

"O Tiber ! Father Tiber !
To whom the Romans pray,
A Roman's life, a Roman's arms,
Take thou in charge this day !"
So he spake, and, speaking, sheathed
The good sword by his side,
And, with his harness on his back,
Plunged headlong in the tide.

No sound of joy or sorrow
Was heard from either bank,
But friends and foes in dumb surprise,
With parted lips and straining eyes,
Stood gazing where he sank ;
And when above the surges
They saw his crest appear,
All Rome sent forth a rapturous cry,
And even the ranks of Tuscany
Could scarce forbear to cheer.

But fiercely ran the current,
Swollen high by months of rain,
And fast his blood was flowing ;
And he was sore in pain,
And heavy with his armor,
And spent with changing blows ;
And oft they thought him sinking,
But still again he rose.

Never, I ween, did swimmer,
In such an evil case,
Struggle through such a raging flood
Safe to the landing-place ;
But his limbs were borne up bravely
By the brave heart within,
And our good Father Tiber
Bare bravely up his chin.

"Curse on him !" quoth false Sextus, —
"Will not the villain drown ?
But for this stay, ere close of day
We should have sacked the town !"
"Heaven help him !" quoth Lars Porsena,
"And bring him safe to shore ;
For such a gallant feat of arms
Was never seen before."

And now he feels the bottom ;
Now on dry earth he stands ;
Now round him throng the fathers
To press his gory hands ;
And now, with shouts and clapping,
And noise of weeping loud,
He enters through the river-gate,
Borne by the joyous crowd.

They gave him of the corn-land,
That was of public right,
As much as two strong oxen
Could plough from morn till night ;
And they made a molten image,
And set it up on high, —
And there it stands unto this day
To witness if I lie.

It stands in the comitium,
Plain for all folk to see, —
Horatius in his harness,
Halting upon one knee ;
And underneath is written,
In letters all of gold,
How valiantly he kept the bridge
In the brave days of old.

And still his name sounds stirring
Unto the men of Rome,
As the trumpet-blast that cries to them
To charge the Volscian home ;
And wives still pray to Juno
For boys with hearts as bold
As his who kept the bridge so well
In the brave days of old.

And in the nights of winter,
When the cold north-winds blow,
And the long howling of the wolves
Is heard amidst the snow ;
When round the lonely cottage
Roars loud the tempest's din,
And the good logs of Algidus
Roar louder yet within ;

When the oldest cask is opened,
And the largest lamp is lit ;
When the chestnuts glow in the embers,
And the kid turns on the spit ;

When young and old in circle
　Around the firebrands close ;
When the girls are weaving baskets,
　And the lads are shaping bows ;

When the goodman mends his armor,
　And trims his helmet's plume ;
When the goodwife's shuttle merrily
　Goes flashing through the loom ;
With weeping and with laughter
　Still is the story told,
How well Horatius kept the bridge
　In the brave days of old.

　　　　　THOMAS BABINGTON MACAULAY.

SEMPRONIUS'S SPEECH FOR WAR.

My voice is still for war.
Gods ! can a Roman senate long debate
Which of the two to choose, slavery or death ?
No ; let us rise at once, gird on our swords,
And at the head of our remaining troops
Attack the foe, break through the thick array
Of his thronged legions, and charge home upon
　him.
Perhaps some arm, more lucky than the rest,
May reach his heart, and free the world from bond-
　age.
Rise ! Fathers, rise ! 'tis Rome demands your help :
Rise, and revenge her slaughtered citizens,
Or share their fate ! The corpse of half her senate
Manures the fields of Thessaly, while we
Sit here deliberating, in cold debates,
If we should sacrifice our lives to honor,
Or wear them out in servitude and chains.
Rouse up, for shame ! Our brothers of Pharsalia
Point out their wounds, and cry aloud, — " To
　battle ! "
Great Pompey's shade complains that we are slow,
And Scipio's ghost walks unrevenged among us.

　　　　　JOSEPH ADDISON.

BOADICEA.

WHEN the British warrior queen,
　Bleeding from the Roman rods,
Sought, with an indignant mien,
　Counsel of her country's gods,

Sage beneath the spreading oak
　Sat the druid, hoary chief ;
Every burning word he spoke
　Full of rage and full of grief.

" Princess ! if our aged eyes
　Weep upon thy matchless wrongs,

'Tis because resentment ties
　All the terrors of our tongues.

" Rome shall perish — write that word
　In the blood that she has spilt —
Perish, hopeless and abhorred,
　Deep in ruin as in guilt.

" Rome, for empire far renowned,
　Tramples on a thousand states ;
Soon her pride shall kiss the ground, —
　Hark ! the Gaul is at her gates !

" Other Romans shall arise,
　Heedless of a soldier's name ;
Sounds, not arms, shall win the prize,
　Harmony the path to fame.

" Then the progeny that springs
　From the forests of our land,
Armed with thunder, clad with wings,
　Shall a wider world command.

" Regions Cæsar never knew
　Thy posterity shall sway ;
Where his eagles never flew,
　None invincible as they."

Such the bard's prophetic words,
　Pregnant with celestial fire,
Bending as he swept the chords
　Of his sweet but awful lyre.

She, with all a monarch's pride,
　Felt them in her bosom glow ;
Rushed to battle, fought, and died, —
　Dying, hurled them at the foe.

Ruffians, pitiless as proud,
　Heaven awards the vengeance due ;
Empire is on us bestowed,
　Shame and ruin wait for you.

　　　　　WILLIAM COWPER.

HERMANN AND THUSNELDA.

[Hermann, or, as the Roman historians call him, Arminius, was a chieftain of the Cheruscans, a tribe in Northern Germany. After serving in Illyria, and there learning the Roman arts of warfare, he came back to his native country, and fought successfully for its independence. He defeated beside a defile near Detmold, in Westphalia, the Roman legions under Varus, with a slaughter so mortifying that the Proconsul is said to have killed himself, and Augustus to have received the catastrophe with indecorous expressions of grief.]

HA ! there comes he, with sweat, with blood of
　Romans,
And with dust of the fight all stained ! O, never
　Saw I Hermann so lovely !
　Never such fire in his eyes !

Come ! I tremble for joy ; hand me the Eagle,
And the red, dripping sword ! come, breathe, and
    rest thee ;
      Rest thee here in my bosom ;
      Rest from the terrible fight !

Rest thee, while from thy brow I wipe the big
    drops,
And the blood from thy cheek ! — that cheek,
    how glowing !
      Hermann ! Hermann ! Thusnelda
      Never so loved thee before !

No, not then when thou first, in old oak-shadows,
With that manly brown arm didst wildly grasp me !
      Spell-bound I read in thy look
      That immortality, then,

Which thou now hast won. Tell to the forests,
Great Augustus, with trembling, amidst his gods
    now,
      Drinks his nectar ; for Hermann,
      Hermann immortal is found !

"Wherefore curl'st thou my hair ? Lies not our
    father
Cold and silent in death ? O, had Augustus
      Only headed his army, —
      He should lie bloodier there !"

Let me lift up thy hair ; 't is sinking, Hermann ;
Proudly thy locks should curl above the crown
    now !
      Sigmar is with the immortals !
      Follow, and mourn him no more !
          KLOPSTOCK.   Translation of
            CHARLES T. BROOKS.

RIENZI TO THE ROMANS.

FRIENDS !
I came not here to talk. Ye know too well
The story of our thraldom. We are slaves !
The bright sun rises to his course, and lights
A race of slaves ! he sets, and his last beam
Falls on a slave ! Not such as, swept along
By the full tide of power, the conqueror leads
To crimson glory and undying fame,
But base, ignoble slaves ! — slaves to a horde
Of petty tyrants, feudal despots ; lords
Rich in some dozen paltry villages,
Strong in some hundred spearmen, only great
In that strange spell, — a name ! Each hour, dark
    fraud,
Or open rapine, or protected murder,
Cries out against them. But this very day
An honest man, my neighbor, — there he stands, —

Was struck — struck like a dog — by one who wore
The badge of Ursini ! because, forsooth,
He tossed not high his ready cap in air,
Nor lifted up his voice in servile shouts,
At sight of that great ruffian ! Be we men,
And suffer such dishonor ? men, and wash not
The stain away in blood ? such shames are common.
I have known deeper wrongs. I that speak to
    ye —
I had a brother once, a gracious boy,
Full of all gentleness, of calmest hope,
Of sweet and quiet joy ; there was the look
Of Heaven upon his face which limners give
To the beloved disciple. How I loved
That gracious boy ! younger by fifteen years,
Brother at once and son ! He left my side, —
A summer bloom on his fair cheeks, a smile
Parting his innocent lips. In one short hour
The pretty, harmless boy was slain ! I saw
The corse, the mangled corse, and then I cried
For vengeance ! Rouse, ye Romans ! Rouse,
    ye slaves !
Have ye brave sons ? — Look in the next fierce
    brawl
To see them die ! Have ye fair daughters ? — Look
To see them live, torn from your arms, disdained,
Dishonored ; and, if ye dare call for justice,
Be answered by the lash ! Yet this is Rome,
That sate on her seven hills, and from her throne
Of beauty ruled the world ! Yet we are Romans.
Why, in that elder day to be a Roman
Was greater than a king ! And once again —
Hear me, ye walls, that echoed to the tread
Of either Brutus ! — once again I swear
The eternal city shall be free !
             MARY RUSSELL MITFORD.

MAKE WAY FOR LIBERTY !

[On the exploit of Arnold Winkelried at the battle of Sempach, in
which the Swiss, fighting for their independence, totally defeated
the Austrians, in the fourteenth century.]

"MAKE way for Liberty !" — he cried ;
Made way for Liberty, and died !

In arms the Austrian phalanx stood,
A living wall, a human wood !
A wall, where every conscious stone
Seemed to its kindred thousands grown ;
A rampart all assaults to bear,
Till time to dust their frames should wear ;
A wood, like that enchanted grove
In which with fiends Rinaldo strove,
Where every silent tree possessed
A spirit prisoned in its breast,
Which the first stroke of coming strife
Would startle into hideous life ;

So dense, so still, the Austrians stood,
A living wall, a human wood !
Impregnable their front appears,
All horrent with projected spears,
Whose polished points before them shine,
From flank to flank, one brilliant line,
Bright as the breakers' splendors run
Along the billows to the sun.

  Opposed to these, a hovering band
Contended for their native land :
Peasants, whose new-found strength had broke
From manly necks the ignoble yoke,
And forged their fetters into swords,
On equal terms to fight their lords,
And what insurgent rage had gained
In many a mortal fray maintained ;
Marshalled once more at Freedom's call,
They came to conquer or to fall,
Where he who conquered, he who fell,
Was deemed a dead, or living Tell !
Such virtue had that patriot breathed,
So to the soil his soul bequeathed,
That wheresoe'er his arrows flew
Heroes in his own likeness grew,
And warriors sprang from every sod
Which his awakening footstep trod.

  And now the work of life and death
Hung on the passing of a breath ;
The fire of conflict burnt within,
The battle trembled to begin ;
Yet, while the Austrians held their ground,
Point for attack was nowhere found,
Where'er the impatient Switzers gazed,
The unbroken line of lances blazed ;
That line 't were suicide to meet,
And perish at their tyrants' feet, —
How could they rest within their graves,
And leave their homes the homes of slaves ?
Would they not feel their children tread
With clanging chains above their head ?

  It must not be : this day, this hour,
Annihilates the oppressor's power ;
All Switzerland is in the field,
She will not fly, she cannot yield, —
She must not fall ; her better fate
Here gives her an immortal date.
Few were the number she could boast ;
But every freeman was a host,
And felt as though himself were he
On whose sole arm hung victory.

  It did depend on *one* indeed ;
Behold him, — Arnold Winkelried !
There sounds not to the trump of fame
The echo of a nobler name.

Unmarked he stood amid the throng,
In rumination deep and long,
Till you might see, with sudden grace,
The very thought come o'er his face,
And by the motion of his form
Anticipate the bursting storm,
And by the uplifting of his brow
Tell where the bolt would strike, and how.

  But 't was no sooner thought than done,
The field was in a moment won : —

  "Make way for Liberty !" he cried,
Then ran, with arms extended wide,
As if his dearest friend to clasp ;
Ten spears he swept within his grasp.

  "Make way for Liberty !" he cried ;
Their keen points met from side to side ;
He bowed amongst them like a tree,
And thus made way for Liberty.

  Swift to the breach his comrades fly ;
"Make way for Liberty !" they cry,
And through the Austrian phalanx dart,
As rushed the spears through Arnold's heart ;
While, instantaneous as his fall,
Rout, ruin, panic, scattered all :
An earthquake could not overthrow
A city with a surer blow.

  Thus Switzerland again was free ;
Thus death made way for Liberty !
                    JAMES MONTGOMERY.

SWITZERLAND.

WILLIAM TELL.

ONCE Switzerland was free ! With what a pride
I used to walk these hills, — look up to heaven,
And bless God that it was so ! It was free
From end to end, from cliff to lake 't was free !
Free as our torrents are, that leap our rocks,
And plough our valleys, without asking leave ;
Or as our peaks, that wear their caps of snow
In very presence of the regal sun !
How happy was I in it, then ! I loved
Its very storms.   Ay, often have I sat
In my boat at night, when midway o'er the lake,
The stars went out, and down the mountain
    gorge
The wind came roaring, — I have sat and eyed
The thunder breaking from his cloud, and smiled
To see him shake his lightnings o'er my head,
And think I had no master save his own.
                    JAMES SHERIDAN KNOWLES.

MONCONTOUR.

O, WEEP for Moncontour! O, weep for the hour
When the children of darkness and evil had
power;
When the horsemen of Valois triumphantly trod
On the bosoms that bled for their rights and
their God.

O, weep for Moncontour! O, weep for the slain
Who for faith and for freedom lay slaughtered in
vain!
O, weep for the living, who linger to bear
The renegade's shame or the exile's despair!

One look, one last look, to the cots and the
towers,
To the rows of our vines and the beds of our
flowers;
To the church where the bones of our fathers
decayed,
Where we fondly had deemed that our own should
be laid.

Alas! we must leave thee, dear desolate home,
To the spearmen of Uri, the shavelings of Rome;
To the serpent of Florence, the sultan of Spain;
To the pride of Anjou, and the guile of Lorraine.

Farewell to thy fountains, farewell to thy shades,
To the song of thy youths, the dance of thy
maids;
To the breath of thy gardens, the hum of thy
bees,
And the long waving line of the blue Pyrenees!

Farewell and forever! The priest and the slave
May rule in the halls of the free and the brave;
Our hearths we abandon, — our lands we resign, —
But, Father, we kneel to no altar but thine.
                    THOMAS BABINGTON MACAULAY.

NASEBY.

O, WHEREFORE come ye forth in triumph from
the north,
With your hands, and your feet, and your rai-
ment all red?
And wherefore doth your rout send forth a joy-
ous shout?
And whence be the grapes of the wine-press that
ye tread?

O, evil was the root, and bitter was the fruit,
And crimson was the juice of the vintage that
we trod;

For we trampled on the throng of the haughty
and the strong,
Who sate in the high places and slew the saints
of God.

It was about the noon of a glorious day of June
That we saw their banners dance and their
cuirasses shine,
And the man of blood was there, with his long
essenced hair,
And Astley, and Sir Marmaduke, and Rupert of
the Rhine.

Like a servant of the Lord, with his Bible and
his sword,
The General rode along us to form us for the fight;
When a murmuring sound broke out, and swelled
into a shout
Among the godless horsemen upon the tyrant's
right.

And hark! like the roar of the billows on the
shore,
The cry of battle rises along their charging line:
For God! for the cause! for the Church! for the
laws!
For Charles, king of England, and Rupert of the
Rhine!

The furious German comes, with his clarions and
his drums,
His bravoes of Alsatia and pages of Whitehall;
They are bursting on our flanks! Grasp your
pikes! Close your ranks!
For Rupert never comes but to conquer, or to
fall.

They are here, — they rush on, — we are broken,
— we are gone, —
Our left is borne before them like stubble on the
blast.
O Lord, put forth thy might! O Lord, defend
the right!
Stand back to back, in God's name! and fight
it to the last!

Stout Skippen hath a wound, — the centre hath
given ground.
Hark! hark! what means the trampling of
horsemen on our rear?
Whose banner do I see, boys? 'T is he! thank
God! 't is he, boys!
Bear up another minute! Brave Oliver is here!

Their heads all stooping low, their points all in
a row,
Like a whirlwind on the trees, like a deluge on
the dikes,

Our cuirassiers have burst on the ranks of the accurst,
And at a shock have scattered the forest of his pikes.

Fast, fast the gallants ride, in some safe nook to hide
Their coward heads, predestined to rot on Temple Bar ;
And he — he turns ! he flies ! shame on those cruel eyes
That bore to look on torture, and dare not look on war !

Ho, comrades ! scour the plain ; and ere ye strip the slain,
First give another stab to make your search secure ;
Then shake from sleeves and pockets their broad-pieces and lockets,
The tokens of the wanton, the plunder of the poor.

Fools ! your doublets shone with gold, and your hearts were gay and bold,
When you kissed your lily hands to your le-mans to-day ;
And to-morrow shall the fox from her chambers in the rocks
Lead forth her tawny cubs to howl above the prey.

Where be your tongues, that late mocked at heaven and hell and fate ?
And the fingers that once were so busy with your blades ?
Your perfumed satin clothes, your catches and your oaths ?
Your stage-plays and your sonnets, your dia-monds and your spades ?

Down ! down ! forever down, with the mitre and the crown !
With the Belial of the court, and the Mammon of the Pope !
There is woe in Oxford halls, there is wail in Durham's stalls ;
The Jesuit smites his bosom, the bishop rends his cope.

And she of the seven hills shall mourn her chil-dren's ills,
And tremble when she thinks on the edge of England's sword ;
And the kings of earth in fear shall shudder when they hear
What the hand of God hath wrought for the houses and the word !

THOMAS BABINGTON MACAULAY.

BRUCE AND THE SPIDER.

FOR Scotland's and for freedom's right
  The Bruce his part had played,
In five successive fields of fight
  Been conquered and dismayed ;
Once more against the English host
His band he led, and once more lost
  The meed for which he fought ;
And now from battle, faint and worn,
The homeless fugitive forlorn
  A hut's lone shelter sought.

And cheerless was that resting-place
  For him who claimed a throne :
His canopy, devoid of grace,
  The rude, rough beams alone ;
The heather couch his only bed, —
Yet well I ween had slumber fled
  From couch of eider-down !
Through darksome night till dawn of day,
Absorbed in wakeful thought he lay
  Of Scotland and her crown.

The sun rose brightly, and its gleam
  Fell on that hapless bed,
And tinged with light each shapeless beam
  Which roofed the lowly shed ;
When, looking up with wistful eye,
The Bruce beheld a spider try
  His filmy thread to fling
From beam to beam of that rude cot ;
And well the insect's toilsome lot
  Taught Scotland's future king.

Six times his gossamery thread
  The wary spider threw ;
In vain the filmy line was sped,
  For powerless or untrue
Each aim appeared, and back recoiled
The patient insect, six times foiled,
  And yet unconquered still ;
And soon the Bruce, with eager eye,
Saw him prepare once more to try
  His courage, strength, and skill.

One effort more, his seventh and last !
  The hero hailed the sign !
And on the wished-for beam hung fast
  That slender, silken line ;
Slight as it was, his spirit caught
The more than omen, for his thought
  The lesson well could trace,
Which even "he who runs may read,"
That Perseverance gains its meed,
  And Patience wins the race.

BERNARD ARTON.

BANNOCKBURN.

At Bannockburn the English lay, —
The Scots they were na far away,
But waited for the break o' day
    That glinted in the east.

But soon the sun broke through the heath
And lighted up that field o' death,
When Bruce, wi' saul-inspiring breath,
    His heralds thus addressed : —

" Scots, wha hae wi' Wallace bled,
Scots, wham Bruce has often led,
Welcome to your gory bed,
    Or to glorious victory !

" Now 's the day, and now 's the hour ;
See the front o' battle lour ;
See approach proud Edward's power, —
    Edward ! chains and slavery !

" Wha will be a traitor knave ?
Wha can fill a coward's grave ?
Wha sae base as be a slave ?
    Traitor ! coward ! turn and flee !

" Wha for Scotland's king and law
Freedom's sword will strongly draw,
Freeman stand, or freeman fa',
    Caledonia ! on wi' me !

" By oppression's woes and pains !
By your sons in servile chains !
We will drain our dearest veins,
    But they shall be — shall be free !

" Lay the proud usurpers low !
Tyrants fall in every foe !
Liberty 's in every blow !
    Forward ! let us do, or die ! "
            ROBERT BURNS.

LOCHIEL'S WARNING.

WIZARD. — LOCHIEL.

WIZARD.

Lochiel, Lochiel ! beware of the day
When the Lowlands shall meet thee in battle array,
For a field of the dead rushes red on my sight,
And the clans of Culloden are scattered in fight.
They rally, they bleed, for their kingdom and
    crown,
Woe, woe to the riders that trample them down !
Proud Cumberland prances, insulting the slain,
And their hoof-beaten bosoms are trod to the plain.

But hark ! through the fast-flashing lightning of
    war,
What steed to the desert flies frantic and far ?
'T is thine, O Glenullin ! whose bride shall await,
Like a love-lighted watch-fire, all night at the gate.
A steed comes at morning : no rider is there ;
But its bridle is red with the sign of despair.
Weep, Albin ! to death and captivity led !
O, weep ! but thy tears cannot number the dead ;
For a merciless sword on Culloden shall wave,
Culloden ! that reeks with the blood of the brave.

LOCHIEL.

Go, preach to the coward, thou death-telling seer !
Or, if gory Culloden so dreadful appear,
Draw, dotard, around thy old wavering sight
This mantle, to cover the phantoms of fright.

WIZARD.

Ha ! laugh'st thou, Lochiel, my vision to scorn ?
Proud bird of the mountain, thy plume shall be
    torn !
Say, rushed the bold eagle exultingly forth
From his home in the dark rolling clouds of the
    north !
Lo ! the death-shot of foemen outspeeding, he rode
Companionless, bearing destruction abroad ;
But down let him stoop from his havoc on high !
Ah ! home let him speed, — for the spoiler is nigh.
Why flames the far summit ? Why shoot to the
    blast
Those embers, like stars from the firmament cast ?
'T is the fire-shower of ruin, all dreadfully driven
From his eyry, that beacons the darkness of
    heaven.
O crested Lochiel ! the peerless in might,
Whose banners arise on the battlements' height,
Heaven's fire is around thee, to blast and to burn ;
Return to thy dwelling ! all lonely return !
For the blackness of ashes shall mark where it
    stood,
And a wild mother scream o'er her famishing brood.

LOCHIEL.

False Wizard, avaunt ! I have marshalled my clan,
Their swords are a thousand, their bosoms are one !
They are true to the last of their blood and their
    breath,
And like reapers descend to the harvest of death.
Then welcome be Cumberland's steed to the shock !
Let him dash his proud foam like a wave on the
    rock !
But woe to his kindred, and woe to his cause,
When Albin her claymore indignantly draws ;
When her bonneted chieftains to victory crowd,
Clanronald the dauntless, and Moray the proud,
All plaided and plumed in their tartan array —

Etch'd by H.B. Hall's N.Y. 12

Walter Scott

FORDS, HOWARD & HULBERT, N.Y.

WIZARD.

—Lochiel, Lochiel ! beware of the day ;
For, dark and despairing, my sight I may seal,
But man cannot cover what God would reveal ;
'T is the sunset of life gives me mystical lore,
And coming events cast their shadows before.
I tell thee, Culloden's dread echoes shall ring
With the bloodhounds that bark for thy fugitive
        king.
Lo ! anointed by Heaven with the phials of wrath,
Behold where he flies on his desolate path !
Now in darkness and billows he sweeps from my
        sight.
Rise, rise ! ye wild tempests, and cover his flight !
'T is finished.   Their thunders are hushed on the
        moors. .
Culloden is lost, and my country deplores,
But where is the iron-bound prisoner ? Where ?
For the red eye of battle is shut in despair.
Say, mounts he the ocean-wave, banished, forlorn,
Like a limb from his country cast bleeding and
        torn ?
Ah no ! for a darker departure is near ;
The war-drum is muffled, and black is the bier ;
His death-bell is tolling : O mercy, dispel
Yon sight, that it freezes my spirit to tell !
Life flutters convulsed in his quivering limbs,
And his blood-streaming nostril in agony swims.
Accursed be the fagots that blaze at his feet,
Where his heart shall be thrown ere it ceases to
        beat,
With the smoke of its ashes to poison the gale —

LOCHIEL.

— Down, soothless insulter ! I trust not the tale ;
For never shall Albin a destiny meet,
So black with dishonor, so foul with retreat.
Though my perishing ranks should be strewed in
        their gore,
Like ocean-weeds heaped on the surf-beaten shore,
Lochiel, untainted by flight or by chains,
While the kindling of life in his bosom remains,
Shall victor exult, or in death be laid low,
With his back to the field, and his feet to the foe !
And leaving in battle no blot on his name,
Look proudly to Heaven from the death-bed of
        fame.   THOMAS CAMPBELL.

SCOTLAND.

O CALEDONIA ! stern and wild,
Meet nurse for a poetic child !
Land of brown heath and shaggy wood,
Land of the mountain and the flood,
Land of my sires ! what mortal hand
Can e'er untie the filial band

That knits me to thy rugged strand ?
Still, as I view each well-known scene,
Think what is now, and what hath been,
Seems as, to me, of all bereft,
Sole friends thy woods and streams were left ;
And thus I love them better still,
Even in extremity of ill.
By Yarrow's stream still let me stray,
Though none should guide my feeble way ;
Still feel the breeze down Ettrick break,
Although it chill my withered cheek ;
Still lay my head by Teviot stone,
Though there, forgotten and alone,
The bard may draw his parting groan.
                           SIR WALTER SCOTT.

MACGREGOR'S GATHERING.

Air, "THAIN' A GRIGALACH."

[These verses are adapted to a very wild, yet lively, gathering
tune, used by the Macgregors.   The severe treatment of this clan,
their outlawry, and the proscription of their very name, are alluded
to in the ballad.]

THE moon 's on the lake, and the mist 's on the
        brae,
And the clan has a name that is nameless by day ;
    Then gather, gather, gather, Grigalach !
    Gather, gather, gather, etc.

Our signal for fight, that from monarchs we drew,
Must be heard but by night in our vengeful haloo !
    Then haloo, Grigalach ! haloo, Grigalach !
    Haloo, haloo, haloo, Grigalach, etc.

Glen Orchy's proud mountains, Coalchurn and
        her towers,
Glenstrae and Glenlyon no longer are ours :
    We 're landless, landless, landless, Grigalach !
    Landless, landless, landless, etc.

But doomed and devoted by vassal and lord
Macgregor has still both his heart and his sword !
    Then courage, courage, courage, Grigalach !
    Courage, courage, courage, etc.

If they rob us of name, and pursue us with beagles,
Give their roofs to the flame, and their flesh to
        the eagles !
    Then vengeance, vengeance, vengeance,
        Grigalach !
    Vengeance, vengeance, vengeance, etc.

While there 's leaves in the forest, and foam on
        the river,
Macgregor, despite them, shall flourish forever !
    Come then, Grigalach ! come then, Griga-
        lach !
    Come then, come then, come then, etc.

Through the depths of Loch Katrine the steed
  shall career,
O'er the peak of Ben Lomond the galley shall steer,
And the rocks of Craig-Royston like icicles melt,
Ere our wrongs be forgot or our vengeance unfelt !
    Then gather, gather, gather, Grigalach !
    Gather, gather, gather, etc.
                              SIR WALTER SCOTT.

ENGLAND.

I TRAVELLED among unknown men
  In lands beyond the sea ;
Nor, England ! did I know till then
  What love I bore to thee.

'T is past, that melancholy dream !
  Nor will I quit thy shore
A second time, for still I seem
  To love thee more and more.

Among thy mountains did I feel
  The joy of my desire ;
And she I cherished turned her wheel
  Beside an English fire.

Thy mornings showed, thy nights concealed,
  The bowers where Lucy played ;
And thine too is the last green field
  That Lucy's eyes surveyed.
                          WILLIAM WORDSWORTH.

MY COUNTRY.

FROM "THE TIMEPIECE."

ENGLAND, with all thy faults, I love thee still, —
My country ! and, while yet a nook is left
Where English minds and manners may be found,
Shall be constrained to love thee. Though thy
  clime
Be fickle, and thy year most part deformed
With dripping rains, or withered by a frost,
I would not yet exchange thy sullen skies,
And fields without a flower, for warmer France
With all her vines ; nor for Ausonia's groves
Of golden fruitage and her myrtle bowers.
To shake thy senate, and from height sublime
Of patriot eloquence to flash down fire
Upon thy foes, was never meant my task :
But I can feel thy fortunes, and partake
Thy joys and sorrows with as true a heart
As any thunderer there.   And I can feel
Thy follies too ; and with a just disdain
Frown at effeminates whose very looks
Reflect dishonor on the land I love.

How, in the name of soldiership and sense,
Should England prosper, when such things, as
  smooth
And tender as a girl, all essenced o'er
With odors, and as profligate as sweet,
Who sell their laurel for a myrtle wreath,
And love when they should fight, — when such as
  these
Presume to lay their hand upon the ark
Of her magnificent and awful cause ?
Time was when it was praise and boast enough
In every clime, and travel where we might,
That we were born her children. Praise enough
To fill the ambition of a private man,
That Chatham's language was his mother tongue,
And Wolfe's great name compatriot with his own.
                              WILLIAM COWPER.

RULE BRITANNIA!

WHEN Britain first, at Heaven's command,
  Arose from out the azure main,
This was the charter of the land,
  And guardian angels sing the strain :
    Rule Britannia ! Britannia rules the waves !
    Britons never will be slaves.

The nations not so blest as thee,
  Must, in their turn, to tyrants fall ;
Whilst thou shalt flourish, great and free,
  The dread and envy of them all.
    Rule Britannia ! etc.

Still more majestic shalt thou rise,
  More dreadful from each foreign stroke ;
As the loud blasts that tear thy skies
  Serve but to root thy native oak.
    Rule Britannia ! etc.

Thee haughty tyrants ne'er shall tame ;
  All their attempts to hurl thee down
Will but arouse thy generous flame,
  And work their woe — but thy renown.
    Rule Britannia ! etc.

To thee belongs the rural reign ;
  Thy cities shall with commerce shine ;
All thine shall be the subject main,
  And every shore encircle thine.
    Rule Britannia ! etc.

The Muses, still with Freedom found,
  Shall to thy happy coast repair ;
Blest Isle ! with matchless beauty crowned,
  And manly hearts to guard the fair.
    Rule Britannia ! etc.
                              JAMES THOMSON.

THE ENGLISHMAN.

THERE 's a land that bears a world-known name,
Though it is but a little spot;
I say 't is first on the scroll of fame,
And who shall aver it is not?
Of the deathless ones who shine and live
In arms, in arts, or song,
The brightest the whole wide world can give
To that little land belong.
'T is the star of earth, deny it who can,
The island home of an Englishman.

There 's a flag that waves o'er every sea,
No matter when or where;
And to treat that flag as aught but the free
Is more than the strongest dare.
For the lion spirits that tread the deck
Have carried the palm of the brave;
And that flag *may* sink with a shot-torn wreck,
But never float over a slave.
Its honor is stainless, deny it who can,
And this is the flag of an Englishman.

There 's a heart that leaps with burning glow
The wronged and the weak to defend;
And strikes as soon for a trampled foe
As it does for a soul-bound friend.
It nurtures a deep and honest love,
The passions of faith and pride,
And yearns with the fondness of a dove
For the light of its own fireside.
'T is a rich rough gem, deny it who can,
And this is the heart of an Englishman.

The Briton may traverse the pole or the zone,
And boldly claim his right;
For he calls such a vast domain his own
That the sun never sets on his might.
Let the haughty stranger seek to know
The place of his home and birth,
And a flush will pour from cheek to brow
While he tells his native earth.
For a glorious charter, deny it who can,
Is breathed in the words "I 'm an Englishman."
ELIZA COOK.

THE SNUG LITTLE ISLAND.

DADDY NEPTUNE, one day, to Freedom did say,
If ever I lived upon dry land,
The spot I should hit on would be little Britain!
Says Freedom, "Why, that's my own island!"
O, it 's a snug little island!
A right little, tight little island!
Search the globe round, none can be found
So happy as this little island.

Julius Cæsar, the Roman, who yielded to no
man,
Came by water, — he could n't come by land;
And Dane, Pict, and Saxon, their homes turned
their backs on,
And all for the sake of our island.
O, what a snug little island!
They 'd all have a touch at the island!
Some were shot dead, some of them fled,
And some stayed to live on the island.

Then a very great war-man, called Billy the Nor-
man,
Cried, "Drat it, I never liked my land.
It would be much more handy to leave this
Normandy,
And live on your beautiful island."
Says he, "'T is a snug little island;
Sha' n't us go visit the island?"
Hop, skip, and jump, there he was plump,
And he kicked up a dust in the island.

But party deceit helped the Normans to beat;
Of traitors they managed to buy land;
By Dane, Saxon, or Pict, Britons ne'er had been
licked,
Had they stuck to the king of their island.
Poor Harold, the king of our island!
He lost both his life and his island.
That 's all very true: what more could he
do?
Like a Briton he died for his island!

The Spanish armada set out to invade — a,
'T will sure, if they ever come nigh land.
They could n't do less than tuck up Queen Bess,
And take their full swing on the island.
O the poor queen of the island!
The Dons came to plunder the island;
But snug in her hive the queen was alive,
And "buzz" was the word of the island.

These proud puffed-up cakes thought to make
ducks and drakes
Of our wealth; but they hardly could spy land,
When our Drake had the luck to make their
pride duck
And stoop to the lads of the island!
The good wooden walls of the island;
Devil or Don, let them come on;
And see how they 'd come off the island!

Since Freedom and Neptune have hitherto kept
time,
In each saying, "This shall be my land";
Should the "Army of England," or all it could
bring, land,
We 'd show 'em some play for the island.

We 'd fight for our right to the island ;
We 'd give them enough of the island ;
Invaders should just — bite once at the dust,
But not a bit more of the island.

THOMAS DIBDIN.

THE LAND, BOYS, WE LIVE IN.

FROM "THE MYRTLE AND THE VINE."

SINCE our foes to invade us have long been pre-
paring,
'T is clear they consider we 've something worth
sharing,
And for that mean to visit our shore ;
It behooves us, however, with spirit to meet 'em,
And though 't will be nothing uncommon to
beat 'em,
We must try how they 'll take it once more :
So fill, fill your glasses, be this the toast given, —
Here 's England forever, the land, boys, we live
in !
So fill, fill your glasses, be this the toast given, —
Here 's England forever, huzza !

Here 's a health to our tars on the wide ocean
ranging,
Perhaps even now some broadsides are exchang-
ing,
We 'll on shipboard and join in the fight ;
And when with the foe we are firmly engaging,
Till the fire of our guns lulls the sea in its raging,
On our country we 'll think with delight.
So fill, fill your glasses, etc.

On that throne where once Alfred in glory was
seated,
Long, long may our king by his people be greeted ;
O, to guard him we 'll be of one mind !
May religion, law, order, be strictly defended,
And continue the blessings they first were in-
tended,
In union the nation to bind !
So fill, fill your glasses, etc.

ANONYMOUS.

AMERICA TO GREAT BRITAIN.

ALL hail ! thou noble land,
Our Fathers' native soil !
O, stretch thy mighty hand,
Gigantic grown by toil,
O'er the vast Atlantic wave to our shore !
For thou with magic might
Canst reach to where the light
Of Phœbus travels bright
The world o'er !

The Genius of our clime
From his pine-embattled steep
Shall hail the guest sublime ;
While the Tritons of the deep
With their conchs the kindred league shall pro-
claim.
Then let the world combine, —
O'er the main our naval line
Like the Milky Way shall shine
Bright in fame !

Though ages long have past
Since our Fathers left their home,
Their pilot in the blast,
O'er untravelled seas to roam,
Yet lives the blood of England in our veins !
And shall we not proclaim
That blood of honest fame
Which no tyranny can tame
By its chains ?

While the language free and bold
Which the Bard of Avon sung,
In which our Milton told
How the vault of heaven rung
When Satan, blasted, fell with his host ;
While this, with reverence meet,
Ten thousand echoes greet,
From rock to rock repeat
Round our coast ;

While the manners, while the arts,
That mould a nation's soul,
Still cling around our hearts, —
Between let Ocean roll,
Our joint communion breaking with the Sun :
Yet still from either beach
The voice of blood shall reach,
More audible than speech,
"We are One."

WASHINGTON ALLSTON.

AMERICA.

O MOTHER of a mighty race,
Yet lovely in thy youthful gráce !
The elder dames, thy haughty peers,
Admire and hate thy blooming years ;
With words of shame
And taunts of scorn they join thy name.

For on thy cheeks the glow is spread
That tints thy morning hills with red ;
Thy step, — the wild deer's rustling feet
Within thy woods are not more fleet ;
Thy hopeful eye
Is bright as thine own sunny sky.

Ay, let them rail, those haughty ones,
While safe thou dwellest with thy sons.
They do not know how loved thou art,
How many a fond and fearless heart
    Would rise to throw
Its life between thee and the foe.

They know not, in their hate and pride,
What virtues with thy children bide, —
How true, how good, thy graceful maids
Make bright, like flowers, the valley shades ;
    What generous men
Spring, like thine oaks, by hill and glen ;

What cordial welcomes greet the guest
By thy lone rivers of the west ;
How faith is kept, and truth revered,
And man is loved, and God is feared,
    In woodland homes,
And where the ocean border foams.

There's freedom at thy gates, and rest
For earth's down-trodden and opprest,
A shelter for the hunted head,
For the starved laborer toil and bread.
    Power, at thy bounds,
Stops, and calls back his baffled hounds.

O fair young mother ! on thy brow
Shall sit a nobler grace than now.
Deep in the brightness of thy skies,
The thronging years in glory rise,
    And, as they fleet,
Drop strength and riches at thy feet.

Thine eye, with every coming hour,
Shall brighten, and thy form shall tower ;
And when thy sisters, elder born,
Would brand thy name with words of scorn,
    Before thine eye
Upon their lips the taunt shall die.
            WILLIAM CULLEN BRYANT.

COLUMBIA.

COLUMBIA, Columbia, to glory arise,
The queen of the world, and child of the skies !
Thy genius commands thee ; with rapture behold,
While ages on ages thy splendors unfold.
Thy reign is the last and the noblest of time,
Most fruitful thy soil, most inviting thy clime ;
Let the crimes of the east ne'er encrimson thy name,
Be freedom and science and virtue thy fame.

To conquest and slaughter let Europe aspire ;
Whelm nations in blood, and wrap cities in fire ;
Thy heroes the rights of mankind shall defend,
And triumph pursue them, and glory attend.

A world is thy realm ; for a world be thy laws,
Enlarged as thine empire, and just as thy cause ;
On Freedom's broad basis that empire shall rise,
Extend with the main, and dissolve with the skies.

Fair Science her gates to thy sons shall unbar,
And the east see thy morn hide the beams of her star.
New bards and new sages unrivalled shall soar
To fame unextinguished when time is no more ;
To thee, the last refuge of virtue designed,
Shall fly from all nations the best of mankind ;
Here grateful to heaven, with transport shall bring
Their incense, more fragrant than odors of spring.

Nor less shall thy fair ones to glory ascend,
And genius and beauty in harmony blend ;
The graces of form shall awake pure desire,
And the charms of the soul ever cherish the fire ;
Their sweetness unmingled, their manners refined,
And virtue's bright image, enstamped on the mind,
With peace and soft rapture shall teach life to
    glow,
And light up a smile on the aspect of woe.

Thy fleets to all regions thy power shall display,
The nations admire, and the ocean obey ;
Each shore to thy glory its tribute unfold,
And the east and the south yield their spices and
    gold.
As the dayspring unbounded thy splendor shall
    flow,
And earth's little kingdoms before thee shall bow,
While the ensigns of union, in triumph unfurled,
Hush the tumult of war, and give peace to the
    world.

Thus, as down a lone valley, with cedars o'er-
    spread,
From war's dread confusion, I pensively strayed, —
The gloom from the face of fair heaven retired ;
The winds ceased to murmur, the thunders
    expired ;
Perfumes, as of Eden, flowed sweetly along,
And a voice, as of angels, enchantingly sung :
"Columbia, Columbia, to glory arise,
The queen of the world, and the child of the skies."
            TIMOTHY DWIGHT.

SONG OF MARION'S MEN.

OUR band is few, but true and tried,
  Our leader frank and bold ;
The British soldier trembles
  When Marion's name is told.
Our fortress is the good greenwood,
  Our tent the cypress-tree ;
We know the forest round us,
  As seamen know the sea ;

We know its walls of thorny vines,
  Its glades of reedy grass,
Its safe and silent islands
  Within the dark morass.

Woe to the English soldiery
  That little dread us near !
On them shall light at midnight
  A strange and sudden fear ;
When, waking to their tents on fire,
  They grasp their arms in vain,
And they who stand to face us
  Are beat to earth again ;
And they who fly in terror deem
  A mighty host behind,
And hear the tramp of thousands
  Upon the hollow wind.

Then sweet the hour that brings release
  From danger and from toil ;
We talk the battle over,
  And share the battle's spoil.
The woodland rings with laugh and shout,
  As if a hunt were up,
And woodland flowers are gathered
  To crown the soldier's cup.
With merry songs we mock the wind
  That in the pine-top grieves,
And slumber long and sweetly
  On beds of oaken leaves.

Well knows the fair and friendly moon
  The band that Marion leads, —
The glitter of their rifles,
  The scampering of their steeds.
'T is life to guide the fiery barb
  Across the moonlight plain ;
'T is life to feel the night-wind
  That lifts his tossing mane.
A moment in the British camp —
  A moment — and away
Back to the pathless forest,
  Before the peep of day.

Grave men there are by broad Santee,
  Grave men with hoary hairs ;
Their hearts are all with Marion,
  For Marion are their prayers.
And lovely ladies greet our band
  With kindliest welcoming,
With smiles like those of summer,
  And tears like those of spring.
For them we wear these trusty arms,
  And lay them down no more
Till we have driven the Briton
  Forever from our shore.
                WILLIAM CULLEN BRYANT.

WARREN'S ADDRESS.

STAND ! the ground 's your own, my braves !
Will ye give it up to slaves ?
Will ye look for greener graves ?
  Hope ye mercy still ?
What 's the mercy despots feel ?
Hear it in that battle-peal !
Read it on yon bristling steel !
  Ask it, — ye who will.

Fear ye foes who kill for hire ?
Will ye to your *homes* retire ?
Look behind you ! — they 're afire !
  And, before you, see
Who have done it ! From the vale
On they come ! — and will ye quail ?
Leaden rain and iron hail
  Let their welcome be !

In the God of battles trust !
Die we may, — and die we must ?
But, O, where can dust to dust
  Be consigned so well,
As where heaven its dews shall shed
On the martyred patriot's bed,
And the rocks shall raise their head,
  Of his deeds to tell ?
                JOHN PIERPONT.

———◆———

THE OLD CONTINENTALS.

IN their ragged regimentals
Stood the old continentals,
    Yielding not,
When the grenadiers were lungeing,
And like hail fell the plunging
    Cannon-shot ;
    When the files
    Of the isles,
From the smoky night encampment, bore the ban-
    ner of the rampant
    Unicorn,
And grummer, grummer, grummer rolled the roll
    of the drummer,
    Through the morn !

Then with eyes to the front all,
And with guns horizontal,
    Stood our sires ;
And the balls whistled deadly,
And in streams flashing redly
    Blazed the fires ;
    As the roar
    On the shore,

Swept the strong battle-breakers o'er the green-
sodded acres
Of the plain ;
And louder, louder, louder, cracked the black
gunpowder,
Cracking amain !

Now like smiths at their forges
Worked the red St. George's
Cannoneers ;
And the "villanous saltpetre"
Rung a fierce, discordant metre
Round their ears ;
As the swift
Storm-drift,
With hot sweeping anger, came the horseguards'
clangor
On our flanks.
Then higher, higher, higher, burned the old-fash-
ioned fire
Through the ranks !

Then the old-fashioned colonel
Galloped through the white infernal
Powder-cloud ;
And his broad sword was swinging,
And his brazen throat was ringing
Trumpet loud.
Then the blue
Bullets flew,
And the trooper-jackets redden at the touch of
the leaden
Rifle-breath ;
And rounder, rounder, rounder, roared the iron
six-pounder,
Hurling death !
GUY HUMPHREY MCMASTER.

THE AMERICAN FLAG.

WHEN Freedom, from her mountain height,
Unfurled her standard to the air,
She tore the azure robe of night,
And set the stars of glory there !
She mingled with its gorgeous dyes
The milky baldric of the skies,
And striped its pure, celestial white
With streakings of the morning light,
Then, from his mansion in the sun,
She called her eagle-bearer down,
And gave into his mighty hand
The symbol of her chosen land !

Majestic monarch of the cloud !
Who rear'st aloft thy regal form,
To hear the tempest-trumpings loud,
And see the lightning lances driven,

When strive the warriors of the storm,
And rolls the thunder-drum of heaven, —
Child of the Sun ! to thee 't is given
To guard the banner of the free,
To hover in the sulphur smoke,
To ward away the battle-stroke,
And bid its blendings shine afar,
Like rainbows on the cloud of war,
The harbingers of victory !

Flag of the brave ! thy folds shall fly,
The sign of hope and triumph high !
When speaks the signal-trumpet tone,
And the long line comes gleaming on,
Ere yet the life-blood, warm and wet,
Has dimmed the glistening bayonet,
Each soldier's eye shall brightly turn
To where thy sky-born glories burn,
And, as his springing steps advance,
Catch war and vengeance from the glance.
And when the cannon-mouthings loud
Heave in wild wreaths the battle shroud,
And gory sabres rise and fall
Like shoots of flame on midnight's pall,
Then shall thy meteor glances glow,
And cowering foes shall shrink beneath
Each gallant arm that strikes below
That lovely messenger of death.

Flag of the seas ! on ocean wave
Thy stars shall glitter o'er the brave ;
When death, careering on the gale,
Sweeps darkly round the bellied sail,
And frighted waves rush wildly back
Before the broadside's reeling rack,
Each dying wanderer of the sea
Shall look at once to heaven and thee,
And smile to see thy splendors fly
In triumph o'er his closing eye.

Flag of the free heart's hope and home,
By angel hands to valor given,
Thy stars have lit the welkin dome,
And all thy hues were born in heaven.
Forever float that standard sheet !
Where breathes the foe but falls before us,
With Freedom's soil beneath our feet,
And Freedom's banner streaming o'er us ?
JOSEPH RODMAN DRAKE.

THE STAR-SPANGLED BANNER.

O SAY, can you see by the dawn's early light
What so proudly we hailed at the twilight's last
gleaming ? —
Whose broad stripes and bright stars through
the perilous fight,

O'er the ramparts we watched were so gallantly
   streaming !
And the rocket's red glare, the bombs bursting
   in air,
Gave proof through the night that our flag was
   still there ;
O say, does that star-spangled banner yet wave
O'er the land of the free and the home of the
   brave ?

On that shore, dimly seen through the mists of
   the deep,
Where the foe's haughty host in dread silence
   reposes,
What is that which the breeze, o'er the towering
   steep,
As it fitfully blows, now conceals, now discloses ?
Now it catches the gleam of the morning's first
   beam,
In full glory reflected, now shines on the stream ;
'T is the star-spangled banner ! O, long may it
   wave
O'er the land of the free and the home of the
   brave !

And where is that band who so vauntingly swore
That the havoc of war and the battle's confusion
A home and a country should leave us no more ?
Their blood has washed out their foul footsteps'
   pollution.
No refuge could save the hireling and slave
From the terror of flight or the gloom of the
   grave ;
And the star-spangled banner in triumph doth
   wave
O'er the land of the free and the home of the
   brave !

O, thus be it ever when freemen shall stand
Between their loved homes and the war's desola-
   tion !
Blest with victory and peace, may the heaven-
   rescued land
Praise the Power that hath made and preserved
   us a nation.
Then conquer we must, when our cause it is just,
And this be our motto, "In God is our trust" ;
And the star-spangled banner in triumph shall
   wave
O'er the land of the free and the home of the
   brave !
                              FRANCIS SCOTT KEY.

———◆———

BARBARA FRIETCHIE.

UP from the meadows rich with corn,
Clear in the cool September morn,

The clustered spires of Frederick stand
Green-walled by the hills of Maryland.

Round about them orchards sweep,
Apple and peach tree fruited deep,

Fair as a garden of the Lord
To the eyes of the famished rebel horde ;

On that pleasant morn of the early fall
When Lee marched over the mountain wall,—

Over the mountains, winding down,
Horse and foot into Frederick town.

Forty flags with their silver stars,
Forty flags with their crimson bars,

Flapped in the morning wind ; the sun
Of noon looked down, and saw not one.

Up rose old Barbara Frietchie then,
Bowed with her fourscore years and ten ;

Bravest of all in Frederick town,
She took up the flag the men hauled down ;

In her attic-window the staff she set,
To show that one heart was loyal yet.

Up the street came the rebel tread,
Stonewall Jackson riding ahead.

Under his slouched hat left and right
He glanced : the old flag met his sight.

"Halt !"— the dust-brown ranks stood fast ;
"Fire !"— out blazed the rifle-blast.

It shivered the window, pane and sash ;
It rent the banner with seam and gash.

Quick, as it fell, from the broken staff
Dame Barbara snatched the silken scarf ;

She leaned far out on the window-sill,
And shook it forth with a royal will.

"Shoot, if you must, this old gray head,
But spare your country's flag," she said.

A shade of sadness, a blush of shame,
Over the face of the leader came ;

The nobler nature within him stirred
To life at that woman's deed and word :

"Who touches a hair of yon gray head
Dies like a dog ! March on !" he said.

All day long through Frederick street
Sounded the tread of marching feet ;

All day long that free flag tost
Over the heads of the rebel host.

Ever its torn folds rose and fell
On the loyal winds that loved it well ;

And through the hill-gaps sunset light
Shone over it with a warm good-night.

Barbara Frietchie's work is o'er,
And the rebel rides on his raids no more.

Honor to her ! and let a tear
Fall, for her sake, on Stonewall's bier.

Over Barbara Frietchie's grave,
Flag of freedom and union, wave !

Peace and order and beauty draw
Round thy symbol of light and law ;

And ever the stars above look down
On thy stars below in Frederick town !

JOHN GREENLEAF WHITTIER.

THE BLACK REGIMENT.

[May 27, 1863.]

DARK as the clouds of even,
Ranked in the western heaven,
Waiting the breath that lifts
All the dead mass, and drifts
Tempest and falling brand
Over a ruined land, —
So still and orderly,
Arm to arm, knee to knee,
Waiting the great event,
Stands the black regiment.

Down the long dusky line
Teeth gleam and eyeballs shine ;
And the bright bayonet,
Bristling and firmly set,
Flashed with a purpose grand,
Long ere the sharp command
Of the fierce rolling drum
Told them their time had come,
Told them what work was sent
For the black regiment.

"Now," the flag-sergeant cried,
"Though death and hell betide,
Let the whole nation see
If we are fit to be
Free in this land ; or bound
Down, like the whining hound, —
Bound with red stripes of pain
In our cold chains again ! "

O, what a shout there went
From the black regiment !

"Charge !" Trump and drum awoke ;
Onward the bondmen broke ;
Bayonet and sabre-stroke
Vainly opposed their rush.
Through the wild battle's crush,
With but one thought aflush,
Driving their lords like chaff,
In the guns' mouths they laugh ;
Or at the slippery brands
Leaping with open hands,
Down they tear man and horse,
Down in their awful course ;
Trampling with bloody heel
Over the crashing steel, —
All their eyes forward bent,
Rushed the black regiment.

"Freedom !" their battle-cry, —
"Freedom ! or leave to die ! "
Ah ! and they meant the word,
Not as with us 't is heard,
Not a mere party shout ;
They gave their spirits out,
Trusted the end to God,
And on the gory sod
Rolled in triumphant blood.
Glad to strike one free blow,
Whether for weal or woe ;
Glad to breathe one free breath,
Though on the lips of death ;
Praying, — alas ! in vain ! —
That they might fall again,
So they could once more see
That burst to liberty !
This was what "freedom" lent
To the black regiment.

Hundreds on hundreds fell ;
But they are resting well ;
Scourges and shackles strong
Never shall do them wrong.
O, to the living few,
Soldiers, be just and true !
Hail them as comrades tried ;
Fight with them side by side ;
Never, in field or tent,
Scorn the black regiment !

GEORGE HENRY BOKER.

SHERIDAN'S RIDE.

UP from the South at break of day,
Bringing to Winchester fresh dismay,
The affrighted air with a shudder bore,
Like a herald in haste, to the chieftain's door,

The terrible grumble and rumble and roar,
Telling the battle was on once more,
And Sheridan twenty miles away.

And wider still those billows of war
Thundered along the horizon's bar,
And louder yet into Winchester rolled
The roar of that red sea uncontrolled,
Making the blood of the listener cold
As he thought of the stake in that fiery fray,
With Sheridan twenty miles away.

But there is a road from Winchester town,
A good, broad highway leading down ;
And there through the flash of the morning light,
A steed as black as the steeds of night,
Was seen to pass as with eagle flight.
As if he knew the terrible need,
He stretched away with the utmost speed ;
Hills rose and fell, — but his heart was gay,
With Sheridan fifteen miles away.

Under his spurning feet the road
Like an arrowy Alpine river flowed,
And the landscape sped away behind
Like an ocean flying before the wind ;
And the steed, like a bark fed with furnace ire,
Swept on with his wild eyes full of fire ;
But, lo ! he is nearing his heart's desire,
He is snuffing the smoke of the roaring fray,
With Sheridan only five miles away.

The first that the General saw were the groups
Of stragglers, and then the retreating troops ;
What was done, — what to do, — a glance told
        him both,
And, striking his spurs with a terrible oath,
He dashed down the line mid a storm of huzzas,
And the wave of retreat checked its course there
        because
The sight of the master compelled it to pause.
With foam and with dust the black charger was
        gray,
By the flash of his eye, and his nostril's play
He seemed to the whole great army to say,
" I have brought you Sheridan all the way
From Winchester, down to save the day ! "

Hurrah, hurrah for Sheridan !
Hurrah, hurrah for horse and man !
And when their statues are placed on high,
Under the dome of the Union sky, —
The American soldier's Temple of Fame, —
There with the glorious General's name
Be it said in letters both bold and bright :
" Here is the steed that saved the day
By carrying Sheridan into the fight,
From Winchester, — twenty miles away ! "
                THOMAS BUCHANAN READ.

THE LITTLE CLOUD.

[Written in 1853.]

As when, on Carmel's sterile steep,
    The ancient prophet bowed the knee,
And seven times sent his servant forth
    To look toward the distant sea ;

There came at last a little cloud,
    Scarce larger than the human hand,
Spreading and swelling till it broke
    In showers on all the herbless land.

And hearts were glad, and shouts went up,
    And praise to Israel's mighty God,
As the sear hills grew bright with flowers,
    And verdure clothed the valley sod.

Even so our eyes have waited long ;
    But now a little cloud appears,
Spreading and swelling as it glides
    Onward into the coming years.

Bright cloud of Liberty ! full soon,
    Far stretching from the ocean strand,
Thy glorious folds shall spread abroad,
    Encircling our beloved land.

Like the sweet rain on Judah's hills,
    The glorious boon of love shall fall,
And our bond millions shall arise,
    As at an angel's trumpet-call.

Then shall a shout of joy go up,
    The wild, glad cry of freedom come
From hearts long crushed by cruel hands,
    And songs from lips long sealed and dumb.

And every bondman's chain be broke,
    And every soul that moves abroad
In this wide realm shall know and feel
    The blessed Liberty of God.
                JOHN HOWARD BRYANT.

————◆————

MARCO BOZZARIS.

[Marco Bozzaris, the Epaminondas of modern Greece, fell in a night attack upon the Turkish camp at Laspi, the site of the ancient Platæa, August 20, 1823, and expired in the moment of victory. His last words were : " To die for liberty is a pleasure, and not a pain."]

At midnight, in his guarded tent,
    The Turk was dreaming of the hour
When Greece, her knee in suppliance bent,
    Should tremble at his power.
In dreams, through camp and court, he bore
The trophies of a conqueror ;
    In dreams his song of triumph heard ;

Then wore his monarch's signet-ring,
Then pressed that monarch's throne — a king;
As wild his thoughts, and gay of wing,
  As Eden's garden bird.

At midnight, in the forest shades,
  Bozzaris ranged his Suliote band, —
True as the steel of their tried blades,
  Heroes in heart and hand.
There had the Persian's thousands stood,
There had the glad earth drunk their blood,
  On old Platæa's day;
And now there breathed that haunted air
The sons of sires who conquered there,
With arms to strike, and soul to dare,
  As quick, as far, as they.

An hour passed on, the Turk awoke:
  That bright dream was his last;
He woke — to hear his sentries shriek,
  "To arms! they come! the Greek! the Greek!"
He woke — to die midst flame, and smoke,
And shout, and groan, and sabre-stroke,
  And death-shots falling thick and fast
As lightnings from the mountain-cloud;
And heard, with voice as trumpet loud,
  Bozzaris cheer his band:
"Strike — till the last armed foe expires;
Strike — for your altars and your fires;
Strike — for the green graves of your sires,
  God, and your native land!"

They fought — like brave men, long and well;
  They piled that ground with Moslem slain:
They conquered — but Bozzaris fell,
  Bleeding at every vein.
His few surviving comrades saw
His smile when rang their proud hurrah,
  And the red field was won;
Then saw in death his eyelids close
Calmly, as to a night's repose.
  Like flowers at set of sun.

Come to the bridal chamber, death,
  Come to the mother's, when she feels,
For the first time, her first-born's breath;
  Come when the blessed seals
That close the pestilence are broke,
And crowded cities wail its stroke;
Come in consumption's ghastly form,
The earthquake shock, the ocean storm;
Come when the heart beats high and warm,
  With banquet song and dance and wine, —
And thou art terrible; the tear,
The groan, the knell, the pall, the bier,
And all we know, or dream, or fear
  Of agony, are thine.

But to the hero, when his sword
  Has won the battle for the free,

Thy voice sounds like a prophet's word,
And in its hollow tones are heard
  The thanks of millions yet to be.
Come when his task of fame is wrought;
Come with her laurel-leaf, blood-bought;
  Come in her crowning hour, — and then
Thy sunken eye's unearthly light
To him is welcome as the sight
  Of sky and stars to prisoned men;
Thy grasp is welcome as the hand
Of brother in a foreign land;
Thy summons welcome as the cry
That told the Indian isles were nigh
  To the world-seeking Genoese,
When the land-wind, from woods of palm,
And orange-groves, and fields of balm,
  Blew o'er the Haytian seas.

Bozzaris! with the storied brave
  Greece nurtured in her glory's time,
Rest thee; there is no prouder grave,
  Even in her own proud clime.
She wore no funeral weeds for thee,
  Nor bade the dark hearse wave its plume,
Like torn branch from death's leafless tree,
In sorrow's pomp and pageantry,
  The heartless luxury of the tomb.
But she remembers thee as one
Long loved, and for a season gone.
For thee her poet's lyre is wreathed,
Her marble wrought, her music breathed;
For thee she rings the birthday bells;
Of thee her babes' first lisping tells;
For thine her evening prayer is said
At palace couch and cottage bed.
Her soldier, closing with the foe,
Gives for thy sake a deadlier blow;
His plighted maiden, when she fears
For him, the joy of her young years,
Thinks of thy fate, and checks her tears.
  And she, the mother of thy boys,
Though in her eye and faded cheek
Is read the grief she will not speak,
  The memory of her buried joys, —
And even she who gave thee birth, —
Will, by her pilgrim-circled hearth,
  Talk of thy doom without a sigh;
For thou art freedom's now, and fame's, —
One of the few, the immortal names
  That were not born to die.
             FITZ-GREENE HALLECK.

GREECE.

THE "GIAOUR."

CLIME of the unforgotten brave!
Whose land from plain to mountain-cave

Was Freedom's home or Glory's grave !
Shrine of the mighty ! can it be
That this is all remains of thee ?
Approach, thou craven, crouching slave ;
　Say, is not this Thermopylæ ?
These waters blue that round you lave,
　O servile offspring of the free,
Pronounce what sea, what shore is this ?
The gulf, the rock of Salamis !
These scenes, their story not unknown,
Arise and make again your own ;
Snatch from the ashes of your sires
The embers of their former fires ;
And he who in the strife expires
Will add to theirs a name of fear
That Tyranny shall quake to hear,
And leave his sons a hope, a fame,
They too will rather die than shame ;
For Freedom's battle once begun,
Bequeathed by bleeding sire to son,
Though baffled oft is ever won.
Bear witness, Greece, thy living page,
Attest it, many a deathless age :
While kings, in dusty darkness hid,
Have left a nameless pyramid,
Thy heroes, though the general doom
Have swept the column from their tomb,
A mightier monument command,
The mountains of their native land !
There points thy muse to stranger's eye
The graves of those that cannot die !
'T were long to tell, and sad to trace,
Each step from splendor to disgrace :
Enough, — no foreign foe could quell
Thy soul, till from itself it fell ;
Yes ! self-abasement paved the way
To villain-bonds and despot sway.
What can he tell who treads thy shore ?
　No legend of thine olden time,
No theme on which the muse might soar,
High as thine own in days of yore,
　When man was worthy of thy clime.
The hearts within thy valleys bred,
The fiery souls that might have led
　Thy sons to deeds sublime,
Now crawl from cradle to the grave,
Slaves — nay, the bondsmen of a slave,
　And callous save to crime.
　　　　　　　　　　　　BYRON.

POLAND.

FROM "THE PLEASURES OF MEMORY."

WARSAW's last champion from her height sur-
　veyed,
Wide o'er the fields, a waste of ruin laid ;
"O Heaven !" he cried, "my bleeding country
　save ! —

Is there no hand on high to shield the brave ?
Yet, though destruction sweep those lovely plains,
Rise, fellow-men ! our country yet remains !
By that dread name, we wave the sword on high,
And swear for her to live — with her to die !"
He said, and on the rampart-heights arrayed
His trusty warriors, few, but undismayed ;
Firm-paced and slow, a horrid front they form,
Still as the breeze, but dreadful as the storm ;
Low murmuring sounds along their banners fly,
Revenge, or death, — the watchword and reply ;
Then pealed the notes, omnipotent to charm,
And the loud tocsin tolled their last alarm ! —
　In vain, alas ! in vain, ye gallant few !
From rank to rank your volleyed thunder flew : —
O, bloodiest picture in the book of Time !
Sarmatia fell, unwept, without a crime ;
Found not a generous friend, a pitying foe,
Strength in her arms, nor mercy in her woe !
Dropped from her nerveless grasp the shattered
　spear,
Closed her bright eye, and curbed her high ca-
　reer ;
Hope, for a season, bade the world farewell,
And Freedom shrieked — as Kosciusko fell !
　　　　　　　　　　　THOMAS CAMPBELL.

MEN AND BOYS.

THE storm is out ; the land is roused ;
Where is the coward who sits well housed ?
Fie on thee, boy, disguised in curls,
Behind the stove, 'mong gluttons and girls,
　A graceless, worthless wight thou must be ;
　No German maid desires thee,
　No German song inspires thee,
　No German Rhine-wine fires thee.
　　　Forth in the van,
　　　Man by man,
　Swing the battle-sword who can.

When, we stand watching, the livelong night,
Through piping storms, till morning light,
Thou to thy downy bed canst creep,
And there in dreams of rapture sleep.
　A graceless, worthless wight, etc.

When hoarse and shrill, the trumpet's blast,
Like the thunder of God, makes our hearts beat
　fast,
Thou in the theatre lov'st to appear,
Where trills and quavers tickle the ear.
　A graceless, worthless wight, etc.

When the glare of noonday scorches the brain,
When our parchéd lips seek water in vain,
Thou canst make champagne corks fly
At the groaning tables of luxury.
　A graceless, worthless wight, etc.

When we, as we rush to the strangling fight,
Send home to our true-loves a long "Good-night,"
Thou canst hie thee where love is sold,
And buy thy pleasure with paltry gold.
   A graceless, worthless wight, etc.

When lance and bullet come whistling by,
And death in a thousand shapes draws nigh,
Thou canst sit at thy cards, and kill
King, queen, and knave with thy spadille.
   A graceless, worthless wight, etc.

If on the red field our bell should toll,
Then welcome be death to the patriot's soul.
Thy pampered flesh shall quake at its doom,
And crawl in silk to a hopeless tomb.
   A pitiful exit thine shall be ;
   No German maid shall weep for thee,
   No German song shall they sing for thee,
   No German goblets shall ring for thee.
         Forth in the van,
         Man for man,
   Swing the battle-sword who can !
         KÖRNER. Translation of
         CHARLES T. BROOKS.

ITALY.

FROM "CASA GUIDI WINDOWS."

" LESS wretched if less fair." Perhaps a truth
Is so far plain in this, — that Italy,
   Long trammelled with the purple of her youth
Against her age's ripe activity,
   Sits still upon her tombs, without death's ruth,
But also without life's brave energy.
   " Now tell us what is Italy ?" men ask :
And others answer, " Virgil, Cicero,
   Catullus, Cæsar." What beside ? to task
The memory closer, — " Why, Boccaccio,
   Dante, Petrarca," — and if still the flask
Appears to yield its wine by drops too slow, —
   " Angelo, Raffael, Pergolese," — all
Whose strong hearts beat through stone, or
         charged again
   The paints with fire of souls electrical,
Or broke up heaven for music. What more then ?
   Why, then, no more. The chaplet's last beads
         fall
In naming the last saintship within ken,
   And, after that, none prayeth in the land.
Alas, this Italy has too long swept
   Heroic ashes up for hour-glass sand ;
Of her own past, impassioned nympholept !
   Consenting to be nailed here by the hand
To the very bay-tree under which she stepped
   A queen of old, and plucked a leafy branch.
And, licensing the world too long indeed
   To use her broad phylacteries to stanch

And stop her bloody lips, she takes no heed
   How one clear word would draw an avalanche
Of living sons around her, to succeed
   The vanished generations.   Can she count
These oil-eaters, with large, live, mobile mouths
   Agape for macaroni, in the amount
Of consecrated heroes of her south's
   Bright rosary ?   The pitcher at the fount,
The gift of gods, being broken, she much loathes
   To let the ground-leaves of the place confer
A natural bowl.   So henceforth she would seem
   No nation, but the poet's pensioner,
With alms from every land of song and dream,
   While aye her pipers sadly pipe of her,
Until their proper breaths, in that extreme
   Of sighing, split the reed on which they played !
         ELIZABETH BARRETT BROWNING.

A COURT LADY.

I.

HER hair was tawny with gold, her eyes with
         purple were dark,
Her cheeks' pale opal burnt with a red and rest-
         less spark.

II.

Never was lady of Milan nobler in name and in
         race ;
Never was lady of Italy fairer to see in the face.

III.

Never was lady on earth more true as woman and
         wife,
Larger in judgment and instinct, prouder in
         manners and life.

IV.

She stood in the early morning, and said to her
         maidens, " Bring
That silken robe made ready to wear at the court
         of the king.

V.

" Bring me the clasps of diamond, lucid, clear
         of the mote,
Clasp me the large at the waist, and clasp me the
         small at the throat.

VI.

" Diamonds to fasten the hair, and diamonds to
         fasten the sleeves,
Laces to drop from their rays, like a powder of
         snow from the eaves."

VII.

Gorgeous she entered the sunlight which gath-
         ered her up in a flame,
While, straight in her open carriage, she to the
         hospital came.

VIII.

In she went at the door, and gazing, from end to end,
"Many and low are the pallets, but each is the place of a friend."

IX.

Up she passed through the wards, and stood at a young man's bed :
Bloody the band on his brow, and livid the droop of his head.

X.

"Art thou a Lombard, my brother ? Happy art thou !" she cried,
And smiled like Italy on him : he dreamed in her face and died.

XI.

Pale with his passing soul, she went on still to a second :
He was a grave, hard man, whose years by dungeons were reckoned.

XII.

Wounds in his body were sore, wounds in his life were sorer.
"Art thou a Romagnole ?" Her eyes drove lightnings before her.

XIII.

"Austrian and priest had joined to double and tighten the cord
Able to bind thee, O strong one, — free by the stroke of a sword.

XIV.

"Now be grave for the rest of us, using the life overcast
To ripen our wine of the present (too new) in glooms of the past."

XV.

Down she stepped to a pallet where lay a face like a girl's,
Young, and pathetic with dying, — a deep black hole in the curls.

XVI.

"Art thou from Tuscany, brother ? and seest thou, dreaming in pain,
Thy mother stand in the piazza, searching the list of the slain ?"

XVII.

Kind as a mother herself, she touched his cheeks with her hands :
"Blessed is she who has borne thee, although she should weep as she stands."

XVIII.

On she passed to a Frenchman, his arm carried off by a ball :
Kneeling, . . "O more than my brother ! how shall I thank thee for all ?

XIX.

"Each of the heroes around us has fought for his land and line,
But *thou* hast fought for a stranger, in hate of a wrong not thine.

XX.

Happy are all free peoples, too strong to be dispossessed.
But blessed are those among nations who dare to be strong for the rest !"

XXI.

Ever she passed on her way, and came to a couch where pined
One with a face from Venetia, white with a hope out of mind.

XXII.

Long she stood and gazed, and twice she tried at the name,
But two great crystal tears were all that faltered and came.

XXIII.

Only a tear for Venice ? — she turned as in passion and loss,
And stooped to his forehead and kissed it, as if she were kissing the cross.

XXIV.

Faint with that strain of heart, she moved on then to another,
Stern and strong in his death. "And dost thou suffer, my brother ?"

XXV.

Holding his hands in hers : — "Out of the Piedmont lion
Cometh the sweetness of freedom ! sweetest to live or to die on."

XXVI.

Holding his cold rough hands, — "Well, O, well have ye done
In noble, noble Piedmont, who would not be noble alone."

XXVII.

Back he fell while she spoke. She rose to her feet with a spring, —
"That was a Piedmontese ! and this is the Court of the King."

ELIZABETH BARRETT BROWNING.

THE MINSTREL BOY.

THE minstrel boy to the war is gone,
  In the ranks of death you 'll find him,
His father's sword he has girded on,
  And his wild harp slung behind him.
" Land of song ! " said the warrior bard,
  " Though all the world betrays thee,
One sword, at least, thy rights shall guard,
  One faithful harp shall praise thee ! "

The minstrel fell ! — but the foeman's chain
  Could not bring his proud soul under ;
The harp he loved ne'er spoke again,
  For he tore its chords asunder,
And said, " No chains shall sully thee,
  Thou soul of love and bravery !
Thy songs were made for the pure and free,
  They shall never sound in slavery ! "
        THOMAS MOORE (" *Irish Melodies* ").

LET ERIN REMEMBER THE DAYS OF OLD.

LET Erin remember the days of old,
  Ere her faithless sons betrayed her ;
When Malachi wore the collar of gold
  Which he won from her proud invader ;
When her kings with standard of green unfurled
  Led the Red-Branch Knights to danger,
Ere the emerald gem of the western world
  Was set in the crown of a stranger.

On Lough Neagh's bank as the fisherman strays,
  When the clear cold eve 's declining,
He sees the round towers of other days
  In the wave beneath him shining !
Thus shall memory often, in dreams sublime,
  Catch a glimpse of the days that are over,
Thus, sighing, look through the waves of time
  For the long-faded glories they cover !
        THOMAS MOORE (" *Irish Melodies* ").

THE HARP THAT ONCE THROUGH TARA'S HALLS.

THE harp that once through Tara's halls
  The soul of music shed,
Now hangs as mute on Tara's walls
  As if that soul were fled.
So sleeps the pride of former days,
  So glory's thrill is o'er,
And hearts that once beat high for praise
  Now feel that pulse no more !

No more to chiefs and ladies bright
  The harp of Tara swells ;
The chord alone that breaks at night
  Its tale of ruin tells.
Thus Freedom now so seldom wakes,
  The only throb she gives
Is when some heart indignant breaks,
  To show that still she lives.
        THOMAS MOORE (" *Irish Melodies* ").

O, BREATHE NOT HIS NAME!

(ROBERT EMMETT.)

O, BREATHE not his name ! let it sleep in the shade,
Where cold and unhonored his relics are laid ;
Sad, silent, and dark be the tears that we shed,
As the night dew that falls on the grave o'er his head.

But the night dew that falls, though in silence it weeps,
Shall brighten with verdure the grave where he sleeps ;
And the tear that we shed, though in secret it rolls,
Shall long keep his memory green in our souls.
        THOMAS MOORE.

SHAN VAN VOCHT.

O, THE French are on the say !
  Says the Shan Van Vocht ;
The French are on the say,
  Says the Shan Van Vocht ;
O, the French are in the bay !
They 'll be here without delay,
And the Orange will decay,
  Says the Shan Van Vocht.
    O, the French are in the bay !
    They 'll be here by break of day,
    And the Orange will decay,
    Says the Shan Van Vocht.

And where will they have their camp ?
  Says the Shan Van Vocht ;
Where will they have their camp ?
  Says the Shan Van Vocht ;
On the Currach of Kildare,
The boys they will be there
With their pikes in good repair,
  Says the Shan Van Vocht.
    To the Currach of Kildare
    The boys they will repair,
    And Lord Edward will be there,
    Says the Shan Van Vocht.

Then what will the yeomen do ?
Says the Shan Van Vocht ;
What will the yeomen do ?
Says the Shan Van Vocht ;
What should the yeomen do,
But throw off the red and blue,
And swear that they 'll be true
To the Shan Van Vocht ?
What should the yeomen do,
But throw off the red and blue,
And swear that they'll be true
To the Shan Van Vocht ?

And what color will they wear ?
Says the Shan Van Vocht ;
What color will they wear ?
Says the Shan Van Vocht ;
What color should be seen,
Where our fathers' homes have been,
But our own immortal green ?
Says the Shan Van Vocht.
What color should be seen,
Where our fathers' homes have been,
But our own immortal green ?
Says the Shan Van Vocht.

And will Ireland then be free ?
Says the Shan Van Vocht ;
Will Ireland then be free ?
Says the Shan Van Vocht ;
Yes ! Ireland shall be free,
From the centre to the sea ;
Then hurrah for liberty !
Says the Shan Van Vocht.
Yes ! Ireland shall be free,
From the centre to the sea ;
Then hurrah for liberty !
Says the Shan Van Vocht.

ANONYMOUS.

AS BY THE SHORE AT BREAK OF DAY.

As by the shore, at break of day,
A vanquished chief expiring lay,
Upon the sands, with broken sword,
  He traced his farewell to the free ;
And there the last unfinished word
  He dying wrote, was " Liberty ! "

At night a sea-bird shrieked the knell
Of him who thus for freedom fell ;
The words he wrote, ere evening came,
  Were covered by the sounding sea ; —
So pass away the cause and name
Of him who dies for liberty !

THOMAS MOORE.

GOUGAUNE BARRA.

[The Lake of Gougaune Barra, i. e. the hollow, or recess of St. Finn Bar, in the rugged territory of Ibh-Laoghaire (the O'Learys' country), in the west end of the county of Cork, is the parent of the river Lee. Its waters embrace a small but verdant island of about half an acre in extent, which approaches its eastern shore. The lake, as its name implies, is situate in a deep hollow, surrounded on every side (save the east, where its superabundant waters are discharged) by vast and almost perpendicular mountains, whose dark inverted shadows are gloomily reflected in its still waters beneath.]

THERE is a green island in lone Gougaune Barra,
Where Allua of songs rushes forth as an arrow ;
In deep-valleyed Desmond — a thousand wild
    fountains
Come down to that lake from their home in the
    mountains.
There grows the wild ash, and a time-stricken
    willow
Looks chidingly down on the mirth of the billow ;
As, like some gay child, that sad monitor scorning,
It lightly laughs back to the laugh of the morning.

And its zone of dark hills, — O, to see them all
    brightening,
When the tempest flings out its red banner of
    lightning,
And the waters rush down, mid the thunder's
    deep rattle,
Like clans from their hills at the voice of the battle ;
And brightly the fire-crested billows are gleaming,
And wildly from Mullagh the eagles are screaming !
O, where is the dwelling, in valley or highland,
So meet for a bard as this lone little island ?

How oft when the summer sun rested on Clara,
And lit the dark heath on the hills of Ivera,
Have I sought thee, sweet spot, from my home
    by the ocean,
And trod all thy wilds with a minstrel's devotion,
And thought of thy bards, when assembling to-
    gether,
In the cleft of thy rocks, or the depth of thy
    heather ;
They fled from the Saxon's dark bondage and
    slaughter,
And waked their last song by the rush of thy water.

High sons of the lyre, O, how proud was the
    feeling,
To think while alone through that solitude steal-
    ing,
Though loftier minstrels green Erin can number,
I only awoke your wild harp from its slumber,
And mingled once more with the voice of those
    fountains
The songs even Echo forgot on her mountains ;
And gleaned each gray legend that darkly was
    sleeping
Where the mist and the rain o'er their beauty
    were creeping !

Least bard of the hills ! were it mine to inherit
The fire of thy harp and the wing of thy spirit,
With the wrongs which like thee to our country
    have bound me,
Did your mantle of song fling its radiance around
    me,
Still, still in those wilds might young Liberty rally,
And send her strong shout over mountain and
    valley,
The star of the west might yet rise in its glory,
And the land that was darkest be brightest in story.

I too shall be gone ; — but my name shall be spoken
When Erin awakes and her fetters are broken.
Some minstrel will come, in the summer eve's
    gleaming,
When Freedom's young light on his spirit is
    beaming,
And bend o'er my grave with a tear of emotion,
Where calm Avon-Buee seeks the kisses of ocean,
Or plant a wild wreath, from the banks of that river,
O'er the heart and the harp that are sleeping for-
    ever.
                    J. J. CALLANAN.

EXILE OF ERIN.

THERE came to the beach a poor exile of Erin,
    The dew on his thin robe was heavy and chill ;
For his country he sighed, when at twilight
    repairing
To wander alone by the wind-beaten hill.
But the day-star attracted his eye's sad devotion,
For it rose o'er his own native isle of the ocean,
Where once, in the fire of his youthful emotion,
He sang the bold anthem of Erin go bragh.

Sad is my fate ! said the heart-broken stranger ;
    The wild deer and wolf to a covert can flee,
But I have no refuge from famine and danger,
    A home and a country remain not to me.
Never again in the green sunny bowers
Where my forefathers lived shall I spend the
    sweet hours,
Or cover my harp with the wild-woven flowers,
    And strike to the numbers of Erin go bragh !

Erin, my country ! though sad and forsaken,
    In dreams I revisit thy sea-beaten shore ;
But, alas ! in a far foreign land I awaken,
    And sigh for the friends who can meet me no
    more !
O cruel fate ! wilt thou never replace me
In a mansion of peace, where no perils can chase
    me ?
Never again shall my brothers embrace me ?
    They died to defend me, or live to deplore !

Where is my cabin door, fast by the wildwood ?
    Sisters and sire, did ye weep for its fall ?
Where is the mother that looked on my childhood ?
    And where is the bosom-friend, dearer than all ?
O my sad heart ! long abandoned by pleasure,
Why did it dote on a fast-fading treasure ?
Tears, like the rain-drop, may fall without
    measure,
But rapture and beauty they cannot recall.

Yet, all its sad recollections suppressing,
    One dying wish my lone bosom can draw, —
Erin, an exile bequeaths thee his blessing !
    Land of my forefathers, Erin go bragh !
Buried and cold, when my heart stills her motion,
Green be thy fields, sweetest isle of the ocean !
And thy harp-striking bards sing aloud with
    devotion, —
Erin mavourneen, Erin go bragh !
                    THOMAS CAMPBELL.

IRELAND.

THEY are dying ! they are dying ! where the
    golden corn is growing ;
They are dying ! they are dying ! where the
    crowded herds are lowing ;
They are gasping for existence where the streams
    of life are flowing,
And they perish of the plague where the breeze
    of health is blowing !

God of justice ! God of power !
    Do we dream ? Can it be,
In this land, at this hour,
    With the blossom on the tree,
In the gladsome month of May,
When the young lambs play,
When Nature looks around
    On her waking children now,
The seed within the ground,
    The bud upon the bough ?
Is it right, is it fair,
That we perish of despair
In this land, on this soil,
    Where our destiny is set,
Which we cultured with our toil,
    And watered with our sweat ?

We have ploughed, we have sown,
But the crop was not our own ;
We have reaped, but harpy hands
Swept the harvest from our lands ;
We were perishing for food,
When lo ! in pitying mood,
Our kindly rulers gave
The fat fluid of the slave,
While our corn filled the manger
Of the war-horse of the stranger !

God of mercy ! must this last ?
  Is this land preordained,
For the present and the past
    And the future, to be chained, —
      To be ravaged, to be drained,
  To be robbed, to be spoiled,
    To be hushed, to be whipt,
    Its soaring pinions clipt,
  And its every effort foiled ?

Do our numbers multiply
  But to perish and to die ?
    Is this all our destiny below,
  That our bodies, as they rot,
  May fertilize the spot
    Where the harvests of the stranger grow ?

If this be, indeed, our fate,
  Far, far better now, though late,
That we seek some other land and try some
    other zone ;
    The coldest, bleakest shore
    Will surely yield us more
Than the storehouse of the stranger that we dare
    not call our own.

Kindly brothers of the West,
  Who from Liberty's full breast
Have fed us, who are orphans beneath a step-dame's
    frown,
    Behold our happy state,
    And weep your wretched fate
That you share not in the splendors of our empire
    and our crown!

Kindly brothers of the East, —
  Thou great tiara'd priest,
Thou sanctified Rienzi of Rome and of the earth, —
    Or thou who bear'st control
    Over golden Istambol,
Who felt for our misfortunes and helped us in
    our dearth, —

Turn here your wondering eyes,
  Call your wisest of the wise,
Your muftis and your ministers, your men of
    deepest lore ;
    Let the sagest of your sages
    Ope our island's mystic pages,
And explain unto your highness the wonders of
    our shore.

A fruitful, teeming soil,
  Where the patient peasants toil
Beneath the summer's sun and the watery winter
    sky ;
    Where they tend the golden grain
    Till it bends upon the plain,
Then reap it for the stranger, and turn aside to die.

Where they watch their flocks increase,
  And store the snowy fleece
Till they send it to their masters to be woven
    o'er the waves ;
    Where, having sent their meat
    For the foreigner to eat,
Their mission is fulfilled, and they creep into
    their graves.

'T is for this they are dying where the golden
    corn is growing,
'T is for this they are dying where the crowded
    herds are lowing,
'T is for this they are dying where the streams
    of life are flowing,
And they perish of the plague where the breeze
    of health is blowing !

DENIS FLORENCE MAC-CARTHY.

1847.

GIVE ME THREE GRAINS OF CORN, MOTHER.

THE IRISH FAMINE.

Give me three grains of corn, mother, —
  Only three grains of corn ;
It will keep the little life I have
  Till the coming of the morn.
I am dying of hunger and cold, mother —
  Dying of hunger and cold ;
And half the agony of such a death
  My lips have never told.

It has gnawed like a wolf, at my heart, mother, —
  A wolf that is fierce for blood ;
All the livelong day, and the night beside,
  Gnawing for lack of food.
I dreamed of bread in my sleep, mother,
  And the sight was heaven to see ;
I awoke with an eager, famishing lip,
  But you had no bread for me.

How could I look to you, mother, —
  How could I look to you,
For bread to give to your starving boy,
  When you were starving too ?
For I read the famine in your cheek,
  And in your eyes so wild,
And I felt it in your bony hand,
  As you laid it on your child.

The Queen has lands and gold, mother, —
  The Queen has lands and gold,
While you are forced to your empty breast
  A skeleton babe to hold, —
A babe that is dying of want, mother,
  As I am dying now,
With a ghastly look in its sunken eye,
  And famine upon its brow.

What has poor Ireland done, mother, —
  What has poor Ireland done,
That the world looks on, and sees us starve,
  Perishing, one by one ?
Do the men of England care not, mother, —
  The great men and the high,
For the suffering sons of Erin's isle,
  Whether they live or die ?

There is many a brave heart here, mother,
  Dying of want and cold,
While only across the Channel, mother,
  Are many that roll in gold ;
There are rich and proud men there, mother,
  With wondrous wealth to view,
And the bread they fling to their dogs to-night
  Would give life to *me* and *you.*

Come nearer to my side, mother,
  Come nearer to my side,
And hold me fondly, as you held
  My father when *he* died ;
Quick, for I cannot see you, mother,
  My breath is almost gone ;
Mother ! dear mother ! ere I die,
  Give me three grains of corn.
                  MISS EDWARDS.

WHAT CONSTITUTES A STATE?

WHAT constitutes a state ?
Not high-raised battlement or labored mound,
  Thick wall or moated gate ;
Not cities proud with spires and turrets crowned ;
  Not bays and broad-armed ports,
Where, laughing at the storm, rich navies ride ;
  Not starred and spangled courts,
Where low-browed baseness wafts perfume to
    pride.
  No : — men, high-minded men,
With powers as far above dull brutes endued
  In forest, brake, or den,
As beasts excel cold rocks and brambles rude, —
  Men who their duties know,
But know their rights, and, knowing, dare main-
    tain,
  Prevent the long-aimed blow,
And crush the tyrant while they rend the chain ;
  These constitute a state ;
And sovereign law, that state's collected will,
  O'er thrones and globes elate
Sits empress, crowning good, repressing ill.
  Smit by her sacred frown,
The fiend, Dissension, like a vapor sinks ;
  And e'en the all-dazzling crown
Hides his faint rays, and at her bidding shrinks ;
  Such was this heaven-loved isle,

Than Lesbos fairer and the Cretan shore !
  No more shall freedom smile ?
Shall Britons languish, and be men no more ?
  Since all must life resign,
Those sweet rewards which decorate the brave
  'T is folly to decline,
And steal inglorious to the silent grave.
             SIR WILLIAM JONES.

CARACTACUS.

BEFORE proud Rome's imperial throne
  In mind's unconquered mood,
As if the triumph were his own,
  The dauntless captive stood.
None, to have seen his freeborn air,
Had fancied him a captive there.

Though through the crowded streets of Rome,
  With slow and stately tread,
Far from his own loved island home,
  That day in triumph led, —
Unbound his head, unbent his knee,
Undimmed his eye, his aspect free.

A free and fearless glance he cast
  On temple, arch, and tower,
By which the long procession passed
  Of Rome's victorious power ;
And somewhat of a scornful smile
Upcurled his haughty lip the while.

And now he stood, with brow serene,
  Where slaves might prostrate fall,
Bearing a Briton's manly mien
  In Cæsar's palace hall ;
Claiming, with kindled brow and cheek,
The liberty e'en there to speak.

Nor could Rome's haughty lord withstand
  The claim that look preferred,
But motioned with uplifted hand
  The suppliant should be heard, —
If he indeed a suppliant were
Whose glance demanded audience there.

Deep stillness fell on all the crowd,
  From Claudius on his throne
Down to the meanest slave that bowed
  At his imperial throne ;
Silent his fellow-captive's grief
As fearless spoke the Island Chief.

"Think not, thou eagle Lord of Rome,
  And master of the world,
Though victory's banner o'er thy dome
  In triumph now is furled,
I would address thee as thy slave,
But as the bold should greet the brave !

"I might perchance, could I have deigned,
    To hold a vassal's throne,
E'en now in Britain's isle have reigned
    A king in name alone,
Yet holding, as thy meek ally,
A monarch's mimic pageantry.

"Then through Rome's crowded streets to-day
    I might have rode with thee,
Not in a captive's base array,
    But fetterless and free, —
If freedom he could hope to find,
Whose bondage is of heart and mind.

"But canst thou marvel that, freeborn,
    With heart and soul unquelled,
Throne, crown, and sceptre I should scorn,
    By thy permission held?
Or that I should retain my right
Till wrested by a conqueror's might?

"Rome, with her palaces and towers,
    By us unwished, unreft,
Her homely huts and woodland bowers
    To Britain might have left;
Worthless to you their wealth must be,
But dear to us, for they were free!

"I might have bowed before, but where
    Had been thy triumph now?
To my resolve no yoke to bear
    Thou ow'st thy laurelled brow;
Inglorious victory had been thine,
And more inglorious bondage mine.

"Now I have spoken, do thy will;
    Be life or death my lot,
Since Britain's throne no more I fill,
    To me it matters not.
My fame is clear; but on my fate
Thy glory or thy shame must wait."

He ceased; from all around upsprung
    A murmur of applause,
For well had truth and freedom's tongue
    Maintained their holy cause.
Their conqueror was their captive then,
He bade the slave be free again.
                    BERNARD BARTON.

———

BOSTON HYMN.

READ IN MUSIC HALL, JANUARY 1, 1863.

THE word of the Lord by night
To the watching Pilgrims came,
As they sat by the seaside,
And filled their hearts with flame.

God said, I am tired of kings,
I suffer them no more;
Up to my ear the morning brings
The outrage of the poor.

Think ye I made this ball
A field of havoc and war,
Where tyrants great and tyrants small
Might harry the weak and poor?

My angel, — his name is Freedom, —
Choose him to be your king;
He shall cut pathways east and west,
And fend you with his wing.

Lo! I uncover the land
Which I hid of old time in the West,
As the sculptor uncovers the statue
When he has wrought his best;

I show Columbia, of the rocks
Which dip their foot in the seas,
And soar to the air-borne flocks
Of clouds, and the boreal fleece.

I will divide my goods;
Call in the wretch and slave:
None shall rule but the humble,
And none but Toil shall have.

I will have never a noble,
No lineage counted great;
Fishers and choppers and ploughmen
Shall constitute a state.

Go, cut down trees in the forest,
And trim the straightest boughs;
Cut down trees in the forest,
And build me a wooden house.

Call the people together,
The young men and the sires,
The digger in the harvest-field,
Hireling, and him that hires;

And here in a pine state-house
They shall choose men to rule
In every needful faculty,
In church and state and school.

Lo, now! if these poor men
Can govern the land and sea,
And make just laws below the sun,
As planets faithful be.

And ye shall succor men;
'T is nobleness to serve;
Help them who cannot help again:
Beware from right to swerve.

I break your bonds and masterships,
And I unchain the slave :
Free be his heart and hand henceforth
As wind and wandering wave.

I cause from every creature
His proper good to flow ;
As much as he is and doeth,
So much he shall bestow.

But, laying hands on another
To coin his labor and sweat,
He goes in pawn to his victim
For eternal years in debt.

To-day unbind the captive,
So only are ye unbound ;
Lift up a people from the dust,
Trump of their rescue, sound !

Pay ransom to the owner,
And fill the bag to the brim.
Who is the owner ?   The slave is owner,
And ever was.   Pay him.

O North ! give him beauty for rags,
And honor, O South ! for his shame ;
Nevada ! coin thy golden crags
With Freedom's image and name.

Up ! and the dusky race
That sat in darkness long,
Be swift their feet as antelopes,
And as behemoth strong.

Come, East and West and North,
By races, as snow-flakes,
And carry my purpose forth,
Which neither halts nor shakes.

My will fulfilled shall be,
For, in daylight or in dark,
My thunderbolt has eyes to see
His way home to the mark.
                    RALPH WALDO EMERSON.

THE LANDING OF THE PILGRIM FA-THERS IN NEW ENGLAND.

THE breaking waves dashed high
    On a stern and rock-bound coast,
And the woods against a stormy sky
    Their giant branches tossed ;

And the heavy night hung dark
    The hills and waters o'er,
When a band of exiles moored their bark
    On the wild New England shore.

Not as the conqueror comes,
    They, the true-hearted, came ;
Not with the roll of the stirring drums,
    And the trumpet that sings of fame ;

Not as the flying come,
    In silence and in fear ; —
They shook the depths of the desert gloom
    With their hymns of lofty cheer.

Amidst the storm they sang,
    And the stars heard, and the sea ;
And the sounding aisles of the dim woods rang
    To the anthem of the free.

The ocean eagle soared
    From his nest by the white wave's foam,
And the rocking pines of the forest roared, —
    This was their welcome home.

There were men with hoary hair
    Amidst that pilgrim-band :
Why had they come to wither there,
    Away from their childhood's land ?

There was woman's fearless eye,
    Lit by her deep love's truth ;
There was manhood's brow serenely high,
    And the fiery heart of youth.

What sought they thus afar ?
    Bright jewels of the mine ?
The wealth of seas, the spoils of war ? —
    They sought a faith's pure shrine !

Ay, call it holy ground,
    The soil where first they trod ;
They have left unstained what there they found, —
    Freedom to worship God.
                    FELICIA HEMANS.

THE FREEMAN.

FROM "THE WINTER MORNING WALK."

HE is the freeman whom the truth makes free,
And all are slaves beside.   There 's not a chain
That hellish foes confederate for his harm
Can wind around him, but he casts it off
With as much ease as Samson his green withes.
He looks abroad into the varied field
Of nature ; and though poor, perhaps, compared
With those whose mansions glitter in his sight,
Calls the delightful scenery all his own.
His are the mountains, and the valley his,
And the resplendent rivers.   His to enjoy
With a propriety that none can feel,
But who, with filial confidence inspired,

Can lift to heaven an unpresumptuous eye,
And smiling say, "My Father made them all!"
Are they not his by a peculiar right,
And by an emphasis of interest his,
Whose eyes they fill with tears of holy joy,
Whose heart with praise, and whose exalted mind
With worthy thoughts of that unwearied love
That planned and built, and still upholds, a world
So clothed with beauty for rebellious man?
Yes, ye may fill your garners, ye that reap
The loaded soil, and ye may waste much good
In senseless riot; but ye will not find
In feast, or in the chase, in song or dance,
A liberty like his, who, unimpeached
Of usurpation, and to no man's wrong,
Appropriates nature as his Father's work,
And has a richer use of yours than you.
He is indeed a freeman.   Free by birth
Of no mean city, planned or e'er the hills
Were built, the fountains opened, or the sea
With all his roaring multitude of waves.
His freedom is the same in every state;
And no condition of this changeful life,
So manifold in cares, whose every day
Bring its own evil with it, makes it less.
For he has wings that neither sickness, pain,
Nor penury can cripple or confine;
No nook so narrow but he spreads them there
With ease, and is at large.   The oppressor holds
His body bound; but knows not what a range
His spirit takes, unconscious of a chain;
And that to bind him is a vain attempt,
Whom God delights in, and in whom he dwells.
                              WILLIAM COWPER.

SLAVERY.

FROM "THE TIMEPIECE."

O FOR a lodge in some vast wilderness,
Some boundless contiguity of shade,
Where rumor of oppression and deceit,
Of unsuccessful or successful war,
Might never reach me more! My ear is pained,
My soul is sick, with every day's report
Of wrong and outrage with which earth is filled.
There is no flesh in man's obdurate heart;
It does not feel for man; the natural bond
Of brotherhood is severed as the flax,
That falls asunder at the touch of fire.
He finds his fellow guilty of a skin
Not colored like his own, and, having power
To enforce the wrong, for such a worthy cause
Dooms and devotes him as his lawful prey.
Lands intersected by a narrow frith
Abhor each other.   Mountains interposed
Make enemies of nations, who had else

Like kindred drops been mingled into one.
Thus man devotes his brother, and destroys;
And, worse than all, and most to be deplored
As human nature's broadest, foulest blot,
Chains him, and tasks him, and exacts his sweat
With stripes, that Mercy, with a bleeding heart,
Weeps, when she sees inflicted on a beast.
Then what is man? And what man, seeing this,
And having human feelings, does not blush,
And hang his head, to think himself a man?
I would not have a slave to till my ground,
To carry me, to fan me while I sleep,
And tremble when I wake, for all the wealth
That sinews bought and sold have ever earned.
No; dear as freedom is, and in my heart's
Just estimation prized above all price,
I had much rather be myself the slave,
And wear the bonds, than fasten them on him.
We have no slaves at home. — Then why abroad?
And they themselves once ferried o'er the wave
That parts us are emancipate and loosed.
Slaves cannot breathe in England; if their lungs
Receive our air, that moment they are free;
They touch our country, and their shackles fall.
That 's noble, and bespeaks a nation proud
And jealous of the blessing.   Spread it then,
And let it circulate through every vein
Of all your empire; that, where Britain's power
Is felt, mankind may feel her mercy too.
                              WILLIAM COWPER.

BATTLE—HYMN OF THE REPUBLIC.

MINE eyes have seen the glory of the coming of
        the Lord:
He is trampling out the vintage where the grapes
        of wrath are stored;
He hath loosed the fateful lightning of his terri-
        ble swift sword.
        His truth is marching on.

I have seen him in the watch-fires of a hundred
        circling camps;
They have builded him an altar in the evening
        dews and damps;
I can read his righteous sentence by the dim and
        flaring lamps.
        His day is marching on.

I have read a fiery gospel, writ in burnished rows
        of steel:
"As ye deal with my contemners, so with you
        my grace shall deal;
Let the Hero, born of woman, crush the serpent
        with his heel,
        Since God is marching on."

He has sounded forth the trumpet that shall
    never call retreat ;
He is sifting out the hearts of men before his
    judgment-seat :
O, be swift, my soul, to answer him ! be jubilant
    my feet !
    Our God is marching on.

In the beauty of the lilies Christ was born across
    the sea,
With a glory in his bosom that transfigures you
    and me ;
As he died to make men holy, let us die to make
    men free,
    While God is marching on.
                        JULIA WARD HOWE.

LAUS DEO !

[On hearing the bells ring on the passage of the Constitutional
Amendment abolishing slavery.]

    It is done !
    Clang of bell and roar of gun
Send the tidings up and down.
    How the belfries rock and reel !
    How the great guns, peal on peal,
Fling the joy from town to town !

    Ring, O bells !
    Every stroke exulting tells
Of the burial hour of crime.
    Loud and long, that all may hear,
    Ring for every listening ear
Of Eternity and Time !

    Let us kneel :
    God's own voice is in that peal,
And this spot is holy ground.
    Lord, forgive us !   What are we,
    That our eyes this glory see,
That our ears have heard the sound !

    For the Lord
    On the whirlwind is abroad ;
In the earthquake he has spoken ;
    He has smitten with his thunder
    The iron walls asunder,
And the gates of brass are broken !

    Loud and long
    Lift the old exulting song ;
Sing with Miriam by the sea :
    He has cast the mighty down ;
    Horse and rider sink and drown ;
He has triumphed gloriously !

    Did we dare,
    In our agony of prayer,
Ask for more than He has done ?

When was ever his right hand
    Over any time or land
Stretched as now beneath the sun ?

    How they pale,
    Ancient myth and song and tale,
In this wonder of our days,
    When the cruel rod of war
    Blossoms white with righteous law,
And the wrath of man is praise !

    Blotted out !
    All within and all about
Shall a fresher life begin ;
    Freer breathe the universe
    As it rolls its heavy curse
On the dead and buried sin.

    It is done !
    In the circuit of the sun
Shall the sound thereof go forth.
    It shall bid the sad rejoice,
    It shall give the dumb a voice,
It shall belt with joy the earth !

    Ring and swing,
    Bells of joy !   On morning's wing
Send the song of praise abroad !
    With a sound of broken chains,
    Tell the nations that He reigns,
Who alone is Lord and God !
                    JOHN GREENLEAF WHITTIER.

GREECE.

FROM "CHILDE HAROLD."

FAIR Greece ! sad relic of departed worth !
Immortal, though no more ; though fallen,
    great !
Who now shall lead thy scattered children
    forth,
And long-accustomed bondage uncreate ?
Not such thy sons who whilome did await,
The hopeless warriors of a willing doom,
In bleak Thermopylæ's sepulchral strait, —
O, who that gallant spirit shall resume,
Leap from Eurotas' banks, and call thee from
    the tomb ?

Spirit of Freedom ! when on Phyle's brow
Thou sat'st with Thrasybulus and his train,
Couldst thou forbode the dismal hour which
    now
Dims the green beauties of thine Attic plain ?
Not thirty tyrants now enforce the chain,
But every carle can lord it o'er thy land ;
Nor rise thy sons, but idly rail in vain,

Trembling beneath the scourge of Turkish hand,
From birth till death enslaved ; in word, in deed, unmanned.

In all save form alone, how changed ! and who
That marks the fire still sparkling in each eye,
Who but would deem their bosoms burned anew
With thy unquenchéd beam, lost Liberty !
And many dream withal the hour is nigh
That gives them back their fathers' heritage ;
For foreign arms and aid they fondly sigh,
Nor solely dare encounter hostile rage,
Or tear their name defiled from Slavery's mournful page.

Hereditary bondsmen ! know ye not
Who would be free themselves must strike the blow ?
By their right arms the conquest must be wrought ?
Will Gaul or Muscovite redress ye ? no !
True, they may lay your proud despoilers low,
But not for you will Freedom's altars flame.
Shades of the Helots ! triumph o'er your foe !
Greece ! change thy lords, thy state is still the same ;
Thy glorious day is o'er, but not thine years of shame !   BYRON.

SONG OF THE GREEK POET.

FROM "DON JUAN."

THE isles of Greece, the isles of Greece !
   Where burning Sappho loved and sung, —
Where grew the arts of war and peace, —
   Where Delos rose, and Phœbus sprung !
Eternal summer gilds them yet ;
But all, except their sun, is set.

The Scian and the Teian muse,
   The hero's harp, the lover's lute,
Have found the fame your shores refuse ;
   Their place of birth alone is mute
To sounds which echo farther west
Than your sires' "Islands of the Blest."

The mountains look on Marathon,
   And Marathon looks on the sea ;
And musing there an hour alone,
   I dreamed that Greece might still be free ;
For, standing on the Persians' grave,
I could not deem myself a slave.

A king sat on the rocky brow
   Which looks o'er sea-born Salamis ;

And ships by thousands lay below,
   And men in nations, — all were his ?
He counted them at break of day, —
   And when the sun set, where were they ?

And where are they ? and where art thou,
   My country ?   On thy voiceless shore
The heroic lay is tuneless now, —
   The heroic bosom beats no more !
And must thy lyre, so long divine,
Degenerate into hands like mine ?

'T is something, in the dearth of fame,
   Though linked among a fettered race,
To feel at least a patriot's shame,
   Even as I sing, suffuse my face ;
For what is left the poet here ?
For Greeks a blush, — for Greece a tear.

Must we but weep o'er days more blest ?
   Must we but blush ? — our fathers bled.
Earth ! render back from out thy breast
   A remnant of our Spartan dead !
Of the three hundred, grant but three
To make a new Thermopylæ !

What, silent still ? and silent all ?
   Ah no ! the voices of the dead
Sound like a distant torrent's fall,
   And answer, "Let one living head,
But one, arise, — we come, we come !"
'T is but the living who are dumb.

In vain, — in vain ; strike other chords ;
   Fill high the cup with Samian wine !
Leave battles to the Turkish hordes,
   And shed the blood of Scio's vine !
Hark ! rising to the ignoble call,
How answers each bold Bacchanal !

You have the Pyrrhic dance as yet,
   Where is the Pyrrhic phalanx gone ?
Of two such lessons, why forget
   The nobler and the manlier one ?
You have the letters Cadmus gave, —
Think ye he meant them for a slave ?

Fill high the bowl with Samian wine !
   We will not think of themes like these !
It made Anacreon's song divine ;
   He served, but served Polycrates, —
A tyrant ; but our masters then
Were still, at least, our countrymen.

The tyrant of the Chersonese
   Was freedom's best and bravest friend ;
That tyrant was Miltiades !
   O that the present hour would lend

Another despot of the kind !
Such chains as his were sure to bind.

Fill high the bowl with Samian wine !
  On Suli's rock and Parga's shore
Exists the remnant of a line
  Such as the Doric mothers bore ;
And there perhaps some seed is sown
The Heracleidan blood might own.

Trust not for freedom to the Franks, —
  They have a king who buys and sells.
In native swords and native ranks
  The only hope of courage dwells ;
But Turkish force and Latin fraud
Would break your shield, however broad.

Fill high the bowl with Samian wine !
  Our virgins dance beneath the shade, —
I see their glorious black eyes shine ;
  But, gazing on each glowing maid,
My own the burning tear-drop laves,
To think such breasts must suckle slaves.

Place me on Sunium's marbled steep,
  Where nothing, save the waves and I,
May hear our mutual murmurs sweep ;
  There, swan-like, let me sing and die.
A land of slaves shall ne'er be mine, —
Dash down yon cup of Samian wine !

BYRON.

O THE PLEASANT DAYS OF OLD !

O THE pleasant days of old, which so often peo-
    ple praise !
True, they wanted all the luxuries that grace our
    modern days :
Bare floors were strewed with rushes, the walls
    let in the cold ;
O, how they must have shivered in those pleasant
    days of old !

O those ancient lords of old, how magnificent
    they were !
They threw down and imprisoned kings, — to
    thwart them who might dare ?
They ruled their serfs right sternly ; they took
    from Jews their gold, —
Above both law and equity were those great lords
    of old !

O the gallant knights of old, for their valor so
    renowned !
With sword and lance and armor strong they
    scoured the country round ;

And whenever aught to tempt them they met by
    wood or wold,
By right of sword they seized the prize, — those
    gallant knights of old !

O the gentle dames of old ! who, quite free from
    fear or pain,
Could gaze on joust and tournament, and see
    their champions slain ;
They lived on good beefsteaks and ale, which
    made them strong and bold, —
O, more like men than women were those gentle
    dames of old !

O those mighty towers of old ! with their turrets,
    moat, and keep,
Their battlements and bastions, their dungeons
    dark and deep.
Full many a baron held his court within the
    castle hold ;
And many a captive languished there, in those
    strong towers of old.

O the troubadours of old ! with the gentle min-
    strelsie
Of hope and joy, or deep despair, whiche'er their
    lot might be ;
For years they served their ladye-love ere they
    their passions told, —
O, wondrous patience must have had those trou-
    badours of old !

O those blessed times of old, with their chivalry
    and state !
I love to read their chronicles, which such brave
    deeds relate ;
I love to sing their ancient rhymes, to hear their
    legends told, —
But, Heaven be thanked ! I live not in those
    blessed times of old !

FRANCES BROWN.

THE REFORMER.

ALL grim and soiled and brown with tan,
  I saw a Strong One, in his wrath,
Smiting the godless shrines of man
      Along his path.

The Church beneath her trembling dome
  Essayed in vain her ghostly charm :
Wealth shook within his gilded home
      With strange alarm.

Fraud from his secret chambers fled
  Before the sunlight bursting in :
Sloth drew her pillow o'er her head
      To drown the din.

"Spare," Art implored, "yon holy pile ;
  That grand old time-worn turret spare" :
Meek Reverence, kneeling in the aisle,
  Cried out, "Forbear !"

Gray-bearded Use, who, deaf and blind,
  Groped for his old accustomed stone,
Leaned on his staff, and wept to find
  His seat o'erthrown.

Young Romance raised his dreamy eyes,
  O'erhung with paly locks of gold, —
"Why smite," he asked in sad surprise,
  "The fair, the old ?"

Yet louder rang the Strong One's stroke,
  Yet nearer flashed his axe's gleam ;
Shuddering and sick of heart I woke,
  As from a dream.

I looked : aside the dust-cloud rolled, —
  The Waster seemed the Builder too ;
Up springing from the ruined Old
  I saw the New.

'T was but the ruin of the bad, —
  The wasting of the wrong and ill ;
Whate'er of good the old time had
  Was living still.

Calm grew the brows of him I feared ;
  The frown which awed me passed away,
And left behind a smile which cheered
  Like breaking day.

The grain grew green on battle-plains,
  O'er swarded war-mounds grazed the cow ;
The slave stood forging from his chains
  The spade and plough.

Where frowned the fort, pavilions gay
  And cottage windows, flower-intwined,
Looked out upon the peaceful bay
  And hills behind.

Through vine-wreathed cups with wine once red,
  The lights on brimming crystal fell,
Drawn, sparkling, from the rivulet head
  And mossy well.

Through prison walls, like Heaven-sent hope,
  Fresh breezes blew, and sunbeams strayed,

And with the idle gallows-rope
  The young child played.

Where the doomed victim in his cell
  Had counted o'er the weary hours,
Glad school-girls, answering to the bell,
  Came crowned with flowers.

Grown wiser for the lesson given,
  I fear no longer, for I know
That where the share is deepest driven
  The best fruits grow.

The outworn rite, the old abuse,
  The pious fraud transparent grown,
The good held captive in the use
  Of wrong alone, —

These wait their doom, from that great law
  Which makes the past time serve to-day ;
And fresher life the world shall draw
  From their decay.

O backward-looking son of time !
  The new is old, the old is new,
The cycle of a change sublime
  Still sweeping through.

So wisely taught the Indian seer ;
  Destroying Seva, forming Brahm,
Who wake by turn Earth's love and fear,
  Are one, the same.

Idly as thou, in that old day
  Thou mournest, did thy sire repine ;
So, in his time, thy child grown gray
  Shall sigh for thine.

But life shall on and upward go ;
  Th' eternal step of Progress beats
To that great anthem, calm and slow,
  Which God repeats.

Take heart ! — the Waster builds again, —
  A charméd life old Goodness hath ;
The tares may perish, — but the grain
  Is not for death.

God works in all things ; all obey
  His first propulsion from the night :
Wake thou and watch ! — the world is gray
  With morning light !
  JOHN GREENLEAF WHITTIER.

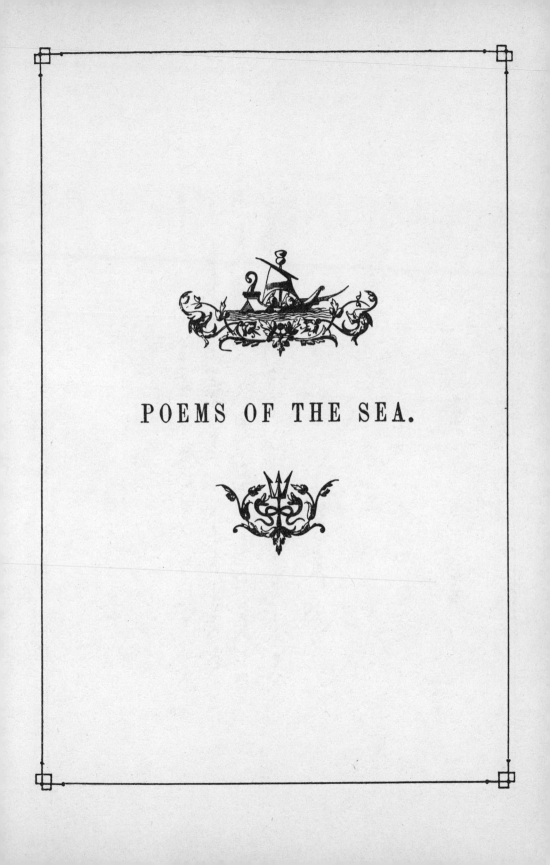

POEMS OF THE SEA.

They turned to the "Earth," but she frowns on her child;
They turned to the "Sea," and he smiled as of old:
Sweeter was the peril of the breakers white and wild,
Sweeter than the land, with its bondage and gold!

Bayard Taylor

POEMS OF THE SEA.

THE SEA.

FROM "CHILDE HAROLD."

THERE is a pleasure in the pathless woods,
There is a rapture on the lonely shore,
There is society where none intrudes
By the deep sea, and music in its roar:
I love not man the less, but nature more,
From these our interviews, in which I steal
From all I may be, or have been before,
To mingle with the universe, and feel
What I can ne'er express, yet cannot all conceal.

Roll on, thou deep and dark blue ocean, — roll !
Ten thousand fleets sweep over thee in vain ;
Man marks the earth with ruin, — his control
Stops with the shore ; — upon the watery plain
The wrecks are all thy deed, nor doth remain
A shadow of man's ravage save his own,
When, for a moment, like a drop of rain,
He sinks into thy depths with bubbling groan,
Without a grave, unknelled, uncoffined, and un-
    known.

His steps are not upon thy paths, — thy fields
Are not a spoil for him, — thou dost arise
And shake him from thee; the vile strength he
    wields
For earth's destruction thou dost all despise,
Spurning him from thy bosom to the skies,
And send'st him, shivering in thy playful spray
And howling, to his gods, where haply lies
His petty hope in some near port or bay,
And dashest him again to earth : — there let him
    lay.

The armaments which thunderstrike the walls
Of rock-built cities, bidding nations quake
And monarchs tremble in their capitals,
The oak leviathans, whose huge ribs make
Their clay creator the vain title take
Of lord of thee and arbiter of war, —
These are thy toys, and, as the snowy flake,
They melt into thy yeast of waves, which mar
Alike the Armada's pride or spoils of Trafalgar.

Thy shores are empires, changed in all save
    thee ;
Assyria, Greece, Rome, Carthage, what are they ?
Thy waters washed them power while they
    were free,
And many a tyrant since ; their shores obey
The stranger, slave, or savage ; their decay
Has dried up realms to deserts : not so thou ;
Unchangeable save to thy wild waves' play,
Time writes no wrinkles on thine azure brow ;
Such as creation's dawn beheld, thou rollest now.

Thou glorious mirror, where the Almighty's
    form
Glasses itself in tempests ; in all time,
Calm or convulsed, — in breeze, or gale, or
    storm,
Icing the pole, or in the torrid clime
Dark - heaving ; boundless, endless, and sub-
    lime,
The image of Eternity, — the throne
Of the Invisible ! even from out thy slime
The monsters of the deep are made ; each zone
Obeys thee ; thou goest forth, dread, fathomless,
    alone.

And I have loved thee, Ocean ! and my joy
Of youthful sports was on thy breast to be
Borne, like thy bubbles, onward ; from a boy
I wantoned with thy breakers, — they to me
Were a delight ; and if the freshening sea
Made them a terror, 't was a pleasing fear ;
For I was as it were a child of thee,
And trusted to thy billows far and near,
And laid my hand upon thy mane, — as I do here.
                                        BYRON.

THE SEA.

THE sea, the sea, the open sea,
The blue, the fresh, the ever free ;
Without a mark, without a bound,
It runneth the earth's wide regions round ;

It plays with the clouds, it mocks the skies,
Or like a cradled creature lies.
I 'm on the sea, I 'm on the sea,
I am where I would ever be,
With the blue above and the blue below,
And silence wheresoe'er I go.
If a storm should come and awake the deep,
What matter? I shall ride and sleep.

I love, O, how I love to ride
On the fierce, foaming, bursting tide,
Where every mad wave drowns the moon,
And whistles aloft its tempest tune,
And tells how goeth the world below,
And why the southwest wind doth blow!
I never was on the dull, tame shore
But I loved the great sea more and more,
And backward flew to her billowy breast,
Like a bird that seeketh her mother's nest, —
And a mother she was and is to me,
For I was born on the open sea.

The waves were white, and red the morn,
In the noisy hour when I was born;
The whale it whistled, the porpoise rolled,
And the dolphins bared their backs of gold;
And never was heard such an outcry wild,
As welcomed to life the ocean child.
I have lived since then, in calm and strife,
Full fifty summers a rover's life,
With wealth to spend, and a power to range,
But never have sought or sighed for change :
And death, whenever he comes to me,
Shall come on the wide, unbounded sea !

BARRY CORNWALL.

A HYMN OF THE SEA.

The sea is mighty, but a mightier sways
His restless billows. Thou, whose hands have
　　scooped
His boundless gulfs and built his shore, thy
　　breath,
That moved in the beginning o'er his face,
Moves o'er it evermore. The obedient waves
To its strong motion roll, and rise and fall.
Still from that realm of rain thy cloud goes up,
As at the first, to water the great earth,
And keep her valleys green. A hundred realms
Watch its broad shadow warping on the wind,
And in the dropping shower with gladness hear
Thy promise of the harvest. I look forth
Over the boundless blue, where joyously
The bright crests of innumerable waves
Glance to the sun at once, as when the hands
Of a great multitude are upward flung

In acclamation. I behold the ships
Gliding from cape to cape, from isle to isle,
Or stemming toward far lands, or hastening
　　home
From the Old World. It is thy friendly breeze
That bears them, with the riches of the land,
And treasure of dear lives, till, in the port,
The shouting seaman climbs and furls the sail.

But who shall bide thy tempest, who shall
　　face
The blast that wakes the fury of the sea ?
O God ! thy justice makes the world turn pale,
When on the arméd fleet, that royally
Bears down the surges, carrying war, to smite
Some city or invade some thoughtless realm,
Descends the fierce tornado. The vast hulks
Are whirled like chaff upon the waves ; the
　　sails
Fly, rent like webs of gossamer ; the masts
Are snapped asunder ; downward from the decks
Downward are slung, into the fathomless gulf,
Their cruel engines ; and their hosts, arrayed
In trappings of the battle-field, are whelmed
By whirlpools or dashed dead upon the rocks.
Then stand the nations still with awe, and
　　pause
A moment from the bloody work of war.

These restless surges eat away the shores
Of earth's old continents ; the fertile plain
Welters in shallows, headlands crumble down,
And the tide drifts the sea-sand in the streets
Of the drowned city. Thou, meanwhile, afar
In the green chambers of the middle sea,
Where broadest spread the waters and the line
Sinks deepest, while no eye beholds thy work,
Creator ! thou dost teach the coral worm
To lay his mighty reefs. From age to age,
He builds beneath the waters, till, at last,
His bulwarks overtop the brine, and check
The long wave rolling from the southern pole
To break upon Japan. Thou bid'st the fires,
That smoulder under ocean, heave on high
The new-made mountains, and uplift their peaks,
A place of refuge for the storm-driven bird.
The birds and wafting billows plant the rifts
With herb and tree ; sweet fountains gush ;
　　sweet airs
Ripple the living lakes that, fringed with flow-
　　ers,
Are gathered in the hollows. Thou dost look
On thy creation and pronounce it good.
Its valleys, glorious with their summer green,
Praise thee in silent beauty ; and its woods
Swept by the murmuring winds of ocean, join
The murmuring shores in a perpetual hymn.

WILLIAM CULLEN BRYANT.

THE SEA.

BEAUTIFUL, sublime, and glorious;
　Mild, majestic, foaming, free, —
Over time itself victorious,
　Image of eternity!

Sun and moon and stars shine o'er thee,
　See thy surface ebb and flow,
Yet attempt not to explore thee
　In thy soundless depths below.

Whether morning's splendors steep thee
　With the rainbow's glowing grace,
Tempests rouse, or navies sweep thee,
　'T is but for a moment's space.

Earth, — her valleys and her mountains,
　Mortal man's behests obey;
The unfathomable fountains
　Scoff his search and scorn his sway.

Such art thou, stupendous ocean!
　But, if overwhelmed by thee,
Can we think, without emotion,
　What must thy Creator be?
　　　　　　　　　BERNARD BARTON.

THE OCEAN.

[Written at Scarborough, in the summer of 1805.]

ALL hail to the ruins, the rocks, and the shores!
Thou wide-rolling Ocean, all hail!
Now brilliant with sunbeams and dimpled with
　　oars,
Now dark with the fresh-blowing gale,
While soft o'er thy bosom the cloud-shadows sail,
And the silver-winged sea-fowl on high,
Like meteors bespangle the sky,
Or dive in the gulf, or triumphantly ride,
Like foam on the surges, the swans of the tide.

From the tumult and smoke of the city set free,
With eager and awful delight,
From the crest of the mountain I gaze upon thee,
I gaze, — and am changed at the sight;
For mine eye is illumined, my genius takes flight,
My soul, like the sun, with a glance
Embraces the boundless expanse,
And moves on thy waters, wherever they roll,
From the day-darting zone to the night-shadowed
　　pole.

My spirit descends where the day-spring is born,
Where the billows are rubies on fire,
And the breezes that rock the light cradle of morn
Are sweet as the Phœnix's pyre.
O regions of beauty, of love and desire!

O gardens of Eden! in vain
Placed far on the fathomless main,
Where Nature with Innocence dwelt in her youth,
When pure was her heart and unbroken her truth.

But now the fair rivers of Paradise wind
Through countries and kingdoms o'erthrown;
Where the giant of tyranny crushes mankind,
Where he reigns, — and will soon reign alone;
For wide and more wide, o'er the sunbeaming zone
He stretches his hundred-fold arms,
Despoiling, destroying its charms;
Beneath his broad footstep the Ganges is dry,
And the mountains recoil from the flash of his eye.

Thus the pestilent Upas, the demon of trees,
Its boughs o'er the wilderness spreads,
And with livid contagion polluting the breeze,
Its mildewing influence sheds;
The birds on the wing, and the flowers in their beds,
Are slain by its venomous breath,
That darkens the noonday with death,
And pale ghosts of travellers wander around,
While their mouldering skeletons whiten the
　　ground.

Ah! why hath Jehovah, in forming the world,
With the waters divided the land,
His ramparts of rocks round the continent hurled,
And cradled the deep in his hand,
If man may transgress his eternal command,
And leap o'er the bounds of his birth,
To ravage the uttermost earth,
And violate nations and realms that should be
Distinct as the billows, yet one as the sea?

There are, gloomy Ocean, a brotherless clan,
Who traverse thy banishing waves,
The poor disinherited outcasts of man,
Whom Avarice coins into slaves.
From the homes of their kindred, their fore-
　　fathers' graves,
Love, friendship, and conjugal bliss,
They are dragged on the hoary abyss;
The shark hears their shrieks, and, ascending to-
　　day,
Demands of the spoiler his share of the prey.

Then joy to the tempest that whelms them beneath,
And makes their destruction its sport;
But woe to the winds that propitiously breathe,
And waft them in safety to port,
Where the vultures and vampires of Mammon
　　resort;
Where Europe exultingly drains
The life-blood from Africa's veins;
Where man rules o'er man with a merciless rod,
And spurns at his footstool the image of God!

The hour is approaching, — a terrible hour !
And Vengeance is bending her bow ;
Already the clouds of the hurricane lower,
And the rock-rending whirlwinds blow ;
Back rolls the huge Ocean, hell opens below ;
The floods return headlong, — they sweep
The slave-cultured lands to the deep,
In a moment entombed in the horrible void,
By their Maker himself in his anger destroyed.

Shall this be the fate of the cane-planted isles,
More lovely than clouds in the west,
When the sun o'er the ocean descending in smiles,
Sinks softly and sweetly to rest ?
No ! — Father of mercy ! befriend the opprest ;
At the voice of thy gospel of peace
May the sorrows of Africa cease ;
And slave and his master devoutly unite
To walk in thy freedom and dwell in thy light !

As homeward my weary-winged Fancy extends
Her star-lighted course through the skies,
High over the mighty Atlantic ascends,
And turns upon Europe her eyes :
Ah me ! what new prospects, new horrors arise ?
I see the war-tempested flood
All foaming, and panting with blood ;
The panic-struck Ocean in agony roars,
Rebounds from the battle, and flies to his shores.

For Britannia is wielding the trident to-day,
Consuming her foes in her ire,
And hurling her thunder with absolute sway
From her wave-ruling chariots of fire.
She triumphs ; the winds and the waters con-
spire
To spread her invincible name ;
The universe rings with her fame ;
But the cries of the fatherless mix with her
praise,
And the tears of the widow are shed on her bays.

O Britain, dear Britain ! the land of my birth ;
O Isle most enchantingly fair !
Thou Pearl of the Ocean ! thou Gem of the Earth !
O my Mother, my Mother, beware,
For wealth is a phantom, and empire a snare !
O, let not thy birthright be sold
For reprobate glory and gold !
Thy distant dominions like wild graftings shoot,
They weigh down thy trunk, they will tear up
thy root, —

The root of thine oak, O my country ! that
stands
Rock-planted and flourishing free ;
Its branches are stretched o'er the uttermost lands,
And its shadow eclipses the sea.

The blood of our ancestors nourished the tree ;
From their tombs, from their ashes, it sprung ;
Its boughs with their trophies are hung ;
Their spirit dwells in it, and — hark ! for it
spoke,
The voice of our fathers ascends from their oak.

"Ye Britons, who dwell where we conquered of
old,
Who inherit our battle-field graves ;
Though poor were your fathers, — gigantic and
bold,
We were not, we could not be, slaves ;
But firm as our rocks, and as free as our waves,
The spears of the Romans we broke,
We never stooped under their yoke.
In the shipwreck of nations we stood up alone, —
The world was great Cæsar's, but Britain our own.

JAMES MONTGOMERY.

ADDRESS TO THE OCEAN.

O THOU vast Ocean ! ever-sounding Sea !
Thou symbol of a drear immensity !
Thou thing that windest round the solid world
Like a huge animal, which, downward hurled
From the black clouds, lies weltering and alone,
Lashing and writhing till its strength be gone !
Thy voice is like the thunder, and thy sleep
Is as a giant's slumber, loud and deep.
Thou speakest in the east and in the west
At once, and on thy heavily laden breast
Fleets come and go, and shapes that have no life
Or motion, yet are moved and meet in strife.
The earth has naught of this : no chance or change
Ruffles its surface, and no spirits dare
Give answer to the tempest-wakened air ;
But o'er its wastes the weakly tenants range
At will, and wound its bosom as they go :
Ever the same, it hath no ebb, no flow :
But in their stated rounds the seasons come,
And pass like visions to their wonted home ;
And come again, and vanish ; the young Spring
Looks ever bright with leaves and blossoming ;
And Winter always winds his sullen horn,
When the wild Autumn, with a look forlorn,
Dies in his stormy manhood ; and the skies
Weep, and flowers sicken, when the summer flies.
O, wonderful thou art, great element,
And fearful in thy spleeny humors bent,
And lovely in repose ! thy summer form
Is beautiful, and when thy silver waves
Make music in earth's dark and winding caves,
I love to wander on thy pebbled beach,
Marking the sunlight at the evening hour,
And hearken to the thoughts thy waters teach, —
Eternity — Eternity — and Power.

BARRY CORNWALL.

THE EQUINOX.

"*Landward in his wrath he scourges
The toiling surges.*"

HAMPTON BEACH.

THE sunlight glitters keen and bright,
　　Where, miles away,
Lies stretching to my dazzled sight
A luminous belt, a misty light,
Beyond the dark pine bluffs and wastes of sandy
　　gray.

The tremulous shadow of the sea !
　　Against its ground
Of silvery light, rock, hill, and tree,
Still as a picture, clear and free,
With varying outline mark the coast for miles
　　around.

On — on — we tread with loose-flung rein
　　Our seaward way,
Through dark-green fields and blossoming
　　grain,
Where the wild brier-rose skirts the lane,
And bends above our heads the flowering locust
　　spray.

Ha ! like a kind hand on my brow
　　Comes this fresh breeze,
Cooling its dull and feverish glow,
While through my being seems to flow
The breath of a new life, — the healing of the
　　seas !

Now rest we, where this grassy mound
　　His feet hath set
In the great waters, which have bound
His granite ankles greenly round
With long and tangled moss, and weeds with
　　cool spray wet.

Good by to pain and care ! I take
　　Mine ease to-day ;
Here, where the sunny waters break,
And ripples this keen breeze, I shake
All burdens from the heart, all weary thoughts
　　away.

I draw a freer breath — I seem
　　Like all I see —
Waves in the sun — the white-winged gleam
Of sea-birds in the slanting beam —
And far-off sails which flit before the south-wind
　　free :

So when Time's veil shall fall asunder,
　　The soul may know
No fearful change, nor sudden wonder,
Nor sink the weight of mystery under,
But with the upward rise, and with the vastness
　　grow.

And all we shrink from now may seem
　　No new revealing, —
Familiar as our childhood's stream,
Or pleasant memory of a dream,
The loved and cherished Past upon the new life
　　stealing.

Serene and mild, the untried light
　　May have its dawning ;
And, as in summer's northern night
The evening and the dawn unite,
The sunset hues of Time blend with the soul's
　　new morning.

I sit alone ; in foam and spray
　　Wave after wave
Breaks on the rocks which, stern and gray,
Shoulder the broken tide away,
Or murmurs hoarse and strong through mossy
　　cleft and cave.

What heed I of the dusty land
　　And noisy town !
I see the mighty deep expand
From its white line of glimmering sand
To where the blue of heaven on bluer waves
　　shuts down !

In listless quietude of mind,
　　I yield to all
The change of cloud and wave and wind ;
And passive on the flood reclined,
I wander with the waves, and with them rise
　　and fall.

But look, thou dreamer ! — wave and shore
　　In shadow lie ;
The night-wind warns me back once more
To where, my native hill-tops o'er,
Bends like an arch of fire the glowing sunset
　　sky !

So then, beach, bluff, and wave, farewell !
　　I bear with me
No token stone nor glittering shell,
But long and oft shall Memory tell
Of this brief thoughtful hour of musing by the
　　sea.
　　　　　JOHN GREENLEAF WHITTIER.

SEA-WEED.

WHEN descends on the Atlantic
　　The gigantic
Storm-wind of the equinox,
Landward in his wrath he scourges
　　The toiling surges,
Laden with sea-weed from the rocks :

From Bermuda's reefs ; from ed
  Of sunken ledges,
In some far-off, bright Azore
From Bahama, and the das¹
  Silver-flashing
Surges of San Salvador ;

From the tumbling sur   aries
  The Orkneyan skerries,
Answering the hoarse Hebrides ;
And from wrecks of ships, and drifting
  Spars, uplifting
On the desolate, rainy seas ; —

Ever drifting, drifting, drifting
  On the shifting
Currents of the restless main ;
Till in sheltered coves, and reaches
  Of sandy beaches,
All have found repose again.

So when storms of wild emotion
  Strike the ocean
Of the poet's soul, erelong,
From each cave and rocky fastness
  In its vastness,
Floats some fragment of a song :

From the far-off isles enchanted
  Heaven has planted
With the golden fruit of Truth ;
From the flashing surf, whose vision
  Gleams Elysian
In the tropic clime of Youth ;

From the strong Will, and the Endeavor
  That forever
Wrestles with the tides of Fate ;
From the wreck of Hopes far-scattered,
  Tempest-shattered,
Floating waste and desolate ; —

Ever drifting, drifting, drifting
  On the shifting
Currents of the restless heart ;
Till at length in books recorded,
  They, like hoarded
Household words, no more depart.
        HENRY WADSWORTH LONGFELLOW.

GULF—WEED.

A WEARY weed, tossed to and fro,
  Drearily drenched in the ocean brine,
Soaring high and sinking low,
  Lashed along without will of mine ;

Sport of the spume of the surging sea ;
  Flung on the foam, afar and anear,
Mark my manifold mystery, —
  Growth and grace in their place appear.

I bear round berries, gray and red,
  Rootless and rover though I be ;
My spangled leaves, when nicely spread,
  Arboresce as a trunkless tree ;
Corals curious coat me o'er,
  White and hard in apt array ;
Mid the wild waves' rude uproar
  Gracefully grow I, night and day.

Hearts there are on the sounding shore,
  Something whispers soft to me,
Restless and roaming forevermore,
  Like this weary weed of the sea ;
Bear they yet on each beating breast
  The eternal type of the wondrous whole,
Growth unfolding amidst unrest,
  Grace informing with silent soul.
        CORNELIUS GEORGE FENNER.

SEA LIFE.

FROM "THE PELICAN ISLAND."

LIGHT as a flake of foam upon the wind
Keel-upward from the deep emerged a shell,
Shaped like the moon ere half her horn is filled :
Fraught with young life, it righted as it rose,
And moved at will along the yielding water.
The native pilot of this little bark
Put out a tier of oars on either side,
Spread to the wafting breeze a twofold sail,
And mounted up and glided down the billow
In happy freedom, pleased to feel the air,
And wander in the luxury of light.
Worth all the dead creation, in that hour,
To me appeared this lonely Nautilus,
My fellow-being, like myself, *alive.*
Entranced in contemplation, vague yet sweet,
I watched its vagrant course and rippling wake,
Till I forgot the sun amidst the heavens.
  It closed, sunk, dwindled to a point, then
    nothing ;
While the last bubble crowned the dimpling eddy,
Through which mine eyes still giddily pursued it,
A joyous creature vaulted through the air, —
The aspiring fish that fain would be a bird,
On long, light wings, that flung a diamond-
    shower
Of dew-drops round its evanescent form,
Sprang into light, and instantly descended.
Ere I could greet the stranger as a friend,
Or mourn his quick departure on the surge,

A shoal of dolphins tumbling in wild glee,
Glowed with such orient tints, they might have been
The rainbow's offspring, when it met the ocean
In that resplendent vision I had seen.
While yet in ecstasy, I hung o'er these,
With every motion pouring out fresh beauties,
As though the conscious colors came and went
At pleasure, glorying in their subtle changes, —
Enormous o'er the flood, Leviathan
Looked forth, and from his roaring nostrils sent
Two fountains to the sky, then plunged amain
In headlong pastime through the closing gulf.
These were but preludes to the revelry
That reigned at sunset : then the deep let loose
Its blithe adventurers to sport at large,
As kindly instinct taught them ; buoyant shells,
On stormless voyages, in fleets or single,
Wherried their tiny mariners ; aloof,
On wing-like fins, in bow-and-arrow figures,
The flying-fishes darted to and fro ;
While spouting whales projected watery columns,
That turned to arches at their height, and seemed
The skeletons of crystal palaces
Built on the blue expanse, then perishing,
Frail as the element which they were made of :
Dolphins, in gambols, lent the lucid brine
Hues richer than the canopy of eve,
That overhung the scene with gorgeous clouds,
Decaying into gloom more beautiful
Than the sun's golden liveries which they lost :
Till light that hides, and darkness that reveals
The stars, — exchanging guard, like sentinels
Of day and night, — transformed the face of nature ;
Above was wakefulness, silence around,
Beneath, repose, — repose that reached even me.
Power, will, sensation, memory, failed in turn ;
My very essence seemed to pass away,
Like a thin cloud that melts across the moon,
Lost in the blue immensity of heaven.
JAMES MONTGOMERY.

THE CORAL INSECT.

TOIL on ! toil on ! ye ephemeral train,
Who build in the tossing and treacherous main ;
Toil on ! for the wisdom of man ye mock,
With your sand-based structures and domes of rock,
Your columns the fathomless fountains' cave,
And your arches spring up to the crested wave ;
Ye 're a puny race thus to boldly rear
A fabric so vast in a realm so drear.

Ye bind the deep with your secret zone, —
The ocean is sealed, and the surge a stone,

Fresh wreaths from the coral pavement spring,
Like the terraced pride of Assyria's king ;
The turf looks green where the breakers rolled ;
O'er the whirlpool ripens the rind of gold ;
The sea-snatched isle is the home of men,
And mountains exult where the wave hath been.

But why do ye plant, 'neath the billows dark,
The wrecking reef for the gallant bark ?
There are snares enough on the tented field,
Mid the blossomed sweets that the valleys yield ;
There are serpents to coil ere the flowers are up,
There 's a poison drop in man's purest cup,
There are foes that watch for his cradle breath,
And why need ye sow the floods with death ?

With mouldering bones the deeps are white,
From the ice-clad pole to the tropics bright ;
The mermaid hath twisted her fingers cold
With the mesh of the sea-boy's curls of gold,
And the gods of the ocean have frowned to see
The mariner's bed in their halls of glee ;
Hath earth no graves, that ye thus must spread
The boundless sea for the thronging dead ?

Ye build — ye build — but ye enter not in,
Like the tribes whom the desert devoured in their sin ;
From the land of promise ye fade and die
Ere its verdure gleams forth on your weary eye ;
As the kings of the cloud-crowned pyramid,
Their noiseless bones in oblivion hid,
Ye slumber unmarked mid the desolate main,
While the wonder and pride of your works remain.
LYDIA H. SIGOURNEY.

THE CORAL INSECT.

FROM "THE PELICAN ISLAND."

. . . . EVERY one,
By instinct taught, performed its little task,
To build its dwelling and its sepulchre,
From its own essence exquisitely modelled ;
There breed, and die, and leave a progeny,
Still multiplied beyond the reach of numbers,
To frame new cells and tombs, then breed and die
As all their ancestors had done, — and rest,
Hermetically sealed, each in its shrine,
A statue in this temple of oblivion !
Millions of millions thus, from age to age,
With simplest skill and toil unweariable,
No moment and no movement unimproved,
Laid line on line, on terrace terrace spread,
To swell the heightening, brightening, gradual mound,
By marvellous structure climbing towards the day.

A point at first
It peered above those waves ; a point so small
I just perceived it, fixed where all was floating ;
And when a bubble crossed it, the blue film
Expanded like a sky above the speck ;
That speck became a hand-breadth ; day and night
It spread, accumulated, and erelong
Presented to my view a dazzling plain,
White as the moon amid the sapphire sea ;
Bare at low water, and as still as death,
But when the tide came gurgling o'er the surface
'T was like a resurrection of the dead :
From graves innumerable, punctures fine
In the close coral, capillary swarms
Covered the bald-pate reef ;

       .   .

Erelong the reef o'ertopt the spring-flood's height,
And mocked the billows when they leapt upon it,
Unable to maintain their slippery hold,
And falling down in foam-wreaths round its verge.
Steep were the flanks, with precipices sharp,
Descending to their base in ocean gloom.
Chasms few and narrow and irregular
Formed harbors, safe at once and perilous, —
Safe for defence, but perilous to enter.
A sea-lake shone amidst the fossil isle,
Reflecting in a ring its cliffs and caverns,
With heaven itself seen like a lake below.

Compared with this amazing edifice,
Raised by the weakest creatures in existence,
What are the works of intellectual man ?
Towers, temples, palaces, and sepulchres ;
Ideal images in sculptured forms,
Thoughts hewn in columns, or in domes expanded,
Fancies through every maze of beauty shown ;
Pride, gratitude, affection turned to marble,
In honor of the living or the dead ;
What are they ? — fine-wrought miniatures of art,
Too exquisite to bear the weight of dew,
Which every morn lets fall in pearls upon them,
Till all their pomp sinks down in mouldering relics,
Yet in their ruin lovelier than their prime ! —
Dust in the balance, atoms in the gale,
Compared with these achievements in the deep,
Were all the monuments of olden time,
In days when there were giants on the earth. —
Babel's stupendous folly, though it aimed
To scale heaven's battlements, was but a toy,
The plaything of the world in infancy ;
The ramparts, towers, and gates of Babylon,
Built for eternity, — though, where they stood,
Ruin itself stands still for lack of work,
And Desolation keeps unbroken Sabbath ;
Great Babylon, in its full moon of empire,
Even when its "head of gold" was smitten off
And from a monarch changed into a brute —
Great Babylon was like a wreath of sand,

Left by one tide and cancelled by the next ;
Egypt's dread wonders, still defying Time,
Where cities have been crumbled into sand,
Scattered by winds beyond the Libyan desert,
Or melted down into the mud of Nile,
And cast in tillage o'er the corn-sown fields,
Where Memphis flourished, and the Pharaohs
    reigned ;
Egypt's gray piles of hieroglyphic grandeur,
That have survived the language which they speak,
Preserving its dead emblems to the eye,
Yet hiding from the mind what these reveal ; —
Her pyramids would be mere pinnacles,
Her giant statues, wrought from rocks of granite
But puny ornaments for such a pile
As this stupendous mound of catacombs,
Filled with dry mummies of the builder-worms.
                     JAMES MONTGOMERY.

———

THE CORAL GROVE.

DEEP in the wave is a coral grove,
Where the purple mullet and gold-fish rove ;
Where the sea-flower spreads its leaves of blue
That never are wet with falling dew,
But in bright and changeful beauty shine
Far down in the green and glassy brine.
The floor is of sand, like the mountain drift,
And the pearl-shells spangle the flinty snow ;
From coral rocks the sea-plants lift
Their boughs, where the tides and billows flow ;
The water is calm and still below,
For the winds and waves are absent there,
And the sands are bright as the stars that glow
In the motionless fields of upper air.
There, with its waving blade of green,
The sea-flag streams through the silent water,
And the crimson leaf of the dulse is seen
To blush, like a banner bathed in slaughter.
There, with a light and easy motion,
The fan-coral sweeps through the clear, deep sea ;
And the yellow and scarlet tufts of ocean
Are bending like corn on the upland lea.
And life, in rare and beautiful forms,
Is sporting amid those bowers of stone,
And is safe when the wrathful spirit of storms
Has made the top of the wave his own.
And when the ship from his fury flies,
Where the myriad voices of ocean roar,
When the wind-god frowns in the murky skies,
And demons are waiting the wreck on shore,
Then, far below, in the peaceful sea,
The purple mullet and gold-fish rove,
Where the waters murmur tranquilly,
Through the bending twigs of the coral grove.
                 JAMES GATES PERCIVAL.

"What hid'st thou in thy treasure-caves and cells?
Thou hollow-sounding and mysterious main!"

THE TREASURES OF THE DEEP.

WHAT hid'st thou in thy treasure-caves and cells?
  Thou hollow-sounding and mysterious main!—
Pale glistening pearls and rainbow-colored shells,
  Bright things which gleam unrecked of and
    in vain!—
Keep, keep thy riches, melancholy sea!
  We ask not such from thee.

Yet more, the depths have more!—what wealth
    untold,
  Far down, and shining through their stillness
    lies!
Thou hast the starry gems, the burning gold,
  Won from ten thousand royal argosies!—
Sweep o'er thy spoils, thou wild and wrathful main!
  Earth claims not *these* again.

Yet more, the depths have more!—thy waves
    have rolled
  Above the cities of a world gone by!
Sand hath filled up the palaces of old,
  Sea-weed o'ergrown the halls of revelry.—
Dash o'er them, Ocean, in thy scornful play!
  Man yields them to decay.

Yet more, the billows and the depths have more!
  High hearts and brave are gathered to thy breast!
They hear not now the booming waters roar,
  The battle-thunders will not break their rest.—
Keep thy red gold and gems, thou stormy grave!
  Give back the true and brave!

Give back the lost and lovely!—those for whom
  The place was kept at board and hearth so long!
The prayer went up through midnight's breathless
    gloom,
  And the vain yearning woke midst festal song!
Hold fast thy buried isles, thy towers o'erthrown,—
  But all is not thine own.

To thee the love of woman hath gone down,
  Dark flow thy tides o'er manhood's noble head,
O'er youth's bright locks, and beauty's flowery
    crown;
  Yet must thou hear a voice,—Restore the dead!
Earth shall reclaim her precious things from
    thee!—
  Restore the dead, thou sea!
                    FELICIA HEMANS.

TACKING SHIP OFF SHORE.

THE weather leach of the topsail shivers,
  The bowlines strain and the lee shrouds
    slacken,
The braces are taut and the lithe boom quivers,
  And the waves with the coming squall-cloud
    blacken.

Open one point on the weather bow
  Is the lighthouse tall on Fire Island head;
There's a shade of doubt on the captain's brow,
  And the pilot watches the heaving lead.

I stand at the wheel and with eager eye
  To sea and to sky and to shore I gaze,
Till the muttered order of "FULL AND BY!"
  Is suddenly changed to "FULL FOR STAYS!"

The ship bends lower before the breeze,
  As her broadside fair to the blast she lays;
And she swifter springs to the rising seas
  As the pilot calls "STAND BY FOR STAYS!"

It is silence all, as each in his place,
  With the gathered coils in his hardened hands,
By tack and bowline, by sheet and brace,
  Waiting the watchword impatient stands.

And the light on Fire Island head draws near,
  As, trumpet-winged, the pilot's shout
From his post on the bowsprit's heel I hear,
  With the welcome call of "READY! ABOUT!"

No time to spare! it is touch and go,
  And the captain growls "DOWN HELM! HARD
    DOWN!"
As my weight on the whirling spokes I throw,
  While heaven grows black with the storm-
    cloud's frown.

High o'er the knight-heads flies the spray,
  As we meet the shock of the plunging sea;
And my shoulder stiff to the wheel I lay,
  As I answer, "AY, AY, SIR! HARD A LEE!"

With the swerving leap of a startled steed
  The ship flies fast in the eye of the wind,
The dangerous shoals on the lee recede,
  And the headland white we have left behind.

The topsails flutter, the jibs collapse
  And belly and tug at the groaning cleats;
The spanker slaps and the mainsail flaps,
  And thunders the order, "TACKS AND SHEETS!"

'Mid the rattle of blocks and the tramp of the
    crew
  Hisses the rain of the rushing squall;
The sails are aback from clew to clew,
  And now is the moment for "MAINSAIL,
    HAUL!"

And the heavy yards like a baby's toy
  By fifty strong arms are swiftly swung;
She holds her way, and I look with joy
  For the first white spray o'er the bulwarks
    flung.

"LET GO, AND HAUL!" 't is the last command,
 And the head-sails fill to the blast once more;
Astern and to leeward lies the land,
 With its breakers white on the shingly shore.

What matters the reef, or the rain, or the squall?
 I steady the helm for the open sea;
The first-mate clamors, BELAY THERE, ALL!"
 And the captain's breath once more comes free.

And so off shore let the good ship fly;
 Little care I how the gusts may blow,
In my fo'castle-bunk in a jacket dry, —
 Eight bells have struck, and my watch is below.
                                MRS. CELIA THAXTER.

SONG OF THE EMIGRANTS IN BER-MUDA.

WHERE the remote Bermudas ride
In the ocean's bosom unespied,
From a small boat that rowed along
The listening winds received this song:
"What should we do but sing His praise
That led us through the watery maze
Where he the huge sea monsters wracks,
That lift the deep upon their backs,
Unto an isle so long unknown,
And yet far kinder than our own?
He lands us on a grassy stage,
Safe from the storms, and prelate's rage;
He gave us this eternal spring
Which here enamels everything,
And sends the fowls to us in care
On daily visits through the air.
He hangs in shades the orange bright
Like golden lamps in a green night,
And does in the pomegranates close
Jewels more rich than Ormus shows:
He makes the figs our mouths to meet,
And throws the melons at our feet;
But apples, plants of such a price,
No tree could ever bear them twice.
With cedars chosen by his hand
From Lebanon he stores the land;
And makes the hollow seas that roar
Proclaim the ambergris on shore.
He cast (of which we rather boast)
The gospel's pearl upon our coast;
And in these rocks for us did frame
A temple where to sound his name.
O let our voice his praise exalt
Till it arrive at heaven's vault,
Which then perhaps rebounding may
Echo beyond the Mexique bay!" —
Thus sung they in the English boat
A holy and a cheerful note;
And all the way, to guide their chime,
With falling oars they kept the time.
                                ANDREW MARVELL.

A WET SHEET AND A FLOWING SEA.

A WET sheet and a flowing sea, —
 A wind that follows fast,
And fills the white and rustling sail,
 And bends the gallant mast, —
And bends the gallant mast, my boys,
 While, like the eagle free,
Away the good ship flies, and leaves
 Old England on the lee.

O for a soft and gentle wind!
 I heard a fair one cry;
But give to me the snoring breeze
 And white waves heaving high, —
And white waves heaving high, my boys,
 The good ship tight and free;
The world of waters is our home,
 And merry men are we.

There 's tempest in yon hornéd moon,
 And lightning in yon cloud;
And hark the music, mariners!
 The wind is piping loud, —
The wind is piping loud, my boys,
 The lightning flashing free;
While the hollow oak our palace is,
 Our heritage the sea.
                                ALLAN CUNNINGHAM.

SONG OF THE ROVER.

FROM "THE CORSAIR."

O'ER the glad waters of the dark blue sea,
Our thoughts as boundless and our souls as free,
Far as the breeze can bear, the billows foam,
Survey our empire, and behold our home!
These are our realms, no limits to their sway, —
Our flag the sceptre all who meet obey.
Ours the wild life in tumult still to range
From toil to rest, and joy in every change.
O, who can tell? not thou, luxurious slave!
Whose soul would sicken o'er the heaving wave;
Not thou, vain lord of wantonness and ease!
Whom slumber soothes not, — pleasure cannot
         please. —
O, who can tell save he whose heart hath tried,
And danced in triumph o'er the waters wide,
The exulting sense, the pulse's maddening play,
That thrills the wanderer of that trackless way?
That for itself can woo the approaching fight,
And turn what some deem danger to delight;
That seeks what cravens shun with more than
         zeal,
And where the feebler faint can only feel —
Feel to the rising bosom's inmost core,
Its hope awaken and its spirit soar?

No dread of death — if with us die our foes —
Save that it seems even duller than repose :
Come when it will — we snatch the life of life —
When lost — what recks it — by disease or strife ?
Let him who crawls enamored of decay,
Cling to his couch and sicken years away ;
Heave his thick breath, and shake his palsied
    head :
Ours — the fresh turf, and not the feverish bed,
While gasp by gasp he falters forth his soul,
Ours with one pang — one bound — escapes con-
    trol.
His corse may boast its urn and narrow cave,
And they who loathed his life may gild his grave :
Ours are the tears, though few, sincerely shed,
When Ocean shrouds and sepulchres our dead.
For us, even banquets fond regrets supply
In the red cup that crowns our memory ;
And the brief epitaph in danger's day,
When those who win at length divide the prey,
And cry, Remembrance saddening o'er each brow,
How had the brave who fell exulted *now!*
BYRON.

MY BRIGANTINE.

JUST in thy mould and beauteous in thy form,
Gentle in roll and buoyant on the surge,
Light as the sea-fowl rocking in the storm,
In breeze and gale thy onward course we urge,
    My water-queen !
    Lady of mine,
More light and swift than thou none thread the
    sea,
With surer keel or steadier on its path,
We brave each waste of ocean-mystery
And laugh to hear the howling tempest's wrath,
    For we are thine.
    " My brigantine !
Trust to the mystic power that points thy way,
Trust to the eye that pierces from afar ;
Trust the red meteors that around thee play,
And, fearless, trust the Sea-Green Lady's Star,
    Thou bark divine !"
JAMES FENIMORE COOPER.

ALL'S WELL.

FROM "THE BRITISH FLEET."

DESERTED by the waning moon,
When skies proclaim night's cheerless noon,
On tower, or fort, or tented ground
The sentry walks his lonely round ;
And should a footstep haply stray
Where caution marks the guarded way,

Who goes there ? Stranger, quickly tell ;
A friend, — the word. Good night ; all's well.

Or sailing on the midnight deep,
When weary messmates soundly sleep,
The careful watch patrols the deck,
To guard the ship from foes or wreck ;
And while his thoughts oft homewards veer,
Some friendly voice salutes his ear, —
What cheer ? brother, quickly tell ;
Above, — below. Good night ; all's well.
THOMAS DIBDIN.

HEAVING OF THE LEAD.

FOR England when with favoring gale
    Our gallant ship up channel steered,
And, scudding under easy sail,
    The high blue western land appeared ;
To heave the lead the seaman sprung,
And to the pilot cheerly sung,
        " By the deep — nine !"

And bearing up to gain the port,
    Some well-known object kept in view, —
An abbey-tower, a harbor-fort,
    Or beacon to the vessel true ;
While oft the lead the seaman flung,
And to the pilot cheerly sung,
        " By the mark — seven !"

And as the much-loved shore we near,
    With transport we behold the roof
Where dwelt a friend or partner dear,
    Of faith and love a matchless proof.
The lead once more the seaman flung,
And to the watchful pilot sung,
        " Quarter less — five !"

Now to her berth the ship draws nigh :
    We shorten sail, — she feels the tide, —
"Stand clear the cable" is the cry, —
    The anchor's gone ; we safely ride.
The watch is set, and through the night
We hear the seamen with delight
        Proclaim, — "All's well !"
CHARLES DIBDIN.

THE WHITE SQUALL.

IN THE MEDITERRANEAN.

ON deck, beneath the awning,
I dozing lay and yawning ;
It was the gray of dawning.
Ere yet the sun arose ·

And above the funnel's roaring,
And the fitful wind's deploring,
I heard the cabin snoring
 With universal nose.
I could hear the passengers snorting, —
I envied their disporting, —
Vainly I was courting
 The pleasure of a doze.

So I lay, and wondered why light
Came not, and watched the twilight,
And the glimmer of the skylight,
 That shot across the deck ;
And the binnacle pale and steady,
And the dull glimpse of the dead-eye,
And the sparks in fiery eddy
 That whirled from the chimney neck.
In our jovial floating prison
There was sleep from fore to mizzen,
And never a star had risen
 The hazy sky to speck.
Strange company we harbored :
We 'd a hundred Jews to larboard,
Unwashed, uncombed, unbarbered, —
 Jews black and brown and gray.

With terror it would seize ye,
And make your souls uneasy,
To see those Rabbis greasy,
 Who did naught but scratch and pray.
Their dirty children puking, —
Their dirty saucepans cooking, —
Their dirty fingers hooking
 Their swarming fleas away.

To starboard Turks and Greeks were, —
Whiskered and brown their cheeks were, —
Enormous wide their breeks were, —
 Their pipes did puff away ;
Each on his mat allotted
In silence smoked and squatted,
Whilst round their children trotted
 In pretty, pleasant play.
He can't but smile who traces
The smiles on those brown faces,
And the pretty, prattling graces
 Of those small heathens gay.

And so the hours kept tolling ;
And through the ocean rolling
Went the brave Iberia bowling,
 Before the break of day, —

When a squall, upon a sudden,
Came o'er the waters scudding ;
And the clouds began to gather,
And the sea was lashed to lather,
And the lowering thunder grumbled,
And the lightning jumped and tumbled,

And the ship, and all the ocean,
Woke up in wild commotion.
Then the wind set up a howling,
And the poodle dog a yowling,
And the cocks began a crowing,
And the old cow raised a lowing,
As she heard the tempest blowing ;
And fowls and geese did cackle,
And the cordage and the tackle
Began to shriek and crackle ;
And the spray dashed o'er the funnels,
And down the deck in runnels ;
And the rushing water soaks all,
From the seamen in the fo'ksal
To the stokers, whose black faces
Peer out of their bed-places ;
And the captain he was bawling,
And the sailors pulling, hauling,
And the quarter-deck tarpauling
Was shivered in the squalling ;
And the passengers awaken,
Most pitifully shaken ;
And the steward jumps up, and hastens
For the necessary basins.

Then the Greeks they groaned and quivered.
And they knelt and moaned and shivered,
As the plunging waters met them,
And splashed and overset them ;
And they called in their emergence
Upon countless saints and virgins ;
And their marrowbones are bended,
And they think the world is ended.
And the Turkish women for'ard
Were frightened and behorrored ;
And, shrieking and bewildering,
The mothers clutched their children ;
The men sang "Allah ! Illah !
Mashallah Bismillah !"
As the warring waters doused them,
And splashed them and soused them ;
And they called upon the Prophet,
Who thought but little of it.

Then all the fleas in Jewry
Jumped up and bit like fury ;
And the progeny of Jacob
Did on the main-deck wake up,
(I wot those greasy Rabbins
Would never pay for cabins ;)
And each man moaned and jabbered in
His filthy Jewish gabardine,
In woe and lamentation,
And howling consternation.
And the splashing water drenches
Their dirty brats and wenches ;
And they crawl from bales and benches,
In a hundred thousand stenches.

This was the white squall famous,
Which latterly o'ercame us,
And which all will well remember,
On the 28th September;
When a Prussian captain of Lancers
(Those tight-laced, whiskered prancers)
Came on the deck astonished,
By that wild squall admonished,
And wondering cried, "Potz tausend,
Wie ist der Stürm jetzt brausend?"
And looked at Captain Lewis,
Who calmly stood and blew his
Cigar in all the bustle,
And scorned the tempest's tussle.
And oft we've thought hereafter
How he beat the storm to laughter;
For well he knew his vessel
With that vain wind could wrestle;
And when a wreck we thought her,
And doomed ourselves to slaughter,
How gayly he fought her,
And through the hubbub brought her,
And as the tempest caught her,
Cried, "George, some brandy and water!"

And when, its force expended,
The harmless storm was ended,
And as the sunrise splendid
    Came blushing o'er the sea, —
I thought, as day was breaking,
My little girls were waking,
And smiling, and making
    A prayer at home for me.
                WILLIAM MAKEPEACE THACKERAY.

THE TEMPEST.

WE were crowded in the cabin,
    Not a soul would dare to sleep, —
It was midnight on the waters
    And a storm was on the deep.

'T is a fearful thing in winter
    To be shattered by the blast,
And to hear the rattling trumpet
    Thunder, "Cut away the mast!"

So we shuddered there in silence, —
    For the stoutest held his breath,
While the hungry sea was roaring,
    And the breakers talked with Death.

As thus we sat in darkness,
    Each one busy in his prayers,
"We are lost!" the captain shouted
    As he staggered down the stairs.

But his little daughter whispered,
    As she took his icy hand,
"Is n't God upon the ocean
    Just the same as on the land?"

Then we kissed the little maiden,
    And we spoke in better cheer,
And we anchored safe in harbor
    When the morn was shining clear.
                JAMES T. FIELDS.

THE MINUTE-GUN.

WHEN in the storm on Albion's coast,
The night-watch guards his wary post,
    From thoughts of danger free,
He marks some vessel's dusky form,
And hears, amid the howling storm,
    The minute-gun at sea.

Swift on the shore a hardy few
The life-boat man with gallant crew
    And dare the dangerous wave;
Through the wild surf they cleave their way,
Lost in the foam, nor know dismay,
    For they go the crew to save.

But, O, what rapture fills each breast
Of the hopeless crew of the ship distressed!
Then, landed safe, what joy to tell
Of all the dangers that befell!
Then is heard no more,
By the watch on shore,
    The minute-gun at sea.
                R. S. SHARPE.

THE BAY OF BISCAY, O!

LOUD roared the dreadful thunder,
    The rain a deluge showers,
The clouds were rent asunder
    By lightning's vivid powers;
The night both drear and dark,
Our poor devoted bark,
Till next day, there she lay,
    In the Bay of Biscay, O!

Now dashed upon the billow,
    Our opening timbers creak,
Each fears a watery pillow,
    None stops the dreadful leak;
To cling to slippery shrouds
Each breathless seaman crowds,
As she lay, till the day,
    In the Bay of Biscay, O!

At length the wished-for morrow
  Broke through the hazy sky,
Absorbed in silent sorrow,
  Each heaved a bitter sigh ;
The dismal wreck to view
  Struck horror to the crew,
As she lay, on that day,
  In the Bay of Biscay, O !

Her yielding timbers sever,
  Her pitchy seams are rent,
When Heaven, all bounteous ever,
  Its boundless mercy sent, —
A sail in sight appears ;
  We hail her with three cheers;
Now we sail, with the gale,
  From the Bay of Biscay, O !
            ANDREW CHERRY.

THE STORM.

CEASE, rude Boreas, blustering railer !
  List, ye landsmen, all to me,
Messmates, hear a brother sailor
  Sing the dangers of the sea ;

From bounding billows, first in motion,
  When the distant whirlwinds rise,
To the tempest-troubled ocean,
  Where the seas contend with skies.

Hark ! the boatswain hoarsely bawling,
  By topsail sheets and halyards stand !
Down top-gallants quick be hauling !
  Down your stay-sails, hand, boys, hand !

Now it freshens, set the braces,
  Quick the topsail sheets let go ;
Luff, boys, luff ! don't make wry faces,
  Up your topsails nimbly clew.

Round us roars the tempest louder,
  Think what fear our minds inthralls !
Harder yet, it yet blows harder,
  Now again the boatswain calls.

The topsail yard point to the wind, boys,
  See all clear to reef each course ;
Let the fore sheet go, don't mind, boys,
  Though the weather should be worse.

Fore and aft the sprit-sail yard get,
  Reef the mizzen, see all clear ;
Hands up ! each preventive brace set !
  Man the fore yard, cheer, lads, cheer !

Now the dreadful thunder 's roaring
  Peal on peal contending clash,
On our heads fierce rain falls pouring,
  In our eyes blue lightnings flash.

One wide water all around us,
  All above us one black sky ;
Different deaths at once surround us :
  Hark ! what means that dreadful cry ?

The foremast 's gone, cries every tongue out,
  O'er the lee twelve feet 'bove deck ;
A leak beneath the chest-tree 's sprung out,
  Call all hands to clear the wreck.

Quick the lanyards cut to pieces ;
  Come, my hearts, be stout and bold ;
Plumb the well, — the leak increases,
  Four feet water in the hold !

While o'er the ship wild waves are beating,
  We our wives and children mourn ;
Alas ! from hence there 's no retreating,
  Alas ! to them there 's no return !

Still the leak is gaining on us !
  Both chain-pumps are choked below :
Heaven have mercy here upon us !
  For only that can save us now.

O'er the lee-beam is the land, boys,
  Let the guns o'erboard be thrown ;
To the pumps call every hand, boys,
  See ! our mizzen-mast is gone.

The leak we've found, it cannot pour fast ;
  We 've lighted her a foot or more ;
Up and rig a jury foremast,
  She rights ! she rights, boys ! we 're off shore.
           GEORGE ALEXANDER STEVENS.

THE INCHCAPE ROCK.

No stir in the air, no stir in the sea, —
The ship was still as she might be ;
Her sails from heaven received no motion ;
Her keel was steady in the ocean.

Without either sign or sound of their shock,
The waves flowed over the Inchcape rock ;
So little they rose, so little they fell,
They did not move the Inchcape bell.

The holy abbot of Aberbrothok
Had floated that bell on the Inchcape rock ;
On the waves of the storm it floated and swung,
And louder and louder its warning rung.

When the rock was hid by the tempest's swell,
The mariners heard the warning bell ;
And then they knew the perilous rock,
And blessed the priest of Aberbrothok.

The sun in heaven shone so gay, —
All things were joyful on that day;
The sea-birds screamed as they sported round,
And there was pleasure in their sound.

The float of the Inchcape bell was seen,
A darker speck on the ocean green;
Sir Ralph, the rover, walked his deck,
And he fixed his eye on the darker speck.

He felt the cheering power of spring, —
It made him whistle, it made him sing;
His heart was mirthful to excess;
But the rover's mirth was wickedness.

His eye was on the bell and float:
Quoth he, "My men, pull out the boat;
And row me to the Inchcape rock,
And I 'll plague the priest of Aberbrothok."

The boat is lowered, the boatmen row,
And to the Inchcape rock they go;
Sir Ralph bent over from the boat,
And cut the warning bell from the float.

Down sank the bell with a gurgling sound;
The bubbles rose, and burst around.
Quoth Sir Ralph, "The next who comes to the
    rock
Will not bless the priest of Aberbrothok."

Sir Ralph, the rover, sailed away, —
He scoured the seas for many a day;
And now, grown rich with plundered store,
His steers his course to Scotland's shore.

So thick a haze o'erspreads the sky
They could not see the sun on high;
The wind had blown a gale all day;
At evening it hath died away.

On the deck the rover takes his stand;
So dark it is they see no land.
Quoth Sir Ralph, "It will be lighter soon,
For there is the dawn of the rising moon."

"Canst hear," said one, "the breakers roar?
For yonder, methinks, should be the shore.
Now where we are I cannot tell,
But I wish we could hear the Inchcape bell."

They hear no sound; the swell is strong;
Though the wind hath fallen, they drift along;
Till the vessel strikes with a shivering shock, —
Alas! it is the Inchcape rock!

Sir Ralph, the rover, tore his hair;
He beat himself in wild despair.
The waves rush in on every side;
The ship is sinking beneath the tide.

But ever in his dying fear
One dreadful sound he seemed to hear, —
A sound as if with the Inchcape bell
The evil spirit was ringing his knell.
                                    ROBERT SOUTHEY.

THE FISHERMEN.

THREE fishers went sailing out into the west —
    Out into the west as the sun went down;
Each thought of the woman who loved him the
        best,
    And the children stood watching them out of
        the town;
For men must work, and women must weep;
And there 's little to earn, and many to keep,
    Though the harbor bar be moaning.

Three wives sat up in the lighthouse tower,
    And trimmed the lamps as the sun went down;
And they looked at the squall, and they looked
        at the shower,
    And the rack it came rolling up, ragged and
        brown;
But men must work, and women must weep,
Though storms be sudden, and waters deep,
    And the harbor bar be moaning.

Three corpses lay out on the shining sands
    In the morning gleam as the tide went down,
And the women are watching and wringing their
        hands,
    For those who will never come back to the town;
For men must work, and women must weep, —
And the sooner it 's over, the sooner to sleep, —
    And good by to the bar and its moaning.
                                    CHARLES KINGSLEY.

O MARY, GO AND CALL THE CATTLE HOME!

"O MARY, go and call the cattle home,
        And call the cattle home,
        And call the cattle home,
    Across the sands o' Dee!"
The western wind was wild and dank wi' foam,
        And all alone went she.

The creeping tide came up along the sand,
        And o'er and o'er the sand,
        And round and round the sand,
    As far as eye could see;
The blinding mist came down and hid the land:
        And never home came she.

" O, is it weed, or fish, or floating hair, —
 A tress o' golden hair,
 O' drowned maiden's hair, —
Above the nets at sea ?
Was never salmon yet that shone so fair,
 Among the stakes on Dee."

They rowed her in across the rolling foam, —
 The cruel, crawling foam,
 The cruel, hungry foam, —
 To her grave beside the sea ;
But still the boatmen hear her call the cattle home
 Across the sands o' Dee.
     CHARLES KINGSLEY.

THE MARINER'S DREAM.

IN slumbers of midnight the sailor-boy lay ;
 His hammock swung loose at the sport of the
  wind ;
But watch-worn and weary, his cares flew away,
 And visions of happiness danced o'er his mind.

He dreamt of his home, of his dear native bowers,
 And pleasures that waited on life's merry morn ;
While memory stood sideways half covered with
  flowers,
And restored every rose, but secreted its thorn.

Then Fancy her magical pinions spread wide,
 And bade the young dreamer in ecstasy rise ;
Now far, far behind him the green waters glide,
 And the cot of his forefathers blesses his eyes.

The jessamine clambers in flowers o'er the thatch,
 And the swallow chirps sweet from her nest in
  the wall ;
All trembling with transport he raises the latch,
 And the voices of loved ones reply to his call.

A father bends o'er him with looks of delight ;
 His cheek is impearled with a mother's warm
  tear ;
And the lips of the boy in a love-kiss unite
 With the lips of the maid whom his bosom
  holds dear.

The heart of the sleeper beats high in his breast ;
 Joy quickens his pulses, — his hardships seem
  o'er ;
And a murmur of happiness steals through his
  rest, —
 "O God ! thou hast blest me, — I ask for no
  more."

Ah ! whence is that flame which now bursts on
  his eye ?
Ah ! what is that sound which now 'larms on
  his ear ?

'T is the lightning's red gleam, painting hell on
  the sky !
'T is the crashing of thunders, the groan of the
  sphere !

He springs from his hammock, he flies to the
  deck ;
 Amazement confronts him with images dire ;
Wild winds and mad waves drive the vessel a
  wreck ;
 The masts fly in splinters ; the shrouds are on
  fire.

Like mountains the billows tremendously swell ;
 In vain the lost wretch calls on mercy to save ;
Unseen hands of spirits are ringing his knell,
 And the death-angel flaps his broad wings o'er
  the wave !

O sailor-boy, woe to thy dream of delight !
 In darkness dissolves the gay frost-work of
  bliss.
Where now is the picture that fancy touched
  bright, —
 Thy parents' fond pressure, and love's honeyed
  kiss ?

O sailor-boy ! sailor-boy ! never again
 Shall home, love, or kindred thy wishes repay ;
Unblessed and unhonored, down deep in the main,
 Full many a fathom, thy frame shall decay.

No tomb shall e'er plead to remembrance for thee,
 Or redeem form or fame from the merciless surge,
But the white foam of waves shall thy winding-
  sheet be,
 And winds in the midnight of winter thy dirge !

On a bed of green sea-flowers thy limbs shall be
  laid, —
 Around thy white bones the red coral shall
  grow ;
Of thy fair yellow locks threads of amber be made,
 And every part suit to thy mansion below.

Days, months, years, and ages shall circle away,
 And still the vast waters above thee shall roll ;
Earth loses thy pattern forever and aye, —
 O sailor-boy ! sailor-boy ! peace to thy soul !
     WILLIAM DIMOND.

ON THE LOSS OF THE ROYAL GEORGE.

WRITTEN WHEN THE NEWS ARRIVED ; 1782.

 TOLL for the brave, —
  The brave that are no more !
 All sunk beneath the wave,
  Fast by their native shore.

Eight hundred of the brave,
  Whose courage well was tried.
Had made the vessel heel,
  And laid her on her side.

A land-breeze shook the shrouds,
  And she was overset ;
Down went the Royal George,
  With all her crew complete.

Toll for the brave !
  Brave Kempenfelt is gone ;
His last sea-fight is fought,
  His work of glory done.

It was not in the battle ;
  No tempest gave the shock ;
She sprang no fatal leak ;
  She ran upon no rock.

His sword was in its sheath ;
  His fingers held the pen,
When Kempenfelt went down
  With twice four hundred men.

Weigh the vessel up,
  Once dreaded by our foes !
And mingle with our cup
  The tear that England owes.

Her timbers yet are sound,
  And she may float again,
Full charged with England's thunder,
  And plough the distant main.

But Kempenfelt is gone ;
  His victories are o'er ;
And he and his eight hundred
  Shall plough the wave no more.
                    WILLIAM COWPER.

THE SHIPWRECK.

In vain the cords and axes were prepared,
For now the audacious seas insult the yard ;
High o'er the ship they throw a horrid shade,
And o'er her burst in terrible cascade.
Uplifted on the surge, to heaven she flies,
Her shattered top half-buried in the skies,
Then headlong plunging thunders on the ground ;
Earth groans ! air trembles ! and the deeps re-
  sound !
Her giant-bulk the dread concussion feels,
And quivering with the wound in torment reels.
So reels, convulsed with agonizing throes,
The bleeding bull beneath the murderer's blows.
Again she plunges ! hark ! a second shock
Tears her strong bottom on the marble rock :

Down on the vale of death, with dismal cries,
The fated victims, shuddering, roll their eyes
In wild despair ; while yet another stroke,
With deep convulsion, rends the solid oak ;
Till like the mine, in whose infernal cell
The lurking demons of destruction dwell,
At length asunder torn her frame divides,
And, crashing, spreads in ruin o'er the tides.
  O, were it mine with tuneful Maro's art
To wake to sympathy the feeling heart ;
Like him the smooth and mournful verse to dress
In all the pomp of exquisite distress,
Then too severely taught by cruel fate,
To share in all the perils I relate,
Then might I, with unrivalled strains deplore
The impervious horrors of a leeward shore !
  As o'er the surge the stooping mainmast hung,
Still on the rigging thirty seamen clung ;
Some, struggling, on a broken crag were cast,
And there by oozy tangles grappled fast.
Awhile they bore the o'erwhelming billows' rage,
Unequal combat with their fate to wage ;
Till, all benumbed and feeble, they forego
Their slippery hold, and sink to shades below.
Some, from the main-yard-arm impetuous thrown
On marble ridges, die without a groan.
Three with Palemon on their skill depend,
And from the wreck on oars and rafts descend.
Now on the mountain wave on high they ride,
Then downward plunge beneath the involving
  tide,
Till one, who seems in agony to strive,
The whirling breakers heave on shore alive ;
The rest a speedier end of anguish knew,
And prest the stony beach, a lifeless crew !
                    WILLIAM FALCONER.

YE MARINERS OF ENGLAND.

A NAVAL ODE.

I.

Ye mariners of England,
That guard our native seas ;
Whose flag has braved, a thousand years,
The battle and the breeze !
Your glorious standard launch again
To match another foe !
And sweep through the deep,
While the stormy winds do blow ;
While the battle rages loud and long,
And the stormy winds do blow.

II.

The spirits of your fathers
Shall start from every wave ;
For the deck it was their field of fame,
And Ocean was their grave.

Where Blake and mighty Nelson fell,
Your manly hearts shall glow,
As ye sweep through the deep,
While the stormy winds do blow;
While the battle rages loud and long,
And the stormy winds do blow.

III.

Britannia needs no bulwarks,
No towers along the steep;
Her march is o'er the mountain-waves,
Her home is on the deep.
With thunders from her native oak,
She quells the floods below, —
As they roar on the shore,
When the stormy winds do blow;
When the battle rages loud and long
And the stormy winds do blow.

IV.

The meteor flag of England
Shall yet terrific burn;
Till danger's troubled night depart,
And the star of peace return.
Then, then, ye ocean warriors!
Our song and feast shall flow
To the fame of your name,
When the storm has ceased to blow;
When the fiery fight is heard no more
And the storm has ceased to blow.

THOMAS CAMPBELL.

BATTLE OF THE BALTIC.

"Look to the Baltic, — blazing from afar,
Your old ally yet mourns perfidious war."
BYRON.

I.

OF Nelson and the North
Sing the glorious day's renown,
When to battle fierce came forth
All the might of Denmark's crown,
And her arms along the deep proudly shone;
By each gun the lighted brand,
In a bold, determined hand,
And the prince of all the land
Led them on.

II.

Like leviathans afloat,
Lay their bulwarks on the brine;
While the sign of battle flew
On the lofty British line;
It was ten of April morn by the chime:
As they drifted on their path,
There was silence deep as death;
And the boldest held his breath
For a time.

III.

But the might of England flushed
To anticipate the scene;
And her van the fleeter rushed
O'er the deadly space between.
"Hearts of oak!" our captains cried; when
each gun
From its adamantine lips
Spread a death-shade round the ships,
Like the hurricane eclipse
Of the sun.

IV.

Again! again! again!
And the havoc did not slack,
Till a feeble cheer the Dane
To our cheering sent us back;
Their shots along the deep slowly boom: —
Then ceased, — and all is wail,
As they strike the shattered sail;
Or, in conflagration pale,
Light the gloom.

V.

Outspoke the victor then,
As he hailed them o'er the wave;
"Ye are brothers! ye are men!
And we conquer but to save!
So peace instead of death let us bring;
But yield, proud foe, thy fleet,
With the crews, at England's feet,
And make submission meet
To our King."

VI.

Then Denmark blessed our chief,
That he gave her wounds repose;
And the sounds of joy and grief
From her people wildly rose,
As Death withdrew his shades from the day
While the sun looked smiling bright
O'er a wide and woful sight,
Where the fires of funeral light
Died away.

VII.

Now joy, Old England, raise!
For the tidings of thy might,
By the festal cities' blaze,
Whilst the wine-cup shines in light;
And yet, amidst that joy and uproar,
Let us think of them that sleep,
Full many a fathom deep,
By thy wild and stormy steep,
Elsinore!

VIII.

Brave hearts! to Britain's pride
Once so faithful and so true,
On the deck of fame that died
With the gallant good Riou:

Soft sigh the winds of heaven o'er their grave,
While the billow mournful rolls
And the mermaid's song condoles,
Singing glory to the souls
Of the brave !
                              THOMAS CAMPBELL.

With shroud and mast and pennon fair,
    That well had borne their part, —
But the noblest thing that perished there
    Was that young, faithful heart.
                              FELICIA HEMANS.

CASABIANCA.

[Young Casabianca, a boy about thirteen years old, son of the Admiral of the Orient, remained at his post (in the Battle of the Nile) after the ship had taken fire and all the guns had been abandoned, and perished in the explosion of the vessel, when the flames had reached the powder.]

THE boy stood on the burning deck,
    Whence all but him had fled ;
The flame that lit the battle's wreck
    Shone round him o'er the dead.

Yet beautiful and bright he stood,
    As born to rule the storm ;
A creature of heroic blood,
    A proud though childlike form.

The flames rolled on ; he would not go
    Without his father's word ;
That father, faint in death below,
    His voice no longer heard.

He called aloud, "Say, father, say,
    If yet my task be done ?"
He knew not that the chieftain lay
    Unconscious of his son.

"Speak, father !" once again he cried,
    "If I may yet be gone !"
And but the booming shots replied,
    And fast the flames rolled on.

Upon his brow he felt their breath,
    And in his waving hair,
And looked from that lone post of death
    In still yet brave despair ;

And shouted but once more aloud,
    "My father ! must I stay ?"
While o'er him fast, through sail and shroud,
    The wreathing fires made way.

They wrapt the ship in splendor wild,
    They caught the flag on high,
And streamed above the gallant child,
    Like banners in the sky.

There came a burst of thunder sound ;
    The boy, — Oh ! where was *he ?*
Ask of the winds, that far around
    With fragments strewed the sea, —

THE SEA FIGHT.

AS TOLD BY AN ANCIENT MARINER.

AH, yes, — the fight ! Well, messmates, well,
    I served on board that Ninety-eight ;
Yet what I saw I loathe to tell.
    To-night be sure a crushing weight
Upon my sleeping breast, a hell
    Of dread, will sit. At any rate,
Though land-locked here, a watch I'll keep, —
Grog cheers us still. Who cares for sleep ?

That Ninety-eight I sailed on board ;
    Along the Frenchman's coast we flew ;
Right aft the rising tempest roared ;
    A noble first-rate hove in view ;
And soon high in the gale there soared
    Her streamed-out bunting, — red, white, blue !
We cleared for fight, and landward bore,
To get between the chase and shore.

Masters, I cannot spin a yarn
    Twice laid with words of silken stuff.
A fact's a fact ; and ye may larn
    The rights o' this, though wild and rough
My words may loom. 'T is your consarn,
    Not mine, to understand. Enough ; —
We neared the Frenchman where he lay,
And as we neared, he blazed away.

We tacked, hove to ; we filled, we wore ;
    Did all that seamanship could do
To rake him aft, or by the fore, —
    Now rounded off, and now broached to ;
And now our starboard broadside bore,
    And showers of iron through and through
His vast hull hissed ; our larboard then
Swept from his threefold decks his men.

As we, like a huge serpent, toiled,
    And wound about, through that wild sea,
The Frenchman each manœuvre foiled, —
    'Vantage to neither there could be.
Whilst thus the waves between us boiled,
    We both resolved right manfully
To fight it side by side ; — began
Then the fierce strife of man to man.

Gun bellows forth to gun, and pain
    Rings out her wild, delirious scream !
Redoubling thunders shake the main ;
    Loud crashing, falls the shot-rent beam.

The timbers with the broadsides strain ;
　The slippery decks send up a steam
From hot and living blood, and high
　And shrill is heard the death-pang cry.

The shredded limb, the splintered bone,
　The unstiffened corpse, now block the way !
Who now can hear the dying groan ?
　The trumpet of the judgment-day,
Had it pealed forth its mighty tone,
　We should not then have heard, — to say
Would be rank sin ; but this I tell,
That could alone our madness quell.

Upon the forecastle I fought
　As captain of the for'ad gun.
A scattering shot the carriage caught !
　What mother then had known her son
Of those who stood around ? — distraught,
　And smeared with gore, about they run,
Then fall, and writhe, and howling die !
But one escaped, — that one was I !

Night darkened round, and the storm pealed ;
　To windward of us lay the foe.
As he to leeward over keeled,
　He could not fight his guns below ;
So just was going to strike, — when reeled
　Our vessel, as if some vast blow
From an Almighty hand had rent
The huge ship from her element.

Then howled the thunder.　Tumult then
　Had stunned herself to silence.　Round
Were scattered lightning-blasted men !
　Our mainmast went.　All stifled, drowned,
Arose the Frenchman's shout.　Again
　The bolt burst on us, and we found
Our masts all gone, — our decks all riven :
Man's war mocks faintly that of heaven !

Just then, — nay, messmates, laugh not now, —
　As I, amazed, one minute stood
Amidst that rout, — I know not how, —
　'T was silence all, — the raving flood,
The guns that pealed from stem to bow,
　And God's own thunder, — nothing could
I then of all that tumult hear,
Or see aught of that scene of fear, —

My aged mother at her door
　Sat mildly o'er her humming wheel ;
The cottage, orchard, and the moor, —
　I saw them plainly all.　I 'll kneel,
And swear I saw them !　O, they wore
　A look all peace ?　Could I but feel
Again that bliss that then I felt,
That made my heart, like childhood's, melt !

The blessed tear was on my cheek,
　She smiled with that old smile I know :
" Turn to me, mother, turn and speak,"
　Was on my quivering lips, — when lo !
All vanished, and a dark, red streak
　Glared wild and vivid from the foe,
That flashed upon the blood-stained water, —
For fore and aft the flames had caught her.

She struck and hailed us.　On us fast
　All burning, helplessly, she came, —
Near, and more near ; and not a mast
　Had we to help us from that flame.
'T was then the bravest stood aghast, —
　'T was then the wicked, on the name
(With danger and with guilt appalled)
Of God, too long neglected, called.

The eddying flames with ravening tongue
　Now on our ship's dark bulwarks dash, —
We almost touched, — when ocean rung
　Down to its depths with one loud crash !
In heaven's top vault one instant hung
　The vast, intense, and blinding flash !
Then all was darkness, stillness, dread, —
The wave moaned o'er the valiant dead.

She 's gone ! blown up ! that gallant foe !
　And though she left us in a plight,
We floated still ; long were, I know,
　And hard, the labors of that night
To clear the wreck.　At length in tow
　A frigate took us, when 't was light ;
And soon an English port we gained, —
A hulk all battered and blood-stained.

So many slain, — so many drowned !
　I like not of that fight to tell.
Come, let the cheerful grog go round !
　Messmates, I 've done.　A spell, ho ! spell, —
Though a pressed man, I 'll still be found
　To do a seaman's duty well.
I wish our brother landsmen knew
One half we jolly tars go through.
ANONYMOUS.

THE SAILOR'S WIFE.

AND are ye sure the news is true ?
　And are ye sure he 's weel ?
Is this a time to think o' wark ?
　Ye jades, lay by your wheel ,
Is this the time to spin a thread,
　When Colin 's at the door ?
Reach down my cloak, I 'll to the quay,
　And see him come ashore.
For there 's nae luck about the house,
　There 's nae luck at a' ;
There 's little pleasure in the house
　When our gudeman 's awa'.

And gie to me my bigonet,
  My bishop's satin gown ;
For I maun tell the baillie's wife
  That Colin 's in the town.
My Turkey slippers maun gae on,
  My stockin's pearly blue ;
It 's a' to pleasure our gudeman,
  For he 's baith leal and true.

Rise, lass, and mak a clean fireside,
  Put on the muckle pot ;
Gie little Kate her button gown,
  And Jock his Sunday coat ;
And mak their shoon as black as slaes,
  Their hose as white as snaw ;
It 's a' to please my ain gudeman,
  For he 's been long awa'.

There 's twa fat hens upo' the coop
  Been fed this month and mair ;
Mak haste and thraw their necks about,
  That Colin weel may fare ;
And spread the table neat and clean,
  Gar ilka thing look braw,
For wha can tell how Colin fared
  When he was far awa' ?

Sae true his heart, sae smooth his speech,
  His breath like caller air ;
His very foot has music in 't
  As he comes up the stair, —
And will I see his face again ?
  And will I hear him speak ?
I 'm downright dizzy wi' the thought,
  In troth I 'm like to greet !

If Colin 's weel, and weel content,
  I hae nae mair to crave :
And gin I live to keep him sae
  I 'm blest aboon the lave :
And will I see his face again ?
  And will I hear him speak ?
I 'm downright dizzy wi' the thought,
  In troth I 'm like to greet.
For there 's nae luck about the house,
  There 's nae luck at a' ;
There 's little pleasure in the house
  When our gudeman 's awa'.

W. J. MICKLE.

SIR SIDNEY SMITH.

GENTLEFOLKS, in my time, I 've made many a
    rhyme,
But the song I now trouble you with,
Lays some claim to applause, and you 'll grant
    it, because
The subject 's Sir Sidney Smith, it is ;
The subject 's Sir Sidney Smith.

We all know Sir Sidney, a man of such kidney,
He 'd fight every foe he could meet ;
Give him one ship for two, and without more ado,
He 'd engage if he met a whole fleet, he would,
He 'd engage if he met a whole fleet.

Thus he took, every day, all that came in his way,
Till fortune, that changeable elf,
Ordered accidents so, that while taking the foe,
Sir Sidney got taken himself, he did,
Sir Sidney got taken himself.

His captors, right glad of the prize they now had,
Rejected each offer we bid,
And swore he should stay locked up till doomsday ;
But he swore he 'd be d——d if he did, he did,
But he swore he 'd be hanged if he did.

So Sir Sid got away, and his jailer next day
Cried, " Sacre, diable, morbleu,
Mon prisonnier 'scape ; I 'ave got in von scrape,
And I fear I must run away too, I must,
I fear I must run away too ! "

If Sir Sidney was wrong, why then blackball my
    song,
E'en his foes he would scorn to deceive ;
His escape was but just, and confess it you must,
For it only was taking French leave, you know,
It only was taking French leave.

CHARLES DIBDIN.

NAPOLEON AND THE BRITISH SAILOR.

I LOVE contemplating — apart
  From all his homicidal glory —
The traits that soften to our heart
  Napoleon's glory !

'T was when his banners at Boulogne
  Armed in our island every freeman,
His navy chanced to capture one
  Poor British seaman.

They suffered him — I know not how —
  Unprisoned on the shore to roam ;
And aye was bent his longing brow
  On England's home.

His eye, methinks ! pursued the flight
  Of birds to Britain half-way over ;
With envy *they* could reach the white
  Dear cliffs of Dover.

A stormy midnight watch, he thought,
  Than this sojourn would have been dearer,
If but the storm his vessel brought
  To England nearer.

At last, when care had banished sleep,
    He saw one morning, dreaming, doting,
An empty hogshead from the deep
    Come shoreward floating ;

He hid it in a cave, and wrought
    The live-long day laborious ; lurking
Until he launched a tiny boat
    By mighty working.

Heaven help us ! 't was a thing beyond
    Description wretched ; such a wherry
Perhaps ne'er ventured on a pond,
    Or crossed a ferry.

For ploughing in the salt-sea field,
    It would have made the boldest shudder ;
Untarred, uncompassed, and unkeeled, —
    No sail, no rudder.

From neighboring woods he interlaced
    His sorry skiff with wattled willows ;
And thus equipped he would have passed
    The foaming billows, —

But Frenchmen caught him on the beach,
    His little Argus sorely jeering ;
Till tidings of him chanced to reach
    Napoleon's hearing.

With folded arms Napoleon stood,
    Serene alike in peace and danger ;
And, in his wonted attitude,
    Addressed the stranger : —

"Rash man, that wouldst yon Channel pass
    On twigs and staves so rudely fashioned,
Thy heart with some sweet British lass
    Must be impassioned."

"I have no sweetheart," said the lad ;
    "But — absent long from one another —
Great was the longing that I had
    To see my mother."

"And so thou shalt," Napoleon said,
    "Ye've both my favor fairly won ;
A noble mother must have bred
    So brave a son."

He gave the tar a piece of gold,
    And, with a flag of truce, commanded
He should be shipped to England Old,
    And safely landed.

Our sailor oft could scantly shift
    To find a dinner, plain and hearty,
But *never* changed the coin and gift
    Of Bonaparté.

                         THOMAS CAMPBELL.

HOW 'S MY BOY ?

"Ho, sailor of the sea !
How 's my boy — my boy ?"
"What 's your boy's name, good wife,
And in what ship sailed he ?"

"My boy John —
He that went to sea —
What care I for the ship, sailor ?
My boy 's my boy to me.

"You come back from sea,
And not know my John ?
I might as well have asked some landsman,
Yonder down in the town.
There 's not an ass in all the parish
But knows my John.

"How 's my boy — my boy ?
And unless you let me know,
I 'll swear you are no sailor,
Blue jacket or no, —
Brass buttons or no, sailor,
Anchor and crown or no, —
Sure his ship was the 'Jolly Briton' "—
"Speak low, woman, speak low !"

"And why should I speak low, sailor,
About my own boy John ?
If I was loud as I am proud
I 'd sing him over the town !
Why should I speak low, sailor ?"
"That good ship went down."

"How 's my boy — my boy ?
What care I for the ship, sailor ?
I was never aboard her.
Be she afloat or be she aground,
Sinking or swimming, I 'll be bound
Her owners can afford her !
I say, how 's my John ?"
"Every man on board went down,
Every man aboard her."

"How 's my boy — my boy ?
What care I for the men, sailor ?
I 'm not their mother —
How 's my boy — my boy ?
Tell me of him and no other !
How 's my boy — my boy ?"

                         SYDNEY DOBELL.

POEMS OF ADVENTURE AND RURAL SPORTS.

O Victor Emmanuel the King,
    The sword be for thee, and the deed,
And nought for the alien, next spring,
    Nought for Hapsburg and Bourbon agreed,
    But, for us, a great Italy freed,
With a hero to head us, .. our King

                    Elizabeth Barrett Browning.

POEMS OF ADVENTURE AND RURAL SPORTS.

CHEVY-CHASE.

[Percy, Earl of Northumberland, had vowed to hunt for three days in the Scottish border, without condescending to ask leave from Earl Douglas, who was either lord of the soil or lord warden of the Marches. This provoked the conflict which was celebrated in the old ballad of the "Hunting a' the Cheviot." The circumstances of the battle of Otterbourne (A. D. 1388) are woven into the ballad and the affairs of the two events confounded. The ballad preserved in the Percy Reliques is probably as old as 1574. The one following is a modernized form of the time of James I.]

GOD prosper long our noble king,
　Our lives and safeties all ;
A woful hunting once there did
　In Chevy-Chase befall.

To drive the deer with hound and horn
　Earl Percy took his way ;
The child may rue that is unborn
　The hunting of that day.

The stout Earl of Northumberland
　A vow to God did make,
His pleasure in the Scottish woods
　Three summer days to take, —

The chiefest harts in Chevy-Chase
　To kill and bear away.
These tidings to Earl Douglas came,
　In Scotland where he lay ;

Who sent Earl Percy present word
　He would prevent his sport.
The English earl, not fearing that,
　Did to the woods resort,

With fifteen hundred bowmen bold,
　All chosen men of might,
Who knew full well in time of need
　To aim their shafts aright.

The gallant greyhounds swiftly ran
　To chase the fallow deer ;
On Monday they began to hunt
　When daylight did appear ;

And long before high noon they had
　A hundred fat bucks slain ;
Then, having dined, the drovers went
　To rouse the deer again.

The bowmen mustered on the hills,
　Well able to endure ;
And all their rear, with special care,
　That day was guarded sure.

The hounds ran swiftly through the woods
　The nimble deer to take,
That with their cries the hills and dales
　An echo shrill did make.

Lord Percy to the quarry went,
　To view the slaughtered deer ;
Quoth he, "Earl Douglas promised
　This day to meet me here ;

"But if I thought he would not come,
　No longer would I stay" ;
With that a brave young gentleman
　Thus to the earl did say : —

"Lo, yonder doth Earl Douglas come, —
　His men in armor bright ;
Full twenty hundred Scottish spears
　All marching in our sight ;

"All men of pleasant Teviotdale,
　Fast by the river. Tweed " ;
"Then cease your sports," Earl Percy said,
　"And take your bows with speed ;

"And now with me, my countrymen,
　Your courage forth advance ;
For never was there champion yet,
　In Scotland or in France,

"That ever did on horseback come,
　But if my hap it were,
I durst encounter man for man,
　With him to break a spear."

Earl Douglas on his milk-white steed,
　Most like a baron bold,
Rode foremost of his company,
　Whose armor shone like gold.

"Show me," said he, "whose men you be,
　That hunt so boldly here,
That, without my consent, do chase
　And kill my fallow-deer."

The first man that did answer make,
  Was noble Percy he —
Who said, " We list not to declare,
  Nor show whose men we be:

" Yet will we spend our dearest blood
  Thy chiefest harts to slay."
Then Douglas swore a solemn oath,
  And thus in rage did say :

" Ere thus I will out-braved be,
  One of us two shall die ;
I know thee well, an earl thou art, —
  Lord Percy, so am I.

" But trust me, Percy, pity it were,
  And great offence, to kill
Any of these our guiltless men,
  For they have done no ill.

" Let you and me the battle try,
  And set our men aside."
" Accursed be he," Earl Percy said,
  " By whom this is denied."

Then stepped a gallant squire forth,
  Witherington was his name,
Who said, "I would not have it told
  To Henry, our king, for shame,

" That e'er my captain fought on foot,
  And I stood looking on.
You two be earls," said Witherington,
  " And I a squire alone ;

" I'll do the best that do I may,
  While I have power to stand ;
While I have power to wield my sword
  I 'll fight with heart and hand."

Our English archers bent their bows, —
  Their hearts were good and true ;
At the first flight of arrows sent,
  Full fourscore Scots they slew.

Yet stays Earl Douglas on the bent,
  As chieftain stout and good ;
As valiant captain, all unmoved,
  The shock he firmly stood.

His host he parted had in three,
  As leader ware and tried ;
And soon his spearmen on their foes
  Bore down on every side.

Throughout the English archery
  They dealt full many a wound ;
But still our valiant Englishmen
  All firmly kept their ground.

And throwing straight their bows away,
  They grasped their swords so bright ;
And now sharp blows, a heavy shower,
  On shields and helmets light.

They closed full fast on every side, —
  No slackness there was found ;
And many a gallant gentleman
  Lay gasping on the ground.

In truth, it was a grief to see
  How each one chose his spear,
And how the blood out of their breasts
  Did gush like water clear.

At last these two stout earls did meet ;
  Like captains of great might,
Like lions wode, they laid on lode,
  And made a cruel fight.

They fought until they both did sweat,
  With swords of tempered steel,
Until the blood, like drops of rain,
  They trickling down did feel.

" Yield thee, Lord Percy," Douglas said,
  " In faith I will thee bring
Where thou shalt high advancéd be
  By James, our Scottish king.

" Thy ransom I will freely give,
  And this report of thee, —
Thou art the most courageous knight
  That ever I did see."

" No, Douglas," saith Earl Percy then,
  " Thy proffer I do scorn ;
I will not yield to any Scot
  That ever yet was born."

With that there came an arrow keen
  Out of an English bow,
Which struck Earl Douglas to the heart, —
  A deep and deadly blow ;

Who never spake more words than these :
  " Fight on, my merry men all ;
For why, my life is at an end ;
  Lord Percy sees my fall."

Then leaving life, Earl Percy took
  The dead man by the hand ;
And said, " Earl Douglas, for thy life
  Would I had lost my land.

" In truth, my very heart doth bleed
  With sorrow for thy sake ;
For sure a more redoubted knight
  Mischance did never take."

A knight amongst the Scots there was
　Who saw Earl Douglas die,
Who straight in wrath did vow revenge
　Upon the Earl Percy.

Sir Hugh Mountgomery was he called,
　Who, with a spear full bright,
Well mounted on a gallant steed,
　Ran fiercely through the fight ;

And past the English archers all,
　Without a dread or fear ;
And through Earl Percy's body then
　He thrust his hateful spear ;

With such vehement force and might
　He did his body gore,
The staff ran through the other side
　A large cloth-yard and more.

So thus did both these nobles die,
　Whose courage none could stain.
An English archer then perceived
　The noble earl was slain.

He had a bow bent in his hand,
　Made of a trusty tree ;
An arrow of a cloth-yard long
　To the hard head haled he.

Against Sir Hugh Mountgomery
　So right the shaft he set,
The gray goose wing that was thereon
　In his heart's blood was wet.

This fight did last from break of day
　Till setting of the sun ;
For when they rung the evening-bell
　The battle scarce was done.

With stout Earl Percy there were slain
　Sir John of Egerton,
Sir Robert Ratcliff, and Sir John,
　Sir James, that bold baron.

And with Sir George and stout Sir James,
　Both knights of good account,
Good Sir Ralph Raby there was slain,
　Whose prowess did surmount.

For Witherington my heart is woe
　That ever he slain should be,
For when his legs were hewn in two,
　He knelt and fought on his knee.

And with Earl Douglas there were slain
　Sir Hugh Mountgomery,
Sir Charles Murray, that from the field
　One foot would never flee.

Sir Charles Murray of Ratcliff, too, —
　His sister's son was he ;
Sir David Lamb, so well esteemed,
　But saved he could not be.

And the Lord Maxwell in like case
　Did with Earl Douglas die :
Of twenty hundred Scottish spears,
　Scarce fifty-five did fly.

Of fifteen hundred Englishmen,
　Went home but fifty-three ;
The rest in Chevy-Chase were slain,
　Under the greenwood tree.

Next day did many widows come,
　Their husbands to bewail ;
They washed their wounds in brinish tears,
　But all would not prevail.

Their bodies, bathed in purple blood,
　They bore with them away ;
They kissed them dead a thousand times,
　Ere they were clad in clay.

The news was brought to Edinburgh,
　Where Scotland's king did reign,
That brave Earl Douglas suddenly
　Was with an arrow slain :

"O heavy news," King James did say ;
　"Scotland can witness be
I have not any captain more
　Of such account as he."

Like tidings to King Henry came
　Within as short a space,
That Percy of Northumberland
　Was slain in Chevy-Chase :

"Now God be with him," said our King,
　"Since 't will no better be ;
I trust I have within my realm
　Five hundred as good as he :

"Yet shall not Scots or Scotland say
　But I will vengeance take ;
I 'll be revengéd on them all
　For brave Earl Percy's sake."

This vow full well the King performed
　After at Humbledown ;
In one day fifty knights were slain
　With lords of high renown ;

And of the rest, of small account,
　Did many hundreds die :
Thus endeth the hunting of Chevy-Chase,
　Made by the Earl Percy.

God save the king, and bless this land,
With plenty, joy, and peace ;
And grant, henceforth, that foul debate
'Twixt noblemen may cease.

RICHARD SHEALE.

ROBIN HOOD AND ALLEN–A–DALE.

[Of Robin Hood, the famous outlaw of Sherwood Forest, and his merry men, there are a large number of ballads ; but the limits of this volume necessitate our giving a selection only.
Various periods, ranging from the time of Richard I. to the end of the reign of Edward II., have been assigned as the age in which Robin Hood lived. He is usually described as a yeoman, and his place of abode Sherwood Forest, in Nottinghamshire. His most noted followers, and those generally spoken of in the ballads, are Little John, Friar Tuck, his chaplain, and his maid Marian. Nearly all the legends extol his courage, generosity, humanity, and skill as an archer. He robbed the rich only, who could afford to lose, and gave freely to the poor. He protected the needy, was a champion of the fair sex, and took great delight in robbing prelates. The following ballad exhibits the outlaw in one of his most attractive aspects, — affording assistance to a distressed lover.]

COME, listen to me, you gallants so free,
All you that love mirth for to hear,
And I will tell you of a bold outlaw,
That lived in Nottinghamshire.

As Robin Hood in the forest stood,
All under the greenwood tree,
There he was aware of a brave young man,
As fine as fine might be.

The youngster was clad in scarlet red,
In scarlet fine and gay ;
And he did frisk it over the plain,
And chanted a roundelay.

As Robin Hood next morning stood
Amongst the leaves so gay,
There did he espy the same young man
Come drooping along the way.

The scarlet he wore the day before
It was clean cast away ;
And at every step he fetched a sigh,
" Alas ! and a well-a-day ! "

Then steppéd forth brave Little John,
And Midge, the miller's son ;
Which made the young man bend his bow,
Whenas he see them come.

" Stand off ! stand off ! " the young man said,
" What is your will with me ? "
" You must come before our master straight,
Under yon greenwood tree."

And when he came bold Robin before,
Robin asked him courteously,
" O, hast thou any money to spare,
For my merry men and me ? "

" I have no money," the young man said,
" But five shillings and a ring ;
And that I have kept these seven long years,
To have at my wedding.

" Yesterday I should have married a maid,
But she was from me ta'en,
And chosen to be an old knight's delight,
Whereby my poor heart is slain."

" What is thy name ? " then said Robin Hood,
" Come tell me without any fail."
" By the faith of my body," then said the young man,
" My name it is Allen-a-Dale."

" What wilt thou give me," said Robin Hood,
" In ready gold or fee,
To help thee to thy true-love again,
And deliver her unto thee ? "

" I have no money," then quoth the young man,
" No ready gold nor fee,
But I will swear upon a book
Thy true servant for to be."

" How many miles is it to thy true-love ?
Come tell me without guile."
" By the faith of my body," then said the young man,
" It is but five little mile."

Then Robin he hasted over the plain,
He did neither stint nor linn,*
Until he came unto the church
Where Allen should keep his weddin'.

" What hast thou here ? " the bishop then said,
" I prithee now tell unto me."
" I am a bold harper," quoth Robin Hood,
" And the best in the north country."

" O. welcome, O, welcome," the bishop he said,
" That music best pleaseth me."
" You shall have no music," quoth Robin Hood,
" Till the bride and bridegroom I see."

With that came in a wealthy knight,
Which was both grave and old ;
And after him a finikin lass,
Did shine like the glistering gold.

" This is not a fit match," quoth Robin Hood,
" That you do seem to make here ;
For since we are come into the church,
The bride shall chuse her own dear."

Then Robin Hood put his horn to his mouth,
And blew blasts two and three ;
When four-and-twenty yeomen bold
Come leaping over the lea.

* Stop nor stay.

And when they came into the churchyard,
 Marching all in a row,
The first man was Allen-a-Dale,
 To give bold Robin his bow.

"This is thy true-love," Robin he said,
 "Young Allen, as I hear say ;
And you shall be married this same time,
 Before we depart away."

"That shall not be," the bishop he cried,
 "For thy word shall not stand ;
They shall be three times asked in the church,
 As the law is of our land."

Robin Hood pulled off the bishop's coat,
 And put it upon Little John ;
"By the faith of my body," then Robin said,
 "This cloth doth make thee a man."

When Little John went into the quire,
 The people began to laugh ;
He asked them seven times into church
 Lest three times should not be enough.

"Who gives me this maid ?" said Little John,
 Quoth Robin Hood, "That do I ;
And he that takes her from Allen-a-Dale,
 Full dearly he shall her buy."

And then, having ended this merry wedding,
 The bride looked like a queen ;
And so they returned to the merry greenwood,
 Amongst the leaves so green.
 ANONYMOUS.

THE KING AND THE MILLER OF MANSFIELD.

HENRY, our royall king, would ride a-hunting
 To the grene forest so pleasant and faire ;
To see the harts skipping, and dainty does tripping :
 Unto merry Sherwood his nobles repaire :
Hawke and hound were unbound, all things
 prepared
For the game, in the same, with good regard.

All a long summer's day rode the king pleasantlye
 With all his princes and nobles eche one ;
Chasing the hart and hind, and the bucke gal-
 lantlye,
 Till the dark evening forced all to turne home.
Then at last, riding fast, he had lost quite
All his lords in the wood, late in the night.

Wandering thus wearilye, all alone, up and downe,
 With a rude miller he mett at the last ;
Asking the ready way unto faire Nottingham,
 "Sir," quoth the miller, "I meane not to jest,

Yet I thinke, what I thinke, sooth for to say,
Yo doe not lightlye ride out of your way."

"Why, what dost thou think of me," quoth our
 king, merrily,
 "Passing thy judgment upon me so briefe ?"
"Good faith," sayd the miller, "I meane not to
 flatter thee ;
I guess thee to be but some gentleman thefe :
Stand thee backe in the dark ; light not adowne,
Lest that I presentlye crack thy knave's crowne."

"Thou dost abuse me much," quoth the king,
 "saying thus ;
I am a gentleman ; lodging I lacke."
"Thou hast not," quoth the miller, "one grot
 in thy purse ;
All thy inheritance hanges on thy backe."
"I have gold to discharge all that I call ;
If it be but forty pence, I will pay all."

Thus they went all along unto the miller's house,
 Where they were seething of puddings and
 souse ;
The miller first entered in ; after him went the king ;
 Never came hee in soe smoakye a house.
"Now," quoth hee, "let me see here what you
 are."
Quoth our king, "Looke your fill, and doe not
 spare."

"I like well thy countenance ; thou hast an
 honest face ;
With my son Richard this night thou shalt lye."
Quoth his wife, "By my troth, it is a handsome
 youth ;
Yet it's best, husband, to deal warilye.
Art thou no runaway ; prythee, youth, tell ?
Show me thy passport, and all shall be well."

Then our king, presentlye making lowe courtesye,
 With his hatt in his hand, thus he did say :
"I have no passport, nor never was servitor,
 But a poor courtier, rode out of my way ;
And for your kindness here offered to mee,
I will requite you in everye degree."

Then to the miller his wife whispered secretlye,
 Saying, "It seemeth this youth's of good kin,
Both by his apparel, and eke by his manners ;
 To turne him out, certainlye, were a great sin."
"Yea," quoth hee, "you may see he hath some
 grace
When he doth speake to his betters in place."

"Well," quoth the miller's wife, "young man,
 ye're welcome here ;
And, though I say it, well lodgéd shall be ;

Fresh straw will I have laid on thy bed so brave,
  And good brown hempen sheets likewise,"
    quoth shee.
"Aye," quoth the goodman, "and when that is
    done,
Thou shalt lye with no worse than our own sonne."

"Nay, first," quoth Richard, "good fellowe, tell
    me true,
Hast thou no creepers within thy gay hose?
Or art thou not troubled with the scabbado?"
  "I pray," quoth the king, "what creatures
    are those?"
"Art thou not lousy, nor scabby?" quoth he:
"If thou beest, surely thou lyest not with mee."

This caused the king suddenlye to laugh most
    heartilye,
  Till the teares trickled fast downe from his eyes.
Then to their supper were they set orderlye,
  With hot bag-puddings and good apple-pyes;
Nappy ale, good and stale, in a browne bowle,
Which did about the board merrilye trowle.

"Here," quoth the miller, "good fellowe, I
    drinke to thee,
  And to all 'cuckholds, wherever they bee.'"
"I pledge thee," quoth our king, "and thanke
    thee heartilye
  For mye welcome in every good degree;
And here, in like manner, I drinke to thy sonne."
"Do, then," quoth Richard, "and quicke let it
    come."

"Wife," quoth the miller, "fetch me forth
    lightfoote,
  And of his sweetnesse a little we'll taste."
A fair ven'son pastye brought she out presently.
  "Eate," quoth the miller; "but, sir, make no
    waste.
Here's dainty lightfoote!" — "In faith," sayd
    the king,
"I never before eat so daintye a thing."

"I wis," quoth Richard, "no daintye at all it is;
  For we doe eate of it everye day."
"In what place," sayd our king, "may be
    bought like to this?"
  "We never pay penny for itt, by my fay:
From merry Sherwood we fetch it home here;
  Now and then we make bold with our kinge's
    deer."

"Then I thinke," sayd our king, "that it is
    venison."
  "Eche foole," quoth Richard, "full well may
    know that;
Never are wee without two or three in the roof,
  Very well fleshed, and excellent fat:

But, prythee, say nothing wherever thou goe;
  We would not, for twopence, the king should it
    knowe."

"Doubt not," then sayd the king, "my promist
    secresye;
  The king shall never know more on't for me."
A cupp of lamb's-wool they dranke unto him then,
  And to their bedds they past presentlye.
The nobles, next morning, went all up and down,
For to seeke out the king in every towne.

At last, at the miller's "cott," soon they espied
    him out,
  As he was mounting upon his faire steede;
To whom they came presently, falling down on
    their knee,
  Which made the miller's heart wofully bleede;
Shaking and quaking, before him he stood,
Thinking he should have been hanged by the Rood.

The king perceiving him fearfully trembling,
  Drew forth his sword, but nothing he sed;
The miller downe did fall, crying before them all,
  Doubting the king would have cut off his head.
But he, his kind courtesye for to requite,
Gave him great living and dubbed him a knight.
    ANONYMOUS.

THE RETURN OF BEPPO.

WHILE Laura thus was seen, and seeing, smiling,
  Talking, she knew not why, and cared not what,
So that her female friends, with envy broiling,
  Beheld her airs and triumph, and all that;
And well-dressed males still kept before her filing,
  And passing bowed and mingled with her chat;
More than the rest one person seemed to stare
With pertinacity that's rather rare.

He was a Turk, the color of mahogany;
  And Laura saw him, and at first was glad,
Because the Turks so much admire philogyny,
  Although their usage of their wives is sad;
'T is said they use no better than a dog any
  Poor woman, whom they purchase like a pad;
They have a number, though they ne'er exhibit 'em,
Four wives by law, and concubines "ad libitum."

They lock them up, and veil, and guard them daily,
  They scarcely can behold their male relations,
So that their moments do not pass so gayly
  As is supposed the case with northern nations;
Confinement, too, must make them look quite
    palely;
  And as the Turks abhor long conversations,
Their days are either passed in doing nothing,
Or bathing, nursing, making love, and clothing.

•   •   •   •   •   •

Our Laura's Turk still kept his eyes upon her,
　Less in the Mussulman than Christian way,
Which seems to say, "Madam, I do you honor,
　And while I please to stare, you'll please to stay."
Could staring win a woman, this had won her,
　But Laura could not thus be led astray ;
She had stood fire too long and well to boggle
Even at this stranger's most outlandish ogle.

.　　.　　.　　.　　.

Laura, who knew it would not do at all
　To meet the daylight after seven hours' sitting
Among three thousand people at a ball,
　To make her courtesy thought it right and fit-
　　ting :
The Count was at her elbow with her shawl,
　And they the room were on the point of quitting,
When lo ! those cursed gondoliers had got
Just in the very place where they *should not*.

.　　.　　.　　.　　.

The Count and Laura found their boat at last,
　And homeward floated o'er the silent tide,
Discussing all the dances gone and past ;
　The dancers and their dresses, too, beside ;
Some little scandals eke : but all aghast
　(As to their palace stairs the rowers glide)
Sate Laura by the side of her Adorer,
When lo ! the Mussulman was there before her.

"Sir," said the Count, with brow exceeding grave,
　"Your unexpected presence here will make
It necessary for myself to crave
　Its import ?　But perhaps 't is a mistake ;
I hope it is so ; and at once to waive
　All compliment, I hope so for *your* sake :
You understand my meaning, or you *shall*."
"Sir" (quoth the Turk), "'t is no mistake at all.

"That lady is *my wife !*"　Much wonder paints
　The lady's changing cheek, as well it might ;
But where an English woman sometimes faints,
　Italian females don't do so outright.
They only call a little on their saints,
　And then come to themselves, almost or quite ;
Which saves much hartshorn, salts, and sprink-
　　ling faces,
And cutting stays, as usual in such cases.

She said, — what could she say ?　Why, not a
　　word ;
　But the Count courteously invited in
The stranger, much appeased by what he heard :
　"Such things, perhaps, we'd best discuss
　　within,"
Said he ; "don't let us make ourselves absurd
　In public, by a scene, nor raise a din,
For then the chief and only satisfaction
Will be much quizzing on the whole transaction."

They entered, and for coffee called, — it came,
　A beverage for Turks and Christians both,
Although the way they make it's not the same.
　Now Laura, much recovered, or less loath
To speak, cries, "Beppo ! what's your pagan name ?
　Bless me ! your beard is of amazing growth !
And how came you to keep away so long ?
Are you not sensible 't was very wrong ?

"And are you *really*, *truly*, now a Turk ?
　With any other women did you wive ?
Is 't true they use their fingers for a fork ?
　Well, that's the prettiest shawl — as I'm alive !
You'll give it me ?　They say you eat no pork.
　And how so many years did you contrive
To —　Bless me ! Did I ever ?　No, I never
Saw a man grown so yellow ! How's your liver ?

"Beppo, that beard of yours becomes you not ;
　It shall be shaved before you're a day older ;
Why do you wear it ?　O, I had forgot —
　Pray, don't you think the weather here is colder ?
How do I look ?　You sha'n't stir from this spot
　In that queer dress, for fear that some beholder
Should find you out, and make the story known.
How short your hair is ! Lord ! how gray it's
　　grown ! "

What answer Beppo made to these démands
　Is more than I know.　He was cast away
About where Troy stood once, and nothing stands ;
　Became a slave, of course, and for his pay
Had bread and bastinadoes, till some bands
　Of pirates landing in a neighboring bay,
He joined the rogues and prospered, and became
A renegado of indifferent fame.

But he grew rich, and with his riches grew so
　Keen the desire to see his home again,
He thought himself in duty bound to do so,
　And not be always thieving on the main ;
Lonely he felt, at times, as Robin Crusoe,
　And so he hired a vessel come from Spain,
Bound for Corfu : she was a fine polacca,
Manned with twelve hands, and laden with to-
　　bacco.

Himself, and much (Heaven knows how gotten !)
　　cash,
　He then embarked, with risk of life and limb,
And got clear off, although the attempt was rash ;
　He said that *Providence* protected him, —
For my part, I say nothing, lest we clash
　In our opinions : — well, the ship was trim,
Set sail, and kept her reckoning fairly on,
Except three days of calm when off Cape Bonn.

They reached the island, he transferred his lading,
　And self and live stock, to another bottom,

And passed for a true Turkey merchant, trading
  With goods of various names, but I 've forgot 'em.
However, he got off by this evading,
    Or else the people would perhaps have shot
      him ;
And thus at Venice landed to reclaim
His wife, religion, house, and Christian name.

His wife received, the patriarch rebaptized him
  (He made the church a present, by the way) ;
He then threw off the garments which disguised
    him,
    And borrowed the Count's small-clothes for a
      day ;
His friends the more for his long absence prized
    him,
    Finding he 'd wherewithal to make them gay
With dinners, where he oft became the laugh of
    them,
For stories, — but *I* don't believe the half of them.

Whate'er his youth had suffered, his old age
  With wealth and talking made him some
    amends ;
Though Laura sometimes put him in a rage,
  I 've heard the Count and he were always friends.
My pen is at the bottom of a page,
  Which being finished, here the story ends ;
'T is to be wished it had been sooner done,
But stories somehow lengthen when begun.
                                        BYRON.

———◆———

JOCK JOHNSTONE, THE TINKLER.

"O, CAME ye ower by the Yoke-burn Ford,
  Or down the King's Road of the cleuch ? *
Or saw ye a knight and a lady bright,
  Wha ha'e gane the gate they baith shall rue ?"

"I saw a knight and a lady bright
  Ride up the cleuch at the break of day ;
The knight upon a coal-black steed,
  And the dame on one of the silver-gray.

"And the lady's palfrey flew the first,
  With many a clang of silver bell :
Swift as the raven's morning flight
  The two went scouring ower the fell.

"By this time they are man and wife,
  And standing in St. Mary's fane ;
And the lady in the grass-green silk
  A maid you will never see again."

"But I can tell thee, saucy wight, —
  And that the runaway shall prove, —
Revenge to a Douglas is as sweet
  As maiden charms or maiden's love."

        * Dell.

"Since thou say'st that, my Lord Douglas,
  Good faith some clinking there will be ;
Beshrew my heart, but and my sword,
  If I winna turn and ride with thee !"

They whipped out ower the Shepherd Cleuch,
  And doun the links o' the Corsecleuch Burn ;
And aye the Douglas swore by his sword
  To win his love, or ne'er return.

"First fight your rival, Lord Douglas,
  And then brag after, if you may ;
For the Earl of Ross is as brave a lord
  As ever gave good weapon sway.

"But I for ae poor siller merk,
  Or thirteen pennies and a bawbee,
Will tak in hand to fight you baith,
  Or beat the winner, whiche'er it be."

The Douglas turned him on his steed,
  And I wat a loud laughter leuch he :
"Of a' the fools I have ever met,
  Man, I ha'e never met ane like thee.

"Art thou akin to lord or knight,
  Or courtly squire or warrior leal ?."
"I am a tinkler," quo' the wight,
  "But I like crown-cracking unco weel."

When they came to St. Mary's kirk,
  The chaplain shook for very fear ;
And aye he kissed the cross, and said,
  "What deevil has sent that Douglas here !

"He neither values book nor ban,
  But curses all without demur ;
And cares nae mair for a holy man
  Than I do for a worthless cur."

"Come here, thou bland and brittle priest,
  And tell to me without delay
Where you have hid the lord of Ross
  And the lady that came at the break of day."

"No knight or lady, good Lord Douglas,
  Have I beheld since break of morn ;
And I never saw the lord of Ross
  Since the woful day that I was born."

Lord Douglas turned him round about,
  And looked the Tinkler in the face ;
Where he beheld a lurking smile,
  And a deevil of a dour grimace.

"How 's this, how 's this, thou Tinkler loun ?
  Hast thou presumed to lie on me ?"
"Faith that I have !" the Tinkler said,
  "And a right good turn I have done to thee ,

"For the lord of Ross and thy own true-love,
  The beauteous Harriet of Thirlestane,
Rade west away, ere the break of day;
  And you 'll never see the dear maid again;

"So I thought it best to bring you here,
  On a wrang scent, of my own accord;
For had you met the Johnstone clan,
  They wad ha'e made mince-meat of a lord."

At this the Douglas was so wroth
  He wist not what to say or do;
But he strak the Tinkler o'er the croun,
  Till the blood came dreeping ower his brow.

"Beshrew my heart," quo' the Tinkler lad,
  "Thou bear'st thee most ungallantlye!
If these are the manners of a lord,
  They are manners that winna gang doun wi' me."

"Hold up thy hand," the Douglas cried,
  "And keep thy distance, Tinkler loun!"
"That will I not," the Tinkler said,
  "Though I and my mare should both go down!"

"I have armor on," cried the Lord Douglas,
  "Cuirass and helm, as you may see."
"The deil me care!" quo' the Tinkler lad;
  "I shall have a skelp at them and thee."

"You are not horsed," quo' the Lord Douglas,
  "And no remorse this weapon brooks."
"Mine 's a right good yaud," quo' the Tinkler lad,
  "And a great deal better nor she looks.

"So stand to thy weapons, thou haughty lord,
  What I have taken I needs must give;
Thou shalt never strike a tinkler again,
  For the langest day thou hast to live."

Then to it they fell, both sharp and snell,
  Till the fire from both their weapons flew;
But the very first shock that they met with,
  The Douglas his rashness 'gan to rue.

For though he had on a sark of mail,
  And a cuirass on his breast wore he,
With a good steel bonnet on his head,
  Yet the blood ran trinkling to his knee.

The Douglas sat upright and firm,
  Aye as together their horses ran;
But the Tinkler laid on like a very deil, —
  Siccan strokes were never laid on by man.

"Hold up thy hand, thou Tinkler loun,"
  Cried the poor priest, with whining din;
"If thou hurt the brave Lord James Douglas,
  A curse be on thee and all thy kin!"

"I care no more for Lord James Douglas
  Than Lord James Douglas cares for me;
But I want to let his proud heart know
  That a tinkler 's a man as well as he."

So they fought on, and they fought on,
  Till good Lord Douglas' breath was gone;
And the Tinkler bore him to the ground,
  With rush, with rattle, and with groan.

"O hon! O hon!" cried the proud Douglas,
  "That I this day should have lived to see!
For sure my honor I have lost,
  And a leader again I can never be!

"But tell me of thy kith and kin,
  And where was bred thy weapon hand?
For thou art the wale of tinkler loons
  That ever was born in fair Scotland."

"My name 's Jock Johnstone," quo' the wight;
  "I winna keep in my name frae thee;
And here, tak thou thy sword again,
  And better friends we two shall be."

But the Douglas swore a solemn oath,
  That was a debt he could never owe;
He would rather die at the back of the dike
  Than owe his sword to a man so low.

"But if thou wilt ride under my banner,
  And bear my livery and my name,
My right-hand warrior thou shalt be
  And I 'll knight thee on the field of fame."

"Woe worth thy wit, good Lord Douglas,
  To think I 'd change my trade for thine;
Far better and wiser would you be,
  To live a journeyman of mine,

"To mend a kettle or a casque,
  Or clout a goodwife's yettlin' pan, —
Upon my life, good Lord Douglas,
  You 'd make a noble tinkler-man!

"I would give you drammock twice a day,
  And sunkets on a Sunday morn,
And you should be a rare adept
  In steel and copper, brass and horn!

"I 'll fight you every day you rise,
  Till you can act the hero's part;
Therefore, I pray you, think of this,
  And lay it seriously to heart."

The Douglas writhed beneath the lash,
  Answering with an inward curse, —
Like salmon wriggling on a spear,
  That makes his deadly wound the worse.

But up there came two squires renowned ;
  In search of Lord Douglas they came ;
And when they saw their master down,
  Their spirits mounted in a flame.

And they flew upon the Tinkler wight,
  Like perfect tigers on their prey :
But the Tinkler heaved his trusty sword,
  And made him ready for the fray.

"Come one to one, ye coward knaves, —
  Come hand to hand, and steed to steed ;
I would that ye were better men,
  For this is glorious work indeed !"

Before you could have counted twelve,
  The Tinkler's wondrous chivalrye
Had both the squires upon the sward,
  And their horses galloping o'er the lea.

The Tinkler tied them neck and heel,
  And mony a biting jest gave he :
"O fie, for shame !" said the Tinkler lad ;
  "Siccan fighters I did never see !"

He slit one of their bridle reins, —
  O, what disgrace the conquered feels ! —
And he skelpit the squires with that good tawse,
  Till the blood ran off at baith their heels.

The Douglas he was forced to laugh
  Till down his cheek the salt tear ran :
"I think the deevil be come here
  In the likeness of a tinkler man !"

Then he has to Lord Douglas gone,
  And he raised him kindly by the hand,
And he set him on his gallant steed,
  And bore him away to Henderland :

"Be not cast down, my Lord Douglas,
  Nor writhe beneath a broken bane ;
For the leech's art will mend the part,
  And your honor lost will spring again.

"'T is true, Jock Johnstone is my name ;
  I'm a right good tinkler, as you see ;
For I can crack a casque betimes,
  Or clout one, as my need may be.

"Jock Johnstone is my name, 't is true, —
  But noble hearts are allied to me ;
For I am the lord of Annandale,
  And a knight and earl as well as thee."

Then Douglas strained the hero's hand,
  And took from it his sword again :
"Since thou art the lord of Annandale,
  Thou hast eased my heart of meikle pain.

"I might have known thy noble form
  In that disguise thou 'rt pleased to wear ;
All Scotland knows thy matchless arm,
  And England by experience dear.

"We have been foes as well as friends,
  And jealous of each other's sway ;
But little can I comprehend
  Thy motive for these pranks to-day."

"Sooth, my good lord, the truth to tell,
  'T was I that stole your love away,
And gave her to the lord of Ross
  An hour before the break of day ;

"For the lord of Ross is my brother,
  By all the laws of chivalrye ;
And I brought with me a thousand men
  To guard him to my ain countrye.

"But I thought meet to stay behind,
  And try your lordship to waylay,
Resolved to breed some noble sport,
  By leading you so far astray.

"Judging it better some lives to spare, —
  Which fancy takes me now and then, —
And settle our quarrel hand to hand,
  Than each with our ten thousand men.

"God send you soon, my Lord Douglas,
  To Border foray sound and haill !
But never strike a tinkler again,
  If he be a Johnstone of Annandale."
               JAMES HOGG.

NORVAL.

My name is Norval : on the Grampian hills
My father feeds his flocks ; a frugal swain,
Whose constant cares were to increase his store,
And keep his only son, myself, at home.
For I had heard of battles, and I longed
To follow to the field some warlike lord :
And Heaven soon granted what my sire denied.
This moon which rose last night, round as my
    shield,
Had not yet filled her horns, when, by her light
A band of fierce barbarians, from the hills,
Rushed like a torrent down upon the vale,
Sweeping our flocks and herds. The shepherds
    fled
For safety and for succor. I alone,
With bended bow, and quiver full of arrows,
Hovered about the enemy, and marked
The road he took, then hastened to my friends.
Whom, with a troop of fifty chosen men,
I met advancing. The pursuit I led,

Till we o'ertook the spoil-encumbered foe.
We fought and conquered. Ere a sword was
　　drawn
An arrow from my bow had pierced their chief,
Who wore that day the arms which now I wear.
Returning home in triumph, I disdained
The shepherd's slothful life; and having heard
That our good king had summoned his bold peers
To lead their warriors to the Carron side,
I left my father's house, and took with me
A chosen servant to conduct my steps, —
Yon trembling coward, who forsook his master.
Journeying with this intent, I passed these towers,
And, Heaven-directed, came this day to do
The happy deed that gilds my humble name.

JOHN HOME.

JORASSE.

Jorasse was in his three-and-twentieth year;
Graceful and active as a stag just roused;
Gentle withal, and pleasant in his speech,
Yet seldom seen to smile. He had grown up
Among the hunters of the Higher Alps;
Had caught their starts and fits of thoughtful-
　　ness,
Their haggard looks, and strange soliloquies.

. 　 . 　 . 　 . 　 . 　 .

　　　　　　　　　Once, nor long before,
Alone at daybreak on the Mettenberg,
He slipped, he fell; and, through a fearful cleft
Gliding from ledge to ledge, from deep to deeper,
Went to the under-world! Long-while he lay
Upon his rugged bed, — then waked like one
Wishing to sleep again and sleep forever!
For, looking round, he saw, or thought he saw,
Innumerable branches of a cavern,
Winding beneath a solid crust of ice;
With here and there a rent that showed the
　　stars !
What then, alas, was left him but to die?
What else in those immeasurable chambers,
Strewn with the bones of miserable men,
Lost like himself? Yet must he wander on,
Till cold and hunger set his spirit free!
And, rising, he began his dreary round;
When hark, the noise as of some mighty river
Working its way to light! Back he withdrew,
But soon returned, and, fearless from despair,
Dashed down the dismal channel; and all day,
If day could be where utter darkness was,
Travelled incessantly, the craggy roof
Just overhead, and the impetuous waves,
Nor broad nor deep, yet with a giant's strength,
Lashing him on. At last the water slept
In a dead lake, — at the third step he took,
Unfathomable, — and the roof, that long

Had threatened, suddenly descending, lay
Flat on the surface. Statue-like he stood,
His journey ended, when a ray divine
Shot through his soul. Breathing a prayer to
　　her
Whose ears are never shut, the Blessed Virgin,
He plunged, he swam, — and in an instant rose,
The barrier past, in light, in sunshine ! Through
A smiling valley, full of cottages,
Glittering the river ran ; and on the bank
The young were dancing ('t was a festival-day)
All in their best attire. There first he saw
His Madelaine. In the crowd she stood to hear,
When all drew round, inquiring; and her face,
Seen behind all, and varying, as he spoke,
With hope and fear and generous sympathy,
Subdued him. From that very hour he loved.

SAMUEL ROGERS.

PRINCE ADEB.

In Sana, O, in Sana, God, the Lord,
Was very kind and merciful to me !
Forth from the Desert in my rags I came,
Weary and sore of foot. I saw the spires
And swelling bubbles of the golden domes
Rise through the trees of Sana, and my heart
Grew great within me with the strength of God;
And I cried out, " Now shall I right myself, —
I, Adeb the despised, — for God is just !"
There he who wronged my father dwelt in
　　peace, —
My warlike father, who, when gray hairs crept
Around his forehead, as on Lebanon
The whitening snows of winter, was betrayed
To the sly Imam, and his tented wealth
Swept from him, 'twixt the roosting of the cock
And his first crowing, — in a single night :
And I, poor Adeb, sole of all my race,
Smeared with my father's and my kinsmen's
　　blood,
Fled through the Desert, till one day a tribe
Of hungry Bedouins found me in the sand,
Half mad with famine, and they took me up,
And made a slave of me, — of me, a prince !
All was fulfilled at last. I fled from them,
In rags and sorrow. Nothing but my heart,
Like a strong swimmer, bore me up against
The howling sea of my adversity.
At length o'er Sana, in the act to swoop,
I stood like a young eagle on a crag.
The traveller passed me with suspicious fear :
I asked for nothing ; I was not a thief.
The lean dogs snuffed around me: my lank bones
Fed on the berries and the crusted pools,
Were a scant morsel. Once a brown-skinned
　　girl

Called me a little from the common path,
And gave me figs and barley in a bag.
I paid her with a kiss, with nothing more,
And she looked glad ; for I was beautiful,
And virgin as a fountain, and as cold.
I stretched her bounty, pecking like a bird,
Her figs and barley, till my strength returned.
So when rich Sana lay beneath my eyes,
My foot was as the leopard's, and my hand
As heavy as the lion's brandished paw :
And underneath my burnished skin the veins
And stretching muscles played, at every step,
In wondrous motion.   I was very strong.
I looked upon my body, as a bird
That bills his feathers ere he takes to flight, —
I, watching over Sana.   Then I prayed ;
And on a soft stone, wetted in the brook,
Ground my long knife ; and then I prayed
     again.
God heard my voice, preparing all for me,
As, softly stepping down the hills, I saw
The Imam's summer-palace all ablaze
In the last flash of sunset.   Every fount
Was spouting fire, and all the orange-trees
Bore blazing coals, and from the marble walls
And gilded spires and columns, strangely
     wrought,
Glared the red light, until my eyes were pained
With the fierce splendor.   Till the night grew
     thick,
I lay within the bushes, next the door,
Still as a serpent, as invisible.
The guard hung round the portal.   Man by man
They dropped away, save one lone sentinel,
And on his eyes God's finger lightly fell ;
He slept half standing.   Like a summer wind
That threads the grove, yet never turns a leaf,
I stole from shadow unto shadow forth ;
Crossed all the marble court-yard, swung the door,
Like a soft gust, a little way ajar, —
My body's narrow width, no more, — and stood
Beneath the cresset in the painted hall.
I marvelled at the riches of my foe ;
I marvelled at God's ways with wicked men.
Then I reached forth, and took God's waiting
     hand :
And so he led me over mossy floors,
Flowered with the silken summer of Shiraz,
Straight to the Imam's chamber.   At the door
Stretched a brawn eunuch, blacker than my eyes :
His woolly head lay like the Kaba-stone
In Mecca's mosque, as silent and as huge.
I stepped across it, with my pointed knife
Just missing a full vein along his neck,
And, pushing by the curtains, there I was, —
I, Adeb the despised, — upon the spot
That, next to heaven, I longed for most of all.
I could have shouted for the joy in me.

Fierce pangs and flashes of bewildering light
Leaped through my brain and danced before my
     eyes.
So loud my heart beat, that I feared its sound
Would wake the sleeper ; and the bubbling blood
Choked in my throat till, weaker than a child,
I reeled against a column, and there hung
In a blind stupor.   Then I prayed again :
And, sense by sense, I was made whole once more.
I touched myself ; I was the same ; I knew
Myself to be lone Adeb, young and strong,
With nothing but a stride of empty air
Between me and God's justice.   In a sleep,
Thick with the fumes of the accursèd grape,
Sprawled the false Imam.   On his shaggy breast,
Like a white lily heaving on the tide
Of some foul stream, the fairest woman slept
These roving eyes have ever looked upon.
Almost a child, her bosom barely showed
The change beyond her girlhood.   All her charms
Were budding, but half opened ; for I saw
Not only beauty wondrous in itself,
But possibility of more to be
In the full process of her blooming days.
I gazed upon her, and my heart grew soft,
As a parched pasture with the dew of heaven.
While thus I gazed she smiled, and slowly raised
The long curve of her lashes ; and we looked
Each upon each in wonder, not alarm, —
Not eye to eye, but soul to soul, we held
Each other for a moment.   All her life
Seemed centred in the circle of her eyes.
She stirred no limb ; her long-drawn, equal
     breath
Swelled out and ebbed away beneath her breast,
In calm unbroken.   Not a sign of fear
Touched the faint color on her oval cheek,
Or pinched the arches of her tender mouth.
She took me for a vision, and she lay
With her sleep's smile unaltered, as in doubt
Whether real life had stolen into her dreams,
Or dreaming stretched into her outer life.
I was not graceless to a woman's eyes.
The girls of Damar paused to see me pass,
I walking in my rags, yet beautiful.
One maiden said, " He has a prince's air ! "
I am a prince ; the air was all my own.
So thought the lily on the Imam's breast ;
And lightly as a summer mist, that lifts
Before the morning, so she floated up,
Without a sound or rustle of a robe,
From her coarse pillow, and before me stood
With asking eyes.   The Imam never moved.
A stride and blow were all my need, and they
Were wholly in my power.   I took her hand,
I held a warning finger to my lips,
And whispered in her small, expectant ear,
" Adeb, the son of Akem ! "   She replied

In a low murmur whose bewildering sound
Almost lulled wakeful me to sleep, and sealed
The sleeper's lids in tenfold slumber, "Prince,
Lord of the Imam's life and of my heart,
Take all thou seest, — it is thy right, I know, —
But spare the Imam for thy own soul's sake!"
Then I arrayed me in a robe of state,
Shining with gold and jewels; and I bound
In my long turban gems that might have bought
The lands 'twixt Babelmandeb and Sahan.
I girt about me, with a blazing belt,
A scimitar o'er which the sweating smiths
In far Damascus hammered for long years,
Whose hilt and scabbard shot a trembling light
From diamonds and rubies. And she smiled,
As piece by piece I put the treasures on,
To see me look so fair, — in pride she smiled.
I hung long purses at my side. I scooped,
From off a table, figs and dates and rice,
And bound them to my girdle in a sack.
Then over all I flung a snowy cloak,
And beckoned to the maiden. So she stole
Forth like my shadow, past the sleeping wolf
Who wronged my father, o'er the woolly head
Of the swart eunuch, down the painted court,
And by the sentinel who standing slept.
Strongly against the portal, through my rags, —
My old base rags, — and through the maiden's
        veil,
I pressed my knife, — upon the wooden hilt
Was "Adeb, son of Akem," carved by me
In my long slavehood, — as a passing sign
To wait the Imam's waking. Shadows cast
From two high-sailing clouds upon the sand
Passed not more noiseless than we two, as one,
Glided beneath the moonlight, till I smelt
The fragrance of the stables. As I slid
The wide doors open, with a sudden bound
Uprose the startled horses: but they stood
Still as the man who in a foreign land
Hears his strange language, when my Desert call,
As low and plaintive as the nested dove's,
Fell on their listening ears. From stall to stall,
Feeling the horses with my groping hands,
I crept in darkness; and at length I came
Upon two sister mares whose rounded sides,
Fine muzzles, and small heads, and pointed ears,
And foreheads spreading 'twixt their eyelids wide,
Long slender tails, thin manes, and coats of silk,
Told me, that, of the hundred steeds there stalled,
My hand was on the treasures. O'er and o'er
I felt their bony joints, and down their legs
To the cool hoofs; — no blemish anywhere:
These I led forth and saddled. Upon one
I set the lily, gathered now for me, —
My own, henceforth, forever. So we rode
Across the grass, beside the stony path,
Until we gained the highway that is lost,

Leading from Sana, in the eastern sands:
When, with a cry that both the desert-born
Knew without hint from whip or goading spur,
We dashed into a gallop. Far behind
In sparks and smoke the dusty highway rose;
And ever on the maiden's face I saw,
When the moon flashed upon it, the strange smile
It wore on waking. Once I kissed her mouth,
When she grew weary, and her strength returned.
All through the night we scoured between the hills:
The moon went down behind us, and the stars
Dropped after her; but long before I saw
A planet blazing straight against our eyes,
The road had softened, and the shadowy hills
Had flattened out, and I could hear the hiss
Of sand spurned backward by the flying mares.
Glory to God! I was at home again!
The sun rose on us; far and near I saw
The level Desert; sky met sand all round.
We paused at mid-day by a palm-crowned well,
And ate and slumbered. Somewhat, too, was
        said:
The words have slipped my memory. That same
        eve
We rode sedately through a Hamoum camp, —
I, Adeb, prince amongst them, and my bride.
And ever since amongst them I have ridden,
A head and shoulders taller than the best;
And ever since my days have been of gold,
My nights have been of silver, — God is just!
                        GEORGE HENRY BOKER.

MAZEPPA'S RIDE.

"'BRING forth the horse!'—the horse was
        brought,
  In truth, he was a noble steed,
  A Tartar of the Ukraine breed,
Who looked as though the speed of thought
Were in his limbs; but he was wild,
  Wild as the wild deer, and untaught,
With spur and bridle undefiled, —
  'T was but a day he had been caught;
And snorting, with erected mane,
And struggling fiercely, but in vain,
In the full foam of wrath and dread
To me the desert-born was led;
They bound me on, that menial throng,
Upon his back with many a thong;
Then loosed him with a sudden lash, —
Away!—away!—and on we dash!
Torrents less rapid and less rash.

  "Away!—away!—My breath was gone, —
I saw not where he hurried on;
'T was scarcely yet the break of day,
And on he foamed, — away!—away!—

The last of human sounds which rose,
As I was darted from my foes,
Was the wild shout of savage laughter,
Which on the wind came roaring after
A moment from that rabble rout ;
With sudden wrath I wrenched my head,
    And snapped the cord which to the mane
    Had bound my neck in lieu of rein,
And, writhing half my form about,
Howled back my curse ; but midst the tread,
The thunder of my courser's speed,
Perchance they did not hear nor heed :

    .   .   .   .   .

"Away, away, my steed and I,
    Upon the pinions of the wind,
    All human dwellings left behind ;
We sped like meteors through the sky,
When with its crackling sound the night
Is checkered with the northern light :
Town, — village, — none were on our track,
    But a wild plain of far extent,
And bounded by a forest black ;
    And, save the scarce seen battlement
On distant heights of some strong hold,
Against the Tartars built of old,

    .   .   .   .   .

"But fast we fled, away, away,
And I could neither sigh nor pray ;
And my cold sweat-drops fell like rain
Upon the courser's bristling mane ;
But, snorting still with rage and fear,
He flew upon his far career ;
At times I almost thought, indeed,
He must have slackened in his speed ;
But no, — my bound and slender frame
    Was nothing to his angry might,
And merely like a spur became :
Each motion which I made to free
My swoln limbs from their agony
    Increased his fury and affright :
I tried my voice, — 't was faint and low,
But yet he swerved as from a blow ;
And, starting to each accent, sprang
As from a sudden trumpet's clang ;
Meantime my cords were wet with gore,
Which, oozing through my limbs, ran o'er ;
And in my tongue the thirst became
A something fierier far than flame.

"We neared the wild wood, — 't was so wide,
I saw no bounds on either side ;
'T was studded with old sturdy trees,
That bent not to the roughest breeze
Which howls down from Siberia's waste,
And strips the forest in its haste, —
But these were few and far between,
Set thick with shrubs more young and green,
Luxuriant with their annual leaves,

Ere strown by those autumnal eves
That nip the forest's foliage dead,
Discolored with a lifeless red,
Which stands thereon like stiffened gore
Upon the slain when battle 's o'er,
And some long winter's night hath shed
Its frost o'er every tombless head,
So cold and stark the raven's beak
May peck unpierced each frozen cheek :
'T was a wild waste of underwood,
And here and there a chestnut stood,
The strong oak, and the hardy pine ;
    But far apart, — and well it were,
Or else a different lot were mine, —
    The boughs gave way, and did not tear
My limbs ; and I found strength to bear
My wounds, already scarred with cold, —
My bonds forbade to loose my hold.
We rustled through the leaves like wind,
Left shrubs and trees and wolves behind ;
By night I heard them on the track,
Their troop came hard upon our back
With their long gallop, which can tire
The hound's deep hate, and hunter's fire ;
Where'er we flew they followed on,
Nor left us with the morning sun ;
Behind I saw them, scarce a rood,
At daybreak winding through the wood,
And through the night had heard their feet
Their stealing, rustling step repeat.
O, how I wished for spear or sword,
At least to die amidst the horde,
And perish — if it must be so —
At bay, destroying many a foe !
When first my courser's race begun
I wished the goal already won ;
But now I doubted strength and speed.
Vain doubt ! his swift and savage breed
Had nerved him like the mountain roe ;

    .   .   .   .   .

"The wood was passed ; 't was more than noon,
But chill the air, although in June ;
Or it might be my veins ran cold, —
Prolonged endurance tames the bold ;

    .   .   .   .   .

"What marvel if this worn-out trunk
Beneath its woes a moment sunk ?
The earth gave way, the skies rolled round,
I seemed to sink upon the ground ;
But erred, for I was fastly bound.
My heart turned sick, my brain grew sore,
And throbbed awhile, then beat no more ;
The skies spun like a mighty wheel ;
I saw the trees like drunkards reel,
And a slight flash sprang o'er my eyes,
Which saw no farther ; he who dies
Can die no more than then I died.
O'ertortured by that ghastly ride,

I felt the blackness come and go,
   And strove to wake ; but could not make
My senses climb up from below ;
I felt as on a plank at sea,
When all the waves that dash o'er thee,
At the same time upheave and whelm,
And hurl thee towards a desert realm.
My undulating life was as
The fancied lights that flitting pass
Our shut eyes in deep midnight, when
Fever begins upon the brain ;
But soon it passed, with little pain,
   But a confusion worse than such ;
   I own that I should deem it much,
Dying, to feel the same again ;
And yet I do suppose we must
Feel far more ere we turn to dust :
No matter ; I have bared my brow
Full in Death's face — before — and now.

"My thoughts came back : where was I ? Cold
   And numb and giddy : pulse by pulse
Life reassumed its lingering hold,
And throb by throb, — till grown a pang
   Which for a moment would convulse,
   My blood reflowed, though thick and chill ;
My ear with uncouth noises rang ;
   My heart began once more to thrill ;
My sight returned, though dim ; alas !
And thickened, as it were, with glass.
Methought the dash of waves was nigh ;
There was a gleam too of the sky,
Studded with stars ; — it is no dream ;
The wild horse swims the wilder stream !
The bright, broad river's gushing tide
Sweeps, winding onward, far and wide,
And we are half-way, struggling o'er
To yon unknown and silent shore.
The waters broke my hollow trance,
And with a temporary strength
   My stiffened limbs were rebaptized,
My courser's broad breast proudly braves,
And dashes off the ascending waves,
And onward we advance !
We reach the slippery shore at length,
   A haven I but little prized,
For all behind was dark and drear,
And all before was night and fear.
How many hours of night or day
In those suspended pangs I lay,
I could not tell ; I scarcely knew
If this were human breath I drew.

"With glossy skin, and dripping mane,
   And reeling limbs, and reeking flank,
The wild steed's sinewy nerves still strain
   Up the repelling bank.
We gain the top ; a boundless plain
Spreads through the shadow of the night,

And onward, onward, onward, seems,
Like precipices in our dreams,
To stretch beyond the sight ;
And here and there a speck of white,
   Or scattered spot of dusky green,
In masses broke into the light
   As rose the moon upon my right.
   But naught distinctly seen
In the dim waste would indicate
The omen of a cottage gate ;
No twinkling taper from afar
Stood like a hospitable star ;
Not even an *ignis-fatuus* rose
To make him merry with my woes ;
   That very cheat had cheered me then !
Although detected, welcome still,
Reminding me, through every ill,
   Of the abodes of men.

"Onward we went, — but slack and slow ;
   His savage force at length o'erspent,
The drooping courser, faint and low,
   All feebly foaming went.
A sickly infant had had power
To guide him forward in that hour ;
   But useless all to me.
His new-born tameness naught availed, —
My limbs were bound ; my force had failed,
   Perchance, had they been free.
With feeble efforts still I tried
To rend the bonds so starkly tied,
   But still it was in vain ;
My limbs were only wrung the more,
And soon the idle strife gave o'er,
   Which but prolonged their pain ;
The dizzy race seemed almost done,
Although no goal was nearly won ;
Some streaks announced the coming sun, —
   How slow, alas ! he came !
Methought that mist of dawning gray
Would never dapple into day ;
How heavily it rolled away, —
   Before the eastern flame
Rose crimson, and deposed the stars,
And called the radiance from their cars,
And filled the earth, from his deep throne,
With lonely lustre, all his own.

"Up rose the sun ; the mists were curled
Back from the solitary world
Which lay around — behind — before.
What booted it to traverse o'er
Plain, forest, river ?   Man nor brute,
Nor dint of hoof, nor print of foot,
Lay in the wild luxuriant soil ;
No sign of travel, — none of toil ;
The very air was mute ;
And not an insect's shrill small horn,

Nor matin bird's new voice, was borne
From herb nor thicket.   Many a werst,
Panting as if his heart would burst,
The weary brute still staggered on ;
And still we were, or seemed, alone.
At length, while reeling on our way,
Methought I heard a courser neigh
From out yon tuft of blackening firs.
Is it the wind those branches stirs ?.
No, no ! from out the forest prance
    A trampling troop ; I see them come !
In one vast squadron they advance !
    I strove to cry, — my lips were dumb.
The steeds rush on in plunging pride ;
But where are they the reins to guide ?
A thousand horse, — and none to ride !
With flowing tail, and flying mane,
Wide nostrils, never stretched by pain,
Mouths bloodless to the bit or rein,
And feet that iron never shod,
And flanks unscarred by spur or rod,
A thousand horse, the wild, the free,
Like waves that follow o'er the sea,
    Came thickly thundering on,
As if our faint approach to meet ;
The sight renerved my courser's feet,
A moment staggering, feebly fleet,
A moment, with a faint low neigh,
He answered and then fell :
With gasps and glazing eyes he lay,
    And reeking limbs immovable,
    His first and last career is done !
On came the troop, — they saw him stoop,
    They saw me strangely bound along
    His back with many a bloody thong :
They stop, — they start, — they snuff the air,
Gallop a moment here and there,
Approach, retire, wheel round and round,
Then plunging back with sudden bound,
Headed by one black mighty steed,
Who seemed the patriarch of his breed,
    Without a single speck or hair
Of white upon his shaggy hide ;
They snort, they foam, neigh, swerve aside,
And backward to the forest fly,
By instinct, from a human eye.
    They left me there to my despair,
Linked to the dead and stiffening wretch,
Whose lifeless limbs beneath me stretch,
Relieved from that unwonted weight,
From whence I could not extricate
Nor him nor me, and there we lay
    The dying on the dead !
I little deemed another day
Would see my houseless, helpless head.

"And there from morn till twilight bound,
I felt the heavy hours toil round,

With just enough of life to see
My last of suns go down on me.

    .   .   .   .

"The sun was sinking, — still I lay
Chained to the chill and stiffening steed ;
I thought to mingle there our clay ;
    And my dim eyes of death had need.
    No hope arose of being freed :
I cast my last looks up the sky,
    And there between me and the sun
I saw the expecting raven fly,
Who scarce would wait till both should die
    Ere his repast begun ;
He flew, and perched, then flew once more,
And each time nearer than before ;
I saw his wing through twilight flit,
And once so near me he alit
    I could have smote, but lacked the strength ;
But the slight motion of my hand,
And feeble scratching of the sand,
The exerted throat's faint struggling noise,
Which scarcely could be called a voice,
    Together scared him off at length.
I know no more, — my latest dream
    Is something of a lovely star
    Which fixed my dull eyes from afar,
And went and came with wandering beam,
And of the cold, dull, swimming, dense
Sensation of recurring sense,
And then subiding back to death,
And then again a little breath,
A little thrill, a short suspense,
    An icy sickness curdling o'er
My heart, and sparks that crossed my brain, —
A gasp, a throb, a start of pain,
A sigh, and nothing more.

"I woke. — Where was I ? — Do I see
A human face look down on me ?
And doth a roof above me close ?
Do these limbs on a couch repose ?
Is this a chamber where I lie ?
And is it mortal yon bright eye,
That watches me with gentle glance ?
    I closed my own again once more,
As doubtful that the former trance
    Could not as yet be o'er.
A slender girl, long-haired and tall,
Sate watching by the cottage wall ;
The sparkle of her eye I caught,
Even with my first return of thought ;
For ever and anon she threw
    A prying, pitying glance on me
    With her black eyes so wild and free :
I gazed and gazed, until I knew
    No vision it could be, —
But that I lived, and was released
From adding to the vulture's feast :

And when the Cossack maid beheld
My heavy eyes at length unsealed,
She smiled, — and I essayed to speak,
   But failed, — and she approached, and made
With lip and finger signs that said,
I must not strive as yet to break
The silence, till my strength should be
Enough to leave my accents free ;
And then her hand on mine she laid,
And smoothed the pillow for my head,
And stole along on tiptoe tread,
   And gently oped the door, and spake
In whispers, — ne'er was voice so sweet !
Even music followed her light feet ;
   But those she called were not awake,
And she went forth ; but, ere she passed,
Another look on me she cast,
   Another sign she made, to say,
That I had naught to fear, that all
Were near, at my command or call,
   And she would not delay
Her due return : while she was gone,
Methought I felt too much alone.

"She came with mother and with sire, —
What need of more ? — I will not tire
With long recital of the rest,
Since I became the Cossack's guest.
They found me senseless on the plain, —
   They bore me to the nearest hut, —
They brought me into life again, —
Me, — one day o'er their realm to reign !
   Thus the vain fool who strove to glut
   His rage, refining on my pain,
Sent me forth to the wilderness,
Bound, naked, bleeding, and alone,
To pass the desert to a throne, —
   What mortal his own doom may guess ?"
                    BYRON.

THE CHILD OF ELLE.

On yonder hill a castle stands,
   With walls and towers bedight,
And yonder lives the Child of Elle,
   A young and comely knight.

The Child of Elle to his garden went,
   And stood at his garden pale,
When, lo ! he beheld fair Emmeline's page
   Come tripping down the dale.

The Child of Elle he hied him thence,
   I wis he stood not still,
And soon he met fair Emmeline's page
   Come climbing up the hill.

"Now Christ thee save, thou little foot-page,
   Now Christ thee save and see !

O, tell me how does thy lady gay,
   And what may thy tidings be ?"

"My lady she is all woe-begone,
   And the tears they fall from her eyne ;
And aye she laments the deadly feud
   Between her house and thine.

"And here she sends thee a silken scarf
   Bedewed with many a tear,
And bids thee sometimes think on her,
   Who lovéd thee so dear.

"And here she sends thee a ring of gold,
   The last boon thou mayst have,
And bids thee wear it for her sake,
   When she is laid in grave.

"For, ah ! her gentle heart is broke,
   And in grave soon must she be,
Sith her father hath chose her a new, new love,
   And forbid her to think of thee.

"Her father hath brought her a carlish knight,
   Sir John of the north countréy,
And within three days she must him wed,
   Or he vows he will her slay."

"Now hie thee back, thou little foot-page,
   And greet thy lady from me,
And tell her that I, her own true-love,
   Will die, or set her free.

"Now hie thee back, thou little foot-page,
   And let thy fair lady know
This night will I be at her bower windów,
   Betide me weal or woe."

The boy he tripped, the boy he ran,
   He neither stint nor stayed
Until he came to fair Emmeline's bower,
   When kneeling down he said, —

"O lady, I 've been with thy own true-love,
   And he greets thee well by me ;
This night will he be at thy bower windów,
   And die, or set thee free."

Now day was gone, and night was come,
   And all was fast asleep,
All save the Lady Emmeline,
   Who sat in her bower to weep :

And soon she heard her true-love's voice
   Low whispering at the wall,
"Awake, awake, my dear ladyé,
   'T is I, thy true-love, call.

"Awake, awake, my lady dear,
   Come, mount this fair palfráy !
This ladder of ropes will let thee down,
   I 'll carry thee hence away."

" Now nay, now nay, thou gentle knight,
    Now nay, this may not be ;
For aye should I tint my maiden fame,
    If alone I should wend with thee."

"O lady, thou with a knight so true
    Mayst safely wend alone,
To my lady mother I will thee bring,
    Where marriage shall make us one."

" My father he is a baron bold,
    Of lineage proud and hie ;
And what would he say if his daughtér
    Away with a knight should fly ?

" Ah ! well I wot, he never would rest,
    Nor his meat should do him no good,
Until he had slain thee, Child of Elle,
    And seen thy dear heart's blood."

" O lady, wert thou in thy saddle set,
    And a little space him fro,
I would not care for thy cruel fathér,
    Nor the worst that he could do.

" O lady, wert thou in thy saddle set,
    And once without this wall,
I would not care for thy cruel fathér,
    Nor the worst that might befall."

Fair Emmeline sighed, fair Emmeline wept,
    And aye her heart was woe ;
At length he seized her lily-white hand,
    And down the ladder he drew :

And thrice he clasped her to his breast,
    And kissed her tenderlíe ;
The tears that fell from her fair eyes
    Ran like the fountain free.

He mounted himself on his steed so tall,
    And her on a fair palfráy,
And slung his bugle about his neck,
    And roundly they rode away.

All this beheard her own damsél,
    In her bed whereon she lay,
Quoth she, " My lord shall know of this,
    So I shall have gold and fee.

" Awake, awake, thou baron bold !
    Awake, my noble dame !
Your daughter is fled with the Child of Elle
    To do the deed of shame."

The baron he woke, the baron he rose,
    And called his merry men all :
" And come thou forth, Sir John the knight,
    Thy lady is carried to thrall."

Fair Emmeline scant had ridden a mile,
    A mile forth of the town,
When she was aware of her father's men
    Come galloping over the down :

And foremost came the carlish knight,
    Sir John of the north countréy :
" Now stop, now stop, thou false traitór,
    Nor carry that lady away.

" For she is come of hie lineáge,
    And was of a lady born,
And ill it beseems thee, a false churl's son,
    To carry her hence to scorn."

" Now loud thy liest, Sir John the knight,
    Now thou doest lie of me ;
A knight me got, and a lady me bore,
    So never did none by thee.

" But light now down, my lady fair,
    Light down, and hold my steed,
While I and this discourteous knight
    Do try this arduous deed.

" But light now down, my dear ladyé.
    Light down, and hold my horse,
While I and this discourteous knight
    Do try our valor's force."

Fair Emmeline sighed, fair Emmeline wept,
    And aye her heart was woe,
While 'twixt her love and the carlish knight
    Past many a baleful blow.

The Child of Elle he fought so well,
    As his weapon he waved amain,
That soon he had slain the carlish knight,
    And laid him upon the plain.

And now the baron and all his men
    Full fast approachéd nigh :
Ah ! what may Lady Emmeline do ?
    'T were now no boot to fly.

Her lover, he put his horn to his mouth,
    And blew both loud and shrill,
And soon he saw his own merry men
    Come riding over the hill.

" Now hold thy hand, thou bold barón,
    I pray thee hold thy hand,
Nor ruthless rend two gentle hearts
    Fast knit in true love's band.

" Thy daughter I have dearly loved
    Full long and many a day ;
But with such love as holy kirk
    Hath freely said we may.

"O, give consent she may be mine,
　And bless a faithful pair ;
My lands and livings are not small,
　My house and lineage fair ;

"My mother she was an earl's daughtér,
　And a noble knight my sire."—
The baron he frowned, and turned away
　With mickle dole and ire.

Fair Emmeline sighed, fair Emmeline wept,
　And did all trembling stand :
At length she sprang upon her knee,
　And held his lifted hand.

"Pardon, my lord and father dear,
　This fair young knight and me :
Trust me, but for the carlish knight
　I never had fled from thee.

"Oft have you called your Emmeline
　Your darling and your joy ;
O, let not then your harsh resolves
　Your Emmeline destroy ! "

The baron he stroked his dark-brown cheek,
　And turned his head aside,
To wipe away the starting tear
　He proudly strove to hide.

In deep revolving thought he stood,
　And mused a little space ;
Then raised fair Emmeline from the ground,
　With many a fond embrace.

"Here take her, Child of Elle," he said,
　And gave her lily-white hand :
"Here take my dear and only child,
　And with her half my land.

"Thy father once mine honor wronged
　In days of youthful pride ;
Do thou the injury repair
　In fondness for thy bride.

"And as thou love her, and hold her dear,
　Heaven prosper thee and thine :
And now my blessing wend wi' thee,
　My lovely Emmeline."

　　　　　　　　　　　　ANONYMOUS.

JAMES FITZ–JAMES AND RODERICK DHU.

　　. . . . "I AM by promise tied
To match me with this man of pride :
Twice have I sought Clan-Alpine's glen
In peace ; but when I come again,
I come with banner, brand, and bow,
As leader seeks his mortal foe.

For love-lorn swain, in lady's bower,
Ne'er panted for the appointed hour,
As I, until before me stand
This rebel Chieftain and his band."

"Have, then, thy wish !"—He whistled shrill,
And he was answered from the hill ;
Wild as the scream of the curlew,
From crag to crag the signal flew.
Instant, through copse and heath, arose
Bonnets and spears and bended bows ;
On right, on left, above, below,
Sprung up at once the lurking foe ;
From shingles gray their lances start,
The bracken bush sends forth the dart,
The rushes and the willow-wand
Are bristling into axe and brand,
And every tuft of broom gives life
To plaided warrior armed for strife.
That whistle garrisoned the glen
At once with full five hundred men,
As if the yawning hill to heaven
A subterranean host had given.
Watching their leader's beck and will,
All silent there they stood, and still.
Like the loose crags whose threatening mass
Lay tottering o'er the hollow pass,
As if an infant's touch could urge
Their headlong passage down the verge,
With step and weapon forward flung,
Upon the mountain-side they hung.
The Mountaineer cast glance of pride
Along Benledi's living side,
Then fixed his eye and sable brow
Full on Fitz-James : " How say'st thou now?
These are Clan-Alpine's warriors true ;
And, Saxon,—I am Roderick Dhu ! "

Fitz-James was brave ;—though to his heart
The life-blood thrilled with sudden start,
He manned himself with dauntless air,
Returned the Chief his haughty stare,
His back against a rock he bore,
And firmly placed his foot before :—
"Come one, come all ! this rock shall fly
From its firm base as soon as I."
Sir Roderick marked,—and in his eyes
Respect was mingled with surprise,
And the stern joy which warriors feel
In foemen worthy of their steel.
Short space he stood,—then waved his hand :
Down sunk the disappearing band ;
Each warrior vanished where he stood,
In broom or bracken, heath or wood :
Sunk brand and spear, and bended bow,
In osiers pale and copses low :
It seemed as if their mother Earth
Had swallowed up her warlike birth.

The wind's last breath had tossed in air
Pennon and plaid and plumage fair, —
The next but swept a lone hillside,
Where heath and fern were waving wide ;
The sun's last glance was glinted back,
From spear and glaive, from targe and jack, —
The next, all unreflected, shone
On bracken green, and cold gray stone.

Fitz-James looked round, — yet scarce believed
The witness that his sight received ;
Such apparition well might seem
Delusion of a dreadful dream.
Sir Roderick in suspense he eyed,
And to his look the Chief replied :
" Fear naught — nay, that I need not say —
But — doubt not aught from mine array.
Thou art my guest ; — I pledged my word
As far as Coilantogle ford :
Nor would I call a clansman's brand
For aid against one valiant hand,
Though on our strife lay every vale
Rent by the Saxon from the Gael.
So move we on ; — I only meant
To show the reed on which you leant,
Deeming this path you might pursue
Without a pass from Roderick Dhu."
They moved ; — I said Fitz-James was brave,
As ever knight that belted glaive ;
Yet dare not say that now his blood
Kept on its wont and tempered flood,
As, following Roderick's stride, he drew
That seeming lonesome pathway through,
Which yet, by fearful proof, was rife
With lances, that, to take his life,
Waited but signal from a guide,
So late dishonored and defied.
Ever, by stealth, his eye sought round
The vanished guardians of the ground,
And still, from copse and heather deep,
Fancy saw spear and broadsword peep,
And in the plover's shrilly strain
The signal whistle heard again.
Nor breathed he free till far behind
The pass was left ; for then they wind
Along a wide and level green,
Where neither tree nor tuft was seen,
Nor rush nor bush of broom was near,
To hide a bonnet or a spear.

The Chief in silence strode before,
And reached that torrent's sounding shore,
Which, daughter of three mighty lakes,
From Vennachar in silver breaks,
Sweeps through the plain, and ceaseless mines
On Bochastle the mouldering lines,
Where Rome, the Empress of the world,
Of yore her eagle wings unfurled,
And here his course the Chieftain stayed,

Threw down his target and his plaid,
And to the Lowland warrior said :
" Bold Saxon ! to his promise just,
Vich-Alpine has discharged his trust.
This murderous Chief, this ruthless man,
This head of a rebellious clan,
Hath led thee safe through watch and ward,
Far past Clan-Alpine's outmost guard.
Now, man to man, and steel to steel,
A Chieftain's vengeance thou shalt feel.
See, here, all vantageless I stand,
Armed, like thyself, with single brand ;
For this is Coilantogle ford,
And thou must keep thee with thy sword."

The Saxon paused : " I ne'er delayed,
When foeman bade me draw my blade ;
Nay more, brave Chief, I vowed thy death :
Yet sure thy fair and generous faith,
And my deep debt for life preserved,
A better meed have well deserved :
Can naught but blood our feud atone ?
Are there no means ?" " No, Stranger, none .
And hear, — to fire thy flagging zeal, —
The Saxon cause rests on thy steel ;
For thus spoke Fate, by prophet bred
Between the living and the dead :
' Who spills the foremost foeman's life,
His party conquers in the strife.' "
" Then, by my word," the Saxon said,
" The riddle is already read.
Seek yonder brake beneath the cliff, —
There lies Red Murdoch, stark and stiff.
Thus Fate hath solved her prophecy,
Then yield to Fate, and not to me.
To James, at Stirling, let us go,
When, if thou wilt be still his foe,
Or if the King shall not agree
To grant thee grace and favor free,
I plight mine honor, oath, and word,
That, to thy native strengths restored,
With each advantage shalt thou stand,
That aids thee now to guard thy land."

Dark lightning flashed from Roderick's eye :
" Soars thy presumption, then, so high,
Because a wretched kern ye slew,
Homage to name to Roderick Dhu ?
He yields not, he, to man nor fate !
Thou add'st but fuel to my hate : —
My clansman's blood demands revenge.
Not yet prepared ? — By Heaven I change
My thought, and hold thy valor light
As that of some vain carpet knight,
Who ill deserved my courteous care,
And whose best boast is but to wear
A braid of his fair lady's hair."
" I thank thee, Roderick, for the word !
It nerves my heart, it steels my sword ;

For I have sworn this braid to stain
In the best blood that warms thy vein.
Now, truce, farewell ! and ruth, begone ! —
Yet think not that by thee alone,
Proud Chief ! can courtesy be shown ;
Though not from copse, or heath, or cairn,
Start at my whistle clansmen stern,
Of this small horn one feeble blast
Would fearful odds against thee cast.
But fear not — doubt not — which thou wilt —
We try this quarrel hilt to hilt."
Then each at once his falchion drew,
Each on the ground his scabbard threw,
Each looked to sun and stream and plain,
As what they ne'er might see again ;
Then, foot and point and eye opposed,
In dubious strife they darkly closed.

Ill fared it then with Roderick Dhu,
That on the field his targe he threw,
Whose brazen studs and tough bull-hide
Had death so often dashed aside ;
For, trained abroad his arms to wield,
Fitz-James's blade was sword and shield.
He practised every pass and ward,
To thrust, to strike, to feint, to guard ;
While less expert, though stronger far,
The Gael maintained unequal war.
Three times in closing strife they stood,
And thrice the Saxon blade drank blood :
No stinted draught, no scanty tide,
The gushing floods the tartans dyed.
Fierce Roderick felt the fatal drain,
And showered his blows like wintry rain ;
And, as firm rock or castle-roof
Against the winter shower is proof,
The foe, invulnerable still,
Foiled his wild rage by steady skill ;
Till, at advantage ta'en, his brand
Forced Roderick's weapon from his hand,
And, backwards borne upon the lea,
Brought the proud Chieftain to his knee.

"Now yield thee, or, by Him who made
The world, thy heart's blood dyes my blade ! "
"Thy threats, thy mercy, I defy !
Let recreant yield, who fears to die."
Like adder darting from his coil,
Like wolf that dashes through the toil,
Like mountain-cat who guards her young,
Full at Fitz-James's throat he sprung ;
Received, but recked not of a wound,
And locked his arms his foeman round.
Now, gallant Saxon, hold thine own !
No maiden's hand is round thee thrown !
That desperate grasp thy frame might feel
Through bars of brass and triple steel !
They tug, they strain ! down, down they go,
The Gael above, Fitz-James below.

The Chieftain's gripe his throat compressed,
His knee was planted in his breast ;
His clotted locks he backward threw,
Across his brow his hand he drew,
From blood and mist to clear his sight,
Then gleamed aloft his dagger bright !
But hate and fury ill supplied
The stream of life's exhausted tide,
And all too late the advantage came,
To turn the odds of deadly game ;
For, while the dagger gleamed on high,
Reeled soul and sense, reeled brain and eye.
Down came the blow ! but in the heath
The erring blade found bloodless sheath.
The struggling foe may now unclasp
The fainting Chief's relaxing grasp ;
Unwounded from the dreadful close,
But breathless all, Fitz-James arose.

He faltered thanks to Heaven for life,
Redeemed, unhoped, from desperate strife ;
Next on his foe his look he cast,
Whose every gasp appeared his last ;
In Roderick's gore he dipped the braid, —
"Poor Blanche ! thy wrongs are dearly paid ·
Yet with thy foe must die, or live,
The praise that faith and valor give."
With that he blew a bugle note,
Undid the collar from his throat,
Unbonneted, and by the wave
Sat down his brow and hands to lave.
Then faint afar are heard the feet
Of rushing steeds in gallop fleet ;
The sounds increase, and now are seen
Four mounted squires in Lincoln green ;
Two who bear lance, and two who lead,
By loosened rein, a saddled steed ;
Each onward held his headlong course,
And by Fitz-James reined up his horse, —
With wonder viewed the bloody spot, —
"Exclaim not, gallants ! question not, —
You, Herbert and Luffness, alight,
And bind the wounds of yonder knight ;
Let the gray palfrey bear his weight,
We destined for a fairer freight,
And bring him on to Stirling straight ;
I will before at better speed,
To seek fresh horse and fitting weed.
The sun rides high ; — I must be boune
To see the archer-game at noon ;
But lightly Bayard clears the lea.
De Vaux and Herries, follow me.
                              SIR WALTER SCOTT.

WAKEN, LORDS AND LADIES GAY.

WAKEN, lords and ladies gay,
On the mountain dawns the day ;

All the jolly chase is here,
  With hawk and horse and hunting-spear !
Hounds are in their couples yelling,
Hawks are whistling, horns are knelling,
  Merrily, merrily mingle they,
  "Waken, lords and ladies gay."

Waken, lords and ladies gay,
The mist has left the mountain gray,
  Springlets in the dawn are steaming,
  Diamonds on the brake are gleaming,
And foresters have busy been
To track the buck in thicket green ;
  Now we come to chant our lay,
  "Waken, lords and ladies gay."

Waken, lords and ladies gay,
To the greenwood haste away ;
  We can show you where he lies,
  Fleet of foot and tall of size ;
We can show the marks he made
When 'gainst the oak his antlers frayed ;
  You shall see him brought to bay ;
  Waken, lords and ladies gay.

Louder, louder chant the lay
Waken, lords and ladies gay !
  Tell them youth and mirth and glee
  Run a course as well as we ;
Time, stern huntsman ! who can balk,
Stanch as hound and fleet as hawk ?
  Think of this, and rise with day,
  Gentle lords and ladies gay !
                 SIR WALTER SCOTT.

MY HEART'S IN THE HIGHLANDS.

My heart's in the Highlands, my heart is not
    here ;
My heart's in the Highlands a-chasing the deer ;
Chasing the wild deer, and following the roe,
My heart's in the Highlands wherever I go.
Farewell to the Highlands, farewell to the North,
The birthplace of valor, the country of worth ;
Wherever I wander, wherever I rove,
The hills of the Highlands forever I love.

Farewell to the mountains high covered with
    snow ;
Farewell to the straths and green valleys below ;
Farewell to the forests and wild-hanging woods ;
Farewell to the torrents and loud-pouring floods.
My heart's in the Highlands, my heart is not
    here ;
My heart's in the Highlands a-chasing the deer ;
Chasing the wild deer, and following the roe,
My heart's in the Highlands wherever I go.
                 ROBERT BURNS.

THE HUNTER'S SONG.

RISE ! Sleep no more ! 'T is a noble morn.
The dews hang thick on the fringéd thorn,
And the frost shrinks back, like a beaten hound,
Under the steaming, steaming ground.
Behold where the billowy clouds flow by,
And leave us alone in the clear gray sky !
Our horses are ready and steady. — So, ho !
I'm gone, like a dart from the Tartar's bow.
Hark, hark ! — Who calleth the maiden Morn
From her sleep in the woods and the stubble corn ?
    The horn, — the horn !
The merry, sweet ring of the hunter's horn.

Now, through the copse where the fox is found,
And over the stream at a mighty bound,
And over the high lands, and over the low,
O'er furrows, o'er meadows, the hunters go !
Away ! — as a hawk flies full at his prey,
So flieth the hunter, away, — away !
From the burst at the cover till set of sun,
When the red fox dies, and — the day is done !
Hark, hark ! — What sound on the wind is borne ?
'T is the conquering voice of the hunter's horn !
    The horn, — the horn !
The merry, bold voice of the hunter's horn.

Sound ! Sound the horn ! To the hunter good
What's the gully deep or the roaring flood ?
Right over he bounds, as the wild stag bounds,
At the heels of his swift, sure, silent hounds.
O, what delight can a mortal lack,
When he once is firm on his horse's back,
With his stirrups short, and his snaffle strong,
And the blast of the horn for his morning song ?
Hark, hark ! — Now, home ! and dream till morn
Of the bold, sweet sound of the hunter's horn !
    The horn, — the horn !
O, the sound of all sounds is the hunter's horn !
                 BARRY CORNWALL.

THE STAG HUNT.

FROM "THE SEASONS."

THE stag too, singled from the herd where long
He ranged the branching monarch of the shades,
Before the tempest drives. At first, in speed
He, sprightly, puts his faith ; and, roused by fear,
Gives all his swift aerial soul to flight.
Against the breeze he darts, that way the more
To leave the lessening murderous cry behind :
Deception short ! though fleeter than the winds
Blown o'er the keen-aired mountain by the north,
He bursts the thickets, glances through the glades,
And plunges deep into the wildest wood, —
If slow, yet sure, adhesive to the track.

Hot-steaming, up behind him come again
The inhuman rout, and from the shady depth
Expel him, circling through his every shift.
He sweeps the forest oft ; and sobbing sees
The glades, mild opening to the golden day,
Where, in kind contest, with his butting friends
He wont to struggle, or his loves enjoy.
Oft in the full-descending flood he tries
To lose the scent, and lave his burning sides ;
Oft seeks the herd ; the watchful herd, alarmed,
With selfish care avoid a brother's woe.
What shall he do ? His once so vivid nerves,
So full of buoyant spirit, now no more
Inspire the course ; but fainting breathless toil,
Sick, seizes on his heart : he stands at bay ;
And puts his last weak refuge in despair.
The big round tears run down his dappled face ;
He groans in anguish ; while the growling pack,
Blood-happy, hang at his fair jutting chest,
And mark his beauteous checkered sides with gore.

JAMES THOMSON.

BETH GELERT.

THE spearmen heard the bugle sound,
  And cheerily smiled the morn ;
And many a brach, and many a hound,
  Obeyed Llewelyn's horn.

And still he blew a louder blast,
  And gave a lustier cheer,
" Come, Gêlert, come, wert never last
  Llewelyn's horn to hear.

" O, where does faithful Gêlert roam,
  The flower of all his race ;
So true, so brave, — a lamb at home,
  A lion in the chase ?"

In sooth, he was a peerless hound,
  The gift of royal John ;
But now no Gêlert could be found,
  And all the chase rode on.

That day Llewelyn little loved
  The chase of hart and hare ;
And scant and small the booty proved,
  For Gêlert was not there.

Unpleased, Llewelyn homeward hied,
  When, near the portal seat,
His truant Gêlert he espied,
  Bounding his lord to greet.

But, when he gained his castle-door,
  Aghast the chieftain stood ;
The hound all o'er was smeared with gore ;
  His lips, his fangs, ran blood.

Llewelyn gazed with fierce surprise ;
  Unused such looks to meet,
His favorite checked his joyful guise,
  And crouched, and licked his feet.

Onward, in haste, Llewelyn passed,
  And on went Gêlert too ;
And still, where'er his eyes he cast,
  Fresh blood-gouts shocked his view.

O'erturned his infant's bed he found,
  With blood-stained covert rent ;
And all around the walls and ground
  With recent blood besprent.

He called his child, — no voice replied, —
  He searched with terror wild ;
Blood, blood he found on every side,
  But nowhere found his child.

" Hell-hound ! my child 's by thee devoured,"
  The frantic father cried ;
And to the hilt his vengeful sword
  He plunged in Gêlert's side.

Aroused by Gêlert's dying yell,
  Some slumberer wakened nigh :
What words the parent's joy could tell
  To hear his infant's cry !

Concealed beneath a tumbled heap
  His hurried search had missed,
All glowing from his rosy sleep,
  The cherub boy he kissed.

Nor scathe had he, nor harm, nor dread,
  But, the same couch beneath,
Lay a gaunt wolf, all torn and dead,
  Tremendous still in death.

Ah, what was then Llewelyn's pain !
  For now the truth was clear ;
His gallant hound the wolf had slain
  To save Llewelyn's heir.

WILLIAM R. SPENCER.

THE STAG HUNT.

FROM "THE LADY OF THE LAKE."

THE stag at eve had drunk his fill,
Where danced the moon on Monan's rill,
And deep his midnight lair had made
In lone Glenartney's hazel shade ;
But, when the sun his beacon red
Had kindled on Benvoirlich's head,
The deep-mouthed bloodhound's heavy bay
Resounded up the rocky way,
And faint, from farther distance borne,
Were heard the clanging hoof and horn.

As Chief who hears his warder call,
" To arms ! the foemen storm the wall,"
The antlered monarch of the waste
Sprung from his heathery couch in haste.
But, ere his fleet career he took,
The dew-drops from his flanks he shook ;
Like crested leader proud and high
Tossed his beamed frontlet to the sky ;
A moment gazed adown the dale,
A moment snuffed the tainted gale,
A moment listened to the cry,
That thickened as the chase drew nigh ;
Then, as the headmost foes appeared,
With one brave bound the copse he cleared,
And, stretching forward free and far,
Sought the wild heaths of Uam-Var.

Yelled on the view the opening pack ;
Rock, glen, and cavern paid them back ;
To many a mingled sound at once
The awakened mountain gave response.
A hundred dogs bayed deep and strong,
Clattered a hundred steeds along,
Their peal the merry horns rung out,
A hundred voices joined the shout ;
With hark and whoop and wild halloo.
No rest Benvoirlich's echoes knew.
Far from the tumult fled the roe ;
Close in her covert cowered the doe ;
The falcon, from her cairn on high,
Cast on the rout a wondering eye,
Till far beyond her piercing ken
The hurricane had swept the glen.
Faint, and more faint, its failing din
Returned from cavern, cliff, and linn,
And silence settled, wide and still,
On the lone wood and mighty hill.

Less loud the sounds of sylvan war
Disturbed the heights of Uam-Var,
And roused the cavern, where, 't is told,
A giant made his den of old ;
For ere that steep ascent was won,
High in his pathway hung the sun,
And many a gallant, stayed perforce,
Was fain to breathe his faltering horse,
And of the trackers of the deer,
Scarce half the lessening pack was near ;
So shrewdly on the mountain-side
Had the bold burst their mettle tried.

The noble stag was pausing now
Upon the mountain's southern brow,
Where broad extended, far beneath,
The varied realms of fair Menteith.
With anxious eye he wandered o'er
Mountain and meadow, moss and moor,
And pondered refuge from his toil,
By far Lochard or Aberfoyle.

But nearer was the copsewood gray
That waved and wept on Loch-Achray,
And mingled with the pine-trees blue
On the bold cliffs of Benvenue.
Fresh vigor with the hope returned,
With flying foot the heath he spurned,
Held westward with unwearied race,
And left behind the panting chase.

'T were long to tell what steeds gave o'er,
As swept the hunt through Cambus-more ;
What reins were tightened in despair,
When rose Benledi's ridge in air ;
Who flagged upon Bochastle's heath,
Who shunned to stem the flooded Teith, —
For twice that day, from shore to shore,
The gallant stag swam stoutly o'er.
Few were the stragglers, following far,
That reached the lake of Vennachar ;
And when the Brigg of Turk was won,
The headmost horseman rode alone.

Alone, but with unbated zeal,
That horseman piled the scourge and steel ;
For, jaded now, and spent with toil,
Embossed with foam, and dark with soil,
While every gasp with sobs he drew,
The laboring stag strained full in view.
Two dogs of black St. Hubert's breed,
Unmatched for courage, breath, and speed,
Fast on his flying traces came,
And all but won that desperate game ;
For, scarce a spear's length from his haunch,
Vindictive toiled the bloodhounds stanch ;
Nor nearer might the dogs attain,
Nor farther might the quarry strain.
Thus up the margin of the lake,
Between the precipice and brake,
O'er stock and rock their race they take.

The Hunter marked that mountain high,
The lone lake's western boundary,
And deemed the stag must turn to bay,
Where that huge rampart barred the way ;
Already glorying in the prize,
Measured his antlers with his eyes ;
For the death-wound and death-halloo
Mustered his breath, his whinyard drew ;
But thundering as he came prepared,
With ready arm and weapon bared,
The wily quarry shunned the shock,
And turned him from the opposing rock ;
Then, dashing down a darksome glen,
Soon lost to hound and hunter's ken,
In the deep Trosachs' wildest nook
His solitary refuge took.
There, while close couched, the thicket shed
Cold dews and wild flowers on his head,

He heard the baffled dogs in vain
Rave through the hollow pass amain,
Chiding the rocks that yelled again.

Close on the hounds the hunter came,
To cheer them on the vanished game ;
But, stumbling in the rugged dell,
The gallant horse exhausted fell.
The impatient rider strove in vain
To rouse him with the spur and rein,
For the good steed, his labors o'er,
Stretched his stiff limbs, to rise no more ;
Then, touched with pity and remorse,
He sorrowed o'er the expiring horse.
"I little thought, when first thy rein
I slacked upon the banks of Seine,
That Highland eagle e'er should feed
On thy fleet limbs, my matchless steed !
Woe worth the chase, woe worth the day,
That costs thy life, my gallant gray ! "

Then through the dell his horn resounds,
From vain pursuit to call the hounds.
Back limped, with slow and crippled pace,
The sulky leaders of the chase ;
Close to their master's side they pressed,
With drooping tail and humbled crest ;
But still the dingle's hollow throat
Prolonged the swelling bugle-note.
The owlets started from their dream,
The eagles answered with their scream,
Round and around the sounds were cast,
Till echo seemed an answering blast ;
And on the Hunter hied his way,
To join some comrades of the day ;
Yet often paused, so strange the road,
So wondrous were the scenes it showed.

SIR WALTER SCOTT.

LAY OF THE IMPRISONED HUNTSMAN.

My hawk is tired of perch and hood,
My idle greyhound loathes his food,
My horse is weary of his stall,
And I am sick of captive thrall.
I wish I were as I have been,
Hunting the hart in forest green,
With bended bow and bloodhound free,
For that 's the life is meet for me.

I hate to learn the ebb of time
From yon dull steeple's drowsy chime,
Or mark it as the sunbeams crawl,
Inch after inch, along the wall.
The lark was wont my matins ring,
The sable rook my vespers sing ;
These towers, although a king's they be,
Have not a hall of joy for me.

No more at dawning morn I rise,
And sun myself in Ellen's eyes,
Drive the fleet deer the forest through,
And homeward wend with evening dew ;
A blithesome welcome blithely meet,
And lay my trophies at her feet,
While fled the eve on wing of glee, —
That life is lost to love and me !

SIR WALTER SCOTT.

THE ARAB TO HIS FAVORITE STEED.

I.

My beautiful ! my beautiful ! that standest meek-
ly by,
With thy proudly arched and glossy neck, and
dark and fiery eye,
Fret not to roam the desert now, with all thy
wingéd speed ;
I may not mount on thee again, — thou 'rt sold,
my Arab steed !
Fret not with that impatient hoof, — snuff not the
breezy wind, —
The farther that thou fliest now, so far am I behind ;
The stranger hath thy bridle-rein, — thy master
hath *his* gold, —
Fleet-limbed and beautiful, farewell ; thou 'rt
sold, my steed, thou 'rt sold.

II.

Farewell ! those free, untiréd limbs full many a
mile must roam,
To reach the chill and wintry sky which clouds
the stranger's home ;
Some other hand, less fond, must now thy corn
and bed prepare,
Thy silky mane, I braided once, must be another's
care !
The morning sun shall dawn again, but never
more with thee
Shall I gallop through the desert paths, where
we were wont to be ;
Evening shall darken on the earth, and o'er the
sandy plain
Some other steed, with slower step, shall bear me
home again.

III.

Yes, thou must go ! the wild, free breeze, the bril-
liant sun and sky,
Thy master's house, — from all of these my exiled
one must fly ;
Thy proud dark eye will grow less proud, thy
step become less fleet,
And vainly shalt thou arch thy neck, thy mas-
ter's hand to meet.

Only in sleep shall I behold that dark eye,
  glancing bright ; —
Only in sleep shall hear again that step so firm
  and light ;
And when I raise my dreaming arm to check or
  cheer thy speed,
Then must I, starting, wake to feel, — thou 'rt
  sold, my Arab steed !

IV.

Ah ! rudely, then, unseen by me, some cruel hand
  may chide,
Till foam-wreaths lie, like crested waves, along
  thy panting side :
And the rich blood that 's in thee swells, in thy
  indignant pain,
Till careless eyes, which rest on thee, may count
  each starting vein.
Will they ill-use thee ? If I thought — but no,
  it cannot be, —
Thou art so swift, yet easy curbed ; so gentle,
  yet so free :
And yet, if haply, when thou 'rt gone, my lonely
  heart should yearn, —
Can the hand which casts thee from it now com-
  mand thee to return ?

V.

Return ! alas ! my Arab steed ! what shall thy
  master do,
When thou, who wast his all of joy, hast vanished
  from his view ?
When the dim distance cheats mine eye, and
  through the gathering tears
Thy bright form, for a moment, like the false
  mirage appears ;
Slow and unmounted shall I roam, with weary
  step alone,
Where, with fleet step and joyous bound, thou
  oft hast borne me on ;
And sitting down by that green well, I 'll pause
  and sadly think,
" It was here he bowed his glossy neck when last
  I saw him drink ! "

VI.

When last I saw thee drink ! — Away ! the fevered
  dream is o'er, —
I could not live a day, and *know* that we should
  meet no more !
They tempted me, my beautiful ! — for hunger's
  power is strong, —
They tempted me, my beautiful ! but I have
  loved too long.
Who said that I had given thee up ? who said
  that thou wast sold ?
'T is false, — 't is false, my Arab steed ! I fling
  them back their gold !

Thus, *thus*, I leap upon thy back, and scour the
  distant plains ;
Away ! who overtakes us now shall claim thee for
  his pains !

CAROLINE E. NORTON.

SLEIGH SONG.

JINGLE, jingle, clear the way,
'T is the merry, merry sleigh,
As it swiftly scuds along
Hear the burst of happy song,
See the gleam of glances bright,
Flashing o'er the pathway white.
Jingle, jingle, past it flies,
Sending shafts from hooded eyes, —
Roguish archers, I ll be bound,
Little heeding who they wound ;
See them, with capricious pranks,
Ploughing now the drifted banks ;
Jingle, jingle, mid the glee
Who among them cares for me ?
Jingle, jingle, on they go,
Capes and bonnets white with snow,
Not a single robe they fold
To protect them from the cold ;
Jingle, jingle, mid the storm,
Fun and frolic keep them warm ;
Jingle, jingle, down the hills,
O'er the meadows, past the mills,
Now 't is slow, and now 't is fast ;
Winter will not always last.
Jingle, jingle, clear the way,
'T is the merry, merry sleigh.

G. W. PETTEE.

OUR SKATER BELLE.

ALONG the frozen lake she comes
  In linking crescents, light and fleet ;
The ice-imprisoned Undine hums
  A welcome to her little feet.

I see the jaunty hat, the plume
  Swerve bird-like in the joyous gale, —
The cheeks lit up to burning bloom,
  The young eyes sparkling through the veil.

The quick breath parts her laughing lips,
  The white neck shines through tossing curls ;
Her vesture gently sways and dips,
  As on she speeds in shell-like whorls.

Men stop and smile to see her go ;
  They gaze, they smile in pleased surprise ;
They ask her name ; they long to show
  Some silent friendship in their eyes.

She glances not ; she passes on ;
  Her steely footfall quicker rings ;
She guesses not the benison
  Which follows her on noiseless wings.

Smooth be her ways, secure her tread
  Along the devious lines of life,
From grace to grace successive led, —
  A noble maiden, nobler wife !
                                ANONYMOUS.

A CANADIAN BOAT-SONG.

FAINTLY as tolls the evening chime,
Our voices keep tune, and our oars keep time.
Soon as the woods on shore look dim,
We 'll sing at St. Ann's our parting hymn.
Row, brothers, row ! the stream runs fast,
The rapids are near, and the daylight 's past !

Why should we yet our sail unfurl ? —
There is not a breath the blue wave to curl.
But when the wind blows off the shore
O, sweetly we 'll rest our weary oar !
Blow, breezes, blow ! the stream runs fast,
The rapids are near, and the daylight 's past !

Utawa's tide ! this trembling moon
Shall see us float over thy surges soon.
Saint of this green isle, hear our prayers, —
O, grant us cool heavens and favoring airs !
Blow, breezes, blow ! the stream runs fast,
The rapids are near, and the daylight 's past !
                                THOMAS MOORE.

THE PLEASURE-BOAT.

COME, hoist the sail, the fast let go !
  They 're seated side by side ;
Wave chases wave in pleasant flow ;
  The bay is fair and wide.

The ripples lightly tap the boat,
  Loose ! Give her to the wind !
She shoots ahead ; they 're all afloat ;
  The strand is far behind.

No danger reach so fair a crew !
  Thou goddess of the foam,
I 'll ever pay thee worship due,
  If thou wilt bring them home.

Fair ladies, fairer than the spray
  The prow is dashing wide,
Soft breezes take you on your way,
  Soft flow the blessèd tide.

O, might I like those breezes be,
  And touch that arching brow,
I 'd dwell forever on the sea
  Where ye are floating now.

The boat goes tilting on the waves ;
  The waves go tilting by ;
There dips the duck, — her back she laves ;
  O'erhead the sea-gulls fly.

Now, like the gulls that dart for prey,
  The little vessel stoops ;
Now, rising, shoots along her way,
  Like them, in easy swoops.

The sunlight falling on her sheet,
  It glitters like the drift,
Sparkling, in scorn of summer's heat,
  High up some mountain rift.

The winds are fresh ; she 's driving fast
  Upon the bending tide ;
The crinkling sail, and crinkling mast,
  Go with her side by side.

Why dies the breeze away so soon ?
  Why hangs the pennant down ?
The sea is glass ; the sun at noon. —
  Nay, lady, do not frown ;

For, see, the wingèd fisher's plume
  Is painted on the sea ;
Below, a cheek of lovely bloom
  Whose eyes look up to thee.

She smiles ; thou need'st must smile on her.
  And, see, beside her face
A rich, white cloud that doth not stir :
  What beauty, and what grace !

And pictured beach of yellow sand,
  And peakèd rock and hill,
Change the smooth sea to fairy-land ;
  How lovely and how still !

From that far isle the thresher's flail
  Strikes close upon the ear ;
The leaping fish, the swinging sail
  Of yonder sloop, sound near.

The parting sun sends out a glow
  Across the placid bay,
Touching with glory all the show, —
  A breeze ! Up helm ! Away !

Careening to the wind, they reach,
  With laugh and call, the shore.
They 've left their footprints on the beach,
  But them I hear no more.
                                RICHARD HENRY DANA.

THE ANGLER'S WISH.

I IN these flowery meads would be,
These crystal streams should solace me ;
To whose harmonious bubbling noise
I, with my angle, would rejoice,
    Sit here, and see the turtle-dove
    Court his chaste mate to acts of love ;

Or, on that bank, feel the west-wind
Breathe health and plenty ; please my mind,
To see sweet dew-drops kiss these flowers,
And then washed off by April showers ;
    Here, hear my kenna sing a song :
    There, see a blackbird feed her young,

Or a laverock build her nest ;
Here, give my weary spirits rest,
And raise my low-pitched thoughts above
Earth, or what poor mortals love.
    Thus, free from lawsuits, and the noise
    Of princes' courts, I would rejoice ;

Or, with my Bryan and a book,
Loiter long days near Shawford brook ;
There sit by him, and eat my meat ;
There see the sun both rise and set ;
There bid good morning to next day ;
There meditate my time away ;
    And angle on ; and beg to have
    A quiet passage to a welcome grave.
                IZAAK WALTON.

ANGLING.

FROM " THE SEASONS."

JUST in the dubious point, where with the pool
Is mixed the trembling stream, or where it boils
Around the stone, or from the hollowed bank
Reverted plays in undulating flow,
There throw, nice-judging, the delusive fly ;
And, as you lead it round in artful curve,
With eye attentive mark the springing game.
Straight as above the surface of the flood
They wanton rise, or urged by hunger leap,
Then fix, with gentle twitch, the barbéd hook ;
Some lightly tossing to the grassy bank,
And to the shelving shore slow dragging some,
With various hand proportioned to their force.
If yet too young, and easily deceived,
A worthless prey scarce bends your pliant rod,
Him, piteous of his youth, and the short space
He has enjoyed the vital light of heaven,
Soft disengage, and back into the stream
The speckled infant throw.   But should you lure
From his dark haunt, beneath the tangled roots

Of pendent trees, the monarch of the brook,
Behooves you then to ply your finest art.
Long time he, following cautious, scans the fly ;
And oft attempts to seize it, but as oft
The dimpled water speaks his jealous fear.
At last, while haply o'er the shaded sun
Passes a cloud, he desperate takes the death,
With sullen plunge.   At once he darts along,
Deep-struck, and runs out all the lengthened line ;
Then seeks the farthest ooze, the sheltering weed,
The caverned bank, his old secure abode ;
And flies aloft, and flounces round the pool,
Indignant of the guile.   With yielding hand,
That feels him still, yet to his furious course
Gives way, you, now retiring, following now
Across the stream, exhaust his idle rage ;
Till, floating broad upon his breathless side,
And to his fate abandoned, to the shore
You gayly drag your unresisting prize.
                JAMES THOMSON.

THE ANGLER.

BUT look ! o'er the fall see the angler stand,
Swinging his rod with skilful hand ;
The fly at the end of his gossamer line
    Swims through the sun like a summer moth,
Till, dropt with a careful precision fine,
    It touches the pool beyond the froth.
A-sudden, the speckled hawk of the brook
Darts from his covert and seizes the hook.
Swift spins the reel ; with easy slip
The line pays out, and the rod like a whip,
Lithe and arrowy, tapering, slim,
Is bent to a bow o'er the brooklet's brim,
Till the trout leaps up in the sun, and flings
The spray from the flash of his finny wings ;
Then falls on his side, and, drunken with fright,
    Is towed to the shore like a staggering barge,
    Till beached at last on the sandy marge,
Where he dies with the hues of the morning light,
While his sides with a cluster of stars are bright.
The angler in his basket lays
The constellation, and goes his ways.
              THOMAS BUCHANAN READ.

THE ANGLER'S TRYSTING-TREE.

SING, sweet thrushes, forth and sing !
    Meet the morn upon the lea ;
Are the emeralds of the spring
    On the angler's trysting-tree ?
    Tell, sweet thrushes, tell to me !

Are there buds on our willow-tree?
Buds and birds on our trysting-tree?

Sing, sweet thrushes, forth and sing!
Have you met the honey-bee,
Circling upon rapid wing,
    Round the angler's trysting-tree?
Up, sweet thrushes, up and see!
Are there bees at our willow-tree?
Birds and bees at the trysting-tree?

Sing, sweet thrushes, forth and sing!
Are the fountains gushing free?
Is the south-wind wandering
    Through the angler's trysting-tree?
Up, sweet thrushes, tell to me!
Is there wind up our willow-tree?
Wind or calm at our trysting-tree?

Sing, sweet thrushes, forth and sing!
Wile us with a merry glee;
To the flowery haunts of spring, —
    To the angler's trysting-tree.
Tell, sweet thrushes, tell to me!
Are there flowers 'neath our willow-tree?
Spring and flowers at the trysting-tree?
                    THOMAS TOD STODDART.

THE ANGLER.

O THE gallant fisher's life,
    It is the best of any!
T is full of pleasure, void of strife,
    And 't is beloved by many;
        Other joys
        Are but toys;
        Only this
        Lawful is;
        For our skill
        Breeds no ill,
    But content and pleasure.

In a morning, up we rise,
    Ere Aurora's peeping;
Drink a cup to wash our eyes,
    Leave the sluggard sleeping;
        Then we go
        To and fro,
        With our knacks
        At our backs,
        To such streams
        As the Thames,
    If we have the leisure.

When we please to walk abroad
    For our recreation,
In the fields is our abode,
    Full of delectation,

Where, in a brook,
    With a hook, —
    Or a lake, —
    Fish we take;
    There we sit,
    For a bit,
Till we fish entangle.

We have gentles in a horn,
    We have paste and worms too;
We can watch both night and morn,
    Suffer rain and storms too;
        None do here
        Use to swear:
        Oaths do fray
        Fish away;
        We sit still,
        Watch our quill:
    Fishers must not wrangle.

If the sun's excessive heat
    Make our bodies swelter,
To an osier hedge we get,
    For a friendly shelter;
        Where, in a dike,
        Perch or pike,
        Roach or dace,
        We do chase,
        Bleak or gudgeon,
        Without grudging;
    We are still contented.

Or we sometimes pass an hour
    Under a green willow,
That defends us from a shower,
    Making earth our pillow;
        Where we may
        Think and pray,
        Before death
        Stops our breath;
        Other joys
        Are but toys,
    And to be lamented.
                    JOHN CHALKHILL.

VERSES IN PRAISE OF ANGLING.

QUIVERING fears, heart-tearing cares,
Anxious sighs, untimely tears,
    Fly, fly to courts,
    Fly to fond worldlings' sports,
Where strained sardonic smiles are glosing still,
And grief is forced to laugh against her will,
    Where mirth 's but mummery,
    And sorrows only real be.

Fly from our country pastimes, fly,
Sad troops of human misery,
    Come, serene looks,
    Clear as the crystal brooks,
Or the pure azured heaven that smiles to see
The rich attendance on our poverty ;
    Peace and a secure mind,
    Which all men seek, we only find.

Abused mortals ! did you know
Where joy, heart's ease, and comforts grow,
    You 'd scorn proud towers
    And seek them in these bowers,
Where winds, sometimes, our woods perhaps may
    shake,
But blustering care could never tempest make ;
    Nor murmurs e'er come nigh us,
    Saving of fountains that glide by us.

Here 's no fantastic mask nor dance,
But of our kids that frisk and prance ;
    Nor wars are seen,
    Unless upon the green
Two harmless lambs are butting one the other,
Which done, both bleating run, each to his mother ;
    And wounds are never found,
    Save what the ploughshare gives the
    ground.

Here are no entrapping baits
To hasten to, too hasty fates ;
    Unless it be
    The fond credulity
Of silly fish, which (worlding like) still look
Upon the bait, but never on the hook ;
    Nor envy, 'less among
    The birds, for price of their sweet song.

Go, let the diving negro seek
For gems, hid in some forlorn creek :
    We all pearls scorn
    Save what the dewy morn
Congeals upon each little spire of grass,
Which careless shepherds beat down as they pass ;
    And gold ne'er here appears,
    Save what the yellow Ceres bears.

Blest silent groves, O, may you be,
Forever, mirth's best nursery !
    May pure contents
    Forever pitch their tents
Upon these downs, these meads, these rocks, these
    mountains !
And peace still slumber by these purling fountains,
    Which we may every year
    Meet, when we come a-fishing here.
                SIR HENRY WOTTON.

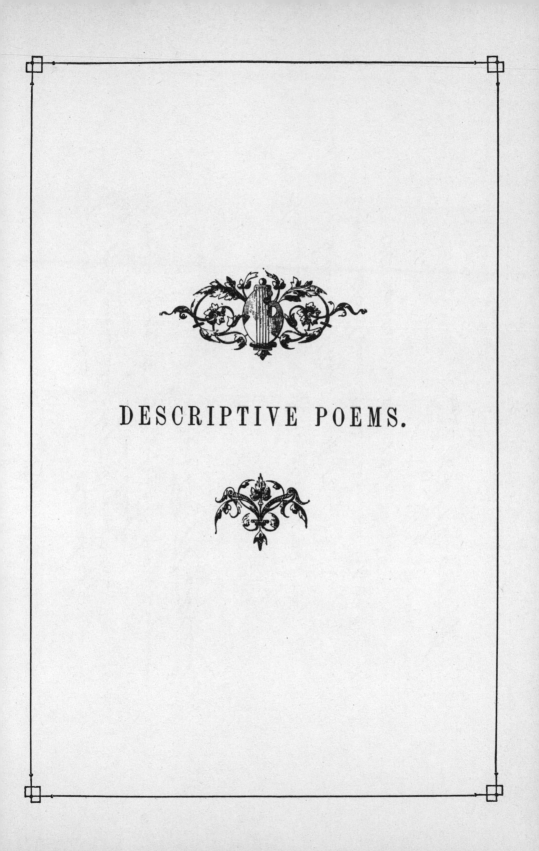

DESCRIPTIVE POEMS.

The star of love now shines above,
    Cool zephyrs crisp the sea;
Among the leaves the wind-harp weaves
    Its serenade for thee.

Geo. P. Morris.

DESCRIPTIVE POEMS.

NORHAM CASTLE.

[The ruinous castle of Norham (anciently called Ubbanford) is situated on the southern bank of the Tweed, about six miles above Berwick, and where that river is still the boundary between England and Scotland. The extent of its ruins, as well as its historical importance, shows it to have been a place of magnificence as well as strength. Edward I. resided there when he was created umpire of the dispute concerning the Scottish succession. It was repeatedly taken and retaken during the wars between England and Scotland, and, indeed, scarce any happened in which it had not a principal share. Norham Castle is situated on a steep bank, which overhangs the river. The ruins of the castle are at present considerable, as well as picturesque. They consist of a large shattered tower, with many vaults, and fragments of other edifices, inclosed within an outward wall of great circuit.]

DAY set on Norham's castled steep,
And Tweed's fair river, broad and deep,
 And Cheviot's mountains lone :
The battled towers, the donjon keep,
The loop-hole grates where captives weep,
The flanking walls that round it sweep,
 In yellow lustre shone.
The warriors on the turrets high,
Moving athwart the evening sky,
 Seemed forms of giant height ;
Their armor, as it caught the rays,
Flashed back again the western blaze,
 In lines of dazzling light.

St. George's banner, broad and gay,
Now faded, as the fading ray
 Less bright, and less, was flung ;
The evening gale had scarce the power
To wave it on the donjon tower,
 So heavily it hung.
The scouts had parted on their search,
 The castle gates were barred ;
Above the gloomy portal arch,
Timing his footsteps to a march,
 The warder kept his guard ;
Low humming, as he paced along,
Some ancient Border gathering-song.

A distant trampling sound he hears ;
He looks abroad, and soon appears,
O'er Horncliff hill, a plump of spears,
 Beneath a pennon gay ;

A horseman, darting from the crowd,
Like lightning from a summer cloud,
Spurs on his mettled courser proud
 Before the dark array.
Beneath the sable palisade,
That closed the castle barricade,
 His bugle-horn he blew ;
The warder hasted from the wall,
And warned the captain in the hall,
 For well the blast he knew ;
And joyfully that knight did call
To sewer, squire, and seneschal.

"Now broach ye a pipe of Malvoisie,
 Bring pasties of the doe,
And quickly make the entrance free,
And bid my heralds ready be,
And every minstrel sound his glee,
 And all our trumpets blow ;
And, from the platform, spare ye not
To fire a noble salvo-shot :
 Lord Marmion waits below."
Then to the castle's lower ward
 Sped forty yeomen tall,
The iron-studded gates unbarred,
Raised the portcullis' ponderous guard,
The lofty palisade unsparred,
 And let the drawbridge fall.

Along the bridge Lord Marmion rode,
Proudly his red-roan charger trode,
His helm hung at the saddle-bow ;
Well by his visage you might know
He was a stalworth knight, and keen,
And had in many a battle been.
The scar on his brown cheek revealed
A token true of Bosworth field ;
His eyebrow dark, and eye of fire,
Showed spirit proud, and prompt to ire.
Yet lines of thought upon his cheek
Did deep design and counsel speak.
His forehead, by his casque worn bare,
His thick mustache, and curly hair,
Coal-black, and grizzled here and there,
 But more through toil than age ;

His square-turned joints, and strength of limb,
Showed him no carpet-knight so trim,
But in close fight a champion grim,
   In camps a leader sage.

Well was he armed from head to heel,
In mail and plate of Milan steel ;
But his strong helm, of mighty cost,
Was all with burnished gold embossed ;
Amid the plumage of the crest,
A falcon hovered on her nest,
With wings outspread, and forward breast ;
E'en such a falcon, on his shield,
Soared sable in an azure field :
The golden legend bore aright,
𝕿𝖍𝖔 𝖈𝖍𝖊𝖈𝖐𝖘 𝖆𝖙 𝖒𝖊 𝖙𝖔 𝖉𝖊𝖆𝖙𝖍 𝖎𝖘 𝖉𝖎𝖌𝖍𝖙.
Blue was the charger's broidered rein ;
Blue ribbons decked his arching mane ;
The knightly housing's ample fold
Was velvet blue, and trapped with gold.

Behind him rode two gallant squires
Of noble name and knightly sires ;
They burned the gilded spurs to claim ;
For well could each a war-horse tame,
Could draw the bow, the sword could sway,
And lightly bear the ring away ;
Nor less with courteous precepts stored,
Could dance in hall, and carve at board,
And frame love-ditties passing rare,
And sing them to a lady fair.

Four men-at-arms came at their backs,
With halbert, bill, and battle-axe ;
They bore Lord Marmion's lance so strong,
And led his sumpter-mules along,
And ambling palfrey, when at need
Him listed ease his battle-steed.
The last and trustiest of the four
On high his forky pennon bore ;
Like swallow's tail, in shape and hue,
Fluttered the streamer glossy blue,
Where, blazoned sable, as before,
The towering falcon seemed to soar.
Last, twenty yeomen, two and two,
In hosen black, and jerkins blue,
With falcons broidered on each breast,
Attended on their lord's behest :
Each, chosen for an archer good,
Knew hunting-craft by lake or wood ;
Each one a six-foot bow could bend,
And far a cloth-yard shaft could send ;
Each held a boar-spear tough and strong,
And at their belts their quivers rung.
Their dusty palfreys and array
Showed they had marched a weary way.
            SIR WALTER SCOTT.

MELROSE ABBEY.

IF thou wouldst view fair Melrose aright,
Go visit it by the pale moonlight ;
For the gay beams of lightsome day
Gild, but to flout, the ruins gray.
When the broken arches are black in night,
And each shafted oriel glimmers white ;
When the cold light's uncertain shower
Streams on the ruined central tower ;
When buttress and buttress, alternately,
Seem framed of ebon and ivory ;
When silver edges the imagery,
And the scrolls that teach thee to live and die ;
When distant Tweed is heard to rave,
And the owlet to hoot o'er the dead man's grave,
Then go, — but go alone the while, —
Then view St. David's ruined pile ;
And, home returning, soothly swear,
Was never scene so sad and fair !

. . . . . .

The pillared arches were over their head,
And beneath their feet were the bones of the dead.

Spreading herbs and flowerets bright
Glistened with the dew of night ;
Nor herb nor floweret glistened there,
But was carved in the cloister-arches as fair.
   The monk gazed long on the lovely moon,
     Then into the night he looked forth ;
   And red and bright the streamers light
     Were dancing in the glowing north.

. . . . . .

He knew, by the streamers that shot so bright,
That spirits were riding the northern light.

By a steel-clenched postern door,
   They entered now the chancel tall ;
The darkened roof rose high aloof
   On pillars lofty and light and small ;
The keystone, that locked each ribbed aisle,
Was a fleur-de-lis, or a quatre-feuille :
The corbells were carved grotesque and grim ;
And the pillars, with clustered shafts so trim,
With base and with capital flourished around,
Seemed bundles of lances which garlands had
     bound.

Full many a scutcheon and banner, riven,
Shook to the cold night-wind of heaven,
   Around the screened altar's pale ;
And there the dying lamps did burn,
Before thy low and lonely urn,
O gallant chief of Otterburne !
   And thine, dark Knight of Liddesdale !
O fading honors of the dead !
O high ambition, lowly laid !

The moon on the east oriel shone
Through slender shafts of shapely stone,
　By foliaged tracery combined ;
Thou wouldst have thought some fairy's hand
'Twixt poplars straight the osier wand
　In many a freakish knot had twined ;
Then framed a spell, when the work was done.
And changed the willow wreaths to stone.
The silver light, so pale and faint,
Showed many a prophet, and many a saint,
　Whose image on the glass was dyed ;
Full in the midst, his Cross of Red
Triumphant Michael brandished,
　And trampled the Apostate's pride.
The moonbeam kissed the holy pane,
And threw on the pavement a bloody stain.
SIR WALTER SCOTT.

CHRISTMAS IN OLDEN TIME.

HEAP on more wood ! — the wind is chill ;
But let it whistle as it will,
We 'll keep our Christmas merry still.
Each age has deemed the new-born year
The fittest time for festal cheer :
Even, heathen yet, the savage Dane
At Iol more deep the mead did drain ;
High on the beach his galleys drew,
And feasted all his pirate crew ;
Then in his low and pine-built hall,
Where shields and axes decked the wall,
They gorged upon the half-dressed steer ;
Caroused in seas of sable beer ;
While round, in brutal jest, were thrown
The half-gnawed rib and marrow-bone,
Or listened all, in grim delight,
While scalds yelled out the joys of fight.
Then forth in frenzy would they hie,
While wildly loose their red locks fly,
And dancing round the blazing pile
They make such barbarous mirth the while,
As best might to the mind recall
The boisterous joys of Odin's hall.

　And well our Christian sires of old
Loved when the year its course had rolled,
And brought blithe Christmas back again,
With all its hospitable train.
Domestic and religious rite
Gave honor to the holy night ;
On Christmas eve the bells were rung :
On Christmas eve the mass was sung;
That only night in all the year,
Saw the stoled priest the chalice rear.
The damsel donned her kirtle sheen ;
The hall was dressed with holly green ;
Forth to the wood did merry-men go,
To gather in the mistletoe.

Then opened wide the baron's hall
To vassal, tenant, serf, and all ;
Power laid his rod of rule aside,
And Ceremony doffed his pride ;
The heir, with roses in his shoes,
That night might village partner choose ;
The lord, underogating, share
The vulgar game of " post and pair."
All hailed with uncontrolled delight
And general voice the happy night
That to the cottage, as the crown,
Brought tidings of salvation down.

　The fire, with well-dried logs supplied,
Went roaring up the chimney wide ;
The huge hall table's oaken face,
Scrubbed till it shone the day to grace,
Bore then upon its massive board
No mark to part the squire and lord ;
Then was brought in the lusty brawn,
By old blue-coated serving-man ;
Then the grim boar's head frowned on high,
Crested with bays and rosemary.
Well can the green-garbed ranger tell
How, when, and where the monster fell,
What dogs before his death he tore,
And all the baiting of the boar.
The wassail round, in good brown bowls,
Garnished with ribbons, blithely trowls,
There the huge sirloin reeked ; hard by
Plum-porridge stood, and Christmas pie,
Nor failed old Scotland to produce
At such high tide, her savory goose.
Then came the merry maskers in ;
And carols roared with blithesome din,
If unmelodious was the song,
It was a hearty note, and strong.
Who lists may in their mumming see
Traces of ancient mystery ;
White skirts supplied the masquerade,
And smutted cheeks the visors made ;
But, oh ! what maskers, richly dight,
Can boast of bosoms half so light ?
England was merry England, when
Old Christmas brought his sports again.
'T was Christmas broached the mightiest ale !
'T was Christmas told the merriest tale ;
A Christmas gambol oft could cheer
The poor man's heart through half the year.
SIR WALTER SCOTT.

DIVINA COMMEDIA.

I.

OFT have I seen, at some cathedral door,
　A laborer, pausing in the dust and heat,
　Lay down his burden, and with reverent feet
　Enter, and cross himself, and on the floor

Kneel to repeat his paternoster o'er ;
  Far off the noises of the world retreat ;
  The loud vociferations of the street
  Become an undistinguishable roar.
So, as I enter here from day to day,
  And leave my burden at this minster gate,
  Kneeling in prayer, and not ashamed to pray,
The tumult of the time disconsolate
  To inarticulate murmurs dies away,
  While the eternal ages watch and wait.

II.

How strange the sculptures that adorn these
      towers !
  This crowd of statues, in whose folded sleeves
  Birds build their nests ; while canopied with
      leaves
Parvis and portal bloom like trellised bowers,
And the vast minster seems a cross of flowers !
  But fiends and dragons on the gargoyled eaves
  Watch the dead Christ between the living
      thieves,
And, underneath, the traitor Judas lowers !
Ah ! from what agonies of heart and brain,
  What exultations trampling on despair,
  What tenderness, what tears, what hate of
      wrong,
What passionate outcry of a soul in pain,
  Uprose this poem of the earth and air,
  This mediæval miracle of song !

III.

I enter, and I see thee in the gloom
  Of the long aisles, O poet saturnine !
  And strive to make my steps keep pace with
      thine.
The air is filled with some unknown perfume ;
The congregation of the dead make room
  For thee to pass ; the votive tapers shine ;
  Like rooks that haunt Ravenna's groves of pine
The hovering echoes fly from tomb to tomb.
From the confessionals I hear arise
  Rehearsals of forgotten tragedies,
  And lamentations from the crypts below ;
And then a voice celestial, that begins
  With the pathetic words, " Although your sins
As scarlet be," and ends with " as the snow."

IV.

I lift mine eyes, and all the windows blaze
  With forms of saints and holy men who died,
  Here martyred and hereafter glorified ;
And the great Rose upon its leaves displays
Christ's Triumph, and the angelic roundelays,
  With splendor upon splendor multiplied ;
  And Beatrice again at Dante's side
No more rebukes, but smiles her words of
      praise.

And then the organ sounds, and unseen choirs
  Sing the old Latin hymns of peace and love,
  And benedictions of the Holy Ghost ;
And the melodious bells among the spires
  O'er all the house-tops and through heaven
      above
Proclaim the elevation of the Host !

V.

O star of morning and of liberty !
  O bringer of the light, whose splendor shines
  Above the darkness of the Apennines,
Forerunner of the day that is to be !
The voices of the city and the sea,
  The voices of the mountains and the pines,
  Repeat thy song, till the familiar lines
Are footpaths for the thought of Italy !
Thy fame is blown abroad from all the heights,
  Through all the nations, and a sound is heard,
  As of a mighty wind, and men devout,
Strangers of Rome, and the new proselytes,
  In their own language hear thy wondrous word,
  And many are amazed and many doubt.
                    HENRY WADSWORTH LONGFELLOW.

WESTMINSTER BRIDGE.

EARTH has not anything to show more fair ;
Dull would he be of soul who could pass by
A sight so touching in its majesty :
This City now doth, like a garment, wear

The beauty of the morning ; silent, bare,
Ships, towers, domes, theatres, and temples lie
Open unto the fields, and to the sky,
All bright and glittering in the smokeless air.

Never did sun more beautifully steep
In his first splendor valley, rock, or hill ;
Ne'er saw I, never felt, a calm so deep !
The river glideth at his own sweet will.
Dear God ! the very houses seem asleep ;
And all that mighty heart is lying still !
                        WILLIAM WORDSWORTH.
1802.

ALNWICK CASTLE.

HOME of the Percy's high-born race,
  Home of their beautiful and brave,
Alike their birth and burial place,
  Their cradle and their grave !
Still sternly o'er the castle gate
Their house's Lion stands in state,
  As in his proud departed hours ;
And warriors frown in stone on high,
And feudal banners "flout the sky"
  Above his princely towers.

FISHER'S ROCK.

" We sat by the fisher's cottage
And looked at the stormy tide "

A gentle hill its side inclines,
  Lovely in England's fadeless green,
To meet the quiet stream which winds
  Through this romantic scene
As silently and sweetly still
As when, at evening, on that hill,
  While summer's wind blew soft and low,
Seated by gallant Hotspur's side,
His Katherine was a happy bride,
  A thousand years ago.

I wandered through the lofty halls
  Trod by the Percys of old fame,
And traced upon the chapel walls
  Each high, heroic name,
From him who once his standard set
Where now, o'er mosque and minaret,
  Glitter the Sultan's crescent moons,
To him who, when a younger son,
Fought for King George at Lexington,
  A major of dragoons.

That last half-stanza, — it has dashed
  From my warm lip the sparkling cup ;
The light that o'er my eyebeam flashed,
  The power that bore my spirit up
Above this bank-note world, is gone ;
And Alnwick 's but a market town,
And this, alas ! its market day,
And beasts and borderers throng the way ;
Oxen and bleating lambs in lots,
Northumbrian boors and plaided Scots,
  Men in the coal and cattle line ;
From Teviot's bard and hero land,
From royal Berwick's beach of sand,
From Wooller, Morpeth, Hexham, and
  Newcastle-upon-Tyne.

These are not the romantic times
So beautiful in Spenser's rhymes,
  So dazzling to the dreaming boy ;
Ours are the days of fact, not fable,
Of knights, but not of the round table,
  Of Bailie Jarvie, not Rob Roy ;
'T is what "Our President," Monroe,
  Has called "the era of good feeling" ;
The Highlander, the bitterest foe
To modern laws, has felt their blow,
Consented to be taxed, and vote,
And put on pantaloons and coat,
  And leave off cattle-stealing :
Lord Stafford mines for coal and salt,
The Duke of Norfolk deals in malt,
  The Douglass in red herrings ;
And noble name and cultured land,
Palace, and park, and vassal band,
Are powerless to the notes of hand
  Of Rothschild or the Barings.

The age of bargaining, said Burke,
Has come : to-day the turbaned Turk
(Sleep, Richard of the lion heart !
Sleep on, nor from your cerements start)
  Is England's friend and fast ally ;
The Moslem tramples on the Greek,
  And on the Cross and altar-stone,
  And Christendom looks tamely on,
And hears the Christian maiden shriek,
  And sees the Christian father die ;
And not a sabre-blow is given
For Greece and fame, for faith and heaven,
  By Europe's craven chivalry.

You 'll ask if yet the Percy lives
  In the armed pomp of feudal state ?
The present representatives
  Of Hotspur and his "gentle Kate,"
Are some half-dozen serving-men
In the drab coat of William Penn ;
  A chambermaid, whose lip and eye,
And check, and brown hair, bright and curling,
  Spoke nature's aristocracy ;
And one, half groom, half seneschal,
Who bowed me through court, bower, and hall,
From donjon keep to turret wall,
  For ten-and-sixpence sterling.
                    FITZ-GREENE HALLECK.

THE FISHER'S COTTAGE.

WE sat by the fisher's cottage,
  And looked at the stormy tide ;
The evening mist came rising,
  And floating far and wide.

One by one in the lighthouse
  The lamps shone out on high ;
And far on the dim horizon
  A ship went sailing by.

We spoke of storm and shipwreck, —
  Of sailors, and how they live ;
Of journeys 'twixt sky and water,
  And the sorrows and joys they give.

We spoke of distant countries,
  In regions strange and fair,
And of the wondrous beings
  And curious customs there ;

Of perfumed lamps on the Ganges,
  Which are launched in the twilight hour ;
And the dark and silent Brahmins,
  Who worship the lotos flower.

Of the wretched dwarfs of Lapland, —
  Broad-headed, wide-mouthed, and small, —
Who crouch round their oil-fires, cooking,
  And chatter and scream and bawl.

And the maidens earnestly listened,
  Till at last we spoke no more ;
The ship like a shadow had vanished,
  And darkness fell deep on the shore.
      HENRY HEINE (German). Translation
        of CHARLES G. LELAND.

THE HURRICANE.

LORD of the winds ! I feel thee nigh,
I know thy breath in the burning sky !
And I wait, with a thrill in every vein,
For the coming of the hurricane !

And lo ! on the wing of the heavy gales,
Through the boundless arch of heaven he sails.
Silent and slow, and terribly strong,
The mighty shadow is borne along,
Like the dark eternity to come ;
While the world below, dismayed and dumb,
Through the calm of the thick hot atmosphere
Looks up at its gloomy folds with fear.

They darken fast ; and the golden blaze
Of the sun is quenched in the lurid haze,
And he sends through the shade a funeral ray —
A glare that is neither night nor day,
A beam that touches, with hues of death,
The clouds above and the earth beneath.
To its covert glides the silent bird,
While the hurricane's distant voice is heard
Uplifted among the mountains round,
And the forests hear and answer the sound.

He is come ! he is come ! do ye not behold
His ample robes on the wind unrolled ?
Giant of air ! we bid thee hail ! —
How his gray skirts toss in the whirling gale ;
How his huge and writhing arms are bent
To clasp the zone of the firmament,
And fold at length, in their dark embrace,
From mountain to mountain the visible space.

Darker, — still darker ! the whirlwinds bear
The dust of the plains to the middle air ;
And hark to the crashing, long and loud,
Of the chariot of God in the thunder-cloud !
You may trace its path by the flashes that start
From the rapid wheels where'er they dart,
As the fire-bolts leap to the world below,
And flood the skies with a lurid glow.

What roar is that ? — 't is the rain that breaks
In torrents away from the airy lakes,
Heavily poured on the shuddering ground,
And shedding a nameless horror round.
Ah ! well-known woods, and mountains, and skies,
With the very clouds ! — ye are lost to my eyes.

I seek ye vainly, and see in your place
The shadowy tempest that sweeps through space,
A whirling ocean that fills the wall
Of the crystal heaven, and buries all.
And I, cut off from the world, remain
Alone with the terrible hurricane.
      WILLIAM CULLEN BRYANT.

HOLLAND.

FROM "THE TRAVELLER."

To men of other minds my fancy flies,
Embosomed in the deep where Holland lies.
Methinks her patient sons before me stand,
Where the broad ocean leans against the land,
And, sedulous to stop the coming tide,
Lift the tall rampire's artificial pride.
Onward methinks, and diligently slow,
The firm connected bulwark seems to grow ;
Spreads its long arms amidst the watery roar,
Scoops out an empire, and usurps the shore.
While the pent ocean, rising o'er the pile,
Sees an amphibious world beneath him smile ;
The slow canal, the yellow-blossomed vale
The willow-tufted bank, the gliding sail,
The crowded mart, the cultivated plain,
A new creation rescued from his reign.
  Thus while around the wave-subjected soil
Impels the native to repeated toil,
Industrious habits in each bosom reign,
And industry begets a love of gain.
Hence all the good from opulence that springs,
With all those ills superfluous treasure brings,
Are here displayed.
      OLIVER GOLDSMITH.

ITALY AND SWITZERLAND.

FROM "THE TRAVELLER."

FAR to the right where Apennine ascends,
Bright as the summer, Italy extends.
Its uplands sloping deck the mountain's side,
Woods over woods, in gay theatric pride ;
While oft some temple's mouldering tops between
With venerable grandeur mark the scene.
  Could nature's bounty satisfy the breast,
The sons of Italy were surely blest.
Whatever fruits in different climes were found,
That proudly rise, or humbly court the ground ;
Whatever blooms in torrid tracts appear,
Whose bright succession decks the varied year ;
Whatever sweets salute the northern sky
With vernal lives, that blossom but to die ;
These here disporting own the kindred soil,
Nor ask luxurance from the planter's toil ;

While sea-born gales their gelid wings expand
To winnow fragrance round the smiling land.

But small the bliss that sense alone bestows,
And sensual bliss is all the nation knows.
In florid beauty groves and fields appear,
Man seems the only growth that dwindles here.
Contrasted faults through all his manners reign ;
Though poor, luxurious ; though submissive, vain ;
Though grave, yet trifling ; zealous, yet untrue ;
And e'en in penance planning sins anew.
All evils here contaminate the mind,
That opulence departed leaves behind ;
For wealth was theirs ; not far removed the date
When commerce proudly flourished through the
        state ;
At her command the palace learnt to rise,
Again the long-fallen column sought the skies ;
The canvas glowed beyond e'en Nature warm,
The pregnant quarry teemed with human form.
Till, more unsteady than the southern gale,
Commerce on other shores displayed her sail ;
While naught remained of all that riches gave,
But towns unmanned, and lords without a slave :
And late the nation found with fruitless skill
Its former strength was but plethoric ill.

Yet still the loss of wealth is here supplied
By arts, the splendid wrecks of former pride ;
From these the feeble heart and long-fallen mind
An easy compensation seem to find.
Here may be seen, in bloodless pomp arrayed,
The pasteboard triumph and the cavalcade ;
Processions formed for piety and love,
A mistress or a saint in every grove.
By sports like these are all their cares beguiled,
The sports of children satisfy the child ;
Each nobler aim, represt by long control,
Now sinks at last, or feebly mans the soul ;
While low delights succeeding fast behind,
In happier meanness occupy the mind ;
As in those domes where Cæsars once bore sway,
Defaced by time and tottering in decay,
There in the ruin, heedless of the dead,
The shelter-seeking peasant builds his shed,
And, wondering man could want the larger pile,
Exults, and owns his cottage with a smile.

My soul, turn from them, turn we to survey,
Where rougher climes a nobler race display,
Where the bleak Swiss their stormy mansion
        tread,
And force a churlish soil for scanty bread ;
No product here the barren hills afford,
But man and steel, the soldier and his sword.
No vernal blooms their torpid rocks array,
But winter lingering chills the lap of May ;
No zephyr fondly sues the mountain's breast,
But meteors glare, and stormy glooms invest.

Yet still, e'en here, content can spread a charm,
Redress the clime, and all its rage disarm,

Though poor the peasant's hut, his feasts though
        small,
He sees his little lot the lot of all ;
Sees no contiguous palace rear its head
To shame the meanness of his humble shed,
No costly lord the sumptuous banquet deal
To make him loathe his vegetable meal ;
But calm, and bred in ignorance and toil,
Each wish contracting, fits him to the soil.
Cheerful at morn, he wakes from short repose,
Breathes the keen air, and carols as he goes ;
With patient angle trolls the finny deep,
Or drives his venturous ploughshare to the steep ;
Or seeks the den where snow-tracks mark the way,
And drags the struggling savage into day.
At night returning, every labor sped,
He sits him down the monarch of a shed :
Smiles by his cheerful fire, and round surveys
His children's looks, that brighten at the blaze ;
While his loved partner, boastful of her hoard,
Displays her cleanly platter on the board ;
And haply too some pilgrim, thither led,
With many a tale repays the nightly bed.

                            OLIVER GOLDSMITH.

ITALY.

O ITALY, how beautiful thou art !
Yet I could weep, — for thou art lying, alas !
Low in the dust ; and they who come admire thee
As we admire the beautiful in death.
Thine was a dangerous gift, the gift of beauty.
Would thou hadst less, or wert as once thou wast,
Inspiring awe in those who now enslave thee !
But why despair ? Twice hast thou lived already,
Twice shone among the nations of the world,
As the sun shines among the lesser lights
Of heaven ; and shalt again. The hour shall come,
When they who think to bind the ethereal spirit,
Who, like the eagle cowering o'er his prey,
Watch with quick eye, and strike and strike again
If but a sinew vibrate, shall confess
Their wisdom folly.

                            SAMUEL ROGERS.

VENICE.

THERE is a glorious City in the Sea.
The Sea is in the broad, the narrow streets,
Ebbing and flowing ; and the salt sea-weed
Clings to the marble of her palaces.
No track of men, no footsteps to and fro,
Lead to her gates. The path lies o'er the Sea,
Invisible ; and from the land we went,
As to a floating City, — steering in,
And gliding up her streets as in a dream,

So smoothly, silently, — by many a dome
Mosque-like, and many a stately portico,
The statues ranged along an azure sky;
By many a pile in more than Eastern splendor,
Of old the residence of merchant kings;
The fronts of some, though Time had shattered
    them,
Still glowing with the richest hues of art,
As though the wealth within them had run o'er.

·   ·   ·   ·   ·

                        A few in fear,
Flying away from him whose boast it was
That the grass grew not where his horse had trod,
Gave birth to Venice.   Like the water-fowl,
They built their nests among the ocean waves;
And where the sands were shifting, as the wind
Blew from the north, the south; where they that
    came,
Had to make sure the ground they stood upon,
Rose, like an exhalation, from the deep,
A vast Metropolis, with glittering spires,
With theatres, basilicas adorned;
A scene of light and glory, a dominion,
That has endured the longest among men.

   And whence the talisman by which she rose
Towering? 'T was found there in the barren sea.
Want led to Enterprise; and, far or near,
Who met not the Venetian? — now in Cairo;
Ere yet the Califa came, listening to hear
Its bells approaching from the Red Sea coast;
Now on the Euxine, on the Sea of Azoph,
In converse with the Persian, with the Russ,
The Tartar; on his lowly deck receiving
Pearls from the gulf of Ormus, gems from Bagdad,
Eyes brighter yet, that shed the light of love
From Georgia, from Circassia. Wandering round,
When in the rich bazaar he saw, displayed,
Treasures from unknown climes, away he went,
And, travelling slowly upward, drew erelong
From the well-head supplying all below;
Making the Imperial City of the East
Herself his tributary.

·   ·   ·   ·   ·

                    Thus did Venice rise,
Thus flourish, till the unwelcome tidings came,
That in the Tagus had arrived a fleet
From India, from the region of the Sun,
Fragrant with spices, — that a way was found,
A channel opened, and the golden stream
Turned to enrich another.   Then she felt
Her strength departing, and at last she fell,
Fell in an instant, blotted out and razed;
She who had stood yet longer than the longest
Of the Four Kingdoms, — who, as in an Ark,
Had floated down amid a thousand wrecks,
Uninjured, from the Old World to the New.
                              SAMUEL ROGERS.

ROME.

I AM in Rome! Oft as the morning ray
Visits these eyes, waking at once I cry,
Whence this excess of joy? What has befallen
    me?
And from within a thrilling voice replies,
Thou art in Rome! A thousand busy thoughts
Rush on my mind, a thousand images;
And I spring up as girt to run a race!

Thou art in Rome! the City that so long
Reigned absolute, the mistress of the world;
The mighty vision that the prophets saw,
And trembled; that from nothing, from the least,
The lowliest village (what but here and there
A reed-roofed cabin by a river-side?)
Grew into everything; and, year by year,
Patiently, fearlessly working her way
O'er brook and field, o'er continent and sea,
Not like the merchant with his merchandise,
Or traveller with staff and scrip exploring,
But hand to hand and foot to foot through hosts,
Through nations numberless in battle array,
Each behind each, each, when the other fell,
Up and in arms, at length subdued them all.
                              SAMUEL ROGERS.

THE GRECIAN TEMPLES AT PÆSTUM.

In Pæstum's ancient fanes I trod,
And mused on those strange men of old,
Whose dark religion could infold
So many gods, and yet no God!

Did they to human feelings own,
And had they human souls indeed,
Or did the sternness of their creed
Frown their faint spirits into stone?

The southern breezes fan my face; —
I hear the hum of bees arise,
And lizards dart, with mystic eyes,
That shrine the secret of the place!

These silent columns speak of dread,
Of lovely worship without love;
And yet the warm, deep heaven above
Whispers a softer tale instead!
                        ROSSITER W. RAYMOND.

COLISEUM BY MOONLIGHT.

FROM "MANFRED."

THE stars are forth, the moon above the tops
Of the snow-shining mountains. — Beautiful!

I linger yet with Nature, for the night
Hath been to me a more familiar face
Than that of man ; and in her starry shade
Of dim and solitary loveliness
I learned the language of another world.
I do remember me, that in my youth,
When I was wandering, — upon such a night
I stood within the Coliseum's wall,
Midst the chief relics of almighty Rome.
The trees which grew along the broken arches
Waved dark in the blue midnight, and the stars
Shone through the rents of ruin ; from afar
The watch-dog bayed beyond the Tiber ; and
More near from out the Cæsars' palace came
The owl's long cry, and, interruptedly,
Of distant sentinels the fitful song
Begun and died upon the gentle wind.
Some cypresses beyond the time-worn breach
Appeared to skirt the horizon, yet they stood
Within a bowshot, — where the Cæsars dwelt,
And dwell the tuneless birds of night, amidst
A grove which springs through levelled battle-
    ments,
And twines its roots with the imperial hearths.
Ivy usurps the laurel's place of growth ; —
But the gladiators' bloody Circus stands,
A noble wreck in ruinous perfection,
While Cæsar's chambers and the Augustan halls
Grovel on earth in indistinct decay. —
And thou didst shine, thou rolling moon, upon
All this, and cast a wide and tender light,
Which softened down the hoar austerity
Of rugged desolation, and filled up,
As 't were anew, the gaps of centuries,
Leaving that beautiful which still was so,
And making that which was not, till the place
Became religion, and the heart ran o'er
With silent worship of the great of old ! —
The dead, but sceptred sovereigns, who still rule
Our spirits from their urns.

                                        BYRON.

THE COLISEUM.

FROM "CHILDE HAROLD."

ARCHES on arches ! as it were that Rome,
Collecting the chief trophies of her line,
Would build up all her triumphs in one dome,
Her Coliseum stands ; the moonbeams shine
As 't were its natural torches, for divine
Should be the light which streams here, to illume
This long-explored, but still exhaustless, mine
Of contemplation ; and the azure gloom
Of an Italian night, where the deep skies assume

Hues which have words, and speak to ye of
    heaven,
Floats o'er this vast and wondrous monument,
And shadows forth its glory.   There is given
Unto the things of earth, which Time hath bent,
A spirit's feeling, and where he hath leant
His hand, but broke his scythe, there is a power
And magic in the ruined battlement,
For which the palace of the present hour
Must yield its pomp, and wait till ages are its dower.

And here the buzz of eager nations ran,
In murmured pity, or loud-roared applause,
As man was slaughtered by his fellow-man.
And wherefore slaughtered ? wherefore, but
    because
Such were the bloody Circus' genial laws,
And the imperial pleasure. — Wherefore not ?
What matters where we fall to fill the maws
Of worms, — on battle-plains or listed spot ?
Both are but theatres where the chief actors rot.

I see before me the Gladiator lie ;
He leans upon his hand, — his manly brow
Consents to death, but conquers agony,
And his drooped head sinks gradually low, —
And through his side the last drops, ebbing slow
From the red gash, fall heavy, one by one,
Like the first of a thunder-shower ; and now
The arena swims around him, — he is gone,
Ere ceased the inhuman shout which hailed the
    wretch who won.

He heard it, but he heeded not, — his eyes
Were with his heart, and that was far away.
He recked not of the life he lost nor prize,
But where his rude hut by the Danube lay,
There were his young barbarians all at play,
There was their Dacian mother, — he, their sire,
Butchered to make a Roman holiday ! —
All this rushed with his blood. — Shall he expire
And unavenged ?   Arise, ye Goths, and glut your
    ire !

But here, where Murder breathed her bloody
    steam,
And here, where buzzing nations choked the
    ways,
And roared or murmured like a mountain stream
Dashing or winding as its torrent strays ;
Here, where the Roman millions' blame or praise
Was death or life, the playthings of a crowd,
My voice sounds much, — and fall the stars'
    faint rays
On the arena void, seats crushed, walls bowed,
And galleries, where my steps seem echoes strange-
    ly loud.

A ruin, — yet what ruin ! from its mass
Walls, palaces, half-cities, have been reared ;

Yet oft the enormous skeleton ye pass,
And marvel where the spoil could have appeared.
Hath it indeed been plundered, or but cleared ?
Alas ! developed, opens the decay,
When the colossal fabric's form is neared ;
It will not bear the brightness of the day,
Which streams too much on all years, man, have
    reft away.

But when the rising moon begins to climb
Its topmost arch, and gently pauses there ;
When the stars twinkle through the loops of
    time,
And the low night-breeze waves along the air
The garland-forest, which the gray walls wear,
Like laurels on the bald first Cæsar's head ;
When the light shines serene, but doth not
    glare, —
Then in this magic circle raise the dead ;
Heroes have trod this spot, — 't is on their dust
    ye tread.

"While stands the Coliseum, Rome shall stand ;
When falls the Coliseum, Rome shall fall ;
And when Rome falls — the World." From
    our own land
Thus spake the pilgrims o'er this mighty wall
In Saxon times, which we are wont to call
Ancient ; and these three mortal things are still
On their foundations, and unaltered all ;
Rome and her Ruin past Redemption's skill,
The World, the same wide den — of thieves, or
    what ye will.

Simple, erect, severe, austere, sublime, —
Shrine of all saints and temple of all gods,
From Jove to Jesus, — spared and blest by time ;
Looking tranquillity, while falls or nods
Arch, empire, each thing round thee, and man
    plods
His way through thorns to ashes, — glorious
    dome !
Shalt thou not last ? Time's scythe and tyrants'
    rods
Shiver upon thee, — sanctuary and home
Of art and piety, — Pantheon ! — pride of Rome !

Relic of nobler days and noblest arts !
Despoiled yet perfect, with thy circle spreads
A holiness appealing to all hearts.
To art a model ; and to him who treads
Rome for the sake of ages, Glory sheds
Her light through thy sole aperture ; to those
Who worship, here are altars for their beads ;
And they who feel for genius may repose
Their eyes on honored forms, whose busts around
    them close.

                    BYRON.

A DAY IN THE PAMFILI DORIA.

ROME.

THOUGH the hills are cold and snowy,
    And the wind drives chill to-day,
My heart goes back to a spring-time,
    Far, far in the past away.

And I see a quaint old city,
    Weary and worn and brown,
Where the spring and the birds are so early
    And the sun in such light goes down.

I remember that old-times villa
    Where our afternoons went by,
Where the suns of March flushed warmly,
    And spring was in earth and sky.

Out of the mouldering city, —
    Mouldering, old, and gray, —
We sped, with a lightsome heart-thrill,
    For a sunny, gladsome day, —

For a revel of fresh spring verdure,
    For a race mid springing flowers,
For a vision of plashing fountains,
    Of birds and blossoming bowers.

There were violet banks in the shadows,
    Violets white and blue ;
And a world of bright anemones,
    That over the terrace grew, —

Blue and orange and purple,
    Rosy and yellow and white,
Rising in rainbow bubbles,
    Streaking the lawns with light.

And down from the old stone-pine trees,
    Those far-off islands of air,
The birds are flinging the tidings
    Of a joyful revel up there.

And now for the grand old fountains,
    Tossing their silvery spray, —
Those fountains, so quaint and so many,
    That are leaping and singing all day.

Those fountains of strange weird sculpture,
    With lichens and moss o'ergrown,
Are they marble greening in moss-wreaths,
    Or moss-wreaths whitening to stone ?

Down many a wild, dim pathway
    We ramble from morning till noon ;
We linger, unheeding the hours,
    Till evening comes all too soon.

And from out the ilex alleys,
    Where lengthening shadows play,

We look on the dreamy Campagna,
  All glowing with setting day, —

All melting in bands of purple,
  In swathings and foldings of gold,
In ribbons of azure and lilac,
  Like a princely banner unrolled.

And the smoke of each distant cottage,
  And the flash of each villa white,
Shines out with an opal glimmer,
  Like gems in a casket of light.

And the dome of old St. Peter's
  With a strange translucence glows,
Like a mighty bubble of amethyst
  Floating in waves of rose.

In a trance of dreamy vagueness,
  We, gazing and yearning, behold
That city beheld by the prophet,
  Whose walls were transparent gold.

And, dropping all solemn and slowly,
  To hallow the softening spell,
There falls on the dying twilight
  The Ave Maria bell.

With a mournful, motherly softness,
  With a weird and weary care,
That strange and ancient city
  Seems calling the nations to prayer.

And the words that of old the angel
  To the mother of Jesus brought
Rise like a new evangel,
  To hallow the trance of our thought.

With the smoke of the evening incense
  Our thoughts are ascending, then,
To Mary, the mother of Jesus,
  To Jesus, the Master of men.

O city of prophets and martyrs !
  O shrines of the sainted dead !
When, when shall the living day-spring
  Once more on your towers be spread ?

When He who is meek and lowly
  Shall rule in those lordly halls,
And shall stand and feed as a shepherd
  The flock which his mercy calls, —

O, then to those noble churches,
  To picture and statue and gem,
To the pageant of solemn worship,
  Shall the *meaning* come back again.

And this strange and ancient city,
  In that reign of his truth and love,
Shall *be* what it *seems* in the twilight,
  The type of that City above.

HARRIET BEECHER STOWE.

ROMAN GIRL'S SONG.

" Roma, Roma, Roma !
  Non è più come era prima."

ROME, Rome ! thou art no more
  As thou hast been !
On thy seven hills of yore
  Thou sat'st a queen.

Thou hadst thy triumphs then
  Purpling the street,
Leaders and sceptred men
  Bowed at thy feet.

They that thy mantle wore,
  As gods were seen, —
Rome, Rome ! thou art no more
  As thou hast been !

Rome ! thine imperial brow
  Never shall rise :
What hast thou left thee now ? —
  Thou hast thy skies !

Blue, deeply blue, they are,
  Gloriously bright !
Veiling thy wastes afar
  With colored light.

Thou hast the sunset's glow
  Rome, for thy dower,
Flushing tall cypress bough,
  Temple and tower !

And all sweet sounds are thine
  Lovely to hear,
While night, o'er tomb and shrine,
  Rests darkly clear.

Many a solemn hymn,
  By starlight sung,
Sweeps through the arches dim,
  Thy wrecks among.

Many a flute's low swell
  On thy soft air
Lingers, and loves to dwell
  With summer there.

Thou hast the south's rich gift
  Of sudden song, —
A charméd fountain, swift,
  Joyous, and strong.

Thou hast fair forms that move
  With queenly tread ;
Thou hast proud fanes above
  Thy mighty dead.

Yet wears thy Tiber's shore
  A mournful mien : —
Rome, Rome ! thou art no more
  As thou hast been !

FELICIA HEMANS.

NAPLES.

THIS region, surely, is not of the earth.
Was it not dropt from heaven? Not a grove,
Citron, or pine, or cedar, not a grot
Sea-worn and mantled with the gadding vine,
But breathes enchantment. Not a cliff but flings
On the clear wave some image of delight,
Some cabin-roof glowing with crimson flowers,
Some ruined temple or fallen monument,
To muse on as the bark is gliding by,
And be it mine to muse there, mine to glide,
From daybreak, when the mountain pales his fire
Yet more and more, and from the mountain-top,
Till then invisible, a smoke ascends,
Solemn and slow, as erst from Ararat,
When he, the Patriarch, who escaped the Flood,
Was with his household sacrificing there, —
From daybreak to that hour, the last and best,
When, one by one, the fishing-boats come forth,
Each with its glimmering lantern at the prow,
And, when the nets are thrown, the evening hymn
Steals o'er the trembling waters.
                              Everywhere
Fable and Truth have shed, in rivalry,
Each her peculiar influence. Fable came,
And laughed and sung, arraying Truth in flowers,
Like a young child her grandam. Fable came;
Earth, sea and sky reflecting, as she flew,
A thousand, thousand colors not their own:
And at her bidding, lo! a dark descent
To Tartarus, and those thrice happy fields,
Those fields with ether pure and purple light
Ever invested, scenes by him described
Who here was wont to wander, record
What they revealed, and on the western shore
Sleeps in a silent grove, o'erlooking thee,
Beloved Parthenope.
                    Yet here, methinks,
Truth wants no ornament, in her own shape
Filling the mind by turns with awe and love,
By turns inclining to wild ecstasy
And soberest meditation.
                              SAMUEL ROGERS.

GREAT BRITAIN.

FROM "THE TRAVELLER."

    .... My genius spreads her wing,
And flies where Britain courts the western spring;
Where lawns extend that scorn Arcadian pride,
And brighter streams than famed Hydaspes glide;
There all around the gentlest breezes stray,
There gentle music melts on every spray;
Creation's mildest charms are there combined,
Extremes are only in the master's mind!
Stern o'er each bosom Reason holds her state,

With daring aims irregularly great;
Pride in their port, defiance in their eye,
I see the lords of human-kind pass by;
Intent on high designs, a thoughtful band,
By forms unfashioned, fresh from Nature's hand,
Fierce in their native hardiness of soul,
True to imagined right, above control,
While e'en the peasant boasts these rights to scan,
And learns to venerate himself as man.
Thine, Freedom, thine the blessings pictured here,
Thine are those charms that dazzle and endear.
                              OLIVER GOLDSMITH.

THE LEPER.

"Room for the leper! Room!" And as he came
The cry passed on, — "Room for the leper!
    Room!"
   .   .   .   .   .   .
                    And aside they stood,
Matron, and child, and pitiless manhood, — all
Who met him on his way, — and let him pass.
And onward through the open gate he came
A leper with the ashes on his brow,
Sackcloth about his loins, and on his lip
A covering, stepping painfully and slow,
And with a difficult utterance, like one
Whose heart is with an iron nerve put down,
Crying, — "Unclean! unclean!"
   .   .   .   .   .   .
                    Day was breaking
When at the altar of the temple stood
The holy priest of God. The incense-lamp
Burned with a struggling light, and a low chant
Swelled through the hollow arches of the roof,
Like an articulate wail, and there, alone,
Wasted to ghastly thinness, Helon knelt.
The echoes of the melancholy strain
Died in the distant aisles, and he rose up,
Struggling with weakness, and bowed down his
    head
Unto the sprinkled ashes, and put off
His costly raiment for the leper's garb,
And with the sackcloth round him, and his lip
Hid in a loathsome covering, stood still,
Waiting to hear his doom: —

    "Depart! depart, O child
Of Israel, from the temple of thy God,
For he has smote thee with his chastening rod,
    And to the desert wild
From all thou lov'st away thy feet must flee,
That from thy plague his people may be free.

    "Depart! and come not near
The busy mart, the crowded city, more;
Nor set thy foot a human threshold o'er;
    And stay thou not to hear

Voices that call thee in the way ; and fly
From all who in the wilderness pass by.

"Wet not thy burning lip
In streams that to a human dwelling glide ;
Nor rest thee where the covert fountains hide,
   Nor kneel thee down to dip
The water where the pilgrim bends to drink,
By desert well, or river's grassy brink.

"And pass not thou between
The weary traveller and the cooling breeze,
And lie not down to sleep beneath the trees
   Where human tracks are seen ;
Nor milk the goat that browseth on the plain,
Nor pluck the standing corn, or yellow grain.

"And now depart ! and when
Thy heart is heavy, and thine eyes are dim,
Lift up thy prayer beseechingly to Him
   Who, from the tribes of men,
Selected thee to feel his chastening rod.
Depart ! O leper ! and forget not God !"

And he went forth — alone ! not one of all
The many whom he loved, nor she whose name
Was woven in the fibres of the heart
Breaking within him now, to come and speak
Comfort unto him.   Yea, he went his way,
Sick and heart-broken, and alone, — to die !
For God had cursed the leper !

              It was noon,
And Helon knelt beside a stagnant pool
In the lone wilderness, and bathed his brow,
Hot with the burning leprosy, and touched
The loathsome water to his fevered lips,
Praying that he might be so blest, — to die !
Footsteps approached, and with no strength to flee,
He drew the covering closer on his lip,
Crying, "Unclean ! unclean !" and in the folds
Of the coarse sackcloth shrouding up his face,
He fell upon the earth till they should pass.
Nearer the stranger came, and bending o'er
The leper's prostrate form, pronounced his name.
— "Helon !" — the voice was like the master-
   tone
Of a rich instrument, — most strangely sweet ;
And the dull pulses of disease awoke,
And for a moment beat beneath the hot
And leprous scales with a restoring thrill.
"Helon ! arise !" and he forgot his curse,
And rose and stood before him.

             Love and awe
Mingled in the regard of Helon's eye
As he beheld the stranger.   He was not
In costly raiment clad, nor on his brow
The symbol of a princely lineage wore ;

No followers at his back, nor in his hand
Buckler, or sword, or spear, — yet in his mien
Command sat throned serene, and if he smiled,
A kingly condescension graced his lips,
The lion would have crouched to in his lair.
His garb was simple, and his sandals worn ;
His stature modelled with a perfect grace ;
His countenance, the impress of a God,
Touched with the open innocence of a child ;
His eye was blue and calm, as is the sky
In the serenest noon ; his hair unshorn
Fell to his shoulders ; and his curling beard
The fulness of perfected manhood bore.
He looked on Helon earnestly awhile,
As if his heart was moved, and, stooping down,
He took a little water in his hand
And laid it on his brow, and said, "Be clean !"
And lo ! the scales fell from him, and his blood
Coursed with delicious coolness through his veins,
And his dry palms grew moist, and on his brow
The dewy softness of an infant's stole.
His leprosy was cleansed, and he fell down
Prostrate at Jesus' feet, and worshipped him.
            NATHANIEL PARKER WILLIS.

THE MINSTREL.

FROM "THE MINSTREL EDWIN."

THERE lived in Gothic days, as legends tell,
A shepherd swain, a man of low degree ;
Whose sires, perchance, in Fairy-land might
   dwell,
Sicilian groves, or vales of Arcady ;
But he, I ween, was of the north countrie, —
A nation famed for song, and beauty's charms ;
Zealous, yet modest ; innocent, though free ;
Patient of toil ; serene amidst alarms ;
Inflexible in faith ; invincible in arms.

The shepherd swain, of whom I mention made,
On Scotia's mountains fed his little flock ;
The sickle, scythe, or plough he never swayed ;
An honest heart was almost all his stock ;
His drink the living water from the rock ;
The milky dams supplied his board, and lent
Their kindly fleece to baffle winter's shock ;
And he, though oft with dust and sweat be-
   sprent,
Did guide and guard their wanderings, where-
   soe'er they went.

From labor health, from health contentment
   springs ;
Contentment opes the source of every joy.
He envied not, he never thought of, kings ;
Nor from those appetites sustained annoy,
That chance may frustrate, or indulgence cloy :

Nor Fate his calm and humble hopes beguiled ;
He mourned no recreant friend nor mistress coy,
For on his vows the blameless Phœbe smiled,
And her alone he loved, and loved her from a child.

No jealousy their dawn of love o'ercast,
Nor blasted were their wedded days with strife ;
Each season looked delightful, as it passed,
To the fond husband and the faithful wife.
Beyond the lowly vale of shepherd life
They never roamed ; secure beneath the storm
Which in Ambition's lofty land is rife,
Where peace and love are cankered by the worm
Of pride, each bud of joy industrious to deform.

The wight, whose tale these artless lines unfold,
Was all the offspring of this humble pair ;
His birth no oracle or seer foretold ;
No prodigy appeared in earth or air,
Nor aught that might a strange event declare.
You guess each circumstance of Edwin's birth ;
The parent's transport and the parent's care ;
The gossip's prayer for wealth and wit and worth ;
And one long summer day of indolence and mirth.

And yet poor Edwin was no vulgar boy ;
Deep thought oft seemed to fix his infant eye.
Dainties he heeded not, nor gaud, nor toy,
Save one short pipe of rudest minstrelsy ;
Silent when glad ; affectionate though shy ;
And now his look was most demurely sad ;
And now he laughed aloud, yet none knew why.
The neighbors stared and sighed, yet blessed the lad :
Some deemed him wondrous wise, and some believed him mad.

But why should I his childish feats display ?
Concourse and noise and toil he ever fled ;
Nor cared to mingle in the clamorous fray
Of squabbling imps ; but to the forest sped,
Or roamed at large the lonely mountain's head,
Or, where the maze of some bewildered stream
To deep untrodden groves his footsteps led,
There would he wander wild, till Phœbus' beam,
Shot from the western cliff, released the weary team.

The exploit of strength, dexterity, or speed,
To him nor vanity nor joy could bring ;
His heart, from cruel sport estranged, would bleed
To work the woe of any living thing,
By trap or net, by arrow or by sling ;
These he detested ; those he scorned to wield ;
He wished to be the guardian, not the king,

Tyrant far less, or traitor of the field ;
And sure the sylvan reign unbloody joy might yield.

Lo ! where the stripling, rapt in wonder, roves
Beneath the precipice o'erhung with pine ;
And sees, on high, amidst the encircling groves,
From cliff to cliff the foaming torrents shine,
While waters, woods, and winds, in concert join,
And Echo swells the chorus to the skies.
Would Edwin this majestic scene resign
For aught the huntsman's puny craft supplies ?
Ah ! no : he better knows great Nature's charms to prize.

And oft he traced the uplands, to survey,
When o'er the sky advanced the kindling dawn,
The crimson cloud, blue main, and mountain gray,
And lake, dim gleaming on the smoky lawn :
Far to the west the long, long vale withdrawn,
While twilight loves to linger for a while ;
And now he faintly kens the bounding fawn,
And villager abroad at early toil.
But, lo ! the Sun appears ! and heaven, earth, ocean, smile.

And oft the craggy cliff he loved to climb,
When all in mist the world below was lost.
What dreadful pleasure ! there to stand sublime,
Like shipwrecked mariner on desert coast,
And view the enormous waste of vapor, tossed
In billows, lengthening to the horizon round,
Now scooped in gulfs, with mountains now embossed !
And hear the voice of mirth and song rebound,
Flocks, herds, and waterfalls, along the hoar profound !

In truth he was a strange and wayward wight,
Fond of each gentle and each dreadful scene.
In darkness and in storm he found delight ;
Nor less, than when on ocean wave serene
The southern sun diffused his dazzling shene.*
Even sad vicissitude amused his soul ;
And if a sigh would sometimes intervene,
And down his cheek a tear of pity roll,
A sigh, a tear, so sweet, he wished not to control.

JAMES BEATTIE.

THE BELLS.

I.

HEAR the sledges with the bells, —
Silver bells, —
What a world of merriment their melody foretells !

---

* Brightness, splendor. The word is used by some late writers, as well as by Milton.

How they tinkle, tinkle, tinkle,
  In the icy air of night!
While the stars that oversprinkle
All the heavens seem to twinkle
  With a crystalline delight, —
Keeping time, time, time,
In a sort of Runic rhyme,
To the tintinnabulation that so musically wells
  From the bells, bells, bells, bells,
      Bells, bells, bells, —
From the jingling and the tinkling of the bells.

II.

Hear the mellow wedding bells, —
      Golden bells!
What a world of happiness their harmony foretells!
  Through the balmy air of night
  How they ring out their delight!
      From the molten-golden notes,
          And all in tune,
      What a liquid ditty floats
To the turtle-dove that listens, while she gloats
      On the moon!
O, from out the sounding cells,
What a gush of euphony voluminously wells!
      How it swells!
      How it dwells
    On the Future! how it tells
    Of the rapture that impels
  To the swinging and the ringing
  Of the bells, bells, bells,
  Of the bells, bells, bells, bells,
      Bells, bells, bells, —
To the rhyming and the chiming of the bells.

III.

Hear the loud alarum bells, —
      Brazen bells!
What a tale of terror, now, their turbulency tells!
  In the startled ear of night
  How they scream out their affright!
      Too much horrified to speak,
      They can only shriek, shriek,
          Out of tune,
In the clamorous appealing to the mercy of the fire,
In a mad expostulation with the deaf and frantic
          fire
    Leaping higher, higher, higher,
      With a desperate desire,
    And a resolute endeavor,
    Now — now to sit or never,
  By the side of the pale-faced moon.
    O the bells, bells, bells,
    What a tale their terror tells
          Of despair!
  How they clang and clash and roar!
    What a horror they outpour
On the bosom of the palpitating air!

    Yet the ear it fully knows,
          By the twanging,
          And the clanging,
  How the danger ebbs and flows;
  Yet the ear distinctly tells,
          In the jangling,
          And the wrangling,
    How the danger sinks and swells,
By the sinking or the swelling in the anger of the
          bells, —
      Of the bells, —
    Of the bells, bells, bells, bells,
      Bells, bells, bells, —
In the clamor and the clangor of the bells!

IV.

Hear the tolling of the bells, —
      Iron bells!
What a world of solemn thought their monody
          compels!
  In the silence of the night,
  How we shiver with affright
At the melancholy menace of their tone!
  For every sound that floats
  From the rust within their throats
          Is a groan.
  And the people, — ah, the people, —
  They that dwell up in the steeple,
          All alone,
  And who tolling, tolling, tolling,
    In that muffled monotone,
  Feel a glory in so rolling
    On the human heart a stone, —
  They are neither man nor woman, —
  They are neither brute nor human, —
          They are ghouls:
  And their king it is who tolls;
  And he rolls, rolls, rolls,
          Rolls,
    A pæan from the bells!
  And his merry bosom swells
    With the pæan of the bells!
  And he dances and he yells;
  Keeping time, time, time,
  In a sort of Runic rhyme,
    To the pæan of the bells, —
          Of the bells:
  Keeping time, time, time,
  In a sort of Runic rhyme,
    To the throbbing of the bells, —
  Of the bells, bells, bells, —
    To the sobbing of the bells;
  Keeping time, time, time,
    As he knells, knells, knells,
  In a happy Runic rhyme,
    To the rolling of the bells, —
  Of the bells, bells, bells, —
    To the tolling of the bells,

Of the bells, bells, bells, bells, —
    Bells, bells, bells, —
To the moaning and the groaning of the bells.
              EDGAR ALLAN POE.

THE BELLS OF SHANDON.

      Sabbata pango ;
      Funera plango ;
      Solemnia clango.
        INSCRIPTION ON AN OLD BELL.

WITH deep affection
And recollection
I often think of
    Those Shandon bells,
Whose sounds so wild would,
In the days of childhood,
Fling round my cradle
    Their magic spells.

On this I ponder
Where'er I wander,
And thus grow fonder,
    Sweet Cork, of thee, —
With thy bells of Shandon,
That sound so grand on
The pleasant waters
    Of the river Lee.

I 've heard bells chiming
Full many a clime in,
Tolling sublime in
    Cathedral shrine,
While at a glibe rate
Brass tongues would vibrate ;
But all their music
    Spoke naught like thine.

For memory, dwelling
On each proud swelling
Of thy belfry, knelling
    Its bold notes free,
Made the bells of Shandon
Sound far more grand on
The pleasant waters
    Of the river Lee.

I 've heard bells tolling
Old Adrian's Mole in,
Their thunder rolling
    From the Vatican, —
And cymbals glorious
Swinging uproarious
In the gorgeous turrets
    Of Notre Dame ;

But thy sounds were sweeter
Than the dome of Peter

Flings o'er the Tiber,
    Pealing solemnly.
Oh ! the bells of Shandon
Sound far more grand on
The pleasant waters
    Of the river Lee.

There 's a bell in Moscow ;
While on tower and kiosk O
In St. Sophia
    The Turkman gets,
And loud in air
Calls men to prayer,
From the tapering summit
    Of tall minarets.

Such empty phantom
I freely grant them ;
But there 's an anthem
    More dear to me, —
'T is the bells of Shandon,
That sound so grand on
The pleasant waters
    Of the river Lee.
         FATHER PROUT (Francis Mahony).

THE GREAT BELL ROLAND.

    TOLL ! Roland, toll !
— High in St. Bavon's tower,
At midnight hour,
The great bell Roland spoke,
And all who slept in Ghent awoke.
— What meant its iron stroke ?
Why caught each man his blade ?
Why the hot haste he made ?
Why echoed every street
With tramp of thronging feet, —
All flying to the city's wall ?
It was the call,
Known well to all,
That Freedom stood in peril of some foe ;
And even timid hearts grew bold,
Whenever Roland tolled,
And every hand a sword could hold ; —
For men
Were patriots then,
Three hundred years ago !

    Toll ! Roland, toll !
Bell never yet was hung,
Between whose lips there swung
So true and brave a tongue !
— If men be patriots still,
    At thy first sound
    True hearts will bound,
Great souls will thrill, —
Then toll ! and wake the test

In each man's breast,
And let him stand confessed !

　Toll ! Roland, toll !
— Not in St. Bavon's tower,
At midnight hour, —
Nor by the Scheldt, nor far off Zuyder Zee ;
But here, — this side the sea !
And here, in broad, bright day !
　Toll ! Roland, toll !
For not by night awaits
A brave foe at the gates,
But Treason stalks abroad — inside ! — at noon !
Toll !　Thy alarm is not too soon !
To arms !　Ring out the Leader's call !
Re-echo it from east to west,
Till every dauntless breast
Swell beneath plume and crest !
Till swords from scabbards leap !
— What tears can widows weep
Less bitter than when brave men fall ?
　Toll ! Roland, toll !
Till cottager from cottage wall
Snatch pouch and powder-horn and gun, —
The heritage of sire to son,
Ere half of Freedom's work was done !
　Toll !　Roland, toll !
Till son, in memory of his sire,
Once more shall load and fire !
　Toll ! Roland, toll !
Till volunteers find out the art
Of aiming at a traitor's heart !

　Toll ! Roland, toll !
— St. Bavon's stately tower
Stands to this hour, —
And by its side stands Freedom yet in Ghent ;
　For when the bells now ring,
　Men shout, "God save the king !"
Until the air is rent !
— Amen ! — So let it be ;
For a true king is he
Who keeps his people free.
　Toll ! Roland, toll !
This side the sea !
No longer they, but we,
Have now such need of thee !
　Toll ! Roland, toll !
And let thy iron throat
Ring out its warning note,
Till Freedom's perils be outbraved,
And Freedom's flag, wherever waved,
Shall overshadow none enslaved !
Toll ! till from either ocean's strand
Brave men shall clasp each other's hand,
And shout, "God save our native land !"
— And love the land which God hath saved !
　Toll ! Roland, toll !
　　　　　THEODORE TILTON.

TOLL, THEN, NO MORE !

　Toll for the dead, toll, toll !
No, no !　Ring out, ye bells, ring out and shout.
For they the pearly gates have entered in,
And they no more shall sin, —
　Ring out, ye bells, ring, ring !

　Toll for the living, toll !
No, no !　Ring out, ye bells, ring out and shout,
For they do His work tho' midst toil and din,
They, too, the goal shall win, —
　Ring out, ye bells, ring, ring !

　Toll for the coming, toll !
No, no !　Ring out, ye bells, ring out and shout,
For it is theirs to conquer, theirs to win
The final entering in, —
　Ring out, ye bells, ring, ring !

　Toll, then, no more, ye bells !
No, no !　Ring out, O bells, ring out and shout :
The Was, the Is, the Shall Be, and all men
Are in His hand !　Amen !
　Ring out, ye bells, ring, ring !
　　　　　R. R. BOWKER.

CITY BELLS.

FROM THE LAY OF ST. ALOY'S.

　　Loud and clear
From the St. Nicholas' tower, on the listening ear,
　　With solemn swell,
　　The deep-toned bell
Flings to the gale a funeral knell ;
　　And hark ! — at its sound,
　　As a cunning old hound,
When he opens, at once causes all the young whelps
Of the cry to put in their less dignified yelps,
　　So — the ltitle bells all,
　　No matter how small,
From the steeples both inside and outside the wall,
　　With bell-metal throat
　　Respond to the note,
And join the lament that a prelate so pious is
Forced thus to leave his disconsolate diocese,
　　Or, as Blois' Lord May'r
　　Is heard to declare,
"Should leave this here world for to go to that
　　there."
　　　　　RICHARD HARRIS BARHAM.

SEVEN TIMES TWO.

ROMANCE.

You bells in the steeple, ring, ring out your
　changes,
How many soever they be,

And let the brown meadow-lark's note as he ranges
　　Come over, come over to me.

Yet birds' clearest carol by fall or by swelling
　　No magical sense conveys,
And bells have forgotten their old art of telling
　　The fortune of future days.

"Turn again, turn again," once they rang cheerily
　　While a boy listened alone :
Made his heart yearn again, musing so wearily
　　All by himself on a stone.

Poor bells ! I forgive you ; your good days are
　　　over,
　　And mine, they are yet to be ;
No listening, no longing, shall aught, aught dis-
　　　cover :
　　You leave the story to me.
　　　　　　　　　　JEAN INGELOW.

———◆———

OZYMANDIAS OF EGYPT.

I MET a traveller from an antique land
Who said : Two vast and trunkless legs of stone
Stand in the desert.   Near them on the sand,
Half sunk, a shattered visage lies, whose frown
And wrinkled lip and sneer of cold command
Tell that its sculptor well those passions read
Which yet survive, stamped on these lifeless things,
The hand that mocked them and the heart that
　　fed ;
And on the pedestal these words appear :
"My name is Ozymandias, king of kings :
Look on my works, ye Mighty, and despair !"
Nothing beside remains.   Round the decay
Of that colossal wreck, boundless and bare,
The lone and level sands stretch far away.
　　　　　　　　　PERCY BYSSHE SHELLEY.

———◆———

ADDRESS TO THE MUMMY AT BEL-
ZONI'S EXHIBITION.

AND thou hast walked about, (how strange a
　　　story !)
　　In Thebes's streets three thousand years ago,
When the Memnonium was in all its glory,
　　And time had not begun to overthrow
Those temples, palaces, and piles stupendous,
Of which the very ruins are tremendous.

Speak ! for thou long enough hast acted dummy ;
　　Thou hast a tongue, — come, let us hear its
　　　tune ;
Thou 'rt standing on thy legs, above ground,
　　　mummy !
　　Revisiting the glimpses of the moon, —

Not like thin ghosts or disembodied creatures,
　　But with thy bones, and flesh, and limbs, and
　　　features.

Tell us — for doubtless thou canst recollect —
　　To whom should we assign the Sphinx's fame ?
Was Cheops or Cephrenes architect
　　Of either pyramid that bears his name ?
Is Pompey's Pillar really a misnomer ?
Had Thebes a hundred gates, as sung by Homer ?

Perhaps thou wert a Mason, and forbidden
　　By oath to tell the secrets of thy trade, —
Then say what secret melody was hidden
　　In Memnon's statue, which at sunrise played ?
Perhaps thou wert a priest, — if so, my struggles
Are vain, for priestcraft never owns its juggles.

Perhaps that very hand, now pinioned flat,
　　Has hob-a-nobbed with Pharaoh, glass to glass ;
Or dropped a halfpenny in Homer's hat ;
　　Or doffed thine own to let Queen Dido pass ;
Or held, by Solomon's own invitation,
A torch at the great temple's dedication.

I need not ask thee if that hand, when armed,
　　Has any Roman soldier mauled and knuckled ;
For thou wert dead, and buried, and embalmed,
　　Ere Romulus and Remus had been suckled :
Antiquity appears to have begun
Long after thy primeval race was run.

Thou couldst develop — if that withered tongue
　　Might tell us what those sightless orbs have
　　　seen —
How the world looked when it was fresh and
　　　young,
　　And the great deluge still had left it green ;
Or was it then so old that history's pages
Contained no record of its early ages ?

Still silent ! incommunicative elf !
　　Art sworn to secrecy ? then keep thy vows ;
But prithee tell us something of thyself, —
　　Reveal the secrets of thy prison-house ;
Since in the world of spirits thou hast slum-
　　　bered, —
What hast thou seen, — what strange adventures
　　　numbered ?

Since first thy form was in this box extended
　　We have, above ground, seen some strange
　　　mutations ;
The Roman empire has begun and ended, —
　　New worlds have risen, — we have lost old na-
　　　tions ;
And countless kings have into dust been humbled,
While not a fragment of thy flesh has crumbled.

Etch⁺ by H.B. Hall N.Y. 1876.

Percy B Shelley.

FORDS, HOWARD & HULBERT, N.Y.

Didst thou not hear the pother o'er thy head,
  When the great Persian conqueror, Cambyses,
Marched armies o'er thy tomb with thundering
    tread, —
  O'erthrew Osiris, Orus, Apis, Isis ;
And shook the pyramids with fear and wonder,
  When the gigantic Memnon fell asunder ?

If the tomb's secrets may not be confessed,
  The nature of thy private life unfold :
A heart has throbbed beneath that leathern
    breast,
  And tears adown that dusty cheek have rolled ;
Have children climbed those knees, and kissed
    that face ?
What was thy name and station, age and race ?

Statue of flesh, — immortal of the dead !
  Imperishable type of evanescence !
Posthumous man, — who quit'st thy narrow bed,
  And standest undecayed within our presence !
Thou wilt hear nothing till the judgment morning,
When the great trump shall thrill thee with its
    warning.

Why should this worthless tegument endure,
  If its undying guest be lost forever ?
O, let us keep the soul embalmed and pure
  In living virtue, — that when both must sever,
Although corruption may our frame consume,
The immortal spirit in the skies may bloom !
                              HORACE SMITH.

───◆───

ANSWER OF THE MUMMY AT BELZO-NI'S EXHIBITION.

CHILD of the later days ! thy words have broken
  A spell that long has bound these lungs of clay,
For since this smoke-dried tongue of mine hath
    spoken
  Three thousand tedious years have rolled away.
Unswathed at length, I "stand at ease" before ye.
List, then, O list, while I unfold my story.

Thebes was my birthplace, — an unrivalled city
  With many gates, — but here I might declare
Some strange, plain truths, except that it were pity
  To blow a poet's fabric into air ;
O, I could read you quite a Theban lecture,
And give a deadly finish to conjecture.

But then you would not have me throw discredit
  On grave historians, — or on him who sung
The Iliad, — true it is I never read it,
  But heard it read, when I was very young.
An old blind minstrel for a trifling profit
Recited parts, — I think the author of it.

All that I know about the town of Homer
  Is that they scarce would own him in his day,
Were glad, too, when he proudly turned a roamer,
  Because by this they saved their parish pay.
His townsmen would have been ashamed to flout
    him,
Had they foreseen the fuss since made about him.

One blunder I can fairly set at rest :
  He says that men were once more big and bony
Than now, which is a bouncer at the best ;
  I 'll just refer you to our friend Belzoni,
Near seven feet high ; in truth a lofty figure.
Now look at me, — and tell me, — am I bigger ?

Not half the size, but then I 'm sadly dwindled,
  Three thousand years with that embalming glue
Have made a serious difference, and have swindled
  My face of all its beauty ; there were few
Egyptian youths more gay, — behold the sequel.
Nay, smile not ; you and I may soon be equal.

For this lean hand did one day hurl the lance
  With mortal aim ; this light, fantastic toe
Threaded the mystic mazes of the dance ;
  This heart has throbbed at tales of love and woe ;
These shreds of raven hair once set the fashion ;
This withered form inspired the tender passion.

In vain ; the skilful hand and feelings warm,
  The foot that figured in the bright quadrille,
The palm of genius and the manly form,
  All bowed at once to Death's mysterious will,
Who sealed me up where mummies sound are
    sleeping,
In cerecloth and in tolerable keeping ;

Where cows and monkeys squat in rich brocade,
  And well-dressed crocodiles in painted cases,
Rats, bats, and owls, and cats in masquerade,
  With scarlet flounces, and with varnished faces ;
Then birds, brutes, reptiles, fish, all crammed
    together,
With ladies that might pass for well-tanned
    leather ;

Where Rameses and Sabacon lie down,
  And splendid Psammis in his hide of crust,
Princes and heroes, — men of high renown,
  Who in their day kicked up a mighty dust.
Their swarthy mummies kicked up dust in num-
    ber,
When huge Belzoni came to scare their slumber.

Who 'd think these rusty hams of mine were seated
  At Dido's table, when the wondrous tale
Of "Juno's hatred" was so well repeated ?
  And ever and anon the Queen turned pale.
Meanwhile the brilliant gaslights hung above her
Threw a wild glare upon her shipwrecked lover.

Ay, gaslights !   Mock me not, — we men of yore
  Were versed in all the knowledge you can men-
    tion ;
Who hath not heard of Egypt's peerless lore,
  Her patient toil, acuteness of invention ?
Survey the proofs, — the pyramids are thriving,
Old Memnon still looks young, and I 'm surviving.

A land in arts and sciences prolific,
  O block gigantic, building up her fame,
Crowded with signs and letters hieroglyphic,
  Temples and obelisks her skill proclaim !
Yet though her art and toil unearthly seem,
Those blocks were brought on railroads and by
    steam !

How, when, and why our people came to rear
  The pyramid of Cheops, — mighty pile ? —
This, and the other secrets, thou shalt hear ;
  I will unfold, if thou wilt stay awhile,
The history of the Sphinx, and who began it,
Our mystic works, and monsters made of granite.

Well, then, in grievous times, when King Ce-
    phrenes,
  But ah ! — What 's this ! the shades of bards
    and kings
Press on my lips their fingers ! What they mean is,
  I am not to reveal these hidden things.
Mortal, farewell ! Till Science' self unbind them,
Men must e'en take these secrets as they find them.
                        ANONYMOUS.

ADDRESS TO THE ALABASTER SAR-
COPHAGUS

LATELY DEPOSITED IN THE BRITISH MUSEUM.

THOU alabaster relic ! while I hold
  My hand upon thy sculptured margin thrown,
Let me recall the scenes thou couldst unfold,
  Mightst thou relate the changes thou hast
    known,
For thou wert primitive in thy formation,
Launched from the Almighty's hand at the Crea-
    tion.

Yes, — thou wert present when the stars and skies
  And worlds unnumbered rolled into their places ;
When God from Chaos bade the spheres arise,
  And fixed the blazing sun upon its basis,
And with his finger on the bounds of space
Marked out each planet's everlasting race.

How many thousand ages from thy birth
  Thou slept'st in darkness, it were vain to ask,
Till Egypt's sons upheaved thee from the earth,
  And year by year pursued their patient task ;

Till thou wert carved and decorated thus,
Worthy to be a king's sarcophagus.

What time Elijah to the skies ascended,
  Or David reigned in holy Palestine,
Some ancient Theban monarch was extended
  Beneath the lid of this emblazoned shrine,
And to that subterranean palace borne
Which toiling ages in the rock had worn.

Thebes from her hundred portals filled the plain
  To see the car on which thou wert upheld : —
What funeral pomps extended in thy train,
  What banners waved, what mighty music
    swelled,
As armies, priests, and crowds bewailed in chorus
Their King, — their God, — their Serapis, — their
    Orus !

Thus to thy second quarry did they trust
  Thee and the Lord of all the nations round.
Grim King of Silence ! Monarch of the Dust !
  Embalmed, anointed, jewelled, sceptred,
    crowned,
Here did he lie in state, cold, stiff, and stark,
A leathern Pharaoh grinning in the dark.

Thus ages rolled, but their dissolving breath
  Could only blacken that imprisoned thing
Which wore a ghastly royalty in death,
  As if it struggled still to be a king ;
And each revolving century, like the last,
Just dropped its dust upon thy lid — and passed.

The Persian conqueror o'er Egypt poured
  His devastating host, — a motley crew ;
The steel-clad horseman, — the barbarian horde, —
  Music and men of every sound and hue, —
Priests, archers, eunuchs, concubines, and brutes, —
Gongs, trumpets, cymbals, dulcimers, and lutes.

Then did the fierce Cambyses tear away
  The ponderous rock that sealed the sacred tomb ;
Then did the slowly penetrating ray
  Redeem thee from long centuries of gloom,
And lowered torches flashed against thy side
As Asia's king thy blazoned trophies eyed.

Plucked from his grave, with sacrilegious taunt,
  The features of the royal corpse they scanned : —
Dashing the diadem from his temple gaunt,
  They tore the sceptre from his graspless hand,
And on those fields, where once his will was law,
Left him for winds to waste and beasts to gnaw.

Some pious Thebans, when the storm was past,
  Unclosed the sepulchre with cunning skill,
And nature, aiding their devotion, cast
  Over its entrance a concealing rill,
Then thy third darkness came, and thou didst sleep
Twenty-three centuries in silence deep.

But he from whom nor pyramid nor Sphinx
　　Can hide its secrecies, Belzoni, came ;
From the tomb's mouth unloosed the granite links,
　　Gave thee again to light and life and fame.
And brought thee from the sands and desert forth
To charm the pallid children of the North.

Thou art in London, which, when thou wert new,
　　Was, what Thebes is, a wilderness and waste,
Where savage beasts more savage men pursue, —
　　A scene by nature cursed, — by man disgraced.
Now — 't is the world's metropolis — the high
Queen of arms, learning, arts, and luxury.

Here, where I hold my hand, 't is strange to think
　　What other hands perchance preceded mine ;
Others have also stood beside thy brink,
　　And vainly conned the moralizing line.
Kings, sages, chiefs, that touched this stone, like me,
Where are ye now ? — where all must shortly be !

All is mutation ; — he within this stone
　　Was once the greatest monarch of the hour : —
His bones are dust, — his very name unknown.
　　Go, — learn from him the vanity of power :
Seek not the frame's corruption to control,
But build a lasting mansion for thy soul.
HORACE SMITH.

THE DESERTED VILLAGE.

SWEET Auburn ! loveliest village of the plain,
Where health and plenty cheered the laboring swain,
Where smiling spring its earliest visit paid,
And parting summer's lingering blooms delayed.
Dear lovely bowers of innocence and ease,
Seats of my youth, when every sport could please,
How often have I loitered o'er thy green,
Where humble happiness endeared each scene !
How often have I paused on every charm,
The sheltered cot, the cultivated farm,
The never-failing brook, the busy mill,
The decent church that topped the neighboring hill,
The hawthorn bush, with seats beneath the shade,
For talking age and whispering lovers made !
How often have I blessed the coming day,
When toil remitting lent its turn to play,
And all the village train, from labor free,
Led up their sports beneath the spreading tree,
While many a pastime circled in the shade,
The young contending as the old surveyed ;
And many a gambol frolicked o'er the ground,
And sleights of art and feats of strength went round;
And still as each repeated pleasure tired,
Succeeding sports the mirthful band inspired ;

The dancing pair that simply sought renown,
By holding out, to tire each other down ;
The swain mistrustless of his smutted face,
While secret laughter tittered round the place ;
The bashful virgin's sidelong looks of love,
The matron's glance that would those looks reprove, —
These were thy charms, sweet village ! sports like these,
With sweet succession, taught e'en toil to please ;
These round thy bowers their cheerful influence shed,
These were thy charms, — but all these charms are fled !
　Sweet smiling village, loveliest of the lawn,
Thy sports are fled, and all thy charms withdrawn ;
Amidst thy bowers the tyrant's hand is seen,
And desolation saddens all thy green ;
One only master grasps the whole domain,
And half a tillage stints thy smiling plain ;
No more thy glassy brook reflects the day,
But, choked with sedges, works its weedy way ;
Along thy glades, a solitary guest,
The hollow-sounding bittern guards its nest ;
Amidst thy desert walks the lapwing flies,
And tires their echoes with unvaried cries.
Sunk are thy bowers in shapeless ruin all,
And the long grass o'ertops the mouldering wall,
And, trembling, shrinking from the spoiler's hand,
Far, far away thy children leave the land.
　Ill fares the land, to hastening ills a prey,
Where wealth accumulates and men decay :
Princes and lords may flourish, or may fade ;
A breath can make them, as a breath has made ;
But a bold peasantry, their country's pride,
When once destroyed, can never be supplied.
　A time there was, ere England's griefs began,
When every rood of ground maintained its man ;
For him light Labor spread her wholesome store,
Just gave what life required, but gave no more :
His best companions, innocence and health ;
And his best riches, ignorance of wealth.
　But times are altered ; trade's unfeeling train
Usurp the land and dispossess the swain ;
Along the lawn, where scattered hamlets rose,
Unwieldy wealth and cumberous pomp repose,
And every want to luxury allied,
And every pang that folly pays to pride.
Those gentle hours that plenty bade to bloom,
Those calm desires that asked but little room,
Those healthful sports that graced the peaceful scene,
Lived in each look, and brightened all the green, —
These, far departing, seek a kinder shore,
And rural mirth and manners are no more.

·　　·　　·　　·　　·　　·

Sweet was the sound, when oft, at evening's close,

Up yonder hill the village murmur rose ;
There, as I passed with careless steps and slow,
The mingling notes came softened from below ;
The swain responsive as the milk-maid sung,
The sober herd that lowed to meet their young ;
The noisy geese that gabbled o'er the pool,
The playful children just let loose from school ;
The watch-dog's voice that bayed the whispering
wind,
And the loud laugh that spoke the vacant mind, —
These all in sweet confusion sought the shade,
And filled each pause the nightingale had made.
But now the sounds of population fail,
No cheerful murmurs fluctuate in the gale,
No busy steps the grass-grown foot-way tread,
But all the bloomy flush of life is fled.
All but yon widowed, solitary thing,
That feebly bends beside the plashy spring ;
She, wretched matron, forced in age, for bread,
To strip the brook with mantling cresses spread,
To pick her wintry fagot from the thorn,
To seek her nightly shed, and weep till morn ;
She only left of all the harmless train,
The sad historian of the pensive plain.

Near yonder copse, where once the garden
smiled,
And still where many a garden-flower grows wild ;
There, where a few torn shrubs the place disclose,
The village preacher's modest mansion rose.
A man he was to all the country dear,
And passing rich with forty pounds a year ;
Remote from towns he ran his godly race,
Nor e'er had changed, nor wished to change, his
place ;
Unskilful he to fawn, or seek for power,
By doctrines fashioned to the varying hour ;
Far other aims his heart had learned to prize,
More bent to raise the wretched than to rise.
His house was known to all the vagrant train,
He chid their wanderings, but relieved their pain ;
The long-remembered beggar was his guest,
Whose beard descending swept his aged breast.
The ruined spendthrift, now no longer proud,
Claimed kindred there, and had his claims allowed ;
The broken soldier, kindly bade to stay,
Sate by his fire, and talked the night away ;
Wept o'er his wounds, or tales of sorrow done,
Shouldered his crutch, and showed how fields
were won.
Pleased with his guests, the good man learned to
glow,
And quite forgot their vices in their woe ;
Careless their merits or their faults to scan,
His pity gave ere charity began.

Thus to relieve the wretched was his pride,
And e'en his failings leaned to Virtue's side ;
But in his duty prompt at every call,
He watched and wept, he prayed and felt for all ;

And, as a bird each fond endearment tries,
To tempt its new-fledged offspring to the skies,
He tried each art, reproved each dull delay,
Allured to brighter worlds, and led the way.

Beside the bed where parting life was laid,
And sorrow, guilt, and pain by turns dismayed,
The reverend champion stood.   At his control,
Despair and anguish fled the struggling soul ;
Comfort came down the trembling wretch to raise.
And his last faltering accents whispered praise.

At church, with meek and unaffected grace,
His looks adorned the venerable place ;
Truth from his lips prevailed with double sway,
And fools, who came to scoff, remained to pray.
The service past, around the pious man,
With steady zeal, each honest rustic ran ;
E'en children followed with endearing wile,
And plucked his gown, to share the good man's
smile.
His ready smile a parent's warmth expressed,
Their welfare pleased him, and their cares dis-
tressed ;
To them his heart, his love, his griefs were given,
But all his serious thoughts had rest in heaven.
As some tall cliff, that lifts its awful form,
Swells from the vale, and midway leaves the storm,
Though round its breast the rolling clouds are
spread,
Eternal sunshine settles on its head.

Beside yon straggling fence that skirts the way,
With blossomed furze unprofitable gay,
There, in his noisy mansion, skilled to rule,
The village master taught his little school ;
A man severe he was, and stern to view,
I knew him well, and every truant knew ;
Well had the boding tremblers learned to trace
The day's disasters in his morning face ;
Full well they laughed with counterfeited glee
At all his jokes, for many a joke had he ;
Full well the busy whisper circling round
Conveyed the dismal tidings when he frowned ;
Yet he was kind, or if severe in aught,
The love he bore to learning was in fault.
The village all declared how much he knew,
'T was certain he could write, and cipher too ;
Lands he could measure, times and tides presage,
And e'en the story ran that he could gauge ;
In arguing too, the parson owned his skill,
For, e'en though vanquished, he could argue still,
While words of learned length and thundering
sound
Amazed the gazing rustics ranged around ;
And still they gazed, and still the wonder grew
That one small head could carry all he knew.

But past is all his fame.   The very spot
Where many a time he triumphed is forgot,
Near yonder thorn, that lifts its head on high,
Where once the sign-post caught the passing eye.

Low lies that house where nut-brown draughts inspired,
Where gray-beard mirth and smiling toil retired,
Where village statesmen talked with looks profound,
And news much older than their ale went round.
Imagination fondly stoops to trace
The parlor splendors of that festive place, —
The whitewashed wall; the nicely sanded floor;
The varnished clock that clicked behind the door;
The chest, contrived a double debt to pay,
A bed by night, a chest of drawers by day;
The pictures placed for ornament and use;
The twelve good rules; the royal game of goose;
The hearth, except when winter chilled the day,
With aspen boughs and flowers and fennel gay;
While broken teacups, wisely kept for show,
Ranged o'er the chimney, glistened in a row,

. . . . . .

As some fair female unadorned and plain,
Secure to please while youth confirms her reign,
Slights every borrowed charm that dress supplies,
Nor shares with art the triumph of her eyes,
But when those charms are past, — for charms are frail, —
When time advances, and when lovers fail,
She then shines forth, solicitous to bless,
In all the glaring impotence of dress;
Thus fares the land by luxury betrayed,
In nature's simplest charms at first arrayed,
But verging to decline, its splendors rise,
Its vistas strike, its palaces surprise;
While, scourged by famine from the smiling land,
The mournful peasant leads his humble band;
And while he sinks, without one arm to save,
The country blooms, — a garden and a grave.

Where then, ah! where shall poverty reside,
To 'scape the pressure of contiguous pride?
If to some common's fenceless limits strayed
He drives his flock to pick the scanty blade,
Those fenceless fields the sons of wealth divide,
And e'en the bare-worn common is denied.

If to the city sped, — what waits him there?
To see profusion that he must not share;
To see ten thousand baneful arts combined
To pamper luxury and thin mankind;
To see each joy the sons of pleasure know
Extorted from his fellow-creature's woe.
Here, while the courtier glitters in brocade,
There the pale artist plies the sickly trade;
Here, while the proud their long-drawn pomps display,
There the black gibbet glooms beside the way.
The dome where Pleasure holds her midnight reign,
Here, richly decked, admits the gorgeous train:
Tumultuous grandeur crowds the blazing square,
The rattling chariots clash, the torches glare.

Sure scenes like these no troubles e'er annoy!
Sure these denote one universal joy!
Are these thy serious thoughts? — Ah, turn thine eyes
Where the poor houseless shivering female lies.
She once, perhaps, in village plenty blest,
Has wept at tales of innocence distrest;
Her modest looks the cottage might adorn,
Sweet as the primrose peeps beneath the thorn
Now lost to all: her friends, her virtue fled,
Near her betrayer's door she lays her head,
And, pinched with cold, and shrinking from the shower,
With heavy heart deplores that luckless hour,
When idly first, ambitious of the town,
She left her wheel and robes of country brown.

Do thine, sweet AUBURN, thine, the loveliest train,
Do thy fair tribes participate her pain?
E'en now, perhaps, by cold and hunger led,
At proud men's doors they ask a little bread!
Ah, no! To distant climes, a dreary scene,
Where half the convex world intrudes between,
Through torrid tracks with fainting steps they go,
Where wild Altama murmurs to their woe.
Far different there from all that charmed before,
The various terrors of that horrid shore, —
Those blazing suns that dart a downward ray,
And fiercely shed intolerable day;
Those matted woods where birds forget to sing,
But silent bats in drowsy clusters cling;
Those poisonous fields with rank luxuriance crowned,
Where the dark scorpion gathers death around;
Where at each step the stranger fears to wake
The rattling terrors of the vengeful snake;
Where crouching tigers wait their hapless prey,
And savage men more murderous still then they;
While oft in whirls the mad tornado flies,
Mingling the ravaged landscape with the skies.
Far different these from every former scene,
The cooling brook, the grassy vested green,
The breezy covert of the warbling grove,
That only sheltered thefts of harmless love.

Good Heaven! what sorrows gloomed that parting day
That called them from their native walks away;
When the poor exiles, every pleasure past,
Hung round the bowers, and fondly looked their last,
And took a long farewell, and wished in vain
For seats like these beyond the western main;
And shuddering still to face the distant deep,
Returned and wept, and still returned to weep.
The good old sire, the first prepared to go
To new-found worlds, and wept for others' woe;
But for himself in conscious virtue brave,
He only wished for worlds beyond the grave.

His lovely daughter, lovelier in her tears,
The fond companion of his helpless years,
Silent went next, neglectful of her charms,
And left a lover's for her father's arms.
With louder plaints the mother spoke her woes,
And blessed the cot where every pleasure rose ;
And kissed her thoughtless babes with many a
    tear,
And clasped them close, in sorrow doubly dear ;
Whilst her fond husband strove to lend relief
In all the silent manliness of grief.
               OLIVER GOLDSMITH.

THE CLOSING SCENE.

WITHIN the sober realm of leafless trees,
  The russet year inhaled the dreamy air ;
Like some tanned reaper, in his hour of ease,
  When all the fields are lying brown and bare.

The gray barns looking from their hazy hills,
  O'er the dun waters widening in the vales,
Sent down the air a greeting to the mills,
  On the dull thunder of alternate flails.

All sights were mellowed and all sounds subdued,
  The hills seemed further and the stream sang
    low,
As in a dream the distant woodman hewed
  His winter log with many a muffled blow.

The embattled forests, erewhile armed with gold,
  Their banners bright with every martial hue,
Now stood like some sad, beaten host of old,
  Withdrawn afar in Time's remotest blue.

On sombre wings the vulture tried his flight ;
  The dove scarce heard his sighing mate's com-
    plaint ;
And, like a star slow drowning in the light,
  The village church vane seemed to pale and
    faint.

The sentinel cock upon the hillside crew, —
  Crew thrice, — and all was stiller than before ;
Silent, till some replying warden blew
  His alien horn, and then was heard no more.

Where erst the jay, within the elm's tall crest,
  Made garrulous trouble round her unfledged
    young ;
And where the oriole hung her swaying nest,
  By every light wind like a censer swung ;

Where sang the noisy martens of the eves,
  The busy swallows circling ever near, —
Foreboding, as the rustic mind believes,
  An early harvest and a plenteous year ;

Where every bird that waked the vernal feast
  Shook the sweet slumber from its wings at
    morn,
To warn the reaper of the rosy east ; —
  All now was sunless, empty, and forlorn.

Alone, from out the stubble, piped the quail ;
  And croaked the crow through all the dreary
    gloom ;
Alone, the pheasant, drumming in the vale,
  Made echo in the distance to the cottage-loom.

There was no bud, no bloom upon the bowers ;
  The spiders moved their thin shrouds night by
    night,
The thistle-down, the only ghost of flowers,
  Sailed slowly by, — passed noiseless out of sight.

Amid all this — in this most dreary air,
  And where the woodbine shed upon the porch
Its crimson leaves, as if the year stood there,
  Firing the floor with its inverted torch, —

Amid all this, the centre of the scene,
  The white-haired matron, with monotonous
    tread,
Plied the swift wheel, and with her joyless mien
  Sat like a fate, and watched the flying thread.

She had known Sorrow. He had walked with her,
  Oft supped, and broke with her the ashen
    crust,
And in the dead leaves still she heard the stir
  Of his thick mantle trailing in the dust.

While yet her cheek was bright with summer
    bloom,
  Her country summoned and she gave her all ;
And twice War bowed to her his sable plume, —
  Re-gave the sword to rust upon the wall.

Re-gave the sword, but not the hand that drew
  And struck for liberty the dying blow ;
Nor him who, to his sire and country true,
  Fell 'mid the ranks of the invading foe.

Long, but not loud, the droning wheel went on,
  Like the low murmur of a hive at noon ;
Long, but not loud, the memory of the gone
  Breathed through her lips a sad and tremulous
    tune.

At last the thread was snapped, — her head was
    bowed ;
  Life dropped the distaff through her hands
    serene ;
And loving neighbors smoothed her careful
    shroud,
  While death and winter closed the autumn
    scene.
             THOMAS BUCHANAN READ.

PEACE IN ACADIE.

FROM "EVANGELINE."

THIS is the forest primeval. The murmuring pines and the hemlocks,
Bearded with moss, and in garments green, indistinct in the twilight,
Stand like Druids of eld, with voices sad and prophetic,
Stand like harpers hoar, with beards that rest on their bosoms.
Loud from its rocky caverns, the deep-voiced neighboring ocean
Speaks, and in accents disconsolate answers the wail of the forest.

This is the forest primeval; but where are the hearts that beneath it
Leaped like the roe, when he hears in the woodland the voice of the huntsman?

. . . . . .

In the Acadian land, on the shores of the Basin of Minas,
Distant, secluded, still, the little village of Grand-Pré
Lay in the fruitful valley. Vast meadows stretched to the eastward,
Giving the village its name, and pasture to flocks without number.
Dikes, that the hands of the farmers had raised with labor incessant,
Shut out the turbulent tides; but at stated seasons the flood-gates
Opened, and welcomed the sea to wander at will o'er the meadows.
West and south there were fields of flax, and orchards and cornfields
Spreading afar and unfenced o'er the plain; and away to the northward
Blomidon rose, and the forests old, and aloft on the mountains
Sea-fogs pitched their tents, and mists from the mighty Atlantic
Looked on the happy valley, but ne'er from their station descended.
There, in the midst of its farms, reposed the Acadian village.
Strongly built were the houses, with frames of oak and of chestnut,
Such as the peasants of Normandy built in the reign of the Henries.
Thatched were the roofs, with dormer-windows; and gables projecting
Over the basement below protected and shaded the doorway.
There in the tranquil evenings of summer, when brightly the sunset
Lighted the village street, and gilded the vanes on the chimneys,
Matrons and maidens sat in snow-white caps and in kirtles
Scarlet and blue and green, with distaffs spinning the golden
Flax for the gossiping looms, whose noisy shuttles within doors
Mingled their sound with the whir of the wheels and the songs of the maidens.
Solemnly down the street came the parish priest, and the children
Paused in their play to kiss the hand he extended to bless them.
Reverend walked he among them; and up rose matrons and maidens,
Hailing his slow approach with words of affectionate welcome.
Then came the laborers home from the field, and serenely the sun sank
Down to his rest, and twilight prevailed. Anon from the belfry
Softly the Angelus sounded, and over the roofs of the village
Columns of pale blue smoke, like clouds of incense ascending,
Rose from a hundred hearths, the homes of peace and contentment.
Thus dwelt together in love these simple Acadian farmers, —
Dwelt in the love of God and of man. Alike were they free from
Fear, that reigns with the tyrant, and envy, the vice of republics.
Neither locks had they to their doors, nor bars to their windows;
But their dwellings were open as day and the hearts of the owners;
There the richest were poor, and the poorest lived in abundance.

Somewhat apart from the village, and nearer the Basin of Minas,
Benedict Bellefontaine, the wealthiest farmer of Grand-Pré,
Dwelt on his goodly acres; and with him, directing his household,
Gentle Evangeline lived, his child, and the pride of the village.
Stalworth and stately in form was the man of seventy winters;
Hearty and hale was he, an oak that is covered with snow-flakes;
White as the snow were his locks, and his cheeks as brown as the oak-leaves.
Fair was she to behold, that maiden of seventeen summers.
Black were her eyes as the berry that grows on the thorn by the wayside,
Black, yet how softly they gleamed beneath the brown shade of her tresses!

Sweet was her breath as the breath of kine that feed in the meadows,

When in the harvest heat she bore to the reapers at noontide

Flagons of home-brewed ale, ah! fair in sooth was the maiden.

Fairer was she when, on Sunday morn, while the bell from its turret

Sprinkled with holy sounds the air, as the priest with his hyssop

Sprinkles the congregation, and scatters blessings upon them,

Down the long street she passed, with her chaplet of beads and her missal,

Wearing her Norman cap, and her kirtle of blue, and the ear-rings,

Brought in the olden time from France, and since, as an heirloom,

Handed down from mother to child, through long generations.

But a celestial brightness, a more ethereal beauty,

Shone on her face and encircled her form, when, after confession,

Homeward serenely she walked with God's benediction upon her.

When she had passed, it seemed like the ceasing of exquisite music.

HENRY WADSWORTH LONGFELLOW.

EVANGELINE ON THE PRAIRIE.

BEAUTIFUL was the night. Behind the black wall of the forest,

Tipping its summit with silver, arose the moon. On the river

Fell here and there through the branches a tremulous gleam of the moonlight,

Like the sweet thoughts of love on a darkened and devious spirit.

Nearer and round about her, the manifold flowers of the garden

Poured out their souls in odors, that were their prayers and confessions

Unto the night, as it went its way, like a silent Carthusian.

Fuller of fragrance than they, and as heavy with shadows and night-dews,

Hung the heart of the maiden. The calm and the magical moonlight

Seemed to inundate her soul with indefinable longings,

As, through the garden gate, and beneath the shade of the oak-trees,

Passed she along the path to the edge of the measureless prairie.

Silent it lay, with a silvery haze upon it, and fire-flies

Gleaming and floating away in mingled and infinite numbers.

Over her head the stars, the thoughts of God in the heavens,

Shone on the eyes of man, who had ceased to marvel and worship,

Save when a blazing comet was seen on the walls of that temple,

As if a hand had appeared and written upon them, "Upharsin."

And the soul of the maiden, between the stars and the fire-flies,

Wandered alone, and she cried, "O Gabriel! O my beloved!

Art thou so near unto me, and yet I cannot behold thee?

Art thou so near unto me, and yet thy voice does not reach me?

Ah! how often thy feet have trod this path to the prairie!

Ah! how often thine eyes have looked on the woodlands around me!

Ah! how often beneath this oak, returning from labor,

Thou hast lain down to rest, and to dream of me in thy slumbers.

When shall these eyes behold, these arms be folded about thee?"

Loud and sudden and near the note of a whippoorwill sounded

Like a flute in the woods; and anon, through the neighboring thickets,

Farther and farther away it floated and dropped into silence.

"Patience!" whispered the oaks from oracular caverns of darkness;

And, from the moonlit meadow, a sigh responded, "To-morrow!"

HENRY WADSWORTH LONGFELLOW.

WEEHAWKEN AND THE BAY OF NEW YORK.

FROM "FANNY."

. . . .

WEEHAWKEN! In thy mountain scenery yet,
  All we adore of Nature in her wild
And frolic hour of infancy is met;
  And never has a summer's morning smiled
Upon a lovelier scene than the full eye
Of the enthusiast revels on, — when high

Amid thy forest solitudes he climbs
  O'er crags that proudly tower above the deep,
And knows that sense of danger which sublimes
  The breathless moment, — when his daring step

Henry W. Longfellow

FORDS, HOWARD & HULBERT, N.Y.

Is on the verge of the cliff, and he can hear
The low dash of the wave with startled ear,

Like the death-music of his coming doom,
    And clings to the green turf with desperate force,
As the heart clings to life ; and when resume
    The currents in his veins their wonted course,
There lingers a deep feeling, — like the moan
Of wearied ocean when the storm is gone.

In such an hour he turns, and on his view,
    Ocean and earth and heaven burst before him ;
Clouds slumbering at his feet, and the clear blue
    Of summer's sky in beauty bending o'er him, —
The city bright below ; and far away,
Sparkling in golden light, his own romantic bay.

Tall spire, and glittering roof, and battlement,
    And banners floating in the sunny air ;
And white sails o'er the calm blue waters bent,
    Green isle, and circling shore, are blended there
In wild reality.   When life is old,
And many a scene forgot, the heart will hold

Its memory of this ; nor lives there one
    Whose infant breath was drawn, or boyhood's
        days
Of happiness were passed beneath that sun,
    That in his manhood's prime can calmly gaze
Upon that bay, or on that mountain stand,
Nor feel the prouder of his native land.

·   ·   ·   ·   ·

                                    FITZ-GREENE HALLECK.

———◆———

THE PRISONER OF CHILLON.

[Francois de Bonnivard was born 1496, and was educated for the church. He stood forward in the defence of Geneva against the Duke of Savoy and the Bishop. He was imprisoned for two years (1519–21) at Grolée, and again at the Château of Chillon, 1530–36. He was much honored by his townsmen, the Genevese, and died in 1570. The castle stands on the margin of the Lake of Geneva.]

I.

My hair is gray, but not with years,
        Nor grew it white
        In a single night,
As men's have grown from sudden fears :
My limbs are bowed, though not with toil,
    But rusted with a vile repose,
For they have been a dungeon's spoil,
    And mine has been the fate of those
To whom the goodly earth and air
Are banned, and barred, — forbidden fare ;
But this was for my father's faith
I suffered chains and courted death ;
That father perished at the stake
For tenets he would not forsake ;

And for the same his lineal race
In darkness found a dwelling-place ;
We were seven, — who now are one,
    Six in youth, and one in age,
Finished as they had begun,
    Proud of Persecution's rage ;
One in fire, and two in field,
Their belief with blood have sealed !
Dying as their father died,
For the God their foes denied ;
Three were in a dungeon cast,
Of whom this wreck is left the last.

II.

There are seven pillars of Gothic mould
In Chillon's dungeons deep and old,
There are seven columns, massy and gray,
Dim with a dull imprisoned ray, —
A sunbeam which hath lost its way,
And through the crevice and the cleft
Of the thick wall is fallen and left,
Creeping o'er the floor so damp,
Like a marsh's meteor lamp, —
And in each pillar there is a ring,
    And in each ring there is a chain ;
That iron is a cankering thing,
    For in these limbs its teeth remain
With marks that will not wear away,
Till I have done with this new day,
Which now is painful to these eyes,
Which have not seen the sun to rise
For years, — I cannot count them o'er,
I lost their long and heavy score
When my last brother drooped and died,
And I lay living by his side.

III.

They chained us each to a column stone,
And we were three, yet each alone ;
We could not move a single pace,
We could not see each other's face,
But with that pale and livid light
That made us strangers in our sight ;
And thus together, yet apart,
Fettered in hand, but pined in heart ;
'T was still some solace, in the dearth
Of the pure elements of earth,
To hearken to each other's speech,
And each turn comforter to each
With some new hope, or legend old,
Or song heroically bold ;
But even these at length grew cold.
Our voices took a dreary tone,
An echo of the dungeon-stone,
    A grating sound, — not full and free
As they of yore were wont to be ;
    It might be fancy, — but to me
They never sounded like our own.

IV.

I was the eldest of the three,
  And to uphold and cheer the rest
  I ought to do — and did — my best,
And each did well in his degree.
  The youngest, whom my father loved,
Because our mother's brow was given
To him, with eyes as blue as heaven, —
  For him my soul was sorely moved ;
And truly might it be distrest
To see such bird in such a nest ;
For he was beautiful as day
  (When day was beautiful to me
  As to young eagles, being free), —
A polar day, which will not see
A sunset till its summer 's gone,
  Its sleepless summer of long light,
The snow-clad offspring of the sun ;
  And thus he was as pure and bright,
And in his natural spirit gay,
With tears for naught but others' ills,
'And then they flowed like mountain rills,
Unless he could assuage the woe
Which he abhorred to view below.

V.

The other was as pure of mind,
But formed to combat with his kind ;
Strong in his frame, and of a mood
Which 'gainst the world in war had stood,
And perished in the foremost rank
  With joy ; — but not in chains to pine ;
His spirit withered with their clank,
  I saw it silently decline, —
  And so perchance in sooth did mine ;
But yet I forced it on to cheer
Those relics of a home so dear.
He was a hunter of the hills,
  Had followed there the deer and wolf ;
  To him this dungeon was a gulf
And fettered feet the worst of ills.

VI.

Lake Leman lies by Chillon's walls :
A thousand feet in depth below
Its massy waters meet and flow ;
Thus much the fathom-line was sent
From Chillon's snow-white battlement,
  Which round about the wave inthralls ;
A double dungeon wall and wave
Have made, — and like a living grave.
Below the surface of the lake
The dark vault lies wherein we lay,
We heard it ripple night and day ;
  Sounding o'er our heads it knocked ;
And I have felt the winter's spray
Wash through the bars when winds were high
And wanton in the happy sky ;

And then the very rock hath rocked,
  And I have felt it shake, unshocked,
Because I could have smiled to see
The death that would have set me free.

VII.

I said my nearer brother pined,
I said his mighty heart declined,
He loathed and put away his food ;
It was not that 't was coarse and rude,
For we were used to hunter's fare,
And for the like had little care ;
The milk drawn from the mountain goat
Was changed for water from the moat.
Our bread was such as captives' tears
Have moistened many a thousand years,
Since man first pent his fellow-men
Like brutes within an iron den ;
But what were these to us or him ?
These wasted not his heart or limb ;
My brother's soul was of that mould
Which in a palace had grown cold,
Had his free breathing been denied
The range of the steep mountain's side ;
But why delay the truth ? — he died.
I saw, and could not hold his head,
Nor reach his dying hand, — nor dead, —
Though hard I strove, but strove in vain,
To rend and gnash my bonds in twain.
He died, — and they unlocked his chain,
And scooped for him a shallow grave
Even from the cold earth of our cave.
I begged them, as a boon, to lay
His corse in dust whereon the day
Might shine, — it was a foolish thought,
But then within my brain it wrought,
That even in death his freeborn breast
In such a dungeon could not rest.
I might have spared my idle prayer, —
They coldly laughed, and laid him there.
The flat and turfless earth above
The being we so much did love ;
His empty chain above it leant,
Such murder's fitting monument !

VIII.

But he, the favorite and the flower,
Most cherished since his natal hour,
His mother's image in fair face,
The infant love of all his race,
His martyred father's dearest thought,
My latest care, for whom I sought
To hoard my life, that his might be
Less wretched now, and one day free ;
He, too, who yet had held untired
A spirit natural or inspired, —
He, too, was struck, and day by day
Was withered on the stalk away.
O God ! it is a fearful thing

To see the human soul take wing
In any shape, in any mood : —
I 've seen it rushing forth in blood,
I 've seen it on the breaking ocean
Strive with a swoln convulsive motion,
I 've seen the sick and ghastly bed
Of Sin delirious with its dread :
But these were horrors, — this was woe
Unmixed with such, — but sure and slow :
He faded, and so calm and meek,
So softly worn, so sweetly weak,
So tearless, yet so tender, — kind,
And grieved for those he left behind ;
With all the while a cheek whose bloom
Was as a mockery of the tomb,
Whose tints as gently sunk away
As a departing rainbow's ray, —
An eye of most transparent light,
That almost made the dungeon bright,
And not a word of murmur, — not
A groan o'er his untimely lot, —
A little talk of better days,
A little hope my own to raise,
For I was sunk in silence, — lost
In this last loss, of all the most ;
And then the sighs he would suppress
Of fainting nature's feebleness,
More slowly drawn, grew less and less :
I listened, but I could not hear, —
I called, for I was wild with fear ;
I knew 't was hopeless, but my dread
Would not be thus admonishéd ;
I called, and thought I heard a sound, —
I burst my chain with one strong bound,
And rushed to him : — I found him not,
I only stirred in this black spot,
I only lived, — *I* only drew
The accurséd breath of dungeon-dew ;
The last — the sole — the dearest link
Between me and the eternal brink,
Which bound me to my failing race,
Was broken in this fatal place.
One on the earth, and one beneath, —
My brothers — both had ceased to breathe.
I took that hand which lay so still,
Alas ! my own was full as chill ;
I had not strength to stir or strive,
But felt that I was still alive, —
A frantic feeling when we know
That what we love shall ne'er be so.
  I know not why
  I could not die,
I had no earthly hope, — but faith,
And that forbade a selfish death.

IX.

What next befell me then and there
 I know not well, — I never knew.

First came the loss of light and air,
 And then of darkness too ;
I had no thought, no feeling, — none, —
Among the stones I stood a stone,
And was, scarce conscious what I wist,
As shrubless crags within the mist ;
For all was blank and bleak and gray,
It was not night, — it was not day,
It was not even the dungeon-light,
So hateful to my heavy sight,
But vacancy absorbing space,
And fixedness, — without a place :
There were no stars — no earth — no time —
No check — no change — no good — no crime ;
But silence, and a stirless breath
Which neither was of life nor death :
A sea of stagnant idleness,
Blind, boundless, mute, and motionless !

X.

A light broke in upon my brain, —
 It was the carol of a bird ;
It ceased, and then it came again,
 The sweetest song ear ever heard,
And mine was thankful till my eyes
Ran over with the glad surprise,
And they that moment could not see
I was the mate of misery ;
But then by dull degrees came back
My senses to their wonted track,
I saw the dungeon walls and floor
Close slowly round me as before,
I saw the glimmer of the sun
Creeping as it before had done,
But through the crevice where it came
That bird was perched, as fond and tame,
 And tamer than upon the tree ;
A lovely bird, with azure wings,
And song that said a thousand things,
 And seemed to say them all for me !
I never saw its like before,
I ne'er shall see its likeness more.
It seemed, like me, to want a mate,
But was not half so desolate,
And it was come to love me when
None lived to love me so again,
And cheering from my dungeon's brink,
Had brought me back to feel and think.
I know not if it late were free,
 Or broke its cage to perch on mine,
But knowing well captivity,
 Sweet bird ! I could not wish for thine !
Or if it were, in wingéd guise,
A visitant from Paradise :
For — Heaven forgive that thought ! the while
Which made me both to weep and smile —
I sometimes deemed that it might be
My brother's soul come down to me ;

But then at last away it flew,
And then 't was mortal, — well I knew,
For he would never thus have flown,
And left me twice so doubly lone, —
Lone — as the corse within its shroud,
Lone — as a solitary cloud,
  A single cloud on a sunny day,
While all the rest of heaven is clear,
A frown upon the atmosphere,
That hath no business to appear
  When skies are blue and earth is gay.

XI.

A kind of change came in my fate,
My keepers grew compassionate ;
I know not what had made them so,
They were inured to sights of woe,
But so it was : — my broken chain
With links unfastened did remain,
And it was liberty to stride
Along my cell from side to side,
And up and down, and then athwart,
And tread it over every part ;
And round the pillars one by one,
Returning where my walk begun,
Avoiding only, as I trod,
My brothers' graves without a sod ;
For if I thought with heedless tread
My step profaned their lowly bed,
My breath came gaspingly and thick,
And my crushed heart fell blind and sick.

XII.

I made a footing in the wall,
  It was not therefrom to escape,
For I had buried one and all
  Who loved me in a human shape :
And the whole earth would henceforth be
A wider prison unto me :
No child, — no sire, — no kin had I,
No partner in my misery ;
I thought of this and I was glad,
For thought of them had made me mad ;
But I was curious to ascend
To my barred windows, and to bend
Once more, upon the mountains high,
The quiet of a loving eye.

XIII.

I saw them, — and they were the same,
They were not changed like me in frame ;
I saw their thousand years of snow
On high, — their wide long lake below,
And the blue Rhone in fullest flow ;
I heard the torrents leap and gush
O'er channelled rock and broken bush ;

I saw the white-walled distant town,
And whiter sails go skimming down ;
And then there was a little isle,
Which in my very face did smile,
  The only one in view ;
A small green isle, it seemed no more,
Scarce broader than my dungeon floor,
But in it there were three tall trees,
And o'er it blew the mountain breeze,
And by it there were waters flowing,
And on it there were young flowers growing,
  Of gentle breath and hue.
The fish swam by the castle wall,
And they seemed joyous each and all ;
The eagle rode the rising blast, .
Methought he never flew so fast
As then to me he seemed to fly,
And then new tears came in my eye,
And I felt troubled, — and would fain
I had not left my recent chain ;
And when I did descend again,
The darkness of my dim abode
Fell on me as a heavy load ;
It was as in a new-dug grave
Closing o'er one we sought to save,
And yet my glance, too much oppressed,
Had almost need of such a rest.

XIV.

It might be months, or years, or days,
  I kept no count, — I took no note,
I had no hope my eyes to raise,
  And clear them of their dreary mote ;
At last men came to set me free,
  I asked not why and recked not where,
It was at length the same to me,
Fettered or fetterless to be,
  I learned to love despair.
And thus when they appeared at last,
And all my bonds aside were cast,
These heavy walls to me had grown
A hermitage, and all my own !
And half I felt as they were come
To tear me from a second home ;
With spiders I had friendship made,
And watched them in their sullen trade,
Had seen the mice by moonlight play,
And why should I feel less than they ?
We were all inmates of one place,
And I, the monarch of each race,
Had power to kill, — yet, strange to tell !
In quiet we had learned to dwell, —
My very chains and I grew friends,
So much a long communion tends
To make us what we are : — even I
Regained my freedom with a sigh.

                                    BYRON.

LAMBRO'S RETURN.

FROM "DON JUAN."

LAMBRO, our sea-solicitor, who had
Much less experience of dry land than ocean,
On seeing his own chimney-smoke, felt glad;
But, not knowing metaphysics, had no notion
Of the true reason of his not being sad,
Or that of any other strong emotion;
He loved his child, and would have wept the loss
of her,
But knew the cause no more than a philosopher.

He saw his white walls shining in the sun,
His garden trees all shadowy and green;
He heard his rivulet's light bubbling run,
The distant dog-bark; and perceived, between
The umbrage of the wood, so cool and dun,
The moving figures, and the sparkling sheen
Of arms (in the East all arm),— and various dyes
Of colored garbs, as bright as butterflies.

And as the spot where they appear he nears,
Surprised at these unwonted signs of idling,
He hears — alas! no music of the spheres,
But an unhallowed earthly sound of fiddling!
A melody which made him doubt his ears,
The cause being past his guessing or unriddling;
A pipe, too, and a drum, and, shortly after,
A most unoriental roar of laughter.

* * * * *

Old Lambro passed unseen a private gate,
And stood within his hall at eventide;
Meantime the lady and her lover sate
At wassail in their beauty and their pride:
An ivory inlaid table spread with state
Before them, and fair slaves on every side;
Gems, gold, and silver formed the service mostly,
Mother-of-pearl and coral the less costly.

Haidee and Juan carpeted their feet
On crimson satin, bordered with pale blue;
Their sofa occupied three parts complete
Of the apartment, — and appeared quite new;
The velvet cushions (for a throne more meet)
Were scarlet, from whose glowing centre grew
A sun embossed in gold, whose rays of tissue,
Meridian-like, were seen all light to issue.

* * * * *

Of all the dresses I select Haidee's;
She wore two jellicks, — one was of pale yellow;
Of azure, pink, and white was her chemise, —
'Neath which her breast heaved like a little bil-
low;
With buttons formed of pearls as large as peas,
All gold and crimson shone her jellick's fellow;
And the striped white gauze baracan that bound
her,
Like fleecy clouds about the moon, flowed round
her.

One large gold bracelet clasped each lovely arm,
Lockless, — so pliable from the pure gold
That the hand stretched and shut it without harm;
The limb which it adorned its only mould:
So beautiful, — its very shape would charm,
And clinging as if loath to lose its hold,
The purest ore enclosed the whitest skin
That e'er by precious metal was held in.

Around, as princess of her father's land,
A liko gold bar, above her instep rolled,
Announced her rank; twelve rings were on her
hand;
Her hair was starred with gems; her veil's fine
fold
Below her breast was fastened with a band
Of lavish pearls, whose worth could scarce be told;
Her orange-silk full Turkish trousers furled
Above the prettiest ankle in the world.

Round her she made an atmosphere of life,
The very air seemed lighter from her eyes,
They were so soft and beautiful, and rife
With all we can imagine of the skies.
And pure as Psyche ere she grew a wife, —
Too pure even for the purest human ties,
Her overpowering presence made you feel
It would not be idolatry to kneel.

Juan had on a shawl of black and gold,
But a white baracan, and so transparent,
The sparkling gems beneath you might behold,
Like small stars through the Milky Way ap-
parent;
His turban, furled in many a graceful fold,
An emerald aigrette, with Haidee's hair in't
Surmounted; at its clasp a glowing crescent,
Whose rays shone ever trembling, but incessant.

* * * * *

They were alone once more; for them to be
Thus was another Eden: they were never
Weary, unless when separate: the tree
Cut from its forest root of years, the river
Dammed from its fountain, the child from the knee
And breast maternal weaned at once forever,
Would wither less than these two torn apart;
Alas! there is no instinct like the heart.

* * * * *

They gazed upon the sunset; 't is an hour
Dear unto all, but dearest to *their* eyes,
For it had made them what they were: the power
Of love had first o'erwhelmed them from such
skies,
When happiness had been their only dower,
And twilight saw them linked in passion's ties;
Charmed with each other, all things charmed that
brought
The past still welcome as the present thought.

* * * * *

Now pillowed cheek to cheek, in loving sleep,
  Haidee and Juan their siesta took, —
A gentle slumber, but it was not deep,
  For ever and anon a something shook
Juan, and shuddering o'er his frame would creep ;
  And Haidee's sweet lips murmured like a brook,
A wordless music, and her face so fair
Stirred with her dream, as rose-leaves with the air.

   .   .   .

She dreamed of being alone on the sea-shore
  Chained to a rock : she knew not how, but stir
She could not from the spot, and the loud roar
  Grew, and each wave rose roughly, threatening
    her ;
And o'er her upper lip they seemed to pour
  Until she sobbed for breath, and soon they were
Foaming o'er her lone head, so fierce and high, —
Each broke to drown her, yet she could not die.

   .   .   .

And wet and cold and lifeless at her feet,
  Pale as the foam that frothed on his dead brow,
Which she essayed in vain to clear, (how sweet
  Were once her cares, how idle seemed they now !)
Lay Juan, nor could aught renew the beat
  Of his quenched heart ; and the sea-dirges low
Rang in her sad ears like a mermaid's song,
And that brief dream appeared a life too long.

And gazing on the dead, she thought his face
  Faded, or altered into something new, —
Like to her father's features, till each trace
  More like and like to Lambro's aspect grew, —
With all his keen worn look and Grecian grace ;
  And, starting, she awoke, and what to view ?
O powers of heaven ! what dark eye meets she there ?
'T is — 't is her father's—fixed upon the pair !

Then shrieking, she arose, and shrieking fell,
  With joy and sorrow, hope and fear, to see
Him whom she deemed a habitant where dwell
  The ocean-buried, risen from death to be
Perchance the death of one she loved too well :
  Dear as her father had been to Haidee,
It was a moment of that awful kind, —
I have seen such, — but must not call to mind.

Up Juan sprung to Haidee's bitter shriek,
  And caught her falling, and from off the wall
Snatched down his sabre, in hot haste to wreak
  Vengeance on him who was the cause of all :
Then Lambro, who till now forbore to speak,
  Smiled scornfully, and said, " Within my call,
A thousand scimitars await the word ;
Put up, young man, put up your silly sword."

And Haidee clung around him : "Juan, 't is—
  Tis Lambro,—'t is my father ! Kneel with me,—
He will forgive us, —yes, —it must be, —yes.
  O dearest father, in this agony

Of pleasure and of pain, —even while I kiss
  Thy garment's hem with transport, can it be
That doubt should mingle with my filial joy ?
Deal with me as thou wilt, but spare this boy."

High and inscrutable the old man stood,
  Calm in his voice, and calm within his eye, —
Not always signs with him of calmest mood :
  He looked upon her, but gave no reply ;
Then turned to Juan, in whose cheek the blood
  Oft came and went, as there resolved to die,
In arms, at least, he stood in act to spring
On the first foe whom Lambro's call might bring.

"Young man, your sword"; so Lambro once more
    said :
  Juan replied, "Not while this arm is free."
The old man's cheek grew pale, but not with dread,
  And drawing from his belt a pistol, he
Replied, "Your blood be then on your own head."
  Then looked close at the flint, as if to see
'T was fresh, — for he had lately used the lock, —
And next proceeded quietly to cock.

   .   .   .

Lambro presented, and one instant more
  Had stopped this canto, and Don Juan's breath,
When Haidee threw herself her boy before ;
  Stern as her sire : "On me," she cried, " let death
Descend, — the fault is mine ; this fatal shore
  He found, — but sought not.   I have pledged
    my faith ;
I love him, — I will die with him : I knew
Your nature's firmness, — know your daughter's
    too."

A minute past, and she had been all tears
  And tenderness and infancy ; but now
She stood as one who championed human fears, —
  Pale, statue-like, and stern, she wooed the blow ;
And tall beyond her sex, and their compeers,
  She drew up to her height, as if to show
A fairer mark ; and with a fixed eye, scanned
Her father's face, — but never stopped his hand.

   .   .   .

The father paused a moment, then withdrew
  His weapon, and replaced it ; but stood still,
And looking on her, as to look her through :
  "Not I," he said, "have sought this stranger's
    ill ;
Not I have made this desolation : few
  Would bear such outrage, and forbear to kill ;
But I must do my duty, — how thou hast
Done thine, the present vouches for the past.

"Let him disarm ; or, by my father's head,
  His own shall roll before you like a ball !"
He raised his whistle, as the word he said,
  And blew ; another answered to the call,
And, rushing in disorderly, though led,
  And armed from boot to turban, one and all,

Some twenty of his train came, rank on rank ;
He gave the word, — "Arrest, or slay, the Frank."

Then, with a sudden movement, he withdrew
    His daughter ; while compressed within his
        clasp,
'Twixt her and Juan interposed the crew ;
    In vain she struggled in her father's grasp, —
His arms were like a serpent's coil : then flew
    Upon their prey, as darts an angry asp,
The file of pirates ; save the foremost, who
Had fallen, with his right shoulder half cut
        through.

The second had his cheek laid open ; but
    The third, a wary, cool, old sworder, took
The blows upon his cutlass, and then put
    His own well in : so well, ere you could look,
His man was floored, and helpless, at his foot,
    With the blood running, like a little brook,
From two smart sabre-gashes, deep and red, —
One on the arm, the other on the head.

And then they bound him where he fell, and bore
    Juan from the apartment : with a sign,
Old Lambro bade them take him to the shore,
    Where lay some ships which were to sail at nine.
They laid him in a boat, and plied the oar
    Until they reached some galliots, placed in line ;
On board of one of these, and under hatches,
They stowed him, with strict orders to the watches.

The last sight Haidee saw was Juan's gore,
    And he himself o'ermastered and cut down :
His blood was running on the very floor,
    Where late he trod, her beautiful, her own ;
Thus much she viewed an instant and no more, —
    Her struggles ceased with one convulsive groan ;
On her sire's arm, which until now scarce held
Her, writhing, fell she, like a cedar felled.

A vein had burst, and her sweet lips' pure dyes
    Were dabbled with the deep blood which ran
        o'er ;
And her head drooped, as when the lily lies
    O'ercharged with rain : her summoned hand-
        maids bore
Their lady to her couch, with gushing eyes ;
    Of herbs and cordials they produced their store,
But she defied all means they could employ,
Like one life could not hold, nor death destroy.

Days lay she in that state, unchanged, though
        chill,
    With nothing livid, still her lips were red ;
She had no pulse, but death seemed absent still ;
    No hideous sign proclaimed her surely dead ;
Corruption came not, in each mind to kill
    All hope ; to look upon her sweet face bred

New thoughts of life, for it seemed full of soul, —
She had so much, earth could not claim the whole.

        .   .   .   .   .

She woke at length, but not as sleepers wake,
    Rather the dead, for life seemed something new,
A strange sensation which she must partake
    Perforce, since whatsoever met her view
Struck not her memory, though a heavy ache
    Lay at her heart, whose earliest beat, still true,
Brought back the sense of pain without the cause,
For, for a while, the furies made a pause.

She looked on many a face with vacant eye,
    On many a token without knowing what ;
She saw them watch her without asking why ;
    And recked not who around her pillow sat ;
Not speechless, though she spoke not ; not a sigh
    Relieved her thoughts ; dull silence and quick
        chat
Were tried in vain by those who served ; she gave
No sign, save breath, of having left the grave.

Her handmaids tended, but she heeded not ;
    Her father watched, she turned her eyes away ;
She recognized no being, and no spot,
    However dear, or cherished in their day ;
They changed from room to room, but all forgot,
    Gentle, but without memory, she lay ;
At length those eyes, which they would fain be
        weaning
Back to old thoughts, waxed full of fearful mean-
        ing.

And then a slave bethought her of a harp ;
    The harper came, and tuned his instrument ;
At the first notes, irregular and sharp,
    On him her flashing eyes a moment bent,
Then to the wall she turned, as if to warp
    Her thoughts from sorrow, through her heart
        re-sent ;
And he began a long low island-song
Of ancient days, ere tyranny grew strong.

Anon her thin wan fingers beat the wall,
    In time to his old tune ; he changed the theme,
And sung of love ; the fierce name struck through
        all
    Her recollection ; on her flashed the dream
Of what she was, and is, if ye could call
    To be so being ; in a gushing stream
The tears rushed forth from her o'erclouded brain,
Like mountain mists at length dissolved in rain.

Short solace, vain relief ! — thought came too
        quick,
    And whirled her brain to madness ; she arose,
As one who ne'er had dwelt among the sick,
    And flew at all she met, as on her foes ;

But no one ever heard her speak or shriek,
  Although her paroxysm drew towards its
    close ; —
Hers was a frenzy which disdained to rave,
Even when they smote her, in the hope to save.

Yet she betrayed at times a gleam of sense ;
  Nothing could make her meet her father's face,
Though on all other things with looks intense
  She gazed, but none she ever could retrace ;
Food she refused, and raiment ; no pretence
  Availed for either ; neither change of place,
Nor time, nor skill, nor remedy, could give her
Senses to sleep, — the power seemed gone forever.

Twelve days and nights she withered thus ; at last,
  Without a groan or sigh or glance to show
A parting pang, the spirit from her past ;
  And they who watched her nearest could not
    know
The very instant, till the change that cast
  Her sweet face into shadow, dull and slow,
Glazed o'er her eyes, — the beautiful, the black, —
O, to possess such lustre, — and then lack !

She died, but not alone ; she held within
  A second principle of life, which might
Have dawned a fair and sinless child of sin ;
  But closed its little being without light,
And went down to the grave unborn, wherein
  Blossom and bough lie withered with one
    blight ;
In vain the dews of heaven descend above
The bleeding flower and blasted fruit of love.

Thus lived, thus died she ; nevermore on her,
  Shall sorrow light, or shame. She was not made
Through years or moons the inner weight to bear,
  Which colder hearts endure till they are laid
By age in earth ; her days and pleasures were
  Brief, but delightful, — such as had not stayed
Long with her destiny ; but she sleeps well
By the sea-shore, whereon she loved to dwell.

That isle is now all desolate and bare,
  Its dwellings down, its tenants passed away ;
None but her own and father's grave is there,
  And nothing outward tells of human clay ;
Ye could not know where lies a thing so fair,
  No stone is there to show, no tongue to say,
What was ; no dirge, except the hollow sea's,
Mourns o'er the beauty of the Cyclades.
BYRON.

CLEOPATRA.

FROM " ANTONY AND CLEOPATRA."

ENOBARBUS. The barge she sat in, like a bur-
  nished throne,
Burned on the water : the poop was beaten gold ;

Purple the sails, and so perfuméd, that
The winds were love-sick with them ; the oars
  were silver ;
Which to the tune of flutes kept stroke, and made
The water, which they beat, to follow faster,
As amorous of their strokes. For her own person,
It beggared all description : she did lie
In her pavilion (cloth of gold of tissue),
O'erpicturing that Venus, where we see,
The fancy out-work nature ; on each side her
Stood pretty dimpled boys, like smiling Cupids,
With divers-colored fans, whose wind did seem
To glow the delicate cheeks which they did cool,
And what they undid, did.

AGRIPPA.   O, rare for Antony !
  ENO. Her gentlewomen, like the Nereids,
So many mermaids, tendered her i' the eyes,
And made their bends adornings : at the helm
A seeming mermaid steers : the silken tackle
Swell with the touches of those flower-soft hands,
That yarely frame the office. From the barge
A strange invisible perfume hits the sense
Of the adjacent wharfs. The city cast
Her people out upon her ; and Antony,
Enthronéd i' the market-place, did sit alone,
Whistling to the air ; which, but for vacancy,
Had gone to gaze on Cleopatra too,
And made a gap in nature.

AGR.   Rare Egyptian !
  ENO. Upon her landing, Antony sent to her,
Invited her to supper : she replied,
It should be better he became her guest ;
Which she entreated : our courteous Antony,
Whom ne'er the word of " No " woman heard
  speak,
Being barbered ten times o'er, goes to the feast ;
And, for his ordinary, pays his heart
For what his eyes eat only.

AGR.   Royal wench !
  MECÆNAS. Now Antony must leave her utterly.
  ENO. Never ; he will not :
Age cannot wither her, nor custom stale
Her infinite variety : other women cloy
The appetites they feed, but she makes hungry
Where most she satisfies : for vilest things
Become themselves in her ; that the holy priests
Bless her when she is riggish.
SHAKESPEARE.

GODIVA.

NOT only we, the latest seed of Time,
New men, that in the flying of a wheel
Cry down the past ; not only we, that prate
Of rights and wrongs, have loved the people well,
And loathed to see them overtaxed ; but she
Did more, and underwent, and overcame,

Etch.d by H. B. Hall N.Y. 1876.

Geoffrey Chaucer.

FORDS, HOWARD & HULBERT, N.Y.

The woman of a thousand summers back,
Godiva, wife to that grim Earl who ruled
In Coventry : for when he laid a tax
Upon his town, and all the mothers brought
Their children, clamoring, "If we pay, we
　　starve !"
She sought her lord, and found him, where he strode
About the hall, among his dogs, alone,
His beard a foot before him, and his hair
A yard behind. She told him of their tears,
And prayed him, "If they pay this tax, they
　　starve."
Whereat he stared, replying, half amazed,
"You would not let your little finger ache
For such as *these*?"— "But I would die," said
　　she.
He laughed, and swore by Peter and by Paul :
Then filliped at the diamond in her ear ;
"O, ay, ay, ay, you talk !"— "Alas !" she said,
"But prove me what it is I would not do."
And from a heart as rough as Esau's hand,
He answered, "Ride you naked through the town,
And I repeal it" ; and nodding, as in scorn,
He parted, with great strides among his dogs.

So left alone, the passions of her mind,
As winds from all the compass shift and blow,
Made war upon each other for an hour,
Till pity won. She sent a herald forth,
And bade him cry, with sound of trumpet, all
The hard condition ; but that she would loose
The people : therefore, as they loved her well,
From then till noon no foot should pace the street,
No eye look down, she passing ; but that all
Should keep within, door shut and window barred.

Then fled she to her inmost bower, and there
Unclasped the wedded eagles of her belt,
The grim Earl's gift ; but ever at a breath
She lingered, looking like a summer moon
Half dipt in cloud : anon she shook her head,
And showered the rippled ringlets to her knee ;
Unclad herself in haste ; adown the stair
Stole on ; and, like a creeping sunbeam, slid
From pillar unto pillar, until she reached
The gateway ; there she found her palfrey trapt
In purple blazoned with armorial gold.

Then she rode forth, clothed on with chastity :
The deep air listened round her as she rode,
And all the low wind hardly breathed for fear.
The little wide-mouthed heads upon the spout
Had cunning eyes to see : the barking cur
Made her cheek flame : her palfrey's footfall shot
Light horrors through her pulses : the blind
　　walls
Were full of chinks and holes ; and overhead
Fantastic gables, crowding, stared : but she
Not less through all bore up, till, last, she saw
The white-flowered elder-thicket from the field
Gleam through the Gothic archways in the wall.

Then she rode back, clothed on with chastity :
And one low churl, compact of thankless earth,
The fatal byword of all years to come,
Boring a little auger-hole in fear,
Peeped — but his eyes, before they had their
　　will,
Were shrivelled into darkness in his head,
And dropt before him. So the Powers, who wait
On noble deeds, cancelled a sense misused ;
And she, that knew not, passed : and all at once,
With twelve great shocks of sound, the shameless
　　noon
Was clashed and hammered from a hundred towers,
One after one : but even then she gained
Her bower ; whence re-issuing, robed and crowned,
To meet her lord, she took the tax away,
And built herself an everlasting name.
　　　　　　　　　ALFRED TENNYSON.

THE CANTERBURY PILGRIMS.

THERE also was a NUN, a Prioress,
That in her smiling was full simple and coy ;
Her greatest oath was but by Saint Eloy ;
And she was cleped Madame Eglantine.
Full well she sang the service divine,
Entuned in her nose full sweetly ;
And French she spake full faire and fetisly,
After the school of Stratford at Bow,
For French of Paris was to her unknowe.
At meat was she well ytaught withall ;
She let no morsel from her lips fall,
Nor wet her fingers in her sauce deep ;
Well could she carry a morsel, and well keep,
That no drop neer fell upon her breast.
In courtesie was set full much her lest.
　　.　　　.　　　.　　　.　　　.
And certainly she was of great disport,
And full pleasant, and amiable of port,
　　.　　　.　　　.　　　.　　　.
And took much pains to imitate the air
Of court, and hold a stately manner,
And to be thoughten high of reverence.
But for to speaken of her conscience,
She was so charitable and so piteous,
She would weep if that she saw a mouse
Caught in a trap, if it were dead or bled ;
Two small hounds had she that she fed
With roasted flesh, and milk, and wasted bread,
But sore she wept if one of them were dead,
Or if men smote it with a staff smarte :
She was all conscience and tender heart.
Full seemely her wimple pinched was ;
Her nose was strait ; her eyes were grey as
　　glass,
Her mouth full small, and thereto soft and red ;
But certainly she had a fair forehead.

It was almost a span broad I trow,
For certainly she was not undergrowne.

Full handsome was her cloak, as I was 'ware
Of small coral about her arm she bare
A pair of beads, gauded all with green ;
And thereon hung a broach of gold full shene,
On which was first ywritten a crowned A,
And after, *Amor vincit omnia*.

Another NUN also with her had she
That was her chaplain, and of PRIESTS three.

. . . . .

A good man there was of religion,
That was a poor PARSONE of a town ;
But rich he was in holy thought and work,
He was also a learned man, a clerk,
That Christ's gospel truely would preach.
His parishens devoutly would he teach,
Benigne he was and wondrous diligent,
And in adversity full patient :
And such he was yproved often times ;
Full loth were he to cursen for his tithes,
But rather would he given, out of doubt,
Unto his poor parishioners about,
Of his offering, and eke of his substance ;
He could in little thing have suffisance.
Wide was his parish, and houses far asunder,
But he nor felt nor thought of rain or thunder,
In sickness and in mischief to visit
The farthest in his parish, much and oft,
Upon his feet, and in his hand a staff.
This noble ensample to his sheep he gave.
That first he wrought, and afterward he taught,
Out of the gospel he the words caught,
And this figure he added yet thereto,
That if gold rust, what should iron do ?
And if a priest be foul, on whom we trust,
No wonder if a common man do rust ;
Well ought a priest ensample for to give,
By his cleanness, how his sheep should live.
He set not his benefice to hire,
Or left his sheep bewildered in the mire,
And ran unto London, unto Saint Paul's,
To seeken him a chanterie for souls,
Or with a brotherhood to be withold :
But dwelt at home, and kept well his fold,
So that the wolf ne made it not miscarry.
He was a shepherd and no mercenarie,
And though he holy were, and virtuous,
He was to sinful men not dispiteous,
Nor of his speech dangerous nor high,
But in his teaching discrete and benigne.
To draw his folk to heaven, with fairness,
By good ensample, was his business :
But if were any person obstinate,
Whether he were of high or low estate,
Him would he reprove sharply for the nones,
A better priest I trow that nowhere is.
He waited after neither pomp ne reverence,

Nor maked him no spiced conscience,
But Christ's lore and his Apostles twelve
He taught, but first he followed it himselve.
                                   CHAUCER.

———◆———

THE VICAR.

SOME years ago, ere time and taste
    Had turned our parish topsy-turvy,
When Darnel park was Darnel waste,
    And roads as little known as scurvy,
The man who lost his way between
    St. Mary's Hill and Sandy Thicket
Was always shown across the green,
    And guided to the parson's wicket.

Back flew the bolt of lissom lath ;
    Fair Margaret, in her tidy kirtle,
Led the lorn traveller up the path,
    Through clean-clipt rows of box and myrtle,
And Don and Sancho, Tramp and Tray,
    Upon the parlor steps collected,
Wagged all their tails, and seemed to say,
    "Our master knows you ; you 're expected."

Up rose the reverend Doctor Brown,
    Up rose the doctor's "winsome marrow";
The lady laid her knitting down,
    Her husband clasped his ponderous Barrow.
Whate'er the stranger's caste or creed,
    Pundit or papist, saint or sinner,
He found a stable for his steed,
    And welcome for himself, and dinner.

If, when he reached his journey's end,
    And warmed himself in court or college,
He had not gained an honest friend,
    And twenty curious scraps of knowledge ;
If he departed as he came,
    With no new light on love or liquor,
Good sooth, the traveller was to blame,
    And not the vicarage or the vicar.

His talk was like a stream which runs
    With rapid change from rocks to roses ;
It slipped from politics to puns ;
    It passed from Mahomet to Moses ;
Beginning with the laws which keep
    The planets in their radiant courses,
And ending with some precept deep
    For dressing eels or shoeing horses.

He was a shrewd and sound divine,
    Of loud dissent the mortal terror ;
And when, by dint of page and line,
    He 'stablished truth or startled error,
The Baptist found him far too deep,
    The Deist sighed with saving sorrow,
And the lean Levite went to sleep
    And dreamt of eating pork to-morrow.

His sermon never said or showed
    That earth is foul, that heaven is gracious.
Without refreshment on the road,
    From Jerome or from Athanasius ;
And sure a righteous zeal inspired
    The hand and head that penned and planned
       them,
For all who understood admired,
    And some who did not understand them.

He wrote too, in a quiet way,
    Small treatises, and smaller verses,
And sage remarks on chalk and clay,
    And hints to noble lords and nurses ;
True histories of last year's ghost ;
    Lines to a ringlet or a turban ;
And trifles for the "Morning Post" ;
    And nothings for Sylvanus Urban.

He did not think all mischief fair,
    Although he had a knack of joking ;
He did not make himself a bear,
    Although he had a taste for smoking ;
And when religious sects ran mad,
    He held, in spite of all his learning,
That if a man's belief is bad,
    It will not be improved by burning.

And he was kind, and loved to sit
    In the low hut or garnished cottage,
And praise the farmer's homely wit,
    And share the widow's homelier pottage.
At his approach complaint grew mild,
    And when his hand unbarred the shutter
The clammy lips of fever smiled
    The welcome that they could not utter.

He always had a tale for me
    Of Julius Cæsar or of Venus ;
From him I learned the rule of three,
    Cat's-cradle, leap-frog, and *Quæ genus.*
I used to singe his powdered wig,
    To steal the staff he put such trust in,
And make the puppy dance a jig
    When he began to quote Augustine.

Alack, the change ! In vain I look
    For haunts in which my boyhood trifled ;
The level lawn, the trickling brook,
    The trees I climbed, the beds I rifled !
The church is larger than before,
    You reach it by a carriage entry ;
It holds three hundred people more,
    And pews are fitted for the gentry.

Sit in the vicar's seat ; you'll hear
    The doctrine of a gentle Johnian,
Whose hand is white, whose voice is clear,
    Whose tone is very Ciceronian.

Where is the old man laid ? Look down
    And construe on the slab before you, —
"*Hic jacet Gulielmus Brown,*
    Vir nullâ non donandus lauro."
              WINTHROP MACKWORTH PRAED.

FORTUNE-TELLER.

FROM "THE COMEDY OF ERRORS."

    A HUNGRY lean-faced villain,
A mere anatomy, a mountebank,
A thread-bare juggler, and a fortune-teller,
A needy, hollow-eyed, sharp-looking wretch,
A living dead man. This pernicious slave,
Forsooth, took on him as a conjurer ;
And, gazing in mine eyes, feeling my pulse,
And with no face, as 't were, outfacing me,
Cries out, I was possessed.
              SHAKESPEARE.

SWAGGER.

FROM "MERCHANT OF VENICE."

    I'LL hold thee any wager,
When we are both accoutred like young men,
I'll prove the prettier fellow of the two,
And wear my dagger with the braver grace ;
And speak between the change of man and boy,
With a reed voice ; and turn two mincing steps
Into a manly stride ; and speak of frays,
Like a fine bragging youth ; and tell quaint lies,
How honorable ladies sought my love,
Which I denying, they fell sick and died, —
I could not do withal ; — then I'll repent,
And wish, for all that, that I had not killed them .
And twenty of these puny lies I'll tell ;
That men shall swear I have discontinued school
Above a twelvemonth : I have within my mind
A thousand raw tricks of these bragging Jacks,
Which I will practise.
              SHAKESPEARE.

THE TOILET.

FROM "THE RAPE OF THE LOCK."

    AND now, unveiled, the toilet stands displayed,
Each silver vase in mystic order laid.
First, robed in white, the nymph intent adores,
With head uncovered, the cosmetic powers.
A heavenly image in the glass appears,
To that she bends, to that her eyes she rears ;
The inferior priestess, at her altar's side
Trembling begins the sacred rites of pride.
Unnumbered treasures ope at once, and here
The various offerings of the world appear ;

From each she nicely culls with curious toil,
And decks the goddess with the glittering spoil.
This casket India's glowing gems unlocks,
And all Arabia breathes from yonder box.
The tortoise here and elephant unite,
Transformed to combs, the speckled and the white.
Here files of pins extend their shining rows,
Puffs, powders, patches, bibles, billets-doux.
Now awful beauty puts on all its arms ;
The fair each moment rises in her charms,
Repairs her smiles, awakens every grace,
And calls forth all the wonders of her face ;
Sees by degrees a purer blush arise,
And keener lightnings quicken in her eyes.
The busy sylphs surround their darling care,
These set the head, and those divide the hair,
Some fold the sleeve, whilst others plait the gown ;
And Betty 's praised for labors not her own.

ALEXANDER POPE.

A RECEIPT FOR SALAD.

To make this condiment your poet begs
The pounded yellow of two hard-boiled eggs ;
Two boiled potatoes, passed through kitchen sieve,
Smoothness and softness to the salad give ;
Let onion atoms lurk within the bowl,
And, half suspected, animate the whole ;
Of mordent mustard add a single spoon,
Distrust the condiment that bites so soon ;
But deem it not, thou man of herbs, a fault
To add a double quantity of salt ;
Four times the spoon with oil from Lucca crown,
And twice with vinegar, procured from town ;
And lastly, o'er the flavored compound toss
A magic soupçon of anchovy sauce.
O green and glorious ! O herbaceous treat !
'T would tempt the dying anchorite to eat ;
Back to the world he 'd turn his fleeting soul,
And plunge his fingers in the salad-bowl ;

Serenely full, the epicure would say,
" Fate cannot harm me, — I have dined to-day."

SYDNEY SMITH.

THE PEDLER'S PACK.

FROM " THE WINTER'S TALE."

Enter AUTOLYCUS, *singing.*

LAWN as white as driven snow ;
Cyprus black as e'er was crow ;
Gloves as sweet as damask roses ;
Masks for faces and for noses ;
Bugle bracelet, necklace-amber,
Perfume for a lady's chamber :
Golden quoifs and stomachers,
For my lads to give their dears ;
Pins and poking-sticks of steel,
What maids lack from head to heel :
Come buy of me, come ; come buy, come buy ;
Buy, lads, or else your lasses cry :
Come buy.

SHAKESPEARE.

METRICAL FEET.

TROCHEE trips from long to short ;
From long to long in solemn sort
Slow Spondee stalks ; strong foot ! yet ill able
Ever to come up with Dactyl trisyllable.
Iambics march from short to long ; —
With a leap and a bound the swift Anapæsts
    throng ;
One syllable long, with one short at each side,
Amphibrachys hastes with a stately stride ; —
First and last being long, middle short, Amphi-
    macer
Strikes his thundering hoofs like a proud high-
    bred racer.

SAMUEL TAYLOR COLERIDGE.

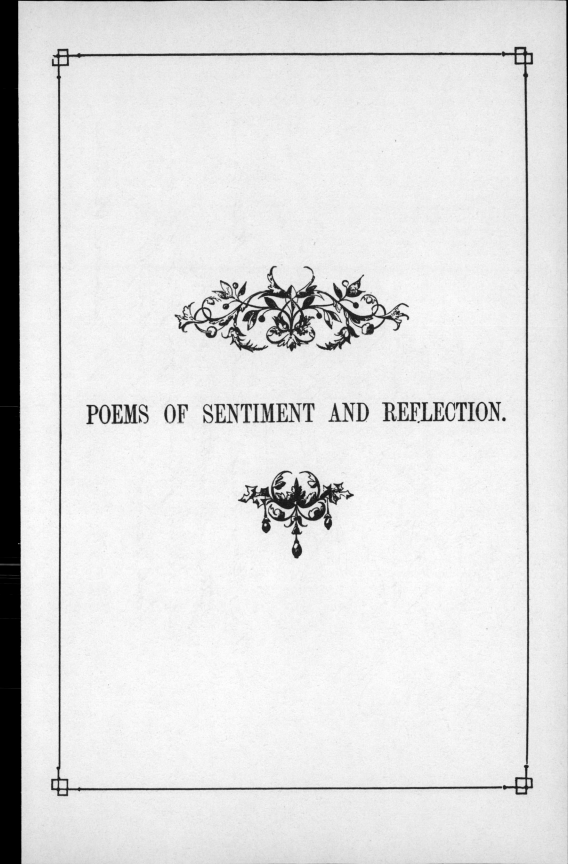

POEMS OF SENTIMENT AND REFLECTION.

They ... hath thy life, thy play ...
... grief or form,
... cheer the living & brave to-day!
They may wait the glad to-morrow,

Fitz-Greene Halleck

———

'Twas ever thus! – Each hour that came,
Still unremitting, brought.
Some newer form of grief or shame,
Some newer cause for thought.

W. Gilmore Simms

POEMS OF SENTIMENT AND REFLECTION.

THE NOBLE NATURE.

It is not growing like a tree
In bulk, doth make man better be;
Or standing long an oak, three hundred year,
To fall a log at last, dry, bald, and sear:
    A lily of a day
    Is fairer far in May,
Although it fall and die that night, —
It was the plant and flower of Light.
In small proportions we just beauties see;
And in short measures life may perfect be.
              BEN JONSON.

MY MINDE TO ME A KINGDOM IS.

My minde to me a kingdom is;
  Such perfect joy therein I finde
As farre exceeds all earthly blisse
  That God or nature hath assignde;
Though much I want that would have,
Yet still my minde forbids to crave.

Content I live; this is my stay, —
  I seek no more than may suffice.
I presse to beare no haughtie sway;
  Look, what I lack my mind supplies.
Loe, thus I triumph like a king,
Content with that my mind doth bring.

I see how plentie surfets oft,
  And hastie clymbers soonest fall;
I see that such as sit aloft
  Mishap doth threaten most of all.
These get with toile, and keepe with feare;
Such cares my mind could never beare.

No princely pompe nor welthie store,
  No force to win the victorie,
No wylie wit to salve a sore,
  No shape to winne a lover's eye, —
To none of these I yeeld as thrall;
For why, my mind despiseth all.

Some have too much, yet still they crave;
  I little have, yet seek no more.
They are but poore, though much they have,
  And I am rich with little store.
They poor, I rich; they beg, I give;
They lacke, I lend; they pine, I live.

I laugh not at another's losse,
  I grudge not at another's gaine;
No worldly wave my mind can tosse;
  I brooke that is another's bane.
I feare no foe, nor fawne on friend;
I lothe not life, nor dread mine end.

I joy not in no earthly blisse;
  I weigh not Cresus' wealth a straw;
For care, I care not what it is;
  I feare not fortune's fatal law;
My mind is such as may not move
For beautie bright, or force of love.

I wish but what I have at will;
  I wander not to seeke for more;
I like the plaine, I clime no hill;
  In greatest stormes I sitte on shore,
And laugh at them that toile in vaine
To get what must be lost againe.

I kisse not where I wish to kill;
  I feigne not love where most I hate;
I breake no sleepe to winne my will;
  I wayte not at the mightie's gate.
I scorne no poore, I feare no rich;
I feele no want, nor have too much.

The court ne cart I like ne loath, —
  Extreames are counted worst of all;
The golden meane betwixt them both
  Doth surest sit, and feares no fall;
This is my choyce; for why, I finde
No wealth is like a quiet minde.

My wealth is health and perfect ease;
  My conscience clere my chiefe defence;
I never seeke by bribes to please,
  Nor by desert to give offence.
Thus do I live, thus will I die;
Would all did so as well as I!
              WILLIAM BYRD.

BEAUTY.

'T is much immortal beauty to admire,
But more immortal beauty to withstand ;
The perfect soul can overcome desire,
If beauty with divine delight be scanned.
For what is beauty but the blooming child
Of fair Olympus, that in night must end,
And be forever from that bliss exiled,
If admiration stand too much its friend ?
The wind may be enamored of a flower,
The ocean of the green and laughing shore,
The silver lightning of a lofty tower, —
But must not with too near a love adore ;
Or flower and margin and cloud-capped tower
Love and delight shall with delight devour !
LORD THURLOW.

THOUGHT.

THOUGHT is deeper than all speech,
  Feeling deeper than all thought;
Souls to souls can never teach
  What unto themselves was taught.

We are spirits clad in veils ;
  Man by man was never seen ;
All our deep communing fails
  To remove the shadowy screen.

Heart to heart was never known ;
  Mind with mind did never meet ;
We are columns left alone
  Of a temple once complete.

Like the stars that gem the sky,
  Far apart though seeming near,
In our light we scattered lie ;
  All is thus but starlight here.

What is social company
  But a babbling summer stream ?
What our wise philosophy
  But the glancing of a dream ?

Only when the sun of love
  Melts the scattered stars of thought,
Only when we live above
  What the dim-eyed world hath taught.

Only when our souls are fed
  By the fount which gave them birth,
And by inspiration led
  Which they never drew from earth,

We, like parted drops of rain,
  Swelling till they meet and run,
Shall be all absorbed again,
  Melting, flowing into one.
CHRISTOPHER PEARSE CRANCH.

PRELUDE TO THE VOICES OF THE NIGHT.

PLEASANT it was, when woods were green,
  And winds were soft and low,
To lie amid some sylvan scene,
Where, the long drooping boughs between,
Shadows dark and sunlight sheen
  Alternate come and go ;

Or where the denser grove receives
  No sunlight from above,
But the dark foliage interweaves
In one unbroken roof of leaves,
Underneath whose sloping eaves
  The shadows hardly move.

Beneath some patriarchal tree
  I lay upon the ground ;
His hoary arms uplifted he,
And all the broad leaves over me
Clapped their little hands in glee,
  With one continuous sound ; —

A slumberous sound, a sound that brings
  The feelings of a dream,
As of innumerable wings,
As, when a bell no longer swings,
Faint the hollow murmur rings
  O'er meadow, lake, and stream.

And dreams of that which cannot die,
  Bright visions, came to me,
As lapped in thought I used to lie,
And gaze into the summer sky,
Where the sailing clouds went by,
  Like ships upon the sea ;

Dreams that the soul of youth engage
  Ere Fancy has been quelled ;
Old legends of the monkish page,
Traditions of the saint and sage,
Tales that have the rime of age,
  And chronicles of eld.

And, loving still these quaint old themes,
  Even in the city's throng
I feel the freshness of the streams
That, crossed by shades and sunny gleams,
Water the green land of dreams,
  The holy land of song.
HENRY WADSWORTH LONGFELLOW.

THE INNER VISION.

MOST sweet it is with unuplifted eyes
To pace the ground, if path there be or none,
While a fair region round the Traveller lies
Which he forbears again to look upon ;

Pleased rather with some soft ideal scene,
The work of Fancy, or some happy tone
Of meditation, slipping in between
The beauty coming and the beauty gone.

If Thought and Love desert us, from that day
Let us break off all commerce with the Muse :
With Thought and Love companions of our way, —

Whate'er the senses take or may refuse, —
The Mind's internal heaven shall shed her dews
Of inspiration on the humblest lay.
WILLIAM WORDSWORTH.

THE POET'S REWARD.

FROM "SNOW-BOUND."

THANKS untraced to lips unknown
Shall greet me like the odors blown
From unseen meadows newly mown,
Or lilies floating in some pond,
Wood-fringed, the wayside gaze beyond ;
The traveller owns the grateful sense
Of sweetness near, he knows not whence,
And, pausing, takes with forehead bare
The benediction of the air.
JOHN GREENLEAF WHITTIER.

IMAGINATION.

FROM "MIDSUMMER NIGHT'S DREAM."

THESEUS. More strange than true : I never may
        believe
These antique fables, nor these fairy toys.
Lovers and madmen have such seething brains,
Such shaping fantasies, that apprehend
More than cool reason ever comprehends.
The lunatic, the lover, and the poet
Are of imagination all compact :
One sees more devils than vast hell can hold, —
That is, the madman ; the lover, all as frantic,
Sees Helen's beauty in a brow of Egypt ;
The poet's eye, in a fine frenzy rolling,
Doth glance from heaven to earth, from earth to
        heaven ;
And, as imagination bodies forth
The forms of things unknown, the poet's pen
Turns them to shapes, and gives to airy nothing
A local habitation and a name.
SHAKESPEARE.

CONTENTMENT.

I WEIGH not fortune's frown or smile ;
  I joy not much in earthly joys ;
I seek not state, I reck not style ;
  I am not fond of fancy's toys :

I rest so pleased with what I have
I wish no more, no more I crave.

I quake not at the thunder's crack ;
  I tremble not at news of war ;
I swound not at the news of wrack ;
  I shrink not at a blazing star ;
I fear not loss, I hope not gain,
I envy none, I none disdain.

I see ambition never pleased ;
  I see some Tantals starved in store ;
I see gold's dropsy seldom eased ;
  I see even Midas gape for more ;
I neither want nor yet abound, —
Enough 's a feast, content is crowned.

I feign not friendship where I hate ;
  I fawn not on the great (in show) ;
I prize, I praise a mean estate, —
  Neither too lofty nor too low :
This, this is all my choice, my cheer, —
A mind content, a conscience clear.
JOSHUA SYLVESTER.

THE WANTS OF MAN.

"MAN wants but little here below,
  Nor wants that little long."
'T is not with me exactly so ;
  But 't is so in the song.
My wants are many and, if told,
  Would muster many a score ;
And were each wish a mint of gold,
  I still should long for more.

What first I want is daily bread —
  And canvas-backs — and wine —
And all the realms of nature spread
  Before me, when I dine.
Four courses scarcely can provide
  My appetite to quell ;
With four choice cooks from France beside,
  To dress my dinner well.

What next I want, at princely cost,
  Is elegant attire :
Black sable furs for winter's frost,
  And silks for summer's fire,
And Cashmere shawls, and Brussels lace
  My bosom's front to deck, —
And diamond rings my hands to grace,
  And rubies for my neck.

I want (who does not want ?) a wife, —
  Affectionate and fair ;
To solace all the woes of life,
  And all its joys to share.

Of temper sweet, of yielding will,
　Of firm, yet placid mind, —
With all my faults to love me still
　With sentiment refined.

And as Time's car incessant runs,
　And Fortune fills my store,
I want of daughters and of sons
　From eight to half a score.
I want (alas ! can mortal dare
　Such bliss on earth to crave ?)
That all the girls be chaste and fair, —
　The boys all wise and brave.

I want a warm and faithful friend,
　To cheer the adverse hour ;
Who ne'er to flatter will descend,
　Nor bend the knee to power, —
A friend to chide me when I 'm wrong,
　My inmost soul to see ;
And that my friendship prove as strong
　For him as his for me.

I want the scals of power and place,
　The ensigns of command ;
Charged by the People's unbought grace
　To rule my native land.
Nor crown nor sceptre would I ask
　But from my country's will,
By day, by night, to ply the task
　Her cup of bliss to fill.

I want the voice of honest praise
　To follow me behind,
And to be thought in future days
　The friend of human-kind,
That after ages, as they rise,
　Exulting may proclaim
In choral union to the skies
　Their blessings on my name.

These are the *Wants* of mortal *Man,* —
　I cannot want them long,
For life itself is but a span,
　And earthly bliss — a song.
My last great *Want* — absorbing all —
　Is, when beneath the sod,
And summoned to my final call,
　The *Mercy of my God.*

JOHN QUINCY ADAMS.

WASHINGTON, August 31, 1841.

CONTENTMENT.

"Man wants but little here below."

LITTLE I ask ; my wants are few ;
　I only wish a hut of stone,
(A *very plain* brown stone will do,)
　That I may call my own ;

And close at hand is such a one,
　In yonder street that fronts the sun.

Plain food is quite enough for me ;
　Three courses are as good as ten ; —
If nature can subsist on three,
　　Thank Heaven for three.　Amen !
I always thought cold victual nice ; —
My *choice* would be vanilla-ice.

I care not much for gold or land ; —
　Give me a mortgage here and there, —
Some good bank-stock, — some note of hand,
　Or trifling railroad share, —
I only ask that Fortune send
A *little* more than I shall spend.

Honors are silly toys, I know,
　And titles are but empty names ;
I would, *perhaps,* be Plenipo, —
　But only near St. James ;
I 'm very sure I should not care
To fill our Gubernator's chair.

Jewels are bawbles ; 't is a sin
　To care for such unfruitful things ; —
One good-sized diamond in a pin, —
　Some, *not so large,* in rings, —
A ruby, and a pearl or so,
Will do for me ; — I laugh at show.

My dame should dress in cheap attire ;
　(Good heavy silks are never dear ;) —
I own perhaps I *might* desire
　Some shawls of true Cashmere, —
Some marrowy crapes of China silk,
Like wrinkled skins on scalded milk.

I would not have the horse I drive
　So fast that folks must stop and stare ;
An easy gait, — two, forty-five, —
　Suits me ; I do not care ; —
Perhaps, for just a *single spurt,*
Some seconds less would do no hurt.

Of pictures, I should like to own
　Titians and Raphaels three or four, —
I love so much their style and tone, —
　One Turner, and no more,
(A landscape, — foreground golden dirt, —
The sunshine painted with a squirt.)

Of books but few, — some fifty score
　For daily use, and bound for wear ;
The rest upon an upper floor ; —
　Some *little* luxury *there*
Of red morocco's gilded gleam,
And vellum rich as country cream.

Busts, cameos, gems, — such things as these,
 Which others often show for pride,
I value for their power to please,
 And selfish churls deride ; —
One Stradivarius, I confess,
Two Meerschaums, I would fain possess.

Wealth's wasteful tricks I will not learn,
 Nor ape the glittering upstart fool ; —
Shall not carved tables serve my turn,
 But *all* must be of buhl ?
Give grasping pomp its double share, —
I ask but *one* recumbent chair.

Thus humble let me live and die,
 Nor long for Midas' golden touch ;
If Heaven more generous gifts deny,
 I shall not miss them *much*, —
Too grateful for the blessing lent
Of simple tastes and mind content !
 OLIVER WENDELL HOLMES.

CONTENTATION.

DIRECTED TO MY DEAR FATHER, AND MOST WORTHY
FRIEND, MR. ISAAC WALTON.

HEAVEN, what an age is this ! what race
 Of giants are sprung up, that dare
Thus fly in the Almighty's face,
 And with his providence make war !

I can go nowhere but I meet
 With malecontents and mutineers,
As if in life was nothing sweet,
 And we must blessings reap in tears.

O senseless man ! that murmurs still
 For happiness, and does not know,
Even though he might enjoy his will,
 What he would have to make him so.

Is it true happiness to be
 By undiscerning Fortune placed
In the most eminent degree,
 Where few arrive, and none stand fast ?

Titles and wealth are Fortune's toils,
 Wherewith the vain themselves insnare :
The great are proud of borrowed spoils,
 The miser's plenty breeds his care.

The one supinely vawns at rest,
 The other eternally doth toil ;
Each of them equally a beast,
 A pampered horse, or laboring moil :

The titulados oft disgraced
 By public hate or private frown,

And he whose hand the creature raised
 Has yet a foot to kick him down.

The drudge who would all get, all save,
 Like a brute beast, both feeds and lies ;
Prone to the earth, he digs his grave,
 And in the very labor dies.

Excess of ill-got, ill-kept pelf
 Does only death and danger breed ;
Whilst one rich worldling starves himself
 With what would thousand others feed.

By which we see that wealth and power,
 Although they make men rich and great,
The sweets of life do often sour,
 And gull ambition with a cheat.

Nor is he happier than these,
 Who, in a moderate estate,
Where he might safely live at ease,
 Has lusts that are immoderate.

For he, by those desires misled,
 Quits his own vine's securing shade,
To expose his naked, empty head
 To all the storms man's peace invade.

Nor is he happy who is trim,
 Tricked up in favors of the fair,
Mirrors, with every breath made dim,
 Birds, caught in every wanton snare.

Woman, man's greatest woe or bliss,
 Does oftener far than serve, enslave
And with the magic of a kiss
 Destroys whom she was made to save.

O fruitful grief, the world's disease !
 And vainer man, to make it so,
Who gives his miseries increase
 By cultivating his own woe.

There are no ills but what we make
 By giving shapes and names to things, —
Which is the dangerous mistake
 That causes all our sufferings.

We call that sickness which is health,
 That persecution which is grace,
That poverty which is true wealth,
 And that dishonor which is praise.

Alas ! our time is here so short
 That in what state soe'er 't is spent,
Of joy or woe, does not import,
 Provided it be innocent.

But we may make it pleasant too,
 If we will take our measures right,

And not what Heaven has done undo
By an unruly appetite.

The world is full of beaten roads,
But yet so slippery withal,
That where one walks secure 't is odds
A hundred and a hundred fall.

Untrodden paths are then the best,
Where the frequented are unsure ;
And he comes soonest to his rest
Whose journey has been most secure.

It is content alone that makes
Our pilgrimage a pleasure here ;
And who buys sorrow cheapest takes
An ill commodity too dear.

CHARLES COTTON.

THE REAPER.

BEHOLD her single in the field,
Yon solitary Highland Lass !
Reaping and singing by herself ;
Stop here, or gently pass !
Alone she cuts and binds the grain,
And sings a melancholy strain ;
O listen ! for the vale profound
Is overflowing with the sound.

No nightingale did ever chaunt
More welcome notes to weary bands
Of travellers in some shady haunt
Among Arabian sands ;
No sweeter voice was ever heard
In spring-time from the cuckoo-bird,
Breaking the silence of the seas
Among the farthest Hebrides.

Will no one tell me what she sings ?
Perhaps the plaintive numbers flow
For old, unhappy, far-off things,
And battles long ago :
Or is it some more humble lay,
Familiar matter of to-day ?
Some natural sorrow, loss, or pain,
That has been, and may be again !

Whate'er the theme, the maiden sang
As if her song could have no ending ;
I saw her singing at her work,
And o'er the sickle bending ;
I listened till I had my fill ;
And as I mounted up the hill
The music in my heart I bore
Long after it was heard no more.

WILLIAM WORDSWORTH.

THE PEASANT.

FROM " THE PARISH REGISTER."

A NOBLE peasant, Isaac Ashford, died.
Noble he was, contemning all things mean,
His truth unquestioned and his soul serene.
Of no man's presence Isaac felt afraid ;
At no man's question Isaac looked dismayed ;
Shame knew him not, he dreaded no disgrace ;
Truth, simple truth, was written in his face ;
Yet while the serious thought his soul approved,
Cheerful he seemed, and gentleness he loved ;
To bliss domestic he his heart resigned,
And with the firmest had the fondest mind ;
Were others joyful, he looked smiling on,
And gave allowance where he needed none ;
Good he refused with future ill to buy,
Nor knew a joy that caused reflection's sigh ;
A friend to virtue, his unclouded breast
No envy stung, no jealousy distressed ;
(Bane of the poor ! it wounds their weaker mind
To miss one favor which their neighbors find ;)
Yet far was he from Stoic pride removed ;
He felt humanely, and he warmly loved.
I marked his action, when his infant died,
And his old neighbor for offence was tried ;
The still tears, stealing down that furrowed cheek,
Spoke pity plainer than the tongue can speak.
If pride were his, 't was not their vulgar pride
Who in their base contempt the great deride ;
Nor pride in learning, though my clerk agreed,
If fate should call him, Ashford might succeed ;
Nor pride in rustic skill, although we knew
None his superior, and his equals few ; —
But if that spirit in his soul had place,
It was the jealous pride that shuns disgrace ;
A pride in honest fame, by virtue gained
In sturdy boys to virtuous labors trained ;
Pride in the power that guards his country's coast,
And all that Englishmen enjoy and boast ;
Pride in a life that slander's tongue defied, —
In fact, a noble passion misnamed pride.

GEORGE CRABBE.

THE HAPPY MAN.

FROM " THE WINTER WALK AT NOON."

HE is the happy man whose life even now
Shows somewhat of that happier life to come ;
Who, doomed to an obscure but tranquil state,
Is pleased with it, and, were he free to choose,
Would make his fate his choice ; whom peace,
the fruit
Of virtue, and whom virtue, fruit of faith,
Prepare for happiness ; bespeak him one
Content indeed to sojourn while he must
Below the skies, but having there his home.

The world o'erlooks him in her busy search
Of objects, more illustrious in her view;
And, occupied as earnestly as she,
Though more sublimely, he o'erlooks the world.
She scorns his pleasures, for she knows them not;
He seeks not hers, for he has proved them vain.
He cannot skim the ground like summer birds
Pursuing gilded flies; and such he deems
Her honors, her emoluments, her joys.
Therefore in contemplation is his bliss,
Whose power is such that whom she lifts from earth
She makes familiar with a heaven unseen,
And shows him glories yet to be revealed.
Not slothful he, though seeming unemployed,
And censured oft as useless.   Stillest streams
Oft water fairest meadows, and the bird
That flutters least is longest on the wing.

WILLIAM COWPER.

HAPPINESS.

FROM THE "ESSAY ON MAN."

O HAPPINESS! our being's end and aim!
Good, pleasure, ease, content! whate'er thy name:
That something still which prompts the eternal
   sigh
For which we bear to live or dare to die,
Which still so near us, yet beyond us lies,
O'erlooked, seen double, by the fool, and wise.
Plant of celestial seed! if dropped below,
Say, in what mortal soil thou deign'st to grow?
Fair opening to some court's propitious shrine,
Or deep with diamonds in the flaming mine?
Twined with the wreaths Parnassian laurels yield,
Or reaped in iron harvests of the field?
Where grows? — where grows it not? If vain
   our toil,
We ought to blame the culture, not the soil:
Fixed to no spot is happiness sincere,
'T is nowhere to be found, or everywhere:
'T is never to be bought, but always free,
And fled from monarchs, St. John! dwells with
   thee.
   Ask of the learned the way? The learned are
   blind;
This bids to serve, and that to shun mankind;
Some place the bliss in action, some in ease,
Those call it pleasure, and contentment these;
Some, sunk to beasts, find pleasure end in pain;
Some, swelled to gods, confess even virtue vain!
Or, indolent, to each extreme they fall, —
To trust in everything, or doubt of all.
   Who thus define it, say they more or less
Than this, that happiness is happiness?
   Take nature's path, and mad opinion's leave;
All states can reach it, and all heads conceive;

Obvious her goods, in no extreme they dwell;
There needs but thinking right and meaning well;
And mourn our various portions as we please,
Equal is common sense and common ease.

ALEXANDER POPE.

A HAPPY LIFE.

How happy is he born and taught
   That serveth not another's will;
Whose armor is his honest thought,
   And simple truth his utmost skill!

Whose passions not his masters are,
   Whose soul is still prepared for death,
Not tied unto the world with care
   Of public fame or private breath;

Who envies none that chance doth raise,
   Or vice; who never understood
How deepest wounds are given by praise;
   Nor rules of state, but rules of good;

Who hath his life from rumors freed,
   Whose conscience is his strong retreat;
Whose state can neither flatterers feed,
   Nor ruin make accusers great;

Who God doth late and early pray
   More of his grace than gifts to lend;
And entertains the harmless day
   With a well-chosen book or friend, —

This man is freed from servile bands
   Of hope to rise, or fear to fall;
Lord of himself, though not of lands;
   And, having nothing, yet hath all.

SIR HENRY WOTTON.

THE HERMIT.

AT the close of the day, when the hamlet is still,
And mortals the sweets of forgetfulness prove,
When naught but the torrent is heard on the hill,
And naught but the nightingale's song in the grove,
'T was thus, by the cave of the mountain afar,
While his harp rung symphonious, a hermit began;
No more with himself or with nature at war,
He thought as a sage, though he felt as a man:

"Ah! why, all abandoned to darkness and woe,
Why, lone Philomela, that languishing fall?
For spring shall return, and a lover bestow,
And sorrow no longer thy bosom inthrall.
But, if pity inspire thee, renew the sad lay, —
Mourn, sweetest complainer, man calls thee to
   mourn!
O, soothe him whose pleasures like thine pass away!
Full quickly they pass, — but they never return.

"Now, gliding remote on the verge of the sky,
The moon, half extinguished, her crescent dis-
    plays;
But lately I marked when majestic on high
She shone, and the planets were lost in her blaze.
Roll on, thou fair orb, and with gladness pursue
The path that conducts thee to splendor again!
But man's faded glory what change shall renew?
Ah, fool! to exult in a glory so vain!

"'T is night, and the landscape is lovely no more.
I mourn,—but, ye woodlands, I mourn not for you;
For morn is approaching your charms to restore,
Perfumed with fresh fragrance, and glittering
    with dew.
Nor yet for the ravage of winter I mourn, —
Kind nature the embryo blossom will save;
But when shall spring visit the mouldering urn?
O, when shall day dawn on the night of the grave?

"'T was thus, by the glare of false science betrayed,
That leads to bewilder, and dazzles to blind,
My thoughts wont to roam from shade onward to
    shade,
Destruction before me, and sorrow behind.
'O pity, great Father of light,' then I cried,
'Thy creature, who fain would not wander from
    thee!
Lo, humbled in dust, I relinquish my pride;
From doubt and from darkness thou only canst
    free.'

"And darkness and doubt are now flying away;
No longer I roam in conjecture forlorn.
So breaks on the traveller, faint and astray,
The bright and the balmy effulgence of morn.
See truth, love, and mercy in triumph descending,
And nature all glowing in Eden's first bloom!
On the cold cheek of death smiles and roses are
    blending,
And beauty immortal awakes from the tomb."
                            JAMES BEATTIE.

THE CROWDED STREET.

LET me move slowly through the street,
    Filled with an ever-shifting train,
Amid the sound of steps that beat
    The murmuring walks like autumn rain.

How fast the flitting figures come!
    The mild, the fierce, the stony face, —
Some bright with thoughtless smiles, and some
    Where secret tears have left their trace.

They pass — to toil, to strife, to rest;
    To halls in which the feast is spread;
To chambers where the funeral guest
    In silence sits beside the dead.

And some to happy homes repair,
    Where children, pressing cheek to cheek,
With mute caresses shall declare
    The tenderness they cannot speak.

And some, who walk in calmness here,
    Shall shudder as they reach the door
Where one who made their dwelling dear,
    Its flower, its light, is seen no more.

Youth, with pale cheek and slender frame,
    And dreams of greatness in thine eye!
Go'st thou to build an early name,
    Or early in the task to die?

Keen son of trade, with eager brow!
    Who is now fluttering in thy snare?
Thy golden fortunes, tower they now,
    Or melt the glittering spires in air?

Who of this crowd to-night shall tread
    The dance till daylight gleam again?
Who sorrow o'er the untimely dead?
    Who writhe in throes of mortal pain?

Some, famine-struck, shall think how long
    The cold, dark hours, how slow the light;
And some, who flaunt amid the throng,
    Shall hide in dens of shame to-night.

Each where his tasks or pleasures call,
    They pass, and heed each other not.
There is who heeds, who holds them all
    In His large love and boundless thought.

These struggling tides of life, that seem
    In wayward, aimless course to tend,
Are eddies of the mighty stream
    That rolls to its appointed end.
                    WILLIAM CULLEN BRYANT.

RETIREMENT.

FAREWELL, thou busy world, and may
    We never meet again;
Here I can eat and sleep and pray,
And do more good in one short day
Then he who his whole age outwears
Upon the most conspicuous theatres,
Where naught but vanity and vice appears.

Good God! how sweet are all things here!
How beautiful the fields appear!
    How cleanly do we feed and lie!
Lord! what good hours do we keep!
How quietly we sleep!
    What peace, what unanimity!
How innocent from the lewd fashion
Is all our business, all our recreation.

O, how happy here 's our leisure !
O, how innocent our pleasure !
O ye valleys ! O ye mountains !
O ye groves and crystal fountains !
How I love, at liberty,
By turns to come and visit ye !

Dear solitude, the soul's best friend,
That man acquainted with himself dost make,
And all his Maker's wonders to intend,
    With thee I here converse at will,
    And would be glad to do so still,
For is it thou alone that keep'st the soul awake.

    How calm and quiet a delight
        Is it, alone
    To read and meditate and write,
        By none offended, and offending none !
    To walk, ride, sit, or sleep at one's own case ;
And, pleasing a man's self, none other to displease.

    O my beloved nymph, fair Dove,
    Princess of rivers, how I love
        Upon thy flowery banks to lie,
        And view thy silver stream,
    When gilded by a summer's beam !
        And in it all thy wanton fry
            Playing at liberty,
    And with my angle upon them
        The all of treachery
    I ever learned industriously to try !

Such streams Rome's yellow Tiber cannot show,
The Iberian Tagus, or Ligurian Po ;
The Maese, the Danube, and the Rhine,
Are puddle-water, all, compared with thine ;
And Loire's pure streams yet too polluted are
With thine, much purer, to compare ;
The rapid Garonne and the winding Seine
        Are both too mean,
        Beloved Dove, with thee
        To vie priority ;
Nay, Tame and Isis, when conjoined, submit,
And lay their trophies at thy silver feet.

O my belovéd rocks, that rise
To awe the earth and brave the skies !
From some aspiring mountain's crown
        How dearly do I love,
Giddy with pleasure, to look down,
And from the vales to view the noble heights
            above !
O my beloved caves ! from dog-star's heat,
And all anxieties, my safe retreat ;
What safety, privacy, what true delight,
        In the artificial night
        Your gloomy entrails make,
        Have I taken, do I take !
How oft, when grief has made me fly,
To hide me from society

E'en of my dearest friends, have I,
        In your recesses' friendly shade,
    All my sorrows open laid,
And my most secret woes intrusted to your
            privacy !

Lord ! would men let me alone,
What an over-happy one
        Should I think myself to be, —
Might I in this desert place,
(Which most men in discourse disgrace,)
        Live but undisturbed and free !
Here in this despised recess,
        Would I, maugre winter's cold
And the summer's worst excess,
Try to live out to sixty full years old ;
        And, all the while,
            Without an envious eye
    On any thriving under Fortune's smile,
Contented live, and then contented die.
                        CHARLES COTTON.

───────

VERSES

SUPPOSED TO BE WRITTEN BY ALEXANDER SELKIRK,
DURING HIS SOLITARY ABODE IN THE ISLAND OF
JUAN FERNANDEZ.

I AM monarch of all I survey, —
    My right there is none to dispute ;
From the centre all round to the sea,
    I am lord of the fowl and the brute.
O Solitude ! where are the charms
    That sages have seen in thy face ?
Better dwell in the midst of alarms
    Than reign in this horrible place.

I am out of humanity's reach ;
    I must finish my journey alone,
Never hear the sweet music of speech, —
    I start at the sound of my own.
The beasts that roam over the plain
    My form with indifference see ;
They are so unacquainted with man,
    Their tameness is shocking to me.

Society, friendship, and love,
    Divinely bestowed upon man !
O, had I the wings of a dove,
    How soon would I taste you again !
My sorrows I then might assuage
    In the ways of religion and truth, —
Might learn from the wisdom of age,
    And be cheered by the sallies of youth.

Religion ! what treasure untold
    Resides in that heavenly word ! —
More precious than silver and gold,
    Or all that this earth can afford ;

But the sound of the church-going bell
   These valleys and rocks never heard,
Never sighed at the sound of a knell,
   Or smiled when a sabbath appeared.

Ye winds that have made me your sport,
   Convey to this desolate shore
Some cordial, endearing report
   Of a land I shall visit no more !
My friends, — do they now and then send
   A wish or a thought after me ?
O, tell me I yet have a friend,
   Though a friend I am never to see.

How fleet is a glance of the mind !
   Compared with the speed of its flight,
The tempest itself lags behind,
   And the swift-winged arrows of light.
When I think of my own native land,
   In a moment I seem to be there ;
But, alas ! recollection at hand
   Soon hurries me back to despair.

But the sea-fowl is gone to her nest,
   The beast is laid down in his lair ;
Even here is a season of rest,
   And I to my cabin repair.
There 's mercy in every place,
   And mercy — encouraging thought ! —
Gives even affliction a grace,
   And reconciles man to his lot.
WILLIAM COWPER.

THE GOOD GREAT MAN.

How seldom, friend, a good great man inherits
   Honor and wealth, with all his worth and pains !
It seems a story from the world of spirits
When any man obtains that which he merits,
   Or any merits that which he obtains.

For shame, my friend ! renounce this idle strain !
What wouldst thou have a good great man obtain ?
Wealth, title, dignity, a golden chain,
Or heap of corses which his sword hath slain ?
Goodness and greatness are not means, but ends.

Hath he not always treasures, always friends,
The great good man ? Three treasures, — love, and light,
   And calm thoughts, equable as infant's breath ;
And three fast friends, more sure than day or night, —
   Himself, his Maker, and the angel Death.
SAMUEL TAYLOR COLERIDGE.

EXAMPLE.

WE scatter seeds with careless hand,
   And dream we ne'er shall see them more ;
     But for a thousand years
     Their fruit appears,
In weeds that mar the land,
   Or healthful store.

The deeds we do, the words we say, —
   Into still air they seem to fleet,
     We count them ever past ;
     But they shall last, —
In the dread judgment they
   And we shall meet !

I charge thee by the years gone by,
   For the love's sake of brethren dear,
     Keep thou the one true way,
     In work and play,
Lest in that world their cry
   Of woe thou hear.
JOHN KEBLE.

MERCY.

FROM "MERCHANT OF VENICE."

THE quality of mercy is not strained, —
It droppeth as the gentle rain from heaven
Upon the place beneath : it is twice blessed, —
It blesseth him that gives, and him that takes :
'T is mightiest in the mightiest ; it becomes
The thronéd monarch better than his crown ;
His sceptre shows the force of temporal power,
The attribute to awe and majesty,
Wherein doth sit the dread and fear of kings :
But mercy is above this sceptred sway, —
It is enthronéd in the hearts of kings,
It is an attribute to God himself ;
And earthly power doth then show likest God's,
When mercy seasons justice.
SHAKESPEARE.

THE GLOVE AND THE LIONS.

KING FRANCIS was a hearty king, and loved a
   royal sport,
And one day, as his lions fought, sat looking on
   the court.
The nobles filled the benches, with the ladies in
   their pride,
And 'mongst them sat the Count de Lorge, with
   one for whom he sighed :
And truly 't was a gallant thing to see that
   crowning show,
Valor and love, and a king above, and the royal
   beasts below.

Ramped and roared the lions, with horrid laugh-
    ing jaws ;
They bit, they glared, gave blows like beams, a
    wind went with their paws ;
With wallowing might and stifled roar they rolled
    on one another,
Till all the pit with sand and mane was in a
    thunderous smother ;
The bloody foam above the bars came whisking
    through the air ;
Said Francis then, "Faith, gentlemen, we 're
    better here than there."

De Lorge's love o'erheard the King, a beauteous
    lively dame,
With smiling lips and sharp bright eyes, which
    always seemed the same ;
She thought, The Count my lover is brave as
    brave can be ;
He surely would do wondrous things to show his
    love of me ;
King, ladies, lovers, all look on ; the occasion is
    divine ;
I 'll drop my glove, to prove his love ; great glory
    will be mine.

She dropped her glove, to prove his love, then
    looked at him and smiled ;
He bowed, and in a moment leaped among the
    lions wild :
The leap was quick, return was quick, he has re-
    gained his place,
Then threw the glove, but not with love, right
    in the lady's face.
"By Heaven," said Francis, "rightly done !"
    and he rose from where he sat ;
"No love," quoth he, "but vanity, sets love a
    task like that."
               LEIGH HUNT.

PERFECTION.

FROM "KING JOHN."

To gild refined gold, to paint the lily,
To throw a perfume on the violet,
To smooth the ice, or add another hue
Unto the rainbow, or with taper-light
To seek the beauteous eye of heaven to garnish,
Is wasteful, and ridiculous excess.
               SHAKSPEARE.

REPUTATION.

FROM "OTHELLO."

GOOD name in man and woman, dear my lord,
Is the immediate jewel of their souls :

Who steals my purse, steals trash ; 't is some-
    thing, nothing ;
'T was mine, 't is his, and has been slave to
    thousands ;
But he that filches from me my good name
Robs me of that which not enriches him,
And makes me poor indeed.
               SHAKSPEARE.

SLEEP.

WEEP ye no more, sad fountains !
    What need you flow so fast ?
Look how the snowy mountains
    Heaven's sun doth gently waste.
But my sun's heavenly eyes
    View not your weeping,
    That now lies sleeping
Softly, now softly lies
        Sleeping

Sleep is a reconciling, —
    A rest that peace begets ;
Doth not the sun rise smiling,
    When fair at even he sets ?
Rest you then, rest, sad eyes, —
    Melt not in weeping,
    While she lies sleeping
Softly, now softly lies
        Sleeping.
             JOHN DOWLAND.

INVOCATION TO SLEEP.

COME, Sleep, and with thy sweet deceiving
    Lock me in delight awhile ;
    Let some pleasing dreams beguile
    All my fancies, that from thence
    I may feel an influence,
All my powers of care bereaving !

Though but a shadow, but a sliding,
    Let me know some little joy !
    We that suffer long annoy
    Are contented with a thought,
    Through an idle fancy wrought : .
O, let my joys have some abiding !
          BEAUMONT and FLETCHER.

SLEEP.

COME, Sleep, O Sleep, the certain knot of peace,
The baiting-place of wit, the balm of woe,
The poor man's wealth, the prisoner's release,
The indifferent judge between the high and low,

With shield of proof shield me from out the prease
Of those fierce darts Despair at me doth throw ;
O, make in me those civil wars to cease :
I will good tribute pay, if thou do so.
Take thou of me smooth pillows, sweetest bed ;
A chamber deaf to noise, and blind to light ;
A rosy garland, and a weary head.
And if these things, as being thine by right,
Move not thy heavy grace, thou shalt in me
Livelier than elsewhere Stella's image see.

SIR PHILIP SIDNEY.

SLEEP.

OF all the thoughts of God that are
Borne inward unto souls afar,
Among the Psalmist's music deep,
Now tell me if that any is
For gift or grace surpassing this, —
"He giveth his beloved sleep" ?

What would we give to our beloved ?
The hero's heart, to be unmoved, —
The poet's star-tuned harp, to sweep, —
The patriot's voice, to teach and rouse, —
The monarch's crown, to light the brows ?
"He giveth his beloved sleep."

What do we give to our beloved ?
A little faith, all undisproved, —
A little dust, to overweep, —
And bitter memories, to make
The whole earth blasted for our sake,
"He giveth his beloved sleep."

"Sleep soft, beloved !" we sometimes say,
But have no tune to charm away
Sad dreams that through the eyelids creep ;
But never doleful dream again
Shall break the happy slumber when
"He giveth his beloved sleep."

O earth, so full of dreary noise !
O men, with wailing in your voice !
O delvéd gold the wailers heap !
O strife, O curse, that o'er it fall !
God strikes a silence through you all,
And "giveth his beloved sleep."

His dews drop mutely on the hill,
His cloud above it saileth still,
Though on its slope men sow and reap ;
More softly than the dew is shed,
Or cloud is floated overhead,
"He giveth his beloved sleep."

For me, my heart, that erst did go
Most like a tired child at a show,

That sees through tears the mummers leap,
Would now its wearied vision close,
Would childlike on His love repose
Who "giveth his beloved sleep."

ELIZABETH BARRETT BROWNING.

SLEEP.

FROM "SECOND PART OF HENRY IV."

KING HENRY. How many thousand of my
    poorest subjects
Are at this hour asleep ! — O sleep ! O gentle
    sleep !
Nature's soft nurse, how have I frighted thee,
That thou no more wilt weigh my eyelids down,
And steep my senses in forgetfulness ?
Why rather, sleep, liest thou in smoky cribs,
Upon uneasy pallets stretching thee,
And hushed with buzzing night-flies to thy
    slumber,
Than in the perfumed chambers of the great,
Under the canopies of costly state,
And lulled with sounds of sweetest melody ?
O thou dull god ! why liest thou with the vile,
In loathsome beds, and leav'st the kingly couch,
A watch-case, or a common 'larum-bell ?
Wilt thou upon the high and giddy mast
Seal up the ship-boy's eyes, and rock his brains
In cradle of the rude imperious surge,
And in the visitation of the winds,
Who take the ruffian billows by the top,
Curling their monstrous heads, and hanging them
With deafening clamors in the slippery clouds,
That, with the hurly, death itself awakes ?
Canst thou, O partial sleep ! give thy repose
To the wet sea-boy in an hour so rude ;
And in the calmest and most stillest night,
With all appliances and means to boot,
Deny it to a king ?   Then, happy low, lie down,
Uneasy lies the head that wears a crown.

FROM "FIRST PART OF HENRY IV."

GLENDOWER. She bids you on the wanton
    rushes lay you down,
And rest your gentle head upon her lap,
And she will sing the song that pleaseth you,
And on your eyelids crown the god of sleep,
Charming your blood with pleasing heaviness ;
Making such difference betwixt wake and sleep,
As is the difference betwixt day and night,
The hour before the heavenly-harnessed team
Begins his golden progress in the east.

FROM "CYMBELINE."

Weariness

Can snore upon the flint, when restive sloth
Finds the down pillow hard.

FROM " MACBETH."

Macbeth does murder sleep, — the innocent sleep,
Sleep that knits up the ravelled sleave of care,
The death of each day's life, sore labor's bath,
Balm of hurt minds, great nature's second course,
Chief nourisher in life's feast.

FROM " THE TEMPEST."

We are such stuff
As dreams are made of, and our little life
Is rounded with a sleep.
SHAKESPEARE.

———◆———

IANTHE, SLEEPING.

How wonderful is Death !
Death and his brother Sleep !
'One, pale as yonder waning moon,
With lips of lurid blue ;
The other, rosy as the morn
When, throned on ocean's wave,
It blushes o'er the world :
Yet both so passing wonderful !

Hath then the gloomy Power
Whose reign is in the tainted sepulchres
Seized on her sinless soul ?
Must then that peerless form
Which love and admiration cannot view
Without a beating heart, those azure veins
Which steal like streams along a field of snow,
That lovely outline which is fair
As breathing marble, perish ?
Must putrefaction's breath
Leave nothing of this heavenly sight
But loathsomeness and ruin ?
Spare nothing but a gloomy theme,
On which the lightest heart might moralize ?
Or is it only a sweet slumber
Stealing o'er sensation,
Which the breath of roseate morning
Chaseth into darkness ?
Will Ianthe wake again,
And give that faithful bosom joy,
Whose sleepless spirit waits to catch
Light, life, and rapture from her smile ?

Yes ! she will wake again,
Although her glowing limbs are motionless,
And silent those sweet lips,
Once breathing eloquence
That might have soothed a tiger's rage,
Or thawed the cold heart of a conqueror.
Her dewy eyes are closed,
And on their lids, whose texture fine

Scarce hides the dark blue orbs beneath,
The baby Sleep is pillowed :
Her golden tresses shade
The bosom's stainless pride,
Curling like tendrils of the parasite
Around a marble column.

. . . . . .

A gentle start convulsed Ianthe's frame :
Her veiny eyelids quietly unclosed ;
Moveless awhile the dark blue orbs remained.
She looked around in wonder, and beheld
Henry, who kneeled in silence by her couch,
Watching her sleep with looks of speechless love,
And the bright-beaming stars
That through the casement shone.
PERCY BYSSHE SHELLEY.

———◆———

SLEEPLESSNESS.

A FLOCK of sheep that leisurely pass by
One after one ; the sound of rain, and bees
Murmuring ; the fall of rivers, winds and seas,
Smooth fields, white sheets of water, and pure sky ;

I 've thought of all by turns, and still I lie
Sleepless ; and soon the small birds' melodies
Must hear, first uttered from my orchard trees,
And the first cuckoo's melancholy cry.

Even thus last night, and two nights more I lay,
And could not win thee, Sleep ! by any stealth :
So do not let me wear to-night away :
Without thee what is all the morning's wealth ?
Come, blessèd barrier between day and day,
Dear mother of fresh thoughts and joyous health !
WILLIAM WORDSWORTH.

———◆———

CARILLON.

IN the ancient town of Bruges,
In the quaint old Flemish city,
As the evening shades descended,
Low and loud and sweetly blended,
Low at times and loud at times,
And changing like a poet's rhymes,
Rang the beautiful wild chimes
From the Belfry in the market
Of the ancient town of Bruges.

Then, with deep sonorous clangor
Calmly answering their sweet anger,
When the wrangling bells had ended,
Slowly struck the clock eleven,
And, from out the silent heaven,
Silence on the town descended.
Silence, silence everywhere,

On the earth and in the air,
Save that footsteps here and there
Of some burgher home returning,
By the street lamps faintly burning,
For a moment woke the echoes
Of the ancient town of Bruges.

But amid my broken slumbers
Still I heard those magic numbers,
As they loud proclaimed the flight
And stole marches of the night ;
Till their chimes in sweet collision
Mingled with each wandering vision,
Mingled with the fortune-telling
Gypsy-bands of dreams and fancies,
Which amid the waste expanses
Of the silent land of trances
Have their solitary dwelling ;
All else seemed asleep in Bruges,
In the quaint old Flemish city.

And I thought how like these chimes
Are the poet's airy rhymes,
All his rhymes and roundelays,
His conceits, and songs, and ditties,
From the belfry of his brain,
Scattered downward, though in vain,
On the roofs and stones of cities !
For by night the drowsy ear
Under its curtains cannot hear,
And by day men go their ways,
Hearing the music as they pass,
But deeming it no more, alas !
Than the hollow sound of brass.

Yet perchance a sleepless wight,
Lodging at some humble inn
In the narrow lanes of life,
When the dusk and hush of night
Shut out the incessant din
Of daylight and its toil and strife,
May listen with a calm delight
To the poet's melodies,
Till he hears, or dreams he hears,
Intermingled with the song,
Thoughts that he has cherished long ;
Hears amid the chime and singing
The bells of his own village ringing,
And wakes, and finds his slumberous eyes
Wet with most delicious tears.

Thus dreamed I, as by night I lay
In Bruges, at the Fleur-de-Blé,
Listening with a wild delight
To the chimes that, through the night,
Rang their changes from the Belfry
Of that quaint old Flemish city.

HENRY WADSWORTH LONGFELLOW.

THE DREAM OF CLARENCE.

FROM "RICHARD III."

CLARENCE. O, I have passed a miserable night !
So full of fearful dreams, of ugly sights,
That, as I am a Christian faithful man,
I would not spend another such a night,
Though 't were to buy a world of happy days, —
So full of dismal terror was the time !
Methought that I had broken from the Tower,
And was embarked to cross to Burgundy,
And, in my company, my brother Gloster,
Who from my cabin tempted me to walk
Upon the hatches ; thence we looked toward
     England,
And cited up a thousand heavy times,
During the wars of York and Lancaster,
That had befallen us.   As we paced along
Upon the giddy footing of the hatches,
Methought that Gloster stumbled ; and, in fall-
     ing,
Struck me, that thought to stay him, overboard,
Into the tumbling billows of the main.
O Lord ! methought what pain it was to drown !
What dreadful noise of water in mine ears !
What sights of ugly death within mine eyes !
Methought I saw a thousand fearful wrecks ;
A thousand men that fishes gnawed upon ;
Wedges of gold, great anchors, heaps of pearl,
Inestimable stones, unvalued jewels,
All scattered in the bottom of the sea :
Some lay in dead men's skulls ; and in those holes
Where eyes did once inhabit, there were crept
(As 't were in scorn of eyes) reflecting gems,
That wooed the slimy bottom of the deep,
And mocked the dead bones that lay scattered by.
   BRAKENBURY. Had you such leisure, in the
     time of death,
To gaze upon these secrets of the deep ?
   CLAR. Methought I had ; and often did I strive
To yield the ghost : but still the envious flood
Stopt in my soul, and would not let it forth
To seek the empty, vast, and wandering air ;
But smothered it within my panting bulk,
Which almost burst to belch it in the sea.
   BRAK. Awaked you not with this sore agony ?
   CLAR. No, no, my dream was lengthened after
     life :
O, then began the tempest to my soul !
I passed, methought, the melancholy flood,
With that grim ferryman which poets write of,
Unto the kingdom of perpetual night.
The first that there did greet my stranger soul
Was my great father-in-law, renownéd Warwick ;
Who cried aloud, "What scourge for perjury
Can this dark monarchy afford false Clarence ?"
And so he vanished : then came wandering by
A shadow like an angel, with bright hair

Dabbled in blood ; and he shrieked out aloud,
"Clarence is come, — false, fleeting, perjured
    Clarence, —
That stabbed me in the field by Tewksbury ; —
Seize on him, Furies ! take him to your torments !"
With that, methought, a legion of foul fiends
Environed me, and howléd in mine ears
Such hideous cries, that, with the very noise,
I trembling waked, and, for a season after,
Could not believe but that I was in hell, —
Such terrible impression made my dream.

SHAKESPEARE.

THE DREAM.

I.

OUR life is twofold ; sleep hath its own world,
A boundary between the things misnamed
Death and existence : sleep hath its own world,
And a wide realm of wild reality,
And dreams in their development have breath,
And tears, and tortures, and the touch of joy ;
They leave a weight upon our waking thoughts,
They take a weight from off waking toils,
They do divide our being ; they become
A portion of ourselves as of our time,
And look like heralds of eternity ;
They pass like spirits of the past, — they speak
Like sibyls of the future ; they have power, —
The tyranny of pleasure and of pain ;
They make us what we were not, — what they
    will,
And shake us with the vision that 's gone by,
The dread of vanished shadows. — Are they so ?
Is not the past all shadow ? What are they ?
Creations of the mind ? — The mind can make
Substances, and people planets of its own
With beings brighter than have been, and give
A breath to forms which can outlive all flesh.
I would recall a vision which I dreamed
Perchance in sleep, — for in itself a thought,
A slumbering thought, is capable of years,
And curdles a long life into one hour.

II.

I saw two beings in the hues of youth
Standing upon a hill, a gentle hill,
Green and of a mild declivity, the last
As 't were the cape of a long ridge of such,
Save that there was no sea to lave its base,
But a most living landscape, and the wave
Of woods and cornfields, and the abodes of men
Scattered at intervals, and wreathing smoke
Arising from such rustic roofs ; the hill
Was crowned with a peculiar diadem
Of trees, in circular array, so fixed,

Not by the sport of nature, but of man :
These two, a maiden and a youth, were there
Gazing, — the one on all that was beneath
Fair as herself, — but the boy gazed on her ;
And both were young, and one was beautiful .
And both were young, — yet not alike in youth.
As the sweet moon on the horizon's verge,
The maid was on the eve of womanhood ;
The boy had fewer summers, but his heart
Had far outgrown his years, and to his eye
There was but one belovéd face on earth,
And that was shining on him ; he had looked
Upon it till it could not pass away ;
He had no breath, no being, but in hers ;
She was his voice ; he did not speak to her,
But trembled on her words ; she was his sight,
For his eye followed hers, and saw with hers,
Which colored all his objects ; — he had ceased
To live within himself : she was his life,
The ocean to the river of his thoughts,
Which terminated all ; upon a tone,
A touch of hers, his blood would ebb and flow,
And his cheek change tempestuously, — his heart
Unknowing of its cause of agony.
But she in these fond feelings had no share :
Her sighs were not for him ; to her he was
Even as a brother, — but no more ; 't was much,
For brotherless she was, save in the name
Her infant friendship had bestowéd on him ;
Herself the solitary scion left
Of a time-honored race. It was a name
Which pleased him, and yet pleased him not, —
    and why ?
Time taught him a deep answer — when she loved
Another ; even *now* she loved another,
And on the summit of that hill she stood
Looking afar if yet her lover's steed
Kept pace with her expectancy, and flew.

III.

A change came o'er the spirit of my dream.
There was an ancient mansion, and before
Its walls there was a steed caparisoned ;
Within an antique oratory stood
The boy of whom I spake ; — he was alone,
And pale, and pacing to and fro : anon
He sate him down, and seized a pen, and traced
Words which I could not guess of ; then he leaned
His bowed head on his hands and shook, as 't
    were
With a convulsion, — then rose again,
And with his teeth and quivering hands did tear
What he had written, but he shed no tears.
And he did calm himself, and fix his brow
Into a kind of quiet ; as he paused,
The lady of his love re-entered there ;
She was serene and smiling then, and yet
She knew she was by him beloved ; she knew —

For quickly comes such knowledge, that his
    heart
Was darkened with her shadow, and she saw
That he was wretched, but she saw not all.
He rose, and with a cold and gentle grasp
He took her hand; a moment o'er his face
A tablet of unutterable thoughts
Was traced, and then it faded, as it came;
He dropped the hand he held, and with slow steps
Retired, but not as bidding her adieu,
For they did part with mutual smiles; he passed
From out the massy gate of that old Hall.
And mounting on his steed he went his way;
And ne'er repassed that hoary threshold more.

IV.

A change came o'er the spirit of my dream.
The boy was sprung to manhood; in the wilds
Of fiery climes he made himself a home,
And his soul drank their sunbeams; he was girt
With strange and dusky aspects; he was not
Himself like what he had been; on the sea
And on the shore he was a wanderer;
There was a mass of many images
Crowded like waves upon me, but he was
A part of all; and in the last he lay
Reposing from the noontide sultriness,
Couched among fallen columns, in the shade
Of ruined walls that had survived the names
Of those who reared them; by his sleeping side
Stood camels grazing, and some goodly steeds
Were fastened near a fountain; and a man,
Clad in a flowing garb, did watch the while,
While many of his tribe slumbered around:
And they were canopied by the blue sky,
So cloudless, clear, and purely beautiful,
That God alone was to be seen in heaven.

V.

A change came o'er the spirit of my dream.
The lady of his love was wed with one
Who did not love her better: in her home,
A thousand leagues from his, — her native home,
She dwelt, begirt with growing infancy,
Daughters and sons of beauty, — but behold!
Upon her face there was the tint of grief,
The settled shadow of an inward strife,
And an unquiet drooping of the eye,
As if its lid were charged with unshed tears.
What could her grief be? — she had all she loved,
And he who had so loved her was not there
To trouble with bad hopes, or evil wish,
Or ill-repressed affliction, her pure thoughts.
What could her grief be? — she had loved him
    not,
Nor given him cause to deem himself beloved,
Nor could he be a part of that which preyed
Upon her mind — a spectre of the past.

VI.

A change came o'er the spirit of my dream.
The wanderer was returned. — I saw him stand
Before an altar — with a gentle bride;
Her face was fair, but was not that which made
The starlight of his boyhood; — as he stood
Even at the altar, o'er his brow there came
The selfsame aspect and the quivering shock
That in the antique oratory shook
His bosom in its solitude; and then —
As in that hour — a moment o'er his face
The tablet of unutterable thoughts
Was traced, — and then it faded as it came,
And he stood calm and quiet, and he spoke
The fitting vows, but heard not his own words,
And all things reeled around him; he could see
Not that which was, nor that which should have
    been, —
But the old mansion, and the accustomed hall,
And the remembered chambers, and the place,
The day, the hour, the sunshine, and the shade,
All things pertaining to that place and hour,
And her who was his destiny, came back
And thrust themselves between him and the light;
What business had they there at such a time?

VII.

A change came o'er the spirit of my dream.
The lady of his love; — O, she was changed,
As by the sickness of the soul! her mind
Had wandered from its dwelling, and her eyes,
They had not their own lustre, but the look
Which is not of the earth; she was become
The queen of a fantastic realm; her thoughts
Were combinations of disjointed things;
And forms impalpable and unperceived
Of others' sight familiar were to hers.
And this the world calls frenzy; but the wise
Have a far deeper madness, and the glance
Of melancholy is a fearful gift;
What is it but the telescope of truth?
Which strips the distance of its fantasies,
And brings life near in utter nakedness,
Making the cold reality too real!

VIII.

A change came o'er the spirit of my dream.
The wanderer was alone as heretofore,
The beings which surrounded him were gone,
Or were at war with him; he was a mark
For blight and desolation, compassed round
With hatred and contention; pain was mixed
In all which was served up to him, until,
Like to the Pontiac monarch of old days,
He fed on poisons, and they had no power,
But were a kind of nutriment; he lived
Through that which had been death to many men.

And made him friends of mountains ; with the
    stars
And the quick Spirit of the universe
He held his dialogues : and they did teach
To him the magic of their mysteries ;
To him the book of Night was opened wide,
And voices from the deep abyss revealed
A marvel and a secret. — Be it so.

IX.

My dream was past ; it had no further change.
It was of a strange order, that the doom
Of these two creatures should be thus traced out
Almost like a reality, — the one
To end in madness, — both in misery.
                       BYRON.

YUSSOUF.

A STRANGER came one night to Yussouf's tent,
Saying, " Behold one outcast and in dread,
Against whose life the bow of power is bent,
Who flies, and hath not where to lay his head ;
I come to thee for shelter and for food,
To Yussouf, called through all our tribes 'The
    Good.' "

"This tent is mine," said Yussouf, "but no more
Than it is God's ; come in, and be at peace ;
Freely shalt thou partake of all my store
As I of His who buildeth over these
Our tents his glorious roof of night and day,
And at whose door none ever yet heard Nay."

So Yussouf entertained his guest that night,
And, waking him ere day, said : " Here is gold,
My swiftest horse is saddled for thy flight,
Depart before the prying day grow bold."
As one lamp lights another, nor grows less,
So nobleness enkindleth nobleness.

That inward light the stranger's face made grand,
Which shines from all self-conquest ; kneeling low,
He bowed his forehead upon Yussouf's hand,
Sobbing : "O Sheik, I cannot leave thee so ;
I will repay thee ; all this thou hast done
Unto that Ibrahim who slew thy son !"

"Take thrice the gold," said Yussouf, "for with
    thee
Into the desert, never to return,
My one black thought shall ride away from me ;
First-born, for whom by day and night I yearn,
Balanced and just are all of God's decrees ;
Thou art avenged, my first-born, sleep in peace !"
           JAMES RUSSELL LOWELL.

JAFFAR.

JAFFAR, the Barmecide, the good vizier,
The poor man's hope, the friend without a peer,
Jaffar was dead, slain by a doom unjust ;
And guilty Haroun, sullen with mistrust
Of what the good, and e'en the bad, might say,
Ordained that no man living from that day
Should dare to speak his name on pain of death.
All Araby and Persia held their breath ;

All but the brave Mondeer : he, proud to show
How far for love a grateful soul could go,
And facing death for very scorn and grief
(For his great heart wanted a great relief),
Stood forth in Bagdad daily, in the square
Where once had stood a happy house, and there
Harangued the tremblers at the scymitar
On all they owed to the divine Jaffar.

"Bring me this man," the caliph cried ; the man
Was brought, was gazed upon. The mutes began
To bind his arms. "Welcome, brave cords,"
    cried he ;
"From bonds far worse Jaffar delivered me ;
From wants, from shames, from loveless house-
    hold fears ;
Made a man's eyes friends with delicious tears ;
Restored me, loved me, put me on a par
With his great self. How can I pay Jaffar ?"

Haroun, who felt that on a soul like this
The mightiest vengeance could but fall amiss,
Now deigned to smile, as one great lord of fate
Might smile upon another half as great.
He said, "Let worth grow frenzied if it will ;
The caliph's judgment shall be master still.
Go, and since gifts so move thee, take this gem,
The richest in the Tartar's diadem,
And hold the giver as thou deemest fit !"
"Gifts !" cried the friend ; he took, and hold-
    ing it
High toward the heavens, as though to meet his
    star,
Exclaimed, "This, too, I owe to thee, Jaffar !"
               LEIGH HUNT.

HARMOSAN.

Now the third and fatal conflict for the Persian
    throne was done,
And the Moslem's fiery valor had the crowning
    victory won.

Harmosan, the last and boldest the invader to
    defy,
Captive, overborne by numbers, they were bring-
    ing forth to die.

Then exclaimed that noble captive: "Lo, I per-
    ish in my thirst ;
Give me but one drink of water, and let then
    arrive the worst ! "

In his hand he took the goblet; but awhile the
    draught forbore,
Seeming doubtfully the purpose of the foeman to
    explore.

Well might then have paused the bravest, — for,
    around him, angry foes
With a hedge of naked weapons did that lonely
    man enclose.

"But what fear'st thou ?" cried the caliph; "is
    it, friend, a secret blow ?
Fear it not ! our gallant Moslems no such
    treacherous dealing know.

"Thou mayst quench thy thirst securely, for
    thou shalt not die before
Thou hast drunk that cup of water, — this reprieve
    is thine — no more ! "

Quick the satrap dashed the goblet down to
    earth with ready hand,
And the liquid sank forever, lost amid the burn-
    ing sand.

"Thou hast said that mine my life is, till the
    water of that cup
I have drained ; then bid thy servants that
    spilled water gather up ! "

For a moment stood the caliph as by doubtful
    passions stirred ;
Then exclaimed, "Forever sacred must remain
    a monarch's word.

"Bring another cup, and straightway to the
    noble Persian give :
Drink, I said before, and perish, — now I bid
    thee drink and live ! "
                RICHARD CHENEVIX TRENCH.

ABOU BEN ADHEM.

ABOU BEN ADHEM (may his tribe increase !)
Awoke one night from a deep dream of peace,
And saw within the moonlight in his room,
Making it rich and like a lily in bloom,
An angel writing in a book of gold :
Exceeding peace had made Ben Adhem bold,
And to the presence in the room he said,
"What writest thou ?" — The vision raised its
    head,
And, with a look made of all sweet accord,
Answered, "The names of those who love the
    Lord."

"And is mine one ?" said Abou. "Nay, not
    so,"
Replied the angel. — Abou spoke more low,
But cheerly still ; and said, "I pray thee, then,
Write me as one that loves his fellow-men."

The angel wrote, and vanished.   The next night
It came again, with a great wakening light,
And showed the names whom love of God had
    blessed, —
And, lo ! Ben Adhem's name led all the rest !
                LEIGH HUNT.

A PSALM OF LIFE.

TELL me not, in mournful numbers,
    Life is but an empty dream !
For the soul is dead that slumbers,
    And things are not what they seem.

Life is real ! Life is earnest !
    And the grave is not its goal ;
Dust thou art, to dust returnest,
    Was not spoken of the soul.

Not enjoyment, and not sorrow,
    Is our destined end or way ;
But to act, that each to-morrow
    Find us farther than to-day.

Art is long, and Time is fleeting,
    And our hearts, though stout and brave,
Still, like muffled drums, are beating
    Funeral marches to the grave.

In the world's broad field of battle,
    In the bivouac of Life,
Be not like dumb, driven cattle !
    Be a hero in the strife !

Trust no Future, howe'er pleasant !
    Let the dead Past bury its dead !
Act, — act in the living Present !
    Heart within, and God o'erhead !

Lives of great men all remind us
    We can make our lives sublime,
And, departing, leave behind us
    Footprints on the sands of time ; —

Footprints, that perhaps another,
    Sailing o'er life's solemn main,
A forlorn and shipwrecked brother,
    Seeing, shall take heart again.

Let us, then, be up and doing,
    With a heart for any fate ;
Still achieving, still pursuing,
    Learn to labor and to wait.
           HENRY WADSWORTH LONGFELLOW.

To Thee, I fondly hoped to cleave,
A forever whom Death alone could sever
But only with malignant Grasp,
Has torn thee from my Breast forever

FROM PHILASTER.

I FOUND him sitting by a fountain-side,
Of which he borrowed some to quench his thirst,
And paid the nymph again as much in tears.
A garland lay him by, made by himself,
Of many several flowers, bred in the bay,
Stuck in that mystic order, that the rareness
Delighted me : but ever when he turned
His tender eyes upon them he would weep,
As if he meant to make them grow again.
Seeing such pretty helpless innocence
Dwell in his face, I asked him all his story.
He told me that his parents gentle died,
Leaving him to the mercy of the fields,
Which gave him roots ; and of the crystal springs,
Which did not stop their courses ; and the sun,
Which still, he thanked him, yielded him his light.
Then took he up his garland, and did show
What every flower, as country people hold,
Did signify ; and how all, ordered thus,
Expressed his grief ; and to my thoughts did read
The prettiest lecture of his country art
That could be wished ; so that methought I could
Have studied it.   I gladly entertained him,
Who was as glad to follow.

                    BEAUMONT and FLETCHER.

WHY THUS LONGING?

WHY thus longing, thus forever sighing,
    For the far-off, unattained and dim,
While the beautiful, all round thee lying,
    Offers up its low, perpetual hymn?

Wouldst thou listen to its gentle teaching,
    All thy restless yearnings it would still ;
Leaf and flower and laden bee are preaching
    Thine own sphere, though humble, first to fill.

Poor indeed thou must be, if around thee
    Thou no ray of light and joy canst throw,
If no silken cord of love hath bound thee
    To some little world through weal and woe ;

If no dear eyes thy fond love can brighten, —
    No fond voices answer to thine own ;
If no brother's sorrow thou canst lighten,
    By daily sympathy and gentle tone.

                    HARRIET WINSLOW.

'T IS SWEET.

FROM "DON JUAN.

            . . . . 'T is sweet to hear,
At midnight on the blue and moonlit deep,
The song and oar of Adria's gondolier,
    By distance mellowed, o'er the waters sweep;

'T is sweet to see the evening star appear ;
    'T is sweet to listen as the night-winds creep
From leaf to leaf ; 't is sweet to view on high
The rainbow, based on ocean, span the sky.

'T is sweet to hear the watch-dog's honest bark
    Bay deep-mouthed welcome as we draw near
        home ;
'T is sweet to know there is an eye will mark
    Our coming, and look brighter when we come ;
'T is sweet to be awakened by the lark,
    Or lulled by falling waters ; sweet the hum
Of bees, the voice of girls, the song of birds,
The lisp of children, and their earliest words.

Sweet is the vintage, when the showering grapes
    In Bacchanal profusion reel to earth,
Purple and gushing : sweet are our escapes
    From civic revelry to rural mirth ;
Sweet to the miser are his glittering heaps ;
    Sweet to the father is his first-born's birth ;
Sweet is revenge, — especially to women,
Pillage to soldiers, prize-money to seamen.

.   .   .   .

'T is sweet to win, no matter how, one's laurels,
    By blood or ink ; 't is sweet to put an end
To strife ; 't is sometimes sweet to have our
        quarrels,
    Particularly with a tiresome friend ;
Sweet is old wine in bottles, ale in barrels ;
    Dear is the helpless creature we defend
Against the world ; and dear the school-boy spot
We ne'er forget, though there we are forgot.

But sweeter still than this, than these, than all,
    Is first and passionate love, — it stands alone,
Like Adam's recollection of his fall ;
    The tree of knowledge has been plucked, — all 's
        known, —
And life yields nothing further to recall
    Worthy of this ambrosial sin, so shown,
No doubt in fable, as the unforgiven
Fire which Prometheus filched for us from heaven.

                    BYRON.

L' ALLEGRO.

HENCE, loathed Melancholy,
    Of Cerberus and blackest Midnight born !
    In Stygian cave forlorn,
'Mongst horrid shapes, and shrieks, and sights
        unholy,
    Find out some uncouth cell,
Where brooding darkness spreads his jealous
        wings,
And the night-raven sings ;
There under ebon shades, and low-browed rocks,

As ragged as thy locks,
  In dark Cimmerian desert ever dwell.
But come, thou goddess fair and free,
In heaven ycleped Euphrosyne,
And, by men, heart-easing Mirth !
Whom lovely Venus, at a birth,
With two sister Graces more,
To ivy-crowned Bacchus bore ;
Or whether (as some sages sing)
The frolic wind that breathes the spring,
Zephyr, with Aurora playing, —
As he met her once a-Maying, —
There, on beds of violets blue
And fresh-blown roses washed in dew,
Filled her with thee, a daughter fair,
So buxom, blithe, and debonair.

  Haste thee, nymph, and bring with thee
Jest, and youthful Jollity, —
Quips and cranks and wanton wiles,
Nods and becks and wreathéd smiles,
Such as hang on Hebe's cheek,
And love to live in dimple sleek, —
Sport, that wrinkled Care derides,
And Laughter, holding both his sides.
Come ! and trip it, as you go,
On the light fantastic toe ;
And in thy right hand lead with thee
The mountain nymph, sweet Liberty;
And if I give thee honor due,
Mirth, admit me of thy crew,
To live with her, and live with thee,
In unreprovéd pleasures free, —
To hear the lark begin his flight,
And singing startle the dull Night,
From his watch-tower in the skies,
Till the dappled Dawn doth rise ;
Then to come, in spite of Sorrow,
And at my window bid good morrow,
Through the sweet-brier, or the vine,
Or the twisted eglantine ;
While the cock with lively din
Scatters the rear of darkness thin,
And to the stack, or the barn door,
Stoutly struts his dames before ;
Oft listening how the hounds and horn
Cheerly rouse the slumbering morn,
From the side of some hoar hill
Through the high wood echoing shrill ;
Sometime walking, not unseen,
By hedge-row elms, on hillocks green,
Right against the eastern gate,
Where the great sun begins his state,
Robed in flames, and amber light,
The clouds in thousand liveries dight ;
While the ploughman near at hand
Whistles o'er the furrowed land,
And the milkmaid singeth blithe,

And the mower whets his scythe,
And every shepherd tells his tale
Under the hawthorn in the dale.

  Straight mine eye hath caught new pleasures,
Whilst the landscape round it measures
Russet lawns, and fallows gray,
Where the nibbling flocks do stray, —
Mountains, on whose barren breast
The laboring clouds do often rest, —
Meadows trim with daisies pied,
Shallow brooks, and rivers wide.
Towers and battlements it sees
Bosomed high in tufted trees,
Where perhaps some beauty lies,
The cynosure of neighboring eyes.
Hard by, a cottage chimney smokes
From betwixt two aged oaks,
Where Corydon and Thyrsis met,
Are at their savory dinner set
Of herbs, and other country messes,
Which the neat-handed Phillis dresses ;
And then in haste her bower she leaves,
With Thestylis to bind the sheaves ;
Or, if the earlier season lead,
To the tanned haycock in the mead.
Sometimes with secure delight
The upland hamlets will invite,
When the merry bells ring round,
And the jocund rebecks sound
To many a youth, and many a maid,
Dancing in the checkered shade ;
And young and old come forth to play
On a sunshine holiday,
Till the livelong daylight fail ;
Then to the spicy nut-brown ale
With stories told of many a feat :
How fairy Mab the junkets eat, —
She was pinched and pulled, she said,
And he, by friar's lantern led ;
Tells how the drudging goblin sweat
To earn his cream-bowl duly set,
When in one night, ere glimpse of morn,
His shadowy flail hath threshed the corn
That ten day-laborers could not end ;
Then lies him down the lubber fiend,
And, stretched out all the chimney's length,
Basks at the fire his hairy strength,
And, crop-full, out of doors he flings
Ere the first cock his matin rings.

  Thus done the tales, to bed they creep,
By whispering winds soon lulled asleep.
Towered cities please us then,
And the busy hum of men,
Where throngs of knights and barons bold
In weeds of peace high triumphs hold, —
With store of ladies, whose bright eyes
Rain influence, and judge the prize

Of wit or arms, while both contend
To win her grace whom all commend.
There let Hymen oft appear
In saffron robe, with taper clear,
And pomp and feast and revelry,
With mask, and antique pageantry, —
Such sights as youthful poets dream
On summer eves by haunted stream ;
Then to the well-trod stage anon,
If Johnson's learnéd sock be on,
Or sweetest Shakespeare, fancy's child,
Warble his native wood-notes wild.

And ever, against eating cares,
Lap me in soft Lydian airs,
Married to immortal verse,
Such as the meeting soul may pierce,
In notes with many a winding bout
Of linkéd sweetness long drawn out,
With wanton heed and giddy cunning
The melting voice through mazes running,
Untwisting all the chains that tie
The hidden soul of harmony, —
That Orpheus' self may heave his head
From golden slumber on a bed
Of heaped Elysian flowers, and hear
Such strains as would have won the ear
Of Pluto, to have quite set free
His half-regained Eurydice.

These delights if thou canst give,
Mirth, with thee I mean to live.
                              JOHN MILTON.

MUSIC.

FROM "TWELFTH NIGHT."

DUKE. IF music be the food of love, play on ;
Give me excess of it, that, surfeiting,
The appetite may sicken, and so die.
That strain again ; — it had a dying fall :
O, it came o'er my ear like the sweet south,
That breathes upon a bank of violets,
Stealing, and giving odor.
                              SHAKESPEARE.

THE soul of music slumbers in the shell,
Till waked and kindled by the master's spell ;
And feeling hearts — touch them but rightly —
         pour
A thousand melodies unheard before !
                              SAMUEL ROGERS.

FROM "MERCHANT OF VENICE."

LORENZO. How sweet the moonlight sleeps
      upon this bank !
Here will we sit, and let the sounds of music
Creep in our ears : soft stillness, and the night,
Become the touches of sweet harmony.
Sit, Jessica : look, how the floor of heaven
Is thick inlaid with patines of bright gold :
There 's not the smallest orb which thou be-
      hold'st,
But in his motion like an angel sings,
Still quiring to the young-eyed cherubins ;
Such harmony is in immortal souls :
But whilst this muddy vesture of decay
Doth grossly close it in, we cannot hear it.

JESSICA. I am never merry when I hear sweet
      music.
LOR. The reason is your spirits are attentive.

                              Therefore the poet
Did feign that Orpheus drew trees, stones, and
      floods ;
Since naught so stockish, hard, and full of rage,
But music for the time doth change his nature.
The man that hath no music in himself,
Nor is not moved with concord of sweet sounds,
Is fit for treasons, stratagems, and spoils ;
The motions of his spirit are dull as night,
And his affections dark as Erebus :
Let no such man be trusted.
                              SHAKESPEARE.

MUSIC, when soft voices die,
Vibrates in the memory, —
Odors, when sweet violets sicken,
Live within the sense they quicken.

Rose-leaves, when the rose is dead,
Are heaped for the belovéd's bed ;
And so thy thoughts, when thou art gone,
Love itself shall slumber on.
                              SHELLEY.

            WHERE music dwells
Lingering, and wandering on, as loath to die,
Like thoughts whose very sweetness yieldeth proof
That they were born for immortality.
                              WORDSWORTH.

MUSIC hath charms to soothe the savage breast,
To soften rocks, or bend a knotted oak.
                              CONGREVE.

ALEXANDER'S FEAST; OR THE POWER OF MUSIC.

AN ODE.

'T WAS at the royal feast, for Persia won
      By Philip's warlike son :
      Aloft in awful state
      The godlike hero sate

On his imperial throne :
His valiant peers were placed around,
Their brows with roses and with myrtles bound ;
(So should desert in arms be crowned.)
The lovely Thais, by his side,
Sate like a blooming Eastern bride
In flower of youth and beauty's pride.
Happy, happy, happy pair !
None but the brave,
None but the brave,
None but the brave deserves the fair.

CHORUS.

Happy, happy, happy pair !
None but the brave,
None but the brave,
None but the brave deserves the fair.

Timotheus, placed on high
Amid the tuneful choir,
With flying fingers touched the lyre ;
The trembling notes ascend the sky,
And heavenly joys inspire.
The song began from Jove,
Who left his blissful seats above,
(Such is the power of mighty love.)
A dragon's fiery form belied the god ;
Sublime on radiant spires he rode,
When he to fair Olympia pressed ;
And while he sought her snowy breast ;
Then round her slender waist he curled,
And stamped an image of himself, a sovereign
of the world.
The listening crowd admire the lofty sound,
A present deity ! they shout around ;
A present deity ! the vaulted roofs rebound.
With ravished ears
The monarch hears,
Assumes the god,
Affects to nod,
And seems to shake the spheres.

CHORUS.

With ravished ears
The monarch hears,
Assumes the god,
Affects to nod,
And seems to shake the spheres.

The praise of Bacchus then the sweet musician
sung,
Of Bacchus — ever fair and ever young :
The jolly god in triumph comes ;
Sound the trumpets ; beat the drums :
Flushed with a purple grace
He shows his honest face :
Now give the hautboys breath. He comes ! he
comes !
Bacchus, ever fair and young,
Drinking joys did first ordain ;

Bacchus' blessings are a treasure,
Drinking is the soldier's pleasure ;
Rich the treasure,
Sweet the pleasure,
Sweet is pleasure after pain.

CHORUS.

Bacchus' blessings are a treasure,
Drinking is the soldier's pleasure ;
Rich the treasure,
Sweet the pleasure,
Sweet is pleasure after pain.

Soothed with the sound the king grew vain ;
Fought all his battles o'er again ;
And thrice he routed all his foes ; and thrice he
slew the slain.
The master saw the madness rise ;
His glowing cheeks, his ardent eyes ;
And, while he heaven and earth defied,
Changed his hand, and checked his pride.
He chose a mournful muse
Soft pity to infuse :
He sung Darius, great and good ;
By too severe a fate,
Fallen, fallen, fallen, fallen,
Fallen from his high estate,
And weltering in his blood ;
Deserted, at his utmost need,
By those his former bounty fed ;
On the bare earth exposed he lies,
With not a friend to close his eyes.
With downcast looks the joyless victor sate,
Revolving in his altered soul
The various turns of chance below ;
And, now and then, a sigh he stole ;
And tears began to flow.

CHORUS.

Revolving in his altered soul
The various turns of chance below ;
And, now and then, a sigh he stole ;
And tears began to flow.

The mighty master smiled, to see
That love was in the next degree ;
'T was but a kindred sound to move,
For pity melts the mind to love.
Softly sweet, in Lydian measures,
Soon he soothed his soul to pleasures.
War, he sung, is toil and trouble ;
Honor, but an empty bubble ;
Never ending, still beginning,
Fighting still, and still destroying :
If the world be worth thy winning,
Think, O, think it worth enjoying !
Lovely Thais sits beside thee,
Take the good the gods provide thee.

The many rend the skies with loud applause ;
So Love was crowned, but Music won the cause.
The prince, unable to conceal his pain,
Gazed on the fair
Who caused his care,
And sighed and looked, sighed and looked,
Sighed and looked, and sighed again :
At length, with love and wine at once oppressed,
The vanquished victor sunk upon her breast.

CHORUS.

The prince, unable to conceal his pain,
Gazed on the fair
Who caused his care,
And sighed and looked, sighed and looked,
Sighed and looked, and sighed again :
At length, with love and wine at once oppressed,
The vanquished victor sunk upon her breast.

Now strike the golden lyre again :
A louder yet, and yet a louder strain.
Break his bands of sleep asunder,
And rouse him, like a rattling peal of thunder.
Hark, hark, the horrid sound
Has raised up his head ;
As awaked from the dead,
And amazed, he stares around.
Revenge ! revenge ! Timotheus cries,
See the furies arise !
See the snakes that they rear,
How they hiss in their hair !
And the sparkles that flash from their eyes !
Behold a ghastly band,
Each a torch in his hand !
Those are Grecian ghosts, that in battle were slain,
And unburied remain,
Inglorious on the plain :
Give the vengeance due
To the valiant crew.
Behold how they toss their torches on high,
How they point to the Persian abodes,
And glittering temples of their hostile gods.
The princes applaud with a furious joy ;
And the king seized a flambeau with zeal to destroy ;
Thais led the way,
To light him to his prey,
And, like another Helen, fired another Troy !

CHORUS.

And the king seized a flambeau with zeal to destroy ;
Thais led the way,
To light him to his prey,
And, like another Helen, fired another Troy !

Thus long ago,
Ere heaving bellows learned to blow,
While organs yet were mute ;
Timotheus, to his breathing flute,

And sounding lyre,
Could swell the soul to rage, or kindle soft desire.
At last divine Cecilia came,
Inventress of the vocal frame ;
The sweet enthusiast, from her sacred store,
Enlarged the former narrow bounds,
And added length to solemn sounds,
With nature's mother-wit, and arts unknown
before,
Let old Timotheus yield the prize,
Or both divide the crown ;
He raised a mortal to the skies.
She drew an angel down.

GRAND CHORUS.

At last divine Cecilia came,
Inventress of the vocal frame ;
The sweet enthusiast, from her sacred store,
Enlarged the former narrow bounds,
And added length to solemn sounds,
With nature's mother-wit, and arts unknown
before.
Let old Timotheus yield the prize,
Or both divide the crown ;
He raised a mortal to the skies,
She drew an angel down.

JOHN DRYDEN.

THE PASSIONS.

AN ODE FOR MUSIC.

When Music, heavenly maid, was young,
While yet in early Greece she sung,
The Passions oft, to hear her shell,
Thronged around her magic cell, —
Exulting, trembling, raging, fainting, —
Possest beyond the muse's painting ;
By turns they felt the glowing mind
Disturbed, delighted, raised, refined ;
Till once, 't is said, when all were fired,
Filled with fury, rapt, inspired,
From the supporting myrtles round
They snatched her instruments of sound ;
And, as they oft had heard apart
Sweet lessons of her forceful art,
Each (for madness ruled the hour)
Would prove his own expressive power.

First Fear his hand, its skill to try,
Amid the cords bewildered laid,
And back recoiled, he knew not why,
E'en at the sound himself had made.

Next Anger rushed ; his eyes, on fire,
In lightnings owned his secret stings ;
In one rude clash he struck the lyre,
And swept with hurried hand the strings.

With woful measures wan Despair,
　Low, sullen sounds, his grief beguiled, —
A solemn, strange, and mingled air ;
　'T was sad by fits, by starts 't was wild.

But thou, O Hope, with eyes so fair, —
　What was thy delightful measure ?
Still it whispered promised pleasure,
　And bade the lovely scenes at distance hail !
Still would her touch the strain prolong ;
　And from the rocks, the woods, the vale,
She called on Echo still, through all the song ;
　And where her sweetest theme she chose,
A soft responsive voice was heard at every close ;
　And Hope, enchanted, smiled, and waved her
　　golden hair.
And longer had she sung — but, with a frown,
　Revenge impatient rose ;
He threw his blood-stained sword in thunder down;
　And, with a withering look,
　The war-denouncing trumpet took,
And blew a blast so loud and dread,
Were ne'er prophetic sounds so full of woe !
　And ever and anon he beat
　The doubling drum with furious heat ;
And though sometimes, each dreary pause between,
　Dejected Pity, at his side,
　Her soul-subduing voice applied,
Yet still he kept his wild, unaltered mien,
While each strained ball of sight seemed bursting
　　from his head.

Thy numbers, Jealousy, to naught were fixed, —
　Sad proof of thy distressful state ;
Of differing themes the veering song was mixed ;
　And now it courted love, — now, raving,
　　called on Hate.

With eyes upraised, as one inspired,
Pale Melancholy sate retired ;
And from her wild sequestered seat,
In notes by distance made more sweet,
　Poured through the mellow horn her pensive
　　soul ;
　And, dashing soft from rocks around,
　Bubbling runnels joined the sound ;
Through glades and glooms the mingled meas-
　　ure stole ;
　Or o'er some haunted stream, with fond delay,
　　Round an holy calm diffusing,
　　Love of peace, and lonely musing,
　In hollow murmurs died away.

But O, how altered was its sprightlier tone
When Cheerfulness, a nymph of healthiest hue,
　Her bow across her shoulder flung,
　Her buskins gemmed with morning dew,
Blew an inspiring air, that dale and thicket rung, —
　The hunter's call, to faun and dryad known !

The oak-crowned sisters, and their chaste-eyed
　　queen,
　Satyrs and sylvan boys, were seen
　Peeping from forth their alleys green ;
Brown Exercise rejoiced to hear ;
　And Sport leapt up, and seized his beechen spear.

Last came Joy's ecstatic trial :
He, with viny crown advancing,
　First to the lively pipe his hand addrest ;
But soon he saw the brisk-awakening viol,
　Whose sweet entrancing voice he loved the best ;
They would have thought who heard the strain,
　They saw, in Tempe's vale, her native maids,
　Amidst the festal-sounding shades,
To some unwearied minstrel dancing,
While, as his flying fingers kissed the strings,
Love framed with Mirth a gay fantastic round :
Loose were her tresses seen, her zone unbound ;
　And he, amidst his frolic play,
　As if he would the charming air repay,
Shook thousand odors from his dewy wings.

O Music ! sphere-descended maid,
Friend of pleasure, wisdom's aid !
Why, goddess ! why, to us denied,
Lay'st thou thy ancient lyre aside ?
As, in that loved Athenian bower,
You learned an all-commanding power,
Thy mimic soul, O nymph endeared,
Can well recall what then it heard ;
Where is thy native simple heart,
Devote to virtue, fancy, art ?
Arise, as in that elder time,
Warm, energetic, chaste, sublime !
Thy wonders, in that godlike age,
Fill thy recording sister's page ;
'T is said — and I believe the tale —
Thy humblest reed could more prevail,
Had more of strength, diviner rage,
Than all which charms this laggard age, —
E'en all at once together found, —
Cecilia's mingled world of sound.
O, bid our vain endeavors cease ;
Revive the just designs of Greece !
Return in all thy simple state, —
Confirm the tales her sons relate !
　　　　　　　　　　　　　WILLIAM COLLINS.

———◆———

A SONG FOR ST. CECILIA'S DAY, 1687.

From harmony, from heavenly harmony,
　This universal frame began ;
　When Nature underneath a heap
　　Of jarring atoms lay,
　And could not heave her head,

The tuneful voice was heard from high,
 Arise, ye more than dead !
Then cold and hot and moist and dry
 In order to their stations leap,
 And Music's power obey.
From harmony, from heavenly harmony,
 This universal frame began :
 From harmony to harmony,
Through all the compass of the notes it ran,
 The diapason closing full in man.

What passion cannot Music raise and quell ?
 When Jubal struck the chorded shell,
 His listening brethren stood around,
 And, wondering, on their faces fell
 To worship that celestial sound.
Less than a God they thought there could not dwell
 Within the hollow of that shell,
 That spoke so sweetly and so well.
What passion cannot Music raise and quell ?

 The trumpet's loud clangor
  Excites us to arms,
 With shrill notes of anger,
  And mortal alarms,
 The double double double beat
  Of the thundering drum
  Cries, hark ! the foes come ;
Charge, charge, 't is too late to retreat.

 The soft complaining flute
 In dying notes discovers
 The woes of hopeless lovers,
Whose dirge is whispered by the warbling lute.

 Sharp violins proclaim
Their jealous pangs, and desperation,
Fury, frantic indignation,
Depth of pains, and height of passion,
 For the fair, disdainful dame.

 But O, what art can teach,
  What human voice can reach,
 The sacred organ's praise ?
 Notes inspiring holy love,
Notes that wing their heavenly ways
 To mend the choirs above.

Orpheus could lead the savage race ;
And trees uprooted left their place,
 Sequacious of the lyre ;
But bright Cecilia raised the wonder higher ;
When to her organ vocal breath was given,
An angel heard, and straight appeared
 Mistaking earth for heaven.

GRAND CHORUS.

As from the power of sacred lays
 The spheres began to move,

And sung the great Creator's praise
 To all the blessed above ;
So when the last and dreadful hour
This crumbling pageant shall devour,
The trumpet shall be heard on high,
The dead shall live, the living die,
And Music shall untune the sky.
JOHN DRYDEN.

MAN.

How poor, how rich, how abject, how august,
How complicate, how wonderful, is man !
How passing wonder He who made him such !
Who centred in our make such strange extremes,
From different natures marvellously mixed,
Connection exquisite of distant worlds !
Distinguished link in being's endless chain !
Midway from nothing to the Deity !
A beam ethereal, sullied, and absorpt !
Though sullied and dishonored, still divine !
Dim miniature of greatness absolute !
An heir of glory ! a frail child of dust !
Helpless immortal ! insect infinite !
A worm ! a God ! — I tremble at myself,
And in myself am lost.   At home, a stranger,
Thought wanders up and down, surprised, aghast,
And wondering at her own.   How reason reels !
O, what a miracle to man is man !
Triumphantly distressed ! What joy ! what dread !
Alternately transported and alarmed !
What can preserve my life ? or what destroy ?
An angel's arm can't snatch me from the grave ;
Legions of angels can't confine me there.
DR. EDWARD YOUNG.

MAN — WOMAN.

Man's home is everywhere.   On ocean's flood,
Where the strong ship with storm-defying tether
 Doth link in stormy brotherhood
  Earth's utmost zones together,
Where'er the red gold glows, the spice-trees wave,
Where the rich diamond ripens, mid the flame
 Of vertic suns that ope the stranger's grave,
  He with bronzed cheek and daring step doth
   rove ;
  He with short pang and slight
 Doth turn him from the checkered light
Of the fair moon through his own forests dancing,
 Where music, joy, and love
  Were his young hours entrancing ;
 And where ambition's thunder-claim
  Points out his lot,
Or fitful wealth allures to roam,
  There doth he make his home,
   Repining not.

It is not thus with Woman. The far halls,
Though ruinous and lone,
Where first her pleased ear drank a nursing-
mother's tone ;
The home with humble walls,
Where breathed a parent's prayer around her
bed ;
The valley where, with playmates true,
She culled the strawberry, bright with dew ;
The bower where Love her timid footsteps led ;
The hearthstone where her children grew ;
The damp soil where she cast
The flower-seeds of her hope, and saw them bide
the blast, —
Affection with unfading tint recalls,
Lingering round the ivied walls,
Where every rose hath in its cup a bee,
Making fresh honey of remembered things,
Each rose without a thorn, each bee bereft of
stings.   LYDIA H. SIGOURNEY.

MAN — WOMAN.

FROM "DON JUAN."

" MAN's love is of man's life a thing apart ;
'T is woman's whole existence. Man may range
The court, camp, church, the vessel, and the mart,
Sword, gown, gain, glory, offer in exchange
Pride, fame, ambition, to fill up his heart,
And few there are whom these cannot estrange :
Men have all these resources, we but one, —
To love again, and be again undone."
            BYRON.

TO A SLEEPING CHILD.

ART thou a thing of mortal birth
Whose happy home is on our earth ?
Does human blood with life imbue
Those wandering veins of heavenly blue
That stray along thy forehead fair,
Lost mid a gleam of golden hair ?
O, can that light and airy breath
Steal from a being doomed to death ?
Those features to the grave be sent
In sleep thus mutely eloquent ?
Or art thou, what thy form would seem,
The phantom of a blessèd dream ?
A human shape I feel thou art
I feel it at my beating heart,
Those tremors both of soul and sense
Awoke by infant innocence !
Though dear the forms by fancy wove,
We love them with a transient love ;
Thoughts from the living world intrude
Even on our deepest solitude ;

But, lovely child ! thy magic stole
At once into my inmost soul,
With feelings as thy beauty fair,
And left no other vision there.

To me thy parents are unknown ;
Glad would they be their child to own !
And well they must have loved before,
If since thy birth they loved not more.
Thou art a branch of noble stem,
And seeing thee I figure them.
What many a childless one would give,
If thou in their still home wouldst live,
Though in thy face no family-line
Might sweetly say, "This babe is mine" !
In time thou wouldst become the same
As their own child, — all but the name !
            JOHN WILSON.

MOTHER AND CHILD.

THE wind blew wide the casement, and within —
It was the loveliest picture ! — a sweet child
Lay in its mother's arms, and drew its life,
In pauses, from the fountain, — the white round
Part shaded by loose tresses, soft and dark,
Concealing, but still showing, the fair realm
Of so much rapture, as green shadowing trees
With beauty shroud the brooklet. The red lips
Were parted, and the cheek upon the breast
Lay close, and, like the young leaf of the flower,
Wore the same color, rich and warm and fresh : —
And such alone are beautiful. Its eye,
A full blue gem, most exquisitely set,
Looked archly on its world, — the little imp,
As if it knew even then that such a wreath
Were not for all ; and with its playful hands
It drew aside the robe that hid its realm,
And peeped and laughed aloud, and so it laid
Its head upon the shrine of such pure joys,
And, laughing, slept. And while it slept, the tears
Of the sweet mother fell upon its cheek, —
Tears such as fall from April skies, and bring
The sunlight after. They were tears of joy ;
And the true heart of that young mother then
Grew lighter, and she sang unconsciously
The silliest ballad-song that ever yet
Subdued the nursery's voices, and brought sleep
To fold her sabbath wings above its couch.
            WILLIAM GILMORE SIMMS.

FORTUNE.

FRAGMENT FROM "FANNY."

BUT Fortune, like some others of her sex,
Delights in tantalizing and tormenting.

One day we feed upon their smiles, — the next
 Is spent in swearing, sorrowing, and repenting.

Eve never walked in Paradise more pure
 Than on that morn when Satan played the devil
With her and all her race. A lovesick wooer
 Ne'er asked a kinder maiden, or more civil,
Than Cleopatra was to Antony
The day she left him on the Ionian sea.

The serpent — loveliest in his coiléd ring,
 With eye that charms, and beauty that outvies
The tints of the rainbow — bears upon his sting
 The deadliest venom. Ere the dolphin dies
Its hues are brightest. Like an infant's breath
Are tropic winds before the voice of death

Is heard upon the waters, summoning
 The midnight earthquake from its sleep of years
To do its task of woe. The clouds that fling
 The lightning brighten ere the bolt appears ;
The pantings of the warrior's heart are proud
Upon that battle-morn whose night-dews wet his
   shroud ;
The sun is loveliest as he sinks to rest;
 The leaves of Autumn smile when fading fast ;
The swan's last song is sweetest.
                    FITZ-GREENE HALLECK.

FORTUNE.
ENID'S SONG.

TURN, Fortune, turn thy wheel and lower the
   proud ;
Turn thy wild wheel through sunshine, storm,
   and cloud ;
Thy wheel and thee we neither love nor hate.

 Turn, Fortune, turn thy wheel with smile or
   frown ;
With that wild wheel we go not up or down ;
Our hoard is little, but our hearts are great.

 Smile and we smile, the lords of many lands ;
Frown and we smile, the lords of our own hands ;
For man is man and master of his fate.

 Turn, turn thy wheel above the staring crowd ;
Thy wheel and thou are shadows in the cloud ;
Thy wheel and thee we neither love nor hate.
                    ALFRED TENNYSON.

THE GIFTS OF GOD.

WHEN God at first made man,
Having a glass of blessings standing by,
Let us (said he) pour on him all we can :
Let the world's riches, which disperséd lie,
   Contract into a span.

So strength first made a way ;
Then beauty flowed, then wisdom, honor, pleasure :
When almost all was out, God made a stay,
Perceiving that alone, of all his treasure,
   Rest in the bottom lay.

 For if I should (said he)
Bestow this jewel also on my creature,
He would adore my gifts instead of me,
And rest in Nature, not the God of Nature :
   So both should losers be.

 Yet let him keep the rest,
But keep them with repining restlessness :
Let him be rich and weary, that at least,
If goodness lead him not, yet weariness
   May toss him to my breast.
                    GEORGE HERBERT.

ENIGMA.
THE LETTER " H."

'T WAS whispered in heaven, and muttered in hell,
And echo caught faintly the sound as it fell ;
On the confines of earth 't was permitted to rest,
And the depths of the ocean its presence confessed ;
'T was seen in the lightning, and heard in the
   thunder ;
'T will be found in the spheres, when riven
   asunder ;
'T was given to man with his earliest breath,
Assists at his birth, and attends him in death ;
Presides o'er his happiness, honor, and health,
Is the prop of his house, and the end of his wealth.

It begins every hope, every wish it must bound,
And though unassuming, with monarchs is
   crowned.
In the heaps of the miser 't is hoarded with care,
But is sure to be lost in his prodigal heir.
Without it the soldier and sailor may roam,
But woe to the wretch who expels it from home !
In the whispers of conscience its voice will be found,
Nor e'er in the whirlwind of passion be drowned.
It softens the heart ; and, though deaf to the ear,
It will make it acutely and instantly hear.
But in shade let it rest, like a delicate flower, —
O, breathe on it softly ; it dies in an hour.
                    MISS FANSHAWE.

FATHER LAND AND MOTHER TONGUE.

OUR Father Land ! and wouldst thou know
   Why we should call it Father Land ?
It is that Adam here below
   Was made of earth by Nature's hand.

And he, our father made of earth,
　Hath peopled earth on every hand;
And we, in memory of his birth,
　Do call our country Father Land.

At first in Eden's bowers, they say,
　No sound of speech had Adam caught,
But whistled like a bird all day, —
　And maybe 't was for want of thought.
But Nature, with resistless laws,
Made Adam soon surpass the birds;
She gave him lovely Eve because
　If he 'd a wife they must *have words*.

And so the native land, I hold,
　By male descent is proudly mine;
The language, as the tale hath told,
　Was given in the female line.
And thus we see on either hand
　We name our blessings whence they've sprung;
We call our country Father Land,
　We call our language Mother Tongue.
　　　　　　　　　　SAMUEL LOVER.

SMALL BEGINNINGS.

A TRAVELLER through a dusty road strewed
　acorns on the lea;
And one took root and sprouted up, and grew
　into a tree.
Love sought its shade, at evening time, to breathe
　its early vows;
And age was pleased, in heats of noon, to bask
　beneath its boughs;
The dormouse loved its dangling twigs, the birds
　sweet music bore;
It stood a glory in its place, a blessing evermore.

A little spring had lost its way amid the grass
　and fern,
A passing stranger scooped a well, where weary
　men might turn;
He walled it in, and hung with care a ladle at
　the brink;
He thought not of the deed he did, but judged
　that toil might drink.
He passed again, and lo! the well, by summers
　never dried,
Had cooled ten thousand parching tongues, and
　saved a life beside.

A dreamer dropped a random thought; 't was
　old, and yet 't was new;
A simple fancy of the brain, but strong in being
　true.
It shone upon a genial mind, and lo! its light
　became
A lamp of life, a beacon ray, a monitory flame.

The thought was small; its issue great; a watch-
　fire on the hill;
It sheds its radiance far adown, and cheers the
　valley still!

A nameless man, amid a crowd that thronged
　the daily mart,
Let fall a word of Hope and Love, unstudied,
　from the heart;
A whisper on the tumult thrown, — a transitory
　breath, —
It raised a brother from the dust; it saved a
　soul from death.
O germ! O fount! O word of love! O thought
　at random cast!
Ye were but little at the first, but mighty at the
　last.　　　　　　　　CHARLES MACKAY.

RAIN ON THE ROOF.

WHEN the showery vapors gather over all the
　starry spheres,
And the melancholy darkness gently weeps in
　rainy tears,
'T is a joy to press the pillow of a cottage cham-
　ber bed,
And listen to the patter of the soft rain overhead.

Every tinkle on the shingles has an echo in the
　heart,
And a thousand dreary fancies into busy being
　start;
And a thousand recollections weave their bright
　hues into woof,
As I listen to the patter of the soft rain on the roof.

There in fancy comes my mother, as she used to
　years agone,
To survey the infant sleepers ere she left them
　till the dawn.
I can see her bending o'er me, as I listen to the
　strain
Which is played upon the shingles by the patter
　of the rain. ʻ

Then my little seraph sister, with her wings and
　waving hair,
And her bright-eyed cherub brother, — a serene,
　angelic pair, —
Glide around my wakeful pillow with their praise
　or mild reproof,
As I listen to the murmur of the soft rain on the
　roof.

And another comes to thrill me with her eyes'
　delicious blue.
I forget, as gazing on her, that her heart was all
　untrue;

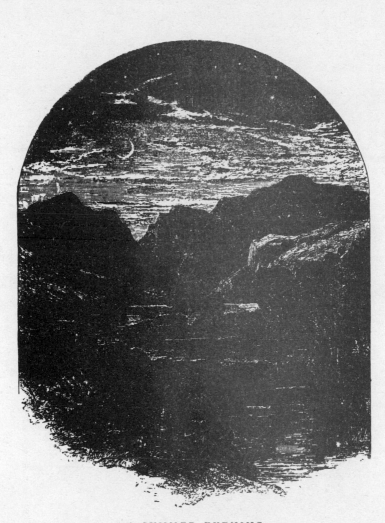

A SUMMER EVENING.

*"Long had I watched the glory moving on
O'er the still radiance of the lake below."*

I remember that I loved her as I ne'er may love
    again,
And my heart's quick pulses vibrate to the patter
    of the rain.

There is naught in art's bravuras that can work
    with such a spell,
In the spirit's pure, deep fountains, whence the
    holy passions swell,
As that melody of nature,—that subdued, sub-
    duing strain,
Which is played upon the shingles by the patter
    of the rain.   COATES KINNEY.

THE EVENING CLOUD.

A CLOUD lay cradled near the setting sun,
  A gleam of crimson tinged its braided snow ;
Long had I watched the glory moving on
  O'er the still radiance of the lake below.
Tranquil its spirit seemed, and floated slow !
  Even in its very motion there was rest ;
While every breath of eve that chanced to blow
  Wafted the traveller to the beauteous west.
Emblem, methought, of the departed soul !
  To whose white robe the gleam of bliss is given
And by the breath of mercy made to roll
  Right onwards to the golden gates of heaven,
Where to the eye of faith it peaceful lies,
And tells to man his glorious destinies.
        JOHN WILSON.

INSIGNIFICANT EXISTENCE.

THERE are a number of us creep
Into this world, to eat and sleep ;
And know no reason why we 're born,
But only to consume the corn,
Devour the cattle, fowl, and fish,
And leave behind an empty dish.
The crows and ravens do the same,
Unlucky birds of hateful name ;
Ravens or crows might fill their place,
And swallow corn and carcasses,
Then if their tombstone, when they die,
Be n't taught to flatter and to lie,
There 's nothing better will be said
Than that "they 've eat up all their bread,
Drunk up their drink, and gone to bed."
        ISAAC WATTS.

LIVING WATERS.

THERE are some hearts like wells, green-mossed
    and deep
    As ever Summer saw ;

And cool their water is,—yea, cool and sweet ;—
    But you must come to draw.
They hoard not, yet they rest in calm content,
    And not unsought will give ;
They can be quiet with their wealth unspent,
    So self-contained they live.

And there are some like springs, that bubbling
    burst
    To follow dusty ways,
And run with offered cup to quench his thirst
    Where the tired traveller strays ;
That never ask the meadows if they want
    What is their joy to give ;—
Unasked, their lives to other life they grant,
    So self-bestowed they live !

And ONE is like the ocean, deep and wide,
    Wherein all waters fall ;
That girdles the broad earth, and draws the tide,
    Feeding and bearing all ;
That broods the mists, that sends the clouds
    abroad,
    That takes, again to give ;—
Even the great and loving heart of God,
    Whereby all love doth live.
        CAROLINE SPENCER.

FREEDOM IN DRESS.

STILL to be neat, still to be drest,
As you were going to a feast ;
Still to be powdered, still perfumed,—
Lady, it is to be presumed,
Though art's hid causes are not found,
All is not sweet, all is not sound.

Give me a look, give me a face,
That makes simplicity a grace ;
Robes loosely flowing, hair as free,—
Such sweet neglect more taketh me
Than all the adulteries of art ;
They strike mine eyes, but not my heart.
        BEN JONSON.

A SWEET DISORDER IN THE DRESS—

A SWEET disorder in the dress
Kindles in clothes a wantonness :
A lawn about the shoulders thrown
Into a fine distraction ;
An erring lace, which here and there
Inthralls the crimson stomacher ;
A cuff neglectful, and thereby
Ribbons to flow confusedly ;
A winning wave, deserving note,
In the tempestuous petticoat ;

A careless shoe-string, in whose tie
I see a wild civility, —
Do more bewitch me than when art
Is too precise in every part.

ROBERT HERRICK.

CONTRADICTION.

FROM "CONVERSATION."

YE powers who rule the tongue, if such there
        are,
And make colloquial happiness your care,
Preserve me from the thing I dread and hate,
A duel in the form of a debate.
The clash of arguments and jar of words,
Worse than the mortal blunt of rival swords,
Decide no question with their tedious length,
For opposition gives opinion strength.
Divert the champions prodigal of breath ;
And put the peaceably disposed to death.
O, thwart me not, Sir Soph, at every turn,
Nor carp at every flaw you may discern !
Though syllogisms hang not on my tongue,
I am not surely always in the wrong ;
'T is hard if all is false that I advance,
A fool must now and then be right by chance.
Not that all freedom of dissent I blame ;
No, — there I grant the privilege I claim.
A disputable point is no man's ground ;
Rove where you please, 't is common all around.
Discourse may want an animated No
To brush the surface, and to make it flow ;
But still remember, if you mean to please,
To press your point with modesty and ease.
The mark at which my juster aim I take,
Is contradiction for its own dear sake.
Set your opinion at whatever pitch,
Knots and impediments make something hitch ;
Adopt his own, 't is equally in vain,
Your thread of argument is snapped again.
The wrangler, rather than accord with you,
Will judge himself deceived and prove it too.
Vociferated logic kills me quite,
A noisy man is always in the right.
I twirl my thumbs, fall back into my chair,
Fix on the wainscot a distressful stare,
And, when I hope his blunders are all out,
Reply discreetly, — To be sure — no doubt !

WILLIAM COWPER.

OATHS.

FROM "CONVERSATION."

OATHS terminate, as Paul observes, all strife, —
Some men have surely then a peaceful life.
Whatever subject occupy discourse,
The feats of Vestris, or the naval force,

Asseveration ,blustering in your face
Makes contradiction such a hopeless case ;
In every tale they tell, or false or true,
Well known, or such as no man ever knew,
They fix attention, heedless of your pain,
With oaths like rivets forced into the brain ;
And even when sober truth prevails throughout,
They swear it, till affirmance breeds a doubt.
A Persian, humble servant of the sun,
Who, though devout, yet bigotry had none,
Hearing a lawyer, grave in his address,
With adjurations every word impress,
Supposed the man a bishop, or, at least,
God's name so much upon his lips, a priest ;
Bowed at the close with all his graceful airs,
And begged an interest in his frequent prayers.

WILLIAM COWPER.

FAME.

FROM THE "ESSAY ON MAN."

WHAT's fame ? — a fancied life in others' breath,
A thing beyond us, e'en before our death.
Just what you hear, you have, and what 's un-
        known
The same (my lord) if Tully's, or your own.
All that we feel of it begins and ends
In the small circle of our foes or friends ;
To all beside as much an empty shade
A Eugene living as a Cæsar dead ;
Alike or when or where they shone or shine,
Or on the Rubicon, or on the Rhine.
A wit 's a feather, and a chief a rod ;
An honest man 's the noblest work of God.
Fame but from death a villain's name can save,
As justice tears his body from the grave ;
When what to oblivion better were resigned
Is hung on high, to poison half mankind.
All fame is foreign, but of true desert ;
Plays round the head, but comes not to the heart :
One self-approving hour whole years outweighs
Of stupid starers and of loud huzzas ;
And more true joy Marcellus exiled feels
Than Cæsar with a senate at his heels.

ALEXANDER POPE.

GREATNESS.

FROM THE "ESSAY ON MAN."

HONOR and shame from no condition rise ;
Act well your part, there all the honor lies.
Fortune in men has some small difference made,
One flaunts in rags, one flutters in brocade ;
The cobbler aproned, and the parson gowned,
The friar hooded, and the monarch crowned.

"What differ more (you cry) than crown and
     cowl ? "
I 'll tell you, friend ! a wise man and a fool.
You 'll find, if once the monarch acts the monk,
Or, cobbler-like, the parson will be drunk,
Worth makes the man, and want of it the fellow ;
The rest is all but leather or prunella.
     Stuck o'er with titles, and hung round with
          strings,
That thou mayst be by kings, or whores of kings ;
Boast the pure blood of an illustrious race,
In quiet flow from Lucrece to Lucrece ;
But by your fathers' worth if yours you rate,
Count me those only who were good and great.
Go ! if your ancient but ignoble blood
Has crept through scoundrels ever since the
     flood.
Go ! and pretend your family is young,
Nor own your fathers have been fools so long.
What can ennoble sots or slaves or cowards ?
Alas ! not all the blood of all the Howards.
     Look next on greatness ! say where greatness
          lies ?
"Where, but among the heroes and the wise ? "
Heroes are much the same, the point 's agreed,
From Macedonia's madman to the Swede ;
The whole strange purpose of their lives, to find
Or make an enemy of all mankind !
Not one looks backward, onward still he goes,
Yet ne'er looks forward farther than his nose.
No less alike the politic and wise ;
All sly slow things, with circumspective eyes :
Men in their loose unguarded hours they take,
Not that themselves are wise, but others weak.
But grant that those can conquer, these can
     cheat ;
'T is phrase absurd to call a villain great :
Who wickedly is wise, or madly brave,
Is but the more a fool, the more a knave.
Who noble ends by noble means obtains,
Or, failing, smiles in exile or in chains,
Like good Aurelius let him reign, or bleed
Like Socrates, that man is great indeed.

ALEXANDER POPE.

OPPORTUNITY.

FROM "JULIUS CÆSAR."

THERE is a tide in the affairs of men,
Which, taken at the flood, leads on to fortune ;
Omitted, all the voyage of their life
Is bound in shallows, and in miseries.
On such a full sea are we now afloat ;
And we must take the current when it serves,
Or lose our ventures.

SHAKESPEARE.

REASON AND INSTINCT.

FROM THE "ESSAY ON MAN."

WHETHER with reason or with instinct blest,
Know all enjoy that power which suits them best ;
To bliss alike by that direction tend,
And find the means proportioned to their end.
Say, where full instinct is the unerring guide,
What pope or council can they need beside ?
Reason, however able, cool at best,
Cares not for service, or but serves when prest,
Stays till we call, and then not often near ;
But honest instinct comes a volunteer,
Sure never to o'ershoot, but just to hit ;
While still too wide or short is human wit,
Sure by quick nature happiness to gain,
Which heavier reason labors at in vain.
This too serves always, reason never long ;
One must go right, the other may go wrong.
See then the acting and comparing powers
One in their nature, which are two in ours ;
And reason raise o'er instinct as you can,
In this 't is God directs, in that 't is man.
     Who taught the nations of the field and wood
To shun their poison and to choose their food ?
Prescient, the tides or tempests to withstand,
Build on the wave, or arch beneath the sand ?
Who made the spider parallels design,
Sure as De Moivre, without rule or line ?
Who bid the stork, Columbus-like, explore
Heavens not his own, and worlds unknown before ?
Who calls the council, states the certain day,
Who forms the phalanx, and who points the way ?

ALEXANDER POPE.

ABUSE OF AUTHORITY.

FROM "MEASURE FOR MEASURE."

ISABEL.   Oh ! it is excellent
To have a giant's strength ; but it is tyrannous
To use it like a giant.
Could great men thunder
As Jove himself does, Jove would ne'er be quiet ;
For every pelting, petty officer
Would use his heaven for thunder, —
Nothing but thunder.   Merciful Heaven !
Thou rather, with thy sharp and sulphurous bolt,
Split'st the unwedgeable and gnarléd oak,
Than the soft myrtle : but man, proud man !
Drest in a little brief authority, —
Most ignorant of what he 's most assured,
His glassy essence, — like an angry ape,
Plays such fantastic tricks before high heaven,
As make the angels weep ; who, with our spleens,
Would all themselves laugh mortal.

SHAKESPEARE.

THE SEASIDE WELL.

"Waters flowed over mine head; then I said, I am cut off."
—LAM. iii. 54.

ONE day I wandered where the salt sea-tide
    Backward had drawn its wave,
And found a spring as sweet as e'er hillside
    To wild flowers gave.
Freshly it sparkled in the sun's bright look,
    And 'mid its pebbles strayed,
As if it thought to join a happy brook
    In some green glade.

But soon the heavy sea's resistless swell
    Came rolling in once more;
Spreading its bitter o'er the clear sweet well
    And pebbled shore.
Like a fair star thick buried in a cloud,
    Or life in the grave's gloom,
The well, enwrapped in a deep watery shroud,
    Sunk to its tomb.

As one who by the beach roams far and wide,
    Remnant of wreck to save,
Again I wandered when the salt sea-tide
    Withdrew its wave.
And there, unchanged, no taint in all its sweet,
    No anger in its tone,
Still as it thought some happy brook to meet,
    The spring flowed on.

While waves of bitterness rolled o'er its head,
    Its heart had folded deep
Within itself, and quiet fancies led,
    As in a sleep.
Till when the ocean loosed his heavy chain,
    And gave it back to day,
Calmly it turned to its own life again
    And gentle way.

Happy, I thought, that which can draw its life
    Deep from the nether springs,
Safe 'neath the pressure, tranquil 'mid the strife,
    Of surface things.
Safe — for the sources of the nether springs
    Up in the far hills lie ;
Calm — for the life its power and freshness
    brings
    Down from the sky.

So, should temptations threaten, and should sin
    Roll in its whelming flood,
Make strong the fountain of thy grace within
    My soul, O God !
If bitter scorn, and looks, once kind, grown
    strange,
    With crushing chillness fall,
From secret wells let sweetness rise, nor change
    my heart to gall !

When sore thy hand doth press, and waves of
    thine
    Afflict me like a sea, —
Deep calling deep, — infuse from source divine
    Thy peace in me !
And when death's tide, as with a brimful cup,
    Over my soul doth pour,
Let hope survive, — a well that springeth up
    Forevermore !

Above my head the waves may come and go,
    Long brood the deluge dire,
But life lies hidden in the depths below
    Till waves retire, —
Till death, that reigns with overflowing flood,
    At length withdraw its sway,
And life rise sparkling in the sight of God
    And endless day.
                  ANONYMOUS.

SCANDAL.

FROM THE "PROLOGUE TO THE SATIRES."

CURSED be the verse, how well soe'er it flow,
That tends to make one worthy man my foe,
Give virtue scandal, innocence a fear,
Or from the soft-eyed virgin steal a tear !
But he who hurts a harmless neighbor's peace,
Insults fallen worth, or beauty in distress,
Who loves a lie, lame slander helps about,
Who writes a libel, or who copies out ;
That fop whose pride affects a patron's name,
Yet absent wounds an author's honest fame :
Who can your merit selfishly approve,
And show the sense of it without the love ;
Who has the vanity to call you friend,
Yet wants the honor, injured, to defend ;
Who tells whate'er you think, whate'er you say,
And, if he lie not, must at least betray ;
Who to the Dean and silver bell can swear,
And sees at Canons what was never there ;
Who reads but with a lust to misapply,
Make satire a lampoon, and fiction lie ;
A lash like mine no honest man shall dread,
But all such babbling blockheads in his stead.
                  ALEXANDER POPE.

PROFUSION.

TIMON.

FROM "MORAL ESSAYS."

AT Timon's villa let us pass a day,
Where all cry out, "What sums are thrown
    away !"

So proud, so grand; of that stupendous air,
Soft and agreeable come never there.
Greatness, with Timon, dwells in such a draught
As brings all Brobdingnag before your thought.
To compass this, his building is a town,
His pond an ocean, his parterre a down :
Who but must laugh, the master when he sees,
A puny insect, shivering at a breeze !
Lo, what huge heaps of littleness around !
The whole, a labored quarry above ground.
Two Cupids squirt before : a lake behind
Improves the keenness of the northern wind.
His gardens next your admiration call,
On every side you look, behold the wall !
No pleasing intricacies intervene,
No artful wildness to perplex the scene ;
Grove nods at grove, each alley has a brother,
And half the platform just reflects the other.
The suffering eye inverted nature sees,
Trees cut to statues, statues thick as trees ;
With here a fountain, never to be played ;
And there a summer-house, that knows no shade;
Here Amphitrite sails through myrtle bowers ;
There gladiators fight, or die in flowers ;
Unwatered see the drooping sea-horse mourn,
And swallows roost in Nilus' dusty urn.

My lord advances with majestic mien,
Smit with the mighty pleasure, to be seen ;
But soft — by regular approach — not yet —
First through the length of yon hot terrace sweat ;
And when up ten steep slopes you 've dragged
　　　your thighs,
Just at his study door he 'll bless your eyes.

His study ! with what authors is it stored ?
In books, not authors, curious is my lord ;
To all their dated backs he turns you round ;
These Aldus printed, those Du Suéil has bound !
Lo, some are vellum, and the rest as good
For all his lordship knows, but they are wood.
For Locke or Milton 't is in vain to look,
These shelves admit not any modern book.

And now the chapel's silver bell you hear,
That summons you to all the pride of prayer :
Light quirks of music, broken and uneven,
Make the soul dance upon a jig to heaven.
On painted ceilings you devoutly stare,
Where sprawl the saints of Verrio or Laguerre,
On gilded clouds in fair expansion lie,
And bring all paradise before your eye.
To rest the cushion and soft dean invite,
Who never mentions hell to ears polite.

But hark ! the chiming clocks to dinner call ;
A hundred footsteps scrape the marble hall :
The rich buffet well-colored serpents grace,
And gaping Tritons spue to wash your face.
Is this a dinner ? this a genial room ?
No, 't is a temple, and a hecatomb.
A solemn sacrifice, performed in state,

You drink by measure, and to minutes eat.
So quick retires each flying course, you 'd swear
Sancho's dread doctor and his wand were there.
Between each act the trembling salvers ring,
From soup to sweet wine, and God bless the king.
In plenty starving, tantalized in state,
And complaisantly helped to all I hate,
Treated, caressed, and tired, I take my leave,
Sick of his civil pride from morn to eve ;
I curse such lavish cost, and little skill,
And swear no day was ever passed so ill.

　　　　　　　　　ALEXANDER POPE.

THE WOUNDED STAG.

FROM "AS YOU LIKE IT."

DUKE S.　Come, shall we go and kill us veni-
　　　son ?
And yet it irks me, the poor dappled fools,
Being native burghers of this desert city,
Should, in their own confines, with forkéd heads
Have their round haunches gored.
　1 LORD.　　　　　Indeed, my lord,
The melancholy Jaques grieves at that ;
And, in that kind, swears you do more usurp
Than doth your brother that hath banished you.
To-day my lord of Amiens and myself,
Did steal behind him, as he lay along
Under an oak, whose antique root peeps out
Upon the brook that brawls along this wood :
To the which place a poor sequestered stag,
That from the hunters' aim had ta'en a hurt,
Did come to languish ; and, indeed, my lord,
The wretched animal heaved forth such groans,
That his discharge did stretch his leathern coat
Almost to bursting ; and the big round tears
Coursed one another down his innocent nose
In piteous chase ; and thus the hairy fool,
Much markéd of the melancholy Jaques,
Stood on the extremest verge of the swift brook,
Augmenting it with tears.
　DUKE S.　　　　But what said Jaques ?
Did he not moralize this spectacle ?
　1 LORD.　　O yes, into a thousand similes.
First, for his weeping into the needless stream ;
"Poor deer," quoth he, " thou mak'st a testament
As wordlings do, giving thy sum of more
To that which had too much " : then being there
　　　alone,
Left and abandoned of his velvet friends ;
" 'T is right," quoth he ; " thus misery doth part
The flux of company " : anon, a careless herd,
Full of the pasture, jumps along by him,
And never stays to greet him ; "Ay," quoth
　　　Jaques,
"Sweep on, you fat and greasy citizens ;
'T is just the fashion : wherefore do you look

Upon that poor and broken bankrupt there ?"
Thus most invectively he pierceth through
The body of the country, city, court,
Yea, and of this our life ; swearing that we
Are mere usurpers, tyrants, and what 's worse,
To fright the animals, and to kill them up,
In their assigned and native dwelling-place.

SHAKESPEARE.

HUMANITY.

FROM "THE WINTER WALK AT NOON."

I WOULD not enter on my list of friends
(Though graced with polished manners and fine
sense,
Yet wanting sensibility) the man
Who needlessly sets foot upon a worm.
An inadvertent step may crush the snail
That crawls at evening in the public path ;
But he that has humanity, forewarned,
Will tread aside, and let the reptile live.
The creeping vermin, loathsome to the sight,
And charged perhaps with venom, that intrudes,
A visitor unwelcome, into scenes
Sacred to neatness and repose, the alcove,
The chamber, or refectory, may die :
A necessary act incurs no blame.
Not so when, held within their proper.bounds,
And guiltless of offence, they range the air,
Or take their pastime in the spacious field :
There they are privileged ; and he that hunts
Or harms them there is guilty of a wrong,
Disturbs the economy of Nature's realm,
Who, when she formed, designed them an abode
The sum is this : If man's convenience, health,
Or safety interfere, his rights and claims
Are paramount, and must extinguish theirs.
Else they are all — the meanest things that are —
As free to live, and to enjoy that life,
As God was free to form them at the first,
Who in his sovereign wisdom made them all.
Ye, therefore, who love mercy, teach your sons
To love it too.

WILLIAM COWPER.

OF CRUELTY TO ANIMALS.

SHAME upon thee, savage monarch-man, proud
monopolist of reason ;
Shame upon creation's lord, the fierce ensanguined
despot :
What, man ! are there not enough, hunger and
diseases and fatigue, —
And yet must thy goad or thy thong add another
sorrow to existence ?
What ! art thou not content thy sin hath dragged
down suffering and death

On the poor dumb servants of thy comfort, and
yet must thou rack them with thy spite ?
The prodigal heir of creation hath gambled away
his all, —
Shall he add torment to the bondage that is galling
his forfeit serfs ?
The leader in nature's pæan himself hath marred
her psaltery,
Shall he multiply the din of discord by over-
straining all the strings ?
The rebel hath fortified his stronghold, shutting
in his vassals with him, —
Shall he aggravate the woes of the besieged by
oppression from within ?
Thou twice-deformed image of thy Maker, thou
hateful representative of Love,
For very shame be merciful, be kind unto the
creatures thou hast ruined ;
Earth and her million tribes are cursed for thy sake,
Earth and her million tribes still writhe beneath
thy cruelty :
Liveth there but one among the million that shall
not bear witness against thee,
A pensioner of land or air or sea that hath not
whereof it will accuse thee ?
From the elephant toiling at a launch, to the
shrew-mouse in the harvest-field,
From the whale which the harpooner hath stricken,
to the minnow caught upon a pin,
From the albatross wearied in its flight, to the
wren in her covered nest,
From the death-moth and lace-winged dragon-fly,
to the lady-bird and the gnat,
The verdict of all things is unanimous, finding
their master cruel :
The dog, thy humble friend, thy trusting, honest
friend ;
The ass, thine uncomplaining slave, drudging
from morn to even ;
The lamb, and the timorous hare, and the labor-
ing ox at plough ;
The speckled trout basking in the shallow, and
the partridge gleaming in the stubble,
And the stag at bay, and the worm in thy path,
and the wild bird pining in captivity,
And all things that minister alike to thy life and
thy comfort and thy pride,
Testify with one sad voice that man is a cruel
master.

Verily, they are all thine : freely mayst thou
serve thee of them all :
They are thine by gift for thy needs, to be used
in all gratitude and kindness ;
Gratitude to their God and thine, — their Father
and thy Father,
Kindness to them who toil for thee, and help
thee with their all :

For meat, but not by wantonness of slaying : for
  burden, but with limits of humanity ;
For luxury, but not through torture : for draught,
  but according to the strength :
For a dog cannot plead his own right, nor render
  a reason for exemption,
Nor give a soft answer unto wrath, to turn aside
  the undeserved lash ;
The galled ox cannot complain, nor supplicate a
  moment's respite ;
The spent horse hideth his distress, till he panteth
  out his spirit at the goal ;
Also, in the winter of life, when worn by constant
  toil,
If ingratitude forget his services, he cannot bring
  them to remembrance ;
Behold, he is faint with hunger ; the big tear
  standeth in his eye ;
His skin is sore with stripes, and he tottereth
  beneath his burden ;
His limbs are stiff with age, his sinews have lost
  their vigor,
And pain is stamped upon his face, while he
  wrestleth unequally with toil ;
Yet once more mutely and meekly endureth he
  the crushing blow ;
That struggle hath cracked his heart-strings, —
  the generous brute is dead !
Liveth there no advocate for him ? no judge to
  avenge his wrongs ?
No voice that shall be heard in his defence ? no
  sentence to be passed on his oppressor ?
Yea, the sad eye of the tortured pleadeth patheti-
  cally for him ;
Yea, all the justice in heaven is roused in indig-
  nation at his woes ;
Yea, all the pity upon earth shall call down a
  curse upon the cruel ;
Yea, the burning malice of the wicked is their
  own exceeding punishment.
The Angel of Mercy stoppeth not to comfort, but
  passeth by on the other side,
And hath no tear to shed, when a cruel man is
  damned.

MARTIN FARQUHAR TUPPER.

PLEA FOR THE ANIMALS.

FROM "THE SEASONS."

.... ENSANGUINED man
Is now become the lion of the plain,
And worse. The wolf, who from the nightly fold
Fierce drags the bleating prey, ne'er drunk her
  milk,
Nor wore her warming fleece ; nor has the steer,
At whose strong chest the deadly tiger hangs,

E'er ploughed for him. They too are tempered
  high,
With hunger stung and wild necessity ;
Nor lodges pity in their shaggy breast.
But man, whom Nature formed of milder clay,
With every kind emotion in his heart,
And taught alone to weep, — while from her lap
She pours ten thousand delicacies, herbs,
And fruits as numerous as the drops of rain
Or beams that gave them birth, — shall he, fair
  form !
Who wears sweet smiles, and looks erect on heaven,
E'er stoop to mingle with the prowling herd,
And dip his tongue in gore ? The beast of prey,
Blood-stained, deserves to bleed ; but you, ye
  flocks,
What have ye done ? ye peaceful people, what,
To merit death ? you who have given us milk
In luscious streams, and lent us your own coat
Against the winter's cold ? And the plain ox,
That harmless, honest, guileless animal,
In what has he offended ? he whose toil,
Patient and ever-ready, clothes the land
With all the pomp of harvest, — shall he bleed,
And struggling groan beneath the cruel hand,
Even of the clown he feeds ? and that, perhaps,
To swell the riot of the autumnal feast,
Won by his labor ?

JAMES THOMSON.

DUELLING.

FROM "CONVERSATION."

THE point of honor has been deemed of use,
To teach good manners, and to curb abuse ;
Admit it true, the consequence is clear,
Our polished manners are a mask we wear,
And, at the bottom, barbarous still and rude,
We are restrained, indeed, but not subdued.
The very remedy, however sure,
Springs from the mischief it intends to cure,
And savage in its principle appears,
Tried, as it should be, by the fruit it bears.
'T is hard, indeed, if nothing will defend
Mankind from quarrels but their fatal end ;
That now and then a hero must decease,
That the surviving world may live in peace.
Perhaps at last close scrutiny may show
The practice dastardly and mean and low ;
That men engage in it compelled by force,
And fear, not courage, is its proper source ;
The fear of tyrant custom, and the fear
Lest fops should censure us, and fools should sneer ;
At least, to trample on our Maker's laws,
And hazard life for any or no cause,
To rush into a fixed eternal state
Out of the very flames of rage and hate,

Or send another shivering to the bar
With all the guilt of such unnatural war,
Whatever Use may urge, or Honor plead,
On Reason's verdict is a madman's deed.
Am I to set my life upon a throw
Because a bear is rude and surly ? No, —
A moral, sensible, and well-bred man
Will not affront me ; and no other can.
Were I empowered to regulate the lists,
They should encounter with well-loaded fists ;
A Trojan combat would be something new,
Let *Dares* beat *Entellus* black and blue ;
Then each might show, to his admiring friends,
In honorable bumps his rich amends,
And carry, in contusions of his skull,
A satisfactory receipt in full.

WILLIAM COWPER.

GOLD.

GOLD ! gold ! gold ! gold !
Bright and yellow, hard and cold,
Molten, graven, hammered and rolled ;
Heavy to get, and light to hold ;
Hoarded, bartered, bought, and sold,
Stolen, borrowed, squandered, doled :
Spurned by the young, but hugged by the old
To the very verge of the churchyard mould ;
Price of many a crime untold :
Gold ! gold ! gold ! gold !
Good or bad a thousand-fold !
    How widely its agencies vary, —
To save, — to ruin, — to curse, — to bless, —
As even its minted coins express,
Now stamped with the image of good Queen Bess,
    And now of a Bloody Mary.

THOMAS HOOD.

LAW.

LAWS, as we read in ancient sages,
Have been like cobwebs in all ages.
Cobwebs for little flies are spread,
And laws for little folks are made ;
But if an insect of renown,
Hornet or beetle, wasp or drone,
Be caught in quest of sport or plunder,
The flimsy fetter flies in sunder.

JAMES BEATTIE.

QUACK MEDICINES.

FROM " THE BOROUGH."

BUT now our Quacks are gamesters, and they
    play
With craft and skill to ruin and betray ;

With monstrous promise they delude the mind,
And thrive on all that tortures human-kind.
    Void of all honor, avaricious, rash,
The daring tribe compound their boasted trash, —
Tincture or syrup, lotion, drop or pill ;
All tempt the sick to trust the lying bill ;
And twenty names of cobblers turned to squires
Aid the bold language of these blushless liars.
There are among them those who cannot read,
And yet they 'll buy a patent, and succeed ;
Will dare to promise dying sufferers aid,
For who, when dead, can threaten or upbraid ?
With cruel avarice still they recommend
More draughts, more syrup, to the journey's end.
" I feel it not." — " Then take it every hour."
" It makes me worse." — " Why, then it shows
        its power."
" I fear to die." — " Let not your spirits sink,
You 're always safe while you believe and drink."
    How strange to add, in this nefarious trade,
That men of parts are dupes by dunces made :
That creatures nature meant should clean our
        streets
Have purchased lands and mansions, parks and
        seats :
Wretches with conscience so obtuse, they leave
Their untaught sons their parents to deceive ;
And when they 're laid upon their dying bed,
No thought of murder comes into their head ;

.   .   .   .   .

And then in many a paper through the year,
Must cures and cases, oaths and proofs, appear ;
Men snatched from graves as they were dropping
        in,
Their lungs coughed up, their bones pierced
        through their skin ;
Their liver all one scirrhus, and the frame
Poisoned with evils which they dare not name ;
Men who spent all upon physicians' fees,
Who never slept, nor had a moment's ease,
Are now as roaches sound, and all as brisk as
        bees.

.   .   .   .   .

    Troubled with something in your bile or blood,
You think your doctor does you little good ;
And, grown impatient, you require in haste
The nervous cordial, nor dislike the taste ;
It comforts, heals, and strengthens ; nay, you
        think
It makes you better every time you drink ;
Who tipples brandy will some comfort feel,
But will he to the medicine set his seal ?

.   .   .   .   .

No class escapes them — from the poor man's
        pay
The nostrum takes no trifling part away ;
See ! those square patent bottles from the shop
Now decoration to the cupboard's top ;

And there a favorite hoard you 'll find within,
Companions meet ! the julep and the gin.

Suppose the case surpasses human skill,
There comes a quack to flatter weakness still ;
What greater evil can a flatterer do,
Than from himself to take the sufferer's view ?
To turn from sacred thoughts his reasoning
    powers,
And rob a sinner of his dying hours ?
Yet this they dare, and, craving to the last,
In hope's strong bondage hold their victim
    fast:
For soul or body no concern have they,
All their inquiry, " Can the patient pay ?
And will he swallow draughts until his dying
    day ?"
  Observe what ills to nervous females flow,
When the heart flutters and the pulse is low ;
If once induced these cordial sips to try,
All feel the ease, and few the danger fly ;
For, while obtained, of drams they 've all the
    force,
And when denied, then drams are the resource.
  Who would not lend a sympathizing sigh,
To hear yon infant's pity-moving cry ?
Then the good nurse (who, had she borne a
    brain,
Had sought the cause that made her babe com-
    plain)
Has all her efforts, loving soul ! applied
To set the cry, and not the cause, aside ;
She gave her powerful sweet without remorse,
The sleeping cordial, — she had tried its force,
Repeating oft ; the infant, freed from pain,
Rejected food, but took the dose again,
Sinking to sleep, while she her joy expressed,
That her dear charge could sweetly take his rest.
Soon may she spare her cordial ; not a doubt
Remains but quickly he will rest without.
  What then our hopes ? — perhaps there may
    by law
Be method found these pests to curb and awe ;
Yet, in this land of freedom, law is slack
With any being to commence attack :
Then let us trust to science, — there are those
Who can their falsehoods and their frauds dis-
    close,
All their vile trash detect, and their low tricks
    expose.
Perhaps their numbers may in time confound
Their arts, — as scorpions give themselves the
    wound ;
For when these curers dwell in every place,
While of the cured we not a man can trace,
Strong truth may then the public mind persuade,
And spoil the fruits of this nefarious trade.
                 GEORGE CRABBE.

THE RULING PASSION.

FROM " MORAL ESSAYS."

IN this one passion man can strength enjoy,
As fits give vigor just when they destroy.
Time, that on all things lays his lenient hand,
Yet tames not this ; it sticks to our last sand.
Consistent in our follies and our sins,
Here honest Nature ends as she begins.
  Old politicians chew on wisdom past,
And totter on in business to the last ;
As weak, as earnest ; and as gravely out,
As sober Lanesb'row dancing in the gout.
  Behold a reverend sire, whom want of grace
Has made the father of a nameless race,
Shoved from the wall perhaps, or rudely pressed
By his own son, that passes by unblessed :
Still to his wench he crawls on knocking knees,
And envies every sparrow that he sees.
  A salmon's belly, Helluo, was thy fate.
The doctor called, declares all help too late.
"Mercy !" cries Helluo, "mercy on my soul ;
Is there no hope ? — Alas ! — then bring the jowl."
  The frugal crone, whom praying priests attend,
Still tries to save the hallowed taper's end,
Collects her breath, as ebbing life retires,
For one puff more, and in that puff expires.
  "Odious ! in woollen ! 't would a saint pro-
    voke,"
(Were the last words that poor Narcissa spoke ;)
"No, let a charming chintz and Brussels lace
Wrap my cold limbs, and shade my lifeless face :
One would not, sure, be frightful when one 's
    dead, —
And — Betty — give this cheek a little red."
  The courtier smooth, who forty years had shined
An humble servant to all human-kind,
Just brought out this, when scarce his tongue
    could stir,
"If — where I'm going — I could serve you, sir ?"
  "I give and I devise " (old Euclio said,
And sighed) " my lands and tenements to Ned."
Your money, sir ? " My money, sir ! what, all ?
Why — if I must — (then wept) I give it Paul."
The manor, sir ? "The manor ! hold," he cried,
"Not that, — I cannot part with that," — and
    died.   ALEXANDER POPE.

THE FICKLE MOB.

FROM " CORIOLANUS."

CAIUS MARCIUS. What would you have, you
    curs,
That like not peace, nor war ? the one affrights you,
The other makes you proud. He that trusts to you,
Where he should find you lions, finds you hares ;

Where foxes, geese : you are no surer, no,
Than is the coal of fire upon the ice,
Or hailstone in the sun. Your virtue is,
To make him worthy whose offence subdues
    him,
And curse that justice did it. Who deserves great-
    ness,
Deserves your hate ; and your affections are
A sick man's appetite, who desires most that
Which would increase his evil. He that depends
Upon your favors swims with fins of lead,
And hews down oaks with rushes. Hang ye !
    Trust ye ?
With every minute you do change a mind ;
And call him noble that was now your hate,
Him vile that was your garland. What 's the
    matter,
That in these several places of the city
You cry against the noble senate, who,
Under the gods, keep you in awe, which else
Would feed on one another ?

     *   *   *   *

    CORIOLANUS. You common cry of curs ! whose
           breath I hate
As reek o' the rotten fens, whose loves I prize
As the dead carcasses of unburied men
That do corrupt my air, — I banish you ;
And here remain with your uncertainty !
Let every feeble rumor shake your hearts !
Your enemies, with nodding of their plumes,
Fan you into despair ! Have the power still
To banish your defenders ; till at length,
Your ignorance, (which finds not, till it feels,)
Making but reservation of yourselves,
(Still your own foes,) deliver you, as most
Abated captives, to some nation
That won you without blows ! Despising,
For you, the city, thus I turn my back :
There is a world elsewhere.
                  SHAKESPEARE.

ADDRESS TO THE TOOTHACHE.

My curse upon thy venomed stang,
That shoots my tortured gums alang ;
An' through my lugs gies mony a twang,
      Wi' gnawing vengeance !
Tearing my nerves wi' bitter pang,
         Like racking engines.

When fevers burn, or ague freezes,
Rheumatics gnaw, or cholic squeezes ;
Our neighbor's sympathy may ease us,
      Wi' pitying moan ;
But thee, — thou hell o' a' diseases,
         Aye mocks our groan.

Adown my beard the slavers trickle ;
I throw the wee stools o'er the mickle,
As round the fire the giglets keckle
      To see me loup ;
While, raving mad, I wish a heckle
         Were in their doup.

O' a' the numerous human dools,
Ill har'sts, daft bargains, cutty-stools,
Or worthy friends raked i' the mools,
      Sad sight to see !
The tricks o' knaves or fash o' fools,
         Thou bear'st the gree.

     *   *   *

                  ROBERT BURNS.

THE AUTHOR'S MISERIES.

FROM THE "PROLOGUE TO THE SATIRES."

SHUT, shut the door, good John ! fatigued I said,
Tie up the knocker, say I 'm sick, I 'm dead.
The Dog-star rages ! nay, 't is past a doubt,
All Bedlam, or Parnassus, is let out :
Fire in each eye, and papers in each hand,
They rave, recite, and madden round the land.
What walls can guard me, or what shades can hide ?
They pierce my thickets, through my grot they
      glide,
By land, by water, they renew the charge,
They stop the chariot, and they board the barge.
No place is sacred, not the church is free,
Even Sunday shines no Sabbath-day to me :
Then from the Mint walks forth the man of rhyme,
Happy ! to catch me, just at dinner-time.
   Is there a parson much be-mused in beer,
A maudlin poetess, a rhyming peer,
A clerk, foredoomed his father's soul to cross,
Who pens a stanza, when he should engross ?
Is there, who, locked from ink and paper, scrawls
With desperate charcoal round his darkened walls ?
All fly to TWIC'NAM, and in humble strain
Apply to me, to keep them mad or vain.
A dire dilemma ! either way I 'm sped,
If foes, they write, — if friends, they read me dead.
Seized and tied down to judge, how wretched I !
Who can't be silent, and who will not lie :
To laugh were want of goodness and of grace,
And to be grave exceeds all power of face.
I sit with sad civility, I read
With honest anguish and an aching head ;
And drop at last, but in unwilling ears,
This saving counsel, "Keep your piece nine years."
   "Nine years!" cries he who high in Drury Lane,
Lulled by soft zephyrs through the broken pane,
Rhymes ere he wakes, and prints before Term ends,
Obliged by hunger, and request of friends, —
"The piece, you think, is incorrect ? why, take it,

I'm all submission; what you'd have it, make it."
Three things another's modest wishes bound,
My friendship, and a prologue, and ten pound.
  Pitholeon sends to me : " You know his Grace,
I want a patron ; ask him for a place."
Pitholeon libelled me — " But here 's a letter
Informs you, sir, 't was when he knew no better.
Dare you refuse him ? Curl invites to dine,
He 'll write a *journal*, or he 'll turn divine."
Bless me ! a packet. — " 'T is a stranger sues,
A virgin tragedy, an orphan muse."
If I dislike it, " Furies, death, and rage ! "
If I approve, "Commend it to the stage."
There (thank my stars) my whole commission ends,
The players and I are, luckily, no friends.
Fired that the house reject him, " 'Sdeath, I 'll
    print it,
And shame the fools. — Your interest, sir, with
    Lintot."
Lintot, dull rogue ! will think your price too much:
" Not, sir, if you revise it, and retouch."
All my demurs but double his attacks ;
At last he whispers, "Do ; and we go snacks."
Glad of a quarrel, straight I clap the door,
Sir, let me see your works and you no more.
Who shames a scribbler ? break one cobweb
    through,
He spins the slight, self-pleasing thread anew :
Destroy his fib or sophistry, in vain,
The creature 's at his dirty work again,
Throned in the centre of his thin designs,
Proud of a vast extent of flimsy lines !
Of all mad creatures, if the learned are right,
It is the slaver kills, and not the bite.
A fool quite angry is quite innocent,
Alas ! 't is ten times worse when they *repent*.
  One dedicates in high heroic prose,
And ridicules beyond a hundred foes :
One from all Grub Street will my fame defend,
And, more abusive, calls himself my friend.
This prints my *Letters*, that expects a bribe,
And others roar aloud, "Subscribe, subscribe."
  There are, who to my person pay their court :
I cough like *Horace*, and, though lean, am short;
Ammon's great son one shoulder had too high,
Such *Ovid's* nose, and "Sir ! you have an eye."—
Go on, obliging creatures, make me see,
All that disgraced my betters met in me.
Say for my comfort, languishing in bed,
"Just so immortal *Maro* held his head" :
And when I die, be sure you let me know
Great *Homer* died three thousand years ago.
  Why did I write ? what sin to me unknown
Dipped me in ink, — my parents', or my own ?
As yet a child, nor yet a fool to fame,
I lisped in numbers, for the numbers came.
I left no calling for this idle trade,
No duty broke, no father disobeyed.

The muse but served to ease some friend, not
    wife,
To help me through this long disease, my life.
  Soft were my numbers ; who could take offence
While pure description held the place of sense ?
Like gentle *Fanny's* was my flowery theme,
A painted mistress, or a purling stream.
Yet then did *Gildon* draw his venal quill ;
I wished the man a dinner, and sate still.
Yet then did *Dennis* rave in furious fret ;
I never answered, I was not in debt.
  Did some more sober critic come abroad ;
If wrong, I smiled ; if right, I kissed the rod.
Pains, reading, study, are their just pretence,
And all they want is spirit, taste, and sense.
Commas and points they set exactly right,
And 't were a sin to rob them of their mite.
Yet ne'er one sprig of laurel graced these ribalds,
From slashing *Bentley* down to piddling *Tibbalds :*
Each wight who reads not, and but scans and
    spells,
Each word-catcher that lives on syllables,
Even such small critics some regard may claim,
Preserved in *Milton's* or in *Shakespeare's* name.
Pretty ! in amber to observe the forms
Of hairs, or straws, or dirt, or grubs, or worms !
The things, we know, are neither rich nor rare,
But wonder how the devil they got there.
The bard whom pilfered pastorals renown,
Who turns a Persian tale for half a crown,
Just writes to make his barrenness appear,
And strains, from hard-bound brains, eight lines
    a year ;
He who still wanting, though he lives on theft,
Steals much, spends little, yet has nothing left ;
And he who now to sense, now nonsense, lean-
    ing,
Means not, but blunders round about a meaning :
And he whose fustian 's so sublimely bad,
It is not poetry, but prose run mad :
All these my modest satire bade translate,
And owned that nine such Poets made a Tate.
  Peace to all such ! but were there one whose
    fires
True genius kindles, and fair fame inspires ;
Blest with each talent and each art to please,
And born to write, converse, and live with ease
Should such a man, too fond to rule alone,
Bear, like the Turk, no brother near the throne,
View him with scornful, yet with jealous eyes,
And hate for arts that caused himself to rise ;
Damn with faint praise, assent with civil leer,
And, without sneering, teach the rest to sneer ;
Willing to wound, and yet afraid to strike ;
Just hint a fault, and hesitate dislike ;
Alike reserved to blame or to commend,
A timorous foe, and a suspicious friend.

ALEXANDER POPE.

RHYMERS.

FROM "FIRST PART OF HENRY IV."

I HAD rather be a kitten, and cry, mew,
Than one of these same metre ballad-mongers;
I had rather hear a brazen canstick turned,
Or a dry wheel grate on an axletree;
And that would set my teeth nothing on edge,
Nothing so much as mincing poetry:
'T is like the forced gait of a shuffling nag.

SHAKESPEARE.

TO THE UNCO GUID.

"My son, these maxims make a rule
And lump them aye thegither:
The Rigid Righteous is a fool,
The Rigid Wise anither;
The cleanest corn that e'er was dight
May hae some pyles o' caff in;
Sae ne'er a fellow-creature slight
For random fits o' daffin."

SOLOMON. — *Eccles.* vii. 16.

O YE wha are sae guid yoursel'
Sae pious and sae holy,
Ye 've nought to do but mark and tell
Your neebor's fauts and folly: —
Whase life is like a weel-gaun mill,
Supplied wi' store o' water,
The heapéd happer 's ebbing still,
And still the clap plays clatter.

Hear me, ye venerable core,
As counsel for poor mortals,
That frequent pass douce Wisdom's door
For glaikit Folly's portals!
I, for their thoughtless, careless sakes,
Would here propone defences,
Their donsie tricks, their black mistakes,
Their failings and mischances.

Ye see your state wi' theirs compared,
And shudder at the niffer;
But cast a moment's fair regard,
What maks the mighty differ?
Discount what scant occasion gave
That purity ye pride in,
And (what 's aft mair than a' the lave)
Your better art o' hidin'.

Think, when your castigated pulse
Gies now and then a wallop,
What ragings must his veins convulse,
That still eternal gallop!
Wi' wind and tide fair i' your tail,
Right on ye scud your sea-way;
But in the teeth o' baith to sail,
It makes an unco leeway.

.   .   .   .   .

Ye high, exalted, virtuous dames,
Tied up in godly laces,
Before ye gie poor Frailty names,
Suppose a change o' cases;
A dear-loved lad, convenience snug,
A treacherous inclination, —
But, let me whisper i' your lug,
Ye 're aiblins nae temptation.

Then gently scan your brother man,
Still gentler sister woman;
Though they may gang a kennin' wrang,
To step aside is human.
One point must still be greatly dark,
The moving why they do it;
And just as lamely can ye mark
How far perhaps they rue it.

Who made the heart, 't is He alone
Decidedly can try us;
He knows each chord, — its various tone,
Each spring, — its various bias:
Then at the balance let 's be mute,
We never can adjust it;
What 's done we partly may compute,
But know not what 's resisted.

ROBERT BURNS.

IL PENSEROSO.

HENCE, vain deluding joys,
The brood of Folly without father bred!
How little you bestead,
Or fill the fixéd mind with all your toys!
Dwell in some idle brain,
And fancies fond with gaudy shapes possess,
As thick and numberless
As the gay motes that people the sunbeams,—
Or likest hovering dreams,
The fickle pensioners of Morpheus' train.
But hail, thou goddess, sage and holy!
Hail, divinest Melancholy!
Whose saintly visage is too bright
To hit the sense of human sight,
And therefore, to our weaker view,
O'erlaid with black, staid wisdom's hue, —
Black, but such as in esteem
Prince Memnon's sister might beseem,
Or that starred Ethiop queen that strove
To set her beauty's praise above
The sea-nymphs, and their powers offended.
Yet thou art higher far descended;
Thee bright-haired Vesta, long of yore,
To solitary Saturn bore, —
His daughter she (in Saturn's reign
Such mixture was not held a stain).
Oft in glimmering bowers and glades

He met her, and in secret shades
Of woody Ida's inmost grove,
While yet there was no fear of Jove.
  Come, pensive nun, devout and pure,
Sober, steadfast, and demure,
All in a robe of darkest grain
Flowing with majestic train,
And sable stole of cyprus lawn
Over thy decent shoulders drawn !
Come, but keep thy wonted state,
With even step, and musing gait,
And looks commercing with the skies,
Thy rapt soul sitting in thine eyes ;
There held in holy passion still,
Forget thyself to marble, till
With a sad, leaden, downward cast
Thou fix them on the earth as fast ;
And join with thee calm Peace, and Quiet, —
Spare Fast, that oft with gods doth diet,
And hears the Muses in a ring
Aye round about Jove's altar sing.
And add to these retired Leisure,
That in trim gardens takes his pleasure ;
But first and chiefest, with thee bring
Him that yon soars on golden wing,
Guiding the fiery-wheeled throne, —
The cherub Contemplation ;
And the mute Silence hist along,
'Less Philomel will deign a song
In her sweetest, saddest plight,
Smoothing the rugged brow of Night,
While Cynthia checks her dragon yoke
Gently o'er the accustomed oak.
Sweet bird, that shun'st the noise of folly, —
Most musical, most melancholy !
Thee, chantress, oft, the woods among,
I woo, to hear thy even-song :
And, missing thee, I walk unseen
On the dry, smooth-shaven green,
To behold the wandering moon
Riding near her highest noon,
Like one that had been led astray
Through the heaven's wide pathless way ;
And oft, as if her head she bowed,
Stooping through a fleecy cloud.
Oft, on a plat of rising ground,
I hear the far-off curfew sound
Over some wide-watered shore,
Swinging slow with sullen roar ;
Or if the air will not permit,
Some still removéd place will fit,
Where glowing embers through the room
Teach light to counterfeit a gloom, —
Far from all resort of mirth,
Save the cricket on the hearth,
Or the bellman's drowsy charm,
To bless the doors from nightly harm ;
Or let my lamp at midnight hour

Be seen in some high lonely tower,
Where I may oft out-watch the Bear
With thrice-great Hermes, or unsphere
The spirit of Plato, to unfold
What worlds or what vast regions hold
The immortal mind that hath forsook
Her mansion in this fleshly nook ;
And of those demons that are found
In fire, air, flood, or under ground,
Whose power hath a true consent
With planet or with element.
Sometime let gorgeous Tragedy
In sceptred pall come sweeping by,
Presenting Thebes, or Pelops' line,
Or the tale of Troy divine,
Or what (though rare) of later age
Ennobled hath the buskined stage.

  But, O sad virgin, that thy power
Might raise Musæus from his bower !
Or bid the soul of Orpheus sing
Such notes as, warbled to the string,
Drew iron tears down Pluto's cheek,
And made hell grant what love did seek !
Or call up him that left half told
The story of Cambuscan bold, —
Of Camball, and of Algarsife, —
And who had Canace to wife,
That owned the virtuous ring and glass, —
And of the wondrous horse of brass,
On which the Tartar king did ride !
And, if aught else great bards beside
In sage and solemn tunes have sung, —
Of tourneys and of trophies hung,
Of forests, and enchantments drear,
Where more is meant than meets the ear.

  Thus, Night, oft see me in thy pale career,
Till civil-suited Morn appear, —
Not tricked and frounced, as she was wont
With the Attic boy to hunt,
But kerchiefed in a comely cloud,
While rocking winds are piping loud,
Or ushered with a shower still
When the gust hath blown his fill,
Ending on the rustling leaves,
With minute drops from off the eaves.
And when the sun begins to fling
His flaring beams, me, goddess, bring
To archéd walks of twilight groves,
And shadows brown, that Sylvan loves,
Of pine, or monumental oak,
Where the rude axe with heavéd stroke
Was never heard the Nymphs to daunt,
Or fright them from their hallowed haunt.
There in close covert by some brook,
Where no profaner eye may look,
Hide me from day's garish eye,

While the bee with honeyed thigh,
That at her flowery work doth sing,
And the waters murmuring
With such consort as they keep,
Entice the dewy-feathered Sleep ;
And let some strange mysterious dream
Wave at his wings, in airy stream
Of lively portraiture displayed,
Softly on my eyelids laid ;
And, as I wake, sweet music breathe
Above, about, or underneath,
Sent by some spirit to mortals good,
Or the unseen genius of the wood.

But let my due feet never fail
To walk the studious cloisters pale,
And love the high embowèd roof,
With antic pillars massy proof,
And storied windows, richly dight,
Casting a dim religious light.
There let the pealing organ blow
To the full-voiced quire below,
In service high and anthems clear,
As may with sweetness, through mine ear,
Dissolve me into ecstasies,
And bring all heaven before mine eyes.

And may at last my weary age
Find out the peaceful hermitage,
The hairy gown and mossy cell,
Where I may sit and rightly spell
Of every star that heaven doth shew,
And every herb that sips the dew,
Till old experience do attain
To something like prophetic strain.

These pleasures, Melancholy, give,
And I with thee will choose to live.
JOHN MILTON.

HALLOWED GROUND.

WHAT's hallowed ground ?   Has earth a clod
Its Maker meant not should be trod
By man, the image of his God,
　　Erect and free,
Unscourged by Superstition's rod
　　To bow the knee ?

That 's hallowed ground — where, mourned and
　　missed,
The lips repose our love has kissed ; —
But where 's their memory's mansion ?   Is 't
　　Yon churchyard's bowers ?
No ! in ourselves their souls exist,
　　A part of ours.

A kiss can consecrate the ground
Where mated hearts are mutual bound :
The spot where love's first links were wound,
　　That ne'er are riven,
Is hallowed down to earth's profound,
　　And up to heaven !

For time makes all but true love old ;
The burning thoughts that then were told
Run molten still in memory's mould ;
　　And will not cool,
Until the heart itself be cold
　　In Lethe's pool.

What hallows ground where heroes sleep ?
'T is not the sculptured piles you heap !
In dews that heavens far distant weep
　　Their turf may bloom ;
Or Genii twine beneath the deep
　　Their coral tomb.

But strew his ashes to the wind
Whose sword or voice has served mankind,
And is he dead, whose glorious mind
　　Lifts thine on high ?
To live in hearts we leave behind
　　Is not to die.

Is 't death to fall for Freedom's right ?
He 's dead alone that lacks her light !
And murder sullies in Heaven's sight
　　The sword he draws : —
What can alone ennoble fight ?
　　A noble cause !

Give that ! and welcome War to brace
Her drums ! and rend heaven's reeking space !
The colors planted face to face,
　　The charging cheer,
Though Death's pale horse lead on the chase,
　　Shall still be dear.

And place our trophies where men kneel
To Heaven ! — but Heaven rebukes my zeal !
The cause of Truth and human weal,
　　O God above !
Transfer it from the sword's appeal
　　To Peace and Love.

Peace, Love ! the cherubim, that join
Their spread wings o'er Devotion's shrine,
Prayers sound in vain, and temples shine,
　　Where they are not, —
The heart alone can make divine
　　Religion's spot.

To incantations dost thou trust,
And pompous rites in domes august ?

See mouldering stones and metal's rust
  Belie the vaunt,
That man can bless one pile of dust
  With chime or chant.

The ticking wood-worm mocks thee, man !
Thy temples, — creeds themselves grow wan !
But there 's a dome of nobler span,
  A temple given
Thy faith, that bigots dare not ban, —
  Its space is heaven !

Its roof star-pictured Nature's ceiling,
Where trancing the rapt spirit's feeling,
And God himself to man revealing,
  The harmonious spheres
Make music, though unheard their pealing
  By mortal ears.

Fair stars ! are not your beings pure ?
Can sin, can death, your worlds obscure ?
Else why so swell the thoughts at your
  Aspect above ?
Ye must be heavens that make us sure
  Of heavenly love !

And in your harmony sublime
I read the doom of distant time ;
That man's regenerate soul from crime
  Shall yet be drawn,
And reason on his mortal clime
  Immortal dawn.

What 's hallowed ground ? 'T is what gives birth
To sacred thoughts in souls of worth ! —
Peace ! Independence ! Truth ! go forth
  Earth's compass round ;
And your high-priesthood shall make earth
  All hallowed ground.
           THOMAS CAMPBELL.

A TEAR.

O THAT the chemist's magic art
  Could crystallize this sacred treasure ! .
Long should it glitter near my heart,
  A secret source of pensive pleasure.

The little brilliant, ere it fell,
  Its lustre caught from Chloe's eye ;
Then, trembling, left its coral cell, —
  The spring of Sensibility !

Sweet drop of pure and pearly light !
  In thee the rays of Virtue shine,
More calmly clear, more mildly bright,
  Than any gem that gilds the mine.

Benign restorer of the soul !
  Who ever fliest to bring relief,
When first we feel the rude control
  Of Love or Pity, Joy or Grief.

The sage's and the poet's theme,
  In every clime, in every age,
Thou charm'st in Fancy's idle dream,
  In Reason's philosophic page.

That very law which moulds a tear,
  And bids it trickle from its source,
That law preserves the earth a sphere,
  And guides the planets in their course.
           SAMUEL ROGERS.

THE GARDEN OF LOVE.

I WENT to the garden of love,
And saw what I never had seen ;
A chapel was built in the midst,
Where I used to play on the green.

And the gate of this chapel was shut,
And "thou shalt not " writ over the door ;
So I turned to the garden of love,
That so many sweet flowers bore.

And I saw it was filled with graves,
And tombstones where flowers should be ;
And priests in black gowns were walking their
  rounds,
And binding with briers my joys and desires.
           WILLIAM BLAKE.

INVOCATION TO RAIN IN SUMMER.

O GENTLE, gentle summer rain,
  Let not the silver lily pine,
The drooping lily pine in vain
  To feel that dewy touch of thine, —
To drink thy freshness once again,
O gentle, gentle summer rain !

In heat the landscape quivering lies ;
  The cattle pant beneath the tree ;
Through parching air and purple skies
  The earth looks up, in vain, for thee ;
For thee — for thee, it looks in vain,
O gentle, gentle summer rain.

Come thou, and brim the meadow streams,
  And soften all the hills with mist,
O falling dew ! from burning dreams
  By thee shall herb and flower be kissed,
And Earth shall bless thee yet again,
O gentle, gentle summer rain.
         WILLIAM COX BENNETT.

IF WOMEN COULD BE FAIR.

FROM BYRD'S "SONGS AND SONNETS," 1588.

IF women could be fair and never fond,
  Or that their beauty might continue still,
I would not marvel though they made men bond,
  By service long to purchase their good-will ;
But when I see how frail these creatures are,
I laugh that men forget themselves so far.

To mark what choice they make, and how they
    change,
  How, leaving best, the worst they choose out
    still,
And how, like haggards, wild about they range,
  Scorning the reason to follow after will ;
Who would not shake such buzzards from the fist,
And let them fly, fair fools, what way they list ?

Yet for our sport we fawn and flatter both,
  To pass the time when nothing else can please,
And train them on to yield, by subtle oath,
  The sweet content that gives such humor ease ;
And then we say, when we their follies try,
To play with fools, O, what a fool was I !
                                      ANONYMOUS.

THE ONE GRAY HAIR.

THE wisest of the wise
Listen to pretty lies,
    And love to hear them told ;
Doubt not that Solomon
Listened to many a one, —
Some in his youth, and more when he grew old.

I never sat among
The choir of wisdom's song,
    But pretty lies loved I
As much as any king, —
When youth was on the wing,
And (must it then be told ?) when youth had quite
    gone by.

Alas ! and I have not
The pleasant hour forgot,
    When one pert lady said, —
"O Landor ! I am quite
Bewildered with affright ;
I see (sit quiet now !) a white hair on your head !"

Another, more benign,
Drew out that hair of mine,
    And in her own dark hair
Pretended she had found
That one, and twirled it round. —
Fair as she was, she never was so fair.
                          WALTER SAVAGE LANDOR.

DRINK TO ME ONLY WITH THINE EYES.

FROM "THE FOREST."

DRINK to me only with thine eyes,
  And I will pledge with mine ;
Or leave a kiss but in the cup,
  And I 'll not look for wine.
The thirst that from the soul doth rise
  Doth ask a drink divine ;
But might I of Jove's nectar sup,
  I would not change for thine.

I sent thee late a rosy wreath,
  Not so much honoring thee
As giving it a hope that there
  It could not withered be ;
But thou thereon didst only breathe
  And sent'st it back to me ;
Since when it grows, and smells, I swear,
  Not of itself but thee !
          PHILOSTRATUS (Greek). Trans-
          lation of BEN JONSON.

THE MAHOGANY-TREE.

CHRISTMAS is here ;
Winds whistle shrill,
Icy and chill,
Little care we ;
Little we fear
Weather without,
Sheltered about
The mahogany-tree.

Once on the boughs
Birds of rare plume
Sang, in its bloom ;
Night-birds are we ;
Here we carouse,
Singing, like them,
Perched round the stem
Of the jolly old tree.

Here let us sport,
Boys, as we sit, —
Laughter and wit
Flashing so free.
Life is but short, —
When we are gone,
Let them sing on,
Round the old tree.

Evenings we knew,
Happy as this ;
Faces we miss,
Pleasant to see.

Kind hearts and true,
Gentle and just,
Peace to your dust !
We sing round the tree.

Care, like a dun,
Lurks at the gate :
Let the dog wait ;
Happy we 'll be !
Drink, every one ;
Pile up the coals ;
Fill the red bowls,
Round the old tree !

Drain we the cup. —
Friend, art afraid ?
Spirits are laid
In the Red Sea.
Mantle it up ;
Empty it yet ;
Let us forget,
Round the old tree !

Sorrows, begone !
Life and its ills,
Duns and their bills,
Bid we to flee.
Come with the dawn,
Blue-devil sprite ;
Leave us to-night,
Round the old tree !

WILLIAM MAKEPEACE THACKERAY.

THE OLD FOGY.

OLD WINE TO DRINK, OLD WOOD TO BURN, OLD BOOKS
TO READ, AND OLD FRIENDS TO CONVERSE WITH.

I.

OLD wine to drink ! —
Ay, give the slippery juice
That drippeth from the grape thrown loose
Within the tun ;
Plucked from beneath the cliff
Of sunny-sided Teneriffe,
And ripened 'neath the blink
Of India's sun !
Peat whiskey hot,
Tempered with well-boiled water !
These make the long night shorter, —
Forgetting not
Good stout old English porter.

II.

Old wood to burn ! —
Ay, bring the hillside beech
From where the owlets meet and screech,
And ravens croak ;

The crackling pine, and cedar sweet ;
Bring too a clump of fragrant peat,
Dug 'neath the fern ;
The knotted oak,
A fagot too, perhaps,
Whose bright flame, dancing, winking,
Shall light us at our drinking ;
While the oozing sap
Shall make sweet music to our thinking.

III.

Old books to read ! —
Ay, bring those nodes of wit,
The brazen-clasped, the vellum writ,
Time-honored tomes !
The same my sire scanned before,
The same my grandsire thumbed o'er,
The same his sire from college bore,
The well-earned meed
Of Oxford's domes ;
Old Homer blind,
Old Horace, rake Anacreon, by
Old Tully, Plautus, Terence lie ;
Mort Arthur's olden minstrelsie,
Quaint Burton, quainter Spenser, ay !
And Gervase Markham's venerie, —
Nor leave behind
The Holye Book by which we live and die.

IV.

Old friends to talk ! —
Ay, bring those chosen few,
The wise, the courtly, and the true,
So rarely found ;
Him for my wine, him for my stud,
Him for my easel, distich, bud
In mountain walk !
Bring Walter good :
With soulful Fred ; and learned Will,
And thee, my *alter ego* (dearer still
For every mood).

ROBERT HINCHLEY MESSENGER.

AULD LANG SYNE.

SHOULD auld acquaintance be forgot,
And never brought to min' ?
Should auld acquaintance be forgot,
And days o' lang syne ?

CHORUS.

For auld lang syne, my dear,
For auld lang syne,
We 'll tak a cup o' kindness yet,
For auld lang syne.

We twa hae run about the braes,
  And pou'd the gowans fine ;
But we 've wandered mony a weary foot
Sin' auld lang syne.
        For auld, etc.

We twa hae paidl't i' the burn,
  Frae mornin' sun till dine ;
But seas between us braid hae roared
Sin' auld lang syne.
        For auld, etc.

And here's a hand, my trusty fiere,
  And gie's a hand o' thine ;
And we 'll tak a right guid willie-waught
For auld lang syne.
        For auld, etc.

And surely ye 'll be your pint-stoup,
  And surely I 'll be mine ;
And we 'll tak a cup o' kindness yet
For auld lang syne.
        For auld, etc.

          ROBERT BURNS.

LIFE.

I MADE a posie, while the day ran by :
Here will I smell my remnant out, and tie
    My life within this band.
But time did beckon to the flowers, and they
By noon most cunningly did steal away,
    And withered in my hand.

My hand was next to them, and then my heart ;
I took, without more thinking, in good part
    Time's gentle admonition ;
Who did so sweetly death's sad taste convey,
Making my minde to smell my fatall day,
    Yet sugring the suspicion.

Farewell, dear flowers, sweetly your time ye spent,
Fit, while ye lived, for smell or ornament,
    And after death for cures.
I follow straight without complaints or grief,
Since, if my scent be good, I care not, if
    It be as short as yours.
          GEORGE HERBERT.

LIFE.

MY life is like the summer rose
That opens to the morning sky,
But, ere the shades of evening close,
Is scattered on the ground, — to die !
Yet on the rose's humble bed
The sweetest dews of night are shed,

As if she wept the waste to see, —
But none shall weep a tear for me !

My life is like the autumn leaf
That trembles in the moon's pale ray ;
Its hold is frail, — its date is brief,
Restless, — and soon to pass away !
Yet, ere that leaf shall fall and fade,
The parent tree will mourn its shade,
The winds bewail the leafless tree, —
But none shall breathe a sigh for me !

My life is like the prints which feet
Have left on Tampa's desert strand ;
Soon as the rising tide shall beat,
All trace will vanish from the sand ;
Yet, as if grieving to efface
All vestige of the human race,
On that lone shore loud moans the sea, —
But none, alas ! shall mourn for me !
          RICHARD HENRY WILDE.

"BLESSED ARE THEY THAT MOURN."

O, DEEM not they are blest alone
  Whose lives a peaceful tenor keep ;
The Power who pities man has shown
  A blessing for the eyes that weep.

The light of smiles shall fill again
  The lids that overflow with tears ;
And weary hours of woe and pain
  Are promises of happier years.

There is a day of sunny rest
  For every dark and troubled night ;
And grief may bide an evening guest,
  But joy shall come with early light.

And thou, who, o'er thy friend's low bier,
  Sheddest the bitter drops like rain,
Hope that a brighter, happier sphere
  Will give him to thy arms again.

Nor let the good man's trust depart,
  Though life its common gifts deny, —
Though with a pierced and bleeding heart,
  And spurned of men, he goes to die.

For God hath marked each sorrowing day
  And numbered every secret tear,
And heaven's long age of bliss shall pay
  For all his children suffer here.
          WILLIAM CULLEN BRYANT.

LIFE.

This life, sae far 's I understand,
Is a' enchanted fairy land,
Where Pleasure is the magic wand,
    That, wielded right,
Maks hours like minutes, hand in hand,
    Dance by fu' light.

The magic wand then let us wield ;
For, ance that five-an'-forty 's speeled,
See crazy, weary, joyless eild,
    Wi' wrinkled face,
Comes hostin', hirplin', owre the field,
    Wi' creepin' pace.

When ance life's day draws near the gloamin',
Then fareweel vacant careless roamin' ;
An' fareweel cheerfu' tankards foamin',
    An' social noise ;
An' fareweel dear, deluding woman !
    The joy of joys !

O Life ! how pleasant in thy morning,
Young Fancy's rays the hills adorning !
Cold-pausing Caution's lesson scorning,
    We frisk away,
Like school-boys, at the expected warning,
    To joy and play.

We wander there, we wander here,
We eye the rose upon the brier,
Unmindful that the thorn is near,
    Amang the leaves :
And though the puny wound appear,
    Short while it grieves.

Some, lucky, find a flowery spot,
For which they never toiled nor swat ;
They drink the sweet and eat the fat,
    But care or pain ;
And, haply, eye the barren hut
    With high disdain.

With steady aim some Fortune chase ;
Keen Hope does every sinew brace ;
Through fair, through foul, they urge the race,
    And seize the prey :
Then cannie, in some cozie place,
    They close the day.

An' others, like your humble servan',
Poor wights ! nae rules nor roads observin',
To right or left, eternal swervin',
    They zig-zag on ;
Till curst wi' age, obscure an' starvin',
    They aften groan.

ROBERT BURNS.

THE RIVER OF LIFE.

The more we live, more brief appear
Our life's succeeding stages ;
A day to childhood seems a year,
And years like passing ages.

The gladsome current of our youth,
Ere passion yet disorders,
Steals lingering like a river smooth
Along its grassy borders.

But as the careworn cheek grows wan,
And sorrow's shafts fly thicker,
Ye stars, that measure life to man,
Why seem your courses quicker ?

When joys have lost their bloom and breath,
And life itself is vapid,
Why, as we near the Falls of Death,
Feel we its tide more rapid ?

It may be strange, — yet who would change
Time's course to slower speeding,
When one by one our friends have gone
And left our bosoms bleeding ?

Heaven gives our years of fading strength
Indemnifying fleetness ;
And those of youth, a seeming length,
Proportioned to their sweetness.

THOMAS CAMPBELL.

A MEDITATION ON THE FRAILTY OF THIS LIFE.

O trifling toys that toss the brains
    While loathsome life doth last ;
O wishéd wealth, O sugared joys,
    O life when death is past !
Who loathes exchange of loss with gain ?
    Yet loathe we death as hell.
What woful wight would wish his woe ?
    Yet wish we here to dwell.
O Fancy frail, that feeds on earth,
    And stays on slippery joys !
O noble mind, O happy man,
    That can contemn such toys !

Such toys as neither perfect are,
    And cannot long endure ;
Our greatest skill, our sweetest joy,
    Uncertain and unsure.
For life is short, and learning long,
    All pleasure mixt with woe ;
Sickness and sleep steal time unseen,
    And joys do come and go.

Thus learning is but learned by halves,
    And joy enjoyed no while ;
That serves to show thee what thou want'st,
    This helps thee to beguile.

But after death is perfect skill,
    And joy without decay ;
When sin is gone, that blinds our eyes,
    And steals our joys away.
No crowing cock shall raise us up
    To spend the day in vain ;
No weary labor shall us drive
    To go to bed again.
But — for we feel not what we want,
    Nor know not what we have —
    We love to keep the body's life,
    We loathe the soul to save.
                        ANONYMOUS.

THE EBB-TIDE.

SLOWLY thy flowing tide
Came in, old Avon ! Scarcely did mine eyes,
As watchfully I roamed thy greenwood side,
    Perceive its gentle rise.

With many a stroke and strong
The laboring boatmen upward plied their oars ;
Yet little way they made, though laboring long
    Between thy winding shores.

Now down thine ebbing tide
The unlabored boat falls rapidly along ;
The solitary helmsman sits to guide,
    And sings an idle song.

Now o'er the rocks that lay
So silent late the shallow current roars ;
Fast flow thy waters on their seaward way,
    Through wider-spreading shores.

Avon, I gaze and know
The lesson emblemed in thy varying way ;
It speaks of human joys that rise so slow,
    So rapidly decay.

Kingdoms which long have stood
And slow to strength and power attained at last,
Thus from the summit of high Fortune's flood,
    They ebb to ruin fast.

Thus like thy flow appears
Time's tardy course to manhood's envied stage.
Alas ! how hurryingly the ebbing years
    Then hasten to old age !
                        ROBERT SOUTHEY.

BUSY, CURIOUS, THIRSTY FLY.

[Last verse added by Rev. J. Plumtree.]

BUSY, curious, thirsty fly,
Drink with me, and drink as I ;
Freely welcome to my cup,
Couldst thou sip and sip it up.
Make the most of life you may ;
Life is short, and wears away.

Both alike are mine and thine,
Hastening quick to their decline ;
Thine's a summer, mine no more,
Though repeated to threescore.
Threescore summers, when they're gone,
Will appear as short as one.

Yet this difference we may see
'Twixt the life of man and thee, —
Thou art for this life alone,
Man seeks another when 't is gone ;
And though allowed its joys to share,
Tries virtue here, hopes pleasure there.
                        VINCENT BOURNE.

THE VANITY OF THE WORLD.

FALSE world, thou ly'st : thou canst not lend
        The least delight :
Thy favors cannot gain a friend,
        They are so slight :
Thy morning pleasures make an end
        To please at night :
Poor are the wants that thou supply'st,
And yet thou vaunt'st, and yet thou vy'st
With heaven ; fond earth, thou boasts ; false
        world, thou ly'st.

Thy babbling tongue tells golden tales
        Of endless treasure ;
Thy bounty offers easy sales
        Of lasting pleasure ;
Thou ask'st the conscience what she ails,
        And swear'st to ease her ;
There's none can want where thou supply'st :
There's none can give where thou deny'st.
Alas ! fond world, thou boasts ; false world, thou
        ly'st.

What well-advisèd ear regards
        What earth can say ?
Thy words are gold, but thy rewards
        Are painted clay :
Thy cunning can but pack the cards,
        Thou canst not play :
Thy game at weakest, still thou vy'st ;
If seen, and then revy'd, deny'st :
Thou art not what thou seem'st ; false world,
        thou ly'st.

Thy tinsel bosom seems a mint
    Of new-coined treasure ;
A paradise, that has no stint,
    No change, no measure ;
A painted cask, but nothing in 't,
    Nor wealth, nor pleasure :
Vain earth ! that falsely thus comply'st
With man ; vain man ! that thou rely'st
On earth ; vain man, thou dot'st ; vain earth,
    thou ly'st.

What mean dull souls, in this high measure,
    To haberdash
In earth's base wares, whose greatest treasure
    Is dross and trash ?
The height of whose enchanting pleasure
    Is but a flash ?
Are these the goods that thou supply'st
Us mortals with ?   Are these the high'st ?
Can these bring cordial peace ? false world, thou
    ly'st.   FRANCIS QUARLES.

THE NEVERMORE.

LOOK in my face ; my name is Might-have-been ;
  I am also called No-more, Too-late, Farewell ;
  Unto thine ear I hold the dead-sea shell
Cast up thy Life's foam-fretted feet between ;
Unto thine eyes the glass where that is seen
  Which had Life's form and Love's, but by my
    spell
Is now a shaken shadow intolerable,
Of ultimate things unuttered the frail screen.

Mark me, how still I am ! But should there dart
One moment through my soul the soft surprise
Of that winged Peace which lulls the breath of
    sighs, —
Then shalt thou see me smile, and turn apart
Thy visage to mine ambush at thy heart
Sleepless with cold commemorative eyes.
        DANTE GABRIEL ROSSETTI.

THE GENIUS OF DEATH.

WHAT is death ? 'T is to be free,
  No more to love or hope or fear,
To join the great equality ;
  All, all alike are humbled there.
    The mighty grave
    Wraps lord and slave ;
Nor pride nor poverty dares come
Within that refuge-house, — the tomb.

Spirit with the drooping wing
And the ever-weeping eye,

Thou of all earth's kings art king ;
  Empires at thy footstool lie ;
    Beneath thee strewed,
    Their multitude
Sink like waves upon the shore ;
Storms shall never raise them more.

What 's the grandeur of the earth
  To the grandeur round thy throne ?
Riches, glory, beauty, birth,
  To thy kingdom all have gone.
    Before thee stand
    The wondrous band, —
Bards, heroes, sages, side by side,
Who darkened nations when they died.

Earth has hosts, but thou canst show
  Many a million for her one ;
Through thy gates the mortal flow
  Hath for countless years rolled on.
    Back from the tomb
    No step has come,
There fixed till the last thunder's sound
Shall bid thy prisoners be unbound.
        GEORGE CROLY.

LINES

WRITTEN BY ONE IN THE TOWER, BEING YOUNG AND
CONDEMNED TO DIE.

My prime of youth is but a frost of cares ;
  My feast of joy is but a dish of pain ;
My crop of corn is but a field of tares ;
  And all my good is but vain hope of gain :
The day.is [fled], and yet I saw no sun ;
And now I live, and now my life is done !

The spring is past, and yet it hath not sprung ;
  The fruit is dead, and yet the leaves are green ;
My youth is gone, and yet I am but young ;
  I saw the world, and yet I was not seen :
My thread is cut, and yet it is not spun ;
And now I live, and now my life is done !

I sought my death, and found it in my womb ;
  I looked for life, and saw it was a shade ;
I trod the earth, and knew it was my tomb ;
  And now I die, and now I am but made ;
The glass is full, and now my glass is run ;
And now I live, and now my life is done !
        CHIDIOCK TYCHBORN.

LINES

WRITTEN THE NIGHT BEFORE HIS EXECUTION.

E'EN such is time ; which takes on trust
  Our youth, our joys, our all we have,
And pays us but with earth and dust ;
  Which in the dark and silent grave,

When we have wandered all our ways,
Shuts up the story of our days :
But from this earth, this grave, this dust,
My God shall raise me up, I trust.

SIR WALTER RALEIGH.

THE LIE.

Go, soul, the body's guest,
  Upon a thankless errand ;
Fear not to touch the best,
  The truth shall be thy warrant :
    Go, since I needs must die,
    And give the world the lie.

Go, tell the court it glows
  And shines like rotten wood ;
Go, tell the church it shows
  What 's good, and doth no good.
    If church and court reply,
    Then give them both the lie.

Tell potentates they live
  Acting by others' action,
Not loved unless they give,
  Not strong but by a faction.
    If potentates reply,
    Give potentates the lie.

Tell men of high condition
  That rule affairs of state,
Their purpose is ambition,
  Their practice only hate.
    And if they once reply,
    Then give them all the lie.

Tell them that brave it most,
  They beg for more by spending,
Who in their greatest cost,
  Seek nothing but commending.
    And if they make reply,
    Then give them all the lie.

Tell zeal it lacks devotion,
  Tell love it is but lust,
Tell time it is but motion,
  Tell flesh it is but dust ;
    And wish them not reply,
    For thou must give the lie.

Tell age it daily wasteth,
  Tell honor how it alters,
Tell beauty how she blasteth,
  Tell favor how it falters.
    And as they shall reply,
    Give every one the lie.

Tell wit how much it wrangles
  In tickle points of niceness ;
Tell wisdom she entangles
  Herself in over-wiseness.
    And when they do reply,
    Straight give them both the lie.

Tell physic of her boldness,
  Tell skill it is pretension,
Tell charity of coldness,
  Tell law it is contention.
    And as they do reply,
    So give them still the lie.

Tell fortune of her blindness,
  Tell nature of decay,
Tell friendship of unkindness,
  Tell justice of delay.
    And if they will reply,
    Then give them all the lie.

Tell arts they have no soundness,
  But vary by esteeming ;
Tell schools they want profoundness,
  And stand too much on seeming.
    If arts and schools reply,
    Give arts and schools the lie.

Tell faith it fled the city ;
  Tell how the country erreth ;
Tell, manhood shakes off pity ;
  Tell, virtue least preferreth.
    And if they do reply,
    Spare not to give the lie.

So when thou hast, as I
  Commanded thee, done blabbing,
Although to give the lie
  Deserves no less than stabbing,
    Yet, stab at thee who will,
    No stab the soul can kill.

SIR WALTER RALEIGH.

LETTERS.

EVERY day brings a ship,
Every ship brings a word ;
Well for those who have no fear,
Looking seaward well assured
That the word the vessel brings
Is the word they wish to hear.

RALPH WALDO EMERSON.

BRAHMA.

IF the red slayer think he slays,
  Or if the slain think he is slain,
They know not well the subtle ways
  I keep, and pass, and turn again.

Far or forgot to me is near ;
　Shadow and sunlight are the same ;
The vanished gods to me appear ;
　And one to me are shame and fame.

They reckon ill who leave me out ;
　When me they fly, I am the wings ;
I am the doubter and the doubt,
　And I the hymn the Brahmin sings.

The strong gods pine for my abode,
　And pine in vain the sacred Seven ;
But thou, meek lover of the good !
　Find me, and turn thy back on heaven.
　　　　　RALPH WALDO EMERSON.

RETRIBUTION.

THOUGH the mills of God grind slowly,
　Yet they grind exceeding small ;
Though with patience he stands waiting,
　With exactness grinds he all.
　　　　　HENRY WADSWORTH LONGFELLOW.

THE FUTURE.

FROM THE "ESSAY ON MAN."

HEAVEN from all creatures hides the book of fate,
All but the page prescribed, their present state :
From brutes what men, from men what spirits
　　know :
Or who could suffer being here below ?
The lamb thy riot dooms to bleed to-day,
Had he thy reason, would he skip and play ?
Pleased to the last, he crops the flowery food,
And licks the hand just raised to shed his blood.
O blindness to the future ! kindly given,
That each may fill the circle marked by Heaven :
Who sees with equal eye, as God of all,
A hero perish, or a sparrow fall,
Atoms or systems into ruin hurled,
And now a bubble burst, and now a world.
　Hope humbly then ; with trembling pinions
　　soar ;
Wait the great teacher Death, and God adore.
What future bliss, he gives not thee to know,
But gives that hope to be thy blessing now.
Hope springs eternal in the human breast :
Man never is, but always to be blest.
The soul, uneasy and confined from home,
Rests and expatiates in a life to come.
Lo, the poor Indian ! whose untutored mind
Sees God in clouds, or hears him in the wind ;
His soul, proud science never taught to stray
Far as the solar walk, or milky way ;

Yet simple nature to his hope has given,
Behind the cloud-topped hill, an humbler heaven ;
Some safer world, in depth of woods embraced,
Some happier island in the watery waste,
Where slaves once more their native land behold,
No fiends torment, no Christians thirst for gold :
To be, contents his natural desire,
He asks no angel's wing, no seraph's fire ;
But thinks, admitted to that equal sky,
His faithful dog shall bear him company.
　　　　　ALEXANDER POPE.

SEVEN AGES OF MAN.

FROM "AS YOU LIKE IT."

ALL the world 's a stage,
And all the men and women merely players :
They have their exits and their entrances ;
And one man in his time plays many parts,
His acts being seven ages.　At first the infant,
Mewling and puking in the nurse's arms.
Then the whining school-boy, with his satchel,
And shining morning face, creeping like snail
Unwillingly to school.　And then the lover,
Sighing like furnace, with a woful ballad
Made to his mistress' eyebrow.　Then a soldier,
Full of strange oaths, and bearded like the pard,
Jealous in honor, sudden and quick in quarrel,
Seeking the bubble reputation
Even in the cannon's mouth.　And then the justice,
In fair round belly with good capon lined,
With eyes severe, and beard of formal cut,
Full of wise saws and modern instances ;
And so he plays his part : the sixth age shifts
Into the lean and slippered pantaloon,
With spectacles on nose, and pouch on side ;
His youthful hose, well saved, a world too wide
For his shrunk shank ; and his big manly voice,
Turning again toward childish treble, pipes
And whistles in his sound.　Last scene of all,
That ends this strange eventful history,
Is second childishness, and mere oblivion, —
Sans teeth, sans eyes, sans taste, sans everything.
　　　　　SHAKESPEARE.

PROCRASTINATION.

BE wise to-day ; 't is madness to defer ;
Next day the fatal precedent will plead ;
Thus on, till wisdom is pushed out of life.
Procrastination is the thief of time ;
Year after year it steals, till all are fled,
And to the mercies of a moment leaves
The vast concerns of an eternal scene.
　Of man's miraculous mistakes this bears
The palm, "That all men are about to live,"

Forever on the brink of being born.
All pay themselves the compliment to think
They one day shall not drivel : and their pride
On this reversion takes up ready praise :
At least their own ; their future selves applaud :
How excellent that life they ne'er will lead !
Time lodged in their own hands is Folly's veils ;
That lodged in Fate's to wisdom they consign ;
The thing they can't but purpose, they postpone :
'T is not in folly not to scorn a fool,
And scarce in human wisdom to do more.
All promise is poor dilatory man,
And that through every stage.   When young, indeed,
In full content we sometimes nobly rest,
Unanxious for ourselves, and only wish,
As duteous sons, our fathers were more wise.
At thirty man suspects himself a fool ;
Knows it at forty, and reforms his plan ;
At fifty chides his infamous delay,
Pushes his prudent purpose to resolve ;
In all the magnanimity of thought
Resolves, and re-resolves ; then dies the same.
And why ? Because he thinks himself immortal.
All men think all men mortal but themselves ;
Themselves, when some alarming shock of fate
Strikes through their wounded hearts the sudden dread ;
But their hearts wounded, like the wounded air,
Soon close ; where passed the shaft no trace is found.
As from the wing no scar the sky retains,
The parted wave no furrow from the keel,
So dies in human hearts the thought of death ;
Even with the tender tears which Nature sheds
O'er those we love, we drop it in their grave.
DR.-EDWARD YOUNG.

DEFER not till to-morrow to be wise,
To-morrow's sun to thee may never rise.
CONGREVE.

TIME.

THE bell strikes one : we take no note of time,
But from its loss.   To give it, then, a tongue,
Is wise in man.   As if an angel spoke,
I feel the solemn sound.   If heard aright,
It is the knell of my departed hours :
Where are they ? with the years beyond the flood ?
It is the signal that demands despatch ;
How much is to be done ! my hopes and fears
Start up alarmed, and o'er life's narrow verge
Look down — on what ? a fathomless abyss ;
A dread eternity ! how surely mine !
And can eternity belong to me,
Poor pensioner on the bounties of an hour ?

Time the supreme ! — Time is eternity ;
Pregnant with all eternity can give ;
Pregnant with all that makes archangels smile.
Who murders time, he crushes in the birth
A power ethereal, only not adored.
Ah ! how unjust to nature and himself,
Is thoughtless, thankless, inconsistent man !
Like children babbling nonsense in their sports,
We censure nature for a span too short :
That span too short, we tax as tedious too ;
Torture invention, all expedients tire,
To lash the lingering moments into speed,
And whirl us (happy riddance !) from ourselves.
Art, brainless art ! our furious charioteer
(For nature's voice, unstifled, would recall)
Drives headlong towards the precipice of death !
Death, most our dread ; death, thus more dreadful made :
O, what a riddle of absurdity !
Leisure is pain ; takes off our chariot wheels :
How heavily we drag the load of life !
Blessed leisure is our curse : like that of Cain,
It makes us wander ; wander earth around
To fly that tyrant, thought.   As Atlas groaned
The world beneath, we groan beneath an hour.
We cry for mercy to the next amusement :
The next amusement mortgages our fields ;
Slight inconvenience ! prisons hardly frown,
From hateful time if prisons set us free.
Yet when Death kindly tenders us relief,
We call him cruel ; years to moments shrink,
Ages to years.   The telescope is turned.
To man's false optics (from his folly false)
Time, in advance, behind him hides his wings,
And seems to creep, decrepit with his age ;
Behold him when passed by ; what then is seen
But his broad pinions, swifter than the winds ?
And all mankind, in contradiction strong,
Rueful, aghast ! cry out on his career.

Ye well arrayed ! ye lilies of our land !
Ye lilies male ! who neither toil nor spin ;
(As sister-lilies might ;) if not so wise
As Solomon, more sumptuous to the sight !
Ye delicate ; who nothing can support,
Yourselves most insupportable ! for whom
The winter rose must blow, the sun put on
A brighter beam in Leo ; silky-soft
Favonius ! breathe still softer, or be chid ;
And other worlds send odors, sauce, and song,
And robes, and notions, framed in foreign looms !
O ye Lorenzos of our age ! who deem
One moment unamused a misery
Not made for feeble man ! who call aloud
For every bawble drivelled o'er by sense ;
For rattles and conceits of every cast,
For change of follies and relays of joy,

HARVEST TIME.

" And summer's green, all girded up in sheaves,
Borne on the bier with white and bristly beard."

To drag you patient through the tedious length
Of a short winter's day, — say, sages ! say,
Wit's oracles ! say, dreamers of gay dreams !
How will you weather an eternal night
Where such expedients fail ?

DR. EDWARD YOUNG.

NEW YEAR'S EVE.

RING out, wild bells, to the wild sky,
  The flying cloud, the frosty light ;
  The year is dying in the night ;
Ring out, wild bells, and let him die.

Ring out the old, ring in the new ;
  Ring, happy bells, across the snow ;
  The year is going, let him go ;
Ring out the false, ring in the true.

Ring out the grief that saps the mind,
  For those that here we see no more ;
  Ring out the feud of rich and poor,
Ring in redress to all mankind.

Ring out a slowly dying cause,
  And ancient forms of party strife ;
  Ring in the nobler modes of life,
With sweeter manners, purer laws.

Ring out false pride in place and blood,
  The civic slander and the spite ;
  Ring in the love of truth and right,
Ring in the common love of good.

Ring out old shapes of foul disease,
  Ring out the narrowing lust of gold ;
  Ring out the thousand wars of old,
Ring in the thousand years of peace.

Ring in the valiant man and free,
  The larger heart, the kindlier hand ;
  Ring out the darkness of the land,
Ring in the Christ that is to be.

ALFRED TENNYSON.

WHEN I DO COUNT THE CLOCK.

SONNET.

WHEN I do count the clock that tells the time,
And see the brave day sunk in hideous night ;
When I behold the violet past prime,
And sable curls all silvered o'er with white ;
When lofty trees I see barren of leaves,
Which erst from heat did canopy the herd,
And summer's green, all girded up in sheaves,
Borne on the bier with white and bristly beard ;
Then of thy beauty do I question make,

That thou among the wastes of time must go,
Since sweets and beauties do themselves forsake,
And die as fast as they see others grow ;
  And nothing 'gainst Time's scythe can make
    defence,
  Save breed, to brave him when he takes thee
    hence.

SHAKESPEARE.

TIME.

GATHER ye rosebuds as ye may,
  Old Time is still a flying ;
And this same flower that smiles to-day
  To-morrow will be dying.

The glorious lamp of heaven, the sun,
  The higher he 's a getting,
The sooner will his race be run,
  And nearer he 's to setting.

The age is best which is the first,
  When youth and blood are warmer ;
But being spent, the worse and worst
  Time still succeed the former.

Then be not coy, but use your time,
  And while ye may, go marry ;
For having lost but once your prime,
  You may forever tarry.

ROBERT HERRICK.

TOO LATE I STAYED.

Too late I stayed, — forgive the crime !
  Unheeded flew the hours :
How noiseless falls the foot of Time
  That only treads on flowers !

And who, with clear account, remarks
  The ebbings of his glass,
When all its sands are diamond sparks,
  That dazzle as they pass ?

O, who to sober measurement
  Time's happy swiftness brings,
When birds of paradise have lent
  Their plumage to his wings ?

WILLIAM R. SPENCER.

WHAT IS TIME?

I ASKED an aged man, with hoary hairs,
Wrinkled and curved with worldly cares :
" Time is the warp of life," said he ; " O, tell
The young, the fair, the gay, to weave it well !"

I asked the ancient, venerable dead,
Sages who wrote, and warriors who bled :
From the cold grave a hollow murmur flowed,
"Time sowed the seed we reap in this abode !"
I asked a dying sinner, ere the tide
Of life had left his veins : "Time !" he replied ;
"I 've lost it ! ah, the treasure !" — and he died.
I asked the golden sun and silver spheres,
Those bright chronometers of days and years :
They answered, "Time is but a meteor glare," ' !
And bade me for eternity prepare.
I asked the Seasons, in their annual round,
Which beautify or desolate the ground ;
And they replied (no oracle more wise),
"'Tis Folly's blank, and Wisdom's highest prize !"
I asked a spirit lost, — but O the shriek
That pierced my soul ! I shudder while I speak.
It cried, "A particle ! a speck ! a mite
Of endless years, duration infinite !"
Of things inanimate my dial I
Consulted, and it made me this reply, —
"Time is the season fair of living well,
The path of glory or the path of hell."
I asked my Bible, and methinks it said,
"Time is the present hour, the past has fled ;
Live ! live to-day ! to-morrow never yet
On any human being rose or set."
I asked old Father Time himself at last ;
But in a moment he flew swiftly past,
His chariot was a cloud, the viewless wind
His noiseless steeds, which left no trace behind.
I asked the mighty angel who shall stand
One foot on sea and one on solid land :
"Mortal !" he cried, "the mystery now is o'er ;
Time was, Time is, but Time shall be no more !"
MARSDEN.

FOOL MORALIZING ON TIME.

FROM "AS YOU LIKE IT."

JAQUES. "Good morrow, fool," quoth I.
    "No, sir," quoth he,
"Call me not fool, till heaven hath sent me for-
    tune."
And then he drew a dial from his poke,
And, looking on it with lack-lustre eye,
Says very wisely, "It is ten o'clock :
Thus may we see," quoth he, "how the world wags :
'T is but an hour ago since it was nine ;
And after one hour more 't will be eleven ;
And so, from hour to hour, we ripe and ripe,
And then, from hour to hour, we rot and rot ;
And thereby hangs a tale." When I did hear
The motley fool thus moral on the time,
My lungs began to crow like chanticleer,
That fools should be so deep contemplative ;

And I did laugh, sans intermission,
An hour by his dial. — O noble fool !
A worthy fool ! — Motley 's the only wear.
    DUKE S. What fool is this ?
    JAQUES. O worthy fool ! — One that hath been
        a courtier ;
And says, if ladies be but young and fair,
They have the gift to know it : and in his brain—
Which is as dry as the remainder biscuit
After a voyage—he hath strange places crammed
With observation, the which he vents
In mangled forms.
SHAKESPEARE.

THE JESTER'S SERMON.

THE Jester shook his hood and bells, and leaped
    upon a chair,
The pages laughed, the women screamed, and
    tossed their scented hair ;
The falcon whistled, staghounds bayed, the lap-
    dog barked without,
The scullion dropped the pitcher brown, the cook
    railed at the lout !
The steward, counting out his gold, let pouch and
    money fall,
And why ? because the Jester rose to say grace in
    the hall !

The page played with the heron's plume, the
    steward with his chain,
The butler drummed upon the board, and laughed
    with might and main ;
The grooms beat on their metal cans, and roared
    till they were red,
But still the Jester shut his eyes and rolled his
    witty head ;
And when they grew a little still, read half a yard
    of text,
And, waving hand, struck on the desk, then
    frowned like one perplexed.

"Dear sinners all," the fool began, "man's life
    is but a jest,
A dream, a shadow, bubble, air, a vapor at the best,
In a thousand pounds of law I find not a single
    ounce of love ;
A blind man killed the parson's cow in shooting
    at the dove ;
The fool that eats till he is sick must fast till he
    is well ;
The wooer who can flatter most will bear away
    the belle.

"Let no man halloo he is safe till he is through
    the wood ;
He who will not when he may, must tarry when
    he should.

He who laughs at crooked men should need walk
    very straight ;
O, he who once has won a name may lie abed
    till eight !
Make haste to purchase house and land, be very
    slow to wed ;
True coral needs no painter's brush, nor need be
    daubed with red.

" The friar, preaching, cursed the thief (the pud-
    ding in his sleeve).
To fish for sprats with golden hooks is foolish, by
    your leave,
To travel well, — an ass's ears, ape's face, hog's
    mouth, and ostrich legs.
He does not care a pin for thieves who limps
    about and begs.
Be always first man at a feast and last man at a
    fray ;
The short way round, in spite of all, is still the
    longest way.
When the hungry curate licks the knife, there 's
    not much for the clerk ;
When the pilot, turning pale and sick, looks up
    — the storm grows dark."

Then loud they laughed, the fat cook's tears ran
    down into the pan :
The steward shook, that he was forced to drop
    the brimming can ;
And then again the women screamed, and every
    staghound bayed, —
And why ? because the motley fool so wise a
    sermon made.

                            G. W. THORNBURY.

THE DEATH OF THE OLD YEAR.

FULL knee-deep lies the winter snow,
And the winter winds are wearily sighing :
Toll ye the church-bell sad and slow,
And tread softly and speak low,
For the old year lies a-dying.
    Old year, you must not die ;
    You came to us so readily,
    You lived with us so steadily,
    Old year, you shall not die.

He lieth still : he doth not move :
He will not see the dawn of day.
He hath no other life above.
He gave me a friend, and a true true-love,
And the New-year will take 'em away.
    Old year, you must not go ;
    So long as you have been with us,
    Such joy as you have seen with us,
    Old year, you shall not go.

He frothed his bumpers to the brim ;
A jollier year we shall not see.
But though his eyes are waxing dim,
And though his foes speak ill of him,
He was a friend to me.
    Old year, you shall not die ;
    We did so laugh and cry with you,
    I 've half a mind to die with you,
    Old year, if you must die.

He was full of joke and jest,
But all his merry quips are o'er.
To see him die across the waste
His son and heir doth ride post-haste,
But he 'll be dead before.
    Every one for his own.
    The night is starry and cold, my friend,
    And the New-year blithe and bold, my friend,
    Comes up to take his own.

How hard he breathes ! over the snow
I heard just now the crowing cock.
The shadows flicker to and fro :
The cricket chirps : the light burns low :
'T is nearly twelve o'clock.
    Shake hands before you die.
    Old year, we 'll dearly rue for you :
    What is it we can do for you ?
    Speak out before you die.

His face is growing sharp and thin.
Alack ! our friend is gone,
Close up his eyes : tie up his chin :
Step from the corpse, and let him in
That standeth there alone,
    And waiteth at the door.
    There 's a new foot on the floor, my friend,
    And a new face at the door, my friend,
    A new face at the door.

                            ALFRED TENNYSON.

THE DOORSTEP.

THE conference-meeting through at last,
    We boys around the vestry waited
To see the girls come tripping past
    Like snowbirds willing to be mated.

Not braver he that leaps the wall
    By level musket-flashes litten,
Than I, who stepped before them all,
    Who longed to see me get the mitten.

But no ; she blushed, and took my arm !
    We let the old folks have the highway,
And started toward the Maple Farm
    Along a kind of lover's by-way.

I can't remember what we said,
  'T was nothing worth a song or story ;
Yet that rude path by which we sped
  Seemed all transformed and in a glory.

The snow was crisp beneath our feet,
  The moon was full, the fields were gleaming ;
By hood and tippet sheltered sweet,
  Her face with youth and health was beaming.

The little hand outside her muff —
  O sculptor, if you could but mould it ! —
So lightly touched my jacket-cuff,
  To keep it warm I had to hold it.

To have her with me there alone, —
  'T was love and fear and triumph blended.
At last we reached the foot-worn stone
  Where that delicious journey ended.

The old folks, too, were almost home ;
  Her dimpled hand the latches fingered,
We heard the voices nearer come,
  Yet on the doorstep still we lingered.

She shook her ringlets from her hood,
  And with a "Thank you, Ned," dissembled,
But yet I knew she understood ,
  With what a daring wish I trembled.

A cloud passed kindly overhead,
  The moon was slyly peeping through it,
Yet hid its face, as if it said,
  "Come, now or never ! do it ! do it !"

My lips till then had only known
  The kiss of mother and of sister,
But somehow, full upon her own
  Sweet, rosy, darling mouth — I kissed her !

Perhaps 't was boyish love, yet still,
  O listless woman, weary lover !
To feel once more that fresh, wild thrill
  I'd give — But who can live youth over ?
                    EDMUND CLARENCE STEDMAN.

THE OLD MAID.

WHY sits she thus in solitude ? Her heart
  Seems melting in her eyes' delicious blue ;
And as it heaves, her ripe lips lie apart,
  As if to let its heavy throbbings through ;
In her dark eye a depth of softness swells,
  Deeper than that her careless girlhood wore ;
And her cheek crimsons with the hue that tells
  The rich, fair fruit is ripened to the core.

It is her thirtieth birthday ! With a sigh
  Her soul hath turned from youth's luxuriant
    bowers,
And her heart taken up the last sweet tie
  That measured out its links of golden hours !
She feels her inmost soul within her stir
  With thoughts too wild and passionate to
    speak ;
Yet her full heart — its own interpreter —
  Translates itself in silence on her cheek.

Joy's opening buds, affection's glowing flowers,
  Once lightly sprang within her beaming track ;
O, life was beautiful in those lost hours !
  And yet she does not wish to wander back ;
No ! she but loves in loneliness to think
  On pleasures past, though nevermore to be ;
Hope links her to the future, — but the link
  That binds her to the past is memory.
                    AMELIA B. WELBY.

THE PETRIFED FERN.

IN a valley, centuries ago,
  Grew a little fern-leaf, green and slender,
  Veining delicate and fibres tender ;
Waving when the wind crept down so low.
  Rushes tall, and moss, and grass grew round it,
  Playful sunbeams darted in and found it,
  Drops of dew stole in by night, and crowned it,
  But no foot of man e'er trod that way ;
  Earth was young, and keeping holiday.

Monster fishes swam the silent main,
  Stately forests waved their giant branches,
  Mountains hurled their snowy avalanches,
Mammoth creatures stalked across the plain ;
  Nature revelled in grand mysteries,
  But the little fern was not of these,
  Did not number with the hills and trees ;
  Only grew and waved its wild sweet way,
  None ever came to note it day by day.

Earth one time put on a frolic mood,
  Heaved the rocks and changed the mighty mo-
    tion
  Of the deep, strong currents of the ocean ;
Moved the plain and shook the haughty wood,
  Crushed the little fern in soft moist clay, —
  Covered it, and hid it safe away.
O the long, long centuries since that day !
  O the agony ! O life's bitter cost,
  Since that useless little fern was lost !

Useless ? Lost ? There came a thoughtful man
  Searching Nature's secrets, far and deep ;

From a fissure in a rocky steep
He withdrew a stone, o'er which there ran
 Fairy pencillings, a quaint design,
 Veinings, leafage, fibres clear and fine,
And the fern's life lay in every line !
So, I think, God hides some souls away,
Sweetly to surprise us, the last day.
ANONYMOUS.

THANATOPSIS.

To him who, in the love of Nature, holds
Communion with her visible forms, she speaks
A various language : for his gayer hours
She has a voice of gladness, and a smile
And eloquence of beauty ; and she glides
Into his darker musings with a mild
And gentle sympathy, that steals away
Their sharpness, ere he is aware.   When thoughts
Of the last bitter hour come like a blight
Over thy spirit, and sad images
Of the stern agony, and shroud, and pall,
And breathless darkness, and the narrow house,
Make thee to shudder, and grow sick at heart,
Go forth under the open sky, and list
To Nature's teachings, while from all around —
Earth and her waters, and the depths of air —
Comes a still voice, — Yet a few days, and thee
The all-beholding sun shall see no more
In all his course ; nor yet in the cold ground,
Where thy pale form was laid, with many tears,
Nor in the embrace of ocean, shall exist
Thy image.   Earth, that nourished thee, shall claim
Thy growth, to be resolved to earth again ;
And, lost each human trace, surrendering up
Thine individual being, shalt thou go
To mix forever with the elements ;
To be a brother to the insensible rock,
And to the sluggish clod, which the rude swain
Turns with his share, and treads upon.   The oak
Shall send his roots abroad, and pierce thy mould.
 Yet not to thine eternal resting-place
Shalt thou retire alone, — nor couldst thou wish
Couch more magnificent.   Thou shalt lie down
With patriarchs of the infant world, — with kings,
The powerful of the earth, — the wise, the good,
Fair forms, and hoary seers of ages past,
All in one mighty sepulchre.   The hills,
Rock-ribbed, and ancient as the sun ; the vales
Stretching in pensive quietness between ;
The venerable woods ; rivers that move
In majesty, and the complaining brooks,
That make the meadows green ; and, poured
    round all,
Old ocean's gray and melancholy waste, —
Are but the solemn decorations all

Of the great tomb of man !   The golden sun,
The planets, all the infinite host of heaven,
Are shining on the sad abodes of death,
Through the still lapse of ages.   All that tread
The globe are but a handful to the tribes
That slumber in its bosom.   Take the wings
Of morning, traverse Barca's desert sands,
Or lose thyself in the continuous woods
Where rolls the Oregon, and hears no sound
Save his own dashings, — yet the dead are there !
And millions in those solitudes, since first
The flight of years began, have laid them down
In their last sleep, — the dead reign there alone !
So shalt thou rest ; and what if thou withdraw
In silence from the living, and no friend
Take note of thy departure ?   All that breathe
Will share thy destiny.   The gay will laugh
When thou art gone, the solemn brood of care
Plod on, and each one, as before, will chase
His favorite phantom ; yet all these shall leave
Their mirth and their employments, and shall
    come
And make their bed with thee.   As the long train
Of ages glide away, the sons of men —
The youth in life's green spring, and he who goes
In the full strength of years, matron and maid,
And the sweet babe, and the gray-headed man —
Shall, one by one, be gathered to thy side
By those who in their turn shall follow them.

So live, that when thy summons comes to join
The innumerable caravan that moves
To the pale realms of shade, where each shall take
His chamber in the silent halls of death,
Thou go not, like the quarry-slave at night,
Scourged to his dungeon, but, sustained and
    soothed
By an unfaltering trust, approach thy grave
Like one who wraps the drapery of his couch
About him, and lies down to pleasant dreams.
WILLIAM CULLEN BRYANT.

A HUNDRED YEARS TO COME.

Who 'll press for gold this crowded street,
 A hundred years to come ?
Who 'll tread yon church with willing feet,
 A hundred years to come ?
Pale, trembling age and fiery youth,
And childhood with his brow of truth,
The rich and poor, on land, on sea,
Where will the mighty millions be,
 A hundred years to come ?

We all within our graves shall sleep,
 A hundred years to come ;
No living soul for us will weep,
 A hundred years to come.

But other men our land will till,
And others then our streets will fill,
And other words will sing as gay,
And bright the sunshine as to-day,
   A hundred years to come.

ANONYMOUS.

NEWPORT BEACH.

WAVE after wave successively rolls on
And dies along the shore, until more loud
One billow with concentrate force is heard
To swell prophetic, and exultant rears
A lucent form above its pioneers,
And rushes past them to the farthest goal.
Thus our unuttered feelings rise and fall,
And thought will follow thought in equal waves,
Until reflection nerves design to will,
Or sentiment o'er chance emotion reigns,
And all its wayward undulations blends
In one o'erwhelming surge !

HENRY THEODORE TUCKERMAN.

TO A SKELETON.

[The MSS. of this poem, which appeared during the first quarter of the present century, was said to have been found in the Museum of the Royal College of Surgeons, in London, near a perfect human skeleton, and to have been sent by the curator to the Morning Chronicle for publication. It excited so much attention that every effort was made to discover the author, and a responsible party went so far as to offer a reward of fifty guineas for information that would discover its origin. The author preserved his *incognito*, and, we believe, has never been discovered.]

BEHOLD this ruin ! 'T was a skull
Once of ethereal spirit full.
This narrow cell was Life's retreat,
This space was Thought's mysterious seat.
What beauteous visions filled this spot,
What dreams of pleasure long forgot ?
Nor hope, nor joy, nor love, nor fear,
Have left one trace of record here.

Beneath this mouldering canopy
Once shone the bright and busy eye,
But start not at the dismal void, —
If social love that eye employed,
If with no lawless fire it gleamed,
But through the dews of kindness beamed,
That eye shall be forever bright
When stars and sun are sunk in night.

Within this hollow cavern hung
The ready, swift, and tuneful tongue ;
If Falsehood's honey it disdained,
And when it could not praise was chained ;
If bold in Virtue's cause it spoke,
Yet gentle concord never broke, —
This silent tongue shall plead for thee
When Time unveils Eternity !

Say, did these fingers delve the mine ?
Or with the envied rubies shine ?
To hew the rock or wear a gem
Can little now avail to them.
But if the page of Truth they sought,
Or comfort to the mourner brought,
These hands a richer meed shall claim
Than all that wait on Wealth and Fame.

Avails it whether bare or shod
These feet the paths of duty trod ?
If from the bowers of Ease they fled,
To seek Affliction's humble shed ;
If Grandeur's guilty bribe they spurned,
And home to Virtue's cot returned, —
These feet with angel wings shall vie,
And tread the palace of the sky !

ANONYMOUS.

ODE.

INTIMATIONS OF IMMORTALITY FROM RECOLLECTIONS OF EARLY CHILDHOOD.

I.

THERE was a time when meadow, grove, and stream,
The earth, and every common sight,
   To me did seem
   Apparelled in celestial light, —
The glory and the freshness of a dream.
It is not now as it hath been of yore :
   Turn wheresoe'er I may,
    By night or day,
The things which I have seen I now can see no
     more.

II.

   The rainbow comes and goes,
   And lovely is the rose ;
   The moon doth with delight
Look round her when the heavens are bare ;
   Waters on a starry night
   Are beautiful and fair ;
   The sunshine is a glorious birth ;
   But yet I know, where'er I go,
That there hath passed away a glory from the earth.

III.

Now, while the birds thus sing a joyous song,
   And while the young lambs bound
   As to the tabor's sound,
To me alone there came a thought of grief ;
A timely utterance gave that thought relief,
   And I again am strong.
The cataracts blow their trumpets from the
    steep, —
No more shall grief of mine the season wrong :
I hear the echoes through the mountains throng ;
The winds come to me from the fields of sleep,
   And all the earth is gay ;
    Land and sea
   Give themselves up to jollity ;

And with the heart of May
Doth every beast keep holiday ; —
Thou child of joy,
Shout round me, let me hear thy shouts, thou
    happy shepherd boy !

IV.

Ye blessèd creatures ! I have heard the call
    Ye to each other make ; I see
The heavens laugh with you in your jubilee ;
    My heart is at your festival,
    My head hath its coronal, —
The fulness of your bliss, I feel, I feel it all.
    O evil day ! if I were sullen
    While earth herself is adorning,
        This sweet May morning,
    And the children are culling
        On every side,
In a thousand valleys far and wide,
Fresh flowers; while the sun shines warm,
And the babe leaps up on his mother's arm, —
    I hear, I hear, with joy I hear ! —
    But there 's a tree, of many one,
A single field which I have looked upon, —
Both of them speak of something that is gone ;
    The pansy at my feet
    Doth the same tale repeat.
Whither is fled the visionary gleam ?
Where is it now, the glory and the dream ?

V.

Our birth is but a sleep and a forgetting ;
The soul that rises with us, our life's star,
    Hath had elsewhere its setting,
    And cometh from afar.
    Not in entire forgetfulness,
    And not in utter nakedness,
But trailing clouds of glory, do we come
    From God, who is our home.
Heaven lies about us in our infancy !
Shades of the prison-house begin to close
    Upon the growing boy ;
But he beholds the light, and whence it flows, —
    He sees it in his joy.
The youth who daily farther from the east
    Must travel, still is nature's priest,
    And by the vision splendid
    Is on his way attended :
At length the man perceives it die away,
And fade into the light of common day.

VI.

Earth fills her lap with pleasures of her own.
Yearnings she hath in her own natural kind ;
And even with something of a mother's mind,
    And no unworthy aim,
    The homely nurse doth all she can
To make her foster-child, her inmate man,

Forget the glories he hath known,
And that imperial palace whence he came.

VII.

Behold the child among his new-born blisses, —
A six years' darling of a pygmy size !
See, where mid work of his own hand he lies,
Fretted by sallies of his mother's kisses,
With light upon him from his father's eyes !
See at his feet some little plan or chart,
Some fragment from his dream of human life,
Shaped by himself with newly learnéd art, —
        A wedding or a festival,
        A mourning or a funeral, —
        And this hath now his heart,
    And unto this he frames his song.
        Then will he fit his tongue
To dialogues of business, love, or strife ;
        But it will not be long
        Ere this be thrown aside,
        And with new joy and pride
The little actor cons another part, —
Filling from time to time his "humorous stage"
With all the persons, down to palsied age,
That life brings with her in her equipage ;
        As if his whole vocation
        Were endless imitation.

VIII.

Thou, whose exterior semblance doth belie
        Thy soul's immensity !
Thou best philosopher, who yet dost keep
Thy heritage ! thou eye among the blind,
That, deaf and silent, read'st the eternal deep,
Haunted forever by the eternal mind ! —
        Mighty prophet ! Seer blest,
        On whom those truths do rest
Which we are toiling all our lives to find,
In darkness lost, the darkness of the grave !
Thou over whom thy immortality
Broods like the day, a master o'er a slave,
A presence which is not to be put by !
Thou little child, yet glorious in the might
Of heaven-born freedom on thy being's height,
Why with such earnest pains dost thou provoke
The years to bring the inevitable yoke,
Thus blindly with thy blessedness at strife ?
Full soon thy soul shall have her earthly freight,
And custom lie upon thee with a weight
Heavy as frost, and deep almost as life !

IX.

        O joy ! that in our embers
        Is something that doth live,
        That nature yet remembers
        What was so fugitive !
The thought of our past years in me doth breed
Perpetual benediction : not, indeed,
For that which is most worthy to be blest, —

Delight and liberty, the simple creed
Of childhood, whether busy or at rest,
With new-fledged hope still fluttering in his
    breast, —
    Not for these I raise
    The song of thanks and praise ;
    But for those obstinate questionings
    Of sense and outward things,
    Fallings from us, vanishings,
    Blank misgivings of a creature
Moving about in worlds not realized,
High instincts, before which our mortal nature
Did tremble like a guilty thing surprised, —
    But for those first affections,
    Those shadowy recollections,
    Which, be they what they may,
Are yet the fountain-light of all our day,
Are yet a master light of all our seeing,
    Uphold us, cherish, and have power to make
Our noisy years seem moments in the being
Of the eternal silence : truths that wake,
    To perish never, —
Which neither listlessness, nor mad endeavor,
    Nor man nor boy,
Nor all that is at enmity with joy,
Can utterly abolish or destroy !
    Hence in a season of calm weather,
    Though inland far we be,
Our souls have sight of that immortal sea
    Which brought us hither, —
    Can in a moment travel thither,
And see the children sport upon the shore,
And hear the mighty waters rolling evermore.

x.

Then sing, ye birds, sing, sing a joyous song !
    And let the young lambs bound
    As to the tabor's sound !
We in thought will join your throng,
    Ye that pipe and ye that play,
    Ye that through your hearts to-day
    Feel the gladness of the May !
What though the radiance which was once so
    bright
Be now forever taken from my sight,
    Though nothing can bring back the hour
Of splendor in the grass, of glory in the flower, —
    We will grieve not, rather find
    Strength in what remains behind ;
    In the primal sympathy
    Which, having been, must ever be ;
    In the soothing thoughts that spring
    Out of human suffering ;
    In the faith that looks through death,
In years that bring the philosophic mind.

XI.

And O ye fountains, meadows, hills, and groves,
Forebode not any severing of our loves.

Yet in my heart of hearts I feel your might ;
I only have relinquished one delight
To live beneath your more habitual sway.
I love the brooks which down their channels fret,
Even more than when I tripped lightly as they ;
The innocent brightness of a new-born day
    Is lovely yet ;
The clouds that gather round the setting sun
Do take a sober coloring from an eye
That hath kept watch o'er man's mortality ;
Another race hath been, and other palms are won.
Thanks to the human heart by which we live,
Thanks to its tenderness, its joys, and fears, —
To me the meanest flower that blows can give
Thoughts that do often lie too deep for tears.
WILLIAM WORDSWORTH.

SOLILOQUY : ON IMMORTALITY.

SCENE. — CATO *sitting in a thoughtful posture, with Plato's book on the Immortality of the Soul in his hand, and a drawn sword on the table by him.*

IT must be so. — Plato, thou reasonest well !
Else whence this pleasing hope, this fond desire,
This longing after immortality ?
Or whence this secret dread, and inward horror,
Of falling into naught ? Why shrinks the soul
Back on herself, and startles at destruction ?
'T is the divinity that stirs within us ;
'T is Heaven itself, that points out a hereafter,
And intimates eternity to man.
Eternity ! — thou pleasing, dreadful thought !
Through what variety of untried being,
Through what new scenes and changes must we
    pass !
The wide, the unbounded prospect lies before me ;
But shadows, clouds, and darkness rest upon it.
Here will I hold. If there 's a Power above us
(And that there is, all Nature cries aloud
Through all her works), he must delight in virtue ;
And that which he delights in must be happy.
But when ? or where ? This world was made for
    Cæsar.
I 'm weary of conjectures, — this must end them.
    [*Laying his hand on his sword.*
    Thus am I doubly armed : my death and life,
My bane and antidote, are both before me.
This in a moment brings me to an end ;
But this informs me I shall never die.
The soul, secured in her existence, smiles
At the drawn dagger, and defies its point.
The stars shall fade away, the sun himself
Grow dim with age, and Nature sink in years ;
But thou shalt flourish in immortal youth,
Unhurt amid the war of elements,
The wreck of matter, and the crash of worlds !
JOSEPH ADDISON.

R.W. Emerson

FORDS, HOWARD & HULBERT, N.Y.

QUATRAINS AND FRAGMENTS.

FROM R. W. EMERSON.

NORTHMAN.

THE gale that wrecked you on the sand,
    It helped my rowers to row ;
The storm is my best galley-hand,
    And drives me where I go.

POET.

To clothe the fiery thought
    In simple words succeeds,
For still the craft of genius is
    To mask a king in weeds.

JUSTICE.

WHOEVER fights, whoever falls,
Justice conquers evermore,
Justice after as before, —
And he who battles on her side,
God, though he were ten times slain,
Crowns him victor glorified, —
Victor over death and pain,
    Forever.

HEROISM.

So nigh is grandeur to our dust,
So near is God to man,
When Duty whispers low, *Thou must,*
The youth replies, *I can.*

THE SEA.

                        BEHOLD the Sea,
The opaline, the plentiful and strong,
Yet beautiful as is the rose in June,
Fresh as the trickling rainbow of July :
Sea full of food, the nourisher of kinds,
Purger of earth, and medicine of men ;
Creating a sweet climate by my breath,
Washing out harms and griefs from memory,
And, in my mathematic ebb and flow,
Giving a hint of that which changes not.
Rich are the sea-gods : — who gives gifts but they ?
They grope the sea for pearls, but more than pearls :
They pluck Force thence, and give it to the wise.
For every wave is wealth to Dædalus,
Wealth to the cunning artist who can work
This matchless strength.   Where shall he find,
        O waves !
A load your Atlas shoulders cannot lift ?
    I with my hammer pounding evermore
The rocky coast, smite Andes into dust,
Strewing my bed, and, in another age,
Rebuild a continent of better men.
Then I unbar the doors : my paths lead out
The exodus of nations : I disperse
Men to all shores that front the hoary main.

BORROWING.

FROM THE FRENCH.

SOME of your hurts you have cured,
    And the sharpest you still have survived,
But what torments of grief you endured
    From evils which never arrived !

HERI, CRAS, HODIE.

SHINES the last age, the next with hope is seen,
To-day slinks poorly off unmarked between ;
Future or Past no richer secret folds,
O friendless Present ! than thy bosom holds.

LINES AND COUPLETS.

FROM POPE.

WHAT, and how great the virtue and the art,
To live on little with a cheerful heart.

Between excess and famine lies a mean,
Plain, but not sordid, though not splendid, clean.

Its proper power to hurt each creature feels :
Bulls aim their horns, and asses kick their heels.

Here Wisdom calls, "Seek virtue first, be bold ;
As gold to silver, virtue is to gold."

Let lands and houses have what lords they will,
Let us be fixed and our own masters still.

'T is the first virtue vices to abhor,
And the first wisdom to be fool no more.

Long as to him who works for debt, the day.

Not to go back is somewhat to advance,
And men must walk, at least, before they dance.

True, conscious honor is to feel no sin ;
He 's armed without that 's innocent within.

For virtue's self may too much zeal be had,
The worst of madmen is a saint run mad.

If wealth alone can make and keep us blest,
Still, still be getting ; never, never rest.

That God of nature who within us still
Inclines our actions, not constrains our will.

It is not poetry, but prose run mad.

Pretty in amber to observe the forms
Of hair, or straws, or dirt, or grubs, or worms :
The things, we know, are neither rich nor rare,
But wonder how the mischief they got there !

Do good by stealth, and blush to find it fame.

Curst be the verse, how well soe'er it flow,
That tends to make one honest man my foe.

Who shames a scribbler? Break one cobweb
    through,
He spins the slight, self-pleasing thread anew;
Destroy his fib or sophistry, in vain,
The creature's at his dirty work again,
Throned in the centre of his thin designs,
Proud of a vast extent of flimsy lines.

He who, still wanting, though he lives on theft,
Steals much, spends little, yet has nothing left.

What future bliss He gives thee not to know,
But gives that hope to be thy blessing now.

All nature is but art, unknown to thee,
All chance, direction which thou canst not see.

'T is education forms the common mind;
Just as the twig is bent the tree's inclined.

Manners with fortunes, humors turn with climes,
Tenets with books, and principles with times.

Who shall decide when doctors disagree?

And then mistook reverse of wrong for right.

That secret rare between the extremes to move,
Of mad good-nature and of mean self-love.

Ye little stars, hide your diminished rays.

Who builds a church to God, and not to fame,
Will never mark the marble with his name.

'T is strange the music should his cares employ
To gain those riches he can ne'er enjoy.

Something there is more needful than expense,
And something previous e'en to taste, — 't is sense.

In all let Nature never be forgot,
But treat the goddess like a modest fair,
Not over-dress nor leave her wholly bare;
Let not each beauty everywhere be spied,
Where half the skill is decently to hide.

Light quirks of music, broken and uneven,
Make the soul dance upon a jig to heaven.

'T is use alone that sanctifies expense,
And splendor borrows all her rays from sense.

To rest the cushion and soft dean invite,
Who never mentions hell to ears polite.

And knows where faith, law, morals, all began,
All end, — in love of God and love of man.

Know then this truth, enough for man to know,
Virtue alone is happiness below.

Happier as kinder in whate'er degree,
And height of bliss but height of charity.

If then to all men happiness was meant,
God in externals could not place content.

Order is Heaven's first law, and, this confest,
Some are, and must be, greater than the rest.

Reason's whole pleasure, all the joys of sense,
Lie in three words, — health, peace, and compe-
    tence.
But health consists with temperance alone,
And peace, O Virtue! peace is all thine own.

Fortune her gifts may variously dispose,
And these be happy called, unhappy those;
But Heaven's just balance equal will appear,
When those are placed in *hope*, and these in *fear*.

"But sometimes virtue starves, while vice is fed";
"What then, is the reward of virtue, — bread?
That vice may merit, 't is the price of toil,
The knave deserves it when he tills the soil."

What nothing earthly gives or can destroy, —
The soul's calm sunshine, and the heartfelt joy.

Honor and shame from no condition rise;
Act well your part, there all the honor lies.

Who wickedly is wise, or madly brave,
Is but the more a fool, the more a knave.

Who noble ends by noble means obtains,
Or, failing, smiles in exile or in chains,
Like good Aurelius let him reign, or bleed
Like Socrates, that man is great indeed.

What's fame? A fancied life in others' breath.

One self-approving hour whole years outweighs
Of stupid starers and of loud huzzas.

As heaven's blest beam turns vinegar more sour.

Lust through some certain strainers well refined
Is gentle love, and charms all womankind.

Vice is a monster of such hideous mien
That to be hated needs but to be seen;
Yet seen too oft, familiar with her face,
We first endure, then pity, then embrace.

Behold the child, by Nature's kindly law,
Pleased with a rattle, tickled with a straw;
Some livelier plaything gives his youth delight,
A little louder, but as empty quite.

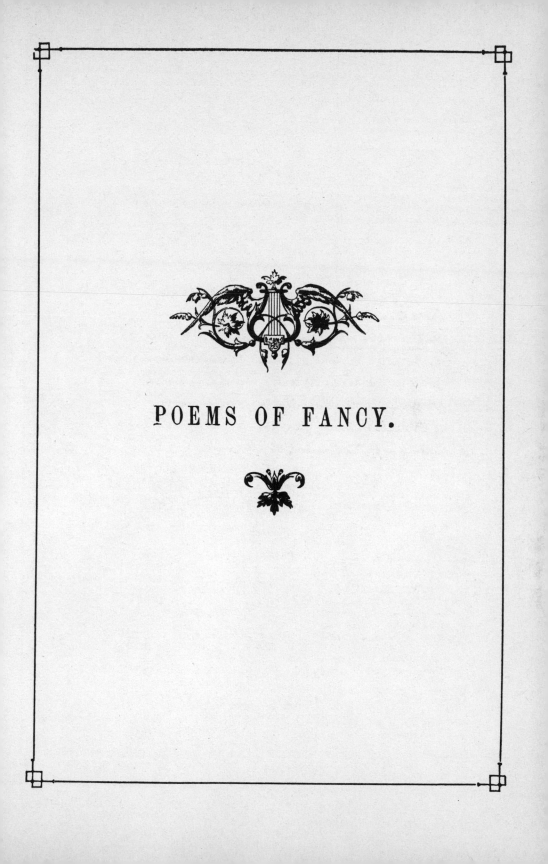

POEMS OF FANCY.

An angel face : — its sunny wealth of hair
In radiant ripples bathed the graceful throat
And dimpled shoulders ; round the rosy curve
Of the sweet mouth a smile seemed wandering ever;
While in the depths of azure fire that gleamed
Beneath the drooping lashes, slept a world
Of eloquent meaning, passionate yet pure —
Dreamy — subdued — but oh, how beautiful !

Edgar A Poe.

POEMS OF FANCY.

FANCY.

FROM "THE MERCHANT OF VENICE."

TELL me where is Fancy bred,
Or in the heart, or in the head?
How begot, how nourishéd?
   Reply, reply.

It is engendered in the eyes,
With gazing fed; and Fancy dies
In the cradle where it lies.
   Let us all ring Fancy's knell;
   I 'll begin it, — Ding, dong, bell.
Ding, dong, bell.
                SHAKESPEARE.

THE REALM OF FANCY.

EVER let the Fancy roam!
Pleasure never is at home:
At a touch sweet Pleasure melteth,
Like to bubbles when rain pelteth;
Then let wingéd Fancy wander
Through the thought still spread beyond her:
Open wide the mind's cage-door,
She 'll dart forth, and cloudward soar.
O sweet Fancy! let her loose;
Summer's joys are spoilt by use,
And the enjoying of the spring
Fades as does its blossoming;
Autumn's red-lipped fruitage too,
Blushing through the mist and dew,
Cloys with tasting: What do then?
Sit thee by the ingle, when
The sear fagot blazes bright,
Spirit of a winter's night;
When the soundless earth is muffled,
And the cakéd snow is shuffled
From the plough-boy's heavy shoon;
When the Night doth meet the Noon
In a dark conspiracy
To banish Even from her sky.
Sit thee there, and send abroad
With a mind self-overawed

Fancy, high-commissioned; — send her!
She has vassals to attend her;
She will bring, in spite of frost,
Beauties that the earth hath lost;
She will bring thee, all together,
All delights of summer weather;
All the buds and bells of May
From dewy sward or thorny spray;
All the heapéd autumn's wealth,
With a still, mysterious stealth;
She will mix these pleasures up
Like three fit wines in a cup,
And thou shalt quaff it; — thou shalt hear
Distant harvest-carols clear;
Rustle of the reapéd corn;
Sweet birds antheming the morn;
And in the same moment — hark!
'T is the early April lark,
Or the rooks, with busy caw,
Foraging for sticks and straw.
Thou shalt, at one glance, behold
The daisy and the marigold;
White-plumed lilies, and the first
Hedge-grown primrose that hath burst;
Shaded hyacinth, alway
Sapphire queen of the mid-May;
And every leaf and every flower
Pearléd with the self-same shower.
Thou shalt see the field-mouse peep
Meagre from its celléd sleep;
And the snake all winter-thin
Cast on sunny bank its skin;
Freckled nest-eggs thou shalt see
Hatching in the hawthorn-tree,
When the hen-bird's wing doth rest
Quíet on her mossy nest;
Then the hurry and alarm
When the beehive casts its swarm;
Acorns ripe down-pattering
While the autumn breezes sing.

O sweet Fancy! let her loose;
Everything is spoilt by use:
Where 's the cheek that doth not fade,
Too much gazed at? Where 's the maid

Whose lip mature is ever new ?
Where 's the eye, however blue,
Doth not weary ?   Where 's the face
One would meet in every place ?
Where 's the voice, however soft,
One would hear so very oft ?
At a touch sweet Pleasure melteth
Like to bubbles when rain pelteth.
Let then wingéd Fancy find
Thee a mistress to thy mind ;
Dulcet-eyed as Ceres' daughter,
Ere the God of Torment taught her
How to frown and how to chide ;
With a waist and with a side
White as Hebe's, when her zone
Slipt its golden clasp, and down
Fell her kirtle to her feet,
While she held the goblet sweet,
And Jove grew languid. — Break the mesh
Of the Fancy's silken leash ;
Quickly break her prison-string,
And such joys as these she 'll bring :
Let the wingéd Fancy roam !
Pleasure never is at home.

JOHN KEATS.

IMAGINATION.

FROM " PLEASURES OF IMAGINATION."

O BLEST of heaven, whom not the languid
      songs
Of luxury, the siren ! not the bribes
Of sordid wealth, nor all the gaudy spoils
Of pageant honor, can seduce to leave
Those ever-blooming sweets, which from the store
Of nature fair imagination culls
To charm the enlivened soul ! What though not
      all
Of mortal offspring can attain the heights
Of envied life ; though only few possess
Patrician treasures or imperial state ;
Yet nature's care, to all her children just,
With richer treasures and an ampler state,
Endows at large whatever happy man
Will deign to use them.   His the city's pomp,
The rural honors his.   Whate'er adorns
The princely dome, the column and the arch,
The breathing marble and the sculptured gold
Beyond the proud possessor's narrow claim,
His tuneful breast enjoys.   For him the Spring
Distils her dews, and from the silken gem
Its lucid leaves unfolds ; for him the hand
Of Autumn tinges every fertile branch
With blooming gold, and blushes like the morn.
Each passing hour sheds tribute from her wings ;
And still new beauties meet his lonely walk,
And loves unfelt attract him.   Not a breeze

Flies o'er the meadow, not a cloud imbibes
The setting sun's effulgence, not a strain
From all the tenants of the warbling shade
Ascends, but whence his bosom can partake
Fresh pleasure, unreproved. Nor thence partakes
Fresh pleasure only ; for the attentive mind,
By this harmonious action on her powers,
Becomes herself harmonious : wont so oft
On outward things to meditate the charm
Of sacred order, soon she seeks at home
To find a kindred order, to exert
Within herself this elegance of love,
This fair-inspired delight : her tempered powers
Refine at length, and every passion wears
A chaster, milder, more attractive mien.

MARK AKENSIDE.

A DREAM OF THE UNKNOWN.

I DREAMED that as I wandered by the way
    Bare winter suddenly was changed to spring,
And gentle odors led my steps astray,
    Mixed with a sound of waters murmuring
Along a shelving bank of turf, which lay
    Under a copse, and hardly dared to fling
Its green arms round the bosom of the stream,
But kissed it and then fled, as Thou mightest in
      dream.

There grew pied wind-flowers and violets,
    Daisies, those pearled Arcturi of the earth,
The constellated flower that never sets ;
    Faint ox-lips ; tender bluebells, at whose birth
The sod scarce heaved ; and that tall flower that
      wets
Its mother's face with heaven-collected tears,
When the low wind, its playmate's voice, it hears.

And in the warm hedge grew lush eglantine,
    Green cow-bind and the moonlight-colored May,
And cherry-blossoms, and white cups, whose wine
    Was the bright dew yet drained not by the day ;
And wild roses, and ivy serpentine
    With its dark buds and leaves, wandering
      astray ;
And flowers azure, black, and streaked with gold,
Fairer than any wakened eyes behold.

And nearer to the river's trembling edge
    There grew broad flag-flowers, purple prankt
      with white,
And starry river-buds among the sedge,
    And floating water-lilies, broad and bright,
Which lit the oak that overhung the hedge
    With moonlight beams of their own watery
      light ;
And bulrushes, and reeds of such deep green
As soothed the dazzled eye with sober sheen.

Methought that of these visionary flowers
  I made a nosegay, bound in such a way
That the same hues, which in their natural bowers
  Were mingled or opposed, the like array
Kept these imprisoned children of the Hours
  Within my hand, — and then, elate and gay,
I hastened to the spot whence I had come
That I might there present it — Oh! to Whom?
PERCY BYSSHE SHELLEY.

DRIFTING.

My soul to-day
  Is far away,
Sailing the Vesuvian Bay;
  My wingéd boat,
  A bird afloat,
Swims round the purple peaks remote : —

Round purple peaks
  It sails, and seeks
Blue inlets and their crystal creeks,
  Where high rocks throw,
  Through deeps below,
A duplicated golden glow.

Far, vague, and dim
  The mountains swim;
While on Vesuvius' misty brim,
  With outstretched hands,
  The gray smoke stands
O'erlooking the volcanic lands.

Here Ischia smiles
  O'er liquid miles;
And yonder, bluest of the isles,
  Calm Capri waits,
  Her sapphire gates
Beguiling to her bright estates.

I heed not, if
  My rippling skiff
Float swift or slow from cliff to cliff; —
  With dreamful eyes
  My spirit lies
Under the walls of Paradise.

Under the walls
  Where swells and falls
The Bay's deep breast at intervals
  At peace I lie,
  Blown softly by,
A cloud upon this liquid sky.

The day, so mild,
  Is Heaven's own child,
With Earth and Ocean reconciled; —

The airs I feel
  Around me steal
Are murmuring to the murmuring keel.

Over the rail
  My hand I trail
Within the shadow of the sail,
  A joy intense,
  The cooling sense
Glides down my drowsy indolence.

Her children, hid
  The cliffs amid,
Are gambolling with the gambolling kid;
  Or down the walls,
  With tipsy calls,
Laugh on the rocks like waterfalls.

The fisher's child,
  With tresses wild,
Unto the smooth, bright sand beguiled,
  With glowing lips
  Sings as she skips,
Or gazes at the far-off ships.

Yon deep bark goes
  Where Traffic blows,
From lands of sun to lands of snows; —
  This happier one,
  Its course is run
From lands of snow to lands of sun.

O happy ship,
  To rise and dip,
With the blue crystal at your lip!
  O happy crew,
  My heart with you
Sails, and sails, and sings anew!

No more, no more
  The worldly shore
Upbraids me with its loud uproar!
  With dreamful eyes
  My spirit lies
Under the walls of Paradise!
THOMAS BUCHANAN READ.

LITTLE BELL.

PIPED the blackbird on the beechwood spray,
  "Pretty maid, slow wandering this way,
  What's your name?" quoth he, —
"What's your name? O, stop and straight unfold,
Pretty maid with showery curls of gold." —
  "Little Bell," said she.

Little Bell sat down beneath the rocks,
Tossed aside her gleaming golden locks, —

"Bonny bird," quoth she,
"Sing me your best song before I go."
"Here's the very finest song I know,
  Little Bell," said he.

And the blackbird piped ; you never heard
Half so gay a song from any bird, —
  Full of quips and wiles,
Now so round and rich, now soft and slow,
All for love of that sweet face below,
  Dimpled o'er with smiles.

And the while the bonny bird did pour
His full heart freely o'er and o'er
  'Neath the morning skies,
In the little childish heart below
All the sweetness seemed to grow and grow,
And shine forth in happy overflow
  From the blue, bright eyes.

Down the dell she tripped and through the glade,
Peeped the squirrel from the hazel shade,
  And from out the tree
Swung, and leaped, and frolicked, void of fear ;
While bold blackbird piped that all might hear,—
  "Little Bell," piped he.

Little Bell sat down amid the fern, —
"Squirrel, squirrel, to your task return ;
  Bring me nuts," quoth she.
Up away the frisky squirrel hies, —
Golden wood-lights glancing in his eyes, —
  And adown the tree
Great ripe nuts, kissed brown by July sun,
In the little lap dropped one by one.
Hark, how blackbird pipes to see the fun !
  "Happy Bell," pipes he.

Little Bell looked up and down the glade, —
"Squirrel, squirrel, if you're not afraid,
  Come and share with me ! "
Down came squirrel eager for his fare,
Down came bonny blackbird, I declare ;
Little Bell gave each his honest share, —
  Ah the merry three !
And the while these frolic playmates twain
Piped and frisked from bough to bough again,
  'Neath the morning skies,
In the little childish heart below
All the sweetness seemed to grow and grow,
And shine out in happy overflow
  From her blue, bright eyes.

By her snow-white cot at close of day,
Knelt sweet Bell, with folded palms, to pray ;
  Very calm and clear
Rose the praying voice to where, unseen,
In blue heaven, an angel shape serene

Paused awhile to hear.
"What good child is this," the angel said,
"That with happy heart beside her bed
  Prays so lovingly ? "
Low and soft, O, very low and soft,
Crooned the blackbird in the orchard croft,
  "Bell, dear Bell ! " crooned he.

"Whom God's creatures love," the angel fair
Murmured, "God doth bless with angels' care ;
  Child, thy bed shall be
Folded safe from harm. Love, deep and kind,
Shall watch around and leave good gifts behind,
  Little Bell, for thee ! "
                                        THOMAS WESTWOOD.

A VISIT FROM ST. NICHOLAS.

'Twas the night before Christmas, when all
      through the house
Not a creature was stirring, not even a mouse ;
The stockings were hung by the chimney with care,
In hopes that St. Nicholas soon would be there ;
The children were nestled all snug in their beds,
While visions of sugar-plums danced in their
      heads ;
And mamma in her kerchief, and I in my cap,
Had just settled our brains for a long winter's
      nap, —
When out on the lawn there arose such a clatter,
I sprang from my bed to see what was the matter.
Away to the window I flew like a flash,
Tore open the shutters and threw up the sash.
The moon on the breast of the new-fallen snow
Gave a lustre of midday to objects below ;
When, what to my wondering eyes should ap-
      pear,
But a miniature sleigh and eight tiny reindeer,
With a little old driver, so lively and quick
I knew in a moment it must be St. Nick.
More rapid than eagles his coursers they came,
And he whistled, and shouted, and called them
      by name :
"Now, Dasher ! now, Dancer ! now, Prancer
      and Vixen !
On, Comet ! on, Cupid ! on, Donder and
      Blitzen !
To the top of the porch, to the top of the wall !
Now dash away, dash away, dash away all ! "
As dry leaves that before the wild hurricane fly,
When they meet with an obstacle, mount to the
      sky,
So up to the house-top the coursers they flew,
With the sleigh full of toys, — and St. Nicholas
      too.
And then in a twinkling I heard on the roof
The prancing and pawing of each little hoof.

As I drew in my head, and was turning around,
Down the chimney St. Nicholas came with a
   bound.
He was dressed all in fur from his head to his
   foot,
And his clothes were all tarnished with ashes
   and soot;
A bundle of toys he had flung on his back,
And he looked like a pedler just opening his pack.
His eyes how they twinkled! his dimples how
   merry!
His cheeks were like roses, his nose like a cherry;
His droll little mouth was drawn up like a bow,
And the beard on his chin was as white as the
   snow.
The stump of a pipe he held tight in his teeth,
And the smoke it encircled his head like a wreath.
He had a broad face and a little round belly
That shook, when he laughed, like a bowl full of
   jelly.
He was chubby and plump, — a right jolly old elf;
And I laughed, when I saw him, in spite of my-
   self.
A wink of his eye and a twist of his head
Soon gave me to know I had nothing to dread.
He spoke not a word, but went straight to his
   work,
And filled all the stockings; then turned with a
   jerk,
And laying his finger aside of his nose,
And giving a nod, up the chimney he rose.
He sprang to his sleigh, to his team gave a whistle,
And away they all flew like the down of a thistle;
But I heard him exclaim, ere he drove out of sight,
"Happy Christmas to all, and to all a good-night!"
                  CLEMENT C. MOORE.

THE FROST.

THE Frost looked forth, one still, clear night,
And he said, "Now I shall be out of sight;
So through the valley and over the height
   In silence I'll take my way.
I will not go like that blustering train,
The wind and the snow, the hail and the rain,
Who make so much bustle and noise in vain,
   But I'll be as busy as they!"

Then he went to the mountain, and powdered its
   crest,
He climbed up the trees, and their boughs he
   dressed
With diamonds and pearls, and over the breast
Of the quivering lake he spread
A coat of mail, that it need not fear
The downward point of many a spear
That he hung on its margin, far and near,
   Where a rock could rear its head.

He went to the windows of those who slept,
And over each pane like a fairy crept,
Wherever he breathed, wherever he stepped,
   By the light of the moon were seen
Most beautiful things. There were flowers and
   trees,
There were bevies of birds and swarms of bees,
There were cities, thrones, temples, and towers,
   and these
   All pictured in silver sheen!

But he did one thing that was hardly fair, —
He peeped in the cupboard, and, finding there
That all had forgotten for him to prepare, —
   "Now, just to set them a thinking,
I'll bite this basket of fruit," said he;
"This costly pitcher I'll burst in three,
And the glass of water they've left for me
   Shall ' *tchick!* ' to tell them I'm drinking."
                  MISS GOULD.

THE CLOUD.

I BRING fresh showers for the thirsting flowers,
   From the seas and the streams;
I bear light shade for the leaves when laid
   In their noonday dreams.
From my wings are shaken the dews that waken
   The sweet birds every one,
When rocked to rest on their mother's breast,
   As she dances about the sun.
I wield the flail of the lashing hail,
   And whiten the green plains under;
And then again I dissolve it in rain;
   And laugh as I pass in thunder.

I sift the snow on the mountains below,
   And their great pines groan aghast;
And all the night 't is my pillow white,
   While I sleep in the arms of the blast.
Sublime on the towers of my skyey bowers
   Lightning, my pilot, sits;
In a cavern under is fettered the thunder;
   It struggles and howls at fits.
Over earth and ocean, with gentle motion,
   This pilot is guiding me,
Lured by the love of the genii that move
   In the depths of the purple sea;
Over the rills and the crags and the hills,
   Over the lakes and the plains,
Wherever he dream, under mountain or stream,
   The spirit he loves remains;
And I all the while bask in heaven's blue smile,
   Whilst he is dissolving in rains.

The sanguine sunrise, with his meteor eyes,
   And his burning plumes outspread,
Leaps on the back of my sailing rack,
   When the morning star shines dead.

As, on the jag of a mountain crag
   Which an earthquake rocks and swings,
An eagle, alit, one moment may sit
   In the light of its golden wings ;
And when sunset may breathe, from the lit sea
      beneath,
   Its ardors of rest and of love,
And the crimson pall of eve may fall
   From the depth of heaven above,
With wings folded I rest on mine airy nest,
   As still as a brooding dove.

That orbéd maiden with white fire laden,
   Whom mortals call the moon,
Glides glimmering o'er my fleece-like floor
   By the midnight breezes strewn ;
And wherever the beat of her unseen feet,
   Which only the angels hear,
May have broken the woof of my tent's thin roof,
   The stars peep behind her and peer ;
And I laugh to see them whirl and flee,
   Like a swarm of golden bees,
When I widen the rent in my wind-built tent,
   Till the calm river, lakes, and seas,
Like strips of the sky fallen through me on high,
   Are each paved with the moon and these.

I bind the sun's throne with a burning zone,
   And the moon's with a girdle of pearl ;
The volcanoes are dim, and the stars reel and swim,
   When the whirlwinds my banner unfurl.
From cape to cape, with a bridge-like shape,
   Over a torrent sea,
Sunbeam-proof, I hang like a roof,
   The mountains its columns be.
The triumphal arch, through which I march,
   With hurricane, fire, and snow,
When the powers of the air are chained to my chair,
   Is the million-colored bow ;
The sphere-fire above its soft colors wove,
   While the moist earth was laughing below.

I am the daughter of the earth and water,
   And the nursling of the sky ;
I pass through the pores of the ocean and shores ;
   I change, but I cannot die.
For after the rain, when, with never a stain,
   The pavilion of heaven is bare,
And the winds and sunbeams, with their convex
      gleams,
   Build up the blue dome of air, —
I silently laugh at my own cenotaph,
   And out of the caverns of rain,
Like a child from the womb, like a ghost from
     the tomb,
   I rise and upbuild it again.
           PERCY BYSSHE SHELLEY.

FANCY IN NUBIBUS.

O, IT is pleasant, with a heart at ease,
Just after sunset, or by moonlight skies,
To make the shifting clouds be what you please,
Or let the easily persuaded eyes
Own each quaint likeness issuing from the mould
Of a friend's fancy ; or, with head bent low,
And cheek aslant, see rivers flow of gold,
'Twixt crimson banks ; and then a traveller go
From mount to mount, through Cloudland, gor-
      geous land !
Or, listening to the tide with closéd sight,
Be that blind Bard, who on the Chian strand,
By those deep sounds possessèd with inward light,
Beheld the Iliad and the Odysse
Rise to the swelling of the voiceful sea.
         SAMUEL TAYLOR COLERIDGE.

ODE ON A GRECIAN URN.

THOU still unravished bride of quietness !
   Thou foster-child of Silence and slow Time,
Sylvan historian, who canst thus express
   A flowery tale more sweetly than our rhyme :
What leaf-fringed legend haunts about thy shape
   Of deities or mortals, or of both,
     In Tempe or the dales of Arcady ?
What men or gods are these ? What maidens
     loath ?
What mad pursuit ? What struggles to escape ?
   What pipes and timbrels ? What wild ecstasy ?

Heard melodies are sweet, but those unheard
   Are sweeter ; therefore, ye soft pipes, play on ;
Not to the sensual ear, but, more endeared,
   Pipe to the spirit ditties of no tone.
Fair youth beneath the trees, thou canst not leave
   Thy song, nor ever can those trees be bare.
     Bold lover, never, never canst thou kiss,
Though winning near the goal, — yet do not grieve :
     She cannot fade, though thou hast not thy
     bliss ;
   Forever wilt thou love, and she be fair !

Ah, happy, happy boughs ! that cannot shed
   Your leaves, nor ever bid the spring adieu ;
And happy melodist, unwearied,
   Forever piping songs forever new ;
More happy love ! more happy, happy love !
   Forever warm and still to be enjoyed,
     Forever panting and forever young ;
All breathing human passion far above,
   That leaves a heart high-sorrowful and cloyed,
     A burning forehead, and a parching tongue.

Who are these coming to the sacrifice?
  To what green altar, O mysterious priest,
Lead'st thou that heifer lowing at the skies,
  And all her silken flanks with garlands drest?
What little town by river or sea-shore,
  Or mountain-built with peaceful citadel,
    Is emptied of its folk, this pious morn?
And, little town, thy streets forevermore
  Will silent be, and not a soul to tell
    Why thou art desolate can e'er return.

O Attic shape! Fair attitude! with brede
  Of marble men and maidens overwrought,
With forest branches and the trodden weed;
  Thou silent form! dost tease us out of thought
As doth eternity. Cold Pastoral!
  When old age shall this generation waste,
    Thou shalt remain, in midst of other woe
Than ours, a friend to man, to whom thou say'st,
"Beauty is truth, truth beauty," — that is all
  Ye know on earth, and all ye need to know.
                                    JOHN KEATS.

THE SUNKEN CITY.

HARK! the faint bells of the sunken city
  Peal once more their wonted evening chime!
From the deep abysses floats a ditty,
  Wild and wondrous, of the olden time.

Temples, towers, and domes of many stories
  There lie buried in an ocean grave, —
Undescried, save when their golden glories
  Gleam, at sunset, through the lighted wave.

And the mariner who had seen them glisten,
  In whose ears those magic bells do sound,
Night by night bides there to watch and listen,
  Though death lurks behind each dark rock
    round.

So the bells of memory's wonder-city
  Peal for me their old melodious chime;
So my heart pours forth a changeful ditty,
  Sad and pleasant, from the bygone time.

Domes and towers and castles, fancy-builded,
  There lie lost to daylight's garish beams, —
There lie hidden till unveiled and gilded,
  Glory-gilded, by my nightly dreams!

And then hear I music sweet upknelling
  From many a well-known phantom band,
And, through tears, can see my natural dwelling
  Far off in the spirit's luminous land!
          WILHELM MUELLER (German). Translation
                    of JAMES CLARENCE MANGAN.

THE BOWER OF BLISS.

FROM THE "FAERIE QUEENE."

THERE the most daintie paradise on ground
Itselfe doth offer to his sober eye,
In which all pleasures plenteously abownd,
And none does others happinesse envye;
The painted flowres; the trees upshooting hye;
The dales for shade; the hilles for breathing
    space;
The trembling groves; the christall running by;
And, that which all faire workes doth most
    aggrace,
The art, which all that wrought, appeared in no
    place.

One would have thought (so cunningly the rude
And scorned partes were mingled with the fine)
That Nature had for wantonesse ensude
Art, and that Art at Nature did repine;
So striving each th' other to undermine,
Each did the others worke more beautify;
So diff'ring both in willes agreed in fine:
So all agreed, through sweete diversity,
This gardin to adorne with all variety.

And in the midst of all a fountaine stood,
Of richest substance that on earth might bee,
So pure and shiny that the silver flood
Through every channell running one might see;
Most goodly it with curious ymageree
Was over-wrought, and shapes of naked boyes,
Of which some seemed with lively iollitee
To fly about, playing their wanton toyes,
Whylest others did themselves embay in liquid
    ioyes.

And over all of purest gold was spred
A trayle of yvie in his native hew;
For the rich metall was so coloured,
That wight, who did not well avis'd it vew,
Would surely deeme it to bee yvie trew:
Low his lascivious armes adown did creepe,
That, themselves dipping in the silver dew
Their fleecy flowres they fearefully did steepe,
Which drops of christall seemed for wantones to
    weep.

Infinit streames continually did well
Out of this fountaine, sweet and faire to see,
The which into an ample laver fell,
And shortly grew to so great quantitie,
That like a little lake it seemd to bee;
Whose depth exceeded not three cubits hight,
That through the waves one might the bottom
    see,
All pav'd beneath with iaspar shining bright,
That seemd the fountaine in that sea did sayle
    upright.

Eftsoones they heard a most melodious sound,
Of all that mote delight a daintie eare,
Such as attonce might not on living ground,
Save in this paradise, be heard elsewhere :
Right hard it was for wight which did it heare,
To read what manner musicke that mote bee ;
For all that pleasing is to living eare,
Was there consorted in one harmonee ;
Birdes, voices, instruments, windes, waters, all
    agree :

The ioyous birdes, shrouded in chearefull shade,
Their notes unto the voice attempred sweet ;
Th' angelicall soft trembling voyces made
To th' instruments divine respondence meet ;
The silver-sounding instruments did meet
With the base murmure of the waters fall ;
The waters fall, with difference discreet,
Now soft, now loud, unto the wind did call ;
The gentle warbling wind low answered to all.
                          EDMUND SPENSER.

THE CAVE OF SLEEP.

FROM THE "FAERIE QUEENE."

HE, making speedy way through spersed ayre,
And through the world of waters wide and deepe,
To Morpheus house doth hastily repaire,
Amid the bowels of the earth full steepe,
And low, where dawning day doth never peepe,
His dwelling is ; there Tethys his wet bed
Doth ever wash, and Cynthia still doth steepe
In silver deaw his ever-drouping hed,
Whiles sad Night over him her mantle black doth
    spred.

And, more, to lulle him in his slumber soft,
A trickling streame from high rock tumbling
    downe,
And ever-drizling raine upon the loft,
Mixt with a murmuring winde, much like the
    sowne
Of swarming bees, did cast him in a swowne.
No other noyse, nor peoples troublous cryes,
As still are wont t' annoy the walled towne,
Might there be heard ; but carelesse Quiet lyes
Wrapt in eternall silence, farre from enimyes.
                          EDMUND SPENSER.

SIR CALEPINE RESCUES SERENA.

FROM THE "FAERIE QUEENE."

THO, when as all things readie were aright,
The damzell was before the altar set,
Being alreadie dead with fearefull fright :
To whom the priest with naked armes full net

Approching nigh, and murdrous knife well whet,
Gan mutter close a certaine secret charme,
With other divelish ceremonies met :
Which doen, he gan aloft t' advance his arme,
Whereat they shouted all, and made a loud alarme.

Then gan the bagpypes and the hornes to shrill
And shrieke aloud, that, with the people's voyce
Confused, did the ayre with terror fill,
And made the wood to tremble at the noyce :
The whyles she wayld, the more they did reioyce.
Now mote ye understand that to this grove
Sir Calepine, by chaunce more then by choyce,
The selfe same evening fortune hether drove,
As he to seeke Serena through the woods did rove.

Long had he sought her, and through many a
    soyle
Had traveld still on foot in heavie armes,
Ne ought was tyred with his endlesse toyle,
Ne ought was feared of his certaine harmes :
And now, all weetlesse of the wretched stormes
In which his love was lost, he slept full fast ;
Till, being waked with these loud alarmes,
He lightly started up like one aghast,
And, catching up his armes, streight to the noise
    forth past.

There by th' uncertaine glims of starry night,
And by the twinkling of their sacred fire,
He mote perceive a litle dawning sight
Of all which there was doing in that quire :
Mongst whom a woman spoyled of all attire
He spyde, lamenting her unluckie strife,
And groning sore from grieved hart entire :
Eftsoones he saw one with a naked knife
Readie to launch her brest, and let out loved life.

With that he thrusts into the thickest throng ;
And, even as his right hand adowne descends,
He him preventing layes on earth along,
And sacrifizeth to th' infernall feends :
Then to the rest his wrathfull hand he bends ;
Of whom he makes such havocke and such hew,
That swarmes of damned soules to hell he sends :
The rest, that scape his sword and death eschew,
Fly like a flocke of doves before a faulcons vew.

From them returning to that ladie backe,
Whom by the altar he doth sitting find
Yet fearing death, and next to death the lacke
Of clothes to cover what they ought by kind ;
He first her hands beginneth to unbind,
And then to question of her present woe ;
And afterwards to cheare with speaches kind :
But she, for nought that he could say or doe,
One word durst speake, or answere him a whit
    thereto.

So inward shame of her uncomely case
She did conceive, through care of womanhood,
That though the night did cover her disgrace,
Yet she in so unwomanly a mood
Would not bewray the state in which she stood :
So all that night to him unknowen she past :
But day, that doth discover bad and good,
Ensewing, made her knowen to him at last :
The end whereof Ile keepe untill another cast.

EDMUND SPENSER.

UNA AND THE LION.

FROM THE "FAERIE QUEENE."

ONE day, nigh wearie of the yrkesome way,
From her unhastie beast she did alight ;
And on the grasse her dainty limbs did lay
In secrete shadow, far from all mens sight ;
From her fayre head her fillet she undight,
And layd her stole aside.   Her angels face,
As the great eye of heaven, shyned bright,
And made a sunshine in the shady place ;
Did never mortall eye behold such heavenly grace.

It fortuned, out of the thickest wood
A ramping lyon rushed suddeinly,
Hunting full greedy after salvage blood :
Soone as the royall virgin he did spy,
With gaping mouth at her ran greedily,
To have attonce devourd her tender corse ;
But to the pray whenas he drew more ny,
His bloody rage aswaged with remorse,
And, with the sight amazd, forgat his furious forse.

Instead thereof, he kist her wearie feet,
And lickt her lilly hands with fawning tong ;
As he her wronged innocence did weet.
O how can beautie maister the most strong,
And simple truth subdue avenging wrong !
Whose yielded pryde and proud submission,
Still dreading death, when she had marked long,
Her hart gan melt in great compassion ;
And drizling teares did shed for pure affection.

"The lyon, lord of everie beast in field,
Quoth she, "his princely puissance doth abate,
And mightie proud to humble weake does yield,
Forgetfull of the hungry rage, which late
Him prickt, in pittie of my sad estate :—
But he, my lyon, and my noble lord,
How does he find in cruell hart to hate
Her, that him lov'd, and ever most adord
As the god of my life ? why hath he me abhord ?"

Redounding tears did choke th' end of her plaint,
Which softly ecchoed from the neighbour wood ;
And, sad to see her sorrowfull constraint,
The kingly beast upon her gazing stood ;

With pittie calmd, downe fell his angry mood.
At last, in close hart shutting up her payne,
Arose the virgin borne of heavenly brood,
And to her snowy palfrey got agayne,
To seeke her strayed champion if she might attayne.

The lyon would not leave her desolate,
But with her went along, as a strong gard
Of her chast person, and a faythfull mate
Of her sad troubles and misfortunes hard :.
Still, when she slept, he kept both watch and
        ward ;
And, when she wakt, he wayted diligent,
With humble service to her will prepard ;
From her fayre eyes he took commandément,
And ever by her lookes conceived her intent.

EDMUND SPENSER.

SCENES FROM "COMUS."

THE LADY LOST IN THE WOOD.

THIS way the noise was, if mine ear be true,
My best guide now ; methought it was the sound
Of riot and ill-managed merriment,
Such as the jocund flute or gamesome pipe
Stirs up amongst the loose, unlettered hinds,
When for their teeming flocks and granges full
In wanton dance they praise the bounteous Pan,
And thank the gods amiss.   I should be loath
To meet the rudeness and swilled insolence
Of such late wassailers ; yet O, where else
Shall I inform my unacquainted feet
In the blind mazes of this tangled wood ?
My brothers, when they saw me wearied out
With this long way, resolving here to lodge
Under the spreading favor of these pines,
Stepped, as they said, to the next thicket side
To bring me berries, or such cooling fruit
As the kind, hospitable woods provide.
They left me then, when the gray-hooded even,
Like a sad votarist in palmer's weed,
Rose from the hindmost wheels of Phœbus' wain.
But where they are, and why they came not back,
Is now the labor of my thoughts : 't is likeliest
They had engaged their wandering steps too far,
And envious darkness, ere they could return,
Had stole them from me ; else, O thievish night,
Why shouldst thou, but for some felonious end,
In thy dark lantern thus close up the stars,
That nature hung in heaven, and filled their
        lamps
With everlasting oil, to give due light
To the misled and lonely traveller ?
This is the place, as well as I may guess,
Whence even now the tumult of loud mirth
Was rife, and perfect in my listening ear,
Yet naught but single darkness do I find.

What might this be ?   A thousand fantasies
Begin to throng into my memory,
Of calling shapes, and beckoning shadows dire,
And airy tongues, that syllable men's names
On sands and shores and desert wildernesses.
These thoughts may startle well, but not astound
The virtuous mind, that ever walks attended
By a strong siding champion, Conscience.
O welcome, pure-eyed Faith, white-handed Hope,
Thou hovering angel girt with golden wings,
And thou unblemished form of Chastity ;
I see you visibly, and now believe
That he, the Supreme Good, to whom all things
        ill
Are but as slavish officers of vengeance,
Would send a glistering guardian, if need were,
To keep my life and honor unassailed.

THE LADY TO COMUS.

IMPOSTOR, do not charge most innocent Nature,
As if she would her children should be riotous
With her abundance ; she, good cateress,
Means her provision only to the good,
That live according to her sober laws,
And holy dictate of spare temperance :
If every just man, that now pines with want,
Had but a moderate and beseeming share
Of that which lewdly pampered luxury
Now heaps upon some few with vast excess,
Nature's full blessings would be well dispensed
In unsuperfluous even proportion,
And she no whit encumbered with her store ;
And then the Giver would be better thanked,
His praise due paid ; for swinish gluttony
Ne'er looks to Heaven amidst his gorgeous feast,
But with besotted, base ingratitude
Crams, and blasphemes his Feeder.

                                    MILTON.

TAM O'SHANTER.

A TALE.

"Of Brownyis and of Bogillis full is this Buke."
                                    GAWIN DOUGLASS.

WHEN chapman billies leave the street,
And drouthy neebors neebors meet,
As market-days are wearing late,
An' folk begin to tak the gate ;
While we sit bousing at the nappy,
An' getting fou and unco happy,
We think na on the lang Scots miles,
The mosses, waters, slaps, and styles,
That lie between us and our hame,
Whare sits our sulky, sullen dame,
Gathering her brows like gathering storm,
Nursing her wrath to keep it warm.

This truth fand honest Tam O' Shanter,
As he, frae Ayr, ae night did canter,
(Auld Ayr, wham ne'er a town surpasses,
For honest men and bonnie lasses.)
O Tam ! hadst thou been but sae wise
As taen thy ain wife Kate's advice !
She tauld thee weel thou was a skellum,
A bleth'ring, blust'ring, drunken blellum ;
That frae November till October,
Ae market-day thou was na sober ;
That ilka melder, wi' the miller,
Thou sat as lang as thou had siller ;
That every naig was ca'd a shoe on,
The smith and thee gat roaring fou on ;
That at the L—d's house, ev'n on Sunday,
Thou drank wi' Kirten Jean till Monday.
She prophesied that, late or soon,
Thou would be found deep drowned in Doon ;
Or catched wi' warlocks in the mirk,
By Alloway's auld haunted kirk.

Ah, gentle dames ! it gars me greet
To think how monie counsels sweet,
How monie lengthened sage advices,
The husband frae the wife despises !
But to our tale : Ae market night
Tam had got planted unco right,
Fast by an ingle, bleezing finely,
Wi' reaming swats, that drank divinely ;
And at his elbow souter Johnny,
His ancient, trusty, drouthy crony, —
Tam lo'ed him like a vera brither, —
They had been fou for weeks thegither.
The night drave on wi' sangs and clatter,
And ay the ale was growing better ;
The landlady and Tam grew gracious,
Wi' favors secret, sweet, and precious ;
The souter tauld his queerest stories ;
The landlord's laugh was ready chorus ;
The storm without might rair and rustle,
Tam did na mind the storm a whistle.

Care, mad to see a man sae happy,
E'en drowned himself amang the nappy ;
As bees flee hame wi' lades o' treasure,
The minutes winged their way wi' pleasure ;
Kings may be blest, but Tam was glorious,
O'er a' the ills o' life victorious.

But pleasures are like poppies spread,
You seize the flower, its bloom is shed ;
Or like the snow-fall in the river,
A moment white, — then melts forever ;
Or like the borealis race,
That flit ere you can point their place ;
Or like the rainbow's lovely form
Evanishing amid the storm.
Nae man can tether time or tide ;
The hour approaches Tam maun ride, —
That hour o' night's black arch the keystane,
That dreary hour he mounts his beast in ;

And sic a night he takes the road in
As ne'er poor sinner was abroad in.

   The wind blew as 't wad blawn its last ;
The rattling showers rose on the blast ;
The speedy gleams the darkness swallowed ;
Loud, deep, and lang the thunder bellowed ;
That night a child might understand
The Deil had business on his hand.

   Weel mounted on his gray mare, Meg,
(A better never lifted leg,)
Tam skelpit on thro' dub and mire,
Despising wind and rain and fire, —
Whyles holding fast his guid blue bonnet,
Whyles crooning o'er some auld Scots sonnet,
Whyles glowering round wi' prudent cares,
Lest bogles catch him unawares ;
Kirk-Alloway was drawing nigh,
Where ghaists and houlets nightly cry.

   By this time he was cross the ford,
Whare in the snaw the chapman smoored ;
And past the birks and meikle stane,
Whare drunken Charlie brak 's neck-bane ;
And through the whins, and by the cairn,
Whare hunters fand the murdered bairn ;
And near the thorn, aboon the well,
Where Mungo's mither hanged hersel'.
Before him Doon pours all his floods ;
The doubling storm roars through the woods ;
The lightnings flash from pole to pole ;
Near and more near the thunders roll ;
When, glimmering through the groaning trees,
Kirk-Alloway seemed in a bleeze !
Through ilka bore the beams were glancing,
And loud resounded mirth and dancing.

   Inspiring bold John Barleycorn !
What dangers thou canst make us scorn !
Wi' tippenny we fear nae evil ;
Wi' usquebae we 'll face the Devil ! —
The swats sae reamed in Tammie's noddle,
Fair play, he cared na Deils a bodle.
But Maggie stood right sair astonished,
Till, by the heel and hand admonished,
She ventured forward on the light ;
And, wow ! Tam saw an unco sight !
Warlocks and witches in a dance :
Nae cotillon brent new frae France,
But hornpipes, jigs, strathspeys, and reels
Put life and mettle in their heels.
A winnock-bunker in the east,
There sat auld Nick, in shape o' beast, —
A towzie tyke, black, grim, and large, —
To gie them music was his charge ;
He screwed the pipes and gart them skirl
Till roof an' rafter a' did dirl.
Coffins stood round like open presses,
That shawed the dead in their last dresses ;
And by some devilish cantrip sleight,
Each in its cauld hand held a light, —

By which heroic Tam was able
To note, upon the haly table,
A murderer's banes in gibbet airns ;
Twa span-lang, wee, unchristened bairns ;
A thief, new cutted frae a rape,
Wi' his last gasp his gab did gape ;
Five tomahawks, wi' bluid red rusted ;
Five scymitars, wi' murder crusted ;
A garter which a babe had strangled ;
A knife a father's throat had mangled,
Whom his ain son o' life bereft, —
The gray hairs yet stack to the heft ;
Three lawyers' tongues turned inside out,
Wi' lies seamed like a beggar's clout ;
And priests' hearts, rotten, black as muck,
Lay stinking, vile, in every neuk :
Wi' mair o' horrible and awfu'
Which even to name wad be unlawfu'.

   As Tammie glowered, amazed and curious,
The mirth and fun grew fast and furious ;
The piper loud and louder blew ;
The dancers quick and quicker flew ;
They reeled, they set, they crossed, they cleekit,
Till ilka carlin swat and reekit,
And coost her duddies to the wark,
And linket at it in her sark !

   Now Tam, O Tam ! had they been queans,
A' plump and strapping in their teens :
Their sarks, instead of creeshie flannen,
Been snaw-white seventeen-hunder linen ;
Thir breeks o' mine, my only pair,
That ance were plush, o' guid blue hair,
I wad hae gi'en them aff my hurdies
For ae blink o' the bonnie burdies !

   But withered beldams, auld and droll,
Rigwoodie hags wad spean a foal,
Lowping an' flinging on a crummock, —
I wonder didna turn thy stomach.

   But Tam kenn'd what was what fu' brawlie.
There was ae winsome wench and walie,
That night inlisted in the core,
(Lang after kenn'd on Carrick shore !
For monie a beast to dead she shot,
And perished monie a bonnie boat,
And shook baith meikle corn and bear,
And kept the country-side in fear,)
Her cutty-sark o' Paisley harn,
That while a lassie she had worn —
In longitude though sorely scanty,
It was her best, and she was vaunty.
Ah ! little kenned thy reverend grannie
That sark she coft for her wee Nannie
Wi' twa pund Scots (twas a' her riches) —
Wad ever graced a dance o' witches !

   But here my Muse her wing maun cower,
Sic flights are far beyond her power ;
To sing how Nannie lap and flang
(A souple jad she was and strang),

And how Tam stood like ane bewitched,
And thought his very een enriched.
Ev'n Satan glowered, and fidged fu' fain,
And hotched and blew wi' might and main ;
Till first ae caper, syne anither, —
Tam tint his reason a' thegither,
And roars out, "Weel done, Cutty-sark !"
And in an instant a' was dark ;
And scarcely had he Maggie rallied,
When out the hellish legion sallied.

As bees bizz out wi' angry fyke,
When plundering herds assail their byke ;
As open pussie's mortal foes,
When, pop ! she starts before their nose ;
As eager runs the market-crowd,
When *Catch the thief !* resounds aloud ;
So Maggie runs, — the witches follow,
Wi' monie an eldritch skreech and hollow.

Ah, Tam ! ah, Tam ! thou 'll get thy fairin'!
In hell they 'll roast thee like a herrin !
In vain thy Kate awaits thy comin' —
Kate soon will be a woefu' woman !
Now, do thy speedy utmost, Meg,
And win the key-stane of the brig ;
There at them thou thy tail may toss, —
A running stream they dare na cross.
But ere the key-stane she could make,
The fient a tail she had to shake ;
For Nannie, far before the rest,
Hard upon noble Maggie prest,
And flew at Tam wi' furious ettle :
But little wist she Maggie's mettle, —
Ae spring brought aff her master hale,
But left behind her ain gray tail :
The carlin claught her by the rump,
And left poor Maggie scarce a stump.

Now, wha this tale o' truth shall read,
Ilk man and mother's son take heed ;
Whene'er to drink you are inclined,
Or cutty-sarks run in your mind,
Think, ye may buy the joys o'er dear,
Remember Tam O' Shanter's mare.

ROBERT BURNS.

——◆——

THE PIED PIPER OF HAMELIN.

HAMELIN Town 's in Brunswick,
By famous Hanover City ;
  The river Weser, deep and wide,
  Washes its wall on the southern side ;
  A pleasanter spot you never spied ;
But when begins my ditty,
  Almost five hundred years ago,
  To see the townsfolk suffer so
From vermin was a pity.

  Rats !
They fought the dogs, and killed the cats,

And bit the babies in the cradles,
And ate the cheeses out of the vats,
  And licked the soup from the cook's own ladles,
Split open the kegs of salted sprats,
Made nests inside men's Sunday hats,
And even spoiled the women's chats,
  By drowning their speaking
  With shrieking and squeaking
In fifty different sharps and flats.

At last the people in a body
  To the Town Hall came flocking :
"'Tis clear," cried they, "our Mayor 's a noddy ;
  And as for our Corporation, — shocking
To think we buy gowns lined with ermine
For dolts that can't or won't determine
What 's best to rid us of our vermin !
At this the Mayor and Corporation
Quaked with a mighty consternation.

An hour they sate in counsel, —
  At length the Mayor broke silence :
"For a guilder I 'd my ermine gown sell ;
  I wish I were a mile hence !
It 's easy to bid one rack one's brain, —
I 'm sure my poor head aches again.
I 've scratched it so, and all in vain.
O for a trap, a trap, a trap !"
Just as he said this, what should hap
At the chamber door but a gentle tap ?
"Bless us," cried the Mayor, "what 's that ?"
"Come in !" — the Mayor cried, looking bigger ;
And in did come the strangest figure ;
He advanced to the council-table :
And, "Please your honors," said he, "I 'm able,
By means of a secret charm, to draw
All creatures living beneath the sun,
That creep or swim or fly or run,
After me so as you never saw !
Yet," said he, "poor piper as I am,
In Tartary I freed the Cham,
Last June, from his huge swarm of gnats ;
I eased in Asia the Nizam
Of a monstrous brood of vampire-bats ;
And as for what your brain bewilders, —
If I can rid your town of rats,
Will you give me a thousand guilders ?"
"One ? fifty thousand !" — was the exclamation
Of the astonished Mayor and Corporation.

Into the street the piper stept,
  Smiling first a little smile,
As if he knew what magic slept
  In his quiet pipe the while ;
Then, like a musical adept,
To blow the pipe his lips he wrinkled,
And green and blue his sharp eyes twinkled,
Like a candle flame where salt is sprinkled ;

And ere three shrill notes the pipe uttered,
You heard as if an army muttered ;
And the muttering grew to a grumbling ;
And the grumbling grew to a mighty rumbling ;
And out of the houses the rats came tumbling.
Great rats, small rats, lean rats, brawny rats,
Brown rats, black rats, gray rats, tawny rats,
Grave old plodders, gay young friskers,
    Fathers, mothers, uncles, cousins,
Cocking tails and pricking whiskers ;
    Families by tens and dozens,
Brothers, sisters, husbands, wives, —
Followed the piper for their lives.
From street to street he piped advancing,
And step for step they followed dancing,
Until they came to the river Weser,
Wherein all plunged and perished
Save one who, stout as Julius Cæsar,
Swam across and lived to carry
(As he the manuscript he cherished)
To Rat-land home his commentary,
Which was : " At the first shrill notes of the pipe,
I heard a sound as of scraping tripe,
And putting apples, wondrous ripe,
Into a cider-press's gripe, —
And a moving away of pickle-tub-boards,
And a leaving ajar of conserve-cupboards,
And a drawing the corks of train-oil-flasks,
And a breaking the hoops of butter-casks ;
And it seemed as if a voice
(Sweeter far than by harp or by psaltery
Is breathed) called out, O rats, rejoice !
The world is grown to one vast drysaltery !
So munch on, crunch on, take your nuncheon,
Breakfast, supper, dinner, luncheon !
And just as a bulky sugar-puncheon,
All ready staved, like a great sun shone
Glorious scarce an inch before me,
Just as methought it said, Come, bore me ! —
I found the Weser rolling o'er me."

You should have heard the Hamelin people
Ringing the bells till they rocked the steeple ,
" Go," cried the Mayor, " and get long poles !
Poke out the nests and block up the holes !
Consult with carpenters and builders
And leave in our town not even a trace
Of the rats ! " — when suddenly, up the face
Of the piper perked in the market-place,
With a " First, if you please, my thousand
    guilders ! "

A thousand guilders ! The Mayor looked blue ;
So did the Corporation too.
For council-dinners made rare havock
With Claret, Moselle, Vin-de-Grave, Hock ;
And half the money would replenish
Their cellar's biggest butt with Rhenish.

To pay this sum to a wandering fellow
With a gypsy coat of red and yellow !
" Beside," quoth the Mayor, with a knowing wink,
" Our business was done at the river's brink ;
We saw with our eyes the vermin sink,
And what 's dead can't come to life, I think.
So, friend, we 're not the folks to shrink
From the duty of giving you something for drink,
And a matter of money to put in your poke ;
But as for the guilders, what we spoke
Of them, as you very well know, was in joke.
Beside, our losses have made us thrifty ;
A thousand guilders ! Come, take fifty ! "

The piper's face fell, and he cried,
" No trifling ! I can't wait ! beside,
I 've promised to visit by dinner time
Bagdat, and accept the prime
Of the head cook's pottage, all he 's rich in,
For having left, in the Caliph's kitchen,
Of a nest of scorpions no survivor, —
With him I proved no bargain-driver ;
With you, don't think I 'll bate a stiver !
And folks who put me in a passion
May find me pipe to another fashion."

" How ? " cried the Mayor, " d' ye think I 'll brook
Being worse treated than a cook ?
Insulted by a lazy ribald
With idle pipe and vesture piebald ?
You threaten us, fellow ? Do your worst,
Blow your pipe there till you burst ! "

Once more he stept into the street ;
    And to his lips again
Laid his long pipe of smooth straight cane ;
    And ere he blew three notes (such sweet
Soft notes as yet musician's cunning
    Never gave the enraptured air)
There was a rustling that seemed like a bustling
Of merry crowds justling at pitching and hustling ;
Small feet were pattering, wooden shoes clattering,
Little hands clapping, and little tongues chatter-
    ing ;
And, like fowls in a farm-yard when barley is
    scattering,
Out came the children running :
All the little boys and girls,
With rosy cheeks and flaxen curls,
And sparkling eyes and teeth like pearls,
Tripping and skipping, ran merrily after
The wonderful music with shouting and laughter.

The Mayor was dumb, and the Council stood
As if they were changed into blocks of wood,
Unable to move a step, or cry
To the children merrily skipping by, —
And could only follow with the eye
That joyous crowd at the piper's back.

But how the Mayor was on the rack,
And the wretched Council's bosoms beat,
As the piper turned from the High Street
To where the Weser rolled its waters
Right in the way of their sons and daughters !
However, he turned from south to west,
And to Koppelberg Hill his steps addressed,
And after him the children pressed ;
Great was the joy in every breast.
" He never can cross that mighty top !
He 's forced to let the piping drop,
And we shall see our children stop ! "
When, lo, as they reached the mountain's side,
A wondrous portal opened wide,
As if a cavern was suddenly hollowed ;
And the piper advanced and the children followed ;
And when all were in, to the very last,
The door in the mountain-side shut fast.
Did I say all ? No ! One was lame,
And could not dance the whole of the way ;
And in after years, if you would blame
His sadness, he was used to say, —
" It 's dull in our town since my playmates left !
I can't forget that I 'm bereft
Of all the pleasant sights they see,
Which the piper also promised me ;
For he led us, he said, to a joyous land,
Joining the town and just at hand,
Where waters gushed and fruit-trees grew,
And flowers put forth a fairer hue,
And everything was strange and new ;
The sparrows were brighter than peacocks here,
And their dogs outran our fallow deer,
And honey-bees had lost their stings,
And horses were born with eagles' wings ;
And just as I became assured
My lame foot would be speedily cured,
The music stopped and I stood still,
And found myself outside the Hill,
Left alone against my will,
To go now limping as before,
And never hear of that country more ! "

ROBERT BROWNING.

RHŒCUS.

A YOUTH named Rhœcus, wandering in the wood,
Saw an old oak just trembling to its fall,
And, feeling pity of so fair a tree,
He propped its gray trunk with admiring care,
And with a thoughtless footstep loitered on.
But, as he turned, he heard a voice behind
That murmured " Rhœcus ! " 'T was as if the leaves,
Stirred by a passing breath, had murmured it,
And, while he paused bewildered, yet again
It murmured " Rhœcus ! " softer than a breeze.

He started and beheld with dizzy eyes
What seemed the substance of a happy dream
Stand there before him, spreading a warm glow
Within the green glooms of the shadowy oak.
It seemed a woman's shape, yet all too fair
To be a woman, and with eyes too meek
For any that were wont to mate with gods.
All naked like a goddess stood she there,
And like a goddess all too beautiful
To feel the guilt-born earthliness of shame.
" Rhœcus, I am the Dryad of this tree,"
Thus she began, dropping her low-toned words
Serene, and full, and clear, as drops of dew,
" And with it I am doomed to live and die ;
The rain and sunshine are my caterers,
Nor have I other bliss than simple life ;
Now ask me what thou wilt, that I can give,
And with a thankful joy it shall be thine."

Then Rhœcus, with a flutter at the heart,
Yet, by the prompting of such beauty, bold,
Answered : " What is there that can satisfy
The endless craving of the soul but love ?
Give me thy love, or but the hope of that
Which must be evermore my spirit's goal."
After a little pause she said again,
But with a glimpse of sadness in her tone,
" I give it, Rhœcus, though a perilous gift ;
An hour before the sunset meet me here."
And straightway there was nothing he could see
But the green glooms beneath the shadowy oak,
And not a sound came to his straining ears
But the low trickling rustle of the leaves,
And far away upon an emerald slope
The falter of an idle shepherd's pipe.

Young Rhœcus had a faithful heart enough,
But one that in the present dwelt too much,
And, taking with blithe welcome whatsoe'er
Chance gave of joy, was wholly bound in that,
Like the contented peasant of a vale,
Deemed it the world, and never looked beyond.
So, haply meeting in the afternoon
Some comrades who were playing at the dice,
He joined them, and forgot all else beside.

The dice were rattling at the merriest,
And Rhœcus, who had met but sorry luck,
Just laughed in triumph at a happy throw,
When through the room there hummed a yellow bee
That buzzed about his ear with down-dropped legs
As if to light. And Rhœcus laughed and said,
Feeling how red and flushed he was with loss,
" By Venus ! does he take me for a rose ? "
And brushed him off with rough, impatient hand.
But still the bee came back, and thrice again
Rhœcus did beat him off with growing wrath.

Then through the window flew the wounded bee,
And Rhœcus, tracking him with angry eyes
Saw a sharp mountain-peak of Thessaly
Against the red disk of the setting sun, —
And instantly the blood sank from his heart,
As if its very walls had caved away.
Without a word he turned, and, rushing forth,
Ran madly through the city and the gate,
And o'er the plain, which now the wood's long
    shade,
By the low sun thrown forward broad and dim,
Darkened wellnigh unto the city's wall.

Quite spent and out of breath he reached the tree,
And, listening fearfully, he heard once more
The low voice murmur "Rhœcus!" close at hand:
Whereat he looked around him, but could see
Naught but the deepening glooms beneath the oak.
Then sighed the voice, "O Rhœcus! nevermore
Shalt thou behold me or by day or night,
Me, who would fain have blessed thee with a love
More ripe and bounteous than ever yet
Filled up with nectar any mortal heart;
But thou didst scorn my humble messenger,
And sent'st him back to me with bruiséd wings.
We spirits only show to gentle eyes,
We ever ask an undivided love.
And he who scorns the least of Nature's works
Is thenceforth exiled and shut out from all.
Farewell! for thou canst never see me more."
                JAMES RUSSELL LOWELL.

KUBLA KHAN.

IN Xanadu did Kubla Khan
A stately pleasure-dome decree
Where Alph, the sacred river, ran,
Through caverns measureless to man,
    Down to a sunless sea.
So twice five miles of fertile ground
With walls and towers were girdled round;
And there were gardens, bright with sinuous rills,
Where blossomed many an incense-bearing tree;
And here were forests ancient as the hills,
Infolding sunny spots of greenery.

But O that deep romantic chasm, which slanted
Down the green hill athwart a cedarn cover!
A savage place! as holy and enchanted
As e'er beneath a waning moon was haunted
By woman wailing for her demon-lover!
And from this chasm, with ceaseless turmoil
    seething,
As if this earth in fast thick pants were breathing,
A mighty fountain momently was forced,
Amid whose swift, half-intermitted burst
Huge fragments vaulted like rebounding hail,
Or chaffy grain beneath the thresher's flail;

And 'mid these dancing rocks at once and ever
It flung up momently the sacred river.
Five miles, meandering with a mazy motion
Through wood and dale, the sacred river ran, —
Then reached the caverns measureless to man,
And sank in tumult to a lifeless ocean,
And 'mid this tumult Kubla heard from far
Ancestral voices prophesying war.

    The shadow of the dome of pleasure
    Floated midway on the waves
    Where was heard the mingled measure
    From the fountain and the caves.
It was a miracle of rare device, —
A sunny pleasure-dome with caves of ice!
    A damsel with a dulcimer
    In a vision once I saw;
It was an Abyssinian maid,
And on her dulcimer she played,
Singing of Mount Abora.
Could I revive within me
Her symphony and song,
To such a deep delight 't would win me
That, with music loud and long,
I would build that dome in air, —
That sunny dome! those caves of ice!
And all who heard should see them there,
And all should cry, Beware! beware
His flashing eyes, his floating hair!
Weave a circle round him thrice,
And close your eyes with holy dread,
For he on honey-dew hath fed,
And drunk the milk of Paradise.
              SAMUEL TAYLOR COLERIDGE.

THE LAKE OF THE DISMAL SWAMP.

WRITTEN AT NORFOLK IN VIRGINIA.

"They tell of a young man who lost his mind upon the death of
a girl he loved, and who, suddenly disappearing from his friends,
was never afterwards heard of. As he had frequently said in his
ravings that the girl was not dead, but gone to the Dismal Swamp,
it is supposed he had wandered into that dreary wilderness,
and had died of hunger, or been lost in some of its dreadful
morasses." — ANONYMOUS.

The Great Dismal Swamp is ten or twelve miles distant from
Norfolk, and the lake in the middle of it (about seven miles long)
is called Drummond's Pond.

"THEY made her a grave too cold and damp
    For a soul so warm and true;
And she's gone to the Lake of the Dismal Swamp,
Where all night long, by a firefly lamp,
    She paddles her white canoe.

And her firefly lamp I soon shall see,
    And her paddle I soon shall hear;
Long and loving our life shall be,
And I'll hide the maid in a cypress-tree,
When the footstep of death is near!"

Away to the Dismal Swamp he speeds, —
　His path was rugged and sore,
Through tangled juniper, beds of reeds,
Through many a fen where the serpent feeds,
　And man never trod before !

And when on the earth he sunk to sleep,
　If slumber his eyelids knew,
He lay where the deadly vine doth weep
Its venomous tear, and nightly steep
　The flesh with blistering dew !

And near him the she-wolf stirred the brake,
　And the copper-snake breathed in his ear,
Till he starting cried, from his dream awake,
"O, when shall I see the dusky Lake,
　And the white canoe of my dear ? "

He saw the Lake, and a meteor bright
　Quick over its surface played, —
"Welcome," he said, "my dear one's light ! "
And the dim shore echoed for many a night
　The name of the death-cold maid !

Till he hollowed a boat of the birchen bark,
　Which carried him off from shore ;
Far he followed the meteor spark,
The wind was high and the clouds were dark,
　And the boat returned no more.

But oft, from the Indian hunter's camp,
　This lover and maid so true
Are seen, at the hour of midnight damp,
To cross the Lake by a firefly lamp,
　And paddle their white canoe !
　　　　　　　　　　　THOMAS MOORE.

THE BLESSED DAMOZEL.

THE blessed damozel leaned out
　From the gold bar of heaven ;
Her eyes were deeper than the depth
　Of waters stilled at even ;
She had three lilies in her hand,
　And the stars in her hair were seven.

Her robe, ungirt from clasp to hem,
　No wrought flowers did adorn,
But a white rose of Mary's gift,
　For service neatly worn ;
Her hair that lay along her back
　Was yellow like ripe corn.

Her seemed she scarce had been a day
　One of God's choristers ;
The wonder was not yet quite gone
　From that still look of hers ;
Albeit, to them she left, her day
　Had counted as ten years.

It was the rampart of God's house
　That she was standing on ;
By God built over the sheer depth
　The which is space begun ;
So high, that looking downward thence
　She scarce could see the sun.

It lies in heaven, across the flood
　Of ether, as a bridge.
Beneath, the tides of day and night
　With flame and darkness ridge
The void, as low as where this earth
　Spins like a fretful midge.

Heard hardly, some of her new friends
　Amid their loving games
Spake evermore among themselves
　Their virginal chaste names ;
And the souls mounting up to God
　Went by her like thin flames.

And still she bowed herself and stopped
　Out of the circling charm ;
Until her bosom must have made
　The bar she leaned on warm,
And the lilies lay as if asleep
　Along her bended arm.

From the fixed place of heaven she saw
　Time like a pulse shake fierce
Through all the worlds.　Her gaze still strove
　Within the gulf to pierce
The path ; and now she spoke as when
　The stars sang in their spheres.

.　　.　　.　　.　　.

"I wish that he were come to me,
　For he will come," she said.
"Have I not prayed in heaven ? — on earth,
　Lord, Lord, has he not prayed ?
Are not two prayers a perfect strength ?
　And shall I feel afraid ? "

.　　.　　.　　.　　.

She gazed and listened, and then said,
　Less sad of speech than mild, —
"All this is when he comes."　She ceased.
　The light thrilled toward her, filled
With angels in strong level flight.
　Her eyes prayed, and she smiled.

(I saw her smile.)　But soon their path
　Was vague in distant spheres ;
And then she cast her arms along
　The golden barriers,
And laid her face between her hands,
　And wept.　(I heard her tears.)
　　　　　　　　　DANTE GABRIEL ROSSETTI.

S. T. Coleridge

FORDS, HOWARD, & HULBERT, N.Y.

RIME OF THE ANCIENT MARINER.

IN SEVEN PARTS.

PART I.

An ancient mariner meeteth three gallants bidden to a wedding feast, and detaineth one.

IT is an ancient mariner,
And he stoppeth one of three.
"By thy long gray beard and glittering
    eye,
Now wherefore stopp'st thou me ?

The bridegroom's doors are opened wide,
And I am next of kin ;
The guests are met, the feast is set; —
May'st hear the merry din."

He holds him with his skinny hand :
"There was a ship," quoth he.
"Hold off! unhand me, graybeard
    loon !" —
Eftsoons his hand dropt he.

The wedding-guest is spellbound by the eye of the old seafaring man, and constrained to hear his tale.

He holds him with his glittering eye, —
The wedding-guest stood still ;
He listens like a three years' child ;
The mariner hath his will.

The wedding-guest sat on a stone, —
He cannot choose but hear ;
And thus spake on that ancient man,
The bright-eyed mariner :

"The ship was cheered, the harbor
    cleared ;
Merrily did we drop
Below the kirk, below the hill,
Below the lighthouse top.

The mariner tells how the ship sailed southward, with a good wind and fair weather, till it reached the line.

The sun came up upon the left,
Out of the sea came he ;
And he shone bright, and on the right
Went down into the sea.

Higher and higher every day,
Till over the mast at noon —"
The wedding-guest here beat his breast,
For he heard the loud bassoon.

The wedding-guest heareth the bridal music; but the mariner continueth his tale.

The bride hath paced into the hall, —
Red as a rose is she ;
Nodding their heads before her goes
The merry minstrelsy.

The wedding-guest he beat his breast,
Yet he cannot choose but hear ;
And thus spake on that ancient man,
The bright-eyed mariner :

The ship drawn by a storm toward the south pole.

"And now the storm-blast came, and he
Was tyrannous and strong ;
He struck with his o'ertaking wings,
And chased us south along.

With sloping masts and dipping prow, —
As who pursued with yell and blow
Still treads the shadow of his foe,
And forward bends his head, —
The ship drove fast ; loud roared the
    blast,
And southward aye we fled.

And now there came both mist and snow,
And it grew wondrous cold ;
And ice, mast-high, came floating by,
As green as emerald.

The land of ice and of fearful sounds, where no living thing was to be seen.

And through the drifts the snowy cliffs
Did send a dismal sheen ;
Nor shapes of men nor beasts we ken, —
The ice was all between.

The ice was here, the ice was there,
The ice was all around ;
It cracked and growled, and roared and
    howled,
Like noises in a swound !

Till a great sea-bird, called the albatross, came through the snow-fog, and was received with great joy and hospitality.

At length did cross an albatross, —
Thorough the fog it came ;
As if it had been a Christian soul,
We hailed it in God's name.

It ate the food it ne'er had eat,
And round and round it flew.
The ice did split with a thunder-fit ;
The helmsman steered us through !

And lo! the albatross proveth a bird of good omen, and followeth the ship as it returned northward through fog and floating ice.

And a good south-wind sprung up be-
    hind ;
The albatross did follow,
And every day, for food or play,
Came to the mariners' hollo !

In mist or cloud, on mast or shroud,
It perched for vespers nine ;
Whiles all the night, through fog-smoke
    white,
Glimmered the white moonshine."

The ancient mariner inhospitably killeth the pious bird of good omen.

"God save thee, ancient mariner !
From the fiends that plague thee thus ! —
Why look'st thou so ?" — "With my
    cross-bow
I shot the albatross."

PART II.

"THE sun now rose upon the right, —
Out of the sea came he,
Still hid in mist, and on the left
Went down into the sea.

And the good south-wind still blew be-
    hind ;
But no sweet bird did follow.

Nor any day for food or play
Came to the mariners' hollo.

His ship-mates cry out against the ancient mariner, for killing the bird of good luck.

And I had done a hellish thing,
And it would work 'em woe ;
For all averred I had killed the bird
That made the breeze to blow :
Ah, wretch ! said they, the bird to slay,
That made the breeze to blow !

But when the fog cleared off, they justify the same, and thus make them-selves ac-complices in the crime.

Nor dim nor red, like God's own head
The glorious sun uprist ;
Then all averred I had killed the bird
That brought the fog and mist :
'Twas right, said they, such birds to slay,
That bring the fog and mist.

The fair breeze con-tinues ; the ship enters the Pacific Ocean, and sails north-ward, even till it reaches the line.

The fair breeze blew, the white foam flew,
The furrow followed free ;
We were the first that ever burst
Into that silent sea.

The ship hath been suddenly becalmed.

Down dropt the breeze, the sails dropt
      down, —
'Twas sad as sad could be ;
And we did speak only to break
The silence of the sea.

All in a hot and copper sky
The bloody sun, at noon,
Right up above the mast did stand,
No bigger than the moon.

Day after day, day after day,
We stuck, — nor breath nor motion ;
As idle as a painted ship
Upon a painted ocean.

And the albatross begins to be aven-ged.

Water, water everywhere,
And all the boards did shrink ;
Water, water everywhere,
Nor any drop to drink.

The very deep did rot : O Christ !
That ever this should be !
Yea, slimy things did crawl with legs
Upon the slimy sea !

About, about, in reel and rout,
The death-fires danced at night ;
The water, like a witch's oils,
Burnt green, and blue, and white.

A spirit had fol-lowed them, — one of the invisi-ble inhabit-ants of this planet,

And some in dreams assuréd were
Of the spirit that plagued us so ;
Nine fathom deep he had followed us
From the land of mist and snow.

neither departed souls nor angels ; concerning whom the learned Jew, Josephus, and the Platonic Constantinopolitan, Michael Psellus, may be consulted. They are very numerous, and there is no cli-mate or element without one or more.

And every tongue, through utter
      drought,
Was withered at the root ;
We could not speak, no more than if
We had been choked with soot.

The ship-mates, in thei sore, distress, would fain throw the whole guilt on the an-cient mari-ner : in sign whereof they hang the dead sea-bird round his neck.

Ah ! well-a-day ! what evil looks
Had I from old and young !
Instead of the cross, the albatross
About my neck was hung.

PART III.

THERE passed a weary time. Each throat
Was parched, and glazed each eye, —
A weary time ! a weary time !
How glazed each weary eye ! —
When, looking westward, I beheld
A something in the sky.

The ancient mari-ner behold eth a sign in the ele-ment afar off.

At first it seemed a little speck,
And then it seemed a mist ;
It moved and moved, and took at last
A certain shape, I wist, —

A speck, a mist, a shape, I wist !
And still it neared and neared ;
As if it dodged a water-sprite,
It plunged, and tacked, and veered.

At its near-er ap-proach it seemeth him to be a ship ; and at a dear ransom he freeth his speech from the bonds of thirst.

With throats unslaked, with black lips
      baked,
We could not laugh nor wail ;
Through utter drought all dumb we
      stood ;
I bit my arm, I sucked the blood,
And cried, A sail ! a sail !

A flash of joy.

With throats unslaked, with black lips
      baked,
Agape they heard me call ;
Gramercy ! they for joy did grin,
And all at once their breath drew in,
As they were drinking all.

And horror follows ; for can it be a ship that comes onward without wind or tide ?

See ! see ! I cried, she tacks no more !
Hither, to work us weal, —
Without a breeze, without a tide,
She steadies with upright keel !

The western wave was all aflame ;
The day was wellnigh done ;
Almost upon the western wave
Rested the broad bright sun, —
When that strange shape drove suddenly
Betwixt us and the sun.

It seemeth him but the skeleton of a ship.

And straight the sun was flecked with
      bars,
(Heaven's mother send us grace !)

As if through a dungeon grate he peered
With broad and burning face.

Alas! thought I — and my heart beat
   loud —
How fast she nears and nears!
Are those her sails that glance in the sun
Like restless gossameres?

And its ribs are seen as bars on the face of the setting sun. The spectre-woman and her death-mate, and no other, on board the skeleton ship.
Are those her ribs through which the sun
Did peer, as through a grate?
And is that woman all her crew?
Is that a Death? and are there two?
Is Death that woman's mate?

Like vessel, like crew!
Her lips were red, her looks were free,
Her locks were yellow as gold;
Her skin was as white as leprosy:
The nightmare Life-in-death was she,
Who thicks man's blood with cold.

Death and Life-in-Death have diced for the ship's crew, and she (the latter) winneth the ancient mariner.
The naked hulk alongside came,
And the twain were casting dice:
'The game is done! I've won! I've
   won!'
Quoth she, and whistles thrice.

No twilight within the courts of the sun.
The sun's rim dips, the stars rush out,
At one stride comes the dark;
With far-heard whisper, o'er the sea
Off shot the spectre bark.

At the rising of the moon,
We listened, and looked sideways up;
Fear at my heart, as at a cup,
My life-blood seemed to sip;
The stars were dim, and thick the
   night, —
The steersman's face by his lamp gleamed
   white;
From the sails the dew did drip, —
Till clomb above the eastern bar
The hornèd moon, with one bright star
Within the nether tip.

One after another
One after one, by the star-dogged moon,
Too quick for groan or sigh,
Each turned his face, with a ghastly pang,
And cursed me with his eye.

His shipmates drop down dead;
Four times fifty living men,
(And I heard nor sigh nor groan!)
With heavy thump, a lifeless lump,
They dropped down one by one.

But Life-in-Death begins her work on the ancient mariner.
The souls did from their bodies fly, —
They fled to bliss or woe!
And every soul it passed me by,
Like the whiz of my cross-bow!"

PART IV.

"I FEAR thee, ancient mariner!
I fear thy skinny hand!
And thou art long, and lank, and brown,
As is the ribbed sea-sand.
The wedding-guest feareth that a spirit is talking to him;

I fear thee and thy glittering eye,
And thy skinny hand so brown."
"Fear not, fear not, thou wedding-guest!
This body dropt not down.
But the ancient mariner assureth him of his bodily life, and proceedeth to relate his horrible penance.

Alone, alone, all, all alone,
Alone on a wide, wide sea!
And never a saint took pity on
My soul in agony.

The many men, so beautiful!
And they all dead did lie;
And a thousand thousand slimy things
Lived on, — and so did I.
He despiseth the creatures of the calm;

I looked upon the rotting sea,
And drew my eyes away;
I looked upon the rotting deck,
And there the dead men lay.
And envieth that they should live, and so many lie dead.

I looked to heaven and tried to pray;
But or ever a prayer had gusht
A wicked whisper came, and made
My heart as dry as dust.

I closed my lids, and kept them close,
And the balls like pulses beat;
For the sky and the sea, and the sea and
   the sky,
Lay like a load on my weary eye,
And the dead were at my feet.

The cold sweat melted from their
   limbs, —
Nor rot nor reek did they;
The look with which they looked on me
Had never passed away.
But the curse liveth for him in the eye of the dead men.

An orphan's curse would drag to hell
A spirit from on high;
But O, more horrible than that
Is the curse in a dead man's eye!
Seven days, seven nights, I saw that
   curse, —
And yet I could not die.

The moving moon went up the sky,
And nowhere did abide;
Softly she was going up,
And a star or two beside.
In his loneliness and fixedness he yearneth towards the journeying moon, and the stars that still sojourn, yet still move onward; and everywhere the blue sky belongs to them, and is their appointed rest, and their native country, and their own natural homes, which they enter unannounced, as lords that are certainly expected; and yet there is a silent joy at their arrival.

Her beams bemocked the sultry main,
Like April hoar-frost spread ;
But where the ship's huge shadow lay
The charméd water burnt alway
A still and awful red.

By the light of the moon he beholdeth God's creatures of the great calm.

Beyond the shadow of the ship
I watched the water-snakes ;
They moved in tracks of shining white ;
And when they reared, the elfish light
Fell off in hoary flakes.

Within the shadow of the ship
I watched their rich attire, —
Blue, glossy green, and velvet black,
They coiled and swam ; and every track
Was a flash of golden fire.

Their beauty and their happiness.

O happy living things ! no tongue
Their beauty might declare ;
A spring of love gushed from my heart,

He blesseth them in his heart.

And I blessed them unaware, —
Sure my kind saint took pity on me,
And I blessed them unaware.

The spell begins to break.

The selfsame moment I could pray ;
And from my neck so free
The albatross fell off, and sank
Like lead into the sea.

PART V.

O SLEEP ! it is a gentle thing,
Beloved from pole to pole !
To Mary Queen the praise be given !
She sent the gentle sleep from heaven
That slid into my soul.

By grace of the Holy Mother, the ancient mariner is refreshed with rain.

The silly buckets on the deck,
That had so long remained,
I dreamt that they were filled with dew ;
And when I woke, it rained.

My lips were wet, my throat was cold,
My garments all were dank ;
Sure I had drunken in my dreams,
And still my body drank.

I moved, and could not feel my limbs ;
I was so light — almost
I thought that l had died in sleep,
And was a blesséd ghost.

He heareth sounds and seeth strange sights and commotions in the sky and the element.

And soon I heard a roaring wind, —
It did not come anear ;
But with its sound it shook the sails,
That were so thin and sear.

The upper air burst into life ;
And a hundred fire-flags sheen,
To and fro they were hurried about ;

And to and fro, and in and out,
The wan stars danced between.

And the coming wind did roar more loud,
And the sails did sigh like sedge ;
And the rain poured down from one
    black cloud, —
The moon was at its edge.

The thick black cloud was cleft, and still
The moon was at its side ;
Like waters shot from some high crag,
The lightning fell with never a jag, —
A river steep and wide.

The bodies of the ship's crew are inspired, and the ship moves on.

The loud wind never reached the ship,
Yet now the ship moved on !
Beneath the lightning and the moon
The dead men gave a groan.

They groaned, they stirred, they all
    uprose, —
Nor spake, nor moved their eyes ;
It had been strange, even in a dream,
To have seen those dead men rise.

The helmsman steered, the ship moved
    on ;
Yet never a breeze upblew ;
The mariners all 'gan work the ropes,
Where they were wont to do ;
They raised their limbs like lifeless
    tools, —
We were a ghastly crew.

The body of my brother's son
Stood by me, knée to knee ;
The body and I pulled at one rope,
But he said naught to me."

But not by the souls of the men, nor by demons of earth or middle air, but by a blessed troop of angelic spirits sent down by the invocation of the guardian saint.

"I fear thee, ancient mariner !"
" Be calm, thou wedding-guest !
'T was not those souls that fled in pain,
Which to their corses came again,
But a troop of spirits blest.

For when it dawned they dropped their
    arms,
And clustered round the mast ;
Sweet sounds rose slowly through their
    mouths,
And from their bodies passed.

Around, around flew each sweet sound,
Then darted to the sun ;
Slowly the sounds came back again,
Now mixed, now one by one.

Sometimes, a-dropping from the sky,
I heard the skylark sing;
Sometimes all little birds that are, —
How they seemed to fill the sea and air
With their sweet jargoning!

And now 't was like all instruments,
Now like a lonely flute;
And now it is an angel's song,
That makes the heavens be mute.

It ceased; yet still the sails made on
A pleasant noise till noon, —
A noise like of a hidden brook
In the leafy month of June,
That to the sleeping woods all night
Singeth a quiet tune.

Till noon we quietly sailed on,
Yet never a breeze did breathe;
Slowly and smoothly went the ship,
Moved onward from beneath.

The lonesome spirit from the south pole carries on the ship as far as the line in obedience to the angelic troop; but still requireth vengeance.

Under the keel nine fathom deep,
From the land of mist and snow,
The spirit slid; and it was he
That made the ship to go.
The sails at noon left off their tune,
And the ship stood still alsó.

The sun, right up above the mast,
Had fixed her to the ocean;
But in a minute she 'gan to stir,
With a short uneasy motion, —
Backwards and forwards half her length,
With a short uneasy motion.

Then like a pawing horse let go,
She made a sudden bound, —
It flung the blood into my head,
And I fell down in a swound.

The polar spirit's fellow-demons, the invisible inhabitants of the element, take part in his wrong; and two of them relate, one to the other, that penance, long and heavy for the ancient mariner, hath been accorded to the polar spirit, who returneth southward.

How long in that same fit I lay
I have not to declare;
But ere my living life returned
I heard, and in my soul discerned,
Two voices in the air;

'Is it he?' quoth one, 'Is this the man?
By him who died on cross,
With his cruel bow he laid full low
The harmless albatross!

The spirit who bideth by himself
In the land of mist and snow,
He loved the bird that loved the man
Who shot him with his bow.'

The other was a softer voice,
As soft as honey-dew:
Quoth he, 'The man hath penance done,
And penance more will do.'

PART VI.

FIRST VOICE.

'But tell me, tell me! speak again,
Thy soft response renewing, —
What makes that ship drive on so fast?
What is the ocean doing?'

SECOND VOICE.

'Still as a slave before his lord,
The ocean hath no blast;
His great bright eye most silently
Up to the moon is cast, —

If he may know which way to go;
For she guides him smooth or grim.
See, brother, see! how graciously
She looketh down on him.'

FIRST VOICE.

'But why drives on that ship so fast,
Without or wave or wind?'

SECOND VOICE.

'The air is cut away before,
And closes from behind.

The mariner hath been cast into a trance; for the angelic power causeth the vessel to drive northward faster than human life could endure.

Fly, brother, fly! more high, more high!
Or we shall be belated;
For slow and slow that ship will go,
When the mariner's trance is abated.'

I woke, and we were sailing on
As in a gentle weather;
'T was night, calm night, — the moon
was high;
The dead men stood together.

The supernatural motion is retarded; the mariner awakes, and his penance begins anew.

All stood together on the deck,
For a charnel-dungeon fitter;
All fixed on me their stony eyes,
That in the moon did glitter.

The pang, the curse, with which they
died,
Had never passed away;
I could not draw my eyes from theirs,
Nor turn them up to pray.

And now this spell was snapt; once more
I viewed the ocean green,
And looked far forth, yet little saw
Of what had else been seen, —

The curse is finally expiated.

Like one that on a lonesome road
Doth walk in fear and dread,

And, having once turned round, walks on,
And turns no more his head ;
Because he knows a frightful fiend
Doth close behind him tread.

But soon there breathed a wind on me,
Nor sound nor motion made ;
Its path was not upon the sea,
In ripple or in shade.

It raised my hair, it fanned my cheek,
Like a meadow-gale of spring, —
It mingled strangely with my fears,
Yet it felt like a welcoming.

Swiftly, swiftly flew the ship,
Yet she sailed softly too ;
Sweetly, sweetly blew the breeze, —
On me alone it blew.

And the ancient mariner beholdeth his native country.

O dream of joy ! is this indeed
The lighthouse top I see ?
Is this the hill ? is this the kirk ?
Is this mine own countree ?

We drifted o'er the harbor-bar,
And I with sobs did pray, —
O, let me be awake, my God !
Or let me sleep alway.

The harbor-bay was clear as glass,
So smoothly it was strewn !
And on the bay the moonlight lay,
And the shadow of the moon.

The rock shone bright, the kirk no less,
That stands above the rock ;
The moonlight steeped in silentness
The steady weathercock.

The angelic spirits leave the dead bodies,

And the bay was white with silent light,
Till, rising from the same,
Full many shapes, that shadows were,
In crimson colors came.

And appear in their own forms of light.

A little distance from the prow
Those crimson shadows were ;
I turned my eyes upon the deck, —
O Christ ! what saw I there !

Each corse lay flat, lifeless and flat ;
And, by the holy rood !
A man all light, a seraph man,
On every corse there stood.

This seraph band, each waved his hand, —
It was a heavenly sight !

They stood as signals to the land,
Each one a lovely light ;

This seraph band each waved his hand ;
No voice did they impart, —
No voice ; but O, the silence sank
Like music on my heart !

But soon I heard the dash of oars,
I heard the pilot's cheer ;
My head was turned perforce away,
And I saw a boat appear.

The pilot and the pilot's boy,
I heard them coming fast ;
Dear Lord in heaven ! it was a joy
The dead men could not blast.

I saw a third, — I heard his voice ;
It is the hermit good !
He singeth loud his godly hymns
That he makes in the wood ;
He 'll shrieve my soul, — he 'll wash away
The albatross's blood.

PART VII.

The hermit of the wood

THIS hermit good lives in that wood
Which slopes down to the sea.
How loudly his sweet voice he rears !
He loves to talk with marineres
That come from a far countree.

He kneels at morn and noon and eve, —
He hath a cushion plump ;
It is the moss that wholly hides
The rotted old oak-stump.

The skiff-boat neared, — I heard them talk :
'Why, this is strange, I trow !
Where are those lights, so many and fair,
That signal made but now ?'

Approacheth the ship with wonder.

'Strange, by my faith !' the hermit said, —
'And they answered not our cheer !
The planks looked warped ! and see those sails,
How thin they are and sear !
I never saw aught like to them,
Unless perchance it were

Brown skeletons of leaves that lag
My forest-brook along,
When the ivy-tod is heavy with snow,

And the owlet whoops to the wolf below,
That eats the she-wolf's young.'

'Dear Lord! it hath a fiendish look,'
The pilot made reply, —
'I am a-feared.' — 'Push on, push on!'
Said the hermit cheerily.

The boat came closer to the ship,
But I nor spake nor stirred;
The boat came close beneath the ship,
And straight a sound was heard:

The ship suddenly sinketh.

Under the water it rumbled on,
Still louder and more dread;
It reached the ship, it split the bay;
The ship went down like lead.

The ancient mariner is saved in the pilot's boat.

Stunned by that loud and dreadful sound,
Which sky and ocean smote,
Like one that hath been seven days drowned,
My body lay afloat;
But, swift as dreams, myself I found
Within the pilot's boat.

Upon the whirl where sank the ship
The boat spun round and round;
And all was still, save that the hill
Was telling of the sound.

I moved my lips, — the pilot shrieked,
And fell down in a fit;
The holy hermit raised his eyes,
And prayed where he did sit.

I took the oars; the pilot's boy,
Who now doth crazy go,
Laughed loud and long; and all the while
His eyes went to and fro:
'Ha! ha!' quoth he, 'full plain I see,
The Devil knows how to row.'

And now, all in my own countree,
I stood on the firm land!
The hermit stepped forth from the boat,
And scarcely he could stand.

The ancient mariner earnestly entreateth the hermit to shrieve him; and the penance of life falls on him.

'O, shrieve me, shrieve me, holy man!' —
The hermit crossed his brow:
'Say quick,' quoth he, 'I bid thee say, —
What manner of man art thou?'

Forthwith this frame of mine was wrenched
With a woful agony,

Which forced me to begin my tale, —
And then it left me free.

Since then, at an uncertain hour,
That agony returns;
And till my ghastly tale is told,
This heart within me burns.

And ever and anon, throughout his future life, an agony constraineth him to travel from land to land.

I pass, like night, from land to land;
I have strange power of speech;
That moment that his face I see
I know the man that must hear me, —
To him my tale I teach.

What loud uproar bursts from that door!
The wedding-guests are there;
But in the garden bower the bride
And bridemaids singing are;
And hark the little vesper bell,
Which biddeth me to prayer!

O wedding-guest! this soul hath been
Alone on a wide, wide sea, —
So lonely 't was, that God himself
Scarce seemed there to be.

O, sweeter than the marriage-feast,
'T is sweeter far to me
To walk together to the kirk
With a goodly company! —

To walk together to the kirk,
And all together pray,
While each to his great Father bends, —
Old men, and babes, and loving friends,
And youths and maidens gay!

Farewell! farewell! but this I tell
To thee, thou wedding-guest!
He prayeth well who loveth well
Both man and bird and beast.

And to teach, by his own example love and reverence of all things that God made and loveth.

He prayeth best who loveth best
All things both great and small;
For the dear God who loveth us,
He made and loveth all."

The mariner, whose eye is bright,
Whose beard with age is hoar,
Is gone. And now the wedding-guest
Turned from the bridegroom's door.

He went like one that hath been stunned,
And is of sense forlorn;
A sadder and a wiser man
He rose the morrow morn.

SAMUEL TAYLOR COLERIDGE.

THE RAVEN.

ONCE upon a midnight dreary, while I pondered,
	weak and weary,
Over many a quaint and curious volume of for-
	gotten lore, —
While I nodded, nearly napping, suddenly there
	came a tapping,
As of some one gently rapping, rapping at my
	chamber door.
"'T is some visitor," I muttered, "tapping at
	my chamber door ;
	Only this, and nothing more.'

Ah, distinctly I remember, it was in the bleak
	December,
And each separate dying ember wrought its ghost
	upon the floor.
Eagerly I wished the morrow ; vainly I had
	sought to borrow
From my books surcease of sorrow, — sorrow for
	the lost Lenore, —
For the rare and radiant maiden whom the angels
	named Lenore, —
	Nameless here forevermore.

And the silken, sad, uncertain rustling of each
	purple curtain
Thrilled me, — filled me with fantastic terrors
	never felt before ;
So that now, to still the beating of my heart, I
	stood repeating,
"'T is some visitor entreating entrance at my
	chamber door, —
Some late visitor entreating entrance at my
	chamber door ;
	That it is, and nothing more."

Presently my soul grew stronger ; hesitating then
	no longer,
"Sir," said I, "or madam, truly your forgive-
	ness I implore ;
But the fact is, I was napping, and so gently you
	came rapping,
And so faintly you came tapping, tapping at my
	chamber door,
That I scarce was sure I heard you" — Here I
	opened wide the door ;
	Darkness there, and nothing more.

Deep into that darkness peering, long I stood
	there, wondering, fearing,
Doubting, dreaming dreams no mortal ever dared
	to dream before ;
But the silence was unbroken, and the darkness
	gave no token,
And the only word there spoken was the whis-
	pered word "Lenore !"

This I whispered, and an echo murmured back
	the word "Lenore !"
	Merely this, and nothing more.

Back into the chamber turning, all my soul within
	me burning,
Soon again I heard a tapping, something louder
	than before.
"Surely," said I, "surely that is something at
	my window-lattice ;
Let me see then what there at is, and this
	mystery explore, —
Let my heart be still a moment, and this mystery
	explore ; —
	'T is the wind, and nothing more."

Open then I flung the shutter, when, with many
	a flirt and flutter,
In there stepped a stately raven of the saintly
	days of yore.
Not the least obeisance made he ; not an instant
	stopped or stayed he ;
But, with mien of lord or lady, perched above
	my chamber door, —
Perched upon a bust of Pallas, just above my
	chamber door, —
	Perched, and sat, and nothing more.

Then this ebony bird beguiling my sad fancy into
	smiling,
By the grave and stern decorum of the counte-
	nance it wore,
"Though thy crest be shorn and shaven, thou,"
	I said, "art sure no craven ;
Ghastly, grim, and ancient raven, wandering
	from the nightly shore,
Tell me what thy lordly name is on the night's
	Plutonian shore ?"
	Quoth the raven, "Nevermore !"

Much I marvelled this ungainly fowl to here
	discourse so plainly,
Though its answer little meaning, little rele-
	vancy bore ;
For we cannot help agreeing that no living human
	being
Ever yet was blessed with seeing bird above his
	chamber door,
Bird or beast upon the sculptured bust above his
	chamber door,
	With such name as "Nevermore !"

But the raven, sitting lonely on the placid bust,
	spoke only
That one word, as if his soul in that one word
	he did outpour.
Nothing further then he uttered, — not a feather
	then he fluttered, —

Eng. by H.B.Hall & Sons 11 Barclay S.N.Y.

Edgar A. Poe.

FORDS, HOWARD & HULBERT, N.Y.

Till I scarcely more than muttered, "Other
    friends have flown before, —
On the morrow he will leave me, as my hopes
    have flown before."
    Then the bird said, "Nevermore!"

Startled at the stillness, broken by reply so aptly
    spoken,
"Doubtless," said I, "what it utters is its only
    stock and store,
Caught from some unhappy master, whom un-
    merciful disaster
Followed fast and followed faster, till his song
    one burden bore,
Till the dirges of his hope that melancholy bur-
    den bore, —
    Of 'Nevermore, — nevermore!'"

But the raven still beguiling all my sad soul into
    smiling,
Straight I wheeled a cushioned seat in front of
    bird and bust and door,
Then, upon the velvet sinking, I betook myself
    to linking
Fancy unto fancy, thinking what this ominous
    bird of yore —
What this grim, ungainly, ghastly, gaunt, and
    ominous bird of yore —
    Meant in croaking "Nevermore!"

This I sat engaged in guessing, but no syllable
    expressing
To the fowl whose fiery eyes now burned into
    my bosom's core;
This and more I sat divining, with my head at
    ease reclining
On the cushion's velvet lining that the lamp-
    light gloated o'er,
But whose velvet violet lining, with the lamp-
    light gloating o'er,
    She shall press — ah! nevermore!

Then methought the air grew denser, perfumed
    from an unseen censer,
Swung by seraphim, whose footfalls tinkled on
    the tufted floor.
"Wretch," I cried, "thy God hath lent thee, —
    by these angels he hath sent thee
Respite, — respite and nepenthe from the mem-
    ories of Lenore!
Quaff, O, quaff this kind nepenthe, and forget
    this lost Lenore!"
    Quoth the raven, "Nevermore!"

"Prophet!" said I, "thing of evil! — prophet
    still, if bird or devil!
Whether tempter sent, or whether tempest
    tossed thee here ashore,
Desolate yet all undaunted, on this desert land
    enchanted, —

On this home by horror haunted, — tell me truly,
    I implore, —
Is there — is there balm in Gilead? — tell me,
    — tell me, I implore!"
    Quoth the raven, "Nevermore!"

"Prophet!" said I, "thing of evil! — prophet
    still, if bird or devil!
By that heaven that bends above us, — by that
    God we both adore,
Tell this soul with sorrow laden, if, within the
    distant Aidenn,
It shall clasp a sainted maiden, whom the an-
    gels name Lenore, —
Clasp a fair and radiant maiden, whom the an-
    gels name Lenore!"
    Quoth the raven, "Nevermore!"

"Be that word our sign of parting, bird or
    fiend!" I shrieked, upstarting, —
"Get thee back into the tempest and the night's
    Plutonian shore!
Leave no black plume as a token of that lie thy
    soul hath spoken!
Leave my loneliness unbroken! — quit the bust
    above my door!
Take thy beak from out my heart, and take thy
    form from off my door!"
    Quoth the raven, "Nevermore!"

And the raven, never flitting, still is sitting,
    still is sitting
On the pallid bust of Pallas, just above my
    chamber door;
And his eyes have all the seeming of a demon
    that is dreaming,
And the lamplight o'er him streaming throws
    his shadow on the floor;
And my soul from out that shadow that lies
    floating on the floor
    Shall be lifted — *nevermore!*
               EDGAR ALLAN POE.

SONG OF THE SEA BY THE ROYAL GARDEN AT NAPLES.

I HAVE swung for ages to and fro;
    I have striven in vain to reach thy feet,
O Garden of joy! whose walls are low,
    And odors are so sweet.

I palpitate with fitful love;
    I sigh and sing with changing breath;
I raise my hands to heaven above,
    I smite my shores beneath!

In vain, in vain! while far and fine,
    To curb the madness of my sweep,

Runs the white limit of a line
    I may not overleap.

Once thou wert sleeping on my breast,
    Till fiery Titans lifted thee
From the fair silence of thy rest,
    Out of the loving sea.

And I swing eternal to and fro ;
    I strive in vain to reach thy feet,
O Garden of joy ! whose walls are low,
    And odors are so sweet !
ROSSITER W. RAYMOND.

SONG OF THE LIGHTNING.

"PUCK. I 'll put a girdle round about the earth
In forty minutes."
MIDSUMMER NIGHT'S DREAM.

AWAY ! away ! through the sightless air
    Stretch forth your iron thread !
For I would not dim my sandals fair
    With the dust ye tamely tread !
Ay, rear it up on its million piers,
    Let it circle the world around,
And the journey ye make in a hundred years
    I 'll clear at a single bound !

Though I cannot toil, like the groaning slave
    Ye have fettered with iron skill
To ferry you over the boundless wave,
    Or grind in the noisy mill,
Let him sing his giant strength and speed !
    Why, a single shaft of mine
Would give that monster a flight indeed, —
    To the depths of the ocean's brine !

No ! no ! I 'm the spirit of light and love !
    To my unseen hand 't is given
To pencil the ambient clouds above
    And polish the stars of heaven !
I scatter the golden rays of fire
    On the horizon far below,
And deck the sky where storms expire
    With my red and dazzling glow.

With a glance I cleave the sky in twain ;
    I light it with a glare,
When fall the boding drops of rain
    Through the darkly curtained air !
The rock-built towers, the turrets gray,
    The piles of a thousand years,
Have not the strength of potter's clay
    Beneath my glittering spears.

From the Alps' or the Andes' highest crag,
    From the peaks of eternal snow,
The blazing folds of my fiery flag
    Illume the world below.

The earthquake heralds my coming power,
    The avalanche bounds away,
And howling storms at midnight's hour
    Proclaim my kingly sway.

Ye tremble when my legions come, —
    When my quivering sword leaps out
O'er the hills that echo my thunder drum,
    And rend with my joyous shout.
Ye quail on the land, or upon the seas
    Ye stand in your fear aghast,
To see me burn the stalworth trees,
    Or shiver the stately mast.

The hieroglyphs on the Persian wall, —
    The letters of high command, —
Where the prophet read the tyrant's fall,
    Were traced by my burning hand.
And oft in fire have I wrote since then
    What angry Heaven decreed ;
But the sealéd eyes of sinful men
    Were all too blind to read.

At length the hour of light is here,
    And kings no more shall bind,
Nor bigots crush with craven fear,
    The forward march of mind.
The words of Truth and Freedom's rays
    Are from my pinions hurled ;
And soon the light of better days
    Shall rise upon the world.
GEORGE W. CUTTER.

ORIGIN OF THE OPAL.

A DEW-DROP came, with a spark of flame
    He had caught from the sun's last ray,
To a violet's breast, where he lay at rest
    Till the hours brought back the day.

The rose looked down, with a blush and frown ;
    But she smiled all at once, to view
Her own bright form, with its coloring warm,
    Reflected back by the dew.

Then the stranger took a stolen look
    At the sky, so soft and blue ;
And a leaflet green, with its silver sheen,
    Was seen by the idler too.

A cold north-wind, as he thus reclined,
    Of a sudden raged around ;
And a maiden fair, who was walking there,
    Next morning, an *opal* found.
ANONYMOUS.

THE ORIGIN OF GOLD.

THE Fallen looked on the world and sneered.
" I can guess," he muttered, " why God is feared,

For the eyes of mortal are fain to shun
The midnight heaven that hath no sun.
I will stand on the height of the hills and wait
Where the day goes out at the western gate,
And, reaching up to its crown, will tear
From its plumes of glory the brightest there :
With the stolen ray I will light the sod,
And turn the eyes of the world from God."

He stood on the height when the sun went down,
He tore one plume from the day's bright crown,
The proud beam stooped till he touched its brow,
And the print of his fingers are on it now ;
And the blush of its anger forevermore
Burns red when it passes the western door.
The broken feather above him whirled,
In flames of torture around him curled,
And he dashed it down on the snowy height,
In broken flashes of quivering light.
Ah, more than terrible was the shock
Where the burning splinters struck wave and rock !
The green earth shuddered, and shrank and paled,
The wave sprang up, and the mountain quailed ;
Look on the hills, let the scars they bear
Measure the pain of that hour's despair.

The Fallen watched while the whirlwind fanned
The pulsing splinters that ploughed the sand ;
Sullen he watched while the hissing waves
Bore them away to the ocean caves ;
Sullen he watched while the shining rills
Throbbed through the hearts of the rocky hills ;
Loudly he laughed, " Is the world not mine ?
Proudly the links of its chain shall shine ;
Lighted with gems shall its dungeon be,
But the pride of its beauty shall kneel to me."
That splintered light in the earth grew cold,
And the diction of mortals hath called it gold.
SARAH E. CARMICHAEL, of Utah.

FAIRIES' SONG.

WE the fairies blithe and antic,
Of dimensions not gigantic,
Though the moonshine mostly keep us,
Oft in orchards frisk and peep us.

Stolen sweets are always sweeter ;
Stolen kisses much completer ;
Stolen looks are nice in chapels ;
Stolen, stolen be your apples.

When to bed the world are bobbing,
Then 's the time for orchard-robbing ;
Yet the fruit were scarce worth peeling
Were it not for stealing, stealing.
THOMAS RANDOLPH (Latin). Trans-
lation of LEIGH HUNT.

FAIRY LORE FROM SHAKESPEARE.

THE FAIRIES' LULLABY.

FROM "MIDSUMMER NIGHT'S DREAM."

Enter TITANIA, *with her train.*

TITANIA. Come, now a roundel, and a fairy song;
Then, for the third part of a minute, hence ; —
Some to kill cankers in the musk-rose buds ;
Some, war with rear-mice for their leathern wings,
To make my small elves coats ; and some, keep
    back
The clamorous owl, that nightly hoots, and
    wonders
At our quaint spirits. Sing me now asleep ;
Then to your offices, and let me rest.

SONG.

1 FAIRY. *You spotted snakes, with double tongue,*
    Thorny hedge-hogs, be not seen ;
    Newts, and blind-worms, do no wrong ;
    Come not near our fairy queen.

CHORUS. *Philomel, with melody,*
    Sing in our sweet lullaby ;
Lulla, lulla, lullaby ; lulla, lulla, lullaby :
    Never harm,
    Nor spell nor charm,
    Come our lovely lady nigh ;
    So, good night, with lullaby.

2 FAIRY. *Weaving spiders, come not here ;*
    Hence, you long-legged spinners,
        hence !
    Beetles black, approach not near ;
    Worm, nor snail, do no offence.

CHORUS. *Philomel, with melody,* etc.

MAIDEN MEDITATION, FANCY FREE

FROM "MIDSUMMER NIGHT'S DREAM."

OBERON. My gentle Puck, come hither. Thou
    remember'st
Since once I sat upon a promontory,
And heard a mermaid, on a dolphin's back,
Uttering such a dulcet and harmonious breath,
That the rude sea grew civil at her song,
And certain stars shot madly from their spheres,
To hear the sea-maid's music.
PUCK.   I remember.
OBE. That very time I saw (but thou couldst
    not),
Flying between the cold moon and the earth,
Cupid all armed : a certain aim he took
At a fair vestal throned by the west,

And loosed his love-shaft smartly from his bow,
As it should pierce a hundred thousand hearts :
But I might see young Cupid's fiery shaft
Quenched in the chaste beams of the watery moon,
And the imperial vot'ress passed on,
In maiden meditation, fancy free.
Yet marked I where the bolt of Cupid fell :
It fell upon a little western flower
Before milk-white, now purple with love's
    wound,
And maidens call it, love-in-idleness.

QUEEN MAB.

FROM "ROMEO AND JULIET."

O THEN I see, Queen Mab hath been with you.
She is the fairies' midwife ; and she comes
In shape no bigger than an agate-stone
On the fore-finger of an alderman,
Drawn with a team of little atomies
Athwart men's noses as they lie asleep :
Her wagon-spokes made of long spinners' legs ;
The cover, of the wings of grasshoppers ;
The traces, of the smallest spider's web ;
The collars, of the moonshine's watery beams ;
Her whip, of cricket's bone ; the lash, of film ;
Her wagoner, a small gray-coated gnat,
Not half so big as a round little worm
Pricked from the lazy finger of a maid :
Her chariot is an empty hazel-nut,
Made by the joiner squirrel, or old grub,
Time out of mind the fairies' coach-makers.
And in this state she gallops night by night
Through lovers' brains, and then they dream of
    love ;
On courtiers' knees, that dream on court'sies
    straight ;
O'er lawyers' fingers, who straight dream on fees ;
O'er ladies' lips, who straight on kisses dream, —
Which oft the angry Mab with blisters plagues,
Because their breaths with sweetmeats tainted
    are :
Sometimes she gallops o'er a courtier's nose,
And then dreams he of smelling out a suit ;
And sometimes comes she with a tithe-pig's tail,
Tickling a parson's nose as 'a lies asleep,
Then dreams he of another benefice :
Sometime she driveth o'er a soldier's neck,
And then dreams he of cutting foreign throats,
Of breaches, ambuscades, Spanish blades,
Of healths five fathom deep ; and then anon
Drums in his ear, at which he starts, and wakes ;
And, being thus frighted, swears a prayer or two,
And sleeps again.   This is that very Mab,
That plats the manes of horses in the night ;
And bakes the elf-locks in foul sluttish hairs,
Which, once untangled, much misfortune bodes :

This is the hag, when maids lie on their backs,
That presses them, and learns them first to bear,
Making them women of good carriage.

WHERE THE BEE SUCKS.

FROM "THE TEMPEST."

WHERE the bee sucks, there suck I :
In a cowslip's bell I lie ;
There I couch when owls do cry.
On the bat's back I do fly
After summer, merrily.
Merrily, merrily shall I live now,
Under the blossom that hangs on the bough.

COME UNTO THESE YELLOW SANDS.

FROM "THE TEMPEST."

COME unto these yellow sands,
    And then take hands ;
Court'sied when you have, and kissed
    The wild waves whist,
Foot it featly here and there ;
And, sweet sprites, the burden bear.
    Hark, hark !
        Bowgh, wowgh.
    The watch-dogs bark :
        Bowgh, wowgh.
Hark, hark ! I hear
The strain of strutting chanticleer
Cry, Cock-a-doodle-doo.

OVER HILL, OVER DALE.

FROM "MIDSUMMER NIGHT'S DREAM."

OVER hill, over dale,
    Thorough bush, thorough brier,
Over park, over pale,
    Thorough flood, thorough fire,
I do wander everywhere,
Swifter than the moon's sphere ;
And I serve the fairy queen,
To dew her orbs upon the green :
The cowslips tall her pensioners b.
In their gold coats spots you see ;
Those be rubies, fairy favors,
In those freckles live their savors :
I must go seek some dew-drops here,
And hang a pearl in every cowslip's ear.

FULL FATHOM FIVE.

FROM "THE TEMPEST."

FULL fathom five thy father lies ;
Of his bones are coral made ;

Those are pearls that were his eyes :
   Nothing of him that doth fade,
But doth suffer a sea-change
Into something rich and strange.
Sea-nymphs hourly ring his knell :
Hark ! now I hear them, — ding-dong, bell.

FAIRY SONG.

SHED no tear ! O, shed no tear !
The flower will bloom another year.
Weep no more ! O, weep no more !
Young buds sleep in the root's white core.
Dry your eyes ! O, dry your eyes !
For I was taught in Paradise
To ease my breast of melodies, —
        Shed no tear.

Overhead ! look overhead !
'Mong the blossoms white and red, —
Look up, look up ! I flutter now
On this fresh pomegranate bough.
See me ! 't is this silvery bill
Ever cures the good man's ill,
Shed no tear ! O, shed no tear !
The flower will bloom another year.
Adieu, adieu — I fly — adieu !
I vanish in the heaven's blue, —
      Adieu, adieu !
         JOHN KEATS.

THE SPICE-TREE.

THE spice-tree lives in the garden green ;
  Beside it the fountain flows ;
And a fair bird sits the boughs between,
  And sings his melodious woes.

No greener garden e'er was known
  Within the bounds of an earthly king ;
No lovelier skies have ever shone
  Than those that illumine its constant spring.

That coil-bound stem has branches three ;
  On each a thousand blossoms grow ;
And, old as aught of time can be,
  The root stands fast in the rocks below.

In the spicy shade ne'er seems to tire
  The fount that builds a silvery dome ;
And flakes of purple and ruby fire
  Gush out, and sparkle amid the foam.

The fair white bird of flaming crest,
  And azure wings bedropt with gold,
Ne'er has he known a pause of rest,
  But sings the lament that he framed of old :

"O princess bright ! how long the night
  Since thou art sunk in the waters clear !
How sadly they flow from the depth below, —
  How long must I sing and thou wilt not hear ?

"The waters play, and the flowers are gay,
  And the skies are sunny above ;
I would that all could fade and fall,
  And I, too, cease to mourn my love.

"O, many a year, so wakeful and drear,
  I have sorrowed and watched, beloved, for thee !
But there comes no breath from the chambers of
    death,
  While the lifeless fount gushes under the tree."

The skies grow dark, and they glare with red ;
  The tree shakes off its spicy bloom ;
The waves of the fount in a black pool spread ;
  And in thunder sounds the garden's doom.

Down springs the bird with a long shrill cry,
  Into the sable and angry flood ;
And the face of the pool, as he falls from high,
  Curdles in circling stains of blood.

But sudden again upswells the fount ;
  Higher and higher the waters flow, —
In a glittering diamond arch they mount,
  And round it the colors of morning glow.

Finer and finer the watery mound
  Softens and melts to a thin-spun veil,
And tones of music circle around,
  And bear to the stars the fountain's tale.

And swift the eddying rainbow screen
  Falls in dew on the grassy floor ;
Under the spice-tree the garden's queen
  Sits by her lover, who wails no more.
         JOHN STERLING.

THE VALLEY BROOK.

FRESH from the fountains of the wood
  A rivulet of the valley came,
And glided on for many a rood,
  Flushed with the morning's ruddy flame.

The air was fresh and soft and sweet ;
  The slopes in spring's new verdure lay,
And wet with dew-drops at my feet
  Bloomed the young violets of May.

No sound of busy life was heard
  Amid those pastures lone and still,

Save the faint chip of early bird,
  Or bleat of flocks along the hill.

I traced that rivulet's winding way ;
  New scenes of beauty opened round,
Where meads of brighter verdure lay,
  And lovelier blossoms tinged the ground.

" Ah, happy valley stream ! " I said,
  " Calm glides thy wave amid the flowers,
Whose fragrance round thy path is shed
  Through all the joyous summer hours.

O, could my years, like thine, be passed
  In some remote and silent glen,
Where I could dwell and sleep at last,
  Far from the bustling haunts of men ! "

But what new echoes greet my ear ?
  The village school-boy's merry call ;
And mid the village hum I hear
  The murmur of the waterfall.

I looked ; the widening vale betrayed
  A pool that shone like burnished steel,
Where that bright valley stream was stayed
  To turn the miller's ponderous wheel.

Ah ! why should I, I thought with shame,
  Sigh for a life of solitude,
When even this stream without a name
  Is laboring for the common good.

No longer let me shun my part
  Amid the busy scenes of life,
But with a warm and generous heart
  Press onward in the glorious strife.
          JOHN HOWARD BRYANT.

THE CULPRIT FAY.

'T IS the middle watch of a summer's night, —
The earth is dark, but the heavens are bright ;
Naught is seen in the vault on high
But the moon, and the stars, and the cloudless
    sky,
And the flood which rolls its milky hue,
A river of light on the welkin blue.
The moon looks down on old Cronest ;
She mellows the shades on his shaggy breast,
And seems his huge gray form to throw
In a silver cone on the wave below.
His sides are broken by spots of shade,
By the walnut bough and the cedar made ;
And through their clustering branches dark
Glimmers and dies the firefly's spark, —
Like starry twinkles that momently break
Through the rifts of the gathering tempest's rack.

The stars are on the moving stream,
  And fling, as its ripples gently flow,
A burnished length of wavy beam
  In an eel-like, spiral line below ;
The winds are whist, and the owl is still ;
  The bat in the shelvy rock is hid ;
And naught is heard on the lonely hill
But the cricket's chirp, and the answer shrill
  Of the gauze-winged katydid ;
And the plaint of the wailing whippoorwill,
  Who moans unseen, and ceaseless sings
Ever a note of wail and woe,
  Till morning spreads her rosy wings,
And earth and sky in her glances glow.

'T is the hour of fairy ban and spell :
The wood-tick has kept the minutes well ;
He has counted them all with click and stroke
Deep in the heart of the mountain-oak,
And he has awakened the sentry elve
Who sleeps with him in the haunted tree,
To bid him ring the hour of twelve,
  And call the fays to their revelry ;
Twelve small strokes on his tinkling bell
('T was made of the white snail's pearly shell) :
" Midnight comes, and all is well !
Hither, hither wing your way !
'T is the dawn of the fairy-day."

They come from beds of lichen green,
They creep from the mullein's velvet screen ;
  Some on the backs of beetles fly
From the silver tops of moon-touched trees,
  Where they swung in their cobweb hammocks
    high,
And rocked about in the evening breeze ;
  Some from the hum-bird's downy nest, —
They had driven him out by elfin power,
  And, pillowed on plumes of his rainbow breast,
Had slumbered there till the charméd hour ;
  Some had lain in the scoop of the rock,
With glittering ising-stars inlaid ;
  And some had opened the four-o'-clock,
And stole within its purple shade.
  And now they throng the moonlight glade,
Above, below, on every side,
  Their little minim forms arrayed
In the tricksy pomp of fairy pride !

They come not now to print the lea,
In freak and dance around the tree,
Or at the mushroom board to sup,
And drink the dew from the buttercup :
A scene of sorrow waits them now,
For an ouphe has broken his vestal vow ;
He has loved an earthly maid,
And left for her his woodland shade ;
He has lain upon her lip of dew,

And sunned him in her eye of blue,
Fanned her cheek with his wing of air,
Played in the ringlets of her hair,
And, nestling on her snowy breast,
Forgot the lily-king's behest.
For this the shadowy tribes of air
  To the elfin court must haste away :
And now they stand expectant there,
  To hear the doom of the culprit fay.

The throne was reared upon the grass,
Of spice-wood and of sassafras ;
On pillars of mottled tortoise-shell
  Hung the burnished canopy, —
And o'er it gorgeous curtains fell
  Of the tulip's crimson drapery.
The monarch sat on his judgment-seat,
  On his brow the crown imperial shone,
The prisoner fay was at his feet,
  And his peers were ranged around the throne.
He waved his sceptre in the air,
  He looked around and calmly spoke ;
His brow was grave and his eye severe,
  But his voice in a softened accent broke :

"Fairy ! fairy ! list and mark :
Thou hast broke thine elfin chain ;
Thy flame-wood lamp is quenched and dark,
  And thy wings are dyed with a deadly stain, —
Thou hast sullied thine elfin purity
  In the glance of a mortal maiden's eye ;
Thou hast scorned our dread decree,
  And thou shouldst pay the forfeit high.
But well I know her sinless mind
  Is pure as the angel forms above,
Gentle and meek, and chaste and kind,
  Such as a spirit well might love.
Fairy ! had she spot or taint,
  Bitter had been thy punishment :
Tied to the hornet's shardy wings ;
Tossed on the pricks of nettles' stings ;
Or seven long ages doomed to dwell
  With the lazy worm in the walnut-shell ;
Or every night to writhe and bleed
  Beneath the tread of the centipede ;
Or bound in a cobweb-dungeon dim,
  Your jailor a spider, huge and grim,
Amid the carrion bodies to lie.
Of the worm, and the bug, and the murdered fly :
These it had been your lot to bear,
Had a stain been found on the earthly fair.
Now list, and mark our mild decree, —
  Fairy, this your doom must be :

"Thou shalt seek the beach of sand
Where the water bounds the elfin land ;
Thou shalt watch the oozy brine
Till the sturgeon leaps in the bright moonshine,
Then dart the glistening arch below,

And catch a drop from his silver bow.
The water-sprites will wield their arms
  And dash around, with roar and rave,
And vain are the woodland spirits' charms ;
  They are the imps that rule the wave.
Yet trust thee in thy single might :
If thy heart be pure and thy spirit right,
Thou shalt win the warlock fight.

"If the spray-bead gem be won,
  The stain of thy wing is washed away ;
But another errand must be done
  Ere thy crime be lost for aye :
Thy flame-wood lamp is quenched and dark,
Thou must reillume its spark.
Mount thy steed, and spur him high
To the heaven's blue canopy ;
And when thou seest a shooting star,
Follow it fast, and follow it far, —
The last faint spark of its burning train
Shall light the elfin lamp again.
Thou hast heard our sentence, fay ;
Hence ! to the water-side, away !"

The goblin marked his monarch well ;
  He spake not, but he bowed him low,
Then plucked a crimson colen-bell,
  And turned him round in act to go.
The way is long, he cannot fly,
  His soiléd wing has lost its power,
And he winds adown the mountain high,
  For many a sore and weary hour.
Through dreary beds of tangled fern,
Through groves of nightshade dark and dern,
Over the grass and through the brake,
  Where toils the ant and sleeps the snake ;
Now o'er the violet's azure flush
  He skips along in lightsome mood ;
  And now he thrids the bramble-bush,
Till its points are dyed in fairy blood.
He has leaped the bog, he has pierced the brier,
He has swum the brook, and waded the mire,
Till his spirits sank, and his limbs grew weak,
And the red waxed fainter in his cheek.
He had fallen to the ground outright,
  For rugged and dim was his onward track,
But there came a spotted toad in sight,
  And he laughed as he jumped upon her back ;
He bridled her mouth with a silkweed twist,
  He lashed her sides with an osier thong ;
And now, through evening's dewy mist,
  With leap and spring they bound along,
Till the mountain's magic verge is past,
And the beach of sand is reached at last.

Soft and pale is the moony beam,
Moveless still the glassy stream ;
The wave is clear, the beach is bright

With snowy shells and sparkling stones ;
The shore-surge comes in ripples light,
In murmurings faint and distant moans ;
And ever afar in the silence deep
Is heard the splash of the sturgeon's leap,
And the bend of his graceful bow is seen, —
A glittering arch of silver sheen,
Spanning the wave of burnished blue,
And dripping with gems of the river-dew.

The elfin cast a glance around,
    As he lighted down from his courser toad,
Then round his breast his wings he wound,
    And close to the river's brink he strode ;
He sprang on a rock, he breathed a prayer,
    Above his head his arms he threw,
Then tossed a tiny curve in air,
    And headlong plunged in the waters blue.

Up sprung the spirits of the waves
From the sea-silk beds in their coral caves,
With snail-plate armor, snatched in haste,
They speed their way through the liquid waste ;
Some are rapidly borne along
On the mailed shrimp or the prickly prong ;
Some on the blood-red leeches glide,
Some on the stony star-fish ride,
Some on the back of the lancing squab,
Some on the sideling soldier-crab ;
And some on the jellied quarl, that flings
At once a thousand streamy stings ;
They cut the wave with the living oar,
And hurry on to the moonlight shore,
To guard their realms and chase away
The footsteps of the invading fay.

Fearlessly he skims along,
His hope is high, and his limbs are strong ;
He spreads his arms like the swallow's wing,
And throws his feet with a frog-like fling ;
His locks of gold on the waters shine,
    At his breast the tiny foam-bees rise,
His back gleams bright above the brine,
    And the wake-line foam behind him lies.
But the water-sprites are gathering near
    To check his course along the tide ;
Their warriors come in swift career
    And hem him round on every side ;
On his thigh the leech has fixed his hold,
The quarl's long arms are round him rolled,
The prickly prong has pierced his skin,
And the squab has thrown his javelin ;
The gritty star has rubbed him raw,
And the crab has struck with his giant claw ;
He howls with rage, and he shrieks with pain ;
He strikes around, but his blows are vain ;
Hopeless is the unequal fight,
Fairy ! naught is left but flight.

He turned him round, and fled amain,
With hurry and dash, to the beach again ;
He twisted over from side to side,
And laid his cheek to the cleaving tide ;
The strokes of his plunging arms are fleet,
And with all his might he flings his feet,
But the water-sprites are round him still,
To cross his path and work him ill.
They bade the wave before him rise ;
They flung the sea-fire in his eyes ;
And they stunned his ears with the scallop-stroke,
With the porpoise heave and the drum-fish croak.
O, but a weary wight was he
When he reached the foot of the dogwood-tree.
Gashed and wounded, and stiff and sore,
He laid him down on the sandy shore ;
He blessed the force of the charméd line,
    And he banned the water-goblins' spite,
For he saw around in the sweet moonshine
Their little wee faces above the brine,
    Giggling and laughing with all their might
    At the piteous hap of the fairy wight.

Soon he gathered the balsam dew
    From the sorrel-leaf and the henbane bud ;
Over each wound the balm he drew,
    And with cobweb lint he stanched the blood.
The mild west-wind was soft and low,
It cooled the heat of his burning brow ;
And he felt new life in his sinews shoot,
As he drank the juice of the calamus-root ;
And now he treads the fatal shore
As fresh and vigorous as before.

Wrapped in musing stands the sprite ;
'T is the middle wane of night ;
    His task is hard, his way is far,
But he must do his errand right
    Ere dawning mounts her beamy car,
And rolls her chariot wheels of light ;
And vain are the spells of fairy-land, —
He must work with a human hand.

He cast a saddened look around ;
    But he felt new joy his bosom swell,
When, glittering on the shadowed ground,
    He saw a purple muscle-shell ;
Thither he ran, and he bent him low,
He heaved at the stern and he heaved at the bow,
And he pushed her over the yielding sand
Till he came to the verge of the haunted land.
She was as lovely a pleasure-boat
    As ever fairy had paddled in,
For she glowed with purple paint without,
    And shone with silvery pearl within ;
A sculler's notch in the stern he made,
An oar he shaped of the bootle-blade ;
Then sprung to his seat with a lightsome leap,
And launched afar on the calm, blue deep.

The imps of the river yell and rave.
They had no power above the wave ;
But they heaved the billow before the prow,
  And they dashed the surge against her side,
And they struck her keel with jerk and blow,
  Till the gunwale bent to the rocking tide.
She whimpled about to the pale moonbeam,
Like a feather that floats on a wind-tossed stream ;
And momently athwart her track
The quarl upreared his island back,
And the fluttering scallop behind would float,
And patter the water about the boat ;
But he bailed her out with his colen-bell,
  And he kept her trimmed with a wary tread,
While on every side, like lightning, fell
  The heavy strokes of his bootle-blade.

Onward still he held his way,
Till he came where the column of moonshine lay,
And saw beneath the surface dim
The brown-backed sturgeon slowly swim ;
Around him were the goblin train, —
But he sculled with all his might and main,
And followed wherever the sturgeon led,
Till he saw him upward point his head ;
Then he dropped his paddle-blade,
And held his colen-goblet up
To catch the drop in its crimson cup.

With sweeping tail and quivering fin
  Through the wave the sturgeon flew,
And, like the heaven-shot javelin,
  He sprung above the waters blue.
Instant as the star-fall light
  He plunged him in the deep again,
But he left an arch of silver bright,
  The rainbow of the moony main.
It was a strange and lovely sight
  To see the puny goblin there ;
He seemed an angel form of light,
  With azure wing and sunny hair,
  Throned on a cloud of purple fair,
Circled with blue and edged with white,
And sitting, at the fall of even,
Beneath the bow of summer heaven.

A moment, and its lustre fell ;
  But ere it met the billow blue
He caught within his crimson bell
  A droplet of its sparkling dew, —
Joy to thee, fay ! thy task is done,
Thy wings are pure, for the gem is won, —
Cheerly ply thy dripping oar,
And haste away to the elfin shore.

He turns, and, lo ! on either side
The ripples on his path divide ;
And the track o'er which his boat must pass
Is smooth as a sheet of polished glass.

Around, their limbs the sea-nymphs lave,
  With snowy arms half swelling out,
While on the glossed and gleamy wave
  Their sea-green ringlets loosely float.
They swim around with smile and song ;
  They press the bark with pearly hand,
And gently urge her course along
  Toward the beach of speckled sand,
  And, as he lightly leaped to land,
They bade adieu with nod and bow ;
  Then gayly kissed each little hand,
And dropped in the crystal deep below.

A moment stayed the fairy there ;
He kissed the beach and breathed a prayer ;
Then spread his wings of gilded blue,
And on to the elfin court he flew.
As ever ye saw a bubble rise,
And shine with a thousand changing dyes,
Till, lessening far, through ether driven,
It mingles with the hues of heaven ;
As, at the glimpse of morning pale,
The lance-fly spreads his silken sail,
And gleams with blendings soft and bright
Till lost in the shades of fading night, —
So rose from earth the lovely fay ;
So vanished, far in heaven away !

. . . .

Up, fairy ! quit thy chickweed bower,
The cricket has called the second hour ;
Twice again, and the lark will rise
To kiss the streaking of the skies, —
Up ! thy charméd armor don,
Thou 'lt need it ere the night be gone.

He put his acorn helmet on ;
It was plumed of the silk of the thistle-down ;
The corselet plate that guarded his breast
Was once the wild bee's golden vest ;
His cloak, of a thousand mingled dyes,
Was formed of the wings of butterflies ;
His shield was the shell of a lady-bug queen,
Studs of gold on a ground of green ;
And the quivering lance which he brandished
      bright
Was the sting of a wasp he had slain in fight.
Swift he bestrode his firefly steed ;
  He bared his blade of the bent-grass blue ;
He drove his spurs of the cockle-seed,
  And away like a glance of thought he flew
To skim the heavens, and follow far
The fiery trail of the rocket-star.

The moth-fly, as he shot in air,
Crept under the leaf, and hid her there ;
The katydid forgot its lay,
The prowling gnat fled fast away,
The fell mosquito checked his drone
And folded his wings till the fay was gone,

And the wily beetle dropped his head,
And fell on the ground as if he were dead ;
They crouched them close in the darksome shade,
  They quaked all o'er with awe and fear,
For they had felt the blue-bent blade,
  And writhed at the prick of the elfin spear.
Many a time, on a summer's night,
When the sky was clear, and the moon was bright,
They had been roused from the haunted ground
By the yelp and bay of the fairy hound ;
  They had heard the tiny bugle-horn,
They had heard the twang of the maize-silk string,
When the vine-twig bows were tightly drawn,
  And the needle-shaft through air was borne,
Feathered with down of the hum-bird's wing.
And now they deemed the courier ouphe
Some hunter-sprite of the elfin ground,
And they watched till they saw him mount the roof
  That canopies the world around ;
Then glad they left their covert lair,
And freaked about in the midnight air.

Up to the vaulted firmament
His path the firefly courser bent,
And at every gallop on the wind
He flung a glittering spark behind ;
He flies like a feather in the blast
Till the first light cloud in heaven is past.
  But the shapes of air have begun their work,
And a drizzly mist is round him cast ;
  He cannot see through the mantle murk ;
He shivers with cold, but he urges fast ;
  Through storm and darkness, sleet and shade,
He lashes his steed, and spurs amain, —
For shadowy hands have twitched the rein,
  And flame-shot tongues around him played,
And near him many a fiendish eye
Glared with a fell malignity,
And yells of rage, and shrieks of fear,
Came screaming on his startled ear.

His wings are wet around his breast,
The plume hangs dripping from his crest,
His eyes are blurred with the lightning's glare,
And his ears are stunned with the thunder's blare.
But he gave a shout, and his blade he drew,
  He thrust before and he struck behind,
Till he pierced their cloudy bodies through,
  And gashed their shadowy limbs of wind :
Howling the misty spectres flew,
  They rend the air with frightful cries ;
For he has gained the welkin blue,
  And the land of clouds beneath him lies.

Up to the cope careering swift,
  In breathless motion fast,
Fleet as the swallow cuts the drift,
  Or the sea-roc rides the blast,

The sapphire sheet of eve is shot,
  The sphered moon is past,
The earth but seems a tiny blot
  On a sheet of azure cast.
O, it was sweet, in the clear moonlight,
  To tread the starry plain of even !
To meet the thousand eyes of night,
  And feel the cooling breath of heaven !
But the elfin made no stop or stay
Till he came to the bank of the Milky Way ;
  Then he checked his courser's foot,
And watched for the glimpse of the planet-shoot.

Sudden along the snowy tide
  That swelled to meet their footsteps' fall,
The sylphs of heaven were seen to glide,
  Attired in sunset's crimson pall ;
Around the fay they weave the dance,
  They skip before him on the plain,
And one has taken his wasp-sting lance,
  And one upholds his bridle-rein ;
With warblings wild they lead him on
  To where, through clouds of amber seen,
Studded with stars, resplendent shone
  The palace of the sylphid queen.
Its spiral columns, gleaming bright,
Were streamers of the northern light ;
Its curtain's light and lovely flush
Was of the morning's rosy blush ;
And the ceiling fair that rose aboon,
The white and feathery fleece of noon.

But, O, how fair the shape that lay
  Beneath a rainbow bending bright !
She seemed to the entrancéd fay
  The loveliest of the forms of light ;
Her mantle was the purple rolled
  At twilight in the west afar ;
'T was tied with threads of dawning gold,
  And buttoned with a sparkling star.
Her face was like the lily roon
  That veils the vestal planet's hue ;
Her eyes, two beamlets from the moon,
  Set floating in the welkin blue.
Her hair is like the sunny beam,
And the diamond gems which round it gleam
Are the pure drops of dewy even
That ne'er have left their native heaven.

  .   .   .

She was lovely and fair to see,
And the elfin's heart beat fitfully ;
But lovelier far, and still more fair,
The earthly form imprinted there ;
Naught he saw in the heavens above
Was half so dear as his mortal love,
For he thought upon her looks so meek,
And he thought of the light flush on her cheek.
Never again might he bask and lie

On that sweet cheek and moonlight eye ;
But in his dreams her form to see,
To clasp her in his revery,
To think upon his virgin bride,
Was worth all heaven, and earth beside.

"Lady," he cried, "I have sworn to-night,
On the word of a fairy knight,
To do my sentence, task aright ;
My honor scarce is free from stain, —
I may not soil its snows again ;
Betide me weal, betide me woe,
Its mandate must be answered now."
Her bosom heaved with many a sigh,
The tear was in her drooping eye ;
But she led him to the palace gate,
    And called the sylphs who hovered there,
And bade them fly and bring him straight,
    Of clouds condensed, a sable car.
With charm and spell she blessed it there,
From all the fiends of upper air ;
Then round him cast the shadowy shroud,
And tied his steed behind the cloud ;
And pressed his hand as she bade him fly
Far to the verge of the northern sky,
For by its wane and wavering light
There was a star would fall to-night.

Borne afar on the wings of the blast,
Northward away, he speeds him fast,
And his courser follows the cloudy wain
Till the hoof-strokes fall like pattering rain.
The clouds roll backward as he flies,
Each flickering star behind him lies,
And he has reached the northern plain,
And backed his firefly steed again,
Ready to follow in its flight
The streaming of the rocket-light.

The star is yet in the vault of heaven,
    But it rocks in the summer gale ;
And now 't is fitful and uneven,
    And now 't is deadly pale ;
And now 't is wrapped in sulphur-smoke,
    And quenched is its rayless beam ;
And now with a rattling thunder-stroke
    It bursts in flash and flame.
As swift as the glance of the arrowy lance
    That the storm-spirit flings from high,
The star-shot flew o'er the welkin blue,
    As it fell from the sheeted sky.
As swift as the wind in its train behind
    The elfin gallops along :
The fiends of the clouds are bellowing loud,
    But the sylphid charm is strong ;
He gallops unhurt in the shower of fire,
    While the cloud-fiends fly from the blaze ;
He watches each flake till its sparks expire,

And rides in the light of its rays.
But he drove his steed to the lightning's speed,
    And caught a glimmering spark ;
Then wheeled around to the fairy ground,
    And sped through the midnight dark.
.   .   .   .   .   .
Ouphe and goblin ! imp and sprite !
    Elf of eve ! and starry fay !
Ye that love the moon's soft light,
    Hither, — hither wend your way ;
Twine ye in a jocund ring,
    Sing and trip it merrily,
Hand to hand, and wing to wing,
    Round the wild witch-hazel tree.

Hail the wanderer again
    With dance and song, and lute and lyre ;
Pure his wing and strong his chain,
    And doubly bright his fairy fire.
Twine ye in an airy round,
    Brush the dew and print the lea ;
Skip and gambol, hop and bound,
    Round the wild witch-hazel tree.

The beetle guards our holy ground,
    He flies about the haunted place,
And if mortal there be found,
    He hums in his ears and flaps his face ;
The leaf-harp sounds our roundelay,
    The owlet's eyes our lanterns be ;
Thus we sing and dance and play
    Round the wild witch-hazel tree.

But hark ! from tower to tree-top high,
    The sentry-elf his call has made ;
A streak is in the eastern sky,
    Shapes of moonlight ! flit and fade !
The hill-tops gleam in morning's spring,
The skylark shakes his dappled wing,
The day-glimpse glimmers on the lawn,
The cock has crowed, and the fays are gone.
                    JOSEPH RODMAN DRAKE.

———◆———

SELLA'S FAIRY SLIPPERS.

"SEE, mother dear," she said, "what I have
        found
Upon our rivulet's bank ; two slippers, white
As the midwinter snow, and spangled o'er
With twinkling points, like stars, and on the edge
My name is wrought in silver ; read, I pray,
Sella, the name thy mother, now in heaven,
Gave at my birth ; and, sure, they fit my feet !"
"A dainty pair," the prudent matron said,
"But thine they are not. We must lay them by
For those whose careless hands have left them
        here ;

Or haply they were placed beside the brook
To be a snare.   I cannot see thy name
Upon the border, — only characters
Of mystic look and dim are there, like signs
Of some strange art ; nay, daughter, wear them
        not."
    Then Sella hung the slippers in the porch
Of that broad rustic lodge, and all who passed
Admired their fair contexture, but none knew
Who left them by the brook.   And now, at length,
May, with her flowers and singing birds, had gone,
And on bright streams and into deep wells shone
The high midsummer sun.   One day, at noon,
Sella was missed from the accustomed meal.
They sought her in her favorite haunts, they looked
By the great rock, and far along the stream,
And shouted in the sounding woods her name.
Night came, and forth the sorrowing household
        went
With torches over the wide pasture-grounds
To pool and thicket, marsh and briery dell,
And solitary valley far away.
The morning came, and Sella was not found.
The sun climbed high, they sought her still ;
        the noon,
The hot and silent noon, heard Sella's name
Uttered with a despairing cry to wastes
O'er which the eagle hovered.   As the sun
Stooped toward the amber west to bring the close
Of that sad second day, and, with red eyes,
The mother sat within her home alone,
Sella was at her side.   A shriek of joy
Broke the sad silence ; glad, warm tears were shed,
And words of gladness uttered.   "O, forgive,"
The maiden said, "that I could e'er forget
Thy wishes for a moment.   I just tried
The slippers on, amazed to see them shaped
So fairly to my feet, when, all at once,
I felt my steps upborne and hurried on
Almost as if with wings.   A strange delight,
Blent with a thrill of fear, o'ermastered me,
And, ere I knew, my plashing steps were set
Within the rivulet's pebbly bed, and I
Was rushing down the current.   By my side
Tripped one as beautiful as ever looked
From white clouds in a dream ; and, as we ran,
She talked with musical voice and sweetly laughed.
Gayly we leaped the crag and swam the pool,
And swept with dimpling eddies round the rock,
And glided between shady meadow-banks.
The streamlet, broadening as we went, became
A swelling river, and we shot along
By stately towns, and under leaning masts
Of gallant barks, nor lingered by the shore
Of blooming gardens ; onward, onward still,
The same strong impulse bore me till, at last,
We entered the great deep, and passed below
His billows, into boundless spaces, lit

With a green sunshine.   Here were mighty groves
Far down the ocean-valleys, and between
Lay what might seem fair meadows, softly tinged
With orange and with crimson.   Here arose
Tall stems, that, rooted in the depths below,
Swung idly with the motions of the sea ;
And here were shrubberies in whose mazy screen
The creatures of the deep made haunt.   My friend
Named the strange growths, the pretty coralline,
The dulse with crimson leaves, and, streaming far,
Sea-thong and sea-lace.   Here the tangle spread
Its broad thick fronds, with pleasant bowers be-
        neath ;
And oft we trod a waste of pearly sands,
Spotted with rosy shells, and thence looked in
At caverns of the sea whose rock-roofed halls
Lay in blue twilight.   As we moved along,
The dwellers of the deep, in mighty herds,
Passed by us, reverently they passed us by,
Long trains of dolphins rolling through the brine,
Huge whales, that drew the waters after them,
A torrent-stream, and hideous hammer-sharks,
Chasing their prey ; I shuddered as they came ;
Gently they turned aside and gave us room."
    Hereat broke in the mother, "'Sella, dear,'
This is a dream, — the idlest, vainest dream."
    "Nay, mother, nay ; behold this sea-green scarf,
Woven of such threads as never human hand
Twined from the distaff.   She who led my way
Through the great waters bade me wear it home,
A token that my tale is true.   'And keep,'
She said, 'the slippers thou hast found, for thou,
When shod with them, shalt be like one of us,
With power to walk at will the ocean-floor,
Among its monstrous creatures, unafraid,
And feel no longing for the air of heaven
To fill thy lungs, and send the warm, red blood
Along thy veins.   But thou shalt pass the hours
In dances with the sea-nymphs, or go forth,
To look into the mysteries of the abyss
Where never plummet reached.   And thou shalt
        sleep
Thy weariness away on downy banks
Of sea-moss, where the pulses of the tide
Shall gently lift thy hair, or thou shalt float
On the soft currents that go forth and wind
From isle to isle, and wander through the sea.'
    "So spake my fellow-voyager, her words
Sounding like wavelets on a summer shore,
And then we stopped beside a hanging rock
With a smooth beach of white sands at its foot,
Where three fair creatures like herself were set
At their sea-banquet, crisp and juicy stalks,
Culled from the ocean's meadows, and the sweet
Midrib of pleasant leaves, and golden fruits
Dropped from the trees that edge the southern isles,
And gathered on the waves.   Kindly they prayed
That I would share their meal, and I partook

With eager appetite, for long had been
My journey, and I left the spot refreshed.
   "And then we wandered off amid the groves
Of coral loftier than the growths of earth ;
The mightiest cedar lifts no trunk like theirs,
So huge, so high, toward heaven, nor overhangs
Alleys and bowers so dim.   We moved between
Pinnacles of black rock, which, from beneath,
Molten by inner fires, so said my guide,
Gushed long ago into the hissing brine,
That quenched and hardened them, and now they
         stand
Motionless in the currents of the sea
That part and flow around them.   As we went,
We looked into the hollows of the abyss,
To which the never-resting waters sweep
The skeletons of sharks, the long white spines
Of narwhal and of dolphin, bones of men
Shipwrecked, and mighty ribs of foundered barks ;
Down the blue pits we looked, and hastened on.
   "But beautiful the fountains of the sea
Sprang upward from its bed ; the silvery jets
Shot branching far into the azure brine,
And where they mingled with it, the great deep
Quivered and shook, as shakes the glimmering air
Above a furnace.   So we wandered through
The mighty world of waters, till at length
I wearied of its wonders, and my heart
Began to yearn for my dear mountain-home.
I prayed my gentle guide to lead me back
To the upper air.   'A glorious realm,' I said,
' Is this thou openest to me, but I stray
Bewildered in its vastness, these strange sights
And this strange light oppress me.   I must see
The faces that I love, or I shall die.'
   "She took my hand, and, darting through the
         waves,
Brought me to where the stream, by which we came,
Rushed into the main ocean.   Then began
A slower journey upward.   Wearily
We breasted the strong current, climbing through
The rapids tossing high their foam.   The night
Came down, and, in the clear depth of a pool,
Edged with o'erhanging rock, we took our rest
Till morning ; and I slept, and dreamed of home
And thee. A pleasant sight the morning showed ;
The green fields of this upper world, the herds
That grazed the bank, the light on the red clouds,
The trees, with all their host of trembling leaves,
Lifting and lowering to the restless wind
Their branches.   As I woke I saw them all
From the clear stream ; yet strangely was my heart
Parted between the watery world and this,
And as we journeyed upward, oft I thought
Of marvels I had seen, and stopped and turned,
And lingered, till I thought of thee again ;
And then again I turned and clambered up
The rivulet's murmuring path, until we came

Beside this cottage door.   There tenderly
My fair conductor kissed me, and I saw
Her face no more.   I took the slippers off.
O, with what deep delight my lungs drew in
The air of heaven again, and with what joy
I felt my blood bound with its former glow !
And now I never leave thy side again !"
   So spoke the maiden Sella, with large tears
Standing in her mild eyes, and in the porch
Replaced the slippers.

WILLIAM CULLEN BRYANT.

KILMENY.

Bonny Kilmeny gaed up the glen ;
But it wasna to meet Duneira's men,
Nor the rosy monk of the isle to see,
For Kilmeny was pure as pure could be.
It was only to hear the yorlin sing,
And pu' the cress-flower round the spring, —
The scarlet hypp, and the hind berry,
And the nut that hung frae the hazel-tree ;
For Kilmeny was pure as pure could be.
But lang may her minny look o'er the wa',
And lang may she seek i' the green-wood shaw ;
Lang the laird of Duneira blame,
And lang, lang greet or Kilmeny come hame.

When many a day had come and fled,
When grief grew calm, and hope was dead,
When mass for Kilmeny's soul had been sung,
When the bedesman had prayed, and the dead-
         bell rung ;
Late, late in a gloamin, when all was still,
When the fringe was red on the westlin hill,
The wood was sear, the moon i' the wane,
The reek o' the cot hung over the plain, —
Like a little wee cloud in the world its lane ;
When the ingle lowed with an eiry leme,
Late, late in the gloamin Kilmeny came hame !

   "Kilmeny, Kilmeny, where have you been ?
Lang hae we sought both holt and den, —
By linn, by ford, and green-wood tree ;
Yet you are halesome and fair to see.
Where got you that joup o' the lily sheen ?
That bonny snood of the birk sae green ?
And these roses, the fairest that ever was seen ?
Kilmeny, Kilmeny, where have you been ?"

Kilmeny looked up with a lovely grace,
But nae smile was seen on Kilmeny's face ;
As still was her look, and as still was her ee,
As the stillness that lay on the emerant lea,
Or the mist that sleeps on a waveless sea.
For Kilmeny had been she knew not where,
And Kilmeny had seen what she could not declare.

Kilmeny had been where the cock never crew,
Where the rain never fell, and the wind never blew;
But it seemed as the harp of the sky had rung,
And the airs of heaven played round her tongue,
When she spake of the lovely forms she had seen,
And a land where sin had never been, —
A land of love, and a land of light,
Withouten sun or moon or night;
Where the river swa'd a living stream,
And the light a pure celestial beam:
The land of vision it would seem,
A still, an everlasting dream.

In yon green-wood there is a waik,
And in that waik there is a wene,
And in that wene there is a maike,
That neither has flesh, blood, nor bane;
And down in yon green-wood he walks his lane.

In that green wene Kilmeny lay,
Her bosom happed wi' the flowerets gay;
But the air was soft, and the silence deep,
And bonny Kilmeny fell sound asleep;
She kend nae mair, nor opened her ee,
Till waked by the hymns of a far countrye.

She wakened on a couch of the silk sae slim,
All striped wi' the bars of the rainbow's rim;
And lovely beings around were rife,
Who erst had travelled mortal life;
And aye they smiled, and 'gan to speer:
"What spirit has brought this mortal here?"

"Lang have I journeyed the world wide,"
A meek and reverend fere replied;
"Baith night and day I have watched the fair
Eident a thousand years and mair.
Yes, I have watched o'er ilk degree,
Wherever blooms femenitye;
But sinless virgin, free of stain,
In mind and body, fand I nane.
Never, since the banquet of time,
Found I a virgin in her prime,
Till late this bonny maiden I saw,
As spotless as the morning snaw.
Full twenty years she has lived as free
As the spirits that sojourn in this countrye.
I have brought her away frae the snares of men,
That sin or death she may never ken."

They clasped her waist and her hands sae fair;
They kissed her cheek, and they kemed her hair;
And round came many a blooming fere,
Saying, "Bonny Kilmeny, ye're welcome here;
Women are freed of the littand scorn;
O, blest be the day Kilmeny was born!
Now shall the land of the spirits see,
Now shall it ken, what a woman may be!"

· · · · · ·

They lifted Kilmeny, they led her away,
And she walked in the light of a sunless day;
The sky was a dome of crystal bright,
The fountain of vision, and fountain of light;
The emerald fields were of dazzling glow,
And the flowers of everlasting blow.
Then deep in the stream her body they laid,
That her youth and beauty never might fade;
And they smiled on heaven, when they saw her lie
In the stream of life that wandered by.
And she heard a song, — she heard it sung,
She kend not where; but sae sweetly it rung,
It fell on her ear like a dream of the morn, —
"O, blest be the day Kilmeny was born!
Now shall the land of the spirits see,
Now shall it ken, what a woman may be!"

They bore her far to a mountain green,
To see what mortal never had seen;
And they seated her high on a purple sward,
And bade her heed what she saw and heard,
And note the changes the spirits wrought;
For now she lived in the land of thought. —
She looked, and she saw nor sun nor skies,
But a crystal dome of a thousand dies;
She looked, and she saw nae land aright,
But an endless whirl of glory and light;
And radiant beings went and came,
Far swifter than wind or the linked flame;
She hid her een frae the dazzling view;
She looked again, and the scene was new.

She saw a sun on a summer sky,
And clouds of amber sailing by;
A lovely land beneath her lay,
And that land had glens and mountains gray;
And that land had valleys and hoary piles,
And marled seas, and a thousand isles;
Its fields were speckled, its forests green,
And its lakes were all of the dazzling sheen,
Like magic mirrors, where slumbering lay
The sun and the sky and the cloudlet gray,
Which heaved and trembled, and gently swung;
On every shore they seemed to be hung;
For there they were seen on their downward plain
A thousand times and a thousand again;
In winding lake and placid firth, —
Little peaceful heavens in the bosom of earth.

Kilmeny sighed and seemed to grieve,
For she found her heart to that land did cleave;
She saw the corn wave on the vale;
She saw the deer run down the dale;
She saw the plaid and the broad claymore,
And the brows that the badge of freedom bore;
And she thought she had seen the land before.

· · · · · ·

Then Kilmeny begged again to see
The friends she had left in her own countrye,

To tell of the place where she had been,
And the glories that lay in the land unseen ;
To warn the living maidens fair,
The loved of heaven, the spirits' care,
That all whose minds unmeled remain
Shall bloom in beauty when time is gane.

With distant music, soft and deep,
They lulled Kilmeny sound asleep ;
And when she awakened, she lay her lane,
All happed with flowers in the green-wood wene.
When seven long years had come and fled ;
When grief was calm, and hope was dead ;
When scarce was remembered Kilmeny's name,
Late, late in a gloamin, Kilmeny came hame !
And O, her beauty was fair to see,
But still and steadfast was her ee !
Such beauty bard may never declare,
For there was no pride nor passion there ;
And the soft desire of maidens' een
In that mild face could never be seen.
Her seymar was the lily flower,
And her cheek the moss-rose in the shower ;
And her voice like the distant melodye
That floats along the twilight sea.
But she loved to raike the lanely glen,
And keeped afar frae the haunts of men ;
Her holy hymns unheard to sing,
To suck the flowers and drink the spring.
But wherever her peaceful form appeared,
The wild beasts of the hills were cheered ;
The wolf played blythely round the field ;
The lordly byson lowed and kneeled ;
The dun deer wooed with manner bland,
And cowered aneath her lily hand.
And when at even the woodlands rung,
When hymns of other worlds she sung
In ecstasy of sweet devotion,
O, then the glen was all in motion !
The wild beasts of the forest came,
Broke from their bughts and faulds the tame,
And goved around, charmed and amazed ;
Even the dull cattle crooned and gazed,
And murmured, and looked with anxious pain
For something the mystery to explain.
The buzzard came with the throstle-cock,
The corby left her houf in the rock ;
The blackbird alang wi' the eagle flew ;
The hind came tripping o'er the dew ;
The wolf and the kid their raike began ;
And the tod, and the lamb, and the leveret ran ;
The hawk and the hern attour them hung,
And the merl and the mavis forhooyed their young ;
And all in a peaceful ring were hurled :
It was like an eve in a sinless world !

When a month and day had come and gane,
Kilmeny sought the green-wood wene ;

There laid her down on the leaves sae green,
And Kilmeny on earth was never mair seen.
But O the words that fell from her mouth
Were words of wonder, and words of truth !
But all the land were in fear and dread,
For they kend na whether she was living or dead.
It wasna her hame, and she couldna remain ;
She left this world of sorrow and pain,
And returned to the land of thought again.

JAMES HOGG.

THE FAIRIES.

Up the airy mountain,
    Down the rushy glen,
We dare n't go a hunting
    For fear of little men ;
Wee folk, good folk,
    Trooping all together ;
Green jacket, red cap,
    And white owl's feather !

Down along the rocky shore
    Some make their home, —
They live on crispy pancakes
    Of yellow tide-foam ;
Some in the reeds
    Of the black mountain-lake,
With frogs for their watch-dogs,
    All night awake.

High on the hill-top
    The old king sits ;
He is now so old and gray
    He 's nigh lost his wits.
With a bridge of white mist
    Columbkill he crosses,
On his stately journeys
    From Slieveleague to Rosses ;
Or going up with music
    On cold starry nights,
To sup with the queen
    Of the gay Northern Lights.

They stole little Bridget
    For seven years long ;
When she came down again
    Her friends were all gone.
They took her lightly back,
    Between the night and morrow ;
They thought that she was fast asleep,
    But she was dead with sorrow.
They have kept her ever since
    Deep within the lakes,
On a bed of flag-leaves,
    Watching till she wakes.

By the craggy hillside,
    Through the mosses bare,

They have planted thorn-trees
 For pleasure here and there.
Is any man so daring
 To dig one up in spite,
He shall find the thornies set
 In his bed at night.

Up the airy mountain,
 Down the rushy glen,
We dare n't go a hunting
 For fear of little men ;
Wee folk, good folk,
 Trooping all together ;
Green jacket, red cap,
 And white owl's feather !

WILLIAM ALLINGHAM.

THE FAIRY CHILD.

THE summer sun was sinking
 With a mild light, calm and mellow ;
It shone on my little boy's bonnie cheeks,
 And his loose locks of yellow.

The robin was singing sweetly,
 And his song was sad and tender ;
And my little boy's eyes, while he heard the song,
 Smiled with a sweet, soft splendor.

My little boy lay on my bosom
 While his soul the song was quaffing ;
The joy of his soul had tinged his cheek,
 And his heart and his eye were laughing.

I sate alone in my cottage,
 The midnight needle plying ;
I feared for my child, for the rush's light
 In the socket now was dying !

There came a hand to my lonely latch,
 Like the wind at midnight moaning ;
I knelt to pray, but rose again,
 For I heard my little boy groaning.

I crossed my brow and I crossed my breast,
 But that night my child departed, —
They left a weakling in his stead,
 And I am broken-hearted !

O, it cannot be my own sweet boy,
 For his eyes are dim and hollow ;
My little boy is gone — is gone,
 And his mother soon will follow.

The dirge for the dead will be sung for me,
 And the mass be chanted meetly,
And I shall sleep with my little boy,
 In the moonlight churchyard sweetly.

JOHN ANSTER.

SONG OF WOOD-NYMPHS.

COME here, come here, and dwell
In forest deep !
Come here, come here, and tell
Why thou dost weep !
Is it for love (sweet pain !)
That thus thou dar'st complain
Unto our pleasant shades, our summer leaves,
Where naught else grieves ?

Come here, come here, and lie
By whispering stream !
Here no one dares to die
For love's sweet dream ;
But health all seek, and joy,
And shun perverse annoy,
And race along green paths till close of day,
And laugh — alway !

Or else, through half the year,
On rushy floor,
We lie by waters clear,
While skylarks pour
Their songs into the sun !
And when bright day is done,
We hide 'neath bells of flowers or nodding corn,
And dream — till morn !

BARRY CORNWALL.

THE GREEN GNOME.

A MELODY.

RING, sing ! ring, sing ! pleasant Sabbath bells !
Chime, rhyme ! chime, rhyme ! thorough dales
 and dells !
Rhyme, ring ! chime, sing ! pleasant Sabbath
 bells !
Chime, sing ! rhyme, ring ! over fields and fells !

And I galloped and I galloped on my palfrey
 white as milk,
My robe was of the sea-green woof, my serk was
 of the silk ;
My hair was golden yellow, and it floated to my
 shoe ;
My eyes were like two harebells bathed in little
 drops of dew ;
My palfrey, never stopping, made a music sweetly
 blent
With the leaves of autumn dropping all around me
 as I went ;
And I heard the bells, grown fainter, far behind
 me peal and play,
Fainter, fainter, fainter, till they seemed to die
 away ;
And beside a silver runnel, on a little heap o
 sand,

I saw the green gnome sitting, with his cheek
  upon his hand.
Then he started up to see me, and he ran with
  cry and bound,
And drew me from my palfrey white and set me
  on the ground.
O crimson, crimson were his locks, his face was
  green to see,
But he cried, " O light-haired lassie, you are
  bound to marry me !"
He clasped me round the middle small, he kissed
  me on the cheek,
He kissed me once, he kissed me twice, — I could
  not stir or speak ;
He kissed me twice, he kissed me thrice, — but
  when he kissed again,
I called aloud upon the name of Him who died
  for men.

Sing, sing ! ring, ring ! pleasant Sabbath bells !
Chime, rhyme ! chime, rhyme ! thorough dales
  and dells !
Rhyme, ring ! chime, sing ! pleasant Sabbath
  bells !
Chime, sing ! rhyme, ring ! over fields and fells !

O faintly, faintly, faintly, calling men and maids
  to pray,
So faintly, faintly, faintly rang the bells far
  away ;
And as I named the Blessed Name, as in our
  need we can,
The ugly green green gnome became a tall and
  comely man :
His hands were white, his beard was gold, his
  eyes were black as sloes,
His tunic was of scarlet woof, and silken were his
  hose ;
A pensive light from Faëryland still lingered on
  his cheek,
His voice was like the running brook, when he
  began to speak ;
" O, you have cast away the charm my step-dame
  put on me,
Seven years I dwelt in Faëryland, and you have
  set me free.
O, I will mount thy palfrey white, and ride to
  kirk with thee,
And, by those little dewy eyes, we twain will
  wedded be !"

Back we galloped, never stopping, he before and
  I behind,
And the autumn leaves were dropping, red and
  yellow, in the wind :
And the sun was shining clearer, and my heart
  was high and proud,
As nearer, nearer, nearer rang the kirk bells
  sweet and loud,

And we saw the kirk before us, as we trotted
  down the fells,
And nearer, clearer, o'er us, rang the welcome of
  the bells.

Ring, sing ! ring, sing ! pleasant Sabbath bells !
Chime, rhyme ! chime, rhyme ! thorough dales
  and dells !
Rhyme, ring ! chime, sing ! pleasant Sabbath
  bells !
Chime, sing ! rhyme, ring ! over fields and fells !
ROBERT BUCHANAN.

LA BELLE DAME SANS MERCI.

" O, WHAT can ail thee, knight-at-arms,
  Alone and palely loitering ?
The sedge has withered from the lake,
  And no birds sing.

" O, what can ail thee, knight-at-arms,
  So haggard and so woe-begone ?
The squirrel's granary is full,
  And the harvest 's done.

" I see a lily on thy brow
  With anguish moist and fever-dew,
And on thy cheeks a fading rose
  Fast withereth too."

" I met a lady in the meads,
  Full beautiful, — a fairy's child,
Her hair was long, her foot was light,
  And her eyes were wild.

" I made a garland for her head,
  And bracelets too, and fragrant zone ;
She looked at me as she did love,
  And made sweet moan.

" I set her on my pacing steed,
  And nothing else saw all day long ;
For sidelong would she bend, and sing
  A fairy's song.

" She found me roots of relish sweet,
  And honey wild and manna-dew ;
And sure in language strange she said,
  'I love thee true.'

" She took me to her elfin grot,
  And there she wept, and sighed full sore ;
And there I shut her wild, wild eyes
  With kisses four.

" And there she lullèd me asleep,
  And there I dreamed — ah, woe betide ! —
The latest dream I ever dreamed
  On the cold hill's side.

"I saw pale kings and princes too,
　Pale warriors, — death-pale were they all ;
They cried, 'La belle Dame sans Merci
　Hath thee in thrall !'

"I saw their starved lips in the gloam
　With horrid warning gapéd wide,
And I awoke and found me here
　On the cold hill's side.

"And this is why I sojourn here
　Alone and palely loitering,
Though the sedge is withered from the lake,
　And no birds sing."

JOHN KEATS.

THE WATER-FAY.

THE night comes stealing o'er me,
　And clouds are on the sea ;
While the wavelets rustle before me
　With a mystical melody.

A water-maid rose singing
　Before me, fair and pale ;
And snow-white breasts were springing,
　Like fountains, 'neath her veil.

She kissed me and she pressed me,
　Till I wished her arms away :
"Why hast thou so caressed me,
　Thou lovely water-fay ?"

"O, thou need'st not alarm thee,
　That thus thy form I hold ;
For I only seek to warm me,
　And the night is black and cold."

"The wind to the waves is calling,
　The moonlight is fading away ;
And tears down thy cheek are falling,
　Thou beautiful water-fay ! "

"The wind to the waves is calling,
　And the moonlight grows dim on the rocks ;
But no tears from mine eyes are falling,
　'T is the water which drips from my locks."

"The ocean is heaving and sobbing,
　The sea-mews scream in the spray ;
And thy heart is wildly throbbing,
　Thou beautiful water-fay ! "

"My heart is wildly swelling,
　And it beats in burning truth ;
For I love thee past all telling, —
　Thou beautiful mortal youth."

HENRY HEINE (German). Translation
of CHARLES G. LELAND.

THE WATER LADY.

I.

ALAS, that moon should ever beam
To show what man should never see ! —
I saw a maiden on a stream,
And fair was she !

II.

I stayed awhile to see her throw
Her tresses back, that all beset
The fair horizon of her brow
With clouds of jet.

III.

I stayed a little while to view
Her cheek, that wore, in place of red,
The bloom of water, — tender blue,
Daintily spread.

IV.

I stayed to watch, a little space,
Her parted lips, if she would sing ;
The waters closed above her face
With many a ring.

V.

And still I stayed a little more, —
Alas ! she never comes again !
I throw my flowers from the shore,
And watch in vain.

VI.

I know my life will fade away, —
I know that I must vainly pine ;
For I am made of mortal clay,
But she 's divine !

THOMAS HOOD.

THE FISHER.

THE waters purled, the waters swelled, —
　A fisher sat near by,
And earnestly his line beheld
　With tranquil heart and eye ;
And while he sits and watches there,
　He sees the waves divide,
And, lo ! a maid, with glistening hair,
　Springs from the troubled tide.

She sang to him, she spake to him, —
　"Why lur'st thou from below,
In cruel mood, my tender brood,
　To die in day's fierce glow ?
Ah ! didst thou know how sweetly there
　The little fishes dwell,
Thou wouldst come down their lot to share,
　And be forever well.

"Bathes not the smiling sun at night —
　The moon too — in the waves ?

Comes he not forth more fresh and bright
  From ocean's cooling caves ?
Canst thou unmoved that deep world see,
  That heaven of tranquil blue,
Where thine own face is beckoning thee
  Down to the eternal dew ?

The waters purled, the waters swelled, —
  They kissed his naked feet ;
His heart a nameless transport held,
  As if his love did greet.
She spake to him, she sang to him ;
  Then all with him was o'er, —
Half drew she him, half sank he in, —
  He sank to rise no more.
GOETHE. Translation of CHARLES T. BROOKS.

THE NIGHTINGALE AND GLOW-WORM.

A NIGHTINGALE, that all day long
Had cheered the village with his song,
Nor yet at eve his note suspended,
Nor yet when eventide was ended,
Began to feel — as well he might —
The keen demands of appetite ;
When, looking eagerly around,
He spied, far off, upon the ground,
A something shining in the dark,
And knew the glow-worm by his spark ;
So, stooping down from hawthorn top,
He thought to put him in his crop.
The worm, aware of his intent,
Harangued him thus, quite eloquent, —
  "Did you admire my lamp," quoth he,
"As much as I your minstrelsy,
You would abhor to do me wrong,
As much as I to spoil your song ;
For 't was the self-same Power divine
Taught you to sing, and me to shine ;
That you with music, I with light,
Might beautify and cheer the night."
The songster heard his short oration,
And, warbling out his approbation,
Released him, as my story tells,
And found a supper somewhere else.
WILLIAM COWPER.

THE MILKMAID.

A MILKMAID, who poised a full pail on her head,
Thus mused on her prospects in life, it is said :
"Let me see, — I should think that this milk
  will procure
One hundred good eggs, or fourscore, to be sure.

"Well then, — stop a bit, — it must not be for-
  gotten,

Some of these may be broken, and some may be
  rotten ;
But if twenty for accident should be detached,
It will leave me just sixty sound eggs to be hatched.

"Well, sixty sound eggs, — no, sound chickens,
  I mean :
Of these some may die, — we 'll suppose seventeen,
Seventeen ! not so many, — say ten at the most,
Which will leave fifty chickens to boil or to roast.

"But then there 's their barley : how much will
  they need ?
Why, they take but one grain at a time when
  they feed, —
So that 's a mere trifle ; now then, let us see,
At a fair market price how much money there 'll be.

"Six shillings a pair — five — four — three-and-six,
To prevent all mistakes, that low price I will fix ;
Now what will that make ? fifty chickens, I said, —
Fifty times three-and-sixpence — *I 'll ask Brother
  Ned.*

"O, but stop, — three-and-sixpence a *pair* I
  must sell 'em ;
Well, a pair is a couple, — now then let us tell 'em ;
A couple in fifty will go (my poor brain !)
Why, just a score times, and five pair will remain.

"Twenty-five pair of fowls — now how tiresome
  it is
That I can't reckon up so much money as this !
Well, there 's no use in trying, so let 's give a
  guess, —
I 'll say twenty pounds, *and it can't be no less.*

"Twenty pounds, I am certain, will buy me a cow,
Thirty geese, and two turkeys, — eight pigs and
  a sow ;
Now if these turn out well, at the end of the year,
I shall fill both my pockets with guineas, 't is
  clear."

Forgetting her burden, when this she had said,
The maid superciliously tossed up her head ;
When, alas for her prospects ! her milk-pail
  descended,
And so all her schemes for the future were ended.

This moral, I think, may be safely attached, —
"Reckon not on your chickens before they are
  hatched."
JEFFREYS TAYLOR.

THE TOAD'S JOURNAL

[It is said that Belzoni, the traveller in Egypt, discovered a living
toad in a temple which had been for ages buried in the sand.]

IN a land for antiquities greatly renowned
A traveller had dug wide and deep under ground,

A temple for ages entombed, to disclose, —
When, lo ! he disturbed, in its secret repose,
A toad, from whose journal it plainly appears
It had lodged in that mansion some thousands of
      years.
The roll which this reptile's long history records,
A treat to the sage antiquarian affords:
The sense by obscure hieroglyphics concealed,
Deep learning at length, with long labor, revealed.
The first thousand years as a specimen take, —
The dates are omitted for brevity's sake :
"Crawled forth from some rubbish, and winked
      with one eye ;
Half opened the other, but could not tell why ;
Stretched out my left leg, as it felt rather queer,
Then drew all together and slept for a year.
Awakened, felt chilly, — crept under a stone ;
Was vastly contented with living alone.
One toe became wedged in the stone like a peg,
Could not get it away, — had the cramp in my leg ;
Began half to wish for a neighbor at hand
To loosen the stone, which was fast in the sand ;
Pulled harder, then dozed, as I found 't was no
      use ; —
Awoke the next summer, and lo ! it was loose.
Crawled forth from the stone when completely
      awake ;
Crept into a corner and grinned at a snake.
Retreated, and found that I needed repose ;
Curled up my damp limbs and prepared for a doze ;
Fell sounder to sleep than was usual before,
And did not awake for a century or more ;
But had a sweet dream, as I rather believe :
Methought it was light, and a fine summer's eve ;
And I in some garden deliciously fed
In the pleasant moist shade of a strawberry-bed.
There fine speckled creatures claimed kindred with
      me,
And others that hopped, most enchanting to see.
Here long I regaled with emotion extreme ; —
Awoke, — disconcerted to find it a dream ;
Grew pensive, — discovered that life is a load ;
Began to get weary of being a toad ;
Was fretful at first, and then shed a few tears."—
Here ends the account of the first thousand years.

MORAL.

It seems that life is all a void,
   On selfish thoughts alone employed ;
That length of days is not a good,
   Unless their use be understood.
                                    JANE TAYLOR.

THE PHILOSOPHER TOAD.

Down deep in a hollow, so damp and so cold,
   Where oaks are by ivy o'ergrown,

The gray moss and lichen creep over the mould,
   Lying loose on a ponderous stone.
Now within this huge stone, like a king on his
      throne,
A toad has been sitting more years than is known ;
And strange as it seems, yet he constantly deems
The world standing still while he 's dreaming
      his dreams, —
Does this wonderful toad, in his cheerful abode
In the innermost heart of that flinty old stone,
By the gray-haired moss and the lichen o'ergrown.

Down deep in the hollow, from morning till night,
   Dun shadows glide over the ground,
Where a watercourse once, as it sparkled with
      light,
   Turned a ruined old mill-wheel around :
Long years have passed by since its bed became
      dry,
And the trees grow so close, scarce a glimpse
      of the sky
Is seen in the hollow, so dark and so damp,
Where the glow-worm at noonday is trimming
      his lamp,
And hardly a sound from the thicket around,
Where the rabbit and squirrel leap over the
      ground,
Is heard by the toad in his spacious abode
In the innermost heart of that ponderous stone,
By the gray-haired moss and the lichen o'ergrown.

Down deep in that hollow the bees never
      come,
   The shade is too black for a flower ;
And jewel-winged birds, with their musical hum,
   Never flash in the night of that bower ;
But the cold-blooded snake, in the edge of the
      brake,
Lies amid the rank grass half asleep, half awake ;
And the ashen-white snail, with the slime in
      its trail,
Moves wearily on like a life's tedious tale,
Yet disturbs not the toad in his spacious abode,
In the innermost heart of that flinty old stone,
By the gray-haired moss and the lichen o'ergrown.

Down deep in a hollow some wiseacres sit
   Like the toad in his cell in the stone ;
Around them in daylight the blind owlets flit,
   And their creeds are with ivy o'ergrown ;—
Their streams may go dry, and the wheels cease
      to ply,
And their glimpses be few of the sun and the sky,
Still they hug to their breast every time-hon-
      ored guest,
And slumber and doze in inglorious rest ;
For no progress they find in the wide sphere of
      mind,

And the world's standing still with all of their
    kind ;
Contented to dwell deep down in the well,
Or move like the snail in the crust of his shell,
Or live like the toad in his narrow abode,
With their souls closely wedged in a thick wall
    of stone,
By the gray weeds of prejudice rankly o'ergrown.
                MRS. R. S. NICHOLS.

THE PHILOSOPHER'S SCALES.

A MONK, when his rites sacerdotal were o'er,
In the depth of his cell with his stone-covered floor,
Resigning to thought his chimerical brain,
Once formed the contrivance we now shall explain;
But whether by magic's or alchemy's powers
We know not ; indeed, 't is no business of ours.

Perhaps it was only by patience and care,
At last, that he brought his invention to bear.
In youth 't was projected, but years stole away,
And ere 't was complete he was wrinkled and gray ;
But success is secure, unless energy fails ;
And at length he produced THE PHILOSOPHER'S
    SCALES.

"What were they?" you ask. You shall pres-
    ently see ;
These scales were not made to weigh sugar and tea.
O no ; for such properties wondrous had they,
That qualities, feelings, and thoughts they could
    weigh,
Together with articles small or immense,
From mountains or planets to atoms of sense.

Naught was there so bulky but there it would lay,
And naught so ethereal but there it would stay,
And naught so reluctant but in it must go :
All which some examples more clearly will show.

The first thing he weighed was the head of Voltaire,
Which retained all the wit that had ever been there.
As a weight, he threw in a torn scrap of a leaf,
Containing the prayer of the penitent thief ;
When the skull rose aloft with so sudden a spell
That it bounced like a ball on the roof of the cell.

One time he put in Alexander the Great,
With the garment that Dorcas had made for a
    weight ;
And though clad in armor from sandals to crown,
The hero rose up, and the garment went down.

A long row of almshouses, amply endowed
By a well-esteemed Pharisee, busy and proud,
Next loaded one scale ; while the other was pressed
By those mites the poor widow dropped into the
    chest:

Up flew the endowment, not weighing an ounce,
And down, down the farthing-worth came with
    a bounce.

By further experiments (no matter how)
He found that ten chariots weighed less than
    one plough ;
A sword with gilt trapping rose up in the scale,
Though balanced by only a ten-penny nail ;
A shield and a helmet, a buckler and spear,
Weighed less than a widow's uncrystallized tear.

A lord and a lady went up at full sail,
When a bee chanced to light on the opposite scale;
Ten doctors, ten lawyers, two courtiers, one earl,
Ten counsellors' wigs, full of powder and curl,
All heaped in one balance and swinging from
    thence,
Weighed less than a few grains of candor and sense ;
A first-water diamond, with brilliants begirt,
Than one good potato just washed from the dirt ;
Yet not mountains of silver and gold could suffice
One pearl to outweigh, — 't was THE PEARL OF
    GREAT PRICE.

Last of all, the whole world was bowled in at the
    grate,
With the soul of a beggar to serve for a weight,
When the former sprang up with so strong a re-
    buff
That it made a vast rent and escaped at the roof !
When balanced in air, it ascended on high,
And sailed up aloft, a balloon in the sky ;
While the scale with the soul in 't so mightily fell
That it jerked the philosopher out of his cell.
                JANE TAYLOR.

THE CALIPH AND SATAN.

VERSIFIED FROM THOLUCK'S TRANSLATION OUT OF THE
PERSIAN.

IN heavy sleep the Caliph lay,
When some one called, "Arise, and pray !"

The angry Caliph cried, "Who dare
Rebuke his king for slighted prayer?"

Then, from the corner of the room,
A voice cut sharply through the gloom :

"My name is Satan. Rise ! obey
Mohammed's law ; awake, and pray."

"Thy *words* are good," the Caliph said,
"But their intent I somewhat dread.

For matters cannot well be worse
Than when the thief says, 'Guard your purse !'"

I cannot trust your counsel, friend,
It surely hides some wicked end."

Said Satan, "Near the throne of God,
In ages past, we devils trod ;

Angels of light, to us 't was given
To guide each wandering foot to heaven.

Not wholly lost is that first love,
Nor those pure tastes we knew above.

Roaming across a continent,
The Tartar moves his shifting tent,

But never quite forgets the day
When in his father's arms he lay ;

So we, once bathed in love divine,
Recall the taste of that rich wine.

God's finger rested on my brow, —
That magic touch, I feel it now !

I fell, 't is true — O, ask not why,
For still to God I turn my eye.

It was a chance by which I fell,
Another takes me back from hell.

'T was but my envy of mankind,
The envy of a loving mind.

Jealous of men, I could not bear
God's love with this new race to share.

But yet God's tables open stand,
His guests flock in from every land ;

Some kind act toward the race of men
May toss us into heaven again.

A game of chess is all we see, —
And God the player, pieces we.

White, black — queen, pawn, — 't is all the same,
For on both sides he plays the game.

Moved to and fro, from good to ill,
We rise and fall as suits his will."

The Caliph said, "If this be so,
I know not, but thy guile I know ;

For how can I thy words believe,
When even God thou didst deceive ?

A sea of lies art thou, — our sin
Only a drop that sea within."

"Not so," said Satan, "I serve God,
His angel now, and now his rod.

In tempting I both bless and curse,
Make good men better, bad men worse.

Good coin is mixed with bad, my brother,
I but distinguish one from the other."

"Granted," the Caliph said, "but still
You never tempt to good, but ill.

Tell then the truth, for well I know
You come as my most deadly foe."

Loud laughed the fiend. "You know me well,
Therefore my purpose I will tell.

If you had missed your prayer, I knew
A swift repentance would ensue.

And such repentance would have been
A good, outweighing far the sin.

I chose this humbleness divine,
Borne out of fault, should not be thine,

Preferring prayers elate with pride
To sin with penitence allied."

J. F. C.

AIRY NOTHINGS.

FROM "THE TEMPEST."

OUR revels now are ended. These our actors,
As I foretold you, were all spirits, and
Are melted into air, into thin air ;
And, like the baseless fabric of this vision,
The cloud-capped towers, the gorgeous palaces,
The solemn temples, the great globe itself,
Yea, all which it inherit, shall dissolve,
And, like this insubstantial pageant faded,
Leave not a rack behind. We are such stuff
As dreams are made of, and our little life
Is rounded with a sleep.

SHAKESPEARE.

And through this land is thoroughed again, O Sea,
Strange sadness trickles all that go with thee.
The wild birds plaining notes, the wild sharp call.
Strange things own spirite it is rather all!
How dark & stern upon the waves looks down
(ponder Table Bluff! ~ he with this lion crown.
And I see! These noble Pines along the steep
Are come to join thy regimen, gloomy deep!
Like soldierd monks they stand & chant the hinges
Down the dark math with thy low exciting surge. ~

———

Orient H. Adams

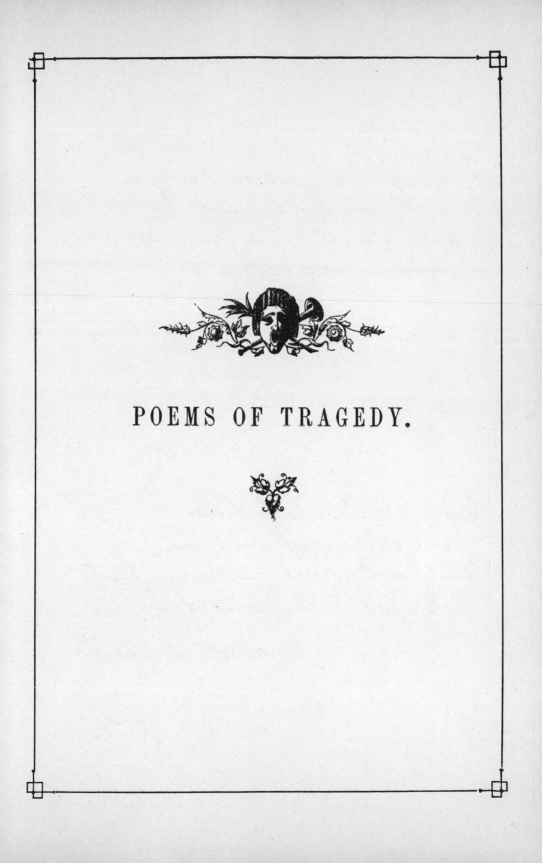

POEMS OF TRAGEDY.

One year, one year one little year
  And so much gone
And yet the even flow of life
  Moves calmly on :

                    H B Stowe

— · —

Hark! to the tolling bells
   In echoes deep and slow.
While on the breeze our banner floats
   Draped in the weeds of woe.

                    L. Huntley Sigourney.

POEMS OF TRAGEDY.

THE EXECUTION OF MONTROSE.

EXECUTED 1650.

THE morning dawned full darkly,
  The rain came flashing down,
And the jagged streak of the levin-bolt
  Lit up the gloomy town.
The thunder crashed across the heaven,
  The fatal hour was come;
Yet aye broke in, with muffled beat,
  The 'larum of the drum.
There was madness on the earth below
  And anger in the sky,
And young and old, and rich and poor,
  Came forth to see him die.

Ah God! that ghastly gibbet!
  How dismal 't is to see
The great tall spectral skeleton,
  The ladder and the tree!
Hark! hark! it is the clash of arms, —
  The bells begin to toll, —
"He is coming! he is coming!
  God's mercy on his soul!"
One last long peal of thunder, —
  The clouds are cleared away,
And the glorious sun once more looks down
  Amidst the dazzling day.

"He is coming! he is coming!"
  Like a bridegroom from his room
Came the hero from his prison
  To the scaffold and the doom.
There was glory on his forehead,
  There was lustre in his eye,
And he never walked to battle
  More proudly than to die.
There was color in his visage,
  Though the cheeks of all were wan;
And they marvelled as they saw him pass,
  That great and goodly man!

He mounted up the scaffold,
  And he turned him to the crowd;
But they dared not trust the people,
So he might not speak aloud.
But he looked upon the heavens,
  And they were clear and blue,
And in the liquid ether
  The eye of God shone through:
Yet a black and murky battlement
  Lay resting on the hill,
As though the thunder slept within, —
  All else was calm and still.

The grim Geneva ministers
  With anxious scowl drew near,
As you have seen the ravens flock
  Around the dying deer.
He would not deign them word nor sign,
  But alone he bent the knee;
And veiled his face for Christ's dear grace
  Beneath the gallows-tree.
Then, radiant and serene, he rose,
  And cast his cloak away;
For he had ta'en his latest look
  Of earth and sun and day.

A beam of light fell o'er him,
  Like a glory·round the shriven,
And he climbed the lofty ladder
  As it were the path to heaven.
Then came a flash from out the cloud,
  And a stunning thunder-roll;
And no man dared to look aloft,
  For fear was on every soul.
There was another heavy sound,
  A hush, and then a groan;
And darkness swept across the sky, —
  The work of death was done!
                    WILLIAM EDMONDSTOUNE AYTOUN.

THE NUN.

FROM "ITALY."

'T IS over; and her lovely cheek is now
On her hard pillow, — there, alas! to be
Nightly, through many and many a dreary hour
Wan, often wet with tears, and (ere at length

Her place is empty, and another comes)
In anguish, in the ghastliness of death ;
Hers nevermore to leave those mournful walls,
Even on her bier.

        'T is over ; and the rite,
With all its pomp and harmony, is now
Floating before her. She arose at home,
To be the show, the idol of the day ;
Her vesture gorgeous, and her starry head, —
No rocket, bursting in the midnight sky,
So dazzling. When to-morrow she awakes,
She will awake as though she still was there,
Still in her father's house ; and lo, a cell
Narrow and dark, naught through the gloom
    discerned, —
Naught save the crucifix and rosary,
And the gray habit lying by to shroud
Her beauty and grace.

        When on her knees she fell,
Entering the solemn place of consecration,
And from the latticed gallery came a chant
Of psalms, most saint-like, most angelical,
Verse after verse sung out, how holily !
The strain returning, and still, still returning,
Methought it acted like a spell upon her,
And she was casting off her earthly dross ;
Yet was it sad and sweet, and, ere it closed,
Came like a dirge. When her fair head was shorn,
And the long tresses in her hands were laid,
That she might fling them from her, saying, —
    "Thus,
Thus I renounce the world and worldly things !"
When, as she stood, her bridal ornaments
Were one by one removed, even to the last,
That she might say, flinging them from her, —
    "Thus,
Thus I renounce the world !" When all was
    changed,
And as a nun in homeliest guise she knelt,
Veiled in her veil, crowned with her silver crown,
Her crown of lilies as the spouse of Christ,
Well might her strength forsake her, and her knees
Fail in that hour ! Well might the holy man,
He at whose foot she knelt, give as by stealth
('T was in her utmost need ; nor, while she lives,
Will it go from her, fleeting as it was)
That faint but fatherly smile, that smile of love
And pity !

        Like a dream the whole is fled ;
And they that came in idleness to gaze
Upon the victim dressed for sacrifice
Are mingling with the world ; thou in thy cell
Forgot, Teresa ! Yet among them all
None were so formed to love and to be loved,
None to delight, adorn ; and on thee now
A curtain, blacker than the night, is dropped
Forever ! In thy gentle bosom sleep
Feelings, affections, destined now to die ;

To wither like the blossom in the bud, —
Those of a wife, a mother ; leaving there
A cheerless void, a chill as of the grave,
A languor and a lethargy of soul,
Death-like, and gathering more and more, till
    Death
Comes to release thee. Ah ! what now to thee,
What now to thee the treasures of thy youth ?
As nothing !   SAMUEL ROGERS.

IPHIGENEIA AND AGAMEMNON.

IPHIGENEIA, when she heard her doom
At Aulis, and when all beside the king
Had gone away, took his right hand, and said :
"O father ! I am young and very happy.
I do not think the pious Calchas heard
Distinctly what the goddess spake ; old age
Obscures the senses. If my nurse, who knew
My voice so well, sometimes misunderstood,
While I was resting on her knee both arms,
And hitting it to make her mind my words,
And looking in her face, and she in mine,
Might not he, also, hear one word amiss,
Spoken from so far off, even from Olympus ?"
The father placed his cheek upon her head,
And tears dropt down it ; but the king of men
Replied not. Then the maiden spake once more :
"O father ! sayest thou nothing ? Hearest thou
    not
Me, whom thou ever hast, until this hour,
Listened to fondly, and awakened me
To hear my voice amid the voice of birds,
When it was inarticulate as theirs,
And the down deadened it within the nest ?"
He moved her gently from him, silent still ;
And this, and this alone, brought tears from her,
Although she saw fate nearer. Then with sighs :
"I thought to have laid down my hair before
Benignant Artemis, and not dimmed
Her polished altar with my virgin blood ;
I thought to have selected the white flowers
To please the nymphs, and to have asked of each
By name, and with no sorrowful regret,
Whether, since both my parents willed the change,
I might at Hymen's feet bend my clipt brow ;
And (after these who mind us girls the most)
Adore our own Athene, that she would
Regard me mildly with her azure eyes, —
But, father, to see you no more, and see
Your love, O father ! go ere I am gone !"
Gently he moved her off, and drew her back,
Bending his lofty head far over hers ;
And the dark depths of nature heaved and burst.
He turned away, — not far, but silent still.
She now first shuddered ; for in him, so nigh,

So long a silence seemed the approach of death,
And like it. Once again she raised her voice :
"O father ! if the ships are now detained,
And all your vows move not the gods above,
When the knife strikes me there will be one prayer
The less to them ; and purer can there be
Any, or more fervent, than the daughter's prayer
For her dear father's safety and success ?"
A groan that shook him shook not his resolve.
An aged man now entered, and without
One word stepped slowly on, and took the wrist
Of the pale maiden. She looked up, and saw
The fillet of the priest and calm, cold eyes.
Then turned she where her parent stood, and cried :
"O father ! grieve no more ; the ships can sail."

WALTER SAVAGE LANDOR.

THE CURSE OF KEHAMA.

I CHARM thy life,
From the weapons of strife,
 From stone and from wood,
 From fire and from flood,
 From the serpent's tooth,
 And the beast of blood.
From sickness I charm thee,
And time shall not harm thee ;
 But earth, which is mine,
 Its fruits shall deny thee ;
 And water shall hear me,
 And know thee and flee thee :
And the winds shall not touch thee
When they pass by thee,
And the dews shall not wet thee
When they fall nigh thee.
 And thou shalt seek death,
 To release thee, in vain ;
 Thou shalt live in thy pain,
 While Kehama shall reign,
 With a fire in thy heart,
And a fire in thy brain.
 And sleep shall obey me,
 And visit thee never,
 And the curse shall be on thee
Forever and ever.

ROBERT SOUTHEY.

HAMLET REPROACHING THE QUEEN.

FROM "HAMLET, PRINCE OF DENMARK."

HAMLET. Leave wringing of your hands :
 peace ! sit you down,
And let me wring your heart : for so I shall,
If it be made of penetrable stuff ;
If damnéd custom have not brazed it so,
That it is proof and bulwark against sense.

QUEEN. What have I done, that thou dar'st
 wag thy tongue
In noise so rude against me ?
HAM. Such an act,
That blurs the grace and blush of modesty ;
Calls virtue, hypocrite ; takes off the rose
From the fair forehead of an innocent love,
And sets a blister there ; makes marriage vows
As false as dicers' oaths : O, such a deed
As from the body of contraction plucks
The very soul ; and sweet religion makes
A rhapsody of words : Heaven's face doth glow ;
Yea, this solidity and compound mass,
With tristful visage, as against the doom,
Is thought-sick at the act.
QUEEN. Ah me, what act,
That roars so loud, and thunders in the index ?
HAM. Look here, upon this picture, and on
 this,—
The counterfeit presentment of two brothers.
See, what a grace was seated on this brow ;
Hyperion's curls ; the front of Jove himself ;
An eye like Mars, to threaten and command ;
A station like the herald Mercury
New-lighted on a heaven-kissing hill ;
A combination, and a form, indeed,
Where every god did seem to set his seal,
To give the world assurance of a man :
This was your husband. Look you now, what
 follows :
Here is your husband ; like a mildewed ear,
Blasting his wholesome brother. Have you eyes ?
Could you on this fair mountain leave to feed,
And batten on this moor ? Ha ! have you eyes ?
You cannot call it love ; for, at your age,
The hey-day in the blood is tame, it 's humble,
And waits upon the judgment : and what judgment
Would step from this to this ? Sense, sure, you
 have,
Else, could you not have motion : but, sure, that
 sense
Is apoplexed : for madness would not err ;
Nor sense to ecstasy was ne'er so thralled
But it reserved some quantity of choice,
To serve in such a difference. What devil was 't
That thus hath cozened you at hoodman-blind ?
Eyes without feeling, feeling without sight,
Ears without hands or eyes, smelling sans all,
Or but a sickly part of one true sense
Could not so mope.
O shame ! where is thy blush ? Rebellious hell,
If thou canst mutine in a matron's bones,
To flaming youth let virtue be as wax,
And melt in her own fire : proclaim no shame
When the compulsive ardor gives the charge,
Since frost itself as actively doth burn,
And reason panders will.
QUEEN. O Hamlet, speak no more :

Thou turn'st mine eyes into my very soul ;
And there I see such black and grainéd spots,
As will not leave their tinct.

      O, speak to me no more ;
These words, like daggers, enter in mine ears ;
No more, sweet Hamlet !

 HAM.   A murderer, and a villain ;
A slave, that is not twentieth part the tithe
Of your precedent lord ; a Vice of kings ;
A cutpurse of the empire and the rule,
That from a shelf the precious diadem stole,
And put it in his pocket !

 QUEEN.   No more.

 HAM. A king of shreds and patches, —

Enter Ghost.

Save me, and hover o'er me with your wings,
You heavenly guards ! — What would your gra-
  cious figure ?

 QUEEN. Alas, he 's mad !

 HAM. Do you not come your tardy son to chide,
That, lapsed in time and passion, lets go by
The important acting of your dread command ?
O, say !

 GHOST. Do not forget : this visitation
Is but to whet thy almost blunted purpose.
But look, amazement on thy mother sits :
O, step between her and her fighting soul, —
Conceit in weakest bodies strongest works, —
Speak to her, Hamlet.

 HAM.   How is it with you, lady ?

 QUEEN. Alas, how is 't with you,
That you do bend your eye on vacancy,
And with the incorporal air do hold discourse ?
Forth at your eyes your spirits wildly peep ;
And, as the sleeping soldiers in the alarm,
Your bedded hair, like life in excrements,
Starts up, and stands on end. O gentle son,
Upon the heat and flame of thy distemper
Sprinkle cool patience. Whereon do you look ?

 HAM. On him ! on him ! Look you, how pale
  he glares !
His form and cause conjoined, preaching to stones,
Would make them capable. — Do not look upon
  me ;
Lest with this piteous action you convert
My stern effects : then, what I have to do
Will want true color ; tears, perchance, for blood.

 QUEEN. To whom do you speak this ?

 HAM.   Do you see nothing there ?

 QUEEN. Nothing at all ; yet all, that is, I see.

 HAM. Nor did you nothing hear ?

 QUEEN.   No, nothing, but ourselves.

 HAM. Why, look you there ! look, how it steals
  away !
My father, in his habit as he lived !
Look, where he goes, even now, out at the portal !
           [*Exit* Ghost.

 QUEEN. This is the very coinage of your brain :
This bodiless creation ecstasy
Is very cunning in.

 HAM. Ecstasy !
My pulse, as yours, doth temperately keep time,
And makes as healthful music : it is not madness
That I have uttered : bring me to the test
And I the matter will re-word ; which madness
Would gambol from. Mother, for love of grace,
Lay not that flattering unction to your soul,
That not your trespass, but my madness, speaks :
It will but skin and film the ulcerous place,
Whilst rank corruption, mining all within,
Infects unseen. Confess yourself to heaven ;
Repent what 's past ; avoid what is to come ;
And do not spread the compost on the weeds,
To make them ranker. Forgive me this my virtue ;
For in the fatness of these pursy times,
Virtue itself of vice must pardon beg,
Yea, curb and woe, for leave to do him good.

 QUEEN. O Hamlet, thou hast cleft my heart
  in twain !

 HAM. O, throw away the worser part of it,
And live the purer with the other half.
Good night : but go not to mine uncle's bed ;
Assume a virtue, if you have it not.
Once more, good night :
And when you are desirous to be blessed,
I 'll blessing beg of you.
I must be cruel, only to be kind :
Thus bad begins, and worse remains behind.
           SHAKESPEARE.

COUNTESS LAURA.

IT was a dreary day in Padua.
The Countess Laura, for a single year
Fernando's wife, upon her bridal bed,
Like an uprooted lily on the snow,
The withered outcast of a festival,
Lay dead. She died of some uncertain ill,
That struck her almost on her wedding day,
And clung to her, and dragged her slowly down,
Thinning her cheeks and pinching her full lips,
Till, in her chance, it seemed that with a year
Full half a century was overpast.
In vain had Paracelsus taxed his art,
And feigned a knowledge of her malady ;
In vain had all the doctors, far and near,
Gathered around the mystery of her bed,
Draining her veins, her husband's treasury,
And physic's jargon, in a fruitless quest
For causes equal to the dread result.
The Countess only smiled when they were gone,
Hugged her fair body with her little hands,
And turned upon her pillows wearily,
As though she fain would sleep no common sleep,
But the long, breathless slumber of the grave.

She hinted nothing. Feeble as she was,
The rack could not have wrung her secret out.
The Bishop, when he shrived her, coming forth,
Cried, in a voice of heavenly ecstasy,
"O blesséd soul ! with nothing to confess
Save virtues and good deeds, which she mis-
     takes —
So humble is she — for our human sins ! "
Praying for death, she tossed upon her bed
Day after day ; as might a shipwrecked bark
That rocks upon one billow, and can make
No onward motion towards her port of hope.
At length, one morn, when those around her said,
"Surely the Countess mends, so fresh a light
Beams from her eyes and beautifies her face," —
One morn in spring, when every flower of earth
Was opening to the sun, and breathing up
Its votive incense, her impatient soul
Opened itself, and so exhaled to heaven.
When the Count heard it, he reeled back a pace ;
Then turned with anger on the messenger ;
Then craved his pardon, and wept out his heart
Before the menial ; tears, ah me ! such tears
As love sheds only, and love only once.
Then he bethought him, "Shall this wonder die,
And leave behind no shadow ? not a trace
Of all the glory that environed her,
That mellow nimbus circling round my star ?"
So, with his sorrow glooming in his face,
He paced along his gallery of art,
And strode among the painters, where they stood,
With Carlo, the Venetian, at their head,
Studying the Masters by the dawning light
Of his transcendent genius. Through the groups
Of gayly-vestured artists moved the Count,
As some lone cloud of thick and leaden hue,
Packed with the secret of a coming storm,
Moves through the gold and crimson evening
     mists,
Deadening their splendor. In a moment still
Was Carlo's voice, and still the prattling crowd ;
And a great shadow overwhelmed them all,
As their white faces and their anxious eyes
Pursued Fernando in his moody walk.
He paused, as one who balances a doubt,
Weighing two courses, then burst out with this :
"Ye all have seen the tidings in my face ;
Or has the dial ceased to register
The workings of my heart ? Then hear the bell,
That almost cracks its frame in utterance ;
The Countess, — she is dead ! " — "Dead ! "
     Carlo groaned.
And if a bolt from middle heaven had struck
His splendid features full upon the brow,
He could not have appeared more scathed and
     blanched.
"Dead ! — dead ! " He staggered to his easel-
     frame,

And clung around it, buffeting the air
With one wild arm, as though a drowning man
Hung to a spar and fought against the waves.
The Count resumed : "I came not here to grieve,
Nor see my sorrow in another's eyes.
Who 'll paint the Countess, as she lies to-night
In state within the chapel ? Shall it be
That earth must lose her wholly ? that no hint
Of her gold tresses, beaming eyes, and lips
That talked in silence, and the eager soul
That ever seemed outbreaking through her clay,
And scattering glory round it, — shall all these
Be dull corruption's heritage, and we,
Poor beggars, have no legacy to show
That love she bore us ? That were shame to love,
And shame to you, my masters." Carlo stalked
Forth from his easel stiffly as a thing
Moved by mechanic impulse. His thin lips,
And sharpened nostrils, and wan, sunken cheeks,
And the cold glimmer in his dusky eyes,
Made him a ghastly sight. The throng drew back
As though they let a spectre through. Then he,
Fronting the Count, and speaking in a voice
Sounding remote and hollow, made reply :
"Count, I shall paint the Countess. 'T is my
     fate, —
Not pleasure, — no, nor duty." But the Count,
Astray in woe, but understood assent,
Not the strange words that bore it ; and he flung
His arm round Carlo, drew him to his breast,
And kissed his forehead. At which Carlo shrank :
Perhaps 't was at the honor. Then the Count,
A little reddening at his public state, —
Unseemly to his near and recent loss, —
Withdrew in haste between the downcast eyes
That did him reverence as he rustled by.

Night fell on Padua. In the chapel lay
The Countess Laura at the altar's foot.
Her coronet glittered on her pallid brows ;
A crimson pall, weighed down with golden work,
Sown thick with pearls, and heaped with early
     flowers,
Draped her still body almost to the chin ;
And over all a thousand candles flamed
Against the winking jewels, or streamed down
The marble aisle, and flashed along the guard
Of men-at-arms that slowly wove their turns,
Backward and forward, through th distant gloom.
When Carlo entered, his unsteady feet
Scarce bore him to the altar, and his head
Drooped down so low that all his shining curls
Poured on his breast, and veiled his countenance.
Upon his easel a half-finished work,
The secret labor of his studio,
Said from the canvas, so that none might err,
"I am the Countess Laura." Carlo kneeled,
And gazed upon the picture ; as if thus,

Through those clear eyes, he saw the way to heaven.
Then he arose ; and as a swimmer comes
Forth from the waves, he shook his locks aside,
Emerging from his dream, and standing firm
Upon a purpose with his sovereign will.
He took his palette, murmuring, "Not yet !"
Confidingly and softly to the corpse ;
And as the veriest drudge, who plies his art
Against his fancy, he addressed himself
With stolid resolution to his task.
Turning his vision on his memory,
And shutting out the present, till the dead,
The gilded pall, the lights, the pacing guard,
And all the meaning of that solemn scene
Became as nothing, and creative Art
Resolved the whole to chaos, and reformed
The elements according to her law :
So Carlo wrought, as though his eye and hand
Were Heaven's unconscious instruments, and
worked
The settled purpose of Omnipotence.
And it was wondrous how the red, the white,
The ochre, and the umber, and the blue,
From mottled blotches, hazy and opaque,
Grew into rounded forms and sensuous lines ;
How just beneath the lucid skin the blood
Glimmered with warmth ; the scarlet lips apart
Bloomed with the moisture of the dews of life ;
How the light glittered through and underneath
The golden tresses, and the deep, soft eyes
Became intelligent with conscious thought,
And somewhat troubled underneath the arch
Of eyebrows but a little too intense
For perfect beauty ; how the pose and poise
Of the lithe figure on its tiny foot
Suggested life just ceased from motion ; so
That any one might cry, in marvelling joy,
"That creature lives, — has senses, mind, a soul
To win God's love or dare hell's subtleties !"
The artist paused. The ratifying "Good !"
Trembled upon his lips. He saw no touch
To give or soften. "It is done," he cried,
"My task, my duty ! Nothing now on earth
Can taunt me with a work left unfulfilled !"
The lofty flame, which bore him up so long,
Died in the ashes of humanity ;
And the mere man rocked to and fro again
Upon the centre of his wavering heart.
He put aside his palette, as if thus
He stepped from sacred vestments, and assumed
A mortal function in the common world.
"Now for my rights !" he muttered, and ap-
proached
The noble body. "O lily of the world !
So withered, yet so lovely ! what wast thou
To those who came thus near thee — for I stood
Without the pale of thy half-royal rank —
When thou wast budding, and the streams of life

Made eager struggles to maintain thy bloom,
And gladdened heaven dropped down in gracious
dews
On its transplanted darling ? Hear me now !
I say this but in justice, not in pride,
Not to insult thy high nobility,
But that the poise of things in God's own sight
May be adjusted ; and hereafter I
May urge a claim that all the powers of heaven
Shall sanction, and with clarions blow abroad. —
Laura, you loved me ! Look not so severe,
With your cold brows, and deadly, close-drawn
lips !
You proved it, Countess, when you died for it, —
Let it consume you in the wearing strife
It fought with duty in your ravaged heart.
I knew it ever since that summer day
I painted Lila, the pale beggar's child,
At rest beside the fountain ; when I felt —
O Heaven ! — the warmth and moisture of your
breath
Blow through my hair, as with your eager soul —
Forgetting soul and body go as one —
You leaned across my easel till our cheeks —
Ah me ! 't was not your purpose — touched, and
clung !
Well, grant 't was genius ; and is genius naught ?
I ween it wears as proud a diadem —
Here, in this very world — as that you wear.
A king has held my palette, a grand-duke
Has picked my brush up, and a pope has begged
The favor of my presence in his Rome.
I did not go ; I put my fortune by.
I need not ask you why : you knew too well.
It was but natural, it was no way strange,
That I should love you. Everything that saw,
Or had its other senses, loved you, sweet,
And I among them. Martyr, holy saint, —
I see the halo curving round your head, —
I loved you once ; but now I worship you,
For the great deed that held my love aloof,
And killed you in the action ! I absolve
Your soul from any taint. For from the day
Of that encounter by the fountain-side
Until this moment, never turned on me
Those tender eyes, unless they did a wrong
To nature by the cold, defiant glare
With which they chilled me. Never heard I word
Of softness spoken by those gentle lips ;
Never received a bounty from that hand
Which gave to all the world. I know the cause.
You did your duty, — not for honor's sake,
Nor to save sin or suffering or remorse,
Or all the ghosts that haunt a woman's shame,
But for the sake of that pure, loyal love
Your husband bore you. Queen, by grace of God,
I bow before the lustre of your throne !
I kiss the edges of your garment-hem,

And hold myself ennobled ! Answer me, —
If I had wronged you, you would answer me
Out of the dusty porches of the tomb : —
Is this a dream, a falsehood ? or have I
Spoken the very truth ?" "The very truth !"
A voice replied ; and at his side he saw
A form, half shadow and half substance, stand,
Or, rather, rest ; for on the solid earth
It had no footing, more than some dense mist
That wavers o'er the surface of the ground
It scarcely touches. With a reverent look
The shadow's waste and wretched face was bent
Above the picture ; as though greater awe
Subdued its awful being, and appalled,
With memories of terrible delight
And fearful wonder, its devouring gaze.
"You make what God makes, — beauty," said
    the shape.
"And might not this, this second Eve, console
The emptiest heart ? Will not this thing outlast
The fairest creature fashioned in the flesh ?
Before that figure, Time, and Death himself,
Stand baffled and disarmed. What would you ask
More than God's power, from nothing to create ?"
The artist gazed upon the boding form,
And answered : "Goblin, if you had a heart,
That were an idle question. What to me
Is my creative power, bereft of love ?
Or what to God would be that selfsame power,
If so bereaved ?" "And yet the love, thus
    mourned,
You calmly forfeited. For had you said
To living Laura — in her burning ears —
One half that you professed to Laura dead,
She would have been your own. These contraries
Sort not with my intelligence. But speak,
Were Laura living, would the same stale play
Of raging passion tearing out its heart
Upon the rock of duty be performed ?"
"The same, O phantom, while the heart I bear
Trembled, but turned not its magnetic faith
From God's fixed centre." "If I wake for you
This Laura, — give her all the bloom and glow
Of that midsummer day you hold so dear, —
The smile, the motion, the impulsive soul,
The love of genius, — yea, the very love,
The mortal, hungry, passionate, hot love,
She bore you, flesh to flesh, — would you receive
That gift, in all its glory, at my hands ?"
A smile of malice curled the tempter's lips,
And glittered in the caverns of his eyes,
Mocking the answer. Carlo paled and shook ;
A woful spasm went shuddering through his
    frame,
Curdling his blood, and twisting his fair face
With nameless torture. But he cried aloud,
Out of the clouds of anguish, from the smoke
Of very martyrdom, "O God, she is thine !

Do with her at thy pleasure !" Something grand,
And radiant as a sunbeam, touched the head
He bent in awful sorrow. "Mortal, see — "
"Dare not ! As Christ was sinless, I abjure
These vile abominations ! Shall she bear
Life's burden twice, and life's temptations twice,
While God is justice ?" "Who has made you
    judge
Of what you call God's good, and what you think
God's evil ? One to him, the source of both,
The God of good and of permitted ill.
Have you no dream of days that might have been,
Had you and Laura filled another fate ? —
Some cottage on the sloping Apennines,
Roses and lilies, and the rest all love ?
I tell you that this tranquil dream may be
Filled to repletion. Speak, and in the shade
Of my dark pinions I shall bear you hence,
And land you where the mountain-goat himself
Struggles for footing." He outspread his wings,
And all the chapel darkened, as though hell
Had swallowed up the tapers ; and the air
Grew thick, and, like a current sensible,
Flowed round the person, with a wash and dash,
As of the waters of a nether sea.
Slowly and calmly through the dense obscure,
Dove-like and gentle, rose the artist's voice :
"I dare not bring her spirit to that shame !
Know my full meaning, — I who neither fear
Your mystic person nor your dreadful power.
Nor shall I now invoke God's potent name
For my deliverance from your toils. I stand
Upon the founded structure of his law,
Established from the first, and thence defy
Your arts, reposing all my trust in that !"
The darkness eddied off ; and Carlo saw
The figure gathering, as from outer space,
Brightness on brightness ; and his former shape
Fell from him, like the ashes that fall off,
And show a core of mellow fire within.
Adown his wings there poured a lambent flood,
That seemed as molten gold, which plashing fell
Upon the floor, enringing him with flame ;
And o'er the tresses of his beaming head
Arose a stream of many-colored light,
Like that which crowns the morning. Carlo stood
Steadfast, for all the splendor, reaching up
The outstretched palms of his untainted soul
Towards heaven for strength. A moment thus ;
    then asked,
With reverential wonder quivering through
His sinking voice, "Who, spirit, and what, art
    thou ?"
"I am that blessing which men fly from, —
    Death."
"Then take my hand, if so God orders it ;
For Laura waits me." "But, bethink thee, man,
What the world loses in the loss of thee !

What wondrous art will suffer with eclipse !
What unwon glories are in store for thee !
What fame, outreaching time and temporal shocks,
Would shine upon the letters of thy name
Graven in marble, or the brazen height
Of columns wise with memories of thee ! "
" Take me ! If I outlived the Patriarchs,
I could but paint those features o'er and o'er :
Lo ! that is done."   A smile of pity lit
The seraph's features, as he looked to heaven,
With deep inquiry in his tender eyes.
The mandate came. He touched with downy wing
The sufferer lightly on his aching heart ;
And gently, as the skylark settles down
Upon the clustered treasures of her nest,
So Carlo softly slid along the prop
Of his tall easel, nestling at the foot
As though he slumbered ; and the morning broke
In silver whiteness over Padua.

GEORGE HENRY BOKER.

THE IMMOLATION OF CONSTANCE DE BEVERLEY.

FROM " MARMION."

THE Abbess was of noble blood,
But early took the veil and hood,
Ere upon life she cast a look,
Or knew the world that she forsook.
Fair too she was, and kind had been
As she was fair, but ne'er had seen
For her a timid lover sigh,
Nor knew the influence of her eye.
Love, to her ear, was but a name,
Combined with vanity and shame ;
Her hopes, her fears, her joys, were all
Bounded within the cloister wall :
The deadliest sin her mind could reach
Was of monastic rule the breach ;
And her ambition's highest aim
To emulate Saint Hilda's fame.
For this she gave her ample dower
To raise the convent's eastern tower ;
For this, with carving rare and quaint,
She decked the chapel of the saint,
And gave the relic-shrine of cost,
With ivory and gems embost.
The poor her convent's bounty blest,
The pilgrim in its halls found rest.

Black was her garb, her rigid rule
Reformed on Benedictine school ;
Her cheek was pale, her form was spare ;
Vigils, and penitence austere,
Had early quenched the light of youth,
But gentle was the dame, in sooth ;

Though, vain of her religious sway,
She loved to see her maids obey ;
Yet nothing stern was she in cell,
And the nuns loved their Abbess well.
Sad was this voyage to the dame ;
Summoned to Lindisfarne, she came,
There, with Saint Cuthbert's Abbot old,
And Tynemouth's Prioress, to hold
A chapter of Saint Benedict,
For inquisition stern and strict,
On two apostates from the faith,
And, if need were, to doom to death.

.   .   .   .   .

    Saint Hilda's nuns would learn.
If, on a rock, by Lindisfarne,
Saint Cuthbert sits, and toils to frame
The sea-born beads that bear his name ;
Such tales had Whitby's fishers told,
And said they might his shape behold,
    And hear his anvil sound ;
A deadened clang, — a huge dim form,
Seen but, and heard, when gathering storm
    And night were closing round.
But this, as tale of idle fame,
The nuns of Lindisfarne disclaim.

While round the fire such legends go,
Far different was the scene of woe,
Where, in a secret aisle beneath,
Council was held of life and death.
    It was more dark and lone, that vault,
        Than the worst dungeon cell ;
    Old Colwulf built it, for his fault
        In penitence to dwell,
When he, for cowl and beads, laid down
The Saxon battle-axe and crown.
This den which, chilling every sense
    Of feeling, hearing, sight,
Was called the Vault of Penitence,
    Excluding air and light,
Was, by the prelate Sexhelm, made
A place of burial for such dead
As, having died in mortal sin,
Might not be laid the church within.
'T was now a place of punishment ;
Whence if so loud a shriek were sent
    As reached the upper air,
The hearers blessed themselves, and said,
The spirits of the sinful dead
    Bemoaned their torments there.

But though, in the monastic pile,
Did of this penitential aisle
    Some vague tradition go,
Few only, save the Abbot, knew
Where the place lay ; and still more few
Were those who had from him the clew
    To that dread vault to go.

THE CONVENT.

"Her hopes, her fears, her joys, were all
Bounded within the cloister wall.

Victim and executioner
Were blindfold when transported there.
In low dark rounds the arches hung,
From the rude rock the side-walls sprung;
The gravestones, rudely sculptured o'er,
Half sunk in earth, by time half wore,
Were all the pavement of the floor;
The mildew-drops fell one by one,
With tinkling splash, upon the stone.
A cresset, in an iron chain,
Which served to light this drear domain,
With damp and darkness seemed to strive,
As if it scarce might keep alive;
And yet it dimly served to show
The awful conclave met below.

There, met to doom in secrecy,
Were placed the heads of convents three:
All servants of Saint Benedict,
The statutes of whose order strict
    On iron table lay;
In long black dress, on seats of stone,
Behind were these three judges shown
    By the pale cresset's ray:
The Abbess of Saint Hilda there
Sate for a pace with visage bare,
Until, to hide her bosom's swell,
And tear-drops that for pity fell,
    She closely drew her veil.
Yon shrouded figure, as I guess,
By her proud mien and flowing dress,
Is Tynemouth's haughty Prioress,
    And she with awe looks pale.
And he, that Ancient Man, whose sight
Has long been quenched by age's night,
Upon whose wrinkled brow alone
Nor ruth nor mercy's trace is shown,
    Whose look is hard and stern, —
Saint Cuthbert's Abbot is his style;
For sanctity called, through the Isle,
    The Saint of Lindisfarne.

Before them stood a guilty pair;
But, though an equal fate they share,
Yet one alone deserves our care.
Her sex a page's dress belied;
The cloak and doublet, loosely tied,
Obscured her charms, but could not hide.
    Her cap down o'er her face she drew;
    And, on her doublet breast,
    She tried to hide the badge of blue,
    Lord Marmion's falcon crest.
But at the Prioress' command,
A monk undid the silken band
    That tied her tresses fair,
And raised the bonnet from her head,
And down her slender form they spread
    In ringlets rich and rare.

Constance de Beverley they know,
Sister professed of Fontevraud,
Whom the church numbered with the dead,
For broken vows, and convent fled.

When thus her face was given to view,
(Although so pallid was her hue,
It did a ghastly contrast bear
To those bright ringlets glistering fair,)
Her look composed, and steady eye,
Bespoke a matchless constancy;
And there she stood so calm and pale
That, but her breathing did not fail,
And motion slight of eye and head,
And of her bosom, warranted
That neither sense nor pulse she lacks,
You might have thought a form of wax,
Wrought to the very life, was there;
So still she was, so pale, so fair.

Her comrade was a sordid soul,
    Such as does murder for a meed;
Who, but of fear, knows no control,
Because his conscience, seared and foul,
    Feels not the import of his deed:
One whose brute feeling ne'er aspires
Beyond his own more brute desires.
Such tools the tempter ever needs
To do the savagest of deeds;
For them no visioned terrors daunt,
Their nights no fancied spectres haunt;
One fear with them, of all most base, —
The fear of death, — alone finds place.
This wretch was clad in frock and cowl,
And shamed not loud to mourn and howl,
His body on the floor to dash,
And crouch, like hound beneath the lash;
While his mute partner, standing near,
Waited her doom without a tear.

Yet well the luckless wretch might shriek,
Well might her paleness terror speak!
For there was seen, in that dark wall,
Two niches, narrow, deep, and tall.
Who enters at such grisly door,
Shall ne'er, I ween, find exit more.
In each a slender meal was laid
Of roots, of water, and of bread:
By each, in Benedictine dress,
Two haggard monks stood motionless,
Who, holding high a blazing torch,
Showed the grim entrance of the porch:
Reflecting back the smoky beam,
The dark red walls and arches gleam.
Hewn stones and cement were displayed,
And building-tools in order laid.

These executioners were chose
As men who were with mankind foes,

And, with despite and envy fired,
Into the cloister had retired ;
  Or who, in desperate doubt of grace,
  Strove, by deep penance, to efface
    Of some foul crime the stain ;
  For, as the vassals of her will,
  Such men the Church selected still,
  As either joyed in doing ill
    Or thought more grace to gain,
If, in her cause, they wrestled down
Feelings their nature strove to own.
By strange device were they brought there,
They knew not how, and knew not where.

And now that blind old Abbot rose,
  To speak the Chapter's doom
On those the wall was to enclose
  Alive within the tomb ;
But stopped, because that woful maid,
Gathering her powers, to speak essayed.
Twice she essayed, and twice in vain ;
Her accents might no utterance gain ;
Naught but imperfect murmurs slip
From her convulsed and quivering lip.
  'Twixt each attempt all was so still,
  You seemed to hear a distant rill, —
    'T was ocean's swell and falls ;
  For though this vault of sin and fear
  Was to the sounding surge so near,
  A tempest there you scarce could hear,
    So massive were the walls.

At length an effort sent apart
The blood that curdled to her heart,
  And light came to her eye,
And color dawned upon her cheek,
A hectic and a fluttered streak,
Like that left on the Cheviot peak
  By autumn's stormy sky ;
And when her silence broke at length,
Still as she spoke she gathered strength,
  And armed herself to bear.
It was a fearful sight to see
Such high resolve and constancy
  In form so soft and fair.

" I speak not to implore your grace ;
Well know I for one minute's space
  Successless might I sue.
Nor do I speak your prayers to gain ;
For if a death of lingering pain
To cleanse my sins be penance vain,
  Vain are your masses too.
I listened to a traitor's tale,
I left the convent and the veil ;
For three long years I bowed my pride,
A horse-boy in his train to ride ;
And well my folly's meed he gave,

Who forfeited, to be his slave,
All here, and all beyond the grave.
He saw young Clara's face more fair,
He knew her of broad lands the heir,
Forgot his vows, his faith forswore,
And Constance was beloved no more.
  'T is an old tale, and often told ;
    But, did my fate and wish agree,
  Ne'er had been read, in story old,
  Of maiden true betrayed for gold,
    That loved, or was avenged, like me.

" The King approved his favorite's aim ;
In vain a rival barred his claim,
  Whose faith with Clare's was plight,
For he attaints that rival's fame
With treason's charge, — and on they came,
  In mortal lists to fight.
    Their oaths are said,
    Their prayers are prayed,
    Their lances in the rest are laid,
  They meet in mortal shock ;
And, hark ! the throng, with thundering cry,
Shout ' Marmion, Marmion, to the sky !
  De Wilton to the block ! '
Say ye, who preach Heaven shall decide,
When in the lists two champions ride,
  Say, was Heaven's justice here,
When, loyal in his love and faith,
Wilton found overthrow or death
  Beneath a traitor's spear ?
How false the charge, how true he fell,
This guilty packet best can tell." —
Then drew a packet from her breast,
Paused, gathered voice, and spoke the rest.

" Still was false Marmion's bridal stayed ;
To Whitby's convent fled the maid,
  The hated match to shun.
' Ho ! shifts she thus ?' King Henry cried ;
' Sir Marmion, she shall be thy bride,
  If she were sworn a nun.'
One way remained, — the King's command
Sent Marmion to the Scottish land ;
I lingered here, and rescue planned
  For Clara and for me.
This caitiff monk for gold did swear
He would to Whitby's shrine repair,
And, by his drugs, my rival fair
  A saint in heaven should be.
But ill the dastard kept his oath,
Whose cowardice hath undone us both.

" And now my tongue the secret tells,
Not that remorse my bosom swells,
But to assure my soul that none
Shall ever wed with Marmion.
Had fortune my last hope betrayed,
This packet, to the King conveyed,

Had given him to the headsman's stroke,
Although my heart that instant broke. —
Now, men of death, work forth your will,
For I can suffer, and be still ;
And come he slow, or come he fast,
It is but Death who comes at last.

"Yet dread me, from my living tomb,
Ye vassal slaves of bloody Rome !
If Marmion's late remorse should wake,
Full soon such vengeance will he take,
That you shall wish the fiery Dane
Had rather been your guest again.
Behind, a darker hour ascends !
The altars quake, the crosier bends,
The ire of a despotic king
Rides forth upon destruction's wing ;
Then shall these vaults, so strong and deep,
Burst open to the sea-winds' sweep.
Some traveller then shall find my bones
Whitening amid disjointed stones,
And, ignorant of priests' cruelty,
Marvel such relics here should be."

Fixed was her look, and stern her air,
Back from her shoulders streamed her hair ;
The locks, that wont her brow to shade,
Stared up erectly from her head ;
Her figure seemed to rise more high ;
Her voice, despair's wild energy
Had given a tone of prophecy.
Appalled the astonished conclave sate ;
With stupid eyes the men of fate
Gazed on the light inspired form,
And listened for the avenging storm.
The judges felt the victim's dread ;
No hand was moved, no word was said,
Till thus the Abbot's doom was given,
Raising his sightless balls to heaven : —
"Sister, let thy sorrows cease ;
Sinful brother, part in peace !"
From that dire dungeon, place of doom,
Of execution too, and tomb,
    Paced forth the judges three ;
Sorrow it were, and shame, to tell
The butcher-work that there befell,
When they had glided from the cell
    Of sin and misery.

An hundred winding steps convey
That conclave to the upper day ;
But, ere they breathed the fresher air,
They heard the shriekings of despair,
    And many a stifled groan ;
With speed their upward way they take
(Such speed as age and fear can make),
And crossed themselves for terror's sake,
    As hurrying, tottering on ;

Even in the vesper's heavenly tone
They seemed to hear a dying groan,
And bade the passing knell to toll
For welfare of a parting soul.
Slow o'er the midnight wave it swung,
Northumbrian rocks in answer rung ;
To Warkworth cell the echoes rolled,
His beads the wakeful hermit told ;
The Bamborough peasant raised his head,
But slept ere half a prayer he said ;
So far was heard the mighty knell,
The stag sprung up on Cheviot Fell,
Spread his broad nostril to the wind,
Listed before, aside, behind,
Then couched him down beside the hind,
And quaked among the mountain fern,
To hear that sound so dull and stern.
                    SIR WALTER SCOTT.

THE SACK OF BALTIMORE.

[Baltimore is a small seaport in the barony of Carbery, in South Munster. It grew up round a castle of O'Driscoll's, and was, after his ruin, colonized by the English. On the 20th of June, 1631, the crew of two Algerine galleys landed in the dead of the night, sacked the town, and bore off into slavery all who were not too old, or too young, or too fierce, for their purpose. The pirates were steered up the intricate channel by one Hackett, a Dungarvan fisherman, whom they had taken at sea for their purpose. Two years after he was convicted, and executed for the crime. Baltimore never recovered from this.]

THE summer sun is falling soft on Carbery's hundred isles,
The summer's sun is gleaming still through Gabriel's rough defiles, —
Old Inisherkin's crumbled fane looks like a moulting bird ;
And in a calm and sleepy swell the ocean tide is heard :
The hookers lie upon the beach ; the children cease their play ;
The gossips leave the little inn ; the households kneel to pray, —
And full of love and peace and rest, — its daily labor o'er, —
Upon that cosey creek there lay the town of Baltimore.

A deeper rest, a starry trance, has come with midnight there ;
No sound, except that throbbing wave, in earth or sea or air.
The massive capes and ruined towers seem conscious of the calm ;
The fibrous sod and stunted trees are breathing heavy balm.
So still the night, these two long barks round Dunashad that glide
Must trust their oars — methinks not few — against the ebbing tide, —

O, some sweet mission of true love must urge
    them to the shore, —
They bring some lover to his bride, who sighs in
    Baltimore !

All, all asleep within each roof along that rocky
    street,
And these must be the lover's friends, with gently
    gliding feet.
A stifled gasp ! a dreamy noise ! "The roof is in
    a flame !"
From out their beds, and to their doors, rush
    maid and sire and dame,
And meet, upon the threshold stone, the gleam-
    ing sabre's fall,
And o'er each black and bearded face the white
    or crimson shawl ;
The yell of "Allah !" breaks above the prayer
    and shriek and roar.
O blesséd God, the Algerine is lord of Baltimore !

Then flung the youth his naked hand against the
    shearing sword ;
Then sprung the mother on the brand with which
    her son was gored ;
Then sunk the grandsire on the floor, his grand-
    babes clutching wild ;
Then fled the maiden moaning faint, and nestled
    with the child.
But see, yon pirate strangling lies, and crushed
    with splashing heel,
While o'er him in an Irish hand there sweeps his
    Syrian steel ;
Though virtue sink, and courage fail, and misers
    yield their store,
There 's *one* hearth well avengéd in the sack of
    Baltimore !

Midsummer morn, in woodland nigh, the birds
    begin to sing ;
They see not now the milking-maids, deserted is
    the spring !
Midsummer day, this gallant rides from distant
    Bandon's town,
These hookers crossed from stormy Skull, that
    skiff from Affadown.
They only found the smoking walls with neigh-
    bors' blood besprent,
And on the strewed and trampled beach awhile
    they wildly went,
Then dashed to sea, and passed Cape Clear, and
    saw, five leagues before,
The pirate-galleys vanishing that ravaged Balti-
    more.

O, some must tug the galley's oar, and some must
    tend the steed, —
This boy will bear a Scheik's chibouk, and that
    a Bey's jerreed.

O, some are for the arsenals by beauteous Dar-
    danelles,
And some are in the caravan to Mecca's sandy dells.
The maid that Bandon gallant sought is chosen
    for the Dey, —
She 's safe, — she 's dead, — she stabbed him in
    the midst of his Serai ;
And when to die a death of fire that noble maid
    they bore,
She only smiled, — O'Driscoll's child, — she
    thought of Baltimore.

'T is two long years since sunk the town beneath
    that bloody band,
And all around its trampled hearths a larger con-
    course stand,
Where high upon a gallows-tree a yelling wretch
    is seen, —
'T is Hackett of Dungarvan, — he who steered
    the Algerine !
He fell amid a sullen shout, with scarce a passing
    prayer,
For he had slain the kith and kin of many a hun-
    dred there :
Some muttered of MacMorrogh, who had brought
    the Norman o'er,
Some cursed him with Iscariot, that day in Balti-
    more.   THOMAS DAVIS.

GOD'S JUDGMENT ON HATTO.

[Hatto, Archbishop of Mentz, in the year 914 barbarously mur-
dered a number of poor people to prevent their consuming a por-
tion of the food during that year of famine. He was afterwards
devoured by rats in his tower on an island in the Rhine. —
Old Legend.]

THE summer and autumn had been so wet,
That in winter the corn was growing yet.
'T was a piteous sight to see all around
The grain lie rotting on the ground.

Every day the starving poor
They crowded around Bishop Hatto's door;
For he had a plentiful last-year's store,
And all the neighborhood could tell
His granaries were furnished well.

At last Bishop Hatto appointed a day
To quiet the poor without delay ;
He bade them to his great barn repair,
And they should have food for the winter there.

Rejoiced the tidings good to hear,
The poor folks flocked from far and near;
The great barn was full as it could hold
Of women and children, and young and old.

Then, when he saw it could hold no more,
Bishop Hatto he made fast the door ;

And whilst for mercy on Christ they call,
He set fire to the barn, and burnt them all.

"I' faith 't is an excellent bonfire!" quoth he;
"And the country is greatly obliged to me
For ridding it, in these times forlorn,
Of rats that only consume the corn."

So then to his palace returned he,
And he sate down to supper merrily,
And he slept that night like an innocent man;
But Bishop Hatto never slept again.

In the morning, as he entered the hall,
Where his picture hung against the wall,
A sweat like death all over him came,
For the rats had eaten it out of the frame.

As he looked, there came a man from his farm, —
He had a countenance white with alarm:
"My lord, I opened your granaries this morn,
And the rats had eaten all your corn."

Another came running presently,
And he was pale as pale could be.
"Fly! my lord bishop, fly!" quoth he,
"Ten thousand rats are coming this way, —
The Lord forgive you for yesterday!"

"I 'll go to my tower in the Rhine," replied he;
"'T is the safest place in Germany, —
The walls are high, and the shores are steep,
And the tide is strong, and the water deep."

Bishop Hatto fearfully hastened away;
And he crossed the Rhine without delay,
And reached his tower in the island, and barred
All the gates secure and hard.

He laid him down and closed his eyes,
But soon a scream made him arise;
He started, and saw two eyes of flame
On his pillow, from whence the screaming came.

He listened and looked, — it was only the cat;
But the bishop he grew more fearful for that,
For she sate screaming, mad with fear
At the army of rats that were drawing near.

For they have swum over the river so deep,
And they have climbed the shores so steep,
And now by thousands up they crawl
To the holes and the windows in the wall.

Down on his knees the bishop fell,
And faster and faster his beads did he tell,
As louder and louder, drawing near,
The saw of their teeth without he could hear.

And in at the windows, and in at the door,
And through the walls, by thousands they pour;

And down from the ceiling and up through the floor,
From the right and the left, from behind and before,
From within and without, from above and below, —
And all at once to the bishop they go.

They have whetted their teeth against the stones,
And now they pick the bishop's bones;
They gnawed the flesh from every limb,
For they were sent to do judgment on him!
ROBERT SOUTHEY.

PARRHASIUS.

PARRHASIUS stood, gazing forgetfully
Upon the canvas.   There Prometheus lay,
Chained to the cold rocks of Mount Caucasus,
The vulture at his vitals, and the links
Of the lame Lemnian festering in his flesh;
And, as the painter's mind felt through the dim
Rapt mystery, and plucked the shadows forth
With its far-reaching fancy, and with form
And color clad them, his fine, earnest eye
Flashed with a passionate fire, and the quick curl
Of his thin nostril, and his quivering lip,
Were like the winged god's breathing from his flights.

"Bring me the captive now!
My hand feels skilful, and the shadows lift
From my waked spirit airily and swift;
And I could paint the bow
Upon the bended heavens, — around me play
Colors of such divinity to-day.

"Ha! bind him on his back!
Look! as Prometheus in my picture here;
Quick, — or he faints! — stand with the cordial near!
Now, — bend him to the rack!
Press down the poisoned links into his flesh!
And tear agape that healing wound afresh!

"So, — let him writhe! How long
Will he live thus? Quick, my good pencil, now!
What a fine agony works upon his brow!
Ha! gray-haired, and so strong!
How fearfully he stifles that short moan!
Gods! could I but paint a dying groan!

"Pity thee! so I do!
I pity the dumb victim at the altar,
But does the robed priest for his pity falter?
I 'd rack thee, though I knew
A thousand lives were perishing in thine;
What were ten thousand to a fame like mine?

"Ah ! there 's a deathless name ! —
A spirit that the smothering vaults shall spurn,
And, like a steadfast planet, mount and burn ;
    And though its crown of flame
Consumed my brain to ashes as it shone,
By all the fiery stars, I 'd bind it on !

"Ay ! though it bid me rifle
My heart's last fount for its insatiate thirst, —
Though every life-strung nerve be maddened
    first, —
Though it should bid me stifle
The yearnings in my heart for my sweet child,
And taunt its mother till my brain went wild, —

"All, — I would do it all, —
Sooner than die, like a dull worm, to rot
Thrust foully in the earth to be forgot.
    O Heavens ! — but I appall
Your heart, old man ! — forgive — ha ! on your
    lives
Let him not faint ! rack him till he revives !

"Vain, — vain, — give o'er.   His eye
Glazes apace.   He does not feel you now, —
Stand back ! I 'll paint the death-dew on his brow !
    Gods ! if he do not die,
But for one moment — one — till I eclipse
Conception with the scorn of those calm lips !

"Shivering !   Hark ! he mutters
Brokenly now, — that was a difficult breath, —
Another ?   Wilt thou never come, O Death ?
    Look ! how his temple flutters !
Is his heart still ?   Aha ! lift up his head !
He shudders, — gasps, — Jove help him ! — so, —
    he 's dead ! "

How like a mountain devil in the heart
Rules the inreined ambition !   Let it once
But play the monarch, and its haughty brow
Glows with a beauty that bewilders thought
And unthrones peace forever.   Putting on
The very pomp of Lucifer, it turns
The heart to ashes, and with not a spring
Left in the desert for the spirit's lip,
We look upon our splendor, and forget
The thirst of which we perish !
                    NATHANIEL PARKER WILLIS.

SELECTIONS FROM "MACBETH."

THE PARLEY.

MACBETH.   If it were done, when 't is done,
    then 't were well
It were done quickly : if the assassination
Could trammel up the consequence, and catch,

With his surcease, success ; that but this blow
Might be the be-all and the end-all here.
But here, upon this bank and shoal of time, —
We 'd jump the life to come.   But in these cases,
We still have judgment here ; that we but teach
Bloody instructions, which, being taught, return
To plague the inventor : this even-handed justice
Commends the ingredients of our poisoned chalice
To our own lips.   He 's here in double trust :
First, as I am his kinsman and his subject,
Strong both against the deed ; then, as his host,
Who should against his murderer shut the door,
Not bear the knife myself.   Besides, this Dun-
    can
Hath borne his faculties so meek, hath been
So clear in his great office, that his virtues
Will plead like angels, trumpet-tongued, against
The deep damnation of his taking-off ;
And pity, like a naked new-born babe,
Striding the blast, or heaven's cherubin, horsed
Upon the sightless couriers of the air,
Shall blow the horrid deed in every eye,
That tears shall drown the wind.   I have no spur
To prick the sides of my intent, but only
Vaulting ambition, which o'erleaps itself,
And falls on the other.

        .   .   .   .   .

We will proceed no farther in this business :
He hath honored me of late ; and I have bought
Golden opinions from all sorts of people,
Which would be worn now in their newest gloss,
Not cast aside so soon.
    LADY MACBETH.   Was the hope drunk,
Wherein you dressed yourself ? hath it slept since ?
And wakes it now, to look so green and pale
At what it did so freely ?   From this time,
Such I account thy love.   Art thou afeard
To be the same in thine own act and valor,
As thou art in desire ?   Wouldst thou have that
Which thou esteem'st the ornament of life,
And live a coward in thine own esteem,
Letting "I dare not" wait upon "I would,"
Like the poor cat i' the adage ?
    MACB.   Pr'ythee, peace :
I dare do all that may become a man ;
Who dares do more is none.
    LADY M.   What beast was 't, then,
That made you break this enterprise to me ?
When you durst do it, then you were a man ;
And, to be more than what you were, you would
Be so much more the man.   Nor time, nor place,
Did then adhere, and yet you would make both :
They have made themselves, and that their fit-
    ness now
Does unmake you.   I have given suck, and know
How tender 't is to love the babe that milks me :
I would, while it was smiling in my face,
Have plucked my nipple from his boneless gums,

And dashed the brains out, had I so sworn as you
Have done to this.

MACB. If we should fail?

LADY M. We fail!
But screw your courage to the sticking-place,
And we'll not fail.

. . . . .

MACB. I am settled, and bend up
Each corporal agent to this terrible feat.

THE MURDER.

MACBETH. Is this a dagger which I see before
  me,
The handle toward my hand? Come, let me clutch
  thee : —
I have thee not, and yet I see thee still.
Art thou not, fatal vision, sensible
To feeling as to sight? or art thou but
A dagger of the mind, a false creation,
Proceeding from the heat-oppresséd brain?
I see thee yet, in form as palpable
As this which now I draw.
Thou marshall'st me the way that I was going ;
And such an instrument I was to use.
Mine eyes are made the fools o' the other senses,
Or else worth all the rest : I see thee still ;
And on thy blade, and dudgeon gouts of blood,
Which was not so before.—There's no such thing :
It is the bloody business, which informs
Thus to mine eyes. — Now o'er the one half world
Nature seems dead, and wicked dreams abuse
The curtained sleep ; witchcraft celebrates
Pale Hecate's offerings ; and withered murder,
Alarumed by his sentinel, the wolf,
Whose howl's his watch, thus with his stealthy
  pace,
With Tarquin's ravishing strides, towards his
  design
Moves like a ghost. —Thou sure and firm-set earth,
Hear not my steps, which way they walk, for
  fear
The very stones prate of my whereabout,
And take the present horror from the time,
Which now suits with it. — Whiles I threat, he
  lives :
Words to the heat of deeds too cold breath gives.
            [A bell rings.
I go, and it is done ; the bell invites me.
Hear it not, Duncan ; for it is a knell
That summons thee to heaven or to hell.

. . . . .

I have done the deed. —Didst thou not hear a
  noise?

LADY MACBETH. I heard the owl scream, and
  the crickets cry.
Did not you speak?

MACB. When?

LADY M. Now.

MACB. As I descended?

LADY M. Ay.

MACB. Hark! —
Who lies i' the second chamber?

LADY M. Donalbain.

MACB. [Looking on his hands.] This is a sorry
  sight.

LADY M. A foolish thought, to say a sorry sight.

MACB. There's one did laugh in 's sleep, and
  one cried, "murder!"
That they did wake each other : I stood and heard
  them :
But they did say their prayers, and addressed
  them
Again to sleep.

LADY M. There are two lodged together.

MACB. One cried, "God bless us!" and,
  "Amen," the other ;
As they had seen me with these hangman's hands.
Listening their fear, I could not say, "Amen,"
When they did say, "God bless us."

LADY M. Consider it not so deeply.

MACB. But wherefore could not I pronounce
  "Amen"?
I had most need of blessing, and "Amen"
Stuck in my throat.

LADY M. These deeds must not be thought
After these ways ; so, it will make us mad.

MACB. Methought I heard a voice cry "Sleep
  no more!
Macbeth does murder sleep," — the innocent sleep,
Sleep that knits up the ravelled sleave of care,
The death of each day's life, sore labor's bath,
Balm of hurt minds, great nature's second course,
Chief nourisher in life's feast, —

LADY M. What do you mean?

MACB. Still it cried, "Sleep no more!" to all
  the house :
"Glamis hath murdered sleep ; and therefore
  Cawdor
Shall sleep no more, — Macbeth shall sleep no
  more!"

LADY M. Who was it that thus cried? Why,
  worthy thane,
You do unbend your noble strength, to think
So brainsickly of things. — Go, get some water,
And wash this filthy witness from your hand. —
Why did you bring these daggers from the place?
They must lie there : go carry them ; and smear
The sleepy grooms with blood.

MACB. I'll go no more!
I am afraid to think what I have done ;
Look on't again, I dare not.

LADY M. Infirm of purpose!
Give me the daggers : the sleeping, and the dead,
Are but as pictures : 'tis the eye of childhood
That fears a painted devil. If he do bleed,

I 'll gild the faces of the grooms withal ;
For it must seem their guilt.

[Exit. Knocking heard.

MACB. Whence is that knocking ?
How is 't with me, when every noise appalls me ?
What hands are here ! Ha ! they pluck out mine
  eyes !
Will all great Neptune's ocean wash this blood
Clean from my hand ? No ; this my hand will
  rather
The multitudinous seas incarnardine,
Making the green — one red.

Re-enter LADY MACBETH.

LADY M. My hands are of your color ; but I
  shame
To wear a heart so white. [*Knocking.*] I hear a
  knocking
At the south entry : — retire we to our chamber :
A little water clears us of this deed :
How easy is it, then !

THE REMORSE.

LADY MACBETH. Naught 's had, all 's spent,
Where our desire is got without content :
'T is safer to be that which we destroy,
Than, by destruction, dwell in doubtful joy.

Enter MACBETH.

How, now, my lord ? why do you keep alone,
Of sorriest fancies your companions making ;
Using those thoughts, which should indeed have
  died
With them they think on ? Things without
  remedy,
Should be without regard : what 's done, is done.
MACB. We have scotched the snake, not killed it :
She 'll close, and be herself ; whilst our poor malice
Remains in danger of her former tooth.
But let the frame of things disjoint,
Both the worlds suffer,
Ere we will eat our meal in fear, and sleep
In the affliction of these terrible dreams,
That shake us nightly : better be with the dead,
Whom we, to gain our peace, have sent to peace,
Than on the torture of the mind to lie
In restless ecstasy. Duncan is in his grave ;
After life's fitful fever, he sleeps well ;
Treason has done his worst : nor steel, nor poison,
Malice domestic, foreign levy, nothing,
Can touch him farther !
LADY M.   Come on ;
Gentle my lord, sleek o'er your rugged looks ;
Be bright and jovial among your guests to-night.
MACB. So shall I, love ; and so, I pray, be you :
Let your remembrance apply to Banquo ;
Present him eminence, both with eye and tongue ;
Unsafe the while, that we
Must lave our honors in these flattering streams ;

And make our faces vizards to our hearts,
Disguising what they are.

  .   .   .

          Come, seeling night,
Scarf up the tender eye of pitiful day ;
And with thy bloody and invisible hand
Cancel, and tear to pieces, that great bond
Which keeps me pale ! — Light thickens ; and
  the crow
Makes wing to the rooky wood :
Good things of day begin to droop and drowse ;
Whiles night's black agents to their prey do rouse.

Blood hath been shed ere now, i' the olden time,
Ere human statute purged the gentle weal ;
Ay, and since too, murders have been performed
Too terrible for the ear : the times have been,
That, when the brains were out, the man would die,
And there an end ; but now, they rise again,
With twenty mortal murders on their crowns,
And push us from our stools : this is more strange
Than such a murder is.

  .   .   .

          Can such things be,
And overcome us like a summer's cloud,
Without our special wonder ? You make me strange
Even to the disposition that I owe,
When now I think you can behold such sights,
And keep the natural ruby of your cheeks,
When mine are blanched with fear.

  .   .   .

        Seyton ! — I am sick at heart,
When I behold — Seyton, I say ! — This push
Will cheer me ever, or disseat me now.
I have lived long enough : my way of life
Is fallen into the sear, the yellow leaf ;
And that which should accompany old age,
As honor, love, obedience, troops of friends,
I must not look to have ; but, in their stead,
Curses, not loud, but deep, mouth-honor, breath,
Which the poor heart would fain deny, but dare not.

  .   .   .

How does your patient, doctor ?
DOCTOR.   Not so sick, my lord,
As she is troubled with thick-coming fancies,
That keep her from her rest.
MACB.   Cure her of that
Canst thou not minister to a mind diseased ;
Pluck from the memory a rooted sorrow ;
Raze out the written troubles of the brain ;
And, with some sweet oblivious antidote,
Cleanse the stuffed bosom of that perilous stuff,
Which weighs upon the heart ?
DOCT.   Therein the patient
Must minister to himself.
MACB. Throw physic to the dogs, — I 'll none
  of it.

  .   .   .

What is that noise ? [*A cry within of women.*
    SEYTON. It is the cry of women, my good lord.
    MACB. I have almost forgot the taste of fears :
The time has been, my senses would have cooled
To hear a night-shriek : and my fell of hair
Would at a dismal treatise rouse, and stir,
As life were in 't : I have supped full with horrors ;
Direness, familiar to my slaughterous thoughts,
Cannot once start me. — Wherefore was that cry ?
    SEY. The queen, my lord, is dead.
    MACB. She should have died hereafter ;
There would have been a time for such a word. —
To-morrow, and to-morrow, and to-morrow,
Creeps in this petty pace from day to day,
To the last syllable of recorded time ;
And all our yesterdays have lighted fools
The way to dusty death. Out, out, brief candle !
Life 's but a walking shadow ; a poor player,
That struts and frets his hour upon the stage,
And then is heard no more : it is a tale
Told by an idiot, full of sound and fury,
Signifying nothing.   SHAKESPEARE.

LUCIUS JUNIUS BRUTUS'S ORATION OVER THE BODY OF LUCRETIA.

WOULD you know why I summoned you to-
        gether ?
Ask ye what brings me here ? Behold this dagger,
Clotted with gore ! Behold that frozen corse !
See where the lost Lucretia sleeps in death !
She was the mark and model of the time,
The mould in which each female face was formed,
The very shrine and sacristy of virtue !
Fairer than ever was a form created
By youthful fancy when the blood strays wild,
And never-resting thought is all on fire !
The worthiest of the worthy ! Not the nymph
Who met old Numa in his hallowed walks,
And whispered in his ear her strains divine,
Can I conceive beyond her ; — the young choir
Of vestal virgins bent to her. 'T is wonderful
Amid the darnel, hemlock, and base weeds,
Which now spring rife from the luxurious com-
        post
Spread o'er the realm, how this sweet lily rose, —
How from the shade of those ill-neighboring
        plants
Her father sheltered her, that not a leaf
Was blighted, but, arrayed in purest grace,
She bloomed unsullied beauty. Such perfections
Might have called back the torpid breast of age
To long-forgotten rapture ; such a mind
Might have abashed the boldest libertine
And turned desire to reverential love
And holiest affection ! O my countrymen !

You all can witness when that she went forth
It was a holiday in Rome ; old age
Forgot its crutch, labor its task, — all ran,
And mothers, turning to their daughters, cried,
"There, there 's Lucretia !" Now look ye where
        she lies !
That beauteous flower, that innocent sweet rose,
Torn up by ruthless violence, — gone ! gone ! gone !
    Say, would you seek instruction ? would ye ask
What ye should do ? Ask ye yon conscious walls,
Which saw his poisoned brother, —
Ask yon deserted street, where Tullia drove
O'er her dead father's corse, 't will cry, Revenge !
Ask yonder senate-house, whose stones are purple
With human blood, and it will cry, Revenge !
Go to the tomb where lies his murdered wife,
And the poor queen, who loved him as her son,
Their unappeased ghosts will shriek, Revenge !
The temples of the gods, the all-viewing heavens,
The gods themselves, shall justify the cry,
And swell the general sound, Revenge ! Revenge !
    And we will be revenged, my countrymen !
Brutus shall lead you on ; Brutus, a name
Which will, when you 're revenged, be dearer to
        him
Than all the noblest titles earth can boast.
    Brutus your king ! — No, fellow-citizens !
If mad ambition in this guilty frame
Had strung one kingly fibre, yea, but one, —
By all the gods, this dagger which I hold
Should rip it out, though it intwined my heart.
    Now take the body up. Bear it before us
To Tarquin's palace ; there we 'll light our torches,
And in the blazing conflagration rear
A pile, for these chaste relics, that shall send
Her soul amongst the stars. On ! Brutus leads
        you !   JOHN HOWARD PAYNE.

ANTONY'S ORATION OVER THE BODY OF CÆSAR.

FROM "JULIUS CÆSAR."

ANTONY. O mighty Cæsar ! dost thou lie so low ?
Are all thy conquests, glories, triumphs, spoils,
Shrunk to this little measure ? — Fare thee well. —

.   .   .   .

TO THE CONSPIRATORS.

            I doubt not of your wisdom.
Let each man render me his bloody hand :
First, Marcus Brutus, will I shake with you ; —
Next, Caius Cassius, do I take your hand ; —
Now, Decius Brutus, yours ; — now yours, Metellus ;
Yours, Cinna ; — and, my valiant Casca, yours ; —
Though last, not least in love, yours, good Tre-
bonius.

Gentlemen all, — alas ! what shall I say ?
My credit now stands on such slippery ground,
That one of two bad ways you must conceit me,
Either a coward or a flatterer. —
That I did love thee, Cæsar, O, 't is true :
If, then, thy spirit look upon us now,
Shall it not grieve thee dearer than thy death,
To see thy Antony making his peace,
Shaking the bloody fingers of thy foes,
Most noble ! in the presence of thy corse ?
Had I as many eyes as thou hast wounds,
Weeping as fast as they stream forth thy blood,
It would become me better, than to close
In terms of friendship with thine enemies.
Pardon me, Julius ! — Here wast thou bayed, brave
    hart ;
Here didst thou fall ; and here thy hunters stand,
Signed in thy spoil, and crimsoned in thy lethe.
O world, thou wast the forest to this hart ;
And this, indeed, O world, the heart of thee. —
How like a deer, stricken by many princes,
Dost thou here lie ?

.   .   .   .   .

TO THE PEOPLE.

Friends, Romans, countrymen, lend me your
    ears ;
I come to bury Cæsar, not to praise him.
The evil that men do lives after them ;
The good is oft interred with their bones ;
So let it be with Cæsar.   The noble Brutus
Hath told you Cæsar was ambitious :
If it was so, it was a grievous fault ;
And grievously hath Cæsar answered it.
Here, under leave of Brutus and the rest,
(For Brutus is an honorable man ;
So are they all, all honorable men,)
Come I to speak in Cæsar's funeral.
He was my friend, faithful and just to me :
But Brutus says he was ambitious ;
And Brutus is an honorable man.
He hath brought many captives home to Rome,
Whose ransoms did the general coffers fill :
Did this in Cæsar seem ambitious ?
When that the poor have cried, Cæsar hath wept :
Ambition should be made of sterner stuff :
Yet Brutus says he was ambitious ;
And Brutus is an honorable man.
You all did see that on the Lupercal
I thrice presented him a kingly crown,
Which he did thrice refuse : was this ambition ?
Yet Brutus says he was ambitious ;
And, sure, he is an honorable man.
I speak not to disprove what Brutus spoke,
But here I am to speak what I do know.
You all did love him once, — not without cause :
What cause withholds you, then, to mourn for him ?

O judgment, thou art fled to brutish beasts,
And men have lost their reason ! — Bear with me ;
My heart is in the coffin there with Cæsar,
And I must pause till it come back to me.

.   .   .   .   .

But yesterday, the word of Cæsar might
Have stood against the world : now lies he there,
And none so poor to do him reverence.
O masters ! if I were disposed to stir
Your hearts and minds to mutiny and rage,
I should do Brutus wrong, and Cassius wrong,
Who, you all know, are honorable men :
I will not do them wrong ; I rather choose
To wrong the dead, to wrong myself, and you,
Than I will wrong such honorable men.
But here's a parchment, with the seal of Cæsar, —
I found it in his closet, — 't is his will :
Let but the commons hear this testament,
(Which, pardon me, I do not mean to read,)
And they would go and kiss dead Cæsar's wounds,
And dip their napkins in his sacred blood ;
Yea, beg a hair of him for memory,
And, dying, mention it within their wills,
Bequeathing it, as a rich legacy,
Unto their issue.
    4 CITIZEN. We 'll hear the will : read it, Mark
        Antony.
    CITIZENS. The will, the will ! we will hear
        Cæsar's will.
    ANT. Have patience, gentle friends, I must not
        read it ;
It is not meet you know how Cæsar loved you.
You are not wood, you are not stones, but men ;
And, being men, hearing the will of Cæsar,
It will inflame you, it will make you mad :
'T is good you know not that you are his heirs,
For if you should, O, what would come of it !
    4 CIT. Read the will ; we 'll hear it, Antony ;
You shall read us the will, — Cæsar's will.
    ANT. Will you be patient ?   Will you stay a
        while ?
I have o'ershot myself to tell you of it.
I fear I wrong the honorable men
Whose daggers have stabbed Cæsar ; I do fear it.
    4 CIT. They were traitors : honorable men !
    CIT. The will ! the testament !
    2 CIT. They were villains, murderers : the will !
        read the will !
    ANT. You will compel me, then, to read the
        will ?
Then make a ring about the corse of Cæsar,
And let me show you him that made the will.
Shall I descend ? and will you give me leave ?
    CITIZENS. Come down.
    ANT. Nay, press not so upon me ; stand far off.
    CITIZENS. Stand back ; room ; bear back.
    ANT. If you have tears, prepare to shed them
        now.

You all do know this mantle : I remember
The first time ever Cæsar put it on ;
'T was on a summer's evening, in his tent ;
That day he overcame the Nervii : —
Look, in this place ran Cassius' dagger through :
See what a rent the envious Casca made :
Through this the well-belovéd Brutus stabbed ;
And, as he plucked his cursed steel away,
Mark how the blood of Cæsar followed it,
As rushing out of doors, to be resolved
If Brutus so unkindly knocked, or no ;
For Brutus, as you know, was Cæsar's angel :
Judge, O you gods, how dearly Cæsar loved
    him !
This was the most unkindest cut of all ;
For when the noble Cæsar saw him stab,
Ingratitude, more strong than traitors' arms,
Quite vanquished him : then burst his mighty
    heart ;
And, in his mantle muffling up his face,
Even at the base of Pompey's statua,
Which all the while ran blood, great Cæsar fell.
O, what a fall was there, my countrymen !
Then I, and you, and all of us fell down,
Whilst bloody treason flourished over us.
O, now you weep ; and, I perceive, you feel
The dint of pity : these are gracious drops.
Kind souls, what, weep you when you but behold
Our Cæsar's vesture wounded ?   Look you here,
Here is himself, marred, as you see, with traitors.

Good friends, sweet friends, let me not stir
    you up
To such a sudden flood of mutiny.
They that have done this deed are honorable ; —
What private griefs they have, alas, I know not,
That made them do it ; — they are wise and
    honorable,
And will, no doubt, with reasons answer you.
I come not, friends, to steal away your hearts ;
I am no orator, as Brutus is ;
But, as you know me all, a plain blunt man,
That love my friend ; and that they know full
    well
That gave me public leave to speak of him :
For I have neither wit, nor words, nor worth,
Action, nor utterance, nor the power of speech,
To stir men's blood : I only speak right on ;
I tell you that which you yourselves do know ;
Show you sweet Cæsar's wounds, poor, poor dumb
    mouths,
And bid them speak for me : but were I Brutus,
And Brutus Antony, there were an Antony
Would ruffle up your spirits, and put a tongue
In every wound of Cæsar, that should move
The stones of Rome to rise and mutiny.

Here is the will, and under Cæsar's seal : —

To every Roman citizen he gives,
To every several man, seventy-five drachmas.
    2 CIT. Most noble Cæsar ! — we 'll revenge his
        death.
    3 CIT. O royal Cæsar !
    ANT. Hear me with patience.
    CITIZENS. Peace, ho !
    ANT. Moreover, he hath left you all his walks,
His private arbors, and new-planted orchards,
On this side Tiber ; he hath left them you,
And to your heirs forever, — common pleasures,
To walk abroad, and recreate yourselves.
Here was a Cæsar ! when comes such another ?
    1 CIT. Never, never ! — Come away, away !
We 'll burn his body in the holy place,
And with the brands fire the traitors' houses.
Take up the body.   SHAKESPEARE.

BEATRICE CENCI.

FROM "THE CENCI."

    BEATRICE.   O,
My God ! can it be possible I have
To die so suddenly ? So young to go
Under the obscure, cold, rotting, wormy ground !
To be nailed down into a narrow place ;
To see no more sweet sunshine ; hear no more
Blithe voice of living thing ; muse not again
Upon familiar thoughts, sad, yet thus lost, —
How fearful !

    LUCRETIA.   Child, perhaps
It will be granted.   We may all then live
To make these woes a tale for distant years ;
O, what a thought ! It gushes to my heart
Like the warm blood.
    BEATR.   Yet both will soon be cold.
O, trample out that thought ! Worse than despair,
Worse than the bitterness of death, is hope ;
It is the only ill which can find place
Upon the giddy, sharp, and narrow hour
Tottering beneath us. Plead with the swift frost
That it should spare the eldest flower of spring ;
Plead with awakening earthquake, o'er whose
    couch
Even now a city stands, fair, strong, and free ;
Now stench and blackness yawns, like death.
    O, plead
With famine, or wind-walking pestilence,
Blind lightning, or the deaf sea, not with man !
Cruel, cold, formal man ! righteous in words,
In deeds a Cain.   No, mother, we must die,
Since such is the reward of innocent lives,
Such the alleviation of worst wrongs.
And whilst our murderers live, and hard, cold men,
Smiling and slow, walk through a world of tears
To death as to life's sleep, 't were just the grave

Were some strange joy for us. Come, obscure
  Death,
And wind me in thine all-embracing arms !
Like a fond mother hide me in thy bosom,
And rock me to the sleep from which none wake.
                          PERCY BYSSHE SHELLEY.

OTHELLO'S DESPAIR.

FROM "OTHELLO, THE MOOR OF VENICE."

THE LAMENTATION.

O, NOW, forever
Farewell the tranquil mind ! farewell content !
Farewell the pluméd troop, and the big wars,
That make ambition virtue ! O, farewell !
Farewell the neighing steed, and the shrill trump,
The spirit-stirring drum, the ear-piercing fife,
The royal banner, and all quality,
Pride, pomp, and circumstance of glorious war !
And, O you mortal engines, whose rude throats
The immortal Jove's dread clamors counterfeit,
Farewell ! Othello's occupation 's gone !

    .   .   .   .   .

Had it pleased Heaven
To try me with affliction ; had he rained
All kinds of sores, and shames, on my bare head ;
Steeped me in poverty to the very lips ;
Given to captivity me and my utmost hopes ;
I should have found in some part of my soul
A drop of patience : but, alas, to make me
A fixed figure, for the time of scorn
To point his slow unmoving finger at ! —
Yet could I bear that too ; well, very well :
But there, where I have garnered up my heart, —
Where either I must live, or bear no life,
The fountain from the which my current runs,
Or else dries up ; to be discarded thence !

THE MURDER.

It is the cause, it is the cause, my soul, —
Let me not name it to you, you chaste stars ! —
It is the cause. — Yet I 'll not shed her blood ;
Nor scar that whiter skin of hers than snow,
And smooth as monumental alabaster.
Yet she must die, else she 'll betray more men.
Put out the light, and then — Put out the light !
If I quench thee, thou flaming minister,
I can again thy former light restore,
Should I repent me : — but once put out thy light,
Thou cunning'st pattern of excelling nature,
I know not where is that Promethean heat,
That can thy light relume. When I have plucked
  thy rose,
I cannot give it vital growth again,
It needs must wither : — I 'll smell it on the tree. —
                          [Kissing her.

O balmy breath, that dost almost persuade
Justice to break her sword ! — One more, one
  more : —
Be thus when thou art dead, and I will kill thee,
And love thee after : — one more, and this the last :
So sweet was ne'er so fatal. I must weep,
But they are cruel tears : this sorrow 's heavenly :
It strikes, where it doth love.

THE REMORSE.

                          Behold, I have a weapon ;
A better never did itself sustain
Upon a soldier's thigh : I have seen the day,
That, with this little arm and this good sword,
I have made my way through more impediments
Than twenty times your stop : — but, O vain boast !
Who can control his fate ? 't is not so now. —
Be not afraid, though you do see me weaponed ;
Here is my journey's end, here is my butt,
And very sea-mark of my utmost sail.
Do you go back dismayed ? 't is a lost fear ;
Man but a rush against Othello's breast,
And he retires : — where should Othello go ? —
Now, how dost thou look now ? O ill-starred wench !
Pale as thy smock ! when we shall meet at compt,
This look of thine will hurl my soul from heaven,
And fiends will snatch at it. Cold, cold, my girl ?
Even like thy chastity. —
O cursed, cursed slave ! — Whip me, ye devils,
From the possession of this heavenly sight !
Blow me about in winds ! roast me in sulphur !
Wash me in steep-down gulfs of liquid fire ! —
O Desdemona ! Desdemona ! dead ! Oh ! Oh ! Oh !

THE SUICIDE.

Soft you ; a word or two, before you go.
I have done the state some service, and they know
  it ; —
No more of that. — I pray you, in your letters,
When you shall these unlucky deeds relate,
Speak of me as I am ; nothing extenuate,
Nor set down aught in malice : then, must you
  speak
Of one that loved, not wisely, but too well :
Of one not easily jealous, but, being wrought,
Perplexed in the extreme ; of one, whose hand,
Like the base Indian, threw a pearl away,
Richer than all his tribe ; of one, whose subdued
  eyes,
Albeit unused to the melting mood,
Drop tears as fast as the Arabian trees
Their medicinal gum. Set you down this ;
And say, besides, — that in Aleppo once,
Where a malignant and a turbaned Turk
Beat a Venetian, and traduced the state,
I took by the throat the circumcised dog,
And smote him — thus.   [Stabs himself.
                          SHAKESPEARE.

THE DREAM OF EUGENE ARAM.

'T was in the prime of summer time,
  An evening calm and cool,
And four-and-twenty happy boys
  Came bounding out of school;
There were some that ran, and some that leapt
  Like troutlets in a pool.

Away they sped with gamesome minds
  And souls untouched by sin;
To a level mead they came, and there
  They drave the wickets in:
Pleasantly shone the setting sun
  Over the town of Lynn.

Like sportive deer they coursed about,
  And shouted as they ran,
Turning to mirth all things of earth
  As only boyhood can;
But the usher sat remote from all,
  A melancholy man!

His hat was off, his vest apart,
  To catch heaven's blessed breeze;
For a burning thought was in his brow,
  And his bosom ill at ease;
So he leaned his head on his hands, and read
  The book between his knees.

Leaf after leaf he turned it o'er,
  Nor ever glanced aside, —
For the peace of his soul he read that book
  In the golden eventide;
Much study had made him very lean,
  And pale, and leaden-eyed.

At last he shut the ponderous tome;
  With a fast and fervent grasp
He strained the dusky covers close,
  And fixed the brazen hasp:
"O God! could I so close my mind,
  And clasp it with a clasp!"

Then leaping on his feet upright,
  Some moody turns he took, —
Now up the mead, then down the mead,
  And past a shady nook, —
And, lo! he saw a little boy
  That pored upon a book.

"My gentle lad, what is 't you read, —
  Romance or fairy fable?
Or is it some historic page,
  Of kings and crowns unstable?"
The young boy gave an upward glance, —
  "It is 'The Death of Abel.'"

The usher took six hasty strides,
  As smit with sudden pain, —
Six hasty strides beyond the place,
  Then slowly back again;
And down he sat beside the lad,
  And talked with him of Cain;

And, long since then, of bloody men,
  Whose deeds tradition saves;
And lonely folk cut off unseen,
  And hid in sudden graves;
And horrid stabs, in groves forlorn;
  And murders done in caves;

And how the sprites of injured men
  Shriek upward from the sod,
Ay, how the ghostly hand will point
  To show the burial clod;
And unknown facts of guilty acts
  Are seen in dreams from God.

He told how murderers walk the earth
  Beneath the curse of Cain, —
With crimson clouds before their eyes,
  And flames about their brain;
For blood has left upon their souls
  Its everlasting stain!

"And well," quoth he, "I know for truth
  Their pangs must be extreme —
Woe, woe, unutterable woe! —
  Who spill life's sacred stream.
For why? Methought, last night I wrought
  A murder, in a dream!

"One that had never done me wrong, —
  A feeble man and old;
I led him to a lonely field, —
  The moon shone clear and cold:
Now here, said I, this man shall die,
  And I will have his gold!

"Two sudden blows with a ragged stick,
  And one with a heavy stone,
One hurried gash with a hasty knife, —
  And then the deed was done:
There was nothing lying at my feet
  But lifeless flesh and bone!

"Nothing but lifeless flesh and bone,
  That could not do me ill;
And yet I feared him all the more
  For lying there so still:
There was a manhood in his look
  That murder could not kill!

"And, lo! the universal air
  Seemed lit with ghastly flame, —
Ten thousand thousand dreadful eyes
  Were looking down in blame;
I took the dead man by his hand,
  And called upon his name.

"O God! it made me quake to see
  Such sense within the slain;
But, when I touched the lifeless clay,
  The blood gushed out amain!
For every clot a burning spot
  Was scorching in my brain!

"My head was like an ardent coal,
  My heart as solid ice ;
My wretched, wretched soul, I knew,
  Was at the Devil's price.
A dozen times I groaned, — the dead
  Had never groaned but twice.

"And now, from forth the frowning sky,
  From the heaven's topmost height,
I heard a voice, — the awful voice
  Of the blood-avenging sprite :
'Thou guilty man ! take up thy dead,
  And hide it from my sight !'

"And I took the dreary body up,
  And cast it in a stream, —
The sluggish water black as ink,
  The depth was so extreme :
My gentle boy, remember, this
  Is nothing but a dream !

"Down went the corse with a hollow plunge,
  And vanished in the pool ;
Anon I cleansed my bloody hands,
  And washed my forehead cool,
And sat among the urchins young,
  That evening, in the school.

"O Heaven ! to think of their white souls,
  And mine so black and grim !
I could not share in childish prayer,
  Nor join in evening hymn ;
Like a devil of the pit I seemed,
  'Mid holy cherubim !

"And Peace went with them, one and all,
  And each calm pillow spread ;
But Guilt was my grim chamberlain,
  That lighted me to bed,
And drew my midnight curtains round
  With fingers bloody red !

"All night I lay in agony,
  In anguish dark and deep ;
My fevered eyes I dared not close,
  But stared aghast at Sleep ;
For Sin had rendered unto her
  The keys of hell to keep !

"All night I lay in agony,
  From weary chime to chime ;
With one besetting horrid hint
  That racked me all the time, —
A mighty yearning, like the first
  Fierce impulse unto crime, —

"One stern tyrannic thought, that made
  All other thoughts its slave !
Stronger and stronger every pulse
  Did that temptation crave, —
Still urging me to go and see
  The dead man in his grave !

"Heavily I rose up, as soon
  As light was in the sky,
And sought the black accursèd pool
  With a wild, misgiving eye ;
And I saw the dead in the river-bed,
  For the faithless stream was dry.

"Merrily rose the lark, and shook
  The dew-drop from its wing ;
But I never marked its morning flight,
  I never heard it sing,
For I was stooping once again
  Under the horrid thing.

"With breathless speed, like a soul in chase,
  I took him up and ran ;
There was no time to dig a grave
  Before the day began, —
In a lonesome wood, with heaps of leaves,
  I hid the murdered man !

"And all that day I read in school,
  But my thought was otherwhere;
As soon as the midday task was done,
  In secret I was there, —
And a mighty wind had swept the leaves,
  And still the corse was bare !

"Then down I cast me on my face,
  And first began to weep,
For I knew my secret then was one
  That earth refused to keep, —
Or land or sea, though he should be
  Ten thousand fathoms deep.

"So wills the fierce avenging sprite,
  Till blood for blood atones !
Ay, though he 's buried in a cave,
  And trodden down with stones,
And years have rotted off his flesh, —
  The world shall see his bones !

"O God ! that horrid, horrid dream
  Besets me now awake !
Again — again, with dizzy brain,
  The human life I take ;
And my red right hand grows raging hot,
  Like Cranmer's at the stake.

"And still no peace for the restless clay
  Will wave or mould allow ;
The horrid thing pursues my soul, —
  It stands before me now !"
The fearful boy looked up, and saw
  Huge drops upon his brow.

That very night, while gentle sleep
  The urchin's eyelids kissed,
Two stern-faced men set out from Lynn
  Through the cold and heavy mist ;
And Eugene Aram walked between,
  With gyves upon his wrist.

                                 THOMAS HOOD.

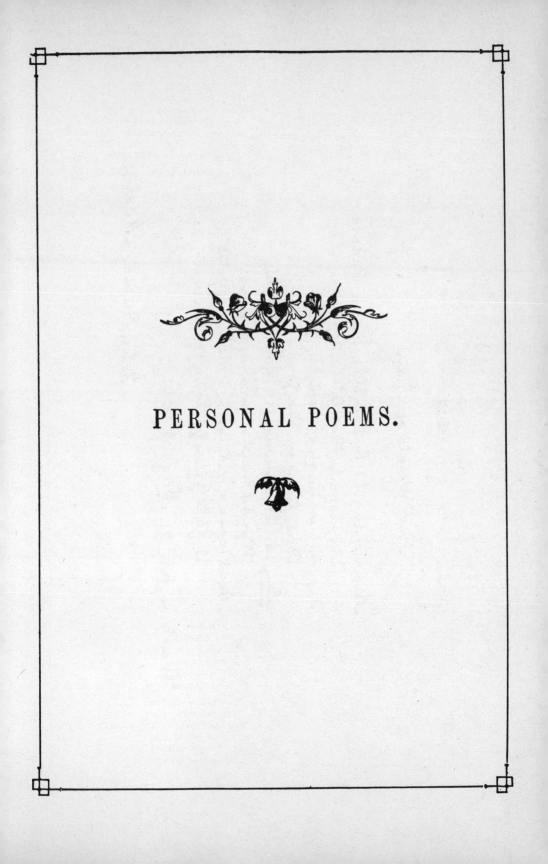

PERSONAL POEMS.

The Wants of Man

"Man wants but little here below:
"Nor wants that little, long".
'Tis not with me exactly so:
But 'tis so, in the song.

My wants are many, and if told,
Would muster many a score;
And were each wish a mint of gold
I still should long for more

Washington 21. August 1841.

John Quincy Adams.

PERSONAL POEMS.

ANNE HATHAWAY.

TO THE IDOL OF MY EYE AND DELIGHT OF MY HEART,
ANNE HATHAWAY.

WOULD ye be taught, ye feathered throng,
With love's sweet notes to grace your song,
To pierce the heart with thrilling lay,
Listen to mine Anne Hathaway!
She hath a way to sing so clear,
Phœbus might wondering stop to hear.
To melt the sad, make blithe the gay,
And nature charm, Anne hath a way;
    She hath a way,
    Anne Hathaway;
To breathe delight Anne hath a way.

When Envy's breath and rancorous tooth
Do soil and bite fair worth and truth,
And merit to distress betray,
To soothe the heart Anne hath a way.
She hath a way to chase despair,
To heal all grief, to cure all care,
Turn foulest night to fairest day.
Thou know'st, fond heart, Anne hath a way;
    She hath a way,
    Anne Hathaway;
To make grief bliss, Anne hath a way.

Talk not of gems, the orient list,
The diamond, topaz, amethyst,
The emerald mild, the ruby gay;
Talk of my gem, Anne Hathaway!
She hath a way, with her bright eye,
Their various lustres to defy, —
The jewels she, and the foil they,
So sweet to look Anne hath a way;
    She hath a way,
    Anne Hathaway;
To shame bright gems, Anne hath a way.

But were it to my fancy given
To rate her charms, I 'd call them heaven;
For though a mortal made of clay,
Angels must love Anne Hathaway;
She hath a way so to control,
To rapture, the imprisoned soul,
And sweetest heaven on earth display,
That to be heaven Anne hath a way;
    She hath a way,
    Anne Hathaway;
To be heaven's self, Anne hath a way.
                    Attributed to SHAKESPEARE.

UNDER THE PORTRAIT OF JOHN MILTON,

PREFIXED TO "PARADISE LOST."

THREE Poets, in three distant ages born,
Greece, Italy, and England did adorn.
The first in loftiness of thought surpassed;
The next in majesty; in both the last.
The force of nature could no further go;
To make a third, she joined the former two.
                    JOHN DRYDEN.

TO THE MEMORY OF BEN JONSON.

THE Muse's fairest light in no dark time,
The wonder of a learnéd age; the line
Which none can pass; the most proportioned
    wit, —
To nature, the best judge of what was fit;
The deepest, plainest, highest, clearest pen;
The voice most echoed by consenting men;
The soul which answered best to all well said
By others, and which most requital made;
Tuned to the highest key of ancient Rome,
Returning all her music with his own;
In whom, with nature, study claimed a part,
And yet who to himself owed all his art:
Here lies Ben Jonson! every age will look
With sorrow here, with wonder on his book.
                    JOHN CLEVELAND.

TO MACAULAY.

THE dreamy rhymer's measured snore
Falls heavy on our ears no more;

And by long strides are left behind
The dear delights of womankind,
Who wage their battles like their loves,
In satin waistcoats and kid gloves,
And have achieved the crowning work
When they have trussed and skewered a Turk.
Another comes with stouter tread,
And stalks among the statelier dead.
He rushes on, and hails by turns
High-crested Scott, broad-breasted Burns;
And shows the British youth, who ne'er
Will lag behind, what Romans were
When all the Tuscans and their Lars
Shouted, and shook the towers of Mars.

WALTER SAVAGE LANDOR.

TO H. W. L.,

ON HIS BIRTHDAY, 27TH FEBRUARY, 1867.

I NEED not praise the sweetness of his song,
　Where limpid verse to limpid verse succeeds
Smooth as our Charles, when, fearing lest he
　　wrong
The new moon's mirrored skiff, he slides along,
　Full without noise, and whispers in his reeds.

With loving breath of all the winds his name
　Is blown about the world, but to his friends
A sweeter secret hides behind his fame,
And Love steals shyly through the loud acclaim
　To murmur a *God bless you!* and there ends.

As I muse backward up the checkered years
　Wherein so much was given, so much was lost,
Blessings in both kinds, such as cheapen tears, —
But hush! this is not for profaner ears;
　Let them drink molten pearls nor dream the
　　cost.

Some suck up poison from a sorrow's core,
　As naught but nightshade grew upon earth's
　　ground;
Love turned all his to heart's-ease, and the more
Fate tried his bastions, she but forced a door,
　Leading to sweeter manhood and more sound.

Even as a wind-waved fountain's swaying shade
　Seems of mixed race, a gray wraith shot with
　　sun,
So through his trial faith translucent rayed
Till darkness, half disnatured so, betrayed
　A heart of sunshine that would fain o'errun.

Surely if skill in song the shears may stay
　And of its purpose cheat the charmed abyss,
If our poor life be lengthened by a lay,
He shall not go, although his presence may,
　And the next age in praise shall double this.

Long days be his, and each as lusty-sweet
　As gracious natures find his song to be;
May Age steal on with softly-cadenced feet
Falling in music, as for him were meet
　Whose choicest verse is harsher-toned than he!

JAMES RUSSELL LOWELL.

VERSES BY HENRY MARTEN,

THE REGICIDE.

[Confined in prison by Charles II., where he died in 1681, after thirty years' imprisonment. The initial letters of the lines form an acrostic.]

HERE or elsewhere (all's one to you — to me!)
Earth, air, or water gripes my ghostless dust,
None knowing when brave fire shall set it free.
Reader, if you an oft-tried rule will trust,
You'll gladly do and suffer what you must.

My life was worn with serving you and you,
And death is my reward, and welcome, too;
Revenge destroying but itself; while I
To birds of prey leave my old cage and fly.
Examples preach to the eye, — care, then, mine
　says
Not how you *end* but how you *spend* your days.

HENRY MARTEN.

INSCRIPTION FOR MARTEN'S PRISON-ROOM.

[The immolation of this republican judge was celebrated in the following lines by the youthful Southey during his short experience as a democratic regenerator. In their original publication they were called: "*Inscription for the Apartment in Cheapstone Castle where Henry Marten the Regicide was imprisoned thirty Years.*" After Southey became Poet Laureate he endeavored to suppress the poem, but unsuccessfully.]

FOR thirty years secluded from mankind,
Here Marten lingered. Often have these walls
Echoed his footsteps, as with even tread
He paced around his prison: not to him
Did nature's fair varieties exist:
He never saw the sun's delightful beams,
Save when through yon high bars it poured a sad
And broken splendor. Dost thou ask his crime?
He had rebelled against the king, and sat
In judgment on him; for his ardent mind
Shaped goodliest plans of happiness on earth,
And peace and liberty. Wild dreams, but such
As Plato loved; such as, with holy zeal,
Our Milton worshipped. Blessed hopes! awhile
From man withheld, even to the latter days,
When Christ shall come and all things be fulfilled.

ROBERT SOUTHEY.

INSCRIPTION FOR BROWNRIGG'S CELL.

A PARODY.

[Canning, who was retained by the other side, parodied Southey's honest lines in the "Anti-Jacobin," November 20, 1797, by the following verses, entitled: "*Inscription for the Door of the Cell in Newgate where Mrs. Brownrigg the 'Prentice-cide was confined previous to her Execution.*"]

FOR one long term, or ere her trial came,
Here Brownrigg lingered. Often have these cells
Echoed her blasphemies, as with shrill voice
She screamed for fresh geneva. Not to her
Did the blithe fields of Tothill, or thy street,
St. Giles, its fair varieties expand;
Till at the last in slow-drawn cart she went
To execution. Dost thou ask her crime?
She whipped two female 'prentices to death,
And hid them in the coal-hole. For her mind
Shaped strictest plans of discipline. Sage schemes!
Such as Lycurgus taught, when at the shrine
Of the Orthyan goddess he bade flog
The little Spartans; such as erst chastised
Our Milton, when at college. For this act
Did Brownrigg swing. Harsh laws! but time shall come
When France shall reign, and laws be all repealed.
GEORGE CANNING.

SMOLLETT.

WHENCE could arise the mighty critic spleen,
The muse a trifler, and her theme so mean?
What had I done that angry heaven should send
The bitterest foe where most I wished a friend?
Oft hath my tongue been wanton at this name,
And hailed the honors of thy matchless fame.
For me let hoary Fielding bite the ground,
So nobler Pickle stands superbly bound;
From Livy's temples tear the historic crown,
Which with more justice blooms upon thy own
Compared with thee, be all life-writers dumb,
But he who wrote the life of Tommy Thumb.
Who ever read the Regicide but sware
The author wrote as man ne'er wrote before?
Others for plots and underplots may call,
Here 's the right method, — have no plot at all!
JOHN CHURCHILL.

TO THE MEMORY OF THOMAS HOOD.

TAKE back into thy bosom, earth,
This joyous, May-eyed morrow,
The gentlest child that ever mirth
Gave to be reared by sorrow!
'T is hard — while rays half green, half gold,
Through vernal bowers are burning,
And streams their diamond mirrors hold
To summer's face returning, —
To say we 're thankful that his sleep
Shall nevermore be lighter,
In whose sweet-tongued companionship
Stream, bower, and beam grew brighter!

But all the more intensely true
His soul gave out each feature
Of elemental love, — each hue
And grace of golden nature, —
The deeper still beneath it all
Lurked the keen jags of anguish;
The more the laurels clasped his brow
Their poison made it languish.
Seemed it that, like the nightingale
Of his own mournful singing,
The tenderer would his song prevail
While most the thorn was stinging.

So never to the desert-worn
Did fount bring freshness deeper
Than that his placid rest this morn
Has brought the shrouded sleeper.
That rest may lap his weary head
Where charnels choke the city,
Or where, mid woodlands, by his bed
The wren shall wake its ditty;
But near or far, while evening's star
Is dear to hearts regretting,
Around that spot admiring thought
Shall hover, unforgetting.

BARTHOLOMEW SIMMONS.

BURNS.

ON RECEIVING A SPRIG OF HEATHER IN BLOSSOM.

No more these simple flowers belong
To Scottish maid and lover;
Sown in the common soil of song,
They bloom the wide world over.

In smiles and tears, in sun and showers,
The minstrel and the heather,
The deathless singer and the flowers
He sang of live together.

Wild heather-bells and Robert Burns!
The moorland flower and peasant!
How, at their mention, memory turns
Her pages old and pleasant!

The gray sky wears again its gold
And purple of adorning,
And manhood's noonday shadows hold
The dews of boyhood's morning.

The dews that washed the dust and soil
From off the wings of pleasure,

The sky, that flecked the ground of toil
  With golden threads of leisure.

I call to mind the summer day,
  The early harvest mowing,
The sky with sun and clouds at play,
  And flowers with breezes blowing.

I hear the blackbird in the corn,
  The locust in the haying ;
And, like the fabled hunter's horn,
  Old tunes my heart is playing.

How oft that day, with fond delay,
  I sought the maple's shadow,
And sang with Burns the hours away,
  Forgetful of the meadow !

Bees hummed, birds twittered, overhead
  I heard the squirrels leaping ;
The good dog listened while I read,
  And wagged his tail in keeping.

I watched him while in sportive mood
  I read "The Twa Dogs'" story,
And half believed he understood
  The poet's allegory.

Sweet day, sweet songs ! — The golden hours
  Grew brighter for that singing,
From brook and bird and meadow flowers
  A dearer welcome bringing.

New light on home-seen Nature beamed,
  New glory over Woman ;
And daily life and duty seemed
  No longer poor and common.

I woke to find the simple truth
  Of fact and feeling better
Than all the dreams that held my youth
  A still repining debtor :

That Nature gives her handmaid, Art,
  The themes of sweet discoursing ;
The tender idyls of the heart
  In every tongue rehearsing.

Why dream of lands of gold and pearl,
  Of loving knight and lady,
When farmer boy and barefoot girl
  Were wandering there already ?

I saw through all familiar things
  The romance underlying ;
The joys and griefs that plume the wings
  Of Fancy skyward flying.

I saw the same blithe day return,
  The same sweet fall of even,
That rose on wooded Craigie-burn,
  And sank on crystal Devon.

I matched with Scotland's heathery hills
  The sweet-brier and the clover ;
With Ayr and Doon, my native rills,
  Their wood-hymns chanting over.

O'er rank and pomp, as he had seen,
  I saw the Man uprising ;
No longer common or unclean,
  The child of God's baptizing.

With clearer eyes I saw the worth
  Of life among the lowly ;
The Bible at his Cotter's hearth
  Had made my own more holy.

And if at times an evil strain,
  To lawless love appealing,
Broke in upon the sweet refrain
  Of pure and healthful feeling,

It died upon the eye and ear,
  No inward answer gaining ;
No heart had I to see or hear
  The discord and the staining.

Let those who never erred forget
  His worth, in vain bewailings ;
Sweet Soul of Song ! — I own my debt
  Uncancelled by his failings !

Lament who will the ribald line
  Which tells his lapse from duty,
How kissed the maddening lips of wine,
  Or wanton ones of beauty ;

But think, while falls that shade between
  The erring one and Heaven,
That he who loved like Magdalen,
  Like her may be forgiven.

Not his the song whose thunderous chime
  Eternal echoes render, —
The mournful Tuscan's haunted rhyme,
  And Milton's starry splendor ;

But who his human heart has laid
  To Nature's bosom nearer ?
Who sweetened toil like him, or paid
  To love a tribute dearer ?

Through all his tuneful art, how strong
  The human feeling gushes !
The very moonlight of his song
  Is warm with smiles and blushes !

Give lettered pomp to teeth of Time,
  So "Bonny Doon" but tarry ;
Blot out the Epic's stately rhyme,
  But spare his Highland Mary !
                    JOHN GREENLEAF WHITTIER.

ROBERT BURNS.

WHAT bird in beauty, flight, or song
  Can with the bard compare,
Who sang as sweet, and soared as strong
  As ever child of air ?

His plume, his note, his form, could Burns
  For whim or pleasure change ;
He was not one, but all by turns,
  With transmigration strange :

The blackbird, oracle of spring,
  When flowed his moral lay ;
The swallow, wheeling on the wing,
  Capriciously at play ;

The humming-bird from bloom to bloom
  Inhaling heavenly balm ;
The raven, in the tempest's gloom ;
  The halcyon, in the calm ;

In "auld Kirk Alloway," the owl,
  At witching time of night ;
By "Bonny Doon," the earliest fowl
  That carolled to the light.

He was the wren amidst the grove,
  When in his homely vein ;
At Bannockburn the bird of Jove,
  With thunder in his train ;

The wood-lark, in his mournful hours ;
  The goldfinch, in his mirth ;
The thrush, a spendthrift of his powers,
  Enrapturing heaven and earth ;

The swan, in majesty and grace,
  Contemplative and still ;
But, roused, — no falcon in the chase
  Could like his satire kill.

The linnet in simplicity,
  In tenderness the dove ;
But more than all beside was he
  The nightingale in love.

O, had he never stooped to shame,
  Nor lent a charm to vice,
How had devotion loved to name
  That bird of paradise !

Peace to the dead ! — In Scotia's choir
  Of minstrels great and small,
He sprang from his spontaneous fire,
  The phœnix of them all.
                    JAMES MONTGOMERY.

BURNS.

A POET'S EPITAPH.

STOP, mortal ! Here thy brother lies, —
  The poet of the poor.
His books were rivers, woods, and skies,
  The meadow and the moor ;
His teachers were the torn heart's wail,
  The tyrant, and the slave,
The street, the factory, the jail,
  The palace, — and the grave !
Sin met thy brother everywhere !
  And is thy brother blamed ?
From passion, danger, doubt, and care
  He no exemption claimed.
The meanest thing, earth's feeblest worm,
  He feared to scorn or hate ;
But, honoring in a peasant's form
  The equal of the great,
He blessed the steward, whose wealth makes
  The poor man's little more ;
Yet loathed the haughty wretch that takes
  From plundered labor's store.
A hand to do, a head to plan,
  A heart to feel and dare, —
Tell man's worst foes, here lies the man
  Who drew them as they are.
                    EBENEZER ELLIOTT.

BURNS.

REAR high thy bleak majestic hills,
  Thy sheltered valleys proudly spread,
And, Scotia, pour thy thousand rills,
  And wave thy heaths with blossoms red ;
But, ah ! what poet now shall tread
  Thy airy heights, thy woodland reign,
Since he, the sweetest bard, is dead,
  That ever breathed the soothing strain !

As green thy towering pines may grow,
  As clear thy streams may speed along,
As bright thy summer suns may glow,
  As gayly charm thy feathery throng ;
But now unheeded is the song,
  And dull and lifeless all around, —
For his wild harp lies all unstrung,
  And cold the hand that waked its sound.

What though thy vigorous offspring rise, —
  In arts, in arms, thy sons excel ;
Though beauty in thy daughters' eyes,
  And health in every feature dwell ;
Yet who shall now their praises tell
  In strains impassioned, fond, and free,
Since he no more the song shall swell
  To love and liberty and thee !

                    WILLIAM ROSCOE.

BURNS.

THAT heaven's beloved die early,
　　Prophetic Pity mourns;
But old as Truth, although in youth,
　　Died giant-hearted Burns.

O that I were the daisy
　　That sank beneath his plough !
Or, "neighbor meet," that "skylark sweet !"
　　Say, are they nothing now ?

That mouse, "our fellow mortal,"
　　Lives deep in Nature's heart ;
Like earth and sky, it cannot die
　　Till earth and sky depart.

Thy Burns, child-honored Scotland !
　　Is many minds in one ;
With thought on thought the name is fraught
　　Of glory's peasant son.

Thy Chaucer is thy Milton,
　　And might have been thy Tell ;
As Hampden fought, thy Sidney wrote,
　　And would have fought as well.

Be proud, man-childed Scotland !
　　Of earth's unpolished gem ;
And "Bonny Doon," and "heaven aboon,"
　　For Burns hath hallowed them.

Be proud, though sin-dishonored
　　And grief-baptized thy child ;
As rivers run, in shade and sun,
　　He ran his courses wild.

Grieve not though savage forests
　　Looked grimly on the wave,
Where dim-eyed flowers and shaded bowers
　　Seemed living in the grave.

Grieve not, though by the torrent
　　Its headlong course was riven,
When o'er it came, in clouds and flame,
　　Niagara from heaven !

For sometimes gently flowing,
　　And sometimes chafed to foam,
O'er slack and deep, by wood and steep,
　　He sought his heavenly home.

EBENEZER ELLIOTT.

BURNS.

His is that language of the heart
　　In which the answering heart would speak,
Thought, word, that bids the warm tear start,
　　Or the smile light the cheek ;

And his that music to whose tone
　　The common pulse of man keeps time,
In cot or castle's mirth or moan,
　　In cold or sunny clime.

Through care and pain and want and woe,
　　With wounds that only death could heal,
Tortures the poor alone can know,
　　The proud alone can feel,

He kept his honesty and truth,
　　His independent tongue and pen,
And moved, in manhood as in youth,
　　Pride of his fellow-men.

Strong sense, deep feeling, passions strong,
　　A hate of tyrant and of knave,
A love of right, a scorn of wrong,
　　Of coward and of slave ;

A kind, true heart, a spirit high,
　　That could not fear and would not bow,
Were written in his manly eye
　　And on his manly brow.

Praise to the bard ! his words are driven,
　　Like flower-seeds by the far winds sown,
Where'er beneath the sky of heaven
　　The birds of fame have flown.

Praise to the man ! a nation stood
　　Beside his coffin with wet eyes, —
Her brave, her beautiful, her good, —
　　As when a loved one dies.

And still, as on his funeral day,
　　Men stand his cold earth-couch around,
With the mute homage that we pay
　　To consecrated ground.

And consecrated ground it is, —
　　The last, the hallowed home of one
Who lives upon all memories,
　　Though with the buried gone.

FITZ-GREENE HALLECK.

BYRON.

FROM "THE COURSE OF TIME."

TAKE one example to our purpose quite.
A man of rank, and of capacious soul,
Who riches had, and fame, beyond desire,
An heir of flattery, to titles born,
And reputation, and luxurious life :
Yet, not content with ancestorial name,
Or to be known because his fathers were,
He on this height hereditary stood,
And, gazing higher, purposed in his heart

To take another step. Above him seemed,
Alone, the mount of song, the lofty seat
Of canonized bards ; and thitherward,
By nature taught, and inward melody,
In prime of youth, he bent his eagle eye.
No cost was spared. What books he wished, he
    read ;
What sage to hear, he heard ; what scenes to see,
He saw. And first in rambling school-boy days,
Britannia's mountain-walks, and heath-girt lakes,
And story-telling glens, and founts, and brooks,
And maids, as dew-drops pure and fair, his soul
With grandeur filled, and melody, and love.
Then travel came, and took him where he wished :
He cities saw, and courts, and princely pomp ;
And mused alone on ancient mountain-brows ;
And mused on battle-fields, where valor fought
In other days ; and mused on ruins gray
With years ; and drank from old and fabulous
    wells,
And plucked the vine that first-born prophets
    plucked ;
And mused on famous tombs, and on the wave
Of ocean mused, and on the desert waste ;
The heavens and earth of every country saw ;
Where'er the old inspiring Genii dwelt ;
Aught that could rouse, expand, refine the soul,
Thither he went, and meditated there.
    He touched his harp, and nations heard en-
      tranced ;
As some vast river of unfailing source,
Rapid, exhaustless, deep, his numbers flowed,
And opened new fountains in the human heart.
Where Fancy halted, weary in her flight,
In other men, his fresh as morning rose,
And soared untrodden heights, and seemed at
    home,
Where angels bashful looked. Others, though
    great,
Beneath their argument seemed struggling whiles ;
He, from above descending, stooped to touch
The loftiest thought ; and proudly stooped, as
    though
It scarce deserved his verse. With Nature's self
He seemed an old acquaintance, free to jest
At will with all her glorious majesty.
He laid his hand upon "the Ocean's mane,"
And played familiar with his hoary locks ;
Stood on the Alps, stood on the Apennines,
And with the thunder talked as friend to friend ;
And wove his garland of the lightning's wing,
In sportive twist, — the lightning's fiery wing,
Which, as the footsteps of the dreadful God,
Marching upon the storm in vengeance seemed ;
Then turned, and with the grasshopper, who sung
His evening song beneath his feet, conversed.
Suns, moons, and stars, and clouds his sisters
    were ;

Rocks, mountains, meteors, seas, and winds, and
    storms
His brothers, younger brothers, whom he scarce
As equals deemed. All passions of all men,
The wild and tame, the gentle and severe ;
All thoughts, all maxims, sacred and profane ;
All creeds, all seasons, time, eternity ;
All that was hated, and all that was dear ;
All that was hoped, all that was feared, by man, —
He tossed about, as tempest-withered leaves ;
Then, smiling, looked upon the wreck he made.
With terror now he froze the cowering blood,
And now dissolved the heart in tenderness ;
Yet would not tremble, would not weep himself ;
But back into his soul retired, alone,
Dark, sullen, proud, gazing contemptuously
On hearts and passions prostrate at his feet.
So Ocean, from the plains his waves had late
To desolation swept, retired in pride,
Exulting in the glory of his might,
And seemed to mock the ruin he had wrought.
    As some fierce comet of tremendous size,
To which the stars did reverence as it passed,
So he, through learning and through fancy, took
His flights sublime, and on the loftiest top
Of Fame's dread mountain sat ; not soiled and worn,
As if he from the earth had labored up,
But as some bird of heavenly plumage fair
He looked, which down from higher regions came,
And perched it there, to see what lay beneath.
    The nations gazed, and wondered much and
      praised.
Critics before him fell in humble plight ;
Confounded fell ; and made debasing signs
To catch his eye ; and stretched and swelled
    themselves
To bursting nigh, to utter bulky words
Of admiration vast ; and many too,
Many that aimed to imitate his flight,
With weaker wing, unearthly fluttering made,
And gave abundant sport to after days.
    Great man ! the nations gazed and wondered
      much,
And praised ; and many called his evil good.
Wits wrote in favor of his wickedness ;
And kings to do him honor took delight.
Thus full of titles, flattery, honor, fame ;
Beyond desire, beyond ambition, full, —
He died, — he died of what ? Of wretchedness ;
Drank every cup of joy, heard every trump
Of fame ; drank early, deeply drank ; drank
    draughts
That common millions might have quenched,
    then died
Of thirst, because there was no more to drink.
His goddess, Nature, wooed, embraced, enjoyed,
Fell from his arms, abhorred ; his passions died,
Died, all but dreary, solitary Pride ;

And all his sympathies in being died.
As some ill-guided bark, well built and tall,
Which angry tides cast out on desert shore,
And then, retiring, left it there to rot
And moulder in the winds and rains of heaven;
So he, cut from the sympathies of life,
And cast ashore from pleasure's boisterous surge,
A wandering, weary, worn, and wretched thing,
Scorched and desolate and blasted soul,
A gloomy wilderness of dying thought, —
Repined, and groaned, and withered from the
    earth.
His groanings filled the land his numbers filled;
And yet he seemed ashamed to groan. — Poor
    man!
Ashamed to ask, and yet he needed help.
ROBERT POLLOK.

CAMP-BELL.

CHARADE.

COME from my first, ay, come!
    The battle dawn is nigh;
And the screaming trump and the thundering
    drum
    Are calling thee to die!

Fight as thy father fought;
    Fall as thy father fell;
Thy task is taught; thy shroud is wrought;
    So forward and farewell!

Toll ye my second! toll!
    Fling high the flambeau's light,
And sing the hymn for a parted soul
    Beneath the silent night!

The wreath upon his head,
    The cross upon his breast;
Let the prayer be said and the tear be shed,
    So, — take him to his rest!

Call ye my whole, — ay, call
    The lord of lute and lay;
And let him greet the sable pall
    With a noble song to-day.

Go, call him by his name!
    No fitter hand may crave
To light the flame of a soldier's fame
    On the turf of a soldier's grave.
WINTHROP MACKWORTH PRAED.

TO THOMAS MOORE.

MY boat is on the shore,
    And my bark is on the sea;

But before I go, Tom Moore,
    Here's a double health to thee!

Here's a sigh to those who love me,
    And a smile to those who hate;
And, whatever sky's above me,
    Here's a heart for every fate!

Though the ocean roar around me,
    Yet it still shall bear me on;
Though a desert should surround me,
    It hath springs that may be won.

Were 't the last drop in the well,
    As I gasped upon the brink,
Ere my fainting spirit fell,
    'T is to thee that I would drink.

With that water, as this wine,
    The libation I would pour
Should be, — Peace with thine and mine,
    And a health to thee, Tom Moore.
BYRON.

A BARD'S EPITAPH.

Is there a whim-inspiréd fool,
Owre fast for thought, owre hot for rule,
Owre blate to seek, owre proud to snool,
    Let him draw near,
And owre this grassy heap sing dool,
    And drap a tear.

Is there a bard of rustic song,
Who, noteless, steals the crowd among,
That weekly this area throng,
    O, pass not by!
But, with a frater-feeling strong,
    Here heave a sigh.

Is there a man whose judgment clear
Can others teach the course to steer,
Yet runs himself life's mad career,
    Wild as the wave;
Here pause, and, through the starting tear,
    Survey this grave.

The poor inhabitant below
Was quick to learn and wise to know,
And keenly felt the friendly glow,
    And sober flame;
But thoughtless follies laid him low,
    And stained his name!

Reader, attend, — whether thy soul
Soars fancy's flights beyond the pole,
Or darkly grubs this earthly hole,
    In low pursuit;
Know prudent, cautious self-control
    Is wisdom's root.
BURNS.

EPITAPH ON THE COUNTESS OF PEMBROKE.

UNDERNEATH this sable hearse
Lies the subject of all verse,
Sidney's sister, Pembroke's mother;
Death! ere thou hast slain another,
Learned and fair and good as she,
Time shall throw a dart at thee.

BEN JONSON.

EPITAPH ON ELIZABETH L. H.

WOULDST thou heare what man can say
In a little?—reader, stay!
Underneath this stone doth lye
As much beauty as could dye,—
Which in life did harbor give
To more vertue than doth live.
If at all she had a fault,
Leave it buried in this vault.
One name was Elizabeth,—
The other, let it sleep with death:
Fitter where it dyed to tell,
Than that it lived at all.   Farewell!

BEN JONSON.

CHARLES XII.

ON what foundations stands the warrior's pride,
How just his hopes, let Swedish Charles decide:
A frame of adamant, a soul of fire,
No dangers fright him, and no labors tire;
O'er love, o'er fear, extends his wide domain,
Unconquered lord of pleasure and of pain.
No joys to him pacific sceptres yield,
War sounds the trump, he rushes to the field;
Behold surrounding kings their power combine,
And one capitulate, and one resign;
Peace courts his hand, but spreads her charms in
    vain;
"Think nothing gained," he cries, "till naught
    remain,
On Moscow's walls till Gothic standards fly,
And all be mine beneath the polar sky."
The march begins in military state,
And nations on his eye suspended wait;
Stern famine guards the solitary coast,
And winter barricades the realms of frost.
He comes, nor want nor cold his course delay;
Hide, blushing glory, hide Pultowa's day!
The vanquished hero leaves his broken bands,
And shows his miseries in distant lands;
Condemned a needy supplicant to wait,
While ladies interpose and slaves debate.

But did not chance at length her error mend?
Did no subverted empire mark his end?
Did rival monarchs give the fatal wound,
Or hostile millions press him to the ground!
His fall was destined to a barren strand,
A petty fortress, and a dubious hand;
He left the name, at which the world grew pale,
To point a moral or adorn a tale.

SAMUEL JOHNSON.

EPISTLE TO ROBERT, EARL OF OXFORD AND EARL OF MORTIMER.

[Sent to the Earl of Oxford with Dr. Parnell's Poems, published by the author after the said earl's imprisonment in the Tower, and retreat into the country, in the year 1721.]

SUCH were the notes thy once-loved poet sung,
Till death untimely stopped his tuneful tongue.
O just beheld, and lost! admired and mourned!
With softest manners, gentlest arts adorned!
Blest in each science, blest in every strain!
Dear to the Muse—to Harley dear—in vain!
    For him, thou oft hast bid the world attend,
Fond to forget the statesman in the friend;
For Swift and him, despised the farce of state,
The sober follies of the wise and great;
Dexterous the craving, fawning crowd to quit,
And pleased to' scape from Flattery to Wit.
    Absent or dead, still let a friend be dear,
(A sigh the absent claims, the dead a tear,)
Recall those nights that closed thy toilsome days,
Still hear thy Parnell in his living lays,
Who, careless now of interest, fame, or fate,
Perhaps forgets that Oxford e'er was great;
Or, deeming meanest what we greatest call,
Beholds thee glorious only in thy fall.
    And sure, if aught below the seats divine
Can touch immortals, 't is a soul like thine,—
A soul supreme, in each hard instance tried,
Above all pain, all passion, and all pride,
The rage of power, the blast of public breath,
The lust of lucre, and the dread of death.
    In vain to deserts thy retreat is made,
The Muse attends thee to thy silent shade:
'Tis hers the brave man's latest steps to trace,
Rejudge his acts, and dignify disgrace.
When interest calls off all her sneaking train,
And all the obliged desert, and all the vain;
She waits, or to the scaffold, or the cell,
When the last lingering friend has bid farewell.
Even now she shades thy evening walk with bays
(No hireling she, no prostitute to praise),
Even now, observant of the parting ray,
Eyes the calm sunset of thy various day;
Through Fortune's cloud one truly great can see,
Nor fears to tell, that Mortimer is he.

ALEXANDER POPE.

THE MAN OF ROSS.

FROM "MORAL ESSAYS."

[Mr. John Kyrle. He died in the year 1724, aged 90, and lies interred in the chancel of the church of Ross in Herefordshire.]

BUT all our praises why should lords engross?
Rise, honest muse ! and sing the Man of Ross ;
Pleased Vaga echoes through her winding bounds,
And rapid Severn hoarse applause resounds.
Who hung with woods yon mountain's sultry
  brow ?
From the dry rock who bade the waters flow ?
Not to the skies in useless columns tost,
Or in proud falls magnificently lost,
But clear and artless, pouring through the plain
Health to the sick, and solace to the swain.
Whose causeway parts the vale with shady rows ?
Whose seats the weary traveller repose ?
Who taught that heaven-directed spire to rise ?
"The Man of Ross !" each lisping babe replies.
Behold the market-place with poor o'erspread !
The Man of Ross divides the weekly bread ;
He feeds yon almshouse, neat, but void of state,
Where age and want sit smiling at the gate :
Him portioned maids, apprenticed orphans
  blest,
The young who labor, and the old who rest.
Is any sick ? the Man of Ross relieves,
Prescribes, attends, the medicine makes and gives.
Is there a variance ? enter but his door,
Balked are the courts, and contest is no more.
Despairing quacks with curses fled the place,
And vile attorneys, now a useless race.
  B. Thrice happy man ! enabled to pursue
What all so wish, but want the power to do !
O say, what sums that generous hand supply ?
What mines to swell that boundless charity ?
  P. Of debts and taxes, wife and children clear,
This man possessed — five hundred pounds a year.
Blush, grandeur, blush ; proud courts, withdraw
  your blaze !
Ye little stars, hide your diminished rays !
  B. And what ? no monument, inscription, stone ?
His race, his form, his name, almost unknown ?
  P. Who builds a church to God, and not to
  fame,
Will never mark the marble with his name :
Go, search it there, where to be born and die,
Of rich and poor makes all the history ;
Enough that virtue filled the space between,
Proved by the ends of being to have been.
                            ALEXANDER POPE.

TO THE LORD-GENERAL CROMWELL.

CROMWELL, our chief of men, who through a cloud,
  Not of war only, but detractions rude,
Guided by faith and matchless fortitude,
To peace and truth thy glorious way hast
  ploughed ;
And on the neck of crownéd fortune proud
  Hast reared God's trophies, and his work pur-
  sued,
  While Darwen stream, with blood of Scots im-
  brued,
  And Dunbar field resounds thy praises loud,
And Worcester's laureate wreath. Yet much re-
  mains
To conquer still ; Peace hath her victories
No less renowned than War : new foes arise,
Threatening to bind our souls with secular chains :
  Help us to save free conscience from the paw
  Of hireling wolves, whose gospel is their maw.
                            MILTON.

THE PRINCESS CHARLOTTE.

FROM "CHILDE HAROLD."

HARK ! forth from the abyss a voice proceeds,
A long, low, distant murmur of dread sound,
Such as arises when a nation bleeds
With some deep and immedicable wound ;
Through storm and darkness yawns the rend-
  ing ground,
The gulf is thick with phantoms, but the chief
Seems royal still, though with her head dis-
  crowned;
And pale, but lovely, with maternal grief
She clasps a babe to whom her breast yields no
  relief.

Scion of chiefs and monarchs, where art thou ?
Fond hope of many nations, art thou dead ?
Could not the grave forget thee, and lay low
Some less majestic, less belovéd head ?
In the sad midnight, while thy heart still bled,
The mother of a moment, o'er thy boy,
Death hushed that pang forever : with thee fled
The present happiness and promised joy
Which filled the imperial isles so full it seemed
  to cloy.

Peasants bring forth in safety. — Can it be,
O thou that wert so happy, so adored !
Those who weep not for kings shall weep for
  thee,
And Freedom's heart, grown heavy, cease to
  hoard
Her many griefs for ONE : for she had poured
Her orisons for thee, and o'er thy head
Beheld her Iris. — Thou, too, lonely lord,
And desolate consort, — vainly wert thou wed !
The husband of a year ! the father of the dead !

Of sackcloth was thy wedding garment made ;
Thy bridal's fruit is ashes ; in the dust
The fair-haired Daughter of the Isles is laid,
The love of millions !   How we did intrust
Futurity to her ! and, though it must
Darken above her bones, yet fondly deemed
Our children should obey her child, and blessed
Her and her hoped-for seed, whose promise
   seemed
Like stars to shepherds' eyes : — 't was but a
   meteor beamed.

Woe unto us, not her ; for she sleeps well :
The fickle reek of popular breath, the tongue
Of hollow counsel, the false oracle,
Which from the birth of monarchy hath rung
Its knell in princely ears, till the o'erstung
Nations have armed in madness, the strange fate
Which tumbles mightiest sovereigns, and hath
   flung
Against their blind omnipotence a weight
Within the opposing scale, which crushes soon
   or late, —

These might have been her destiny ; but no,
Our hearts deny it : and so young, so fair,
Good without effort, great without a foe ;
But now a bride and mother, — and now *there!*
How many ties did that stern moment tear !
From thy sire's to his humblest subject's breast
Is linked the electric chain of that despair,
Whose shock was as an earthquake's, and op-
   prest
The land which loved thee so that none could
   love thee best.
                   BYRON.

DANIEL BOONE.

FROM "DON JUAN."

Of all men, saving Sylla the man-slayer,
   Who passes for in life and death most lucky,
Of the great names which in our faces stare,
   The General Boone, backwoodsman of Kentucky,
Was happiest amongst mortals anywhere ;
   For, killing nothing but a bear or buck, he
Enjoyed the lonely, vigorous, harmless days
Of his old age in wilds of deepest maze.

Crime came not near him, she is not the child
   Of solitude ; Health shrank not from him, for
Her home is in the rarely trodden wild,
   Where if men seek her not, and death be more
Their choice than life, forgive them, as beguiled
   By habit to what their own hearts abhor,
In cities caged.   The present case in point I
Cite is, that Boone lived hunting up to ninety ;

And, what 's still stranger, left behind a name
   For which men vainly decimate the throng,
Not only famous, but of that *good* fame,
   Without which glory 's but a tavern song, —
Simple, serene, the antipodes of shame,
   Which hate nor envy e'er could tinge with
      wrong ;
An active hermit, even in age the child
Of nature, or the Man of Ross run wild.

'T is true he shrank from men, even of his nation,
   When they built up unto his darling trees, —
He moved some hundred miles off, for a station
   Where there were fewer houses and more ease ;
The inconvenience of civilization
   Is that you neither can be pleased nor please ;
But where he met the individual man,
He showed himself as kind as mortal can.

He was not all alone ; around him grew
   A sylvan tribe of children of the chase,
Whose young, unwakened world was ever new :
   Nor sword nor sorrow yet had left a trace
On her unwrinkled brow, nor could you view
   A frown on nature's or on human face ; —
The freeborn forest found and kept them free,
And fresh as is a torrent or a tree.

And tall, and strong, and swift of foot, were they,
   Beyond the dwarfing city's pale abortions,
Because their thoughts had never been the prey
   Of care or gain : the green woods were their
      portions ;
No sinking spirits told them they grew gray ;
   No fashion made them apes of her distortions ;
Simple they were, not savage ; and their rifles,
Though very true, were not yet used for trifles.

Motion was in their days, rest in their slumbers,
   And cheerfulness the handmaid of their toil ;
Nor yet too many nor too few their numbers ;
   Corruption could not make their hearts her soil.
The lust which stings, the splendor which en-
      cumbers,
   With the free foresters divide no spoil ;
Serene, not sullen, were the solitudes
Of this unsighing people of the woods.
                   BYRON.

NAPOLEON.

'T is done, — but yesterday a king !
   And armed with kings to strive, —
And now thou art a nameless thing ;
   So abject, — yet alive !
Is this the man of thousand thrones,
Who strewed our earth with hostile bones,
   And can he thus survive ?

Since he, miscalled the Morning Star,
Nor man nor fiend hath fallen so far.

Ill-minded man ! why scourge thy kind
   Who bowed so low the knee ?
By gazing on thyself grown blind,
   Thou taught'st the rest to see.
With might unquestioned, — power to save, —
Thine only gift hath been the grave
   To those that worshipped thee ;
Nor till thy fall could mortals guess
Ambition's less than littleness !

Thanks for that lesson, — it will teach
   To after warriors more
Than high philosophy can preach,
   And vainly preached before.
That spell upon the minds of men
Breaks never to unite again,
   That led them to adore
Those Pagod things of sabre sway,
With fronts of brass and feet of clay.

The triumph and the vanity,
   The rapture of the strife ;
The earthquake voice of Victory,
   To thee the breath of life ;
The sword, the sceptre, and that sway
Which man seemed made but to obey,
   Wherewith renown was rife, —
All quelled ! — Dark spirit ! what must be
The madness of thy memory !

The desolator desolate !
   The victor overthrown !
The arbiter of others' fate
   A suppliant for his own !
Is it some yet imperial hope,
That with such change can calmly cope ?
   Or dread of death alone ?
To die a prince, or live a slave, —
Thy choice is most ignobly brave !

He who of old would rend the oak
   Dreamed not of the rebound ;
Chained by the trunk he vainly broke, —
   Alone, — how looked he round ?
Thou, in the sternness of thy strength,
An equal deed hast done at length,
   And darker fate hast found :
He fell, the forest-prowlers' prey ;
But thou must eat thy heart away !

The Roman, when his burning heart
   Was slaked with blood of Rome,
Threw down the dagger, dared depart,
   In savage grandeur, home.

He dared depart in utter scorn
Of men that such a yoke had borne,
   Yet left him such a doom !
His only glory was that hour
Of self-upheld abandoned power.

The Spaniard, when the lust of sway
   Had lost its quickening spell,
Cast crowns for rosaries away,
   An empire for a cell ;
A strict accountant of his beads,
A subtle disputant on creeds,
   His dotage trifled well ;
Yet better had he neither known
A bigot's shrine nor despot's throne.

But thou, — from thy reluctant hand
   The thunderbolt is wrung, —
Too late thou leav'st the high command
   To which thy weakness clung.
All evil spirit as thou art,
It is enough to grieve the heart
   To see thine own unstrung ;
To think that God's fair world hath been
The footstool of a thing so mean !

And Earth hath spilt her blood for him,
   Who thus can hoard his own !
And monarchs bowed the trembling limb,
   And thanked him for a throne !
Fair Freedom ! may we hold thee dear,
When thus thy mightiest foes their fear
   In humblest guise have shown.
O, ne'er may tyrant leave behind
A brighter name to lure mankind !

Thine evil deeds are writ in gore,
   Nor written thus in vain ;
Thy triumphs tell of fame no more,
   Or deepen every stain.
If thou hadst died as honor dies,
Some new Napoleon might arise,
   To shame the world again ;
But who would soar the solar height,
To set in such a starless night ?

Weighed in the balance, hero dust
   Is vile as vulgar clay ;
Thy scales, Mortality ! are just
   To all that pass away :
But yet methought the living great
Some higher spark should animate,
   To dazzle and dismay ;
Nor deemed contempt could thus make mirth
Of these, the conquerors of the earth.

And she, proud Austria's mournful flower,
   Thy still imperial bride ;

How bears her breast the torturing hour ?
  Still clings she to thy side ?
Must she, too, bend, — must she, too, share
Thy late repentance, long despair,
  Thou throneless homicide ?
If still she loves thee, hoard that gem ;
'T is worth thy vanished diadem !

Then haste thee to thy sullen Isle,
  And gaze upon the sea ;
That element may meet thy smile, —
  It ne'er was ruled by thee !
Or trace with thine all-idle hand,
In loitering mood, upon the sand,
  That earth is now as free !
That Corinth's pedagogue hath now
Transferred his byword to thy brow.

Thou Timour ! in his captive's cage, —
  What thoughts will there be thine,
While brooding in thy prisoned rage ?
  But one, — " The world *was* mine ! "
Unless, like he of Babylon,
All sense is with thy sceptre gone,
  Life will not long confine
That spirit poured so widely forth, —
So long obeyed, so little worth !

Or, like the thief of fire from heaven,
  Wilt thou withstand the shock ?
And share with him, the unforgiven,
  His vulture and his rock !
Foredoomed by God, by man accurst,
And that last act, though not thy worst,
  The very fiend's arch mock :
He in his fall preserved his pride,
And, if a mortal, had as proudly died !
                              BYRON.

ICHABOD.

DANIEL WEBSTER. 1850.

So fallen ! so lost ! the light withdrawn
  Which once he wore !
The glory from his gray hairs gone
  Forevermore !

Revile him not, — the Tempter hath
  A snare for all !
And pitying tears, not scorn and wrath,
  Befit his fall !

O, dumb be passion's stormy rage,
  When he who might
Have lighted up and led his age
  Falls back in night !

Scorn ! would the angels laugh to mark
  A bright soul driven,

Fiend-goaded, down the endless dark,
  From hope and heaven ?

Let not the land, once proud of him,
  Insult him now ;
Nor brand with deeper shame his dim,
  Dishonored brow.

But let its humbled sons, instead,
  From sea to lake,
A long lament, as for the dead,
  In sadness make.

Of all we loved and honored, naught
  Save power remains, —
A fallen angel's pride of thought,
  Still strong in chains.

All else is gone ; from those great eyes
  The soul has fled :
When faith is lost, when honor dies,
  The man is dead !

Then pay the reverence of old days
  To his dead fame ;
Walk backward, with averted gaze,
  And hide the shame !
                JOHN GREENLEAF WHITTIER.

THE DEAD CZAR NICHOLAS.

LAY him beneath his snows,
The great Norse giant who in these last days
Troubled the nations.   Gather decently
The imperial robes about him. 'T is but man, —
This demi-god.   Or rather it *was* man,
And is — a little dust, that will corrupt
As fast as any nameless dust which sleeps
'Neath Alma's grass or Balaklava's vines.

No vineyard grave for him.   No quiet tomb
By river margin, where across the seas
Children's fond thoughts and women's memories
      come
Like angels, to sit by the sepulchre,
Saying : "All these were men who knew to count,
Front-faced, the cost of honor, nor did shrink
From its full payment ; coming here to die,
They died — like men."

                      But this man ? Ah ! for him
Funereal state, and ceremonial grand,
The stone-engraved sarcophagus, and then
Oblivion.

                      Nay, oblivion were as bliss
To that fierce howl which rolls from land to land
Exulting, — " Art thou fallen, Lucifer,
Son of the morning ? " or condemning, — " Thus

Perish the wicked!" or blaspheming, — "Here
Lies our Belshazzar, our Sennacherib,
Our Pharaoh, — he whose heart God hardenéd,
So that he would not let the people go."

Self-glorifying sinners! Why, this man
Was but like other men : — you, Levite small,
Who shut your saintly ears, and prate of hell
And heretics, because outside church-doors,
Your church-doors, congregations poor and small
Praise Heaven in their own way ; — you, autocrat
Of all the hamlets, who add field to field
And house to house, whose slavish children cower
Before your tyrant footstep ; — you, foul-tongued
Fanatic or ambitious egotist,
Who thinks God stoops from his high majesty
To lay his finger on your puny head,
And crown it, that you henceforth may parade
Your maggotship throughout the wondering
          world, —
"I am the Lord's anointed!"

                              Fools and blind !
This Czar, this emperor, this disthronéd corpse,
Lying so straightly in an icy calm
Grander than sovereignty, was but as ye, —
No better and no worse ; — Heaven mend us all !

Carry him forth and bury him.   Death's peace
Rest on his memory !   Mercy by his bier
Sits silent, or says only these few words, —
"Let him who is without sin 'mongst ye all
Cast the first stone."   DINAH MARIA MULOCK.

ABRAHAM LINCOLN.

FROM THE "COMMEMORATION ODE."

LIFE may be given in many ways,
     And loyalty to Truth be sealed
As bravely in the closet as the field,
     So bountiful is Fate ;
     But then to stand beside her,
     When craven churls deride her,
To front a lie in arms and not to yield,
     This shows, methinks, God's plan
     And measure of a stalwart man,
     Limbed like the old heroic breeds,
     Who stand self-poised on manhood's solid
          earth,
     Not forced to frame excuses for his birth,
Fed from within with all the strength he needs.

Such was he, our Martyr-Chief,
     Whom late the Nation he had led,
     With ashes on her head,
Wept with the passion of an angry grief :

Forgive me, if from present things I turn
To speak what in my heart will beat and burn,
And hang my wreath on his world-honored urn,
     Nature they say, doth dote,
     And cannot make a man
     Save on some worn-out plan,
     Repeating us by rote :
For him her Old World moulds aside she threw,
     And, choosing sweet clay from the breast
     Of the unexhausted West,
With stuff untainted shaped a hero new,
Wise, steadfast in the strength of God, and true.
     How beautiful to see
Once more a shepherd of mankind indeed,
Who loved his charge, but never loved to lead ;
One whose meek flock the people joyed to be,
     Not lured by any cheat of birth,
     But by his clear-grained human worth,
And brave old wisdom of sincerity !
     They knew that outward grace is dust ;
     They could not choose but trust
In that sure-footed mind's unfaltering skill,
     And supple-tempered will
That bent like perfect steel to spring again and
          thrust.

     His was no lonely mountain-peak of mind,
     Thrusting to thin air o'er our cloudy bars,
     A sea-mark now, now lost in vapors blind ;
     Broad prairie rather, genial, level-lined,
     Fruitful and friendly for all human kind,
Yet also nigh to heaven and loved of loftiest stars.
     Nothing of Europe here,
Or, then, of Europe fronting mornward still,
     Ere any names of Serf and Peer
     Could Nature's equal scheme deface ;
     Here was a type of the true elder race,
And one of Plutarch's men talked with us face
          to face.
I praise him not ; it were too late ;
And some innative weakness there must be
In him who condescends to victory
Such as the Present gives, and cannot wait,
     Safe in himself as in a fate.
     So always firmly he :
     He knew to bide his time,
     And can his fame abide,
Still patient in his simple faith sublime,
     Till the wise years decide.
Great captains, with their guns and drums,
     Disturb our judgment for the hour,
     But at last silence comes ;
These all are gone, and, standing like a tower,
Our children shall behold his fame,
     The kindly-earnest, brave, foreseeing man,
Sagacious, patient, dreading praise, not blame,
New birth of our new soil, the first American.

                              JAMES RUSSELL LOWELL.

BURIAL OF LINCOLN.

PEACE ! Let the long procession come,
For hark ! — the mournful, muffled drum,
   The trumpet's wail afar ;
   And see ! the awful car !

Peace ! Let the sad procession go,
While cannon boom, and bells toll slow ;
   And go, thou sacred car,
   Bearing our woe afar !

Go, darkly borne, from State to State,
Whose loyal, sorrowing cities wait
   To honor, all they can,
   The dust of that good man !

Go, grandly borne, with such a train
As greatest kings might die to gain :
   The just, the wise, the brave
   Attend thee to the grave !

And you, the soldiers of our wars,
Bronzed veterans, grim with noble scars,
   Salute him once again,
   Your late commander, — *slain !*

Yes, let your tears indignant fall,
But leave your muskets on the wall ;
   Your country needs you now
   Beside the forge, the plough !
      .   .   .   .

So sweetly, sadly, sternly goes
The fallen to his last repose.
   Beneath no mighty dome,
   But in his modest home,

The churchyard where his children rest,
The quiet spot that suits him best,
   There shall his grave be made,
   And there his bones be laid !

And there his countrymen shall come,
With memory proud, with pity dumb,
   And strangers, far and near,
   For many and many a year !

For many a year and many an age,
While History on her ample page
   The virtues shall enroll
   Of that paternal soul !
                RICHARD HENRY STODDARD.

———◆———

KANE.

DIED FEBRUARY 16, 1857.

ALOFT upon an old basaltic crag,
   Which, scalped by keen winds that defend the
      Pole
   Gazes with dead face on the seas that roll

Around the secret of the mystic zone,
A mighty nation's star-bespangled flag
      Flutters alone,
And underneath, upon the lifeless front
   Of that drear cliff, a simple name is traced ;
Fit type of him who, famishing and gaunt,
   But with a rocky purpose in his soul,
      Breasted the gathering snows,
      Clung to the drifting floes,
By want beleaguered, and by winter chased,
Seeking the brother lost amid that frozen waste.

Not many months ago we greeted him,
   Crowned with the icy honors of the North,
   Across the land his hard-won fame went forth,
And Maine's deep woods were shaken limb by limb.
His own mild Keystone State, sedate and prim,
   Burst from decorous quiet as he came.
   Hot Southern lips, with eloquence aflame,
Sounded his triumph. Texas, wild and grim,
Proffered its horny hand. The large-lunged West,
      From out his giant breast,
Yelled its frank welcome. And from main to main,
      Jubilant to the sky,
      Thundered the mighty cry,
      HONOR TO KANE !

In vain, — in vain beneath his feet we flung
   The reddening roses ! All in vain we poured
   The golden wine, and round the shining board
Sent the toast circling, till the rafters rung
   With the thrice-tripled honors of the feast !
   Scarce the buds wilted and the voices ceased
Ere the pure light that sparkled in his eyes,
Bright as auroral fires in Southern skies,
   Faded and faded ! And the brave young heart
That the relentless Arctic winds had robbed
Of all its vital heat, in that long quest
For the lost captain, now within his breast
   More and more faintly throbbed.
His was the victory ; but as his grasp
Closed on the laurel crown with eager clasp,
      Death launched a whistling dart ;
And ere the thunders of applause were done
His bright eyes closed forever on the sun !
Too late, — too late the splendid prize he won
In the Olympic race of Science and of Art !
Like to some shattered berg that, pale and lone,
Drifts from the white North to a Tropic zone,
      And in the burning day
      Wastes peak by peak away,
      Till on some rosy even
It dies with sunlight blessing it ; so he
Tranquilly floated to a Southern sea,
      And melted into heaven !

He needs no tears who lived a noble life !
   We will not weep for him who died so well ;
   But we will gather round the hearth, and tell

The story of his strife ;
　　Such homage suits him well,
Better than funeral pomp or passing bell !

What tale of peril and self-sacrifice !
Prisoned amid the fastnesses of ice,
　　With hunger howling o'er the wastes of snow !
　　Night lengthening into months ; the ravenous
　　　　floe
Crunching the massive ships, as the white bear
Crunches his prey.   The insufficient share
　　　　Of loathsome food ;
The lethargy of famine ; the despair
　　Urging to labor, nervelessly pursued ;
　　Toil done with skinny arms, and faces hued
Like pallid masks, while dolefully behind
Glimmered the fading embers of a mind !
That awful hour, when through the prostrate band
Delirium stalked, laying his burning hand
　　Upon the ghastly foreheads of the crew ;
　　The whispers of rebellion, faint and few
　　At first, but deepening ever till they grew
Into black thoughts of murder, — such the throng
Of horrors bound the hero.   High the song
Should be that hymns the noble part he played !
Sinking himself, yet ministering aid
　　To all around him.   By a mighty will
　　Living defiant of the wants that kill,
Because his death would seal his comrades' fate ;
　　Cheering with ceaseless and inventive skill
Those polar waters, dark and desolate.
Equal to every trial, every fate,
　　He stands, until spring, tardy with relief,
　　　　Unlocks the icy gate,
And the pale prisoners thread the world once more,
To the steep cliffs of Greenland's pastoral shore
　　　　Bearing their dying chief !

Time was when he should gain his spurs of gold
　　From royal hands, who wooed the knightly state;
The knell of old formalities is tolled,
　　And the world's knights are now self-consecrate.
No grander episode doth chivalry hold
　　In all its annals, back to Charlemagne,
　　Than that lone vigil of unceasing pain,
Faithfully kept through hunger and through cold,
　　By the good Christian knight, Elisha Kane !
　　　　　　　　FITZ-JAMES O'BRIEN.

———◆———

THE OLD ADMIRAL.

ADMIRAL STEWART, U. S. N.

GONE at last,
　　That brave old hero of the past !
His spirit has a second birth,
　　An unknown, grander life ;

All of him that was earth
　　Lies mute and cold,
　　Like a wrinkled sheath and old
Thrown off forever from the shimmering blade
That has good entrance made
　　Upon some distant, glorious strife.

From another generation,
　　A simpler age, to ours Old Ironsides came ;
The morn and noontide of the nation
　　Alike he knew, nor yet outlived his fame, —
　　　O, not outlived his fame !
The dauntless men whose service guards our shore
　　Lengthen still their glory-roll
　　With his name to lead the scroll,
As a flagship at her fore
Carries the Union, with its azure and the stars,
Symbol of times that are no more
　　And the old heroic wars.

He was the one
Whom Death had spared alone
Of all the captains of that lusty age,
Who sought the foeman where he lay,
On sea or sheltering bay,
　　Nor till the prize was theirs repressed their
　　　　rage.
They are gone, — all gone :
　　They rest with glory and the undying Powers ;
　　Only their name and fame, and what they saved,
　　　　are ours !

It was fifty years ago,
　　Upon the Gallic Sea,
He bore the banner of the free,
And fought the fight whereof our children know, —
　　The deathful, desperate fight !
　　Under the fair moon's light
The frigate squared, and yawed to left and right.
　　Every broadside swept to death a score !
Roundly played her guns and well, till their fiery
　　　　ensigns fell,
　　Neither foe replying more.
All in silence, when the night-breeze cleared the
　　　　air,
　　Old Ironsides rested there,
Locked in between the twain, and drenched with
　　　　blood.
　　Then homeward, like an eagle with her prey !
　　O, it was a gallant fray, —
　　That fight in Biscay Bay !
Fearless the captain stood, in his youthful hardi-
　　　　hood :
　　He was the boldest of them all,
　　Our brave old Admiral !

And still our heroes bleed,
Taught by that olden deed.

Whether of iron or of oak
The ships we marshal at our country's need,
  Still speak their cannon now as then they spoke;
Still floats our unstruck banner from the mast
  As in the stormy past.

Lay him in the ground :
  Let him rest where the ancient river rolls ;
Let him sleep beneath the shadow and the sound
  Of the bell whose proclamation, as it tolls,
Is of Freedom and the gift our fathers gave.
  Lay him gently down :
  The clamor of the town
Will not break the slumbers deep, the beautiful
  ripe sleep,
  Of this lion of the wave,
  Will not trouble the old Admiral in his grave.

Earth to earth his dust is laid.
Methinks his stately shade
  On the shadow of a great ship leaves the shore ;
Over cloudless western seas
Seeks the far Hesperides,
  The islands of the blest,
Where no turbulent billows roar, —
  Where is rest.
His ghost upon the shadowy quarter stands
Nearing the deathless lands.
  There all his martial mates, renewed and strong,
  Await his coming long.
  I see the happy Heroes rise
  With gratulation in their eyes :
"Welcome, old comrade," Lawrence cries ;
"Ah, Stewart, tell us of the wars !
Who win the glory and the scars ?
  How floats the skyey flag, — how many stars ?
  Still speak they of Decatur's name,
  Of Bainbridge's and Perry's fame ?
  Of me, who earliest came ?
Make ready, all :
Room for the Admiral !
Come, Stewart, tell us of the wars !"
EDMUND CLARENCE STEDMAN.

DEATH-BED OF BOMBA, KING OF NAPLES, AT BARI. 1859.

COULD I pass those lounging sentries, through
  the aloe-bordered entries, up the sweep of
  squalid stair,
On through chamber after chamber, where the
  sunshine's gold and amber turn decay to
  beauty rare ;
I should reach a guarded portal, where for strife
  of issue mortal, face to face two kings are
  met, —

One the grisly King of Terrors ; one a Bourbon,
  with his errors, late to conscience-clearing
  set.
Well his fevered pulse may flutter, and the priests
  their mass may mutter with such fervor
  as they may :
Cross and chrysm, and genuflection, mop and
  mow, and interjection, will not frighten
  Death away.
By the dying despot sitting, at the hard heart's
  portals hitting, shocking the dull brain
  to work,
Death makes clear what life has hidden, chides
  what life has left unchidden, quickens
  truth life tried to burke.
He but ruled within his borders after Holy
  Church's orders, did what Austria bade
  him do ;
By their guidance flogged and tortured ; high-
  born men and gently nurtured chained
  with crime's felonious crew.
What if summer fevers gripped them, what if
  winter freezings nipped them, till they
  rotted in their chains ?
He had word of Pope and Kaiser ; none could
  holier be or wiser ; theirs the counsel, his
  the reins.
So he pleads excuses eager, clutching, with his
  fingers meagre, at the bedclothes as he
  speaks ;
But King Death sits grimly grinning at the
  Bourbon's cobweb-spinning, — as each cob-
  web-cable breaks.
And the poor soul, from life's eylot, rudderless,
  without a pilot, drifteth slowly down the
  dark ;
While 'mid rolling incense vapor, chanted dirge,
  and flaring taper, lies the body, stiff and
  stark.   PUNCH.

BURIAL OF SIR JOHN MOORE.

NOT a drum was heard, nor a funeral note,
  As his corse to the rampart we hurried ;
Not a soldier discharged his farewell shot
  O'er the grave where our hero we buried.

We buried him darkly, at dead of night,
  The sods with our bayonets turning ;
By the struggling moonbeams' misty light,
  And the lantern dimly burning.

No useless coffin inclosed his breast,
  Nor in sheet nor in shroud we wound him ;
But he lay, like a warrior taking his rest,
  With his martial cloak around him.

Few and short were the prayers we said,
  And we spoke not a word of sorrow ;
But we steadfastly gazed on the face of the dead,
  And we bitterly thought of the morrow.

We thought, as we hollowed his narrow bed,
  And smoothed down his lonely pillow,
That the foe and the stranger would tread o'er
    his head,
  And we far away on the billow !

Lightly they 'll talk of the spirit that 's gone,
  And o'er his cold ashes upbraid him ;
But little he 'll reck, if they let him sleep on,
  In the grave where a Briton has laid him !

But half of our heavy task was done,
  When the clock tolled the hour for retiring ;
And we heard the distant and random gun
  That the foe was sullenly firing.

Slowly and sadly we laid him down,
  From the field of his fame fresh and gory !
We carved not a line, we raised not a stone,
  But we left him alone in his glory.
                              CHARLES WOLFE.

ZIMRI.

GEORGE VILLIERS, DUKE OF BUCKINGHAM. 1682.

SOME of their chiefs were princes of the land ;
In the first rank of these did Zimri stand ;
A man so various, that he seemed to be
Not one, but all mankind's epitome :
Stiff in opinions, always in the wrong ;
Was everything by starts, and nothing long ;
But, in the course of one revolving moon,
Was chymist, fiddler, statesman, and buffoon ;
Then all for women, painting, rhyming, drinking,
Besides ten thousand freaks that died in thinking.
Blest madman, who could every hour employ,
With something new to wish or to enjoy !
Railing and praising were his usual themes ;
And both, to show his judgment, in extremes :
So over-violent or over-civil,
That every man with him was God or Devil.
In squandering wealth was his peculiar art ;
Nothing went unrewarded but desert.
Beggared by fools, whom still he found too late ;
He had his jest, and they had his estate.
He laughed himself from court, then sought relief
By forming parties, but could ne'er be chief ;
For, spite of him, the weight of business fell
On Absalom, and wise Achitophel.
Thus, wicked but in will, of means bereft,
He left no faction, but of that was left.
                              JOHN DRYDEN.

WHITEFIELD.

FROM "HOPE."

LEUCONOMUS (beneath well-sounding Greek
I slur a name a poet may not speak)
Stood pilloried on infamy's high stage,
And bore the pelting storm of half an age ;
The very butt of slander, and the blot
For every dart that malice ever shot.
The man that mentioned him at once dismissed
All mercy from his lips, and sneered and hissed ;
His crimes were such as Sodom never knew,
And perjury stood up to swear all true ;
His aim was mischief, and his zeal pretence,
His speech rebellion against common sense ;
A knave, when tried on honesty's plain rule,
And when by that of reason, a mere fool ;
The world's best comfort was, his doom was past ;
Die when he might, he must be damned at last.
  Now, truth, perform thine office ; waft aside
The curtain drawn by prejudice and pride,
Reveal (the man is dead) to wondering eyes
This more than monster in his proper guise.
  He loved the world that hated him ; the tear
That dropped upon his Bible was sincere ;
Assailed by scandal and the tongue of strife,
His only answer was a blameless life ;
And he that forged and he that threw the dart
Had each a brother's interest in his heart.
Paul's love of Christ and steadiness unbribed
Were copied close in him, and well transcribed.
He followed Paul ; his zeal a kindred flame,
His apostolic charity the same.
Like him crossed cheerfully tempestuous seas,
Forsaking country, kindred, friends, and ease ;
Like him he labored, and like him, content
To bear it, suffered shame where'er he went.
Blush, Calumny ! and write upon his tomb,
If honest Eulogy can spare thee room,
Thy deep repentance of thy thousand lies,
Which, aimed at him, has pierced the offended
      skies ;
And say, Blot out my sin, confessed, deplored,
Against thine image in thy saint, O Lord !
                              WILLIAM COWPER.

SOUTHEY.

FROM "THE VISION OF JUDGMENT."

HE said (I only give the heads), — he said
  He meant no harm in scribbling ; 't was his
      way
Upon all topics ; 't was, besides, his bread,
  Of which he buttered both sides ; 't would
      delay
Too long the assembly (he was pleased to dread),
  And take up rather more time than a day,

Yours very truly

Thos Hood

FORDS, HOWARD & HULBERT. N.Y.

To name his works, — he would but cite a few, —
"Wat Tyler," — "Rhymes on Blenheim," —
"Waterloo."

He had written praises of a regicide;
  He had written praises of all kings whatever;
He had written for republics far and wide,
  And then against them bitterer than ever;
For pantisocracy he once had cried
Aloud, a scheme less moral than 't was clever;
Then grew a hearty anti-jacobin, —
Had turned his coat, — and would have turned
    his skin.

He had sung against all battles, and again
  In their high praise and glory; he had called
Reviewing "the ungentle craft," and then
  Become as base a critic as e'er crawled, —
Fed, paid, and pampered by the very men
By whom his muse and morals had been mauled;
He had written much blank verse, and blanker
    prose,
And more of both than anybody knows.
BYRON.

SPORUS, — LORD HERVEY.

FROM THE "PROLOGUE TO THE SATIRES."

LET Sporus tremble. — A. What? that thing
    of silk,
Sporus, that mere white curd of asses' milk?
Satire of sense, alas! can Sporus feel?
Who breaks a butterfly upon a wheel?
  P. Yet let me flap this bug with gilded wings,
This painted child of dirt that stinks and stings;
Whose buzz the witty and the fair annoys,
Yet wit ne'er tastes, and beauty ne'er enjoys:
So well-bred spaniels civilly delight
In mumbling of the game they dare not bite.
Eternal smiles his emptiness betray,
As shallow streams run dimpling all the way.
Whether in florid impotence he speaks,
And, as the prompter breathes, the puppet squeaks,
Or at the ear of Eve, familiar toad,
Half froth, half venom, spits himself abroad,
In puns, or politics, or tales, or lies,
Or spite, or smut, or rhymes, or blasphemies;
His wit all seesaw, between that and this.
Now high, now low, now master up, now miss,
And he himself one vile antithesis.
Amphibious thing! that, acting either part,
The trifling head, or the corrupted heart,
Fop at the toilet, flatterer at the board,
Now trips a lady, and now struts a lord.
Eve's tempter thus the rabbins have exprest,
A cherub's face, a reptile all the rest;
Beauty that shocks you, parts that none will trust,
Wit that can creep, and pride that licks the dust.
ALEXANDER POPE.

OG.

SHADWELL, THE DRAMATIST.

Now stop your noses, readers, all and some,
For here's a tun of midnight work to come.
Og, from a treason-tavern rolling home
Round as a globe, and liquored every chink,
Goodly and great he sails behind his link:
With all this bulk there's nothing lost in Og,
For every inch that is not fool is rogue;
A monstrous mass of foul, corrupted matter,
As all the devils had spewed to make the batter.
  The midwife laid her hand on his thick skull,
With this prophetic blessing, — "Be thou dull;
Drink, swear, and roar, forbear no lewd delight
Fit for thy bulk; do anything but write:
Thou art of lasting make, like thoughtless men;
A strong nativity — but for the pen!
Eat opium, mingle arsenic in thy drink,
Still thou mayst live, avoiding pen and ink":
I see, I see, 't is counsel given in vain,
For treason botched in rhyme will be thy bane;
Rhyme is the rock on which thou art to wreck,
'T is fatal to thy fame and to thy neck;
Why should thy metre good King David blast?
A psalm of his will surely be thy last.
A double noose thou on thy neck dost pull
For writing treason and for writing dull.
To die for faction is a common evil,
But to be hanged for nonsense is the devil.
JOHN DRYDEN.

ODE TO RAE WILSON, ESQUIRE.

A WANDERER, Wilson, from my native land,
Remote, O Rae, from godliness and thee,
Where rolls between us the eternal sea,
Besides some furlongs of a foreign sand, —
Beyond the broadest Scotch of London Wall,
Beyond the loudest Saint that has a call,
Across the wavy waste between us stretched,
A friendly missive warns me of a stricture,
Wherein my likeness you have darkly etched;
And though I have not seen the shadow sketched,
Thus I remark prophetic on the picture.

I guess the features: — in a line to paint
Their moral ugliness, I'm not a saint.
Not one of those self-constituted saints,
Quacks — not physicians — in the cure of souls,
Censors who sniff out moral taints,
And call the devil over his own coals, —
Those pseudo Privy-Councillors of God,
Who write down judgments with a pen hard-
    nibbed;
  Ushers of Beelzebub's Black Rod,
Commending sinners not to ice thick-ribbed,
But endless flames, to scorch them like flax, —

Yet sure of heaven themselves, as if they'd cribbed
The impression of St. Peter's keys in wax !

Of such a character no single trace
Exists, I know, in my fictitious face.
There wants a certain cast about the eye ;
A certain lifting of the nose's tip ;
A certain curling of the nether lip,
In scorn of all that is, beneath the sky ;
In brief, it is an aspect deleterious,
A face decidedly not serious,
A face profane, that would not do at all
To make a face at Exeter Hall, —
That Hall where bigots rant and cant and pray,
And laud each other face to face,
Till every farthing-candle *ray*
Conceives itself a great gaslight of grace !

Well ! — be the graceless lineaments confest !
I do enjoy this bounteous beauteous earth ;
   And dote upon a jest
" Within the limits of becoming mirth " ; —
No solemn sanctimonious face I pull,
Nor think I 'm pious when I 'm only bilious, —
Nor study in my sanctum supercilious
To frame a Sabbath Bill or forge a Bull.
I pray for grace, — repent each sinful act, —
Peruse, but underneath the rose, my Bible ;
And love my neighbor far too well, in fact,
To call and twit him with a godly tract
That 's turned by application to a libel.
My heart ferments not with the bigot's leaven,
All creeds I view with toleration thorough.
And have a horror of regarding heaven
   As anybody's rotten borough.

I 've no ambition to enact the spy
On fellow-souls, a spiritual Pry, —
'T is said that people ought to guard their noses
Who thrust them into matters none of theirs ;
And, though no delicacy discomposes
Your saint, yet I consider faith and prayers
Amongst the privatest of men's affairs.

I do not hash the Gospel in my books,
And thus upon the public mind intrude it,
As if I thought, like Otaheitan cooks,
No food was fit to eat till I had chewed it.

On Bible stilts I don't affect to stalk ;
Nor lard with Scripture my familiar talk, —
   For man may pious texts repeat,
And yet religion have no inward seat ;
'T is not so plain as the old Hill of Howth,
A man has got his belly full of meat
Because he talks with victuals in his mouth !

I honestly confess that I would hinder
The Scottish member's legislative rigs,
   That spiritual Pindar,

Who looks on erring souls as straying pigs,
That must be lashed by law, wherever found,
And driven to church as to the parish pound.
I do confess, without reserve or wheedle,
I view that grovelling idea as one
Worthy some parish clerk's ambitious son,
A charity-boy who longs to be a beadle.
On such a vital topic sure 't is odd
How much a man can differ from his neighbor ;
One wishes worship freely given to God,
Another wants to make it statute-labor, —
The broad distinction in a line to draw,
As means to lead us to the skies above,
You say, — Sir Andrew and his love of law,
And I, — the Saviour with his law of love.

Spontaneously to God should tend the soul,
Like the magnetic needle to the Pole ;
But what were that intrinsic virtue worth,
Suppose some fellow, with more zeal than knowl-
    edge
   Fresh from St. Andrew's college,
Should nail the conscious needle to the north ?
I do confess that I abhor and shrink
From schemes, with a religious willy-nilly,
That frown upon St. Giles's sins, but blink
The peccadilloes of all Piccadilly, —
My soul revolts at such bare hypocrisy,
And will not, dare not, fancy in accord
The Lord of Hosts with an exclusive lord
   Of this world's aristocracy.
It will not own a notion so unholy
As thinking that the rich by easy trips
May go to heaven, whereas the poor and lowly
Must work their passage, as they do in ships.

One place there is, — beneath the burial-sod,
Where all mankind are equalized by death ;
Another place there is, — the fane of God,
Where all are equal who draw living breath ; —
Juggle who will *elsewhere* with his own soul,
Playing the Judas with a temporal dole,
He who can come beneath that awful cope,
In the dread presence of a Maker just,
Who metes to every pinch of human dust
One even measure of immortal hope, —
He who can stand within that holy door,
With soul unbowed by that pure spirit-level,
And frame unequal laws for rich and poor, —
Might sit for Hell, and represent the Devil !

The humble records of my life to search,
I have not herded with mere pagan beasts ;
But sometimes I have " sat at good men's feasts,"
And I have been " where bells have knolled to
    church."
Dear bells ! how sweet the sounds of village bells
When on the undulating air they swim !
Now loud as welcomes ! faint, now, as farewells !

And trembling all about the breezy dells,
As fluttered by the wings of cherubim.
Meanwhile the bees are chanting a low hymn ;
And, lost to sight, the ecstatic lark above
Sings, like a soul beatified, of love,
With, now and then, the coo of the wild pigeon ;—
O pagans, heathens, infidels, and doubters !
If such sweet sounds can't woo you to religion,
Will the harsh voices of church cads and touters ?

A man may cry Church ! Church ! at every word,
With no more piety than other people, —
A daw 's not reckoned a religious bird
Because it keeps a-cawing from a steeple ;
The Temple is a good, a holy place,
But quacking only gives it an ill savor,
While saintly mountebanks the porch disgrace,
And bring religion's self into disfavor !

      .   .   .   .   .

     Church is "a little heaven below,
       I have been there and still would go," —
Yet I am none of those who think it odd
     A man can pray unbidden from the cassock,
     And, passing by the customary hassock,
Kneel down remote upon the simple sod,
And sue *in forma pauperis* to God.

As for the rest, — intolerant to none,
Whatever shape the pious rite may bear,
Even the poor pagan's homage to the sun
I would not harshly scorn, lest even there
I spurned some elements of Christian prayer, —
An aim, though erring, at a "world ayont," —
Acknowledgment of good, — of man's futility,
A sense of need, and weakness, and indeed
That very thing so many Christians want, —
                   Humility.

      .   .   .   .   .

I have not sought, 't is true, the Holy Land,
As full of texts as Cuddie Headrigg's mother,
     The Bible in one hand,
And my own commonplace-book in the other ;
But you have been to Palestine — alas !
Some minds improve by travel ; others, rather,
     Resemble copper wire or brass,
Which gets the narrower by going farther !

Worthless are all such pilgrimages — very !
If Palmers at the Holy Tomb contrive
The human heats and rancor to revive
That at the Sepulchre they ought to bury.
A sorry sight it is to rest the eye on,
To see a Christian creature graze at Sion,
Then homeward, of the saintly pasture full,
Rush bellowing, and breathing fire and smoke,
At crippled Papistry to butt and poke,
Exactly as a skittish Scottish bull
Hunts an old woman in a scarlet cloke.

      .   .   .   .   .

Gifted with noble tendency to climb,
     Yet weak at the same time,
Faith is a kind of parasitic plant,
That grasps the nearest stem with tendril-rings ;
And as the climate and the soil may grant,
So is the sort of tree to which it clings.
Consider, then, before, like Hurlothrumbo,
You aim your club at any creed on earth,
That, by the simple accident of birth,
You might have been High-Priest to Mumbo
     Jumbo.

For me, — through heathen ignorance perchance,
Not having knelt in Palestine, — I feel
None of that griffinish excess of zeal
Some travellers would blaze with here in France.
Dolls I can see in Virgin-like array,
Nor for a scuffle with the idols hanker
Like crazy Quixotte at the puppet's play,
If their "offence be rank," should mine be *rancor*?

      .   .   .   .

Suppose the tender but luxuriant hop
Around a cankered stem should twine,
What Kentish boor would tear away the prop
So roughly as to wound, nay, kill the bine ?

The images, 't is true, are strangely dressed,
With gauds and toys extremely out of season ;
The carving nothing of the very best,
The whole repugnant to the eye of Reason,
Shocking to Taste, and to Fine Arts a treason, —
Yet ne'er o'erlook in bigotry of sect
One truly *Catholic*, one common form,
     At which unchecked
All Christian hearts may kindle or keep warm.

Say, was it to my spirit's gain or loss,
One bright and balmy morning, as I went
From Liege's lovely environs to Ghent,
If hard by the wayside I found a cross,
That made me breathe a prayer upon the spot, —
While Nature of herself, as if to trace
The emblem's use, had trailed around its base
The blue significant Forget-Me-Not ?
Methought, the claims of Charity to urge
More forcibly along with Faith and Hope,
The pious choice had pitched upon the verge
     Of a delicious slope,
Giving the eye much variegated scope ! —
"Look round," it whispered, "on that prospect
     rare,
Those vales so verdant, and those hills so blue ;
Enjoy the sunny world, so fresh and fair,
But" (how the simple legend pierced me through !)
     "Priez pour les Malheureux."

With sweet kind natures, as in honeyed cells,
Religion lives, and feels herself at home ;

But only on a formal visit dwells
Where wasps instead of bees have formed the
    comb.
Shun pride, O Rae ! — whatever sort beside
You take in lieu, shun spiritual pride !
A pride there is of rank, — a pride of birth,
A pride of learning, and a pride of purse,
A London pride, — in short, there be on earth
A host of prides, some better and some worse ;
But of all prides, since Lucifer's attaint,
The proudest swell 's a self-elected Saint.

To picture that cold pride so harsh and hard,
Fancy a peacock in a poultry-yard.
Behold him in conceited circles sail,
Strutting and dancing, and now planted stiff,
In all his pomp of pageantry, as if
He felt "the eyes of Europe " on his tail !
As for the humble breed retained by man,
    He scorns the whole domestic clan, —
        He bows, he bridles,
        He wheels, he sidles,
As last, with stately dodgings in a corner,
He pens a simple russet hen, to scorn her
Full in the blaze of his resplendent fan !

"Look here," he cries, (to give him words,)
"Thou feathered clay, thou scum of birds !" —
Flirting the rustling plumage in her eyes, —
    "Look here, thou vile predestined sinner,
    Doomed to be roasted for a dinner,
Behold these lovely variegated dyes !
These are the rainbow colors of the skies,
That heaven has shed upon me *con amore*, —
A Bird of Paradise ? — a pretty story ! ·
I am that Saintly Fowl, thou paltry chick !
    Look at my crown of glory !
Thou dingy, dirty, dabbled, draggled jill ! "
And off goes Partlett, wriggling from a kick,
With bleeding scalp laid open by his bill !

That little simile exactly paints
How sinners are despised by saints.
By saints ! — the Hypocrites that ope heaven's
    door
Obsequious to the sinful man of riches ;
But put the wicked, naked, barelegged poor
    In parish stocks, instead of breeches.

    .   .   .   .   .   .

Thrice blessed, rather, is the man with whom
The gracious prodigality of nature,
The balm, the bliss, the beauty, and the bloom,
The bounteous providence in every feature,
Recall the good Creator to his creature,
Making all earth a fane, all heaven its dome !

To *his* tuned spirit the wild heather-bells
    Ring Sabbath knells ;
The jubilate of the soaring lark
    Is chant of clerk ;
For choir, the thrush and the gregarious linnet;
The sod 's a cushion for his pious want ;
And, consecrated by the heaven within it,
    The sky-blue pool, a font.
Each cloud-capped mountain is a holy altar ;
    An organ breathes in every grove ;
    And the full heart 's a Psalter,
Rich in deep hymns of gratitude and love !

    .   .   .   .   .   .

Once on a time a certain English lass
Was seized with symptoms of such deep decline,
Cough, hectic flushes, every evil sign,
That, as their wont is at such desperate pass,
The doctors gave her over — to an ass.

Accordingly, the grisly Shade to bilk,
Each morn the patient quaffed a frothy bowl
    Of asinine new milk,
Robbing a shaggy suckling of a foal,
Which got proportionally spare and skinny ;
Meanwhile the neighbors cried, "Poor Mary
    Ann !
She can't get over it ! she never can ! "
When, lo ! to prove each prophet was a ninny,
The one that died was the poor wet-nurse Jenny.

    To aggravate the case,
There were but two grown donkeys in the place ;
And, most unluckily for Eve's sick daughter,
The other long-eared creature was a male,
Who never in his life had given a pail
    Of milk, or even chalk-and-water.
No matter : at the usual hour of eight
Down trots a donkey to the wicket-gate,
With Mister Simon Gubbins on his back : —
"Your sarvant, miss, — a werry springlike
    day, —
Bad time for hasses, though ! good lack ! good
    lack !
Jenny be dead, miss, — but I 'ze brought ye
    Jack, —
He does n't give no milk, — but he can bray."

    So runs the story,
    And, in vain self-glory,
Some Saints would sneer at Gubbins for his blind-
    ness ;
    But what the better are their pious saws
    To ailing souls, than dry hee-haws,
Without the milk of human kindness ?
                            THOMAS HOOD.

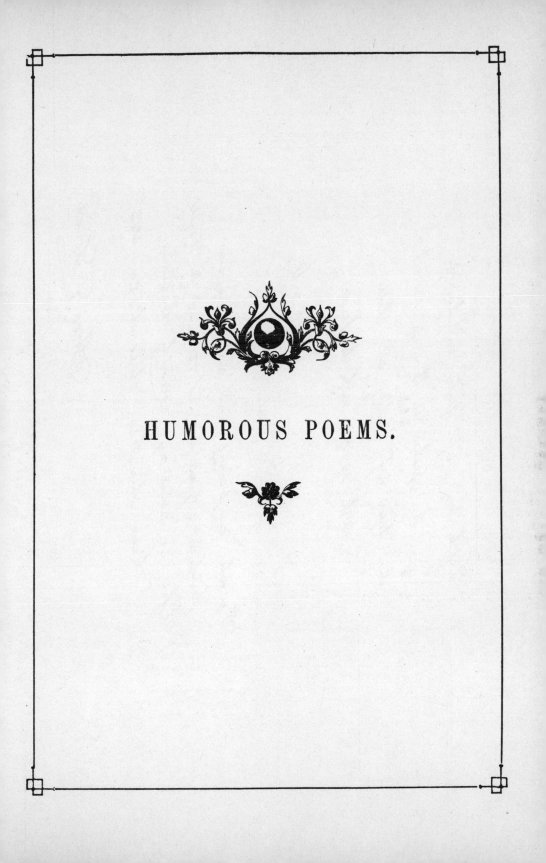

HUMOROUS POEMS.

Let'le boys' up quite underknown
An' pushed in thro' the wrislet
En' thro let shallty all alone
Wilth so me nigh to herdes.

[signature]

—

Such a person is a woman
That, you see, is *must* be true
She is always *exactly* better
Shows the best that she can do!"

Thos. E. Sage.

HUMOROUS POEMS.

QUESTIONS AND ANSWERS.

WHERE, O, where are the visions of morning,
  Fresh as the dews of our prime ?
Gone, like tenants that quit without warning,
  Down the back entry of time.

Where, O, where are life's lilies and roses,
  Nursed in the golden dawn's smile ?
Dead as the bulrushes round little Moses,
  On the old banks of the Nile.

Where are the Marys, and Anns, and Elizas,
  Loving and lovely of yore ?
Look in the columns of old Advertisers, —
  Married and dead by the score.

Where the gray colts and the ten-year-old fillies,
  Saturday's triumph and joy ?
Gone like our friend πόδας ὠκύς Achilles,
  Homer's ferocious old boy.

Die-away dreams of ecstatic emotion,
  Hopes like young eagles at play,
Vows of unheard-of and endless devotion,
  How ye have faded away !

Yet, though the ebbing of Time's mighty river
  Leave our young blossoms to die,
Let him roll smooth in his current forever,
  Till the last pebble is dry.
                    OLIVER WENDELL HOLMES.

METEMPSYCHOSIS.

ROSALIND. Look here what I found on a palm-tree: I was
never so be-rhymed since Pythagoras' time, that I was an Irish
rat, which I can hardly remember. — AS YOU LIKE IT.

I.

I DISTINCTLY remember (and who dares doubt me ?)
  Having been (now, I care not who believes !)
An ape with a forest around about me, —
  Prodigious trees and enormous leaves,
Great bulks of flowers, gigantic grasses,
  Boughs that bent not to any gale ;
And thence I date my contempt for Asses,
  And my deep respect for the Devil's Tail !

II.

I shall never forget the exquisite feeling
  Of elevation, sans thought, sans care,
When I twisted my tail round the wood's bough-
        ceiling,
  And swung, meditatively, in the air. —
There 's an advantage ! — Fairer shapes can
  Aspire, yearn upward, tremble and glow,
But, by means of their posteriority, apes can
  Look down on aspirants that walk below !

III.

There was a life for a calm philosopher,
  Self-supplied with jacket and trousers and
        socks,
Nothing to learn, no hopes to get cross over,
  A head that resisted the hardest knocks,
Liquor and meat in serene fruition,
  A random income from taxes free,
No cares at all, and but one ambition, —
  To swing by the Tail to the bough of a tree !

IV.

Whence I firmly believe, to the consternation
  Of puppies who think monkeyosophy sin,
In gradual human degeneration
  And a general apely origin.
Why, the simple truth 's in a nutshell or thimble,
  Though it rouses the monkey in ignorant elves ;
And the Devil's Tail is a delicate symbol
  Of apehood predominant still in ourselves.

V.

Pure class government, family glory,
  Were the delights of that happy lot ;
My politics were serenely Tory,
  And I claimed old descent from Heaven knows
        what :
Whence I boast extraction loftier, nobler,
  Than the beggarly Poets one often meets,
A boast I am happy to share with the cobbler
  Who whisked his Tail out, — to whip John
        Keats.

VI.

There was a life, I assever ! With reasons
  That lead me to scorn every star-gazing Ass ;
And because I loved it, at certain seasons
  'T is a pleasure to gaze in the looking-glass.
When the bright sun beckons the spring, green-
    deckt, up,
  The Ape swells within me ; whenever I see
Mortals look skyward, walking erect up,
  I long for a Tail and a large strong Tree !
                            ROBERT BUCHANAN.

THE UNIVERSITY OF GOTTINGEN.

BY ONE ELEVEN YEARS IN PRISON.
SONG BY ROGERO IN "THE ROVERS."

WHENE'ER with haggard eyes I view
  This dungeon that I 'm rotting in,
I think of those companions true
  Who studied with me at the U-
                niversity of Gottingen,
                niversity of Gottingen.

[*Weeps, and pulls out a blue kerchief, with which he wipes
his eyes ; gazing tenderly at it, he proceeds :*]

Sweet kerchief, checked with heavenly blue,
  Which once my love sat knotting in —
Alas, Matilda then was true !
  At least I thought so at the U-
                niversity of Gottingen,
                niversity of Gottingen.

Barbs ! barbs ! alas ! how swift you flew,
  Her neat post-wagon trotting in !
Ye bore Matilda from my view ;
  Forlorn I languished at the U-
                niversity of Gottingen,
                niversity of Gottingen.

This faded form ! this pallid hue !
  This blood my veins is clotting in !
My years are many, — they were few
  When first I entered at the U-
                niversity of Gottingen,
                niversity of Gottingen.

There first for thee my passion grew,
  Sweet, sweet Matilda Pottingen !
Thou wast the daughter of my tu-
  tor, law-professor at the U-
                niversity of Gottingen,
                niversity of Gottingen.

Sun, moon, and thou, vain world, adieu,
  That kings and priests are plotting in ;
Here doomed to starve on water gru-
  el, never shall I see the U-
                niversity of Gottingen,
                niversity of Gottingen.
                        GEORGE CANNING.

THE FRIEND OF HUMANITY AND THE KNIFE–GRINDER.

FRIEND OF HUMANITY.

NEEDY knife-grinder ! whither are you going ?
Rough is the road ; your wheel is out of order.
Bleak blows the blast ; — your hat has got a hole
        in 't ;
    So have your breeches !

Weary knife-grinder ! little think the proud ones,
Who in their coaches roll along the turnpike-
road, what hard work 't is crying all day ' Knives
        and
    Scissors to grind O ! '

Tell me, knife-grinder, how came you to grind
        knives ?
Did some rich man tyrannically use you ?
Was it the squire ? or parson of the parish ?
    Or the attorney ?

Was it the squire for killing of his game ? or
Covetous parson for his tithes distraining ?
Or roguish lawyer made you lose your little
    All in a lawsuit ?

(Have you not read the Rights of Man, by Tom
        Paine ?)
Drops of compassion tremble on my eyelids,
Ready to fall as soon as you have told your
    Pitiful story.

KNIFE-GRINDER.

Story ! God bless you ! I have none to tell, sir ;
Only, last night, a-drinking at the Chequers,
This poor old hat and breeches, as you see, were
    Torn in a scuffle.

Constables came up for to take me into
Custody ; they took me before the justice ;
Justice Oldmixon put me in the parish-
    stocks for a vagrant.

I should be glad to drink your honor's health in
A pot of beer, if you will give me sixpence ;
But for my part, I never love to meddle
    With politics, sir.

FRIEND OF HUMANITY.

I give thee sixpence ! I will see thee damned
        first, —
Wretch ! whom no sense of wrongs can rouse to
        vengeance, —
Sordid, unfeeling, reprobate, degraded,
    Spiritless outcast !

[*Kicks the knife-grinder, overturns his wheel, and exit
in a transport of republican enthusiasm and universal
philanthropy*]
                        GEORGE CANNING.

THE SENTIMENTAL GARDENER.

FROM THE GERMAN OF JOHANN MARTIN MILLER.

ONCE there was a gardener,
Who sang all day a dirge to his poor flowers ;
He often stooped and kissed 'em
After thunder-showers :
His nerves were delicate, though fresh air is
      deemed a hardener
Of the human system.

Many a moon went over,
And still his death-bell tale was told and tolled, —
His tears, like rain in winter,
Dribbling slow and cold :
Voici the song itself, — I send it under cover
To my Leipsic printer.

"Weary, I am weary !
No rest from raking till I reach my goal !
Here, like a tulip trampled,
Lose I heart and soul ;
Sure such a death-in-life as mine, so dark, so
      dreary,
Must be unexampled.

"Hence, when droughty weather
Has dulled the spirits of my violets,
Medreams I feel as though I
Should have slight regrets
Were they and I just then to droop and die to-
      gether,
Watched and wept by no eye.

"O gazelle-eyed Princess !
Granddaughter of the Sultan of Cathay !
The knave of spades beseeches
Thee by night and day :
He dies to lay before thee samples of his quinces,
Apricots, and peaches !

"Questionless thy Highness
Must wonder why I play the Absent Man ;
Yet if I pitch my lonely
Tent in Frankistan,
Attribute, O full moon ! the blame, not to my
      shyness,
But to my planet only.

"But enough ! — I 'll smother
My groanings, — and myself. Were I free
Rix baron, or a Markgrave,
I would fly to thee ;
But since — alas, my stars ! — I 'm neither one
      nor t'other,
Here I 'll dig — my dark grave."

                    Translation of JAMES CLARENCE MANGAN.

THE COCKNEY.

IT was in my foreign travel,
At a famous Flemish inn,
That I met a stoutish person
With a very ruddy skin ;
And his hair was something sandy,
And was done in knotty curls,
And was parted in the middle,
In the manner of a girl's.

He was clad in checkered trousers,
And his coat was of a sort
To suggest a scanty pattern,
It was bobbed so very short ;
And his cap was very little,
Such as soldiers often use ;
And he wore a pair of gaiters,
And extremely heavy shoes.

I addressed the man in English,
And he answered in the same,
Though he spoke it in a fashion
That I thought a little lame ;
For the aspirate was missing
Where the letter should have been,
But where'er it was n't wanted,
He was sure to put it in !

When I spoke with admiration
Of St. Peter's mighty dome,
He remarked : " ' T is really nothing
To the sights we 've at 'ome !"
And declared upon his honor, —
Though, of course, 't was very queer, —
That he doubted if the Romans
'Ad the *h*art of making beer !

.   .   .   .   .   .

Then we talked of other countries,
And he said that he had heard
That *h*Americans spoke *h*English,
But he deemed it quite *h*absurd ;
Yet he felt the deepest *h*interest
In the missionary work,
And would like to know if Georgia
Was in Boston or New York !

When I left the man in gaiters,
He was grumbling, o'er his gin,
At the charges of the hostess
Of that famous Flemish inn ;
And he looked a very Briton,
(So, methinks, I see him still,)
As he pocketed the candle
That was mentioned in the bill !

                    JOHN G. SAXE.

THE MODERN BELLE.

SHE sits in a fashionable parlor,
  And rocks in her easy chair ;
She is clad in silks and satins,
  And jewels are in her hair ;
She winks and giggles and simpers,
  And simpers and giggles and winks ;
And though she talks but little,
  'T is a good deal more than she thinks.

She lies abed in the morning
  Till nearly the hour of noon,
Then comes down snapping and snarling
  Because she was called so soon ;
Her hair is still in papers,
  Her cheeks still fresh with paint, —
Remains of her last night's blushes,
  Before she intended to faint.

She dotes upon men unshaven,
  And men with "flowing hair" ;
She 's eloquent over mustaches,
  They give such a foreign air.
She talks of Italian music,
  And falls in love with the moon ;
And, if a mouse were to meet her,
  She would sink away in a swoon.

Her feet are so very little,
  Her hands are so very white,
Her jewels so very heavy,
  And her head so very light ;
Her color is made of cosmetics
  (Though this she will never own),
Her body is made mostly of cotton,
  Her heart is made wholly of stone.

She falls in love with a fellow
  Who swells with a foreign air ;
He marries her for her money,
  She marries him for his hair !
One of the very best matches, —
  Both are well mated in life ;
She 's got a fool for a husband,
  He 's got a fool for a wife !
                              STARK.

HOW IT HAPPENED.

FROM "THE KNIGHT AND THE LADY."

ADAM and Eve were, at the world's beginning,
Ashamed of nothing till they took to sinning ;
But after Adam's slip, — the first was Eve's, —
  With sorrow big,
  They sought the fig,
To cool their blushes with its banging leaves.

Whereby we find
That, when all things were recent,
  (So paradoxical is human kind !)
Till folks grew naughty, they were, *barely*, decent.

Thus, dress may date its origin
  From sin ;
Which proves, beyond the shadow of dispute,
How many owe their livelihoods to fruit ; —

For fruit caused sin, and sin brought shame,
And all through shame our dresses came, —
  With that sad stopper of our breath,
    Death !

Now, had not woman worked our fall,
How many, who have trades and avocations,
Would shut up shop, in these our polished nations,
  And have no business to transact at all !
                              GEORGE COLMAN.

AMERICAN ARISTOCRACY.

OF all the notable things on earth,
The queerest one is pride of birth
  Among our "fierce democracy" !
A bridge across a hundred years,
Without a prop to save it from sneers,
Not even a couple of rotten *peers*, —
A thing for laughter, fleers, and jeers,
  Is American aristocracy !

English and Irish, French and Spanish,
Germans, Italians, Dutch and Danish,
Crossing their veins until they vanish
  In one conglomeration !
So subtle a tangle of blood, indeed,
No Heraldry Harvey will ever succeed
  In finding the circulation.

Depend upon it, my snobbish friend,
Your family thread you can't ascend,
Without good reason to apprehend
You may find it *waxed*, at the farther end,
  By some plebeian vocation !
Or, worse that that, your boasted line
May end in a loop of stronger twine,
  That plagued some worthy relation !
                              JOHN G. SAXE.

PLAIN LANGUAGE FROM TRUTHFUL JAMES.

POPULARLY KNOWN AS "THE HEATHEN CHINEE."

WHICH I wish to remark —
  And my language is plain —
That for ways that are dark

And for tricks that are vain,
The heathen Chinee is peculiar :
    Which the same I would rise to explain.

Ah Sin was his name ;
    And I shall not deny
In regard to the same
    What that name might imply ;
But his smile it was pensive and childlike,
    As I frequent remarked to Bill Nye.

It was August the third,
    And quite soft was the skies,
Which it might be inferred
    That Ah Sin was likewise :
Yet he played it that day upon William
    And me in a way I despise.

Which we had a small game,
    And Ah Sin took a hand :
It was euchre.   The same
    He did not understand ;
But he smiled, as he sat by the table,
    With the smile that was childlike and bland.

Yet the cards they were stocked
    In a way that I grieve,
And my feelings were shocked
    At the state of Nye's sleeve,
Which was stuffed full of aces and bowers,
    And the same with intent to deceive.

But the hands that were played
    By that heathen Chinee,
And the points that he made,
    Were quite frightful to see —
Till at last he put down a right bower,
    Which the same Nye had dealt unto me.

Then I looked up at Nye,
    And he gazed upon me ;
And he rose with a sigh,
    And said, "Can this be ?
We are ruined by Chinese cheap labor," —
    And he went for that heathen Chinee.

In the scene that ensued
    I did not take a hand,
But the floor it was strewed
    Like the leaves on the strand
With the cards that Ah Sin had been hiding
    In the game "he did not understand."

In his sleeves, which were long,
    He had twenty-four packs —
Which was coming it strong,
    Yet I state but the facts.
And we found on his nails, which were taper —
    What is frequent in tapers — that 's wax.

Which is why I remark,
    And my language is plain,
That for ways that are dark,
    And for tricks that are vain,
The heathen Chinee is peculiar —
    Which the same I am free to maintain.
                    FRANCIS BRET HARTE.

NONSENSE.

GOOD reader, if you e'er have seen,
    When Phœbus hastens to his pillow,
The mermaids, with their tresses green,
    Dancing upon the western billow ;
If you have seen at twilight dim,
    When the lone spirit's vesper-hymn
        Floats wild along the winding shore,
If you have seen through mist of eve
    The fairy train their ringlets weave,
Glancing along the spangled green ; —
    If you have seen all this, and more,
God bless me ! what a deal you 've seen !
                    THOMAS MOORE.

WOMAN'S WILL.

AN EPIGRAM.

MEN dying make their wills — but wives
    Escape a work so sad ;
Why should they make what all their lives
    The gentle dames have had ?
                    JOHN GODFREY SAXE.

BACHELOR'S HALL.

BACHELOR'S HALL, what a comical place it is !
    Keep me from such all the days of my life !
Sure but he knows what a burning disgrace it is,
    Never at all to be getting a wife.

See the old bachelor, gloomy and sad enough,
    Fussing around while he 's making his fire ;
His kettle has tipt up, och, honey, he 's mad enough,
    If he were present, to fight with the squire !

Pots, dishes, and pans, and such other com-
        modities,
    Ashes and praty-skins, kiver the floor ;
His cupboard a storehouse of comical oddities,
    Things never thought of as neighbors before.

When his meal it is over, the table 'a left sittin' so ,
    Dishes, take care of yourselves if you can ;
Devil a drop of hot water will visit ye.
    Och, let him alone for a baste of a man !

Now, like a pig in a mortar-bed wallowing,
  See the old bachelor kneading his dough ;
Troth, if his bread he can ate without swallowing,
  How it would help his digestion, ye know !

Late in the night, when he goes to bed shivering,
  Never the bit is his bed made at all ;
So he creeps like a terrapin under the kivering ; —
  Bad luck to the pictur of Bachelor's Hall !
                                    ANONYMOUS.

MR. MOLONY'S ACCOUNT OF THE BALL

GIVEN TO THE NEPAULESE AMBASSADOR BY THE PENIN-
SULAR AND ORIENTAL COMPANY.

O, WILL ye choose to hear the news ?
  Bedad, I cannot pass it o'er :
I 'll tell you all about the ball
  To the Naypaulase Ambassador.
Begor ! this fête all balls does bate,
  At which I worn a pump, and I
Must here relate the splendthor great
  Of th' Oriental Company.

These men of sinse dispoised expinse,
  To fête these black Achilleses.
" We 'll show the blacks," says they, " Almack's,
  And take the rooms at Willis's."
With flags and shawls, for these Nepauls,
  They hung the rooms of Willis up,
And decked the walls and stairs and halls
  With roses and with lilies up.

And Jullien's band it tuck its stand
  So sweetly in the middle there,
And soft bassoons played heavenly chunes,
  And violins did fiddle there.
And when the Coort was tired of spoort,
  I 'd lave you, boys, to think there was
A nate buffet before them set,
  Where lashins of good dhrink there was !

At ten before the ball-room door,
  His moighty Excelléncy was ;
He smoiled and bowed to all the crowd,
  So gorgeous and immense he was.
His dusky shuit, sublime and mute,
  Into the door-way followed him ;
And O the noise of the blackguard boys,
  As they hurrood and hollowed him !

The noble Chair stud at the stair,
  And bade the dthrums to thump ; and he
Did thus evince to that Black Prince
  The welcome of his Company.
O fair the girls, and rich the curls,
  And bright the oys, you saw there, was ;
And fixed each oye, ye there could spoi,
  On Gineral Jung Bahawther was !

This Gineral great then tuck his sate,
  With all the other ginerals,
(Bedad, his troat, his belt, his coat,
  All bleezed with precious minerals ;)
And as he there, with princely air,
  Recloinin on his cushion was,
All round about his royal chair,
  The squeezin and the pushin was.

O Pat, such girls, such Jukes and Earls,
  Such fashion and nobilitee !
Just think of Tim, and fancy him
  Amidst the hoigh gentility !
There was Lord De L'Huys, and the Portygeese
  Ministher and his lady there,
And I reckonized, with much surprise,
  Our messmate, Bob O'Grady, there ;

There was Baroness Brunow, that looked like Juno,
  And Baroness Rehausen there,
And Countess Roullier, that looked peculiar
  Well, in her robes of gauze in there.
There was Lord Crowhurst (I knew him first
  When only Mr. Pips he was),
And Mick O'Toole, the great big fool,
  That after supper tipsy was.

There was Lord Fingall and his ladies all,
  And Lords Killeen and Dufferin,
And Paddy Fife, with his fat wife, —
  I wondther how he could stuff her in.
There was Lord Belfast, that by me past,
  And seemed to ask how should I go there ?
And the Widow Macrae, and Lord A. Hay,
  And the Marchioness of Sligo there.

Yes, Jukes and Earls, and diamonds and pearls,
  And pretty girls, was spoorting there ;
And some beside (the rogues !) I spied,
  Behind the windies, coorting there.
O, there 's one I know, bedad, would show
  As beautiful as any there ;
And I 'd like to hear the pipers blow,
  And shake a fut with Fanny there !
                        WILLIAM MAKEPEACE THACKERAY.

IRISH ASTRONOMY.

A VERITABLE MYTH, TOUCHING THE CONSTELLATION
OF O'RYAN, IGNORANTLY AND FALSELY SPELLED·ORION.

O'RYAN was a man of might
  Whin Ireland was a nation,
But poachin' was his heart's delight
  And constant occupation.
He had an ould militia gun,
  And sartin sure his aim was ;
He gave the keepers many a run,
  And would n't mind the game laws.

St. Pathrick wanst was passin' by
    O'Ryan's little houldin',
And, as the saint felt wake and dhry,
    He thought he'd enther bould in.
"O'Ryan," says the saint, "avick !
    To praich at Thurles I 'm goin' ;
So let me have a rasher quick,
    And a dhrop of Innishowen."

"No rasher will I cook for you
    While betther is to spare, sir,
But here's a jug of mountain dew,
    And there's a rattlin' hare, sir."
St. Pathrick he looked mighty sweet,
    And says he, "Good luck attind you,
And when you're in your windin' sheet,
    It's up to heaven I'll sind you."

O'Ryan gave his pipe a whiff, —
    "Them tidin's is thransportin',
But may I ax your saintship if
    There's any kind of sportin'?"
St. Pathrick said, "A Lion's there,
    Two Bears, a Bull, and Cancer" —
"Bedad," says Mick, "the huntin's rare ;
    St. Pathrick, I'm your man, sir."

So, to conclude my song aright,
    For fear I'd tire your patience,
You'll see O'Ryan any night
    Amid the constellations.
And Venus follows in his track
    Till Mars grows jealous raally,
But, faith, he fears the Irish knack
    Of handling the shillaly.
          CHARLES G. HALPINE.
          (MILES O'REILLY.)

SONG OF THE ICHTHYOSAURUS.

[This curious specimen of German scientific humor refers to the close of the Jurassic (or Liassic) period and the beginning of the Cretaceous, and describes the sad forebodings of a venerable Saurian, who sees in the degeneracy of the times a sign of the coming cataclysm.

The translator says, "Among the many extraordinary liberties which we have felt obliged to take with the letter of the original, in order to preserve as far as possible its spirit and its flowing movement, the most violent is the substitution in the last stanza but one, of an entirely new (and poor) joke for the very neat, but untranslatable *jeu* of the German. The last two lines of the stanza are :

    'Sie kamen zu tief in die Kreide ;
    Da war es natürlich vorbei.'

The literal meaning is, 'They got too deep in the chalk, and it was, of course, all up with them.' The allusion is to the score chalked up by a landlord against some bibulous but impecunious customer ; and the notion that the Saurians ran up so large an account for drinks that the chalk required to mark their indebtedness smothered the whole race, and brought on the Cretaceous or chalk period, is so absurdly funny that it is a pity to sacrifice it."]

THERE's a rustling in the rushes,
    There's a flashing in the sea,
There's a tearful Ichthyosaurus
    Swims hither mournfully !

He weeps o'er the modern corruption,
    Compared with the good old times,
And don't know what is the matter
    With the Upper Jura limes !

The hoary old Plesiosaurus
    Does naught but quaff and roar ;
And the Pterodactylus lately
    Flew drunk to his own front door !

The Iguanodon of the Period
    Grows worse with every stratum ;
He kisses the Ichthyosauresses
    Whenever he can get at 'em !

I feel a catastrophe coming ;
    This epoch will soon be done,
And what will become of the Jura
    If such goings-on go on ?

The groaning Ichthyosaurus
    Turns suddenly chalky pale ;
He sighs from his steaming nostrils,
    He writhes with his dying tail !

In that self-same hour and minute
    Died the whole Saurian stem, —
The fossil-oil in their liquor
    Soon put an end to them !

And the poet found their story
    Which here he doth indite,
In the form of a petrified album-leaf
    Upon a coprolite !
          ROSSITER W. RAYMOND.

TO THE PLIOCENE SKULL.

A GEOLOGICAL ADDRESS.

["A human skull has been found in California, in the pliocene formation. This skull is the remnant, not only of the earliest pioneer of this State, but the oldest known human being. . . . . The skull was found in a shaft one hundred and fifty feet deep, two miles from Angel's, in Calaveras County, by a miner named James Matson, who gave it to Mr. Scribner, a merchant, and he gave it to Dr. Jones, who sent it to the State Geological Survey. . . . . The published volume of the State Survey on the Geology of California states that man existed contemporaneously with the mastodon, but this fossil proves that he was here before the mastodon was known to exist." — *Daily Paper.*]

"SPEAK, O man, less recent ! Fragmentary fossil !
Primal pioneer of pliocene formation,
Hid in lowest drifts below the earliest stratum
    Of volcanic tufa !

Older than the beasts, the oldest Palæotherium ;
Older than the trees, the oldest Cryptogamia ;
Older than the hills, those infant eruptions
    Of earth's epidermis !

Eo — Mio — Plio — whatsoe'er the "cene" was
That those vacant sockets filled with awe and
        wonder, —
Whether shores Devonian or Silurian beaches, —
    Tell us thy strange story !

Or has the Professor slightly antedated
By some thousand years thy advent on this planet,
Giving thee an air that 's somewhat better fitted
    For cold-blooded creatures ?

Wert thou true spectator of that mighty forest
When above thy head the stately Sigillaria
Reared its columned trunks in that remote and
        distant
    Carboniferous epoch ?

Tell us of that scene, — the dim and watery wood-
        land,
Songless, silent, hushed, with never bird or insect,
Veiled with spreading fronds and screened with
        tall club-mosses,
    Lycopodiacea —

When beside thee walked the solemn Plesiosaurus,
And around thee crept the festive Ichthyosaurus,
While from time to time above thee flew and circled
    Cheerful Pterodactyls.

Tell us of thy food, — those half-marine refections,
Crinoids on the shell, and Brachipods *au naturel*, —
Cuttle-fish to which the *pieuvre* of Victor Hugo
    Seems a periwinkle.

Speak, thou awful vestige of the earth's creation, —
Solitary fragment of remains organic !
Tell the wondrous secrets of thy past existence, —
    Speak ! thou oldest primate ! "

Even as I gazed, a thrill of the maxilla
And a lateral movement of the condyloid process,
With post-pliocene sounds of healthy mastication,
    Ground the teeth together.

And from that imperfect dental exhibition,
Stained with expressed juices of the weed Nicotian,
Came those hollow accents, blent with softer
        murmurs
    Of expectoration :

"Which my name is Bowers, and my crust was
        busted
Falling down a shaft, in Calaveras County,
But I 'd take it kindly if you 'd send the pieces
    Home to old Missouri ! "
              FRANCIS BRET HARTE.

THE JOVIAL BEGGAR.

THERE was a jovial beggar,
    He had a wooden leg ;
Lame from his cradle,
    And forced for to beg.
        And a-begging we will go,
          Will go, will go,
        And a-begging we will go.

A bag for his oatmeal,
    Another for his salt,
And a long pair of crutches,
    To show that he can halt.
        And a-begging we will go, etc.

A bag for his wheat,
    Another for his rye,
And a little bottle by his side,
    To drink when he 's a-dry.
        And a-begging we will go, etc.

Seven years I begged
    For my old master Wilde ;
He taught me how to beg
    When I was but a child.
        And a-begging we will go, etc.

I begged for my master,
    And got him store of pelf ;
But, goodness now be praised !
    I 'm begging for myself.
        And a-begging we will go, etc.

In a hollow tree
    I live, and pay no rent ;
Providence provides for me,
    And I am well content.
        And a-begging we will go, etc.

Of all the occupations
    A beggar's is the best,
For whenever he 's a-weary,
    He can lay him down to rest.
        And a-begging we will go, etc.

I fear no plots against me,
    I live in open cell ;
Then who would be a king, lads,
    When the beggar lives so well ?
        And a-begging we will go,
          Will go, will go,
        And a-begging we will go.
              ANONYMOUS.

GOOD ALE.

I CANNOT eat but little meat, —
    My stomach is not good ;

But, sure, I think that I can drink
  With any that wears a hood.
Though I go bare, take ye no care ;
  I am nothing a-cold, —
I stuff my skin so full within
  Of jolly good ale and old.
Back and side go bare, go bare ;
  Both foot and hand go cold ;
But, belly, God send thee good ale enough,
  Whether it be new or old !

I love no roast but a nut-brown toast,
  And a crab laid in the fire ;
A little bread shall do me stead, —
  Much bread I not desire.
No frost nor snow, nor wind, I trow,
  Can hurt me if I wold, —
I am so wrapt, and thorowly lapt
  Of jolly good ale and old.
Back and side go bare, go bare, etc.

And Tyb, my wife, that as her life
  Loveth well good ale to seek,
Full oft drinks she, till you may see
  The tears run down her cheek ;
Then doth she trowl to me the bowl,
  Even as a malt-worm should ;
And saith, "Sweetheart, I took my part
  Of this jolly good ale and old."
Back and side go bare, go bare, etc.

Now let them drink till they nod and wink,
  Even as good fellows should do ;
They shall not miss to have the bliss
  Good ale doth bring men to ;
And all poor souls that have scoured bowls,
  Or have them lustily trowled,
God save the lives of them and their wives,
  Whether they be young or old !
Back and side go bare, go bare ;
  Both foot and hand go cold ;
But, belly, God send thee good ale enough,
  Whether it be new or old !
                                    JOHN STILL.

GLUGGITY GLUG.

FROM "THE MYRTLE AND THE VINE."

A JOLLY fat friar loved liquor good store,
  And he had drunk stoutly at supper ;
He mounted his horse in the night at the door,
  And sat with his face to the crupper :
"Some rogue," quoth the friar, "quite dead to
    remorse,
Some thief, whom a halter will throttle,
Some scoundrel has cut off the head of my horse,
  While I was engaged at the bottle,
    Which went gluggity, gluggity — glug
    — glug — glug."

The tail of the steed pointed south on the dale,
  'T was the friar's road home, straight and
    level ;
But, when spurred, a horse follows his nose, not
    his tail,
  So he scampered due north, like a devil :
"This new mode of docking," the friar then said,
  "I perceive does n't make a horse trot ill ;
And 't is cheap, — for he never can eat off his head
  While I am engaged at the bottle,
    Which goes gluggity, gluggity — glug
    — glug — glug."

The steed made a stop, — in a pond he had got,
  He was rather for drinking than grazing ;
Quoth the friar, "'T is strange headless horses
    should trot,
  But to drink with their tails is amazing !"
Turning round to see whence this phenomenon
    rose,
  In the pond fell this son of a pottle ;
Quoth he, "The head 's found, for I 'm under his
    nose, —
  I wish I were over a bottle,
    Which goes gluggity, gluggity — glug
    — glug — glug."
                                    ANONYMOUS.

ODE FOR A SOCIAL MEETING.

WITH SLIGHT ALTERATIONS BY A TEETOTALER.

COME ! fill a fresh bumper, — for why should we
    go
            logwood
While the ~~nectar~~ still reddens our cups as they
    flow ?
            decoction
Pour out the ~~rich juices~~ still bright with the sun,
                              dye-stuff
Till o'er the brimmed crystal the ~~rubies~~ shall run.

            half-ripened apples
The ~~purple-globed clusters~~ their life-dews have
    bled ;
              taste   sugar of lead
How sweet is ~~the breath~~ of the ~~fragrance they shed~~ !
      rank poisons   wines ! ! !
For summer's ~~last roses~~ lie hid in the ~~wines~~
                        stable-boys smoking long-nines
That were garnered by ~~maidens who laughed~~
    ~~through the vines.~~

        scowl   howl   scoff   sneer
Then a ~~smile,~~ and a ~~glass,~~ and a ~~toast,~~ and a ~~cheer,~~
            strychnine and whiskey, and ratsbane and beer
For ~~all the good wine, and we 've some of it here~~ !
In cellar, in pantry, in attic, in hall,
      Down, down with the tyrant that masters us all !
~~Long live the gay servant that laughs for us all~~ !
                          OLIVER WENDELL HOLMES.

A NOSEGAY.

A SIMILE FOR REVIEWERS.

YE overseers and reviewers
Of all the Muses' sinks and sewers,
Who dwell on high,
Enthroned among your peers
The garreteers,
That border on the sky :
Who hear the music of the spheres,
Ye have such ears
And dwell so high !
I thank you for your criticism,
Which you have ushered in
With a delightful witticism
That tastes like rotten fruit preserved in gin ;
And therefore marvel not that my two ballads,
Which are but like two salads,
By no means suit,
Like your fruit,
With your palates.
I do admire your dealings,
To speak according to your feelings,
And do believe if you had withal
You would drop honey,
And that you overflow with gall
Because you do not overflow with money.
Thence all your spite
Against a poor conundrumite,
Whose only business is to watch
Where the conundrums lie,
And be upon the watch,
As they go by ;
To make a simile in no feature
Resembling the creature
That he has in his eye,
Just as a fisher shoots an owl,
Or a sea-fowl,
To make the likeness of a fly ;
Just as you look into the fire,
For any likeness you desire.
Simile-making is an undertaking,
In which the undertaker
Resembles the marriage-contract maker ;
A poor industrious man who means no ill,
But does the best he can
With a quill,
In that he does according to his skill.
If matters can be brought to bear
So as to tie the knot,
He does not care
Whether they are a happy pair or not ;
And, as I said at first,
Nothing could make you all so keen
And curst,
But that which makes you all so lean, —
Hunger and thirst.
So now and then a judge

Consigns a wretch
To Master Ketch,
Having no grudge ;
No reason clear can be assigned,
Only, like you, he has not dined.
So far from wishing your allowance shorter,
I wish, for all your sakes,
You may never want beefsteaks
And porter,
And for your merits
A dram of British spirits.
And so I leave you with a fable
Designed, without a sneer,
To exhilarate your table
And give a relish to your beer.
I beg my compliments to all your ladies
The revieweresses—
Hark ! ! !
And, if you please take warning,
My fable is concerning
A cuckoo and a lark.
If I had said a nightingale,
You would have cried —
You could not fail,
That it was pride,
And naught beside,
That made me think of such a tale.
Upon a tree as they were sitting
They fell into a warm dispute,
Warmer than was fitting,
Which of them was the better flute.
After much prating
And debating,
Not worth relating,
Things came to such a pass,
They both agree
To take an ass
For referee :
The ass was studying botany and grass
Under the tree.
What do you think was the decree ?
"Why," said the ass, "the question is not hard:"
And so he made an excellent award,
As you shall see.
"The lark," says he,
"Has got a wild fantastic pipe,
But no more music than a snipe ;
It gives one pain
And turns one's brain,
One can't keep time to such a strain ;
Whereas the cuckoo's note
Is measured and composed with thought ;
His method is distinct and clear,
And dwells
Like bells
Upon the ear,
Which is the sweetest music one can hear.
I can distinguish, I 'll lay a wager,

His manner and expression,
From every forester and cager
Of the profession."
Thus ended the dispute :
The cuckoo was quite mute
With admiration,
The lark stood laughing at the brute
Affecting so much penetration.
The ass was so intoxicated
And shallow-pated,
That ever since
He's got a fancy in his skull,
That he's a commission from his prince,
Dated when the moon's at full ;
To summon every soul,
Every ass and ass's foal,
To try the quick and dull ;
Trumpeting through the fields and streets,
Stopping and jading all he meets,
Pronouncing with an air
Of one pronouncing from the chair,
"Here's a beauty, this is new, —
And that's a blemish
For which I have no relish," —
Just like the Critical Review.

STERNE.

THE YARN OF THE "NANCY BELL."

FROM "THE BAB BALLADS."

'T WAS on the shores that round our coast
From Deal to Ramsgate span,
That I found alone, on a piece of stone,
An elderly naval man.

His hair was weedy, his beard was long,
And weedy and long was he ;
And I heard this wight on the shore recite,
In a singular minor key : —

"O, I am a cook and a captain bold,
And the mate of the Nancy brig,
And a bo'sun tight, and a midshipmite,
And the crew of the captain's gig."

And he shook his fists and he tore his hair,
Till I really felt afraid,
For I could n't help thinking the man had been drinking,
And so I simply said : —

"O elderly man, it 's little I know
Of the duties of men of the sea,
And I 'll eat my hand if I understand
How you can possibly be

"At once a cook and a captain bold,
And the mate of the Nancy brig,

And a bo'sun tight, and a midshipmite,
And the crew of the captain's gig!"

Then he gave a hitch to his trousers, which
Is a trick all seamen larn,
And having got rid of a thumping quid
He spun this painful yarn : —

"'T was in the good ship Nancy Bell
That we sailed to the Indian sea,
And there on a reef we come to grief,
Which has often-occurred to me.

"And pretty nigh all o' the crew was drowned
(There was seventy-seven o' soul) ;
And only ten of the Nancy's men
Said ' Here ' to the muster-roll.

"There was me, and the cook, and the captain bold,
And the mate of the Nancy brig,
And a bo'sun tight and a midshipmite,
And the crew of the captain's gig.

"For a month we 'd neither wittles nor drink,
Till a hungry we did feel,
So we drawed a lot, and, accordin', shot
The captain for our meal.

"The next lot fell to the Nancy's mate,
And a delicate dish he made ;
Then our appetite with the midshipmite
We seven survivors stayed.

"And then we murdered the bo'sun tight,
And he much resembled pig ;
Then we wittled free, did the cook and me,
On the crew of the captain's gig.

"Then only the cook and me was left,
And the delicate question, ' Which
Of us two goes to the kettle ?' arose,
And we argued it out as sich.

"For I loved that cook as a brother, I did,
And the cook he worshipped me ;
But we 'd both be blowed if we 'd either be stowed
In the other chap's hold, you see.

"' I 'll be eat if you dines off me,' says Tom.
' Yes, that,' says I, ' you 'll be.
I 'm boiled if I die, my friend,' quoth I ;
And ' Exactly so,' quoth he.

"Says he : ' Dear James, to murder me
Were a foolish thing to do,
For don't you see that you can't cook me,
While I can — and will — cook you ?'

"So he boils the water, and takes the salt
And the pepper in portions true
(Which he never forgot), and some chopped shalot,
And some sage and parsley too.

" ' Come here,' says he, with a proper pride,
    Which his smiling features tell ;
" 'T will soothing be if I let you see
    How extremely nice you 'll smell.'

" And he stirred it round, and round, and round,
    And he sniffed at the foaming froth ;
When I ups with his heels, and smothers his
        squeals
    In the scum of the boiling broth.

" And I eat that cook in a week or less,
    And as I eating be
The last of his chops, why I almost drops,
    For a wessel in sight I see.

.   .   .   .   .   .

" And I never larf, and I never smile,
    And I never lark nor play ;
But I sit and croak, and a single joke
    I have — which is to say :

" O, I am a cook and a captain bold
    And the mate of the Nancy brig,
And a bo'sun tight, and a midshipmite,
    And the crew of the captain's gig ! "
                            W. S. GILBERT.

COLOGNE.

In Köln, a town of monks and bones,
And pavements fanged with murderous stones,
And rags, and hags, and hideous wenches, —
I counted two-and-seventy stenches,
All well-defined and several stinks !
Ye nymphs that reign o'er sewers and sinks,
The river Rhine, it is well known,
Doth wash your city of Cologne ;
But tell me, nymphs ! what power divine
Shall henceforth wash the river Rhine ?
                    SAMUEL TAYLOR COLERIDGE.

THE WILL.

[The following will, by which a large fortune was bequeathed, was proved in Doctors' Commons, London, in 1737.]

The fifth day of May
Being airy and gay,
And to hyp. not inclined,
But of vigorous mind,
And my body in health,
I 'll dispose of my wealth,
And all I 'm to leave
On this side of the grave,
To some one or other,
And I think to my brother,
Because I foresaw
That my brethren in law,

If I did not take care,
Would come in for a share ;
Which I no wise intended
Till their manners were mended.
Of that there 's no sign,
I do therefore enjoin,
And do strictly command,
Of which witness my hand,
That naught I have got
Be brought to hotch-pot ;
But I give and devise
As much as in me lies
To the son of my mother,
My own dear brother,
To have and to hold,
All my silver and gold,
Both sutton and potten,
Until the world 's rotten,
As the affectionate pledges
Of his brother.
                            JOHN HEDGES.

ECHO.

I asked of Echo, 't other day,
    (Whose words are few and often funny,)
What to a novice she could say
    Of courtship, love, and matrimony ?
    Quoth Echo, plainly, — " Matter-o'-money ! "

Whom should I marry ? — should it be
    A dashing damsel, gay and pért,
A pattern of inconstancy ;
    Or selfish, mercenary flirt ?
    Quoth Echo, sharply, — " Nary flirt ! "

What if, aweary of the strife
    That long has lured the dear deceiver,
She promise to amend her life,
    And sin no more ; can I believe her ?
    Quoth Echo, very promptly, — " Leave her ! "

But if some maiden with a heart
    On me should venture to bestow it,
Pray, should I act the wiser part
    To take the treasure, or forego it ?
    Quoth Echo, with decision, — " Go it ! "

But what if, seemingly afraid
    To bind her fate in Hymen's fetter,
She vow she means to die a maid,
    In answer to my loving letter ?
    Quoth Echo, rather coolly, — " Let her ! "

What if, in spite of her disdain,
    I find my heart intwined about
With Cupid's dear delicious chain
    So closely that I can't get out ?
    Quoth Echo, laughingly, — " Get out ! "

But if some maid with beauty blest,
    As pure and fair as Heaven can make her,
Will share my labor and my rest
    Till envious Death shall overtake her?
    Quoth Echo (*sotto voce*), — "Take her!"
                    JOHN G. SAXE.

PHILOSOPHY OF HUDIBRAS.

BESIDE, he was a shrewd philosopher,
And had read every text and gloss over;
Whate'er the crabbed'st author hath,
He understood b' implicit faith.
Whatever sceptic could inquire for,
For every why he had a wherefore;
Knew more than forty of them do,
As far as words and terms could go:
All which he understood by rote,
And, as occasion served, would quote;
No matter whether right or wrong;
They might be either said or sung.
His notions fitted things so well
That which was which he could not tell;
But oftentimes mistook the one
For the other, as great clerks have done.
He could reduce all things to acts,
And knew their natures by abstracts;
Where entity and quiddity,
The ghosts of defunct bodies, fly;
Where truth in person does appear,
Like words congealed in northern air:
He knew what's what, and that's as high
As metaphysic wit can fly.
                    SAMUEL BUTLER.

LOGIC OF HUDIBRAS.

HE was in logic a great critic,
Profoundly skilled in analytic;
He could distinguish and divide
A hair 'twixt south and southwest side;
On either which he would dispute,
Confute, change hands, and still confute:
He 'd undertake to prove, by force
Of argument, a man 's no horse;
He 'd prove a buzzard is no fowl,
And that a lord may be an owl,
A calf an alderman, a goose a justice,
And rooks committee-men and trustees.
He 'd run in debt by disputation,
And pay with ratiocination:
All this by syllogism true,
In mood and figure he would do.
                    SAMUEL BUTLER.

THE VIRTUOSO.

IN IMITATION OF SPENSER'S STYLE AND STANZA.

" . . . . Videmus
Nugari solitos."— PERSIUS.

WHILOM by silver Thames's gentle stream,
    In London town there dwelt a subtle wight, —
A wight of mickle wealth, and mickle fame,
    Book-learned and quaint: a Virtuoso hight.
Uncommon things, and rare, were his delight;
    From musings deep his brain ne'er gotten ease,
Nor ceaséd he from study, day or night;
    Until (advancing onward by degrees)
He knew whatever breeds on earth or air or seas.

He many a creature did anatomize,
    Almost unpeopling water, air, and land;
Beasts, fishes, birds, snails, caterpillars, flies,
    Were laid full low by his relentless hand,
That oft with gory crimson was distained;
    He many a dog destroyed, and many a cat;
Of fleas his bed, of frogs the marshes drained,
    Could tellen if a mite were lean or fat,
And read a lecture o'er the entrails of a gnat.

He knew the various modes of ancient times,
    Their arts and fashions of each different guise,
Their weddings, funerals, punishments for crimes,
    Their strength, their learning eke, and rarities;
Of old habiliments, each sort and size,
    Male, female, high and low, to him were known;
Each gladiator dress, and stage disguise;
    With learnéd, clerkly phrase he could have shown
How the Greek tunic differed from the Roman gown.

A curious medallist, I wot, he was,
    And boasted many a course of ancient coin;
Well as his wife's he knewen every face,
    From Julius Cæsar down to Constantine:
For some rare sculpture he would oft ypine,
    (As green-sick damosels for husbands do;)
And when obtainéd, with enraptured eyne,
    He 'd run it o'er and o'er with greedy view,
And look, and look again, as he would look it through.

His rich museum, of dimensions fair,
    With goods that spoke the owner's mind was fraught:
Things ancient, curious, value-worth, and rare,
    From sea and land, from Greece and Rome, were brought;
Which he with mighty sums of gold had bought:
    On these all tides with joyous eyes he pored;
And, sooth to say, himself he greater thought,

When he beheld his cabinets thus stored,
Than if he'd been of Albion's wealthy cities lord.

.   .   .   .   .   .

MARK AKENSIDE.

KING CANUTE AND HIS NOBLES.

CANUTE was by his nobles taught to fancy,
That, by a kind of royal necromancy,
  He had the power Old Ocean to control.
Down rushed the royal Dane upon the strand,
And issued, like a Solomon, command, —
    Poor soul.

"Go back, ye waves, you blustering rogues,"
    quoth he ;
"Touch not your lord and master, Sea ;
For by my power almighty, if you do — "
Then, staring vengeance, out he held a stick,
Vowing to drive Old Ocean to Old Nick,
  Should he even wet the latchet of his shoe.

The Sea retired, — the monarch fierce rushed on,
  And looked as if he'd drive him from the land ;
But Sea, not caring to be put upon,
    Made for a moment a bold stand :

Not only made a stand did Mr. Ocean,
But to his honest waves he made a motion,
  And bid them give the king a hearty trim-
    ming.
The orders seemed a deal the waves to tickle,
For soon they put his majesty in pickle,
  And sat his royalties, like geese, a swimming.

All hands aloft, with one tremendous roar,
Sound did they make him wish himself on shore ;
  His head and ears most handsomely they
    doused, —
Just like a porpoise, with one general shout,
The waves so tumbled the poor king about, —
  No anabaptist e'er was half so soused.

At length to land he crawled, a half-drowned thing,
Indeed more like a crab than like a king,
  And found his courtiers making rueful faces :
But what said Canute to the lords and gentry,
Who hailed him from the water, on his entry,
  All trembling for their lives or places ?

"My lords and gentlemen, by your advice,
I 've had with Mr. Sea a pretty bustle ;
My treatment from my foe not over nice,
  Just made a jest for every shrimp and muscle :

A pretty trick for one of my dominion ! —
My lords, I thank you for your great opinion.

You 'll tell me, p'rhaps, I 've only lost one
    game,
  And bid me try another — for the rubber ;
Permit me to inform you all, with shame,
  That you 're a set of knaves, and I 'm a lubber."

DR. WOLCOTT (PETER PINDAR).

LET US ALONE.

A REMINISCENCE OF " THE LATE ONPLEASANTNESS."

As vonce I valked by a dismal swamp,
There sot an Old Cove in the dark and damp,
  And at everybody as passed that road
A stick or a stone this Old Cove throwed ;
And venever he flung his stick or his stone,
He 'd set up a song of " Let me alone."

"Let me alone, for I loves to shy
These bits of things at the passers-by ;
Let me alone, for I 've got your tin,
And lots of other traps snugly in ;
Let me alone, — I am rigging a boat
To grab votever you 've got afloat ;
In a veek or so I expects to come
And turn you out of your 'ouse and 'ome ;
I 'm a quiet Old Cove," says he, with a groan ;
  "All I axes is, Let me alone."

Just then came along, on the self-same vay,
Another Old Cove, and began for to say, —
" Let you alone !   That 's comin' it strong !
You 've *ben* let alone — a darned site too long !
Of all the sarce that ever I heerd !
Put down that stick ! (You may well look skeered.)
Let go that stone !   If you once show fight,
I 'll knock you higher than any kite.
You must have a lesson to stop your tricks,
And cure you of shying them stones and sticks ;
And I 'll have my hardware back, and my
    cash,
And knock your scow into tarnal smash ;
And if ever I catches you round my ranch,
I 'll string you up to the nearest branch.
The best you can do is to go to bed,
And keep a decent tongue in your head ;
For I reckon, before you and I are done,
You 'll wish you had let honest folks alone."

The Old Cove stopped, and t'other Old Cove,
He sot quite still in his cypress grove,
And he looked at his stick, revolvin' slow,
Vether 't were safe to shy it, or no ;
And he grumbled on, in an injured tone,
" All that I axed vos, *Let me alone.*"

H. P. H. BROWNELL.

EVENING.

BY A TAILOR.

DAY hath put on his jacket, and around
His burning bosom buttoned it with stars.
Here will I lay me on the velvet grass,
That is like padding to earth's meagre ribs,
And hold communion with the things about me.
Ah me! how lovely is the golden braid
That binds the skirt of night's descending robe!
The thin leaves, quivering on their silken threads,
Do make a music like to rustling satin,
As the light breezes smooth their downy nap.

Ha! what is this that rises to my touch,
So like a cushion? Can it be a cabbage?
It is, it is that deeply injured flower,
Which boys do flout us with; — but yet I love thee,
Thou giant rose, wrapped in a green surtout.
Doubtless in Eden thou didst blush as bright
As these, thy puny brethren; and thy breath
Sweetened the fragrance of her spicy air;
But now thou seemest like a bankrupt beau,
Stripped of his gaudy hues and essences,
And growing portly in his sober garments.

Is that a swan that rides upon the water?
O no, it is that other gentle bird,
Which is the patron of our noble calling.
I well remember, in my early years,
When these young hands first closed upon a goose;
I have a scar upon my thimble finger,
Which chronicles the hour of young ambition.
My father was a tailor, and his father,
And my sire's grandsire, all of them were tailors;
They had an ancient goose, — it was an heir-loom
From some remoter tailor of our race.
It happened I did see it on a time
When none was near, and I did deal with it,
And it did burn me, — O, most fearfully!

It is a joy to straighten out one's limbs,
And leap elastic from the level counter,
Leaving the petty grievances of earth,
The breaking thread, the din of clashing shears,
And all the needles that do wound the spirit,
For such a pensive hour of soothing silence.
Kind Nature, shuffling in her loose undress,
Lays bare her shady bosom; — I can feel
With all around me; — I can hail the flowers
That sprig earth's mantle, — and yon quiet bird,
That rides the stream, is to me as a brother.
The vulgar know not all the hidden pockets,
Where Nature stows away her loveliness.
But this unnatural posture of the legs
Cramps my extended calves, and I must go
Where I can coil them in their wonted fashion.

OLIVER WENDELL HOLMES.

THE PILGRIMS AND THE PEAS.

A BRACE of sinners, for no good,
  Were ordered to the Virgin Mary's shrine,
Who at Loretto dwelt, in wax, stone, wood,
  And in a fair white wig looked wondrous fine.

Fifty long miles had those sad rogues to travel,
With something in their shoes much worse than
    gravel;
In short, their toes so gentle to amuse,
The priest had ordered peas into their shoes:
A nostrum famous in old popish times
For purifying souls that stunk of crimes:
    A sort of apostolic salt,
    Which popish parsons for its powers exalt,
For keeping souls of sinners sweet,
Just as our kitchen salt keeps meat.

The knaves set off on the same day,
Peas in their shoes, to go and pray;
  But very different was their speed, I wot:
One of the sinners galloped on,
Swift as a bullet from a gun;
  The other limped, as if he had been shot.
One saw the Virgin soon, Peccavi cried,
  Had his soul whitewashed all so clever;
Then home again he nimbly hied,
  Made fit with saints above to live forever.

In coming back, however, let me say,
He met his brother rogue about half-way, —
Hobbling, with outstretched arms and bended
    knees,
Cursing the souls and bodies of the peas;
His eyes in tears, his cheeks and brow in sweat,
Deep sympathizing with his groaning feet.
"How now," the light-toed, whitewashed pil-
    grim broke,
    "You lazy lubber!"
"Ods curse it!" cried the other, "'t is no joke;
My feet, once hard as any rock,
  Are now as soft as blubber."

"Excuse me, Virgin Mary, that I swear,
As for Loretto, I shall not get there;
No, to the Devil my sinful soul must go,
For damme if I ha' n't lost every toe.
But, brother sinner, pray explain
How 't is that you are not in pain.
What power hath worked a wonder for your toes
Whilst I just like a snail am crawling,
Now swearing, now on saints devoutly bawling,
  Whilst not a rascal comes to ease my woes?

"How is 't that you can like a greyhound go,
  Merry as if that naught had happened, burn ye!"
"Why," cried the other, grinning, "you must
    know,

That just before I ventured on my journey,
  To walk a little more at ease,
I took the liberty to *boil my peas.*"
                    DR. WOLCOTT (PETER PINDAR).

THE RAZOR–SELLER.

A fellow in a market-town,
Most musical, cried razors up and down,
  And offered twelve for eighteen pence ;
Which certainly seemed wondrous cheap,
And, for the money, quite a heap,
  As every man would buy, with cash and sense.

A country bumpkin the great offer heard, —
Poor Hodge, who suffered by a broad black beard,
  That seemed a shoe-brush stuck beneath his
    nose :
With cheerfulness the eighteen pence he paid,
And proudly to himself in whispers said,
  "This rascal stole the razors, I suppose.

"No matter if the fellow *be* a knave,
Provided that the razors *shave ;*
  It certainly will be a monstrous prize."
So home the clown, with his good fortune, went,
Smiling, in heart and soul content,
  And quickly soaped himself to ears and eyes.

Being well lathered from a dish or tub,
Hodge now began with grinning pain to grub,
  Just like a hedger cutting furze ;
'T was a vile razor ! — then the rest he tried, —
All were impostors.   "Ah !" Hodge sighed,
  "I wish my eighteen pence within my purse."

In vain to chase his beard, and bring the graces,
  He cut, and dug, and winced, and stamped,
    and swore ;
Brought blood, and danced, blasphemed, and
    made wry faces,
  And cursed each razor's body o'er and o'er :

His muzzle formed of *opposition* stuff,
Firm as a Foxite, would not lose its ruff ;
  So kept it, — laughing at the steel and suds.
Hodge, in a passion, stretched his angry jaws,
Vowing the direst vengeance with clenched claws,
  On the vile cheat that sold the goods.
"Razors ! a mean, confounded dog,
Not fit to scrape a hog !"

Hodge sought the fellow, — found him, — and
    begun :
"P'rhaps, Master Razor-rogue, to you 't is fun,
  That people flay themselves out of their lives.
You rascal ! for an hour have I been grubbing,
Giving my crying whiskers here a scrubbing,
  With razors just like oyster-knives.

Sirrah ! I tell you you 're a knave,
To cry up razors that can't shave !"

"Friend," quoth the razor-man, "I 'm not a
    knave ;
  As for the razors you have bought,
  Upon my soul, I never thought
That they would *shave.*"
"Not think they 'd *shave !*" quoth Hodge, with
    wondering eyes,
  And voice not much unlike an Indian yell ;
"What were they made for, then, you dog ?"
  he cries.
  "*Made,*" quoth the fellow with a smile, —
    "*to sell.*"
                    DR. WOLCOTT (PETER PINDAR).

THE NEWCASTLE APOTHECARY.

A MAN in many a country town we know,
  Professing openly with death to wrestle ;
Entering the field against the grimly foe,
  Armed with a mortar and a pestle.
Yet some affirm no enemies they are,
But meet just like prize-fighters at a fair,
Who first shake hands before they box,
Then give each other plaguy knocks,
  With all the love and kindness of a brother ;
So, (many a suffering patient saith,)
Though the apothecary fights with death,
  Still they 're sworn friends with one another.

A member of this Esculapian race
Lived in Newcastle-upon-Tyne ;
  No man could better gild a pill,
    Or make a bill,
Or mix a draught, or bleed, or blister,
Or draw a tooth out of your head,
Or chatter scandal by your bed,
    Or tell a twister.

Of occupations these were *quantum suff.*,
Yet still he thought the list not long enough,
And therefore surgery he chose to pin to 't ; —
This balanced things ; for if he hurled
A few more mortals from the world,
He made amends by keeping others in it.
His fame full six miles round the country ran,
  In short, in reputation he was *solus ;*
All the old women called him "a fine man !"
    His name was Bolus.

Benjamin Bolus, though in trade,
  Which oftentimes will genius flatter,
Read works of fancy, it is said,
  And cultivated the belles-lettres.

And why should this be thought so odd ?
Can't men have taste to cure a phthisic ?
Of poetry, though patron god,
Apollo patronizes physic.

Bolus loved verse, and took so much delight in 't,
That his prescriptions he resolved to write in 't ;
No opportunity he e'er let pass
Of writing the directions on his labels
In dapper couplets, — like Gay's fables,
Or rather like the lines in Hudibras.
Apothecary's verse ! — and where 's the treason ?
'T is simply honest dealing, — not a crime :
When patients swallow physic without reason,
It is but fair to give a little rhyme.

He had a patient lying at death's door,
Some three miles from the town, — it might be
        four, —
To whom, one evening, Bolus sent an article
In pharmacy, that 's called cathartical ;
And on the label of the stuff
        He wrote verse,
Which, one would think, was clear enough,
        And terse : —
            "When taken,
            To be well shaken."

Next morning, early, Bolus rose,
And to the patient's house he goes,
        Upon his pad,
Who a vile trick of stumbling had :
    It was, indeed, a very sorry hack ;
        But that 's of course, —
For what 's expected of a horse
    With an apothecary upon his back ?
Bolus arrived, and gave a loudish tap,
Between a single and a double rap.

    Knocks of this kind
Are given by gentlemen who teach to dance,
    By fiddlers, and by opera-singers ;
One loud, and then a little one behind,
    As if the knocker fell by chance
        Out of their fingers.
The servant lets him in with dismal face,
Long as a courtier's out of place,
        Portending some disaster ;
John's countenance as rueful looked, and grim,
As if the apothecary had physicked him,
        And not his master.

"Well, how 's the patient ?" Bolus said :
        John shook his head.
"Indeed ! — hum ! — ha ! — that 's very odd !
He took the draught ?" John gave a nod.
"Well, how ? — what then ? Speak out, you
        dunce !"
"Why, then," says John, "we shook him once."

"Shook him ! — how ?" Bolus stammered out.
    "We jolted him about."

"What ! shake a patient, man ! — a shake won't
        do."
"No, sir, — and so we gave him two."
    "Two shakes ! Foul nurse,
    'T would make the patient worse !"
"It did so, sir, — and so a third we tried."
"Well, and what then ?" "Then, sir, my mas-
        ter died !"

GEORGE COLMAN.

MORNING MEDITATIONS.

LET Taylor preach, upon a morning breezy,
How well to rise while nights and larks are fly-
        ing, —
For my part, getting up seems not so easy
        By half as *lying*.

What if the lark does carol in the sky,
Soaring beyond the sight to find him out, —
Wherefore am I to rise at such a fly ?
        I 'm not a trout.

Talk not to me of bees and such-like hums,
The smell of sweet herbs at the morning prime, —
Only lie long enough, and bed becomes
        A bed of *time*.

To me Dan Phœbus and his car are naught,
His steeds that paw impatiently about, —
Let them enjoy, say I, as horses ought,
        The first turn-out !

Right beautiful the dewy meads appear
Besprinkled by the rosy-fingered girl ;
What then, — if I prefer my pillow-beer
        To early pearl ?

My stomach is not ruled by other men's,
And, grumbling for a reason, quaintly begs
Wherefore should master rise before the hens
        Have laid their eggs ?

Why from a comfortable pillow start
To see faint flushes in the east awaken ?
A fig, say I, for any streaky part,
        Excepting bacon.

An early riser Mr. Gray has drawn,
Who used to haste the dewy grass among,
"To meet the sun upon the upland lawn," —
        Well, — he died young.

With charwomen such early hours agree,
And sweeps that earn betimes their bit and sup ;
But I 'm no climbing boy, and need not be
        All up, — all up !

So here I lie, my morning calls deferring,
Till something nearer to the stroke of noon ; —
A man that 's fond precociously of *stirring*
        Must be a spoon.
                THOMAS HOOD.

EARLY RISING.

"Now blessings light on him that first invented sleep ! It covers a man all over, thoughts and all, like a cloak ; it is meat for the hungry, drink for the thirsty, heat for the cold, and cold for the hot." — DON QUIXOTE. Part II. ch. 67.

"GOD bless the man who first invented sleep !"
  So Sancho Panza said, and so say I ;
And bless him, also, that he did n't keep
  His great discovery to himself, nor try
To make it — as the lucky fellow might —
A close monopoly by patent-right !

Yes, — bless the man who first invented sleep,
  (I really can't avoid the iteration ;)
But blast the man with curses loud and deep,
  Whate'er the rascal's name or age or station,
Who first invented, and went round advising,
That artificial cut-off, — Early Rising !

"Rise with the lark, and with the lark to bed,"
  Observes some solemn, sentimental owl ;
Maxims like these are very cheaply said ;
  But, ere you make yourself a fool or fowl,
Pray just inquire about his rise and fall,
And whether larks have any beds at all !

"The time for honest folks to be abed
  Is in the morning, if I reason right ;
And he who cannot keep his precious head
  Upon his pillow till it 's fairly light,
And so enjoy his forty morning winks,
Is up to knavery, or else — he drinks !

Thomson, who sung about the "Seasons," said
  It was a glorious thing to *rise* in season ;
But then he said it — lying — in his bed,
  At ten o'clock A. M., — the very reason
He wrote so charmingly.   The simple fact is,
His preaching was n't sanctioned by his practice.

'T is, doubtless, well to be sometimes awake, —
  Awake to duty, and awake to truth, —
But when, alas ! a nice review we take
  Of our best deeds and days, we find, in sooth,
The hours that leave the slightest cause to weep
Are those we passed in childhood or asleep !

'T is beautiful to leave the world awhile
  For the soft visions of the gentle night ;
And free, at last, from mortal care or guile,
  To live as only in the angels' sight,
In sleep's sweet realm so cosely shut in,
Where, at the worst, we only *dream* of sin !

So let us sleep, and give the Maker praise.
  I like the lad who, when his father thought
To clip his morning nap by hackneyed phrase
  Of vagrant worm by early songster caught,
Cried, "Served him right ! — it 's not at all sur-
    prising ;
The worm was punished, sir, for early rising !"
                JOHN G. SAXE.

SWELL'S SOLILOQUY.

I DON'T appwove this hawid waw ;
  Those dweadful bannahs hawt my eyes ;
And guns and dwums are such a baw, —
  Why don't the pawties compwamise ?

Of cawce, the twoilet has its chawms ;
  But why must all the vulgah cwowd
Pawsist in spawting unifawms,
  In cullahs so extwemely loud ?

And then the ladies, — pwecious deahs ! —
  I mawk the change on ev'wy bwow ;
Bai Jove !   I weally have my feahs
  They wathah like the hawid wow !

To heah the chawming cweatures talk,
  Like patwons of the bloody wing,
Of waw and all its dawty wawk, —
  It does n't seem a pwappah thing !

I called at Mrs. Gweene's last night,
  To see her niece, Miss Mawy Hertz,
And found her making — cwushing sight ! —
  The weddest kind of flannel shirts !

Of cawce, I wose, and sought the daw,
  With fawyah flashing from my eyes !
I can't appwove this hawid waw ; —
  Why don't the pawties compwamise ?
                ANONYMOUS.

TOBY TOSSPOT.

ALAS ! what pity 't is that regularity,
Like Isaac Shove's, is such a rarity !
But there are swilling wights in London town,
Termed jolly dogs, choice spirits, alias swine,
Who pour, in midnight revel, bumpers down,
  Making their throats a thoroughfare for wine.

These spendthrifts, who life's pleasures thus
  run on,
  Dozing with headaches till the afternoon,
Lose half men's regular estate of sun,
  By borrowing too largely of the moon.

Eng^d by H.B.Hall & Sons 18 Barclay St.N.Y.

Oliver Wendell Holmes

FORDS, HOWARD & HULBERT, N.Y.

One of this kidney — Toby Tosspot hight —
Was coming from the Bedford late at night ;
  And being Bacchi plenus, full of wine,
  Although he had a tolerable notion
  Of aiming at progressive motion,
'T was n't direct, —'t was serpentine.
He worked with sinuosities, along,
Like Monsieur Corkscrew, worming through a
      cork,
Not straight, like Corkscrew's proxy, stiff Don
      Prong, — a fork.

At length, with near four bottles in his pate,
He saw the moon shining on Shove's brass plate,
When reading, "Please to ring the bell,"
  And being civil beyond measure,
"Ring it !" says Toby, — "very well ;
  I 'll ring it with a deal of pleasure."
Toby, the kindest soul in all the town,
Gave it a jerk that almost jerked it down.

He waited full two minutes, — no one came ;
  He waited full two minutes more ; — and then
Says Toby, "If he 's deaf, I 'm not to blame ;
  I 'll pull it for the gentleman again."

But the first peal woke Isaac in a fright,
  Who, quick as lightning, popping up his head,
  Sat on his head's antipodes, in bed,
Pale as a parsnip, — bolt upright.

At length he wisely to himself doth say, calming
      his fears, —
"Tush ! 't is some fool has rung and run away " ;
When peal the second rattled in his ears.

Shove jumped into the middle of the floor ;
  And, trembling at each breath of air that stirred,
He groped down stairs, and opened the street
      door,
  While Toby was performing peal the third.

Isaac eyed Toby, fearfully askant,
  And saw he was a strapper, stout and tall ;
Then put this question, "Pray, sir, what d' ye
      want ?"
  Says Toby, "I want nothing, sir, at all."

"Want nothing ! Sir, you 've pulled my bell, I
      vow,
  As if you 'd jerk it off the wire."
Quoth Toby, gravely making him a bow,
  "I pulled it, sir, at your desire."

"At mine ?" "Yes, yours ; I hope I 've done
      it well.
  High time for bed, sir ; I was hastening to it ;
But if you write up, 'Please to ring the bell,'
  Common politeness makes me stop and do it."
                              GEORGE COLMAN.

THE ONE-HOSS SHAY ;

OR THE DEACON'S MASTERPIECE.

A LOGICAL STORY.

HAVE you heard of the wonderful one-hoss shay,
That was built in such a logical way
It ran a hundred years to a day,
And then of a sudden, it — ah, but stay,
I 'll tell you what happened without delay,
Scaring the parson into fits,
Frightening people out of their wits, —
Have you ever heard of that, I say ?

Seventeen hundred and fifty-five.
Georgius Secundus was then alive, —
Snuffy old drone from the German hive.
That was the year when Lisbon-town
Saw the earth open and gulp her down,
And Braddock's army was done so brown,
Left without a scalp to its crown.
It was on the terrible Earthquake-day
That the Deacon finished the one-hoss shay.

Now in building of chaises, I tell you what,
There is always *somewhere* a weakest spot, —
In hub, tire, felloe, in spring or thill,
In panel, or crossbar, or floor, or sill,
In screw, bolt, thoroughbrace, — lurking still,
Find it somewhere you must and will, —
Above or below, or within or without, —
And that 's the reason, beyond a doubt,
A chaise *breaks down*, but does n't *wear out*.

But the Deacon swore, (as Deacons do,
With an "I dew vum," or an "I tell *yeou*,")
He would build one shay to beat the taown
'n' the keounty 'n' all the kentry raoun' ;
It should be so built that it *could n'* break daown ;
— "Fur," said the Deacon, "'t 's mighty plain
Thut the weakes' place mus' stan' the strain ;
'n' the way t' fix it, uz I maintain,
          Is only jest
T' make that place uz strong uz the rest."

So the Deacon inquired of the village folk
Where he could find the strongest oak,
That could n't be split nor bent nor broke, —
That was for spokes and floor and sills ;
He sent for lancewood to make the thills ;
The crossbars were ash, from the straightest trees ;
The panels of whitewood, that cuts like cheese,
But lasts like iron for things like these ;
The hubs of logs from the "Settler's ellum," —
Last of its timber, — they could n't sell 'em,
Never an axe had seen their chips,
And the wedges flew from between their lips,
Their blunt ends frizzled like celery-tips ;
Step and prop-iron, bolt and screw,
Spring, tire, axle, and linchpin too,
Steel of the finest, bright and blue ;

Thoroughbrace bison-skin, thick and wide ;
Boot, top, dasher, from tough old hide
Found in the pit when the tanner died.
That was the way he " put her through." —
" There ! ' said the Deacon, " naow she 'll dew ! "

Do ! I tell you, I rather guess
She was a wonder, and nothing less !
Colts grew horses, beards turned gray,
Deacon and deaconess dropped away,
Children and grandchildren, — where were they ?
But there stood the stout old one-hoss shay
As fresh as on Lisbon-earthquake-day !

EIGHTEEN HUNDRED ; — it came and found
The Deacon's masterpiece strong and sound.
Eighteen hundred increased by ten ; —
" Hahnsum kerridge " they called it then.
Eighteen hundred and twenty came ; —
Running as usual ; much the same.
Thirty and forty at last arrive,
And then come fifty, and FIFTY-FIVE.

Little of all we value here
Wakes on the morn of its hundredth year
Without both feeling and looking queer.
In fact, there 's nothing that keeps its youth,
So far as I know, but a tree and truth.
(This is a moral that runs at large ;
Take it. — You 're welcome. — No extra charge.)

FIRST OF NOVEMBER, — the Earthquake-day. —
There are traces of age in the one-hoss shay,
A general flavor of mild decay,
But nothing local as one may say.
There could n't be, — for the Deacon's art
Had made it so like in every part
That there was n't a chance for one to start.
For the wheels were just as strong as the thills,
And the floor was just as strong as the sills,
And the panels just as strong as the floor,
And the whippletree neither less nor more,
And the back-crossbar as strong as the fore,
And spring and axle and hub *encore.*
And yet, *as a whole*, it is past a doubt
In another hour it will be *worn out !*

First of November, 'Fifty-five !
This morning the parson takes a drive.
Now, small boys, get out of the way !
Here comes the wonderful one-hoss shay,
Drawn by a rat-tailed, ewe-necked bay.
" Huddup ! " said the parson. — Off went they.
The parson was working his Sunday's text, —
Had got to *fifthly*, and stopped perplexed
At what the — Moses — was coming next.
All at once the horse stood still,
Close by the meet'n'-house on the hill.
— First a shiver, and then a thrill,
Then something decidedly like a spill, —

And the parson was sitting upon a rock,
At half past nine by the meet'n'-house clock, —
Just the hour of the Earthquake shock !
— What do you think the parson found,
When he got up and stared around ?
The poor old chaise in a heap or mound,
As if it had been to the mill and ground !
You see, of course, if you 're not a dunce,
How it went to pieces all at once, —
All at once, and nothing first, —
Just as bubbles do when they burst.

End of the wonderful one-hoss shay.
Logic is logic.   That 's all I say.
                              OLIVER WENDELL HOLMES.

RAILROAD RHYME.

SINGING through the forests,
  Rattling over ridges ;
Shooting under arches,
  Rumbling over bridges ;
Whizzing through the mountains,
  Buzzing o'er the vale, —
Bless me ! this is pleasant,
  Riding on the rail !

Men of different " stations "
  In the eye of fame,
Here are very quickly
  Coming to the same ;
High and lowly people,
  Birds of every feather,
On a common level,
  Travelling together.

Gentleman in shorts,
  Looming very tall ;
Gentleman at large,
  Talking very small ;
Gentleman in tights,
  With a loose-ish mien ;
Gentleman in gray,
  Looking rather green ;

Gentleman quite old,
  Asking for the news ;
Gentleman in black,
  In a fit of blues ;
Gentleman in claret,
  Sober as a vicar ;
Gentleman in tweed,
  Dreadfully in liquor !

Stranger on the right
  Looking very sunny,
Obviously reading
  Something rather funny.

Now the smiles are thicker, —
  Wonder what they mean ?
Faith, he 's got the Knicker-
  bocker Magazine !

Stranger on the left
  Closing up his peepers ;
Now he snores amain,
  Like the Seven Sleepers ;
At his feet a volume
  Gives the explanation,
How the man grew stupid
  From "Association ! "

Ancient maiden lady
  Anxiously remarks,
That there must be peril
  'Mong so many sparks ;
Roguish-looking fellow,
  Turning to the stranger,
Says it 's his opinion
  She is out of danger !

Woman with her baby,
  Sitting *vis-à-vis ;*
Baby keeps a-squalling,
  Woman looks at me ;
Asks about the distance,
  Says it 's tiresome talking,
Noises of the cars
  Are so very shocking !

Market-woman, careful
  Of the precious casket,
Knowing eggs are eggs,
  Tightly holds her basket ;
Feeling that a smash,
  If it came, would surely
Send her eggs to pot,
  Rather prematurely.

Singing through the forests,
  Rattling over ridges ;
Shooting under arches,
  Rumbling over bridges ;
Whizzing through the mountains,
  Buzzing o'er the vale, —
Bless me ! this is pleasant,
  Riding on the rail !

          JOHN G. SAXE.

———◆———

THE RAIL.

I MET him in the cars,
  Where resignedly he sat ;
His hair was full of dust,
  And so was his cravat ;

He was furthermore embellished
  By a ticket in his hat.

The conductor touched his arm,
  And awoke him from a nap ;
When he gave the feeding flies
  An admonitory slap,
And his ticket to the man
  In the yellow-lettered cap.

So, launching into talk,
  We rattled on our way,
With allusions to the crops
  That along the meadows lay, —
Whereupon his eyes were lit
  With a speculative ray.

The heads of many men
  Were bobbing as in sleep,
And many babies lifted
  Their voices up to weep ;
While the coal-dust darkly fell
  On bonnets in a heap.

All the while the swaying cars
  Kept rumbling o'er the rail,
And the frequent whistle sent
  Shrieks of anguish to the gale,
And the cinders pattered down
  On the grimy floor like hail.

When suddenly a jar,
  And a thrice-repeated bump,
Made the people in alarm
  From their easy cushions jump ;
For they deemed the sounds to be
  The inevitable trump.

A splintering crash below,
  A doom-foreboding twitch,
As the tender gave a lurch
  Beyond the flying switch, —
And a mangled mass of men
  Lay writhing in the ditch.

With a palpitating heart
  My friend essayed to rise ;
There were bruises on his limbs
  And stars before his eyes,
And his face was of the hue
  Of the dolphin when it dies.

   .   .   .   .   .

I was very well content
  In escaping with my life ;
But my mutilated friend
  Commenced a legal strife, —
Being thereunto incited
  By his lawyer and his wife.

And he writes me the result,
 In his quiet way as follows:
That his case came up before
 A bench of legal scholars,
Who awarded him his claim,
 Of $1500 !

GEORGE H. CLARK.

SALLY SIMPKIN'S LAMENT;

OR, JOHN JONES'S KIT-CAT-ASTROPHE.

"He left his body to the sea,
And made a shark his legatee."
BRYAN and PERENNE.

"O WHAT is that comes gliding in,
 And quite in middling haste ?
It is the picture of my Jones,
 And painted to the waist.

It is not painted to the life,
 For where's the trousers blue ?
O Jones, my dear ! — O dear ! my Jones,
 What is become of you ?"

"O Sally dear, it is too true, —
 The half that you remark
Is come to say my other half
 Is bit off by a shark !

"O Sally, sharks do things by halves,
 Yet most completely do !
A bite in one place seems enough,
 But I 've been bit in two.

"You know I once was all your own,
 But now a shark must share !
But let that pass, — for now to you
 I 'm neither here nor there.

"Alas ! death has a strange divorce
 Effected in the sea :
It has divided me from you,
 And even me from me !

"Don't fear my ghost will walk o' nights
 To haunt, as people say ;
My ghost can't walk, for, O, my legs
 Are many leagues away !

"Lord ! think when I am swimming round,
 And looking where the boat is,
A shark just snaps away a half,
 Without ' a quarter's notice.'

"One half is here, the other half
 Is near Columbia placed ;
O Sally, I have got the whole
 Atlantic for my waist.

"But now, adieu, — a long adieu !
 I 've solved death's awful riddle,
And would say more, but I am doomed
 To break off in the middle !"

THOMAS HOOD.

FAITHLESS SALLY BROWN.

AN OLD BALLAD.

YOUNG BEN he was a nice young man,
 A carpenter by trade ;
And he fell in love with Sally Brown,
 That was a lady's maid.

But as they fetched a walk one day,
 They met a press-gang crew ;
And Sally she did faint away,
 Whilst Ben he was brought to.

The boatswain swore with wicked words
 Enough to shock a saint,
That, though she did seem in a fit,
 'T was nothing but a feint.

"Come, girl," said he, "hold up your head,
 He 'll be as good as me ;
For when your swain is in our boat
 A boatswain he will be."

So when they 'd made their game of her,
 And taken off her elf,
She roused, and found she only was
 A coming to herself.

"And is he gone, and is he gone ?"
 She cried and wept outright ;
"Then I will to the water-side,
 And see him out of sight."

A waterman came up to her ;
 "Now, young woman," said he,
"If you weep on so, you will make
 Eye-water in the sea."

"Alas ! they 've taken my beau, Ben,
 To sail with old Benbow" ;
And her woe began to run afresh,
 As if she 'd said, Gee woe !

Says he, "They 've only taken him
 To the tender-ship, you see."
"The tender-ship," cried Sally Brown, —
 "What a hard-ship that must be !"

"O, would I were a mermaid now,
 For then I 'd follow him !
But O, I 'm not a fish-woman,
 And so I cannot swim.

"Alas! I was not born beneath
  The Virgin and the Scales,
So I must curse my cruel stars,
  And walk about in Wales."

Now Ben had sailed to many a place
  That's underneath the world;
But in two years the ship came home,
  And all her sails were furled.

But when he called on Sally Brown,
  To see how she got on,
He found she'd got another Ben,
  Whose Christian-name was John.

"O Sally Brown! O Sally Brown!
  How could you serve me so?
I've met with many a breeze before,
  But never such a blow!"

Then, reading on his 'bacco box,
  He heaved a heavy sigh,
And then began to eye his pipe,
  And then to pipe his eye.

And then he tried to sing "All's Well!"
  But could not, though he tried;
His head was turned, — and so he chewed
  His pigtail till he died.

His death, which happened in his berth,
  At forty-odd befell;
They went and told the sexton, and
  The sexton tolled the bell.
                        THOMAS HOOD.

———◆———

FAITHLESS NELLY GRAY.

A PATHETIC BALLAD.

BEN BATTLE was a soldier bold,
  And used to war's alarms;
But a cannon-ball took off his legs,
  So he laid down his arms.

Now as they bore him off the field,
  Said he, "Let others shoot;
For here I leave my second leg,
  And the Forty-second Foot."

The army-surgeons made him limbs:
  Said he, "They're only pegs;
But there's as wooden members quite,
  As represent my legs."

Now Ben he loved a pretty maid, —
  Her name was Nelly Gray;
So he went to pay her his devours,
  When he devoured his pay.

But when he called on Nelly Gray,
  She made him quite a scoff;
And when she saw his wooden legs,
  Began to take them off.

"O Nelly Gray! O Nelly Gray!
  Is this your love so warm?
The love that loves a scarlet coat
  Should be more uniform."

Said she, "I loved a soldier once,
  For he was blithe and brave;
But I will never have a man
  With both legs in the grave.

"Before you had those timber toes
  Your love I did allow;
But then, you know, you stand upon
  Another footing now."

"O Nelly Gray! O Nelly Gray!
  For all your jeering speeches,
At duty's call I left my legs
  In Badajos's breaches."

"Why, then," said she, "you've lost the feet
  Of legs in war's alarms,
And now you cannot wear your shoes
  Upon your feats of arms!"

"O false and fickle Nelly Gray!
  I know why you refuse:
Though I've no feet, some other man
  Is standing in my shoes.

"I wish I ne'er had seen your face;
  But, now, a long farewell!
For you will be my death; — alas!
  You will not be my Nell!"

Now when he went from Nelly Gray
  His heart so heavy got,
And life was such a burden grown,
  It made him take a knot.

So round his melancholy neck
  A rope he did intwine,
And, for his second time in life,
  Enlisted in the Line.

One end he tied around a beam,
  And then removed his pegs;
And, as his legs were off, — of course
  He soon was off his legs.

And there he hung till he was dead
  As any nail in town;
For, though distress had cut him up,
  It could not cut him down.

A dozen men sat on his corpse,
　　To find out why he died, —
And they buried Ben in four cross-roads,
　　With a stake in his inside.

THOMAS HOOD.

A LEGEND OF A SHIRT.

I SING of a Shirt that *never was* new !
In the course of the year Eighteen hundred and two
　　Aunt Fanny began,
　　Upon Grandmamma's plan,
To make one for me, then her "dear little man."
At the epoch I speak about, I was between
　　A man and a boy,
　　A hobble-de-hoy,
A fat, little, punchy concern of sixteen, —
　　Just beginning to flirt
　　And ogle, — so pert,
I'd been whipt every day had I had my desert, —
And Aunt Fan volunteered to make me a shirt !

　　I've said she *began* it, —
　　Some unlucky planet
No doubt interfered, — for, before she and Janet
Completed the "cutting-out," "hemming," and
　　　　"stitching,"
A tall Irish footman appeared in the kitchen ;
　　This took off the maid, —
　　And I'm sadly afraid
My respected Aunt Fanny's attention, too, strayed;
For, about the same period, a gay son of Mars,
Cornet Jones of the Tenth (then the Prince's)
　　　　Hussars,
　　With his fine dark eyelashes,
　　And finer mustaches,
And the ostrich plume worked on the corps'
　　sabre-taches,
She had even resolved to say "Yes" should he
　　ask it,
And I — and my Shirt — were both left in the
　　basket.

　　To her grief and dismay
　　She discovered one day
Cornet Jones of the Tenth was a little too gay ;
For, besides that she saw him — he could not
　　say nay —
Wink at one of the actresses capering away
In a Spanish *bolero*, one night at the play,
She found he'd already a wife at Cambray ;
One at Paris, — a nymph of the *corps de ballet ;*
And a third down in Kent, at a place called Foot's
　　Cray.
　　He was "viler than dirt !"
　　Fanny vowed to exert
All her powers to forget him, — and finish my
　　Shirt.

But, O, lack-a-day !
　　How time slips away ! —
Who'd have thought that while Cupid was play-
　　ing these tricks
Ten years had elapsed, and — I'd turned twenty-
　　six ?

　　"I care not a whit,
　　He's not grown a bit,"
Says my 'Aunt ; "it will still be a very good fit."
　　So Janet and She,
　　Now about thirty-three,
(The maid had been jilted by Mr. Magee,)
Each taking one end of "the Shirt" on her knee,
Again began working with hearty good-will,
"Felling the Seams," and "whipping the Frill,"—
For, twenty years since, though the Ruffle had
　　vanished,
A Frill like a fan had by no means been banished ;
People wore them at playhouses, parties, and
　　churches,
Like overgrown fins of overgrown perches.

Now, then, by these two thus laying their caps
Together, my "Shirt" had been finished, perhaps,
But for one of those queer little three-cornered
　　straps,
Which the ladies call "Side-bits," that sever
　　the "Flaps" ;
　　Here unlucky Janet
　　Took her needle, and ran it
Right into her thumb, and cried loudly, "Ad's
　　cuss it !
I've spoiled myself now by that 'ere nasty Gusset !"

　　For a month to come
　　Poor dear Janet's thumb
Was in that sort of state vulgar people call "Rum."
　　At the end of that time,
　　A youth, still in his prime,
The Doctor's fat Errand-boy — just such a dolt
　　as is
Kept to mix draughts, and spread plasters and
　　poultices,
Who a bread-cataplasm each morning had carried
　　her —
Sighed, — ogled, — proposed, — was accepted, —
　　and married her !

　　Ten years, or nigh,
　　Had again gone by,
When Fan, accidentally casting her eye
On a dirty old work-basket, hung up on high
In the store-closet where herbs were put by to dry,
Took it down to explore it, — she didn't know why.

Within, a pea-soup-colored fragment she spied,
Of the hue of a November fog in Cheapside,
Or a bad piece of gingerbread spoilt in the baking.

I still hear her cry, —
"I wish I may die
If here is n't Tom's Shirt, that's been so long
   amaking !
My gracious me !
Well, — only to see !
I declare it 's as yellow as yellow can be !
Why, it looks just as though 't had been soaked
   in green tea !
Dear me, *did* you *ever* ! —
But come, 't will be clever
To bring matters round ; so I 'll do my endeavor.
' Better Late,' says an excellent proverb, ' than
   Never !'
It *is* stained, to be sure, but ' grass-bleaching '
   will bring it
To rights 'in a jiffy.' We 'll wash it, and wring it ;
Or, stay, — ' Hudson's Liquor '
Will do it still quicker,
And — " Here the new maid chimed in, " Ma'am,
   Salt of Lemon
Will make it, in no time, quite fit for the Gemman !"
So they " set in the gathers," — the large round
   the collar,
While those at the wristbands of course were
   much smaller, —
The button-holes now were at length "overcast."
Then a button itself was sewn on, — 't was the
   last !

All 's done !
All 's won !
Never under the sun
Was Shirt so late finished, so early begun !
The work would defy
The most critical eye.
It was " bleached," — it was washed, — it was
   hung out to dry, —
It was marked on the tail with a T, and an I !
On the back of a chair it
Was placed, — just to air it,
In front of the fire. — " Tom to-morrow shall
   wear it !"
O cœca mens hominum ! — Fanny, good soul,
Left her charge for one moment, — but one, — a
   vile coal
Bounced out from the grate, and set fire to the
   whole !   RICHARD HARRIS BARHAM.
                (THOMAS INGOLDSBY, ESQ.)

MISADVENTURES AT MARGATE.

A LEGEND OF JARVIS'S JETTY.

MR. SIMPKINSON (*loquitur*).

I WAS in Margate last July, I walked upon the pier,
I saw a little vulgar Boy, — I said, " What make
   you here ?

The gloom upon your youthful cheek speaks
   anything but joy " ;
Again I said, " What make you here, you little
   vulgar Boy ? "
He frowned, that little vulgar Boy, — he deemed
   I meant to scoff, —
And when the little heart is big, a little "sets
   it off."
He put his finger in his mouth, his little bosom
   rose, —
He had no little handkerchief to wipe his little nose !

" Hark ! don't you hear, my little man ? — it 's
   striking Nine," I said,
" An hour when all good little boys and girls
   should be in bed.
Run home and get your supper, else your Ma
   will scold, — O fie !
It 's very wrong indeed for little boys to stand
   and cry ! "

The tear-drop in his little eye again began to spring,
His bosom throbbed with agony, — he cried like
   anything !
I stooped, and thus amidst his sobs I heard him
   murmur, — " Ah !
I have n't got no supper ! and I have n't got
   no Ma ! " —

" My father, he is on the seas, — my mother 's
   dead and gone !
And I am here, on this here pier, to roam the
   world alone ;
I have not had, this livelong day, one drop to
   cheer my heart,
Nor ' brown ' to buy a bit of bread with, — let
   alone a tart.

" If there 's a soul will give me food, or find me
   in employ,
By day or night, then blow me tight ! " (he was
   a vulgar Boy ;)
" And now I 'm here, from this here pier it is
   my fixed intent
To jump as Mister Levi did from off the Monu-
   ment ! "

" Cheer up ! cheer up ! my little man, — cheer
   up ! " I kindly said,
" You are a naughty boy to take such things into
   your head ;
If you should jump from off the pier, you 'd
   surely break your legs,
Perhaps your neck, — then Bogey 'd have you,
   sure as eggs are eggs !

" Come home with me, my little man, come
   home with me and sup ;
My landlady is Mrs. Jones, — we must not keep
   her up, —

There's roast potatoes at the fire, — enough for
　　me and you, —
Come home, you little vulgar Boy, — I lodge at
　　Number 2."

I took him home to Number 2, the house beside
　　" The Foy,"
I bade him wipe his dirty shoes, — that little
　　vulgar Boy, —
And then I said to Mistress Jones, the kindest of
　　her sex,
"Pray be so good as go and fetch a pint of
　　double X ! "

But Mrs. Jones was rather cross, she made a little
　　noise,
She said she "did not like to wait on little vul-
　　gar Boys."
She with her apron wiped the plates, and, as she
　　rubbed the delf,
Said I might " go to Jericho, and fetch my beer
　　myself ! "

I did not go to Jericho, — I went to Mr. Cobb, —
I changed a shilling (which in town the people
　　call a Bob,) —
It was not so much for myself as for that vulgar
　　child, —
And I said, " A pint of double X, and please to
　　draw it mild ! "

When I came back I gazed about, — I gazed on
　　stool and chair, —
I could not see my little friend, because he
　　was not there !
I peeped beneath the table-cloth, beneath the
　　sofa too, —
I said, " You little vulgar Boy ! why, what 's be-
　　come of you ? "

I could not see my table-spoons, — I looked, but
　　could not see
The little fiddle-patterned ones I use when I 'm
　　at tea ;
I could not see my sugar - tongs, my silver
　　watch, — O, dear !
I know 't was on the mantel-piece when I went
　　out for beer.

I could not see my Macintosh, — it was not to be
　　seen !
Nor yet my best white beaver hat, broad-brimmed
　　and lined with green ;
My carpet-bag, — my cruet-stand, that holds my
　　sauce and soy, —
My roast potatoes ! — all are gone ! — and so 's
　　that vulgar Boy !

I rang the bell for Mrs. Jones, for she was down
　　below,
" O Mrs. Jones, what *do* you think ? — ain't this
　　a pretty go ?
That horrid little vulgar Boy whom I brought
　　here to-night
He 's stolen my things and run away ! " Says
　　she, " And sarve you right ! "

Next morning I was up betimes, — I sent the
　　Crier round,
All with his bell and gold-laced hat, to say, I 'd
　　give a pound
To find that little vulgar Boy, who 'd gone and
　　used me so ;
But when the Crier cried, " O Yes ! " the people
　　cried, " O No ! "

I went to " Jarvis' Landing-place," the glory of
　　the town,
There was a common sailor-man a walking up and
　　down,
I told my tale, — he seemed to think I 'd not
　　been treated well,
And called me " Poor old Buffer ! " — what that
　　means I cannot tell.

That Sailor-man, he said he 'd seen that morning
　　on the shore,
A son of — something — 't was a name I 'd never
　　heard before, —
A little " gallows-looking chap" — dear me,
　　what could he mean ? —
With a " carpet-swab " and " mucking-togs,"
　　and a hat turned up with green.

He spoke about his " precious eyes," and said
　　he 'd seen him " sheer," —
It 's very odd that Sailor-men should talk so
　　very queer ;
And then he hitched his trousers up, as is, I 'm
　　told, their use, —
It 's very odd that Sailor-men should wear those
　　things so loose.

I did not understand him well, but think he meant
　　to say
He 'd seen that little vulgar Boy, that morning,
　　swim away
In Captain Large's Royal George, about an hour
　　before,
And they were now, as he supposed, "some*wheres*"
　　about the Nore.

A landsman said, " I *twig* the chap, — he 's been
　　upon the Mill, —
And 'cause he *gammons* so the *flats*, ve calls him
　　Veeping Bill ! "

He said " he 'd done me werry brown," and nicely
" *stowed* the *swag*," —
That 's French, I fancy, for a hat, or else a carpet-
bag.

I went and told the constable my property to track ;
He asked me if " I did not wish that I might get
it back."
I answered, "To be sure I do ! — it 's what I 'm
come about."
He smiled and said, " Sir, does your mother
know that you are out ?"

Not knowing what to do, I thought I 'd hasten
back to town,
And beg our own Lord Mayor to catch the boy
who 'd "done me brown."
His Lordship very kindly said he 'd try and find
him out,
But he " rather thought that there were several
vulgar boys about."

He sent for Mr. Whithair then, and I described
" the swag,"
My Macintosh, my sugar-tongs, my spoons, and
carpet-bag ;
He promised that the New Police should all their
powers employ,
But never to this hour have I beheld that vulgar
Boy !

MORAL.

Remember, then, what when a boy I 've heard
my Grandma tell,
" BE WARNED IN TIME BY OTHERS' HARM, AND
YOU SHALL DO FULL WELL !"
Don't link yourself with vulgar folks, who 've got
no fixed abode,
Tell lies, use naughty words, and say they " wish
they may be blowed !"

Don't take too much of double X ! — and don't
at night go out
To fetch your beer yourself, but make the pot
boy bring your stout !
And when you go to Margate next, just stop, and
ring the bell,
Give my respects to Mrs. Jones, and say I 'm
pretty well !
RICHARD HARRIS BARHAM.
(THOMAS INGOLDSBY, ESQ.)

"LOOK AT THE CLOCK!"

FYTTE I.

" LOOK at the Clock !" quoth Winifred Pryce,
As she opened the door to her husband's knock,
Then paused to give him a piece of advice,
" You nasty Warmint, look at the Clock !

Is this the way, you
Wretch, every day you
Treat her who vowed to love and obey you ? —
Out all night !
Me in a fright ;
Staggering home as it 's just getting light !
You intoxified brute ! — you insensible block ! —
Look at the Clock ! — Do ! — Look at the Clock ! "

Winifred Pryce was tidy and clean,
Her gown was a flowered one, her petticoat green,
Her buckles were bright as her milking-cans,
And her hat was a beaver, and made like a man's ;
Her little red eyes were deep set in their socket-
holes,
Her gown-tail was turned up, and tucked through
the pocket-holes ;
A face like a ferret
Betokened her spirit :
To conclude, Mrs. Pryce was not over young,
Had very short legs, and a very long tongue.

Now David Pryce
Had one darling vice ;
Remarkably partial to anything nice,
Naught that was good to him came amiss,
Whether to eat, or to drink, or to kiss !
Especially ale, —
If it was not too stale
I really believe he 'd have emptied a pail ;
Not that in Wales·
They talk of their Ales ;
To pronounce the word they make use of might
trouble you,
Being spelt with a C, two Rs, and a W.

That particular day,
As I 've heard people say,
Mr. David Pryce had been soaking his clay,
And amusing himself with his pipe and cheroots,
The whole afternoon at the Goat-in-Boots,
With a couple more soakers,
Thoroughbred smokers,
Both, like himself, prime singers and jokers ;
And, long after day had drawn to a close,
And the rest of the world was wrapped in repose,
They were roaring out " Shenkin !" and " Ar
hydd y nos" ;
While David himself, to a Sassenach tune,
Sang, " We 've drunk down the Sun, boys !
let 's drink down the Moon !
What have we with day to do ?
Mrs. Winifred Pryce, 't was made
for you ! "
At length, when they could n't well drink any more,
Old " Goat-in-Boots" showed them the door ;
And then came that knock,
And the sensible shock·

David felt when his wife cried, "Look at the Clock !"
For the hands stood as crooked as crooked might be,
The long at the Twelve, and the short at the Three !

That self-same clock had long been a bone
Of contention between this Darby and Joan ;
And often, among their pother and rout,
When this otherwise amiable couple fell out,
   Pryce would drop a cool hint
   With an ominous squint
At its case, of an "Uncle" of his, who'd a "Spout."
   That horrid word "Spout"
   No sooner came out,
Than Winifred Pryce would turn her about,
   And with scorn on her lip,
   And a hand on each hip,
"Spout" herself till her nose grew red at the tip,
   "You thundering Willin,
   I know you'd be killing
Your wife —ay, a dozen of wives — for a shilling !
   You may do what you please,
   You may sell my chemise,
(Mrs. P. was too well bred to mention her stock,)
But I never will part with my Grandmother's Clock !"

Mrs. Pryce's tongue ran long and ran fast ;
But patience is apt to wear out at last,
And David Pryce in temper was quick,
So he stretched out his hand, and caught hold of a stick.
Perhaps in its use he might mean to be lenient,
But walking just then wasn't very convenient,
   So he threw it, instead,
   Direct at her head ;
   It knocked off her hat ;
   Down she fell flat ;
Her case, perhaps, was not much mended by that ;
But whatever it was, — whether rage and pain
Produced apoplexy, or burst a vein,
Or her tumble induced a concussion of brain,
I can't say for certain, — but *this* I can,
When, sobered by fright, to assist her he ran,
Mrs. Winifred Pryce was as dead as Queen Anne.

And then came Mr. Ap Thomas, the Coroner,
With his jury to sit, some dozen or more, on her.
   Mr. Pryce, to commence
   His "ingenious defence,"
Made a "powerful appeal" to the jury's "good sense," —
   The unlucky lick
   From the end of his stick
He "deplored," — he was "apt to be rather too quick" ;
   But, really, her prating
   Was so aggravating :

Some trifling correction was just what he meant ;—all
The rest, he assured them, was "quite accidental !"

The jury, in fine, having sat on the body
The whole day, discussing the case and gin toddy,
Returned about half past eleven at night
The following verdict, "We find, *Sarve her right !*"

Mr. David has since had a "serious call,"
He never drinks ale, wine, or spirits, at all,
And they say he is going to Exeter Hall
   To make a grand speech,
   And to preach and to teach
People that "they can't brew their malt liquor too small !"
That an ancient Welsh Poet, one PYNDAR AP TUDOR,
Was right in proclaiming "ARISTON MEN UDOR !"
   Which means "The pure Element
   Is for Man's belly meant !"
And that *Gin*'s but a *Snare* of Old Nick the deluder !

And "still on each evening when pleasure fills up,"
At the old Goat-in-Boots, with Metheglin, each cup,
   Mr. Pryce, if he's there,
   Will get into "The Chair,"
And make all his *quondam* associates stare
By calling aloud to the Landlady's daughter,
"Patty, bring a cigar, and a glass of Spring Water !"
The dial he constantly watches ; and when
The long hand's at the "XII," and the short at the "X,"
   He gets on his legs,
   Drains his glass to the dregs,
Takes his hat and great-coat off their several pegs,
With his President's hammer bestows his last knock,
And says solemnly, — "Gentlemen ! LOOK AT THE CLOCK ! ! !"
     RICHARD HARRIS BARHAM.
     (THOMAS INGOLDSBY, ESQ.)

THE JACKDAW OF RHEIMS.

THE Jackdaw sat on the Cardinal's chair !
Bishop and abbot and prior were there ;
   Many a monk, and many a friar,
   Many a knight, and many a squire,
With a great many more of lesser degree, —
In sooth, a goodly company ;
And they served the Lord Primate on bended knee.
   Never, I ween,
   Was a prouder seen,

Read of in books, or dreamt of in dreams,
Than the Cardinal Lord Archbishop of Rheims !
    In and out
    Through the motley rout,
That little Jackdaw kept hopping about :
    Here and there,
    Like a dog in a fair,
    Over comfits and cates,
    And dishes and plates,
Cowl and cope, and rochet and pall !
Mitre and crosier ! he hopped upon all.
    With a saucy air,
    He perched on the chair
Where, in state, the great Lord Cardinal sat,
In the great Lord Cardinal's great red hat ;
    And he peered in the face
    Of his Lordship's Grace,
With a satisfied look, as if he would say,
" We Two are the greatest folks here to-day ! "
    And the priests, with awe,
    As such freaks they saw,
Said, "The Devil must be in that little Jackdaw !"

The feast was over, the board was cleared,
The flawns and the custards had all disappeared,
And six little Singing-boys — dear little souls !
In nice clean faces, and nice white stoles —
    Came, in order due,
    Two by two,
Marching that grand refectory through !
A nice little boy held a golden ewer,
Embossed and filled with water, as pure
As any that flows between Rheims and Namur,
Which a nice little boy stood ready to catch
In a fine golden hand-basin made to match.
Two nice little boys, rather more grown,
Carried lavender-water and eau de Cologne ;
And a nice little boy had a nice cake of soap,
Worthy of washing the hands of the Pope.
    One little boy more
    A napkin bore,
Of the best white diaper, fringed with pink,
And a Cardinal's Hat marked in "permanent ink."

The great Lord Cardinal turns at the sight
Of these nice little boys dressed all in white ;
    From his finger he draws
    His costly turquoise :
And, not thinking at all about little Jackdaws,
    Deposits it straight
    By the side of his plate,
While the nice little boys on his Eminence wait ;
Till, when nobody 's dreaming of any such thing,
That little Jackdaw hops off with the ring !

    There 's a cry and a shout,
    And a deuce of a rout,

And nobody seems to know what they 're about,
But the monks have their pockets all turned in-
    side out ;
    The friars are kneeling,
    And hunting and feeling
The carpet, the floor, and the walls, and the ceiling.
    The Cardinal drew
    Off each plum-colored shoe,
And left his red stockings exposed to the view ;
    He peeps, and he feels
    In the toes and the heels.
They turn up the dishes, — they turn up the
    plates, —
They take up the poker and poke out the grates,
    — They turn up the rugs, .
    They examine the mugs ;
    But, no ! — no such thing, —
    They can't find THE RING !
And the Abbot declared that "when nobody
    twigged it,
Some rascal or other had popped in and prigged it !"

The Cardinal rose with a dignified look,
He called for his candle, his bell, and his book !
    In holy anger and pious grief
    He solemnly cursed that rascally thief !
He cursed him at board, he cursed him in bed ;
From the sole of his foot to the crown of his head ;
He cursed him in sleeping, that every night
He should dream of the devil, and wake in a fright.
He cursed him in eating, he cursed him in
    drinking,
He cursed him in coughing, in sneezing, in
    winking ;
He cursed him in sitting, in standing, in lying ;
He cursed him in walking, in riding, in flying ;
He cursed him living, he cursed him dying ! —
Never was heard such a terrible curse !
    But what gave rise
    To no little surprise,
Nobody seemed one penny the worse !

    The day was gone,
    The night came on,
The Monks and the Friars they searched till dawn ;
    When the Sacristan saw,
    On crumpled claw,
Come limping a poor little lame Jackdaw !
    No longer gay,
    As on yesterday ;
His feathers all seemed to be turned the wrong
    way ; —
His pinions drooped, — he could hardly stand, —
His head was as bald as the palm of your hand ;
    His eye so dim,
    So wasted each limb,
That, heedless of grammar, they all cried, "THAT
    'S HIM ! —

That 's the scamp that has done this scandalous
      thing,
That 's the thief that has got my Lord Cardinal's
      Ring ! "
      The poor little Jackdaw,
      When the Monks he saw,
Feebly gave vent to the ghost of a caw ;
And turned his bald head as much as to say,
" Pray be so good as to walk this way ! "
      Slower and slower
      He limped on before,
Till they came to the back of the belfry-door,
      Where the first thing they saw,
      Midst the sticks and the straw,
Was the RING, in the nest of that little Jack-
      daw !

Then the great Lord Cardinal called for his book,
And off that terrible curse he took ;
      The mute expression
      Served in lieu of confession,
And, being thus coupled with full restitution,
The Jackdaw got plenary absolution !
      — When those words were heard,
      That poor little bird
Was so changed in a moment, 't was really absurd :
      He grew sleek and fat ;
      In addition to that,
A fresh crop of feathers came thick as a mat !
      His tail waggled more
      Even than before ;
But no longer it wagged with an impudent air,
No longer he perched on the Cardinal's chair.
      He hopped now about
      With a gait devout ;
At Matins, at Vespers, he never was out ;
And, so far from any more pilfering deeds,
He always seemed telling the Confessor's beads.
If any one lied, or if any one swore,
Or slumbered in prayer-time and happened to
      snore,
      That good Jackdaw
      Would give a great "Caw ! "
As much as to say, " Don't do so any more ! "
While many remarked, as his manners they saw,
That they " never had known such a pious Jack-
      daw ! "
      He long lived the pride
      Of that country side,
And at last in the odor of sanctity died ;
      When, as words were too faint
      His merits to paint,
The Conclave determined to make him a Saint.
And on newly made Saints and Popes, as you know,
It 's the custom at Rome new names to bestow,
So they canonized him by the name of Jem Crow !

RICHARD HARRIS BARHAM.
(THOMAS INGOLDSBY, ESQ.)

I AM A FRIAR OF ORDERS GRAY.

I AM a friar of orders gray,
And down in the valleys I take my way ;
I pull not blackberry, haw, or hip, —
Good store of venison fills my scrip ;
My long bead-roll I merrily chant ;
Where'er I walk no money I want ;
And why I 'm so plump the reason I tell, —
Who leads a good life is sure to live well.
      What baron or squire,
      Or knight of the shire,
      Lives half so well as a holy friar ?

After supper of heaven I dream,
But that is a pullet and clouted cream ;
Myself, by denial, I mortify —
With a dainty bit of a warden-pie ;
I 'm clothed in sackcloth for my sin, —
With old sack wine I 'm lined within ;
A chirping cup is my matin song,
And the vesper's bell is my bowl, ding dong.
      What baron or squire,
      Or knight of the shire,
      Lives half so well as a holy friar ?

JOHN O'KEEFE.

THE VICAR OF BRAY.

[" The Vicar of Bray in Berkshire, England, was Simon Alleyn, or Allen, and held his place from 1540 to 1588. He was a Papist under the reign of Henry the Eighth, and a Protestant under Edward the Sixth. He was a Papist again under Mary, and once more became a Protestant in the reign of Elizabeth. When this scandal to the gown was reproached for his versatility of religious creeds, and taxed for being a turn-coat and an inconstant changeling, as Fuller expresses it, he replied : " Not so, neither ; for if I changed my religion, I am sure I kept true to my principle, which is to live and die the Vicar of Bray." — D'ISRAELI.
The idea seems to have been adapted to some changelings of a later date. In a note in Nichols's " Select Poems," 1782, Vol. VIII. p. 234, it is stated that "the song of the Vicar of Bray" is said to have been written by an officer in Colonel Fuller's regiment, in the reign of King George the First. It is founded on an historical fact ; and though it reflects no great honor on the hero of the poem, is humorously expressive of the complexion of the times, in the successive reigns from Charles the Second to George the First."]

IN good King Charles's golden days,
      When loyalty no harm meant,
A zealous high-churchman was I,
      And so I got preferment.
To teach my flock I never missed :
      Kings were by God appointed,
And lost are those that dare resist
      Or touch the Lord's anointed.
    And this is law that I'll maintain
      Until my dying day, sir,
    That whatsoever king shall reign,
      Still I'll be the Vicar of Bray, sir.

When royal James possessed the crown,
      And popery grew in fashion,

The penal laws I hooted down,
   And read the declaration ;
The Church of Rome I found would fit
   Full well my constitution ;
And I had been a Jesuit
   But for the revolution.
     And this is law that I'll maintain, etc.

When William was our king declared,
   To ease the nation's grievance ;
With this new wind about I steered,
   And swore to him allegiance ;
Old principles I did revoke,
   Set conscience at a distance ;
Passive obedience was a joke,
   A jest was non-resistance.
     And this is law that I'll maintain, etc.

When royal Anne became our queen,
   The Church of England's glory,
Another face of things was seen,
   And I became a Tory ;
Occasional conformists base,
   I blamed their moderation ;
And thought the church in danger was,
   By such prevarication.
     And this is law that I'll maintain, etc.

When George in pudding-time came o'er,
   And moderate men looked big, sir,
My principles I changed once more,
   And so became a Whig, sir ;
And thus preferment I procured
   From our new faith's defender ;
And almost every day abjured
   The pope and the pretender.
     And this is law that I'll maintain, etc.

The illustrious house of Hanover,
   And Protestant succession,
To these I do allegiance swear —
   While they can keep possession :
For in my faith and loyalty
   I nevermore will falter,
And George my lawful king shall be —
   Until the times do alter.
     And this is law that I'll maintain, etc.
       ANONYMOUS.

THE KNIGHT AND THE LADY.

A DOMESTIC LEGEND OF THE REIGN OF QUEEN ANNE.

  "Hail, wedded love ! mysterious tie !"
       Thomson — or Somebody.

THE Lady Jane was tall and slim,
   The Lady Jane was fair,
And Sir Thomas, her lord, was stout of limb,
And his cough was short, and his eyes were dim,

And he wore green "specs," with a tortoise-
    shell rim,
And his hat was remarkably broad in the brim,
And she was uncommonly fond of him, —
   And they were a loving pair ! —
   And the name and the fame
   Of the Knight and his Dame,
Were everywhere hailed with the loudest acclaim.

.   .   .   .   .

   Now Sir Thomas the Good,
   Be it well understood,
Was a man of very contemplative mood, —
   He would pore by the hour,
   O'er a weed or a flower,
Or the slugs that come crawling out after a
    shower ;
Black-beetles and Bumble-bees, Blue-bottle flies
And Moths, were of no small account in his
    eyes ;
An "Industrious Flea" he'd by no means despise,
While an "Old Daddy-long-legs," whose "long
    legs" and thighs
Passed the common in shape or in color or size,
He was wont to consider an absolute prize.
   Well, it happened one day, —
   I really can't say
The particular month ; but I *think* 't was in
    May, —
'T was, I *know*, in the Springtime, — when
    "Nature looks gay,"
As the Poet observes, — and on tree-top and spray
The dear little dickey-birds carol away ;
When the grass is so green, and the sun is so
    bright,
And all things are teeming with life and with
    light, —
That the whole of the house was thrown into
    affright,
For no soul could conceive what was gone with
    the Knight !

   It seems he had taken
   A light breakfast, — bacon,
An egg, — with a little broiled haddock, — at most
A round and a half of some hot buttered toast,
With a slice of cold sirloin from yesterday's roast.
   And then — let me see ! —
   He had two, perhaps three,
Cups (with sugar and cream) of strong gunpowder
    tea,
With a spoonful in each of some choice *eau de vie*, —
Which with nine out of ten would perhaps dis-
    agree. —
   In fact, I and my son
   Mix "black" with our "Hyson,"
Neither having the nerves of a bull or a bison,
And both hating brandy like what some call
    "pison."

No matter for that, —
He had called for his hat,
With the brim that I 've said was so broad and
so flat,
And his "specs" with the tortoise-shell rim,
and his cane
With the crutch-handled top, which he used to
sustain
His steps in his walks, and to poke in the shrubs
And the grass, when unearthing his worms and
his grubs.
Thus armed, he set out on a ramble, — alack !
He *set out*, poor dear soul ! — but he never came
back !

The morning dawned, — and the next, — and
the next,
And all in the mansion were still perplexed ;

. . . . . .

Up came running a man, at a deuce of a pace,
With that very peculiar expression of face
Which always betokens dismay or disaster,
Crying out, — 't was the gardener, — "O Ma'am !
we 've found Master ! "
"Where ? where ? " screamed the lady ; and
Echo screamed, "Where ? "
The man could n't say " There ! "
He had no breath to spare,
But, gasping for air, he could only respond
By pointing, — he pointed, alas ! TO THE POND.
'T was e'en so, — poor dear knight ! — with his
"specs" and his hat
He 'd gone poking his nose into this and to that,
When, close to the side
Of the bank, he espied
An "uncommon fine" tadpole, remarkably fat !
He stooped ; — and he thought her
His own ; — he had caught her !
Got hold of her tail, — and to land almost brought
her,
When — he plumped head and heels into, fifteen
feet water !

The Lady Jane was tall and slim,
The Lady Jane was fair,
Alas, for Sir Thomas ! — she grieved for him.
As she saw two serving-men, sturdy of limb,
His body between them bear :
She sobbed and she sighed, she lamented and
cried,
For of sorrow brimful was her cup ;
She swooned, and I think she 'd have fallen down
and died
If Captain MacBride
Had not been by her side,
With the gardener ; they both their assistance
supplied,
And managed to hold her up.

But, when she " comes to,"
O, 't is shocking to view
The sight which the corpse reveals !
Sir Thomas's body,
It looked so odd, — he
Was half eaten up by the eels !
His waistcoat and hose, and the rest of his
clothes,
Were all gnawled through and through !
And out of each shoe
An eel they drew ;
And from each of his pockets they pulled out
two !
And the gardener himself had secreted a few,
As well we may suppose ;
For when he came running to give the alarm
He had six in the basket that hung on his
arm.

Good Father John
Was summoned anon ;
Holy water was sprinkled,
And little bells tinkled,
And tapers were lighted,
And incense ignited,
And masses were sung, and masses were said,
All day, for the quiet repose of the dead,
And all night no one thought about going to bed.

But Lady Jane was tall and slim,
And Lady Jane was fair, —
And, ere morning came, that winsome dame
Had made up her mind, — or what 's much the
same,
Had *thought about* — once more "changing her
name."
And she said, with a pensive air,
To Thompson the valet, while taking away,
When supper was over, the cloth and the
tray, —
" Eels a many
I 've ate ; but any
So good ne'er tasted before ! —
They 're a fish, too, of which I 'm remarkably
fond. —
Go, pop Sir Thomas again in the pond ;
Poor dear ! — HE 'LL CATCH US SOME
MORE ! "

RICHARD HARRIS BARHAM.
(THOMAS INGOLDSBY.

SIR MARMADUKE.

SIR MARMADUKE was a hearty knight, —
Good man ! old man !
He 's painted standing bolt upright,
With his hose rolled over his knee ;

His periwig 's as white as chalk,
And on his fist he holds a hawk ;
    And he looks like the head
      Of an ancient family.

His dining-room was long and wide, —
    Good man ! old man !
His spaniels lay by the fireside ;
    And in other parts, d' ye see,
Cross-bows, tobacco-pipes, old hats,
A saddle, his wife, and a litter of cats ;
    And he looked like the head
      Of an ancient family.

He never turned the poor from the gate, —
    Good man ! old man !
But was always ready to break the pate
    Of his country's enemy.
What knight could do a better thing
Than serve the poor and fight for his king ?
    And so may every head
      Of an ancient family.
                 GEORGE COLMAN.

LITTLE BREECHES.

A PIKE COUNTY VIEW OF SPECIAL PROVIDENCE.

I DON'T go much on religion,
    I never ain't had no show ;
But I 've got a middlin' tight grip, sir,
    On the handful o' things I know.
I don't pan out on the prophets
    And free-will, and that sort of thing, —
But I b'lieve in God and the angels,
    Ever sence one night last spring.

I come into town with some turnips,
    And my little Gabe come along, —
No four-year-old in the county
    Could beat him for pretty and strong,
Peart and chipper and sassy,
    Always ready to swear and fight, —
And I 'd larnt him ter chaw terbacker,
    Jest to keep his milk-teeth white.

The snow come down like a blanket
    As I passed by Taggart's store ;
I went in for a jug of molasses
    And left the team at the door.
They scared at something and started, —
    I heard one little squall,
And hell-to-split over the prairie
    Went team, Little Breeches and all.

Hell-to-split over the prairie !
    I was almost froze with skeer ;
But we rousted up some torches,
    And sarched for 'em far and near.
At last we struck hosses and wagon,
    Snowed under a soft white mound,
Upsot, dead beat, — but of little Gabe
    No hide nor hair was found.

And here all hope soured on me
    Of my fellow-critter's aid, —
I jest flopped down on my marrow-bones,
    Crotch-deep in the snow, and prayed.

   *   *   *   *   *

By this, the torches was played out,
    And me and Isrul Parr
Went off for some wood to a sheepfold
    That he said was somewhar thar.

We found it at last, and a little shed
    Where they shut up the lambs at night.
We looked in, and seen them huddled thar,
    So warm and sleepy and white ;
And THAR sot Little Breeches and chirped,
    As peart as ever you see,
"I want a chaw of terbacker,
    And that 's what 's the matter of me."

How did he git thar ? Angels.
    He could never have walked in that storm.
They jest scooped down and toted him
    To whar it was safe and warm.
And I think that saving a little child,
    And bringing him to his own,
Is a derned sight better business
    Than loafing around The Throne.
                 JOHN HAY.

THE COMET.

THE comet ! he is on his way,
    And singing as he flies ;
The whizzing planets shrink before
    The spectre of the skies.
Ah, well may regal orbs burn blue,
    And satellites turn pale, —
Ten million cubic miles of head,
    Ten billion leagues of tail !

On, on by whistling spheres of light,
    He flashes and he flames ;
He turns not to the left nor right,
    He asks them not their names.

One spurn from his demoniac heel, —
　Away, away they fly,
Where darkness might be bottled up
　And sold for "Tyrian dye."

And what would happen to the land,
　And how would look the sea,
If in the bearded devil's path
　Our earth should chance to be?
Full hot and high the sea would boil,
　Full red the forests gleam ;
Methought I saw and heard it all
　In a dyspeptic dream !

I saw a tutor take his tube
　The comet's course to spy ;
I heard a scream, — the gathered rays
　Had stewed the tutor's eye !
I saw a fort, — the soldiers all
　Were armed with goggles green ;
Pop cracked the guns ! whiz flew the balls !
　Bang went the magazine !

I saw a poet dip a scroll
　Each moment in a tub ;
I read upon the warping back,
　"The Dream of Beelzebub."
He could not see his verses burn,
　Although his brain was fried,
And ever and anon he bent
　To wet them as they dried.

I saw the scalding pitch roll down
　The crackling, sweating pines,
And streams of smoke, like water-spouts,
　Burst through the rumbling mines.
I asked the firemen why they made
　Such noise about the town ;
They answered not, but all the while
　The brakes went up and down.

I saw a roasting pullet sit
　Upon a baking egg ;
I saw a cripple scorch his hand
　Extinguishing his leg.
I saw nine geese upon the wing
　Towards the frozen pole,
And every mother's gosling fell
　Crisped to a crackling coal.

I saw the ox that browsed the grass
　Writhe in the blistering rays,
The herbage in his shrinking jaws
　Was all a fiery blaze ;
I saw huge fishes, boiled to rags,
　Bob through the bubbling brine ;
And thoughts of supper crossed my soul, —
　I had been rash at mine.

Strange sights ! strange sounds ! O fearful dream !
　Its memory haunts me still,
The steaming sea, the crimson glare,
　That wreathed each wooded hill ;
Stranger, if through thy reeling brain
　Such midnight visions sweep,
Spare, spare, O spare thine evening meal,
　And sweet shall be thy sleep !
　　　　　　　　　OLIVER WENDELL HOLMES.

SPRING.

A FRAGMENT.

IN the merry month of May the jocund bee pro-
　claims the spring,
The verdant fields give hopes of hay, the house-fly
　now is on the wing,
The nettle now puts forth her charms, the thistle
　tempts the patient ass,
Black beetles walk about in swarms, and from
　the kitchens upward pass.
　　　　　　　　　PUNCH.

THE LAWYER'S INVOCATION TO SPRING.

WHEREAS, on certain boughs and sprays
　Now divers birds are heard to sing,
And sundry flowers their heads upraise,
　Hail to the coming on of Spring !

The songs of those said birds arouse
　The memory of our youthful hours,
As green as those said sprays and boughs,
　As fresh and sweet as those said flowers.

The birds aforesaid — happy pairs —
　Love, 'mid the aforesaid boughs, inshrines
In freehold nests ; themselves their heirs,
　Administrators, and assigns.

O busiest term of Cupid's Court,
　Where tender plaintiffs actions bring, —
Season of frolic and of sport,
　Hail, as aforesaid, coming Spring !
　　　　　　　　　H. P. H. BROWNELL.

DOUBLE BLESSEDNESS.

FROM "MISS KILMANSEGG."

O, HAPPY, happy, thrice happy state,
When such a bright Planet governs the fate
　Of a pair of united lovers !
'Tis theirs, in spite of the Serpent's hiss,
To enjoy the pure primeval kiss
With as much of the old original bliss
　As mortality ever recovers !

There 's strength in double joints, no doubt,
In Double X Ale, and Dublin Stout,
That the single sorts know nothing about, —
    And a fist is strongest when doubled, —
And double aqua-fortis, of course,
And double soda-water, perforce,
    Are the strongest that ever bubbled !

There 's double beauty whenever a Swan
Swims on a Lake with her double thereon ;
And ask the gardener, Luke or John,
    Of the beauty of double-blowing, —
A double dahlia delights the eye ;
And it 's far the loveliest sight in the sky
    When a double rainbow is glowing !

There 's warmth in a pair of double soles,
As well as a double allowance of coals, —
    In a coat that is double-breasted, —
In double windows and double doors,
And a double U wind is blest by scores
    For its warmth to the tender-chested.

There 's a twofold sweetness in double pipes,
And a double barrel and double snipes
    Give the sportsman a duplicate pleasure :
There 's double safety in double locks ;
And double letters bring cash for the box ;
And all the world knows that double knocks
    Are gentility's double measure.

There 's a double chuck at a double chin,
And of course there 's a double pleasure therein,
    If the parties were brought to telling :
And however our Dennisses take offence,
A double meaning shows double sense :
    And if proverbs tell truth,
        A double tooth
Is Wisdom's adopted dwelling.

But double wisdom, and pleasure, and sense,
Beauty, respect, strength, comfort, and thence
    Through whatever the list discovers,
They are all in the double blessedness summed,
Of what was formerly double-drummed,
    The Marriage of two true Lovers !
                              THOMAS HOOD.

THE HOUSEKEEPER.

THE frugal snail, with forecast of repose,
Carries his house with him where'er he goes ;
Peeps out, — and if there comes a shower of rain,
Retreats to his small domicile again.
Touch but a tip of him, a horn, — 't is well, —
He curls up in his sanctuary Shell,
He 's his own landlord, his own tenant ; stay
Long as he will, he dreads no Quarter Day.

Himself he boards and lodges ; both invites
And feasts himself ; sleeps with himself o' nights.
He spares the upholsterer trouble to procure
Chattels ; himself is his own furniture,
And his sole riches.   Wheresoe'er he roam —
Knock when you will — he 's sure to be at home.
                              CHARLES LAMB.

NEWTON'S PRINCIPIA.

GREAT Newton's self, to whom the world 's in debt,
Owed to School Mistress sage his Alphabet ;
But quickly wiser than his Teacher grown,
Discovered properties to her unknown ;
Of A *plus* B, or *minus*, learned the use,
Known Quantities from unknown to educe ;
And made — no doubt to that old dame's sur-
        prise —
The Christ-Cross-Row his ladder to the skies.
Yet, whatsoe'er Geometricians say,
Her lessons were his true PRINCIPIA !
                              CHARLES LAMB.

THE EGGS AND THE HORSES.

A MATRIMONIAL EPIC.

JOHN DOBBINS was so captivated
By Mary Trueman's fortune, face, and cap,
(With near two thousand pounds the hook was
        baited,)
That in he popped to matrimony's trap.

One small ingredient towards happiness,
It seems, ne'er occupied a single thought ;
    For his accomplished bride
    Appearing well supplied
With the three charms of riches, beauty, dress,
    He did not, as he ought,
    Think of aught else ; so no inquiry made he
    As to the temper of the lady.

And here was certainly a great omission ;
None should accept of Hymen's gentle fetter,
    "For worse or better,"
Whatever be their prospect or condition,
Without acquaintance with each other's nature ;
    For many a mild and quiet creature
    Of charming disposition,
Alas ! by thoughtless marriage has destroyed it.
So take advice ; let girls dress e'er so tastily,
    Don't enter into wedlock hastily
        Unless you can't avoid it.

Week followed week, and, it must be confest,
The bridegroom and the bride had both been
        blest :

Month after month had languidly transpired,
   Both parties became tired :
   Year after year dragged on ;
    Their happiness was gone.

Ah ! foolish pair !
  "Bear and forbear"
Should be the rule for married folks to take.
But blind mankind (poor discontented elves !)
  Too often make
  The misery of themselves.

At length the husband said, "This will not do !
Mary, I never will be ruled by you :
  So, wife, d' ye see ?
To live together as we can't agree,
   Suppose we part !"
    With woman's pride,
    Mary replied,
   "With all my heart !"

John Dobbins then to Mary's father goes,
And gives the list of his imagined woes.

"Dear son-in-law !" the father said, "I see
All is quite true that you 've been telling me ;
Yet there in marriage is such strange fatality,
   That when as much of life
    You will have seen
    As it has been
My lot to see, I think you 'll own your wife
As good or better than the generality.

"An interest in your case I really take,
And therefore gladly this agreement make :
An hundred eggs within this basket lie,
With which your 'uck, to-morrow, you shall try ;
Also my five best horses, with my cart ;
And from the farm at dawn you shall depart.
   All round the country go,
    And be particular, I beg ;
  Where husbands rule, a horse bestow,
  But where the wives, an egg.
And if the horses go before the eggs,
I 'll ease you of your wife, — I will, — I fegs !"

Away the married man departed,
   Brisk and light-hearted :
   Not doubting that, of course,
The first five houses each would take a horse.
   At the first house he knocked,
   He felt a little shocked
To hear a female voice, with angry roar,
  Scream out, — "Hullo !
  Who 's there below ?
Why, husband, are you deaf ? go to the door,
  See who it is, I beg."
    Our poor friend John
    ·Trudged quickly on,
But first laid at the door an egg.

I will not, all his journey through
  The discontented traveller pursue ;
   Suffice it here to say
That when his first day's task was nearly done,
He 'd seen an hundred husbands, minus one,
And eggs just ninety-nine had given away.
"Ha ! there 's a house where he I seek must
     dwell,"
At length cried John ; "I 'll go and ring the bell."

The servant came, — John asked him, "Pray,
   Friend, is your master in the way ?"
   "No," said the man, with smiling phiz,
"My master is not, but my mistress is ;
Walk in that parlor, sir, my lady 's in it :
Master will be himself there — in a minute."
The lady said her husband then was dressing,
And, if his business was not very pressing,
She would prefer that he should wait until
   His toilet was completed ;
  Adding, "Pray, sir, be seated."
    "Madam, I will,"
Said John, with great politeness ; "but I own
   That you alone
Can tell me all I wish to know ;
   Will you do so ?
   Pardon my rudeness,
   And just have the goodness
(A wager to decide) to tell me — do —
Who governs in this house, — your spouse or
    you ?"

"Sir," said the lady, with a doubting nod,
  "Your question 's very odd ;
But as I think none ought to be
Ashamed to do their duty (do you see ?)
On that account I scruple not to say
It always is my pleasure to obey.
But here 's my husband (always sad without
    me) ;
Take not my word, but ask him, if you
    doubt me."

"Sir," said the husband, "'t is most true ;
   I promise you,
A more obedient, kind, and gentle woman
  Does not exist.
  "Give us your fist,"
Said John, "and, as the case is something more
   than common,
  Allow me to present you with a beast
  Worth fifty guineas at the very least.

There 's Smiler, sir, a beauty, you must own,
  There 's Prince, that handsome black,
Ball the gray mare, and Saladin the roan,
   Besides old Dunn ;
   Come, sir, choose one ;

But take advice from me,
Let Prince be he ;
Why, sir, you 'll look the hero on his back."

" I 'll take the black, and thank you too."
"Nay, husband, that will never do ;
You know, you 've often heard me say
How much I long to have a gray ;
And this one will exactly do for me."
"No, no," said he,
" Friend, take the four others back,
And only leave the black."
"Nay, husband, I declare
I must have the gray mare."
Adding (with gentle force),
" The gray mare is, I 'm sure, the better horse."

"Well, if it must be so, — good sir,
The gray mare we prefer ;
So we accept your gift." John made a feg :
" Allow me to present you with an egg ;
'T is my last egg remaining,
The cause of my regaining,
I trust, the fond affection of my wife,
Whom I will love the better all my life.

Home to content has her kind father brought me ;
I thank him for the lesson he has taught me."
ANONYMOUS.

THE INDIAN CHIEFTAIN.

'T was late in the autumn of '53
That, making some business-like excuse,
I left New York, which is home to me,
And went on the cars to Syracuse.

Born and cradled in Maiden Lane,
I went to school in Battery Row,
Till when, my daily bread to obtain,
They made me clerk to Muggins & Co.

But I belonged to a genteel set
Of clerks with souls above their sphere,
Who night after night together met
To feast on intellectual cheer.

We talked of Irving and Bryant and Spratt, —
Of Willis, and how much they pay him per
page, —
Of Sontag and Julien and Art, and all that, —
And what d' ye call it ? — the Voice of the Age !

We wrote little pieces on purling brooks,
And meadow, and zephyr, and sea, and sky, —
Things of which we had seen good descriptions
in books,
And the last, between houses some sixty feet
high !

Somehow in this way my soul got fired ;
I wanted to see and hear and know
The glorious things that our hearts inspired, —
The things that sparkled in poetry so !

And I had heard of the dark-browed braves
Of the famous Onondaga race,
Who once paddled the birch o'er Mohawk's waves,
Or swept his shores in war and the chase.

I 'd see that warrior stern and fleet !
Ay, bowed though he be with oppression's
abuse :
I 'd grasp his hand ! — so in Chambers Street
I took my passage for Syracuse.

Arrived at last, I gazed upon
The smoke-dried wigwam of the tribe :
" The depot, sir," suggested one, —
I smiled to scorn the idle gibe.

Then to the baggage-man I cried,
"O, point me an Indian chieftain out !"
Rudely he grinned as he replied,
" You 'll see 'em loafin' all about !"

Wounded I turn, — when lo, e'en now
Before me stands the sight I crave !
I know him by his swarthy brow ;
It is an Onondaga brave !

I know him by his falcon eye,
His raven tress and mien of pride ;
Those dingy draperies, as they fly,
Tell that a great soul throbs inside !

No eagle-feathered crown he wears,
Capping in pride his kingly brow ;
But his crownless hat in grief declares,
" I am an unthroned monarch now !"

"O noble son of a royal line !"
I exclaim, as I gaze into his face,
" How shall I knit my soul to thine ?
How right the wrongs of thine injured race ?

" What shall I do for thee, glorious one ?
To soothe thy sorrows my soul aspires.
Speak ! and say how the Saxon's son
May atone for the wrongs of his ruthless sires !"

He speaks, he speaks ! — that noble chief !
From his marble lips deep accents come ;
And I catch the sound of his mighty grief, —
" Ple' gi' me tree cent for git some rum !"
ANONYMOUS.

ROPRECHT THE ROBBER.

ROPRECHT the Robber is taken at last ;
In Cologne they have him fast ;
Trial is over, and sentence past ;

And hopes of escape were vain, he knew ;
For the gallows now must have its due.

But buried Roprecht must not be ;
He is to be left on the triple tree ;
That they who pass along may spy
Where the famous robber is hanging on high.

It will be a comfortable sight
To see him there by day and by night ;
For Roprecht the Robber many a year
Had kept the country round in fear.

In his suit of irons he was hung ;
They sprinkled him then, and their psalm they
        sung ;
And, turning away when this duty was paid,
They said, — "What a goodly end he had made !"

The crowd broke up, and went their way ;
All were gone by the close of day ;
And Roprecht the Robber was left there,
Hanging alone in the moonlight air.

The stir in Cologne is greater to-day
Than all the bustle of yesterday ;
Hundreds and thousands went out to see ;
The irons and chains, as well as he,
Were gone, but the rope was left on the tree.

A wonderful thing ! for every one said
He had hung till he was dead, dead, dead ;
And on the gallows was seen, from noon
Till ten o'clock, in the light of the moon.

Moreover, the hangman was ready to swear
He had done his part with all due care ;
And that certainly better hanged than he
No one ever was, or ever *could* be.

So 't was thought, because he had died so well,
He was taken away by miracle.
But would he again alive be found ?
Or had he been laid in holy ground ?

'T was a whole week's wonder in that great town,
And in all places, up the river and down ;
But a greater wonder took place of it then,
For Roprecht was found on the gallows again.

With that the whole city flocked out to see ;
There Roprecht was on the triple tree,
Dead, past all doubt, as dead could be ;
But fresh he was, as if spells had charmed him,
And neither wind nor weather had harmed him.

While the multitude stood in a muse,
One said, " I 'm sure he was hanged in shoes."
In this the hangman and all concurred ;
But now, behold, he was booted and spurred !

Plainly, therefore, it was to be seen,
That somewhere on horseback he had been ;
And at this the people marvelled more
Than at anything which had happened before.

For not in riding trim was he
When he disappeared from the triple tree ;
And his suit of irons he still was in,
With the collar that clipped him under the chin.

Roprecht the Robber had long been their curse,
And hanging had only made him worse ;
For bad as he was when living, they said
They had rather meet him alive than dead.

.   .   .   .   .

Pieter Snoye was a boor of good renown,
Who dwelt about an hour and a half from the town;
And he, while the people were all in debate,
Went quietly in at the city gate.

For Father Kijf he sought about,
His Confessor, till he found him out ;
But the Father Confessor wondered to see
The old man, and what his errand might be.

" I and my son, Piet Pieterszoon,
Were returning home, by the light of the moon,
From this good city of Cologne,
On the night of the execution day ;
And hard by the gibbet was our way.

" About midnight it was we were passing by,
My son, Piet Pieterszoon, and I,
When we heard a moaning as we came near,
Which made us quake, at first, for fear.

" But the moaning was presently heard again,
And we knew it was nothing ghostly then ;
' Lord help us, father !' Piet Pieterszoon said,
' Roprecht, for certain, is not dead.'

" So under the gallows our cart we drive,
And, sure enough, the man was alive.
Because of the irons that he was in,
He was hanging, not by the *neck*, but the *chin*.

" The reason why things had got thus wrong
Was that the rope had been left too long ;
The hangman's fault, — a clumsy rogue,
He is not fit to hang a dog.

" My son, Piet Pieterszoon, and I,
We took him down, seeing none was nigh ;
And we took off his suit of irons with care,
When we got him home, and we hid him there.

" Well, Father, we kept him at bed and board
Till his neck was cured and his strength restored,
And we should have sent him off this day
With something to help him on his way ;

"But this wicked Roprecht, what did he,
Though he had been saved thus mercifully?
Hanging had done him so little good,
That he took to his old ways as soon as he could.

"Last night, when we were all asleep,
Out of his bed did this gallows-bird creep;
Piet Pieterszoon's boots and spurs he put on,
And stole my best horse, and away he was gone.

"Now Alit, my wife, did not sleep so hard
But she heard the horse's feet in the yard;
And when she jogged me, and bade me wake,
My mind misgave me as soon as she spake.

"To the window my good woman went,
And watched which way his course he bent;
And in such time as a pipe can be lit,
Our horses were ready with bridle and bit.

"Away, as fast as we could hie,
We went, Piet Pieterszoon and I;
And still on the plain we had him in sight;
The moon did not shine for nothing that night.

"Knowing the ground and riding fast,
We came up with him at last;
And — would you believe it? — Father Kijf,
The ungrateful wretch would have taken my life,
If he had not missed his stroke with a knife.

"When we had got him on the ground,
We fastened his hands, and his legs we bound;
And across the horse we laid him then,
And brought him back to the house again.

"'We have robbed the gallows, and that was ill
done,'
Said I to Pieterszoon, my son,
'And restitution we must make
To that same gallows, for justice' sake.'

"In his suit of irons the rogue we arrayed,
And once again in the cart he was laid;
Night not yet so far was spent
But there was time enough for our intent;
And back to the triple tree we went.

"His own rope was ready there,
To measure the length we took good care;
And the job which the bungling hangman begun,
This time, I think, was properly done,
By me and Piet Pieterszoon, my son."
ROBERT SOUTHEY.

SNEEZING.

WHAT a moment, what a doubt!
All my nose is inside out, —
All my thrilling, tickling caustic,
Pyramid rhinocerostic,

Wants to sneeze and cannot do it!
How it yearns me, thrills me, stings me,
How with rapturous torment fills me!
Now says, "Sneeze, you fool, — get through it."
Shee — shee — oh! 't is most del-ishi —
Ishi — ishi — most del-ishi!
(Hang it, I shall sneeze till spring!)
Snuff is a delicious thing.
ANONYMOUS.

CARMEN.

CANO carmen sixpence, a corbis plena rye,
Multas aves atras percoctas in a pie;
Ubi pie apertus tum canit avium grex;
Nonne suavis cibus hoc locari ante rex?
Fuisset rex in parlor, multo de nummo tumens;
Regina in culina, bread and mel consumens;
Ancilla was in horto, dependens out her clothes,
Quum venit parva cornix demorsa est her nose."
MATER ANSER'S MELODIES.

NOCTURNAL SKETCH.

EVEN is come; and from the dark Park, hark,
The signal of the setting sun — one gun!
And six is sounding from the chime, prime time
To go and see the Drury-Lane Dane slain, —
Or hear Othello's jealous doubt spout out, —
Or Macbeth raving at that shade-made blade,
Denying to his frantic clutch much touch; —
Or else to see Ducrow with wide stride ride
Four horses as no other man can span;
Or in the small Olympic Pitt sit split
Laughing at Liston, while you quiz his phiz.

Anon Night comes, and with her wings brings
things
Such as, with his poetic tongue, Young sung;
The gas up-blazes with its bright white light,
And paralytic watchmen prowl, howl, growl,
About the streets and take up Pall-Mall Sal,
Who, hasting to her nightly jobs, robs fobs.

Now thieves to enter for your cash, smash, crash,
Past drowsy Charley, in a deep sleep, creep,
But, frightened by Policeman B. 3, flee,
And while they're going, whisper low, "No go!"

Now puss, while folks are in their beds, treads leads,
And sleepers waking, grumble, — "Drat that cat!"
Who in the gutter caterwauls, squalls, mauls,
Some feline foe, and screams in shrill ill-will.

Now Bulls of Bashan, of a prize size, rise
In childish dreams, and with a roar gore poor

Georgy, or Charley, or Billy, willy-nilly ; —
But Nursemaid in a nightmare rest, chest-pressed,
Dreameth of one of her old flames, James Games,
And that she hears — what faith is man's — Ann's
   banns
And his, from Reverend Mr. Rice, twice, thrice ;
White ribbons flourish, and a stout shout out,
That upward goes, shows Rose knows those beaux'
   woes !
                        THOMAS HOOD.

SORROWS OF WERTHER.

WERTHER had a love for Charlotte
  Such as words could never utter ;
Would you know how first he met her ?
  She was cutting bread and butter.

Charlotte was a married lady,
  And a moral man was Werther,
And for all the wealth of Indies
  Would do nothing for to hurt her.

So he sighed and pined and ogled,
  And his passion boiled and bubbled,
Till he blew his silly brains out,
  And no more was by it troubled.

Charlotte, having seen his body
  Borne before her on a shutter,
Like a well-conducted person,
  Went on cutting bread and butter.
       WILLIAM MAKEPEACE THACKERAY.

TOO FULL OF BEER.

A SONG OF THE ENGLISH WORKING CLASSES.

Air, — "POOR MARY ANNE."

FOR Reform we feels too lazy ;
    Too full o' beer.
Much malt liquor makes us hazy,
    Too full o' beer.
We don't want no alteration
Of the present Legislation ;
'T won't affect our sittiwation,
    Too full o' beer.

We 've the means to bile our kettles,
    Too full o' beer.
Not bad off for drink and wittles,
    Too full o' beer.
When we 've got no work nor wages
Politics our minds engages,
Till such time we never rages,
    Too full o' beer.

Will this here Reform, we axes,
    Too full o' beer.
Clear us quite of rates and taxes,
    Too full o' beer ?
Income-Tax the middlin' classes
Loads unequal, — patient asses ! —
But it don't oppress the masses,
    Too full o' beer.

We be willin' to be quiet,
    Too full o' beer.
Not a bit inclined to riot,
    Too full o' beer.
From the ale that 's sound and nappy,
Him as wants a change is sappy ;
Wot 's the odds so long 's you 're happy,
    Too full o' beer ?
               PUNCH.

DOW'S FLAT.

1856.

Dow's Flat. That 's its name.
  And I reckon that you
Are a stranger ? The same ?
  Well, I thought it was true,
For thar is n't a man on the river as can't spot the
    place at first view.

It was called after Dow, —
  Which the same was an ass ;
And as to the how
  Thet the thing kem to pass, —
Jest tie up your hoss to that buckeye, and sit ye
    down here in the grass.

You see this yer Dow
  Hed the worst kind of luck ;
He slipped up somehow
  On each thing thet he struck.
Why, ef he 'd a' straddled thet fence-rail the
    derned thing 'ed get up and buck.

He mined on the bar
  Till he could n't pay rates ;
He was smashed by a car
  When he tunnelled with Bates ;
And right on the top of his trouble kem his wife
    and five kids from the States.

It was rough, — mighty rough ;
  But the boys they stood by,
And they brought him the stuff
  For a house, on the sly ;
And the old woman, — well, she did washing,
    and took on when no one was nigh.

But this yer luck of Dow's
  Was so powerful mean
That the spring near his house
  Dried right up on the green ;
And he sunk forty feet down for water, but nary
  a drop to be seen.

Then the bar petered out,
  And the boys would n't stay ;
And the chills got about,
  And his wife fell away ;
But Dow, in his well, kept a peggin' in his
  usual ridikilous way.

One day, — it was June, —
  And a year ago, jest, —
This Dow kem at noon
  To his work like the rest,
With a shovel and pick on his shoulder, and a
  derringer hid in his breast.

He goes to the well,
  And he stands on the brink,
And stops for a spell
  Jest to listen and think :
For the sun in his eyes, (jest like this, sir !) you
  see, kinder made the cuss blink.

His two ragged gals
  In the gulch were at play,
And a gownd that was Sal's
  Kinder flapped on a bay :
Not much for a man to be leavin', but his all, —
  as I 've heer'd the folks say.

And — that 's a peart hoss
  Thet you 've got — ain't it now ?
What might be her cost ?
  Eh ? Oh ! — Well then, Dow —
Let's see, — well, that forty-foot grave was n't
  his, sir, that day, anyhow.

For a blow of his pick
  Sorter caved in the side,
And he looked and turned sick,
  Then he trembled and cried.
For you see the dern cuss had struck — " Wa-
  ter ?" — beg your parding, young man,
  there you lied !

It was *gold*, — in the quartz,
  And it ran all alike ;
And I reckon five oughts
  Was the worth of that strike ;
And that house with the coopilow 's his'n, —
  which the same is n't bad for a Pike.

Thet 's why it 's Dow's Flat ;
  And the thing of it is
That he kinder got that

Through sheer contrairiness :
For 't was *water* the derned cuss was seekin', and
  his luck made him certain to miss.

Thet 's so. Thar 's your way
  To the left of yon tree ;
But — a — look h'yur, say,
  Won't you come up to tea ?
No ? Well, then the next time you 're passin' ;
  and ask after Dow, — and thet 's *me*.

FRANCIS BRET HARTE.

CHIQUITA.

BEAUTIFUL ! Sir, you may say so. Thar is n't
  her match in the county, —
Is thar, old gal ? Chiquita, my darling, my
  beauty !
Feel of that neck, sir, — thar 's velvet ! Whoa !
  Steady — ah, will you ? you vixen !
Whoa ! I say. Jack, trot her out ; let the gen-
  tleman look at her paces.

Morgan ! — She ain't nothin' else, and I 've got
  the papers to prove it.
Sired by Chippewa Chief, and twelve hundred
  dollars won't buy her.
Briggs of Tuolumne owned her. Did you know
  Briggs of Tuolumne ? —
Busted hisself in White Pine, and blew out his
  brains down in 'Frisco ?

Hed n't no savey, — hed Briggs. Thar, Jack !
  that 'll do, — quit that foolin' !
Nothin' to what she kin do when she 's got her
  work cut out before her.
Hosses is hosses, you know, and likewise, too,
  jockeys is jockeys ;
And 't ain't every man as can ride as knows what
  a hoss has got in him.

Know the old ford on the Fork, that nearly got
  Flanigan's leaders ?
Nasty in daylight, you bet, and a mighty rough
  ford in low water !
Well, it ain't six weeks ago that me and the
  Jedge, and his nevey,
Struck for that ford in the night, in the rain, and
  the water all round us ;

Up to our flanks in the gulch, and Rattlesnake
  Creek just a bilin',
Not a plank left in the dam, and nary a bridge
  on the river.
I had the gray, and the Jedge had his roan, and
  his nevey, Chiquita ;
And after us trundled the rocks jest loosed from
  the top of the cañon.

Lickity, lickity, switch, we came to the ford,
　　and Chiquita
Buckled right down to her work, and afore I could
　　yell to her rider,
Took water jest at the ford, and there was the
　　Jedge and me standing,
And twelve hundred dollars of hoss-flesh afloat,
　　and a driftin' to thunder!

Would ye b'lieve it, that night, that hoss, — that
　　ar' filly, — Chiquita, —
Walked herself into her stall, and stood there all
　　quiet and dripping!
Clean as a beaver or rat, with nary a buckle of
　　harness,
Just as she swam the Fork, — that hoss, that ar'
　　filly, Chiquita.

That's what I call a hoss! and — what did you
　　say? — O, the nevey?
Drownded, I reckon, — leastways, he never kem
　　back to deny it.
Ye see the derned fool had no seat, — ye could n't
　　have made him a rider;
And then, ye know, boys will be boys, and hosses
　　— well, hosses is hosses!

　　　　　　　　　　FRANCIS BRET HARTE.

LITTLE BILLEE.

THERE were three sailors of Bristol City
　　Who took a boat and went to sea,
But first with beef and captain's biscuits
　　And pickled pork they loaded she.

There was gorging Jack, and guzzling Jimmy,
　　And the youngest he was little Billee;
Now when they'd got as far as the Equator
　　They'd nothing left but one split pea.

Says gorging Jack to guzzling Jimmy,
　　"I am extremely hungaree."
To gorging Jack says guzzling Jimmy,
　　"We've nothing left, us must eat we."

Says gorging Jack to guzzling Jimmy,
　　"With one another we should n't agree!
There's little Bill, he's young and tender,
　　We're old and tough, so let's eat he."

"O Billy! we're going to kill and eat you,
　　So undo the button of your chemie."
When Bill received this information,
　　He used his pocket-handkerchie.

"First let me say my catechism
　　Which my poor mother taught to me."

"Make haste! make haste!" says guzzling Jimmy,
　　While Jack pulled out his snickersnee.

Billy went up to the main-top-gallant mast,
　　And down he fell on his bended 'knee,
He scarce had come to the Twelfth Commandment
　　When up he jumps — "There's land I see!"

"Jerusalem and Madagascar
　　And North and South Amerikee,
There's the British flag a riding at anchor,
　　With Admiral Napier, K. C. B."

So when they got aboard of the Admiral's,
　　He hanged fat Jack and flogged Jimmee,
But as for little Bill he made him
　　The Captain of a Seventy-three.

　　　　　WILLIAM MAKEPEACE THACKERAY.

SEBASTOPOL TAKEN — IN AND DONE FOR.

Air, — "BOW, WOW, WOW."

I SING about a subject now, of which each paper
　　has its full, —
The glorious deed so lately done, — the taking of
　　Sebastopol;
That is, — they would have taken it, as such
　　was their intention, yet
They have n't, so this latest joke I hope you will
　　not mention yet.
　　　　　　　　Bosh, bosh, bosh!
　　All the wires are telegraphing bosh, bosh, bosh.

With fifty thousand men, and more, and cannon
　　primed and loaded, sirs,
They smashed and crashed each standing stone,
　　and all the Russians goaded, sirs;
That is, — they would have done that same, and
　　left them not a jot at all,
But it happened neither guns nor men were ever
　　near the spot at all.
　　　　　　　　Bosh, bosh, bosh.

They slew full twenty thousand foes, and took
　　as many living, sirs,
And seized on everything they saw, not waiting
　　for the giving, sirs;
That is, — all this they would have done, your
　　growlers I will bet 'em,
But a trifling thing prevented it, — the Russians
　　would n't let 'em.
　　　　　　　　Bosh, bosh, bosh.

They took at least five hundred sail, and steam-
　　ers nine-and-sixty, too,
Blew up and sunk and fired the rest; most prop-
　　erly they "fixed it," too;

That is, — they would have shaved the coast as
 clean as any barber, sir,
But it so happened that the fleet lay snugly in
 the harbor, sir.

    Bosh, bosh, bosh.

Prince Menschikoff one Jack Tar took, all singly,
 with no aid alive,
Requesting which he'd rather be, stuck, stran-
 gled, drowned, or flayed alive ;
That is, — there cannot be a doubt the Prince
 would have been taken,
But he's no rasher than he should be, — so he
 saved his bacon.

    Bosh, bosh, bosh.

Lord Raglan slew, with his own hand, of Rus-
 sians full a hundred, sirs ;
St. Arnaud kept the game alive, and eighty
 wesands sundered, sirs ;
That is, — they would have killed them all, and
 left each corse behind 'em,
But as they were not there to kill, in course
 they couldn't find 'em.

    Bosh, bosh, bosh.

At night, according to the Times, that surest of
 all staters,
The Allies supped within the walls, on tripe and
 baked potatoes ;
That is, — they would have had that fare, and,
 doubtless, keenly relished it,
But they had junk outside the walls and noth-
 ing else embellished it !

    Bosh, bosh, bosh.

Now when the next news come to hand, we hope
 it will be true, sirs,
Assuring us of something done, and not a public
 "do," sirs ;
And if there is, why then we'll shout, "Well
 done, my lads !" that's poz, sirs,
And if there isn't, why then things ar'n't as
 they used to was, sirs.

    Bosh, bosh, bosh.
       LONDON DIOGENES.

THE INEBRIATE.

PARODY.

NOT a *sous* had he got, — not a guinea or note,
  And he looked confoundedly flurried,
As he bolted away without paying his shot,
  And the Landlady after him hurried.

We saw him again at dead of night,
  When home from the Club returning ;
We twigged the Doctor beneath the light
  Of the gas-lamp brilliantly burning.

All bare, and exposed to the midnight dews,
  Reclined in the gutter we found him ;
And he looked like a gentleman taking a snooze,
  With his *Marshall* cloak around him.

"The Doctor's as drunk as the d——," we said,
  And we managed a shutter to borrow ;
We raised him, and sighed at the thought that
   his head
  Would "consumedly ache" on the morrow.

We bore him home, and we put him to bed,
  And we told his wife and his daughter
To give him, next morning, a couple of red
  Herrings, with soda-water.

Loudly they talked of his money that's gone,
  And his Lady began to upbraid him ;
But little he recked, so they let him snore on
  'Neath the counterpane just as we laid him.

We tucked him in, and had hardly done
  When, beneath the window calling,
We heard the rough voice of a son of a gun
  Of a watchman "One o'clock !" bawling.

Slowly and sadly we all walked down
  From his room in the uppermost story ;
A rushlight we placed on the cold hearthstone,
  And we left him alone in his glory !
      RICHARD HARRIS BARHAM.
      (THOMAS INGOLDSBY.)

PERILS OF THE PAVE.

JUMPING over gutters,
  Wading through the flood,
Ploughing through the slush,
  Tumbling in the mud,
Squatting in the puddles, —
  Bless me ! this is nice,
Slopping through the water,
  Slipping on the ice.

Men of every class,
  In such falling weather,
Find it very easy,
  Tumbling down together.
Pillars of the church,
  Servants of the devil,
Here they very quickly
  Find a common level.

Very sharp young fellow
  Makes a perfect flat,
Rusty, fusty bachelor
  Tumbles on his hat.

Strictly temperate man,
　　Who has ne'er been fuddled,
Staggers here and falls,
　　Dreadfully be-muddled.

Corpulent old lady,
　　Radiant with blushes,
Ere she can cry "Ned,"
　　To the pavement rushes.
Affluent old butcher,
　　With a solemn frown,
Says "he's very sorry
　　Beef is going down."

Antiquated maiden,
　　Easy to disturb,
Violently seats her
　　On the filthy curb.
Witty man assisting,
　　Says, "Trust you have n't hurt you ;
Judging from position,
　　You must be gutta-percha."

Policeman on corner,
　　Holding up the wall,
Suddenly, in slipping,
　　Can't arrest his fall.
Curious little boy,
　　Walking with his par,
Anxiously inquires
　　"If that's a falling star."

Yellow-kidded dandy,
　　Dressed in height of fashion,
Falls into a puddle,
　　And then into a passion ;
Finding that he's going,
　　In his wild alarm
Tries to break his tumble, —
　　Only breaks his arm.

Here a robust, sober,
　　Hearty-looking Quaker
Lays himself out flat
　　Sans an undertaker.
Then a jolly soul,
　　Full of gin and porter,
Quickly drops his rum
　　And takes to dirty water.

Smiling little girls,
　　Charming little trippers,
Slip along the pave
　　As if they had on slippers ;
Skipping over streams
　　No wider than their thumbs,
Show their pretty teeth
　　And horrid ugly gums.

Broken-winded horses,
　　Pulling all they're able,
Frequently get stalled,
　　But seldom in the stable.
Passengers in 'busses,
　　Dreadfully aggravated,
From their fellow-creatures
　　Are wholly isolated.

Jumping over gutters,
　　Wading through the flood,
Ploughing through the slush,
　　Tumbling in the mud,
Squatting in the puddles, —
　　Bless me ! this is nice,
Slopping through the water,
　　Slipping on the ice.
　　　　　　　　　　　　ANONYMOUS.

WIDOW BEDOTT TO ELDER SNIFFLES.

FROM "THE WIDOW BEDOTT PAPERS."

O REVEREND sir, I do declare
　　It drives me most to frenzy,
To think of you a lying there
　　Down sick with influenzy.

A body'd thought it was enough
　　To mourn your wive's departer,
Without sich trouble as this ere
　　To come a follerin' arter.

But sickness and affliction
　　Are sent by a wise creation,
And always ought to be underwent
　　By patience and resignation.

O, I could to your bedside fly,
　　And wipe your weeping eyes,
And do my best to cure you up,
　　If 't would n't create surprise.

It's a world of trouble we tarry in,
　　But, Elder, don't despair ;
That you may soon be movin' again
　　Is constantly my prayer.

Both sick and well, you may depend
　　You 'll never be forgot
By your faithful and affectionate friend,
　　　　PRISCILLA POOL BEDOTT.
　　　　FRANCES MIRIAM WHITCHER.

DEBORAH LEE.

PARODY.

'T IS a dozen or so of years ago,
　　Somewhere in the West countree,
That a nice girl lived, as ye Hoosiers know
　　By the name of Deborah Lee ;

Her sister was loved by Edgar Poe,
　But Deborah by me.

Now I was green, and she was green,
　As a summer's squash might be;
And we loved as warmly as other folks, —
　I and my Deborah Lee, —
With a love that the lasses of Hoosierdom
　Coveted her and me.

But somehow it happened a long time ago,
　In the aguish West countree,
That a chill March morning gave the *shakes*
　To my beautiful Deborah Lee;
And the grim steam-doctor (drat him!) came,
　And bore her away from me, —
The doctor and death, old partners they, —
　In the aguish countree.

The angels wanted her in heaven
　(But they never asked for me),
And that is the reason, I rather guess,
　In the aguish West countree,
That the cold March wind, and the doctor, and
　death,
　Took off my Deborah Lee —
　My beautiful Deborah Lee —
From the warm sunshine and the opening flower,
　And bore her away from me.

Our love was as strong as a six-horse team,
　Or the love of folks older than we,
　Or possibly wiser than we;
But death, with the aid of doctor and steam,
　Was rather too many for me;
He closed the peepers and silenced the breath
　Of my sweetheart Deborah Lee,
And her form lies cold in the prairie mould,
　Silent and cold, — ah me!

The foot of the hunter shall press her grave,
　And the prairie's sweet wild flowers
In their odorous beauty around it wave
　Through all the sunny hours, —
　The still, bright summer hours;
And the birds shall sing in the tufted grass,
　And the nectar-laden bee,
With his dreamy hum, on his gauze wings pass, —
　She wakes no more to me;
　Ah, nevermore to me!
Though the wild birds sing and the wild flowers
　spring,
　She wakes no more to me.

Yet oft in the hush of the dim, still night,
　A vision of beauty I see
Gliding soft to my bedside, — a phantom of light,
　Dear, beautiful Deborah Lee, —
　My bride that was to be;

And I wake to mourn that the doctor, and death,
And the cold March wind, should stop the breath
　Of my darling Deborah Lee, —
　Adorable Deborah Lee, —
That angels should want her up in heaven
　Before they wanted me.

ANONYMOUS.

WHAT MR. ROBINSON THINKS.

FROM "THE BIGLOW PAPERS."

Guvener B. is a sensible man;
　He stays to his home an' looks arter his folks;
He draws his furrer ez straight ez he can,
　An' into nobody's tater-patch pokes; —
　　　But John P.
　　　Robinson he
　Sez he wunt vote fer Guvener B.

My! aint it terrible? Wut shall we du?
　We can't never choose him o' course, — thet's
　　flat;
Guess we shall hev to come round, (don't you?)
　An' go in fer thunder an' guns, an' all that;
　　　Fer John P.
　　　Robinson he
　Sez he wunt vote fer Guvener B.

Gineral C. is a dreffle smart man:
　He's ben on all sides thet give places or pelf;
But consistency still wuz a part of his plan, —
　He's ben true to *one* party, — an' thet is him-
　　self; —
　　　So John P.
　　　Robinson he
　Sez he shall vote fer Gineral C.

Gineral C. he goes in fer the war;[*]
　He don't vally principle more 'n an old cud;
Wut did God make us raytional creeturs fer,
　But glory an' gunpowder, plunder an' blood?
　　　So John P.
　　　Robinson he
　Sez he shall vote fer Gineral C.

We were gittin' on nicely up here to our village,
　With good old idees o' wut's right an' wut aint,
We kind o' thought Christ went agin war an'
　　pillage,
　An' thet eppyletts worn't the best mark of a
　　saint;
　　　But John P.
　　　Robinson he
　Sez this kind o' thing's an exploded idee.

* Written at the time of the Mexican war, which was strongly
opposed by the Anti-Slavery party as being unnecessary and
wrong.

The side of our country must ollers be took,
　An' Presidunt Polk, you know, *he* is our coun-
　　try ;
An' the angel thet writes all our sins in a book
　Puts the *debit* to him, an' to us the *per con-
　　try ;*
　　　An' John P.
　　　Robinson he
　Sez this is his view o' the thing. to a T.

Parson Wilbur he calls all these argimunts lies ;
　Sez they 're nothin' on airth but jest *fee, faw,
　　fum :*
And thet all this big talk of our destinies
　Is half ov it ign'ance, an' t'other half rum ;
　　　But John P.
　　　Robinson he
　Sez it aint no sech thing ; an', of course, so
　　must we.

Parson Wilbur sez *he* never heerd in his life
　Thet th' Apostles rigged out in their swaller-
　　tail coats,
An' marched round in front of a drum an' a fife,
　To git some on 'em office, an' some on 'em
　　votes ;
　　　But John P.
　　　Robinson he
　Sez they did n't know everythin' down in
　　Judee.

Wal, it 's a marcy we 've gut folks to tell us
　The rights an' the wrongs o' these matters, I
　　vow, —
God sends country lawyers, an' other wise fel-
　　lers,
　To drive the world's team wen it gits in a
　　slough ;
　　　Fer John P.
　　　Robinson he
　Sez the world 'll go right, ef he hollers out
　　Gee !
　　　　　　　　JAMES RUSSELL LOWELL.

A TALE OF DRURY LANE.

IMITATION OF SIR WALTER SCOTT.

"Thus he went on, stringing one extravagance upon another, in
the style his books of chivalry had taught him, and imitating, as
near as he could, their very phrase."— DON QUIXOTE.

*To be spoken by Mr. Kemble, in a suit of the Black
Prince's armor, borrowed from the Tower.*

REST there awhile, my bearded lance,
While from green curtain I advance
To yon foot-lights, no trivial dance,
And tell the town what sad mischance
　Did Drury Lane befall.

THE NIGHT.

On fair Augusta's towers and trees
Flitted the silent midnight breeze,
Curling the foliage as it past,
Which from the moon-tipped plumage cast
A spangled light, like dancing spray,
Then reassumed its still array ;
When, as night's lamp unclouded hung,
And down its full effulgence flung,
It shed such soft and balmy power,
That cot and castle, hall and bower,
And spire and dome, and turret height,
Appeared to slumbei in the light.
From Henry's Chapel, Rufus' Hall,
To Savoy, Temple, and St. Paul ;
From Knightsbridge, Pancras, Camden Town,
To Redriffe, Shadwell, Horsleydown,
No voice was heard, no eye unclosed,
But all in deepest sleep reposed.
They might have thought who gazed around
Amid a silence so profound
　It made the senses thrill,
That 't was no place inhabited,
But some vast city of the dead, —
　All was so hushed and still.

THE BURNING.

As Chaos, which, by heavenly doom,
Had slept in everlasting gloom,
Started with terror and surprise
When light first flashed upon her eyes, —
So London's sons in nightcap woke,
　In bedgown woke her dames ;
For shouts were heard 'mid fire and smoke,
And twice ten hundred voices spoke, —
　"The playhouse is in flames !"
And, lo ! where Catherine Street extends,
A fiery tail its lustre lends
　To every window-pane ;
Blushes each spout in Martlet Court,
And Barbican, moth-eaten fort,
And Covent Garden kennels sport,
　A bright ensanguined drain ;
Meux's new Brewhouse shows the light,
Rowland Hill's Chapel, and the height
　Where Patent Shot they sell ;
The Tennis Court, so fair and tall,
Partakes the ray, with Surgeons' Hall,
The Ticket-Porters' House of Call,
Old Bedlam, close by London Wall,
Wright's shrimp and oyster shop withal,
　And Richardson's Hotel.
Nor these alone, but far and wide,
Across red Thames's gleaming tide,
To distant fields the blaze was borne,
And daisy white and hoary thorn
In borrowed lustre seemed to sham
The rose or red sweet Wil-li-am.

To those who on the hills around
Beheld the flames from Drury's mound,
    As from a lofty altar rise,
It seemed that nations did conspire
.To offer to the god of fire
    Some vast, stupendous sacrifice !
The summoned firemen woke at call,
And hied them to their stations all :
Starting from short and broken snooze,
Each sought his ponderous hobnailed shoes,
But first his worsted hosen plied ;
Plush breeches next, in crimson dyed,
    His nether bulk embraced ;
Then jacket thick, of red or blue,
Whose massy shoulder gave to view
The badge of each respective crew,
    In tin or copper traced.
The engines thundered through the street,
Fire-hook, pipe, bucket, all complete,
And torches glared, and clattering feet
    Along the pavement paced.
And one, the leader of the band,
From Charing Cross along the Strand,
Like stag by beagles hunted hard,
Ran till he stopped at Vin'gar Yard.
The burning badge his shoulder bore,
The belt and oil-skin hat he wore,
The cane he had, his men to bang,
Showed foreman of the British gang, —
His name was Higginbottom. Now
'T is meet that I should tell you how
    The others came in view :
The Hand-in-Hand the race began,
Then came the Phœnix and the Sun,
The Exchange, where old insurers run,
    The Eagle, where the new ;
With these came Rumford, Bumford, Cole,
Robins from Hockley in the Hole,
Lawson and Dawson, cheek by jowl,
    Crump from St. Giles's Pound :
Whitford and Mitford joined the train,
Huggins and Muggins from Chick Lane,
And Clutterbuck, who got a sprain
    Before the plug was found.
Hobson and Jobson did not sleep,
But ah ! no trophy could they reap,
For both were in the Donjon Keep
    Of Bridewell's gloomy mound !
E'en Higginbottom now was posed,
For sadder scene was ne'er disclosed ;
Without, within, in hideous show,
Devouring flames resistless glow,
And blazing rafters downward go,
And never halloo " Heads below ! "
    Nor notice give at all.
The firemen terrified are slow
To bid the pumping torrent flow,
    For fear the roof should fall.

Back, Robins, back ! Crump, stand aloof !
Whitford, keep near the walls !
Huggins, regard your own behoof,
For, lo ! the blazing rocking roof
Down, down, in thunder falls !
An awful pause succeeds the stroke,
And o'er the ruins volumed smoke,
Rolling around its pitchy shroud,
Concealed them from the astonished crowd.
At length the mist awhile was cleared,
When, lo ! amid the wreck upreared,
Gradual a moving head appeared,
    And Eagle firemen knew
'T was Joseph Muggins, name revered,
    The foreman of their crew.
Loud shouted all in signs of woe,
" A Muggins ! to the rescue, ho ! "
    And poured the hissing tide :
Meanwhile the Muggins fought amain,
And strove and struggled all in vain,
For, rallying but to fall again,
    He tottered, sunk, and died !

Did none attempt, before he fell,
To succor one they loved so well ?
Yes, Higginbottom did aspire
(His fireman's soul was all on fire)
    His brother chief to save ;
But ah ! his reckless generous ire
    Served but to share his grave !
'Mid blazing beams and scalding streams,
Through fire and smoke he dauntless broke,
    Where Muggins broke before.
But sulphury stench and boiling drench,
Destroying sight, o'erwhelmed him quite,
    He sunk to rise no more.
Still o'er his head, while Fate he braved,
His whizzing water-pipe he waved :
" Whitford and Mitford, ply your pumps !
You, Clutterbuck, come, stir your stumps !
Why are you in such doleful dumps ?
A fireman, and afraid of bumps ! —
What are they feared on ? fools ! 'od rot 'em ! "
Were the last words of Higginbottom.
          HORACE SMITH. From the
          Rejected Addresses.

THE THEATRE.

IMITATION OF CRABBE.

Interior of a Theatre described. — Pit gradually fills. — The Check-
taker. — Pit full. — The Orchestra tuned. — One fiddle rather dil-
atory. — Is reproved — and repents. — Evolutions of a Play-bill.
— Its final Settlement on the Spikes. — The Gods taken to task
— and why. — Motley Group of Play-goers. — Holywell Street,
St. Pancras. — Emanuel Jennings binds his Son apprentice — not
in London — and why. — Episode of the Hat.

'T is sweet to view, from half past five to six,
Our long wax-candles, with short cotton wicks,

Touched by the lamplighter's Promethean art,
Start into light, and make the lighter start ;
To see red Phœbus through the gallery-pane
Tinge with his beam the beams of Drury Lane ;
While gradual parties fill our widened pit,
And gape and gaze and wonder ere they sit.

At first, while vacant seats give choice and ease,
Distant or near, they settle where they please ;
But when the multitude contracts the span,
And seats are rare, they settle where they can.

Now the full benches to late-comers doom
No room for standing, miscalled *standing room.*

Hark ! the check-taker moody silence breaks,
And bawling "Pit full !" gives the check he takes ;
Yet onward still the gathering numbers cram,
Contending crowders shout the frequent damn,
And all is bustle, squeeze, row, jabbering, and jam.

See to their desks Apollo's sons repair, —
Swift rides the rosin o'er the horse's hair !
In unison their various tones to tune,
Murmurs the hautboy, growls the hoarse bassoon ;
In soft vibration sighs the whispering lute,
Tang goes the harpsichord, too-too the flute,
Brays the loud trumpet, squeaks the fiddle sharp,
Winds the French horn, and twangs the tingling
        harp ;
Till, like great Jove, the leader, figuring in,
Attunes to order the chaotic din.
Now all seems hushed, — but, no, one fiddle will
Give, half ashamed, a tiny flourish still.
Foiled in his crash, the leader of the clan
Reproves with frowns the dilatory man ;
Then on his candlestick thrice taps his bow,
Nods a new signal, and away they go.

Perchance, while pit and gallery cry "Hats off !"
And awed Consumption checks his chided cough,
Some giggling daughter of the Queen of Love
Drops, reft of pin, her play-bill from above :
Like Icarus, while laughing galleries clap,
Soars, ducks, and dives in air the printed scrap ;
But, wiser far than he, combustion fears,
And, as it flies, eludes the chandeliers ;
Till, sinking gradual, with repeated twirl,
It settles, curling, on a fiddler's curl ;
Who from his powdered pate the intruder strikes,
And, from mere malice, sticks it on the spikes.

Say, why these Babel strains from Babel tongues ?
Who 's that calls " Silence ! " with such leathern
        lungs ?
He who, in quest of quiet, " Silence ! " hoots,
Is apt to make the hubbub he imputes.

What various swains our motley walls contain !—
Fashion from Moorfields, honor from Chick Lane ;

Bankers from Paper Buildings here resort,
Bankrupts from Golden Square and Riches Court ;
From the Haymarket canting rogues in grain,
Gulls from the Poultry, sots from Water Lane ;
The lottery-cormorant, the auction-shark,
The full-price master, and the half-price clerk :
Boys who long linger at the gallery door,
With pence twice five, — they want but twopence
        more ;
Till some Samaritan the twopence spares,
And sends them jumping up the gallery stairs.

Critics we boast who ne'er their malice balk,
But talk their minds, — we wish they 'd mind
        their talk ;
Big-worded bullies, who by quarrels live, —
Who give the lie, and tell the lie they give ;
Jews from St. Mary Axe, for jobs so wary,
That for old clothes they 'd even axe St. Mary ;
And bucks with pockets empty as their pate,
Lax in their gaiters, laxer in their gait ;
Who oft, when we our house lock up, carouse
With tippling tipstaves in a lock-up house.

Yet here, as elsewhere, Chance can joy bestow,
For scowling Fortune seemed to threaten woe.

John Richard William Alexander Dwyer
Was footman to Justinian Stubbs, Esquire ;
But when John Dwyer listed in the Blues,
Emanuel Jennings polished Stubbs's shoes.
Emanuel Jennings brought his youngest boy
Up as a corn-cutter, — a safe employ ;
In Holy-well Street, St. Pancras, he was bred
(At number twenty-seven, it is said),
Facing the pump, and near the Granby's Head ;
He would have bound him to some shop in town,
But with a premium he could not come down.
Pat was the urchin's name, — a red-haired youth,
Fonder of purl and skittle grounds than truth.

Silence, ye gods ! to keep your tongues in awe,
The Muse shall tell an accident she saw.

Pat Jennings in the upper gallery sat,
But, leaning forward, Jennings lost his hat :
Down from the gallery the beaver flew,
And spurned the one to settle in the two.
How shall he act ?   Pay at the gallery-door
Two shillings for what cost, when new, but four ?
Or till half-price, to save his shilling, wait,
And gain his hat again at half past eight ?
Now, while his fears anticipate a thief,
John Mullens whispers, "Take my handkerchief."
"Thank you," cries Pat ; "but one won't make
        a line."
"Take mine," cried Wilson ; and cried Stokes,
        " Take mine."

A motley cable soon Pat Jennings ties,
Where Spitalfields with real India vies.
Like Iris' bow, down darts the painted clew,
Starred, striped, and spotted, yellow, red, and blue,
Old calico, torn silk, and muslin new.
George Green below, with palpitating hand,
Loops the last kerchief to the beaver's band, —
Upsoars the prize ! The youth with joy unfeigned
Regained the felt, and felt what he regained ;
While to the applauding galleries grateful Pat
Made a low bow, and touched the ransomed hat.
                                JAMES SMITH.

THE CATARACT OF LODORE.

DESCRIBED IN RHYMES FOR THE NURSERY.

" How does the water
    Come down at Lodore ?"
My little boy asked me
Thus, once on a time ;
And moreover he tasked me
    To tell him in rhyme.
    Anon at the word,
There first came one daughter,
    And then came another,
    To second and third
The request of their brother,
And to hear how the water
    Comes down at Lodore,
    With its rush and its roar,
    As many a time
    They had seen it before.
So I told them in rhyme,
For of rhymes I had store ;
And 't was in my vocation
    For their recreation
That so I should sing ;
Because I was Laureate
    To them and the King.

From its sources which well
    In the tarn on the fell ;
    From its fountains
    In the mountains,
Its rills and its gills ;
Through moss and through brake,
    It runs and it creeps
    For a while, till it sleeps
    In its own little lake.
And thence at departing,
Awakening and starting,
It runs through the reeds,
    And away it proceeds,
Through meadow and glade,
    In sun and in shade,
And through the wood-shelter,
    Among crags in its flurry,

    Helter-skelter,
    Hurry-skurry.
Here it comes sparkling,
And there it lies darkling ;
Now smoking and frothing
    Its tumult and wrath in,
    Till in this rapid race
    On which it is bent,
    It reaches the place
    Of its steep descent.

    The cataract strong
    Then plunges along,
    Striking and raging
    As if a war waging
Its caverns and rocks among ;
    Rising and leaping,
    Sinking and creeping,
Swelling and sweeping,
Showering and springing,
    Flying and flinging,
Writhing and ringing,
Eddying and whisking,
Spouting and frisking,
Turning and twisting,
    Around and around
With endless rebound :
    Smiting and fighting,
    A sight to delight in ;
    Confounding, astounding,
Dizzying and deafening the ear with its sound.

    Collecting, projecting,
    Receding and speeding,
    And shocking and rocking,
    And darting and parting,
    And threading and spreading,
    And whizzing and hissing,
    And dripping and skipping,
    And hitting and splitting,
    And shining and twining,
    And rattling and battling,
    And shaking and quaking,
    And pouring and roaring,
    And waving and raving,
    And tossing and crossing,
    And flowing and going,
    And running and stunning,
    And foaming and roaming,
    And dinning and spinning,
    And dropping and hopping,
    And working and jerking,
    And guggling and struggling,
    And heaving and cleaving,
    And moaning and groaning ;

    And glittering and frittering,
    And gathering and feathering,

And whitening and brightening,
And quivering and shivering,
And hurrying and skurrying,
And thundering and floundering ;

Dividing and gliding and sliding,
And falling and brawling and sprawling,
And driving and riving and striving,
And sprinkling and twinkling and wrinkling,
And sounding and bounding and rounding,
And bubbling and troubling and doubling,
And grumbling and rumbling and tumbling,
And clattering and battering and shattering ;

Retreating and beating and meeting and sheeting,
Delaying and straying and playing and spraying,
Advancing and prancing and glancing and dan-
    cing,
Recoiling, turmoiling and toiling and boiling,
And gleaming and streaming and steaming and
    beaming,
And rushing and flushing and brushing and gush-
    ing,
And flapping and rapping and clapping and slap-
    ping,
And curling and whirling and purling and
    twirling,
And thumping and plumping and bumping and
    jumping,
And dashing and flashing and splashing and
    clashing ;
And so never ending, but always descending,
Sounds and motions forever and ever are blending,
All at once and all o'er, with a mighty uproar,
And this way the water comes down at Lodore.
            ROBERT SOUTHEY.

POEMS

RECEIVED IN RESPONSE TO AN ADVERTISED
CALL FOR A NATIONAL ANTHEM.

NATIONAL ANTHEM.

BY H. W. L——, OF CAMBRIDGE.

BACK in the years when Phlagstaff, the Dane,
    was monarch
    Over the sea-ribbed land of the fleet-footed
    Norsemen,
Once there went forth young Ursa to gaze at the
    heavens, —
    Ursa, the noblest of all Vikings and horsemen.

Musing he sat in his stirrups and viewed the
    horizon,
    Where the Aurora lapt stars in a north-polar
    manner ;

Wildly he started, — for there in the heavens be-
    fore him
    Fluttered and flew the original star-spangled
    banner.

Two objections are in the way of the acceptance of this anthem
by the committee : in the first place, it is not an anthem at all ; sec-
ondly, it is a gross plagiarism from an old Sclavonic war-song of the
primeval ages.
Next we quote from a

NATIONAL ANTHEM

BY THE HON. EDWARD E——, OF BOSTON.

PONDEROUS projectiles, hurled by heavy hands,
    Fell on our Liberty's poor infant head,
Ere she a stadium had well advanced
    On the great path that to her greatness led ;
Her temple's propylon was shatter-ed ;
    Yet, thanks to saving Grace and Washington,
Her incubus was from her bosom hurled ;
    And, rising like a cloud-dispelling sun,
She took the oil with which her hair was curled
To grease the "hub" round which revolves the
    world.

This fine production is rather heavy for an "anthem," and contains
too much of Boston to be considered strictly national. To set such
an "anthem" to music would require a Wagner ; and even were it
really accommodated to a tune, it could only be whistled by the
populace.
We now come to a

NATIONAL ANTHEM.

BY JOHN GREENLEAF W——.

MY native land, thy Puritanic stock
Still finds its roots firm bound in Plymouth Rock ;
And all thy sons unite in one grand wish, —
To keep the virtues of Preserv-ed Fish.

Preserv-ed Fish, the Deacon stern and true,
Told our New England what her sons should do ;
And, should they swerve from loyalty and right,
Then the whole land were lost indeed in night.

The sectional bias of this "anthem" renders it unsuitable for use
in that small margin of the world situated outside of New England.
Hence the above must be rejected.
Here we have a very curious

NATIONAL ANTHEM.

BY DR. OLIVER WENDELL H——.

A DIAGNOSIS of our history proves
Our native land a land its native loves ;
Its birth a deed obstetric without peer,
Its growth a source of wonder far and near.

To love it more, behold how foreign shores
Sink into nothingness beside its stores.
Hyde Park at best — though counted ultra grand —
The "Boston Common" of Victoria's land —

The committee must not be blamed for rejecting the above after
reading thus far, for such an "anthem" could only be sung by a
college of surgeons or a Beacon Street tea-party.
Turn we now to a

NATIONAL ANTHEM.

BY RALPH WALDO E——.

SOURCE immaterial of material naught,
  Focus of light infinitesimal,
Sum of all things by sleepless Nature wrought,
  Of which abnormal man is decimal.

Refract, in prism immortal, from thy stars
  To the stars blent incipient on our flag,
To beam translucent, neutrifying death,
  And raise to immortality "the rag."

This "anthem" was greatly praised by a celebrated German scholar, but the committee will feel obliged to reject it on account of its too childish simplicity.
Here we have a

NATIONAL ANTHEM.

BY WILLIAM CULLEN B——.

THE sun sinks softly to his evening post,
  The sun swells grandly to his morning crown;
Yet not a star our flag of heaven has lost,
  And not a sunset stripe with him goes down.

So thrones may fall; and from the dust of those
  New thrones may rise, to totter like the last;
But still our country's nobler planet glows,
  While the eternal stars of Heaven are fast.

Upon finding that this does not go well to the air of "Yankee Doodle," the committee feel justified in declining it; being furthermore prejudiced against it by a suspicion that the poet has crowded an advertisement of a paper which he edits into the first line.
Next we quote from a

NATIONAL ANTHEM.

BY GENERAL GEORGE P. M——.

IN the days that tried our fathers,
  Many years ago,
Our fair land achieved her freedom,
  Blood-bought, you know.
Shall we not defend her ever,
  As we 'd defend
That fair maiden, kind and tender,
  Calling us friend?

Yes! Let all the echoes answer,
  From hill and vale;
Yes! Let other nations hearing,
  Joy in the tale.
Our Columbia is a lady,
  High-born and fair;
We have sworn allegiance to her, —
  Touch her who dare.

The tone of this "anthem" not being devotional enough to suit the committee, it should be printed on an edition of linen-cambric handkerchiefs for ladies especially.
Observe this

NATIONAL ANTHEM.

BY N. P. W——.

ONE hue of our flag is taken
  From the cheeks of my blushing pet,
And its stars beat time and sparkle
  Like the studs on her chemisette.

Its blue is the ocean shadow
  That hides in her dreamy eyes,
And it conquers all men, like her,
  And still for a Union flies.

Several members of the committee find that this "anthem" has too much of the Anacreon spice to suit them.
We next peruse a

NATIONAL ANTHEM.

BY THOMAS BAILEY A——.

THE little brown squirrel hops in the corn,
  The cricket quaintly sings;
The emerald pigeon nods his head,
  And the shad in the river springs;
The dainty sunflower hangs its head
  On the shore of the summer sea;
And better far that I were dead,
  If Maud did not love me.

I love the squirrel that hops in the corn,
  And the cricket that quaintly sings;
And the emerald pigeon that nods his head,
  And the shad that gayly springs.
I love the dainty sunflower, too,
  And Maud with her snowy breast;
I love them all; but I love — I love —
  I love my country best.

This is certainly very beautiful, and sounds somewhat like Tennyson. Though it may be rejected by the committee, it can never lose its value as a piece of excellent reading for children. It is calculated to fill the youthful mind with patriotism and natural history, beside touching the youthful heart with an emotion palpitating for all.
We close the list with the following: —

NATIONAL ANTHEM.

BY R. H. STOD——.

BEHOLD the flag! Is it not a flag?
  Deny it, man, if you dare!
And midway spread 'twixt earth and sky
  It hangs like a written prayer.

Would impious hand of foe disturb
  Its memories' holy spell,
And blight it with a dew of blood?
  Ha, tr-r-aitor! . . . . It is well.

R. H. NEWELL.
(ORPHEUS C. KERR.)

In the beauty of the lilies Christ was born
across the sea,
With a glory in his bosom that transfigures you
and me;
As he died to make men holy, let us die to
make men free
While God is marching on.

Julia Ward Howe.

INDEX OF FIRST LINES.